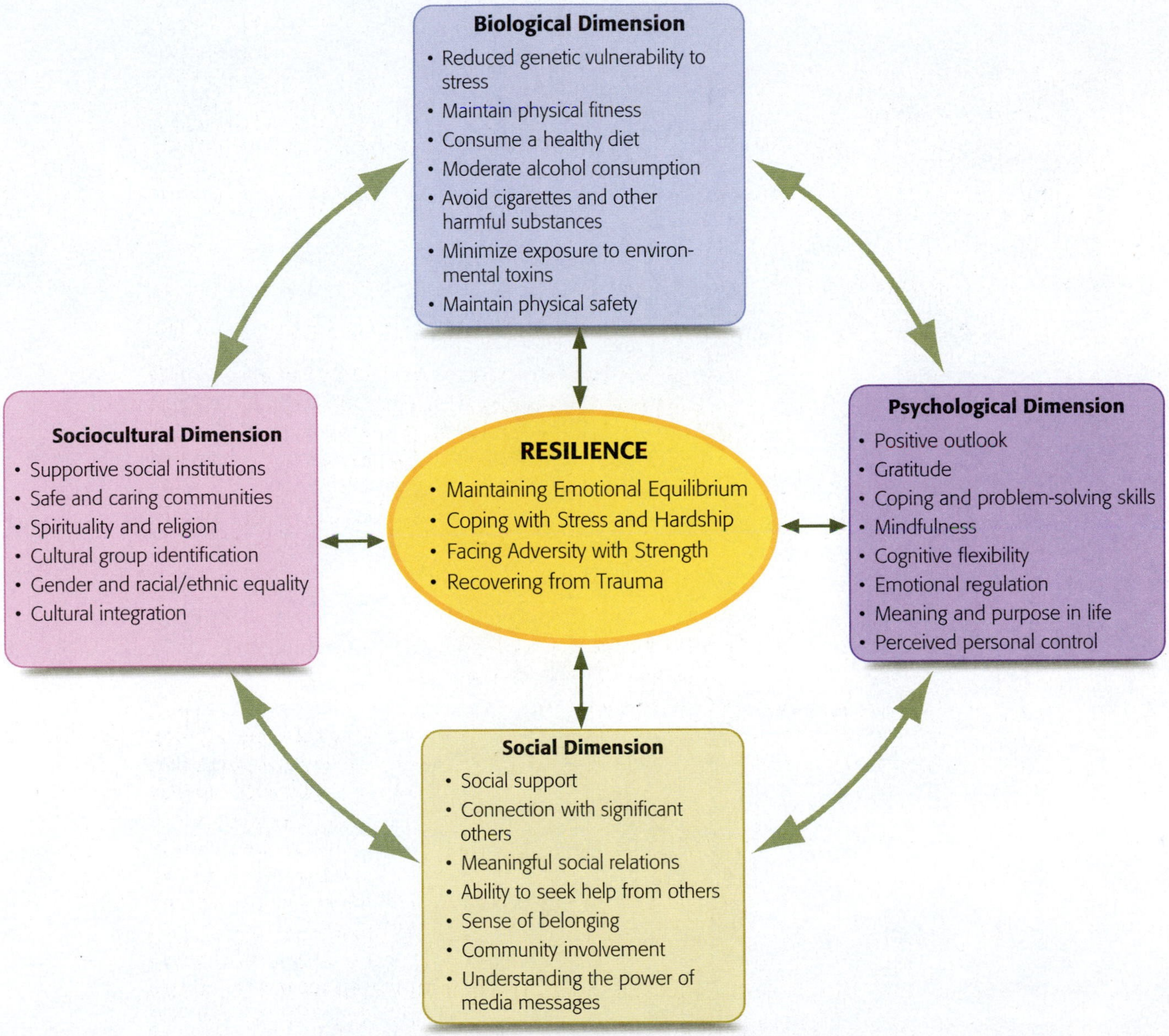

Biological Dimension

- Reduced genetic vulnerability to stress
- Maintain physical fitness
- Consume a healthy diet
- Moderate alcohol consumption
- Avoid cigarettes and other harmful substances
- Minimize exposure to environmental toxins
- Maintain physical safety

Sociocultural Dimension

- Supportive social institutions
- Safe and caring communities
- Spirituality and religion
- Cultural group identification
- Gender and racial/ethnic equality
- Cultural integration

RESILIENCE

- Maintaining Emotional Equilibrium
- Coping with Stress and Hardship
- Facing Adversity with Strength
- Recovering from Trauma

Psychological Dimension

- Positive outlook
- Gratitude
- Coping and problem-solving skills
- Mindfulness
- Cognitive flexibility
- Emotional regulation
- Meaning and purpose in life
- Perceived personal control

Social Dimension

- Social support
- Connection with significant others
- Meaningful social relations
- Ability to seek help from others
- Sense of belonging
- Community involvement
- Understanding the power of media messages

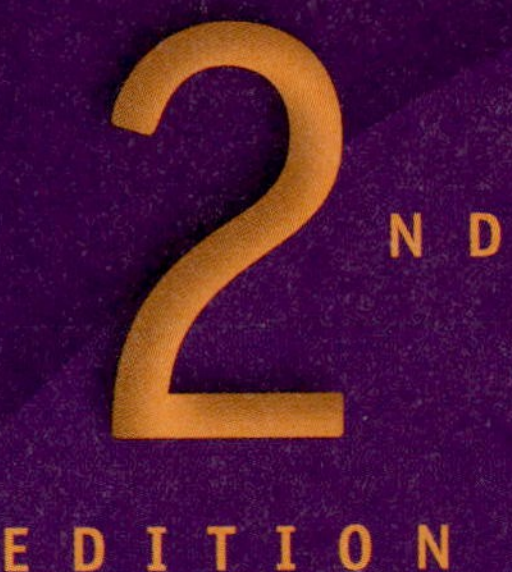

Essentials of Understanding Abnormal Behavior

David Sue
Department of Psychology
Western Washington University

Derald Wing Sue
Department of Counseling and Clinical Psychology
Teachers College, Columbia University

Diane Sue
Private Practice

Stanley Sue
Professor of Psychology
Palo Alto University

Australia • Brazil • Japan • Korea • Mexico • Singapore • Spain • United Kingdom • United States

***Essentials of Understanding Abnormal Behavior*, 2nd Edition**

David Sue, Derald Wing Sue, Diane Sue, Stanley Sue

Acquisitions Editor: Tim Matray

Developmental Editor: Tangelique Williams

Assistant Editor: Jessica Alderman

Editorial Assistant: Audrey Espey

Media Editor: Mary Noel

Senior Brand Manager: Elisabeth Rhoden

Market Development Manager: Christine Sosa

Content Project Manager: Charlene M. Carpentier

Art Director: Vernon Boes

Manufacturing Planner: Karen Hunt

Rights Acquisitions Specialist: Thomas McDonough

Production Service: Graphic World Inc.

Photo Researcher: Q2A/Bill Smith

Text Researcher: Karyn Morrison

Copy Editor: Graphic World Inc.

Text Designer: Diane Beasley

Cover Designer: Roger Knox

Cover Image: Corbin/SuperStock

Compositor: Graphic World Inc.

Library of Congress Control Number: 2012942043

Student Edition:

ISBN-13: 978-1-133-95635-8

ISBN-10: 1-133-95635-1

Loose-leaf Edition:

ISBN-13: 978-1-133-95633-4

ISBN-10: 1-133-95633-5

Wadsworth
20 Davis Drive
Belmont, CA 94002-3098
USA

Cengage Learning is a leading provider of customized learning solutions with office locations around the globe, including Singapore, the United Kingdom, Australia, Mexico, Brazil, and Japan. Locate your local office at **www.cengage.com/global**.

Cengage Learning products are represented in Canada by Nelson Education, Ltd.

To learn more about Wadsworth, visit **www.cengage.com/Wadsworth**

Purchase any of our products at your local college store or at our preferred online store **www.CengageBrain.com**.

Printed in Canada

1 2 3 4 5 6 7 17 16 15 14 13

Brief Contents

Contents

© Rohit Seth/Shutterstock.com

© Frank Renlie/PhotoDisc/Jupiterimages.com

Huan Tran/Ikon Images/Getty

© Wilson Valentin/Shutterstock.com

5 Trauma and Stress-Related Disorders 119

© Jose Luis Pelaez Inc/Jupiterimages.com

6 Somatic Symptom and Dissociative Disorders 147

Fuse/Jupiterimages

LWA/Sharie Kennedy/Blend Images/Jupiterimages

Rob Hainer/Shutterstock.com

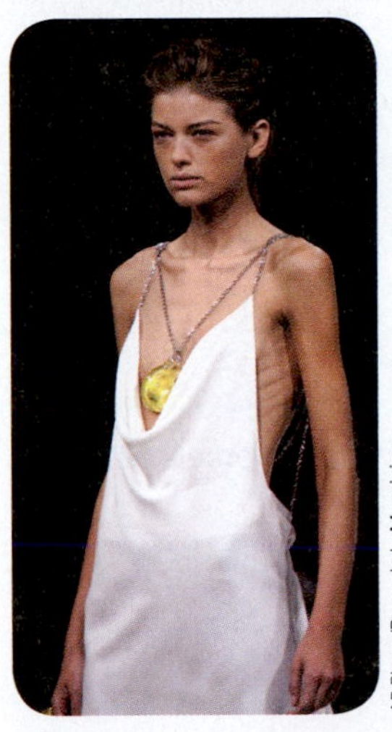
AP Photo/Remy de la Mauviniere

Alina G/Shutterstock.com

11 Schizophrenia and Other Psychotic Disorders 291

iStockphoto.com/Richard Johnson

12 Neurocognitive Disorders 321

David Eulitt/MCT/Newscom

13 Sexual Dysfunction, Gender Dysphoria, and Paraphilic Disorders 347

Medioimages/Photodisc/Jupiterimages

14 Personality Psychopathology 381

Blend Images/DreamPictures/Jupiterimages

15 Disorders of Childhood and Adolescence 411

Jaimie Duplass/Shutterstock.com

Features

Focus on Resilience

Disorders Charts

Controversy

Preface

We are all touched in one way or another by mental health issues, either directly through our own struggles with mental disorders or indirectly through affected friends or relatives. Over the years, major research discoveries in genetics, neuroscience, and psychology have made unprecedented contributions to our understanding of abnormal behaviors. The hope among mental health professionals is that such advances will allow for increased understanding of mental disorders and their subsequent treatments. In addition to tremendous biological breakthroughs, we also know more about how psychological forms of intervention can effectively treat mental disorders. The move to identify evidence-based treatments has taken the profession by storm. Finally, research has revealed great cultural variations in the expression of psychological symptoms and what other cultures consider effective treatments. In the second edition of *Essentials of Understanding Abnormal Behavior*, we explore all of these topics.

The text has been completely revised to accommodate updated research and changes in the classification and diagnosis of mental disorders, including proposed changes in the American Psychiatric Association's *Diagnostic and Statistical Manual* (DSM-5). We have incorporated the latest information from the committee involved in the restructured organization of DSM-5 and the 13 DSM-5 work groups (multidisciplinary groups of professionals who have extensively reviewed scientific research on various mental health conditions) to guide our discussion of disorders throughout the text, including controversies and trends in the field. While research findings and knowledge in the field of psychopathology have grown considerably, we have tried to highlight the most important and significant developments in the field.*

In our revision, we hope to once again engage students in the exciting process of understanding abnormal behavior and the ways that mental health professionals study and attempt to treat various mental conditions. In pursuing this goal, we have focused on five major objectives:

- providing students with scholarship of the highest quality;
- offering an evenhanded treatment of abnormal psychology as both a scientific and a clinical endeavor, giving students the opportunity to explore topics thoroughly and responsibly;
- focusing on the human face of mental illness, including an emphasis on both resilience and recovery;
- translating the concepts and principles of mental health practice into concrete and real-life clinical applications; and
- making our book inviting and stimulating to a wide range of students.

Essentials of Understanding Abnormal Behavior continues to retain the approach, style, and hallmark multicultural emphasis of our comprehensive text, *Understanding Abnormal Behavior*, while providing concise yet thorough coverage in a convenient 16-chapter format. The text is, therefore, manageable for a one-semester or one-quarter class. It presents complex material in a dynamic, highly readable format that challenges students, encourages them to think critically, and provides them with a solid background in the field of abnormal psychology.

---

*Throughout the text, proposed DSM-5 definitions of disorders have been adapted for a student audience. These definitions are intended for educational purposes only.

A distinguishing characteristic of this text is our focus on resilience and positive psychological principles. Throughout this edition we focus on contributions from the field of positive psychology, including the topics of optimal mental health, psychological strengths and protective factors that can help decrease the risk of developing mental disorders, and resilience and recovery for those with mental illness. We believe it is very valuable for students to understand not only what contributes to disorders but also factors (many under their control) that can decrease the likelihood of developing a disorder or minimize the progression and duration of a disorder. Because of recent findings and evolving trends in the field, we have strengthened our coverage of gender issues, disorders of childhood and adolescence, neurocognitive disorders, substance-use disorders, depressive and bipolar disorders, and protective factors and psychological resilience.

Our Approach

We take an eclectic, clinical, research-based, multicultural approach to understanding abnormal behavior, drawing on important contributions from various disciplines and theoretical perspectives. We believe that different combinations of biological strengths and vulnerabilities, personal attributes, and life experiences influence mental disorders, and we project this view throughout the text. This combination of influences is demonstrated in our *multipath model*, a conceptual framework that was introduced in the ninth edition of our full-length text with the goal of helping students understand and conceptually organize the wide array of research pertaining to the causes of specific mental disorders.

There are several elements to our multipath model. First, the multipath model divides etiological explanation into four dimensions: biological, psychological, social, and sociocultural. Different disorders have different etiological explanations under these four dimensions. Second, influences within any of the four dimensions can increase the risk that someone will develop a psychological disorder. For instance, severe depression can be influenced by a single factor, such as a sudden trauma, but is more likely to involve a combination of influences from different dimensions, such as biological vulnerability to depression (biological), residual effects of childhood sexual trauma (psychological), a stressful interpersonal relationship in adulthood (social), and ongoing exposure to discrimination (sociocultural). Thus a disorder such as depression can be caused by different combinations of factors that can vary significantly from person to person.

Third, factors within the four dimensions are viewed as having the potential to interact with and influence each other. For example, childhood sexual abuse can activate biological processes linked with depression. Individuals experiencing depression may develop certain ways of thinking about the world that affect their relationships with others; relationship stress can then influence depression. Fourth, many disorders appear to be heterogeneous in nature. Therefore, there may be very separate types or versions of a disorder, each with distinct etiological influences. Additionally, a disorder may manifest along a continuum that varies in terms of severity and symptom expression. Finally, different disorders may be caused by similar factors. For example, child sexual abuse and interpersonal stress can produce anxiety as well as depression. In fact, people frequently experience anxiety and depression concurrently.

Sociocultural factors, including cultural norms, values, and expectations, are given special attention in our multipath model. Not only do we discuss how changing demographics increase the importance of multicultural psychology, we also introduce multicultural models of psychopathology in the opening chapters and address multicultural issues throughout the text whenever research findings and theoretical formulations allow. Such an approach adds richness to students' understanding of mental disorders.

The text covers the major disorders proposed for inclusion in the updated *Diagnostic and Statistical Manual of Mental Disorders* (DSM-5), but it is not a mechanistic reiteration of the DSM. As psychologists (and professors), we know that learning is enhanced when material is presented in a lively and engaging manner. We therefore provide case vignettes and clients' descriptions of their experiences to complement and illustrate symptoms of various disorders and research-based explanations. Our goal is to encourage students to appreciate the personal challenge experienced by those who have a mental disorder and to think critically rather than to merely assimilate a collection of facts and theories. As a result, we hope that students will develop an appreciation of the study of abnormal behavior.

Organization of the Text

Chapters 1 through 3 provide a context for viewing abnormal behavior and treatment by introducing students to definitions of and historical perspectives regarding abnormal behavior (Chapter 1), models used in the study of psychopathology and psychotherapeutic interventions (Chapter 2), and methods of research, assessment, and diagnosis (Chapter 3). These chapters provide necessary background information, including the different models or perspectives from which we can better understanding mental disorders. The bulk of the text, Chapters 4 through 15, presents the major disorders included in the proposed DSM-5 revision. In each chapter, symptoms, diagnostic issues, and etiological research are presented, followed by a discussion of common treatment approaches. Chapter 16 covers the issues and controversies surrounding topics such as ethics, the insanity defense, patients' rights, confidentiality, and mental health practices in general.

Topics of interest and relevance to college students (e.g., eating disorders, suicide, substance use in college populations, and traumatic brain injuries in sports), as well as contemporary issues in abnormal psychology such as the influence of pharmaceutical companies in the treatment of mental disorders, are presented. This edition of our book provides current information on a variety of topics in the field of abnormal psychology, as illustrated by the new information added to each chapter.

New and Updated Coverage in the Second Edition

Our foremost objective in preparing this edition was to thoroughly update the content of the text and present the latest trends in research and clinical thinking, with a particular emphasis on the DSM revision proposals. This has led to updated coverage of dozens of topics throughout the text, including the following:

Chapter 1—Abnormal Behavior

- Discussion of the proposed DSM-5 definition of mental disorders and its implications
- New statistics on the incidence and prevalence of mental disorders
- Discussion of cultural relativism and cultural universality as well as the contextual, sociopolitical, and cultural limitations involved in defining mental disorders
- Focus on the role of spirituality and religion in mental health care and trends in psychopharmacology
- Discussion of the role of positive psychology and optimal psychological health

Chapter 2—Models of Abnormal Behavior

- Discussion of the inadequacy of single etiological models
- Overview of the multipath model, including a focus on epigenetics and cultural neuroscience

- Presentation of a new resilience model that complements and explores the biological, psychological, social and sociocultural strengths of people.
- Discussion of the universal shamanic tradition and the role ancient healers played in defining and treating abnormal behaviors
- Discussions of implicit bias and the relationship between brain function and aggression

Chapter 3—Clinical Research, Assessment, and Diagnosis in Abnormal Psychology

- Updated discussion of assessment, differential diagnosis, and classification of abnormal behavior
- Discussion of mental status exams and their use, illustrated with a case study
- Discussion of DSM-5 proposals that will affect assessment and controversies regarding the new classification system
- Expanded coverage of assessment of ethnic minorities
- Discussion of the need for strengths assessment in psychopathology
- Updated sections on scientific evidence, the scientific method, and research design

Chapter 4—Anxiety and Obsessive-Compulsive and Related Disorders

- Incorporation of proposed DSM-5 changes including obsessive-compulsive, body dysmorphic, hair-pulling, and skin-picking disorders
- Discussion of hoarding
- Expanded multipath discussion regarding biological, psychological, social, and sociocultural factors involved in these disorders
- Discussion of research on environmental factors that can help guard against developing an anxiety disorder

Chapter 5—Trauma and Stress-Related Disorders

- Expanded discussion of the physiological and psychological effects of stress and biological factors contributing to stress disorders
- New discussion of trauma, post-traumatic stress disorder, and acute stress disorders from a multipath perspective
- Updated section on psychophysiological disorders, including a focus on the relationship between stress and cancer
- Discussion of the positive side of experiencing adverse life events

Chapter 6—Somatic Symptom and Dissociative Disorders

- Overview of proposed DSM-5 changes regarding somatic symptom disorders
- Discussion of proposed DSM-5 changes involving the dissociative disorders including the diagnostic categories of somatic symptom disorders, including conversion disorder (functional neurological symptom disorder), factitious disorder, and factitious disorder imposed on another
- Expanded coverage regarding the validity of diagnosis of some dissociative disorders

Chapter 7—Depressive and Bipolar Disorders

- Discussion of research regarding methods to provide "psychological immunization" against depression

- Expanded discussion of depressive and manic symptoms and of gender differences in depression
- Discussion of the clear division between depressive and bipolar disorders, and the critical importance of assessing for elevated mood episode when making diagnostic decisions
- Overview of new diagnostic categories, including premenstrual dysphoric disorder and categories undergoing research such as seasonal affective disorder and mixed anxiety/depression
- Presentation of updated research on etiological factors and treatment approaches for both depressive and bipolar disorders
- New discussion of the overlap between bipolar disorders and schizophrenia

Chapter 8—Suicide

- Updated statistics on suicide and sociodemographic correlates of suicide risk
- New focus on suicide on college campuses
- New discussion of suicide among youth and children
- Updated presentation of individual rights regarding suicide and legal implications
- Comprehensive multipath analysis of suicide
- Discussion of factors that are especially effective in preventing or immunizing against suicide

Chapter 9—Eating Disorders

- Up-to-date information on eating disorders, including obesity
- New critical analysis of the use of underweight models and digitally "enhanced" photos in advertising
- Increased coverage of muscle dysphoria
- Updated discussion of the Web presence of groups promoting anorexia and bulimia
- Discussion of psychological and social factors that can help promote resilience against eating disorders

Chapter 10—Substance-Use Disorders

- Extensively revised discussion of abuse of alcohol, prescription drugs, and a variety of other substances
- Coverage of new topics, including dissociative anesthetics, inhalants, energy drinks, and caffeinated alcoholic beverages
- Inclusion of many new statistics and charts illustrating the prevalence of substance use and abuse, with a particular focus on alcohol
- Expanded discussion of drug and alcohol use among college students, including the debate regarding cognitive-enhancing drugs and alcohol-abuse prevention programs
- New focus on relapse prevention and the efficacy of treatment for the most commonly abused substances
- Discussion of factors that can help curb the tide of substance abuse

Chapter 11—Schizophrenia and Other Psychotic Disorders

- Updated research on schizophrenia
- Updated discussion of the controversy regarding Morgellons disease

- New critical discussion of the marketing of atypical antipsychotic medications
- Discussion of how the recovery model can help instill optimism and hope after a diagnosis of schizophrenia

Chapter 12—Neurocognitive Disorders

- Completely rewritten and reorganized chapter, including new research and critical discussions related to traumatic brain injury, sports concussions, brain injuries sustained in combat, and genetic testing for neurocognitive disorders
- Discussion of new diagnostic categories (including mild neurocognitive disorder and major neurocognitive disorder) and disorders such as Lewy body dementia
- Continued focus on neurocognitive disorders across the life span, with a strong emphasis on lifestyle changes that can help prevent the development of degenerative disorders such as dementia
- Discussion of preventive efforts that can reduce the likelihood of developing certain neurocognitive disorders

Chapter 13—Sexual Dysfunction, Gender Dysphoria, and Paraphilic Disorders

- New statistics and data on the sexual behavior of men and women in the United States
- Discussion of hypersexual disorder
- Updated terminology related to sexual disorders, gender incongruence, and paraphilias
- New discussion of whether transgender people have a mental disorder
- Resilience discussion focusing on protective factors enhancing the ability to overcome the adversity associated with sexual assault

Chapter 14—Personality Psychopathology

- Discussion of the significant changes proposed in the DSM revision, including a revised definition of personality disorders and the rationale for diagnostic changes in personality psychopathology
- Discussion of six personality types (antisocial, avoidant, borderline, narcissistic, obsessive-compulsive, and schizotypal) and five personality trait domains that form the basis of diagnosing a personality disorder, including application of personality traits to a case vignette
- Discussion of the DSM-5 change of focus from a categorical to a hybrid dimensional-categorical model of personality assessment
- Detailed use of the multipath model to explain the antisocial personality type
- Overview of the resilience demonstrated by an eminent psychologist who overcame a personality disorder and went on to develop a life-changing form of therapy that has helped others with various forms of mental illness
- Overview of factors that can help youth become more resilient to biological vulnerabilities and environmental stressors

Chapter 15—Disorders of Childhood and Adolescence

- Substantially reorganized chapter with multiple case descriptions illustrating various disorders

- New topics, including neurodevelopmental disorders, childhood anxiety, depressive and bipolar disorders, childhood post-traumatic stress disorder, reactive attachment disorder, and tics and Tourette's syndrome; discussion of new diagnostic categories, including nonsuicidal self injury, disruptive mood dysregulation disorder, disinhibited social engagement disorder, and the callous and unemotional subtype of conduct disorder

Chapter 16—Law and Ethics in Abnormal Psychology

- New case studies illustrating dilemmas posed by the interaction of psychology and the law
- Updates on legal rulings that affect criminal commitment, the insanity defense and civil commitment.
- New focus on the therapeutic and legal implications of disclosure by clients in regard to violent behaviors or child abuse
- New findings on therapists predicting dangerousness in clients
- Updated profiles of mass murderers and serial killers

Special Features

Even the most well-aimed textbook will miss its mark if not presented in a way that engages students' interest, follows through with clear explanations, and reinforces concepts to keep students on track. Contributing to the strength of this and previous editions are carefully planned presentation and learning aids that assist students in reflecting on chapter concepts and internalizing the material covered. Most chapters include the following pedagogical elements:

- *Focus on Resilience* boxes provide students with key research from a positive psychology perspective, including aspects of resilience and protective factors associated with specific disorders.
- *Controversy* boxes provide factual evidence and thought-provoking questions that focus on key issues, examine widely held assumptions about abnormal behavior, and challenge the students' own understanding of the text material. They will doubtless stimulate critical thinking, evoke alternative views, provoke discussion, and draw students into issues that help them to better explore the wider meaning of abnormal behavior in our society.
- *Disorder charts* provide information not only about characteristics of various disorders but also about the prevalence, typical age of onset, and course of the disorders. These charts are expressly designed to help students conceptualize, define, and compare disorders.
- *Myth Versus Reality* discussions challenge the many myths and false beliefs that have surrounded the field of abnormal behavior, and help students realize that beliefs—some of which may appear to be common sense—must be checked against scientific facts and knowledge.
- *Did You Know?* boxes found throughout the book provide fascinating, at-a-glance research-based tidbits that add interest and connect with materials covered in the main text.
- *Focus Questions* frame the chapter and stimulate active learning—with these questions in mind, students begin thinking about the concepts they are about to explore within the chapter.
- *Checkpoint Reviews* at the end of each major section provide students with questions they can use to review and check their understanding of the central concepts and key terms covered up to that point. These reviews enable students to digest the material more easily and

efficiently, helping them to form an integrated understanding of the chapter content.

- *Chapter summaries* provide a review of the main concepts addressed in the chapter by answering each of the focus questions.
- *Key terms* are indicated in the text and are defined both in the margins and in the glossary at the end of the book. Ready access to definitions in the text margins facilitates students' comprehension of the terms. A list of all key terms is also provided at the end of each chapter, allowing students to check their recall of key terminology.

Throughout the text we pay special attention to cultural, gender, and diversity phenomena. Research findings include rates of each mental disorder and the prevalence of disorders according to gender, ethnicity, and age. Case studies and up-to-date research findings make issues of mental health and mental disorders come to life for students and instructors. The latest scholarly research is incorporated throughout the text to reflect recent breakthroughs in the etiology and treatment of mental disorders.

The format and design of the book include a new single column design and an upbeat and engaging palette throughout the text, art, and tables. Along with the pedagogical features previously outlined, *Essentials of Understanding Abnormal Behavior* contains numerous tables, illustrations, figures, and photographs to enhance students' understanding of concepts or controversies in the field. In addition to updating the book's coverage, look, and special features, we have focused on concise presentations and have maintained a streamlined organization of the book.

Ancillaries

This text is supported by a rich set of supplementary materials designed to enhance the teaching and learning experience. Several new components make use of new instructional technologies.

For Instructors

- *Instructor's Resource Manual*: The *Instructor's Resource Manual* includes extended chapter outlines, learning objectives, discussion topics, classroom exercises, handouts, and lists of supplementary readings and multimedia resources. The *Instructor's Resource Manual* is available on the instructor Web site (www.cengage.com/psychology/sue) and is also available in print. Please consult your sales representative for further details.
- *Test Bank*: The *Test Bank* contains 100 multiple-choice and three essay questions (with sample answers) per chapter. Each question is labeled with the corresponding text reference as well as the type of question being asked, allowing for easier test creation. The *Test Bank* is also available in print. Please consult your sales representative for further details.
- *CourseMate*: Cengage Learning's Psychology CourseMate brings course concepts to life with interactive learning, study, and exam preparation tools that support the printed textbook. CourseMate includes an integrated eBook, glossaries, flashcards, quizzes, videos, and more—as well as EngagementTracker, a first-of-its-kind tool that monitors student engagement in the course. The accompanying instructor website, available through login.cengage.com, offers access to password-protected resources such as an electronic version of the instructor's manual, test bank files, and PowerPoint® slides. CourseMate can be bundled with the student text. Contact your Cengage sales representative for information on getting access to CourseMate.

- *PowerLecture with ExamView® for Essentials of Understanding Abnormal Behavior*, 2e: The fastest, easiest way to build powerful, customized, media-rich lectures, *PowerLecture* gathers all instructor supplements on one easily accessible DVD. These materials include the *Instructor's Resource Manual*, *Test Bank*, book-specific PowerPoint lectures, and class tools to enhance the educational experience.
- WebTutor™ on Blackboard and WebCT: Jump-start your course with customizable, rich, text-specific content within your course management system. Whether you want to Web-enable your class or put an entire course online, WebTutor delivers. WebTutor offers a wide array of resources, including access to the e-book, glossaries, flashcards, quizzes, videos, and more.
- *ABC Video: Abnormal Psychology*
  Vol 1 978-0-495-59639-4
  Vol 2 978-0-495-60494-5

For Students

- *Case Studies in Abnormal Psychology*: This volume, by Clark Clipson (California School of Professional Psychology) and Jocelyn Steer (San Diego Family Institute), contains 16 studies and can be shrink-wrapped with the text at a discounted package price. Each case represents a major psychological disorder. After a detailed history of each case, critical-thinking questions prompt students to formulate hypotheses and interpretations based on the client's symptoms, family and medical background, and relevant information. The case proceeds with sections on assessment, case conceptualization, diagnosis, and treatment outlook, and is concluded by a final set of discussion questions.
- *CourseMate:* Cengage Learning's Psychology CourseMate brings course concepts to life with interactive learning, study, and exam preparation tools that support the printed textbook. Access an integrated e-book and learning tools including glossaries, flashcards, quizzes, videos, and more in your Psychology CourseMate. Go to **CengageBrain.com** to register or purchase access.

Acknowledgments

We continue to appreciate the critical feedback received from reviewers and colleagues. The following individuals helped us prepare the second edition by sharing valuable insights, opinions, and recommendations.

Edward Change, University of Michigan
Ronald K. Craig, Cincinnati State College
Mocha Dyrud, Northern Virginia Community College
Craig Eben, Kean University
Roy Fish, Zane State College
Tony Fowler, Florence-Darlington Technical College
Kenneth France, Texas State University
Corey Gilbert, Toccoa Falls College
Beth Hopkins, Stanly Community College
Lora L. Jacobi, Stephen F. Austin State University
Jason King, Utah Valley University
Laurel Krautwurst, Blue Ridge Community College
Jan Mendoza, Golden West College
Kristelle Miller, University of Minnesota, Duluth

Rebecca L. Rahschulte, Ivy Tech Community College
Karen Rhines, Northampton Community College
Jaine Stauss, Macalester College
Eugenia Valentine, Xavier University of Louisiana
Glenn White, West Los Angeles College

We also thank the reviewers of the previous editions of *Understanding Abnormal Behavior*.

Julia C. Babcock, University of Houston
Betty Clark, University of Mary Hardin-Baylor
Irvin Cohen, Hawaii Pacific University & Kapiolani Community College
Lorry Cology, Owens Community College
Bonnie J. Ekstrom, Bemidji State University
Greg A. R. Febbraro, Drake University
Kate Flory, University of South Carolina
David M. Fresco, Kent State University
Jerry L. Fryrear, University of Houston, Clear Lake
Michele Galietta, John Jay College of Criminal Justice
Christina Gordon, Fox Valley Technical College
Robert Hoff, Mercyhurst College
George-Harold Jennings, Drew University
Kim L. Krinsky, Georgia Perimeter College
Brian E. Lozano, Virginia Polytechnic Institute and State University
Jan Mohlman, Rutgers University
Sherry Davis Molock, George Washington University
Rebecca L. Motley, University of Toledo
Gilbert R. Parra, University of Memphis
Kimberly Renk, University of Central Florida
Mark Richardson, Boston University
Alan Roberts, Indiana University
Daniel L. Segal, University of Colorado at Colorado Springs
Tom Schoeneman, Lewis & Clark College
Michael D. Spiegler, Providence College
Ma. Teresa G. Tuason, University of North Florida
Theresa A. Wadkins, University of Nebraska, Kearney
Susan Brooks Watson, Hawaii Pacific University
Fred Whitford, Montana State University

We also wish to acknowledge the support of, and high quality of work done by Tangelique Williams, development editor; Jaime Perkins, executive editor; Cassie Carey, production editor; Charlene Carpentier, content project manager; Jessica Alderman, assistant editor; and Vernon Boes, art director. We also thank text designer Cheryl Carrington, text researcher Karyn Morrison, photo researcher Alexa Orr, and copyeditor Jeff Anderson.

D. S.
D. W. S.
D. M. S.
S. S.

About the Authors

David Sue is Professor Emeritus of Psychology at Western Washington University, where he is an associate of the Center for Cross-Cultural Research. He has served as the director of both the Psychology Counseling Clinic and the Mental Health Counseling Program. He coauthored the book *Counseling and Psychotherapy in a Diverse Society* and is a coauthor of *Counseling the Culturally Diverse: Theory and Practice*. He received his PhD in clinical psychology from Washington State University. His research interests revolve around multicultural issues in individual and group counseling. He enjoys hiking, snowshoeing, traveling, and spending time with his family.

Derald Wing Sue is Professor of Psychology and Education in the Department of Counseling and Clinical Psychology at Teachers College, Columbia University. He has written extensively in the field of counseling psychology and multicultural counseling and therapy, and is the author of the best-selling book *Microaggressions in Everyday Life: Race, Gender and Sexual Orientation* and coauthor of the best-selling *Counseling the Culturally Diverse: Theory and Practice*. He has served as president of the Society of Counseling Psychology and the Society for the Psychological Study of Ethnic Minority Issues, and has received numerous awards for teaching and service. He received his doctorate from the University of Oregon and is married and the father of two children. Friends describe him as addicted to exercise and the Internet.

Diane M. Sue received her EdS in school psychology and her PhD in educational psychology from the University of Michigan, Ann Arbor. She has worked as a school psychologist and counselor and with adults needing specialized care for mental illness and neurocognitive disorders. She has taught courses at Western Washington University as an adjunct faculty member. She received the Washington State School Psychologist of the Year Award and the Western Washington University College of Education Professional Excellence Award, and coauthored the book *Counseling and Psychotherapy in a Diverse Society*. Her areas of expertise include child and adolescent psychology, neuropsychology, and interventions with children and adolescents from various ethnic groups. She enjoys traveling and spending time with friends and family.

Stanley Sue is Professor of Psychology and Director of the Center for Excellence in Diversity at Palo Alto University. From 1971 to 1981, he was Assistant and Associate Professor of Psychology at the University of Washington; Professor of Psychology at the University of California, Los Angeles (1981–1996); and Professor of Psychology at the University of California–Davis (1996–2010), where he is now Emeritus Distinguished Professor. He recently served as president of the Western Psychological Association and has received the Award for Distinguished Contributions to Diversity in Clinical Psychology from the American Psychological Association. His hobbies include working on computers and swimming.

1

Abnormal Behavior

CHAPTER OUTLINE

On January 8, 2011, 23-year-old Jared Lee Loughner took a taxi to a Safeway supermarket in Tucson, Arizona, where Democratic representative Gabrielle Giffords was holding a constituents' meeting. It was early in the morning when Loughner used a 9-mm Glock pistol to open fire on Giffords and numerous bystanders. Six people were killed and thirteen injured while attempting to flee the scene. Giffords, who is believed to have been the target, was shot in the head and left in critical condition (Cloud, 2011). She has since made a miraculous recovery from brain injury, but in 2012 decided not to return to her congressional seat.

FOCUS QUESTIONS

1 What is abnormal psychology?

2 What criteria are used to determine normal or abnormal behaviors?

3 How do context, cultural differences, and sociopolitical experiences affect definitions of abnormality?

4 How common are mental disorders?

5 What are some common misconceptions about people who are mentally disturbed?

6 How have explanations of abnormal behavior changed over time?

7 What were early viewpoints on the causes of mental disorders?

8 What are some contemporary trends in abnormal psychology?

In an attempt to make sense out of an apparently "senseless" act, many questions were asked. What could have motivated Loughner to carry out such a heinous deed and take so many innocent lives? Was he a political extremist? Was he deranged, a psychopathic killer, or high on drugs? Were there warning signs that he was homicidal? Did he suffer from a mental disorder? Was he insane?

These questions are extremely difficult to answer for a number of reasons. First, we do not know enough about the causes of abnormal behavior and mental disorders to arrive at a definitive answer. **Psychopathology**, or abnormal behavior, is the result not of any singular cause but of an interaction of many factors. Most mental disorders have multiple contributors, a fact that we discuss in the next chapter.

Second, trying to assess Loughner's state of mind has proven extremely difficult. As of this writing, he has been declared mentally incompetent to stand trial for the crime. In other words, his thinking and reasoning have been found to be so confused that he is unable to assist in his own defense. As a result, we must rely on secondary sources such as school records, observations by family and acquaintances, and other available data (Internet postings and media communications) to construct a portrait of his state of mind.

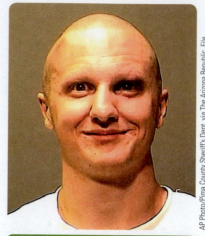

AP Photo/Pima County Sheriff's Dept. via The Arizona Republic, File

Is This the Picture of an Insane Man?

This picture of Jared Lee Loughner was taken after his arrest for shooting Representative Gabrielle Giffords and killing numerous bystanders. His appearance was variously described as "creepy," "frightening," and "smirky," with "hollow eyes ablaze." On August 7, 2012, Loughner pleaded guilty and was sentenced to life imprisonment without the possibility of parole.

The purpose of this book is to help you answer such questions. To do so, however, requires us to first examine basic aspects of the study of abnormal behavior, including some of its history and emerging changes in the field. Periodically, throughout this chapter, we use the Loughner case to illustrate complex issues in the mental health field.

The Concerns of Abnormal Psychology

psychopathology the study of mental or behavioral disorders

abnormal psychology the scientific study whose objectives are to describe, explain, predict, and modify behaviors that are considered strange or unusual

psychodiagnosis assessment and description of an individual's psychological symptoms, including inferences about what might be causing the psychological distress

Abnormal psychology is an area of scientific study that attempts to describe, explain, predict, and modify behaviors that are considered strange or unusual. Its subject matter ranges from behavior that is bizarre and spectacular to the more commonplace—from the violent homicides, suicides, and "perverted" sexual acts that are widely reported by the news media to unsensational (but more prevalent) concerns such as depression, sleep disturbances, and anxiety.

Describing Abnormal Behavior

Understanding a particular case of abnormal behavior begins with systematic observations by an attentive professional. These observations, usually paired with the results of the person's psychological history, become the raw material for a **psychodiagnosis**, an attempt to describe, assess, and systematically draw inferences about an individual's psychological disorder. For example, Loughner received a psychiatric evaluation by a mental health professional while imprisoned. Usually such an evaluation includes a mental status exam to ascertain the degree to which the person is in contact with reality, whether the person suffers from delusions and hallucinations, and whether the person is potentially dangerous. After his evaluation, Loughner was diagnosed as having schizophrenia and being incompetent to stand trial.

In light of the current animosity and antagonism prevalent in our political parties, some have hypothesized that Loughner's act was motivated by extreme political rhetoric. Indeed, his Internet postings and YouTube videos indicate a belief in conspiracy theories, such as that the U.S. government was brainwashing people and a "new world order" was about to come. Can political extremism alone explain Loughner's horrendous actions? Probably not! Extreme delusions such as those possessed by Loughner are usually signs of a mental disturbance.

Explaining Abnormal Behavior

To explain abnormal behavior, a psychologist first identifies possible causes, or the *etiology*, for the described behavior. One popular explanation of Loughner's behavior was that he was a right-wing political extremist who held positions diametrically opposed to those of Representative Giffords. When he attended one of her political events in 2007 and asked the question "What is government if words have no meaning?," Giffords declined to comment (probably because it made no sense to her). Loughner felt slighted and angered by her lack of response. When he received a thank-you letter for attending the event, he wrote "die bitch" on it. From that day forth, his rage and obsession with Giffords seem to have increased.

A closer look at Loughner's background, however, reveals many other possible causes for his rampage:

- Friends noted that he seemed to undergo a personality transformation when he did poorly in high school and dropped out. His sense of academic failure was re-enacted years later when he enrolled in Pima Community College. There he was suspended because of poor academic performance, bizarre erratic behavior, and a YouTube posting in which he described the school as "one of the biggest scams in America." Could his sense of academic failure have contributed to his downward spiral and resultant anger?
- Others have noted that a breakup with a high school girlfriend proved particularly devastating to him. The failed relationship seemed to trigger his drug and alcohol abuse. He is reported to have used LSD, psychedelic mushrooms, marijuana, and other hallucinogens. When he tried to enlist in the U.S. Army, he was deemed unqualified because of his drug use. What roles did the breakup with his girlfriend and drugs play in his actions?
- By all accounts, Loughner was fascinated with lucid dreaming, a state of consciousness where the dreamer is half awake but aware he or she is dreaming. Interest in and practice of lucid dreaming have a long history among some Eastern cultures that believe in altered states of consciousness. The ability to control dreams and to discern meaning is among the goals of those who strive for lucid dreaming. It is reported that Loughner practiced replaying his lucid dreams over and over, became obsessed with them, and kept a dream journal. Could lucid dreaming have caused his break with reality and his paranoid delusions?
- Others have noted that strong biological factors may account for Loughner's psychotic breakdown. He was diagnosed with paranoid schizophrenia, and studies show strong support for a biological explanation (hereditary component, neuroanatomical causes, or biochemical imbalances) for this disorder. Interestingly, the downward spiral of Loughner in his early 20s is very consistent with the onset of schizophrenia, his delusional symptoms, and reported nonsensical speech during this period of his life. What role does biology play in mental disorders?

From these snippets of Loughner's life, many explanations for his actions can be offered. There was something biologically wrong with him; he was spurred on by extremist political rhetoric; he could not cope with the sense of academic failure; he was devastated and angry about breaking up with his girlfriend; his obsession with lucid dreaming caused his break with reality; and his drug and

David Harry Stewart/Stone/Getty Images

Intervening Through Therapy

Group therapy is a widely used form of treatment for many problems, especially those involving interpersonal relationships. In this group session, participants are learning to develop new and adaptive social skills in coping with social problems rather than relying on alcohol or drugs to escape the stresses of life.

alcohol abuse led to his downward spiral. Depending on your viewpoint, some explanations may appear more valid than others. As we will see in the next chapter, no one explanation is sufficient to explain the complexity of the human condition; normal and abnormal behaviors result from a combination of factors: biological, psychological, social, and sociocultural.

Predicting Abnormal Behavior

Many believe that there was sufficient evidence to predict that Loughner was a seriously disturbed young man and potentially dangerous. At Pima Community College, campus police recorded five contacts with Loughner over classroom and library disruptions. His YouTube ranting about the college was described as full of venom and hate, and at least one teacher and one classmate thought he was capable of a school shooting. To protect the campus, the college suspended Loughner with the stipulation that his return depended on his meeting two requirements: (a) he needed to conform his conduct to the codes of the college, and (b) he needed to obtain a mental health clearance testifying that his presence on campus did not constitute a danger to himself or others. In light of these reports, why was it that Loughner never received any type of psychological help or treatment?

Modifying Abnormal Behavior

Abnormal behavior may be modified through **therapy**, which is a program of systematic intervention designed to improve a person's behavioral, affective (emotional), or cognitive state. For example, many therapists believe Loughner could have been helped and the killings prevented if he had received treatment. Allowing Loughner an opportunity to get in touch with and to vent his anger may have reduced his chances of doing harm to others. Some mental health professionals might also recommend family therapy or social skills training. Those who see Loughner's condition as caused by a chemical imbalance might prescribe medication, such as antipsychotic drugs.

Psychologists focus first on understanding the cause of abnormal behavior and then plan treatment. Just as there are many ways to explain abnormal behaviors, there are many ways to conduct therapy and many professional helpers offering their services. Along with the demand for mental health treatment, the numbers and types of qualified helping professionals have grown. Table 1.1 lists the qualifications and training of various mental health professionals.

Determining Abnormality

therapy a program of systematic intervention whose purpose is to improve a person's behavioral, affective (emotional), or cognitive state

abnormal behavior a behavioral or psychological syndrome or pattern that reflects an underlying psychobiological dysfunction, is associated with distress or disability, and is not merely an expectable response to common stressors or losses

Implicit in our discussion is the one overriding concern of abnormal psychology: **abnormal behavior** itself. But what exactly is abnormal behavior, and how do psychologists define a mental disorder? The *Diagnostic and Statistical Manual of Mental Disorders* (DSM), the most widely used classification system of mental disorders, defines abnormal behavior as containing some of the following components: It is (a) a behavioral or psychological syndrome or pattern that reflects an underlying psychobiological dysfunction, (b) associated with distress (e.g., a painful symptom) or disability (i.e., impairment in one or more important areas of functioning) and (c) not merely an expectable response to common stressors or losses (www.dsm5.org).

TABLE 1.1 The Mental Health Professions

Profession	Description
Clinical psychologist	• Must hold a PhD or a PsyD (doctor of psychology) degree, a more practitioner-oriented degree. • Undergoes training that includes course work in psychopathology, personality, diagnosis, psychological testing, psychotherapy, and human physiology.
Counseling psychologist	• Has academic and internship requirements that are similar to those for a clinical psychologist, but with different emphasis. • Is more immediately concerned with the study of life problems in relatively normal people.
Mental health and marriage/family counselor or therapist	• Is a specialist in a distinct field with its own professional organization, journals, and state licensing requirements. • Undergoes training that usually includes a master's degree in counseling or therapy and many hours of supervised clinical experience.
Psychiatrist	• Holds an MD degree. • Undergoes the 4 years of medical school required for an MD, along with an additional 3 or 4 years of training in psychiatry.
Psychiatric social worker	• Is trained in a school of social work, usually in a 2-year graduate program leading to a master's degree. • Works in family counseling services or community agencies, specializing in intake (assessment and screening of clients), taking psychiatric histories, and dealing with other agencies.
School psychologist	• Is concerned with the cognitive and emotional development of students in educational settings. • Focuses on the processes of learning and on human development as it applies to the educational process. • May hold a master's or a doctoral degree. • Is often employed by school districts to assess and intervene with emotional and learning difficulties.

This definition is quite broad and raises many questions. First, when is a syndrome or pattern of behavior significant enough to have meaning? Second, is it possible to have a mental disorder without any signs of distress or discomfort? Third, what criteria do we use in ascertaining that a behavior pattern is a reflection of an underlying psychobiological dysfunction and not merely an expectable response to common stressors?

Despite problems in defining abnormal behavior, practitioners tend to agree that it represents behavior that departs from some norm and that harms the affected individual or others. Nearly all definitions of abnormal behavior use some form of statistical average to gauge deviations from normative standards. The four major factors in judging psychopathology are

- distress,
- deviance (bizarreness),
- dysfunction (inefficiency in behavioral, affective, or cognitive domains), and
- dangerousness.

Distress

Most people who seek the help of therapists are suffering psychological distress that may show up physically, psychologically, or some combination of both. In the psychological realm, distress is also manifested in extreme or prolonged emotional reactions such as anxiety and depression; it may surface physically in conditions like asthma or hypertension and with symptoms like fatigue, pain, or heart palpitations. Of course, it is normal for a person to feel depressed after experiencing a loss or a disappointment. But if the reaction is so intense, exaggerated, and prolonged that it interferes with the person's capacity to function adequately, it is likely to be considered abnormal.

Deviance

Statistical criteria equate normality with those behaviors that occur most frequently in the population. Abnormality is therefore defined in terms of those behaviors that occur least frequently. Bizarre or unusual behavior is an abnormal deviation from an accepted standard of behavior (such as an antisocial act), or a false perception of reality (such as a hallucination or delusion). This criterion can be extremely subjective; it depends on the individual being diagnosed, on the diagnostician, and on the particular cultural context.

Did You Know ? During the Victorian era, women wore six to eight layers to conceal their bodies from the neck down. Exposing an ankle was roughly equivalent to going topless at the beach today. Taboos against publicly recognizing sexuality dictated that words avoid any sexual connotation. Victorians said *limb* instead of *leg* because the word *leg* was considered erotic; even pianos and tables were said to have limbs. People who did not adhere to these codes of conduct were considered at best immoral and at worst abnormal.

Certain sexual acts, criminal behavior, and homicide are examples of acts that our society considers deviant. But social norms are far from static, and behavioral standards are not always absolute. Changes in our attitudes toward human sexuality are a prime example. Many U.S. magazines and films now openly exhibit the naked human body, and topless and bottomless nightclub entertainment is hardly newsworthy. Various sex acts are explicitly portrayed in NC-17-rated movies, and women are freer to question traditional gender roles and to act more assertively in initiating sex. Such changes in attitudes make it difficult to subscribe to absolute standards of normality.

Certain behaviors are judged abnormal in most situations. Among these are severe disorientation, hallucinations, and delusions. *Disorientation* is confusion with regard to identity, place, or time. People who are disoriented may not know who they are, where they are, or what historical era they are living in. *Hallucinations* are false impressions—either pleasant or unpleasant—that involve the senses. People who have hallucinations may hear, feel, or see things that are not really there, such as seeing loved ones who have passed away, hearing voices accusing them of vile deeds, feeling insects crawling on their bodies, or perceiving monstrous apparitions. *Delusions* are false beliefs steadfastly held by the individual despite contradictory objective evidence. A *delusion of grandeur* is a belief that one is an exalted personage, such as Jesus Christ or Joan of Arc; a *delusion of persecution* is a belief that one is controlled by others or is the victim of a conspiracy.

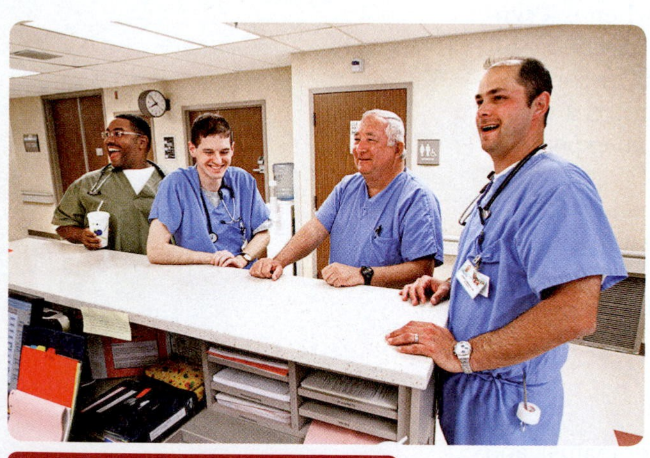
AP Images/Richmond Times-Dispatch/Dean Hoffmeyer

Societal Norms and Deviance

Societal norms often affect our definitions of normality and abnormality. When social norms begin to change, standards used to judge behaviors or roles also shift. Here we see four male nurses—men in an overwhelmingly female occupation. In the past, being a nurse would have been regarded as less than masculine. Role reversals in employment, hobbies, sports, and other activities, however, are becoming more acceptable over time.

Dysfunction

In everyday life, people are expected to fulfill various roles. Emotional problems sometimes interfere with the performance of these roles, and the resulting role dysfunction may be used as an indicator of abnormality. Thus one way to assess dysfunction is to compare an individual's performance with the requirements of a role. A productive employee who suddenly becomes unproductive in fulfilling job demands may be experiencing emotional stress. Another related way to assess dysfunction is to compare an individual's performance with his or her potential. For example, concern develops when an individual with an IQ of 150 is failing in school.

Dangerousness

Predicting the dangerousness of clients to themselves and others has become an inescapable part of clinical practice (Haggard-Grann, 2007; C. Scott & Resnick, 2009). Therapists are required

Determining What Is Abnormal

By most people's standards, the full-body tattoos of these three men would probably be considered unusual at best and bizarre at worst. Yet these three openly and proudly display them at the National Tattoo Association Convention. Such individuals may be very "normal" and functional in their work and personal lives. This leads to an important question: What constitutes abnormal behavior, and how do we recognize it?

by law to take appropriate action when they ascertain that clients may be potentially homicidal or suicidal. In the case of the former, they have a duty to warn or protect the intended victim. It is interesting that some believed Loughner to be homicidal, but he was never referred to or seen by a therapist. Despite the fear that people with mental disorders might become violent, it is a statistical rarity (Corrigan & Watson, 2005).

Cultural Considerations in Abnormality

Psychologists now recognize that all behaviors, whether normal or abnormal, originate from a cultural context. For our purposes, **culture** is the configuration of shared learned behavior that is transmitted from one generation to another by members of a particular group; the components of culture include the values, beliefs, and attitudes embedded in a group's world view and symbolized by artifacts, roles, expectations, and institutions (D. W. Sue & Sue, 2013).

Three important points should be emphasized:

1. *Culture* is not synonymous with *race* or *ethnic group*. Jewish, Polish, Irish, and Italian Americans represent diverse ethnic groups whose individual members may share a common racial classification. Yet their cultural contexts may differ substantially from one another. Likewise, an Irish American and an Italian American, despite their different ethnic heritages, may share the same cultural context.
2. Every society or group that shares and transmits behaviors to its members possesses a culture. European Americans, African Americans, Latino/Hispanic Americans, Asian Americans/Pacific Islanders, Native Americans, and other social groups within the United States each have a culture.

culture the configuration of shared values, beliefs, attitudes, and behaviors that is transmitted from one generation to another by members of a particular group and symbolized by artifacts, roles, expectations, and institutions

3. Culture is a powerful determinant of worldviews (D. W. Sue & Sue, 2013). It affects how we define normal and abnormal behaviors and how we treat disorders encountered by members of that culture.

These three points highlight a major problem with addressing abnormal behavior in a culturally sensitive way. One group's definition of mental illness may not be shared by another. This contradicts the traditional view of abnormal psychology, which is based on **cultural universality**—the assumption that a fixed set of mental disorders exists whose obvious manifestations cut across cultures (Eshun & Gurung, 2009; McGoldrick, Giordano, & Garcia-Preto, 2005). Early research supported the belief that certain mental disorders occurred worldwide, had similar processes, and were more similar than dissimilar (R. Howard, 1992). From this flowed the belief that a disorder such as depression is similar in origin, process, and manifestation in all societies, such as those across Asia, Africa, and Central and South America.

In contrast to the traditional view of cultural universality has been **cultural relativism**—the belief that lifestyles, cultural values, and worldviews affect the expression and determination of abnormal behavior. For example, a body of research supports the conclusion that acting-out behaviors associated with mental disorders are much higher in the United States than in Asia and that even Asian Americans in the United States are less likely to express symptoms via acting out (D. W. Sue & Sue, 2013; Yang & WonPat-Borja, 2007). Researchers have proposed that Asian cultural values (restraint of feelings, emphasis on self-control, and use of subtlety in approaching problems) all contribute to this difference.

Proponents of cultural relativism also point out that cultures vary in what they consider to be normal or abnormal behavior. In some societies and cultural groups, hallucinating (having false sensory impressions) is considered normal in specific situations. Yet in the United States, hallucinating is generally perceived to be a manifestation of a disorder.

cultural universality the assumption that a fixed set of mental disorders exists whose obvious manifestations cut across cultures

cultural relativism the belief that lifestyles, cultural values, and worldviews affect the expression and determination of behavior

Which view is correct? Should the criteria used to determine normality and abnormality be based on cultural universality or cultural relativism? Few mental health professionals today embrace the extreme of either position, although most gravitate toward one or the other. Proponents of cultural universality focus on a specific disorder and minimize cultural factors, while proponents of cultural relativism focus on the culture and on how the disorder is manifested within it.

Sylvain Grandadam/TSI/Getty Images

Mohsen Shandiz/Corbis

Cultural Relativism

Cultural differences often lead to misunderstandings and misinterpretations. In a society that values technological conveniences and clothing that comes from the runways of modern fashion, the lifestyles and cultural values of others may be perceived as strange. The Amish, for example, continue to rely on traditional modes of transportation (horse and buggy). And women in both Amish and Islamic cultures wear simple, concealing clothing; in their circumstances, dressing in any other way would be considered deviant. Revealing clothes are not allowed even in sunbathing or swimming.

Both views have validity. It is naive to believe that no disorders cut across different cultures and share universal characteristics.

A more fruitful approach to studying multicultural criteria of abnormality is to explore two questions:

- What is universal in human behavior that is also relevant to understanding psychopathology?
- What is the relationship between cultural norms, values, and attitudes and the incidence and manifestation of behavior disorders?

These are important questions that we hope you will ask as we continue our journey into the field of abnormal psychology.

Sociopolitical Considerations in Abnormality

The criteria for defining abnormal behavior discussed so far are not without faults. Considering behavior from a sociopolitical perspective, mental illness might instead be called "problems in living" (Ivey, D'Andrea, Ivey, & Simek-Morgan, 2007). Many of these deficiencies are related to sociopolitical implications and have been well articulated by Thomas Szasz (1987). In a radical departure from conventional beliefs, he asserted that mental illness is a myth, a fictional creation by society used to control and change people. According to Szasz, people may have "problems in living," not "mental illness." His argument stems from three beliefs: (a) that abnormal behavior is so labeled because it is different, not necessarily because it is a reflection of illness; (b) that unusual belief systems are not necessarily wrong; and (c) that abnormal behavior is frequently a reflection of something wrong with society rather than with the individual. Laing (1969) echoed a similar sentiment when he asked, Is schizophrenia a "sick" response to a healthy society or is it a "healthy" response to sick society?

According to this line of thought, individuals are labeled mentally ill because their behaviors violate the social order and their beliefs challenge the prevailing wisdom of the times. Szasz finds the concept of mental illness to be dangerous and a form of social control used by those in power. Hitler branded Jews as abnormal; political dissidents in many countries, including both China and the former Soviet Union, have often been cast as mentally ill.

Few mental health professionals would take the extreme position advocated by Szasz, but his arguments highlight an important area of concern. Those who diagnose behavior as abnormal must be sensitive not only to such variables as psychological orientation but also to individual value systems, societal norms and values, and potential sociopolitical ramifications.

In the past, "mentally healthy" African Americans were described as interested in servitude and faithful to their masters. In his article "Diseases and Peculiarities of the Negro Race," Cartwright (1851) described two forms of mental disorders found among black people: (a) those who had an "unnatural desire for freedom" and ran away were considered to have *drapetomania*, and (b) those who resisted slavery, argued, and created disturbances were diagnosed with *dyaesthesia aethiopica*, a term to describe "rascality."

The Frequency and Burden of Mental Disorders

A student once asked one of the authors of this text, "How crazy is this nation?" This question, put in somewhat more scientific terms, has occupied psychologists for some time. **Psychiatric epidemiology**, the study of the prevalence of mental illness in a society, provides insights into factors that contribute to the occurrence of specific mental disorders. To address this question, some terms need to be clarified. The **prevalence** of a disorder indicates the percentage of people in a population who have the disorder at a given point in time. **Incidence** refers to the

psychiatric epidemiology the study of the prevalence of mental illness in a society

prevalence the percentage of individuals in a targeted population who have a particular disorder during a specific period of time

incidence number of new cases of a disorder that appear in an identified population within a specified time period

FIGURE 1.1

1-Year Prevalence of Mental Disorders in Adult Americans and Lifetime Prevalence of Mental Disorders in American Adolescents

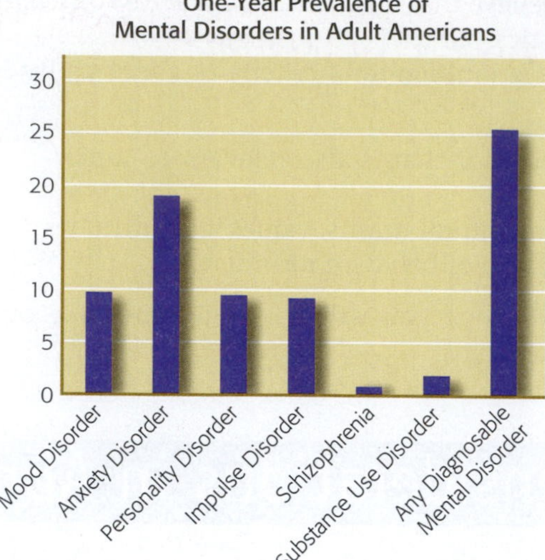

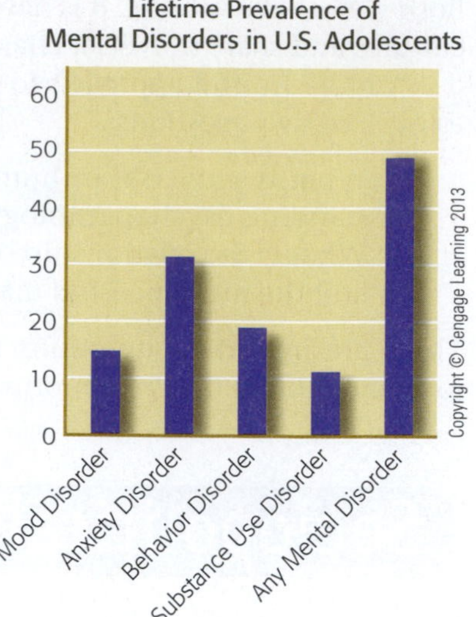

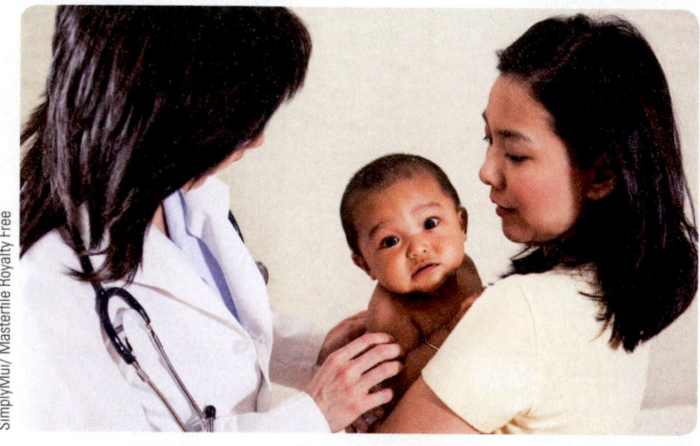

SimplyMui/ Masterfile Royalty Free

Mental disorders are believed to begin early in life. Well baby visits are important to monitor developmental milestones. Identifying possible biological, psychological, and social abnormalities is important to preventing the development of mental disorders in later life.

onset or occurrence of a given disorder over some period of time. From this information, we can find out how frequently or infrequently various disturbances occur in the population. We can also consider how the prevalence of disorders varies by ethnicity, gender, and age, and whether current mental health practices are effective. See Figure 1.1 for the statistical breakdown of 1-year prevalence rates.

In a study investigating the **lifetime prevalence** of mental disorders in U.S. youths (Merikangas, et al., 2010), data from a face-to-face survey of more than 10,000 youths between the ages of 13 and 18 revealed the following: Nearly half of the youths met the criteria for at least one psychological disorder, and of this group, 40 percent met the criteria for an additional disorder. Anxiety disorder was the most common (31.9 percent), followed by behavior disorders (19.1 percent), mood disorders (14.3 percent), and substance-use disorders (11.4 percent). Severe impairment or distress was reported by 22.2 percent of those found to have a mental disorder. Figure 1.1 summarizes prevalence data from these studies.

The cost and burden of mental disorders to our society are indeed a major source of concern. Not only do 25 percent of adults have a diagnosable mental health condition in a given year, but many more people experience "mental health problems" that do not meet the criteria for a mental disorder. These problems may be equally debilitating unless adequately treated.

These epidemiological findings are troubling, to say the least. Clearly, mental disturbances are widespread, and many people currently have them. What is more troubling is that two thirds of all people with diagnosable mental disorders are not receiving or seeking mental health services (President's New Freedom Commission on Mental Health, 2003). In addition, spending on mental health services continues to decline.

Did You Know ?

About 15 percent of Canadians and 20 percent of U.S. Americans stated they would probably not seek care for mental health problems even if they had a severe disorder! Negative attitudes toward help-seeking behavior are most associated with socioeconomically challenged young, single, less-educated men (Jagdeo, Cox, Stein, & Sareen, 2009), antisocial personalities, and those who abuse drugs. Aversion to seeking therapy is associated with social stigma.

lifetime prevalence the percentage of people in the population who have had a disorder at some point in their lives

Stereotypes About People Who Are Mentally Disturbed

U.S. Americans tend to be suspicious of people with mental disorders. Are people with mental illness really maniacs who at any moment may be seized by uncontrollable urges to murder, rape, or maim? Such portrayals seem to emerge from the news media and the entertainment industry, but they are rarely accurate. Indeed, Jared Lee Loughner's actions are a statistical anomaly. Violence in people with a mental disorder is a rarity (Corrigan & Watson, 2005; Grann & Langstrom, 2007). People with mental disturbances are subject to rampant stereotyping and popular misconceptions.

Popular movie portrayals of mental disorders often perpetuate stereotypes and myths by showing the extremes in abnormality. In *Me, Myself, and Irene*, Jim Carrey plays a nice-guy cop with dissociative identity disorder.

MYTH VS REALITY

MYTH People who are mentally disturbed can always be recognized by their abnormal behavior.

REALITY People who are mentally disturbed people are not always distinguishable from others on the basis of consistently unusual behavior. There are two main reasons for this difficulty. First, no sharp dividing line usually exists between normal and abnormal behavior. Second, even when people have some form of emotional disturbance, their difficulties may not always be detectable in their behavior.

MYTH People who are mentally disturbed have inherited their disorders. If one member of a family has an emotional breakdown, other members will probably suffer a similar fate.

REALITY The belief that insanity runs in certain families has caused misery and undue anxiety for many people. Heredity does play a role in some mental disorders, such as schizophrenia and mood disorders. However, even though heredity may predispose an individual to certain disorders, mental problems are the result of an interaction of biological, psychological, social, and cultural factors.

MYTH Mentally disturbed people can never be cured and will never be able to function normally or hold jobs in the community.

REALITY This is an erroneous belief. Nearly three-fourths of people who are hospitalized with severe mental disorders will improve and go on to lead productive lives.

MYTH People become mentally disturbed because they are weak willed. To avoid emotional disorders or cure oneself of them, one need only exercise willpower.

REALITY Needing help to resolve difficulties does not indicate a lack of willpower. In fact, recognizing one's own need for help is a sign of strength rather than a sign of weakness. Many problems stem from situations not under the individual's control, such as the death of a loved one or loss of a job. Other problems stem from lifelong patterns of faulty learning; it is naive to expect that a simple exercise of will can override years of experience.

MYTH Mental illness is always a deficit, and a person who has it can never contribute anything of worth until cured.

REALITY Many people with mental illness were never "cured," but they nevertheless made great contributions to humanity. Ernest Hemingway, one of the great writers of the 20th century and winner of a Nobel Prize for Literature, experienced lifelong depression,

(continued)

MYTH VS REALITY

alcoholism, and frequent hospitalizations. The famous Dutch painter Vincent van Gogh produced great works of art despite the fact that he was severely disturbed. Others, such as Pablo Picasso and Edgar Allan Poe, contributed major artistic and literary works while seriously disturbed.

MYTH Mentally disturbed people are unstable and potentially dangerous.

REALITY The vast majority of individuals who are mentally ill do not commit crimes, do not harm others, and do not get into trouble with the law. According to epidemiologic surveys (Elbogen & Johnson, 2009), there is a small elevation of risk of violence, especially among individuals with a dual diagnosis (a mental disorder and substance abuse), but the risk is minimal (Eronen, Angermeyer, & Schulze, 1998; Swanson, 1994).

CHECKPOINT REVIEW

1. Name and describe the four criteria used by clinicians to determine abnormality.
2. Why must clinicians consider cultural factors in determining abnormal behavior? Can you give examples?
3. Compare and contrast the concepts of cultural universality and cultural relativism.
4. How common or frequent are mental disorders?
5. What are some common stereotypes of people who are mentally disturbed?

Did You Know?

Famous people with mental disorders who have made important contributions to the world include J. K. Rowling, Winston Churchill, and Virginia Woolf, pictured here, as well as Michelangelo, Abraham Lincoln, Isaac Newton, Ludwig van Beethoven, Patrick Kennedy, Buzz Aldrin, and Janet Jackson.

©Presselect/Alamy

©David Cole/Alamy

George C. Beresford/Hulton Archive/Getty Images

Historical Perspectives on Abnormal Behavior

Most ideas about abnormal behavior are firmly rooted in the system of beliefs that operate in a given society at a given time. Much of this history section is based on discussions of deviant behavior by F. G. Alexander and Selesnick (1966), Hunter and Macalpine (1963), Neugebauer (1979), Spanos (1978), and Zilboorg and Henry (1941). We must be aware, however, that our journey is necessarily culture-bound and that other civilizations (non-Western) have histories of their own.

Prehistoric and Ancient Beliefs

Prehistoric societies some half a million years ago did not distinguish sharply between mental and physical disorders. Abnormal behaviors, from simple headaches to convulsive attacks, were attributed to evil spirits that inhabited or controlled the afflicted person's body. According to historians, these ancient peoples attributed many forms of illness to demonic possession, sorcery, or the behest of an offended ancestral spirit. Within this system of belief, called *demonology*, the victim was usually held at least partly responsible for the misfortune.

It has been suggested that Stone Age cave dwellers may have treated behavior disorders with a surgical method called **trephining**, in which part of the skull was chipped away to provide an opening through which the evil spirit could escape. People may have believed that when the evil spirit left, the person would return to his or her normal state. Surprisingly, some trephined skulls have been found to have healed over, indicating that some patients survived this extremely crude operation. Another treatment method used by the early Greeks, Chinese, Hebrews, and Egyptians was exorcism. In an **exorcism**, elaborate prayers, noises, emetics (drugs that induce vomiting), and extreme measures such as flogging and starvation were used to cast evil spirits out of an afflicted person's body.

Trephining: Evidence of Therapy?

Anthropologists speculate that this human skull is evidence of trephining, the centuries-old manner of treating mentally disturbed individuals by chipping a hole in the skull to release the evil spirit causing the bizarre behaviors.

Naturalistic Explanations: Greco-Roman Thought

With the flowering of Greek civilization and its continuation into the era of Roman rule (500 B.C.–A.D. 500), naturalistic explanations gradually became distinct from supernatural ones. Early thinkers, such as Hippocrates (460–370 B.C.), a physician who is often called the father of medicine, actively questioned prevailing superstitious beliefs and proposed much more rational and scientific explanations for mental disorders. He believed that, because the brain was the central organ of intellectual activity, deviant behavior was caused by **brain pathology**, that is, a dysfunction or disease of the brain. He also considered heredity and environment important factors in psychopathology. He classified mental illnesses into three categories—mania, melancholia, and phrenitis (brain fever)—and for each category gave detailed clinical descriptions of such disorders as paranoia, alcoholic delirium, and epilepsy. Many of his descriptions of symptoms are still used today, eloquent testimony to his keen powers of observation.

Other thinkers who contributed to the organic explanation of behavior were the philosopher Plato and the Greek physician Galen, who practiced in Rome. Plato (429–347 B.C.) carried on the thinking of Hippocrates; he insisted that people who were mentally disturbed were the responsibility of their families and should not be punished for their behavior. Galen (A.D. 129–199) made major contributions through his scientific examination of the nervous system and his explanation of the role of the brain and central nervous system in mental functioning. His greatest contribution may have been the codification of all European medical knowledge from Hippocrates's time to his own.

Reversion to Supernatural Explanations: The Middle Ages

With the collapse of the Roman Empire and the rise of Christianity, rational and scientific thought gave way to a re-emphasis on the supernatural. Religious dogma included the beliefs that nature was a reflection of divine will and beyond human reason and that earthly life was a prelude to the "true" life (after death). Scientific inquiry—attempts to understand, classify, explain, and control nature—was less important than accepting nature as a manifestation of God's will.

trephining a surgical method from the Stone Age in which part of the skull was chipped away to provide an opening through which an evil spirit could escape

exorcism treatment method used by the early Greeks, Chinese, Hebrews, and Egyptians in which prayers, noises, emetics, flogging, and starvation were used to cast evil spirits out of an afflicted person's body

brain pathology a dysfunction or disease of the brain

Exorcism of a demon from a possessed woman (oil on panel), Salimbeni, Lorenzo (1374-c.1420)/Museo Horne, Florence, Italy/Giraudon/The Bridgeman Art Library

Casting Out the Cause of Abnormality

During the Middle Ages, people with mental disorders were often perceived as being victims of a demonic possession. The most prevalent form of treatment was exorcism, usually conducted by religious leaders who used prayers, incantations, and sometimes torturous physical techniques to cast the evil spirit from the bodies of the afflicted.

During this period, treatment of people who were mentally ill sometimes consisted of torturous exorcism procedures, seen as appropriate to combat Satan and eject him from the possessed person's body. Prayers, curses, obscene epithets, and the sprinkling of holy water—as well as such drastic and painful "therapy" as flogging, starving, and immersion in hot water—were used to drive out the devil. The humane treatments that Hippocrates had advocated centuries earlier were challenged severely. A time of trouble for everyone, the Middle Ages were especially bleak for the mentally ill.

Belief in the power of the supernatural became so prevalent and intense that it frequently affected whole populations. Beginning in Italy early in the 13th century, large numbers of people were affected by various forms of **mass madness**, or group hysteria, in which a great many people exhibit similar symptoms that have no apparent physical cause. One of the better-known manifestations of this disorder was **tarantism**, a mania characterized by wild raving, jumping, dancing, and convulsing. A person would leap up, believing himself or herself to have been bitten, and run out into the street or marketplace, jumping and raving, to be joined by others who believed that they had also been bitten. The mania soon spread throughout the rest of Europe, where it became known as *Saint Vitus's dance.*

How can these phenomena be explained? Stress and fear are often associated with outbreaks of mass hysteria. During the 13th century, for example, there was enormous social unrest. The bubonic plague had decimated one third of the population of Europe. War, famine, and pestilence were rampant, and the social order of the times was crumbling.

Witchcraft: 15th Through 17th Centuries

Most psychiatric historians argue that mental disorders were at the root of witchcraft persecutions (Alexander & Selesnick, 1966; Deutsch, 1949; Zilboorg & Henry, 1941). Torture was used to obtain confessions from suspected witches, and many victims—most of them with mental disorders—confessed because they preferred death to prolonged agony. Thousands of innocent men, women, and even children were beheaded, burned alive, or mutilated. Witch hunts occurred in both colonial America and Europe. The witchcraft trials of 1692 in Salem, Massachusetts, were infamous. Several hundred people were accused, many were imprisoned and tortured, and 20 were killed. It has been estimated that some 20,000 people (mainly women) were killed as witches in Scotland alone, and that more than 100,000 throughout Europe were executed as witches from the middle of the 15th to the end of the 17th century.

mass madness group hysteria in which a great many people exhibit similar symptoms that have no apparent physical cause

tarantism a mania or form of mass hysteria prevalent during the Middle Ages, characterized by wild raving, jumping, dancing, and convulsing; also known as *St. Vitus's dance*

humanism a philosophical movement that emphasizes human welfare and the worth and uniqueness of the individual

The Rise of Humanism: The Renaissance

A resurgence of rational and scientific inquiry during the Renaissance (14th through 16th centuries) led to great advances in science and **humanism,** a philosophical movement that emphasizes human welfare and the worth and uniqueness of the individual. Until this time, most asylums were at best custodial centers in which people who were mentally disturbed were chained, caged, starved, whipped, and even exhibited to the public for a small fee, much like animals in a zoo. The term *bedlam,* for example, has become synonymous with chaos and disorder; it was the shortened name of Bethlehem Hospital, an asylum in London that has come to symbolize the cruel treatment of people who were mentally ill. Patients were bound by chains, left untreated, and exhibited to the public in the courtyard. They were frequently unfed and left unattended and untreated for physical ailments and starvation, and their cries of pain and neglect were ignored.

But the new way of thinking held that if people were "mentally ill" and not possessed, then they should be treated as though they were sick. A number of new methods for treating people who were mentally ill reflected this humanistic spirit. In 1563 Johann Weyer (1515–1588), a German physician, published a revolutionary book that challenged the foundations of ideas about witchcraft. Weyer asserted that many people who were tortured, imprisoned, and burned as witches were mentally disturbed, not possessed by demons. His book was severely criticized and banned by both church and state, but it proved to be a forerunner of the humanitarian perspective on mental illness. Others eventually followed his lead.

Dorothea Dix (1802–1887)

During a time when women were discouraged from political participation, Dorothea Dix, a New England schoolteacher, worked tirelessly as a social reformer to improve the deplorable conditions in which people who were mentally ill were forced to live.

The Reform Movement: 18th and 19th Centuries

In France, Philippe Pinel (1745–1826), a physician, was put in charge of la Bicêtre, a hospital for insane men in Paris. Pinel instituted what came to be known as the **moral treatment movement**—a shift to more humane treatment of people who were mentally disturbed. He ordered that patients' chains be removed, replaced dungeons with sunny rooms, encouraged exercise outdoors on the hospital grounds, and treated patients with kindness and reason. Surprising many disbelievers, the freed patients did not become violent; instead, this humane treatment seemed to foster recovery and improve behavior. Pinel later instituted similar, equally successful, reforms at la Salpêtrière, a large mental hospital for women in Paris.

In England, William Tuke (1732–1822), a prominent Quaker tea merchant, established a retreat at York for the "moral treatment" of mental patients. At this pleasant country estate, the patients worked, prayed, rested, and talked out their problems—all in an atmosphere of kindness, quite unlike that of the lunatic asylums of the time.

In the United States, three individuals—Benjamin Rush, Dorothea Dix, and Clifford Beers—made important contributions to the moral treatment movement. Rush (1745–1813), widely acclaimed as the father of U.S. psychiatry, attempted to train physicians to treat mental patients and to introduce more humane treatment policies into mental hospitals. He insisted that patients be accorded respect and dignity and that they be gainfully employed while hospitalized, an idea that anticipated the modern concept of work therapy. Yet Rush was not unaffected by the established practices and beliefs of his times: His theories were influenced by astrology, and his remedies included bloodletting and purgatives.

Dorothea Dix (1802–1887), a New England schoolteacher, was the preeminent U.S. social reformer of the 19th century. While teaching Sunday school to female prisoners, she became familiar with the deplorable conditions in which jailed mental patients were forced to live. (Prisons and poorhouses were commonly used to incarcerate these patients.) For the next 40 years, Dix worked tirelessly for people who were mentally ill. She campaigned for reform legislation and funds to establish suitable mental hospitals and asylums. She raised millions of dollars, established more than 30 modern mental hospitals, and greatly improved conditions in countless others. But the struggle for reform was far from over. Although the large hospitals that replaced jails and poorhouses had better physical facilities, the humanistic, personal concern of the moral treatment movement was lacking.

moral treatment movement movement instituted by Philippe Pinel that resulted in a shift to more humane treatment of people who were mentally disturbed

CONTROVERSY:

What Role Should Spirituality and Religion Play in Mental Health Care?

The role of demons, witches, and possession in explaining abnormal behavior has been part and parcel of past religious teachings. Psychology's reluctance to incorporate religion into the profession may be understandable in light of the historical role played by the church in the oppression of people who are mentally ill. Furthermore, psychology as a science stresses objectivity and naturalistic explanations of human behavior; this approach is often at odds with religion as a belief system (Engh, 2006; D. W. Sue & Sue, 2013).

Until recently, the mental health profession had been largely silent about the influence or importance of spirituality and religion in mental health. Thus, during therapy or work with clients, therapists have generally avoided discussing such topics (Saunders, Miller, & Bright, 2010). It has been found, for example, that many therapists (a) do not feel comfortable or competent in discussing spiritual or religious issues with their clients, (b) are concerned they will appear proselytizing or judgmental if they touch on such topics, (c) believe they may usurp the role of the clergy, and (d) may feel inauthentic addressing client concerns, especially if the therapists are atheist or agnostic (Gonsiorek, Richards, Pargament, & McMinn, 2009; Knox, Catlin, Casper, & Schlosser, 2005; Saunders et al., 2010; D. W. Sue & Sue, 2013).

Yet it has been found that more than 80 percent of U.S. Americans say that religion is important in their lives; that in both medical and mental health care, patients express a strong desire for providers to discuss spiritual and faith issues with them; and that racial and ethnic minority groups believe that spiritual issues are intimately linked to their cultural identities (Gallup, 2009; Saunders et al., 2010; D. W. Sue & Sue, 2013). More compelling are findings that reveal a positive association between spirituality or religion and optimal health outcomes, longevity, and lower levels of anxiety, depression, suicide, and substance abuse (Cornah, 2006; Thoresen, 1998). Many mental health professionals are becoming increasingly open to the potential benefits of spirituality in the treatment of patients. As part of that process, psychologists are making distinctions between spirituality and religion. Spirituality is an animating life force that is inclusive of religion and speaks to the thoughts, feelings, and behaviors related to a transcendent state. Religion is narrower, involving a specific doctrine and particular system of beliefs. Spirituality can be pursued outside a specific religion because it is transpersonal and includes one's capacity for creativity, growth, and love (Cornish & Wade, 2010). Mental health professionals are increasingly recognizing that people are thinking, feeling, behaving, social, cultural, and **spiritual beings**.

For Further Consideration

1. What thoughts do you have about the role of spirituality and religion in psychology and mental health?
2. Should therapists avoid discussing these matters with patients and leave it to the clergy?
3. If you were in therapy, how important would it be to discuss your religious or spiritual beliefs?

Did You Know? Although the practice of exorcism is ancient, it is still recognized in Catholicism, the Eastern Orthodox Church, and some Protestant sects. The Church of England has an official exorcist in each diocese. In general, possessed people are not considered evil in themselves, so exorcism is seen as treatment rather than punishment.

That movement was given further impetus in 1908 with the publication of *A Mind That Found Itself*, a book by Clifford Beers (1876–1943) about his own mental collapse. His book describes the terrible treatment he and other patients experienced in three mental institutions, where they were beaten, choked, spat on, and restrained with straitjackets. His vivid account aroused great public sympathy and attracted the interest and support of the psychiatric establishment, including such eminent figures as psychologist-philosopher William James. Beers founded the National Committee for Mental Hygiene (forerunner of the National Mental Health Association, now known as Mental Health America), an organization dedicated to educating the public about mental illness and about the need to treat people who are mentally ill rather than punish them for their unusual behaviors.

It would be naive to believe that these reforms have totally eliminated inhumane treatment of people who are mentally disturbed. Books such as Mary Jane Ward's *The Snake Pit* (1946) and films such as Frederick Wiseman's *Titicut Follies* (1967) continued to document harsh treatment of mental patients. Even the severest critic of the mental health system, however, would have to admit that conditions and treatment for people who are mentally ill have improved in this century.

spiritual being a person's animating life force that speaks to the thoughts, feelings, and behaviors related to a transcendent state or one's capacity for creativity, growth, and love

Causes: Early Viewpoints

Paralleling the rise of humanism in the treatment of mental illness was an inquiry into its causes. Two schools of thought emerged. The **biological (organic) viewpoint** holds that mental disorders are the result of physiological damage or disease; the *psychological viewpoint* stresses an emotional basis for mental illness. It is important to note that most people were not extreme adherents of one or the other. Rather, they tended to combine elements of both.

Emil Kraepelin (1856–1926)

In an 1883 publication, psychiatrist Emil Kraepelin proposed that mental disorders could be directly linked to organic brain disorders and further proposed a diagnostic classification system for all disorders.

The Biological Viewpoint

Hippocrates's suggestion of an organic explanation for abnormal behavior was ignored during the Middle Ages but revived after the Renaissance. Not until the 19th century, however, did the biological or organic view—the belief that mental disorders have a physical or physiological basis—become important. The ideas of Wilhelm Griesinger (1817–1868), a German psychiatrist who believed that all mental disorders had physiological causes, received considerable attention. Emil Kraepelin (1856–1926), a follower of Griesinger, observed that certain symptoms tend to occur regularly in clusters, called **syndromes**. Kraepelin believed that each cluster of symptoms represented a mental disorder with its own unique—and clearly specifiable—cause, course, and outcome. In his *Textbook of Psychiatry* (1883/1923), Kraepelin outlined a system for classifying mental illnesses on the basis of their organic causes. That system was the original basis for the diagnostic categories in the *Diagnostic and Statistical Manual of Mental Disorders* (DSM), the classification system of the American Psychiatric Association. The biological viewpoint gained even greater strength with the discovery of the organic basis of *general paresis*, a progressively degenerative and irreversible physical and mental disorder (paresis is syphilis of the brain). As medical breakthroughs in the study of the nervous system occurred, many scientists were hopeful that a biological basis of all mental disorders could be found.

The Psychological Viewpoint

Some scientists noted, however, that certain types of emotional disorders were not associated with any organic disease in the patient. Such observations led to the **psychological viewpoint**—the belief that mental disorders are caused by psychological and emotional factors rather than organic or biological ones. For example, the inability to attain personal goals and resolve interpersonal conflicts could lead to intense feelings of frustration, depression, failure, and anger, which may consequently lead to disturbed behavior.

Mesmerism and Hypnotism

The unique and exotic techniques of Friedrich Anton Mesmer (1734–1815), an Austrian physician who practiced in Paris, presented an early challenge to the biological point of view. Mesmer developed a highly controversial treatment that came to be called *mesmerism* and that was the forerunner of the modern practice of hypnotism.

Mesmer performed his most miraculous cures in the treatment of *hysteria*—the appearance of symptoms such as blindness, deafness, loss of bodily feeling, and paralysis that seemed to have no organic basis. His techniques for curing this illness

biological (organic) viewpoint the belief that mental disorders have a physical or physiological basis

syndrome certain symptoms that tend to occur regularly in clusters

psychological viewpoint the belief that mental disorders are caused by psychological and emotional factors rather than organic or biological ones

©Everett Collection Inc/Alamy

Friedrich Anton Mesmer (1734–1815)

Mesmer's techniques were a forerunner of modern hypnotism. Although highly controversial and ultimately discredited, Mesmer's efforts stimulated inquiry into psychological and emotional factors, rather than biological factors, as causes of mental disorders.

involved inducing a sleeplike state, during which his patients became highly susceptible to suggestion. During this state, their symptoms often disappeared.

The idea that psychological processes could produce mental and physical disturbances began to gain credence among several physicians who were using hypnosis. Among them was the Viennese doctor Josef Breuer (1842–1925). He discovered accidentally that after one of his female patients spoke quite freely about her past traumatic experiences while in a trance, many of her symptoms abated or disappeared. He achieved even greater success when the patient recalled previously forgotten memories and relived their emotional aspects. This latter technique became known as the **cathartic method**, a therapeutic use of verbal expression to release pent-up emotional conflicts. It foreshadowed psychoanalysis, whose founder, Sigmund Freud (1856–1939), had a great and lasting influence in the field of abnormal psychology.

CHECKPOINT REVIEW

1. Define trephining and exorcism. What belief system do they share in common when used as forms of treatment for the mentally disturbed?
2. Describe how the rise of humanism and the reform movement altered our view and treatment of people who are mentally disturbed.
3. Compare and contrast the basic assumptions of the biological and psychological points of view.
4. In what way did mesmerism or hypnosis reinforce the view that mental disorders could be psychological in nature?

Contemporary Trends in Abnormal Psychology

Our understanding and treatment of psychopathological disorders has changed significantly over the past 30 years. Views of abnormality continue to evolve as they incorporate the effects of several major events and trends in the field: (a) the influence of multicultural psychology, (b) resilience and the focus on positive psychology, and (c) changes in the therapeutic landscape (the drug revolution, prescription privileges for psychiatrists, evidence-based treatments, and managed health care).

The Influence of Multicultural Psychology

Psychological research published in scholarly journals focuses too narrowly on U.S. Americans, who comprise *only 5 percent* of the world's population (Arnett, 2008). Can the findings, principles, and theories of psychology and mental health derived from the United States be applicable to the "neglected" 95 percent of the rest of the world? Are human beings similar enough that studying them in only one part of the world allows us to generalize findings to people residing in other parts of the world? Do stark differences in income, education, health, and life expectancy between developing countries and the United States affect psychological functioning? Furthermore, how important are cultural differences in determining the causes and manifestation of mental disorders?

The answers seem to indicate that U.S. psychology is too insular, that it may not be universally applicable, and that differences in culture, standard of living, and life circumstances have major influence on psychological functioning (Arnett, 2008; Cole, 2006; Valsiner, 2007). Even the DSM recognizes the existence of "culture-bound syndromes," mental disorders unique to certain cultures. The focus on global

cathartic method a therapeutic use of verbal expression to release pent-up emotional conflicts

psychology has reawakened the profession to the importance of cultural and multicultural psychology (Shweder et al., 2006).

As international and global psychology have challenged the universality of Western psychology, so have the changing demographics of the United States. We are fast becoming a multicultural, multiracial, and multilingual society (Figure 1.2). The U.S. Census Bureau reveals that within several decades, members of racial and ethnic minorities will become a numerical majority (D. W. Sue & Sue, 2013). These changes have been referred to as the diversification of the United States or, literally, the changing complexion of society.

Diversity has had a major impact on the mental health profession, creating a new field of study called **multicultural psychology**. Mental health professionals now recognize the need to (a) increase their cultural sensitivity, (b) acquire knowledge of the worldviews and lifestyles of a culturally diverse population, and (c) develop culturally relevant therapy approaches in working with different groups (American Psychological Association, 2003; D. W. Sue & Sue, 2013). Culture, ethnicity, and gender are now increasingly recognized as powerful influences on many aspects of normal and abnormal human development. Four primary dimensions related to cultural diversity—social conditioning, cultural values and influences, sociopolitical influences, and bias in diagnosis—seem to explain how cultural forces exert their influence.

Social Conditioning How we are raised, what values are instilled in us, and how we are expected to behave in fulfilling our roles seem to have a major effect on the types of disorder we are most likely to exhibit. In U.S. culture, men have traditionally been raised to fulfill the masculine role, to be independent, assertive, courageous, active, unsentimental, and objective. Women, in contrast, are commonly raised to be dependent, helpful, fragile, self-deprecating, conforming, empathetic, and emotional. Some mental health professionals believe that, as a result, women are more likely to internalize their conflicts (resulting in anxiety and depression), whereas men are more likely to externalize and act out (resulting in drug or alcohol abuse). Although gender roles have begun to change, their effects continue to be widely felt.

Cultural Values and Influences Mental health professionals now recognize that types of mental disorders differ from country to country and that differences in cultural traditions among various racial and ethnic minority groups in the United States may influence susceptibility to certain emotional disorders. Among Latino/Hispanic Americans and Asian Americans, experiencing physical complaints is a common and culturally accepted means of expressing psychological and emotional stress (Santiago-Rivera, Arredondo, & Gallardo-Cooper, 2002; Yang & WonPat-Borja, 2007). People with these cultural backgrounds believe that physical problems cause emotional distress and that the emotional disturbance will disappear as soon as appropriate treatment for the physical illness is instituted. In addition, mental illness among Asians is seen as a source of shame and disgrace, although physical illness is acceptable (D. W. Sue & Sue, 2013). Asian values also emphasize restraint of strong feelings. Thus, when stress is encountered, mental health professionals are likely to hear complaints involving headaches, fatigue, restlessness, and disturbances of sleep and appetite.

Sociopolitical Influences In response to a history of prejudice, discrimination, and racism, many minorities have adopted various behaviors (in particular, behaviors toward white people) that have proved important for their survival (Ponterotto, Utsey, & Pedersen, 2006; D. W. Sue, 2010). Mental health professionals may define these behaviors as abnormal and deviant, yet from the minority group's perspective, such behaviors may function as healthy survival mechanisms. Early personality studies of African Americans concluded that, as a group, they tend to appear more "suspicious,"

Did You Know?

Psychologically, how different are the rest of the world and the United States? Do these differences influence psychological functioning and mental disorders?

- Half the world's population lives on $2 per day; 80 percent of the world's population lives on a family income of less than $6,000 per year.
- In developing countries, 1 in 5 children do not complete primary school; only half enroll in secondary school.
- About 17 percent of children are malnourished, in comparison to less than 1 percent in the United States.
- Life expectancy in developing countries is 15 years less than in the United States.

Source: Taken from Kent & Haub, 2005; United Nations Development Programme, 2006

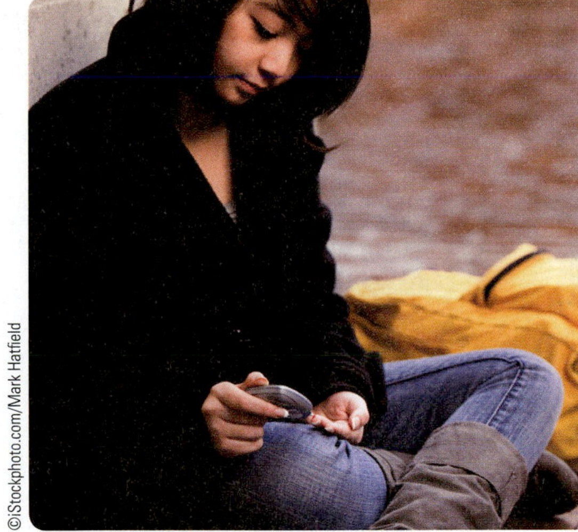

©iStockphoto.com/Mark Hatfield

Diversity a Fact of Life

This Latina student represents the increasing diversity of the United States.

multicultural psychology an approach that stresses the importance of culture, race, ethnicity, gender, age, socioeconomic class, and other similar factors in its effort to understand and treat abnormal behavior

FIGURE 1.2

Census 2010 Racial and Ethnic Composition of the United States

The rapid demographic transformation of the United States is illustrated by the fact that minorities now constitute an increasing proportion of the population. Several trends are evident. First, within several short decades, people of color will constitute a numerical majority. Second, the number of Latino/Hispanic Americans has surpassed the number of African Americans. Third, mental health providers will increasingly be coming into contact with clients who differ from them in race, ethnicity, and culture.

Source: http://www.census.gov/newsroom/release/archives/2010_census/cb11-cn125htm

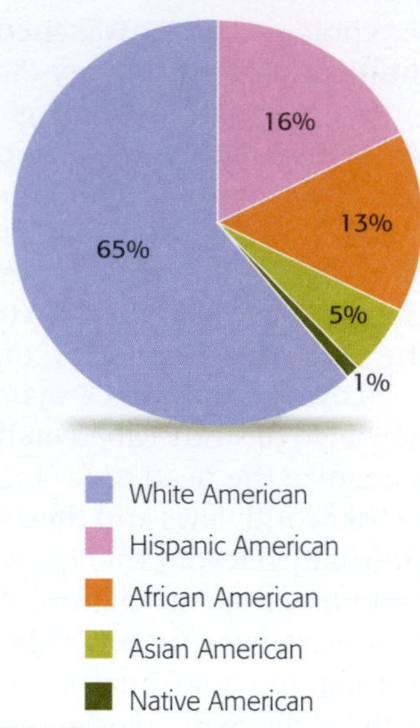

Did You Know?

- More than 50 percent of California's population is composed of people of color.
- Thirty percent of New York City residents were born in other countries.
- Seventy percent of the population of the District of Columbia is African American.
- Thirty-seven percent of the population of San Francisco is Asian American/Pacific Islander.
- Sixty-seven percent of the population of Miami is Latino/Hispanic American.

"mistrustful," and "paranoid" than their white counterparts. But are African Americans inherently pathological, as studies suggest, or are they making healthy, adaptive responses? Members of minority groups who have been victims of discrimination and oppression in a society not yet free of racism have good reason to be suspicious and distrustful of white society. The "paranoid orientation" may reflect not only survival skills but also *accurate reality testing*. Certain behaviors and characteristics need to be evaluated not only by an absolute standard but also by the sociopolitical context in which they arise.

Cultural and Ethnic Bias in Diagnosis Epidemiological studies reporting the distribution and types of mental disorders that occur in the population may be prone to bias on the part of clinicians and researchers. Mental health professionals are not immune to inheriting the prejudicial attitudes, biases, and stereotypes of the larger society. Even the most enlightened and well-intentioned mental health professionals may be victims of race, gender, and social class bias. One source of bias is the tendency to overpathologize—to exaggerate the severity of disorders—among clients from particular socioeconomic, racial, or ethnic groups whose cultural values or lifestyles differ markedly from the clinician's own. The overpathologizing of disorders has been found to occur in psychological evaluations of African Americans, Latino/Hispanic Americans, and women (Lopez & Hernandez, 1987; D. W. Sue & Sue, 2013).

Positive Psychology

positive psychology the philosophical and scientific study of positive human functioning and the strengths and assets of individuals, families, and communities

optimal human functioning qualities such as subjective well-being, happiness, optimism, resilience, hope, courage, ability to cope with stress, self-actualization, and self-determinism

spirituality the animating life force or energy of the human condition that is broader than but inclusive of religion

Positive psychology is a branch of the profession that seeks to add balance to our view of human functioning; its purpose is to study, develop, and achieve scientific understanding of positive human qualities that build thriving individuals, families, and communities (M. E. P. Seligman & Csikszentmihalyi, 2000). Positive psychology and **optimal human functioning** can be divided into three domains (M. E. P. Seligman, 2007; M. E. P. Seligman & Csikszentmihalyi, 2000). First, subjectively, it can be measured in feelings of well-being, contentment, and satisfaction in the past; hope and optimism for the future; and flow and happiness in the present. Second, at the individual level, it is about positive traits such as resilience, capacity for love, courage, interpersonal skills, **spirituality**, and wisdom. Third, at the group level, it is about civic virtues and the institutions that move us toward better citizenship and responsibility. Despite his combat trauma, Randy seems to exhibit many of these traits.

FOCUS ON RESILIENCE

Psychology Is Also the Study of Strengths and Assets

Randy and Billy grew up in the same neighborhood, went to the same high school, joined the army together, and served two tours of duty in Iraq before being honorably discharged. There they encountered constant threat of death, saw many of their buddies killed or wounded, and endured inhuman hardships related to their brief capture by enemy forces. While in the army, Billy used drugs and alcohol as a form of self-medication. Although Randy also used drugs, he never did so excessively.

Upon their return home, Randy and Billy both enrolled in a community college with the hopes of opening a car repair business. However, Billy's mental health deteriorated quickly. He had anxiety, depression, and flashbacks about the war, became heavily involved in drugs, and dropped out of college. As a result, they lost touch with one another. Unlike Billy, however, Randy finished his college training and opened a small, successful automobile repair shop with three employees. He has since married, and he and his wife are expecting their first child. In addition, he has become actively involved in helping other veterans at the local VA hospital.

After years of not seeing his friend Billy, Randy accidentally ran into him late one afternoon. Billy sat on a milk crate on a street corner, talking to himself, and occasionally swore at pedestrians. He had an unkempt appearance and wore dirty clothes. It was obvious he had not bathed for some time. He was begging for handouts and would verbally assail passersby who did not drop money into his hat. Billy did not seem to recognize Randy, even when addressed by name. He avoided eye contact, refused to speak, and simply pointed to his hat. Feeling sorry for his friend, Randy gave him all the cash he had before leaving.

Shutterstock

Billy's mental state and his war trauma are certainly understandable in light of the large numbers of soldiers returning from Iraq with post-traumatic stress disorder, anxiety attacks, drug or alcohol abuse, and depression. The constant threat of bodily harm or death to soldiers serving in war zones is a reality, and the trauma they experience is often beyond human endurance. We know much about war trauma, post-traumatic stress disorders, and about the psychological harm that combat has on soldiers like Billy. In many ways, we know more about pathology than about resilience and strength; we know more about mental illness than mental health, and thus we know more about Billy than we do about Randy.

It may sound strange to ask this question, but what *do* we know about Randy? He seems to have returned from Iraq unscathed, completed his college education, started a successful business, married, and become an active member of the community. Didn't he go through the same war traumas as his friend Billy? Why didn't he show psychological symptoms? What made him appear so mentally healthy? How did he cope with and overcome the hardships of war? What made him strong in the face of adversity?

There are benefits to addressing these questions and realizing that psychology is not just the study of pathology, weakness, and damage but also the study of strength, character and virtue. As such, we are reminded that the other side of mental illness is *mental health* and that it is therefore important for psychologists to consider resilience, assets, strengths, and optimal human functioning (Day & Rottinghaus, 2003; M. E. P. Seligman, 2007). By focusing on the inadequacies, problems, and limitations of people, we inadvertently see a very narrow picture of the human condition.

What are the advantages of positive psychology to mental health?

1. Conceptualizing client strengths and their resilience have become increasingly important in therapeutic assessment and treatment (Gelson & Woodhouse, 2003). Therapists realize that clients are not just passive beings without adaptive skills, helpless to deal with life problems. Identifying strengths has been found to be a positive experience for clients.
2. Positive psychology also focuses on prevention rather than remediation. The goal is to identify the strengths and assets of people, to arm them with adaptive coping skills, and to promote mental health. If the

positive qualities of human functioning and adaptive coping can be identified, then clients are better able to meet adjustment challenges.

3. Positive psychology encourages adaptive, healthy coping and resilience. When one encounters a traumatic stress in life or is a target of violence, abuse, bullying, racism, or discrimination, what distinguishes those who handle adversity well from to those who do not? Are these qualities or life strategies teachable? If so, can we teach people—even children—how to handle life stressors so that they become inoculated to the many demanding challenges of life?

Positive psychology has reawakened the profession's need to present a more balanced picture of the human condition. In most chapters, a section called **Focus on Resilience** covers the positive aspects of resilience, strengths, and assets in successful mental health coping.

Changes in the Therapeutic Landscape

The discovery and introduction of psychiatric drugs, prescription privileges for psychologists, and the need for cost containment of health care services have literally changed the therapeutic landscape of the profession.

The Drug Revolution in Psychiatry Many mental health professionals consider the introduction of psychiatric drugs in the 1950s as one of the great medical advances of the 20th century (Norfleet, 2002). Drug therapy has had an immense impact on mental health. It started when lithium was discovered to radically calm manic patients who had been hospitalized for years. Several years later, the discovery that the drug chlorpromazine (brand name Thorazine) was extremely effective in treating agitated people with schizophrenia was received with great fanfare. Within a matter of years, drugs were developed to treat disorders such as depression, schizophrenia, phobias, obsessive-compulsive disorders, and anxiety.

These drugs were considered revolutionary because they sometimes rapidly and dramatically decreased or eliminated troublesome symptoms experienced by patients. As a result, other forms of therapy became available to those with the most serious mental illnesses, who were then more able to focus their attention on their therapy. Stays in mental hospitals were shortened and treatment became more cost-effective. In addition, many were able to return home while receiving treatment.

The new drug therapies were credited with the depopulation of mental hospitals often referred to as *deinstitutionalization*, which we discuss in more detail in Chapter 16. To handle the large number of patients returning to the community, outpatient treatment became the primary mode of service for those with severe disturbances. In addition to changing the way therapy was dispensed, the introduction of psychiatric drugs revived strong belief in the biological bases of mental disorders.

The Push by Psychologists for Prescription Privileges One of the major features distinguishing psychiatrists from psychologists has been the right to prescribe medication. Should psychologists have a legal right to prescribe medication? Within the mental health field, this controversy has been extremely divisive. Psychologists have increasingly exerted pressure on state legislatures to allow them to prescribe medication in treating mental illnesses. They have argued that such a move would be cost-effective and would benefit the American public by containing escalating health care costs.

The American Medical Association, however, has adamantly opposed any such move. The fear of economic loss and blurring of boundaries between professions, and a concern that psychologists lack medical training, have been given as reasons. Proponents of prescription privileges, on the other hand, present compelling reasons for approval (Foxhall, 2001; Gutierrez & Silk, 1998): (a) studies reveal that psychologists would be more cautious than psychiatrists in prescribing medication, (b) it is a logical extension of the psychologist's role, (c) psychologists are equally if not better trained to understand mind-body relationships than are their psychiatric counterparts, and (d) psychologists wishing to prescribe would be required to master rigorous psychopharmacological training. As of this writing, Guam (a U.S. territory), Louisiana, and New Mexico allow prescription privileges for psychologists.

The Development of Managed Health Care **Managed health care** refers to the industrialization of health care, whereby large organizations in the private sector control the delivery of services. In the past, psychotherapy was carried out primarily by individuals in solo offices or in small group practices. Some clients paid for services out of their own pockets. Others had health plans that covered treatment, generally with minimal restrictions on the number of sessions the client could attend and usually with reimbursable treatment for a broad array of "psychological problems." The fees, number of sessions, and types of treatment were determined by the mental health practitioner. When mental health costs rapidly escalated in the 1980s, attempts were made to contain costs via managed health care or some form of health care reform (Cantor & Fuentes, 2008; Sammons, 2004). This industrialization of health care has brought about major changes in the mental health professions:

- The business interests of health insurers exert increasing control over psychotherapy by determining reimbursable diagnoses, limiting the number of sessions psychologists may offer clients, and imposing other such restrictions.
- Current business practices are depressing the income of practitioners. Some organizations prefer hiring therapists with master's degrees rather than those with doctoral degrees, or they reimburse at rates below those set by the therapist.
- Psychologists are being asked to justify the use of their therapies on the basis of whether the therapies are empirically based—that is, are they using established treatments with research support? This last point is especially important. For example, if research reveals that cognitive-behavioral forms of treatment are more successful than psychodynamic approaches for a certain form of phobia, then therapy using the latter approach might be denied by the insurance carrier.

These trends have alarmed many psychologists, who fear that decisions will be made not so much for health reasons but for business ones, that the need for doctoral-level practitioners will decrease, and that the livelihood of clinicians will be threatened. On a positive note, in 2010, mental health advocates celebrated the enactment of groundbreaking mental health and substance-abuse parity legislation; health insurance organizations can no longer discriminate in the coverage offered to those with addictions or mental illness. Instead of being restricted by arbitrary limits, individuals covered by insurance can now access more comprehensive treatment.

An Increased Appreciation for Research Breakthroughs in neuroscience, identification of the role that neurotransmitters play in mental disorders, and increasing interest in exploring evidence-based forms of psychotherapy have produced another contemporary trend: a heightened appreciation for the role of research in the study of abnormal behavior. The success of psychopharmacology spawned renewed interest and research into brain-behavior relationships. Indeed, more and more researchers are now exploring the biological bases (chemical and structural) of abnormal behavior. Within recent years, biological factors have

managed health care the industrialization of health care, whereby large organizations in the private sector control the delivery of services

been associated with many psychological disorders, such as depression, suicide, schizophrenia, alcoholism, and Alzheimer's disease.

Currently, researchers are seeking insights into the most effective means of understanding and treating specific disorders through studies comparing the effectiveness of drug treatment with that of cognitive treatment and through the development of empirically based treatments (Hays, 2009; La Roche & Christopher, 2009). The move toward empirically based treatments is one of the most visible aspects of the profession's use of research to determine the most effective forms of therapy for various disorders (Norcross, 2004; Wampold, Lichtenberg, & Waehler, 2002).

Although the move to evidence-based practice is accepted as important, it is not without controversy. Some claim that the call for empirically based treatments is biased against certain theoretical orientations. For example, studies reveal that 60 to 80 percent of those treatments identified as most effective are cognitive-behavioral treatments (Norcross, 2004). Others assert that evidence-based practice is too restrictive and does not recognize clinical intuition and the dynamic basis of therapy. Furthermore, the majority of disorders identified for treatment are those that can be easily measured and have a discrete but narrow symptom cluster, such as phobias. What about disorders that are more global and less susceptible to precise description, such as alienation in life, feelings of meaninglessness, and so on (Messer, 2001)? Lastly, as noted earlier, some fear that managed care companies will use this information to place more restrictions on the types of treatments they are willing to reimburse.

CHECKPOINT REVIEW

1. Describe the four major influences of multicultural psychology.
2. Define positive psychology. In what ways does it represent the "other side of mental illness?"
3. How has the drug revolution changed the therapeutic landscape of the helping professions?
4. What is managed care?
5. What is evidence-based treatment?

Summary

1 What is abnormal psychology?

- Abnormal psychology is a scientific study whose objectives are to describe, explain, predict, and modify behaviors that are considered strange or unusual.

2 What criteria are used to determine normal and abnormal behaviors?

- Abnormality is often determined by four criteria: distress, deviance, dysfunction, and dangerousness.

3 How do context, cultural differences, and sociopolitical experiences affect definitions of abnormality?

- Criteria used to define normality or abnormality must be considered in light of community standards, changes over time, cultural values, and sociopolitical experiences.

4 How common are mental disorders?

- Over the course of a year, approximately 25 percent of adults in the United States experience mental health problems.

5 What are some common misconceptions about people who are mentally disturbed?

- Beliefs that mental disorders are inherited, incurable, and the result of a weak will, and that those who have them will never contribute to society, have caused undue worry and harm to many.

6 How have explanations of abnormal behavior changed over time?

- Ancient peoples believed in demonology and attributed abnormal behaviors to evil spirits that inhabited the victim's body. Treatments consisted of trephining, exorcism, and bodily assaults.

- Rational and scientific explanations of abnormality emerged during the Greco-Roman era. Hippocrates believed that abnormal behavior was due to organic, or biological, causes, such as a dysfunction or disease of the brain. Treatment became more humane.
- With the collapse of the Roman Empire and the increased influence of the church, rationalist thought was suppressed and belief in the supernatural again flourished. During the Middle Ages, some of those killed in church-endorsed witch hunts were people we would today call mentally ill.
- The Renaissance brought a return to rational and scientific inquiry, along with a heightened interest in humanitarian methods of treating the mentally ill.

7 What were early viewpoints on the causes of mental disorders?

- In the 19th and 20th centuries, major medical breakthroughs fostered a belief in the biological roots of mental illness. An especially important discovery of this period was the micro-organism that causes general paresis.
- The uncovering of a relationship between hypnosis and hysteria corroborated the belief that psychological processes could produce emotional disturbances.

8 What are some contemporary trends in abnormal psychology?

- Multicultural psychology, resilience and positive psychology, the drug revolution, prescription privileges for psychologists, managed care, and evidence-based practice have all influenced the study and practice of abnormal psychology.

Key Terms

psychopathology 2
abnormal psychology 2
psychodiagnosis 2
therapy 4
abnormal behavior 4
culture 7
cultural universality 8
cultural relativism 8
psychiatric epidemiology 9
prevalence 9
incidence 9
lifetime prevalence 10
trephining 13
exorcism 13
brain pathology 13
mass madness 14
tarantism 14
humanism 14
moral treatment movement 15
spiritual being 16
biological (organic) viewpoint 17
syndrome 17
psychological viewpoint 17
cathartic method 18
multicultural psychology 19
positive psychology 20
optimal human functioning 20
spirituality 20
managed health care 23

Media Resources

Psychology CourseMate

Access an interactive e-Book and chapter-specific interactive learning tools, including:

- flashcards
- quizzes
- videos

and more in your Psychology CourseMate.

Go to **CengageBrain.com.**

2

Models of Abnormal Behavior

CHAPTER OUTLINE

Steve V., a 21-one-year-old college student, has been suffering from a crippling bout of depression. He has a long psychiatric history and was hospitalized twice when he was in high school. In the past, he has been diagnosed as suffering from schizophrenia (paranoid type) and bipolar mood disorder.

FOCUS QUESTIONS

1 What models of psychopathology have been used to explain abnormal behavior?

2 What is the multipath model of mental disorders?

3 How much of mental disorder can be explained through our biological makeup?

4 What psychological models are used to explain the etiology of mental disorders?

5 What role do social factors play in psychopathology?

6 What sociocultural factors may play a role in the etiology of mental disorders?

Steve was born in a suburb of San Francisco, California, the only child of an extremely wealthy couple. His father, who is of Scottish descent, was a prominent businessman who worked long hours and traveled frequently. On those rare occasions when he was at home, Mr. V. was often preoccupied with business matters and held himself quite aloof from his son. The few interactions they had were characterized by his constant ridicule and criticism of Steve. Mr. V. was greatly disappointed that his son seemed so timid, weak, and withdrawn. Although Steve is extremely bright and did well in school, Mr. V. felt that he lacked the "toughness" needed to survive and prosper in today's "dog-eat-dog" world. Once, when Steve was about 10 years old, he came home from school with a bloody nose and bruised face, crying and complaining of being bullied by classmates. His father showed no sympathy but instead berated Steve for losing the fight. Mr. V. often commented that Steve had inherited "bad genes" from his wife's side of the family.

Mrs. V. was very active in civic and social affairs, and she, too, spent relatively little time with her son. Although she treated Steve more warmly and lovingly than her husband, she seldom came to Steve's defense when he was being unfairly criticized. In reality, Mrs. V. was quite lonely. She felt abandoned by Mr. V. and harbored a deep resentment toward him, which she was frightened to express. Mrs. V. often allowed Steve to sleep with her when her husband was away on business trips. She usually dressed minimally on these occasions and was very demonstrative—holding, stroking, and kissing Steve. This behavior continued until Steve was 12, when his mother abruptly refused to let Steve into her bed. Mrs. V. had caught him masturbating under her sheets one morning when she awoke.

Steve was raised, in effect, by a full-time maid. He rarely had playmates of his own age. His birthdays were celebrated with a cake and candles, but the only celebrants were Steve and his mother. By age 10, Steve had learned to keep himself occupied by playing "mind games," letting his imagination carry him off on flights of fancy. He frequently imagined himself as a powerful figure—Superman or Batman. His fantasies were often extremely violent, and his foes were vanquished only after much blood had been spilled.

At age 16, Steve became convinced that external forces were controlling his mind and behavior. Although he was strongly attracted to his fantasy world, he also felt that something was wrong with him. After seeing the movie *The Exorcist*, he became convinced that he was possessed by the devil.

What do you make of Steve? He certainly fulfills our criteria of someone suffering from a mental disorder. Yet how do we make sense of his bizarre behaviors, thoughts, and feelings? Where do they come from? Is Steve correct in his belief that he is possessed by evil spirits? Is his father correct in suggesting that "bad genes" caused his disorder? What role did his upbringing, isolation, and constant criticisms from his father play in the development of his problems? These complex questions lead us into a very important aspect of abnormal psychology: the **etiology**, or causes, of disorders.

One-Dimensional Models of Mental Disorders

Most explanations or causes of abnormal behavior fall into four distinct camps: (a) biological problems (symptoms of physical disease or damage), (b) psychosocial issues, rooted in the invisible complexities of the human mind or in stressful environmental forces, (c) social relationships, with family and peers, that are

etiology cause or origin of a disorder

dysfunctional, and (d) sociocultural influences. Let's look at how each model has traditionally explained Steve's psychopathology.

- **Biological explanations:** Steve's mental disorders are caused by some form of biological malfunctioning. His problems are possibly due to a genetic predisposition to mental disorders, to an imbalance of brain chemistry, or perhaps to structural abnormalities in his neurological makeup. The most effective way to treat this disorder is through drug therapy or some form of somatic intervention.
- **Psychological explanations:** Psychologically, there are a variety of ways to explain Steve's behavior. His problems are due to his (a) early childhood experiences, inability to confront his own intense feelings of hostility toward his father, and unresolved sexual longing toward his mother, (b) isolation from others, which prevented him from developing appropriate social skills and behaviors, or (c) irrational beliefs (that he is worthless and unmanly) and distorted thinking processes that made him lose touch with objective reality.
- **Social explanations:** From a social-relational perspective, Steve's problem resides in a dysfunctional family system and pathological parental upbringing. Parental neglect, rejection, and abuse may explain many of his pathological symptoms. The constant bullying of Steve by his father and the lack of support from his mother are the primary culprits.
- **Sociocultural explanations:** The societal and cultural context in which Steve's problems arise must be considered in understanding his dilemma. He is a white European American of Scottish descent, born to a wealthy family in the upper socioeconomic class. He is a male, raised in a cultural context that values individual achievement, assertiveness, and competitiveness. Because Steve does not live up to his father's benchmarks of masculinity, he is considered a failure not only by his father, but by himself.

Today we realize that these one-dimensional perspectives are overly simplistic because they (a) set up a false "either-or" dichotomy between accepting one explanation or another (e.g., nature vs. nurture), (b) fail to recognize the reciprocal influences of one on the other, and (c) mask the importance of acknowledging the contributions of all four dimensions in the origin of mental disorders (D. W. Sue & Sue, 2013; T.-Y. Zhang & Meaney, 2010).

As evidenced by the preceding analysis of Steve, each explanation seems to contain kernels of truth. But which is more accurate? Does accepting the validity of one perspective pre-empt the applicability of another? Is it possible that combinations of biological, psychological, social, and sociocultural factors all interact and contribute to Steve's mental disorder?

These four explanations, perspectives, or viewpoints of abnormal behavior are referred to as *models* by psychologists. A **model** is an analogy that scientists often use to describe a phenomenon or process that they cannot directly observe. Models help psychologists conceptualize the causes of abnormal behavior, ask probing questions, determine relevant information, and organize information in a meaningful way. In this chapter, we propose a *multipath model* for explaining abnormal behavior that integrates these four major dimensions.

A Multipath Model of Mental Disorders

According to the biopsychosocial model, mental disorders are the result of biological, psychological, and social factors. For instance, in the case of Steve V., genetics and brain functioning (a biological perspective) may interact with ways of thinking

model an analogy used by scientists, usually to describe or explain a phenomenon or process they cannot directly observe

● FIGURE 2.1

The Multipath Model

Each dimension of the multipath model contains factors found to be important in explaining abnormal behavior.

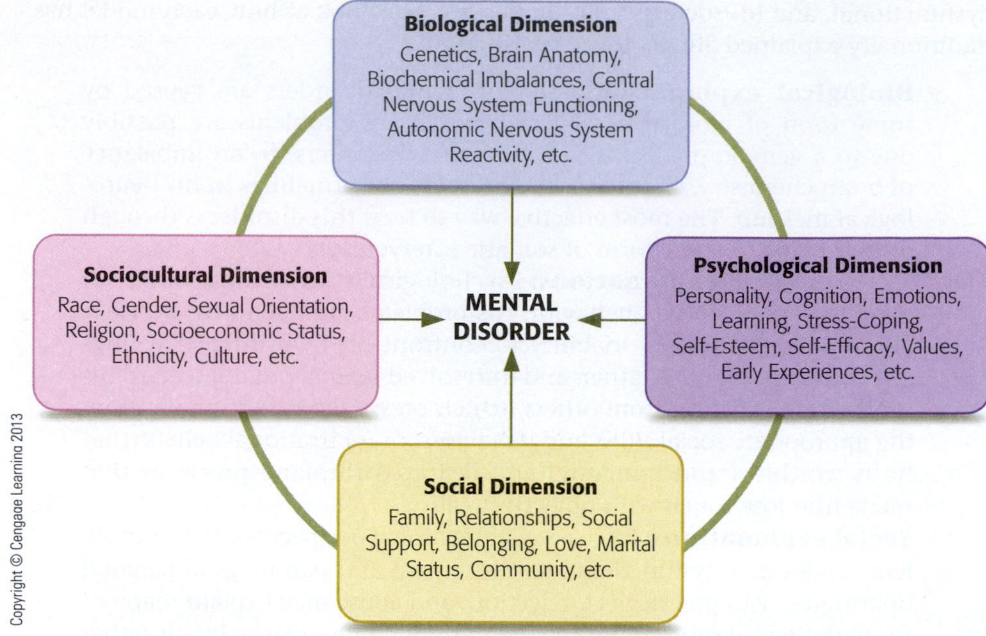

(a cognitive perspective) in a given family environment (a social perspective) to produce abnormal behavior (J. J. Mann & Haghighi, 2010; University of Michigan, 2010). Although a step in the right direction, the model continues to give short shrift to the importance of sociocultural influences in explaining mental disorders.

What, then, is the "best" way to conceptualize the causes of mental disorders? We propose an integrative and interacting **multipath model** as a way of viewing disorders and their causes. The multipath model is not a theory but a way of looking at the variety and complexity of contributors to mental disorders. The multipath model operates under several assumptions:

- No one theoretical perspective is adequate to explain the complexity of the human condition and the development of mental disorders.
- There are multiple pathways to and causes of any single disorder. It is a rarity to find a disorder due to only one cause.
- Explanations of abnormal behavior must consider biological, psychological, social, and sociocultural elements.
- Not all dimensions contribute equally to a disorder. In some cases, greater support for a biological perspective, for example, may be present, but this may evolve as research enlightens us about the contributions of other factors.
- The multipath model is integrative and interactive. It acknowledges that factors may combine in complex and reciprocal ways so that people exposed to the same factors may not develop the same disorder and that different individuals exposed to different factors may develop similar mental disorders.
- Just as weaknesses and liabilities contribute to mental disorders, the strengths and assets of a person may serve as protective factors against psychopathology, minimize its manifestation or severity, or predict resilience in the face of adversity.

multipath model a model of models that provides an organizational framework for understanding the numerous causes of mental disorders, the complexity of their interacting components, and the need to view disorders from a holistic framework

Let's look at how the multipath model operates under these assumptions. The etiology of mental disorders can be subsumed under four dimensions, as shown in Figure 2.1. Each dimension contains both weaknesses or liabilities and strengths or assets. This latter point is important. Because abnormal psychology concentrates on pathology, we often forget or ignore the positive aspects of the human condition. For example, we know more about inadequacies than strengths, anxiety and fear than courage, depression than happiness, selfishness than altruism, hate than love, stagnation than creativity, ignorance than wisdom, and hostility than affiliation. Yet these positive attributes have been found to immunize people against stressors, predict resiliency and recovery, and serve as "protective factors" against mental disorders (see Figure 2.1a) (Geschwind, Peeters, Drukker, Van Os, & Wichers, 2011; Mak, Ivy, Ng, & Wong, 2011; Seery, 2011).

- **Dimension One: Biological Factors**—Genetics, brain anatomy, biochemical imbalances, central nervous system functioning, autonomic nervous system reactivity, and so forth.
- **Dimension Two: Psychological Factors**—Personality, cognition, emotions, learning, stress coping, self-esteem, self-efficacy, values, early experiences, and so forth.
- **Dimension Three: Social Factors**—Family, relationships, social support, belonging, love, marital status, community, and so forth.
- **Dimension Four: Sociocultural Factors**—Race, gender, sexual orientation, spirituality or religion, socioeconomic status, ethnicity, culture, and so forth.

Within each dimension, how the multiplicity of factors is organized to explain abnormal behavior depends on a particular theoretical perspective. First, let's take the psychological dimension as an example. Psychodynamic theories might emphasize the importance of childhood experiences in the formation of abnormal behavior; learning theories would emphasize learning and personality;

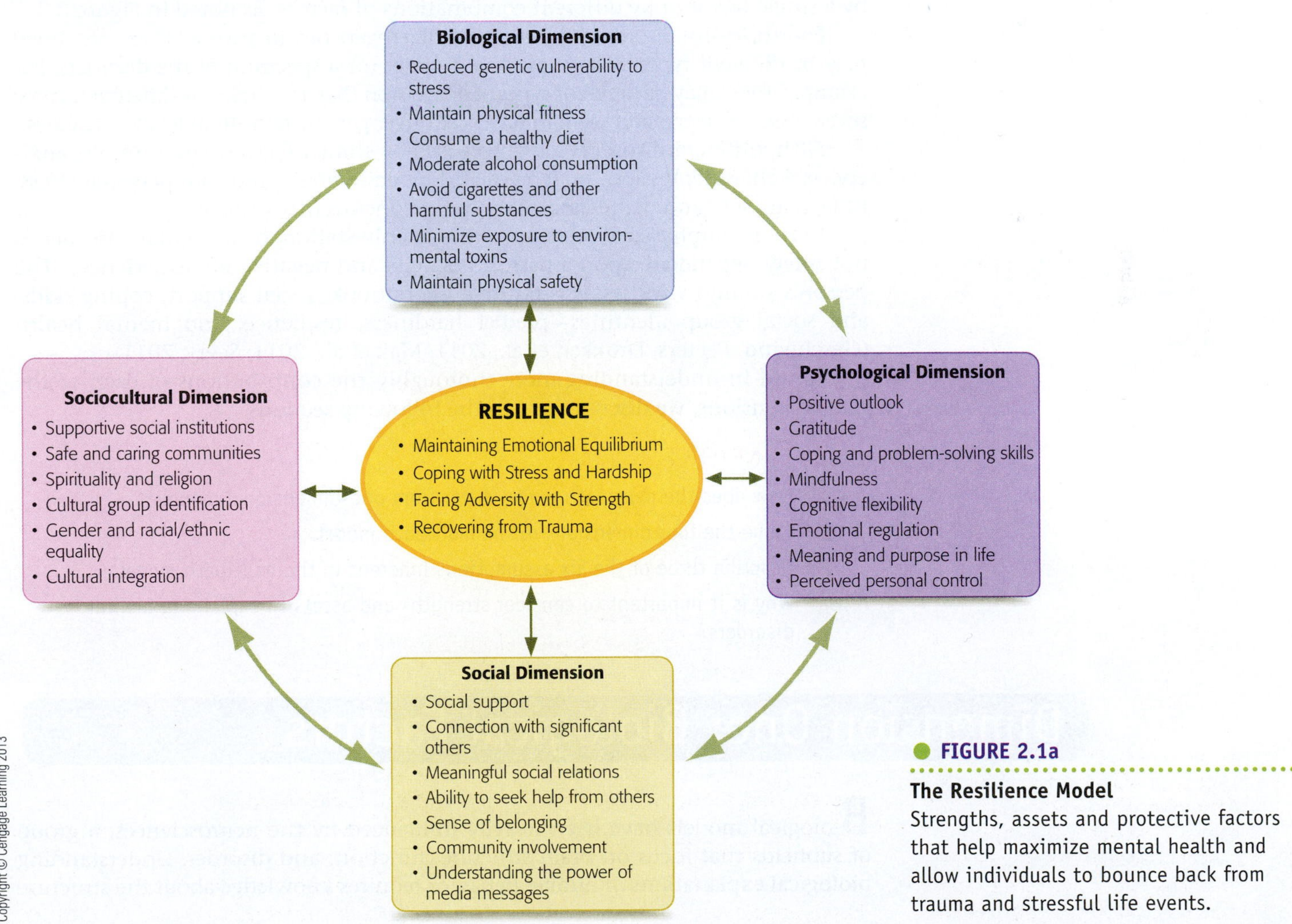

FIGURE 2.1a

The Resilience Model

Strengths, assets and protective factors that help maximize mental health and allow individuals to bounce back from trauma and stressful life events.

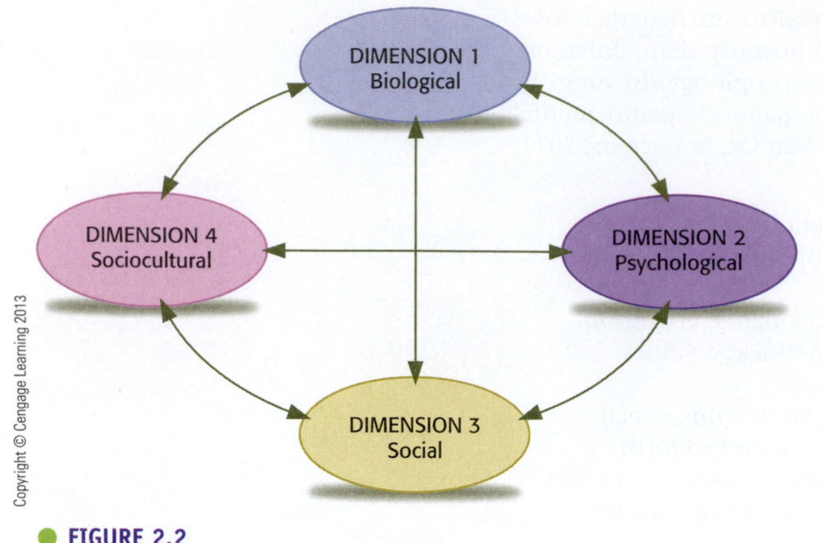

FIGURE 2.2

The Four Dimensions and Possible Pathways of Influence
Abnormal behavior can be conceptualized as arising from four possible dimensions.

and cognitive theories would emphasize cognition and thinking. Thus, it is possible to have considerable differences even within a categorical dimension. Because some explanations, like stress theory, can be categorized in more than one dimension (psychological and social), it is best to view these four dimensions as having permeable boundaries with considerable overlap.

Second, factors in the four dimensions can interact and influence each other in any direction. For example, research shows that brain functioning affects behaviors. However, research also demonstrates that engaging in certain behaviors can affect brain functioning (Pajonk et al., 2010). We also know that sociocultural factors can influence biological factors (Azar, 2010). The actual situation is much more complex because the interaction of factors may involve all four dimensions, as noted in Figure 2.2.

Third, different combinations within the four dimensions may cause abnormal behaviors. For instance, let's assume that a woman suffers from severe depression. Her depression may be caused by a single factor (e.g., the death of a loved one) or by an interaction of factors in different dimensions (e.g., child abuse occurring in early life and stressors in adulthood). Thus, a disorder such as depression may be caused by a single factor or by different combinations of factors, as noted in Figure 2.3.

Fourth, many disorders appear to be heterogeneous in nature. Therefore, there may be different types or versions of a disorder (or a spectrum of the disorder). For example, there may be different types of depression that are caused by different factors; severe cases of depression seem to have a stronger genetic basis than less severe cases.

Fifth, different disorders may be caused by similar factors. For example, anxiety, as well as depression, may be caused by child abuse and interpersonal stress. In fact, anxiety and depression often occur concurrently in people.

Last, as emphasized previously, the manifestation of a mental disorder is not solely dependent upon a person's deficits and negative life experiences. The person's strengths and assets—positive life outlook, social support, coping skills, and social group identities—predict hardiness, resilience, and mental health (Geschwind, Peeters, Drukker, et al., 2011; Mak et al., 2011; Seery, 2011),

To aid in understanding more thoroughly the contributions of each of the four dimensions, we discuss them in the following sections.

CHECKPOINT REVIEW

1. How does the multipath model differ from one-dimensional models?
2. Name the four dimensions of the multipath model.
3. Describe three of the six assumptions inherent in the multipath model.
4. Why is it important to consider strengths and assets in explaining mental disorders?

Dimension One: Biological Factors

Biological models have been heavily influenced by the neurosciences, a group of subfields that focus on brain structure, function, and disorder. Understanding biological explanations of human behavior requires knowledge about the structure and function of the central nervous system (composed of the brain and spinal cord).

The Human Brain

The brain is composed of billions of **neurons**, or nerve cells that transmit messages throughout the body. The brain is responsible for three very important and highly complicated functions. It receives information from the outside world, it uses the information to decide on a course of action, and it implements decisions by commanding muscles to move and glands to secrete. Weighing approximately three pounds, this relatively small organ continues to amaze and mystify biological researchers.

Viewed in cross section, the brain has three parts: forebrain, midbrain, and hindbrain. Although each part is vital for functioning and survival, the forebrain is probably the most relevant to a discussion of abnormality.

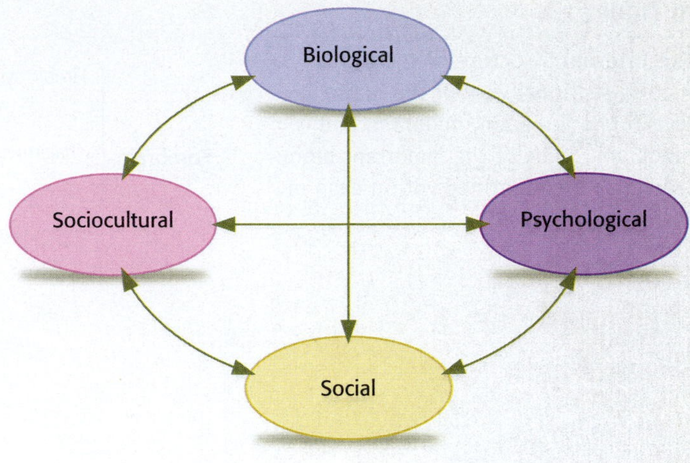

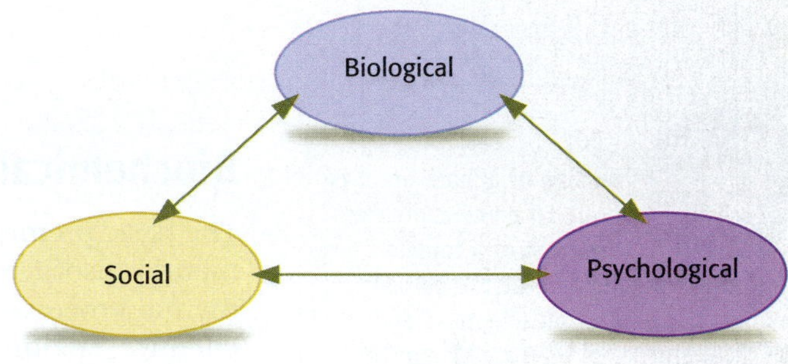

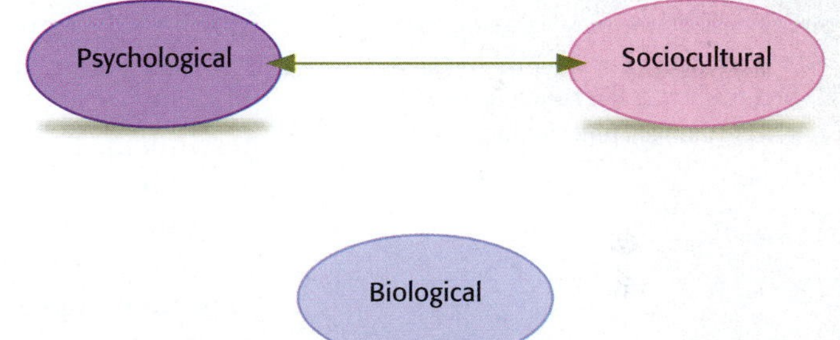

Biological

FIGURE 2.3

The Number of Dimensions That May Lead to Particular Disorders

The dimensions shown are examples only, because any of them can serve to influence a particular disorder.

The Forebrain

The *forebrain* probably controls all the higher mental functions associated with human consciousness, learning, speech, thought, and memory. Within the forebrain are the thalamus, hypothalamus, reticular activating system, limbic system, and cerebrum (Figure 2.4). The specific functions of these structures are still being debated, but we can discuss their more general functions with some confidence.

The *thalamus* appears to serve as a "relay station," transmitting nerve impulses from one part of the brain to another. The *hypothalamus* ("under the thalamus") regulates bodily drives, such as hunger, thirst, and sex, and body conditions, such as temperature and hormone balance. The *limbic system* is involved in experiencing and expressing emotions and motivation—pleasure, fear, aggression, sexual arousal, and pain. The largest structure in the brain is the *cerebrum*, with its most visible part, the *cerebral cortex*, covering the midbrain and thalamus.

The Midbrain and Hindbrain

The midbrain and hindbrain also have distinct functions:

- The *midbrain* is involved in vision and hearing and—along with the hindbrain—in the control of sleep, alertness, and pain. Mental health professionals are especially interested in the midbrain's role in manufacturing chemicals—serotonin, norepinephrine, and dopamine—that have been implicated in certain mental disorders.
- The *hindbrain* also manufactures serotonin. The hindbrain appears to control functions such as heart rate, sleep, and respiration. The *reticular formation*, a network of nerve fibers that controls bodily states such as sleep, alertness, and attention, starts in the hindbrain and threads its way into the midbrain.

Because the brain controls all aspects of human functioning, it is not difficult to conclude that damage or interruption of normal brain function and activity could lead to observable mental disorders.

neuron nerve cell that transmits messages throughout the body

FIGURE 2.4

The Internal Structure of the Brain
A cross-sectional view of the brain reveals the forebrain, midbrain, and hindbrain. Some of the important brain structures are identified within each of the divisions.

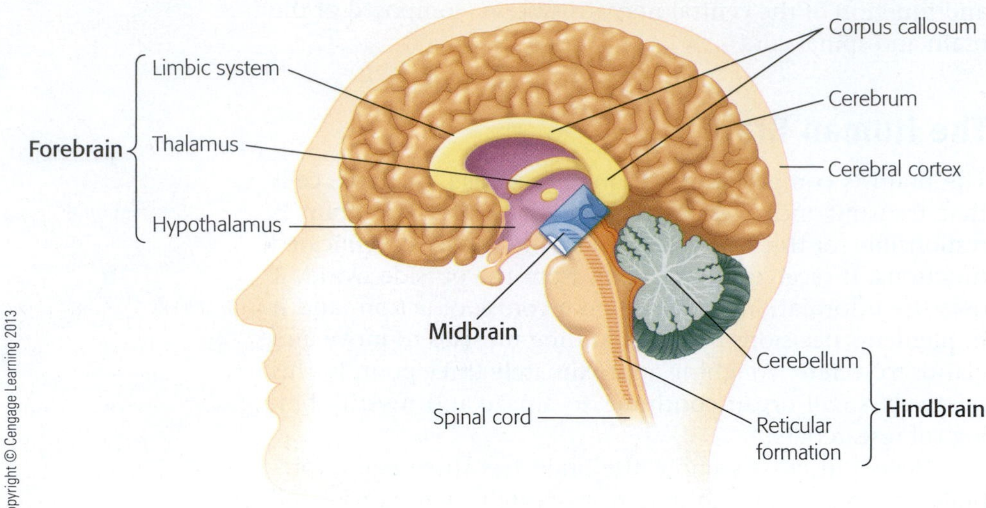

Did You Know? The size of a male brain is about 10 percent greater than that of a female brain; men's heads are also 2 percent bigger. The greater muscle mass and physical stature of men may mean they require more neurons to control their bodies. Other differences between male and female brains may be associated with potential susceptibility to certain disorders such as Alzheimer's disease and other human functioning.

Biochemical Theories

The basic premise of biochemical theories is that chemical imbalances underlie mental disorders. This premise relies on the fact that most physiological and mental processes, from sleeping and digestion to reading and thinking, involve chemical actions within the body. Support for the biochemical theories has been found in research into anxiety disorders, mood disorders (both depression and bipolar disorder), Alzheimer's disease, autism, dyslexia, and schizophrenia (N. C. Andreasen, 2005; Lambert & Kinsley, 2005; Sarter, Bruno, & Parikh, 2007). In fact, it is possible that our gene pool affects such characteristics as alienation, leadership, career choice, risk aversion, religious conviction, and pessimism. To see how biochemical imbalances in the brain can result in abnormal behavior, we need to understand how messages in the brain are transmitted from nerve cell to nerve cell.

Nerve cells (neurons) vary in function throughout the brain; but though they may appear different, they all share certain characteristics. Each neuron possesses a cell membrane that separates it from the outside environment and regulates the chemical contents within it. On one end of the cell body are **dendrites**, numerous short, rootlike structures whose function is to receive signals from other neurons. At the other end is an **axon**, a much longer extension that sends signals to other neurons, some a considerable distance away. Under an electron microscope, dendrites can be distinguished by their many short branches (Figure 2.5).

Messages travel through the brain by electrical impulses via neurons: An incoming message is received by a neuron's dendrites and is sent down the axon to bulblike swellings called *axon terminals*, usually located near dendrites of another neuron. Note that neurons do not touch one another. A minute gap (the **synapse**) exists between the axon of the sending neuron and the dendrites of the receiving neuron (Figure 2.6). The electrical impulse crosses the synapse when the axon releases chemical substances called **neurotransmitters.** When the neurotransmitters reach the dendrites of the receiving neuron, they attach themselves to receptors and, if their "shapes" correspond, bind with them (Figure 2.7). The binding of transmitters to receptors in the neuron triggers either synaptic excitation (encouragement to produce other nerve impulses) or synaptic inhibition (a state preventing production of nerve impulses). The human body has many different

dendrite short, rootlike structure on the neuron cell body whose function is to receive signals from other neurons

axon extension on the neuron cell body that sends signals to other neurons, some a considerable distance away

synapse minute gap that exists between the axon of the sending neuron and the dendrites of the receiving neuron

neurotransmitter any of a group of chemicals that help transmit messages between neurons

chemical transmitters, and their effects on neurons vary (Table 2.1). An imbalance of certain neurotransmitters in the brain is believed to be implicated in mental disorders. Research into biochemical mechanisms holds great promise for our understanding and treatment of mental disorders.

Genetic Explanations

Research strongly indicates that genetic makeup plays an important role in the development of certain abnormal conditions. There is strong evidence that autonomic nervous system (ANS) reactivity is inherited in human beings; that is, a person may be born with an ANS that makes an unusually strong response to stimuli (N. C. Andreasen, 2005). Heredity has been implicated as a causal factor in alcoholism, schizophrenia, and depression.

Biological inheritance is transmitted by genes. A person's genetic makeup is called his or her **genotype**. Interaction between the genotype and the environment results in the person's **phenotype**, or observable physical and behavioral characteristics. At times, however, it is difficult to determine whether genotype or environment is exerting a stronger influence. For example, characteristics such as eye color are determined solely by our genotype—by the coding in our genes. But other physical characteristics, such as height, are determined partly by the genetic code and partly by environmental factors.

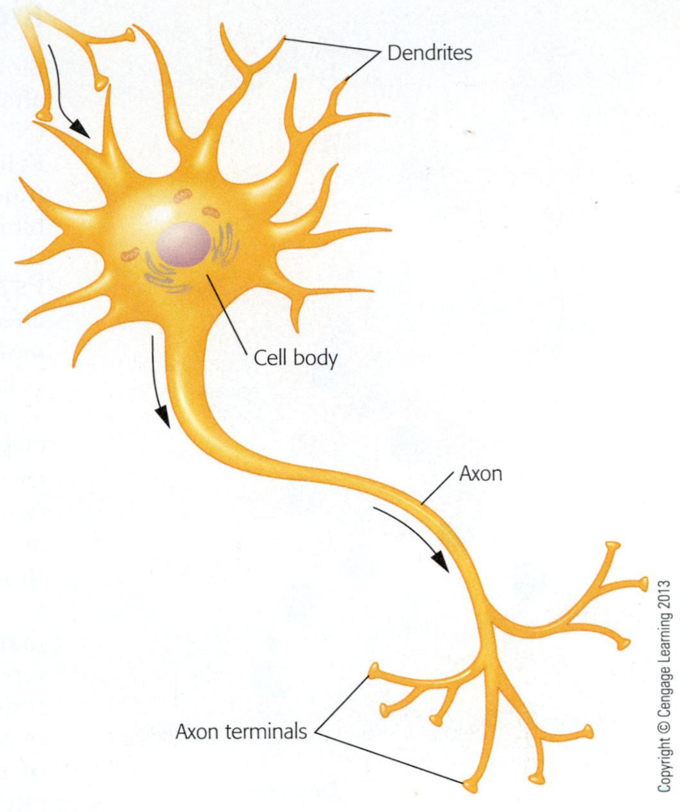

FIGURE 2.5

Major Parts of a Neuron

The major parts of a neuron are dendrites, the cell body, the axon, and the axon terminals.

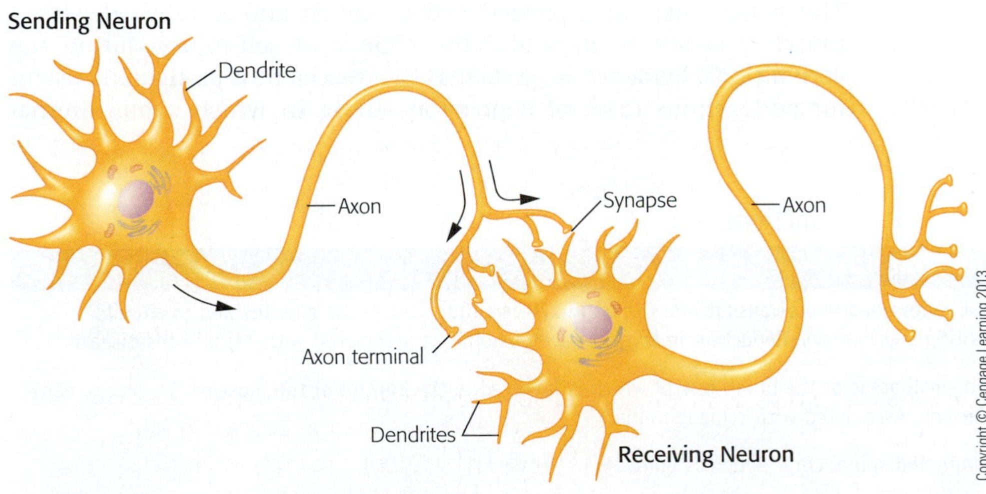

FIGURE 2.6

Synaptic Transmission

Messages travel via electrical impulses from one neuron to another. The impulse crosses the synapse in the form of chemicals called neurotransmitters. Note that the axon terminals and the receiving dendrites do not touch.

genotype a person's genetic makeup

phenotype observable physical and behavioral characteristics caused by the interaction between the genotype and the environment

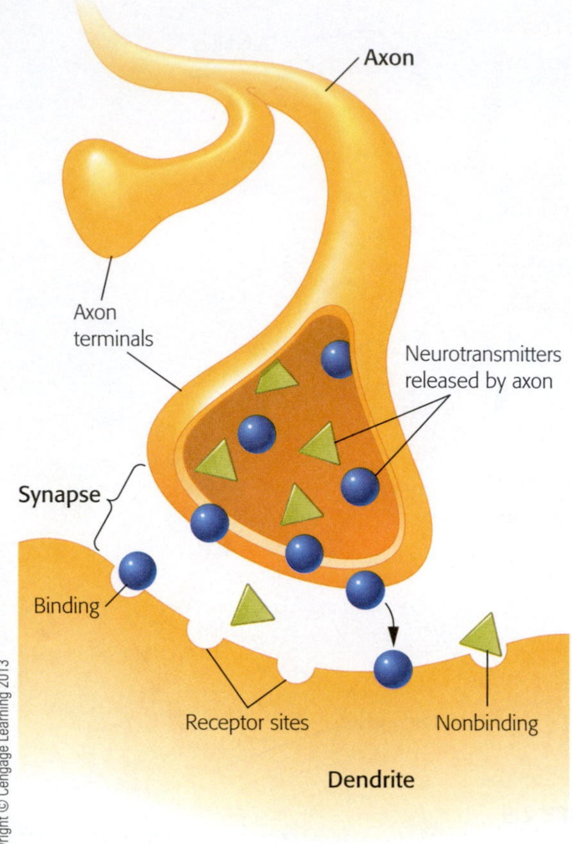

FIGURE 2.7

Neurotransmitter Binding

Neurotransmitters are released into the synapse and travel to the receiving dendrite. Each transmitter has a specific "shape" that corresponds to a receptor site. Like a jigsaw puzzle, binding occurs if the transmitter fits into the receptor site.

Biology-Based Treatment Techniques

Biological or somatic treatment techniques use physical means to alter the patient's physiological state and hence psychological state (N. C. Andreasen, 2005; Kolb, Gibb, & Robinson, 2003; G. A. Miller & Keller, 2000). As our understanding of human physiology and brain functioning has increased, so has our ability to provide more effective biologically based therapies for the mentally ill.

Psychopharmacology *Psychopharmacology* is the study of the effects of drugs on the mind and on behavior; it is also known as *medication* or *drug therapy*. Medication is now widely used throughout the United States: more mental patients receive drug therapy than receive all other forms of therapy combined (Levinthal, 2005). The four major classes of medication are (a) *antianxiety drugs* (or *minor tranquilizers*), (b) *antipsychotic drugs* (or *major tranquilizers*), (c) *antidepressant drugs* (which relieve depression by elevating one's mood), and (d) *antimanic drugs* (such as lithium). Many of these drugs are discussed more thoroughly in the context of specific disorders in forthcoming chapters.

The use of antidepressant, antianxiety, antipsychotic, and antimanic drugs has greatly changed therapy. Patients who take them report that they feel better, that symptoms decline, and that overall functioning improves. Long periods of hospitalization are no longer needed in most cases, and patients are more amenable to other forms of treatment, such as psychotherapy. Medications seem to be most effective in treating "active" symptoms such as delusions, hallucinations, and aggression, and much less effective with "passive" symptoms such as withdrawal, poor interpersonal relationships, and feelings of alienation. Medication does not help patients improve their living skills.

Electroconvulsive Therapy Besides medication, *electroconvulsive therapy* (ECT) can be used to treat certain mental disorders. ECT is the application of electric voltage to the brain to induce convulsions. The patient lies on a padded bed or couch and is injected with a muscle relaxant to minimize the chance of self-injury during the convulsions. Evidence suggests that the treatment is particularly useful for endogenous cases of depression—those in which some internal

TABLE 2.1 Major Neurotransmitters and Their Functions

NEUROTRANSMITTER	LOCATION AND FUNCTION
Acetylcholine (ACH)	One of the most widespread neurotransmitters. Occurs in systems that control the muscles and in circuits related to attention and memory. Reduction in levels of acetylcholine is associated with Alzheimer's disease.
Dopamine	Concentrated in small areas of the brain, one of which is involved in the control of the muscles. In excess, can cause hallucinations. Associated with schizophrenia.
Endorphins	Found in the brain and spinal cord. Suppress pain.
Gamma-aminobutyric acid	Widely distributed in the brain. Works against other neurotransmitters, particularly dopamine.
Norepinephrine	Occurs widely in the central nervous system. Regulates moods and may increase arousal and alertness. Often associated with mood disorders and eating disorders.
Serotonin	Occurs in the brain. Works more or less in opposition to norepinephrine, suppressing activity and causing sleep. Linked with anxiety disorders, mood disorders, and eating disorders.

cause can be determined. But how ECT acts to improve depression is still unclear. Despite its success, the use of ECT has declined significantly since the 1960s and 1970s because of potential permanent damage to the brain and the ethical objections raised by detractors.

Psychosurgery During the 1940s and 1950s, *psychosurgery*—brain surgery performed for the purpose of correcting a severe mental disorder—became increasingly popular. The treatment was used most often with patients suffering from schizophrenia and severe depression, although many who had personality and anxiety disorders also underwent psychosurgery. Critics of psychosurgical procedures have raised both scientific and ethical objections.

Multipath Implications of Biological Explanations

The majority of human diseases are multidimensional and multifactorial, caused by many genes interacting in a cellular environment of hormones, electrical signals, and nutrient supplies, as well as in our physical, psychological, social, and cultural environments. A one-to-one correspondence between a gene and a disorder is a statistical rarity in behavioral genetics. Mental health researchers have increasingly come to reject a simple linear explanation of genetic determinism (Rucker & McGuffin, 2010). Rather, disorders are seen as the result of complex interactive and oftentimes reciprocal processes (J. J. Mann & Haghighi, 2010). The field of **epigenetics** reveals that reciprocal gene × environment interactions actually modify the expression of the **genome**. It has been found, for example, that certain genes or gene combinations may actually promote an environment likely to elicit stressors that negatively affect the individual (Diamond, 2009; Plomin & McGuffin, 2003). Genes may predispose a person to seek out situations that place the person at high risk of experiencing stressors that trigger depression. Adolescent girls prone to depression, for example, may actually seek out situations that promote mood disorders (such as selecting unstable romantic partners, who increase the probability of breakups). Accumulating evidence also strongly suggests that biochemical changes, brain activity, and even the structures of neurological circuitry often occur because of environmental influences (J. A. Foster & MacQueen, 2008; Leonardo & Hen, 2006).

Did You Know? Over the past few years, several major research universities have opened up cultural neuroscience centers to study how biology shapes culture and culture shapes biology. One neuroimaging study found that when Chinese people think about honesty for themselves and honesty for a close relative, their brain activities are nearly identical for each task. When U.S. American people think about honesty for themselves and relatives, their patterns are very different. It appears that U.S. American people see themselves more as individuals, whereas Chinese people view themselves as part of a family. These findings are consistent with the difference between a collectivistic and an individualistic cultural perspective. In other words, culture shapes how the brain functions (Azar, 2010).

CHECKPOINT REVIEW

1. Name the three parts of the brain and their primary functions.
2. Describe the ways in which biology may play a role in mental disorders.
3. Describe three biological treatments for mental disorders.
4. In what ways are biological explanations reciprocal and interactive with environmental influences?

epigenetics field of biological research focused on understanding how environmental factors (e.g., trauma, toxins, or nutrition) influence or program gene expression

genome all the genetic material in the chromosomes of a particular organism

Dimension Two: Psychological Factors

A number of psychological factors have been shown to be important in the etiology of mental disorders, as shown in Figure 2.1. Especially important for the psychological dimension are conflicts in the mind, emotions, learned behavior, and cognitions in personality formation. Psychological theories, like many biological explanations, can also be prone to viewing normal and abnormal human development in a linear and one-dimensional fashion.

Interestingly, psychological explanations of abnormal behavior vary considerably depending on the psychologist's theoretical orientation. In this section, we briefly describe four major psychological perspectives in explaining abnormal behavior: psychodynamic, behavioral, cognitive, and humanistic-existential. We then apply a multipath analysis to these four approaches.

Psychodynamic Models

Psychodynamic models of abnormal behavior view disorders in adults as the result of childhood trauma or anxieties. They hold that many of these childhood-based anxieties operate unconsciously; because experiences are too threatening for the adult to face, they are repressed through mental **defense mechanisms**. As a result, people exhibit symptoms that they are unable to understand. To eliminate the symptoms, therapists must make patients aware of these unconscious anxieties and conflicts.

The early development of psychodynamic theory is credited to Sigmund Freud (1938, 1949). Freud was convinced that powerful mental processes could remain hidden from consciousness and could cause abnormal behaviors. He believed that the therapist's role was to help patients achieve insight into these unconscious processes.

Personality Structure Freud believed that personality is composed of three major components—the id, the ego, and the superego—and that all behavior is a product of their interaction. The *id* is the original component of the personality; it is present at birth, and from it the ego and superego eventually develop. The id operates from the **pleasure principle**—the impulsive, pleasure-seeking aspect of our being—and it seeks immediate gratification of instinctual needs, regardless of moral or realistic concerns. In contrast, the *ego* represents the realistic and rational part of the mind. It is influenced by the **reality principle**—an awareness of the demands of the environment and of the need to adjust behavior to meet these demands. The ego's decisions are dictated by realistic considerations rather than by moral judgments. Moral judgments and moralistic considerations are the domain of the *superego*. The *conscience* is the part of the superego that instills guilt in us when we engage in immoral or unethical behavior.

The energy system from which the personality operates occurs through the interplay of *instincts*. Instincts give rise to our thoughts and actions and fuel their expression. Freud emphasized *sex* (libido) and *aggression* as the dominant human instincts because he recognized that the society in which he lived placed strong prohibitions on these drives and that, as a result, people were taught to inhibit them. A profound need to express one's instincts is often frightening and can lead a person to deny their existence. Most impulses are hidden from one's consciousness; they nonetheless determine human actions.

Psychosexual Stages Human personality develops through a sequence of five **psychosexual stages**, each of which brings a unique challenge. If unfavorable circumstances prevail, the personality may be drastically affected. Because Freud stressed the importance of early childhood experiences, he saw the human personality as largely determined in the first 5 years of life—during the *oral* (first year of life), *anal* (around the second year of life), and *phallic* (beginning around the third or fourth years of life) stages. The last two psychosexual stages are the *latency* (approximately 6 to 12 years of age) and *genital* (beginning in puberty) stages.

The importance of each psychosexual stage for later development lies in whether fixation occurs during that stage. *Fixation* halts emotional development at

psychodynamic model model that views disorders as the result of childhood trauma or anxieties and that holds that many of these childhood-based anxieties operate unconsciously

defense mechanism in psychoanalytic theory, an ego-protection strategy that shelters the individual from anxiety, operates unconsciously, and distorts reality

pleasure principle the impulsive, pleasure-seeking aspect of our being, from which the id operates

reality principle an awareness of the demands of the environment and of the need to adjust behavior to meet these demands, from which the ego operates

psychosexual stages in psychodynamic theory, the sequence of stages—oral, anal, phallic, latency, and genital—through which human personality develops

a particular psychosexual stage. According to the psychodynamic model, each stage is characterized by distinct traits and, should fixation occur, by distinct conflicts.

Defense Mechanisms Neurotic behavior develops from the threat of overwhelming anxiety, which may lead to full-scale panic. To forestall this panic, the ego often resorts to defense mechanisms. Defense mechanisms share three characteristics: they protect the individual from anxiety, they operate unconsciously, and they distort reality.

All individuals use some strategies to reduce anxiety. Defense mechanisms are considered maladaptive, however, when they are overused—that is, when they become the predominant means of coping with stress and when they interfere with one's ability to handle life's everyday demands. The difference is one of degree, not of kind. Table 2.2 lists some common defense mechanisms.

Traditional Psychodynamic Therapy Psychoanalytic therapy, or **psychoanalysis**, seeks to overcome defenses so that repressed material can be uncovered, the client can achieve insight into his or her inner motivations and desires, and unresolved childhood conflicts can be controlled. Psychoanalysts traditionally use four methods to achieve their therapeutic goals: free association, dream analysis, analysis of resistance, and analysis of transference.

- In **free association**, the patient says whatever comes to mind, regardless of how illogical or embarrassing it may seem, for the purpose of revealing the contents of the unconscious. Psychoanalysts believe the material that surfaces in this process is determined by the patient's psychic makeup and can provide understanding of the patient's conflicts, unconscious processes, and personality dynamics.
- Dream analysis is a therapeutic technique that depends on interpretation of hidden meanings in dreams. Psychoanalysts believe that when people sleep, defenses and inhibitions of the ego weaken, allowing unacceptable motives and feelings to surface. The therapist's job is to uncover the disguised symbolic meanings and let the patient achieve insight into the anxiety-provoking implications.
- Analysis of **resistance**—when the patient unconsciously attempts to impede the analysis by preventing the exposure of repressed material—is used to interpret and uncover the repressed material. In free association, for example, the patient may suddenly change the subject, lose his or her train of thought, go blank, or become silent. The therapist can make use of properly interpreted instances of resistance to show the patient that repressed material is coming close to the surface and to suggest means of uncovering it.
- In **transference**, the patient re-enacts early conflicts by applying to the analyst feelings and attitudes that the patient had toward significant others—primarily parents—in the past. Working through transference is considered therapeutic.

Contemporary Psychodynamic Theories Freud's psychoanalytic approach attracted many followers. Some of Freud's disciples, however, came to disagree with his insistence that the sex instinct is the major determinant of behavior. Many of his most gifted adherents broke away from him and formulated psychological models of their own. Today, very few psychodynamic therapists practice traditional psychoanalysis; instead, they emphasize freedom of choice and future goals, ego autonomy, social forces, object relations (past interpersonal relations), and treatment of seriously disturbed people.

Sigmund Freud (1856–1939)

Freud began his career as a neurologist. He became increasingly intrigued with the relationship between illness and mental processes and ultimately developed psychoanalysis, a therapy in which unconscious conflicts are aired so that the patient can become aware of and understand his or her problems.

psychoanalysis therapy whose goals are to uncover repressed material, to help clients achieve insight into inner motivations and desires, and to resolve childhood conflicts that affect current relationships

free association psychoanalytic therapeutic technique in which the patient says whatever comes to mind for the purpose of revealing his or her unconscious

resistance during psychoanalysis, a process in which the patient unconsciously attempts to impede the analysis by preventing the exposure of repressed material

transference process by which a patient in psychoanalysis re-enacts early conflicts by applying to the analyst feelings and attitudes that the patient had toward significant others in the past

TABLE 2.2 Examples of Defense Mechanisms

MECHANISM	DEFINITION	EXAMPLE
Repression	Blocking forbidden or dangerous desires and thoughts to keep them from entering one's consciousness; the most basic defense mechanism.	A soldier who witnesses the horrible death of his friend in combat may force the event out of consciousness because it symbolizes his own mortality.
Reaction formation	Repression of dangerous impulses, followed by conversion of them to their direct opposite.	A woman who gives birth to an unwanted child may become an extremely overprotective mother who is afraid to let the child out of her sight and who showers the child with superficial attention.
Projection	Ridding oneself of threatening desires or thoughts by attributing them to others.	A worker may mask unpleasant feelings of inadequacy by blaming his poor performance on the incompetence of fellow workers or on a conspiracy in which enemies are disrupting his life.
Rationalization	Explaining one's behavior by giving well-thought-out and socially acceptable reasons that do not happen to be the real ones.	A student may explain flunking a test as follows: "I'm not interested in the course and don't really need it to graduate. Besides, I find the teacher extremely dull."
Displacement	Directing an emotion, such as hostility or anxiety, toward a substitute target.	A meek clerk who is constantly belittled by her boss builds up tremendous resentment and snaps at her family members instead of at her boss, who might fire her.
Undoing	Symbolically attempting, often in a ritualistic or repetitive way, to right a wrong or negate some disapproved thought, impulse, or act.	In Shakespeare's play *Macbeth*, Lady Macbeth goads her husband into slaying the king and then tries to cleanse herself of sin by constantly going through the motions of washing her hands.
Regression	Retreating to an earlier developmental level—according to Freud, to one's most fixated stage—that demands less mature responses and aspirations.	A dignified college president drinks too much and sings old school songs at a reunion with college classmates.

Ivan Pavlov (1849–1936)

A Russian physiologist, Pavlov discovered the associative learning process we know as classical conditioning while he was studying salivation in dogs. Pavlov won the Nobel Prize in Physiology or Medicine in 1904 for his work on the principal digestive glands.

Among the ego autonomy theorists were people such as Anna Freud, Heinz Hartmann, and Erik Erikson, who believed that cognitive processes of the ego were often constructive, creative, and productive (independent from the id). Likewise, object relations theorists such as Melanie Klein, Margaret Mahler, Otto Kernberg, and Heinz Kohut stressed the importance of interpersonal relationships and the child's separation from the mother as important in one's psychological growth.

Criticisms of Psychodynamic Models Psychodynamic theory has had a tremendous impact on the field of psychology, but three major criticisms are often leveled at it. First, Freud's observations about human behavior were often made under uncontrolled conditions. For example, he relied heavily on case studies and on his own self-analysis as a basis for formulating theory. Second, his patients, from whom he drew conclusions about universal aspects of personality dynamics and behavior, tended to represent a very narrow spectrum of his society. Third, it cannot be applied to a wide range of disturbed people. Among them are individuals who have speech disturbances or are inarticulate (talking is important in therapy); people who have urgent, immediate problems (classical psychoanalysis requires much time); and people who are very young or old. Last, psychodynamic formulations are very difficult to investigate in a scientific manner because they are ambiguous and loosely formulated.

Behavioral Models

behavioral models models of psychopathology concerned with the role of learning in abnormal behavior

The **behavioral models** of psychopathology are concerned with the role of learning in abnormal behavior. The differences among them lie mainly in their explanations of how learning occurs (Corey, 2013). The three learning paradigms are *classical conditioning*, *operant conditioning*, and *observational learning*.

The Classical Conditioning Paradigm Early in the 20th century, Ivan Pavlov (1849–1936), a Russian physiologist, discovered a process known as **classical conditioning**, in which responses to new stimuli are learned through association. This process involves involuntary responses (such as reflexes, emotional reactions, and sexual arousal), which are controlled by the autonomic nervous system.

Pavlov was measuring dogs' salivation as part of a study of their digestive processes when he noticed that the dogs began to salivate at the sight of an assistant carrying their food. This response led to his formulation of classical conditioning. He reasoned that food is an **unconditioned stimulus (UCS)**, which, in the mouth, automatically elicits salivation; this salivation is an unlearned or **unconditioned response (UCR)** to the food. Pavlov then presented a previously *neutral* stimulus (one, such as the sound of a bell, that does not initially elicit salivation) to the dogs just before presenting the food. He found that, after a number of repetitions, the sound of the bell alone elicited salivation. This learning process is based on association: the neutral stimulus (the bell) acquires some of the properties of the unconditioned stimulus (the food) when they are repeatedly paired. When the bell alone can provoke the salivation, it becomes a **conditioned stimulus (CS)**. The salivation elicited by the bell is a **conditioned response (CR)**—a learned response to a previously neutral stimulus. Each time the conditioned stimulus is paired with the unconditioned stimulus, the conditioned response is *reinforced*, or strengthened. Pavlov's conditioning process is illustrated in Figure 2.8.

In a classic and oft-cited experiment, J. B. Watson (Watson & Rayner, 1920), using classical conditioning principles, was able to demonstrate that the acquisition of a *phobia* (an exaggerated, seemingly illogical fear of a particular object or class of objects) could be explained by classical conditioning. Classical conditioning has provided explanations not only for the acquisition of phobias but also for certain unusual sexual attractions and other extreme emotional reactions.

The Operant Conditioning Paradigm An **operant behavior** is a voluntary and controllable behavior, such as walking or thinking, that "operates" on an individual's environment. In an extremely warm room, for example, you would have difficulty consciously controlling your sweating—willing your body not to perspire. You could, however, simply walk out of the uncomfortably warm room—an operant behavior. Most human behavior is operant in nature.

Operant conditioning differs from classical conditioning in two primary ways. First, classical conditioning is linked to the development of involuntary

classical conditioning a process in which responses to new stimuli are learned through association

unconditioned stimulus (UCS) in classical conditioning, the stimulus that elicits an unconditioned response

unconditioned response (UCR) in classical conditioning, the unlearned response made to an unconditioned stimulus

conditioned stimulus (CS) in classical conditioning, a previously neutral stimulus that has acquired some of the properties of another stimulus with which it has been paired

conditioned response (CR) in classical conditioning, a learned response to a previously neutral stimulus that has acquired some of the properties of another stimulus with which it has been paired

operant behavior voluntary and controllable behavior, such as walking or thinking, that "operates" on an individual's environment

operant conditioning theory of learning that holds that behaviors are controlled by the consequences that follow them

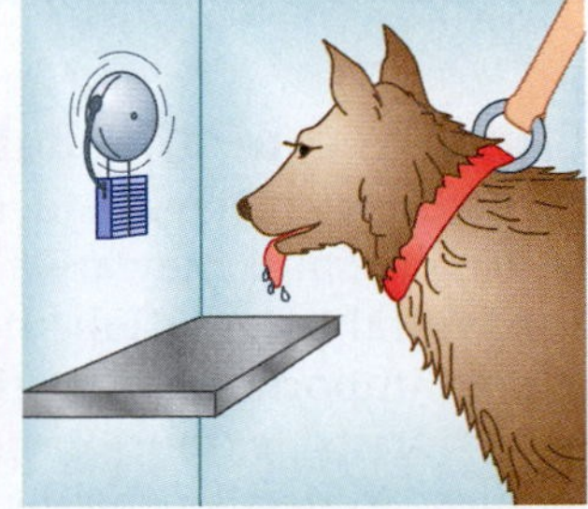

FIGURE 2.8

A Basic Classical Conditioning Process Dogs normally salivate when food is provided (left). With his laboratory dogs, Ivan Pavlov paired the ringing of a bell with the presentation of food (middle). Eventually, the dogs would salivate to the ringing of the bell alone, when no food was near (right).

Steve Warnowski/The Image Works

Operant Conditioning in the Classroom

In operant conditioning, positive consequences increase the likelihood and frequency of a desired response. This is particularly important in teaching young children that appropriate behavior will be rewarded and inappropriate behavior will be punished. These first graders are being treated to a petting zoo for good behavior maintained in the classroom. The reward is changed on a monthly basis.

behaviors, such as fear responses, whereas operant conditioning is related to voluntary behaviors. Second, behaviors based on *classical* conditioning are controlled by stimuli, or events *preceding* the response: Salivation occurs only when it is preceded by a UCS (food in the mouth) or a CS (the thought of a sizzling, juicy steak covered with mushrooms, for example). In *operant* conditioning, however, behaviors are controlled by reinforcers—consequences that influence the frequency or magnitude of the event they follow. Positive consequences increase the likelihood and frequency of a response. But when the consequences are negative, the behavior is less likely to be repeated.

Studies have demonstrated a relationship between environmental reinforcers and certain abnormal behaviors. Self-injurious behavior, such as head banging, is a dramatic form of psychopathology that is often reported in children with psychosis and mental retardation. Parents may unwittingly reinforce a child's self-injurious behaviors by showing greater attention and concern whenever such responses occur. Although positive reinforcement can account for some forms of self-injurious or other undesirable behaviors, in some instances other variables seem more important.

Negative reinforcement (the removal of an aversive stimulus), for example, can also strengthen and maintain unhealthy behaviors. Consider a student who has enrolled in a class in which the instructor requires oral reports. The thought of doing an oral presentation in front of a class produces feelings of anxiety, sweating, an upset stomach, and trembling in the student. Having these feelings is aversive. To stop the unpleasant reaction, the student switches to another section in which the instructor does not require oral presentations. The student's behavior is reinforced by escape from aversive feelings, and such avoidance responses to situations involving "stage fright" will increase in frequency.

AP Photo

B. F. Skinner (1904–1990)

Skinner was a leader in the field of behaviorism. His research and work in operant conditioning started a revolution in applying the principles of learning to the psychology of human behavior. He was also a social philosopher, and many of his ideas fueled debate about the nature of the human condition. These ideas were expressed in his books *Walden Two* and *Beyond Freedom and Dignity*.

The Observational Learning Paradigm

The traditional behavioral theories of learning—classical conditioning and operant conditioning—require that the individual actually perform behaviors to learn them. **Observational learning theory** suggests that an individual can acquire new behaviors simply by watching other people perform them (Bandura, 1997). The process of learning by observing models (and later imitating them) is called *vicarious conditioning* or **modeling**. Direct and tangible reinforcement (such as praise or other rewards) for imitation of the model is not necessary, although reinforcers are necessary to maintain behaviors learned in this manner. Observational learning can involve both respondent and operant behaviors, and its discovery has had such an impact in psychology that it has been proposed as a third form of learning (Bandura, 1997).

In explaining psychopathology, the assumption is that exposure to disturbed models is likely to produce disturbed behaviors. For example, when monkeys watch other monkeys respond with fear to an unfamiliar object, they learn to respond in a similar manner.

Criticisms of the Behavioral Models

Behavioral approaches to psychopathology have had a tremendous impact in the areas of etiology and treatment, and they are a strong force in psychology today. Opponents of the behavioral orientation, however, point out that it often neglects—or places a low importance on—the inner determinants of behavior. They criticize behaviorists' extension to human beings of results obtained from animal studies. Some also charge that because of its lack of attention to human values in relation to behavior, the behaviorist perspective is mechanistic, viewing people as "empty organisms." This specific criticism is less applicable to proponents of modeling.

observational learning theory theory that suggests that an individual can acquire new behaviors by watching other people perform them

modeling process of learning by observing models (and later imitating them)

Cognitive Models

Cognitive models are based on the assumption that conscious thought mediates, or modifies, an individual's emotional state or behavior in response to a stimulus. According to these models, people actually create their own problems (and symptoms) by the ways they interpret events and situations. For example, one person who fails to be hired for a job may become depressed, blaming himself or herself for the failure. Another might become only mildly irritated, believing that failure to get the job had nothing to do with personal inadequacy. How does it happen that the event (not being hired for a job) is identical for both people but the responses are very different?

Observational learning proponents believe that watching violent TV or video games may be harmful to the mental health of teenagers and promote more aggressive behavior. A recent study on teenage boys found a relationship between observing violence, brain function, and aggression (Strenziok et al., 2010). The researchers found that repeated exposure to violence affects neurological reactivity, desensitizes adolescent brains, blunts emotional responses to aggression, and promotes aggressive attitudes and behaviors. Such a finding is very consistent with the reciprocity explanation of the multipath model.

Cognitive Dynamics in Psychopathology Cognitive theories argue that modifying thoughts and feelings is essential to changing behavior. How people label a situation and how they interpret events profoundly affect their emotional reactions and behaviors. Cognitive psychologists usually search for the causes of psychopathology in one of two processes: (a) actual irrational and maladaptive assumptions and thoughts or (b) distortions of the actual thought process.

With respect to the former, cognitive theorists stress that disturbed individuals have both irrational and maladaptive thoughts (A. T. Beck & Weishaar, 2010; A. Ellis, 2008). Aaron Beck (1921–) and Albert Ellis (1913–2007) are cognitive psychologists who have explained psychological problems as being produced by irrational thought patterns that stem from the individual's belief system. Irrational thoughts have been conditioned through early childhood, and these false beliefs are reinstilled in ourselves by autosuggestion and self-repetition (A. Ellis, 2008). Although being accepted and loved by everyone is desirable, it is an unrealistic and irrational idea, and as such it creates dysfunctional feelings and behaviors.

Whereas irrational thoughts may constitute the basis of a mental disorder, psychopathology may also result from distortions in the actual process of thinking. For example, a person's approach to life may involve *catastrophizing*, or thinking about the worst scenario or outcome for situations (having a headache and concluding it is due to a brain tumor). These "logical errors" in thinking distort objective reality and may result in anxiety, depression, or feelings of worthlessness.

Cognitive Approaches to Therapy Certain commonalities characterize almost all cognitive approaches to psychotherapy. These have been summarized by A. T. Beck & Weishaar (2010):

> Cognitive therapy consists of highly specific learning experiences designed to teach patients (1) to monitor their negative, automatic thoughts (cognitions); (2) to recognize the connections between cognition, affect, and behavior; (3) to examine the evidence for and against distorted automatic thoughts; (4) to substitute more reality-oriented interpretations for these biased cognitions; and (5) to learn to identify and alter the beliefs that predispose them to distort their experiences. (p. 308)

Criticisms of the Cognitive Models Some behaviorists remain quite skeptical of the cognitive schools. Just before his death, B. F. Skinner (1990) warned that cognitions are not observable phenomena and cannot form the foundations of empiricism. In this context, he echoed the historical beliefs of John B. Watson, who stated that the science of psychology was about observable behaviors, not "mentalistic concepts." Although Watson's reference was to the intrapsychic dynamics of the mind postulated by Freud, he might have viewed cognitions in the same manner.

Cognitive theories have also been attacked by more humanistically oriented psychologists who believe that human behavior is more than thoughts and beliefs (Corey, 2013. They object to the mechanistic manner by which human beings are reduced to the sum of their cognitive parts. Do thoughts and beliefs

cognitive models models based on the assumption that conscious thought mediates an individual's emotional state or behavior in response to a stimulus

© Bob Daemmrich/The Image Works

Learning by Observing

Observational learning is based on the theory that behavior can be learned by observing it. Although much has been made of the relationship between violence and aggression viewed on television and in movies and violent behavior in real life, observational learning can have positive benefits as well.

really cause disturbances, or do the disturbances themselves distort thinking?

Criticisms have also been leveled at the therapeutic approach taken by cognitive therapists. The nature of the approach makes the therapist a teacher, expert, and authority figure. The therapist is quite direct and confrontive in identifying and attacking irrational beliefs and processes. In such interactions, clients can readily be intimidated into acquiescing to the therapist's power and authority. Thus the therapist may misidentify the client's disorder and the client may be hesitant to challenge the therapist's beliefs.

Humanistic-Existential Models

Applying humanistic-existential approaches to the development of mental disorders is a major challenge. In many respects, humanistic approaches (characterized by a belief in the innate goodness of humanity) are philosophical in nature, deal with values, speak to the nature of the human condition, decry the use of diagnostic labels, and prefer a holistic view of the person. The humanistic and existential approaches evolved as a reaction to the determinism of early models of psychopathology. For example, Freudian theory stressed strongly that personality was developed during the first 5 years of life and relatively unchangeable. Similarly, cognitive-behavioral schools of thought described human beings as "learned responses," "automatic beings," and "deterministic creatures" who were victims of their conditioning histories.

Although the humanistic and existential perspectives represent many schools of thought, they nevertheless share a set of assumptions that distinguishes them from other approaches. The first is that people's realities are products of unique experiences and perceptions of the world. A person's subjective universe—how he or she construes events—is more important than the events themselves. Hence, to understand why people behave as they do, psychologists must reconstruct the world from an individual's vantage point. Second, humanistic-existential theorists assume that individuals have the ability to make free choices and are responsible for their own decisions. Third, they believe in the wholeness or integrity of the person and view as pointless all attempts to reduce human beings to a set of formulas, to explain them simply by measuring responses to certain stimuli. And fourth, they assume that people have the ability to become what they want, to fulfill their capacities, and to lead the lives best suited to them.

The Humanistic Perspective

One of the major contributions of the **humanistic perspective** is its positive view of the individual. Carl Rogers (1902–1987) is perhaps the best-known of the humanistic psychologists. Rogers's theory of personality (C. R. Rogers, 1959, 1961) reflects his concern with human welfare and his deep conviction that humanity is basically good, forward moving, and trustworthy.

The Actualizing Tendency Instead of concentrating exclusively on behavior disorders, the humanistic approach is concerned with helping people *actualize* their potential and with bettering the state of humanity. Humanistic psychological theory is based on the idea that people are motivated not only to satisfy their biological needs (for food, warmth, and sex) but also to cultivate, maintain, and enhance the self.

The quintessence of this view is the concept of **self-actualization**—a term popularized by Abraham Maslow (1954)—which is an inherent tendency to strive toward the realization of one's full potential. This thrust of life that pushes people forward is manifested in such qualities as curiosity, creativity, and joy of discovery.

humanistic perspective the optimistic viewpoint that people are born with the ability to fulfill their potential and that abnormal behavior results from disharmony between a person's potential and his or her self-concept

self-actualization an inherent tendency to strive toward the realization of one's full potential

Development of Abnormal Behavior Rogers believed that if people were left unencumbered by societal restrictions and were allowed to grow and develop freely, the result would be fully functioning people. In such a case, the **self-concept** and the actualizing tendency would be considered congruent.

However, society frequently imposes *conditions of worth* on its members, standards by which people determine whether they have worth. These standards are transmitted via *conditional positive regard*. That is, significant others (such as parents, peers, friends, and spouses) in a person's life accept some but not all of that person's actions, feelings, and attitudes. The person's self-concept becomes defined as having worth only when others approve. But this reliance on others forces the individual to develop a distorted self-concept that is inconsistent with his or her self-actualizing potential, inhibiting that person from being self-actualized. A state of disharmony or *incongruence* is said to exist between the person's inherent potential and his or her self-concept (as determined by significant others). This state of incongruence forms the basis of abnormal behavior.

Rogers believed that fully functioning people have been *allowed to grow* toward their potential. The environmental condition most suitable for this growth is called *unconditional positive regard* (C. R. Rogers, 1951). In essence, people who are significant figures in someone's life value and respect that person *as a person*. Giving unconditional positive regard is valuing and loving regardless of behavior. People may disapprove of someone's actions, but they still respect, love, and care for that someone.

Roger Ressmeyer/Corbis

Carl Rogers (1902–1987)

Rogers believed that people need both positive regard from others and positive self-regard. According to Rogers, when positive regard is given unconditionally, a person can develop freely and become self-actualized.

Person-Centered Therapy

The assumption that humans need unconditional positive regard has many implications for psychotherapy. For therapists, it means fostering conditions that allow clients to grow and fulfill their potential; this approach has become known as *nondirective* or *person-centered therapy*. Rogers emphasized that therapists' attitudes are more important than specific counseling techniques. Therapists cannot help clients by explaining their behavior or by prescribing actions to follow. Therapeutic techniques involve expressing and communicating respect, understanding, and acceptance.

Did You Know?

Perhaps the forerunner of positive psychology comes from the work of humanistic psychologists such as Abraham Maslow and Carl Rogers, who believed that people are basically good and motivated to enhance the self and have inner resources that, if encouraged, will result in self-actualization. Instead of viewing a person's weaknesses and deficits, tapping into the assets and strengths is more important. The more willing a therapist is to rely on a patient's strengths and potential, the more likely it is that the patient will discover such strengths and potential.

The Existential Perspective

The **existential approach** is not a systematized school of thought but a set of attitudes. It shares with humanistic psychology an emphasis on individual uniqueness, a quest for meaning in life and for freedom and responsibility, a phenomenological approach (understanding a person's subjective world of experience) to understanding people, and a belief that the individual has positive attributes that are eventually expressed unless they are distorted by the environment.

The existential and humanistic approaches differ in several dimensions: (a) existentialism is less optimistic than humanism and focuses on the irrationality, difficulties, and suffering all humans encounter in life; (b) humanists attempt to understand the subjective world of their clients through empathy, while existentialists believe the individual must be viewed within the context of the human condition; and (c) humanism stresses the individual's responsibility for what he or she becomes in this life, while existentialists stress responsibility not only to the self but also to others.

Criticisms of the Humanistic and Existential Approaches

Criticisms of the humanistic and existential approaches point to their "fuzzy," ambiguous, and nebulous nature and to the small population in which these approaches can be applied. Although these phenomenological approaches have been extremely creative in describing the human condition, they have been less successful in constructing theory. Moreover, they are not suited to scientific or experimental investigation. The emphasis on subjective understanding rather than prediction and control, on intuition and empathy rather than objective investigation,

self-concept an individual's assessment of his or her own value and worth

existential approach a set of attitudes that has many commonalities with humanism but is less optimistic, focusing (a) on human alienation in an increasingly technological and impersonal world, (b) on the individual in the context of the human condition, and (c) on responsibility to others as well as to oneself

and on the individual rather than the more general category all tend to hinder empirical study.

Carl Rogers certainly expressed many of his ideas as researchable propositions, but it is difficult to verify scientifically the humanistic concept of people as rational, inherently good, and moving toward self-fulfillment. The existential perspective can be similarly criticized for its lack of scientific grounding because of its reliance on the unique subjective experiences of individuals to describe the inner world. Such data are difficult to quantify and test. Nevertheless, the existential concepts of freedom, choice, responsibility, being, and nonbeing have had a profound influence on contemporary thought beyond the field of psychology.

Another major criticism leveled at the humanistic and existential approaches is that they do not work well with severely disturbed clients. They seem to be most effective with intelligent, well-educated, and relatively "normal" individuals who may be suffering adjustment difficulties. This limitation, along with the occasional vagueness of humanistic and existential thought, has hindered broad application of these ideas to abnormal psychology.

Multipath Implications of Psychological Explanations

All the psychological theories discussed have both strengths and weaknesses; no one of them can claim to tell "the whole truth." Each model—whether psychodynamic, behavioral, cognitive, or existential-humanistic—represents different views of pathology. Each details a different perspective from which to interpret reality, the nature of people, the origin of disorders, the standards used for judging normality and abnormality, and the therapeutic cure. Each model has devout supporters.

The multipath model would suggest that we best understand abnormal behavior only by evidence-based integration of the various approaches. It is possible that the psychological models of psychopathology are describing the same phenomena but from different vantage points. Many models of psychopathology focus on one aspect of the human condition to the exclusion of others, overlooking the person as a total package and resulting in a distorted view. Some models emphasize the importance of *history* (psychodynamic), some of *feeling* (humanistic-existential), some of *thinking* (cognitive), and still others of *behaving* (behavioral). A truly comprehensive model of human behavior, normal and abnormal, must address the possibility that people are all of these—*biological*, *historical*, *feeling*, *thinking*, and *behaving* beings—and probably much more: social, cultural, spiritual, and political ones as well.

CHECKPOINT REVIEW

1. Compare and contrast the psychodynamic, behavioral, cognitive and humanistic-existential models with one another.
2. What are the major criticisms associated with each model?
3. How does the multipath model integrate these perspectives?

Dimension Three: Social Factors

Almost all theories of psychopathology discussed so far focus on the individual rather than on the social environment. They are relatively silent in addressing such important aspects of our lives as relationships with people and how such factors as family, social support, love, community, and belonging affect the manifestation and expression of behavior disorders. It is clear that we are social beings and that our relationships can influence the development, manifestation, and amelioration of mental disorders.

Did You Know? People with rich relationships and social networks have greater resilience and positive mental health outcomes: they live longer, are less prone to commit suicide, are less likely to develop psychiatric disorders such as depression and alcoholism, enjoy better physical health, recover more quickly after an illness, and are generally happier and more optimistic (A. L. Berman, 2006; Segrin, Powell, Givertz, & Brackin, 2003; University of Michigan, 2010). It is clear that social relationships are important in places of employment, churches, neighborhoods, schools, communities, and in healthy family relationships.

Social-Relational Models

Studies support the conclusion that social isolation and lack of emotional support and intimacy are correlated with asthma, depression, suicide, lower stress tolerance, and low self-esteem (Collishaw et al., 2007; Elsevier, 2010; Nagano et al., 2010; Smyke et al., 2007). Social-relational explanations of abnormal behavior make several important assumptions (D. W. Johnson & Johnson, 2003): (a) healthy relationships are important for human development and functioning; (b) these relationships provide many intangible health benefits (social support, love, compassion, trust, faith, sense of belonging, resistance to stress, etc.); and (c) when relationships prove dysfunctional or are absent, the individual may be subject to mental disturbances. Treatment of socially produced disorders is most effective by improving interpersonal relationships of patients through a systemic approach.

Family, Couples, and Group Perspectives In contrast to traditional psychological models, social-relational models emphasize how other people, especially significant others, influence our behavior. This viewpoint holds that all people are enmeshed in a network of interdependent roles, statuses, values, and norms. One of these, the **family systems model**, assumes that the behavior of one family member directly affects the entire family system. Correspondingly, people typically behave in ways that reflect family influences (both healthy and unhealthy).

We can identify three distinct characteristics of the family systems approach (Corey, 2013). First, personality development is ruled largely by the attributes of the family, especially by the way parents behave toward and around their children. Second, abnormal behavior in an individual is usually a reflection or "symptom" of unhealthy family dynamics and, more specifically, of poor communication among family members. Third, therapists must focus on the family system, not solely on the individual, and must strive to involve the entire family in therapy. As a result, the locus of disorder is seen to reside not within the individual but within the family system.

Social-Relational Treatment Approaches The family systems model has spawned a number of treatment approaches. One group emphasizes the importance of clear and direct *communications* for healthy family system development (V. Satir, 1967). Virginia Satir's *conjoint family therapeutic approach* stresses the importance of teaching message-sending and message-receiving skills to family members. Like other family therapists, Satir believes that the identified patient is really a reflection of the family system gone awry. *Strategic family approaches* (Haley, 1963, 1987) deal with power struggles that occur among family members by attempting to shift the balance to a more healthy distribution. *Structural family approaches* (Minuchin, 1974) attempt to reorganize family members because they are either too much involved or too little involved with one another. All of these approaches focus on communication, balancing power relationships among family members, and restructuring the troubled family system.

Couples therapy includes both marital relationships and intimate relationships between unmarried partners. It is a treatment aimed at helping couples understand and clarify their communications, role relationships, unfulfilled needs, and unrealistic or unmet expectations. Couples therapy has become an increasingly popular

family systems model model that assumes that the behavior of one family member directly affects the entire family system

couples therapy a treatment aimed at helping couples understand and clarify their communications, role relationships, unfulfilled needs, and unrealistic or unmet expectations

Hill Street Studios/Getty Images

treatment for those who find that the quality of their relationship needs improvement (Nichols & Schwartz, 2005).

Another form of social-relational treatment is **group therapy**. Unlike couples and family therapy, members of the group are initially strangers. Group members may, however, share various characteristics. Groups may be formed to treat older clients, unemployed workers, or pregnant women; to treat clients with similar psychological disturbances; or to treat people with similar therapeutic goals. Most group therapies focus on interrelationships and the dynamics of interaction among members. Despite their wide diversity, successful groups and group approaches share several features that promote change in clients (Corey, 2013; Yalom, 2005): (a) the group experience allows each client to become involved in a social situation and to see how his or her behavior affects others; (b) the therapist can see how clients actually respond in a real-life social and interpersonal context; (c) group members can develop new communication skills, social skills, and insights; (d) groups often help members feel less isolated and less fearful about their problems; and (e) groups can provide members with strong social and emotional support. The feelings of intimacy, belonging, protection, and trust (which members may not be able to experience outside the group) can be a powerful motivation to confront one's problems and seek to overcome them.

Family Dynamics and Positive Self-Image

Family interaction patterns can exert tremendous influence on a child's personality development, determining the child's sense of self-worth and the acquisition of appropriate social skills. This picture shows a Hispanic family preparing dinner together. Notice the attentiveness and obvious expressions of joy by the parents toward their children (communicating a sense of importance to them) and how all family members are actively involved in their respective roles (emphasizing family cohesion and belonging).

Criticisms of Social-Relational Models There is no denying that we are social creatures, and by concentrating on this aspect of human behavior, the social-relational models have added an important social dimension to our understanding of abnormal behavior. Research on the effects of family and couples therapy has been consistent in pointing to the value of therapy compared with no-treatment and alternative-treatment control groups. However, research studies have generally not been rigorous in design; they have often lacked appropriate control groups, follow-up periods of outcome, or good measures of outcome. Further, considerable evidence exists that couples, marital, and family therapy operate under culture-bound definitions (D. W. Sue & Sue, 2013). Other critics have voiced concern that family systems models may have unpleasant consequences. Too often, psychologists have pointed an accusing finger at the parents of children who suffer from certain disorders, despite an abundance of evidence that parental influence may not be a factor in those disorders. The parents are then burdened with unnecessary guilt over a situation they could not have controlled.

CHECKPOINT REVIEW

1. Name several psychological problems that may arise from dysfunctional social relationships.
2. What evidence do we have that positive social relationships foster good mental health?
3. Provide several examples of social-relational treatment approaches.

Dimension Four: Sociocultural Factors

group therapy a form of therapy that involves the simultaneous treatment of two or more clients and may involve more than one therapist

Sociocultural perspectives emphasize the importance of considering race, ethnicity, gender, sexual orientation, religious preference, socioeconomic status, physical disabilities, and other such factors in explaining mental disorders. Research consistently reveals that belonging to specific sociodemographic groups influences the manifestation of behavior disorders and may subject members to unique stressors not experienced by other groups (Keller & Calgay, 2010; L. Smith & Reddington, 2010; D. W. Sue, 2010).

The importance of the sociocultural dimension is clearly evident in the *Diagnostic and Statistical Manual of Mental Disorders* (DSM), in which a number of culture-bound syndromes are listed. These are disorders generally limited to a specific society or cultural group. For example, *taijin kyofusho* is a culture-specific disorder (seen not in the United States but in Japan) in which the individual fears that his or her body parts or function are offensive to other people because of appearance, odor, or movements. *Ataque de nervios* is reported among Latinos from the Caribbean and includes symptoms of uncontrollable shouting, seizure-like episodes, trembling, and crying. It is clear that people's cultural experiences are important factors in the manifestation of mental disorders (D. W. Sue & Sue, 2013). We briefly discuss three major sociocultural factors to illustrate their importance in understanding psychopathology: gender, socioeconomic class, and race and ethnicity.

Gender Factors

The importance of gender in understanding psychopathology is clearly seen in rates of depression among women. Up to seven million women suffer from depression, which is twice the number for men (Schwartzman & Glaus, 2000). Rather than a narrow explanation (biological or psychological alone), it is highly probable that many factors contribute, including sociocultural ones. For example, women are placed in an unenviable position of fulfilling stereotyped feminine social roles defined by our society. In Chapter 9 (on eating disorders), we discuss more fully how stereotyped standards of beauty in advertisements and the mass media can affect the health and self-esteem of girls and women. Body dissatisfaction, eating disorders, and depression are all significantly related to sociocultural standards.

Women are also consistently subjected to greater stressors than their male counterparts (L. Smith, 2010; Spradlin & Parsons, 2008). They carry more of the domestic burden, more responsibility for child care, and more responsibility for social and interpersonal relationships. This is true even if they are employed full-time outside of the home (D. W. Sue, 2010). The plight of women in the United States is well documented (National Academy of Sciences, National Academy of Engineering, & Institute of Medicine, 2006): (a) employed primarily in low-wage, traditionally female occupations; (b) subjected to sexual harassment (81 percent of eighth through 11th graders, 30 percent of undergraduates, and 40 percent of graduate students); (c) paid less than their male counterparts in similar jobs; (d) given less recognition, encouragement, and approval in classrooms than their male counterparts; (e) more likely to live in poverty; (f) faced with more barriers to their career choices; and (g) faced with greater discrimination and victimization. Given these facts, little doubt exists that these stressors have a major impact on female mental health.

Socioeconomic Class

Social class and classism are two frequently overlooked sociodemographic factors in psychology and mental health (L. Smith, 2010). Lower socioeconomic class is related to lower sense of self-control, poorer physical health, and higher incidence of depression (D. W. Sue, 2010). Increasingly, psychologists are beginning to appreciate how poverty subjects people to increased stressors (Smith & Reddington, 2010). Life in poverty is characterized by low wages, unemployment, underemployment, lack of savings, little property ownership, and lack of food reserves. Meeting even the most basic needs of food and shelter becomes a major challenge. In such circumstances, people are likely to experience feelings of hopelessness, helplessness, dependence, and inferiority.

Tim Graham/Getty Images

Amana Productions Inc./Getty Images

Multicultural Perspectives

Multicultural models of human behavior regard race, culture, and ethnicity as central to the understanding of normality and abnormality. In China, children are taught to value group harmony over individual competitiveness. In contrast, in the United States, individual efforts and privacy are valued. Note the common use of cubicles in work settings to separate people from one another.

inferiority model early attempt to explain differences in minority groups that contended that racial and ethnic minorities are inferior in some respect to the majority population

deficit model early attempt to explain differences in minority groups that contended that differences are the result of "cultural deprivation"

universal shamanic tradition (UST) set of beliefs and practices from non-Western indigenous psychologies that assume that special healers are blessed with powers to act as intermediaries or messengers between the human and spirit worlds

Race and Ethnicity: Multicultural Models of Psychopathology

Early attempts to explain differences between various minority groups and their white counterparts tended to adopt one of two models. The first, the **inferiority model**, contended that racial and ethnic minorities are inferior in some respect to the majority population. For example, this model attributes low academic achievement and higher unemployment rates among African Americans and Latinos to low intelligence (heredity). The second model—the deprivations or **deficit model**—explained differences as the result of "cultural deprivation." It implied that minority groups lacked the "right" culture. Both models have been severely criticized as inaccurate, biased, and unsupported in the scientific literature (Ridley, 2005; D. W. Sue & Sue, 2013).

CONTROVERSY:

The Universal Shamanic Tradition: Wizards, Sorcerers, and Witch Doctors

Since the beginning of human existence, all societies and cultural groups have developed their own explanations of abnormal behavior and their own culture-specific ways of dealing with human suffering and distress (Moodley, 2005). A surprising consequence of the multicultural psychology movement has been a revival of interest in non-Western indigenous explanations of human disorders and their treatments. Much of this is due to our changing demographics, with the influx of many immigrants who may hold non-Western beliefs regarding illness, mental disorder, and treatment.

Western science defines reality as grounded in what can be observed and measured through the five senses, whereas many indigenous peoples' explanations believe that the nature of reality transcends the senses (R. Walsh & Shapiro, 2006). The term ***universal shamanic tradition* (UST)** refers to the belief that there are special healers

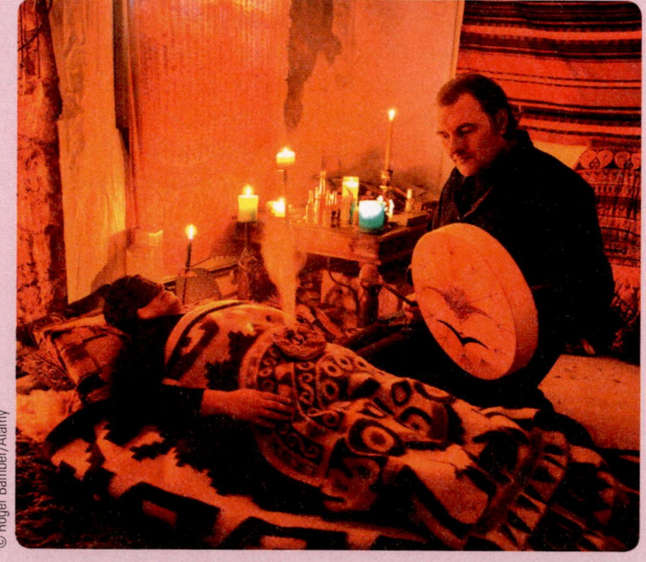

© Roger Bamber/Alamy

(continued)

who are blessed with powers to act as intermediaries or messengers between the human and spirit worlds. Healers are believed to possess unusual powers beyond the sensory and physical planes of existence. They are (a) sanctioned by their communities as extraordinary people; (b) regarded highly, respected, and sometimes feared; (c) keepers of timeless wisdom; and (d) believed to be able to muster up spiritual forces to heal the sick (C. C. Lee & Armstrong, 1995; C. C. Lee, Oh, & Montcastle, 1992; Moodley, 2005).

When a person is afflicted by a mental or physical disorder, treatment may involve special ceremonies that include rituals, prayers, and sacred symbols all aimed at summoning spiritual forces to help in the cure. Shamans are believed to possess the power to enter altered states of consciousness, to journey to an existence beyond the physical world, and to contact and communicate with spirits.

People who study indigenous psychologies and UST do not make an assumption that one particular perspective is superior to another (Mikulas, 2006). Western explanations, however, do consider scientific methods to be more advanced than those found in many cultures (Moodley, 2005). UST shares common beliefs and assumptions in its explanations of disorders and healing:

- Illness, distress, and problematic behaviors are seen as an imbalance in people relationships, a disharmony between the person and the group, or a lack of synchrony with mind, body, spirit, and nature. Illness is seen as a break in the hoop of life, an imbalance, or a separation between these elements. In many respects, Western values of individualism, separation, and autonomy are seen as unhealthy functioning.
- These approaches accept as given the existence of different planes of consciousness, experience, or existence. The causes of illness or problems are believed to reside in a plane of reality separate from the physical world of existence. Shamans or healers have an ability to enter extraordinary reality states that allow them to access an invisible world surrounding the physical one. There they can enlist the aid of spirits or mollify those that are displeased.
- Many cultures believe that accessing higher states of consciousness enhances perceptual sensitivity, clarity, concentration, and emotional well-being. Having patients attain a higher state of consciousness is part of mental and physical health treatments. Interestingly, meditation and yoga are the most widely practiced form of therapy in the world today. They have been shown to reduce anxiety, specific phobias, substance abuse, chronic pain, and high blood pressure, and to enhance self-confidence, marital satisfaction, and sense of control (D. W. Sue & Sue, 2013).
- Spirituality or a belief in an animating life force is a strong component of most non-Western indigenous psychologies. Western science and society operate from the principle of *separation of church and state* and *separation of science and religion*. In contrast, many Native Americans, for example, believe that our spiritual connectedness or lack of connectedness to the universe and the human condition foretells the "good life" or a life filled with troubles. When one falls out of alignment with spirituality, that person travels an unhealthy path (isolation, loss of meaning, selfishness, etc.) that may be characterized by substance abuse, depression, anxiety, and other psychological disorders.

For Further Consideration

1. How valid are shamanic explanations of illness? Are shamans therapists? In what ways do you believe they are the same? Can you identify commonalities between what therapists and shamans do?
2. What can we learn from indigenous forms of healing? In what ways do religion and spirituality affect your life? Do you believe in altered states of consciousness or different planes of existence?
3. Are there dangers or downsides to shamanism as a belief system or form of treatment?

During the late 1980s and early 1990s, a new and conceptually different model emerged in the literature. Often referred to as the **multicultural model** (or the *culturally diverse model*; D. W. Sue & Sue, 2013), the new approach emphasized that being culturally different does not equal being deviant, pathological, or inferior. The model recognizes that each culture has strengths and limitations. Behaviors are to be evaluated from the perspective of a group's value system, as well as by other standards used in determining normality and abnormality (Ivey, D'Andrea, Ivey, & Simek-Morgan, 2007).

multicultural model contemporary attempt to explain differences in minority groups that suggests that behaviors be evaluated from the perspective of a group's value system, as well as by other standards used in determining normality and abnormality

The multicultural model makes an explicit assumption that all theories of human development arise from a particular cultural context (Ivey et al., 2007). Thus, many traditional European American models of psychopathology are culture

Did You Know? Social psychological studies on implicit bias reveal that nearly everyone born and raised in a particular society—like the United States—inherits racial stereotypes, biases, and prejudices. On a conscious level, most of us believe we are good, moral, and decent human beings who would never deliberately or intentionally discriminate against others. Yet many of our stereotypes operate outside the level of conscious awareness and can be expressed in a discriminatory fashion without our knowledge (Dovidio, Kawakami, Smoak, & Gaertner, 2009). Given that we are unaware of our hidden biases, how do we rid ourselves of them?

bound, evaluating and viewing events and processes from a worldview not experienced or shared by other cultural groups. For example, individualism and autonomy are highly valued in the United States and are equated with healthy functioning. Most European American children are raised to become increasingly independent, to be able to make decisions on their own, and to "stand on their own two feet." In contrast, many traditional Asians and Asian Americans place an equally high value on collectivity, in which the psychosocial unit of identity is the family, not the individual. Similarly, whereas European Americans fear the loss of individuality, members of traditional Asian groups fear the loss of belonging.

Given such different experiences and values, unenlightened mental health professionals may make biased assumptions about human behavior—assumptions that may influence their judgments of normality and abnormality among various racial and ethnic minorities. For example, a mental health professional who does not understand that Asian Americans typically value a collectivistic identity might see such clients as overly dependent, immature, and unable to make decisions on their own. Likewise, such a person might perceive restraint of strong feelings—a valued characteristic among some Asian groups—as evidence of being inhibited, unable to express emotions, or repressed.

The multicultural model also suggests that problems in life may be due to sociocultural stressors residing in the social system rather than conflicts within the person. Racism, bias, discrimination, economic hardships, and cultural conflicts are just a few of the sociopolitical realities with which members of racial and ethnic minorities must contend. As a result, the role of therapist may be better served by ameliorating oppressive or detrimental social conditions than by attempting therapy aimed at changing the individual. Appropriate individual therapy may, however, be directed at teaching clients self-help skills and strategies focused on influencing their immediate social situation.

Criticisms of the Multicultural Model In many respects, the multicultural model operates from a relativistic framework; that is, normal and abnormal behavior must be evaluated from a cultural perspective. The reasoning is that behavior considered disordered in one context—seeing a vision of a dead relative, for example—might be considered acceptable in another time or place. As indicated in the DSM, some religious practices and beliefs consider it normal to hear or see a deceased relative during bereavement. In addition, certain groups, including some American Indian and Hispanic/Latino groups, may perceive hallucinations not as disordered but actually as positive events.

Critics of the multicultural model argue that a disorder is a disorder, regardless of the cultural context in which it is considered. For example, a person suffering from schizophrenia and actively hallucinating is evidencing a malfunctioning of the senses (seeing, hearing, or feeling things that are not there) and a lack of contact with reality. Regardless of whether *the person* judges the occurrence to be desirable or undesirable, it nevertheless represents a disorder (biological dysfunction), according to this viewpoint.

Another criticism leveled at the multicultural model is its lack of empirical validation concerning many of its concepts and assumptions. The field of multicultural counseling and therapy, for example, has been accused of not being solidly grounded in research (Ponterotto & Casas, 1991). Most of the underlying concepts of the multicultural model are based on conceptual critiques or formulations that have not been subjected to formal scientific testing. There is generally heavy reliance on case studies, ethnographic analyses, and investigations of a more qualitative type.

Multicultural psychologists respond to such criticisms by noting that they are based on a Western worldview that emphasizes precision and empirical definitions. They point out that there is more than one way to ask and answer questions about the human condition.

Table 2.3 compares and contrasts the most influential models of psychopathology along a number of different categories.

TABLE 2.3 Comparison of the Most Influential Models of Psychopathology

MODEL	MOTIVATION FOR BEHAVIOR	BASIS FOR ASSESSMENT	THEORETICAL FOUNDATION	SOURCE OF ABNORMAL BEHAVIOR	TREATMENT
Biological	State of biological integrity and health	Medical tests, self-reports, observable behaviors	Animal and human research, case studies, other research methods	Internal: biological trauma, heredity, biochemical imbalances	Biological interventions (drugs, ECT, surgery, diet)
Psychodynamic	Unconscious influences	Personal history, oral self-reports	Case studies, correlational methods	Internal: early childhood experiences	Dream analysis, free association, transference, locating unconscious conflict from childhood, resolving problem and reintegrating personality
Behavioral	External influences	Observable, objective data; overt behaviors	Animal research, case studies, experimental methods	External: learning maladaptive responses, not acquiring appropriate responses	Directly modifying problem behavior, analyzing environmental factors controlling behavior, altering contingencies
Cognitive	Interaction of external and cognitive influences	Self-statements, alterations in overt behaviors	Human research, case studies, experimental methods	Internal: learned patterns of irrational or negative self-statements	Understanding relationship between self-statements and problem behavior, modifying internal dialogue
Humanistic	Self-actualization	Subjective data, oral self-reports	Case studies, correlational and experimental methods	Internal: incongruence between self and experiences	Nondirective reflection, no interpretation, providing unconditional positive regard, increasing congruence between self and experience
Existential	Capacity for self-awareness; freedom to decide one's fate; search for meaning	Subjective data, oral self-reports, experiential encounters	An approach to understanding the human condition rather than a firm theoretical model	Internal: failure to actualize human potential, avoidance of choice and responsibility	Providing conditions for maximizing self-awareness and growth to enable patients to be free and responsible
Family Systems	Interaction with significant others	Observation of family dynamics	Case studies, social psychological studies, experimental methods	External: faulty family interactions (family pathology, inconsistent communication patterns)	Treating the entire family, not just the identified patient
Multicultural	Cultural values and norms	Study of group norms and behaviors, understanding of societal values and relations between minority and dominant group	Study of cultural groups; data from anthropology, sociology, and political science	Culture conflicts, oppression	Balancing culture universal and culture specific healing approaches and recognizing that no one approach is adequate for all populations

CHECKPOINT REVIEW

1. How may social class, gender, and race influence the manifestation of mental disorders?
2. Provide an explanation of why women in our society may be subjected to greater stressors than men.
3. In what ways may poverty affect the mental health of those who are less affluent?
4. Compare and contrast the inferiority, deficit, and multicultural models with one another.

Summary

1 What models of psychopathology have been used to explain abnormal behavior?

- One-dimensional models have been traditionally used to explain disorders. They are inadequate because mental disorders are multidimensional.

2 What is the multipath model of mental disorders?

- The multipath model provides a framework for understanding the biological, psychological, social, and sociocultural causes of mental disorders; the complexity of their interacting components; and the need to view disorders from a holistic framework.

3 How much of mental disorder can be explained through our biological makeup?

- Genetics, brain anatomy, biochemical imbalances, central nervous system functioning, and autonomic nervous system reactivity are oftentimes involved. Neurotransmitters seem to play a significant role in abnormal behavior, and there are some correlations between genetic inheritance and certain psychopathologies. More importantly, research reveals that a predisposition to a disorder, not the disorder itself, may be inherited. Gene × environment interactions are a two-way process that is reciprocal in nature.

4 What psychological models are used to explain the etiology of mental disorders?

- Psychodynamic models emphasize childhood experiences and the role of the unconscious in determining adult behavior.
- Behavioral models focus on the role of learning in abnormal behavior. Abnormal behaviors are acquired through association (classical conditioning), reinforcement (operant conditioning), or modeling (observational learning).
- Cognitive models are based on the assumption that mental disorders are due to irrational beliefs or distorted cognitive processes.
- The humanistic-existential models view an individual's reality as a product of personal perception and experience, see people as capable of making free choices and fulfilling their potential, and emphasize the whole person and the individual's ability to fulfill his or her capacities.

5 What role do social factors play in psychopathology?

- Impairment or absence of social relationships has been found to be correlated with increased susceptibility to mental disorders. Good relationships seem to immunize people against stressors.
- Family systems approaches view abnormal behavior as the result of distorted or faulty communication or unbalanced structural relationships within the family.
- Three social treatments described are family therapy, couples therapy, and group therapy.

6 What sociocultural factors may play a role in the etiology of mental disorders?

- Proponents of the sociocultural approach believe that race, culture, ethnicity, gender, sexual orientation, religious preference, socioeconomic status, physical disabilities, and other variables are powerful influences in determining how specific cultural groups manifest disorders.
- Cultural differences have been perceived in three ways: (a) the inferiority model, in which differences are attributed to the interplay of undesirable elements in a person's biological makeup; (b) the deprivation or deficit model, in which differences in traits or behaviors are blamed on not having the "right culture"; and (c) the multicultural model, in which differences do not necessarily equate with deviance.

Key Terms

etiology 28
model 29
multipath model 30
neuron 33
dendrite 34
axon 34
synapse 34
neurotransmitter 34
genotype 35
phenotype 35
epigenetics 37
genome 37
psychodynamic model 38
defense mechanism 38
pleasure principle 38
reality principle 38
psychosexual stages 38
psychoanalysis 39
free association 39
resistance 39
transference 39
behavioral models 40
classical conditioning 41
unconditioned stimulus (UCS) 41
unconditioned response (UCR) 41
conditioned stimulus (CS) 41
conditioned response (CR) 41
operant behavior 41
operant conditioning 41
observational learning theory 42
modeling 42
cognitive models 43
humanistic perspective 44
self-actualization 44
self-concept 45
existential approach 45
family systems model 47
couples therapy 47
group therapy 48
inferiority model 50
deficit model 50
universal shamanic tradition (UST) 50
multicultural model 51

Media Resources

Psychology CourseMate

Access an interactive e-Book and chapter-specific interactive learning tools, including:

- flashcards
- quizzes
- videos

and more in your Psychology CourseMate.

Go to **CengageBrain.com.**

Huan Tran/Ikon Images/Getty

3

Clinical Research, Assessment, and Diagnosis in Abnormal Psychology

CHAPTER OUTLINE

A mysterious illness involving uncontrolled bodily tics and verbal outbursts was first reported in 15 teenagers (14 girls and 1 boy) in upstate New York. All of the afflicted attended Le Roy Junior/Senior High School when they started showing symptoms. One girl spends most of her time in a wheelchair due to the severity of her symptoms. The New York State Department of Health and local physicians have found no medical or environmental explanations for the symptoms (Moisse & Davis, 2012).

FOCUS QUESTIONS

1 What kinds of studies are used in the field of abnormal psychology?

2 What kinds of tools do clinicians use to evaluate a client's mental health?

3 How are mental health problems categorized or classified?

Clinical research, assessment, and diagnosis are critical tools for the study of **psychopathology**. In the case of Le Roy High School, research and the scientific method were utilized to identify possible causes of the sudden *tics* (spasmodic muscular movements). The teenagers were individually assessed to determine possible individual characteristics or exposures that might be consistent with the symptoms; from this information, tentative diagnoses were formulated. In this chapter, we will consider different research methods used in the field of abnormal psychology, the types of assessment used by clinicians to determine the diagnosis and **etiology** (i.e., the cause) for specific symptom patterns shown by a client. We will first begin with a discussion of how science and research inform the study of abnormal behavior.

The Scientific Method in Clinical Research

Scientists are often described as skeptics. Rather than accept the conclusions from a single study, scientists demand that other researchers *replicate* (repeat) the results. Replication reduces the chance that findings are due to experimenter bias, methodological flaws, or sampling errors (LeBel & Peters, 2011). For example, the following findings were initially reported as "conclusive" in the mass media. Note their current status after further investigation:

- *Childhood vaccines may cause autism.* Due to media reports suggesting that childhood vaccines cause autism, half of all parents report concerns about vaccine safety and side effects, and 11 percent of parents have refused at least one recommended vaccine (Freed, Clark, Butchart, Singer, & Davis, 2010).
  Status: There is no research evidence supporting a link between vaccines and autism (Autism Decisions, 2010; Price et al., 2010).
- *Cannabis use leads to the development of psychoses.* Drug prevention efforts nationwide cite this concern regarding marijuana use.
  Status: A number of studies have found that use of marijuana during adolescence is related to an increased risk of adult psychosis, particularly among those with a pre-existing genetic vulnerability (J. McGrath et al., 2010).
- *The majority of sexually abused children exhibit signs or symptoms of trauma that can be reliably detected by experts in the field of child sexual abuse.*
  Status: There are no signs or symptoms that characterize the majority of abused children, and a significant number of abused children have no apparent symptoms (Hagen, 2003; Kuehnle & Connell, 2009).

As you can see, the search for "truth" is often a long journey. Clinical phenomena need to be assessed and evaluated. The **scientific method** is a method of inquiry that provides for the systematic collection of data, controlled observation, and the testing of hypotheses. A **hypothesis** is a conjectural statement (i.e., a tentative explanation) that describes possible reasons for observed phenomena. Examples of hypotheses regarding the cause of the mysterious illness in New York might include (a) an environmental toxin, (b) a common infection or other medical condition, or (c) a psychologically based disorder. Researchers have to determine which of these hypotheses are supported by data. Quality clinical research requires developing a specific hypothesis, defining the variables of interest, using reliable assessments, and determining if the hypothesis is supported.

psychopathology the study of mental or behavioral disorders

etiology cause or origin of a disorder

scientific method method of inquiry that provides for the systematic collection of data, controlled observation, and the testing of hypotheses

hypothesis conjectural statement that usually describes a relationship between two variables

TABLE 3.1 Levels of Scientific Believability for Research Designs

Experimental designs are considered the gold standard in research because they can provide information regarding cause and effect relationships. Correlational and case studies furnish other important information, including ideas for hypotheses that can be tested using an experimental design.
Level 1: Randomized, controlled experimental studies can be used to demonstrate cause and effect relationships.
Level 2: Correlational studies generate moderate levels of scientific proof, but cannot demonstrate cause and effect.
Level 3: Case studies involve the study of a single individual. They can generate hypotheses to be tested but cannot show cause and effect.

Adapted from Ghaemi (2010a).

In investigating mental disorders, we must always consider the adequacy of the method of inquiry. Some types of investigation provide stronger evidence because of their methodological soundness. Understanding different means of investigating clinical phenomena and their relative strengths and weaknesses is necessary when evaluating reported findings in abnormal psychology. Case studies, correlational approaches, and experimental designs are tools used in the field of abnormal psychology to study the characteristics, causes, and appropriate treatments for mental disorders (see Table 3.1). We will begin with the case study method.

The Case Study

In psychology, a **case study** is an intensive study of an individual that relies on clinical data, including observations, medical and psychological tests, and historical and biographical information. Case studies provide detailed information regarding the development and features of psychopathology in a specific individual but lack the control and objectivity of many other methods. A case study is illustrated in the following example.

Case Study

A 24-year-old married Puerto Rican woman, Nayda, reported that she was in "utter anguish" and incapacitated by "epileptic fits." These seizures were preceded by a strong headache and involved a loss of consciousness and convulsions. The neurologist diagnosed her condition as intractable (difficult-to-treat) epilepsy. The psychotherapist, however, believed that some of Nayda's symptoms were not consistent with those seen in epilepsy. First, when regaining consciousness, Nayda sometimes did not recognize her husband or children. Second, during seizures she appeared fearful and would plead to an invisible presence to have mercy and not to kill her. Third, during these episodes Nayda often hit herself and burned items in the house. Her most recent seizures included hallucinations involving blood and an attempt to strangle herself with a rope.

Because Nayda's symptoms were not consistent with those commonly seen in seizures, the therapist wanted to determine if the seizures were psychogenic (generated from psychological causes). He asked if Nayda had suffered any significant trauma in her life. Nayda told of an event that had occurred

Continued

case study intensive study of one individual that relies on clinical data, such as observations, psychological tests, and historical and biographical information

Case Study—cont'd

when she was 17—2 years before the seizures began. She tearfully related that one night at about 2 a.m., she was awakened by the smell of something burning. She was shocked to find her grandmother's house in flames (her grandmother lived in a small house in the backyard). Strangely, she decided to go back to sleep and repeatedly told herself, "Tomorrow I will tell my parents of the fire" (Martinez-Taboas, 2005, p. 8). A few minutes later, the rest of the family was awakened by the smoke. Their attempts to rescue the grandmother failed. It was later determined that the grandmother had set the fire to take her own life. When Nayda was asked about her feelings regarding the incident, she cried profusely and said that it was her fault her grandmother had died. It was highly probable that this event was related to the seizures.

The therapist also wanted to investigate the possibility that cultural influences were contributing to these symptoms. In many Latin American countries, there is a belief in *espiritismo*—the idea that the soul is immortal and, under certain circumstances, able to inhabit or possess a living person. Auditory or visual hallucinations when experiencing episodes related to espiritismo are not uncommon. When asked about what she believed was causing the seizures, Nayda explained that the spirit of her grandmother was not at peace and was causing her seizures and other problems. She believed that her failure to help her grandmother during the fire resulted in a disturbed and revenge-seeking spirit. Through the case study method, the therapist was able to successfully treat Nayda's symptoms by using a therapeutic approach that combined cognitive therapy with her cultural beliefs.

As can be seen in the example of Nayda, a case study allows a clinician to gather comprehensive information regarding possible causes of a client's problem through questions, tests, and direct observation. Clinicians using the case study method develop a strong therapeutic relationship with the client and strive to understand the client's subjective experience of the disorder (Josselson & Matilla, 2012). The therapist can then formulate hypotheses regarding the causes of the client's behaviors and test out different therapeutic strategies. Innovative methods of assessment or treatment often arise from case studies, strategies that can be later evaluated with further research. In this case, the therapist adapted a therapeutic approach to incorporate cultural beliefs. In addition to facilitating new therapeutic or diagnostic approaches, case studies are also used to study rare psychological phenomena.

However, case studies have limitations. First, because the study involves a single individual, questions arise about whether findings can be generalized to other individuals with similar problems. Would the technique devised by Nayda's therapist also work with other clients with psychogenic seizures—even those with the same cultural background? Second, the data gathered in case studies reflect the theoretical perspective or bias of the investigator. The clinician may operate from a biological, psychological, sociocultural, or other perspective and ignore other viewpoints. Third, case studies cannot be used to demonstrate a cause and effect relationship. Because of these problems, group designs such as correlational studies and experimental designs that allow for replication and larger sample sizes provide a more solid research foundation for investigating the causes and treatments of mental disorders.

CONTROVERSY:

Scientific Integrity: Money and Politics

- An internal pharmaceutical company memo concerning a study of antidepressant medication use with children stated it would be "commercially unacceptable" to admit that the medication did not work in children and recommended that the company "effectively manage the dissemination of these data in order to minimize any potential negative impact" (Dyer, 2004, p. 1395).
- About 70 percent of the work group members working on writing the new DSM-5 diagnostic manual have financial ties to pharmaceutical companies, including being paid consultants, researchers, or promoters of certain medications (Cosgrove & Krimsky, 2012).

Do financial ties to drug companies by clinical researchers or practitioners influence opinions regarding the effectiveness of medications for mental disorders? Are DSM-5 work group members with ties to the pharmaceutical industry more likely to broaden diagnostic definitions so that more people receive a psychiatric diagnosis and related medication? The scientific method requires a commitment from researchers to search for the truth and to remain objective. Should professionals be excluded from research or other activities in which they have a financial conflict of interest?

Correlational Studies

Correlational studies allow researchers to look at data from a group to determine if variations in one variable are accompanied by increases or decreases in a second variable. A statistical analysis is performed to determine the relationship between variables. A **positive correlation** means that an increase in one variable is accompanied by an increase in the other. When an increase in one variable is accompanied by a decrease in the other variable, there is a **negative correlation**. The stronger the correlation (positive or negative), the stronger the relationship between the two variables. See Figure 3.1 for examples of correlations. Correlational studies are very important to scientific inquiry because they allow analysis of variables that cannot be controlled—variables such as age, social class, childhood experiences, or ethnicity.

David Sue

Correlational Studies

Identical twins are often used in correlational studies to determine the influence of genetic factors. They tend to show greater behavioral similarities than do fraternal twins or siblings; this similarity is attributed to genetic factors.

Although correlational studies provide data regarding the degree to which two variables are related, they do not explain the reason for the relationship. For example, eating certain processed foods (e.g., sweets, fried foods, refined grains, high-fat dairy) is correlated with increased likelihood of depression (Akbaraly et al., 2009; Sánchez-Villegas et al., 2011). However, because these data come from correlational studies, it is possible that the relationship between dietary patterns and depression is due to variables other than those studied. In other words, we cannot conclude that consuming processed foods *causes* depression; overeating or eating unhealthy foods may, in fact, be a symptom, rather than a cause, of depression.

Let's consider another study. J. G. Johnson, Cohen, Smailes, Kasen, & Brook (2002) assessed the relationship between the number of hours of television viewing and the number of aggressive behaviors by viewers over a 17-year period. A significant correlation was found. The greater the number of hours spent watching television per day, the greater the number of aggressive acts (assaults, robberies, threats to injure someone, or crimes using a weapon). The researchers controlled for possible confounding variables such as childhood neglect, low family income, unsafe neighborhoods, and psychiatric disorders. Because this was a correlational study, the authors cautioned, "It should be noted that a strong inference of causality cannot be made without conducting a controlled experiment, and we cannot rule out the possibility that some other covariates that were not controlled in the present study may have been responsible for these associations" (p. 2470). Such cautions are common with respect to

positive correlation increase in one variable accompanied by an increase in a second variable

negative correlation increase in one variable accompanied by a decrease in a second variable

FIGURE 3.1

Possible Correlation Between Two Variables

The more closely the data points approximate a straight line, the greater the magnitude of the correlation coefficient *r*. The slope of the regression line rising from left to right in example (a) indicates a perfect positive correlation between two variables, whereas example (b) reveals a perfect negative correlation. Example (c) shows a lower positive correlation. Example (d) shows no correlation whatsoever.

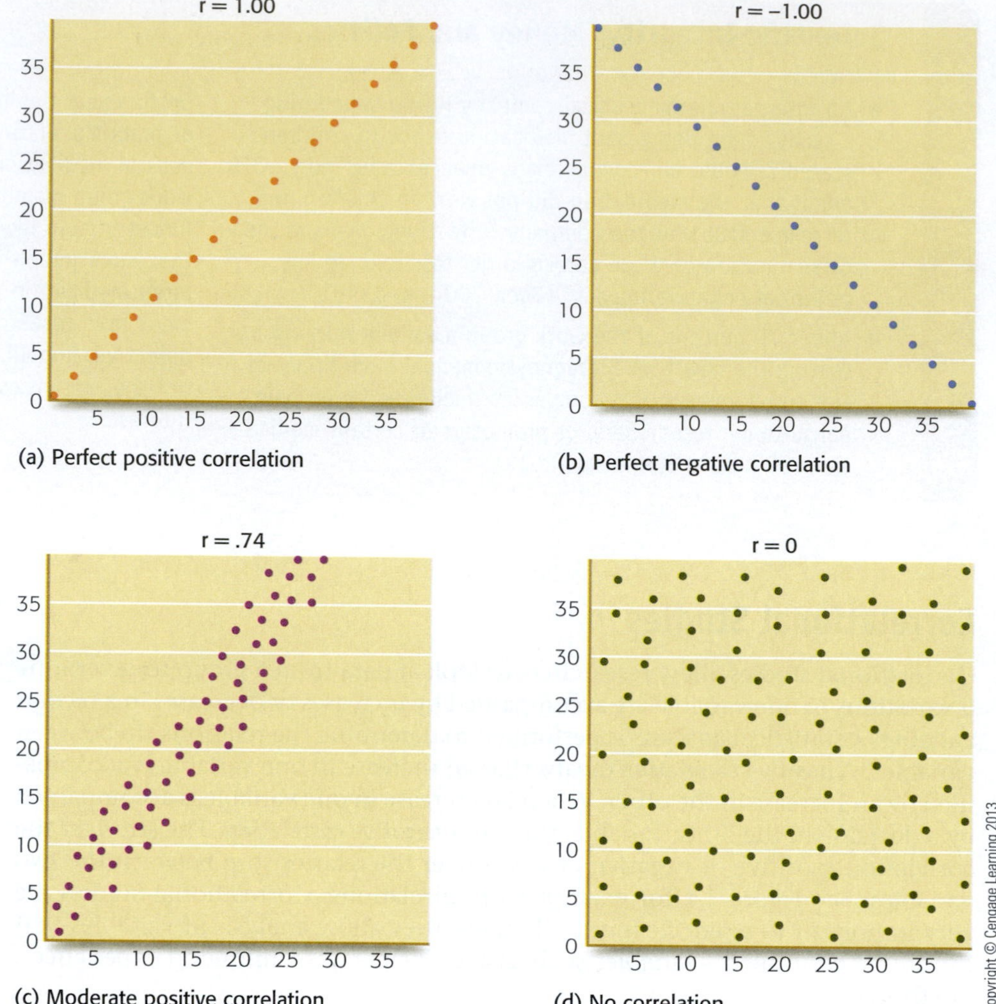

Did You Know?

Adolescent girls with the greatest exposure to televised programs with sexual themes were 2 times more likely to become pregnant within a 3-year period than those with lower levels of exposure (Chandra et al., 2008). What are possible explanations for this finding?

experiment technique of scientific inquiry in which a prediction is made about two variables; the independent variable is then manipulated in a controlled situation and changes in the dependent variable are measured

experimental hypothesis prediction concerning how an independent variable will affect a dependent variable in an experiment

interpreting correlational studies; these studies cannot be used to demonstrate cause and effect.

In summary, correlational studies are a very important method of scientific inquiry. Because samples sizes are large and the research can be replicated, this method of investigation has a broader scientific foundation than case studies. However, interpreting the outcome of correlational studies can be problematic. It is possible that variables that are highly correlated are, in fact, causally unrelated or influenced by an additional, not-yet-identified variable. Even when variables are causally related, the direction of causality may be unclear.

Experiments

The **experiment** is perhaps the best tool for testing cause and effect relationships. As opposed to the case study and correlational method, it can be used to determine causality because variables are manipulated to determine their effect on other variables. In its simplest form, the experiment involves the following:

- an **experimental hypothesis**, which is a prediction concerning how an independent variable will affect a dependent variable;

- an **independent variable** (the possible cause), which the experimenter manipulates to determine its effect on a dependent variable; and
- a **dependent variable**, which is expected to change as a result of changes in the independent variable.

Let's clarify these concepts by examining an actual research study.

© ROB & SAS/Corbis

Correlational Findings

Social contact and support are associated with better mental health. How would you determine the direction of the relationship? Does friendship prevent mental disturbances or do individuals with psychological problems have fewer friends?

Case Study

Melinda N., a 19-year-old sophomore who needed dental treatment for several painful cavities, sought help from a university psychology clinic for dental phobia. Her strong fear of dentists began when she was about 12 years old. Melinda's therapist had heard that antianxiety medication and psychological methods (relaxation training and changing fearful thoughts about the procedure) were both successful in treating dental phobia. Before deciding which treatment to recommend, she reviewed research studies that compared the effectiveness of these approaches.

A study by Thom, Sartory, & Johren (2000) seemed to provide some direction. In that study, 50 individuals with dental phobia who needed dental surgery were assigned to either a psychological, medication, or no-treatment group. The psychological treatment took only one session, involving stress management training (relaxation exercises, visualization of dental work, use of coping thoughts), followed by 1 week of practice of these techniques at home. Those in the medication group received the antianxiety medication 30 minutes before the dental procedure. All participants (including those in the control group) were told that their surgeon specialized in patients with dental anxiety and would treat them carefully.

The Experimental Group An **experimental group** is the group in an experiment that is subjected to the independent variable. In their study, Thom et al. (2000) created two experimental groups: One group received a single-session psychological treatment involving exposure to images of dental scenes, stress management, relaxation, and breathing exercises plus 1 week of daily home-based stress reduction activities. The other experimental group received antianxiety medication.

Because the investigators were interested in how treatment affects level of anxiety and reports of panic, several dependent variables were measured. Pre- and post-treatment self-reports of dental fear were obtained, as well as **subjective**, or personal, ratings of pain during the procedure. The investigators also tabulated how many of the patients completed dental treatment with further appointments. Thus, the dependent variables were self-reports of fear, subjective ratings of pain when undergoing dental surgery, and participation in further dental care.

The Control Group If the participants in the two experimental groups in the study by Thom et al. (2000) showed a reduction in dental fear based on pretesting to post-testing measures, could the researchers conclude that the treatments were effective forms of therapy? The answer would be no, because participants may have shown less anxiety about dental procedures merely due to the passage of time or as a function of completing the assessment measures. The use of a control group enables researchers to eliminate such possibilities.

A **control group** is a group that is similar in every way to the experimental group except that members of the control group are not exposed to the factor

independent variable variable or condition that an experimenter manipulates to determine its effect on a dependent variable

dependent variable variable that is expected to change when an independent variable is manipulated in an experiment

experimental group the group in an experiment that is subjected to the independent variable

subjective taking place in the person's own mind

control group the group in an experiment that is similar to the experimental group except for exposure to the independent variable under study; that is, they are not exposed to the independent variable. In the study by Thom, Sartory, & Johren (2000), the control group took the pretest measures, received dental work, and took the post-test measures. However, those in the control group did not receive any treatment. Because of this, we can be more certain that any differences found between the control and experimental groups were due to the independent variable (i.e., the treatment received).

The findings revealed that the groups treated with either psychological intervention or antianxiety medication had significantly greater reductions in fear and pain when undergoing surgery than the control group. However, those treated with medication continued to display dental phobia following their surgery, whereas those who received psychological intervention showed further improvement and continued dental treatment. Of those who completed additional dental procedures, 70 percent had been in the psychological intervention group, 20 percent in the medication group, and 10 percent in the control group. Given these findings, the therapist told Melinda that both treatments could help her during her dental appointment but that psychological intervention would be more likely to produce long-term effects.

Did You Know?

Many findings are based on research involving undergraduate participants. The following conclusions were reported by the Associated Press (2007b):

- Muscular men were twice as likely as less muscular men to have had more than three sex partners (based on 99 UCLA undergraduates).
- Despite being stereotyped as "chatty," women spoke only 3 percent more per day than men (based on 400 college students).
- Younger individuals were 6 percent more likely to make jokes than those who were older (based on 81 college participants).

R. A. Peterson (2001) raised questions about whether samples of college students are representative of people in general, adults, or even college students in general. In addition, the number of participants is certainly often too low for any conclusions to be meaningful.

The Placebo Group

The results of an experiment are sometimes challenged for another reason. What if the participants in the treated experimental groups improved not because of the treatment, but because they expected that they would improve? Some researchers have found that if participants expect to improve from treatment, this expectation—rather than specific treatment—is responsible for the outcome.

One method by which expectation can be induced without using a specific treatment is to include a **placebo control group**. Thom, Sartory, & Johren (2000) could have given another group a medication capsule containing an inert drug (a placebo) or a single-session intervention (not thought to be effective) with a therapist, such as reading an informational pamphlet and the homework of reviewing the pamphlet daily for 1 week. If the experimental groups (i.e., those receiving medication or psychological treatment) improved more than the placebo control group, then one could be even more confident that therapy, rather than expectation, was responsible for the results.

Additional Controls in Clinical Research

Because experimenter and participant expectations can also influence the outcome of a study, a researcher may use a **blind design**, in which those helping with the experiment are not aware of the purpose of the research. A method to reduce the impact of both experimenter and participant expectations is **double-blind design**. In this procedure, neither the participants nor the individuals working directly with them (such as therapists or physicians) are aware of the experimental conditions. The effectiveness of this design is dependent on whether participants are truly "blind" to the intervention, which may not always be the case. For example, in medication studies, over 75 percent of subjects may correctly guess their treatment assignment due to either the presence or absence of physical symptoms or other side effects (Perlis, Ostacher, et al., 2010). Physicians are also able to distinguish between placebos and actual medications based on patient reactions. Many researchers attempt to design experiments so that the degree of blindness is increased and the expectancy effects are decreased.

Although experimental studies have the greatest credibility with respect to cause and effect relationships, shortcomings also exist. Some variables cannot be manipulated. For example, we cannot experimentally investigate if child abuse increases risk of depression, because we cannot ethically manipulate whether a child is exposed to abuse. To do so would require randomly assigning children to conditions of abuse or no abuse to determine if those in the abuse condition were

placebo control group a group whose members are given either attention equivalent to that given to the experimental group or a medication capsule containing an inert drug

blind design an experimental approach in which those helping are not aware of the details of the research

double-blind design an experimental approach in which neither the participants nor those working directly with them are aware of experimental details

more likely to develop depression. In this case, correlational studies would be the most appropriate method of studying the hypothesis that child abuse increases risk of depression. In addition, questions are sometimes raised about the generalizability of the results of experimental studies. For example, some critics question if findings generated in clinics or research settings are generalizable to other environments. The tight control regarding all variables that might possibly influence the outcome of a study may not resemble problems faced in the real world, where this kind of control does not exist.

Sheff/Shutterstock.com

Double-Blind Design

When researching the effects of a drug, researchers often use a double-blind design to ensure that neither participants nor experimenters are aware of the experimental conditions. Here a physician is holding a bottle containing either medication or placebo pills. Neither she nor the participants in the study will know the type of pill received. This design is used to control for expectancy effects.

Analogue Studies

Ethical, moral, or legal standards may prevent researchers from devising certain studies. Additionally, studying real-life situations is often not feasible because it is difficult to control all possible variables. Therefore, researchers sometimes resort to an **analogue study**—an investigation that attempts to replicate or simulate, under controlled conditions, a situation that occurs in real life. Here are some examples of analogue studies:

- To study the possible effects of a new treatment for anxiety disorders, a researcher experiments with students who have test anxiety rather than with individuals diagnosed with an anxiety disorder.
- To test the hypothesis that sexual sadism is influenced by watching sexually violent media, an experimenter exposes male participants to either a violent or a nonviolent sexual program. The participants then complete a questionnaire assessing their attitudes and values toward women and their likelihood of engaging in violent sexual behaviors.

Obviously, each example is only an approximation of real life. Students with test anxiety may not be equivalent to individuals with anxiety disorders. And exposure to one violent sexual film and the use of a questionnaire may not be sufficient to allow a researcher to draw the conclusion that sexual violence and disrespect toward women are influenced by long-term exposure to such films. However, analogue studies can give researchers insight into the processes that might be involved in abnormal behavior and facilitate the search for effective treatment.

Field Studies

In some cases, analogue studies would be too contrived to accurately reflect a real-life situation. Investigators, therefore, sometimes conduct a **field study**, in which behaviors and events are observed and recorded in their natural environment. Field studies are sometimes used to examine catastrophic events such as wars, floods, and earthquakes, or to study personal crises such as undergoing major surgery or treatment for a terminal illness. Field studies conducted in New York City 3 to 6 months after the September 11, 2001, terrorist attacks on the World Trade Center revealed that although 18.5 percent of individuals interviewed displayed post-traumatic stress disorder symptoms, only 11.3 percent had received any help for the symptoms (DeLisi et al., 2003).

Although field studies offer a more realistic investigative environment than other types of research, they suffer from certain limitations. First, although field studies can yield important data, they are correlational in nature and cannot be used to determine cause and effect relationships. Second, so many factors affect real-life situations that it is impossible to control—or even distinguish—all possible variables. As a result, the findings may be difficult to interpret. Third, observers can never be absolutely sure that their presence did not influence the interactions observed.

analogue study investigative technique that attempts to replicate or simulate, under controlled conditions, a situation that occurs in real life

field study investigative technique in which behaviors and events are observed and recorded in their natural environment

Chen Jianli Xinhua News Agency/Newscom

Field Studies

Over 18,000 people in Japan were killed by a destructive earthquake and ensuing tsunami in March 2011. Here a rescue team is using life detection instruments to attempt to locate survivors. Can social scientists remain detached and objective when recording a tragedy of such magnitude?

Biological Research Strategies

The success of psychopharmacology spawned renewed interest and research into brain-behavior relationships. More recently, breakthroughs in neuroscience such as understanding the role of neurotransmitters and brain structure abnormalities in mental disorders, and research suggesting long-lasting brain changes resulting from some forms of psychotherapy have produced another contemporary trend: a heightened appreciation for the role of physiologically based research in the study of abnormal behavior. Indeed, more and more researchers are now exploring the biological bases (genetic, neurochemical, and neurostructural) of a wide array of mental disorders.

Genetics and Epigenetics Ongoing developments in the field of genetic research are contributing greatly to the field of abnormal psychology. Not only are scientists focusing on the influence of specific genes in the development of psychopathology, but major advances are being made in the field of **epigenetics**. Epigenetic research is shedding light on how the environment affects or "programs" gene expression, thus influencing an individual's risk of developing disorders such as depression, schizophrenia, and phobias (Bale et al., 2010). Researchers are finding that environmental stressors such as trauma, toxins, and dietary variations have the greatest impact on genetic expression during certain sensitive periods in early development (J. J. Mann & Haghighi, 2010).

Did You Know? Although twins have the same genotype, their phenotype can differ. Each fetus is exposed to a slightly different environment, resulting in differences in appearance including different fingerprints; different fingertip patterns develop based on each twin's position in the uterus. (E. P. Richards, 2010).

Source: Tao, Chen, Yang & Tian, 2012

Genetic Linkage Studies **Genetic linkage studies** attempt to determine whether a disorder follows a genetic pattern. If a disorder is genetically linked, individuals closely related to the person with the disorder (who is called the *proband*) are more likely to display that disorder or related disorders (Smoller, Shiedly, & Tsuang, 2008). Genetic studies of psychiatric disorders often employ the following procedure (Smoller et al., 2008):

1. The proband and his or her family members are identified.
2. The proband is asked about the psychiatric history of specific family members.
3. These members are contacted and given some type of assessment, such as psychological or neurological tests, to determine their mental health status.

This research strategy depends on accurate diagnosis of both the proband and the relatives. Caution is needed when using client recall of family history in genetic linkage studies. An individual's psychiatric status ("sick" or "well") may influence the accuracy of the person's assessment or recall of the mental health of relatives. This bias in reporting is reduced when multiple informants are used or when family members are assessed directly.

epigenetics field of biological research focused on understanding how environmental factors (e.g., trauma, toxins, or nutrition) influence or program gene expression

genetic linkage studies investigations regarding whether a disorder follows a genetic pattern

endophenotype measurable characteristics (neurochemical, endocrinological, neuroanatomical, cognitive, or neuropsychological) that can give clues regarding the specific genes involved in a disorder

The Endophenotype Concept **Endophenotypes** are measurable characteristics (e.g., cognitive functioning, anatomical or chemical differences in the brain) that can give clues regarding the genetic pathways involved in a disorder. To be considered an endophenotype, the characteristic must be heritable (able to be inherited), seen in family members who do not have the disorder, and seen more frequently in affected families than in the general population.

For example, it has been found that as many as 80 percent of individuals diagnosed with schizophrenia (a severe mental illness we will discuss in Chapter 11) and 45 percent of their close relatives show irregularities in the way they track objects with their eyes. In families without schizophrenia, only 10 percent have this irregularity. This irregularity thus qualifies as an endophenotype: It is inherited, is seen in families with a particular disorder (schizophrenia), and occurs more often in those families than the general population (Gottesman & Gould, 2003).

Epidemiological Survey Research Surveys are frequently used in **epidemiological research**, which examines the rate and distribution of mental disorders in a population. Two terms, *prevalence* and *incidence*, are used to describe the rates. As noted in Chapter 1, the **prevalence** tells us the percentage of individuals in a targeted population who have a particular disorder during a specific period of time. For example, we might be interested in how many preschool-aged children had a spider phobia during the previous 6 months (6-month prevalence rate), during the previous year (1-year prevalence rate), or at any time during their lives (lifetime prevalence rate). In general, shorter time periods have lower prevalence rates.

The **incidence** tells the number of *new* cases of a disorder that appear in an identified population within a specified time period. The incidence rate is lower than the prevalence rate because incidence involves only new cases, whereas prevalence includes both new and existing. Incidence rates are important for examining hypotheses about the causes or origins of a disorder. For example, if we find an increased incidence of a disorder (i.e., more new cases) in a population exposed to a particular stressor compared with another population not exposed to the stressor, we can hypothesize that the stressor caused the disorder. Epidemiological research, then, is important not only in describing the frequency and distribution of disorders but also in analyzing possible causal factors.

CHECKPOINT REVIEW

1. Describe the different groups used in an experimental study.
2. Compare and contrast case, correlational, experimental, analogue, and field studies.
3. Describe the difference between incidence and prevalence rates.

Assessment of Abnormal Behavior

Case Study

Police were called when Ms. Y. became physically aggressive, breaking several windows and leaving her home in disarray. Police officers described her behavior as threatening and violent. Because Ms. Y. was not in a condition to be interviewed, her boyfriend provided background information. He reported that she had been hospitalized 6 months previously with auditory hallucinations and claims that she was God. She had also been hospitalized on one other occasion when similar symptoms developed after she experimented with drugs. Ms. Y.'s family history includes an aunt diagnosed with schizophrenia (Lavakumar, Garlow, & Schwartz, 2011).

Different conditions can result in psychotic symptoms such as those demonstrated by Ms. Y; a thorough assessment must be performed. A drug screen ruled out alcohol and illicit drugs as causal factors. No infections that might produce delirium or temporary psychosis were found. During questioning about other substances, Ms. Y. volunteered that she had been taking carnitine, an over-the-counter weight-loss supplement. In fact, Ms. Y. had been taking twice the recommended levels of carnitine. In addition, she had been drinking 16-oz. energy drinks that listed the main ingredients as L-carnitine and caffeine. The mental health team concluded that her psychotic symptoms were due to carnitine intoxication.

epidemiological research study of the rate and distribution of mental disorders in a population

prevalence percentage of individuals in a targeted population who have a particular disorder during a specific period of time

incidence number of *new* cases of a disorder that appear in an identified population within a specified time period

In the mental health field, assessment is critical. Therapists collect and organize information about a person's current condition and past history using observations, interviews, psychological and neurological tests, and input from relatives and friends. Data gathered from a variety of sources allow clinicians to better understand the individual's symptoms and mental state. In the case of Ms. Y., the therapists relied on observations, laboratory tests, and interviews to arrive at their diagnosis. With any mental disorder, the first step is to rule out physical or biological causes for the symptoms.

As we noted in Chapter 1, evaluation of gathered information leads to a **psychodiagnosis**, which is a description of the individual's psychological state and inferences about possible causes of the psychological distress. To formulate a diagnosis, the therapist attempts to obtain a clear description of the client's concerns and behavioral patterns and to classify or group them based on the symptom picture that emerges. Psychodiagnosis is usually the first step in the treatment process. In this section, we examine assessment methods and tools clinicians use. We also discuss the most widely employed diagnostic classification system, as well as criticism regarding labeling and the use of classification systems. We begin with a discussion of the reliability and validity of assessment tools and diagnostic systems.

Reliability and Validity

To be useful, assessment tools and classification systems must demonstrate reliability and validity. **Reliability** is the degree to which a procedure or test yields the same results repeatedly under the same circumstances. There are many types of reliability (Coaley, 2010; Golafshani, 2003).

Test-retest reliability determines whether a measure yields the same results when given at two different points in time. For example, if we administer a personality measure to an individual in the morning and then readminister the measure later in the day, the measure is reliable if the results show stability (i.e., are consistent) from one point in time to another. Another measure of reliability, *internal consistency*, requires that various parts of a measure yield similar or consistent results (Kline, 2005). For example, if responses to different items on a measure of anxiety are not related to one another, the test may be unreliable because test items may be measuring different things, not just anxiety. Finally, *inter-rater reliability* determines consistency of responses when different raters administer the measure. For instance, imagine that two clinicians are trained to diagnose individuals according to a certain classification scheme. Yet one clinician presented with a set of symptoms diagnoses an anxiety disorder, whereas another considers the exact same symptoms and diagnoses depression. If this were to occur, there would be poor inter-rater reliability.

Validity is the extent to which a test or procedure actually performs the function it was designed to perform. If a measure that is intended to assess depression instead measures anxiety, the measure is an invalid measure of depression. Two common forms of validity considered in assessment are predictive and construct validity (Weiner & Greene, 2008).

Predictive validity refers to the ability of a test or measure to predict or foretell how a person will behave, respond, or perform. Colleges and universities often use applicants' SAT or ACT scores to predict their future college grades. If the tests have good predictive validity, they should be able to differentiate students who will perform well from those who will perform poorly in college.

Construct validity refers to whether a measure is, in fact, related to the phenomena that are empirically or theoretically related to that measure. Let's say that a researcher has developed a questionnaire to measure anxiety. To determine construct validity, the researcher needs to demonstrate that the questionnaire is correlated with other measures of anxiety. Furthermore, we would have increased confidence that the questionnaire is measuring anxiety if it is related to other phenomena that appear in anxious people, such as muscle tension, sweating, tremors, or startle responses.

psychodiagnosis assessment and description of an individual's psychological symptoms, including inferences about what might be causing the psychological distress

reliability the degree to which a measure or procedure yields the same results repeatedly

validity degree to which an instrument measures what it was developed to measure

Let's look at the use of reliability and validity on a measure developed to assess the unusual thinking patterns and impaired sense of reality seen in psychosis, such as believing that everyday events have personal significance. Cicero, Kerns, & McCarthy (2010) constructed the Aberrant Salience Inventory (ASI) and wanted to determine if the instrument was a valid and reliable measure of individuals' likelihood of developing psychosis. The items for the test were constructed from descriptions of psychosis in the literature, characteristics observed during the early stage of schizophrenia, and interviews with people who had schizophrenia.

The test was found to have high (0.89) internal reliability (i.e., consistency among the items). To determine if the measure actually assessed likelihood of developing psychosis, the inventory was compared to other scales that measure psychosis (construct validity). The ASI was highly correlated to other measures of psychosis, which increased confidence in the validity of the measure. Because the ASI measures the likelihood of developing psychosis, you would also expect that individuals with psychosis would score higher on this test than would individuals with other mental disorders. This was also found. Thus the researchers concluded that the ASI is a useful measure of susceptibility to psychosis in clinical and nonclinical samples.

Reliability and validity are also influenced by the conditions under which a test or measure is administered. **Standardization**, or standard administration, requires that those who administer a test strictly follow common rules or procedures. If an examiner creates a tense and hostile environment for some individuals who are taking a test, for example, the test scores may vary simply because not all examinees were treated in a similar or standard fashion.

An additional concern is the standardization sample—the group of people who originally took the measure and whose performance is used as a standard or norm. Because performance on a measure is subsequently interpreted against this norm, the standardization sample must be representative of the backgrounds of those being evaluated. For example, interpretations may not be valid if the test score of a 20-year-old African American woman is compared with scores from a standardization sample consisting of middle-aged white men.

Assessing Abnormal Behavior

Assessment involves gathering information and drawing conclusions about the traits, skills, abilities, emotional functioning, and psychological problems of an individual; information from assessment is used in developing a diagnosis. Various means of assessment are available to clinicians including observations, interviews, psychological tests and inventories, and neurological tests. Whenever possible, assessment is conducted using several different methods in order to get a more accurate view of the client (Godoy & Haynes, 2011; Kendall, Holmbeck, & Verduin, 2004).

Observations

Case Study

A 9-year-old boy . . . was referred to a neurologist for treatment of "hysterical paralysis." . . . Medical tests indicated no apparent neurological damage. . . . He reported that his legs simply did not work no matter how he tried. As the child was describing his difficulties, we noted that he would shift his feet and legs in his wheelchair so his legs could swing freely. . . . When we asked him to describe his paralysis, he would look at his feet and . . . his leg movements would diminish. However, when we asked him to discuss other topics (e.g., school, friends), he would look up, become engaged in the interview, and his feet would swing. (W. H. O'Brien & Carhart, 2011, p. 14)

standardization the use of identical procedures in the administration of tests, or the establishment of a norm or comparison group to which an individual's test performance can be compared

assessment the process of gathering information and drawing conclusions about the traits, skills, abilities, emotional functioning, and psychological problems of an individual

© Bruce Coleman Inc./Alamy

Controlled Observations

Research on animals can provide clues to the development of emotions in humans. Baby chimpanzees show empathy, curiosity, and the ability to copy facial expressions.

Observations of overt behavior provide the most basic method of assessing symptoms. Clinical observations can be either controlled or naturalistic. *Controlled* (or *analogue*) *observations* occur in a laboratory, clinic, or other contrived (artificial) setting (Haynes, 2001). *Naturalistic observations* (as in the case study) are made in a natural setting—a schoolroom, an office, a hospital ward, or a home—rather than in a laboratory. Observations can be highly structured and specific. For example, an observer may count episodes of off-task behavior and the circumstances under which off-task behaviors occur. On other occasions, observations may be less formal and specific, as when a clinician simply looks for any unusual behaviors when interacting with a client. In such a situation, the observations and interpretations of the behaviors may be quite subjective in nature.

Behavior is usually observed when psychologists interview clients. Psychologists watch for cues that may have diagnostic significance. A client's general mode of dress, significant scars or tattoos, and even choice of jewelry provide information about the client. Similarly, expressive behaviors, such as posture, facial expression, and language and verbal patterns can provide important clues, as seen in the following case study.

Case Study

Margaret was a 37-year-old woman seen by one of the authors of this text for treatment of severe depression. It was obvious from a casual glance that Margaret had not taken care of herself for weeks. Her face, hands, and hair were dirty. Her beat-up tennis shoes were only halfway on her stockingless feet. Her disheveled appearance and stooped body posture made her appear much older than she was.

When first interviewed, Margaret sat as though she did not have the strength to straighten her body. She avoided eye contact and stared at the floor. When asked questions, she responded in short phrases: "yes," "no," "I don't know," "I don't care." There were long pauses between the questions and her answers.

Interviews The clinical interview is a time-honored means of psychological assessment. It allows the therapist to observe the client and collect data about the person's life history, current situation, and personality. Verbal and nonverbal behaviors, as well as the content and process of communications, are important to analyze; therapists listen carefully to what clients are saying and whether they are expressing anxiety, hesitation, anger, or other emotions via their manner of speaking. Interviews can vary in the degree to which they are structured and the formality with which they are conducted (C. E. Hill & Lambert, 2004).

A widely used interview procedure is the **mental status examination**. The intent of this examination is to evaluate the client's cognitive, psychological, and behavioral functioning by means of questions, observations, and tasks posed to the client (C. Goldberg, 2009). The clinician considers the appropriateness and quality of the client's responses (behaviors, speech, emotions, and intellectual functioning) and then attempts to render initial, tentative evaluations of diagnosis, prognosis, and treatment issues (Brannon, 2011). A mental status report on Margaret (described in the previous case study) might indicate:

- Appearance—Poor self-care in grooming; disheveled appearance; shoes halfway off her feet; stooped body posture; avoidance of eye contact.
- Mood—Appears to be depressed, hopeless. Margaret verified that she has felt "depressed," "exhausted," and "worthless" for months.

mental status examination procedure designed to evaluate cognitive, psychological, and behavioral functioning by means of questions, observations, and tasks posed to the client

- Affect—Margaret exhibited constricted emotions and very little affect. Her overall demeanor was suggestive of depression.
- Speech—Margaret spoke slowly, was slow in answering questions, and used short responses or "I don't know" and "I don't care."
- Thought Process—Margaret's lack of responsiveness makes the assessment of thought process difficult. There was no evidence of racing or tangential thinking.
- Thought Content—Margaret denied experiencing any hallucinations or delusions (false beliefs). She indicated that she had been thinking about suicide multiple times each day but denied having a suicide plan or thoughts of hurting someone else. She reported constantly worrying about what others think of her, especially her coworkers.
- Memory—Margaret seemed to have good recall of family background, past events, jobs, and educational background. However, she had difficulty with short-term memory—she was able to recall only one out of three words after a 5-minute delay.
- Abstract Thought—Margaret was slow to respond but was able to explain the proverbs "a rolling stone gathers no moss" and "people in glass houses should not throw stones."
- General Knowledge—Margaret was able to name the last four presidents but gave up before determining the number of nickels in $135, explaining that she "just can't concentrate."

Naturalistic Versus Controlled Observations

Naturalistic observations are made in settings that occur naturally in one's environment. Here a female researcher is taking notes while observing children at play on a playground.

The mental status exam is a useful diagnostic tool that helps clinicians cover areas that are ordinarily not part of a clinical interview. However, many aspects of the exam are subjective, and one's cultural background can influence the assessment. As C. Goldberg (2009) pointed out:

> There is a major distinction between "different" and "abnormal." A "failure" to provide a correct interpretation of a proverb, for example, may have nothing to do with an individual's intellectual function but rather may simply reflect a different upbringing or background. Similarly, tests of memory which require the subject to recite past U.S. presidents may not be an appropriate measuring tool depending on a person's country of origin, language skills, educational level, etc. (p. 3)

Observations regarding a client's eye contact and body posture must also consider possible cultural factors. Individuals from diverse cultural backgrounds may show different patterns of eye contact, dress, and body postures during interviews (D. W. Sue & D. Sue, 2013).

Did You Know? Imaginary friends that appear and disappear are a source of comfort to many children. Children often report hearing voices from these friends. Reports of such friends would be considered a symptom of psychosis in adults, but rarely in children.

Source: Sidhu & Dickey (2010)

Psychological Tests and Inventories

Psychological tests and inventories are standardized instruments that are used to assess a client's characteristics, including personality, maladaptive behavior, social skills, intellectual abilities, vocational interests, and cognitive impairment. Tests differ in form (that is, they may be oral or written and may be administered to groups or to individuals), structure, degree of objectivity, and content. We examine two general types of personality tests and measures (projective and self-report inventories) and tests of intelligence and cognitive impairment.

Projective Personality Tests

In a **projective personality test**, the test taker is presented with ambiguous stimuli, such as inkblots, pictures, or incomplete sentences, and asked to respond to them in some way. The stimuli are generally novel, and the test is relatively unstructured. When responding to such stimuli, people "project" their attitudes, motives, and other personality characteristics onto the situation. Participants are often unaware of the true nature or purpose of the test and usually do not recognize the significance of their responses. Projective tests

projective personality test test involving responses to ambiguous stimuli, such as inkblots, pictures, or incomplete sentences

© Narcisse/Shutterstock.com

The Rorschach Technique

Devised by Swiss psychiatrist Hermann Rorschach in 1921, the Rorschach technique uses a number of cards, each showing a symmetrical inkblot design similar to the one shown here. What do you see in this inkblot?

presumably tap into the individual's unconscious needs and motivations (G. J. Meyer et al., 2001).

Swiss psychiatrist Hermann Rorschach devised the *Rorschach technique* for personality appraisal in 1921. A Rorschach test consists of 10 cards that display symmetrical inkblot designs. The cards are presented one at a time to participants, who are asked (a) what they see in the blots and (b) what characteristics of the blots make them see that. The Rorschach test and the interpretation of the client's responses rely on psychoanalytic theory. For example, seeing eyes or buttocks may imply paranoid tendencies; fierce animals may imply aggressive tendencies; blood may imply strong uncontrolled emotions; food may imply dependency needs; and masks may imply avoidance of personal exposure (Klopfer & Davidson, 1962). However, research has found that interpretation of these "signs" often reflects the bias or cultural expectation of the clinician (L. J. Chapman & Chapman, 1967; Garb, Wood, Lilienfeld, & Nezworski, 2005).

The *Thematic Apperception Test* (TAT), another projective personality test, was developed in 1935 (H. A. Murray & Morgan, 1938). It consists of 30 picture cards, most depicting two human figures. Their poses and actions are vague and ambiguous enough to be open to different interpretations. As with the Rorschach technique, responses to the TAT items indicate underlying motives, drives, and personality processes (Verdon, 2011). Generally, 20 TAT cards are administered, one at a time, with instructions to tell a story about each picture. Typically, the tester says, "I am going to show you some pictures. Tell me a story about what is going on in each one, what led up to it, and what its outcome will be." The purpose is to gain insight into the individual's conflicts and worries, as well as clues about his or her core personality structure.

Other types of projective tests include sentence-completion and draw-a-person tests. In the *sentence-completion test*, the participant is given a list of partial sentences and is asked to complete each of them. Typical partial sentences are "My ambition . . . ," "My mother was always . . . ," and "I can remember . . ." Clinicians try to interpret the meaning of the individual's responses. In *draw-a-person tests*, such as the Machover D-A-P (Machover, 1949), the participant is asked to draw a person. Many clinicians analyze these drawings for size, position, detail, and so on, assuming that the drawings provide diagnostic clues. Well-controlled studies cast doubt on such diagnostic interpretations (Anastasi, 1982; Lilienfeld, Wood, & Garb, 2000).

Support for the TAT and Rorschach interpretations is very limited, and it is even poorer for the draw-a-person test (Lilienfeld et al., 2000). Additionally, the

CONTROVERSY:

Wikipedia and the Rorschach Test

In 2009, editors of the online encyclopedia Wikipedia decided to publish the entire set of Rorschach inkblot plates, the most common responses for each inkblot, and the characteristics each inkblot are purported to measure. One of the inkblots, for example, is considered representative of a "father figure"; responses to this card are supposed to reveal one's attitude toward males and authority figures.

Although there are questions regarding the reliability and validity of the inkblot test, many clinicians still utilize this assessment tool. As Bruce Smith, president of the International Society of the Rorschach and Projective Methods, stated, "The more test materials are promulgated widely, the more possibility there is to game the test" (N. Cohen, 2009). In other words, awareness of answers that are typically given to each inkblot may change the responses of individuals taking the test and invalidate the results.

In defense of their decision to publish the inkblot information, editors at Wikipedia argue that the Rorschach test is in the public domain because intellectual property rights have expired, and it does not have copyright protection. Did Wikipedia go too far in publishing the entire Rorschach inkblot test?

cultural relevance of these tests, developed many decades ago with nondiverse populations, is quite questionable.

Lewis J. Merrim/Photo Researchers

The Thematic Apperception Test

In the Thematic Apperception Test, clients tell a story about each of a series of pictures they are shown. These pictures—often depicting people doing something—are less ambiguous than Rorschach inkblots.

Self-Report Inventories Unlike projective tests, self-report inventories require test takers to answer specific written questions or to select specific responses from a list of alternatives—usually self-descriptive statements. Participants are asked to either agree or disagree with the statement or to indicate the extent to which the statement is true of them. Because a predetermined score is assigned to each possible answer, subjective factors in scoring and interpretation are minimized. In addition, participants' responses and scores can be compared readily with a standardization sample.

Perhaps the most widely used self-report personality inventory is the *Minnesota Multiphasic Personality Inventory*, or MMPI (Hathaway & McKinley, 1943). The MMPI-2, a revision by Butcher and colleagues (see Butcher, 1990; Graham, 2005; Greene, 1991), restandardized the inventory, refined the wording of certain items, eliminated items considered outdated, and attempted to include appropriate representations of ethnic minority groups. The MMPI-2 consists of 567 statements; participants are asked to indicate whether each statement is true or false as it applies to them.

The test taker's MMPI-2 results are rated on 10 clinical scales and a number of validity scales. The 10 clinical scales were originally constructed by analyzing the responses of diagnosed psychiatric patients (and the responses of adults in the general population) to the 567 test items. These analyses allowed researchers to determine what kinds of responses each of the various types of psychiatric patients usually made. The MMPI-2 also has validity scales, which assess factors such as degree of candor, confusion, or falsification on the part of the respondent and help clinicians detect potential faking or symptom exaggeration (Groth-Marnat, 2009; Tolin, Steenkamp, Marx, & Litz, 2010). Figure 3.2 shows 10 sample MMPI-2 items and the responses to those items that contribute to high ratings on the 10 MMPI clinical scales.

Whereas the MMPI-2 assesses a number of different personality characteristics, some self-report inventories or questionnaires focus only on certain kinds of personality traits or emotional problems, such as depression or anxiety. For example, the *Beck Depression Inventory* is composed of 21 items that measure various aspects of depression, such as mood, appetite, functioning at work, suicidal thinking, and sleeping patterns (A. T. Beck, Ward, Mendelson, Mock, & Erbaugh, 1961).

Did You Know?

Two thirds of normal individuals acknowledged having psychotic-like beliefs or thoughts on a psychotic screening questionnaire. Of these individuals, 21.2 percent felt that others were out to harm them, 9 percent felt that their thoughts were interfered with by an outside force or someone else, and 4.2 percent reported hearing or seeing things that others could not.

Source: Johns et al. (2004)

Though widely used, personality inventories have limitations (Sollman, Ranseen, & Berry, 2010). First, the fixed number of alternatives can hinder individuals from presenting an accurate picture of themselves. Being asked to answer "true" or "false" to the statement "I am suspicious of people" does not permit an individual to qualify the item in any way. Second, a person may have a unique response style or **response set** (i.e., a tendency to respond to test items in a certain way regardless of content) that may distort the results. For example, many people have a need to present themselves in a favorable light, and this can cause them to give answers that are socially acceptable but inaccurate. Third, interpretations of responses of people from different cultural groups may be inaccurate if norms for these groups have not been developed (Knabb, Vogt, & Newgren, 2011; Monot, Quirk, Hoerger, & Brewer, 2009). Fourth, cultural factors may shape the way a trait or characteristic is viewed. Asian Americans tend to score higher on measures of social anxiety, but their scores may be a reflection of cultural values of modesty and self-restraint rather than a sign of psychopathology (Melka, Lancaster, Adams, Howarth, & Rodriguez, 2010). African Americans also show a unique pattern of responding to measures of social anxiety (Melka et al., 2010).

response set tendency to respond to test items in a certain way regardless of content

TEN MMPI CLINICAL SCALES WITH SIMPLIFIED DESCRIPTIONS	SAMPLE ITEMS: I like mechanics magazines.	I have a good appetite.	I wake up fresh and rested most mornings.	I think I would like the work of a librarian.	I am easily awakened by noise.	I like to read newspaper articles on crime.	My hands and feet are usually warm enough.	My daily life is full of things that keep me interested.	I am about as able to work as I ever was.	There seems to be a lump in my throat much of the time.
1. **Hypochondriasis (Hs)**—Individuals showing excessive worry about health with reports of obscure pains.		NO	NO				NO		NO	
2. **Depression (D)**—People suffering from chronic depression, feelings of uselessness, and inability to face the future.		NO			YES			NO	NO	
3. **Hysteria (Hy)**—Individuals who react to stress by developing physical symptoms (paralysis, cramps, headaches, etc.).		NO	NO			NO	NO	NO	NO	YES
4. **Psychopathic Deviate (Pd)**—People who show irresponsibility, disregard social conventions, and lack deep emotional responses.								NO		
5. **Masculinity-Femininity (Mf)**—People tending to identify with the opposite sex rather than their own.	NO			YES						
6. **Paranoia (Pa)**—People who are suspicious, sensitive, and feel persecuted.										
7. **Psychasthenia (Pt)**—People troubled with fears (phobias) and compulsive tendencies.			NO					NO		YES
8. **Schizophrenia (Sc)**—People with bizarre and unusual thoughts or behavior.								NO		
9. **Hypomania (Ma)**—People who are physically and mentally overactive and who shift rapidly in ideas and actions.										
10. **Social Introversion (Si)**—People who tend to withdraw from social contacts and responsibilities.										

FIGURE 3.2

The 10 MMPI-2 Clinical Scales and Some MMPI-2 Items

Shown here are the MMPI-2 clinical scales and a few of the items that appear on them. As an example, answering "no" or "false" (rather than "yes" or "true") to the item "I have a good appetite" would result in a higher scale score for hypochondriasis, depression, and hysteria.

Source: Adapted from Dahlstrom & Welsh (1965). These items from the original MMPI remain unchanged in the MMPI-2.

Intelligence Tests Intelligence testing, intended to obtain an estimate of a person's current level of cognitive functioning, results in a score called the *intelligence quotient* (IQ). An IQ score indicates an individual's level of performance relative to that of other people of the same age (see Figure 3.3). As such, an IQ score is an important aid in predicting school performance or detecting intellectual disability. (Through statistical procedures, IQ test results are converted into numbers, with 100 representing the mean, or average, score. An IQ score of about 130 indicates performance exceeding that of 95 percent of all same-age peers.) The two most widely used intelligence tests are the Wechsler scales (Wechsler, 1981) and the Stanford–Binet scales (Terman & Merrill, 1960; Thorndike, Hagen, & Sattler, 1986). The *Wechsler Adult Intelligence Scale* (the WAIS and its revised version, WAIS-IV) is administered to people age 16 and older. The WAIS consists of four factors: verbal comprehension, perceptual organization, working memory, and processing speed (Saklofske, Hildebrand, & Gorsuch, 2000). Table 3.2 shows subtest items similar to those used in the WAIS-IV. The *Stanford–Binet Intelligence Scale*, now in its fifth edition, is used for individuals ages 2 to 85. Much more complicated in administration and scoring, the Stanford–Binet requires considerable skill in its use.

There are various critiques of the use of IQ tests. First, some investigators believe that IQ tests largely reflect cultural and social factors rather than innate intelligence (Sternberg, 2005). Second, the predictive validity of IQ tests has been criticized. That is, IQ test scores do not accurately predict future behaviors or achievements. Many believe that factors such as motivation and work ethic are much better predictors of future success. Third, some researchers have questioned whether our current conceptions of IQ tests and intelligence are adequate. A number of researchers have proposed that intelligence is a multidimensional attribute. E. H. Taylor (1990) stated that an important aspect of intelligence, and one that cannot be adequately assessed using IQ tests, is social intelligence and social competency. Social skills often affect problem solving, adaptation to life, social knowledge, and the ability to use resources effectively.

Tests for Cognitive Impairment Clinical psychologists, especially those who work in a hospital setting, are concerned with detecting and assessing cognitive impairment resulting from brain damage. Such damage can have profound effects both physically and psychologically (I. Grant & Adams, 2009).

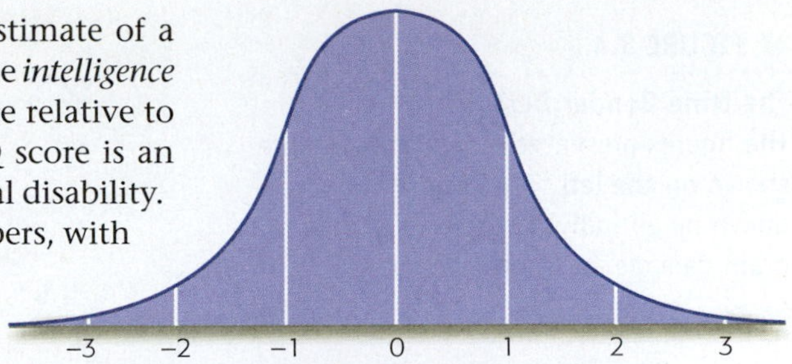

FIGURE 3.3

A Bell Curve Showing Standard Deviations

The distribution of certain traits in a population resembles the shape of a bell, with most scores hovering over the mean and fewer scores falling in the outlying areas of the distribution. IQ scores are generally distributed in this manner. IQ scores are devised so that the mean equals 100, and deviations from the mean are expressed in terms of standard deviations. One standard deviation from the mean (about 15 IQ points above or below the mean, or IQ scores between 85 and 115) encompasses about 68 percent of the scores. Two standard deviations (about 30 IQ points above or below the mean, or IQs between 70 and 130) account for more than 95 percent of the scores.

TABLE 3.2 Items Similar to Those for the Wechsler Adult Intelligence Scale-IV

Information	1. How many pennies make a nickel? 2. What is ice made of?
Comprehension	1. Why do some people save rubber bands? 2. Why is copper often used in water pipes?
Arithmetic (all calculated "in the head")	1. Susan had three pieces of candy and John gave her two more. How many pieces of candy did Susan have altogether? 2. Four women divided 20 pieces of candy equally among themselves. How many pieces of candy did each person receive?
Similarities	In what way are the following alike? 1. horse/zebra 2. rake/lawn mower 3. triangle/rectangle
Vocabulary	This test consists simply of asking, "What is a ___?" or "What does ___ mean?" The words cover a wide range of difficulty.

● **FIGURE 3.4**

The Nine Bender Designs

The figures presented to participants are shown on the left. The distorted figures drawn by an individual with suspected brain damage are shown on the right.

Source: L. Bender (1938)

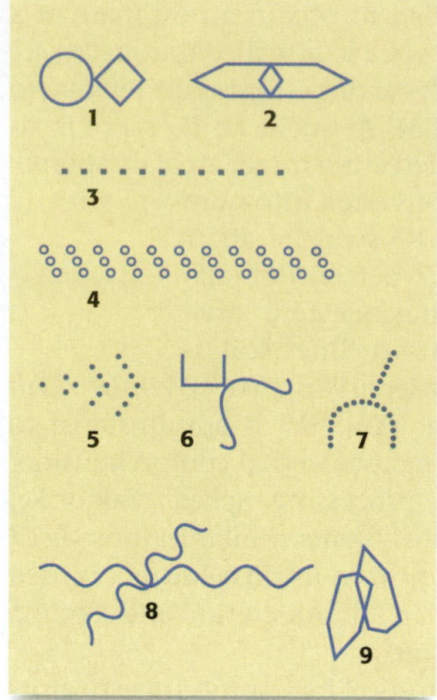

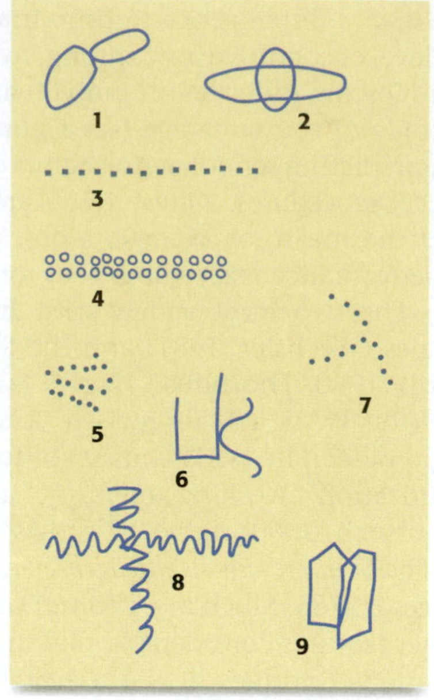

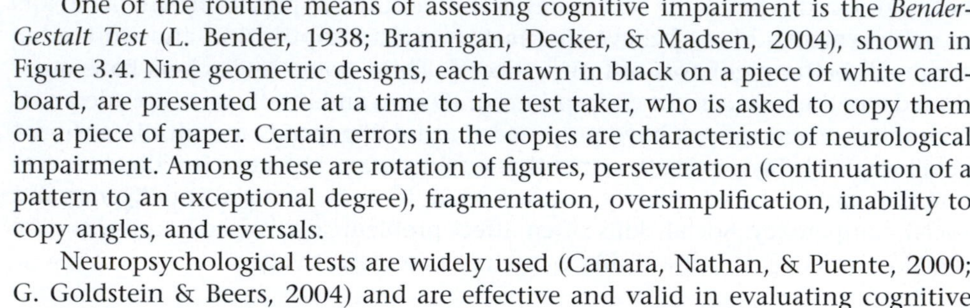

One of the routine means of assessing cognitive impairment is the *Bender-Gestalt Test* (L. Bender, 1938; Brannigan, Decker, & Madsen, 2004), shown in Figure 3.4. Nine geometric designs, each drawn in black on a piece of white cardboard, are presented one at a time to the test taker, who is asked to copy them on a piece of paper. Certain errors in the copies are characteristic of neurological impairment. Among these are rotation of figures, perseveration (continuation of a pattern to an exceptional degree), fragmentation, oversimplification, inability to copy angles, and reversals.

Neuropsychological tests are widely used (Camara, Nathan, & Puente, 2000; G. Goldstein & Beers, 2004) and are effective and valid in evaluating cognitive impairment due to brain damage. In fact, they are far more accurate in documenting cognitive deficits than are interviews or informal observations (Kubiszyn et al., 2000). For example, the *Halstead–Reitan Neuropsychological Test Battery* successfully differentiates patients with brain damage from those without brain damage and can provide valuable information about the type and location of the damage (G. Goldstein & Beers, 2004).

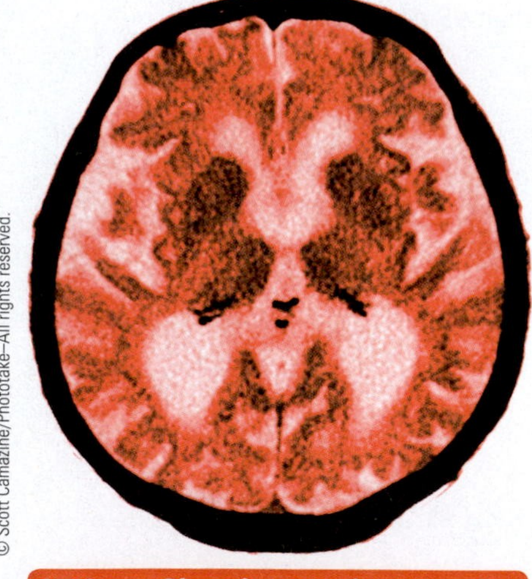

CT Scan Showing Brain Atrophy

Cerebral CT scans, which involve multiple, cross-sectional X-rays of the brain, are able to document a variety of brain changes associated with neurocognitive disorders. This CT scan of the brain of a 94-year-old woman shows enlarged ventricles and atrophy indicative of a loss of neurons in some regions of the brain.

Neurological Tests

In addition to psychological tests, a variety of neurological medical procedures are available for diagnosing cognitive impairments due to brain damage or abnormal brain functioning. The *electroencephalograph* examines the brain by recording brain waves; abnormalities in the activity can provide information about the presence of tumors or other brain conditions. A more sophisticated procedure, the *computerized axial tomography (CT) scan*, produces cross-sectional images of the structure of the brain, allowing for a detailed view of brain deterioration or abnormality. *Magnetic resonance imaging* (MRI) creates a magnetic field around the patient and uses radio waves to detect abnormalities. MRIs can produce an amazingly clear cross-sectional picture of the brain and its tissues. Because of these superior pictures, which are reminiscent of postmortem brain slices, MRIs can often provide more detailed images of lesions than CT scans can (Burghart & Finn, 2010).

The *positron emission tomography (PET) scan* enables noninvasive study of the physiological and biochemical processes of the brain, rather than the anatomical structures seen in the CT scan. In PET scans, a radioactive substance is injected into the patient's bloodstream. The scanner detects the substance as it is metabolized in the brain, yielding information about brain functioning.

CT, PET, and MRI scans are used to study brain tissue abnormalities and metabolic patterns among patients diagnosed with a variety of disorders, including schizophrenia, mood disorders, Alzheimer's disease, and alcoholism (E. C. Lin & Alavi, 2009; Lynch, 2007). These neurological tests (discussed in detail in Chapter 12), coupled with psychological tests, can increase diagnostic accuracy and understanding of many mental disorders. Some researchers predict that in the future such techniques will allow clinicians to make more precise diagnoses and to pinpont precise areas of the brain affected by mental disorders.

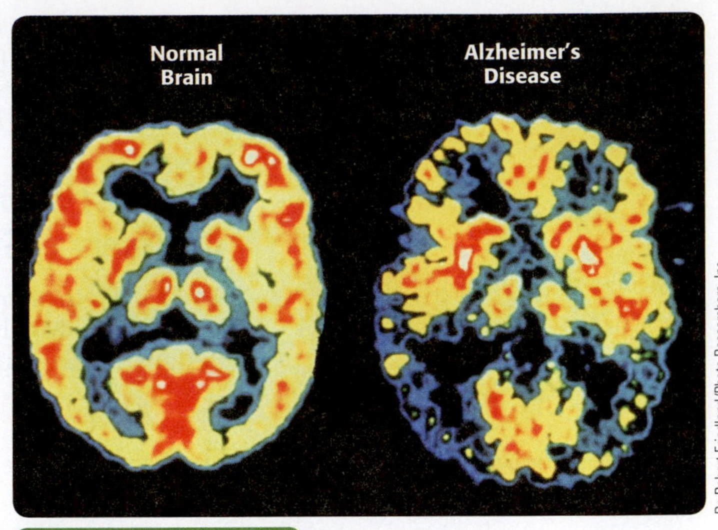

Alzheimer's Disease

As can be seen in these PET scans comparing brain activity between someone with Alzheimer's disease (on the right) and a healthy control, glucose metabolism is reduced in the temporal and parietal lobes of the individual with Alzheimer's disease.

CHECKPOINT REVIEW

1. What kinds of information do psychologists gather when making a diagnosis?
2. Define *reliability* and describe different methods of determining if a test is reliable.
3. Define *validity* and describe different methods of determining if a test is valid.
4. Describe the four principal methods for assessing abnormal behavior.

Diagnosis and Classification of Abnormal Behavior

Clinicians use the data obtained from assessment to formulate a diagnosis using a psychiatric classification system. The goal of having a classification system for abnormal behaviors is to provide distinct categories, indicators, and diagnostic names for particular patterns of behavior, thought processes, and emotional disturbances. Thus, classification systems serve as a means of diagnosing disorders in those seeking mental health treatment. For example, the behaviors classified as *social phobia* are clearly different from the diagnostic category of *major depressive disorder* (DSM-V Work Groups, 2012; National Institute of Mental Health [NIMH], 2010a, 2011a) as seen in the following abbreviated symptom descriptions:

- Social phobia involves (a) a strong fear of being judged by others and of being embarrassed; (b) excessive concern over the reactions of others to one's anxiety; and (c) severe impairment with everyday activities such as going to work or school, shopping, or participating in any social activity.
- Major depressive disorder involves (a) severe and persistent feelings of sadness, hopelessness, or "emptiness," (b) a loss of interest in hobbies or once pleasurable activities, and (c) severe distress and impairment in functioning that lasts for at least 2 weeks.

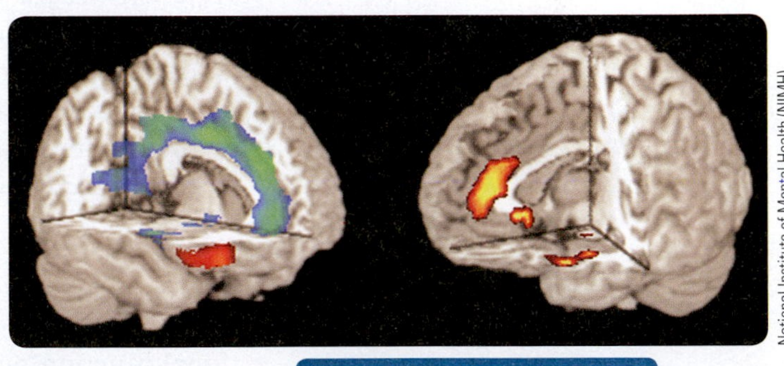

Neuroimaging with MRI

Structural MRI (left) and functional MRI (right) scans reveal that some violent individuals have reduced volume and activity in the anterior cingulate cortex (the blue area in the front part of the brain at left and the corresponding yellow area in the brain at right), which is thought to be the hub of a circuit responsible for regulating impulsive aggression.

Classification systems also facilitate communication between mental health professionals and form a foundation for research on the etiology and treatment of mental disorders. Without the means to identify and group disorders, none of these goals can be accomplished.

Diagnostic and Statistical Manual of Mental Disorders (DSM)

The *Diagnostic and Statistical Manual of Mental Disorders* (DSM) is a classification system widely used by mental health professionals. It lists all officially designated mental disorders and the characteristics or symptoms needed to confirm a diagnosis. The DSM has traditionally been a categorical system: An individual either has or does not have a particular disorder (Shorter, 2010). However, dissatisfaction with the categorical model led to the recent proposal of a dimensional model in which disorders are now seen to lie on a continuum, with "normality" at one end. From this perspective, anxiety, depression, and even psychotic-like experiences are no longer an either-or phenomenon; instead, it is recognized that individuals can experience varying degrees of these conditions (A. L. Pincus, 2011). Let's look at an example of a client and a diagnostic evaluation based on the upcoming DSM-5. We then discuss concerns with labeling and classification systems.

MYTH VS. REALITY

MYTH Psychological tests are less accurate than medical tests because a person's psychological status is more difficult to assess.

REALITY The widely held belief that medical tests are more reliable and valid than psychological tests appears to be false. G. J. Meyer and colleagues (2001) conducted an evaluation of the validity of psychological and medical tests and found that both kinds of tests can vary in reliability and validity. However, many psychological tests were as good as or better than medical tests in detecting conditions. For example, neuropsychological tests were as accurate as the MRI in detecting dementia.

Case Study

Mark is a 50-year-old machine operator referred for treatment by his work supervisor due to concerns about frequent absenteeism, difficulty getting along with others, and suspicion of alcohol use during work hours. Mark acknowledged that he consumes a large quantity of alcohol daily. His wife recently left him, claiming she could no longer tolerate his drinking, extreme jealousy, and unwarranted suspicions concerning her marital fidelity. Coworkers avoid Mark because he is a cold, unemotional person who distrusts others and overreacts to any perceived criticism. Mark has no close friends although he does hang out with "regulars" at a local bar.

Mark's heavy use of alcohol, which interferes with his social and occupational functioning, resulted in a diagnosis of an alcohol-use disorder. Mark also exhibited a personality trait disorder with prominent paranoid features involving suspiciousness, hypervigilance, and hostility toward others. Mark was found to have some mild cognitive deficits (presumably resulting from his heavy alcohol consumption) and moderate depressive symptoms. Cirrhosis of the liver was listed as a significant medical condition. The clinician noted Mark's pending divorce, work difficulties, and poor relationships with coworkers when assessing psychosocial functioning.

Mark's diagnosis, then, was as follows:

- Alcohol-use disorder
- Personality disorder with prominent paranoid traits

- Physical disorder: cirrhosis of the liver
- Causal factors:
  1. *Biological/genetic*—There is a family history of alcohol abuse. The early onset of Mark's heavy drinking may be related to genetic vulnerability to alcohol abuse.
  2. *Environmental*—Mark is in jeopardy of losing his job and is facing financial stress due to his upcoming divorce.
  3. *Developmental*—Mark's father exhibited paranoia, drank heavily, and was physically and verbally abusive throughout Mark's childhood. Mark began drinking in early adolescence; this appears to have affected emotional maturation and social development.
  4. *Social*—There is limited family support. Mark's wife is seeking a divorce. Mark has very few friends other than a few "drinking buddies."
  5. *Cultural*—Mark is very concerned about family reactions to his upcoming divorce, due to his Catholic upbringing.
  6. *Behavioral*—Mark tends to blame others and is often "cold and unemotional" in interactions with others. Mark has a strong tendency to be suspicious of others, a psychological factor that affects all social relationships.

DSM-5 also includes a culturally focused interview that can be used to assess the possible impact of culture on the presenting problem. It can be used with any client and covers areas such as the following (Dowdy, 2000):

- *"What do you think is causing your problem?"* This helps the therapist to understand the client's perception of the factors involved, including interpersonal, social, and cultural influences.
- *"Why is this happening to you?"* This question taps into the issue of causality and possible spiritual or cultural explanations for the problem.
- *"What have you done to treat this condition? Where else have you sought treatment?"* These questions can lead to a discussion of previous interventions, the possible use of home remedies, and the client's evaluation of the usefulness of these treatments.
- *"How has this condition affected your life?"* This question helps identify individual, interpersonal, health, and social issues related to the concern.

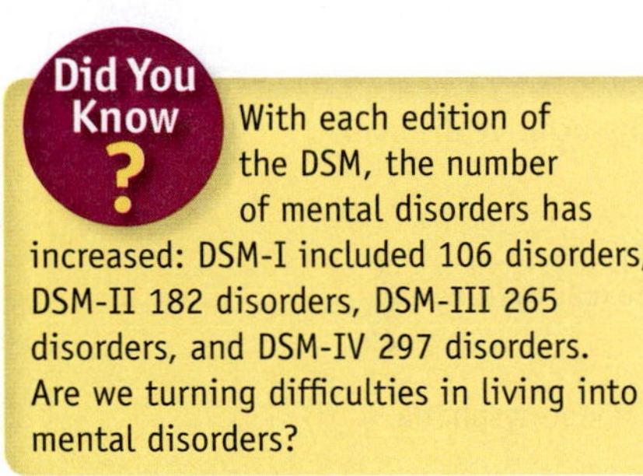

With each edition of the DSM, the number of mental disorders has increased: DSM-I included 106 disorders, DSM-II 182 disorders, DSM-III 265 disorders, and DSM-IV 297 disorders. Are we turning difficulties in living into mental disorders?

It should be noted that many individuals who have one mental disorder also suffer from another. As with Mark, an individual diagnosed with an alcohol-use disorder may also have a second disorder such as a personality disorder. **Comorbidity** is the term for this co-occurrence of different disorders. Physical disorders are also noted during the diagnostic process. Table 3.3 lists the broad categories of mental disorders, most of which are discussed in this book.

Evaluation of the DSM Classification System

As previously mentioned, proposed revisions to the DSM (DSM-5) involve moving away from a categorical system and toward a dimensional system. Research shows that for many disorders, the distinction between major and less severe symptom states is a matter of degree rather than kind (Ruscio & Ruscio, 2000). The move toward dimensional ratings and inclusion of milder forms of disorders in DSM-5 is an attempt to deal with this problem.

Although DSM-5 was developed to increase the reliability and validity of diagnoses, it has been subject to a variety of criticisms that include the lowering of

comorbidity co-occurrence of different disorders

TABLE 3.3 DSM-5 Disorders

CATEGORY OF DISORDERS	FEATURES
Neurodevelopmental disorders	Cognitive, learning, and language disorders, autism spectrum disorder, attention-deficit/hyperactivity disorder, and so on
Neurocognitive disorders	Psychological or behavioral abnormality associated with a dysfunction of the brain, including problems that arise from head injuries, ingestion of toxic or intoxicating substances, brain degeneration or disease, and so on
Mental disorders due to a general medical condition	Medical conditions that cause a disorder; for example, hypothyroidism can cause a major depressive disorder, so the diagnosis would be "major depressive disorder due to a general medical condition (hypothyroidism)"
Substance-use and addictive disorders (including behavioral addictions)	Excessive use of alcohol, illicit drugs, or prescription medications that results in impaired functioning; nonsubstance addictions, including behavioral addictions such as gambling
Schizophrenia spectrum and other psychotic disorders	Disorders marked by severe impairment in thinking and perception, often involving delusions, hallucinations, and inappropriate affect
Bipolar and related disorders	Mania or hypomania, and possibly episodes of depressed mood; bipolar I, bipolar II, and cyclothymic disorders
Depressive disorders	Feelings of sadness, emptiness, and social withdrawal; major depressive disorder and chronic depressive disorder (dysthymia)
Anxiety disorders	Disorders characterized by excessive or irrational anxiety over everyday situations, often accompanied by avoidance behaviors and fearful cognitions or worry
Obsessive-compulsive and related disorders	Disorders characterized by obsessions (recurrent thoughts) or compulsions (repetitive behaviors)
Trauma and stressor-related disorders	Disorders associated with exposure to stressors such as acute stress and post-traumatic stress disorder
Somatic symptom disorders	Physical symptoms that cause distress and disability, bodily dysfunctions, and preoccupation with beliefs of having a health problem; possibly high levels of health anxiety and disproportionate concern
Dissociative disorders	Disturbance or alteration in memory, identity, or consciousness; individuals may not remember who they are, assume new identities, have two or more distinct personalities, or experience feelings of depersonalization
Sexual dysfunctions	Disorders involving the disruption of any stage of a normal sexual response cycle, including desire, arousal, or orgasm
Gender dysphoria	Clinically significant discontentment or conflict with biological sex and gender assigned at birth
Paraphilias	Recurrent, intense sexual fantasies or urges involving nonhuman objects, pain or humiliation, or children
Eating disorders	Disorders characterized by disturbed eating patterns, such as bingeing, purging, excessive dieting, and body dissatisfaction
Sleep–wake disorders	Problems in initiating or maintaining sleep, excessive sleepiness, sleep disruptions, repeated awakening associated with nightmares and sleepwalking
Personality disorders	Stable traits that are inflexible and maladaptive and notably impair functioning or cause subjective distress

diagnostic thresholds, the inclusion of questionable "new disorders," and cultural concerns (Clay, 2012):

- *Lowering of diagnostic thresholds.* Frances (2009), the chair of the previous edition of the DSM (DSM-IV), has expressed concern that viewing mental disorders on a continuum will have the "unintended consequence" of increasing the number of individuals labeled as having a mental disorder. Frances's concerns may have some validity. In one

CONTROVERSY:

Differential Diagnosis: The Case of Charlie Sheen

During the first week of March 2011, actor Charlie Sheen appeared on numerous television and radio shows. He appeared energized and made exaggerated gestures while stating that he had "tiger blood" with "Adonis DNA." Individuals whom he disagreed with were referred to as "trolls," among other terms (Gardner, 2011). Some of the statements he made on mass media included the following (Boudreault, 2011):

- "I am on a drug, it's called Charlie Sheen. It's not available, 'cause if you try it once, you will die. Your face will melt off and your children will weep over your exploded body."
- "I'm tired of pretending like I'm not special. I'm tired of pretending like I'm not bitchin', a total frickin' star from Mars."
- "I have cleansed myself. I closed my eyes and in a nanosecond, I cured myself. . . . The only thing I'm addicted to is winning."

Do you think he has a psychological disorder or is he just an angry individual spouting off? Should allowances be made for his behavior because he is a celebrity?

study that assessed "regular drinkers," use of the DSM-5 criteria for alcohol-use disorder resulted in a nearly two-thirds increase in the number diagnosed with an alcohol-use disorder (Mewton, Slade, McBride, Grove, & Teesson, 2011).

- *Proposed new diagnoses.* More problems have been given a diagnosis of a mental disorder. For example, there is a new category of "behavioral addictions." Although it currently only includes gambling, other possible addictions such as addiction to the Internet, video games, shopping, and

FOCUS ON RESILIENCE

Should Strengths Be Assessed?

A woman who had elevated depression scores on the MMPI-2 and Beck Depression Inventory was treated by therapists (Rashid & Ostermann, 2009). She received a DSM diagnosis of major depression. When talking about her symptoms, she expressed feelings of hopelessness and despair. The clinicians then conducted a strength assessment by asking her to describe a life story that would show her at her best. She relayed a story about defending a boy in school who was being laughed at by other students. As she discussed this story, her face lit up, and she described her strengths as courage and fairness. Other strengths were identified and applied to the problems she was facing. After 20 sessions, the woman no longer met the criteria for major depressive disorder.

PhotoDisc

The DSM-5 classification continues to rely on assessment that emphasizes deficits, symptoms, problem behaviors, and emotional difficulties. The negative picture created by this focus can affect both the client and the therapist's view of the client. Recently it has been argued that it is important to focus not only on problems experienced by clients but also on their strengths, including positive personal characteristics, accomplishments, satisfying relationships, and prior successes in dealing with adversities and stress (Corcoran & Walsh, 2010; Tedeschi & Kilmer, 2005). Strength assessment can provide a more balanced picture for both the mental health professional and the client. Peterson & Seligman (2005) developed a classification system involving character strengths and virtues to complement the DSM; their system focuses on six overarching virtues (wisdom, courage, humanity, justice, temperance, and transcendence), characteristics that are important to assess and consider when working with mental disorders. What are the advantages of assessing client strengths?

D. L. Rosenhan (1973) sent eight "normal" researchers (pseudopatients) to different psychiatric hospitals. Their assignment was first to fake psychiatric symptoms to gain admission into psychiatric wards (i.e., they reported hearing the words *empty*, *hollow*, and *thud*); once admitted, they behaved in a normal manner. Interestingly, no hospital staff detected that the pseudopatients were normal. However, other patients did. What might account for this difference?

eating were also considered for inclusion. Frances (2009) believes that such diagnostic expansion amounts to medicalizing behavioral problems.

- *Cultural concerns.* Although the proposed DSM-5 revisions have sought to strengthen cultural considerations in diagnosis, questions remain regarding the cross-cultural applicability of the system. Are diagnostic criteria developed by Western countries valid for use with other countries? The prevalence of anxiety disorders, for example, differs greatly worldwide. Higher rates of panic disorder, specific phobias, and social anxiety disorder are found in the United States and European countries than in Asian and African countries (Lewis-Fernàndez et al., 2010). The DSM criteria for these disorders may be less valid for cultural groups that place more emphasis on somatic (bodily) symptoms.

CHECKPOINT REVIEW

1. Why are diagnostic and classification systems important?
2. Explain the difference between categorical and dimensional classification.
3. What is the DSM and what are some criticisms of the most recent DSM?

Summary

1 What kinds of studies are used in the field of abnormal psychology?

- A case study is an intensive study of an individual using observations, psychological tests, and biographical information.
- Correlational studies look at the relationship between variables, but cannot be used to determine cause and effect.
- The experiment is a powerful research tool used to test cause and effect relationships. In its simplest form, an experiment involves an experimental hypothesis, an independent variable, and a dependent variable.
- An analogue study is used to replicate a situation as close to real life as possible under controlled conditions.
- Field studies rely primarily on naturalistic observations in real-life situations. As opposed to in analogue studies, events are observed as they naturally occur.
- Epidemiological studies allow researchers to estimate the rate and distribution of mental disorders in a population.
- Biological research strategies focus on genetic and epigenetic factors involved in psychological disorders.

2 What kinds of tools do clinicians use to evaluate a client's mental health?

- Clinicians use assessment tools that are reliable (i.e., yield the same results repeatedly) and valid (i.e., perform the functions they were designed to perform).
- Clinicians primarily use four methods of assessment: observations, interviews, psychological tests and inventories, and neurological tests.
- Observations of external signs and expressive behaviors are often made during an interview and can have diagnostic significance.
- Interviews involve a face-to-face conversation, after which the interviewer differentially weighs and interprets verbal information obtained from the interviewee. The mental status exam is frequently used as an interview tool in clinical assessment.
- Psychological tests and inventories provide a more formalized means of obtaining information.
- Neurological assessment, including X-rays, CT and PET scans, electroencephalography, and MRI, have added highly important and sophisticated means to detect brain abnormalities.

3 How are mental health problems categorized or classified?

- The DSM is moving away from a categorical model (someone either has or does not have the disorder) toward a dimensional system in which disorders are seen to be on a continuum with "normality."

Key Terms

psychopathology 58
etiology 58
scientific method 58
hypothesis 58
case study 59
positive correlation 61
negative correlation 61
experiment 62
experimental hypothesis 62
independent variable 63
dependent variable 63
experimental group 63
subjective 63
control group 63
placebo control group 64
blind design 64
double-blind design 64
analogue study 65
field study 65
epigenetics 66
genetic linkage studies 66
endophenotype 66
epidemiological research 67
prevalence 67
incidence 67
psychodiagnosis 68
reliability 68
validity 68
standardization 69
assessment 69
mental status examination 70
projective personality test 71
response set 73
comorbidity 79

Media Resources

Psychology CourseMate

Access an interactive e-book and chapter-specific interactive learning tools, including:

- flashcards
- quizzes
- videos

and more in your Psychology CourseMate.

Go to **CengageBrain.com**.

4

Anxiety and Obsessive-Compulsive and Related Disorders

CHAPTER OUTLINE

Emily was hiking with her dog when another dog attacked her and bit her wrist. She was terrified. The wound became badly infected and very painful, requiring medical treatment. On another occasion, her sister, Marian, was walking in the fields when three large, growling dogs chased her. The owner heard the commotion and intervened before she was physically injured. Marian developed a fear of dogs, but Emily, who suffered painful injuries, did not. What could account for these differences? (Mineka & Zinbarg, 2006, p. 10)

FOCUS QUESTIONS

1 According to the multipath model, how are biological, psychological, social, and sociocultural factors involved in the development of anxiety disorders?

2 What are phobias, what contributes to their development, and how are they treated?

3 What is panic disorder, what produces it, and how is it treated?

4 What is generalized anxiety disorder, what are its causes, and how is it treated?

5 What are characteristics of obsessive-compulsive and related disorders, what causes these disorders, and how are they treated?

Anxiety, a feeling of uneasiness or apprehension, is a fundamental human emotion that was recognized as much as 5,000 years ago. It is common to experience anxiety. In fact, many observers regard anxiety as a basic condition of modern existence. Anxiety is an anticipatory emotion; the dreaded event or situation has not yet occurred. **Fear** is a more intense emotion experienced in response to a threatening situation. Anxiety appears to have an adaptive function, producing bodily reactions that prepare us for "fight or flight." Mild or moderate anxiety acts as a safeguard to keep us from ignoring danger. Physiological responses associated with anxiety allow us to cope with potentially dangerous situations. In some cases, however, fear or anxiety occurs even when no danger is present, resulting in an **anxiety disorder**. Fear or anxiety symptoms are considered a disorder only when they interfere with an individual's day-to-day functioning.

Anxiety disorders are the most common mental condition in the United States and affect about 40 million adults (approximately 18 percent) in a given year (R. C. Kessler, Chiu, Demler, & Walters, 2005; see Figure 4.1). In a large survey of adolescents, 31.9 percent had experienced an anxiety disorder (lifetime prevalence), with 8.3 percent experiencing severe impairment (Merikangas, He, Burstein, Swanson, et al., 2011). People with anxiety disorders report a lower quality of life than individuals without anxiety symptoms (Barrera & Norton, 2010). Anxiety disorders are responsible for a great deal of distress and dysfunction and are often accompanied by disorders such as depression, substance abuse, or other anxiety disorders.

In this chapter, we discuss three major groups of anxiety disorders—*phobias*, *panic disorder*, and *generalized anxiety disorder*. (The major anxiety disorders are shown in Table 4.1.) Because obsessive-compulsive and related disorders (*obsessive-compulsive disorder, body dysmorphic disorder, hair-pulling disorder, and skin-picking disorder*) have important similarities with anxiety disorders, they are also discussed in this chapter. Acute stress disorder and post-traumatic stress disorder, which are also anxiety disorders, are covered in Chapter 5.

In order to give you an understanding of some of the predisposing factors that can result in an anxiety disorder, we begin our discussion with the multipath model defined in Chapter 2.

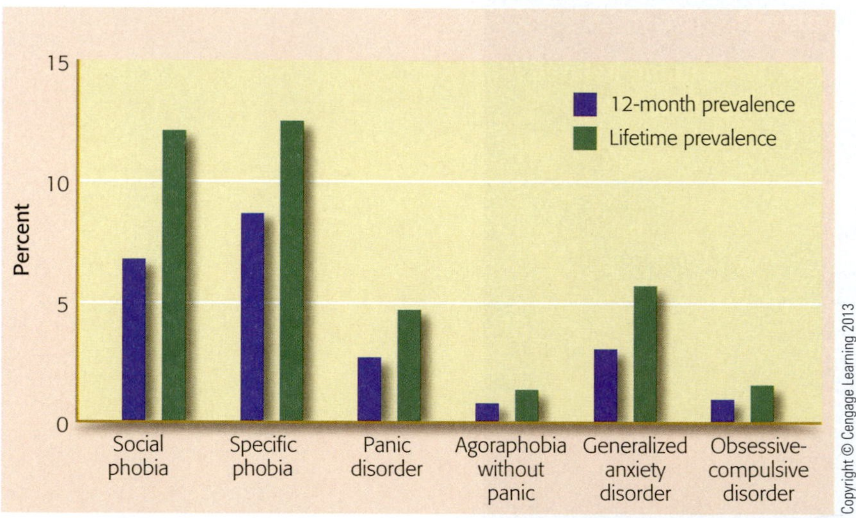

FIGURE 4.1

Prevalence of Anxiety Disorders in the United States

Anxiety disorders are the most common mental condition in the United States.

Source: R. C. Kessler, Berglund, Demler, Jin, Merikangas, et al. (2005); R. C. Kessler, Chiu, Demler, & Walters (2005)

anxiety a fundamental human emotion that produces bodily reactions that prepare us for "fight or flight;" anxiety is anticipatory—the dreaded event or situation has not yet occurred

fear an intense emotion experienced in response to a threatening situation

anxiety disorder fear or anxiety symptoms that interfere with an individual's day-to-day functioning

DISORDERS CHART ANXIETY DISORDERS

TABLE 4.1

Disorder	Symptoms	Gender and Cultural Factors	Age of Onset
Social Anxiety Disorder	• Excessive fear of being watched or judged by others; extreme self-consciousness in social situations • Intense fear or panic produced by the social situation • Worry about being judged that may last for hours after the event	More common in females; in Asian cultures, may involve fear of offending others	Mid-teens
Specific Phobia	• Irrational fear of specific objects or situations where there is little or no threat • Intense fear or panic attacks produced by exposure	Approximately twice as common in females, although it depends on type of phobia	Childhood or early adolescence (depends on type of phobia)
Agoraphobia	• Anxiety or panic in situations where escape is difficult or embarrassing	More prevalent in females	Usually late adolescence, with two thirds before the age of 35
Panic Disorder	• Recurrent and unexpected attacks of terror • Concern about future panic attacks • Can occur with or without agoraphobia	2–3 times more common in females; may involve intense fear of the supernatural in some cultures	Late adolescence and early adulthood
Generalized Anxiety Disorder	• Excessive anxiety and worry over life circumstances (i.e., health, money, family, school, or work) • Vigilance, muscle tension, restlessness, edginess, and difficulty concentrating	Up to 2 times more prevalent in females	Usually childhood or adolescence and middle age

Source: Lewis-Fernández et al. (2010); National Institute of Mental Health (2009a); Wittchen, Gloster, Beesdo-Baum, Fava, & Craske (2010)

Understanding Anxiety Disorders from a Multipath Perspective

In the case at the beginning of the chapter, Emily was exposed to greater trauma when she was attacked by a dog, but it was her sister, Marian, who developed an anxiety disorder. What factors affect the likelihood of someone's developing an anxiety disorder? In general, single **etiological models**, whether biological, psychological, social, or sociocultural, insufficiently explain individual variations in response to fearful situations. A number of different factors play a role in the acquisition of fears or phobias, including biological factors such as genetically based vulnerabilities and psychological factors such as personality variables, an individual's sense of mastery or control, and learning experiences (Mineka & Zinbarg, 2006). In addition, cultural rules and norms or social stressors can influence the expression of anxiety disorders. The multipath model for anxiety disorders is shown in Figure 4.2.

In the next section we consider the biological underpinnings of anxiety disorders, including a discussion of how genes exert their influence and how the environment influences the expression of genes.

Biological Dimension

Two main biological factors affect anxiety disorders: brain function and genetic influences.

etiological model model developed to explain the cause of a disorder

● FIGURE 4.2

Multipath Model of Anxiety Disorders
The dimensions interact with one another and combine in different ways to result in a specific anxiety disorder. The importance and influence of each dimension varies from individual to individual.

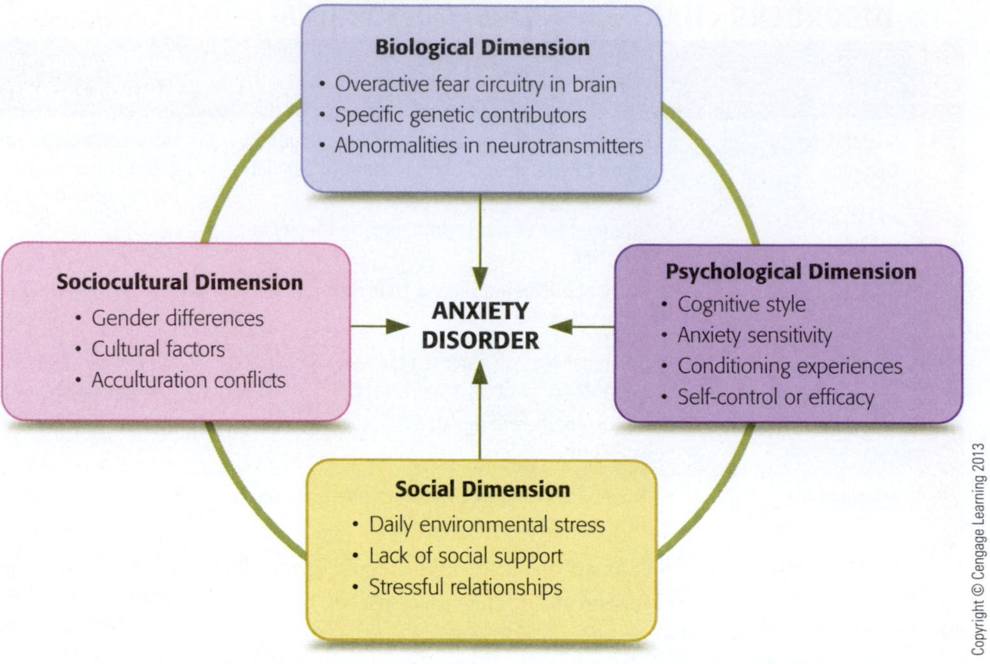

Did You Know? Neuroimaging studies of a woman who was unable to experience fear or recognize dangerous situations revealed bilateral damage to her amygdala; this brain abnormality likely caused her absence of fear.

Source: Feinstein, Adolphs, Damasio, & Tranel, 2011

Brain Function

The **amygdala** (the part of the brain involved in the formation and memory of emotional events) plays a central role in anxiety disorders. In response to potential threats, signals from the amygdala alert other brain structures, such as the **hippocampus** and **prefrontal cortex**, and trigger a fear response. There are two pathways to the amygdala (B. J. Casey et al., 2011; L. Fava & Morton, 2009). In the first, a potentially dangerous sensory stimulus results in *immediate* activation of the amygdala. The second and slower pathway involves signals that travel to the prefrontal cortex, allowing evaluation of the stimulus and an opportunity to override the initial fear response. For example, when passengers in an airplane encounter turbulence, they may initially feel fear. However, when the pilot gives a reassuring explanation for the turbulence, signals from the prefrontal cortex reduce anxiety by inhibiting fear responses from the amygdala.

In some individuals, however, neural structures involved in the fear network appear to be overactive, resulting in symptoms seen in anxiety disorders. Neuroimaging techniques such as positron emission tomography (PET) scans and magnetic resonance imaging (MRI) have documented increased reactivity in the amygdala when individuals with anxiety disorders are exposed to specific emotional stimuli (Sehlmeyer et al., 2011; Stein, Simmons, Feinstein, & Paulus, 2007).

Neuroimaging techniques allow us to observe the effects of both medication and psychotherapy in the treatment of anxiety disorders. Medication appears to "normalize" anxiety circuits in the brain. Interestingly, psychotherapies also produce neurobiological changes similar to those seen with medications (Kumari, 2006). The connections between the amygdala and prefrontal cortex allow us to speculate about why medications and psychotherapy may both be effective in treating anxiety disorders: Each may operate on a different level of the brain. Therapy may reduce arousal by strengthening the ability of the prefrontal cortex to inhibit fear responses from the amygdala. Medication may directly influence or decrease activity in the amygdala and other brain structures (Britton, Lissek, Grillon, Norcross, & Pine, 2011; Gorman, Kent, Sullivan, & Coplan, 2000; see Figure 4.3).

amygdala brain structure associated with the processing, expression and memory of emotions, especially anger and fear

hippocampus the part of the brain involved in forming, organizing, and storing memories

prefrontal cortex the part of the brain involved in abstract thought and complex thinking, personality characteristics, and social functioning

Genetic Influences Genes make a modest contribution to anxiety disorders and interact with other important multipath factors (Bienvenu, Davydow, & Kendler, 2011). Currently, researchers are trying to identify how genes exert their influence. As you learned in Chapter 2, **neurotransmitters** are chemicals that help transmit messages in the brain. One specific neurotransmitter, **serotonin**, is implicated in mood and anxiety disorders. Consequently, a serotonin transporter gene variation (5-HTTLPR) has been the focus of attention. **Alleles** (the gene pair responsible for each trait) influence the expression of genetic characteristics. In the case of the serotonin transporter gene (5-HTTLPR), a **polymorphic variation** (a common DNA mutation) of the gene affects the length of the associated alleles; it is possible to inherit two short alleles, two long alleles, or one short and one long allele of this gene. Researchers have found that short alleles in the serotonin transporter gene are associated with (a) a reduction in serotonin activity and (b) increased fear and anxiety-related behaviors (Pezawas et al., 2005). This means that carriers of the short allele show more reactivity of the amygdala when exposed to threatening stimuli (Pezawas et al., 2005).

Although this research is promising, it is probable that numerous genes affect vulnerability to anxiety disorders. Additionally, identified genes only influence an individual's **predisposition** to develop an anxiety disorder. In most cases, the presence of certain alleles increases the chances that a characteristic is expressed; however, actual expression of the gene depends on interactions between the allele and environmental influences (Klauke, Deckert, Reif, Pauli, & Domschke, 2010; Leonardo & Hen, 2006).

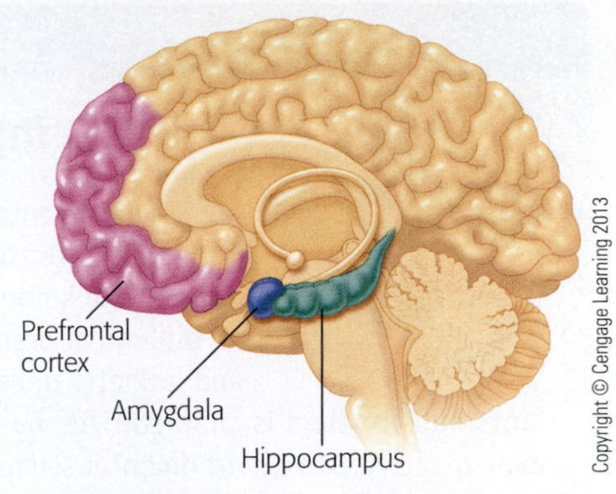

FIGURE 4.3

Neuroanatomical Basis for Panic and Other Anxiety Disorders

The fear network in the brain is centered in the amygdala, which interacts with the hippocampus and areas of the prefrontal cortex. Antianxiety medications appear to desensitize the fear network. Some psychotherapies also affect brain functioning related to anxiety.

Interactions Among Biological, Psychological, and Social and Sociocultural Influences

How do environmental variables affect the influence of genes and alleles? Researchers were initially puzzled by conflicting findings regarding carriers of the short allele of the serotonin transporter gene—the allele associated with anxiety and **behavioral inhibition** (Auerbach, Faroy, Ebstein, Kahana, & Levine, 2001; Leonardo & Hen, 2006). If the short allele of the 5-HTTLPR gene is associated with anxiety, why are only some children who are carriers of this allele behaviorally inhibited (i.e., shy)?

N. A. Fox and colleagues (Nichols & Schwartz 2005) hypothesized that environmental factors such as parental behaviors may interact with a genetic predisposition to produce behavioral inhibition. Using a longitudinal design, 153 children were observed and rated for characteristics of behavioral inhibition at age 14 months and again at 7 years. Mothers were rated in terms of nurturing behaviors and social assistance provided to their children. DNA from each child was analyzed, and children were divided into two groups: those with and those without the short allele of the 5-HTTLPR gene. The researchers found that children with short alleles only showed behavioral inhibition when they were raised in a stressful environment with low levels of maternal social support.

As Fox observed:

> "If you have two short alleles of this serotonin gene, but your mom is not stressed, you will be no more shy than your peers as a school age child. . . . But . . . [i]f you are raised in a stressful environment, and you inherit the short form of the gene, there is a higher likelihood that you will be fearful, anxious or depressed." (Association for Psychological Science, 2007).

Thus, understanding interactions between genetic predisposition and environmental factors yields insight into the causes of anxiety-related behaviors such as shyness.

neurotransmitter any of a group of chemicals that help transmit messages between neurons

serotonin a neurotransmitter that regulates mood, sleep, and appetite

alleles the gene pair responsible for a specific trait

polymorphic variation a common DNA mutation of a gene

predisposition a susceptibility to certain symptoms or disorders

behavioral inhibition shyness

FOCUS ON RESILIENCE

Reducing Risk of Lifelong Anxiety

Environmental factors can both contribute to and protect against anxiety among those with a biological predisposition to shyness and anxiety. Behavioral inhibition in infants and toddlers is characterized by distress and emotional over-reactivity to environmental stimuli. Inhibited children tend to be cautious, shy, and wary of unfamiliar situations or people. Children with these characteristics show negative emotional reactions to novelty, attempt to avoid or escape from social situations, and are at risk for developing social anxiety disorder (Hirshfeld-Becker et al., 2007). Such behavioral inhibition is thought to result from biological predispositions involving heightened fear responses (Auerbach et al., 2001; N. A. Fox, Henderson, et al., 2005).

Additionally, parental behaviors can influence the course of behavioral inhibition in children. Overprotection of socially withdrawn children and lack of support for their independence increase their sense of insecurity and decrease opportunities for them to practice approaching novel situations (K. Burgess, Rubin, Cheah, & Nelson, 2001). The children are thus prevented from developing emotional regulation and coping skills—and anxiety is more likely to continue (Muris & Dietvorst, 2006).

PhotoDisc

However, less than half of children who are biologically predisposed to anxiety continue to be inhibited in middle childhood (Degnan & Fox, 2007). What protective factors enhance the resilience of these children? Nurturing behaviors on the part of parents and other caretakers can help reduce symptoms of inhibition. A warm, sensitive parenting style can help reduce anxiety by building up the child's self-confidence and feelings of mastery; this is important because behavioral inhibition is associated with beliefs that controlling anxiety is not possible (Windsor, Anstey, Butterworth, & Rogers, 2008). Other helpful parental behaviors include encouraging the child to explore new situations by reinforcing independent behaviors, supporting the child's attempts to approach situations that evoke anxiety, and giving comfort when needed (Degnan & Fox, 2007). Such exposure allows children to develop the skills needed to regulate emotional reactivity. As children with anxiety increasingly engage with anxiety-evoking situations, they begin to focus on positive aspects of the situation rather than solely on their anxiety and vigilance to threats (G. E. Miller, Lachman, et al., 2011). When children with behavioral inhibition learn to shift their attention, their emotionality and risk of developing an anxiety disorder decrease (L. White, McDermott, Degnan, Henderson, & Fox, 2011).

Thus, the behaviors of parents or other caretakers can produce adaptive emotional regulation skills in young children and help them overcome their biological predisposition toward behavioral inhibition; in fact, such support has been found to reduce the physiological reactivity and emotional overarousal associated with anxiety disorders (Jaffee, 2007; Maier & Watkins, 2010).

Psychological Dimension

Individual psychological characteristics can also interact with biological predispositions to produce anxiety symptoms. People who tend to interpret events, even ambiguous ones, as threatening are more likely to develop an anxiety disorder. Similarly, those who have **anxiety sensitivity**, which involves interpreting physiological changes as signs of danger, are particularly vulnerable to developing anxiety symptoms (McLaughlin & Hatzenbuehler, 2009). One's sense of control may also be a factor in the development of an anxiety disorder. Young monkeys reared in environments in which they could control access to water and food showed less fear when exposed to anxiety-provoking situations than monkeys without this control. Similarly, children who develop a sense of self-control

anxiety sensitivity trait involving fear of physiological changes within the body

and mastery also appear to be less vulnerable to anxiety (Chorpita & Barlow, 1998). Thus a number of psychological characteristics can affect individual vulnerability to anxiety disorders.

Social and Sociocultural Dimensions

© Ellen B. Senisi/The Image Works

Self-Control and Mastery Decrease Anxiety

Children who develop a sense of control and mastery are less susceptible to anxiety disorders. In this case, the child is allowed to choose her dinner from an assortment of healthy foods and to serve herself.

Any etiological theory of anxiety disorders should consider the impact of social and sociocultural factors and stressors. Daily environmental stress is a social factor that can produce anxiety, especially in individuals who have biological or psychological vulnerabilities. For example, those with lower incomes have higher rates of anxiety disorders (R. C. Kessler, Berglund, Demler, Jin, Merikangas, et al., 2005). Living in poverty or in an unsafe environment can exacerbate both stress and anxiety. Traumatic events such as terrorist attacks, school shootings, and natural disasters also increase rates of anxiety disorders (Palmieri, Weathers, Difede, & King, 2007; Weems, et al., 2007). An individual's social support network (family, friends, and peers) can either exacerbate or mitigate anxiety reactions (Ozer, Best, Lipsey, & Weiss, 2003).

Gender plays a role in the development of anxiety disorders. Females are more likely to experience anxiety disorders than males. Is the reason biological, social, or a combination of the two? Nolen-Hoeksema (2004) has argued that women are more likely to be diagnosed with emotional disorders due to their lack of power and status and to stressors associated with poverty, lack of respect, and limited choices. Stress hormones produced by these social factors may make women more vulnerable to depression and anxiety. Thus interactions between psychological, social, and biological factors may help explain why women are more likely to develop anxiety disorders.

Cultural factors such as acculturation conflicts also contribute to anxiety disorders among ethnic minorities. Among Native Americans and Asian American undergraduate students, there is evidence of high levels of self-reported anxiety (De Coteau, Anderson, & Hope, 2006; Okazaki, Liu, Longworth, & Minn, 2002). Exposure to discrimination and prejudice can increase the anxiety of people who are members of ethnic minorities or other marginalized groups, such as individuals with disabilities or sexual minorities. Culture may influence how anxiety is expressed. Awareness of cultural manifestations of anxiety in different groups is essential for clinicians working with clients from diverse backgrounds.

Biological, psychological, social, and sociocultural explanations can all help answer the question, "What is the cause of this disorder?" Keep this in mind as we now turn our attention to understanding anxiety disorders, beginning with phobias. We conclude the chapter with a focus on obsessive-compulsive and related disorders.

Phobias

The word *phobia* comes from the Greek word for "fear." A **phobia** is a strong, persistent, and unwarranted fear of some specific object or situation. An individual with a phobia often experiences extreme anxiety or panic when

phobia a strong, persistent, and unwarranted fear of a specific object or situation

TABLE 4.2 Examples of Phobias

PHOBIA	OBJECT OF PHOBIA
Acrophobia	Heights
Ailurophobia	Cats
Algophobia	Pain
Astrapophobia	Storms, thunder, lightning
Dementophobia	Insanity
Genophobia	Fear of sexual relations
Hematophobia	Blood
Microphobia	Germs
Monophobia	Being alone
Mysophobia	Contamination/germs
Nyctophobia	Dark
Pathophobia	Disease
Phobophobia	Phobias
Pyrophobia	Fire
Xenophobia	Strangers

encountering the phobic stimulus. Adults with phobias realize that their fear is excessive, although children may not. Many people with phobias also have anxiety, mood, or substance-use disorders (Nedic, Zivanovic, & Lisulov, 2011). Phobias are the most common mental disorder in the United States (see Table 4.2). There are three subcategories of phobias: social anxiety disorder, specific phobias, and agoraphobia.

Social Anxiety Disorder

Case Study

In any social situation, I felt fear. I would be anxious before I even left the house, and it would escalate as I got closer to a college class, a party, or whatever. When I would walk into a room full of people, I'd turn red, and it would feel like everybody's eyes were on me. I was embarrassed to stand off in a corner by myself, but I couldn't think of anything to say. . . . It was humiliating. . . . I couldn't wait to get out. (National Institute of Mental Health [NIMH], 2009a, p. 9)

A **social anxiety disorder (SAD)** is an intense fear of being scrutinized or of doing something embarrassing or humiliating in the presence of others (M. A. Bruch, Fallon, & Heimberg, 2003; Lipsitz, 2006). Social anxiety disorder can involve high levels of anxiety in most social situations (*generalized type*), or can involve very specific anxiety (*performance type*), associated with particular activities such as playing a musical instrument, speaking in public, eating in a restaurant, or using a public restroom.

Individuals with SAD are so self-conscious that they literally feel sick with fear at the prospect of public activities. The most common form of social anxiety disorder involves public speaking and meeting new people.

Social anxiety disorder affects 8.7 percent of adults in a given year. More than 48 percent, however, rate the severity of their symptoms as "mild" (R. C. Kessler, Chiu, et al., 2005). Women are twice as likely as men to have this disorder (R. C. Kessler, Berglund, et al., 2005). SAD is often chronic and disabling, especially for those who develop the disorder early in life (Dalrymple & Zimmerman, 2011; Nedic, et al., 2011). In a 5-year naturalistic follow-up study, only 40 percent of those with SAD disorder recovered (Beard, Moitra, Weisberg, & Keller, 2010). SAD, especially the generalized type, is often **comorbid** with (i.e., often occurs with) major depressive disorders, substance-use disorders, and suicidal thoughts or attempts (El-Gabalawy, Cox, Clara, & Mackenzie, 2010). Individuals with SAD report significant impairment in the quality of interpersonal relationships (Rodebaugh, 2009; Sparrevohn & Rapee, 2009).

Individuals with high social anxiety tend to believe that others view them or their performance negatively (Cody & Teachman, 2011; Wong & Moulds, 2009) and remain alert for "threat" cues such as signs of disapproval or criticism (C. T. Taylor & Alden, 2010). To avoid drawing attention to themselves, they engage in "safety behaviors" such as avoiding eye contact, talking less, sitting alone, holding a glass tightly to prevent tremors, or wearing makeup to hide blushing (Moukheiber et al., 2010; Vassilopoulos, Banerjee, & Prantzalou, 2009) and show high levels of submissiveness in an effort to avoid conflicts with others (Russell, Moskowitz, Zuroff, Bleau, & Young, 2010).

Did You Know?

Women with SAD have a wider variety of social fears and are more likely to receive medications for treatment than men. Men are most likely to report fear regarding dating and to use alcohol and illicit drugs to cope with social anxiety symptoms.

Source: Xu et al. (2012)

social anxiety disorder an intense fear of being scrutinized in one or more social or performance situations

comorbid existing simultaneously with another condition

Specific Phobias

A **specific phobia** is an extreme fear of a specific object (such as snakes) or situation (such as being in an enclosed place). Exposure to the stimulus nearly always produces intense anxiety or panic. The primary types of specific phobias are (LeBeau et al., 2010):

- animal (e.g., spiders, insects, dogs, snakes),
- natural environmental (e.g., heights, earthquakes, thunder, water),
- blood/injections or injury (e.g., needles, dental treatment, invasive medical procedures), and
- situational (e.g., enclosed places, flying, driving, being alone, the dark, or traveling in tunnels or over bridges).

The following case study illustrates a common specific phobia exhibited by a 26-year-old public relations executive.

Case Study

If I see a spider in my house, I get out! I start shaking, and I feel like I'm going to throw up. I get so scared, I have to bolt across the street to drag my neighbor over to get rid of the spider. Even after I know it's gone, I obsess for hours. I check between my sheets 10 times before getting in bed, and I'm so creeped out that I won't get up and go to the bathroom at night, even if my bladder feels like it's about to burst. (Kusek, 2001, p. 183)

Specific phobias are estimated to affect 19 million adults in a given year in the United States (approximately 8.7 percent of the population) and are twice as common in women as in men (R. C. Kessler, Berglund, et al., 2005; NIMH, 2009a). The degree to which they interfere with daily life depends on how easy it is to avoid the feared object or situation. These phobias often begin during childhood. Animal phobias tend to have the earliest onset (age 7), followed by blood phobia (age 9), dental phobia (age 12), and claustrophobia (age 20; Öst, 1987, 1992). Figure 4.4 illustrates ages at which different phobias typically begin.

The most common childhood fears have traditionally included spiders, the dark, frightening movies, and being teased, whereas adolescents most frequently fear heights, animals, and speaking in class or speaking to strangers (Muris, Merckelbach, & Collaris, 1997). However, contemporary fears of students now include "being raped," "terrorist attacks," "having to fight in a war," "drive-by shootings," and "snipers at school" (Burnham, 2009). Most early fears do **remit**, or disappear, without treatment (Broeren, Lester, Muris, & Field, 2011).

Blood phobias differ from other phobias because they are associated with a unique physiological response: fainting in the phobic situation. Fainting appears to result from an initial increase in physiological arousal followed by a sudden drop in blood pressure and heart rate (Ayala, Meuret, & Ritz, 2009). Nearly 70 percent of those with blood phobias report a history of fainting in medical situations (Antony, Brown, & Barlow, 1997); many avoid medical examinations or are unable to care for injured family members (Hellstrom, Fellenius, & Öst, 1996). In one study, over 7 percent of pregnant women receiving prenatal care met the criteria for blood and injection phobia (Lilliecreutz & Josefsson, 2008).

Phobias

Coulrophobia, a fear of clowns, may result from their painted eyes and smiles and never-changing expressions. Celebrities reported to have a fear of clowns include Johnny Depp, Daniel Radcliffe, Billy Bob Thornton, and Sean "P. Diddy" Combs. Uma Thurman is reported to have claustrophobia (fear of enclosed places).

specific phobia an extreme fear of a specific object (such as snakes) or situation (such as being in an enclosed place)

remit diminish or disappear

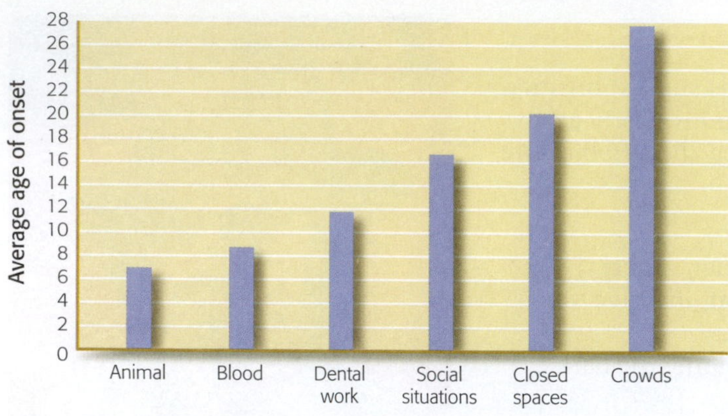

FIGURE 4.4

Phobia Onset

This graph illustrates the average ages at which 370 people said their phobias began. Animal phobias began during childhood, whereas the onset of agoraphobia did not occur until the individuals were in their late 20s. What accounts for the differences reported in the age of onset for the types of phobias?

Source: Based on Öst (1987, 1992)

Agoraphobia

Agoraphobia is an intense fear of at least two of the following situations: (a) being outside of the home alone; (b) traveling in public transportation; (c) being in open spaces (e.g., parking lot or park); (d) being in stores or theaters; or (e) standing in line or being in a crowd. These situations are feared because escape or help may not be readily available (Wittchen, et al., 2010). Agoraphobia arises from a fear that paniclike symptoms, such as fainting, losing control over bodily functions, or displaying excessive fear in public, will incapacitate the person or cause severe embarrassment. Anxiety over having a **panic attack**, which is an episode of intense fear accompanied by various physiological symptoms, can prevent people from leaving their homes. Agoraphobia occurs much more frequently in females than in males. Although this phobia is relatively uncommon (less than 1 percent of U.S. adults in a given year), 41 percent of those affected rate the symptoms as serious (R. C. Kessler, Chiu, et al., 2005).

Individuals who have agoraphobia may misinterpret and overreact to bodily sensations. Normal physiological changes precipitate anxiety; anxiety reactions then further increase bodily sensations (e.g., sweating or heart palpitations), resulting in a vicious cycle that can culminate in a panic attack (Rudaz, Craske, Becker, Ledermann, & Margraf, 2010). In support of this view, Reiss, Peterson, Gursky, & McNally (1986) found that people with agoraphobia scored high on the Anxiety Sensitivity Index (ASI), which measures the degree to which individuals "fear" their physiological reactions.

Fears or Phobias Reported by Celebrities

Jennifer Aniston—Flying (aviophobia)

Pamela Anderson—Mirrors (eisoptrophobia)

Sarah Michelle Gellar—Graveyards (coimetrophobia)

Orlando Bloom—Pigs (swinophobia)

Keanu Reeves—Darkness (nyctophobia)

Tyra Banks—Dolphins and whales (cetaphobia)

Justin Timberlake—Spiders (arachnophobia) and snakes (ophidiophobia)

Etiology of Phobias

How do such strong and "irrational" fears develop? As we indicated at the beginning of the chapter, in most cases, predisposing genetic factors interact with psychological, social, and sociocultural influences. In this section, we examine the factors related to the etiology of phobias, as shown in Figure 4.5.

Biological Dimension Studies on male and female twin pairs have supported a moderate genetic contribution (heritability of 31 percent) for all phobia subtypes (Hettema, Annas, Neale, Kendler, & Frederikson, 2003; Kendler & Prescott, 2006). Individuals with phobias may have an innate tendency to be anxious and respond more strongly to emotional stimuli; thus their chances of developing an irrational fear response are increased. Exaggerated responsiveness of the amygdala and other areas of the brain associated with fear may make an individual more susceptible to developing a phobia (Sehlmeyer et al., 2011). Neuroimaging studies have confirmed that individuals with phobias show increased physiological fear responses in reaction to phobic-related stimuli (Schweckendiek et al., 2011).

A different biological view of the development of fear reactions is that of *preparedness*. Proponents of this position argue that fears do not develop randomly. They believe that it is easier for humans to develop fears to which we are physiologically predisposed, such as a fear of heights or snakes. Such quickly aroused (or "prepared") fears may have been necessary to the survival of pretechnological humanity. In fact, evolutionarily prepared fears (e.g., fear of fire or deep water) occur even without exposure to traumatic conditioning experiences (Forsyth, Eifert, & Thompson, 1996; Muhlberger, Wiedemann, Herrmann, & Pauli, 2006). There is some research to support this view. In one study, participants were able

agoraphobia an intense fear of being in public places where escape or help may not be readily available

panic attack episode of intense fear accompanied by symptoms such as a pounding heart, trembling, shortness of breath, and fear of losing control or dying

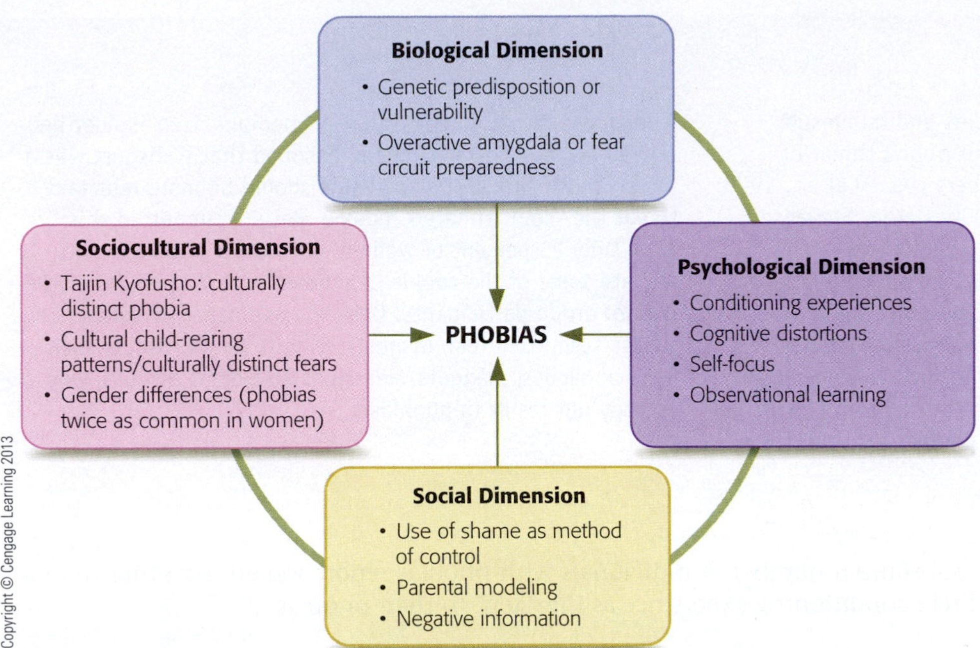

FIGURE 4.5

Multipath Model of Phobias
The dimensions interact with one another and combine in different ways to result in a phobia.

to detect fear-producing stimuli (spiders and snakes) more quickly than neutral stimuli (mushrooms) against a background of fruits (Soares, Esteves, Lundqvist, & Ohman, 2009). Macaque monkeys are also able to rapidly detect pictures of snake stimuli (Shibasaki & Kawai, 2009).

Although preparedness is an interesting theory, it is hard to believe that most phobias stem from prepared fears. Many simply do not fit into the prepared-fear model. It would be difficult, for example, to explain the survival value of social phobias such as fear of using public restrooms, as well as many of the other specific phobias. In addition, prepared fears are relatively easy to eliminate.

- 3.5 percent of Americans have a severe injection phobia.
- 50 percent of individuals who use medications that require self-injections are unable to perform the injections.
- Those with an injection phobia fear pain or have unrealistic thoughts such as "the needle might break off."

Source: Mohr, Cox, & Merluzzi (2005)

Psychological Dimension There are multiple psychological pathways that can lead to the development of phobias: (a) fear conditioning, (b) observational learning or modeling, (c) negative informational effects, and (d) cognitive processes. The pathway involved often depends on the specific type of phobia. For example, modeling—watching someone else display the fear—seems to be more important in spider phobia, whereas direct conditioning plays a major role in blood or injection phobia (Coelho & Purkis, 2009).

Classical Conditioning Perspective The view that phobias are conditioned fear responses evolved from psychologist John B. Watson's classic conditioning experiment with an infant, Little Albert. Watson caused Little Albert to develop a fear of white rats by pairing a white rat with a loud sound (Watson & Rayner, 1920), demonstrating that fears can result through an association process. Similarly, conditioning occurred when women undergoing chemotherapy for breast cancer were given lemon-lime Kool-Aid in a container with a bright orange lid. After repeated pairings of the drink and the chemotherapy, the women indicated emotional distress and nausea when presented with the container (Jacobsen et al., 1995).

Many children with severe phobias report conditioning experiences as the cause (N. J. King, Clowes-Hollins, & Ollendick, 1997; N. J. King, Eleonora, & Ollendick, 1998). Similarly, more adults attribute their phobias to conditioning experiences than to any other factor (Öst, 1987; Öst & Hugdahl, 1981). However,

CONTROVERSY

Fear or Disgust?

Do phobias such as fears of spiders and rats result from disgust evoked rather than from a threat of physical danger? Some researchers (Davey et al., 1998; de Jong, Vorage, & van den Hout, 2000; Oaten, Stevenson, & Case, 2009) have pointed out that spiders and rats are, in general, harmless. These researchers attribute some phobias to an inherent or "prepared" fear of disease or contamination, rather than a threat of physical danger. In an experiment to determine whether disgust is involved in spider phobia, Mulkens, de Jong, and Merckelbach (1996) had women with and without spider phobias indicate their willingness to eat a cookie that a "medium sized" spider had walked across. The researchers reasoned that if disgust was a factor, those with a spider phobia should be more reluctant to eat the "contaminated" cookie. Results supported this idea: Only 25 percent of women with spider phobia eventually ate some of the cookie, compared with 70 percent of the control group participants. Does the avoidance of spiders and snakes stem from fear, disgust, or both? Since insects such as cockroaches, maggots, and slugs also elicit disgust, why do they not result in phobias?

a substantial number of individuals with phobias report something other than a direct conditioning experience as the "key" to their phobias.

Observational Learning, or Modeling, Perspective Fears can develop through observational learning. Participants in a study watched a video of a male involved in a fear conditioning experiment. The video displayed an uncomfortable shock being delivered to the man's wrist in response to a stimulus. The observers were told that they would participate in a similar experiment after viewing the video. When they were shown the same stimulus that had been associated with the shock, the participants responded with fear. Neuroimaging scans of the participants during the conditioning experiment showed activation of the amygdala when participants saw the stimulus (Olsson, Nearing, & Phelps, 2007).

Children can develop fear responses by observing others displaying fear in real life or in the media. In a study (Burstein & Ginsburg, 2010), parents of children aged 8 to 12 were trained to act either anxiously or in a relaxed manner before their child took a spelling test. Children exposed to an anxious-acting parent reported higher anxiety levels, more anxious thoughts, and a greater avoidance of the spelling test than did those in the relaxed parent condition. In another study, watching peers who showed either calm or anxious behaviors in interacting with a novel animal influenced how much fear children displayed when asked to interact with the animal (Broeren et al., 2011). Thus, it appears that observational learning can play a role in the development of fear.

NGS Image Collection

Scary or Cute?

Fears can be induced through negative information. Childrens' reactions to the cuscus depended upon the descriptions furnished to their parents about the unfamiliar animal.

Negative Information Perspective Can information cause someone to fear an object or situation? To determine this, parents were given descriptions regarding an unfamiliar animal (a cuscus) that were (a) negative (has sharp claws and long teeth, can jump at your throat); (b) ambiguous (has white teeth, can jump, likes to drink all sorts of things); or (c) positive (has nice tiny teeth, eats tasty strawberries, likes to play with other animals). Using this information, the parents then described to their children how the cuscus might behave in certain situations. Children whose parents received the negative description reacted with more fear to the cuscus than those whose parents received positive or ambiguous information (Muris, van Zwol, Huijding, & Mayer, 2010). Thus, fears can be induced through negative or threatening information.

Cognitive-Behavioral Perspective Why do individuals with spider phobia react with such terror at the sight of a spider? Some researchers believe that cognitive distortions (including overestimating threat) and catastrophic thoughts may cause strong fears to develop (Rinck & Becker, 2006). For example, people with spider phobia overestimate the size of spiders they encounter (Vasey et al., 2012) and believe that spiders single them out for attack (Riskind, Moore, & Bowley, 1995). Others report thoughts such as the spider "will attack" or "will take revenge" (Mulkens et al., 1996). Individuals with social phobia believe they are being scrutinized by others and think, "Everyone in the room is watching me. I know I am going to do something stupid!" (Schmidt, Richey, Buckner, & Timpano, 2009; Vassilopoulos et al., 2009)

Social Dimension Family interaction patterns are also related to the development of phobias and anxiety disorders. Behavioral inhibition (shyness) and family process variables were measured in a sample of 242 boys and girls at age 3 and again 4 years later. Anxiety symptoms were predicted both by early negative family affect and family stress in middle childhood (Schmidt et al., 2009). A punitive maternal parenting style (based on child report) has been linked with increased tendency to have fearful beliefs (Field, Ball, Kawycz, & Moore, 2007). Victimization by peers during childhood is also associated with increased social anxiety (R. E. McCabe, Miller, Laugesen, Antony, & Young, 2010).

Sociocultural Dimension Females are more likely to have phobias, with the difference showing up as early as 9 years of age. However, this difference is found mainly for repulsive animals, such as snakes, rather than harmless animals such as dogs. Fewer gender differences exist for fears of bodily injury, social fears, and fears of enclosed spaces. Such differences may be due to biological factors, temperamental factors, or social norms and values (C. P. McLean & Anderson, 2009). Some of the gender differences in phobias may be due to the facts that women show a stronger disgust response than men and that some phobic objects produce both fear and disgust responses (Rohrmann, Hopp, & Quirin, 2008).

Social phobias appear to be more common in families who use shame as a method of control and who stress the importance of the opinions of others (M. A. Bruch & Heimberg, 1994). These are common child-rearing practices in Asian families; fear of being evaluated by others is more common in Chinese children and adolescents than in Western comparison groups (Dong, Yang, & Ollendick, 1994).

It is important to note that social fears and other anxiety disorders may be expressed differently in different cultures. *Taijin kyofusho*, for instance, is a culturally distinctive phobia found in Japan that is similar to a social anxiety disorder. However, instead of a fear involving social or performance situations, *taijin kyofusho* is a fear of offending or embarrassing others, a concept consistent with the Japanese cultural emphasis on maintaining interpersonal harmony (Okazaki, 1997; K. Suzuki, Takei, Kawai, Minabe, & Mori, 2003). Individuals with this disorder are fearful that their appearance, facial expression, eye contact, body parts, or body odor are offensive to others. In DSM-5, fear of offending others was added to the description of social anxiety disorder for more cross-cultural relevance.

Treatment of Phobias

For all anxiety disorders, it is first important to rule out possible medical or physical causes of anxiety symptoms, such as hyperthyroidism (overactive thyroid), cardiac arrhythmias, stimulants (e.g., excessive caffeine intake) or asthma medications, or withdrawal from alcohol (Katon, 2006). Phobias have been

The use of antipsychotic medications for anxiety disorders increased from 10.6 percent to 21.3 percent between 1996 and 2007, even though the drugs are not approved for these conditions by the Food and Drug Administration. Could this increase be due to the marketing activities of drug companies?

Source: Breier (2011); Comer, Mojtabai, & Olfson (2011)

successfully treated by both behavioral and pharmacological methods (Koszycki, Taljaard, Segal, & Bradwejn, 2011).

Biochemical Treatments In treating phobias, a number of medications appear to be effective. For social anxiety disorder, both benzodiazepines (a class of antianxiety medication) and the antidepressant selective serotonin reuptake inhibitors (SSRIs) have shown evidence of efficacy, and benzodiazepines have been used with some success in treating specific phobias (Lader & Bond, 1998; M. W. Otto et al., 2010). As with most medications, side effects can occur. Benzodiazepines can produce dependence, withdrawal symptoms, and paradoxical reactions such as increased talkativeness, excessive movement, and even hostility and rage (C. E. Mancuso, Tanzi, & Gabay, 2004). In addition, symptoms often recur when the medication is discontinued (Sundel & Sundel, 1998).

Behavioral Treatments Phobias have also been successfully treated with a variety of behavioral approaches, including exposure therapy, systematic desensitization, cognitive restructuring, and modeling therapy. Most behavioral treatments combine several of these techniques (Lipsitz, 2006).

Exposure Therapy In **exposure therapy**, treatment involves gradual and increasingly difficult encounters with a feared situation. For example, when treating a client with a fear of leaving the house, a therapist may first ask the client to visualize or imagine the anxiety-evoking situation. Eventually, the client might walk outside the home with the therapist until the fear has been eliminated. Exposure therapy is frequently used to treat phobias (Hofmann, Moscovitch, Kim, & Taylor, 2004; Meyerbroker & Emmelkamp, 2010; Schneier, 2006; Vogele et al., 2010).

A variant of exposure therapy has been developed for the treatment of the fainting and drop in blood pressure associated with blood and injection phobia. A procedure known as *applied tension* (described in the following case study), combined with exposure, has proven effective (Hellstrom et al., 1996).

Case Study

Mr. A. reported feeling faint when exposed to any stimuli involving blood, injections, injury, or surgery. Even hearing an instructor discuss the physiology of the heart caused Mr. A. to feel sweaty and faint. Mr. A. was taught to recognize the first signs of a drop in blood pressure and then to combat this autonomic response by tightening (tensing) the muscles of his arms, chest, and legs until his face felt warm. Mr. A. was then taught to stop the tension for about 15 to 20 seconds and then to reapply the tension, repeating the procedure about five times. (The rise in blood pressure that follows this process prevents fainting, and the fear becomes extinguished.) After going through this process, Mr. A. was able to watch a video of thoracic surgery, watch blood being drawn, listen to a talk about cardiovascular disease, and read an anatomy book—stimuli that in the past would have produced fainting (K. W. Anderson, Taylor, & McLean, 1996).

exposure therapy treatment that involves gradually introducing the client to increasingly difficult encounters with a feared situation

systematic desensitization exposure strategy that uses muscle relaxation to reduce the anxiety associated with specific and social phobias

Systematic Desensitization **Systematic desensitization** uses muscle relaxation to reduce the anxiety associated with phobias. Wolpe (1958, 1973), who developed the treatment, first taught clients to relax their muscles. Second, he had them

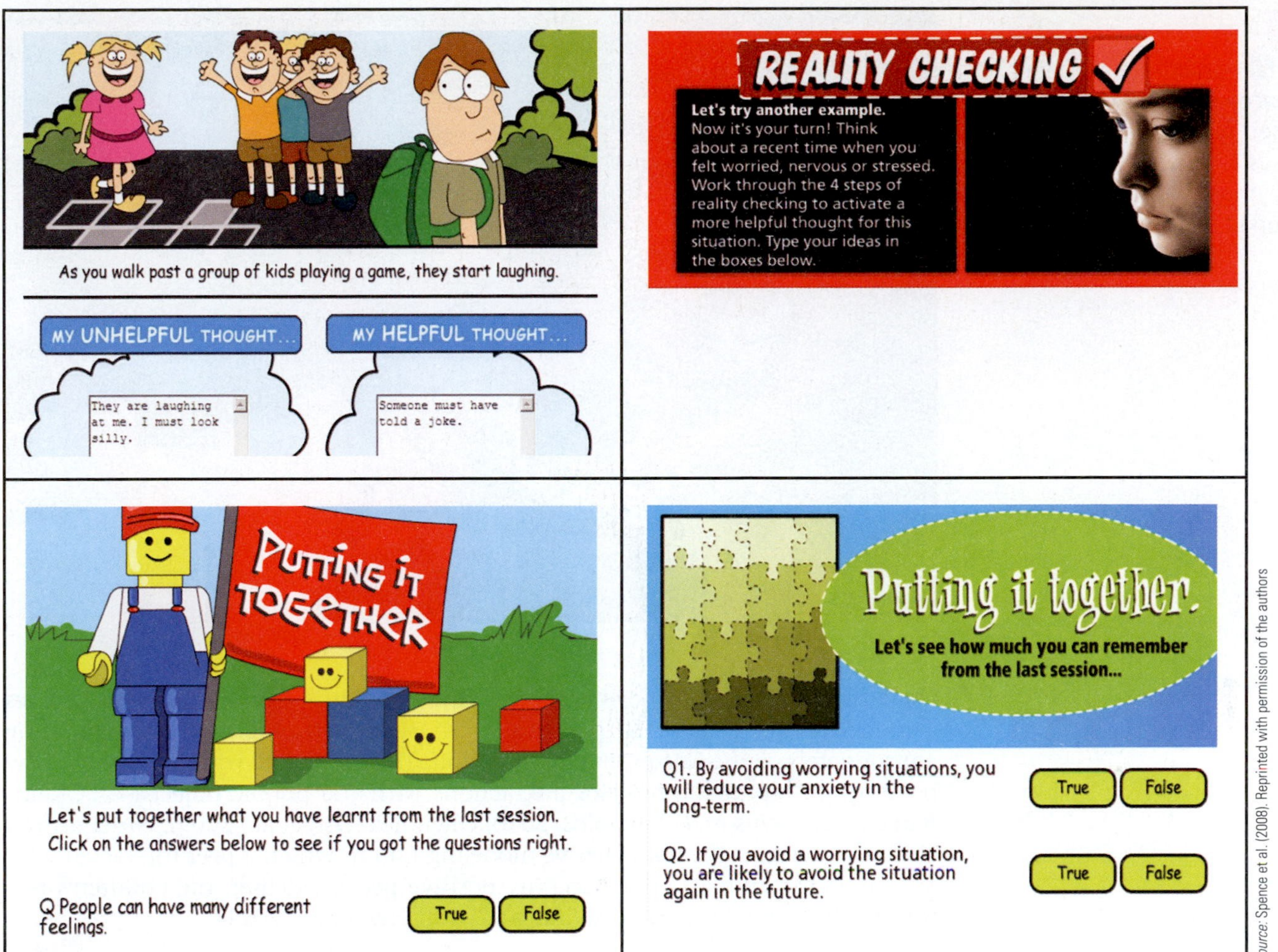

As you walk past a group of kids playing a game, they start laughing.
MY UNHELPFUL THOUGHT...
They are laughing at me. I must look silly.
MY HELPFUL THOUGHT...
Someone must have told a joke.
REALITY CHECKING
Let's try another example.
Now it's your turn! Think about a recent time when you felt worried, nervous or stressed. Work through the 4 steps of reality checking to activate a more helpful thought for this situation. Type your ideas in the boxes below.
PUTTING IT TOGETHER
Let's put together what you have learnt from the last session.
Click on the answers below to see if you got the questions right.
Q People can have many different feelings.
True
False
Putting it together.
Let's see how much you can remember from the last session...
Q1. By avoiding worrying situations, you will reduce your anxiety in the long-term.
True
False
Q2. If you avoid a worrying situation, you are likely to avoid the situation again in the future.
True
False

Source: Spence et al. (2008). Reprinted with permission of the authors

Online Program for Social Anxiety

Pictured are sample items from a computerized treatment program dealing with social phobia in children and adolescents.

visualize feared stimuli (arranged from least to most anxiety provoking) while in the relaxed state. This was continued until the clients reported little or no anxiety with the stimuli. This procedure was adapted for a man who had a fear of urinating in restrooms when others were present. He was trained in muscle relaxation and, while relaxed, learned to urinate under the following conditions: no one in the bathroom, therapist in the stall, therapist washing hands, therapist at adjacent urinal, therapist waiting behind client. The easier items were practiced first until anxiety was sufficiently reduced (McCracken & Larkin, 1991).

Cognitive Restructuring In **cognitive restructuring**, unrealistic thoughts believed to be responsible for phobias are altered (Kendall, Khanna, Edson, Cummings, & Harris, 2011). Individuals with social phobias, for example, tend to be intensely self-focused and fearful that others will see them as anxious, incompetent, or weak. Their own self-criticism is the basis for their phobia (Britton et al., 2011; C. T. Taylor & Alden, 2010). Cognitive strategies can help "normalize" social anxiety by encouraging individuals to interpret emotional and physical tension as "normal anxiety" and by helping them redirect their attention away from themselves in social situations.

cognitive restructuring cognitive strategy that attempts to alter unrealistic thoughts that are believed to be responsible for phobias

Modeling

Watching a fear-producing act being performed successfully can help people overcome their fear. In this photo, a friend exposes a reluctant teen (on the right) to a python. Why do you think modeling works?

Jeff Greenberg/Photo Edit, Inc.

Modeling Therapy In **modeling therapy**, the individual with the phobia observes a model (either in a visual portrayal or in person) coping with or responding appropriately to the fear-producing situation. The individual with the phobia may be asked to repeat the model's interactions with the phobic object (V. L. Kelly, Barker, Field, Wilson, & Reynolds, 2010; Ollendick, Öst, et al., 2009). Ninety-seven children saw a positive or negative modeling film in which a peer interacted with an unfamiliar animal. After watching positive peer modeling, the children's fear toward the animal decreased significantly (Broeren et al., 2011).

CHECKPOINT REVIEW

1. Describe how phobias develop.
2. Give a brief description of the different types of phobias.
3. How are phobias treated?

Panic Disorder

Case Study

For me, a panic attack is almost a violent experience. . . . My heart pounds really hard, I feel like I can't get my breath and there's an overwhelming feeling that things are crashing in on me. . . . In between attacks, there is this dread and anxiety that it's going to happen again. I'm afraid to go back to places where I've had an attack. Unless I get help, there soon won't be any place where I can go and feel safe from panic. (NIMH, 2009a, p. 3)

modeling therapy procedure involving observation of a non-phobic individual successfully coping with the phobic object or situation used to treat certain phobias

panic disorder disorder involving recurrent, unexpected panic attacks with apprehension over future attacks or behavioral changes to avoid attacks

A diagnosis of **panic disorder** involves recurrent unexpected panic attacks in combination with (a) apprehension over having another attack or worry about the consequences of an attack (e.g., feeling a loss of control or inability to breathe) or (b) changes in behavior or activities designed to avoid another panic attack. These reactions must be present for a period of 1 month or more (Craske et al., 2010). The attacks are especially feared because they often occur unpredictably and without warning.

Panic attacks often begin in late adolescence or early adulthood (NIMH, 2009a). Although panic disorder is diagnosed in only a small percentage of individuals, panic attacks appear to be fairly common. Approximately 40 percent of the general population experiences panic attack symptoms at some point in their lifetime. The 12-month prevalence rate for panic disorder is 2.7 percent (R. C. Kessler, Chiu, et al., 2005); it is twice as common in women as in men (NIMH, 2009a). Those who have more recurrent panic symptoms tend to have comorbid depression, generalized anxiety, or substance abuse (Bystritsky et al., 2010). Many individuals diagnosed with a panic disorder also have agoraphobia, caused by fear of having a panic episode in a public place.

Did You Know? The word *panic* originates from Greek mythology. Pan was a Greek demigod who lived in isolated forests. He amused himself by making noises while following travelers who were traveling at night through the woods. He would continue to frighten them until they bolted in *panic*.

Etiology of Panic Disorder

As with the other disorders we have discussed so far, biological, psychological, social, and sociocultural factors and their interactions play a role in the etiology of panic disorder, as shown in Figure 4.6.

Biological Dimension Higher **concordance rates** (i.e., percentages of relatives sharing the same disorder) for panic disorder have been found in monozygotic (identical) twins than in dizygotic (fraternal) twins; heritability is estimated to be about 32 percent, which is considered a modest contribution (Kendler & Prescott, 2006). Research has been directed at identifying specific gene × environment interactions, neural structures, and a neurochemical basis for panic disorder (Klauke et al., 2010).

As we mentioned earlier, brain structures (such as the amygdala) are involved in anxiety disorders (including panic disorder), and neurotransmitters (such as serotonin) play an important role in emotions. Some studies have linked anxiety and fear with a reduction in **GABA** receptors in the hippocampus and amygdala (Roy-Byrne, Craske, & Stein, 2006). Additionally, disturbances or

concordance rate degree of similarity between twins or family members with respect to a trait or disorder

GABA gamma-aminobutyric acid, an inhibitory neurotransmitter involved in inducing sleep and relaxation

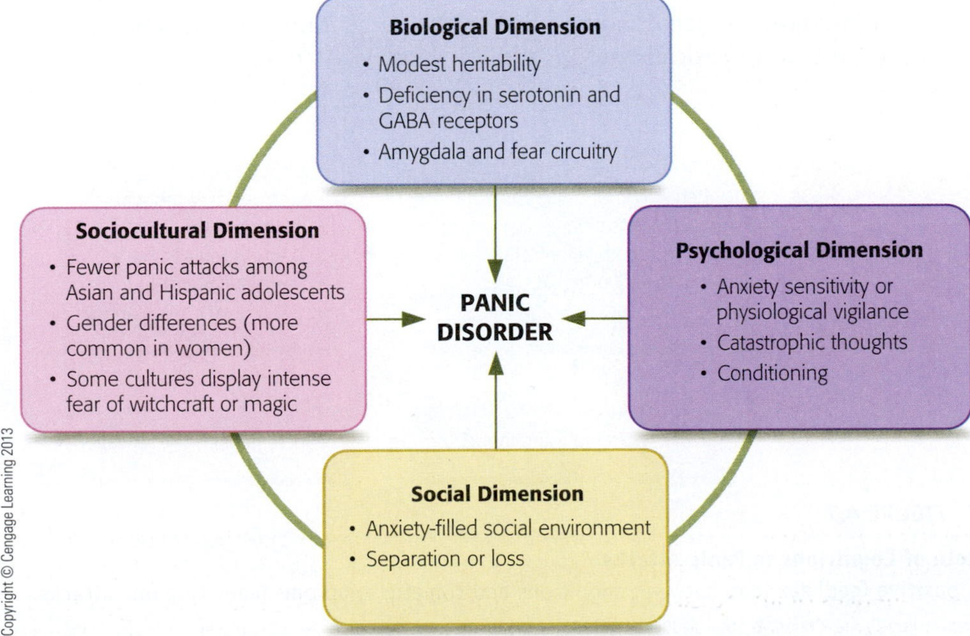

FIGURE 4.6

Multipath Model of Panic Disorder The dimensions interact with one another and combine in different ways to result in panic disorder.

Women diagnosed with panic disorder report more severe premenstrual symptoms; it is possible that premenstrual hormonal fluctuations contribute to panic disorder in women (Nillni, Rohan, Bernstein, & Zvolensky, 2010).

abnormalities in a serotonin receptor gene (5-HT1A) may contribute to panic disorder (Klauke et al., 2010; J. R. Nash et al., 2008). Neuroimaging has revealed that individuals with panic disorder have nearly one-third fewer serotonin 5-HT1A receptors than individuals in a control group (Neumeister et al., 2004); this results in decreased availability of serotonin. It is interesting to note that SSRIs, antidepressant medications designed to increase levels of serotonin in the brain, are effective in treating panic disorders as well as other anxiety disorders.

Psychological Dimension Certain psychological characteristics have been associated with panic disorder. Individuals with panic disorder score high on anxiety sensitivity measures assessing fear responses to bodily sensations (Schmidt, Keough, et al., 2010). They display vigilance over changes in the physiological processes such as heart rate, blood pressure, and respiration (see Figure 4.7). When physical bodily changes are detected, anxiety increases, resulting in even greater physiological responses and more anxiety; this cycle often culminates in a panic attack (Domschke, Stevens, Pfleiderer, & Gerlach, 2010). It is possible that physiological sensitivity is learned by watching parents or friends express fears about physical sensations or witnessing a traumatic event such as a heart attack (Schmidt, Keough, et al., 2010; Schmidt, Lerew, & Jackson, 1997).

Cognitive-Behavioral Perspective The cognitive-behavioral model contends that panic attacks occur when unpleasant bodily sensations are misinterpreted as indicators of an impending disaster. These inaccurate cognitions (see Table 4.3) and somatic symptoms create a feedback loop that results in increasingly higher levels of anxiety. Thus, the following pattern is associated with the development of a panic disorder (Roy-Byrne et al., 2006; Rudaz et al., 2010):

1. A physiological change occurs (e.g., faster breathing or increased heart rate) due to factors such as exercise, excitement, or stress.
2. Catastrophic thoughts develop, such as "Something is wrong," "I'm having a heart attack," or "I'm going to die."
3. These thoughts result in increased apprehension and fear, resulting in even more physiological changes.
4. A circular pattern develops as the amplified bodily changes now result in even more fearful thoughts.
5. This pairing of changes in internal bodily sensations with fear results in **interoceptive conditioning**—that is, the perception of bodily changes begin to automatically produce fear and panic attacks.

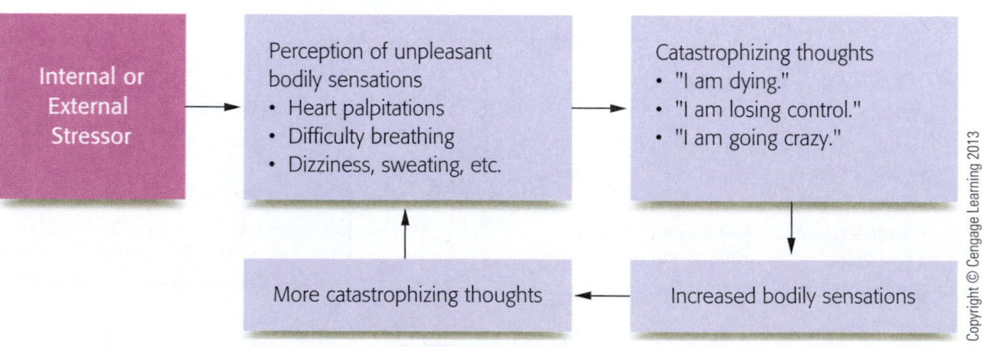

FIGURE 4.7

Role of Cognitions in Panic Attacks

A positive feedback loop between cognitions and somatic symptoms leads to panic attacks.

Source: Roy-Byrne, Craske, & Stein (2006), p. 1027

interoceptive conditioning the production of fear and panic by the perception of bodily changes due to frequent pairing of changes in internal bodily sensations with fear responses

TABLE 4.3 Examples of Catastrophic Thoughts in Panic Disorder

PHYSICAL	MENTAL	SOCIAL
"I will die"	"I will go crazy"	"People will think I'm crazy or weird"
"I will have a heart attack"	"I will become hysterical"	"People will laugh at me"
"I will suffocate"	"I will uncontrollably try to escape"	"People will stare at me"
"I will pass out"		

Source: Hicks, Leitenberg, Barlow & Gorman (2005)

Research support for the cognitive hypothesis includes findings that a reduction in panic-related cognitions (resulting from cognitive-behavioral therapy) is associated with a subsequent reduction in panic symptoms (Hofmann et al., 2007; Teachman, Marker, & Clerkin, 2010).

Social and Sociocultural Dimensions Many individuals with panic disorder report a stressful childhood involving separation anxiety, family conflicts, school problems, or the loss of a loved one (Klauke et al., 2010; Mahoney, 2000). Such environmental stressors may create a predisposition to developing anxiety reactions and subsequently a panic disorder. Some individuals with panic attacks report facing major life changes just before the attacks began (Pollard, Pollard, & Corn, 1989).

Culture can also play a role in panic disorder. Asian and Latino/Hispanic adolescents report higher anxiety sensitivity than white adolescents but are less likely to have panic attacks. This may be due to cultural differences in the way Asian and Latino/Hispanic adolescents interpret anxiety or bodily symptoms (Weems, Hayward, Killen, & Taylor, 2002). Symptom differences are also found in people from India, where panic attacks are associated with physiological symptoms (e.g., increased heart rate, shortness of breath) rather than with catastrophic thoughts (Neerakal & Srinivasan, 2003).

Treatment of Panic Disorder

Both medication and cognitive-behavioral therapies have been effective in treating panic disorder (Hicks, Leitenberg, Barlow, & Gorman, 2005). With either therapy, an important step involves teaching clients about panic disorders and providing reassurance about normal physiological changes.

Biochemical Treatment A number of different classes of medications have been used successfully to treat panic disorder. Benzodiazepines (antianxiety medications) have been found to reduce the number of panic attacks (Nardi et al., 2012). Panic disorder also has been treated with tricyclic antidepressants and SSRI antidepressants (S. M. Marcus et al., 2007); it usually takes 4 to 8 weeks for antidepressants to become fully effective, and some individuals may initially have more panic attacks than usual during the first few weeks. Relapse rates after cessation of drug therapy appear to be quite high (Biondi & Picardi, 2003).

MYTH VS. REALITY

MYTH Because brain activity associated with anxiety disorders can be "normalized" with medication, biological explanations and treatments provide the best alternatives for treatment.

REALITY Psychotherapy is highly effective with anxiety disorders and may also affect brain metabolism. Medications appear to temporarily affect the fear network at the level of the amygdala, whereas cognitive-behavioral therapy leads to changes in the prefrontal cortex and hippocampus.

Cognitive-Behavioral Treatment Cognitive-behavioral treatment is successful in treating panic disorder (Roy-Byrne et al., 2006). Cognitive-behavioral intervention involves extinction of the fear associated with both internal bodily sensations (e.g., heart rate, sweating, dizziness, breathlessness) and fear-producing environmental situations, such as being in crowds or in unfamiliar areas (Hofmann et al., 2007). In general, cognitive-behavioral treatment for panic disorder involves the following steps (Hicks et al., 2005; D. B. Pincus, May, Whitton, Mattis, & Barlow, 2010; Roy-Byrne et al., 2006):

1. educating the client about panic disorder and correcting misconceptions regarding the symptoms;
2. identifying and correcting catastrophic thinking—for example, the therapist might comment, "Maybe you are overreacting to what is going on in your body" or "A panic attack will not stop your breathing";
3. teaching the client to self-induce physiological symptoms associated with panic (such as hyperventilating or breathing through a straw) in order to extinguish panic reactions in response to bodily cues or sensations;
4. encouraging the client to face the symptoms, both within the session and in the outside world, using statements such as "Allow your body to have its reactions and let the reactions pass";
5. teaching coping statements such as "This feeling is not pleasant, but I can handle it"; and
6. helping the client to identify the antecedents of the panic: "What stress am I facing?"

CHECKPOINT REVIEW

1 Describe symptoms of panic disorder.

2 Describe how panic disorder develops.

3 Describe the elements of cognitive-behavioral treatment for panic disorder.

CONTROVERSY:

Panic Disorder Treatment: Should We Focus on Personal Control?

Imagine standing in the middle of a busy mall when suddenly your heart starts to pound and you begin to sweat. Soon you feel nauseated and disoriented, and can barely breathe. You fear you are going to either pass out or die. What is happening to you? What brought on this terrifying experience? Will it happen again? When you regain your composure, you think about what has just happened. You may decide to explore treatment options. If so, what treatment techniques will you choose? Consider the following studies.

Abraham Bakker and his colleagues (Bakker, Spinhoven, Van Balkom, & Van Dyck, 2002) compared two groups of individuals with panic disorder. One group was treated with cognitive-behavioral therapy (CBT)—a therapy that encouraged clients to accept personal control over their panic reactions. The other group was treated with antidepressant medications without psychotherapy. Clients in the CBT group had lower relapse rates than those treated pharmacologically, perhaps because those in the CBT group learned to view their gains as the result of their own efforts rather than due to medication.

Biondi & Picardi (2003) compared medication alone with a combination of medication and CBT. The CBT strategies included sharing information about panic disorders, challenging catastrophic misinterpretations, considering alternative explanations for bodily sensations, practicing relaxation strategies, exposing clients to feared situations, and understanding the implications of having a panic disorder. Before, during, and at the end of treatment, the researchers assessed participants' beliefs concerning what accounted for their recovery. After the treatment, relapse rate was 78.1 percent for those in the medication group, compared with 14.3 percent for the CBT group.

A common factor in the cognitive-behavioral approaches used in both studies was the enhancement of self-efficacy—a belief that recovery and the ability to manage anxiety are under personal control. Individuals who believe (or come to believe) that success is up to them are significantly more likely to reduce anxiety symptoms than those who attribute their improvement to external factors, such as medication. How might therapists help their clients increase self-efficacy?

Generalized Anxiety Disorder

Case Study

Lana, age 12, has worried about many things over the past year, including what will happen if her mother gets sick, if her parents cannot afford their house, or if she fails a math test. She has trouble concentrating and becomes easily fatigued. Usually, if she starts worrying about one issue, she starts thinking about others, and often seeks reassurance from her mother. (Rynn et al., 2011, p. 77)

All of us have had concerns or worries that are specific and time limited. **Generalized anxiety disorder (GAD)**, however, is characterized by persistent, high levels of anxiety and excessive worry over many life circumstances; diagnosis requires that symptoms be present on the majority of days for at least 3 months and be accompanied by physical or somatic symptoms. Worry appears to be the defining characteristic of GAD, and some believe a better term for this disorder would be "pathological worry behavior" (Andrews et al., 2010). The worry produces symptoms such as feeling on edge, muscle tension, restlessness, sleep difficulties, poor concentration, avoidance of situations associated with the worry, and repeated seeking of reassurance concerning the worry.

GAD develops gradually, often beginning in childhood or adolescence (NIMH, 2009a; Rynn et al., 2011). In one study, individuals with GAD reported higher anxiety levels, were more sensitive to bodily changes, and exhibited greater physiological responsiveness than control participants (Hoehn-Saric, McLeod, Funderburk, & Kowalski, 2004). Interestingly, most undergraduates believe that GAD symptoms are just a reaction to life stressors and not signs of an anxiety disorder (Coles & Coleman, 2010). In any given year, about 3.1 percent of the adult U.S. population has GAD (R. C. Kessler, Chiu, et al., 2005); women are twice as likely to receive this diagnosis as men (R. C. Kessler, Berglund, et al., 2005). In medical settings around the world, GAD is the most frequently diagnosed anxiety disorder (D. J. Stein, 2001).

Etiology of Generalized Anxiety Disorder

GAD is the result of biological factors combined with psychosocial stressors, as shown in Figure 4.8. Let's take a look at each of the factors that may contribute to the etiology of GAD.

Biological Dimension There appears to be less support for the role of genetic factors in GAD than in panic disorder. Still, heritability appears to play a small but significant role in the development of GAD (Ehringer, Rhee, Young, Corley, & Hewitt, 2006; Kendler & Prescott, 2006). Genes may be expressed in terms of abnormalities with the GABA receptors, other neurotransmitter abnormalities, or overactivity of the anxiety circuit in the brain.

As mentioned earlier, the prefrontal cortex can modulate the response of the amygdala to threatening situations. GAD may involve a disruption in this system. In an MRI investigation, Monk et al. (2006) exposed 18 adolescents with GAD and 15 without GAD to angry faces. Those with GAD showed greater activation of the prefrontal cortex in response to the faces, perhaps because the prefrontal cortex was attempting to regulate the anxiety aroused by the angry faces.

In a 2-year study of adolescents with GAD or social phobia, the following findings were made:

- GAD (but not social phobia) was associated with increased frequency of underage drinking.
- GAD symptoms preceded alcohol and cannabis use.
- Adolescents with social phobia used less alcohol and cannabis than those with GAD or no anxiety disorder.

Source: Frojd, Ranta, Kaltiala-Heino, & Marttunen (2011)

generalized anxiety disorder (GAD) condition characterized by persistent, high levels of anxiety and excessive worry over many life circumstances

● FIGURE 4.8

Multipath Model of Generalized Anxiety Disorder (GAD)

The dimensions interact with one another and combine in different ways to result in generalized anxiety disorder (GAD).

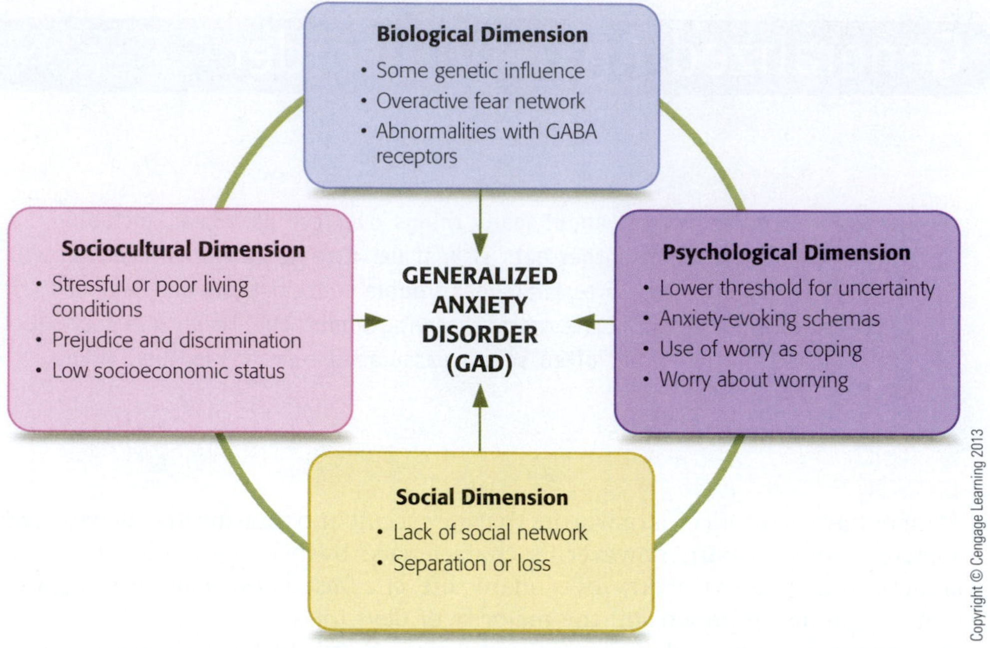

Psychological Dimension Cognitive theories emphasize the role of dysfunctional thinking and beliefs in those who display generalized anxiety. Individuals with GAD have a lower threshold for uncertainty, which leads to worrying. They also have erroneous beliefs regarding worry and assume that "worry is an effective way to deal with problems" or that it prevents some type of negative outcome from occurring (Ladouceur et al., 2000). A. T. Beck (1985) believes that anxiety disorders involving negative **schemas** (mental frameworks for organizing and interpreting information) can be a product of temperament and negative early learning. Schemas may involve beliefs such as "I am incompetent" or "The world is dangerous." The individual interprets events through the filter of the schema so that ambiguous or even positive situations are viewed with concern and apprehension.

A. Wells (2005, 2009) developed another theoretical model of GAD. He believes that the roots of GAD lie in beliefs regarding the function of worrying. In his model, there are two types of worry. The first involves a belief that worry has a positive, coping function; thus, it occurs frequently. However, the stress of constantly generating solutions to "what if" scenarios eventually results in a belief that worry is uncontrollable, harmful, and dangerous. GAD develops when the second type of worry ("worrying about worry") occurs. This worrying about worry leads to increased anxiety and thus reinforces the view that worry has negative effects (D. M. Ellis & Hudson, 2010; McLaughlin, Mennin, & Farach, 2007).

Social and Sociocultural Dimensions Mothers with GAD are sometimes less responsive and engaged with their infants than mothers who are not anxious. These behaviors may result in the development of an anxiety disorder in the child (A. Stein et al., 2012). Stressful conditions such as poverty, poor housing, prejudice, and discrimination also contribute to GAD. The disorder is twice as prevalent among those with low income (R. C. Kessler, Chiu, et al., 2005). It is also seen more frequently in individuals who are separated, divorced, or widowed and in the unemployed (Wittchen & Hoyer, 2001).

schema mental framework for organizing and interpreting information

Treatment of Generalized Anxiety Disorder

Benzodiazepines have been successful in treating GAD, but because it is a chronic condition, drug dependence is a concern (Nutt, 2001). Tricyclic and SSRI antidepressants have been used in treating GAD and are the medications of choice because they do not have the potential for dependence associated with the benzodiazepines (Allgulander et al., 2007; Seidel & Walkup, 2006). A newer antianxiety medication, buspirone, is also used to treat GAD (NIMH, 2009a).

Cognitive-behavioral therapy (CBT) is the only consistently validated psychological treatment for GAD (Ballenger et al., 2000). In an evaluation of 13 controlled clinical trials, cognitive-behavioral strategies were not only effective in treating GAD but also were associated with low dropout rates and long-term improvement (Borkovec & Ruscio, 2001). It has also been found to be effective in treating GAD in older adults (Ayers, Sorrell, Thorp, & Wetherell, 2007; Gonçalves & Byrne, 2012).

This treatment generally involves teaching clients to (Dugas & Ladouceur, 2000; Eisen & Silverman, 1998; Stanley et al., 2003):

- identify worrisome thoughts;
- discriminate between worries that are helpful to problem solving and those that are not;
- evaluate beliefs concerning worry, including evidence for and against any distorted beliefs;
- develop self-control skills to monitor and challenge irrational thoughts and substitute more positive, coping thoughts; and
- use muscle relaxation to deal with somatic symptoms.

We now discuss another set of disorders characterized by persistent troublesome thoughts: obsessive-compulsive and related disorders.

CHECKPOINT REVIEW

1. Describe four characteristics of GAD.
2. Summarize possible factors that cause GAD.
3. What are the different treatment options for GAD?

Obsessive-Compulsive and Related Disorders

Case Study

Mrs. A. is a 32-year-old married mother of two who has been spending increasing amounts of time (approximately 4 hours per day) cleaning and making sure everything in her house is in its perfect place. If Mrs. A. sees or hears words pertaining to death she immediately begins to repeat the Lord's Prayer in her mind 100 times. She believes that failure to perform this ritual will lead to the untimely death of her children (W. M. Greenberg, 2010).

Obsessive-compulsive and related disorders include obsessive-compulsive disorder (illustrated in the preceding case study), body dysmorphic disorder, hair-pulling disorder (trichotillomania), and skin-picking disorder (Table 4.4). These disorders are grouped together because they have similar symptoms, such as repetitive disturbing thoughts and irresistible urges, and are believed to share

DISORDERS CHART OBSESSIVE-COMPULSIVE SPECTRUM DISORDERS

TABLE 4.4

Disorder	Symptoms	Gender and Cultural Factors	Age of Onset
Obsessive-Compulsive Disorder	• Repeated disturbing and intrusive thoughts or impulses • Inability to control or suppress the thoughts or behaviors • Brief relief after performing the behaviors	Equally common in males and females; less prevalent among African Americans, Asian Americans, and Latino/Hispanic Americans	Usually adolescence or early adulthood
Body Dysmorphic Disorder	• Distressing and impairing preoccupation with imagined or slight defects in appearance	Equally common in males and females; prevalence from 5 to 15 percent depending on setting	Early adolescence to 20s; may be sudden or gradual
Hair-Pulling Disorder (Trichotillomania)	• Repeated pulling out of hair, resulting in hair loss	4 times more common in females; prevalence up to 4 percent	Usually before age 17
Skin-Picking Disorder	• Repeated picking at the skin, resulting in lesions	Females are 75 percent of affected population	Childhood through adulthood

Source: Based on Leckman et al. (2010); K. A. Phillips, Stein, et al. (2010); "K. A. Phillips, Wilhelm, et al. (2010)", PubMed Health (2012); Tucker, Woods, Flessner, Franklin, & Franklin (2011)

Did You Know? In the 17th century, obsessions and compulsions were often described as symptoms of religious melancholy (depression). The unusual nature of the intrusive thoughts and compulsions associated with obsessive-compulsive disorder resulted in the disorder being considered a form of insanity until the 1850s (Berrios, 1989).

similar neurobiological causes. They have much in common with anxiety disorders (Mathews & Grados, 2011; K. A. Phillips, Stein, et al., 2010; K. A. Phillips, Wilhelm, et al., 2010).

Obsessive-Compulsive Disorder

Obsessive-compulsive disorder (OCD) involves **obsessions**, which are anxiety-producing, repetitive thoughts or images; **compulsions**, felt needs to perform acts or dwell on thoughts to reduce anxiety; or both. Although obsessions and compulsions sometimes occur separately, they frequently occur together; in fact, only 25 percent of those with OCD report distressing obsessions without compulsive behaviors (Foa & Kozak, 1995; Markarian et al., 2010).

Common themes associated with obsessions include:

- contamination, including concern about dirt, germs, body wastes, or secretions and fear of being polluted by contact with items, places, or people considered to be unclean or harmful (Cisler, Adams, et al., 2011);
- errors or uncertainty, including obsessing over decisions and anxiety regarding locks, appliances, or paperwork;
- unwanted impulses, like thoughts of sexual acts or harming the self or others; and
- orderliness, including striving for perfect order or symmetry (Yadin & Foa, 2009).

Like obsessions, compulsions can occur primarily in the mind and involve mental acts such as praying, counting, or repeating words silently. However, many people with compulsions engage in repetitive behaviors such as hand washing, checking, or ordering objects (Leckman, Denys, et al., 2010). Compulsions are often, but not always, associated with obsessions and, thus, performed to neutralize or counteract a specific obsession. For example, individuals with an obsession about contamination may feel compelled to frequently wash their hands. Distress or anxiety occurs if the behavior is not performed or if it is not done "correctly." Mild examples of compulsive behavior include acts such as refusing to walk under a ladder or step on cracks in a sidewalk, throwing salt over one's shoulder, and

obsessive-compulsive disorder (OCD) condition characterized by intrusive, repetitive anxiety-producing thoughts or a strong need to perform acts or dwell on thoughts to reduce anxiety

obsession intrusive, repetitive thought or image that produces anxiety

compulsion the need to perform acts or dwell on thoughts to reduce anxiety

TABLE 4.5 Clinical Examples of Obsessions and Compulsions

CLIENT AGE	GENDER	DURATION OF OBSESSION IN YEARS	CONTENT OF OBSESSION OR COMPULSION
21	M	6	Teeth are decaying, particles between teeth
55	F	35	Fetuses lying in the street, people buried alive
29	M	14	Shoes dirtied by dog excrement
32	F	7	Contracting AIDS
42	F	17	Hand washing triggered by touching surfaces touched by other people
21	M	2	Intense fear of contamination after touching money
9	M	4	Going back and forth through doorways 500 times

Source: Based on W. M. Greenberg (2010); Jenike (2001); Kraus & Nicholson (1996); Rachman, Marks, & Hodgson (1973); Zerdzinski (2008)

knocking on wood. Table 4.5 contains additional examples of obsessions and compulsions.

Do "normal" people have intrusive, unacceptable thoughts and impulses? Several studies (Edwards & Dickerson, 1987; Freeston & Ladouceur, 1993; Ladouceur et al., 2000) have found that more than 80 percent of respondents without OCD reported the existence of some unpleasant intrusive thoughts and impulses. The content of obsessions reported by individuals with OCD overlap considerably with thoughts reported by the general population. However, individuals with OCD report that their obsessions last longer, are more intense, produce more discomfort, and are more difficult to dismiss (Morillo, Belloch, & Garcia-Soriano, 2007). Intrusive thoughts may increase during times of stress. For example, some women with postpartum mood changes report intrusive thoughts that the baby might stop breathing or that they might scream at, slap, or drop the baby (Abramowitz, Metzer-Brody, et al., 2010).

Compulsions are also common in nonclinical populations (Muris, Merckelbach, & Clavan, 1997). A continuum appears to exist between "normal" rituals and "pathological" compulsions. In individuals with obsessive-compulsive disorder, the compulsions are more frequent and of greater intensity, and they produce more discomfort. In the severe compulsive state, the behaviors become stereotyped and rigid; if compulsive acts are not performed in a certain manner or a specific number of times, the individual is flooded with anxiety.

Individuals with OCD often describe the associated thoughts and actions as being out of character for them and not under their voluntary control. The inability to resist or rid oneself of uncontrollable, unacceptable thoughts or refrain from performing ritualistic acts over and over again arouses intense anxiety. The majority of individuals with OCD recognize that their thoughts and impulses are senseless, yet they feel unable to control them. Failure to engage in specific rituals often results in mounting anxiety and tension. As one individual noted, "The reason I do these kinds of rituals and obsessing is that I have a fear that someone is going to die. This is not rational thinking to me. I know I can't prevent somebody from dying by putting 5 ice cubes in a glass instead of 4" (Jenike, 2001, p. 2122).

In a given year, about 1 percent of the U.S. adult population has OCD significant enough to constitute a disorder. Over half of those affected report the severity

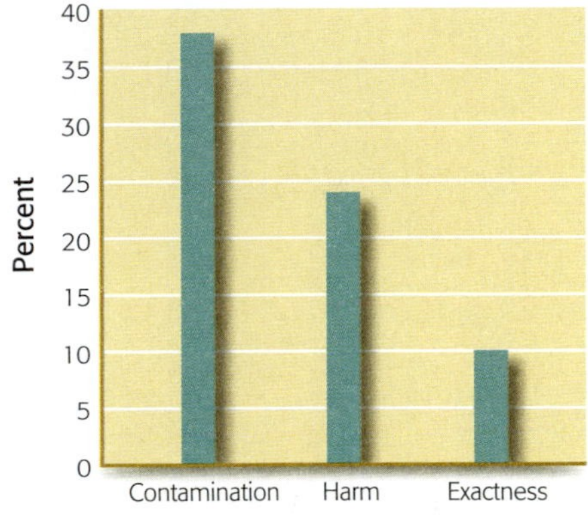

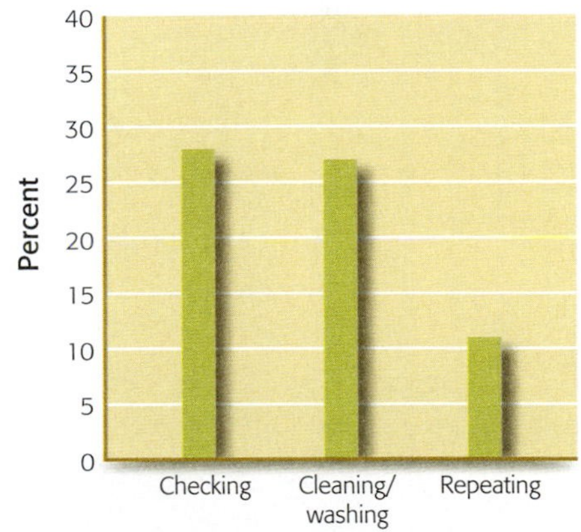

FIGURE 4.9

Common Obsessions and Compulsions
About half of the clients reported both obsessions and compulsions. Twenty-five percent believed that their symptoms were reasonable.

Source: Based on Foa & Kozak (1995)

Did You Know?

- Intrusive thoughts are common among college students.
- 50 percent of men and 42 percent of women have thoughts of hurting a family member.
- 24 percent of men and 14 percent of women have thoughts of indecently exposing themselves.
- 19 percent of men and 7 percent of women have thoughts of sex with a child or minor.

Source: Purdon & Clark (2005)

of the disorder as "serious" (R. C. Kessler, Chiu, et al., 2005). See Figure 4.9 for some examples of disabling obsessions and compulsions. About one fourth of the general population claims to have some OCD symptoms, but without the severity required to meet the diagnostic criteria for OCD (Fullana et al., 2009).

Onset of OCD usually occurs in childhood or adolescence (Yadin & Foa, 2009). Children tend to have poor insight into the nature of their obsessions, which frequently involve themes of harm or separation (D. A. Geller, 2006). The disorder is about equally common in males and females but is less common in African Americans and Hispanic Americans (A. Y. Zhang & Snowden, 1999). Many people with this disorder are depressed and may abuse substances, possibly because of the emotional distress associated with the symptoms of OCD (Canavera, Ollendick, May, & Pincus, 2010).

OCD may be underdiagnosed. If it is suspected, screening questions such as these are asked (Work Group on Obsessive-Compulsive Disorder, 2007, p. 12):

- "Do you have unpleasant thoughts you can't get rid of?"
- "Do you worry that you might impulsively harm someone?"
- "Do you count things, or check things over and over?"
- "Do you worry a lot about whether you performed religious rituals correctly or have been immoral?"
- "Do you need to have things arranged symmetrically or in a very exact order?"

Body Dysmorphic Disorder

Case Study

A twenty-four-year-old Caucasian male in his senior year of college reported, "I've got a physical deformity (small hands) and it makes me very uncomfortable, especially around women with hands bigger than mine. I see my deformity as a sign of weakness; it's like I'm a cripple." He also reported being concerned that women might believe small hands are indicative of having a small penis. (Schmidt & Harrington, 1995, pp. 162–163)

Body dysmorphic disorder (BDD) involves a preoccupation with a perceived physical defect in a normal-appearing person or excessive concern over a slight physical defect, accompanied by repetitive behaviors such as checking one's appearance in mirrors, applying makeup to mask "flaws," and comparing one's appearance to those of others (K. A. Phillips, Wilhelm, et al., 2010). The term comes from the Greek word *dysmorphia*, which means "abnormal shape." The preoccupation produces marked clinical distress and is underdiagnosed because individuals are unwilling to bring attention to their "problem" (J. E. Grant, Kim, & Crow, 2001). Individuals with BDD often engage in compulsive behaviors such as checking mirrors frequently, grooming excessively, or seeking constant reassurance regarding their appearance (K. A. Phillips, Stein, et al., 2010). They regard their "defect" with embarrassment and loathing and are concerned that others may be looking at or thinking about the defect. Some make frequent requests for cosmetic surgery (Fontenelle et al., 2006). Some individuals with BDD recognize that their beliefs are untrue, whereas most maintain strong **delusions** (false beliefs) about their bodies (S. P. Mancuso, Knoesen, & Castle, 2010; H. E. Reese,

body dysmorphic disorder (BDD) condition involving a preoccupation with a perceived physical defect or excessive concern over a slight physical defect; often accompanied by frequently checking appearance, applying makeup to mask "flaws," and comparing appearance to those of others

delusion a firmly held false belief

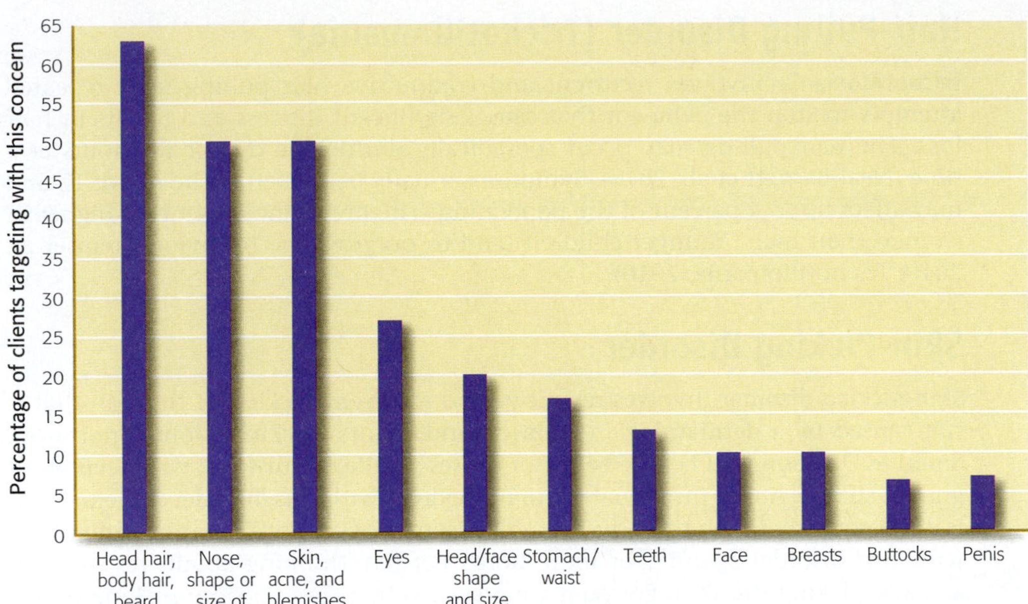

FIGURE 4.10

Imagined Defects in Patients With Body Dysmorphic Disorder

This graph illustrates the percentage of 30 patients who targeted different areas of their body as having "defects." Many of the patients selected more than one body region.

Source: K. A. Phillips, McElroy, Keck, et al. (1993)

McNally, & Wilhelm, 2011). Concern commonly focuses on bodily features such as excessive hair or lack of hair or the size or shape of the nose, face, or eyes (Figure 4.10).

Some questions that may indicate the presence of BDD follow; the more a person answers in the affirmative, the more likely he or she is to have characteristics of this disorder:

- Do you believe that there is a defect in a part of your body or appearance?
- Do you spend considerable time checking this defect?
- Do you attempt to hide or cover up this defect, or remedy it by exercising, dieting, or seeking surgery?
- Does this belief cause you significant distress, embarrassment, or torment?
- Does the defect interfere with your ability to function at school, at social events, or at work?
- Do friends or family members tell you that there is nothing wrong or that the defect is minor?

Did You Know?

In a survey of college students:

- 74 percent were "very concerned" about the appearance of parts of their body,
- 29 percent were preoccupied with a "defective" part,
- 6 percent reported spending from 1 to over 3 hours a day worrying about their perceived defect, and
- 4 percent appeared to meet the criteria for BDD.

Source: A. Bohne, Keuthen, Wilhelm, Deckersbach, & Jenike (2002)

Among individuals with BDD in Brazil, many had other psychiatric disorders, and three quarters had obsessive-compulsive disorder. More than one third had active suicidal ideation, and 30 percent had no insight into their difficulties (Fontenelle et al., 2006). BDD tends to be chronic and difficult to treat. In a 1-year follow-up of 183 individuals with BDD (84 percent had received mental health treatment), only 9 percent had full remission and 21 percent had partial remission of symptoms (K. A. Phillips, Pagano, et al., 2006). However, another study showed a more favorable outcome, with 76 percent recovering over an 8-year period (Bjornsson et al., 2011).

Muscle dysphoria, the belief that one's body is too small or insufficiently muscular, is a form of BDD. Some bodybuilders who show a pathological preoccupation with their muscularity may also suffer from BDD. Researchers identified a subgroup of bodybuilders who scored high in body dissatisfaction, had low self-esteem, and mistakenly believed they were "small" even though they were large and very muscular (Choi, Pope, Olivardia, & Cash, 2002; Olivardia, Pope, & Hudson, 2000).

muscle dysphoria belief that one's body is too small or insufficiently muscular

Hair-Pulling Disorder (Trichotillomania)

Trichotillomania involves recurrent and compulsive hair pulling with repeated attempts to stop the behavior that causes significant distress and results in hair loss. The hair pulling may occur sporadically during the day or for hours at a time (Neal-Barnett et al., 2010). Symptoms usually begin before the age of 17 and may affect up to 4 percent of the population. The prevalence is 4 times higher in women than men. Younger children tend to outgrow the behavior (Stein et al, 2010; Trichotillomania, 2010).

Skin-Picking Disorder

Skin-picking disorder involves repetitive and recurrent picking of the skin that is not caused by a dermatologic condition and results in skin lesions (Snorrason, Smari & Olafsson, 2011). The behavior causes significant distress, with feelings of guilt or shame. About three quarters of individuals with this disorder are females. It is often comorbid with body dysmorphic disorder or trichotillomania. Individuals with this disorder spend 1 or more hours per day thinking about, resisting, or actually picking the skin. Episodes are preceded by rising tension; picking results in feelings of relief or pleasure (Tucker et al 2011). As with trichotillomania, individuals with this disorder report psychosocial impairment and a lower quality of life than individuals without (Odlaug, Kim, & Grant, 2010). CBT and SSRIs have been helpful in treating the condition (Fama, 2010; Martinson, Nangle, Boulard & Sigmon, 2011). Skin picking is also reported in other countries, such as Turkey (Calikusu, Kucukgoncu, Tercer & Bestepe, 2012) and Germany (Bohne, Wilhelm, Keuthen, Baer, & Jenike, 2002).

trichotillomania recurrent and compulsive hair pulling that results in hair loss and causes significant distress

skin-picking disorder distressing and recurrent compulsive picking of the skin resulting in skin lesions

Etiology of Obsessive-Compulsive and Related Disorders

The causes of obsessive-compulsive and related disorders remain speculative. OCD itself may involve distinct disorders with different triggers and etiologies (S. J. Thorpe, Barnett, Friend, & Nottingham, 2011). In this section we examine the biological, psychological, social, and sociocultural dimensions of obsessive-compulsive and related disorders (see Figure 4.11).

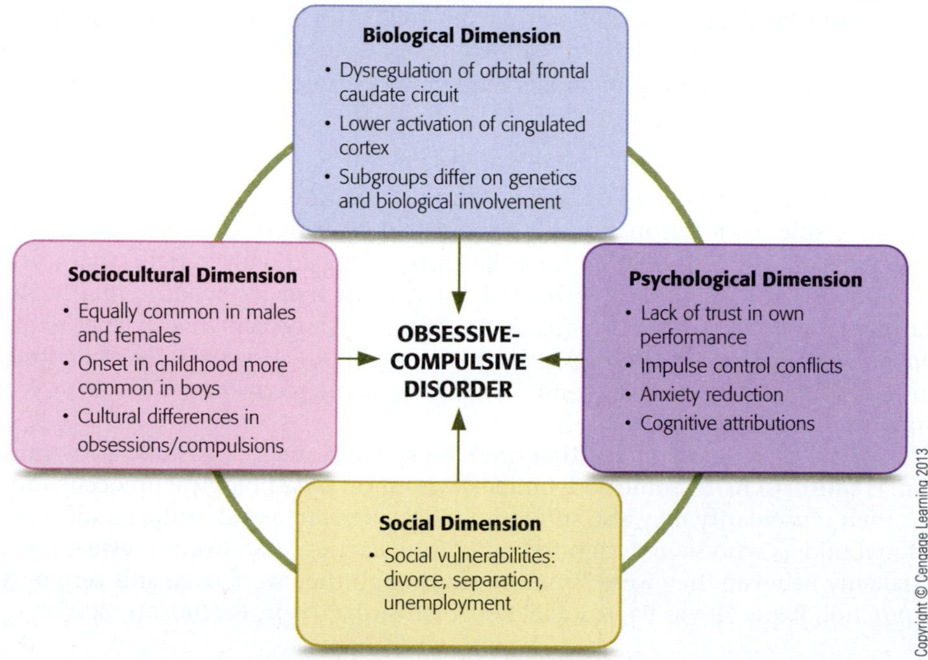

FIGURE 4.11

Multipath Model of Obsessive-Compulsive Disorder

The dimensions interact with one another and combine in different ways to result in obsessive-compulsive disorder.

CONTROVERSY:

Is Hoarding Related to Obsessive-Compulsive Disorder?

In the past, hoarding was believed to be a form of obsessive-compulsive disorder (OCD); some continue to argue that it is closely related to OCD (Phillips, Stein et al., 2010). However, others believe that its characteristics differ from those in the OCD spectrum (Tolin & Villavicencio, 2011). For example, in contrast to the hypermetabolism found in brain regions (e.g., the orbitofrontal cortex) of individuals with OCD, individuals who hoard show a pattern of significantly lower activation of the cingulate cortex (Saxena, 2007).

Compulsive hoarding involves the inability to discard items regardless of their value. Accumulating possessions fill up and clutter the home or workplace, preventing use of the area and increasing the risk of fire, disease, or injury. Social pressure to cease hoarding is distressing to the individual because of an irrational emotional attachment to the items (Rachman, Elliott, Shafran, & Radomsky, 2009). One client collected discarded objects such as soda cans, paper bags, and newspapers, saying she "may need them sometime." Although movement around her house was impeded, she could not decide what to throw away (Samuels, Shugart, et al., 2007).

The prevalence of hoarding disorder ranges from 2 percent to 5 percent of adults (Lervolino et al., 2009; Mueller, Mitchell, Crosby, Glaesmer, & de Zwaan, 2009); up to 25 percent of individuals with anxiety disorders report significant hoarding symptoms (Tolin, Meunier, Frost, & Steketee, 2011). Genetic factors appear to be significantly involved in compulsive hoarding (Lervolino et al., 2009). Cognitive-behavioral therapy can be effective with hoarding disorder, but about half of the individuals do not complete treatment due to their extreme distress at the idea of parting with their possessions (Steketee, Frost, Tolin, Rasmussen, & Brown, 2010). Should hoarding be considered a mental disorder or a bad habit?

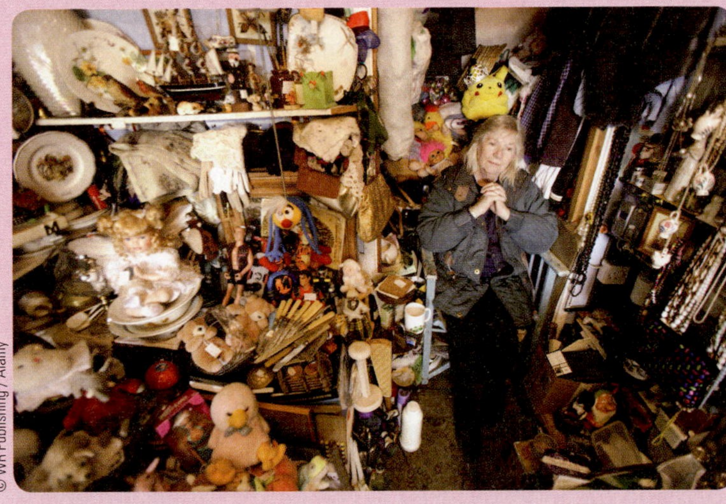

Hoarding

Individuals who hoard believe that the items collected are valuable and resist having them removed, even when the possessions are worthless or unsanitary or create a fire danger.

Biological Dimensions Biological explanations for obsessive-compulsive behaviors are based on data relating to brain structure, genetic studies, and biochemical abnormalities. First-degree relatives of individuals with OCD show impairment in decision making, planning, and mental flexibility, so these cognitive characteristics may be an **endophenotype** for OCD (Cavedini, Zorzi, Piccinni, Cavallini, & Bellodi, 2010).

Neuroimaging has revealed that some people with obsessive-compulsive disorder show increased metabolic activity in the frontal lobe of the left hemisphere of the brain, suggesting that this area—the **orbitofrontal cortex**—is associated with obsessive-compulsive behaviors (Blier, Szabo, Haddjeri, & Dong, 2000; Freyer et al., 2011; see Figure 4.12). Symptoms of obsessive-compulsive disorder similarly suggest dysregulation involving the orbitofrontal-caudate circuit. The orbitofrontal cortex alerts the rest of the brain when something is wrong. When it is

endophenotype measurable characteristics (neurochemical, endocrinological, neuroanatomical, cognitive, or neuropsychological) that can give clues regarding the specific genes involved in a disorder

orbitofrontal cortex brain region associated with planning and decision making

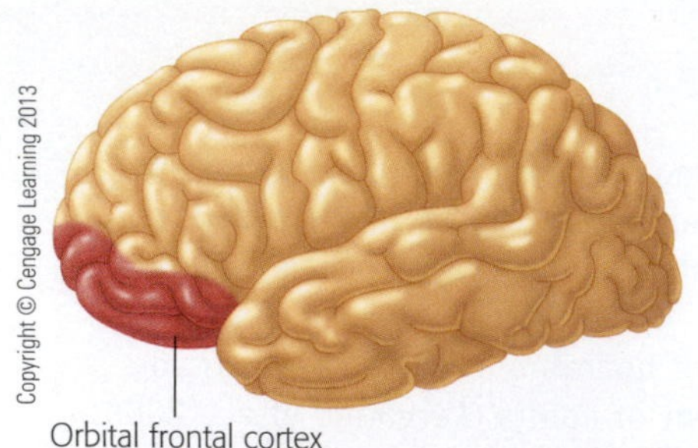

FIGURE 4.12

OrbitoFrontal Cortex
Individuals with untreated obsessive-compulsive disorder show a high metabolism rate in this area of the brain. Certain medications reduce metabolic rates to "normal" levels and also reduce obsessive-compulsive symptoms.

hyperactive, it not only triggers the feeling that something is not right but actually produces the feeling that something is "deadly wrong." Additionally, the brain region that regulates transmission of impulses (the **caudate nuclei**) is weakened in those with OCD, and disturbing thoughts leak through (Markarian et al., 2010; Saxena, Brody, Schwartz, & Baxter, 1998).

Medications that increase the amount of available serotonin in the brain have also been effective in treating many individuals with OCD. When individuals with OCD are given fluoxetine (a medication that increases the availability of serotonin), brain activity in the frontal lobes becomes more similar to that found in individuals without the disorder, and symptoms are reduced (Hoehn-Saric, Pearlson, Harris, Machlin, & Camargo, 1991). Additionally, drugs that are effective with other anxiety disorders but that do not raise serotonin availability show limited success in the treatment of OCD (Zohar, Hollander, Stein, Westenberg, & the Cape Town Consensus Group, 2007). As a result, researchers have hypothesized that the disorder is the result of a serotonin deficiency (B. D. Greenberg, Altemus, & Murphy, 1997; Tollefson et al., 1994). However, similar neurological changes have been reported in individuals treated with cognitive-behavioral therapy (Freyer et al., 2011; Rauch, Shin, & Wright, 2003).

Psychological Dimension

Proponents of the behavioral perspective maintain that obsessive-compulsive behaviors develop because they reduce anxiety. For example, many college students develop mild forms of compulsive behavior during finals week. During this anxiety-filled time, students may find themselves engaging in escape activities such as daydreaming, straightening up their rooms, or eating five or more times a day, all of which serve to shield them from thoughts of the upcoming tests. If the stress (and avoidance behaviors) last a long time, behaviorists believe that OCD could develop.

Psychologists have also studied the cognitive factors that lead to the severe doubts associated with obsessive-compulsive behavior. Individuals with OCD show certain cognitive characteristics in the following areas (D. A. Clark & Beck, 2009):

- Threat estimation (exaggerated estimates regarding the probability of harm)—"If the door isn't locked, I'll be killed by an intruder."
- Control—"If I am not able to control my thoughts, I will be overwhelmed with anxiety."
- Intolerance of uncertainty—"I have to be absolutely certain that I turned off the computer."

These patterns of thoughts can lead to compulsive rituals to reduce anxiety. Individuals with OCD believe that if they don't act in a certain way, negative consequences occur (Ghisi, Chiri, Marchetti, Sanavio, & Sica, 2010).

Individuals with OCD do not trust their own memories and judgment and make futile attempts to determine whether they actually performed the behavior or performed it "correctly." Someone with a compulsive need to check things "may turn the key in the lock over and over again without being able to convince himself or herself that the door has in fact been locked, even though he or she can plainly see that the key is in the proper position, hear it engaging, and feel the lock snapping" (Dar, Rish, Hermesh, Taub, & Fux, 2000, p. 673). Individuals with OCD sometimes have a disconfirmatory bias—that is, they generate a search for evidence that undermines their confidence.

Social and Sociocultural Dimensions

Family variables such as a controlling, overly critical style of parenting, minimal parental warmth, and discouragement of autonomy are related to the development of OCD symptoms (Challacombe & Salkovskis, 2009). Individuals raised in adverse environments may develop

caudate nuclei brain region that regulates transmission of impulses warning that something is not right

maladaptive beliefs relating to personal responsibility; they may believe it is their responsibility to prevent harm to themselves or others and overestimate threats and feeling of responsibility (Briggs & Price, 2009). Individuals with OCD who perceive their relatives to be critical or hostile have more severe symptoms (Van Noppen & Steketee, 2009).

OCD is more common among young people and among individuals who are divorced, separated, or unemployed (Karno & Golding, 1991). African Americans and Latino/Hispanic Americans are less likely to receive a diagnosis of OCD than are European Americans (A. Y. Zhang & Snowden, 1999); people from ethnic minorities with OCD have been underrepresented in clinical outcome studies (M. Williams, Powers, Yun, & Foa, 2010). Culture may affect how the symptoms of OCD are expressed and may not be picked up by current diagnostic systems. For example, African Americans show greater concern about contamination than do white Americans (M. T. Williams, Abramowitz, & Olatunji, 2012).

Treatment of Obsessive-Compulsive and Related Disorders

The primary modes of treatment for obsessive-compulsive and related disorders are either biological or behavioral in nature. Behavioral therapies have been used successfully for many years, but treatment with medication is becoming more common.

Biological Treatments SSRIs are the antidepressants recommended for the treatment of OCD, because they have fewer side effects than older antidepressants and are equally as effective (American Psychiatric Association, 2007). However, only about 60 percent of people with OCD respond to these medications, and often the relief is only partial (Brandl, Muller, & Richter, 2012). In addition, there is a rapid return of symptoms, and relapse occurs within months of stopping the medication (Jenike, 2001). Children with OCD appear to be less responsive to treatment with antidepressants than adults are (Ulloa, Nicolini, Avila, & Fernandez-Guasti, 2007). Nearly two thirds of a sample of individuals with body dysmorphic disorder improved with SSRIs (K. A. Phillips, McElroy, Dwight, Eisen, & Rasmussen, 2001; K. A. Phillips & Rasmussen, 2004), and hair-pulling disorder has also been successfully treated with SSRIs (Trichotillomania, 2010).

Behavioral Treatments The treatment of choice for obsessive-compulsive disorder is a combination of exposure and response prevention (Abramowitz & Larsen, 2007; Valderhaug, Larsson, & Gotestam, 2007). However, dropout rates are high (Mancebo, Eisen, Sibrava, Dyck, & Rasmussen, 2011). In treating OCD, exposure therapy involves continued actual or imagined exposure to a fear-arousing situation; it can involve **flooding**, which is the immediate presentation of the most frightening stimuli, or more gradual exposure. **Response prevention** involves not allowing the individual with OCD to perform the compulsive behavior. The steps in exposure therapy with response prevention generally include (M. E. Franklin, Abramowitz, Kozak, Levitt, & Foa, 2000):

1. education about OCD and the rationale for exposure and response prevention;
2. development of an exposure hierarchy (from somewhat fearful to most-feared situations);
3. exposure to feared situations until anxiety has diminished; and
4. prevention of the performance of compulsive rituals such as hand washing.

flooding a technique that involves inducing a high anxiety level through continued actual or imagined exposure to a fear-arousing situation

response prevention treatment in which an individual with OCD is prevented from performing a compulsive behavior

Cognitive-behavioral therapy has also produced promising results with body dysmorphic disorder (Wilhelm, Phillips, Fama, Greenberg, & Steketee, 2011) and compulsive hoarding (St-Pierre-Delorme, Lalonda, Perreault, Koszegi, & O'Connor, 2011), although attrition rates are high. Combining CBT with SSRIs may be a more effective means of treating hoarding (Saxena, 2011).

CHECKPOINT REVIEW

1. Describe the characteristics of OCD and related disorders.
2. What are some explanations regarding how OCD and related disorders develop?
3. Describe the biological and behavioral treatments for OCD and related disorders.

Summary

1 According to the multipath model, how are biological, psychological, social, and sociocultural factors involved in the development of anxiety disorders?

- The multipath model stresses the importance of considering the contribution of and *interaction* between biological, psychological, social, and sociocultural factors in the etiology of anxiety disorders.
- For example, genetically predisposed individuals (e.g., those with inherited overactivity of the fear circuitry in the brain and neurotransmitter abnormalities) who grow up in a supportive family or social environment may not develop an anxiety disorder. Similarly, although sociocultural factors (e.g., discrimination, poverty) can increase the risk of anxiety disorders, personality variables, such as a sense of control and mastery, can help mitigate the impact of stressors.

2 What are phobias, what are their causes, and how are they treated?

- Phobias are strong, irrational fears. Social anxiety disorder involves anxiety over situations in which others can observe the person. Agoraphobia is an intense fear of being in public places where escape or help may not be possible. Specific phobias include all the irrational fears that are not classed as social phobias or agoraphobia.
- Biological explanations are based on studies of the influence of genetic, biochemical, and neurological factors and on the idea that humans are predisposed to develop certain fears. Psychological explanations include classical conditioning, observational learning, and cognitions that are distorted and frightening.
- The most effective treatments for phobias seem to be biochemical (antidepressants) and cognitive-behavioral (exposure, systematic desensitization, modeling, and graduated exposure).

3 What is panic disorder, what causes it, and how is it treated?

- Panic disorder is marked by episodes of extreme anxiety and feelings of impending doom that seem to occur "out of the blue."
- The causes of panic disorder include biological factors (genetics, neural structures, and neurotransmitters), psychological factors (catastrophic thoughts regarding bodily sensations), and social and sociocultural factors (such as a disturbed childhood environment and gender-related issues).
- Treatments for panic disorder include biochemical treatments (benzodiazepines and antidepressants) and behavioral treatments (identifying catastrophic thoughts, correcting them, and substituting more realistic ones).

4 What is generalized anxiety disorder, what are its causes, and how is it treated?

- Generalized anxiety disorder (GAD) involves chronically high levels of anxiety and excessive worry that are present for 3 months or more.
- There appears to be less support for the role of genetics in GAD than in other anxiety disorders, although there are some reports of overactivity of the anxiety circuitry in the brain. Cognitive-behavioral theorists emphasize erroneous beliefs regarding the purpose of worry or the existence of dysfunctional schemas. Social and sociocultural factors such as poverty and discrimination can also contribute to GAD.
- Antidepressant medications and behavioral therapies have been used to treat this disorder.

5 What are obsessive-compulsive and related disorders, what causes these disorders, and how are they treated?

- Obsessive-compulsive (OCD) and related disorders involve thoughts or actions that are involuntary, intrusive, repetitive, and uncontrollable.
- Neuroimaging shows increased metabolic activity in the orbitofrontal cortex in individuals with OCD. According to the anxiety-reduction hypothesis, obsessions and compulsions develop because they reduce anxiety. Cognitive-behavioral therapists have focused on cognitive factors that lead to doubt such as overestimating the probability of harm or an intolerance of uncertainty. The treatment of choice is a combination of flooding and response prevention, sometimes combined with cognitive therapy.
- Body dysmorphic disorder involves excessive concern or preoccupation with a perceived defect in a part of the body.
- Hair-pulling disorder (trichotillomania) involves the compulsive pulling out of one's hair, resulting in noticeable hair loss.
- Skin-picking disorder involves the repetitive picking of one's skin, resulting in the development of lesions.

Key Terms

anxiety 86
fear 86
anxiety disorder 86
etiological model 87
amygdala 88
hippocampus 88
prefrontal cortex 88
neurotransmitter 89
serotonin 89
alleles 89
polymorphic variation 89
predisposition 89
behavioral inhibition 89
anxiety sensitivity 90
phobia 91
social anxiety disorder 92
comorbid 92
specific phobia 93
remit 93
agoraphobia 94
panic attack 94
exposure therapy 98
systematic desensitization 98
cognitive restructuring 99
modeling therapy 100
panic disorder 100
concordance rate 101
GABA 101
interoceptive conditioning 102
generalized anxiety disorder (GAD) 105
schema 106
obsessive-compulsive disorder (OCD) 108
obsession 108
compulsion 108
body dysmorphic disorder (BDD) 110
delusion 110
muscle dysphoria 111
trichotillomania 112
skin-picking disorder 112
endophenotype 113
orbitofrontal cortex 113
caudate nuclei 114
flooding 115
response prevention 115

Media Resources

Psychology CourseMate

Access an interactive e-Book and chapter-specific interactive learning tools, including:

- flashcards
- quizzes
- videos

and more in your Psychology CourseMate.

Go to **CengageBrain.com.**

5

Trauma and Stress-Related Disorders

CHAPTER OUTLINE

Caroline, a 26-year-old woman, was traumatized by the sexual abuse perpetrated by her grandfather when she was in her early teens. The grandfather was brought to trial on the abuse charges; he was convicted, but died of a heart attack after a few months in prison. This further traumatized Caroline. She continues to experience flashbacks of seeing her grandfather's eyes when she is physically close to her boyfriend (U. Kramer, 2009).

Broken heart syndrome, a reversible cardiac condition, results from toxic levels of epinephrine (i.e., adrenaline) associated with sudden stress. In one study, researchers found 19 adults who thought they had had a massive heart attack following an emotional event (e.g., car accident, news of a death, surprise birthday party, armed robbery, court appearance) but were actually experiencing broken heart syndrome precipitated by their emotional stress (Wittstein et al., 2005). For some unknown reason, this condition is 7.5 times more likely to occur in women. Only about 1 percent of cases are fatal (Deshmukh, 2012).

FOCUS QUESTIONS

1 What are acute and post-traumatic stress disorders, and how are they diagnosed?

2 What causes acute and post-traumatic stress disorders?

3 What are possible treatments for acute and post-traumatic stress disorders?

4 What role does stress play in physical health, and what are psychophysiological disorders?

5 What causes psychophysiological disorders?

6 What methods have been developed to treat psychophysiological disorders?

How does stress affect our mental and physical health? **Stressors** are external events or situations that place physical or psychological demands on a person. They range from chronic irritation and frustration to acute and traumatic events. **Stress** is the internal psychological or physiological response to a stressor. Exposure to worrisome but less traumatic events can also affect our health. According to the Stress in America Survey, 44 percent indicated that their stress levels had increased over the past 5 years. Symptoms such as irritability or anger (45 percent), fatigue (41 percent), feeling nervous or anxious (36 percent), headache (36 percent), feeling depressed (34 percent), and muscle tension (23 percent) were identified as by-products of stress (American Psychological Association, 2010b). Thus, stress can lead to the development of both psychological and physical conditions. But how does this occur? And why are many people who are exposed to stressors, even traumatic ones, able to adjust, whereas others develop intense, long-lasting psychological or physical symptoms? As we will see, this question is best answered by examining the influence of biological, psychological, social, and sociocultural factors (and their interactions) using the multipath model. Exposure to traumatic stressors, such as the death of a loved one, serious injury, or harm, can lead to the development of a stress disorder or physical problems associated with stress. These conditions will be the focus of this chapter.

Acute and Post-Traumatic Stress Disorders

Case Study

I was raped when I was twenty-five years old. For a long time, I spoke about the rape as though it was something that happened to someone else. I was very aware that it had happened to me, but there was just no feeling. Then I started having flashbacks. They kind of came over me like a splash of water. I would be terrified. Suddenly I was reliving the rape. Every instant was startling. I wasn't aware of anything around me. I was in a bubble, just kind of floating. And it was scary. (National Institute of Mental Health [NIMH], 2007a, p. 7)

stressor an external event or situation that places a physical or psychological demand on a person

stress the internal psychological or physiological response to a stressor

acute stress disorder (ASD) disorder characterized by flashbacks, hypervigilance, and avoidance symptoms that occur within 1 month after exposure to a traumatic stressor

post-traumatic stress disorder (PTSD) disorder characterized by flashbacks, hypervigilance, avoidance, and other symptoms that last for more than 1 month and that occur as a result of exposure to extreme trauma

Both **acute stress disorder (ASD)** and **post-traumatic stress disorder (PTSD)** involve heightened anxiety and reactivity to traumatic circumstances. Although these disorders begin with normal responses to extremely upsetting circumstances, those who experience stress disorders remain frightened or alarmed even when the danger has passed. Indirect or "secondhand" exposure to trauma can also lead to ASD or PTSD. In one study, 18 percent of parents who learned that their child was injured in a car accident developed PTSD (Allenou et al., 2010). However, not everyone who faces a psychological or physical trauma develops a stress disorder. The probability of developing either ASD or PTSD depends both on the magnitude and the type of stressor and on risk factors specific to the individual.

Diagnosis of Acute and Post-Traumatic Stress Disorders

Acute stress disorder and post-traumatic stress disorder both involve the following (DSM-5 Work Groups, 2012; NIMH, 2009b):

- Exposure to an actual traumatizing stressor (e.g., serious injury or danger), either directly or indirectly. Indirect exposure can involve witnessing or learning of a traumatic event involving family or loved ones or experiencing repeated, direct exposure to aversive details of a traumatic event.
- Intrusive symptoms including distressing recollections, nightmares, or flashbacks of the trauma accompanied by physical symptoms such as increased heart rate or sweating. One woman who had been forced to play Russian roulette described flashbacks and nightmares of the event: "Different scenes came back, replays of exactly what happened, only the time is drawn out. . . . It seems to take forever for the gun to reach my head" (Hudson, Manoach, Sabo, & Sternbach, 1991, p. 572).
- Avoidance of thoughts, feelings, or physical sensations associated with the trauma, as well as places, events, or objects that are reminders of the experience (Brewin, 2011). One Iraq War veteran avoided social events and cookouts: Even grilling hamburgers reminded him of the burning flesh he had been exposed to in Iraq (Keltner & Dowben, 2007).
- Alterations in cognitions and mood associated with the traumatic event, such as having problems remembering important aspects of the event; feeling emotionally numb, detached, or estranged from others; and being unable to experience positive emotions.
- Changes in reactivity such as difficulty concentrating or sleeping; heightened physiological reactivity; or psychological changes such as **hypervigilance** (i.e., constantly being alert for possible danger), feeling irritable or "on edge," or engaging in aggressive, reckless, or self-destructive behaviors. War veterans can become "unglued" at the sound of a door slamming, a nail gun being used, or a camera clicking. An Iraq War veteran who almost attacked some strangers at a sports event remarked, "When friends say 'I know where you're coming from,' . . . [h]ow could they? They didn't have to deal with insects, the heat, not knowing who the enemy is, not knowing where the bullet is coming from" (Lyke, 2004, p. A8).

Initial stress reactions that occur shortly after a traumatic event and continue for several days are considered normative responses to an overwhelming and threatening stimulus. A diagnosis of ASD is made when these types of symptoms persist for at least 3 days and up to one month after the traumatic event; PTSD is diagnosed when symptoms continue for more than one month (R. A. Bryant, Creamer, O'Donnel, Silove, & McFarlane, 2012). Most individuals who experience such traumas recover, showing a marked decrease or remission in symptoms with time (Delahanty, 2007; Medina, 2008). However, PTSD can be a long-lasting disorder with significant effects on occupational and social functioning (Ravindran & Stein, 2010).

Exposure to trauma is not uncommon. In fact, as many as 85 percent of undergraduate students have experienced a traumatic event sometime in their lifetime (Table 5.1), with exposure to family violence and unwanted sexual attention or assault producing the highest levels of distress. Ethnic minority students report the highest rates of exposure to traumatic events (Frazier et al., 2009). What traumatic situations can cause a stress disorder? Events associated with PTSD include:

- combat (Seal, Bertenthal, Miner, Sen, & Marmar, 2007);
- sexual assaults (Kilpatrick, Amstadter, Resnick, & Ruggiero, 2007);
- violent crime or domestic violence (Zinzow et al., 2010);
- sexual harassment (O'Donohue, Mosco, Bowers, & Avina, 2006);

hypervigilance state of ongoing anxiety in which the person is constantly tense and alert for threats

TABLE 5.1 Undergraduates' Lifetime Exposure to Traumatic Events

	Women	Men
Unexpected death of close friend or loved one	49%	41%
Another's life-threatening event	31%	25%
Witnessing of family violence	25%	20%
Unwanted sexual attention	27%	5%
Severe injury (self or someone else)	18%	22%
Motor vehicle accident	17%	15%
Threat to one's life	11%	19%
Stalking	15%	4%
Childhood physical abuse	7%	7%
Partner violence	7%	3%
Unwanted sexual contact	8%	3%

Source: Frazier et al. (2009)

- natural disasters, such as hurricanes and earthquakes (La Greca, Silverman, Lai, & Jaccard, 2010; Lommen, Sanders, Buck, & Arntz, 2009); and
- car accidents, work-related accidents, or other situations that produce a fear of severe injury or death (Buodo et al., 2011; NIMH, 2007a).

Of those who were in the World Trade Center complex during the September 11, 2001, attacks; experienced injury in the attacks; witnessed people falling or jumping from the towers; were caught in the dust clouds from the collapsing towers; or had friends or relatives killed in the attacks, up to 15 percent developed PTSD (DiGrande, Neria, Brackbill, Pulliam, & Galea, 2011; R. D. Marshall et al., 2007).

Current diagnostic guidelines for ASD and PTSD require that the stressor be "traumatic." Therefore, individuals who experience repeated mild or low-magnitude stressors (e.g., employment problems, marital distress, parental separation, or relationship conflicts) would not receive a stress disorder diagnosis (Copeland, Keeler, Angold, & Costello, 2010; Elwood, Mott, Lohr, & Galovski, 2011). However, some mental health professionals believe that individuals with significant stress symptoms due to milder chronic stressors should be recognized as having a stress disorder even in the absence of a specific trauma (A. Cameron, Palm, & Follette, 2010).

Impact of Natural Catastrophes

Acute stress disorder is often observed among people who experience natural disasters. Here Leona Watts sits in a chair in the wreckage of her home of 61 years. She had returned to look for some of her belongings.

AP Photo/Marcio Jose Sanchez

The lifetime prevalence of PTSD is highest among African Americans (8.7 percent), intermediate among Latino/Hispanic Americans (7 percent) and white Americans (7.4 percent) and lowest among Asian Americans (4 percent). Asian Americans have lower exposure to trauma and are less likely to develop PTSD after exposure (A. L. Roberts, Gilman, Breslau, Breslau, & Koenen, 2010). Women are twice as likely as men to be diagnosed with PTSD (Kessler, Berglund, Demler, Jin, Merikangas, et al., 2005; NIMH, 2007). Of the few studies available on ASD, lifetime prevalence rates ranging from 14 to 33 percent of those exposed to traumatic stress have been reported (American Psychiatric Association, 2000). However, the prevalence of ASD may be underestimated, as many of those with the symptoms may not seek treatment within the 30-day period that defines the disorder.

CHECKPOINT REVIEW

1. What are the major symptoms seen with ASD and PTSD?
2. Compare and contrast PTSD with ASD.
3. What are the findings regarding the prevalence of PTSD in ethnic groups and women?
4. Make an argument for and against a diagnosis of PTSD in individuals who show symptoms of the disorder but have not been exposed to a trauma.

Etiology of Acute and Post-Traumatic Stress Disorders

Not everyone exposed to trauma develops a stress disorder. What factors increase risk? Table 5.2 shows PTSD prevalence associated with specific stressors. Both severe trauma and grave physical injuries are associated with an increased likelihood of PTSD (Kolassa et al., 2010). Approximately one third of individuals hospitalized with major burn injuries demonstrated PTSD symptoms either initially or within the first 2 years after their trauma (McKibben, Bresnick, Wiechman Askay, & Fauerbach, 2008). About 37 percent of the survivors of the World Trade Center attacks met the diagnostic criteria for ASD (Delahanty, 2007). Approximately one third of those who are raped or sexually assaulted develop PTSD (Kilpatrick, Amstadter, Resnick, & Ruggiero, 2007). The impact of a traumatic event is moderated by other factors, including cognitive style, childhood history, genetic vulnerability, and availability of social support (La Greca & Silverman, 2006). In this section we use the multipath model to consider biological, psychological, social, and sociocultural contributors to stress disorders (see Figure 5.1).

Biological Dimension

ASD and PTSD are not biologically normative stress responses. Individuals who develop PTSD have a nervous system that is highly reactive to fear and stress when compared to people who are exposed to trauma but do not develop stress

TABLE 5.2 Lifetime Prevalence of Exposure to Stressors by Gender and PTSD Risk

TRAUMA	LIFETIME PREVALENCE (%)		PTSD RISK	
	Male	**Female**	**Male**	**Female**
Life-threatening accident	25.0	13.8	6.3	8.8
Natural disaster	18.9	15.2	3.7	5.4
Threat with weapon	19.0	6.8	1.9	32.6
Physical attack	11.1	6.9	1.8	21.3
Rape	0.7	9.2	65.0	45.9

Some traumas are more likely to result in PTSD than others. Significant gender differences were found in reactions to "being threatened with a weapon" and "physical attack." What accounts for the differences in risk for developing PTSD among the specific traumas and for the two genders?

Source: Ballenger et al. (2000)

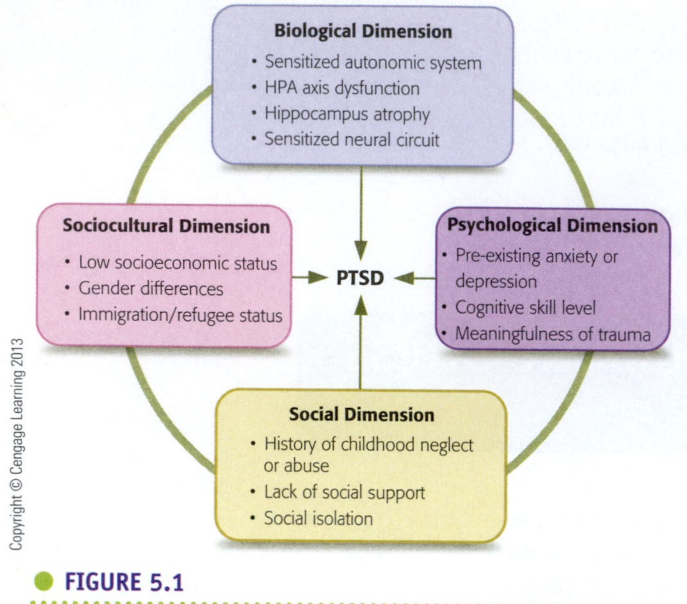

FIGURE 5.1

Multipath Model for Post-Traumatic Stress Disorder
The dimensions interact with one another and combine in different ways to result in post-traumatic stress disorder (PTSD).

disorders (Keltner & Dowben, 2007; Medina, 2008). In PTSD, not only does the individual demonstrate increased overall biological reactivity, but there are also exaggerated sensitivity to stimuli that are similar to the traumatic event and a diminished ability to inhibit fear responses (Ressler, 2010).

The normal response to a fear-producing stimulus is quite rapid, occurring in milliseconds, and involves the **amygdala**, the part of the brain that is the major interface between events occurring in the environment and physiological fear responses. In response to a potentially dangerous situation, the amygdala sends out a signal to the sympathetic nervous system, preparing the body for action (i.e., to fight or to flee). The **hypothalamic-pituitary-adrenal (HPA) axis** (the system involved in stress and trauma reactions and regulation of body processes such as "fight or flight" responses) then releases hormones, including **epinephrine** and **cortisol**. These hormones prepare the body for "fight or flight" by raising blood pressure, blood sugar level, and heart rate; the body is thus prepared to react to the potentially dangerous situation (Stahl & Wise, 2008). Cortisol also helps the body return to normal (i.e., restore **homeostasis**) after the stressor is removed. Individuals with PTSD, however, continue to demonstrate physiological stress reactions even when the stressor is no longer present (Dedovic, D'Aguiar, & Pruessner, 2009; Kendall-Tackett & Klest, 2009).

Why this occurs (i.e., why homeostasis is not restored) is unclear. It is possible that chronic release of cortisol alters the brain structures involved in the fear response. PTSD also appears to affect the medial prefrontal cortex, the part of the brain involved in the inhibition of fear and emotional reactivity (Piefke et al., 2007). Neuroimaging studies of individuals with stress disorders have shown heightened amygdala reactivity in response to fear stimuli along with reduced activity in the medial prefrontal cortex (i.e., less inhibition of fear). The overactive amygdala (which produces an exaggerated fear response) is thus able to overcome the weakened inhibitory influence of the medial prefrontal cortex; the result is the heightened reactivity to fear and stress seen in PTSD (Jovanovic et al., 2010). These changes in sensitivity may not be permanent, as over half of those with PTSD eventually recover (Kolassa, Ertl, Eckart, Kolassa, Onyut, & Elbert, 2010).

Individuals who have certain variations in the serotonin transporter gene (5-HTTLPR) appear to have an increased risk of PTSD symptoms after severe trauma (Mercer et al., 2012). This variation (having a short allele of the serotonin transporter gene) is associated with increased amygdala reactivity (R. A. Bryant, Felmingham, et al., 2010). However, this genetic variation appears to increase the risk of developing PTSD only among individuals exposed to a strong trauma who have little social support (Kilpatrick, Koenen, et al., 2008). In addition, epigenetic factors may be involved; for example, it has been suggested that an environmental event such as childhood trauma can produce changes in biological processes involving the serotonin transporter gene that subsequently increase vulnerability to PTSD (Yehuda, Cai, et al., 2009).

amygdala brain structure associated with the processing, expression and memory of emotions, especially anger and fear

hypothalamic-pituitary-adrenal (HPA) axis the system involved in stress and trauma reactions and regulation of body processes such as "fight or flight" responses

epinephrine hormone released by the adrenal gland in response to physical or mental stress; also known as adrenaline

cortisol hormone released by the adrenal gland in response to stress

homeostasis state of metabolic equilibrium

Psychological Dimension

What psychological factors contribute to the development of a stress disorder? Pre-existing conditions such as anxiety and depression were found to be risk factors for the development of PTSD among youth exposed to Hurricane Katrina (Weems, Pina, et al., 2007). Individuals with higher anxiety may react much more strongly to a traumatic event because they overestimate the probability that aversive events will follow (Engelhard, de Jong, van den Hout, & van Overveld, 2009).

Individuals with specific cognitive styles or dysfunctional thoughts about themselves (e.g., "I am incompetent") or the environment (e.g., "The world is a dangerous place") are more likely to develop PTSD (S. A. Bennett, Beck, & Clapp, 2009). They may interpret stressors in a catastrophic manner and thereby increase the psychological impact of trauma. For example, child and adolescent survivors of assault and motor vehicle accidents with thoughts such as "I will never be the same" were more likely to develop PTSD symptoms (Meiser-Stedman, Dalgleish, Gluckman, Yule, & Smith, 2009). Negative thoughts such as these may produce sustained and heightened physiological reactivity, making the development of ASD or PTSD more likely. On the other hand, positive cognitive styles such as attempting to solve or alter problems (Baschnagel, Gudmundsdottir, Hawk, & Beck, 2009), reframing traumatic events in a more positive light (Gupta & Bonanno, 2010), believing that good things are more likely to happen than bad things (Prati & Pietrantoni, 2009), and believing in one's ability to control both actions and thoughts (Schaubroeck, Riolli, Peng & Spain, 2011; K. H. Walter, Gunstad, & Hobfoll, 2010) increase resilience and reduce risk of PTSD.

Although PTSD was not officially recognized as a diagnosis until 1980, its symptoms have been recorded throughout history and known by different names:

- *soldier's heart* during the Civil War (most prevalent among soldiers ages 9–17),
- *shell shock* during World War I,
- *battle fatigue* during World War II, and
- *post-Vietnam syndrome* after the Vietnam War.

Source: Pizarro, Silver, & Prause (2006)

Social Dimension

Less than optimal social support during childhood and adulthood has also been identified as a possible contributor to the development of stress disorders. Pre-existing family conflict or overprotectiveness may increase the impact of stress following exposure to a traumatic event (Bokszczanin, 2008). Conflicts or maltreatment in an individual's family of origin may increase anxiety, lead to negative cognitive styles, result in HPA axis dysfunction, or "trigger" a genetic predisposition toward greater physiological reactivity and thus increase the risk of developing PTSD (Kidd, Hamer, & Steptoe, 2011). Individuals who are socially isolated and lacking in support systems appear to be more vulnerable to PTSD. Social support may act to dampen the anxiety associated with a trauma or to prevent negative cognitions from occurring. In one study, those who reported low social support in the 6 months prior to exposure to the September 11, 2001, attacks were more than twice as likely as those with high levels of social support to report symptoms of PTSD (Galea et al., 2002).

Sociocultural Dimension

Ethnic differences in stress reactions were seen in a survey of 1,008 adult New York residents following the terrorist attacks of September 11, 2001: 3.2 percent of Asian Americans, 6.5 percent of white Americans, 9.3 percent of African Americans, and 13.4 percent of Latino/Hispanic Americans reported symptoms consistent with PTSD (Galea et al., 2002). Ethnic group differences may be due to pre-existing variables such as differential exposure to previous trauma, childhood environment, or cultural differences in responding to stress (Triffleman & Pole, 2010). For example, African Americans and Latino/Hispanic Americans report higher levels of childhood trauma and interpersonal violence, experiences that can increase risk for PTSD (A. L. Roberts, Austin, Corliss, Vandermorris, & Koenen, 2010; A. L. Roberts, Gilman, et al., 2010). Perceived discrimination based on race or sexual orientation is also associated with increased risk for PTSD (Flores, Tschann, Dimas, Pasch, & de Groat, 2010). Experiences or perceptions of discrimination can lead to higher anxiety levels and the development of negative thoughts about oneself and the world.

Women are also twice as likely as men to suffer from a stress disorder (Galea et al., 2002; NIMH, 2007). This may result from physiological differences or from gender-related increased risk of exposure to stressors that are likely to result in PTSD. In analyzing the data from the National Violence Against Women Survey, Cortina and Kubiak (2006) concluded that the greater prevalence of stress disorders in women was due, in part, to more frequent exposure to violent interpersonal situations.

Post-Traumatic Stress Disorder and Abuse

Women who have been battered or sexually assaulted experience high rates of acute stress or post-traumatic stress disorder. In this photo, women comfort each other during group therapy.

Interestingly, although female police officers face greater assaultive violence than civilian women, they are less likely to have symptoms of PTSD (Lilly, Pole, Best, Metzler, & Marmar, 2009), and female veterans deployed to Iraq and Afghanistan appear to be as resilient as men to combat-related stress (Maguen, Luxton, Skopp, &

Did You Know?

About 5 percent of the 650 military dogs in Afghanistan, exposed to explosions, gunfire, and other combat violence, develop PTSD with symptoms such as hypervigilance, fear, and avoidance.

Source: Dao, 2011

Madden, 2012; Vogt et al., 2011). What accounts for the difference in PTSD prevalence among civilian women and women who join the police force or the military? Women in these groups may differ biologically from civilian women, may engage in emotional suppression to cope with the challenges of their work, or may conform to male norms (Lilly et al., 2009). It is also possible that combat or police training may have increased their resilience.

CHECKPOINT REVIEW

1. Identify three psychological and three social risk factors for PTSD.
2. In what ways do biological factors contribute to stress disorders?
3. What has been found regarding ethnic and gender differences in stress disorders?

FOCUS ON RESILIENCE

Is There a Silver Lining to Adverse Life Events?

Stressful and traumatic life events are common. Although some people develop stress disorders or psychophysiological disorders, most individuals appear to be resilient to stressors—that is, they are able to rebound after exposure to adversity. In fact, many who encounter significant stressors not only show recovery but appear to develop a greater capacity for future resilience (Seery, 2011). We know that resilient individuals are more likely to have good social and family support systems and characteristics such as strong interpersonal skills, a sense of optimism, confidence in their abilities, and a sense of personal control over events (Ahmed, 2007; Alim et al., 2008). Such qualities appear to act as buffers, allowing individuals to show faster physiological and psychological recovery following stress or trauma.

However, are there other factors involved in resilience to stress? Dienstbier (1989) was one of the first to assert that some exposure to adversity can, in fact, produce mental and physiological "toughness" in people by increasing their sense of control and their skill in dealing with difficult situations, as well as decreasing physiological reactivity to stressors. Similarly, the concepts of stress inoculation (Meichenbaum, 2007) and "steeling" (Rutter, 2006) involve the assumption that some exposure to stress can actually strengthen an individual's resilience for encountering future stressors.

In a study to determine the accuracy of these perspectives, Seery, Holman, and Silver (2010) assessed the cumulative lifetime exposure to 37 negative events (e.g., death of family members, serious illness or injury, divorce, physical or sexual assaults, and exposure to natural disasters) experienced by several thousand respondents. Measures of mental health and well-being were also administered, assessing life satisfaction, overall psychological distress and distress during the previous week, any impairment in day-to-day functioning, and posttraumatic stress symptoms. For the next 2 years, respondents were periodically questioned regarding stressors encountered and current mental health. The researchers found an interesting relationship between adversity and mental health: Those who reported a moderate number of prior adverse events showed greater mental health (higher life satisfaction, lower global distress, fewer PTSD symptoms) than those who had either minimal or high levels of prior adversity. In addition, those with moderate exposure to adversity appeared to be more resilient to the adversities encountered within the 2-year follow-up period.

Thus, it does appear that moderate amounts of adversity can generate resiliency to future stressors. This may be because individuals who encounter adversities learn that challenges can be overcome, thereby increasing a sense of mastery and control. These qualities may buffer the impact of stressors and reduce physiological stress reactions. Individuals with very limited exposure to adversity may not have developed the skills necessary for overcoming challenges. Conversely, individuals confronted by multiple adverse events may feel overwhelmed and develop feelings of hopelessness and helplessness. Neither of these situations maximizes resilience or allows "toughness" to develop. Although more research is needed to determine if certain stressors or traumas are more toxic than others, it appears that "in moderation, whatever does not kill us may indeed make us stronger" (Seery, Holman, et al., 2010, p. 1038).

PhotoDisc

Treatment of Acute and Post-Traumatic Stress Disorders

Certain antidepressant medications (selective serotonin reuptake inhibitors) are considered an effective treatment for ASD and PTSD (Nacasch et al., 2007; NIMH, 2009b). These medications appear to help by altering serotonin levels, decreasing overactivation of the amygdala and desensitizing the fear network. However, they are effective in less than 60 percent of people with PTSD, with only about 20–30 percent of those individuals fully recovering (W. Berger et al., 2009).

Psychotherapy strategies have generally focused on extinguishing the fear of trauma-related stimuli or correcting dysfunctional cognitions that are thought to perpetuate PTSD symptoms. Exposure to cues associated with the trauma appears to be effective in treating PTSD (El Khoury-Malhame et al., 2011; Nacasch et al., 2007; S. Taylor, Thordarson, et al., 2003). The process of exposure sometimes involves asking the person to re-create the traumatic event in his or her imagination. For example, female sexual assault victims might be asked to repeatedly imagine and describe the assault "as if it were happening now," verbalizing not only details of the assault, but also their thoughts and emotions regarding the incident. Their descriptions would be recorded, and the process repeated for about an hour. The women would then be instructed to listen to the recordings once a day and, when doing so, to "imagine that the assault is happening now." This kind of exposure process allows extinction of the fear to occur (Foa, Dancu, et al., 1999). In a meta-analytic review of this therapeutic technique, individuals treated using prolonged exposure fared better than 86 percent of individuals in control conditions (Powers, Halpern, Ferenschak, Gillihan, & Foa, 2010). For PTSD resulting from child abuse, a therapeutic focus on helping individuals regulate their emotions appears to augment the effects of exposure therapy (Cloitre et al., 2010). Antidepressant medication has been found to be more effective when combined with exposure therapy (F. R. Schneier et al., 2012).

GARVEY SCOTT/MCT/Landov

Psychiatric Service Dogs

Trained service dogs can mitigate PTSD symptoms in veterans by entering and checking out anxiety-evoking environments before the veteran enters and by reducing panic symptoms by giving the veteran a friendly nudge. Service dogs are also trained to place themselves as a barrier to reduce the chance of the veteran being startled by people unexpectedly approaching.

Some therapists teach their clients to identify and challenge both dysfunctional cognitions about the traumatic event and current beliefs about the self and others, since cognitive factors can affect symptoms of PTSD. For example, battered women with PTSD often have thoughts associated with guilt or self-blame. Cognitions such as "I could have prevented it," "I never should have . . . ," and "I'm so stupid" can maintain PTSD symptoms. Therapy involving acquiring psychoeducation regarding PTSD, developing a solution-oriented focus, reducing negative self-talk, and receiving therapeutic exposure to fear triggers (such as photos of their partner or movies involving domestic violence) reduced PTSD symptoms in 87 percent of battered women receiving this treatment (Kubany et al., 2004).

Mindfulness training, which involves paying attention to emotions and thoughts on a nonjudgmental basis without reacting to symptoms, also shows promise as an intervention for PTSD (Kearney, McDermott, Malte, Martinez, & Simpson, 2012).

CHECKPOINT REVIEW

1. Name three therapeutic interventions that have been successful with PTSD.
2. Describe some of the steps used in exposure approaches to treating PTSD.

Psychological Factors Affecting Medical Conditions: Psychophysiological Disorders

Case Study

Data from 200 patients who happened to have cardiac defibrillators implanted prior to the World Trade Center attack on September 11, 2001, provided interesting information regarding the physiological impact of the stressful event. The defibrillators, which record and respond to serious heart arrhythmias, showed a doubling of life-threatening arrhythmias during the month following the terrorist attacks (Steinberg et al., 2004).

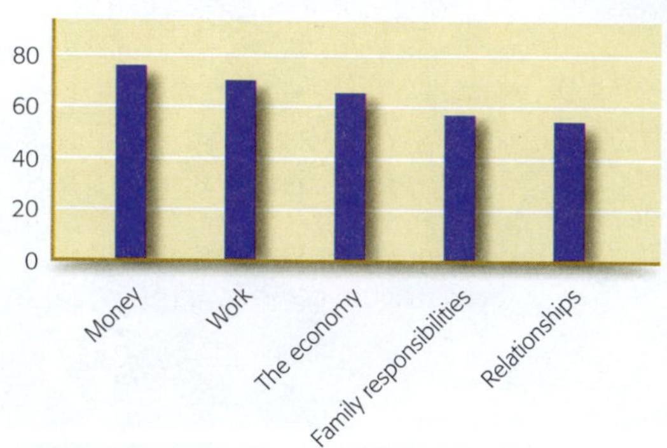

FIGURE 5.2

Five Leading Causes of Stress in America
The Stress in America survey shows that the economic recession has taken a toll on the well-being of adults in the U.S.

Source: American Psychological Association (2010b)

Stress results in a multitude of physiological, psychological, and social changes that influence health conditions. As we mentioned earlier, U.S. adults are quite stressed. (See Figure 5.2 for the major causes of stress.) Stress experienced by parents is often apparent to their children; more than 90 percent of children report that their parents are more likely to argue, yell, or complain when stressed (American Psychological Association, 2010b). In this part of the chapter, we consider the ways in which stress affects physical illness.

Most researchers acknowledge that attitudes and emotional states can have an impact on physical well-being. In the past, physical disorders—such as asthma, hypertension, and headaches—made worse by stressors were referred to as *psychosomatic disorders*. The use of this term was meant to distinguish physical disorders affected by psychological factors from conditions considered strictly physical in nature. Now, however, mental health professionals recognize that almost any physical disorder can have a strong psychological basis. The term *psychosomatic disorder* has been replaced with the term **psychophysiological disorder**, which references any physical disorder that has a strong psychological basis or component.

The diagnostic category "Psychological Factors Affecting Medical Condition" is the newest terminology for medical conditions in which psychological or behavioral factors influence the course or treatment of a medical disorder, constitute an additional risk factor for the medical condition, or make the illness worse (DSM-5 Work Groups, 2012). Emotional states, patterns of interpersonal interaction, and coping styles are examples of psychological or behavioral influences.

MYTH VS REALITY

MYTH Psychophysiological disorders are merely psychological in nature and can be treated with only psychotherapy. Real physical problems are not present.

REALITY Although psychophysiological disorders do have a psychological component, actual physical processes or conditions are involved. Any physical condition can be considered a psychophysiological disorder if psychological factors contribute to the development of the disorder, make the condition worse, or delay improvement. In most cases, both medical and psychological treatments are needed.

Characteristics of Psychophysiological Disorders

Psychophysiological disorders involve actual tissue damage (e.g., coronary heart disease), a disease process (e.g., impairment of the immune system), or physiological dysfunction (e.g., asthma, migraine headaches). Both medical treatment and psychotherapy are usually required. The relative contributions of physical and psychological factors to a physical disorder can vary greatly. Although it is sometimes difficult to determine which psychological factors might be contributing to a disorder, repeated association between a stressor and symptoms of the disorder increases suspicion that a psychological component is involved.

psychophysiological disorder any physical disorder that has a strong psychological basis or component

In this section we discuss several of the more prevalent psychophysiological disorders—coronary heart disease, hypertension (high blood pressure), headaches, and asthma—and then consider the topic of how stress influences the immune system. Research identifying biological, psychological, social, and sociocultural influences on specific psychophysiological disorders is also reviewed.

Did You Know? Within 24 hours of losing a loved one, the risk of a heart attack is over 21 times higher than normal. Grief and stress may produce life-threatening changes in the sympathetic nervous system. Preventative steps such as taking low-dose aspirin or beta blockers have been suggested for this situation.

Source: Mostofsky et al. (2012)

Coronary Heart Disease

Coronary heart disease (CHD) involves the narrowing of cardiac arteries due to **atherosclerosis** (plaque build-up within the arterial walls), resulting in complete or partial blockage of the flow of blood and oxygen to the heart, as seen in Figure 5.3. When coronary arteries are narrowed or blocked, oxygen-rich blood can't reach the heart muscle. This can result in angina (chest pain) or, if blood flow to the heart is significantly blocked, a heart attack.

Approximately 8 percent of U.S. Americans have CHD, and almost 500,000 die of this condition each year. Risk factors for CHD include high cholesterol levels, hypertension, cigarette smoking, obesity, lack of physical activity, and psychosocial factors such as depression, perceived stress, and difficult life events (American Heart Association, 2010). Stress plays both a biological and psychological role in coronary heart disease. Biologically, stress causes the release of hormones that activate the sympathetic nervous system, which can lead to changes in heart rhythm such as *ventricular fibrillation* (rapid, ineffective contractions of the heart), *bradycardia* (slowing of the heartbeat), *tachycardia* (speeding up of the heartbeat), or *arrhythmia* (irregular heartbeat). Figure 5.4 shows an example of ventricular fibrillation.

coronary heart disease (CHD) disease process involving the narrowing of cardiac arteries, resulting in the restriction or partial blockage of the flow of blood and oxygen to the heart

atherosclerosis condition involving the progressive thickening and hardening of the walls of arteries due to an accumulation of fats and cholesterol along their inner linings

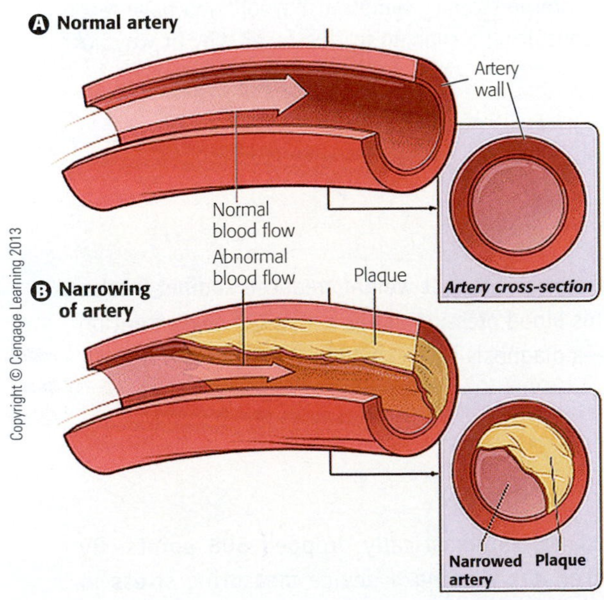

FIGURE 5.3

Atherosclerosis

Atherosclerosis occurs when fat, cholesterol, and other substances build up in arteries and form a hard structure called *plaque*. The plaque can make the artery narrow and can reduce or even stop blood flow.

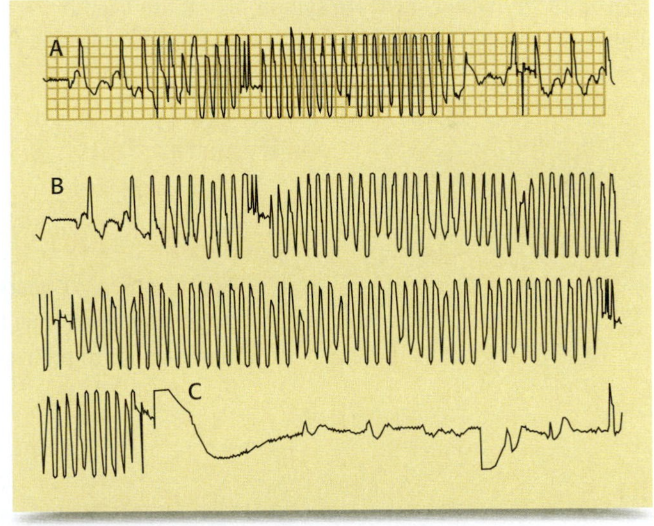

FIGURE 5.4

Ventricular Fibrillation in Sudden Unexplained Death

A Thai man fitted with a defibrillator showed ventricular episodes (rapid spikes on the graph) when asleep. Part A represents a transient episode that resolved itself. Part B depicts a sustained ventricular episode accompanied by labored breathing. Part C shows that the defibrillator was set off, which normalized the heart rate. Is this the explanation for sudden unexplained death syndrome?

Source: Nademanee et al. (1997)

CONTROVERSY:

The Hmong Sudden Death Syndrome

Vang Xiong is a Hmong (Laotian) former soldier who, with his wife and child, resettled in Chicago in 1980. City life in a new country was a significant change from the familiar farm life and rural surroundings of his native village. Vang had experienced the trauma of seeing people killed prior to his escape from Laos, and expressed feelings of guilt about leaving his brothers and sisters behind. His physical difficulties began soon after his move to Chicago:

[He] could not sleep the first night in the apartment, nor the second, nor the third. After three nights of sleeping very little, Vang went to see his resettlement worker, a bilingual Hmong man named Moua Lee. Vang told Moua that the first night he woke suddenly, short of breath, from a dream in which a cat was sitting on his chest. The second night, the room suddenly grew darker, and a figure, like a large black dog, came to his bed and sat on his chest. He could not push the dog off, and he grew quickly and dangerously short of breath. The third night, a tall, white-skinned female spirit came into his bedroom from the kitchen and lay on top of him. Her weight made it increasingly difficult for him to breathe, and as he grew frantic and tried to call out he could manage but a whisper. He attempted to turn onto his side, but found he was pinned down. After fifteen minutes, the spirit left him, and he awoke, screaming.
(Tobin & Friedman, 1983, p. 440)

The terrifying dream-state symptoms experienced by Vang are connected to Hmong sudden death syndrome—the term used to describe hundreds of cases of sudden death involving Southeast Asian refugees. Almost all cases involved men and most occurred within the first 2 years of residence in the United States. Autopsies produced no identifiable cause for the deaths. All of the reports were the same: A person in apparently good health went to sleep and died in his or her sleep. Often, the victim displayed labored breathing, screams, and frantic movements just before death. Some consider the deaths to represent an extreme and very specific example of the impact of psychological stress on physical health (Figure 5.4). Similar cases of sudden unexplained death have also been reported in Asian countries (Aoki et al., 2003).

Vang was one of the lucky people with the syndrome—he survived. He went for treatment to a Hmong woman, a highly respected shaman in Chicago's Hmong community. She interpreted his problem as being caused by unhappy spirits and performed the ceremonies required to release them. After that, Vang reported no more physical problems or nightmares during sleep.

In many non-Western cultures, physical or mental problems are attributed to supernatural forces such as witchcraft or evil spirits (D. W. Sue & Sue, 2013). The spiritual treatment Vang received using non-Western methods seemed to have been successful. How would a doctor practicing Western medicine interpret Vang's symptoms? Would you have recommended consulting a shaman in this case? Why or why not?

Hypertension

Case Study

Scott Cote, a 41-year-old software engineer, lost weight, reduced sodium intake, and began exercising to control his blood pressure, all as a result of new attention being given to prehypertension—a diagnosis he received in 2008 (Landro, 2010).

Case Study

On October 19, 1987, the stock market drastically dropped 508 points. By chance, a 48-year-old stockbroker was wearing a device measuring stress in the work environment on that day. The instrument measured his pulse every 15 minutes. At the beginning of the day, his pulse was 64 beats per minute and his blood pressure was 132 over 87. As stock prices fell dramatically, the man's physiological system surged in the other direction. His heart rate increased to 84 beats per minute and his blood pressure hit a dangerous 181 over 105. His pulse was "pumping adrenaline, flooding his arteries, and maybe slowly killing him in the process" (Tierney, 1988).

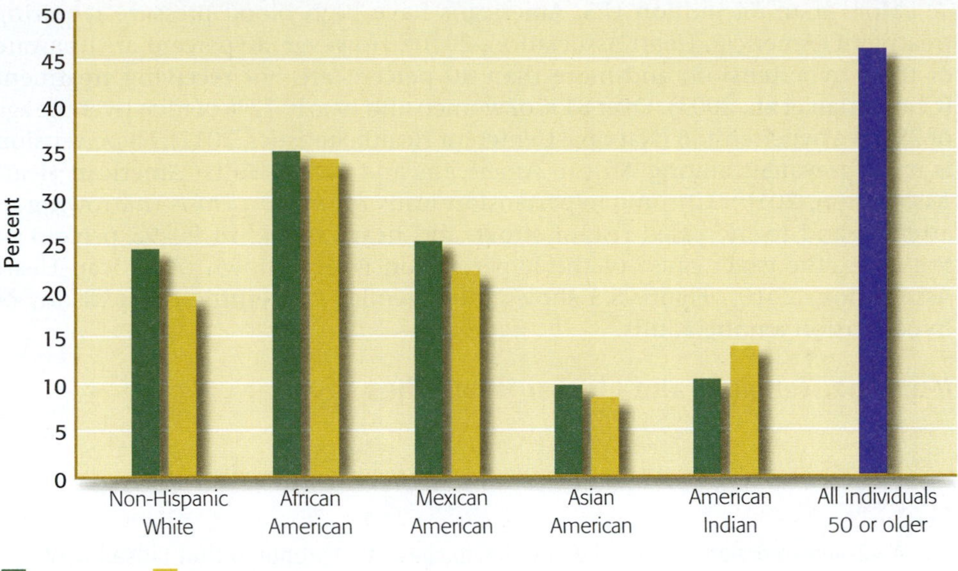

FIGURE 5.5

Gender and Ethnic Differences in Hypertension Among Adults in the United States

The highest prevalence of chronic high blood pressure occurs among African Americans and among all individuals over the age of 50. Women tend to have somewhat lower blood pressure than men.

Source: Data from American Heart Association (2007); Burt et al. (1995)

The stockbroker's reaction in the case study illustrates the impact of a stressor on **blood pressure**, the measurement of the force of blood against the walls of the arteries and veins. **Normal blood pressure** is considered a **systolic pressure** (force when the heart contracts) lower than 120 and a **diastolic pressure** (the arterial pressure that occurs when the heart is relaxed after a contraction) lower than 80. We all experience transient physiological responses to stressors, but some people develop a chronic condition called **hypertension**, in which the systolic blood pressure equals or exceeds 140 and the diastolic pressure is 90 or higher. **Prehypertension**, described in the other case study, involves increases in blood pressure (systolic pressure between 120 and 139 and diastolic pressure between 80 to 89) believed to be a precursor to hypertension, stroke, and heart disease; prehypertension is found in 34 percent of men and 22 percent of women (Ostchega, Yoon, Hughes, & Louis, 2008).

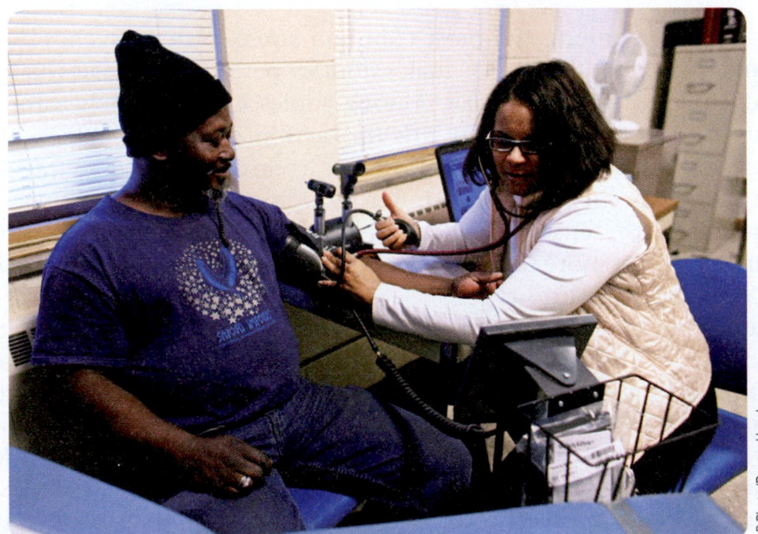
AP Photo/Darren Hauck

Undiagnosed Hypertension

David Thomas was buying groceries and decided to get a blood pressure check at a clinic located in the store. He found that he had high blood pressure and was a prime candidate for a stroke.

blood pressure the measurement of the force of blood against the walls of the arteries and veins

normal blood pressure the normal amount of force exerted by blood against the artery walls; systolic pressure is less than 120 and diastolic pressure is less than 80

systolic pressure force on blood vessels when the heart contracts

diastolic pressure arterial force exerted when the heart is relaxed and the ventricles of the heart are filling with blood

hypertension a chronic condition, which increases risk of stroke and heart disease, characterized by a systolic blood pressure of 140 or higher or a diastolic pressure of 90 or higher

prehypertension a condition believed to be a precursor to hypertension, stroke, and heart disease, characterized by systolic blood pressure of 120 to 139 and diastolic pressure from 80 to 89

More than 74 million U.S. Americans have high blood pressure requiring treatment (American Heart Association, 2010). However, 30 percent are unaware of their hypertension, and more than 40 percent are not receiving treatment (Chobanian et al., 2003). Over 81% of women and nearly 72% of men over the age of 75 have hypertension (National Center for Health Statistics, 2012). Hypertension is most prevalent among African Americans and older adults (American Heart Association, 2010). Chronic hypertension leads to *arteriosclerosis* (narrowing of arteries) and to increased risk of stroke and heart attack. In 90–95 percent of the cases, the exact cause of the hypertension is not known (American Heart Association, 2010). Figure 5.5 shows some gender and ethnic comparisons of hypertension among adults.

Migraine, Tension, and Cluster Headaches

Case Study

A 42-year-old woman described her headaches as a throbbing that pulsed with every heartbeat. Visual effects, such as sparklers flashing across her visual field, accompanied the pain. The symptoms would last for up to 3 days (Adler & Rogers, 1999).

Case Study

A patient seeking help for excruciating headaches described the pain in the following manner: "It feels like someone walked up to me, took a screwdriver and jammed it up in my right eye and kept digging it around for 20 minutes" (Linn, 2004, p. A1).

Headaches are among the most common stress-related psychophysiological complaints. About 90 percent of males and 95 percent of females have at least one headache during a given year. Among adolescents, headaches are common and more prevalent and severe in girls (B. Larsson & Fischtel, 2012). More than 45 million U.S. Americans suffer from chronic, recurring headaches (Meeks, 2004). The pain of a headache can vary in intensity from dull to excruciating. Although we discuss migraine, tension, and cluster headaches separately, the same person can be susceptible to more than one type of headache. (Figure 5.6 illustrates some differences among the three types.)

A number of biological, psychological, social, and sociocultural factors have been associated with the onset of headaches. In addition to stress, headaches can be precipitated by negative emotions, sexual harassment, poor body posture, eyestrain, noise, too much or too little sleep, exposure to smoke or strong odors, the weather, hormonal factors in women, and certain foods (P. R. Martin & MacLeod, 2009; National Institute of Neurological Disorders and Stroke [NINDS], 2009). Headaches have also been reported as a result of coughing, exertion, and sexual activity (S.-J. Wang & Fu, 2010).

migraine headache moderate to severe head pain resulting from abnormal brain activity affecting the cranial blood vessels and nerves

Migraine Headaches **Migraine headaches** are believed to be caused by abnormal brain activity that results in inflammation and dilation of cranial arteries; the pressure on nearby nerves and chemical changes within the brain produce

Headache	Migraine	Tension	Cluster
	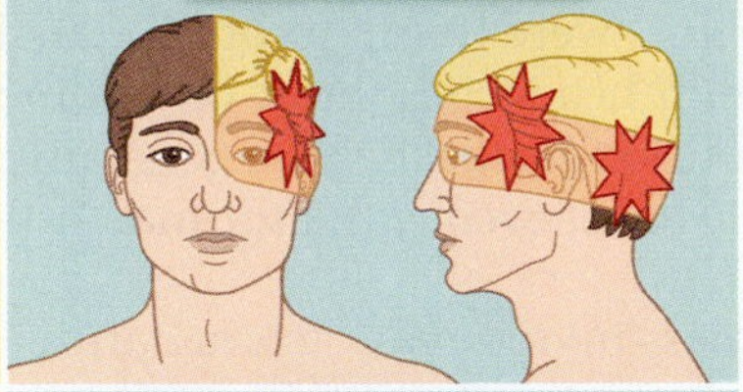	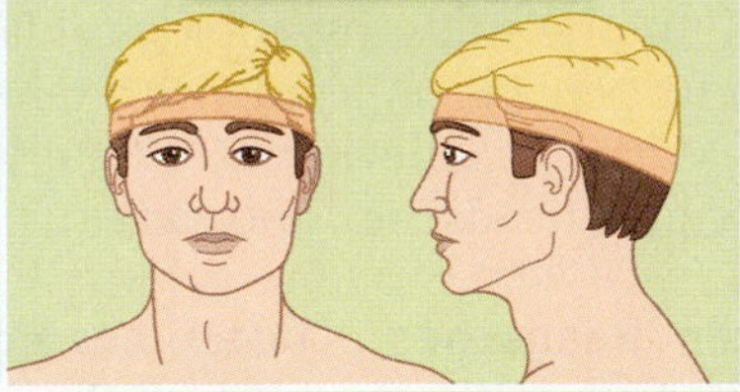	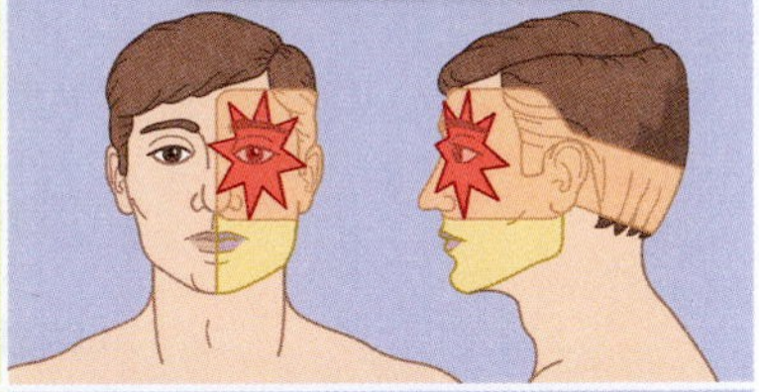
Location	Often one side of head but location varies	Both sides of head, often concentrated	Centered on one eye on same side of head
Duration	Hours to 4 days	Hours to days	Usually less than an hour
Severity of Pain	Mild to severe	Mild to moderate	Excruciating
Symptoms	Nausea, sensitivity to light, sound, odors, and movement	Tightness or pressure around neck, head, or shoulders	Eye often teary, nose clogged on side of head with pain; pacing and rubbing head
Sex Ratio	More common in young adult women	More common in women	More common in men
Heredity	Often hereditary	Probably not hereditary	Not hereditary

FIGURE 5.6

Three Types of Headaches

Some differences in the characteristics of migraine, tension, and cluster headaches have been reported, although similarities between them also exist.

Source: Data adapted from "Headaches" (2006); Silberstein (1998)

pain (National Institute of Neurological Disorders and Stroke [NINDS], 2009). Pain from a migraine headache may be mild, moderate, or severe. Most people with migraines report having them once or twice a month; 10 percent have them weekly, 20 percent have them every 2 or 3 days, and 15 percent have them more than 15 days a month (Dodick & Gargus, 2008). Migraines may last from a few hours to several days and are often accompanied by nausea and vomiting. Up to one third of individuals with migraines experience an **aura**—involving unusual physical sensations or visual symptoms such as flashes of light, unusual visual patterns, or blind spots—prior to the headache (Steiner, MacGregor, & Davies, 2007). The 1-year prevalence of migraine headaches is 11.7 percent (17.1 percent in women and 5.6 percent in men). Prevalence peaks in midlife and is lower in adolescents and those over age 60. Migraine headaches are common not only among women but also among people with lower incomes. They are more common among white Americans than African Americans (Lipton et al., 2007). Genetic factors affecting the release of inflammatory chemicals that affect cranial nerves and blood vessels have been implicated in migraine headaches (Anttila et al., 2010).

Tension Headaches **Tension headaches** are produced when stress creates prolonged contraction of the scalp and neck muscles, resulting in vascular constriction and steady pain. They are the most common form of headache and tend to disappear

aura a visual or physical sensation (e.g., tingling of an extremity or flashes of light) that precedes a headache

tension headache head pain produced by prolonged contraction of the scalp and neck muscles, resulting in constriction of the blood vessels and steady pain once the stress producing the muscle tension is over (NINDS, 2007). Tension headaches are experienced by the vast majority of adults; additionally, about 31 percent of children report having tension headaches (Monteith & Sprenger, 2010). In one study, psychological factors were found to precipitate headaches in up to 61 percent of people with tension headaches, most of whom were women (P. R. Martin & Seneviratne, 1997). Tension headaches are generally not as severe as migraine headaches, and can usually be relieved with aspirin or other analgesics.

Cluster Headaches **Cluster headaches** involve an excruciating stabbing or burning sensation located in the eye or cheek. The symptoms are so severe that 55 percent of individuals experiencing a cluster headache report suicidal thoughts (Rozen & Fishman, 2012). Cluster headaches occur in cycles, and incapacitating attacks can occur a number of times a day (Meeks, 2004). In about 20 percent of cases, the headaches are preceded by an aura (Rozen, 2010). Each attack may last from 15 minutes to 3 hours before ending abruptly. Along with the headache, the individual may experience tears or a stuffy nose on the same side of the head on which the pain is felt. Headache cycles may last from several days to months, followed by pain-free periods. Only about 10 to 20 percent of cluster headaches are chronic. Cluster headaches do not appear to run in families and, in contrast to other headaches, are more common in men (Rozen & Fishman, 2012).

Asthma

Asthma, a chronic inflammatory disease of the lungs, can be significantly affected by stress. During asthma episodes, stress or other triggers result in excessive mucus secretion combined with spasms and swelling of the airways, which reduces the amount of air that can be inhaled (Figure 5.7). Symptoms range from mild and infrequent wheezing or coughing to severe respiratory distress requiring emergency care. In severe asthma attacks, respiratory failure can occur.

In the United States, prevalence of asthma has increased dramatically since the 1980s. It affects up to 8.2 percent of the population, or about 24.6 million individuals, with a disproportionate recent increase among women (Akinbami, Moorman, & Liu, 2011; Asthma and Allergy Foundation of America, 2007). Ethnic minority children living in inner cities and African American, American Indian, and Filipino children are more vulnerable to asthma (Brim, Rudd, Funk, & Callahan, 2008; Forno & Celedón, 2009). Puerto Ricans and African Americans are three times more likely to die from asthma than are other U.S. Americans (Akinbami, 2006). Figure 5.8 shows asthma prevalence among different groups.

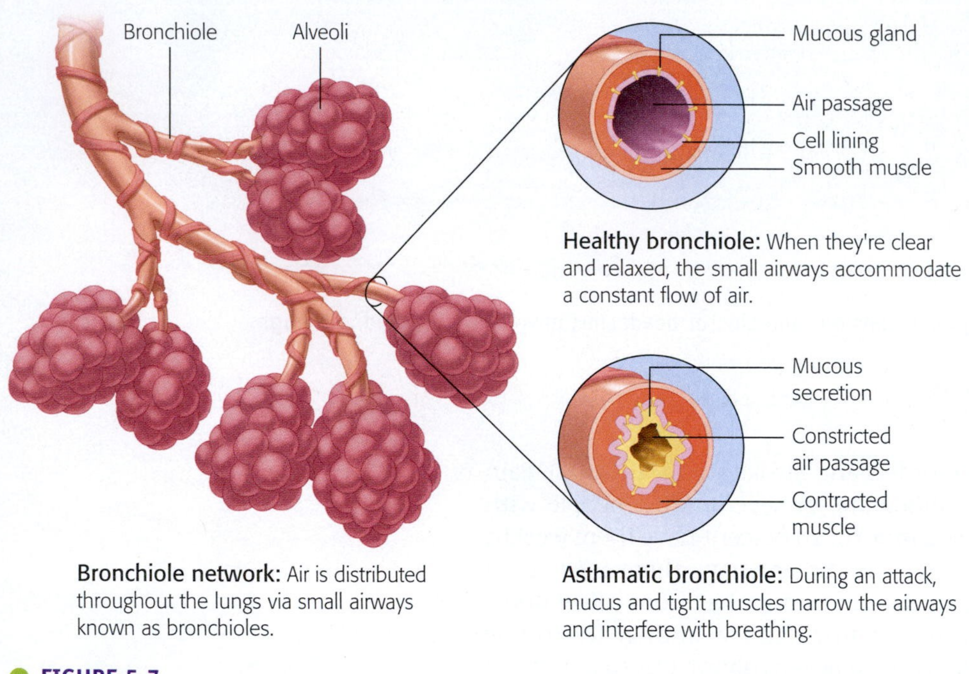

Bronchiole
Alveoli
Mucous gland
Air passage
Cell lining
Smooth muscle
Healthy bronchiole: When they're clear and relaxed, the small airways accommodate a constant flow of air.
Mucous secretion
Constricted air passage
Contracted muscle
Bronchiole network: Air is distributed throughout the lungs via small airways known as bronchioles.
Asthmatic bronchiole: During an attack, mucus and tight muscles narrow the airways and interfere with breathing.

FIGURE 5.7

An Asthma Attack

Asthma attacks and deaths have increased dramatically since the 1980s.

Source: Cowley & Underwood (1997, p. 61)

cluster headache excruciating stabbing or burning sensations located in the eye or cheek

asthma a chronic inflammatory disease of the airways in the lungs

People with asthma often underestimate the magnitude of airflow obstruction during an asthma attack (Janssens, Verleden, De Peuter, Van Diest, & Van den Bergh, 2009). Unfortunately, when there is a delay in seeking emergency assistance, death can result. In fact, asthma is the sixth leading cause of death in children 5–14 years of age (Katon, 2010). Additionally, for reasons that are not

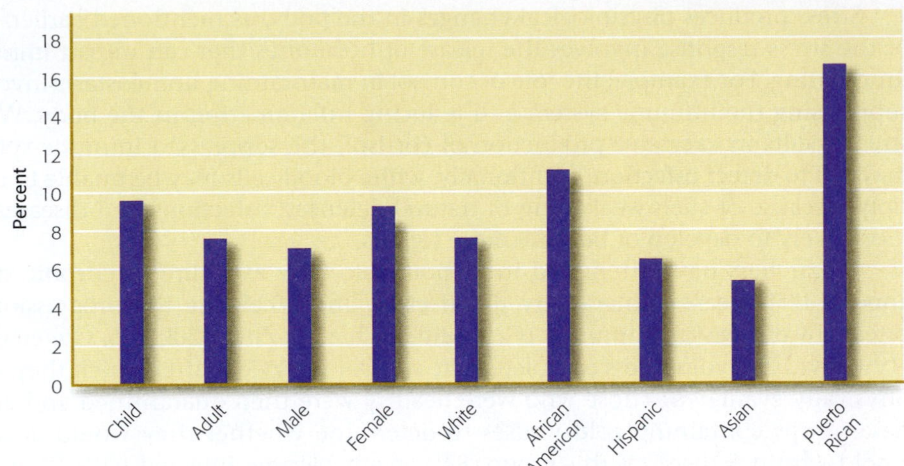

FIGURE 5.8

Asthma Prevalence

This figure shows the prevalence of asthma among adults and children, men and women, and members of different ethnic groups. Of these groups, Puerto Ricans, African Americans, females, and children appear to be especially vulnerable.

Source: Akinbami, Moorman, & Liu (2011)

clearly understood, adolescents with asthma are twice as likely to die from suicide compared to their peers without asthma (C.-J. Kuo et al., 2010).

The recent increase in the number of asthma cases in the United States is puzzling. Suspicion grows that, in addition to increasingly stressful life circumstances, a number of different pollutants (cigarette smoke, industrial toxins, pet hair and dander, indoor molds, and cockroaches) may be responsible (Forno & Celedón, 2009). Rosenstreich, Eggleston, & Kattan (1997) examined 476 children with asthma who lived in inner cities. They found that 23 percent were allergic to pets, 35 percent to dust mites, and 37 percent to cockroaches. Allergy to cockroaches had the highest association with emergency room treatment, hospitalization, and school absences in these children. Programs to eliminate environmental allergens within the homes of children with asthma can successfully reduce asthma symptoms (W. J. Morgan et al., 2004).

Stress and the Immune System

Case Study

Florida was hit by four hurricanes within a 6-week period. One woman was able to deal with the first, even though it smashed her windows, flooded her carpets, and caused her to throw food away. Then a second hurricane struck, causing similar damage. She had to wait in the hot sun to get ice and was without food or water for her children. As she related, "The first one, I stayed strong. But this second one, I started crying and couldn't stop" (Barton, 2004, p. A3).

We have already mentioned the relationship between stress and illness. How do emotional and psychological states influence the disease process? We know that stress is related to illness, but what is the precise relationship between the two? How does stress affect health?

Although stress itself does not cause infections, it does appear to decrease the immune system's efficiency, thereby increasing a person's susceptibility to disease. The white blood cells in the immune system help maintain health by recognizing and destroying pathogens such as bacteria, viruses, fungi, and tumors. In an intact system, more than 600 billion white blood cells circulate through the bloodstream performing this function (Kendall-Tackett, 2009).

Did You Know?

Strong relationships lead to a longer life. Having strong, close relationships can reduce the influence of risk factors such as obesity or lack of exercise, whereas poor or limited social relationships are the equivalent of smoking 15 cigarettes a day or having more than six drinks of alcohol a day.

Source: Holt-Lundstad, Smith, & Layton (2010)

Stress produces physiological changes in the body, as mentioned earlier. Part of the stress response involves the release of hormones that can impair immune functioning. For example, the role of cortisol in maintaining homeostasis involves suppressing the immune system and reducing inflammation in the body. When stress results in excessive production of cortisol, the suppressed immune system may fail to detect infection; additionally, white blood cells may be unable to multiply. Because of such weakening of natural defenses, infections and diseases are more likely to develop or become more serious.

Researchers have attempted to demonstrate how exposure to chronic stress appears to increase vulnerability to infection and accelerate the progression of disease by decreasing immunity (G. E. Miller, Chen, & Zhou, 2007). S. Cohen et al. (1998) had 276 volunteers complete a life stressor interview, after which they were physically evaluated. Those who were healthy were then quarantined and given nasal drops containing cold viruses to determine whether they would develop a cold within 5 days. Of this group, 84 percent became infected with the virus, but only 40 percent developed cold symptoms. Participants who had undergone severe stress (e.g., conflicts with family or friends or unemployment) for one or more months were much more likely to develop colds. Similarly, a group of law students were evaluated five times over a period of 6 months. On each occasion they first indicated how optimistic they were about their law school experience and were then injected with an antigen designed to generate an immune response. When students were more optimistic about law school, greater immune response was noted. Thus, expectations about their performance in school influenced their immunity (Segerstrom & Sephton, 2010). Deterioration in immune system functioning can increase vulnerability to certain illnesses, but can it also lead to the development of diseases such as cancer? Consider the following case study.

Case Study

Anne is an unhappy, passive individual who always accedes to the wishes and demands of her husband. She has difficulty expressing strong emotions, especially anger, and represses her feelings. She has few friends and no one to confide in. She often feels a pervasive sense of hopelessness and depression. During a routine physical exam, Anne's doctor discovers a lump in her breast. A biopsy reveals that the tumor is malignant.

Did Anne's personality or emotional state contribute to the formation or growth of the malignant tumor? Can she now alter the course of her disease by changing her emotional state, thereby improving her immune functioning?

Several problems exist in research investigating the effects of mood and personality on the development of cancer (Honda & Goodwin, 2004). First, *cancer* is a general name for a variety of disease processes, each of which may have a varying susceptibility to emotions. Second, cancer develops over a relatively long period of time. Determining a relationship between its occurrence and a specific mood or personality is not possible. Third, most studies examining the relationship between psychological variables and cancer are retrospective—that is, personality or mood states are usually assessed after the cancer is diagnosed. People who receive the life-threatening diagnosis of cancer may respond with depression, anxiety, and confusion. Thus, instead of being a cause, negative emotions may be an emotional response to having a life-threatening disease.

Do stress, negative emotions, or certain personality characteristics increase susceptibility to cancer or increase the severity of the disease? Certain emotions

CONTROVERSY:

Can Humor Influence the Course of a Disease?

Can humor reduce the severity of or even cure a physical illness? Author Norman Cousins, who suffered from rheumatoid disease, described how he recovered his health through laughter. He claimed that 10 minutes of laughter would provide 2 hours of pain relief (Cousins, 1979). In 1999, Patch Adams, a physician who uses humor with his patients, received an award for "excellence in the field of therapeutic humor." Some research has shown that exposing participants to humorous videos reduces stress and improves immune system functioning (M. P. Bennett, Zeller, Rosenberg, & McCann, 2003). Watching funny videos is associated with improved blood flow (Sugawara, Tarumi, & Tanaka, 2010), and laughter is associated with improved heart functioning (Sakuragi, Sugiyama, & Takeuchi, 2002). However, the overall evidence regarding positive health benefits of humor is mixed and relatively weak (M. P. Bennett & Lengacher, 2006).

How might humor influence the disease process? Several routes are possible:

- Humor may directly affect immune functioning.
- Humor may increase the tendency of individuals to engage in health-promoting behaviors.
- Humor may serve as a psychological buffer to stress, thus reducing the impact of stressors on physical health.
- Humor may increase social connections and enhance social support from friends and family, thus exerting an indirect positive influence on health.

For Further Consideration

1. How would you respond to someone claiming that laughter and humor play no role in slowing the progression of a disease such as cancer?
2. Does promoting laughter and humor give false hope to ill individuals?

and stressors have been associated with decreases in immune system functioning; when the immune system is compromised, it is possible that cancer can gain a foothold (Kiecolt-Glaser, 2009). Nevertheless, the connection between stress and naturally occurring cancers has yet to be demonstrated. In a critical review of the literature on the impact of psychological factors on the progression of cancer, J. C. Coyne, Stefanek, & Palmer (2007) concluded there is little evidence that psychotherapy improves survival after a diagnosis of cancer.

CHECKPOINT REVIEW

1. What is meant by *psychophysiological disorder*?
2. Describe the characteristics of each of the psychophysiological disorders (coronary heart disease, hypertension, headaches, asthma).
3. In what ways are psychological factors involved in coronary heart disease, hypertension, headaches, and asthma?

Etiology of Psychophysiological Disorders

As we have seen, not everyone who faces stressful events develops a psychophysiological disorder or shows reduced immune functioning. For example, men who have governed as president have a longer natural life span than other men (Olshansky, 2011). Daily living involves constant exposure to stressors, including work expectations at school or on the job, relationship problems, and illness, to name a few. Why do only some individuals develop a physical disorder when exposed to stressors? In this section, we use the multipath model to explore some of the biological, psychological, social, and sociocultural dimensions of the disease process, as shown in Figure 5.9. Although we are discussing these dimensions separately, there are significant interactions among the different factors.

FIGURE 5.9

Multipath Model of Psychophysiological Disorders

The dimensions interact with one another and combine in different ways to result in a specific psychophysiological disorder.

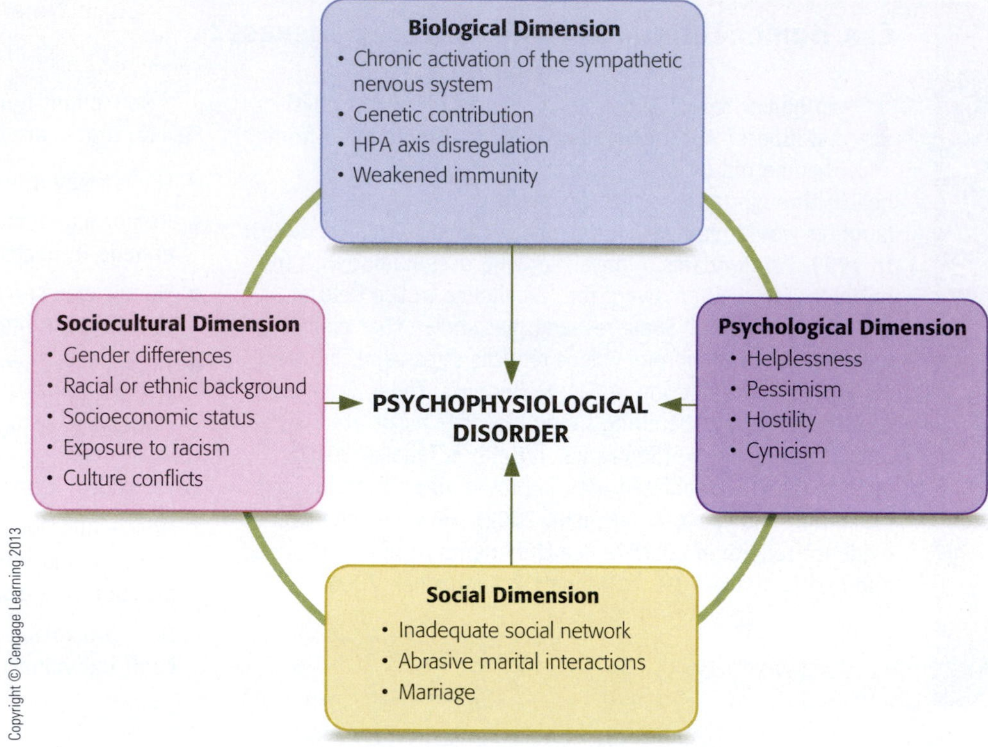

Biological Dimension

Stressors, especially chronic ones, can dysregulate the HPA axis and the **sympathetic nervous system** through the release of hormones such as epinephrine, norepinephrine, and cortisol. These hormones, along with the activation of the sympathetic nervous system, prepare the body for emergency action by increasing heart rate, respiration, and alertness while simultaneously decreasing vulnerability to inflammation. This preparation helps humans respond quickly to a crisis situation. However, when such activation occurs over an extended period of time (i.e., there are chronic stressors), a psychophysiological disorder can develop (Gotlib, Joormann, Minor, & Hallmayer, 2008; Kendall-Tackett, 2009). Research supports the view that brief exposure to stressors enhances immune functioning, whereas long-lasting stress can result in impaired immune response (Schuster, Bornovalova, & Hunt, 2012; Segerstrom & Miller, 2004). Heightened preparedness to face stress results in increased cortisol production: Excess cortisol has been linked with coronary artery calcification, a contributor to coronary heart disease (Hamer, O'Donnell, Lahiri, & Steptoe, 2010). Table 5.3 compares short-term adaptive responses to stress with symptoms that can result from chronic stress.

Early environmental influences such as traumatic childhood experiences may produce changes in brain structure and in the stress-responsive neurobiological systems, resulting in increased vulnerability to the development of a psychophysiological disorder (Anda et al., 2006). Additionally, genetic influences contribute to psychophysiological disorders. For example, cardiovascular stress reactivity as measured by blood pressure is more similar among identical twins than among fraternal twins (De Geus, Kupper, Boomsma, & Snieder, 2007). Genetic factors also appear to play a role in asthma: If one parent has asthma, a child has a 1 in 3 chance of developing asthma; if both parents have asthma, the chances increase to 7 in 10 (Asthma and Allergy Foundation of America, 2007). Migraine headaches may involve a

sympathetic nervous system part of the nervous system that automatically performs functions such as increasing heart rate, constricting blood vessels, and raising blood pressure

biological predisposition that affects the reactivity of brain cells and pain receptors (Dodick & Gargus, 2008). Although genetics and physiological response to chronic stress play a role in physical illness, so do psychological, social, and sociocultural factors.

TABLE 5.3 Adaptive and Maladaptive Responses to Stress

ADAPTIVE RESPONSES (SHORT-TERM STRESS)	MALADAPTIVE RESPONSES (CHRONIC STRESS)
Increased glucose	Hyperglycemia (diabetes)
Increased blood pressure	Hypertension, breakage of plaque in arteries
Increased immunity	Impaired immune response to illnesses
Increased vigilance	Hypervigilance
Diminished interest in sex	Global loss of interest in sex
Improved cognition and memory	Increased focus on traumatic events, lack of attention to current environment
Faster blood clotting	Increased thickness of coronary artery walls (coronary vascular disease, strokes)

Source: Data from Carels et al. (2003); Keltner & Dowben (2007)

Psychological Dimension

Psychological and personality characteristics can also mediate the effects of exposure to stressors. Positive affect, such as optimism, happiness, joy, and contentment, enhances the parasympathetic modulation of heart rate, blood pressure, and other physiological stress reactions, whereas negative emotions accentuate the stress response (K. W. Davidson, Mostofsky, & Whang, 2010). For example, a longitudinal study of employees retained after nearly half of the workforce was laid off showed that although two thirds developed health problems, one third appeared to thrive. The individuals who did well had three characteristics: (1) commitment—they were involved in ongoing changes rather than feeling isolated and helpless; (2) control—they made attempts to influence decisions and refused to feel powerless; and (3) openness to challenge—they viewed changes as opportunities (Maddi, 2002). These characteristics are sometimes together described as "hardiness," a trait which appears to protect people from the harmful effect of stressors (Eschleman, Bowling, & Alarcon, 2010; Hamer et al., 2010).

A number of other psychological attributes also influence health. Control and the perception of control over the environment and its stressors appear to mitigate the effects of stress (Christie & Barling, 2009). Among older adults with physical health problems, those with high levels of control behaviors, such as engaging in health-improving strategies, seeking help, and remaining motivated to address their physical problems, did not show the pattern of biological decline typical of those with health issues (Wrosch, Schulz, Miller, Lupien, & Dunne, 2007). In contrast, those who have limited perception of control over life events ("I have little control over things that happen to me") showed an increased risk of mortality from CHD (Surtees et al., 2010). Similarly, women with demanding jobs involving little personal control had nearly double the chance of having a heart attack compared to women with more personal control over stressful jobs (M. A. Albert, Glynn, & Buring, 2010). In a sample of 335 older adults in Pittsburgh, Pennsylvania, diary ratings of stressful demands and levels of perceived control in daily life were obtained. Individuals who perceived greater daily stress and lower control were found to have thickening of the lining of the carotid artery, a marker of atherosclerosis (Kamarck, Muldoon, Shiffman, & Sutton-Tyrrell, 2007).

Alan CHIN/Gamma-Rapho via Getty Images

Stress and Hypertension

On September 11, 2001, many survivors of the World Trade Center attacks recounted the terror they felt during the attack and their fight for survival. Here ash covered survivors leave the scene dazed and in shock.

Positive emotions may increase heart health. In a study of nearly 10,000 women over an 8-year follow-up period, those who scored high on optimism ("In unclear times, I usually expect the best") had a 9 percent lower risk of developing heart disease and a 14 percent lower risk of dying, whereas cynical women who had hostile thoughts about others ("I often have to take orders from someone who did not know as much as I do") were 16 percent more likely to die during the same time period (Tindle et al., 2009). People who are satisfied with their job, family, sex life, and themselves had less CHD risk than their dissatisfied counterparts (Boehm, Peterson, Kivimaki, & Kubzansky, 2011).

In general, negative emotional states such as depression, hostility, anxiety, and cynicism are related to elevated CHD risk (Low, Thurston, & Matthews, 2010).

Depression can influence both physiological functioning and behaviors that affect health. Depressed individuals show irregularities in the autonomic nervous system. They have elevated levels of adrenal hormones (e.g., epinephrine and norepinephrine), resulting in exaggerated cardiovascular responses to stressors (Carney, Freedland, & Veith, 2005). In addition, an individual who is depressed may sleep more, exercise less, eat unhealthy food, and use caffeine, alcohol, or cigarettes. These behaviors may in turn increase the individual's susceptibility to disease or may prolong an existing illness.

The emotion of hostility has been implicated in several physiological disorders, particularly CHD (Tindle et al., 2009). Several possibilities exist that may explain the relationship between hostility and CHD. First, hostility may increase a person's cardiovascular responsivity, subsequently increasing the risk of developing CHD. At least one study (S. B. Miller et al., 1998) has supported this view. In that study, individuals who scored high on hostility showed exaggerated cardiovascular reactivity to a stressor (verbal harassment) compared with participants with low hostility. Thus, hostility may lead to damaging physiological responses.

Young healthy males who tended to become angry when frustrated or treated unfairly showed elevated cholesterol levels, which is associated with increased risk of developing CHD (J. C. Richards, Alvarenga, & Hof, 2000). Hostility in children and adolescents has also been related to elevated lipids and blood pressure (Raikkonen, Matthews, & Salomon, 2003). Among African American and white adolescents, those who scored low on social skills and high on anger or hostility measures had increased abdominal fat and greater arterial stiffness (hardening of the arteries); these associations were stronger for African American participants (Midei & Matthews, 2009).

Social Dimension

Social stressors have been associated with impaired immunological functioning and other adverse health outcomes (Dickerson & Kemeny, 2004). Childhood adversities such as physical, emotional, or sexual abuse have been linked to adult onset headaches (S. Lee, Tsang, Von Korff, et al., 2009; Tietjen et al., 2010) and hypertension (Kidd et al., 2011; D. J. Stein, Scott, et al., 2010). Those who reported a greater number of childhood adversities had a greater likelihood of developing hypertension in adulthood (S. E. Taylor, 2010). Early childhood or chronic adversities can affect physiological stress reactions and result in the suppression of immune functioning.

Divorced or separated men tend to have more physical illness than their married counterparts (Eaker, Sullivan, Kelly-Hayes, D'Agostino, & Benjamin, 2007). Abrasive marital interactions between long-married men and women have also been associated with negative health changes (Kiecolt-Glaser, Glaser, Cacioppo, et al., 1997). However, having social support (i.e., feelings that one is loved, valued, and cared for) is associated with positive health (S. Cohen & Lemay, 2007; S. E. Taylor, 2010). In fact, good relationships may moderate the link between hostility and poor health. In one study, hostile individuals in high-quality relationships showed reduced physiological reactivity to stress (Guyll, Cutrona, Burzette, & Russell, 2010). Although our discussion has focused on the direct physiological impact of stress on health, indirect pathways must also be considered. For example, an individual with a spouse or a large social network may receive encouragement for healthy eating habits, exercise, and other health-promoting activities, thus increasing resistance to disease.

Did You Know? Spirituality and religion appear to influence physical health. In one study of 5,300 African Americans, a group at risk for high blood pressure, those who were involved in religious activities had significantly lower blood pressure than those who were not. This effect was found even though members of the religious group were more likely to be overweight and less likely to take prescribed medications.

Source: S. Wyatt (2006)

Sociocultural Dimension

Discrimination, cultural expectations, and conflicts with societal standards can have a significant impact on health. Women are more likely to be affected by stress because of their role as caregivers for children, partners, and parents (Stambor, 2006).

Social relationships are very important for women. In a longitudinal study of men and women, high loneliness in women (discrepancy between actual and desired social relationships) was associated with a nearly 80 percent increase in coronary heart disease; this association was not found in men (Thurston & Kubzansky, 2009).

David Sacks/Getty Images

Maintaining Tradition and Reducing Risk

Japanese Americans who maintain traditional lifestyles have a lower rate of coronary heart disease than those who have acculturated to mainstream U.S. culture. The difference does not appear to be due to diet or other investigated risk factors.

Although genetic and other biological factors may perhaps partially explain the high rate of hypertension in African Americans, another line of research supports a sociocultural explanation. Exposure to racism and perceived discrimination can heighten stress responses and elevate blood pressure and heart rate (Pascoe & Richman, 2009). African Americans who watched videos or imagined depictions of social situations involving racism showed increases in heart rate and blood pressure (C. Y. Fang & Myers, 2001; Jones, Harrell, Morris-Prather, Thomas, & Omowale, 1996). Similarly, elevations in cardiovascular responses were observed among a sample of African American men who were exposed to subtle racism (Merritt, Bennett, Williams, Edwards, & Sollers, 2006). Thus, exposure to discrimination may function as a chronic stressor and increase the chances of hypertension (Troxel, Matthews, Bromberger, & Tyrrell, 2003). This relationship may be more complicated, however, at least among African American women. Increases in blood pressure when exposed to racism were found among those who were least likely to seek social support, whereas those who frequently sought social support did not show this tendency (R. Clark, 2006). Thus, coping ability, resources, and social support may mitigate vascular reactivity in response to racism.

Cultural changes have been found to affect health in Samoa. Samoans have a culture that stresses rigid control of behaviors, including strict discipline for children, control of anger for females, and suppression of emotions in adults. M. S. Steele & McGarvey (1997) hypothesized that the Samoan traditional pattern in which women were expected to suppress their emotions might conflict with the expanded roles expected by modern young women, resulting in increases in blood pressure. In support of their hypothesis, the investigators found an interesting contrast: Increases in blood pressure occurred when young women inhibited their anger, whereas among older women, blood pressure increased when they outwardly expressed anger. Thus, the roles or behavior patterns the women were socialized to (modern or traditional) appeared to influence their physiological response to expressions of anger (i.e., blood pressure increased when they behaved in a manner contrary to the way in which they had been socialized).

CHECKPOINT REVIEW

1. In what way do biological stress responses influence different psychophysiological disorders?
2. Which psychological characteristics tend to increase or moderate against psychophysiological reactivity?
3. In what ways do social or sociocultural factors contribute to psychophysiological disorders?

Treatment of Psychophysiological Disorders

Psychotherapy can effectively treat symptoms of psychophysiological disorders. For example, individuals who learn stress management techniques show reductions in stress hormones and report less pain, less anxiety, improved sleep, and a higher quality of life (Mommersteeg, Keijsers, Heijnen, Verbraak, & van Doornen,

2006; Tyre, 2004). Similarly, therapeutic interventions such as relaxation training, cognitive therapy, and biofeedback can reduce headaches (NINDS, 2007). Treatment programs for psychophysiological disorders generally consist of both medical treatment for the physical symptoms and psychological therapy to eliminate stress and anxiety. This combination provides a wide array of treatment options. Psychological approaches for stress management often include relaxation training, biofeedback, or cognitive-behavioral therapy.

Relaxation Training

Relaxation training is a therapeutic technique in which a person acquires the ability to relax the muscles of the body in almost any circumstance. It is possible that this reduces the fight-or-flight reaction triggered by muscle tension (Marr, 2006). Progressive muscle relaxation has been effective in reducing physiological arousal and the impact of stressors (Rausch, Gramling, & Auerbach, 2006; Trautmann & Kroner-Herwig, 2010). Imagine that you are a client who is beginning relaxation training. You are instructed to concentrate on one set of muscles at a time—first tensing them and then relaxing them. First you clench your fists as tightly as possible for approximately 10 seconds, then you release them. As you release your tightened muscles, you are asked to focus on the sensation of warmth and looseness in your hands. You practice this tightening and relaxing cycle several times before proceeding to the next muscle group, in your lower arms. After each muscle group has received individual attention in tensing and relaxing, the trainer asks you to tighten and then relax your entire body. The emphasis throughout the procedure is on the contrast between the feelings produced during tensing and those produced during relaxing. For a novice, the entire exercise lasts about 30 minutes. Relaxation-based treatment such as this has produced "clinically significant" reductions in headache activity among people with recurrent headaches (Trautmann & Kroener-Herwig, 2010).

Biofeedback Training

In **biofeedback training**, the client is taught to *voluntarily* control some physiological functions, such as heart rate or blood pressure. During training, the client receives second-by-second information (feedback) regarding the physiological activity being monitored. For someone attempting to lower high blood pressure, for example, the feedback would involve actual blood pressure readings, which are presented visually on a screen or via auditory signals transmitted through a set of headphones. The biofeedback device helps the client learn to control the targeted physiological function with the goal of continued improvement without relying on the feedback device.

Case Study

A 23-year-old male reported that when he was nervous about exams his resting heart rate increased to 95–120 beats per minute. He sought treatment due to concern that his anxiety might lead to a serious cardiac condition. The treatment consisted of eight sessions of biofeedback training, during which his heart rate was monitored and he was provided with both a visual and an auditory feedback signal. After the treatment, his heart rate had stabilized and was within normal limits (73 beats per minute). Even 1 year later, he was able to control his heart rate during stressful situations by both relaxing and concentrating on reducing the heart rate (Janssen, 1983).

relaxation training a therapeutic technique in which a person acquires the ability to relax the muscles of the body in almost any circumstance

biofeedback training a physiological and behavioral approach in which an individual receives information regarding particular autonomic functions and is rewarded for influencing those functions in a desired direction

Biofeedback works because the feedback received serves as reinforcement. It has been used to help people lower their heart rates and decrease their blood pressure during stressful situations (K. West, 2007), to treat migraine and tension headaches (M. S. Schwartz & Andrasik, 2003), to decrease the need for asthma medication (Lehrer et al., 2004), and to reduce muscle tension (Fogel, 2003).

Michael A. Keller/CORBIS

Controlling Physiological Responses

Meditation is associated with a relaxed bodily state produced by minimizing distractions and focusing on a positive image, mantra, or word. This process has been associated with a reduction in the level of stress hormones and the development of a sense of control.

Cognitive-Behavioral Therapy

Because hostility is associated with hypertension, cognitive-behavioral programs have been developed to reduce the expression of this emotion. In one study, individuals with hypertension participated in a 6-week anger management program (Larkin & Zayfert, 1996). When initially exposed to confrontational role-playing situations, they experienced sharp rises in blood pressure. The participants learned to relax by using muscle relaxation techniques and to change their thoughts about confrontational situations. They also received assertiveness training to learn appropriate ways of expressing disagreements. After the various types of training, their blood pressure was significantly reduced when they again participated in confrontational role-playing scenes.

Social-cognitive processing approaches can help individuals who have been told they have a life-threatening disease attempt to adjust and find validation and meaning in the experience. This approach is helpful for those who may see the world as unfair, who are experiencing reactive depression or avoidance, or who find it difficult to process the disease experience. In a study of 70 female cancer patients, cognitive processing opportunities were found to predict adjustment to cancer (Cordova, Cunningham, Carlson, & Andrykowski, 2001). Those who were unable to cognitively process their diseases because of invalidation ("When I talk about cancer, my husband tells me I'm living in the past") or discomfort ("It's difficult to share with those you love, as they are scared, too"; p. 709) reported more depressive symptoms. In contrast, women who reported being able to talk about cancer were less depressed and better adjusted.

Cognitive strategies to improve coping skills and to manage stress have also been effective in improving both physiological functioning and psychological distress in individuals with chronic illness (Cruess et al., 2000). Improved immune functioning and reduced cortisol levels (associated with a reduction in stress) were found among breast cancer patients who participated in cognitive-behavioral treatment, whereas patients in a control group continued to show deterioration of their immune response (Witek-Janusek et al., 2008). In a 1-year follow-up study, prostate and breast cancer patients who learned techniques to cope with stress showed improved quality of life and cortisol levels suggestive of lower levels of stress (L. E. Carlson, Speca, Faris, & Patel, 2007). With many diseases, having the opportunity to express fears, to cognitively process beliefs, and to develop adaptive strategies appears to improve feelings of well-being and physical health.

CHECKPOINT REVIEW

1. Compare and contrast relaxation therapy and biofeedback training.
2. Describe how cognitive-behavioral interventions are used to treat stress disorders and reactions to serious illness.

Summary

1 What are acute and post-traumatic stress disorders, and how are they diagnosed?

- Acute and post-traumatic stress disorders involve exposure to a traumatic event, resulting in intrusive memories of the occurrence, attempts to forget or repress the memories, emotional withdrawal, and increased arousal.
- In acute stress disorder (ASD) these symptoms last up to 1 month, while in posttraumatic stress disorder (PTSD) the symptoms remain for more than 1 month.

2 What causes acute and post-traumatic stress disorders?

- Possible biological factors involve a sensitized autonomic nervous system, stress hormones, and alterations in the brain. Psychological factors include anxiety, depression, and maladaptive cognitions. Poor or inadequate support during childhood has been identified as a risk factor, as have various sociocultural factors, such as gender and stressful immigration experiences.

3 What are possible treatments for acute and post-traumatic stress disorders?

- Antidepressant medication is somewhat successful in the treatment of ASD and PTSD. Exposure and cognitive-based therapies have also proven effective.

4 What role does stress play in physical health, and what are psychophysiological disorders?

- External events that place a physical or psychological demand on a person can serve as stressors and can affect physical health.
- A psychophysiological disorder is any physical disorder that has a strong psychological component. Psychophysiological disorders involve actual tissue damage (such as coronary heart disease), a disease process (immune impairment), or physiological dysfunction (as in asthma or migraine headaches).
- Not everyone develops an illness when exposed to the same stressor or traumatic event. Individuals may react to the same stressor in very different ways.

5 What causes psychophysiological disorders?

- Biological explanations include (a) chronic activation of the sympathetic nervous system and continual release of stress hormones, and (b) genetic contributions.
- Psychological contributors include characteristics such as helplessness, isolation, cynicism, pessimism, and hostility, as well as feelings of depression or anxiety.
- Social contributors include having an inadequate social network; abrasive interpersonal interactions; childhood maltreatment, a stressful environment, and, for men, being unmarried.
- Sociocultural factors such as gender, racial, and ethnic background are risk factors in certain physiological disorders. Stressful environments associated with poverty, prejudice, racism, and cultural conflicts have been related to illnesses.

6 What methods have been developed to treat psychophysiological disorders?

- These disorders are treated through stress management or anxiety management programs, combined with medical treatment for physical symptoms or conditions.
- Relaxation training and biofeedback training, which help the client learn to control muscular or internal functioning, are usually a part of such programs.
- Cognitive-behavioral interventions, which involve changing anxiety-arousing thoughts, have also been useful.

Key Terms

stressor 120
stress 120
acute stress disorder (ASD) 120
post-traumatic stress disorder (PTSD) 120
hypervigilance 121
amygdala 124
hypothalamic-pituitary-adrenal (HPA) axis 124
epinephrine 124
cortisol 124
homeostasis 124
psychophysiological disorder 128
coronary heart disease (CHD) 129
atherosclerosis 129
blood pressure 131
normal blood pressue 131
systolic pressure 131
diastolic pressure 131
hypertension 131
prehypertension 131
migraine headache 132
aura 133
tension headache 133
cluster headache 134
asthma 134
sympathetic nervous system 138
relaxation training 142
biofeedback training 142

Media Resources

Psychology CourseMate

Access an interactive e-book and chapter-specific interactive learning tools, including:

- flashcards
- quizzes
- videos

and more in your Psychology CourseMate.

Go to **CengageBrain.com**.

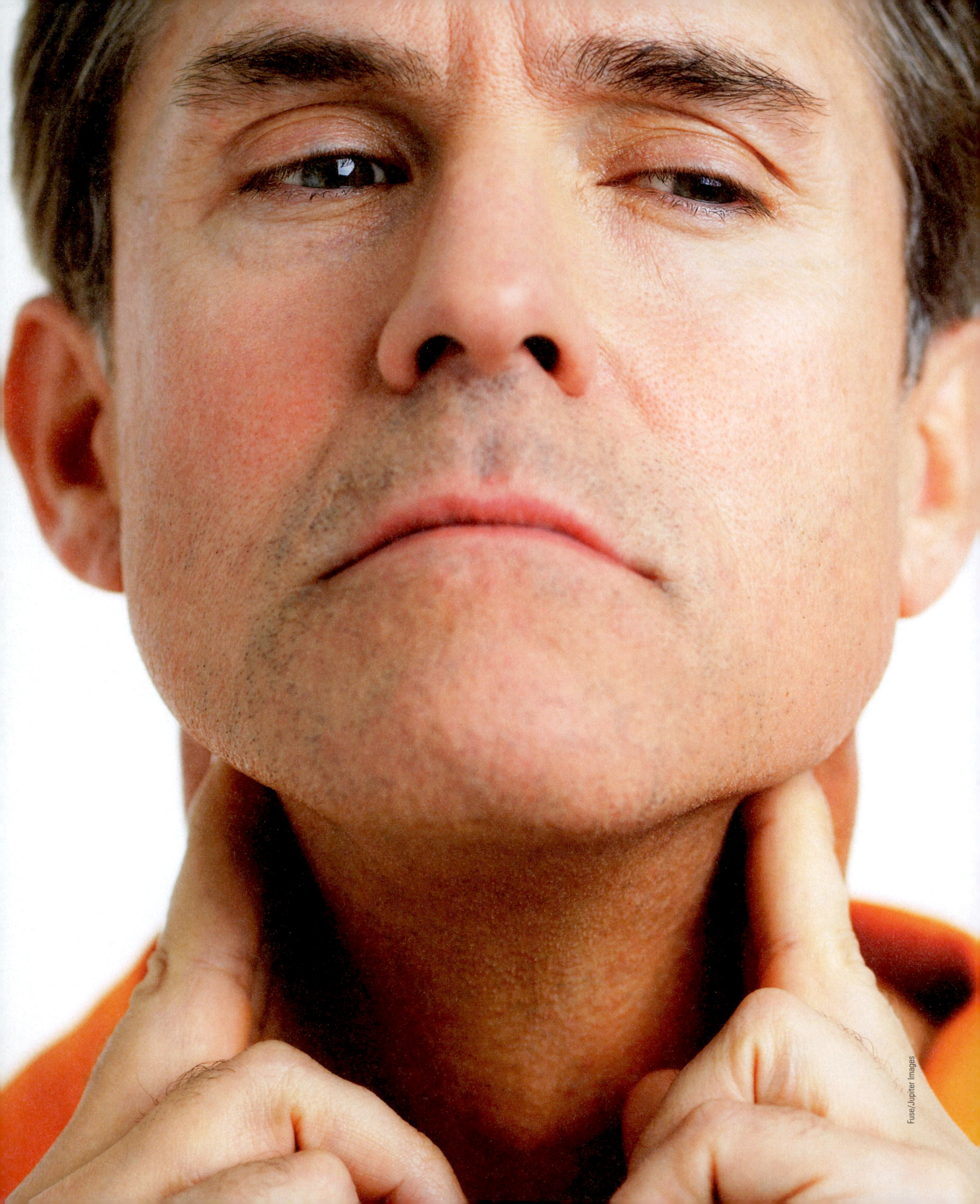

Fuse/Jupiter Images

6

Somatic Symptom and Dissociative Disorders

CHAPTER OUTLINE

A boy of 12 was referred for evaluation because he suddenly began to walk in an unusual staggering manner, which on close inspection appeared to be voluntary and deliberate. A comprehensive clinical examination showed no neurological abnormality. Shortly before his symptoms developed, he was promoted, with his peer group, to an academically rigorous secondary school. He was unable to meet the high academic expectations, and the teacher who taught his favorite subject humiliated him by rejecting classwork he had done and throwing his workbook on the floor (P. M. Leary, 2003, p. 436).

Joe Bieger, a beloved husband, father, grandfather, and high school assistant athletic director, walked out of his front door one morning with his two dogs. Minutes later, his very identity was seemingly wiped from his brain's hard drive. For 25 days he wandered the streets of Dallas, unable to remember what his name was, what he did for a living, or where he lived, until finally a contractor he had been working with happened to recognize him (Associated Press, 2007b).

FOCUS QUESTIONS

1 When do somatic complaints represent a psychological disorder? What are the causes and treatments of these conditions?

2 What are dissociations? What forms can they take? How are they caused, and how are they treated?

In this chapter, we discuss (a) somatic symptom disorders, conditions that involve distressing health anxiety or thoughts related to physical complaints or bodily symptoms; and (b) dissociative disorders, which involve alterations in memory, consciousness, or identity. These disorders, and the genuine distress experienced by those who have them, often occur because of underlying psychological or social factors. We discuss somatic symptom and dissociative disorders together because research shows they have common etiological roots (Farina, Mazzotti, Pasquini, Nijenhuis, & De Giannantonio, 2011). Those with somatic symptom disorders often express stress through physical symptoms, while dissociative disorders are thought to involve psychological mechanisms for coping with stress (Cloninger & Dokucu, 2008). We begin with a discussion of the somatic symptom disorders.

Somatic Symptom Disorders

The somatic symptom disorders are a disparate group of disorders, including somatic symptom disorder, illness anxiety disorder, conversion disorder (functional neurological symptom disorder), and factitious disorder. The somatic symptom disorders are grouped together because they involve expression of physical symptoms or anxiety over illness (DSM-5 Work Groups, 2012). Psychophysiological disorders, discussed in Chapter 5, are also considered part of this category. Differences between the somatic symptom disorders are shown in Table 6.1.

Somatic Symptom Disorder

Case Study

Cheryl, a 38-year-old, separated Italian American woman, was raising her 10-year-old daughter, Melanie, without much support. Cheryl had a history of several abusive relationships and unresolved grief about the loss of her mother. Cheryl became extremely distressed by episodes of vertigo and a variety of vague somatic complaints, including neck pain. When Cheryl was incapacitated, Melanie helped comfort her, providing remedies such as back rubs and hot compresses or taking over activities such as grocery shopping if Cheryl felt dizzy in the store. Cheryl and Melanie both described the efficiency with which Melanie provided comfort and assistance (McDaniel & Speice, 2001).

somatic symptom disorders broad grouping of psychological disorders that involve physical symptoms or anxiety over illness including somatic symptom disorder, illness anxiety disorder, conversion disorder (functional neurological symptom disorder), and factitious disorder

somatic symptom disorder (SSD) condition involving a pattern of reporting distressing physical symptoms combined with extreme concern about health or fears of undiagnosed medical conditions

somatic symptoms distressing physical or bodily symptoms

somatic symptom disorder (SSD) with predominately somatic complaints a subtype of SSD involving chronic complaints of specific bodily symptoms that have no physical basis

Individuals diagnosed with **somatic symptom disorder (SSD)** have a pattern of reporting pain or other distressing physical or bodily symptoms, referred to as **somatic symptoms**, for at least 6 months. They also have excessive, often life-disrupting, responses to these symptoms, including extreme concern about their health or fears that undiagnosed medical conditions are causing their symptoms. SSD involves not only excessive focus on somatic symptoms, but also catastrophic thoughts related to these symptoms (Burton, McGorm, Weller, & Sharpe, 2010; A. Martin & Rief, 2011). See Table 6.2 for types of somatic complaints reported by individuals with SSD.

Individuals with **SSD with predominately somatic complaints** (previously known as *somatization disorder*) report a variety of physical complaints that can involve discomfort in different parts of the body; gastrointestinal symptoms such as nausea, diarrhea, and bloating; sexual symptoms such as sexual indifference, irregular menses, or erectile dysfunction; and pseudoneurological symptoms such as amnesia

DISORDERS CHART SOMATIC SYMPTOM DISORDERS

TABLE 6.1

Disorder	Identifiable Medical Condition?	Voluntarily Produced?	Cognitive Distortions Regarding Illness?
Psychophysiological disorders*	Yes	No	No
Somatic symptom disorder	Sometimes	No	Yes
Illness anxiety disorder	No, but may involve mild somatic symptoms	No	Yes
Conversion disorder	No, but involves physical or mental symptoms	No	No
Factitious disorder	Possibly, but self-induced	Yes	No

*Covered in Chapter 5.

or breathing difficulties (Yates, 2010). Approximately 2 percent of women and less than 0.2 percent of men have been diagnosed with this form of SSD (Yates, 2010). The diagnosis is more prevalent in African Americans and among those with less than a high school education or lower socioeconomic status (Noyes, Stuart, Watson, & Langbehn, 2006). Although it is considered a chronic condition, in one large study only about half of those diagnosed with SSD with predominately somatic complaints met the criteria 12 months later (Steinbrecher & Hiller, 2011).

Somatic symptom disorder (SSD) with pain features, previously known as *pain disorder*, is characterized by reports of severe pain that (a) appears to have no physiological or neurological basis, (b) seems significantly greater than would be expected with an existing physical condition, or (c) lingers long after a physical injury has healed. It is often difficult to determine when pain is "excessive" or "lingering too

TABLE 6.2 Symptoms Reported by Patients With Somatic Symptom Disorder (SSD)

GASTROINTESTINAL SYMPTOMS	PSEUDONEUROLOGICAL SYMPTOMS
Vomiting	Amnesia
Abdominal pain	Difficulty swallowing
Nausea	Loss of voice
Bloating and excessive gas	Difficulty walking
	Seizures
PAIN SYMPTOMS	**REPRODUCTIVE ORGAN SYMPTOMS**
Diffuse pain	Burning sensation in sex organs
Pain in extremities	Pain during intercourse
Joint pain	Irregular menstrual cycles
Headaches	Excessive menstrual bleeding
CARDIOPULMONARY SYMPTOMS	**OTHER SYMPTOMS**
Shortness of breath at rest	Vague food allergies
Palpitations	"Hypoglycemia"
Chest pain	Chronic fatigue
Dizziness	Chemical sensitivity

Source: So (2008)

somatic symptom disorder (SSD) with pain features a subtype of SSD involving severe or lingering pain that appears to have no physical basis

Paul Hakimata Photography/Shutterstock.com

A Physical or Psychological Disorder?

Somatic symptom disorder with pain features is most frequently diagnosed in women, in members of minority groups, and in people living in poverty. How can we determine if the cause of the pain is psychological, physical, or both?

long," or if psychological factors are exacerbating pain sensitivity. Understandably, questioning the veracity of reports of pain can result in feelings of anger and frustration from patients (Furness, Glazebrook, Tay, Abbas, & Slaveska-Hollis, 2009). In one study (J. R. Walker & Furer, 2008), pain complaints included back pain (30 percent), joint pain (25 percent), pain in the extremities (20 percent), headache (19 percent), abdominal pain (11 percent), and chest pain (5 percent). Visits to physicians are frequent and patients sometimes become addicted to pain medication.

Chronic pain is relatively common and affects 30 percent of the U.S. population (B. M. Hoffman, Papas, Chatkoff, & Kerns, 2007; Turk, Swanson, & Tunks, 2008). Higher rates of chronic pain are reported by women, individuals from lower socioeconomic classes, African Americans, and Latinos (Poleshuck et al., 2010). Unexplained physical pain involving the abdomen, head, and limbs is also frequently present in young children (Furness et al., 2009; Hunfeld et al., 2002).

Deciding if someone meets the diagnostic criteria for SSD can be problematic. Depending on the particular primary care setting, 10 to 50 percent of all patients are described as expressing excessive concerns over physical symptoms (I. A. Arnold, de Waal, Eekhoff, & van Hemert, 2006; McCarron, 2006; McGorm, Burton, Weller, Murray, & Sharpe, 2010). Many undergo unnecessary surgical or assessment procedures. Although medical professionals sometimes believe that those with SSD are faking their symptoms (So, 2008), mental health professionals do not consider SSD to be under voluntary or conscious control (Parish & Yutzy, 2011). Reassuring those with SSD that there is no serious medical problem usually does not alleviate their concerns, and their search for answers continues (Lahmann, Loew, Tritt, & Nickel, 2008).

Sykes (2007) points out that it is often difficult to determine whether physical complaints are, in fact, disproportionate or simply not fully explained. Many researchers and clinicians are moving away from the view that SSD is *only* "psychological" in nature and now acknowledge that many people with SSD have accompanying medical conditions (Dimsdale, 2011).

Illness Anxiety Disorder

Case Study

A 41-year-old woman, Linda, reported having a history of concerns about cancer, especially stomach or bowel cancer. Her grandmother had bowel cancer when Linda was 22. Media stories of illness, medical documentaries, or reading about people who are ill triggers her worries: "I notice a feeling of discomfort and bloating in my abdomen. I wonder if this could be an early sign of cancer. Cancer is something that can happen at my age. People can have very few symptoms and then suddenly it is there and a few months later they are gone." (Furer & Walker, 2005, p. 261)

The primary characteristic of **illness anxiety disorder** (previously called *hypochondriasis*) is a chronic pattern (at least 6 months) of significantly distressing and disruptive anxiety about one's health when minimal or no somatic symptoms are present. Individuals with health-related anxiety and fixation over illness would receive the diagnosis of SSD (DSM-5 Work Groups, 2012).

illness anxiety disorder persistent health anxiety and concern that one has an undetected physical illness with no or minimal somatic symptoms

Those with illness anxiety concerns do the following:

- *catastrophize* and view ambiguous or mild somatic symptoms as indications of a severe or catastrophic illness,

TABLE 6.3 Percentage of Adults With Illness Anxiety Disorder Who Endorse Selected Fears Related to Health

ITEM	MUCH AGREE OR VERY MUCH AGREE (%)
When I notice my heart beating rapidly, I worry I might have a heart attack.	51
When I get aches or pains, I worry that there is something wrong with my health.	75
It scares me when I feel "shaky" (trembling).	47
It scares me when I feel tingling or prickling sensations in my hands.	50
When I feel a strong pain in my stomach, I worry it might be cancer.	62

Source: J. R. Walker & Furer (2008)

- *overgeneralize* by believing that serious illness and fatal conditions are prevalent,
- *display all-or-none thinking* by believing they must be symptom free to be healthy, and
- *show selective attention* to medical information and focus primarily on threatening information (Fulton, Marcus, & Merkey, 2011).

Illness anxiety disorder is considered cognitively based because the individual misinterprets bodily variations or sensations as indications of a serious illness or undetected disease (K. S. White, Craft, & Gervino, 2010). When unpleasant or "unusual" symptoms are identified, this bodily focus produces feelings of extreme alarm (Lahmann et al., 2008; Sorensen, Birket-Smith, Wattar, Buemann, & Salkovskis, 2011).

Those with illness anxiety disorder often excessively check for signs of illness or disease, seek reassurance from others or through researching possible diseases, and avoid activities or circumstances they believe might result in an illness. Paradoxically, these behaviors only serve to increase anxiety (Olatunji, Etzel, Tomarken, Ciesielski, & Deacon, 2011). It is estimated that approximately 4 to 6 percent of those who visit doctors have illness anxiety disorder (Yates, 2010). See Table 6.3 for examples of the fears related to health seen in individuals with illness anxiety disorder.

The expression of psychological and social distress through physical symptoms is the norm in many cultures of the world:

- Worldwide, the most common somatic symptoms are gastrointestinal complaints or abnormal skin sensations, whereas in the United States menstrual pain, abdominal pain, and chest pain are the most common somatic symptoms.
- Distinctive cultural somatic symptoms include concerns about body odor (Japan), body heat and coldness (Nigeria), loss of semen while urinating (India), and kidney weakness (China).

Source: B. S. Singh (2007)

Conversion Disorder (Functional Neurological Symptom Disorder)

Case Study

A., a 34-year-old woman, described frequent attacks of sudden onset, often resembling sleep but sometimes involving violent jerking of her arms and legs and arching of her back. She experienced violent outbursts. She viewed herself as disabled and needing constant care and was extremely dependent on her partner and teenage stepsons (Howlett & Reuber, 2009, p. 129). Interviews revealed that she was raped at the age of 13 by her biological father and was very traumatized by the death of her grandparents.

Case Study

A boy, age 10, was first believed to have a case of juvenile myasthenia gravis (weakening of the voluntary muscles). For 5 weeks he had been unable to open his eyes, and the consequent "blindness" had stopped him from attending school. On detailed physical examination, no other abnormalities were found. In the hospital ward it was noted that he did not walk into furniture. He was the village football star and had been blamed for his team's defeat, and from that day he had been unable to open his eyes. (P. M. Leary, 2003, p. 436)

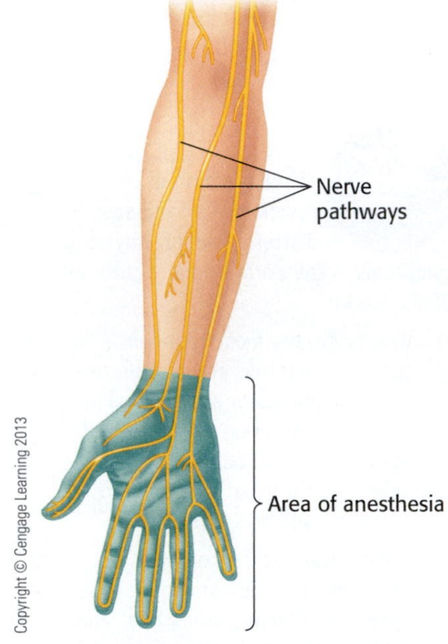

FIGURE 6.1

Glove Anesthesia

In glove anesthesia, the lack of feeling covers the hand in a glovelike shape. It does not correspond to the distribution of nerve pathways. This discrepancy leads to a diagnosis of functional neurological symptom disorder.

conversion disorder (functional neurological symptom disorder) a condition involving sensory or motor impairment suggestive of a neurological disorder but with no underlying medical cause

psychogenic originating from psychological causes

malingering feigning illness for an external purpose

Conversion disorder (functional neurological symptom disorder) involves motor, sensory, or seizurelike symptoms that are incongruent with any recognized neurological or medical disorder. The most common conversion symptoms seen in neurological clinics involve **psychogenic** movement disorders such as disturbances of stance and walking, sensory symptoms such as blindness, loss of voice, motor tics, dizziness, and psychogenic seizures (Hesapcioglu, Aktepe, Zeynep, & Dandil, 2010; J. H. Friedman & LaFrance, 2010; S. A. Marshall, Landau, Carroll, & Schwieters, 2008). Neurologists report that about 2 to 3 percent of new referrals involve cases of conversion disorder (J. H. Friedman & LaFrance, 2010). Individuals with this disorder are not consciously faking symptoms, as are those who are **malingering** (feigning illness for an external purpose such as getting out of work duties). A person with conversion disorder believes that the problem is genuine and not under his or her control (Voon et al., 2010).

As illustrated in the case studies, the appearance of conversion symptoms is often related to traumas or even milder stressors such as the loss of employment or divorce (Jankovic, 2011; S. A. Marshall et al., 2008). Nearly 75 percent of respondents in one sample reported that their conversion symptoms developed after they had experienced a stressor (S. P. Singh & Lee, 1997). In a 10-year follow-up study of individuals diagnosed with conversion disorder, symptoms persisted in about 40 percent of the cases (Mace & Trimble, 1996). Sudden onset, shorter duration of symptoms, and a good premorbid (before the illness) personality are associated with positive outcome (Crimlisk, Bhatia, Cope, & David, 1998; S. P. Singh & Lee, 1997).

In general, individuals with conversion disorder do not incur any physical damage from the symptoms. For example, a person with psychogenic paralysis of the legs rarely shows the atrophy of the lower limbs that occurs when there is an underlying biological cause. In some persistent cases, however, long-term disuse *can* result in atrophy (Schonfeldt-Lecuona, Connemann, Spitzer, & Herwig, 2003). Some symptoms—such as an inability to talk or whisper combined with the ability to cough or *glove anesthesia* (Figure 6.1), which involves a loss of feeling in the hand ending in a straight line at the wrist—are easily diagnosed as symptoms of conversion disorder, because coughing indicates intact vocal cord function and in glove anesthesia, the area of sensory loss does not correspond to the distribution of nerves in the body (R. J. Brown, 2004). Other symptoms may require extensive neurological and physical examinations to rule out a true medical disorder before a diagnosis of conversion disorder can be made. Discriminating between this disorder and actual medical conditions can be difficult, because there are no specific tests to confirm the diagnosis (J. H. Friedman & LaFrance, 2010). For this reason, neurologists and other physicians are reluctant to make a diagnosis of conversion disorder unless they are absolutely certain (Kanaan, Armstrong, & Wessely, 2009).

Factitious Disorder and Factitious Disorder Imposed on Another

Case Study

Mandy was not hesitant to discuss how she was diagnosed with leukemia at the age of 37, right after her husband left her. She shared how chemotherapy damaged her immune system, liver, and heart, resulting in a stroke and weeks in a coma. She posted her story and updates on a Web site and the virtual community rallied to support her as she shared her story of additional surgeries and bouts of life-threatening infections. It was later discovered that Mandy was not sick and had made up the entire story (Kleeman, 2011).

Factitious disorders are mental disorders in which the symptoms of physical or mental illnesses are deliberately induced or simulated with no apparent incentive—other than attention from medical personnel or others (Catalina, Gomez, & de Cos, 2008). Factitious disorder involves inducing or simulating illness in oneself, whereas factitious disorder imposed on another involves inducing or falsifying illness in another. Before we discuss the factitious disorders, we should note that these disorders are completely different from malingering—faking a disorder to achieve some goal, such as an insurance settlement. With malingering, the specific goal is usually evident, and the individual can "turn off" the symptoms whenever they are no longer useful. In factitious disorders, the purpose of the simulated or induced illness is much less apparent. Complex psychological variables are assumed to be involved, and the individual is usually unaware of the motivation for the behavior. Simulation of illness is often done almost compulsively.

Factitious Disorder

Factitious disorder is characterized by the presentation of oneself to others as ill or impaired through the recurrent falsification of physical or psychological symptoms. This is done without any obvious external rewards (DSM-5 Work Groups, 2012). In the past, this condition was called *hospital addiction* or *professional patient syndrome*. In 1951, it was given the name *Munchausen syndrome* after an 18th-century German nobleman who was noted for making up fanciful stories (Bande & Garcia-Alba, 2008).

Signs of factitious disorder may include lingering unexplained illnesses with multiple surgical or complex treatments; "remarkable willingness" to undergo painful or dangerous treatments such as amputations or prophylactic double mastectomy; a tendency to anger if the illness is questioned; and the involvement of multiple doctors (Gregory & Jindal, 2006; Worley, Feldman, & Hamilton, 2009). Depending on the study, the prevalence rate for adults is about 1.3 percent and about 0.7 percent for adolescents (Ehrlich, Pfeiffer, Salbach, Lenz, & Lehmkuhl, 2008).

Factitious Disorder Imposed on Another Person

Case Study

A hidden camera at a children's hospital captured the image of a mother suffocating the baby she had brought in for treatment of breathing problems. In another case, a child was brought in for treatment of ulcerations on his

Continued

factitious disorder a disorder in which symptoms of illness are deliberately induced, simulated, or exaggerated, with no apparent external incentive

Case Study—cont'd

back; hospital staff discovered the mother had been rubbing oven cleaner on his skin. Another "sick" infant had been fed laxatives for nearly 4 months (Wartik, 1994). In each of these cases, no apparent motive was found other than the attention the parent received from the hospital staff caring for the child's "illness."

If an individual deliberately feigns or induces an illness in another person (or even a pet) in the absence of any obvious external rewards, the diagnosis is **factitious disorder imposed on another**; this condition is sometimes referred to as *Munchausen syndrome by proxy* (Brannon & Dunayevich, 2011). In the case examples, the mothers produced symptoms in their children. Because this diagnostic category is somewhat new, little information is available on prevalence, age of onset, or familial patterns. In the vast majority of cases, the individual is a mother who appears to be loving and attentive toward her infant or young child while simultaneously sabotaging the child's health, sometimes by poisoning or suffocation (Kannai, 2009; D. M. Siegel, 2009). Warning signs involve physical symptoms that occur only when the mother or caretaker is around and insistence on medical tests that are unnecessary or invasive. A mortality rate of up to 9 percent of those targeted has been reported either from the abuse itself or from invasive medical procedures (Abdulhamid & Pataki, 2011).

Diagnosis of this condition is difficult, and some believe that the diagnosis is so unclear, unreliable, and subject to misdiagnosis that it should be eliminated as a psychiatric diagnosis (Butz, Evans, & Webber-Dereszynski, 2009). Cases of false accusations against parents have been reported (C. Smith, 2002). What safeguards should be put in place to balance protection of a child with the possibility of a false accusation against a parent?

Etiology of Somatic Symptom Disorders

In the majority of cases, multiple factors contribute to the development of somatic symptom, illness anxiety, conversion, and factitious disorders, as evidenced by the multipath model, which includes biological, psychological, social, and sociocultural dimensions (Figure 6.2).

Biological Dimension Research involving twin (K. Kato, Sullivan, Evengard, & Pedersen, 2009) and family studies (Noyes, Holt, Happel, Kathol, & Yagla, 1997) suggests that genetic factors make only a modest contribution to the somatic symptom disorders. Environmental influences appear to play a much greater role. However, biological vulnerabilities such as lower pain thresholds and heightened sensitivity to pain, as well as greater sensitivity to somatic cues, have been hypothesized to play an important role in the development of somatic symptoms or health anxiety (Katzer, Oberfeld, Hiller, Gerlach, & Witthoft, 2012; Kellner, 1985; Starcevic, 2005). A biological predisposition, hardwired into the central nervous system, can result in (a) hypervigilance or exaggerated focus on bodily sensation, (b) increased sensitivity to even mild bodily changes, and (c) a tendency to react to somatic sensations with alarm (S. Taylor, Jang, Stein, & Asmundson, 2008).

It is also possible that repetitive activation of the sympathetic nervous system due to chronic exposure to stressors can lead to increased sensitivity of the nerves associated with pain and subsequent increases in pain sensation (Farrugia & Fetter, 2009; Sauer, Burris, & Carlson, 2010). The finding that war veterans with combat exposure are more likely to report high levels of somatic symptoms than are veterans

factitious disorder imposed on another a pattern of falsification or production of physical or psychological symptoms in another individual

without exposure to trauma supports this hypothesis (Ginzburg & Solomon, 2010). Conversion disorder may result from abnormal actions of inhibitory neural systems. For example, MRIs were used to examine a patient with "hysterical mutism" before and after successful psychotherapy. Before treatment, there was evidence of impaired connectivity in the speech network; it disappeared after treatment (R. A. Bryant & Das, 2012).

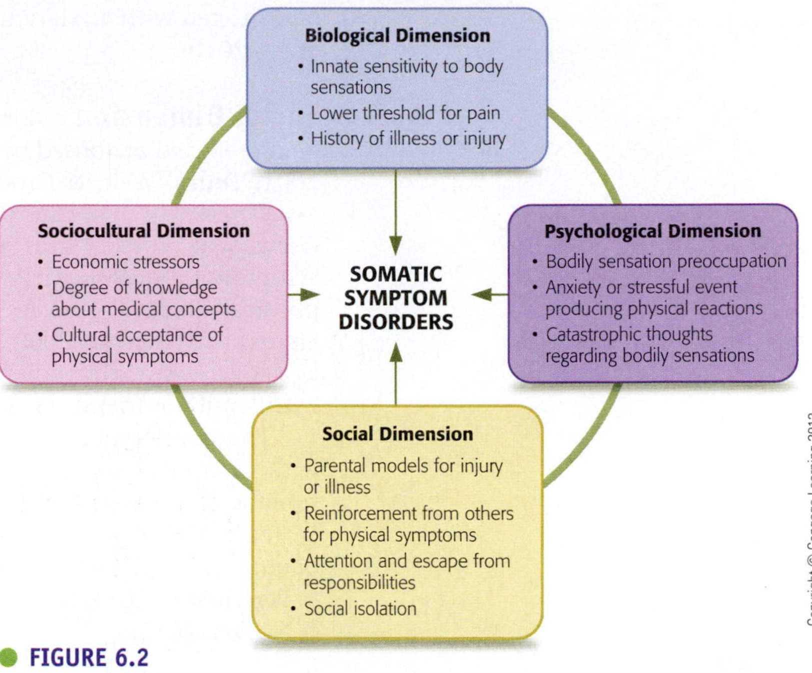

FIGURE 6.2

Multipath Model of Somatic Symptom Disorders

The dimensions interact with one another and combine in different ways to result in a specific somatic symptom disorder.

Psychological Dimension Reinforcement, modeling, catastrophic cognitions, or a combination of these can play a role in the development of somatic symptom disorders. Some researchers contend that people with these disorders assume the "sick role" because it is reinforcing and because it allows them to escape unpleasant circumstances or to avoid responsibilities (Datta, Basu, & Bandyopadhyay, 2011; Turk et al., 2008). Not surprisingly, many individuals with SSDs have experiences associated with convalescence, including serious illness, physical injury, and depression (Burton et al., 2010; Starcevic, 2005); in fact, these situations are all associated with an increased risk of developing SSD (Leiknes, Finset, Moum, & Sandanger, 2008). The importance of reinforcement was evident in a study of male pain patients. Men with wives who were supportive and attentive to pain cues reported significantly greater pain when their wives were present than when their wives were absent. The reverse was true of patients whose wives were nonsupportive: Reports of pain were greater when their wives were absent (D. Williamson, Robinson, & Melamed, 1997).

Cognitive factors are also believed to be important in the etiology of somatic symptom disorders (Avia & Ruiz, 2005; Furer & Walker, 2005; Lipsitt & Starcevic, 2006; Severeijns, Vlaeyen, van den Hout, & Picavet, 2004). According to this perspective, somatic symptoms may develop in individuals who are predisposed—that is, who have somatic sensitivity, a low pain threshold, or a history of illness, or have received parental attention for somatic symptoms—in the following manner (Abramowitz, Taylor, & McKay, 2010; Starcevic, 2005; J. R. Walker & Furer, 2008):

1. External triggers (traumatic or anxiety-evoking stressors) or internal triggers (anxiety-producing thoughts such as "My father died of cancer at age 47") result in physiological arousal.
2. The individual perceives bodily changes such as increased heart rate or respiration.
3. Thoughts and worries about possible disease begin in response to these sensations.
4. Bodily sensations become amplified because of these thoughts, causing even more bodily sensations and concern.
5. Catastrophic thoughts increase in response to the magnified bodily sensations, creating a circular feedback pattern.

Consistent with this perspective, individuals with somatic symptom disorders have been shown to unrealistically interpret and overestimate the dangerousness of bodily symptoms (Haenen, de Jong, Schmidt, Stevens, & Visser, 2000; P. G. Williams, Smith, & Jordan, 2010). Similarly, individuals reporting chest pain in the absence of cardiac pathology were attuned to cardiac-related symptoms and reacted with anxiety to heart palpitations and chest discomfort (K. S. White et al., 2010).

Social Dimension Some individuals with somatic symptom disorders report being rejected or abused by family members and feeling unloved (Rivera & Borda, 2001; Tunks, Weir, & Crook, 2008). A history of sexual abuse or rape has been associated with chronic pelvic pain and gastrointestinal disorders in women (Paras et al., 2009). More than 50 percent of a sample of individuals with somatic symptom, illness anxiety, or conversion disorder had experienced a serious physical illness in the preceding 12 months (G. C. Smith, Clarke, Handrinos, Dunsis, & McKenzie, 2000). Some patients may seek out contact with medical staff as a source of reinforcement because of social isolation or an inability to connect with family or friends (S. Stuart & Noyes, 2005).

The development of illness or injury sensitivity appears to be closely linked with parental characteristics such as being preoccupied with or overly attentive to somatic complaints expressed by their children (Watt, O'Connor, Stewart, Moon, & Terry, 2008). Additionally, individuals with somatic symptom disorders frequently have parents or family members with chronic physical illnesses (Schulte & Petermann, 2011; Starcevic, 2005) or high health anxiety (Schulte, Petermann, & Noeker, 2010).

Did You Know?

In the 2nd century, hysteria in women was believed to be a result of sexual deprivation. Treatment involved marriage or, for women who remained single, vaginal massage by a midwife. Later, physicians treated the condition by producing "hysterical paroxysm," or orgasm, in women. An electric vibrator was advertised in a Sears catalog in 1918 to treat hysteria (Maines, 1999).

Sociocultural Dimension Functional neurological symptom disorder, initially called *hysteria*, was originally viewed as a problem that afflicted only women; in fact, it derived its name from *hystera*, the ancient Greek word for uterus. Hippocrates believed that a shift or movement of the uterus resulted in complaints of breathing difficulties, anesthesia, and seizures. He presumed that the movement was due to the uterus "wanting a child." However, others argued that hysteria was more prevalent in women because social mores did not provide them with appropriate channels for the expression of aggression or sexuality (Satow, 1979).

Cultural factors can influence the frequency, expression, and interpretation of somatic complaints. Risk factors associated with somatic symptom disorders include lower educational levels, ethnicity, and immigrant status (Noyes, Stuart, et al., 2006). Among Asian populations, physical complaints often occur in reaction to stress (Ryder et al., 2008; D. W. Sue & Sue, 2013). Some African groups express somatic complaints, such as feelings of heat, crawling sensations, and numbness, that differ from those expressed in Western cultures (R. J. Brown & Lewis-Fernandez, 2011). Reports of pain also differ between white and Latino patients with Latinos reporting more pain, perhaps due to the cultural acceptance of physical problems as an expression of distress (Hernandez & Sachs-Ericsson, 2006).

Differences such as those just described may reflect different cultural views of the relationship between mind and body. The dominant view in Western culture is the *psychosomatic* perspective: Psychological conflicts are expressed in physical complaints. But many other cultures have a *somatopsychic* perspective: Physical problems are thought to produce psychological and emotional symptoms. Although we probably believe that our psychosomatic view is the correct one, the somatopsychic view is the dominant perspective in most cultures.

Treatment of Somatic Symptom Disorders

Although somatic symptom disorders are considered difficult to treat, newer biological and psychological treatments are showing some success. Therapists now realize that it is necessary to focus on mind-body connections, understand clients' perspectives regarding their somatic symptoms, and acknowledge the role of stressors in the development of physical complaints, as seen in the following case study.

Case Study

Mr. X, a 68-year-old Chinese man, reported sleep disturbance, loss of appetite, dizziness, and a sensation of tightness around his chest. Several episodes of chest pain led to admission and medical evaluation at the local hospital. All results, including tests for heart disease, were normal. He was referred for psychiatric consultation. Because traditional Chinese views of medicine recognize an interconnection between mind and body, the psychiatrist accepted and showed interest in the somatic symptoms, such as their onset, duration, and exacerbating and relieving factors. Medication was provided as a supportive treatment. A stressor was identified that involved arguments with Mr. X's wife. Suggestions were made on how to improve communication, which led to a decrease in physical complaints. (Yeung & Deguang, 2002)

Biological Treatment Antidepressant medications such as selective serotonin reuptake inhibitors are used to treat somatic symptom disorder (S. Taylor, Asmundson, & Coons, 2005) and illness anxiety disorder (Schweitzer, Zafar, Pavlicova, & Fallon, 2011). For conversion disorder, interventions involving increased physical activity are recommended (G. C. Smith et al., 2000).

Psychological Treatments A fundamental focus of treatment involves understanding the client's view regarding his or her problem. Individuals with somatic symptom disorders are often frustrated, disappointed, and angry following years of encounters with the medical profession. They believe that treatment strategies have been ineffective and resent the implication that they are "fakers" or "problem patients" (Frohm & Beehler, 2010; Lipsitt & Starcevic, 2006). Medical personnel often do, in fact, show negative reactions when interacting with individuals with somatic symptom disorders (Merten & Brunnhuber, 2004; P. G. Williams et al., 2010). Because of these reactions, patients and physicians may have a difficult time establishing a positive relationship.

A newer approach involves demonstrating empathy regarding the physical complaints and focusing on helping the individual develop better coping skills, as indicated in the following statement to a patient: "I don't know exactly the cause of your problem, and I'm not certain that I can provide immediate relief. Nevertheless, I will work with you as best I can to find solutions" (Monopoli, 2005, p. 293). Eliciting the patient's views and providing psychoeducation regarding the relationship between somatic symptoms, emotional state, and interpersonal relationships can enhance working relationships between physicians and patients with somatic symptom disorders (Poleshuck et al., 2010).

In another approach, somatic symptom disorders are viewed within a social context—a belief that somatic complaints are a reflection of unsatisfying or inadequate social relationships. Individuals who assume a "sick role" often receive some reinforcement, such as escape from responsibility or control of others through bodily complaints. Therapy is therefore directed toward developing and improving the individual's social network. A therapist may say something such as: "There is treatment available that may be helpful to you, if you would like to participate. This involves learning new ways of understanding and coping with stresses, other than going to the nearest emergency room. Treatment will also involve learning more about yourself and finding out what gets in the way of developing more fulfilling relationships" (Gregory & Jindal, 2006, p. 34).

Because many patients with somatic symptom disorders appear to have cognitive distortions, such as a conviction that they are especially vulnerable to

Did You Know?

A physician was called in to assist woman in labor. She had a melon-sized stomach and was writhing and groaning with pain. The physician later found that the woman was not pregnant but instead had pseudocyesis, a rare somatic symptom disorder involving numerous signs of pregnancy, including abdominal and breast enlargement and cessation of menses. It is believed that emotions can produce abnormal hormone secretions resulting in signs of pregnancy in nonpregnant women (Svoboda, 2006).

disease, cognitive-behavioral approaches focused on correcting these misinterpretations are successful (Abramowitz, Taylor, et al., 2010; Barsky & Ahern, 2004; Buwalda & Bouman, 2008). In one program, individuals with illness anxiety disorder (hypochondriasis) who had fears of having cancer, heart disease, or other fatal diseases were educated about the relationship between misinterpretations of bodily sensations and selective attention to illness themes. Six 2-hour group sessions covered topics such as "What Is Hypochondriasis?," "The Role of Your Thoughts," "Attention and Illness Anxiety," "Stress and Bodily Symptoms," and "Your Own Vicious Cycle." As homework, participants monitored and challenged hypochondriacal thoughts. After completing these sessions, most participants showed considerable improvement or no longer met the criteria for the disorder; the gains were maintained at a 6-month follow-up (Hiller, Leibbrand, Rief, & Fichter, 2002).

Because individuals with somatic symptom disorders often show a fear of internal bodily sensations, cognitive-behavioral therapists have utilized *interoceptive* exposure (exposure to bodily sensations) during treatment. Therapists ask clients to perform activities that typically trigger anxiety, such as breathing through a straw, hyperventilating, spinning, or climbing stairs, until feared reactions such as light-headedness, chest discomfort, or increased heart rate occur. The activities are performed over and over again until the bodily sensations no longer elicit anxiety or fear (Flink, Nicholas, Boersma, & Linton, 2009). Relaxation training can also effectively reduce sympathetic nervous system activity levels (Sauer et al., 2010). Mindfulness-based cognitive therapy, which reduces the impact of distressing thoughts regarding physical symptoms by having the client fully experience and observe the symptoms and thoughts without judgment or emotion, has been effective in treating somatic symptom disorders (Blacker, Herbert, Forman, & Kounios, 2012; Vowles, McCracken, & O'Brien, 2011; M. J. Williams, McManus, Muse, Williams, & Mark, 2011).

CHECKPOINT REVIEW

1. What are four characteristics of somatic symptom disorder?
2. How is illness anxiety disorder similar to and different from somatic symptom disorder?
3. Compare and contrast illness anxiety disorder with factitious disorder.
4. Cite research regarding the contribution of psychological, social, and sociocultural factors to somatic symptom disorders.

Dissociative Disorders

Case Study

A 29-year-old woman who was in China for an academic trip was found unconscious in the hotel bathroom. The woman was unable to remember her identity or any information about her life. Examinations showed no neurological abnormalities or evidence of substance use. She remained in an amnesiac state for 10 months, until blood on her fingers triggered memories of witnessing a murder in China and being unable to help the victim because of her fear. Once this memory surfaced, she began to remember other aspects of her life (Reinhold & Markowitsch, 2009).

The **dissociative disorders**—dissociative amnesia (localized, generalized, and fugue), depersonalization/derealization disorder, and dissociative identity disorder (multiple-personality disorder)—are shown in Table 6.4. Each disorder involves some sort of dissociation, or separation, of a part of the person's consciousness, memory, or identity.

The dissociative disorders are highly publicized and sensationalized; yet except for depersonalization/derealization disorder, they are considered rare. As with the somatic symptom disorders discussed earlier, there are no objective assessments to confirm the existence of a dissociative disorder. Thus, the possibility of feigning must be considered. Among young criminal offenders, 19 percent reported partial amnesia and 1 percent reported complete amnesia for their violent crimes (Evans, Mezey, & Ehlers, 2009). Wadih el Hage, charged as a conspirator with Osama bin Laden in the attacks on the U.S. embassies in Kenya and Tanzania, claimed that he suffered from a loss of memory. Court-appointed experts voiced the opinion that he was "faking the symptoms of amnesia" (Weiser, 2000).

dissociative disorders a group of disorders, including dissociative amnesia, dissociative identity disorder, and depersonalization/derealization disorder, all of which involve some sort of dissociation, or separation, of a part of the person's consciousness, memory, or identity

DISORDERS CHART DISSOCIATIVE DISORDERS

TABLE 6.4

Disorder	Symptoms	Prevalence	Age of Onset	Course
Dissociative amnesia	• Sudden inability to recall information of specific events or of one's identity or life history—not due to ordinary forgetting	Recent increase in prevalence, often involving forgotten early childhood trauma	Any age group	Acute forms may remit spontaneously, whereas others are chronic; usually related to trauma or stress
Dissociative amnesia, fugue subtype	• Inability to recall personal identity and past, with sudden confused wandering to a new area with inability to recall one's past and confusion about personal identity	0.2%; may increase during natural disasters or wartime	Usually adulthood	Related to stress or trauma; recovery is generally rapid
Depersonalization/ derealization disorder	• Persistent symptoms involving changes in perception and detachment from one's own thoughts and body • Possible feeling that things are unreal or a sense of being in a dreamlike state • Intact reality testing	About 1%; 50% to 75% of adults may experience brief episodes of stress-related depersonalization	Adolescence or adulthood	May be short lived or chronic
Dissociative identity disorder (multiple-personality disorder)	• Disruption of identity by the existence of two or more distinct personality states or by the experience of possession • Discontinuities in sense of self, memories, emotions, cognitions, and perceptions • Frequent gaps in memory of everyday events • Inability to recall important personal information	Sharp rise in reported cases since the 1980s; up to 9 times more frequent in women	Childhood to adolescence, but misdiagnosis may result in late reporting	Fluctuating; tends to be chronic and recurrent

Source: Data from DSM-5 Work Groups (2012); Spiegel et al. (2011)

David McNew/Getty Images

Hypnosis as Therapy

Some practitioners continue to use hypnosis to assess and treat dissociative disorders, based on the belief that these disorders may be inadvertently induced by self-hypnosis.

Complex legal debate arises regarding acts performed when an individual with dissociative identity disorder is purportedly in a dissociated state. The following examples offer an additional glimpse into this controversy:

- A therapist claimed that it was one of her client's 24 personalities who kidnapped and sexually assaulted her and that the main personality was not responsible (Haley, 2003).
- A man was charged with the rape of a woman with multiple personalities; one of the personalities said she did not consent.
- A South Carolina woman going through a divorce had 21 personalities. She claimed that she had not committed adultery and that she had tried to stop the responsible personality, "Rosie," from becoming involved in an extramarital affair.
- Individuals believed to have multiple personalities have claimed that they committed violent crimes in a dissociated state or that their alter personality committed the acts (H. M. Farrell, 2011).

Cases such as these raise questions regarding dissociative disorders and responsibility. Does a diagnosis of dissociative identity disorder or dissociative amnesia constitute mitigating circumstances and "diminished capacity"?

Dissociative Amnesia

Dissociative amnesia involves the sudden partial or total loss of important personal information or memory of a specific event following a traumatic event or stressful circumstances (Spiegel et al., 2011). It affects both men and women equally (Staniloiu & Markowitsch, 2010). Although strokes, substance abuse, and other medical conditions can cause amnesia, dissociative amnesia results from psychological factors or stressors (Schauer & Elbert, 2010; Tikhonova, Gnezditskii, Stakhovskaya, & Skvortsova, 2003). Individuals with dissociative amnesia often score high on tests measuring hypnotizability and are likely to report depression, anxiety, or a history of trance states (American Psychiatric Association, 2000a). Dissociative amnesia may also involve a fugue state which involves aimless traveling and identity confusion.

dissociative amnesia sudden partial or total loss of important personal information or recall of events due to psychological factors

localized amnesia lack of memory for a specific event or events

selective amnesia an inability to remember certain details of an event

Localized Amnesia

The most common form of dissociative amnesia, **localized amnesia**, involves an inability to recall events that happened in a specific short period, often centered on some highly painful or disturbing event. The following case study is typical of localized amnesia.

Case Study

An 18-year-old woman who survived a dramatic fire claimed not to remember it or the death of her child and husband in the fire. She claimed her relatives were lying about the fire. She became extremely agitated and emotional several hours later, when her memory abruptly returned.

Did You Know?

Some individuals experience a rare form of amnesia called *continuous amnesia*, which involves an inability to recall any events that occur between a specific time in the past and the present time. The individual remains alert and attentive but forgets each successive event after it occurs (Spiegel et al., 2011).

An affected individual may be unable to recall information such as his or her name, address, or names of relatives, yet remember the necessities of daily life—how to read, write, and drive. People vary in the degree and type of memory that is lost in localized amnesia (Spiegel et al., 2011). Some have **selective amnesia**, an inability to remember certain details of an incident. For example, a man remembered having an automobile accident but could not recall that his child had died in the crash. Selective amnesia is often claimed by people accused of violent criminal offenses; many murderers report that they remember arguments but do not remember killing anyone. However, according to one estimate, about 70 percent of criminals who say they have amnesia regarding their crime are feigning (Merryman, 1997). Some individuals display **systematized amnesia**, which involves the loss of memory for certain categories of information. Individuals may be unable to recall memories of their families or of a particular person. In one case, shortly after the sudden death of her only daughter, an elderly woman had no recall of having had a daughter.

In some cases of localized amnesia, the amnesia comes to light only after the individual begins to recall details of a traumatic event—a **repressed memory**. Cases of repressed memory are generally believed to result from exposure to trauma that is so overwhelming or threatening that the individual represses the event, often for a sustained period of time (McNally, 2007). However, some researchers have questioned whether repressed memories are valid and accurate. Laney & Loftus (2005) point out that memory is changeable, details of events can be distorted, and false memories can develop. Similarly, Pezdek, Blandon-Gitlin, & Gabbay (2006) believe that implausible memories can be unintentionally planted and further strengthened by information provided by parents or therapists. At this point, it is not clear how many cases of genuine repressed memory actually exist, or whether the phenomenon exists at all.

AP Photo/John Froschauer

Dissociative Fugue

Jeff Ingram was on his way to visit a terminally ill friend in Alberta and woke up 4 days later in Denver without any memory of his life. He was without his car or any personal identification. Ingram now wears a necklace flash drive and a bracelet that contains his personal information.

Dissociative Fugue

A subtype of dissociative amnesia is **dissociative fugue**, which involves bewildered wandering or purposeless travel accompanied by amnesia for one's identity and life history. The following case study illustrates the extensive loss of personal identity seen during a dissociative fugue state.

Case Study

An 18-year-old woman was found outside a Manhattan youth center. She claimed to have no memory of her identity, family, or home. When found, she was lying in a fetal position and said she wanted to know who she was. The authorities believe that she was on the streets for quite a while. She was identified when a photo of her aired on CNN. Her father indicated that she had had previous episodes of lost identity (K. Moore, 2009).

Individuals sometimes demonstrate multiple fugue episodes, as seen in the following case study.

Case Study

Mr. A, a 74-year-old man, was brought to the hospital emergency room after awakening on a park bench not knowing who or where he was. He reported having no memory of how he got to the park, nor did he know his name or where he was from (Ballew, Morgan, & Lippmann, 2003, p. 347). Mr. A was treated with an antianxiety medication and recovered his memory. His family was contacted, and his sister reported that Mr. A had disappeared on two other occasions when under stress.

Because of the complete loss of memory of the individual's entire life, law enforcement agencies or hospitals often become involved. However, during a fugue episode, some individuals act completely normal and slowly begin to take

systematized amnesia loss of memory for certain categories of information

repressed memory memory of a traumatic event has been repressed and is, therefore, unavailable for recall

dissociative fugue episode involving complete loss of memory of one's life and identity, unexpected travel to a new location, or assumption of a new identity

Did You Know? Compared to those who attended a lecture on internal medicine, general medical practitioners who attended a lecture on dissociation reported significantly more dissociative experiences and symptoms, more suicidal ideas, and more abuse of alcohol (Damsa et al., 2009). Why might the two groups of physicians differ in their views of dissociative disorders?

on a new identity. Fugue states sometimes last for months. As with other forms of amnesia, recovery from a fugue state is often abrupt and complete, although bits of information about the past may return gradually.

Depersonalization/Derealization Disorder

Depersonalization/derealization disorder is the most common dissociative disorder. It is characterized by feelings of unreality or of detachment from oneself and one's environment (Brand & Loewenstein, 2010; Sierra, 2009). Questions used to screen for this disorder include "Have you had the feeling that things around you are unreal?" and "Have you found yourself somewhere and not known how you got there?" (Armstrong, Putnam, Carlson, Libero, & Smith, 1997). One woman described her depersonalization symptoms this way: "It is as if the real me is taken out and put on a shelf and stored somewhere inside of me. Whatever makes me me is not there" (Simeon, Gross, et al., 1997, p. 1110). Episodes of depersonalization can be fairly intense, and they can produce great anxiety, as the following case study illustrates.

Case Study

Ms. A., age 23, presents to our clinic complaining of feeling detached for the past 4 years. She feels "fuzzy all the time, like I lost touch of reality." She complains of confused thinking: "It feels like I'm watching my life on television; I don't feel any emotions." These symptoms began immediately after a college party, which the police stopped because of underage drinking (Janjua, Rapport, & Ferrara, 2010, p. 62).

A diagnosis of depersonalization/derealization disorder is given only when the feelings of unreality and detachment cause major impairment in social or occupational functioning. The prevalence of this disorder, which typically begins in the teenage years, is about 1 percent. Depersonalization episodes may be short lived

Depersonalization/Derealization Disorder

An individual may feel like an automaton—mechanical and robotic—when experiencing depersonalization/derealization disorder. This painting—*The Subway* (ca. 1950), by George Tooker—captures this feeling.

depersonalization/derealization disorder dissociative condition characterized by feelings of unreality concerning the self and the environment

or may last for decades, depending on individual circumstances. Fleeting experiences of depersonalization are reported in up to 70 percent of college students and 23 percent of the general population. Depersonalization may be a response to extreme stress and is often accompanied by mood and anxiety disorders (Janjua et al., 2010; Simeon, Guralnik, Hazlett, et al., 2000).

Did You Know? Individuals with DID often claim that information about events happening to one personality is unavailable to other personalities. Research, however, has found that learning does in fact transfer between the different personalities (Huntjens, Peters, Woertman, van der Hart, & Postma, 2007; Kong, Allen, & Glisky, 2008).

Dissociative Identity Disorder

Dissociative identity disorder (DID), formerly known as *multiple-personality disorder*, is a disruption of identity as evidenced by two or more distinct personality states or an experience of **possession**, in which one's sense of personal identity is supernaturally replaced. Possession was added to the DID definition in DSM-5 to "provide more cross-cultural utility" (Spiegel et al., 2011). Many individuals with DID also experience trance states, sleepwalking, paranormal and possession episodes (C. A. Ross, 2011), conversion symptoms (DSM-5 Work Groups, 2012), and high rates of post-traumatic stress disorder (Rodewald, Wilhelm-Gobling, Emrich, Reddemann, & Gast, 2011).

In situations in which two or more personalities exist, only one personality is typically evident at any one time, and the alternation of personalities usually produces periods of amnesia in the personality that has been displaced. However, one or several personalities may be aware of the existence of the others. The personalities usually differ from one another and sometimes are direct opposites, as the following case study illustrates.

Case Study

"Little Judy" is a young child who laughs and giggles. "Gravelly Voice" is a man who speaks with a raspy voice. "The one who walks in darkness" is blind and trips over furniture. "Big Judy" is articulate, competent, and funny. These are four of the 44 personalities that exist within Judy Castelli. She was initially diagnosed with schizophrenia but later told that dissociative identity disorder was the appropriate diagnosis. She is a singer, a musician, an inventor, and an artist who has also become a lay expert on mental health issues (Woliver, 2000).

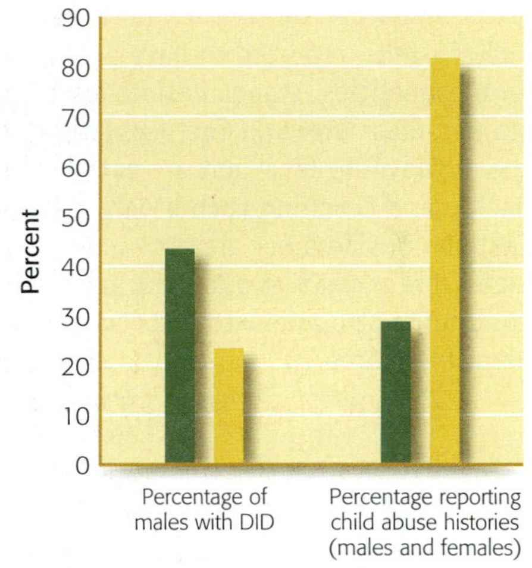

FIGURE 6.3

Comparison of Characteristics of Reported Cases of Dissociative Identity Disorder (Multiple-Personality Disorder) This graph illustrates characteristics of dissociative identity disorder (DID) cases reported in the 1980s versus those reported between 1800 and 1965. What could account for these differences?

Source: Based on Goff & Simms (1993)

The characteristics associated with DID have changed over time. Goff & Simms (1993) compared professional and historical case reports from the years 1800 to 1965 with those from the 1980s. The earlier cases involved an average of three personalities (versus 12 in the more recent cases), a later age of onset of first dissociation (age 20, as opposed to age 11 in the 1980s), a greater proportion of males, and a much lower prevalence of child abuse (Figure 6.3). Similarly, H. G. Pope, Jr., Barry, Bodkin, & Hudson (2006) tracked publications related to DID and dissociative amnesia over a 20-year period. The number of articles related to these disorders was low in the 1980s, rose to a sharp peak in the mid-1990s, and then declined sharply by 2003. No other disorder showed a similar phenomenon. The researchers concluded that both DID and dissociative amnesia "enjoyed a brief period of fashion that has now waned. . . . [T]hese diagnostic entities presently do not command widespread scientific acceptance" (p. 19).

Diagnostic Controversy Before the case of Sybil—a woman who appeared to have 16 different personalities—became popularized in a movie and book in the 1970s, there had been fewer than 200 reported cases of DID worldwide. Now thousands of new cases are reported each year (Milstone, 1997). Foote, Smolin,

dissociative identity disorder (DID) a condition in which two or more relatively independent personality states appear to exist in one person, including experiences of possession; also known as *multiple-personality disorder*

possession the replacement of a person's sense of personal identity with a supernatural spirit or power

Gordon M. Grant Photography

Dissociative Identity Disorder

Judy Castelli, reported to have 44 personalities, stands beside her stained-glass artwork. The people in the art have no faces but are connected and touching each other. Castelli considers her artistic endeavors a creative outlet for her continuing struggle with dissociative identity disorder.

Kaplan, Legatt, & Lipschitz (2006) contend that the condition is relatively common but often not recognized and diagnosed. However, other practitioners believe that DID is rare and that the increase in numbers may be due to clinician bias, the use of faulty assessment, or the use of therapeutic techniques that increase the likelihood of a DID diagnosis (J. F. Cormier & Thelen, 1998; Gharaibeh, 2009).

DID is rarely diagnosed outside the United States and Canada, except in the Netherlands and Turkey (Chaturvedi, Desai, & Shaligram, 2010; Merskey, 1995; B. J. Phelps, 2000; Tutkun, Sar, Yargic, & Ozpulat, 1998). In a study of DID in Switzerland, Modestin (1992) concluded that it is relatively rare and estimated its prevalence rate to be 0.05 to 0.1 percent of patients. He also found that three psychiatrists accounted for more than 50 percent of the patients given this diagnosis. Why is it that some psychiatrists or therapists report treating many patients with DID, whereas the majority do not?

Cases of dissociated states and multiple personalities resulting from the use of hypnosis or suggestion have, in fact, been reported (Coons, 1988; Freeland, Manchanda, Chiu, Sharma, & Merskey, 1993; P. R. McHugh, 2009; Ofshe, 1992). Temporary dissociation symptoms such as alterations in memory, thoughts, and perceptions or a sense of depersonalization (feeling detached or numb) can occur during periods of stress (Cardena & Weiner, 2004; Freinkel, Koopman, & Spiegel, 1994). Some clinicians may mistakenly interpret these symptoms as evidence of DID. Whether the increase in diagnosis of DID is the result of more accurate diagnosis, false positives, hypnosis, or an actual increase in the incidence of the disorder is still being debated.

Etiology of Dissociative Disorders

The possible causes of dissociative disorders are subject to much conjecture. Because diagnosis depends heavily on patients' self-reports, as noted, feigning or faking is always a possibility. Fabricated amnesia, dissociative fugue, or DID can be produced by individuals who "are attempting to flee a situation involving legal, financial, or personal difficulties, as well as in soldiers who are attempting to avoid combat or unpleasant military duties" (American Psychiatric Association, 2000, p. 525). However, true cases of these disorders may also result from these types of stressors. Differentiating between genuine cases of dissociative disorders and faked ones is difficult.

In this section, we consider the multipath dimensions that contribute to the dissociative disorders (Figure 6.4). Although two models—the psychologically based *post-traumatic model* (PTM) and the *sociocognitive model* (SCM)—are currently the most influential etiological perspectives, neither is sufficient to explain why only some individuals develop these disorders. It is likely that biological, psychological, social, and sociocultural vulnerabilities all play a role (Dalenberg, 2012).

MYTH VS REALITY

MYTH Dissociative identity disorder is relatively easy to diagnose, and most mental health professionals accept the category.

REALITY There are no objective measures from which a diagnosis can be made, and cases involving feigning the disorder have been reported. Those who question the category suggest that symptoms of the disorder are inadvertently produced through suggestion or hypnosis.

Biological Dimension Atypical brain functioning has been documented in various dissociative disorders. In dissociative amnesia, MRIs show inhibited neural activity associated with memory repression in the hippocampus (Kikuchi et al., 2010), while PET scans show hypometabolism in an area of the prefrontal cortex that is involved in the retrieval of autobiographical memories (M. Brand et al., 2009). A number of studies using PET scans and MRIs on individuals diagnosed with DID have found variations in

CONTROVERSY:

Culture and Somatic Symptom and Dissociative Disorders

- A 56-year-old Brazilian man requested an evaluation and treatment due to an ongoing somatic complaint. He had the firm belief that his penis was retracting and entering his abdomen, and he was reacting with a great deal of anxiety. He attempted to pull on his penis to prevent the retraction, a strategy he felt had been effective with a previous episode that occurred when he was 19 (Hallak, Crippa, & Zuardi, 2000).
- Dibuk ak Suut, a Malaysian woman, goes into a trancelike state in which she follows commands, blurts out offensive phrases, and mimics the actions of people around her. This happens when she has been suddenly frightened. She displays profuse sweating and increased heart rate, but claims to have no memory of what she says or does (Osbourne, 2001).

The symptoms of the first case study fit the description of *koro*, a culture-bound syndrome that has been reported primarily in Southeast Asia, although cases have also been reported in West Africa (Dzokoto & Adams, 2005) and South America. Symptoms of koro involve an intense fear that the penis—or, in a woman, the labia, nipples, or breasts—is receding into the body. Episodes of koro are usually brief in duration and responsive to positive reassurances. In the second case study, Dibuk is displaying symptoms related to *latah*, a condition found in Malaysia and many other parts of the world that consists of dissociation or a trancelike state associated with mimicking or following the instructions or behaviors of others. Other culture-bound disorders related to either somatic symptom or dissociative disorders include the following:

- *Brain fag.* Found primarily in West Africa, this condition affects high school and college students who report somatic symptoms involving a fatigued brain, neck or head pain, or blurring of vision due to difficult course work or classes.
- *Dhat syndrome.* This is a term used in India to describe hypochondriacal concerns and severe anxiety over the discharge of semen. The condition produces feelings of weakness or exhaustion.
- *Ataque de nervios.* Commonly found in Latino/Hispanic people residing in the United States and Latin America, the somatic symptoms or dissociative symptoms of this condition can include brain aches, stomach disturbances, anxiety symptoms, and trance-like states.
- *Piblokto.* Generally found in Inuit communities, this condition involves dissociative-type episodes accompanied by extreme excitement that are sometimes followed by convulsions and coma. The individual may perform aggressive and dangerous acts and report amnesia after the episode.
- *Zar.* This condition found in Middle Eastern or North African societies involves the experience of being possessed by a spirit. Individuals in a dissociative state may engage in bizarre behaviors, including shouting or hitting their heads against a wall.

Culture-bound syndromes are interesting because they point to the existence of a pattern of symptoms that are associated primarily with specific societies or groups. These "disorders" do not fit easily into the DSM-5 classification or into many of the biological and psychological models used to explain dissociative and somatic symptom disorders. What does it mean when unusual behavioral patterns are discovered that do not fit into Western-developed classification systems?

brain activity when comparing different personalities (Reinders et al., 2003; Sheehan, Sewall, & Thurber, 2005; G. E. Tsai, Condie, Wu, & Chang, 1999). Switching between personalities is associated with activation or inhibition of certain brain regions, particularly the hippocampus (G. E. Tsai et al., 1999), an area involved in memories and hypothesized to be involved in the generation of dissociative states and amnesia (Staniloiu & Markowitsch, 2010; M. H. Teicher, Andersen, Polcari, Anderson, & Navalta, 2002). However, these patterns of brain activity are difficult to interpret because it is unclear what causes them and what specific role they play, if any, in dissociative disorders.

M. H. Teicher et al. (2002) believe that chronic activation of stress responses due to childhood trauma can result in permanent structural changes in the brain. Similarly, Spiegel (2006) has suggested that reduced volume in the hippocampus and amygdala may hamper the ability of the brain to encode, store, and retrieve memory; comprehend contradictory information; and integrate emotional memories. Such alterations may play an etiological role in dissociative amnesia, DID, and depersonalization (Janjua et al., 2010).

Did You Know? Many individuals with DID report hearing voices before the age of 18. They hear two or more voices (often child and adult), and also report tactile and visual hallucinations (Dorahy et al., 2009).

● **FIGURE 6.4**

Multipath Model of Dissociative Identity Disorder

The dimensions interact with one another and combine in different ways to result in dissociative identity disorder.

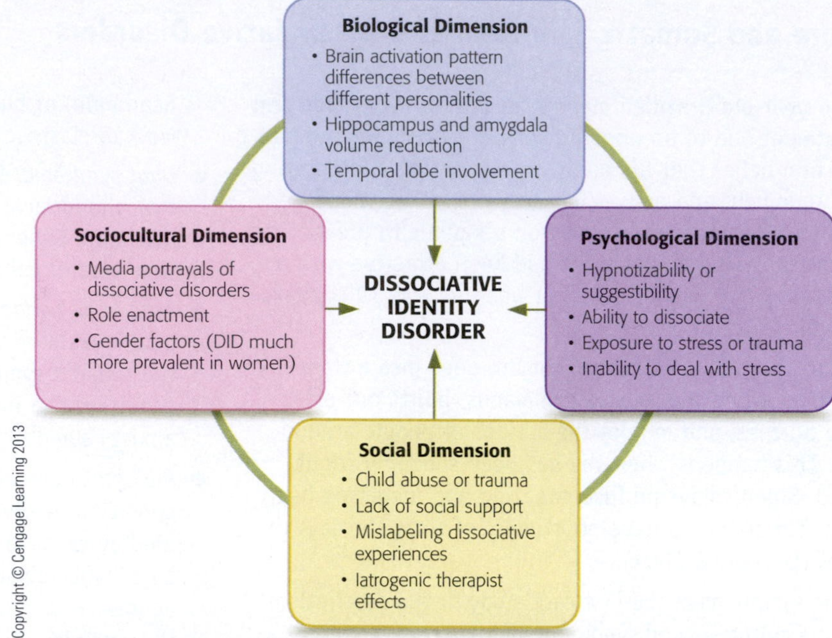

Psychological Dimension The primary psychological explanations for the dissociative disorders come from psychodynamic theory, although individual vulnerabilities such as hypnotizability or suggestibility are also thought to play an important role. According to psychodynamic theory, dissociative disorders are caused by an individual's use of repression to block from consciousness unpleasant or traumatic events (L. F. Richardson, 1998). This process protects the individual from painful memories or conflicts. In dissociative amnesia and fugue, for example, memories of specific events or large parts of the individual's personal identity are no longer available to conscious awareness. Dissociation is carried to an extreme in DID. Here, the splits in mental processes become so extreme that independent identities are formed, each with a unique set of memories (K. Baker, 2010; Gleaves, 1996).

Contemporary psychodynamic perspective suggests that DID results from severe childhood abuse, as illustrated in the PTM. According to Kluft (1987), the four factors necessary for the development of DID are:

1. being exposed to overwhelming childhood stress, such as traumatic physical or sexual abuse;
2. having the capacity to dissociate;
3. encapsulating or walling off the experience; and
4. developing different memory systems.

If a supportive environment is not available or if the personality is not resilient, DID results from these factors (Irwin, 1998; see Figure 6.5).

Thus, according to the PTM, the split in personality develops because of traumatic early experiences combined with an inability to escape them. In the case of Sybil, who was severely abused by her mother, Dr. Wilbur—Sybil's psychiatrist—speculated that "by dividing into different selves [which were] defenses against an intolerable and dangerous reality, Sybil had found a [design] for survival" (F. R. Schreiber, 1973, p. 158). Consistent with this perspective, most individuals diagnosed with DID do report a history of physical or sexual abuse during childhood (Barlow, 2011; Coons, 1994; Foote et al., 2006; Sheehan et al., 2005; Vermetten, Schmahl, Lindner, Loewenstein, & Bremner, 2006).

To develop DID, the individual must have the capacity to dissociate—or separate—certain memories or mental processes in response to traumatic events.

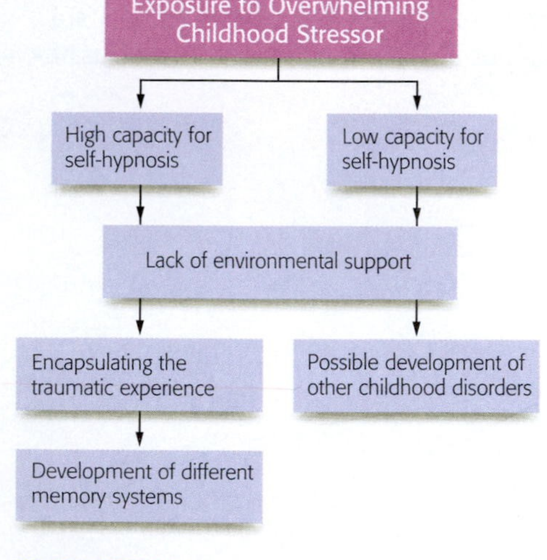

● **FIGURE 6.5**

The Post-Traumatic Model of Dissociative Identity Disorder

Note the importance of each of the factors in the development of dissociative identity disorder.

Source: Adapted from Kluft (1987); Loewenstein (1994)

Some researchers believe that pathological dissociation represents an escape from unpleasant experiences through self-hypnosis (L. D. Butler, Duran, Jasiukaitis, Koopman, & Spiegel, 1996). In fact, people who have DID are very susceptible to hypnotic suggestion. Additionally, females with DID have a history of trance states and sleepwalking and report more alterations in consciousness (International Society for the Study of Dissociation, 2005; Scroppo, Drob, Weinberger, & Eagle, 1998).

As with most psychodynamic conceptualizations, it is difficult to formulate and test hypotheses. In addition, the PTM presupposes exposure to childhood trauma. In most studies, information on child abuse is based on self-reports, is not independently corroborated, and involves varying definitions of abuse (Gharaibeh, 2009; Lilienfeld et al., 1999; A. Piper & Merskey, 2004). Questions have also been raised regarding reports of memories retrieved from very early ages. Clients with DID have reported the emergence of alternate personalities at the age of 2 or earlier (Dell & Eisenhower, 1990), and in one study, 11 percent reported being abused before age 1 (C. A. Ross et al., 1991). Reports regarding memories of events at these ages would be highly suspect.

Social and Sociocultural Dimension An approach that takes both social and sociocultural factors into consideration is the sociocognitive model (SCM) of DID, developed by Spanos (1994) and further elaborated by Lilienfeld, Lynn, Kirsch, et al. (1999). In this perspective, the disorder is conceptualized as

> displays of multiple role enactments that have been created, legitimized, and maintained by social reinforcement. Patients with DID synthesize these role enactments by drawing on a wide variety of sources of information, including the print and broadcast media, cues provided by therapists, personal experiences, and observations of individuals who have enacted multiple identities. (Lilienfeld, Lynn, Kirsch, et al., 1999, p. 507)

According to this model, patients learn about DID and its characteristics through the mass media and, under certain circumstances, begin to act out these roles. Vulnerable individuals may demonstrate these behaviors when therapists inadvertently use questions or techniques that evoke dissociative types of problem descriptions by clients. Proponents of the SCM cite the large increase in DID cases after mass media portrayals of this disorder as support for this perspective. For example, after the 1973 publication of *Sybil*, which detailed her 16 personalities, the mean number of personalities for those diagnosed rose from three to 12 (Goff & Simms, 1993).

Therapists are also exposed to mass media portrayals of DID and may unconsciously encourage reports of DID from clients. This would be referred to as an **iatrogenic disorder**—a condition unintentionally produced by a therapist through mechanisms such as selective attention, suggestion, reinforcement, and expectations that are placed on the client. Could some or even most cases of dissociative identity disorder be iatrogenic? A number of researchers and clinicians say yes. They believe that many of the cases of DID and dissociative amnesia have unwittingly been produced by therapists, self-help books, and the mass media (Aldridge-Morris, 1989; Chodoff, 1987; Goff & Simms, 1993; Lilienfeld, Lynn, & Lohr, 2004; Loftus, Garry, & Feldman, 1994; Ofshe, 1992; Piper & Mersky, 2004; Weissberg, 1993). Clients most sensitive to these influences may have predisposing characteristics. Research findings indicate that individuals who report dissociations score high on fantasy proneness and fantasy susceptibility (Giesbrecht, Lynn, Lilienfeld, & Merckelbach, 2008; McNally, Clancy, Schacter, & Pitman, 2000).

The authenticity of one well-known case of DID—that of Sybil (mentioned earlier)—has also been questioned (Borch-Jacobsen, 1997). Herbert Spiegel, a hypnotist, worked with Sybil and used her to demonstrate hypnotic phenomena in his classes. He described her as a "Grade 5" or "hypnotic virtuoso," something found in only 5 percent of the population. Sybil told Spiegel that her psychiatrist,

iatrogenic disorder a condition unintentionally produced by a therapist's actions and treatment strategies

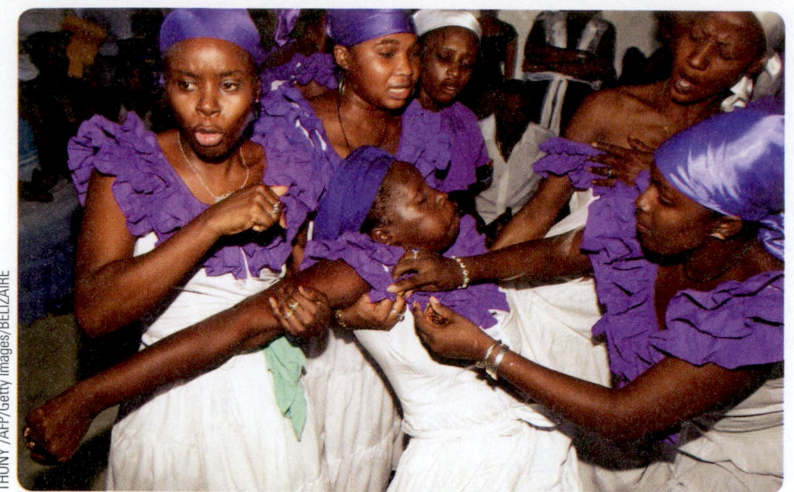

THONY/AFP/Getty Images/BELIZAIRE

Cross-Cultural Factors and Dissociation

Dissociative trance states can be entered voluntarily as part of certain cultural or religious practices, as demonstrated by this Haitian woman during a voodoo ceremony.

Cornelia Wilbur, had wanted her to be "Helen," a name given to a feeling she expressed during therapy. Spiegel later came to believe that Wilbur was using a technique in which different memories or emotions were converted into personalities. Sybil also wrote a letter denying that she had multiple personalities and stating that the "extreme things" she told about her mother were not true. Tapes of sessions between Wilbur and Sybil indicate that Wilbur may have described personalities for Sybil (Rieber, 2006).

Although iatrogenic influences can be found in any disorder, such effects may be more common with dissociative disorders, in part because of the high levels of hypnotizability and suggestibility found in individuals with these conditions. As Goff has stated, it is "no coincidence that the field of [multiple-personality disorder] studies in the United States largely originated among practitioners of hypnosis" (1993, p. 604). Hypnosis and other memory-retrieval methods may *create* rather than uncover personalities in suggestible clients. Although some cases of DID probably are therapist produced, we do not know to what extent iatrogenic influences can account for this disorder.

Treatment of Dissociative Disorders

A variety of treatments for the dissociative disorders have been developed, including supportive counseling and the use of hypnosis and personality reconstruction. Currently, there are no specific medications for the dissociative disorders. Instead, medications are prescribed to treat concurrent anxiety or depression.

CONTROVERSY:

"Suspect" Techniques Used to Treat Dissociative Identity Disorder

Bennett Braun, who founded the International Society for the Study of Multiple Personality and Dissociation and trained many therapists to work with clients with dissociative identity disorder, was brought up on charges by the Illinois Department of Financial and Professional Regulation. A former patient, Patricia Burgus, claimed that Braun inappropriately used hypnotic drugs, hypnosis, and leather strap restraints to stimulate abuse memories. Under this "repressed-memory therapy," Burgus became convinced that she possessed 300 personalities, was a high priestess in a satanic cult, ate meatloaf made of human flesh, and sexually abused her children. Burgus later began to question her "memories." In November 1997, she won a $10.6 million lawsuit, alleging inappropriate treatment and emotional harm (Associated Press, 1998). Braun lost his license to practice for 2 years and was placed on probation for an additional 5 years (Bloomberg, 2000).

Another former patient, Elizabeth Gale, won a $7 million settlement against Braun and other staff at the hospital where he worked. She had been convinced she was raised as a "breeder" to produce babies who would be subjected to sexual abuse. She has since sought to re-establish relationships with family members whom she accused of being part of a cult (Dardick, 2004).

Such lawsuits create a quandary for mental health practitioners. Many feel intimidated by the threat of legal action if they attempt to treat adult survivors of childhood sexual abuse, especially cases involving recovered memories. However, discounting the memories of clients could result in further victimization. Especially worrisome is the use of techniques such as hypnosis, trance work, body memories, and age regression, because they may produce inaccurate "memories" (J. G. Benedict & Donaldson, 1996).

For Further Consideration

1. In the case of repressed memories, should clients be told that some techniques are experimental and may produce inaccurate information?
2. Under what conditions, if any, should a therapist express doubt about information remembered by a client?
3. Given the high prevalence of child sexual abuse and the indefinite nature of repressed memories, how should clinicians proceed if a client discusses early memories of abuse?

Dissociative Amnesia and Dissociative Fugue The symptoms of dissociative amnesia and fugue tend to end, or abate, spontaneously. It has been noted that depression is often associated with the fugue state and that severe stress is often associated with both dissociative amnesia and fugue (Kopelman, 2002). A reasonable therapeutic approach is to treat these dissociative disorders indirectly by alleviating the depression (with antidepressants or cognitive-behavioral therapy) and the stress (through stress management techniques).

Depersonalization/Derealization Disorder Depersonalization/derealization disorder is also subject to spontaneous remission, but at a much slower rate than is seen with dissociative amnesia and fugue. Treatment generally concentrates on alleviating the feelings of anxiety or depression or the fear of going insane. Various antidepressants and antianxiety medications are used to treat the associated symptoms (Janjua et al., 2010).

Dissociative Identity Disorder The mental health literature contains more information on the treatment of dissociative identity disorder than on all of the other dissociative disorders combined.

A major goal in the treatment of DID is the use of trauma-based therapy to develop healthier ways of dealing with stressors. A hierarchical treatment approach involves the following (Brand et al., 2012; Brand & Loewenstein, 2010; International Society for the Study of Dissociation, 2005):

1. working on safety issues, stabilization, and the reduction of symptoms;
2. using trauma-focused cognitive therapy to reduce cognitive distortions;
3. identifying and working through the traumatic memories underlying the disorder;
4. stabilizing and learning to identify and deal with current stressors; and
5. developing healthy relationships and practicing self-care.

Treatment for this disorder is not always successful. Chris Sizemore (who was the inspiration for the book and movie *The Three Faces of Eve*) developed additional personalities after therapy but has now recovered. She is a writer, lecturer, and artist. Sybil also recovered (although questions remain regarding her diagnosis), and eventually became a college art professor (M. Miller & Kantrowitz, 1999). Successful treatment of DID, however, may be difficult to achieve. Coons (1986) conducted a study of

Debra Lex/Time Life Pictures/Getty Images

A Famous Case of Dissociative Identity Disorder

Chris Sizemore, whose experiences with dissociative identity disorder inspired the book and movie *The Three Faces of Eve*, is an artist today and no longer shows any signs of her former disorder.

20 individuals with DID followed for about 39 months after their initial assessment. Nine patients achieved partial or full recovery, but only five patients maintained it—the others dissociated again. A more recent review of 16 treatment outcome studies (B. L. Brand, Classen, McNary, & Zaveri, 2009) found that patients tended to have lower rates of dissociation, suicidality, and depression following treatment. Those who were able to integrate their personalities showed the greatest reduction in symptoms.

CHECKPOINT REVIEW

1. Describe the different types of dissociative amnesia and contrast them with depersonalization/derealization disorder.
2. Discuss evidence for and against the view that DID is a legitimate diagnosis.
3. Compare and contrast the post-traumatic and sociocognitive models of DID.
4. What are the treatment steps for DID?
5. Why is the DID diagnosis so controversial?

Summary

1 When do physical complaints represent a psychological disorder? What are the causes and treatments of these conditions?

- Somatic symptom disorders involve somatic complaints and illness anxiety. The symptoms are distressing and result in significant disruptions in one's life.
- Somatic symptom disorder (SSD) is characterized by chronic multiple physical complaints, sometimes with pain or health anxiety as predominate features.
- Illness anxiety disorder (hypochondriasis) is characterized by health anxiety and a belief that one has a serious and undetected illness or physical problem.
- Functional neurological symptom disorder (conversion disorder) involves neurological-like symptoms that are incompatible with a medical condition.
- Factitious disorders involve self-induced or feigned physical complaints, or symptoms induced in others.
- Biological explanations have suggested that there is increased vulnerability to somatic symptom disorders when individuals have high sensitivity to bodily sensations, a lower pain threshold, or a history of illness or injury.
- Psychological factors include social isolation, high anxiety or stress, and catastrophic thoughts regarding bodily sensations. Social explanations suggest that the role of "being sick" is reinforcing. Parental models for injury or illness can also be influential. From a sociocultural perspective, somatic symptom disorders result from societal restrictions placed on women, who are affected by these disorders to a much greater degree than are men. Additionally, social class, limited knowledge about medical concepts, and cultural acceptance of physical symptoms can play a role.
- Treatment includes the use of antidepressants to improve anxiety and the use of cognitive-behavioral strategies. The process involves psychoeducation about physical complaints, the role of distorted cognitions, and strategies for tolerating changes in bodily sensations.

2 What are dissociations? What forms can they take? How are they caused, and how are they treated?

- Dissociation involves a disruption in consciousness, memory, identity, or perception, and may be transient or chronic.
- Dissociative amnesia, including localized amnesia and dissociative fugue, involves a selective form of forgetting in which the person cannot remember information that is of personal significance. Depersonalization/derealization disorder is characterized by feelings of unreality—distorted perceptions of oneself and one's environment. Dissociative identity disorder (DID) involves the alternation of two or more relatively independent personalities in one individual, or an experience of possession.
- Biological explanations for DID have focused on variations in brain activity during dissociative states. Some researchers believe that childhood trauma and chronic stress can result in permanent structural changes in the brain. Psychoanalytic perspectives attribute these disorders to the repression of impulses that are seeking expression and ways of coping with childhood abuse. Sociocultural explanations for dissociation include exposure to media portrayals of dissociation and role enactment. Social explanations include childhood abuse, subtle reinforcement, mislabeling of dissociative experiences, and responding to the expectations of a therapist.
- Dissociative amnesia and dissociative fugue tend to remit spontaneously; behavioral therapy has also been used successfully. Dissociative identity disorder has most often been treated with trauma-focused and cognitive therapy to reduce cognitive distortions and deal with current stressors.

Key Terms

somatic symptom disorders 148
somatic symptom disorder (SSD) 148
somatic symptoms 148
somatic symptom disorder (SSD) with predominately somatic complaints 148
somatic symptom disorder (SSD) with pain features 149
illness anxiety disorder 150
conversion disorder (functional neurological symptom disorder) 152
malingering 152
psychogenic 152
factitious disorder 153
factitious disorder imposed on another 154
dissociative disorders 159
dissociative amnesia 160
localized amnesia 160
selective amnesia 160
systematized amnesia 161
repressed memory 161
dissociative fugue 161
depersonalization/derealization disorder 162
dissociative identity disorder (DID) 163
possession 163
iatrogenic disorder 167

Media Resources

Psychology CourseMate

Access an interactive e-book and chapter-specific interactive learning tools, including:

- flashcards
- quizzes
- videos

and more, in your Psychology CourseMate.

Go to **CengageBrain.com**.

LWA/Sharie Kennedy/Blend Images/Jupiterimages

7 Depressive and Bipolar Disorders

CHAPTER OUTLINE

Chelsea, raised in a stable and loving family, was an A student and star athlete throughout much of high school. However, in her senior year, she became uncharacteristically irritable, frequently snapping at her parents and sister without reason. She seemed uninterested when friends called or texted. She began to miss swimming practice and fell behind in her school assignments. When her parents tried to talk to her, she asked to be left alone and retreated to her bedroom. She spent most of her weekends sleeping. As graduation approached, Chelsea became increasingly withdrawn from family and friends. She felt guilty about how she was treating everyone and finally agreed to see a therapist. During her first visit she told the therapist. "I don't know what's wrong with me. Everything had seemed so right, and now everything seems so wrong."

FOCUS QUESTIONS

1 What are symptoms of depression and mania?

2 What are depressive disorders, what causes them, and how are they treated?

3 What are bipolar disorders, what causes them, and how are they treated?

Mood refers to a prolonged emotional state. A person's mood can significantly affect his or her perceptions of the world and sense of well-being. Persistent changes in mood, such as those demonstrated by Chelsea, are often difficult to explain. In many cases, there is no single stressor or traumatic experience that causes such changes. A variety of factors, including genetic predisposition, early life events, and other stressors, can interact to produce pervasive mood changes. In this chapter, we first discuss various mood symptoms and then focus on two categories of disorders involving mood changes—depressive and bipolar disorders. While those with depressive disorders experience only one mood extreme (depression), those with bipolar disorder (sometimes called manic depression) often experience both depression and an abnormally "high" mood (i.e., bipolar refers to moods at both "poles"). We include depressive and bipolar disorders in the same chapter because they both involve pervasive, life-altering disturbances in mood that occur in the absence of any physical or mental health condition that could account for the mood change; these disorders can both significantly impair normal functioning across the life span (Figure 7.1). We discuss suicide, a serious problem associated with these disorders, in Chapter 8.

Assessing Mood Symptoms

We have all felt depressed or elated at some time during our lives. The loss of a friendship can produce feelings of sadness, or we may feel energized or even ecstatic when we hear great news. Unlike these temporary emotional reactions, the mood symptoms seen in depressive and bipolar disorders

- affect every part of the person's life,
- continue for weeks or months,
- often occur for no apparent reason, and
- involve extreme reactions that cannot be easily explained by what is happening in the person's life.

Depression and mania, opposite ends of a continuum that extends from deep sadness to wild elation, represent the extremes of mood. Let's begin by looking carefully at the symptoms of these conditions (Table 7.1). We will then discuss how clinicians carefully analyze mood symptoms to determine if someone has a depressive or bipolar disorder.

mood a prolonged emotional state

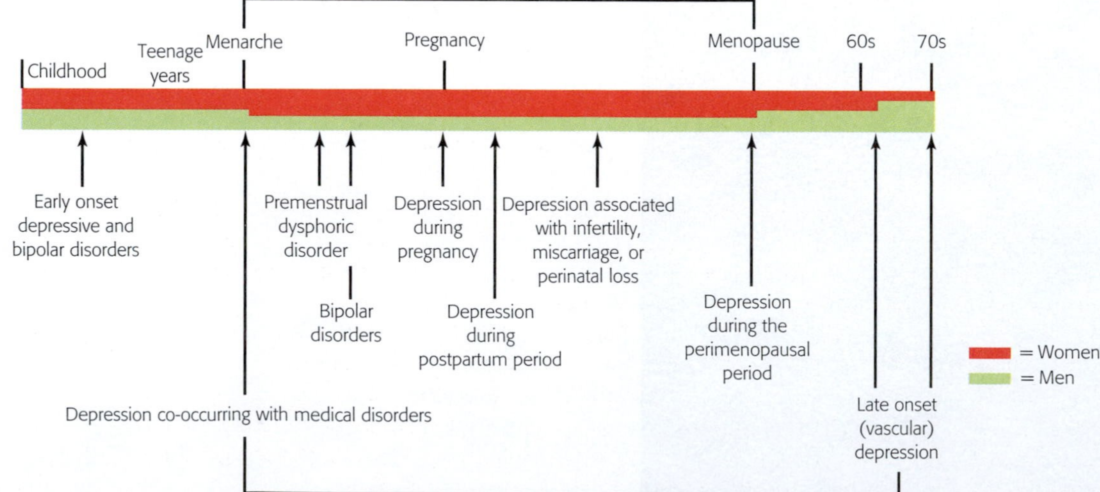

FIGURE 7.1

Depressive and Bipolar Disorders Across the Life Span
Biological, psychological, social, and sociocultural factors increase vulnerability to depressive and bipolar disorders during different life stages.

Source: C. B. Nemeroff. Recent Findings in the Pathophysiology of Depression. Focus, January 1, 2008; 6(1): 3–14. Reprinted with permission from Focus, copyright © 2008. American Psychiatric Association.

TABLE 7.1 Symptoms of Depression and Mania

DOMAIN	DEPRESSION	MANIA
Mood	Feelings of sadness, emptiness and worthlessness, apathy, anxiety, brooding	Elevated mood, grandiosity, irritability, hostility
Cognitive	Pessimism, guilt, difficulty concentrating, negative thinking, suicidal thoughts	Disorientation, racing thoughts, decreased focus and attention and judgment
Behavioral	Social withdrawal, crying, low energy, lowered productivity, agitation	Overactivity, rapid or incoherent speech, impulsivity
Physiological	Appetite and weight changes, sleep disturbance, aches and pain, loss of sex drive	High levels of arousal, decreased sleep, increased sex drive

Symptoms of Depression

Depression, characterized by intense sadness, feelings of futility and worthlessness, and withdrawal from others, is the core feature of depressive disorders and is also commonly seen in bipolar disorders. We can often tell when people are depressed by looking at changes in their mood, thinking, behavior, or bodily functions.

Mood Symptoms The most striking symptom of depression—depressed mood—involves feelings of sadness, emptiness, hopelessness, worthlessness, or low self-esteem. The following case study illustrates the hopelessness and emotional numbness seen with depression.

Case Study

It's hard to describe the state I was in several months ago. The depression was total—it was as if everything that happened to me passed through this dark filter, and I kept seeing the world through this dark cloud. Nothing was exciting. I felt I was no good, completely worthless, and deserving of nothing. The people who tried to cheer me up just couldn't understand how down I felt.

People who are depressed have little enthusiasm for things they once enjoyed, including hanging out with family and friends. Feeling irritable or anxious is also common (M. Fava et al., 2009).

Cognitive Symptoms Certain thoughts and ideas, including pessimistic, self-critical beliefs and thoughts of suicide, are common among people who are depressed. Depression interferes with a person's ability to concentrate, remember things, and make decisions. **Rumination**, continually thinking about certain topics or repeatedly reviewing certain past events, is often reported by those who are depressed. Such rumination frequently involves irrational or unjustified beliefs.

Behavioral Symptoms Behavioral symptoms such as fatigue, social withdrawal, and reduced motivation are common with depression. Daily activities may seem overwhelming. People who are depressed may speak slowly and respond only in short phrases. Some appear agitated and restless. They may cry easily for no particular reason or in reaction to sadness, frustration, or anger. Lack of concern for personal cleanliness may also be evident.

Did You Know? Cultural norms can affect how symptoms of depression are expressed. European Americans tend to show decreased emotional reactivity when depressed (e.g., less smiling), while Asian Americans who are depressed show increased internal physiological reactivity but no significant outward change in emotional expression.

Source: Chentsova-Dutton, Tsai, & Gotlib (2010)

depression a mood state characterized by sadness or despair, feelings of worthlessness, and withdrawal from others

rumination continually thinking about certain topics or reviewing events that have occurred

Physiological Symptoms The following physical symptoms are often seen with depression:

- *Appetite and weight changes*. Depression sometimes causes changes in weight due to either increased or decreased eating. While some people have almost no appetite, others eat even if they are not hungry.
- *Sleep disturbance*. Many people with depression have difficulty falling asleep or staying asleep. They often wake up feeling tired and unrefreshed.
- *Unexplained aches and pain*. Headaches, stomachaches, or other body aches commonly occur during depression (Jain, 2009), especially among those with severe or chronic depression (Huijbregts et al., 2010; P. Lee et al., 2009). In some cultural groups, unexplained aches and pains are the main symptoms of depression (Kung & Lu, 2008).
- *Aversion to sexual activity*. Depression often produces dramatically reduced sexual interest and arousal.

Symptoms of Mania

Case Study

Upon returning to work after a short vacation, Alan, a 26-year-old computer programmer, seemed unusually happy, talkative, and energetic; he bragged that he only needed a few hours of sleep each night. He brought several huge cakes to work and insisted that coworkers eat some of each cake. Initially, everyone was surprised and amused by his antics. However, amusement was soon replaced with irritation at Alan's continual talking and interruptions.

One morning, Alan jumped onto a desk, yelling, "Listen! We aren't working on the most important aspects of our data! Erase, reprogram, you know what I mean. We've got to examine the total picture based on the input!" Alan's speech was so rapid and disjointed that it was difficult to understand him. He then threw chair and began to smash computers. After several coworkers grabbed him, Alan continued to shout and struggle. Police officers were summoned; they handcuffed Alan to restrain his movements and transported him to a psychiatric hospital for observation.

Individuals with bipolar disorder experience elevated mood states characterized by increased energy, changes in mood, and other significant transformations in behavior. There are two levels of manic intensity—hypomania and mania (DSM-5 Work Groups, 2012). The milder form, **hypomania**, is characterized by changes in behavior and mood that can include increased levels of activity or energy (including decreased need for sleep, and increased goal-oriented behavior) combined with an elevated or irritable mood. Someone with hypomania may appear quite distractible, change topics frequently, and have many disconnected ideas. The person may talk excessively, dominate conversations, and act in a self-important manner. The person may feel creative and start many projects. Impulsivity and risk taking are other characteristics of hypomania.

hypomania a milder form of mania involving increased levels of activity and goal-directed behaviors combined with an elevated, expansive, or irritable mood

mania mental state characterized by very exaggerated activity and emotions including euphoria, excessive excitement or irritability, diminished need for sleep and resultant impairment in social or occupational functioning

euphoria exceptionally elevated mood; exaggerated feeling of well-being

Mania is characterized by even more exaggerated activity and emotions including **euphoria** (exceptionally elevated mood), markedly excessive excitement or irritability, diminished need for sleep and clear impairment in social or occupational functioning. When someone is experiencing a manic episode it is clearly evident to others whereas hypomania is much more subtle and may only be evident to those who know the person well. Aside from hypomania being a milder version of mania, another notable difference is that hypomanic episodes do not involve psychosis (loss of contact with reality), nor do they cause marked impairment in social or occupational functioning or a need for hospitalization. As we saw in the case study with Alan, hypomania can progress into a full manic episode involving significant mood, cognitive, behavioral, and physiological changes.

Mood Symptoms People with mania are very emotionally unstable and show mood changes ranging from extreme elation to intense rage. Someone with an **elevated mood** may be in extremely high spirits and full of energy and enthusiasm. Inappropriate use of humor, poor judgment in expressing feelings or opinions, and **grandiosity** (inflated self-esteem and beliefs of being special, chosen, or superior to others) can result in interpersonal conflicts. Mania can also produce extreme irritability, hostility, and agitation.

Cognitive Symptoms People experiencing mania are often disoriented, have difficulty focusing their attention, show poor judgment, and do not recognize the inappropriateness of their behavior. Cognitive difficulties are often apparent from their speech, sometimes referred to as **pressured speech**, which may be rapid, loud, frenzied, and difficult to understand. Those experiencing mania frequently have difficulty maintaining focus and display a **flight of ideas**; that is, they change topics, become distracted with new thoughts, or make irrelevant comments.

Behavioral Symptoms Individuals experiencing mania are often uninhibited, frequently act impulsively (e.g., gamble, drive recklessly, make poor investments, or spend excessively), and have difficulty delaying gratification (Strakowski et al., 2010). Failure to evaluate the consequences of decisions can lead to unsafe sexual practices or illegal activity, behaviors that might be highly uncharacteristic for the individual. Speech is often rapid and incoherent. Wild excitement, ranting, raving (thus the stereotype of a raving "maniac"), constant movement, and agitation characterize severe manic episodes. Psychotic symptoms including paranoia, hallucinations, and delusions (false beliefs) may appear. Individuals experiencing extreme mania are often hospitalized after becoming dangerous to themselves or to others.

Physiological Symptoms Individuals experiencing mania often sleep very little. High levels of physiological arousal can result in ongoing restlessness, intense activity, and impulsive behaviors. Increased libido (sex drive) often leads to reckless sexual behavior. The high energy expenditure and limited sleep characteristic of manic episodes often result in weight loss.

Evaluating Mood Symptoms

Effective treatment of depressive and bipolar disorders requires a clear understanding of the symptoms and an accurate diagnosis. Therefore, clinicians ask many questions and attempt to determine if mood symptoms are mild, moderate, or severe. They also ask about the frequency and duration of any manic or depressive episodes, any seasonal changes in mood, and patterns of alcohol use or other substance use (i.e., illegal drugs or overuse of prescription medications). Other questions involving mood symptoms include:

- During depressive or hypomanic/manic episodes, are there symptoms from the other end of the mood continuum? People who experience manic or depressive episodes sometimes exhibit milder symptoms from

elevated mood a mood state involving exaggerated feelings of energy and well-being

grandiosity an overvaluation of one's significance or importance

pressured speech rapid, frenzied, or loud, disjointed communication

flight of ideas rapidly changing or disjointed thoughts

the opposite pole. For example, someone may cry excessively or talk of suicide during a hypomanic/manic episode or experience extreme restlessness and have racing thoughts when depressed.

- Are there indicators of past or current suicidal thinking or behavior? Mood changes increase risk of suicide. People who feel hopeless, act impulsively, abuse drugs or alcohol, or have previously attempted suicide have the greatest risk of suicide during mania or depression (Fiedorowicz et al., 2009; Swann, Dougherty et al., 2005).
- Was the onset of this mood episode within 6 months of childbirth? Mood symptoms occurring after childbirth can include depressive or hypomanic/manic behaviors as well as mental confusion, anxiety, and insecurity (C. T. Beck & Indman, 2005; V. Sharma, Khan, Corpse, & Sharma, 2008). **Postpartum depression**, an underdiagnosed condition, is estimated to affect as many as 13 percent of women (Breese-McCoy, 2011).

Clinicians evaluating mood symptoms carefully gather information in order to make an accurate diagnosis and plan appropriate intervention. During treatment, individuals with depressive or bipolar disorders are periodically asked about anxiety, suicidality, and substance use, because these conditions so frequently accompany these disorders. Clinicians also look into other possible causes of mood symptoms, such as medication reactions or medical conditions. In some cases, intense depression or hypomania/mania occurs during alcohol or drug intoxication or withdrawal.

When evaluating someone who is depressed, clinicians also determine if the individual has ever had any manic/hypomanic symptoms. Careful symptom evaluation prior to diagnosis (and during treatment) is important because, as you will see, interventions for depressive and bipolar disorders are quite different. In the next section, we focus on depressive disorders; we conclude the chapter with a discussion of bipolar disorders.

CHECKPOINT REVIEW

1. Name four symptoms of depression and four symptoms of mania.
2. Name four ways the symptoms seen in depressive and bipolar disorder differ from temporary emotional reactions.
3. Why is it important for clinicians to gather comprehensive information about mood symptoms before making a diagnosis?

Depressive Disorders

Depressive disorders, a group of related disorders characterized by depressive symptoms, include major depressive disorder, dysthymic disorder, and premenstrual dysphoric disorder, as well as depressive disorders under study including mixed anxiety/depression and seasonal affective disorder (Table 7.2).

Diagnosis and Classification of Depressive Disorders

As previously noted, one important factor in diagnosing a depressive disorder is making sure the person has never experienced a hypomanic or manic episode—the presence of such episodes would lead the clinician to consider a bipolar disorder instead. Clinicians also consider how severe and how chronic the depressive symptoms have been.

postpartum depression depressive symptoms beginning within 6 months of childbirth

DISORDERS CHART DEPRESSIVE DISORDERS

TABLE 7.2

Disorder	Symptoms	Lifetime Prevalence (%)	Gender Difference	Age of Onset
Major depressive disorder	• Occurrence of at least one major depressive episode (2-week duration) • No history of mania or hypomania	8.0–19.0	Much higher in females	Any age; average onset in 20s
Dysthymic disorder	• Depressed mood that has lasted for at least 2 years (with no more than 2 months symptom-free)[a]	6.0	Much higher in females	Often childhood or adolescence
Mixed anxiety depression[b]	• Multiple symptoms of major depression • Anxious distress	No data	More common in females	Often childhood or adolescence
Premenstrual dysphoric disorder	• Severe depression, mood swings, anxiety, or irritability occurring before the onset of menses (this pattern evident for at least 1 year) • Improvement of symptoms within a few days of menstruation and minimal or no symptoms following menstruation	2.0–8.0, among women of reproductive age	Most common in women with personal or family history of depression	Late 20s, although earlier onset is possible
Seasonal affective disorder[b]	• At least two major depressive episodes occurring during fall or winter and remitting in spring or summer • Seasonal episodes of depression outnumbering nonseasonal episodes	0.4–2.9	More common in females	Early adulthood, although earlier onset is possible

Source: Data from DSM-5 Work Groups (2012); R. C. Kessler, Chiu, Demler, & Walters (2005); Merikangas, Akiskal, et al. (2007); National Institutes of Health (2010); N. E. Rosenthal (2009); Westrin & Lam (2007a)

[a]In children and adolescents, mood can be irritable and symptoms must have been present for at least 1 year.

[b]The American Psychiatric Association does not recognize mixed anxiety/depression or seasonal affective disorder as diagnostic categories.

Major Depressive Disorder A diagnosis of major depressive disorder (MDD) requires that the individual experience a **major depressive episode**; that is, *severe* depressive symptoms have impaired functioning most of the day, nearly every day, for at least 2 full weeks. The depressive symptoms seen in MDD include (a) depressed mood, feelings of sadness, or emptiness and/or (b) loss of interest or pleasure in previously enjoyed activities. In addition, weight or appetite changes, changes in sleep patterns, fatigue or loss of energy, observable restlessness or slowing of activity, excessive feelings of guilt or worthlessness, difficulty with concentration and decision making, or recurrent thoughts of death or suicide are often evident (DSM-5 Work Groups, 2012). Nearly one third of those with MDD also have a substance-use disorder; this combination increases suicide risk (L. Davis, Uezato, Newell, & Frazier, 2008). Similarly, persisting depressive symptoms increase risk of suicide (Trivedi, Hollander, Nutt, & Blier, 2008; Witte, Timmons, Fink, Smith, & Joiner, 2009).

Dysthymic Disorder (Chronic Depression) **Dysthymic disorder**, a disorder involving chronic depression, is diagnosed when depressive symptoms are present most of the day for more days than not during a 2-year period (with no more than 2 months symptom-free). Dysthymia involves the ongoing presence of at least two of the following symptoms: feelings of hopelessness, low self-esteem, poor appetite or overeating, low energy or fatigue, difficulty concentrating or making decisions, or sleep difficulties (DSM-5 Work Groups, 2012). Individuals with chronic MDD also fall in this category. Dysthymia is often associated with negative thinking patterns and a pessimistic outlook on the future. For many, dysthymia is a lifelong, pervasive disorder with long periods of depression, few periods without symptoms, and less response to treatment (J. P. McCullough et al., 2008; Torpey & Klein, 2008).

major depressive episode a period involving severe depressive symptoms that have impaired functioning for at least 2 full weeks

dysthymic disorder condition involving chronic depressive symptoms that are present most of the day for more days than not during a 2-year period with no more than 2 months symptom-free

Did You Know? Screening of students who visited university health clinics revealed that about one fourth of the students had significant symptoms of depression.

Source: S. Mackenzie et al. (2011)

Mixed Anxiety/Depression Mixed anxiety/depression is being researched as a possible future diagnostic category that would be used when symptoms of depression are accompanied by **anxious distress** (e.g., pervasive worries, difficulty relaxing); the diagnosis would be used only when neither anxiety nor depression predominates. Individuals with mixed anxiety and depression generally have less severe depressive symptoms compared to MDD and fewer somatic symptoms compared to generalized anxiety disorder (Małyszczak & Pawłowski, 2006). Mixed anxiety/depression is associated with longer depressive episodes and a higher risk of suicide (Boden, Fergusson, & Horwood, 2007; Schmidt, Kotov, et al., 2007).

© Science Museum/SSPL/The Image Works

Seasonal Patterns of Depression

In seasonal affective disorder (SAD), depressive symptoms vary with the seasons. One theory is that inadequate bright light and related circadian-rhythm disruptions during the winter months affect neurotransmitters in the brain and subsequently induce depression. The people in this photo are receiving light therapy through exposure to specially designed light boxes. This treatment is effective for many individuals who experience symptoms of SAD or who have depressive symptoms during the winter months.

Seasonal Affective Disorder Seasonal affective disorder (SAD) involves severe depression that occurs with a seasonal pattern associated with decreasing light. Symptoms typically begin in the fall or winter and remit during the spring or summer. Although SAD is not yet an official diagnostic category (DSM-5 Work Groups, 2012), researchers define it as involving at least two seasonal episodes of severe depression and a pattern of depressive episodes which occur seasonally more than nonseasonally. (Thus, the many people who experience only mild to moderate seasonal mood changes do not have SAD.) Those with SAD typically have a normal mood the rest of the year, although some have mild hypomaniclike symptoms during summer months.

Those experiencing SAD have "vegetative symptoms," including low energy, social withdrawal, increased need for sleep, and carbohydrate craving. SAD occurs most frequently in regions with less light in the winter months and among those who are sensitive to the influence of environmental light on their circadian rhythm (Shirani & St. Louis, 2009). In fact, some individuals with SAD report that overcast skies can produce symptoms any time of the year.

Premenstrual Dysphoric Disorder Premenstrual dysphoric disorder (PMDD) is a controversial diagnostic category involving serious symptoms of depression, irritability, and tension that appear the week before menstruation and disappear soon after menstruation begins. A PMDD diagnosis requires premenstrual symptoms such as significantly depressed mood, mood swings, anger, anxiety, tension, irritability, or increased interpersonal conflict. Other possible symptoms include difficulty concentrating; social withdrawal; lack of energy; food cravings or overeating; insomnia or excessive sleepiness; feeling overwhelmed; or physical symptoms such as bloating, weight gain, or breast tenderness. These are similar to the physical and emotional symptoms of premenstrual syndrome; however, PMDD produces much greater distress and interferes with social, interpersonal, academic, or occupational functioning (DSM-5 Work Groups, 2012). Some researchers have argued against designating symptoms of a normal biological function (menstruation) as a psychiatric disorder (Chekoudjian, 2009; Offman & Kleinplatz, 2004).

Prevalence of Depressive Disorders

Depression is one of the most common psychiatric disorders and a leading cause of disability worldwide (Andrade et al., 2010). Moreover, depression is very costly. It causes people to miss work and to be less productive at work and school. In the United States, about $50 billion is spent annually on health care services and lost workdays due to depression (P. E. Greenberg, Burnham, Lowe, & Corey-Lisle, 2003).

anxious distress symptoms of motor tension, difficulty relaxing, pervasive worries, or feelings that something catastrophic will occur

Nearly 15 million Americans will experience a depressive disorder this year. The prevalence of SAD ranges from 0.4 to 2.9 percent of the general population (N. E. Rosenthal, 2009; Westrin & Lam, 2007a). Approximately 2–8 percent of women in their reproductive years experience PMDD (DSM-5 Work Groups, 2012; National Institutes of Health, 2010; Vigod & Stewart, 2009). It is estimated that between 13 percent (Hasin, Goodwin, Stinson, & Grant, 2005) and 16 percent (R. C. Kessler, Berglund, Demler, Jin, Koretz, et al., 2003) of the U.S. population will experience the severe symptoms of MDD at some point in their lives (Figure 7.2). Being female, Native American, middle aged, widowed, separated, or divorced, or having a low income, increases risk for depression (R. C. Kessler, Berglund, Demler, Jin, Koretz, et al., 2003); women have a 70 percent increased lifetime risk of experiencing a major depressive episode compared to men (R. C. Kessler, Chiu, Demler, & Walters, 2005).

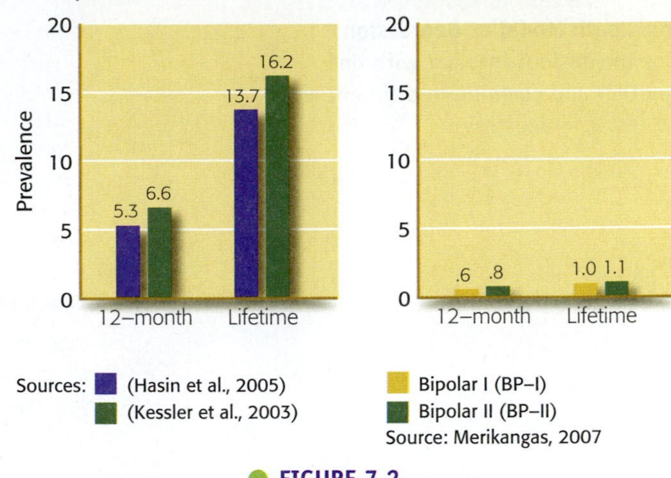

FIGURE 7.2

12-Month and Lifetime Prevalence of Depressive and Bipolar Disorders

Source: Based on Hasin, Goodwin, et al. (2005); R. C. Kessler, Berglund, Demler, Jin, Koretz, et al. (2003); Merikangas, Akiskal, et al. (2007)

After one episode of depression, the likelihood of another is 50 percent; after two episodes, 70 percent; and after three episodes, 90 percent (Muñoz, Ying, et al., 1995). If depressive symptoms do not completely resolve with treatment, the chances of a relapse or chronic depression are greatly increased (Conradi, Ormel, & de Jonge, 2010). The most common lingering symptoms of depression include poor concentration, lack of decisiveness, low energy, and sleep difficulties (Conradi et al., 2010).

Approximately 15 percent of those treated for depression fail to show any significant reduction in symptoms (Berlim & Turecki, 2007); it is believed that many of these cases represent undiagnosed bipolar disorder (Bowden, 2010a; Brunoni, Fraguas, & Fregni, 2009). In an 8-year follow-up of individuals diagnosed with MDD, approximately 10 percent eventually received a bipolar diagnosis, including 25 percent of those who did not improve after taking antidepressant medications (C. T. Li et al., 2012). Those misdiagnosed often experience greater impairment, presumably because they receive ineffective treatment due to the inaccurate diagnosis (Kamat et al., 2008).

Etiology of Depressive Disorders

Over the years, a variety of explanations have been proposed to account for depression. Consistent with our multipath approach, we will discuss how biological, psychological, social, and sociocultural factors interact in complex ways to cause depressive disorders (Figure 7.3). For example, in our discussion of depression occurring with greater frequency in some families, we discuss interactions between genetic susceptibility, timing of stressful life events, and the type of stressors encountered (Pemberton et al., 2010). In general, environmental factors have more influence on childhood depression, whereas hereditary factors have greater influence in adolescence and adulthood (Harold et al., 2010). The transition between middle and late adolescence is considered a time when genetic influences begin to surpass environmental influences (Tully, Iacono, & McGue, 2010).

Biological Dimension Biological explanations regarding depressive disorders generally focus on genetic predisposition, abnormalities involving neurotransmitters, hormones and brain structures, or interactions among these factors.

The Role of Heredity Depression tends to run in families, and the same types of depressive disorders are often found among members of the same family (Hettema, 2010). Among people who are adopted, the likelihood of developing depression is increased when there is a history of depression among biological

● FIGURE 7.3

Multipath Model of Depression

The dimensions interact with one another and combine in different ways to result in depression.

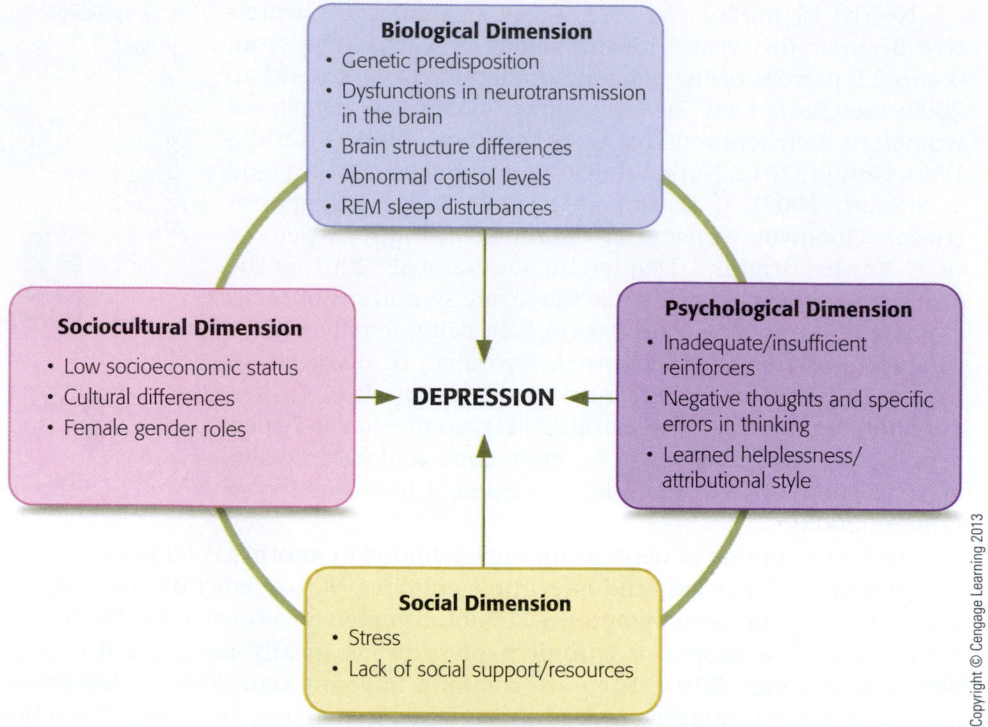

relatives. Studies comparing the incidence of depressive disorders among the biological and adoptive families of individuals with depression indicate that the incidence is significantly higher among biological families than among adoptive families (Levinson, 2006). Interestingly, the chances of inheriting depression are greatest for female twins, suggesting gender differences in heritability (D. Goldberg, 2006).

Genetics also appears to increase anxiety symptoms in some people with depression. An extensive study investigating the contribution of genetic and environmental factors to depressive and anxiety disorders (based on data from more than 4,500 pairs of identical and fraternal twins) concluded that genetics contributes to both depression and anxiety disorders and that many people with depression also have genes associated with anxiety (Kendler & Prescott, 2006).

Many different genes, each with relatively small influence, interact with environmental factors to produce depression (C. M. Lewis et al., 2010; Lohoff, 2010). For example, certain variations in the serotonin transporter gene (5-HTT) increase the likelihood of depression. Carriers of the shorter allele of this gene release more stress hormone (cortisol) and, when mistreated as children, have an increased risk of depression in adulthood (Caspi, Sugden, et al., 2003; Karg, Burmeister, Shedden, & Sen, 2011). Those with this genetic makeup also have more difficulty effectively using the neurotransmitter serotonin (J. M. Miller et al., 2009). This same gene is also associated with changes in brain anatomy seen in some people with depression (K. A. Young, Bonkale, Holcomb, Hicks, & German, 2008). Although depressive disorders are influenced by genetic factors, it is important to remember that the ultimate expression of genes depends upon factors encountered during one's lifetime (Leonardo & Hen, 2006).We now focus on ways that various biological factors—such as circadian cycles, hormones and neurotransmitters, and brain structure abnormalities—contribute to depression.

circadian rhythm an internal clock or daily cycle of internal biological rhythms that influence various bodily processes such as body temperature and sleep–wake cycles

Circadian Rhythm Disturbances in Depression **Circadian rhythms** are internal biological rhythms that influence a number of our bodily processes, including body temperature and sleeping patterns. Depression is associated with disruptions in this system (Monteleone & Maj, 2008). For example, insomnia (difficulty falling or staying asleep) can both cause and worsen depressive symptoms (Howland, 2011; R. W. Lam, 2008). One study found that adolescents who went to sleep at midnight or later were 24 percent more likely to have depression and 20 percent more likely to have suicidal thoughts compared to peers who went to sleep by 10 p.m. (Gangwisch et al., 2010). Disrupted sleep is strongly linked to the onset of postpartum depression (Goyal, Gay, & Lee, 2009). It has long been recognized that people with depression have more rapid eye movement sleep, the stage of sleep during which dreaming occurs (Modell & Lauer, 2007). Interestingly, reducing the rapid eye movement sleep of people with depression can improve depressive symptoms (Howland, 2011).

Shorter sleep duration is associated with chronic psychological distress in young adults; as hours of sleep decrease, levels of distress increase.

Source: Glozier et al. (2010)

Cortisol, Stress, and Depression Abnormalities in hormone regulation associated with the hypothalamic-pituitary-adrenal axis are frequently linked with depression in both youth and adults (Guerry & Hastings, 2011). In explaining stress disorders in Chapter 5, we focused on the stress circuitry of the brain and discussed how stressors can increase levels of *cortisol*, a hormone secreted in response to stress. Interestingly, throughout the world, people with depression have higher blood levels of cortisol (Schnittker, 2010).

Gillespie and Nemeroff (2007) observed that many individuals with depression have early life traumas or stressors such as child abuse, neglect, or loss of a parent. Exposure to stress during early development affects cortisol levels and can increase susceptibility to depression in later life, especially among those who have genetic vulnerability. In fact, researchers have linked depression to an interaction between childhood adversities and certain genes that increase cortisol release once they have been triggered by environmental stressors (R. G. Bradley et al., 2008; H. J. Grabe et al., 2010). Thus, stress, the timing of stress, and genetic predisposition can interact to increase cortisol production and produce depression.

How cortisol might influence depression is still unclear. It affects various brain regions associated with depression, most notably the hippocampus. Chronic stress and associated high levels of cortisol can damage the hippocampus (i.e., neurons die and fail to regenerate) and interfere with systems involved in our stress response. People who have had multiple lifetime stressors, especially stressors early in life, are most likely to have irregularities in their stress response system (Stahl & Wise, 2008).

Overactive stress responses and cortisol production may also cause depressive symptoms by depleting certain neurotransmitters, particularly serotonin (Leonard, 2010). As discussed in Chapter 5, serotonin levels are affected by both chronic and acute stress. In situations involving acute stress, serotonin is released so we can respond to a threatening circumstance. However, chronic stress can deplete serotonin. When levels of serotonin are depleted, depression can occur. Additionally, stress can affect the production of enzymes that are necessary for our brains to use serotonin effectively (J. M. Miller et al., 2009).

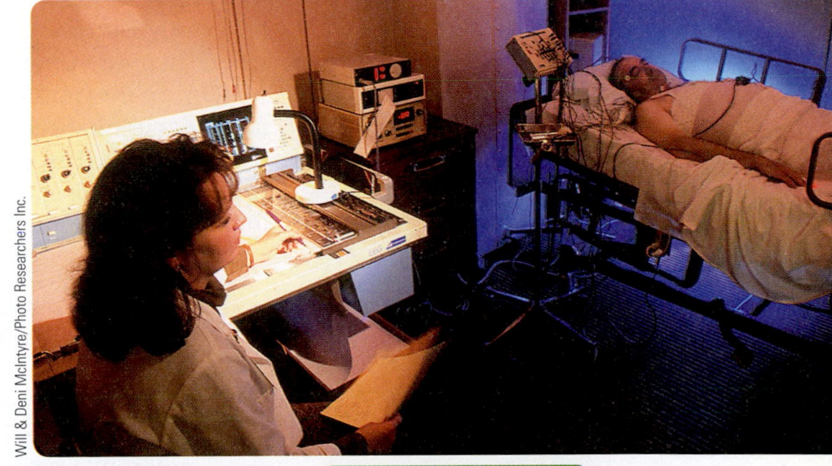

Will & Deni McIntyre/Photo Researchers Inc.

Sleep Disturbances and Depression

Sleep patterns have been linked to depression. For example, rapid eye movement during sleep occurs more often among those who have depression than among those who do not. The reasons for this are unclear. Here, a researcher is monitoring a man's sleep.

Neurotransmitters and Depressive Disorders Abnormalities in the availability of neurotransmitters (including serotonin, norepinephrine, and dopamine) are seen with depression. Evidence regarding the importance of neurotransmitters in depression comes from a variety of sources. Years ago, it was accidentally discovered that when the drug reserpine was used to treat hypertension, many patients became depressed (reserpine depletes neurotransmitters). Similarly, the drug iproniazid, given to patients with tuberculosis, elevated the mood of those who were depressed. (Iproniazid increases the availability of neurotransmitters.) Also, as previously noted, a serotonin transporter allele (5-HTT) is associated with

AP Photo/Karim Kadim

Loss as a Source of Depression

Mourning the death of a loved one occurs in all cultures and societies, as illustrated by these women mourning an Iraqi tae kwon do team who were kidnapped and killed. What characteristics or symptoms would help one to distinguish between "normal" grief and a depressive disorder?

depression (Caspi, Sugden, et al., 2003). More recently, studies of antidepressant medications (which increase the availability of norepinephrine and serotonin) have also pointed to the role of neurotransmission (Stahl & Wise, 2008).

Neuroanatomy and Depression Neuroimaging of individuals with depression has documented decreased brain activity and other brain changes (Leonardo & Hen, 2006; Stahl & Wise, 2008), including abnormalities in brain structures that affect motivation, appetite, sleep, energy level, circadian rhythm, and response to rewarding and aversive stimuli (Nestler et al., 2002).

Whether depressive disorders are caused by circadian system disturbances, hormonal or neurotransmitter abnormalities, or other brain irregularities cannot be resolved at this time. Because depression involves so many different symptoms, it is also possible that no single cause will be isolated. It certainly does appear that complex interactions between genetic makeup, stressful experiences, and psychological, social, and sociocultural factors are involved in depression.

Psychological Dimension

A number of psychological theories have been proposed to account for the development of depression. In this section we look at behavioral and cognitive theories of depression.

Behavioral Explanations Behavioral explanations suggest that depression occurs when people receive insufficient social reinforcement (Lejuez, Hopko, Acierno, Daughters, & Pagoto, 2011). This lack of reinforcement sometimes results from losses such as unemployment, divorce, or the death of a friend or family member. Depression can result from the void created by such losses, including reductions in available reinforcement (e.g., love, affection, companionship). Behaviorists believe that increasing activity that generates environmental reinforcement can reduce depressive symptoms (Gawrysiak, Nicholas, & Hopko, 2009).

One of the most comprehensive behavioral explanations of depression identifies variables that can increase or decrease a person's chances of receiving positive reinforcement (Lewinsohn, 1974; Lewinsohn, Munoz, Youngren, & Zeiss, 1994). A low rate of positive reinforcement due to any of the following factors can increase risk of depression:

- *The number of events and activities that are potentially reinforcing to the person.* This number depends on personal experiences and characteristics (including biological traits). For example, age, gender, or physical attributes can affect the availability of possible reinforcers.
- *The availability of reinforcements in the environment.* Harsh or isolating environments contain fewer possible reinforcers, while warm, nurturing environments increase the likelihood of reinforcement.
- *The behavior of the individual.* Social interaction can bring about or reduce reinforcement. Individuals experiencing depression often show fewer behaviors associated with positive reinforcement (e.g., smiling). They interact with fewer people, respond less, and initiate less conversation. Their behavior may result in subdued responses from others. Interestingly, people with negative personality traits experience depression at an early age and people with few positive personality traits are more likely to have chronic depression (Robison, Shankman, & McFarland, 2009).

Lewinsohn, Hoberman, Teri, and Hautzinger (1985) also proposed that stressful events can produce depression by disrupting predictable behavioral patterns. If these patterns are not reversed, the aftermath of a stressful event can include self-criticism, negative expectancies, and loss of self-confidence, which can then lead to a depressed mood. Once depression sets in, normal functioning is affected; this further increases vulnerability to depression. This model not only addresses behavioral elements but also focuses on the cognitive and emotional consequences of diminished social reinforcement.

Magnification of Events

According to cognitive explanations for depression, people become depressed because of the way they interpret situations. They may overly magnify events that happen to them. In this photo, an adolescent football player sits alone in a locker room after losing a football game.

Cognitive Explanations Cognitive psychologists contend that depression is caused by the way people think and that negative thoughts and errors in thinking result in pessimism, damaging self-views, and feelings of hopelessness. Those who are depressed often see themselves as unworthy and incompetent; personal success may be dismissed as pure luck.

A. T. Beck (1976) proposed that depression is a disturbance in *thinking* rather than a disturbance in *mood* and that it is the way people interpret their experiences that affects their mood. For example, a negative mood is more likely to develop when a situation is viewed as unfair. The tendency to focus on negative information can cause symptoms of depression (Gotlib & Joormann, 2010). Interestingly, carriers of two short alleles of the serotonin transporter gene (associated with increased depression risk following stressful circumstances) show an attentional bias for negative information when undergoing acute stress (Markus & De Raedt, 2011).

According to Beck's theory, individuals experiencing depression tend to have a pessimistic outlook regarding present experiences and future expectations. They may draw sweeping conclusions about their ability, performance, or worth from a single experience or incident, or focus on trivial details taken out of context. For example, if no one initiates conversation at a party, someone with depression may conclude, "People dislike me"; or if a supervisor makes a minor corrective comment, the person may believe that the supervisor is suggesting incompetence, even when the supervisor's overall feedback is highly positive. Similarly, a job loss due to budgetary cuts may lead to self-perceptions of inadequacy or worthlessness. Exaggeration of personal limitations and minimization of accomplishments, achievements, and capabilities is often seen in those with depression. These negative thinking patterns often lead to exaggerated, irrational, or catastrophic thinking involving self-blame and self-criticism (A. Ellis, 1989) as well as increased irritability, a common symptom of depression (M. Fava et al., 2009). Confirming this line of thought, a longitudinal study involving adolescents found that those with negative thinking patterns were much more likely to experience depression in response to high stress (J. S. Carter & Garber, 2011). Individuals with a more negative outlook on life often lack psychological flexibility and get stuck in dysfunctional thinking patterns (Kashdan & Rottenberg, 2010) or have difficulty using positive events to regulate negative mood (Gotlib & Joormann, 2010).

Did You Know ?

In a survey of youth aged 13 to 24, being sexually active and using alcohol or drugs were associated with *less* happiness. What *did* make the youth in this survey happy? Spending time with family was the top answer, followed by time with friends and significant others.

Source: Noveck & Tompson (2007)

Individuals with depression sometimes try to cope with stressful circumstances via rumination (repeatedly thinking about concerns or events) rather than active problem solving. Having a ruminative response style increases the likelihood of depressive symptoms among youth and adults, particularly females and those who tend to be anxious (Hankin, 2008). **Co-rumination**, the process of constantly talking over problems or negative events with others, also increases risk for depression, especially in girls (Stone, Hankin, Gibb, & Abela, 2011; Stone, Uhrlass, & Gibb, 2010). The tendency to ruminate has been associated with early temperament. In a group of youth followed from birth through adolescence, negative emotionality at age one was associated with self-reported rumination at age 13 and depressive symptoms at ages 13 and 26; the link between rumination and depressive symptoms in this group was particularly strong for girls (Mezulis, Priess, & Hyde, 2011).

co-rumination extensively discussing negative feelings or events with peers or others

JOHN ZICH/AFP/Getty Images

Learned Helplessness and Depression

According to Martin Seligman, feelings of helplessness can lead to depression. Former Major League Baseball pitcher Jim Abbott, born without a right hand, fought feelings of helplessness and won multiple awards for overcoming obstacles and adversity through determination and courage.

Learned Helplessness and Attributional Style Martin Seligman and his colleagues (Nolen-Hoeksema, Girgus, & Seligman, 1992; Seligman, 1975) proposed that depression results from thinking patterns related to **learned helplessness**—a belief that one is unable to influence outcomes in one's life. People who feel helpless often make erroneous assumptions about why events occur. For instance, suppose that a student in a math course receives low grades despite studying extensively. A student prone to depression is likely to attribute the low grades to personal factors ("*I* don't do well in math because *I'm* scared of math") rather than external factors ("The *teacher* doesn't like me, so I can't get a good grade"). Someone prone to depression is also more likely to assume that the low grade is due to unchangeable factors ("*I'm the type of person* who can never do well in math") rather than a temporary, changeable situation ("My low math grade was probably due to *my heavy workload this quarter*"). Additionally, someone with depression is more likely to think globally ("I'm a *lousy student*") rather than specifically ("I'm *poor at math but good in other subjects*"). Individuals whose thinking focuses on causes that are internal, stable, and global are more likely to experience depression compared to those whose explanations are external, unstable, and specific (Abramson, Seligman, & Teasdale, 1978; M. C. Morris, Ciesla, & Garber, 2008). These patterns of thinking are referred to as one's attributional style. Cognitive-behavioral theories make an important contribution to understandings of depression, but appear to only partially explain how depression might develop.

Social Dimension

Environmental factors such as maltreatment during childhood, loss of a parent, and stressful life events have moderate effects on the development of depression (Kendler & Prescott, 2006). Parental depression appears to have both a genetic and an environmental influence on intergenerational transmission of depression (Silberg, Maes, & Eaves, 2010). Among children born by assisted conception, depression in either parent (but especially the mother) increases the likelihood of childhood depression even when the children are not biologically related to the depressed parent (Harold et al., 2010; G. Lewis, Rice, Harold, Collishaw, & Thapar, 2011). Similarly, children whose adoptive mothers demonstrate high levels of anxiety and depression show high reactivity to frustrating events, suggesting that they are affected by their adoptive mother's emotional distress (Leve et al., 2010).

What kinds of stressful life events are associated with depression? Severe acute stress (e.g., serious illness, the death of a loved one) often precedes the onset of major depression (Stroud, Davila, Hammen, & Vrshek-Schallhorn, 2011) and is much more likely to cause a first depressive episode than is chronic stress (Muscatell, Slavich, Monroe, & Gotlib, 2009). However, after an initial episode of depression, less severe stressors can trigger further depressive episodes (Stroud et al., 2011). Chronic social stress can also interact with personal vulnerabilities to produce depression (M. C. Morris, Ciesla, & Garber, 2010). For example, individuals who are highly conscientious and who have chronically high levels of work stress coupled with few decision-making opportunities tend to be particularly affected by depression (Bonde, 2008; Verboom et al., 2011). Additionally, *targeted rejection* (active, intentional social exclusion or rejection) has a particularly strong link with depressive symptoms (Slavich, Way, Eisenberger, & Taylor, 2010).

Timing of negative life events is also important. Experiences occurring during childhood, including harsh discipline, are associated with increased severity of depression (Lara, Klein, & Kasch, 2000). Not surprisingly, negative thinking patterns can result from early stressful interactions with parents or caregivers

learned helplessness a learned belief that one is helpless and unable to affect outcomes

(Van Vlierberghe, Braet, Bosmans, Rosseel, & Bogels, 2010; Woolgar & Tranah, 2010). For example, emotional abuse and neglect in childhood is associated with pessimistic thinking, feelings of shame or inadequacy, and beliefs that loving someone will lead to rejection (Eberhart, 2011; M. O. Wright, Crawford, & Del Castillo, 2009).

Why do some people who encounter stressful life events develop depression, whereas others do not? The relationship between stress and depression is complex and interactive. For example, maternal depression has been associated with not only fewer positive but also more negative parent–child interactions; this pattern appears to initiate a cascade of risk factors that culminate in depression (C. J. Foster, Garber, & Durlak, 2008; Garber & Cole, 2010). Similarly, individuals who fail to develop secure attachments and trusting relationships with caregivers early in life have increased vulnerability to depression when confronted with stressful life events (T. E. Morley & Moran, 2011).

Not only can stress cause depression, but depression can also cause stress. Hammen (2006) found that individuals who are depressed are more likely to experience stressors that are within their control (e.g., initiating arguments). She believes that some people who are depressed create and generate stress themselves. R. T. Liu and Alloy (2010) also concluded that *stress generation* (i.e., engaging in behaviors that lead to stressful events) increases depression. Thus the research suggests that stress and depression are bidirectional.

Finally, stress itself may activate a genetic predisposition for depression; as previously discussed, individuals who are predisposed to depression (carriers of the short allele of the serotonin transporter gene) develop depression when exposed to childhood maltreatment (Caspi, Sugden, et al., 2003). This may also explain why some people with genetic predispositions do not develop depression (i.e., significant stressors are absent) and why others who have encountered the same stressors as a person who is depressed do not experience depression (i.e., they do not have the predisposition).

Sociocultural Dimension Sociocultural factors found to be significantly associated with depression include socioeconomic status, culture, race and ethnicity, and gender. For example, individuals living in communities that have high rates of poverty, delinquency, and drug use have increased risk for depression (Cutrona et al., 2005).

Culture, Ethnicity, and Depression Culture influences descriptions of depressive symptoms, decisions about treatment, doctor–patient interactions, and the likelihood of outcomes such as suicide (Kleinman, 2004). In some cultures, depression is experienced largely in the form of somatic or bodily complaints, rather than as sadness. For example, depression is often expressed as "nerves" and headaches in Latino and Mediterranean cultures; weakness, tiredness, or "imbalance" in Chinese and other Asian cultures; problems of the "heart" in Middle Eastern cultures; and being "heartbroken" among the Hopi (American Psychiatric Association, 2000).

Why do depressive reactions and symptoms differ from culture to culture? Greenberger, Chen, Tally, and Dong (2000) gained some insight into this question by comparing factors associated with depressed mood among adolescents in China and the United States. In both cultures, "culture general" stressors such as serious illness or family economic distress had similar effects on depressed mood. However, cultural differences emerged for other variables. For instance, correlations between depressed mood and poor relationships with parents or poor academic achievement were higher for Chinese participants compared to U.S. participants, perhaps reflecting the Chinese cultural emphasis on family and achievement. Similarly, family conflict and intergenerational stress is a risk factor for depression among adolescents with immigrant parents (Fornos et al., 2005;

FOCUS ON RESILIENCE

Can We Immunize People Against Depression?

Just as vaccines can protect people against the flu and other diseases, considerable research now suggests that various interventions can prevent or reduce depressive symptoms. For example, recognizing the strong connection between behaviors associated with depression (withdrawal, listlessness, agitation) and the learned helplessness that develops when aversive situations seem inescapable, positive psychologists have developed programs to "psychologically immunize" children against depression and to combat learned helplessness. Youth who learn to think optimistically (e.g., recognize how their efforts result in successful outcomes) and cope effectively with disappointments and challenges are much less likely to experience depression (Seligman, Reivich, Jaycox, & Gillham, 1995; Seligman, Ernst, Gillham, Reivich & Linkins, 2009).

The Penn Resiliency Program has concentrated on classroom teaching of cognitive-behavioral and social problem-solving skills (Seligman, Ernst, et al., 2009). Premised on understandings that people's beliefs about events play a critical role in their emotional reactions and behaviors, students are taught to evaluate the accuracy of various thoughts, detect inaccurate thoughts (especially negative beliefs), and consider alternate interpretations of events. Youth also practice coping and problem-solving strategies that can be used in stressful situations (e.g., learning to relax, respond assertively, or negotiate resolutions to conflicts). The results have been particularly impressive for high-risk populations, including females and youth displaying high levels of depressive symptoms, and when parents have also been taught depression-prevention strategies or homework has been assigned (Gillham, Hamilton, Freres, Patton, & Gallup, 2006; Gillham, Reivich, et al., 2006; Stice, Shaw, Bohon, Marti, & Rohde, 2009). Programs for adolescent girls target gender-related risk factors such as media messages, body image, and rumination, and teach emotion regulation and strategies for dealing with relational aggression and interpersonal conflicts (Gillham, Chaplin, Reivich, & Hamilton, 2008). In one recent study, adolescents who demonstrated the most optimism were half as likely as others to be depressed and were more able to cope effectively with life challenges (Patton et al., 2011).

PhotoDisc

Other interventions that can help protect against depression include:

- *Mobilizing social support.* Friendships and family support can help youth and adults cope with difficult circumstances (including racism, teenage pregnancy, and serious illness) and decrease the incidence of depression (J. E. Cox et al., 2008; Kollannoor-Samuel et al., 2011; Odom & Vernon-Feagans, 2010). Sports participation has been found to significantly decrease the risk of depression and suicidal thinking in adolescents (Babiss & Gangwisch, 2009). Social support that meets specific needs (e.g., financial support, decreasing loneliness) is particularly protective against depression (Knowlton & Latkin, 2007).
- *Increasing positive emotions.* Participating in enjoyable or meaningful activities, reflecting on personal strengths, focusing on gratitude, and performing acts of kindness can significantly increase positive emotions, particularly when multiple strategies are used on an ongoing basis (Sin & Lyubomirsky, 2009). The ability to boost one's mood by finding pleasure in daily activities ("in-the-moment" pleasure) is also protective against depression (Geschwind, Peeters, Van Os, Drukker, & Wichers, 2011).
- *Exercising, eating, and sleeping properly.* Higher levels of physical activity are associated with lower depression risk (Lucas et al., 2011). Both aerobic and weight-training activities can boost mood (Greer & Trivedi, 2009). Eating a healthy diet has also been linked with better mental health (Jacka, Kremer, et al., 2011), and eating vegetables, fruit, meat, fish, nuts, legumes, and whole grains is associated with a reduced risk of depression (Jacka, Pasco, et al., 2010; Sánchez-Villegas, Delgado-Rodriguez, et al., 2009). Dietary patterns in Japan (high intake of vegetables, fruit, mushrooms, and soy) are considered one of the factors that help protect this population from depression (Nanri et al., 2010). Sufficient sleep (7–9 hours) is also strongly associated with positive mood and psychological well-being (S. Brand & Kirov, 2011).

In summary, just as a variety of factors contribute to the development of depressive illness, a variety of protective factors can reduce the risk of (i.e., immunize against) depression.

Juang, Syed, & Takagi, 2007; S. Y. Kim, Chen, Li, Huang, & Moon, 2009). Perceived discrimination based on gender, race or ethnicity, or sexual orientation, especially among those who do not talk to others about their experiences, is also associated with depression (Juang & Cookston, 2009; McLaughlin, Hatzenbuehler, & Keyes, 2010). Analysis of everyday encounters with discrimination among African American women revealed that those subjected to more frequent discrimination were most likely to have depressive symptoms (Schulz et al., 2006). Another study involving African Americans found perceived discrimination to be related to severity of depressive symptoms; discrimination was more stressful for the women than men in the study (J. Wagner & Abbott, 2007).

Gender and Depressive Disorders Depression is far more common among women than among men, regardless of region of the world, race and ethnicity, or social class (R. C. Kessler, 2003). Some have wondered if women are simply more likely than men to seek treatment or to report their depression to physicians or those conducting surveys regarding emotional well-being. That is, the gender differences may reflect differences in self-report of depressive symptoms or willingness to seek treatment rather than differences in actual depression rates. It is also possible that diagnosticians or diagnostic systems are biased toward finding depression among women (Caplan, 1995). Additionally, depression in men may be hidden by other factors such as substance abuse or other addictive behaviors. However, evidence suggests that women do, in fact, have higher rates of depression than men and that the differences are real rather than an artifact of self-reports or biases (Rieker & Bird, 2005). Gender differences in depression begin appearing during adolescence and are greatest during the reproductive years through menopause. Attempts to explain these differences have focused on physiological and social psychological factors (Table 7.3).

Did You Know?

You could be living in a "depressed" or a "happy" city. The following rankings were based on antidepressant sales, suicide rates, unemployment, and the number of days residents reported being depressed.

DEPRESSED CITIES	HAPPY CITIES
1. St. Petersburg, FL	1. Honolulu, HI
2. Detroit, MI	2. Manchester, NH
3. Memphis, TN	3. Fargo, ND
4. Tampa, FL	4. Omaha, NE
5. Louisville, KY	5. Boston, MA

Source: Sgobba, 2011

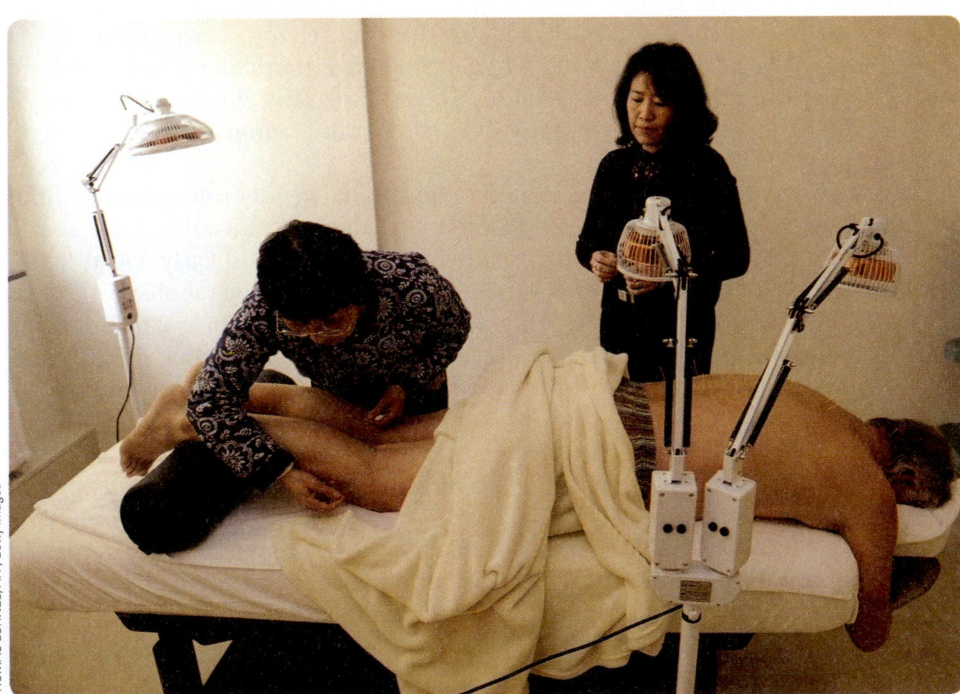

Cultural Differences in Symptoms and Treatment

People from different cultures vary in the way they express depression. Individuals of Chinese descent often report somatic or bodily complaints instead of psychological symptoms, such as sadness or loss of pleasure. They also are more likely to rely on Chinese medicine and acupuncture to treat their symptoms.

TABLE 7.3 Possible Explanations for the Higher Frequency of Depression Among Women

- Women may be more willing to acknowledge and seek help for depression.
- Genetic or hormonal differences may result in higher rates of depression among women.
- Women are subjected to societal factors such as unfulfilling gender roles or limited occupational opportunities that lead to feelings of helplessness and hopelessness.
- Cognitive styles (such as ruminating or co-ruminating) that increase depression are more common in women.
- Women are more likely to have experienced childhood trauma (sexual abuse, childhood maltreatment) and other stressors associated with depression.

Multiple research findings suggest that environmental and sociocultural factors interact with biological factors, such as genetic or hormonal differences, to influence gender differences in depression. Heritability of depression appears to be higher among women than men, as noted earlier (D. Goldberg, 2006). It has been suggested that genetic risk factors associated with depression may, in fact, increase some women's likelihood of encountering other stressors such as trauma or divorce (Kendler & Prescott, 2006). Additionally, changes in hormones and neurotransmitters (specifically serotonin), combined with life stress, history of sexual abuse, and socialization effects, are believed to influence the likelihood of developing depression (Vigod & Stewart, 2009). Sexual abuse has a particularly strong association with lifetime risk of depression (L. P. Chen et al., 2010).

Gender differences in depression are believed to be influenced by the variations in hormone levels that begin in puberty and continue until menopause (Graziottin & Serafini, 2009). Interestingly, girls who experience early physical maturity are at particular risk of depression (Joinson, Heron, Lewis, Croudace & Araya, 2011). Menopause is a time when women are particularly vulnerable to severe depression (Graziottin & Serafini, 2009), especially when menopause is combined with poor health or negative views regarding aging (Woods, Mitchell, Percival, & Smith-DiJulio, 2009).

Social or psychological factors related to traditional gender roles can also influence the development of depressive disorders. Dedovic, Wadiwalla, Engert, and Pruessner (2009) have suggested that gender socialization and early social learning contribute to gender differences in the regulation and metabolism of stress hormones. Specifically, social modeling and socialization practices can influence feelings of self-worth. While males are socialized to value autonomy, self-interest, and achievement-oriented goals, females learn to value social goals and interdependent functioning (e.g., caring about others, not wanting to hurt others). Women's self-perceptions are, therefore, more influenced by the opinions of others, a factor that increases vulnerability to interpersonal stress, particularly stressors involving close friends or family.

Nolen-Hoeksema (1987) has suggested that the way women respond to depressed moods contributes to the severity, chronicity, and frequency of depressive episodes. In her view, women tend to ruminate and amplify their depressive moods, whereas men often find ways to minimize sad feelings. When individuals tracked their depressed moods and responses to these moods for 1 month, women were more likely than men to ruminate when feeling depressed; this tendency to ruminate was a major factor in explaining gender differences in depression (Nolen-Hoeksema, 1991). During adolescence, increases in anxious arousal and rumination increase the likelihood of depressive symptoms among girls (Hankin, 2009). Adolescent girls who are depressed are also more likely to generate interpersonal stress, which in turn often leads to chronic depression (Rudolph, Flynn, Abaied, Groot, & Thompson, 2009).

Treatment for Depression

Finding the correct treatment or combination of treatments is exceptionally important with depression, because longer depressive episodes are associated with negative long-term outcomes, more frequent depressive episodes, and lower likelihood of symptom improvement (Papakostas & Fava, 2008; Shelton, Osuntokun, Heinloth, & Corya, 2010). When someone is not responding to initial treatment, adding on a therapy is generally preferred over switching from one therapy to another, particularly if the initial treatment had some effect (Shelton et al., 2010). If depression does not respond to treatment, it is important to rule out possible misdiagnosis (e.g., asking about manic or hypomanic symptoms to ensure that the person does not, in fact, have a bipolar disorder; Fornaro & Giosue, 2010).We now turn to various treatment strategies used with depressive disorders.

Biomedical Treatments for Depressive Disorders

Biomedical treatments include the use of medication and other interventions that affect various brain systems, such as circadian-related treatments (light therapy and sleep deprivation) and brain stimulation techniques.

Medication Antidepressant medications are believed to work by increasing the availability of neurotransmitters in the brain. Three classes of antidepressants—the *tricyclics, monoamine oxidase inhibitors* (MAOIs), and *serotonin norepinephrine reuptake inhibitors* (SNRIs)—block the reabsorption of norepinephrine and serotonin, whereas the *selective serotonin reuptake inhibitors* (SSRIs) block the reuptake of serotonin. *Atypical antidepressants*, a group of unique medications used to treat depressions, affect other neurotransmitters, including dopamine. MAOIs are the

CONTROVERSY:

Antidepressants and Suicidality: Risk Versus Benefit

In 2004, the U.S. Food and Drug Administration (FDA) required manufacturers of certain antidepressants to provide warnings regarding the possibility of increased risk for suicidal thinking and behavior in children and adolescents taking these medications. In 2007, the warning was expanded to include those aged 18–24. The following is from the FDA (2007):

> Antidepressants increased the risk compared to placebo of suicidal thinking and behavior (suicidality) in children, adolescents, and young adults in short-term studies of major depressive disorder (MDD) and other psychiatric disorders. . . . All patients being treated with antidepressants for any indication should be monitored appropriately and observed closely for clinical worsening, suicidality, and unusual changes in behavior, especially during the initial few months of a course of drug therapy, or at times of dose changes, either increases or decreases.

What is the relationship between suicidal thoughts, suicide, and antidepressant medication? The findings are consistent for children and adolescents and somewhat mixed for older age groups. The data cited by the FDA showed that suicidal thoughts and behaviors occurred among 4 percent of youth taking antidepressants compared to 2 percent of those taking placebo. The risk of suicide associated with antidepressant use appears to be strongly age dependent. When compared to placebo, the risk of suicidal thinking or behaviors associated with antidepressant use in young adults (younger than 25) approached that of children and adolescents (i.e., risk almost doubled), was equivalent among adults aged 25–64, and was decreased in those 65 years of age and older (P. D. Kramer, 2009; Seemüller et al., 2009; M. Stone et al., 2009).

Some believe the FDA warning has resulted in more harm than good, due to the subsequent reduction in the diagnosis and treatment of depression in children, adolescents, and young adults (Brent, 2009b; Cuffe, 2007). In the year following the FDA warning, the suicide rate in children and adolescents increased 18 percent, the first increase in 10 years (Hamilton et al., 2007).

For Further Consideration:

1. Should the FDA warnings regarding antidepressants be reviewed?
2. What factors should be considered when treating children, adolescents, and young adults experiencing depression?

Did You Know? In the United States:

- The rate of antidepressant use has increased almost 400 percent over the last two decades.
- Eleven percent of those aged 12 and older are taking antidepressants.
- Over 60 percent of those taking antidepressants have done so for over 2 years.
- Women are 2.5 times more likely to take antidepressants than men.
- Twenty-three percent of women aged 40–59 take antidepressants.
- The majority of people taking antidepressants are not receiving therapy.

Source: Pratt, Brody, & Gu (2011)

least frequently used, due to concern about serious effects when they are combined with certain foods, beverages, or medications.

Selecting which antidepressant to use to treat depression is often rather arbitrary, but the choice can be influenced by prior response to antidepressants (or family patterns of response), the desire to avoid certain side effects (e.g., weight gain, sexual side effects, or gastrointestinal problems), or the presence of other symptoms, such as anxiety or nicotine addiction, that might also be helped by certain antidepressants (Brunoni, Fraguas, et al., 2009). Those who respond to antidepressants often show increases in positive emotions more than decreases in negative emotions (Geschwind, Nicolson, Peeters, Van Os, & Wichers, 2011). Antidepressant medications help improve mood but do not cure depression; that is, once medication is stopped, symptoms often return (DeRubeis, Siegle, & Hollon, 2008). For this reason, antidepressants are often continued even after symptoms subside. Antidepressants are not addictive, but they do have a variety of potential side effects, including the increases in suicidality seen in those younger than 25 taking certain antidepressants (Berenson, 2006). Additionally, stopping certain antidepressants abruptly (especially those that affect the neurotransmitter serotonin) can produce severe flu-like symptoms, emotionality, and suicidal thinking as the body adjusts to functioning without the medication (Hosenbocus & Chahal, 2011).

Although antidepressants are commonly used in the treatment of depression, questions over their effectiveness remain. Concerns have been raised regarding publication bias in studies on antidepressant medication. One review of studies evaluating the effectiveness of antidepressants found that 94 percent of the studies supportive of antidepressants were submitted for publication and published, whereas many of the studies that did not support the effectiveness of antidepressants were never published or were written to give the impression of a positive antidepressant outcome (E. H. Turner, Matthews, Linardatos, Tell, & Rosenthal, 2008). Even with this publication bias, the evidence for antidepressant efficacy is rather weak. Many individuals affected by depression do not respond to antidepressant medications (M. P. Ward & Irazoqui, 2010); chronic, milder depression and older age are associated with decreased response (Fournier et al., 2010). Placebos are often as effective as antidepressants in treating mild depression (Barbui, Cipriani, Patel, Ayuso-Mateos, & van Ommeren, 2011). A comprehensive study evaluating the effectiveness of antidepressant medication concluded that the benefit of these medications over placebo for treating mild or moderate depression was "minimal or nonexistent." Antidepressants appeared somewhat more effective for those with severe depression (Fournier et al., 2010), with about half showing some response to the first antidepressant prescribed; unfortunately, fewer than one third of those with severe depression make a full recovery (Leuchter, Cook, Hunter, & Korb, 2009).

Exercise and Dietary Changes For many individuals with depression who do not fully respond to antidepressant medication, participating in moderate to intense levels of daily exercise can significantly reduce residual symptoms of depression (Stathopoulou, Powers, Berry, Smits, & Otto, 2006; Trivedi, Greer, et al., 2011). Omega-3 supplementation can also reduce depressive symptoms, particularly for those without concurrent anxiety symptoms (Lespérance et al., 2011).

Circadian-Related Treatments Some treatments for depression involve efforts to reset the circadian clock (McClung, 2007). For example, a night of total sleep deprivation followed by a night of sleep recovery can improve depressive symptoms (Howland, 2011). Additionally, use of specially designed lights is an effective and well-tolerated treatment for those with SAD and other depressive disorders (R. E. Strong et al., 2009; Westrin & Lam, 2007b). This therapy involves dawn-light simulation (timer-activated lights that gradually increase in brightness) or daily use of a box, visor, or lighting system that delivers light of a particular intensity for a designated period of time, usually 20–60 min (Gooley et al., 2010).

Many individuals taking SSRIs report feelings of emotional detachment, indifference, diminished positive and negative emotional responsiveness, and personality changes.

Source: J. Price, Cole, & Goodwin (2009)

A well-designed study evaluating treatment for SAD compared light therapy alone to light therapy combined with antidepressants; both groups made similar improvement (67 percent showed improvement and 50–54 percent showed remission of symptoms), but light therapy produced more rapid treatment response and fewer side effects (R. W. Lam, Levitt, et al., 2006). An analysis of randomized controlled trials suggested that light therapy is as beneficial as antidepressant treatment not only for SAD, but also for nonseasonal depression (R. N. Golden et al., 2005). Light therapy is typically continued throughout the low-light season for people with SAD or for people whose depressive symptoms get worse during the winter (Westrin & Lam, 2007a).

Brain Stimulation Therapies Electroconvulsive therapy, vagus nerve stimulation, and transcranial magnetic stimulation are sometimes used to treat severe or chronic depression, especially when life-threatening symptoms are present (Andrade et al., 2010).

Electroconvulsive therapy (ECT) has FDA approval for treating depression that does not respond to other treatments, and is considered the treatment of choice for profound, life-threatening depression involving refusal to eat or intense suicidal intent (Brunoni, Teng, et al., 2010; Fink, Shorter, & Taylor, 2010; Ungvari, Caroff, & Gerevich, 2009). ECT, which is typically conducted several times weekly, involves application of moderate electrical voltage to the brain in order to produce a convulsion (seizure) lasting at least 15 seconds; appropriate use of anesthetics during ECT minimizes side effects such as headaches, confusion, and memory loss (Mayo, Kaye, Conrad, Baluch, & Frost, 2010). Regularly implemented stimulation of the vagus nerve (approved for use if four prior treatments for chronic, recurrent depression have failed) has helped reduce symptoms of depression both when combined with ECT (Marangell, Martinez, Jurdi, & Zboyan, 2007; A. Sharma, Chaturvedi, Sharma, & Sorrell, 2009) and when used alone (Nemeroff et al., 2006).

Another controversial technique used with treatment-resistant depression is repetitive transcranial magnetic stimulation, in which an electromagnetic field stimulates the brain. Although a recent meta-analysis concluded that this technique has sufficient research to support its use for major depressive disorder and for auditory hallucinations (Slotema, Blom, Hoek, & Sommer, 2010), other literature reviews have expressed more skepticism, in part because of the weak design of many studies evaluating the procedure. A factor confounding the research may be intensity of stimulation; high-intensity stimulation appears to produce the most significant results (Levkovitz et al., 2009).

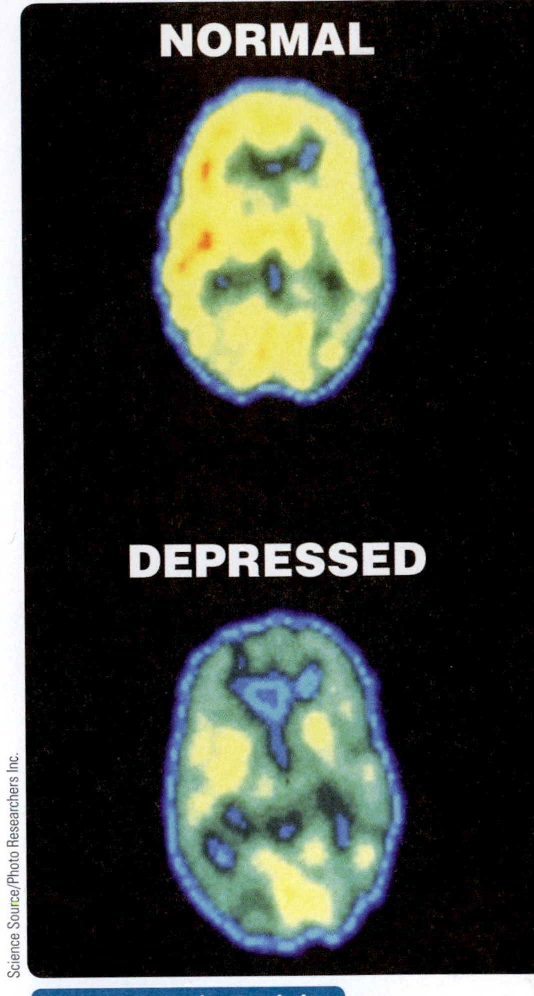

Reduced Brain Activity in Depression

These positron emission tomography scans comparing normal brain activity with the cerebral metabolism of a person with depression show the decreased brain activity seen in depressive disorders. Researchers hope that brain scans will soon guide treatment for disorders such as depression.

Psychological and Behavioral Treatments for Depressive Disorders

Research has supported the effectiveness of a variety of psychological techniques in treating depression. These therapies can be used alone or in conjunction with biomedical interventions. Three particular approaches have received extensive research support (behavioral activation, interpersonal and cognitive-behavioral therapies), and another technique (mindfulness-based cognitive therapy) has shown promise in treating depression.

Behavioral Activation Therapy Behavioral activation therapy is based on the idea that depression results from diminished reinforcement. Consistent with this perspective, treatment focuses on increasing exposure to pleasurable events and activities, improving social skills, and facilitating social interactions. The steps involved in treatment are: (1) identifying and rating different activities in terms of the pleasure or feelings of competence or mastery they might produce; (2) performing some of the selected activities, thereby increasing feelings of pleasure or mastery; (3) identifying day-to-day problems and using behavior techniques to deal with them; and (4) improving social and assertiveness skills (Lejuez et al., 2011). Behavioral activation has been shown in one study to be as effective as antidepressant medication and more effective than cognitive-behavioral therapy (Dimidjian et al., 2006).

Interpersonal Psychotherapy Interpersonal psychotherapy is an evidence-based approach focused on current interpersonal problems. Because this approach presumes that depression occurs within an interpersonal context, therapy focuses on relationship issues. Clients learn to evaluate their role in interpersonal conflict and make positive changes in their relationships. By improving communication with others, identifying role conflicts, and increasing social skills, clients come to find relationships more satisfying and pleasant. Although interpersonal psychotherapy acknowledges the role of early life experiences and trauma, it is oriented primarily toward present, not past, relationships. It has proven to be an efficacious treatment for acute depression (Levenson et al., 2010) and is as effective as continuing use of antidepressant medication in preventing relapse (K. S. Dobson et al., 2008).

Cognitive-Behavioral Therapy Cognitive-behavioral therapy focuses on altering the negative thought patterns and distorted thinking associated with depression. Cognitive therapists teach clients to identify thoughts that precede upsetting emotions, distance themselves from these thoughts, and examine the accuracy of their beliefs (DeRubeis et al., 2008). Clients are taught to identify negative, self-critical thoughts and the connection between negative thoughts and negative feelings. They then learn to replace inaccurate thoughts with realistic interpretations.

Overall, individuals treated with cognitive-behavioral therapy are less likely to relapse after treatment has stopped, compared to individuals taking antidepressants (K. S. Dobson et al., 2008). Changes in explanatory styles and alterations in negative self-biases may help prevent recurrence of depressive symptoms (DeRubeis et al., 2008). Cognitive-behavioral treatment has, in fact, produced changes in the same brain regions affected by the use of antidepressants (Goldapple et al., 2004). It has effectively helped adolescents from diverse backgrounds (E. Marchand, Ng, Rohde, & Stice, 2010), and adapted versions of the therapy are used in non-Western cultures (Naeem, Waheed, Gobbi, Ayub, & Kingdon, 2011). Cognitive-behavioral intervention has also reduced depression risk and symptoms among children whose parents have a history of depression (Compas et al., 2011; Garber et al., 2009).

Mindfulness-Based Cognitive Therapy Mindfulness-based cognitive therapy involves calm awareness of one's present experience, thoughts, and feelings, and promotes an attitude of acceptance rather than judgment, evaluation, or rumination. Mindfulness allows those affected by depression to disrupt the cycle of negative thinking by focusing on the present (B. D. Gilbert & Christopher, 2010). Focusing on experiences with curiosity and without judgment prevents the development of maladaptive beliefs and thus prevents depressive thinking (Frewen, Evans, Maraj, Dozois, & Partridge, 2008). Clinical studies have found that mindfulness-based cognitive therapy reduces residual symptoms in chronic depression, is effective in treatment-resistant depression, and reduces the risk of recurrence of depressive symptoms (Barnhofer et al., 2010; Eisendrath et al., 2008; Godfrin & van Heeringen, 2010; Kenny & Williams, 2007). The increases in positive emotions and appreciation of pleasant daily activities associated with mindfulness-based cognitive therapy may contribute to its protective effects against depressive relapse (Geschwind, Peeters, Van Os, et al., 2011).

Less costly interventions including brief training to reduce negative attentional bias (T. T. Wells & Beevers, 2010), computerized skill-building sessions (Andrews, Cuijpers, Craske, McEvoy, & Titov, 2010), and cognitive-behavioral therapy delivered online (D. Kessler et al., 2009) have also shown promise in the treatment of depression. Participants in treatment focused on anticipation of a more positive future showed significant reductions in depressive symptoms (Vilhauer et al., 2011).

Cognitive bias modification, a guided self-help intervention aimed at minimizing rumination and overgeneralization and enhancing specific problem-solving skills, is another low-cost, accessible treatment for depression (Watkins & Moberly, 2009; Watkins, Taylor, et al., 2012). However, individuals who tend to ruminate have shown an increase in depressive symptoms when using self-directed workbooks; those who ruminate may have difficulty identifying and disputing negative thoughts without the help of a trained professional (Haeffel, 2010).

Combining Biomedical and Psychological Treatments Unfortunately, only one third of those treated for depression achieve sustained recovery from depressive symptoms (DeRubeis et al., 2008). Although there is evidence that antidepressant medications can be beneficial in cases of severe depression (Fournier et al., 2010), psychotherapies appear to have longer-lasting effects. That is, effective psychological treatment appears to produce more enduring results, whereas medication produces relief from depressive symptoms only during active treatment (Hollon, Stewart, & Strunk, 2006). There appears to be some advantage to combining medication and psychotherapy for those with severe depression. Medication can reduce symptoms, whereas psychotherapy can enhance social functioning and reduce risk of relapse (M. A. Friedman et al., 2004).

CHECKPOINT REVIEW

1. Name five depressive disorders and the major symptoms associated with each.
2. Why is premenstrual dysphoric disorder a controversial diagnostic category?
3. Give an example of how genetic factors interact with environmental factors to produce depression.
4. Describe two ways in which biological factors can lead to depression.
5. Describe two ways in which psychological factors can contribute to depression.
6. Describe three different treatment options for depression.

Bipolar Disorders

Up to this point, we have discussed disorders that involve only depressive symptoms. In this section, we discuss bipolar disorders, a group of disorders which involve symptoms of hypomania/mania that may alternate with episodes of depression (see Table 7.4). Although depressive symptoms are often seen in bipolar disorders, depressive and bipolar disorders are very different conditions. As we will discuss, bipolar disorders have a very strong genetic component; in fact, there is strong evidence of physiological overlap (i.e., shared biological etiology) between bipolar disorders and schizophrenia (a severe mental health disorder involving loss of contact with reality, which we discuss extensively in Chapter 11). Also, people with bipolar disorders respond to medications that have little effect with depressive disorders. Additionally, the average age of onset is somewhat earlier for bipolar disorders (teens and early 20s) than for depressive disorders (late 20s). Finally, the prevalence of bipolar disorders is much lower than that seen with depression (see Figure 7.2; Merikangas, Akiskal, et al., 2007).

Diagnosis and Classification of Bipolar Disorders

Bipolar disorders are diagnosed following careful evaluation and confirmation of hypomanic or manic symptoms. The severity and pattern of any depressive symptoms are also reviewed; in fact, severe depression is what causes people with bipolar

DISORDERS CHART BIPOLAR DISORDERS

TABLE 7.4

Disorder	Symptoms	Lifetime Prevalence (%)	Gender Difference	Age of Onset
Bipolar I	• At least one weeklong manic episode • Most recent episode may be manic, hypomanic, or depressed • Mixed or depressive episodes are common, but not required, for diagnosis • Possible psychotic features	0.4–1.0	No major difference, although rapid-cycling is more common in females	Any age; usually late adolescence or early adulthood
Bipolar II	• At least one major depressive episode • At least one hypomanic episode • No history of mania • Most recent episode may be hypomanic or depressed	0.6–1.1	Higher in females	Any age; usually late adolescence or early adulthood
Cyclothymia	• Numerous hypomanic episodes alternating with milder depression for at least 2 years (with no more than 2 months symptom-free)[a] • No history of major depression or mania	0.4–1.0	No difference	Often adolescence

Source: Data from DSM-5 Work Groups (2012); R. C. Kessler, Chiu, Demler, & Walters (2005); Merikangas, Akiskal, et al. (2007); Merikangas, Jin, et al., (2011)
[a]In children and adolescents, mood can be irritable and symptoms must have been present for at least 1 year.

disorders to spend much of the time ill (Altshuler et al., 2010). The three types of bipolar disorders are bipolar I, bipolar II, and cyclothymic disorder. Although clinicians are interested in the frequency of normal mood states, they differentiate between bipolar categories by reviewing the severity of depressive and hypomanic/manic symptoms and the pattern of mood changes (see Figure 7.4).

Bipolar I is diagnosed when someone (with or without a history of severe depression) experiences at least one manic episode. (Manic symptoms need to be present most of the day, nearly every day, for at least 1 week and significantly affect functioning). In addition to this manic episode, those with bipolar I (especially women) often have hypomanic episodes that alternate with depression (Swann, Steinberg, Lijffijt, & Moeller, 2009). Approximately 25 percent of mood episodes among those with bipolar I involve **rapid-cycling**, a pattern where there are four or more significant mood swings per year (D. A. Solomon et al., 2009).

Bipolar II is diagnosed when there has been at least one major depressive episode lasting at least 2 weeks and at least one hypomanic episode lasting at least 4 consecutive days. Depression is the most pronounced feature of bipolar II; depressive symptoms sometimes occur almost simultaneously with hypomanic symptoms. In bipolar II, symptoms are usually most severe during depressive episodes, with almost three fourths of those with bipolar II reporting severe impairment while depressed (Merikangas, Jin, et al., 2011). Bipolar II is considered an underdiagnosed disorder, in part because many physicians prescribe antidepressants without adequately assessing for periods of highly energetic, goal-directed activity and other hypomanic symptoms (Benazzi, 2007). The primary distinction between bipolar I and bipolar II is the severity of the symptoms during energized episodes. A bipolar I diagnosis requires that symptoms be (a) severe enough to be considered manic; (b) ongoing for at least 1 week; and (c) severe enough to significantly impair social or occupational functioning (DSM-5 Work Groups, 2012; Benazzi, 2007).

Approximately one third of those with bipolar disorder exhibit both rapid-cycling and mixed episodes (Koszewska & Rybakowski, 2009). **Mixed episodes** (i.e., three or more symptoms of hypomania/mania or depression occurring during an episode from the opposite pole) are common with both bipolar I

rapid-cycling the occurrence of four or more mood episodes per year

mixed episode concurrent hypomanic/manic and depressive symptoms

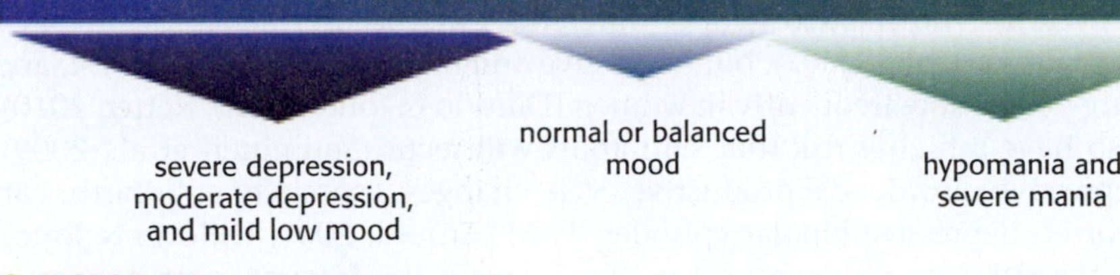

FIGURE 7.4

Mood States Experienced in Bipolar Disorder
All individuals diagnosed with a bipolar disorder have experienced at least one episode of elevated mood (mania or hypomania). Many also experience periods of mild, moderate, or severe depression.

Source: National Institute of Mental Health, 2012. Retrieved from http://www.nimh.nih.gov/health/publications/bipolar-disorder/complete-index.shtml

and bipolar II (Targum & Nierenberg, 2011). Hypomanic/manic symptoms that accompany a depressive episode are of particular concern because they predict a more severe form of the disorder and a need for more intensive treatment (Valentí et al., 2011). Unfortunately, hypomanic symptoms often go unrecognized due to the prominence of depressive features (Frye et al., 2009; J. F. Goldberg et al., 2009). A particular danger of hypomanic/manic symptoms occurring with depressive symptoms is the increased risk of dangerous, impulsive behaviors such as suicidal actions or substance abuse (Swann, Moeller, et al., 2007). Rapid-cycling is more common in those who develop bipolar disorder at an earlier age. Rapid-cycling increases the chance that the disorder will be chronic and that the symptoms of mania, depression, and anxiety will be more severe (Kupka et al., 2005; S. Lee, Tsang, Kessler, et al., 2010; Nierenberg et al., 2010). Both rapid-cycling and anxiety symptoms occur more frequently in women and predict more pervasive depressive episodes (Altshuler et al., 2010). Rapid-cycling can be triggered by a variety of factors, including sleep deprivation, certain antidepressants, and anti-inflammatory medications (Salvadore et al., 2010).

Cyclothymic disorder is diagnosed when hypomanic episodes are consistently interspersed with depressed moods for at least 2 years. (The depressive moods do not reach the level of a severe depression, and the person is never symptom-free for more than 2 months.) Cyclothymic disorder is similar to dysthymic disorder (chronic depression) because the mood symptoms are chronic, but differs because the person experiences periodic hypomanic symptoms. The risk that a person with cyclothymic disorder will subsequently develop bipolar I or II is 15–50 percent (American Psychiatric Association, 2000).

AP Photo/M. Spencer Green, File

Living with Bipolar Disorder
U.S. Rep. Jesse Jackson Jr. took a leave from Congress to undergo treatment for bipolar II disorder at the Mayo Clinic. Jackson was visited by former U.S. Rep. Patrick Kennedy who has been open about his own struggles with bipolar disorder and who is an outspoken advocate for removing the stigma associated with mental disorders.

How Common Are Bipolar Disorders?

A large-scale national survey found that the lifetime prevalence for bipolar I is 1.0 percent and for bipolar II, 1.1 percent (see Figure 7.2). Cyclothymic disorder has a lifetime prevalence rate between 0.4 and 1 percent. Thus, bipolar disorders are far less prevalent than depressive disorders. Although bipolar disorder can begin in childhood, onset more frequently occurs in late adolescence or early adulthood. It is important to recall, however, that bipolar disorder may be underdiagnosed. It is estimated that more than 10 percent of those diagnosed with a depressive disorder will eventually be diagnosed with a bipolar disorder (G. M. Goodwin et al., 2008; C. T. Li et al., 2012); in other words, the diagnosis changes once hypomanic/manic symptoms become evident. Assessment instruments that contain self-ratings of hypomanic/manic symptoms and daily mood monitoring can help avoid misdiagnosis (Picardi, 2009).

Research on gender differences in bipolar disorder is mixed. Most researchers agree that there are no marked gender differences in the prevalence of bipolar I (Merikangas, Akiskal, et al., 2007), but depressive and mixed episodes, bipolar II, and rapid-cycling occur more frequently in women (Diflorio & Jones, 2010; Ketter, 2010). Women also have a higher risk that symptoms will recur (Suominen et al., 2009). As with depressive disorders, reproductive cycle changes, especially childbirth, can cause or worsen depressive bipolar episodes (L. M. Arnold, 2003; Diflorio & Jones, 2010). The transition to menopause can also increase the frequency of depressive episodes in women with bipolar disorder (W. K. Marsh, Ketter, & Rasgon, 2009).

Although bipolar disorders are much less prevalent than depressive disorders, their costs are high. Bipolar disorder is associated with high unemployment and decreased work productivity (Ketter, 2010). Bipolar disorder was associated with 65.5 annual lost workdays per ill worker, compared to 27.2 days for those with major depressive disorder; this is because those with bipolar disorder tend to have more severe and persistent depressive episodes (R. C. Kessler, Akiskal, et al., 2006). Furthermore, those with bipolar disorder often find that their symptoms recur; as the number of bipolar episodes increases, so does the likelihood of future episodes (Hollon, Stewart, et al., 2006).

Those with bipolar disorder are frequently diagnosed with concurrent anxiety disorders (especially panic attacks), attention-deficit/hyperactivity disorder, and substance-use disorders (Merikangas, Jin, et al., 2011). Anxiety (and mixed episodes) appears to increase the severity of both manic and depressive symptoms (Swann, Steinberg, et al., 2009). Those with coexisting conditions tend to develop the disorder earlier and have longer episodes as well as increased suicidal or violent behavior (Baldassano, 2006). Men with a bipolar disorder have an increased likelihood of having a coexisting substance-use disorder, whereas women with a bipolar diagnosis frequently have eating disorders (Kawa et al., 2005; Suominen et al., 2009). Substance abuse is common among those with bipolar disorder and can significantly increase the degree of impairment (Lagerberg et al., 2010). For example, more than half of one sample of individuals diagnosed with a bipolar disorder had a concurrent alcohol-use disorder and suicidal ideation (Oquendo et al., 2010).

Bipolar disorder is also associated with increased rates of physical illnesses such as hypertension, cardiovascular disease, and diabetes, as well as increased rates of death from suicide (Fagiolini, 2008; Ketter, 2010; Leahy, 2007). In fact, bipolar disorder is considered the disorder with the greatest risk of attempted or completed suicide; an estimated 15–19 percent of individuals with bipolar disorder die from suicide (Abreu, Lafer, Baca-Garcia, & Oquendo, 2009). Antidepressant-associated suicidal behavior is most common in those with bipolar disorder; undiagnosed bipolar disorder may be responsible for some cases of antidepressant-associated suicidal behaviors (Rihmer & Gonda, 2011).

Etiology of Bipolar Disorders

What explains the mood roller coaster experienced by those with bipolar disorders? Many of the psychological, social, and sociocultural factors that influence depressive disorders can also contribute to depressive episodes in bipolar disorder. In this section, we primarily focus on factors that contribute to the hypomanic/manic episodes and mood switching seen in bipolar disorder. We conclude with a brief discussion of the overlap between bipolar disorder and another serious mental illness, schizophrenia.

Biological Dimension The contribution of genetic factors to bipolar disorder is well established from twin, adoption, and family studies. For example, the chance of developing bipolar I, bipolar II, or cyclothymic disorder when a twin is diagnosed with the condition is quite high—72 percent for identical twins, compared to 14 percent for fraternal twins (Edvardsen et al., 2008; Kato, 2007). Bipolar disorders are believed to have a complex genetic basis involving interactions among multiple genes, including several genes influenced by the chemical compound lithium (Baum et al., 2008). Because individuals with bipolar disorders (like those with depressive disorders) have abnormalities in their circadian cycles, it is not surprising that genes related to the circadian cycle are linked with vulnerability to bipolar disorder (Lavebratt et al., 2010; Shi et al., 2008; Sjöholm et al., 2010; Soria et al., 2010).

A variety of neurological influences appear to affect bipolar symptoms. Irregularities in the way the brain processes and responds to stimuli associated with reward are associated with both manic and depressive symptoms. Consistent with this dysregulation model, individuals with bipolar disorders show hypomanic/manic symptoms after reaching a goal as well as anger and irritability in response to obstructed goals (Alloy & Abramson, 2010; S. L. Johnson, Cuellar, et al., 2008). Due to this high sensitivity to reward, mania can develop due to overly ambitious pursuit of goals and the brain dysregulation (i.e., excessive brain activation and increased energy output) that occurs when goals are attained (S. L. Johnson, Edge, Holmes, & Carver, 2012). This same hypersensitivity can cause a shutting down (i.e., deactivation) of motivational systems within the brain in response to perceived failures; this deactivation results in symptoms of depression such as decreased goal-directed activity, low energy, loss of interest, hopelessness, and sadness (Alloy & Abramson, 2010). Thus, individuals with hypersensitive neurological systems appear to have a vulnerability to bipolar disorder that is triggered by events that activate or deactivate brain systems involved in regulating energy and motivation.

The likelihood and severity of manic and depressive episodes can be reduced by helping those with bipolar disorder recognize and challenge overly ambitious goal setting as well as the decreased goal striving that occurs in response to perceived failure (Alloy & Abramson, 2010). Additionally, because sleep deprivation is linked with poor emotional regulation and exaggerated brain reactivity to both negative and positive experiences (Gujar, Yoo, Hu, & Walker, 2011), interventions focused on regulating sleep patterns can help stop the vicious cycle involving disrupted sleep and increased emotional reactivity commonly seen in those with bipolar disorder (Eidelman, Talbot, Gruber, & Harvey, 2010; A. G. Harvey, 2008).

In a review of the literature, goal attainment, antidepressant medication use, disrupted circadian rhythm, and spring or summer seasonal conditions were all linked to the onset of hypomanic/manic episodes in certain individuals (Proudfoot, Doran, Manicavasagar, & Parker, 2010). As with depressive disorder, hormonal influences and disruptions in the stress circuitry of the brain appear to contribute to bipolar symptoms. For example, increased levels of glutamate (a neurotransmitter with stimulatory functions) have been found in autopsies of individuals with bipolar disorder (Hashimoto, Sawa, & Iyo, 2007), and brain imaging has documented elevated glutamate neurotransmission in the brains of individuals with bipolar disorder (Eastwood & Harrison, 2010).

Imaging studies have also confirmed brain irregularities in individuals with bipolar disorder (Brambilla, Bellani, Yeh, Soares, & Tansella, 2009; Cerullo, Adler, Delbello, & Strakowski, 2009; Heng, Song, & Sim, 2010; W. R. Marchand et al., 2011; Palaniyappan & Cousins, 2010), including abnormalities in areas involved in the generation and regulation of emotions (Mahon, Burdick, & Szeszko, 2010) and response to emotional stimuli (Ellison-Wright & Bullmore, 2010). Brain injury has been found to precipitate manic episodes, especially in individuals with a family history of bipolar disorder (Mustafa, Evrim, & Sari, 2005); in fact, manic episodes are reported to affect up to 9 percent of those with traumatic brain injury (Oster, Anderson, Filley, Wortzel, & Arciniegas, 2007).

As with depressive disorders, in some cases of bipolar disorder a major stressful event occurs just prior to the onset of symptoms (R. E. Bender & Alloy, 2011). In those with bipolar disorder, a ruminative cognitive style is predictive of depressive episodes, whereas self-focused thinking patterns, perfectionism, and self-criticism are predictive of hypomanic/manic episodes (Alloy, Abramson, Flynn, et al., 2009; Alloy, Abramson, Walshaw, et al., 2009). As indicated earlier, biological factors appear to play a much more prominent role in the development of bipolar disorders than in depressive disorders. Additionally, evidence is mounting regarding common genetic vulnerabilities between bipolar disorders and schizophrenia.

Did You Know?

Individuals with bipolar disorder often possess the positive traits of spirituality, empathy, creativity, and resilience. Researchers are considering ways that these strengths can be tapped to improve outcomes for those with bipolar disorder.

Source: Galvez, Thommi, & Ghaemi (2011)

Commonalities Between Bipolar Disorders and Schizophrenia It is now commonly accepted that bipolar disorder and schizophrenia, both chronic disorders with clear neurological irregularities, share genetic, neuroanatomical, and cognitive abnormalities. In fact, some contend that bipolar disorders (particularly bipolar I) are much more similar to schizophrenia than they are to depressive disorders (D. P. Goldberg, Krueger, Andrews, & Hobbs, 2009). Genome-wide studies have shown that schizophrenia and bipolar disorder have common genetic influences (Goes et al., 2007; Huang et al., 2010). There is substantial overlap in the brain regions affected by schizophrenia and bipolar disorder (Yu et al., 2010). Meta-analytic comparisons of the neuroanatomy of schizophrenia and bipolar disorder reveal similar gray matter abnormalities in two brain regions, although each disorder also is associated with unique deficits in gray matter. In the case of bipolar disorder, the brain regions affected tend to be less extensive and primarily involve areas related to emotional processing (Ellison-Wright & Bullmore, 2010).

Bipolar disorder and schizophrenia also involve similar cognitive deficits, including confused thought processes and difficulty recognizing inappropriate behavior (this is referred to as *poor insight*). In bipolar disorder, this lack of insight into the illness is particularly pronounced during manic episodes, whereas insight is adequate during depressive episodes (F. Cassidy, 2010). Noncompliance with medication regimes is common to both disorders. Poor insight and lack of illness awareness are believed to account for the finding that, on average, those with schizophrenia or bipolar disorder take only 51–70 percent of the medication prescribed for their illness (Velligan et al., 2009). Neurocognitive deficits that affect social competence and daily functioning are also present in both disorders (Bowie et al., 2010), although the deficits are usually more pervasive in schizophrenia (Jabben, Arts, Van Os, & Krabbendam, 2010). Significant psychosocial and vocational impairment linked to cognitive deficits involving attention, processing speed, and memory are common in both disorders (Bearden, Woogen, & Glahn, 2010).

Treatment for Bipolar Disorders

Therapy for bipolar disorders aims to eliminate all symptoms. Lingering or residual symptoms increase the likelihood of relapse and ongoing impairment (Judd et al., 2008; Marangell, Dennehy, et al., 2009). Intervention efforts, therefore, target future hypomanic/manic and depressive episodes. Effective treatment often involves a combination of mood-stabilizing medications and psychoeducation to help the individual (and family members) understand the importance of regular use of prescribed medications and recognize early symptoms of mood episodes.

Mood-stabilizing medications such as lithium are the foundation of treatment for bipolar disorder (Bowden, 2010; J. O. Brooks et al., 2011). Although anticonvulsant medications are sometimes used instead of lithium, lithium is the most effective medication in terms of stabilizing mood and preventing hospitalization (Kessing, Hellmund, Geddes, Goodwin, & Andersen, 2011); lithium also helps decrease suicide risk (J. F. Goldberg, 2007). Lithium and other mood stabilizers are usually used indefinitely to prevent recurrence of hypomania/mania; antidepressants are sometimes added to deal with depressive symptoms (Hollon, Stewart, et al., 2006). However, antidepressants are used cautiously with bipolar disorder—although they target depressive symptoms, they can in fact produce or worsen hypomanic/manic symptoms (Benazzi, 2007).

The generally positive results achieved with lithium are sometimes overshadowed by serious side effects that can occur if blood levels of lithium are not regularly monitored (Wingo, Wingo, Harvey, & Baldessarini, 2009). Fortunately, accurate measurements of blood lithium levels are easily obtained, and dosages can be adjusted accordingly. If medication is taken regularly, symptoms of bipolar disorder can often be effectively controlled (Berk et al., 2010). Unfortunately, noncompliance in taking medication as prescribed is a major problem associated with lithium and other mood stabilizers. Individuals with bipolar disorder often report adjusting their own medication due to weight gain, feelings of sedation, a desire to re-create hypomanic symptoms, a belief that the medication is no longer needed (especially when judgment is impaired by mania), and doubts about the need for continued treatment (Clatworthy et al., 2009; Velligan et al., 2009). Unfortunately, lithium and other mood stabilizers lose their effectiveness when they are not taken as prescribed. When the dosage is decreased, a hypomanic state can quickly progress into a severe manic or depressive state. Drug or alcohol abuse, negative attitudes toward mood-stabilizing medications, and difficulty remembering to take medication also negatively influence compliance (Sajatovic et al., 2009). Psychoeducation that emphasizes the link between the regular use of medication and long-term improvement is an important aspect of treatment (Berk et al., 2010).

Jason Merritt/Getty Images

© Allstar Picture Library/Alamy

Overcoming Bipolar Disorder

Actor Ben Stiller has bipolar disorder, as do other members of his family. Following a stressful year and a brief hospital stay for treatment of bipolar II disorder, award-winning actress Catherine Zeta-Jones expressed hope that telling the public about her diagnosis would encourage others struggling with similar symptoms to seek help rather than suffer silently.

Although pharmacological therapies are critical in the treatment of bipolar disorder, there is strong evidence that psychoeducation, family-focused therapy, interpersonal therapy, and cognitive-behavioral therapy can help reduce symptom severity, prevent relapse, and enhance psychosocial functioning (Rizvi & Zaretsky, 2007). For example, combining family-focused education about bipolar disorder with training in communication and problem-solving skills can reduce the risk of relapse and hospitalization (C. D. Morris, Miklowitz, & Waxmonsky, 2007). Social rhythm therapy, a treatment that avoids disruption of bodily rhythm patterns by developing regular patterns of eating, sleeping, and exercising, also reduces relapse (D. Lam, 2009).

Selecting the most appropriate intervention depending on the symptoms present can significantly affect treatment outcome. When people with bipolar disorder learn to detect triggers or behavior patterns that lead to hypomania/mania (e.g., excessive goal-seeking behavior), full manic episodes can be prevented (Hollon, Stewart, et al., 2006; D. Lam, 2009). Mindfulness interventions have shown success in helping those with bipolar disorder regulate their moods (Chadwick, Kaur, Swelam, Ross, & Ellett, 2011). Light therapy is used cautiously, if at all, in individuals with bipolar disorder, due to concerns about light exposure precipitating hypomanic/manic episodes (McClung, 2007). Finally, ECT is sometimes used to treat severe depression or acute mania.

CHECKPOINT REVIEW

1. Name characteristics of each of the three types of bipolar disorder.
2. What is a primary cause of bipolar disorder?
3. List three similarities between bipolar disorder and schizophrenia.
4. What is a key treatment for bipolar disorder?

Summary

1 What are the symptoms of depression and mania?

- Depression involves feelings of sadness or emptiness, social withdrawal, loss of interest in activities, pessimism, low energy, and sleep and appetite disturbances.
- Mania produces significant impairment and involves high levels of arousal, elevated or irritable mood, increased activity, poor judgment, grandiosity, and decreased need for sleep. Hypomania refers to milder manic symptoms, which are sometimes accompanied by productive, goal-directed behaviors.

2 What are depressive disorders, what causes them, and how are they treated?

- Depressive disorders are diagnosed only when depressive symptoms occur without a history of hypomania/mania. Depressive disorders include major depressive disorder, dysthymic disorder and premenstrual dysphoric disorder. Mixed anxiety/depression and seasonal affective disorder are undergoing further study.
- Biological factors, including heredity, are important in predisposing one to depression. The functioning of neurotransmitters and cortisol levels in the body are associated with depression.
- Behavioral explanations for depression focus on reduced reinforcement following losses. Cognitive explanations focus on negative thinking patterns, irrational beliefs, and rumination.
- Social explanations focus on relationships and interpersonal stressors that make one vulnerable to depression. Early childhood stressors are particularly important.
- Sociocultural explanations have focused on cultural, demographic, and socioeconomic factors, including gender and cultural differences.
- Behavioral activation, cognitive-behavioral, and interpersonal psychotherapy have received extensive research support as treatments for depression; mindfulness-based cognitive therapy has also shown promising results. Biomedical treatments include sleep deprivation, light therapy, and electrical stimulation of the brain. Antidepressant medications are frequently used to treat depression; they are most effective with severe depression, but produce only temporary effects. Psychotherapy is more likely to prevent the return of depressive symptoms.

3 What are bipolar disorders, what causes them, and how are they treated?

- Bipolar disorders involve symptoms of mania or hypomania. Depressive mood episodes are also common in bipolar disorder.
- Bipolar I involves at least one weeklong manic episode. Bipolar II is diagnosed when there is a history of both milder depression and hypomania. Cyclothymic disorder is a chronic bipolar disorder involving hypomanic episodes that alternate with depressed mood for at least 2 years.
- Research has shown that bipolar disorders have a strong genetic basis involving multiple, interacting genes. Biological factors, including neurochemical and neuroanatomical abnormalities and circadian rhythm disturbances, contribute to bipolar disorder. There are many overlaps between bipolar disorder and schizophrenia.
- The most effective treatment for bipolar disorders is ongoing use of mood-stabilizing medication combined with psychotherapy and psychosocial interventions.

Key Terms

mood 174
depression 175
rumination 175
hypomania 176
mania 176
euphoria 176
elevated mood 177
grandiosity 177
pressured speech 177
flight of ideas 177
postpartum depression 178
major depressive episode 179
dysthymic disorder 179
anxious distress 180
circadian rhythm 182
co-rumination 185
learned helplessness 186
rapid-cycling 196
mixed episode 196

Media Resources

Psychology CourseMate

Access an interactive e-Book and chapter-specific interactive learning tools, including:

- flashcards
- quizzes
- videos

and more in your Psychology CourseMate.

Go to **CengageBrain.com.**

Rob Hainer/Shutterstock.com

8

Suicide

CHAPTER OUTLINE

Late one evening, Carl Johnson, MD, left his downtown office, got into his Mercedes-Benz S600, and drove toward his expensive suburban home. He was in no hurry, because the house would be empty anyway; his wife had divorced him and moved back east with their children. Carl was deeply affected. Although he had been drinking heavily for 2 years before the divorce, he had always been able to function at work. For the past several months, however, his private practice had declined dramatically. He had once found his work rewarding, but now his patients bored and irritated him. Although he had suffered from depression in the past, this time it was different. The future had never looked so bleak and hopeless. Carl knew he was in serious trouble—he was, after all, a psychiatrist.

Carl parked carelessly, not bothering to press the switch that closed the garage door. Once in the house, he headed directly for his den. There he pulled out a bottle of bourbon and three glasses, filled each glass to the rim, and lined them up along the bar. He drank them down, one after the other, in rapid succession. For a good half hour he stood at the window, staring out into the night. Then Carl sat down at his mahogany desk and unlocked one of the drawers. Taking a loaded .38-caliber revolver from the desk drawer, Carl held it to his temple and pulled the trigger. He was killed instantly.

FOCUS QUESTIONS

1 What do we know about suicide?

2 What are the major explanations of suicide?

3 How does suicide affect specific populations?

4 How can we intervene or prevent suicides?

5 Are there times and situations in which suicide should be an option?

Why would someone like Dr. Johnson take his own life? Granted, he was depressed and obviously feeling the loss of his family, but most people under similar circumstances are able to cope and choose life over death. Unfortunately, we will never know the answer, but our multipath model, shown in Figure 8.1, does offer clues: a combination of biological, psychological, social, and sociocultural factors possibly contributed to his suicide (Leenaars, 2008).

First, there is evidence that Carl had a history of depression, and strong biological factors (biochemical or genetic) are implicated in suicide (J. J. Mann, Arango, et al., 2009). For example, cerebrospinal fluid levels of people who kill themselves reveal that they have lower levels of 5-HIAA serotonin, found to predict a rate of suicide 10 to 20 times higher (Leonardo & Hen, 2006). Second, psychological factors such as alcohol abuse (Bryan & Rudd, 2006), hopelessness, and depression are often associated with suicide (Jobes, 2006). Third, social factors were evident in Dr. Johnson's pain; a divorce and loss of his family made life no longer meaningful. People who are divorced and lack social relationships are more likely to commit suicide (Rudd, Joiner, & Rajab, 2004). Finally, there are major sociocultural correlates of Dr. Johnson's decision to take his own life. His gender and occupation are significant factors. Men are more likely to kill themselves than women, and occupationally, psychiatrists have among the highest rates of suicide (Comtois & Linehan, 2006; Klott & Jongsma, 2004). It is clear that Dr. Johnson was at high risk for suicide on a number of risk dimensions.

Suicide has been extensively researched, but we know very little about it. Although this may sound contradictory, this chapter is filled with an impressive array of facts, statistics, and information about many aspects of suicide. We are able to construct fairly accurate portraits of individuals who are most at risk, delineate protective factors, and even develop intervention strategies in working with suicidal individuals. But in actuality, we continue to ask: "Why do people kill themselves?"

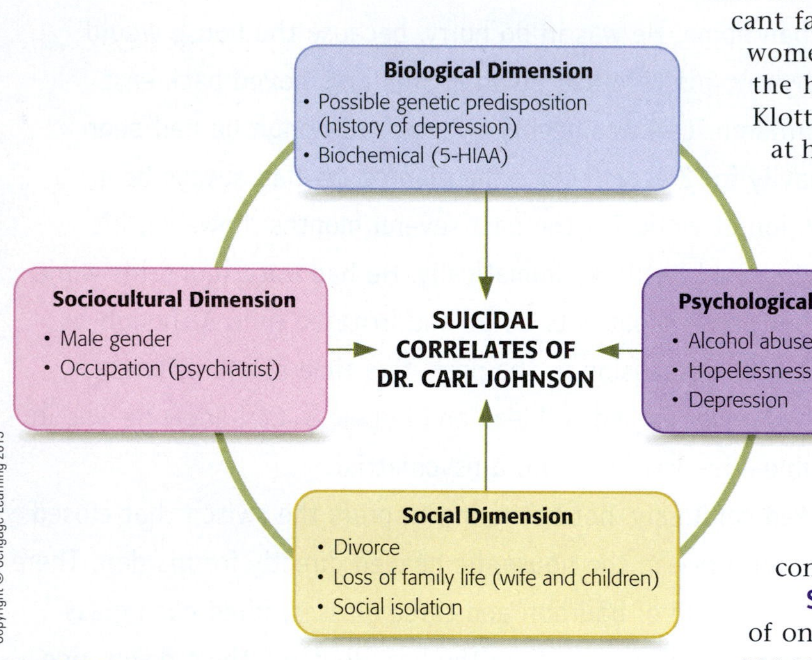

FIGURE 8.1

Multipath Model of the Suicide of Dr. Carl Johnson

Here you see the interacting multipath dimensions that may have contributed to Dr. Carl Johnson's suicide. Their precise relationship to and interaction with one another is difficult to ascertain, but clearly he was at high risk for suicide.

Suicide—the intentional, direct, and conscious taking of one's own life—is not only a tragic act, it is a baffling one as well. Most of us have been raised to believe in the sanctity of life, and we operate under strong moral, religious, and cultural sanctions against taking our own lives. Suicide is as old as human history itself, so its occurrence is not rare. Although explanations abound for suicide, we can never be entirely certain why people knowingly and deliberately end their own lives (Leenaars, 2008; Rudd et al., 2004). The easy and most frequent explanation is that people who kill themselves are suffering from a mental disorder. Research now suggests that suicide has many causes, and people kill themselves for many different reasons (Granello, 2010; Rosenfeld, 2004).

A separate chapter on suicide is provided in this text for several reasons. First, although suicide is not classified as a mental disorder in the *Diagnostic and Statistical Manual of Mental Disorders, Fifth Edition* (DSM-5), people who are suicidal usually have clear psychiatric symptoms. Many people with depression, alcohol dependence, and schizophrenia exhibit suicidal thoughts or behavior (Bryan & Rudd, 2006; Suicide Prevention Resource Center (SPRC), 2012).

suicide the intentional, direct, and conscious taking of one's own life

Yet suicide does not fall neatly into any of the recognized psychiatric disorders. Thus, suicide and **suicidal ideation**—thoughts about suicide—may represent a distinct and separate mental clinical entity from those identified in the DSM-5.

Second, the fact that suicide is the eleventh leading cause of death for all U.S. Americans (Table 8.1) appears to warrant study of this phenomenon in its own right. Every year, there are more deaths due to suicide in the United States than to homicide. However, throughout history, people have traditionally avoided discussing suicide and have participated in a "conspiracy of silence" because of the shame and stigma involved in taking one's life (Maris, Berman, & Silverman, 2000; Rudd et al., 2004). Even mental health professionals find the topic uncomfortable and deeply disturbing (R. A. Friedman, 2004). Nearly all therapists encounter a client in their careers who is suicidal; one fourth will experience an actual client suicide (Granello, 2010).

Finally, we need to recognize that suicide is an irreversible act. Once the action has been taken, there is no going back, no reconsideration, and no reprieve. Regardless of the moral stance one takes on this position, the decision to commit suicide is often an ambivalent one, clouded by many personal and social stressors. Many mental health professionals believe that people who are suicidal, if taught how to deal with personal and social crises, would not consciously take their own lives. Most do not want to die, but simply want the pain to end (Granello & Granello, 2007). As a result, understanding the causes of suicide and what can be done to prevent such an act becomes extremely important to psychologists (A. L. Berman, 2006).

TABLE 8.1 Leading Causes of Death in the United States

1. Diseases of the heart (heart disease)
2. Malignant neoplasms (cancer)
3. Cerebrovascular diseases (stroke)
4. Chronic lower respiratory diseases
5. Accidents (unintentional injuries)
6. Diabetes mellitus (diabetes)
7. Alzheimer's disease
8. Pneumonia and influenza
9. Nephritis and nephrosis (kidney disease)
10. Septicemia (bacterial blood poisoning)
11. Suicide
12. Chronic liver disease and cirrhosis
13. Essential hypertension and renal disease
14. Parkinson's disease
15. Homicide (assault)

Source: Centers for Disease Control and Prevention, Web-Based Injury Statistics Query and Reporting System (2005)

Correlates of Suicide

People who commit suicide—who complete their suicide attempts—can no longer inform us about their motives, frames of mind, and emotional states. We have only indirect information, such as case records and reports by others, to help us understand what led them to their heartrending act. Systematically examining information after a person's death to understand and explain the person's behavior before death is called a **psychological autopsy** (C. A. King & Merchant, 2008). It is patterned on the *medical autopsy*, which is an examination of a dead body to determine the cause or nature of the biological death.

The psychological autopsy attempts to make psychological sense of a suicide or homicide by compiling and analyzing case histories of victims, recollections of therapists, interviews with relatives and friends, information obtained from crisis phone calls, Internet postings (Facebook, YouTube, etc.), and messages left in suicide notes. Unfortunately, these sources are not always available or reliable. Only 12–34 percent of victims leave suicide notes, many have never undergone psychotherapy, and the judgment of loved ones is often clouded by intense feelings (S. T. Black, 1993; Maris, 2001).

Another strategy involves studying those who survive suicide attempts. This method, however, assumes that people who attempt suicide are no different from those who complete the act. Studies suggest that these two populations differ on many important dimensions. Attempters are more likely to be white housewives in their 20s and 30s who are experiencing marital difficulties and use primarily barbiturates to attempt suicide. Those who complete the act are more likely to be men in their 40s or older with poor health and depression; they tend to shoot or

suicidal ideation thoughts about suicide

psychological autopsy the systematic examination of existing information after a person's death for the purpose of understanding and explaining the person's behavior before death

MYTH VS REALITY

MYTH Suicides occur more frequently during the holiday seasons because of depression, loneliness, and a feeling of disconnection from significant others.

REALITY Although depressive feelings and loneliness may increase during holidays, suicides do not. The National Center for Health Statistics reports that suicide rates are actually the lowest in December ("Holiday-Suicide Link," 2009). Suicides are most frequent during the spring and summer months.

hang themselves (Diekstra, Kienhorst, & de Wilde, 1995; Furr, Westefeld, McConnell, & Jenkins, 2001; Shea, 2002).

Facts About Suicide

To understand suicide, researchers have focused on events, characteristics, and demographic variables that recur in psychological autopsies and are highly correlated with the act (Comtois & Linehan, 2006; D. Lester, 2008). Profiles of individuals who are suicidal emerge from our increasing knowledge of facts that are correlated with suicide (A. L. Berman, 2006; Bryan & Rudd, 2006; CDC WISQARS, 2005; Comtois & Linehan, 2006; Karch, Cosby, & Simon, 2006; C. A. King & Merchant, 2008; D. Lester, 2008; Leach, 2006; Substance Abuse and Mental Health Services Administration, 2012). Look at Table 8.2, which examines some of the characteristics shared by individuals who are suicidal.

Frequency Every 15 minutes or so, someone in the United States takes his or her own life. Approximately 34,000 people kill themselves each year. Suicide is among the top 11 causes of death in the industrialized parts of the world; it is the eighth leading cause of death among U.S. American males, the third leading cause of death among young people aged 15–24, and the second leading cause of death among college students (CDC, 2010d; Drum, Brownson, Denmark, & Smith, 2009; Substance Abuse and Mental Health Services Administration, 2010b). Some evidence shows that the number of actual suicides is probably 25–30 percent higher than that recorded. Many deaths that are officially recorded as accidental—such as single-auto crashes, drownings, and falls from great heights—are actually suicides. According to some estimates, 11 people attempt suicide for every one person who completes the act (CDC, 2010d).

Suicide Publicity and Identification With Victims Media reports of suicides, especially by celebrities, seem to spark an increase in suicide (D. S. Bailey, 2003; Gould, 2007). The 12-month period following Marilyn Monroe's suicide saw a 12 percent increase. Suicides by young people in small communities or schools seem to evoke copycat suicides in some students. Publicized murder-suicides also seem to be correlated with an increase in car accidents. Interestingly, publicized natural deaths (as opposed to suicides) of celebrities do not produce similar increases.

Gender The rate of completed suicide for men is about 4 times that for women, although recent findings suggest that the gap is closing, as many more women are now incurring a higher risk (CDC, 2010d). Further, women are more likely to make attempts, but it appears that men are more successful because they use more lethal means. Among people older than 65, the rate of completed suicide for men is 10 times that for women. However, women in the same age range attempt suicide 3 times as often as men.

Marital Status A stable marriage or relationship seems to immunize people against killing themselves, although the precise reason is unclear. Being widowed appears to be associated with higher risk of suicide for white men and women and African American men when compared to people who are divorced. At older ages, however, divorce rather than widowhood increases the risk. The suicide rates for single and widowed or divorced men are about twice those for women of similar marital status. Attempted and completed suicide rates are higher among those who are separated, divorced, or widowed, and they are especially high among single adolescent girls and single men in their 30s.

Chelsea Lauren/WireImage

Celebrity Attempts at Suicide

Here, actor Owen Wilson watches a basketball game between the Miami Heat and the Golden State Warriors on March 7, 2008. About half a year earlier, on August 28, 2007, he had attempted suicide with a drug overdose and slitting his wrists.

TABLE 8.2 10 Common Characteristics of Suicide

1.	The common purpose is to seek a solution. People may believe that suicide represents a solution to an insoluble problem. To people who are suicidal, taking their own lives is not a pointless or accidental occurrence.
2.	The cessation of consciousness is a common goal. Consciousness represents constant psychological pain, and suicide represents a termination of distressing thoughts and feelings.
3.	The stimulus for suicide is generally intolerable psychological pain. Depression, hopelessness, guilt, shame, and other negative emotions are frequently the basis of a suicide.
4.	The common stressor in suicide is frustrated psychological need. The inability to attain high standards or expectations may lead to feelings of frustration, failure, and worthlessness. When progress toward goals is blocked, some individuals become vulnerable to suicide.
5.	A common emotion in suicide is hopelessness or helplessness. Pessimism about the future and a conviction that nothing can be done to improve one's life situation may predispose a person to suicide.
6.	The cognitive state is one of ambivalence. Although people who are suicidal may be strongly motivated to end their lives, there is usually a desire (in varying degrees) to live as well.
7.	The cognitive state is also characterized by "tunnel vision." People who are suicidal have great difficulty seeing the larger picture and can be characterized as suffering from tunnel vision. People intent on suicide seem unable to consider other options or alternatives. Death is the only way out.
8.	The common action in suicide is escape. The goal is egression—escape from an intolerable situation.
9.	The common interpersonal act in suicide is communication of intention. At least 80 percent of suicides are preceded by either verbal or nonverbal behavioral cues indicating the person's intentions.
10.	The common consistency is in the area of lifelong coping patterns. Patterns or habits developed in coping with crisis generally are the same response patterns that are used throughout life. Some patterns may predispose people to suicide.

Source: From DEFINITION OF SUICIDE, E. Shneidman, 1985. By permission of Regina Ryan Publishing Enterprises, Inc.

Occupation Physicians, lawyers, law enforcement personnel, and dentists have higher than average rates of suicide. Among medical professionals, psychiatrists have the highest rate and pediatricians the lowest. One in 16 surgeons in the United States has considered suicide, and researchers speculate that burnout, stress, and guilt over medical errors increase the risk of suicides (Joelving, 2011). Interestingly, the suicide rate of women physicians is 4 times higher than that of a matched general population. We can certainly ask whether the specialty influences susceptibility or whether people who are prone to suicide are more likely to be attracted to certain specialties.

Socioeconomic Level Suicide is represented proportionately among all socioeconomic levels. Level of wealth does not seem to affect the suicide rate as much as do changes in that level. In the Great Depression of the 1930s, suicide was higher among those who had suddenly become impoverished than among those who had always been poor.

Choice of Method More than 50 percent of completed suicides are committed by firearms, and 70 percent of attempts are accounted for by drug overdose. Men most frequently choose firearms as the means of suicide; poisoning and asphyxiation

Cleopatra, Kurt Cobain, Don Cornelius (the host of *Soul Train*), Ernest Hemingway, Margaux Hemingway, Adolf Hitler, Jim Jones (the leader of the Peoples Temple), Marilyn Monroe, Seung-Hui Cho (the perpetrator of the Virginia Tech massacre), Freddie Prinze (the comedian), King Saul of Israel, and Virginia Woolf all have one thing in common. They all committed suicide—the intentional, direct, and conscious taking of one's own life.

Bob Daemmrich/The Image Works

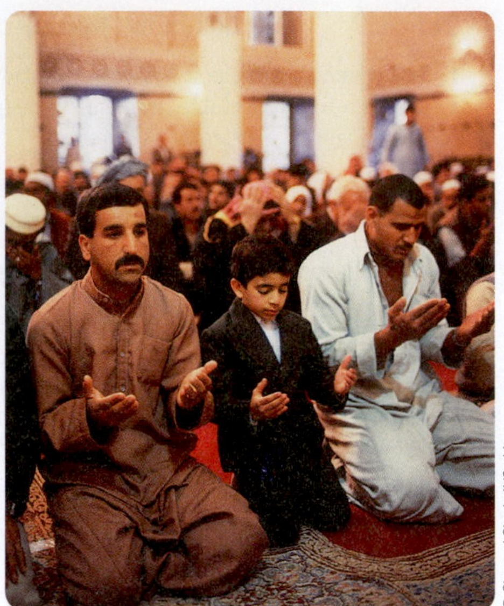

© Shepard Sherbell/Corbis

Religion and Suicide

Many religions have strong taboos and sanctions against suicide. In countries in which Catholicism and Islam are strong, for example, the rates of suicide tend to be lower than in countries in which religious sanctions against suicide are not as deeply held.

via barbiturates are the most common means for women. Because men use more violent means, this may account for why their suicide attempts are more often completed. Recent findings indicate, however, that women are increasingly choosing firearms and explosives as methods (55.9 percent increase; CDC, 2007b).

Among children younger than 15, the most common suicide methods are jumping from buildings and running into traffic. Older children try hanging or drug overdoses. Younger children attempt suicide impulsively and thus use more readily available means.

AP Photo/Billings Gazette, Larry Mayer

American Indian and Proud of It

Suicide rates among American Indian youth are extremely high, due perhaps to a lack of validation of their cultural lifestyle. Here an elder of the tribe helps teens become reacquainted with their cultural heritage and teaches them how spirituality plays a major role in their relationships with one another, mother earth, and the cosmos.

Religious Affiliation Religious affiliation is correlated with suicide rates. Although the U.S. rate is 11.4 per 100,000, in countries in which the influence of the Catholic Church is strong—Brazil, Argentina, Ireland, Spain, and Italy—the suicide rate is relatively low (less than 10 per 100,000; CDC, 2010d). Islam, too, condemns suicide, but the increase in suicide attacks in the Middle East may affect rates in Arab countries, which are generally low. Where religious sanctions against suicide are absent or weaker, as they are in Scandinavian countries and Hungary and were in Czechoslovakia—higher rates are observed (De Leo, 2009). Indeed, rates in Hungary stand at 40.7 per 100,000, and in the former Czechoslovakia they are 22.4 per 100,000.

Ethnic and Cultural Variables Suicide rates vary among ethnic minority groups in the United States. American Indian groups have the highest rate, followed by white Americans, Mexican Americans, African Americans, Japanese Americans, and Chinese Americans. American Indian youngsters have frighteningly high rates (26 per 100,000) as compared with white youths (14 per 100,000). For American Indians, suicide is the second leading cause of death (CDC, 2010d). High rates of alcoholism, a low standard of living, and an invalidation of their cultural lifestyles may all contribute to this misfortune.

FOCUS ON RESILIENCE

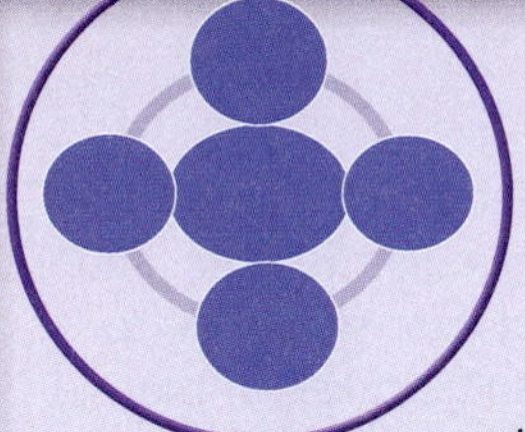

Suicide Prevention: Reinforcing Protective Factors

The majority of people who are suicidal do not truly wish to end their lives (Granello & Granello, 2007). When helped to understand the sources of their distress and the resources and options available to them, they inevitably choose life over death. This, indeed, is one of the primary protective mechanisms for individuals who are suicidal. Reawakening the "desire to live" and using it as an ally in suicide prevention is the task of the clinician. One of the most effective ways to prevent suicide is to utilize a strength-based approach to working with potentially suicidal clients. A strength-based approach does not just look at the person's vulnerabilities, but asks the following questions: "What are the factors that protect or build resilience against suicide? How can a therapist use such an approach to help suicidal clients?"

Four protective techniques have been found to be especially effective in preventing or immunizing against suicide: (1) reawakening and reinforcing the desire to live, (2) expanding perceptual outlook by reducing suicide myopia, (3) enhancing social connectedness, and (4) increasing the repertoire of coping skills.

1. *Reawakening and reinforcing the desire to live.* Most people possess a natural barrier against suicide. Most of us have been socialized to believe that life is better than death and possess a strong barrier against hurting ourselves or taking our own lives. Once a person crosses that barrier, however, it becomes easier to act against one's moral, ethical, or religious upbringing (P. N. Smith, Cukrowicz, Poindexter, Hobson, & Cohen, 2010). Even in clients who are suicidal and have made an attempt, the barrier is never completely gone. Whenever possible, a therapist should immediately and forcefully reinforce the barrier to prevent it from being crossed. This can be done in a number of different ways, but generally it involves concrete actions aimed at reintegrating clients with family, friends, and the community so that purpose and meaning in life can be revived or further developed (Joiner, 2005).

PhotoDisc

2. *Expanding perceptual outlook by reducing suicide myopia.* Most clients contemplating suicide have a very constricted and narrow perception of their problems and options. They see *no* solutions, and feel *hopeless* and *helpless*. Taking their own lives is the only option. Their feelings of hopelessness and futility are difficult to share with family and friends. Worse yet, significant others often communicate to them that such topics are taboo, because only "crazy people" contemplate suicide.

Many beginning counselors are also not comfortable with openly and directly discussing suicide with their clients. They are afraid that, if they open the door to this topic, they will inadvertently encourage a suicidal gesture or their actions will result in a suicide. Nothing could be further from the truth. Clients who are serious about suicide have entertained those thoughts for some time. Indeed, reluctance to discuss their suicidal thoughts or actions can have a most devastating effect: It prevents the clients from examining themselves objectively (fostering myopia and cognitive constriction) and reinforces the belief that only "crazy people" entertain these thoughts.

Asking direct questions such as the following progression is a necessity:

"Are you feeling unhappy and down most of the time?" (If yes. . .)
"Do you feel so unhappy that you sometimes wish you were dead?" (If yes. . .)
"Have you ever thought about taking your own life?" (If yes. . .)
"What methods have you thought about using to kill yourself?" (If the client specifies a method. . .)
"When do you plan to do this?"

Contrary to fears that such an approach will adversely affect clients, it has been found that directness diminishes their distress and frees them to see their problems and situations from a broader perspective. Many clients are relieved to be able to discuss a taboo topic openly and honestly.

3. *Enhancing social connectedness.* Research increasingly reveals that social support, integration with family, and connectedness to schools, peers, and friends are powerful antidotes to suicide (J. Johnson, Gooding, Wood, & Tarrier, 2010; Roy, Carli, & Sarchiapone, 2011; Suicide Prevention Resource Center, 2012). In many cases, individuals who are suicidal feel lonely, isolated, and disconnected from others, especially those who love them. The therapist may represent or symbolize an opportunity for the client to begin the process of learning to reintegrate

Continued

FOCUS ON RESILIENCE

Suicide Prevention: Reinforcing Protective Factors—cont'd

with others. Learning to ask for help and support from others is a major step toward accomplishing that goal. Connecting with a person who is empathetic, willing to listen, and concerned begins the healing process. The most important task, however, is to involve significant others in the therapeutic process so that familial, peer, and community social connections can be re-established and strengthened.

4. *Increasing the repertoire of coping skills.* People with suicidal thoughts usually feel unable to cope with a problematic situation. Research reveals that the greater the repertoire of effective coping skills possessed by a person, the less likely the person is to attempt suicide. It is considered a protective factor. Although effective coping skills can be taught and learned, this requires time. In the case of clients who are suicidal, coping with strong urges to carry out the act requires immediate and concrete action on the part of a therapist.

A therapist must prepare for the eventuality that suicidal thoughts and urges may return when the client is alone and ill-equipped to deal with them. The goal here should be to teach clients short-term actions that can be taken in the immediacy of the situation and act as a buffer to suicide. The therapist can rehearse with the client what actions to take when suicidal thoughts emerge. Here are coping skills a practitioner could convey to suicidal clients:

- Encourage clients (especially youth) to speak with their parents or significant others when such thoughts or urges arise.
- Provide specific phone numbers and contact sources (therapist, school counselor, or suicide prevention center).
- Obtain an agreement with clients (a verbal promise) that they will not make any attempt at suicide that week or for a fixed time period. Although research is mixed on the effectiveness of "no suicide" contracts, some counselors, especially those in schools, continue to use them.

Historical Period Suicide rates tend to decline among the general population during times of war and natural disasters, but they increase during periods of shifting norms and values or social unrest, when traditional expectations no longer apply. Sociologists speculate that during wars, people "pull together" and are less concerned with their own difficulties and conflicts.

Communication of Intent More than two thirds of people who commit suicide communicate their intent to do so within 3 months of the fatal act. The belief that people who threaten suicide are not serious about it or will not actually make such an attempt is ill founded. It is estimated that 20 percent of people who attempt suicide try again within 1 year and that 10 percent of those complete the act. Most people who attempt suicide appear to have been ambivalent about death until the suicide. It has been estimated that fewer than 5 percent unequivocally wish to end their lives.

CHECKPOINT REVIEW

1. Name four factors that seem to be correlated with suicide.
2. Explain why men are more likely to commit suicide even though women attempt it more often.
3. What factors seem to protect against suicide?
4. Is it true that people who make a suicide attempt are not serious about it?

A Multipath Perspective of Suicide

The most viable explanation of mental disorders must come from an integrated and multidimensional analysis. This is truly exemplified in the study of suicide, in which so many different factors seem to be involved (Leong & Leach, 2008;

D. Lester, 2008). Our biological, psychological, social, and sociocultural multipath model seems especially well suited for this purpose, as it acknowledges the multiple pathways to suicide.

Did You Know? The primary risk factors for suicide include: a previous suicide attempt, history of depression or mental illness, alcohol or drug abuse, family history of suicide or violence, physical illness, feelings of aloneness, and being an elderly male (CDC, 2010d; Suicide Prevention Resource Center, 2012).

Biological Dimension

Two sets of findings—from biochemistry and from genetics—suggest that suicide may have a strong biological component (Brent & Melhem, 2008; Brezo, Klempan, & Turecki, 2008; J. J. Mann, Arango, et al., 2009). Just like with the association between neurotransmitters and depression, similar evidence shows that low serotonin levels in the brain influence suicide.

In the mid-1970s, researchers identified a chemical called *5-hydroxyindoleacetic acid* (5-HIAA; Boldrini, Underwood, Mann, & Arango, 2005; J. J. Mann, 2003). This chemical is produced when serotonin, a neurotransmitter that affects mood and emotions, is broken down in the body. The spinal fluid of some patients who were depressed and suicidal has been found to contain abnormally low amounts of 5-HIAA (Laje et al., 2007). Patients with low levels of 5-HIAA are more likely than others to commit suicide; more likely to select violent methods of killing themselves; and more likely to have a history of violence, aggression, and impulsiveness (Brent, 2009a; J. J. Mann, Arango, et al., 2009).

Researchers believe that suicidal tendencies are not simply linked to depression. We already know that patients with depression also exhibit low levels of 5-HIAA. What is startling is that low levels of 5-HIAA have been discovered in people who are suicidal but do not have a history of depression and in individuals who are suicidal and have other mental disorders. Researchers believe that low 5-HIAA content does not cause suicide but may make people more vulnerable to environmental stressors. Further, this evidence is correlational in nature; it does not indicate whether low levels of 5-HIAA are a cause or a result of particular moods and emotions—or even whether the two are directly related.

Genetics is also implicated in suicidal behavior, but the relationship is far from clear. There appears to be a higher rate of suicide and suicide attempts among parents and close relatives of people who attempt or commit suicide than among people who are not suicidal (Brent & Melhem, 2008; Brezo et al., 2008). As always, great care must be used in drawing conclusions, because it can be argued that modeling by a close member of the family might make a relative more prone to find suicide an acceptable alternative.

Psychological Dimension

Findings have consistently revealed that a number of individuals who commit suicide suffer from a mental disorder (Bryan & Rudd, 2006). More than 90 percent of individuals who kill themselves have risk factors associated with mood disorders, schizophrenia, and substance abuse (CDC, 2010d). Those with schizophrenia are most likely to be experiencing an episode of depression, and their suicide methods are usually violent and bizarre; those with personality disorders are usually emotionally immature and have low frustration tolerance, such as those with borderline and antisocial personalities (J. J. Mann, Arango, et al., 2009). Contributing factors to suicide include separation and divorce, academic pressures, shame, serious illness, loss of a job, and other life stressors (Granello & Granello, 2007; Rosenfeld, 2004; Substance Abuse and Mental Health Services Administration, 2010b).

Suicide Methods

Common methods of suicide include:

Firearms: 51.6 percent

Suffocation/hanging: 22.6 percent

Poisoning: 17.9 percent

Cutting/piercing: 1.8 percent

Drowning: 1.1 percent

Other: 5 percent

Source: CDC WISQARS (2007a)

Depression and Hopelessness Perhaps the psychological state of mind most correlated with suicide is depression and hopelessness (A. L. Berman, 2006; Bryan & Rudd, 2006). For example, suicidal thoughts usually develop gradually as a result of pleasure loss and fatigue accompanying a serious depressed mood

(D. Lester, 2008). Shneidman (1993) has described it as a "psychache," an intolerable pain created from an absence of joy. Among both children and adolescents, depression seems to be highly correlated with suicidal behavior (CDC WISQARS, 2005; Eaton et al., 2006).

The role depression plays in suicide is far from simple. For example, clients seldom commit suicide while severely depressed. Such clients generally show motor retardation and low energy, which keep them from reaching the level of activity required for suicide. The danger period often comes after some treatment, when the depression begins to lift. Energy and motivation increase, and patients are more likely to carry out the act.

Although depression is undeniably correlated with suicidal thoughts and behavior, the relationship seems very complex. Why do some people with depression commit suicide, whereas others do not? The answer may be found in the characteristics of depression and in the factors that contribute to it (Jobes, 2006). It has been found that an increase in sadness is a frequent mood indicator of suicide, but heightened feelings of anxiety, anger, and shame are also associated. Some researchers believe that hopelessness, or negative expectations about the future, may be the major catalyst in suicide, possibly an even more important factor than depression and other moods (D. Lester, 2008; Weishaar & Beck, 1992). Some sample statements indicative of hopelessness are "My future seems dark for me," "I might as well give up because there's nothing I can do about making things better for myself," and "I never get anything I want, so it's foolish to want anything."

Alcohol Consumption One of the most consistently reported correlates of suicidal behavior is alcohol consumption (Canapary, Bongar, & Cleary, 2002; Shea, 2002). As many as 70 percent of people who attempt suicide drink alcohol before the act, and autopsies of suicide victims suggest that 25 percent are legally intoxicated (Lejoyeux et al., 2008; McCloud, Barnaby, Omu, Drumond, & Aboud, 2004). Indeed, a successful suicide unconnected to alcohol abuse is rare. Heavy alcohol consumption, such as binge drinking, also seems to deepen feelings of remorse during dry periods, and a person may be at risk even when sober. Many theorists have traditionally argued that alcohol may lower inhibitions related to the fear of death and make it easier to carry out the fatal act.

Several classic studies, however, suggest another explanation of the effects of alcohol: The strength of the relationship between alcohol and suicide is the result of "alcohol-induced myopia," a constriction of cognitive and perceptual processes (J. R. Rogers, 1992; C. M. Steele & Josephs, 1990). Alcohol use by individuals in psychological conflict may increase rather than decrease personal distress by focusing the individuals' thoughts on negative aspects of their personal situations. Alcohol does seem to constrict cognitive and perceptual processes. Although alcohol-induced myopia may relieve depression and anxiety by distracting the person from the problem, it is equally likely to intensify the conflict and distress by narrowing the person's focus on the problem (Cha, Najmi, Park, Finn, & Nock, 2010). Thus, the link between alcohol and suicide may be the result of the myopic qualities of alcohol exaggerating a previously existing constrictive state. If this is true, alcohol is most likely to increase the probability of a suicide in a person who is already suicidal.

Social Dimension

Many suicides are interpersonal in nature and are influenced primarily by relationships involving significant others (Jobes, 2006; Leenaars, 2008). Individuals who are incapacitated or who have a terminal illness are often at higher risk for suicide (Bazalgette, Bradley, & Ousbey, 2011). A desire not to burden family and friends with their increasing dependency and with financial depletion of family resources is a reason often given for the desire to end their lives. Suicides and

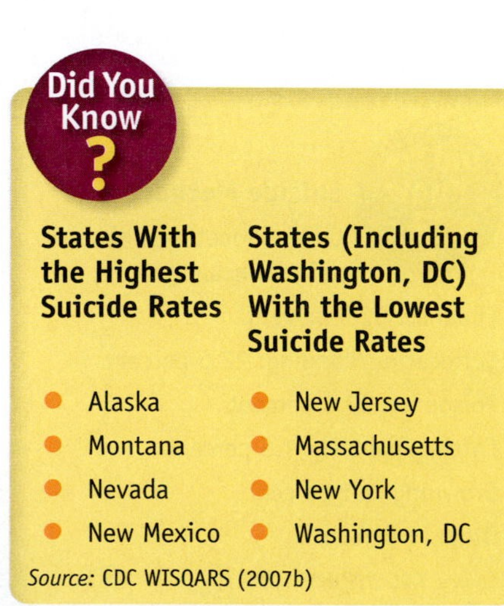

Did You Know?

States With the Highest Suicide Rates	States (Including Washington, DC) With the Lowest Suicide Rates
Alaska	New Jersey
Montana	Massachusetts
Nevada	New York
New Mexico	Washington, DC

Source: CDC WISQARS (2007b)

attempted suicides are often related to the quality and nature of social relationships with people. It has been found that unhappiness over a broken or hopeless love affair, marital discord, disputes with parents, and recent bereavements are correlated with suicides (Rudd et al., 2004). Family instability, stress, and a chaotic family atmosphere are factors in suicide attempts by younger children as well. Children who are suicidal seem to have experienced abuse, unpredictable traumatic events, and the loss of a significant parenting figure before age 12 (C. A. King & Merchant, 2008).

Joiner's interpersonal-psychological theory of suicide (2005) has received considerable attention in the psychological literature. In an attempt to integrate the many factors associated with suicide, he postulated that two social dimensions must be experienced by people before suicide attempts are made: (a) perceived burdensomeness—beliefs or feelings that they are a burden to their family, friends, loved ones, community, and society; and (b) thwarted belongingness—beliefs or feelings that they are not meaningfully connected to others or are alienated from them (Joiner, 2005; Joiner, Van Orden, et al., 2009). Social factors that separate people or make them somehow less connected to other people or to their families, religious institutions, or communities can increase susceptibility to suicide (Alcantara & Gone, 2008).

A unique third condition must exist before a suicide attempt is made, according to Joiner's theory: the acquired capacity for suicide (P. N. Smith et al., 2010). People must experience a reduction in fear of taking their own life sufficient to overcome self-preservation reflexes. Repeated exposure to painful life events (an abusive childhood, physical abuse, emotional abuse, rape, bullying, exposure to wartime atrocities, etc.) results in habituation to painful life circumstances and lowering of fear of inflicting self-injury; this is the acquired capacity for suicide. Studies have found that people who attempt suicide do indeed report the highest levels of fearlessness and pain insensitivity, as well as greater frequency of painful life events (P. N. Smith et al., 2010).

Suicide prevention will be vastly more effective when social support and connectedness are increased and when social isolation is decreased, Joiner's theory predicts. Conversely, it expects rates to be higher among the elderly, as their loved ones and friends die off, they begin to disengage from their work through retirement, and they sense they are a burden to others. It also expects that among people who are divorced, separated, or widowed, suicide rates will be higher than among those who are married. As we have seen, the research literature supports all of these expectations.

Political Protest and Suicide

During the Vietnam War, people were horrified by scenes of self-immolation by Buddhist monks as a form of protest against the government. This altruistic suicide in 1963 was witnessed by passersby in the central market of Saigon.

Sociocultural Dimension

In a pioneering work, the French sociologist Émile Durkheim related differences in suicide rates to the impact of sociocultural forces on the person (Durkheim, 1897/1951). From his detailed study of suicides in different countries and across different periods, he proposed one of the first sociocultural explanations of suicide: It can result from an inability to integrate oneself with society. In Durkheim's view, failing to maintain close ties with the community deprives a person of the support systems that are necessary for adaptive functioning. Without such support, and unable to function adaptively, the person becomes isolated and alienated from other people. Some **suicidologists** believe that modern, mobile, and highly technological society has de-emphasized the importance of extended families and the sense of community. The result, even among young people, has been an increase in suicide rates.

Suicide can also be motivated by a person's desire to further group goals or to achieve some greater good. Someone may give up his or her life for a higher cause (in a religious sacrifice or the ultimate political protest, for example). Group pressures may make such an act highly acceptable and honored. During World War II,

suicidologist a professional who studies the manifestation, dynamics, and prevention of suicides

REUTERS/STR/Landov

Suicide Bombings

These events have become an all too common sight in Iraq. In the aftermath of a suicide bombing in Baghdad in April 2007, two men try desperately to move a car away to clear the way for help. A suicide truck bomb was used in an attempt to destroy a satellite television station and take as many lives as possible.

Japanese kamikaze pilots voluntarily flew their airplanes into enemy warships "for the Emperor and the glory of Japan." The self-immolation of Buddhist monks during the Vietnam War is likewise in this category. Although likely to arouse considerable disagreement and controversy, a strong case can be made that the suicide bombings now so prevalent in the Middle East, Iraq, and Afghanistan—and even the September 11, 2001, terrorist attacks—qualify for this category. From the perspective of those who condone such acts, the perpetrators are not terrorists, but freedom fighters who willingly give their lives for a greater good.

Sociocultural factors have been shown to account for the differential rates and manifestations of suicides among Asian/Pacific Islander Americans (Leong & Leach, 2008), African Americans (Utsey, Stanard, & Hook, 2008), Latino/Hispanic Americans (Duarte-Velez & Bernal, 2008), American Indians (Alcantara & Gone, 2008), and gay men and lesbians (Leach, 2006). American Indians have a 70 percent higher rate of suicide than is found among all other groups in U.S. society, including white Americans (Dorgan, 2010). Rates for Asian Americans and Latino/Hispanic Americans are significantly lower than that for white Americans (Duarte-Velez & Bernal, 2008; Leong & Leach, 2008). Although rates for African American youngsters have also been traditionally lower than for their white counterparts, reports reveal a dramatic increase over the past two decades (Utsey et al., 2008).

Social change and disorganization, which lead to a breakup in integration with one's community, often predispose members of a particular group to suicide. Suicidologists point to the disorganization imposed on American Indians by U.S. society: Deprived of their lands, forced to live on reservations, and trapped on the margins of two different cultural traditions, many American Indians become alienated and isolated from their own communities and the larger society (Goldston et al., 2008).

CHECKPOINT REVIEW

1. What evidence suggests a biological explanation for suicide?
2. Name three proposed psychological factors that may explain suicidal behavior.
3. Explain how social connectedness provides an explanation for suicide.
4. How does a sociocultural explanation account for differential suicide rates among various racial groups?

Suicide and Specific Populations

In this section we briefly discuss three groups of people who are affected by suicide: those who are very young, college students, and those who are elderly. It is important, however, to realize that those who are left behind may be considered victims as well. Indeed, it is estimated that for every suicide, six other people are intimately affected as survivors, such as family members and friends (CDC WISQARS, 2005).

Suicide Among Children and Adolescents

Suicide among young people is an unmentioned tragedy in our society. We have traditionally avoided the idea that some of our young people find life so painful that they consciously and deliberately take their own lives. The suicide rate for children younger than 14 is increasing at an alarming rate, and the rate for adolescents is rising even faster (CDC, 2007b; CDC WISQARS, 2005). Suicide is now the third leading cause of death among teenagers, just behind automobile accidents—some of which may also really be suicides (Iannelli, 2009; Rudd et al., 2004).

After a trend of decreasing rates from 1996 to 2003, teen suicides increased 18 percent in 2004 and 17 percent in 2005; even children from 6–9 years of age showed an increase (Iannelli, 2009). In a study of high school students in grades 9–12 in 2009, the following was found: 13.8 percent had considered suicide in the previous 12 months (17.4 percent of girls and 10.5 percent of boys), 6.3 percent reported making at least one attempt (8.1 percent of girls and 4.5 percent of boys), and 1.9 percent had made an attempt that resulted in an injury, poisoning, or overdose requiring medical attention (2.3 percent of girls and 1.6 percent of boys; CDC, 2010d).

Many reasons have been postulated for the increase of suicide among young children and teenagers: attempts to regain control of their lives, retaliation or revenge against wrongs, reunion fantasies with a loved one, relief from unbearable pain, escape from being a family scapegoat, distracting family from issues such as divorce, and acting out their parents' covert or overt desire to be rid of them. Three, however, seem to have gained considerable attention in recent years (Bates & Bowles, 2012).

AP Photo/Marcio Jose Sanchez

Teens and Suicide

As more and more teens like those shown here find themselves attending the funerals of their peers, it is becoming clear that suicide among high school students is reaching epidemic proportions. To prevent more suicides, schools sometimes initiate programs to help students and faculty cope with their feelings of loss and anger.

The Role of Bullying "Bullycide" is an increasingly used term to describe bullying that leads to suicides among young people (Ollove, 2010). Such was the case of Phoebe Prince, a 15-year-old high school freshman who hanged herself in the stairwell of her home on January 14, 2010. The investigation of her death indicated that she had been subjected to nearly three torturous months of verbally assaultive behavior, threats of physical harm, cyberbullying, and statutory rape before her suicide. Six of her classmates were charged with Prince's death for their part in violating her civil rights with bodily injury, harassment, and stalking. After pleading guilty, the six were given sentences of probation and community service.

In 2009, bullying statistics revealed that one third of teens reported being bullied at school: 20 percent were teased, 18 percent had rumors or gossip spread about them, 11 percent were physically bullied (spat upon, shoved, or tripped), 6 percent were threatened, 5 percent were excluded, 4 percent were coerced, and 4 percent had belongings destroyed ("Bullying Statistics 2009," 2009). It has been found that bullying victims are 2 to 9 times more likely to consider suicide than nonvictims; nearly 50 percent of young people who commit suicide have experienced bullying (Bullying Statistics 2009).

Copycat Suicides Considerable attention has been directed at multiple or so-called copycat suicides (suicide contagion), in which youngsters in a particular school or community seem to mimic a suicide (Alcantara & Gone, 2008; D. P. Phillips, Van Voorhees, & Ruth, 1992). Suggestion and imitation seem to play an especially powerful role. Young people may be especially vulnerable, but studies indicate that highly publicized suicides such as those of a celebrity or other well-known person, and even a close friend, relative, or coworker, can increase the number of subsequent suicide attempts (Gould, 2007; Stack, 1987). When Nirvana's Kurt Cobain committed suicide in 1994, many youth counselors warned about potential imitations by fans. Fans worshiped Cobain, he represented an icon of the "lost generation," and his known psychological problems seemed to endear him to the hearts of many youngsters. According to one study, Cobain's death resulted in an excess of 119 suicides beyond the average number in the 1-month period following his death (Queinec et al., 2010).

Did You Know?

In 2010, 150 workers in China threatened a mass suicide by leaping off the rooftop of Foxconn, the world's largest manufacturer of electronics products for such well-known companies as Apple and Sony. That year, a suicide cluster of 14 deaths occurred when workers, one after another, hurled themselves from the rooftop or windows. The factory owners installed roof nets to catch potential victims and even hired a Buddhist monk to rid the factory of bad karma. Was this a product of copycat suicide? Perhaps that played a role, but it seems more likely that workers were protesting the inhumane working conditions of the factory. Most of the workers were well-educated migrants who were forced to work 15-hour days, 7 days a week, for extremely low pay. The working conditions (dust and chemicals) were hazardous to their health and they became isolated from coworkers. They felt like cogs in a machine where few knew or cared about them.

Source: Barboza, 2010

Although imitative suicides may not be as common as the media suggest, research has indicated that publicizing the event may have the effect of glorifying and drawing attention to it. Thus, people who are depressed may identify with a colorful portrayal, increasing the risk of even more suicides. This pattern appears to be especially true for youngsters who may already be thinking about killing themselves; stable, well-adjusted teenagers do not seem to be at risk in these situations.

Adolescence and young adulthood are often periods of confusing emotions, identity formation, and questioning. It is a difficult and turbulent time for most teenagers, and suicide may seem to be a logical response to the pain and stress of growing up. A suicide that occurs in school brings increased risk of other suicides because of its proximity to students' daily lives. In such instances, a suicide prevention program should be implemented to let students vent their feelings in an environment equipped to respond appropriately—and perhaps even to save their lives. Encouragingly, approximately 41 percent of schools have programs aimed at suicide prevention (professional counseling services, peer counseling, and special seminars). It is no longer unusual to hear about school programs that are immediately implemented when a tragedy strikes, such as student suicide, the violent death of a student or teacher, or a natural disaster (Freiberg, 1991).

Decrease in Antidepressant Medication Another explanation for the increase in youth suicides relates to the 2004 U.S. Food and Drug Administration (FDA) warning of an increased suicide risk for children taking selective serotonin reuptake inhibitor antidepressants. Although antidepressants are found to help people with depression, the FDA noted an increase in suicidal thoughts and actions in adolescents, and required a "black box" warning on all such medication. There is considerable controversy over the actions of the FDA. Research seems to suggest that selective serotonin reuptake inhibitors may increase suicidal thoughts or behaviors for a very select few, that the majority of youths who are depressed benefit from them, and that completed suicides (in contrast to suicidal thoughts) are not increased in young people who take them (Brent, 2009b; Ludwig, Marcotte, & Norberg, 2009). In fact, these investigators observed that suicide rates among young people have increased since the black box warnings were imposed. They reasoned that since the notification requirement, parents and doctors have been less inclined to give antidepressant medication, resulting in the increase in suicides. The issue is far from being resolved.

Suicide Among College Students

Due to high-profile suicide-related events on several college campuses, national interest in college-student suicides has increased (Drum et al., 2009). A wave of suicides at Cornell University, in particular, brought this issue into national consciousness (Spodak, 2010). In 2009, six students committed suicide, a proportion far above the national average. These and a previous cluster of suicides in 1990 have mobilized the Cornell community to institute major suicide prevention and remedial programs on campus.

When you consider how fortunate college students as a group generally are—with youth, intelligence, and boundless opportunity—you might wonder why they would choose to end their lives. Was the major transition of leaving home, family, and friends too stressful? Did college work prove too difficult and act as a "pressure cooker"? Did they have pre-existing mental conditions like depression or hopelessness? Or did loneliness, isolation, and alienation play a role in their suicides? As in all suicides, we can never be certain.

Is there a suicidal crisis on our college campuses? According to a major study on college students, suicide rates among their peers are no higher than among a matched noncollege group (Furr et al., 2001). Indeed, in a study of 12 colleges and universities conducted over a 60-year period, it was found that the rate was nearly half that of a nonstudent group (A. J. Schwartz & Whittaker, 1990).

But these findings do not tell the entire story. First, the lower rates may be a statistical artifact due to limited access to lethal means (such as firearms) for students on campus, and the decreasing proportion of males attending colleges (completed suicides for men are twice that of women students; Drum et al., 2009; A. J. Schwartz, 2006). Second, although suicide is the third leading cause of death for people ages 15–24, it is the second leading cause of death for college students; nearly 1,000 students end their lives in any given year (CDC, 2007c). Third, counseling centers report a 44 percent increase of severe psychiatric disorders in students seeking services over the past 10 years; apparently the effectiveness of psychotropic medication in controlling psychiatric symptoms allows more severely disturbed students to function academically at a marginal level (Gabriel, 2010). Many of these students are considered suicidal. Last, the most recent report by the Substance Abuse and Mental Health Services Administration (2012) revealed that among full-time college students, serious thoughts of suicide rose significantly from 2009 to 2010.

In one of the most comprehensive studies of college student suicides, 70 participating colleges and universities were surveyed on suicidal ideation, attempts, preparation, and other demographic factors (Drum et al., 2009). The study revealed the following:

- More than 50 percent of undergraduate and graduate college students reported suicidal thoughts.
- Eighteen percent of undergraduates and 15 percent of graduate students had *seriously considered* attempting suicide.

Of those who had contemplated suicide seriously in the past 12 months:

- Ninety-two percent of undergraduates and 90 percent of graduate students had a specific plan for killing themselves; most commonly considered was a drug or alcohol overdose.
- Fourteen percent of undergraduates and 8 percent of graduate students had made an attempt.
- Twenty-three percent of undergraduates and 27 percent of graduate students who had made a first attempt were considering a second try.

Approximately 80 percent of students who die by suicide do not go for help on their own to a counseling or psychological services center (Kisch, Leino, & Silverman, 2005), and 45 percent never tell anyone about their serious intentions (Drum et al., 2009). Those who do share their anguish and thoughts of suicide with someone are most likely to do so with a fellow student. It is important to note that verbalizing thoughts of suicide is not the only sign of suicidal potential—there is also withdrawal, depression, giving prized possessions away, etc. Two thirds of those who commit suicide communicate their intent in one way or another.

Campus prevention and remediation efforts are of critical importance in identifying students at risk for suicide. Many colleges and universities have begun to develop programs and resources to (1) identify warning signs related to suicide; (2) have well-established procedures for counselors, faculty, staff, and students in suicide intervention; and (3) clearly identify campus and community resources with expertise in a suicidal crisis.

In order of frequency, the following were listed as contributing to suicidal thoughts and attempts for undergraduates:

- emotional or physical pain,
- problems with romantic relations,
- a desire to end one's life,
- school problems,
- friend problems,
- family problems, and
- financial problems.

Source: Drum, et al, (2009)

Suicide Among the Elderly

Aging inevitably results in generally unwelcome physical changes, such as wrinkling and thickening skin, graying hair, and diminishing physical strength. In addition, we all encounter a succession of stressful life changes as we grow older. Friends and relatives die, social isolation may increase, and the prospect of death becomes more real. Mandatory retirement rules may lead to the need for financial

Christiana Dittmann/Rainbow

A Matter of Respect

Suicide is less likely to occur among the elderly in cultures that revere, respect, and esteem people of increasing age. In Asian and African countries, increasing age is equated with greater privilege and status, such as that shown for this elderly Ghanaian chief; in contrast, in the United States, growing old is often associated with declining worth and social isolation.

assistance and the difficulties of living on a fixed and inadequate income. Such conditions make depression one of the most common psychiatric complaints of elderly people. And their depression seems to be involved more with "feeling old" than with their actual age or poor physical health (Rosenfeld, 2004).

Suicide seems to accompany depression for older people. Their suicide rates (especially rates for elderly white U.S. men) are higher than those for the general population; indeed, suicide rates for elderly white men are the highest for any age group (CDC WISQARS, 2005). From 1980 through 1997, the largest relative increases in suicide rates occurred among those ages 80–84. Firearms were the most common method of suicide for both men and women 65 years or older. People who are elderly make fewer attempts per completed suicide, being among the most likely to succeed in taking their lives. In one study comparing rates of suicide among different ethnic groups, it was found that elderly white Americans committed almost 18 percent of all suicides, although they composed only about 11 percent of the population (Leong & Leach, 2008). Suicide rates for elderly Chinese Americans, Japanese Americans, and Filipino Americans were even higher than the rate for elderly white Americans. American Indians and African Americans showed the lowest rates of suicide among older adults (although both groups are at high risk for suicide during young adulthood).

Of the Asian American groups, first-generation immigrants were at greatest risk of suicide. One possible explanation for this finding is that newly arrived Asian immigrants intended to earn money and then return to their native countries. When they found they were unable to earn enough either to return home or to bring their families to the United States, they developed feelings of isolation that increased their risk of suicide. This risk has decreased among subsequent generations of Asian Americans (and probably among other immigrant groups as well) because of acculturation and the creation of strong family ties.

CHECKPOINT REVIEW

1. Explain the role that bullying and victim identification have in suicide among young people.
2. What do we know about suicide among college students?
3. Why may elderly people be prone to suicide?

Preventing Suicide

In almost every case of suicide, there are hints that the act is about to occur. Suicide is irreversible, of course, so preventing it depends very much on early detection and successful intervention (Comtois & Linehan, 2006; Granello, 2010). Mental health professionals involved in suicide prevention efforts operate under the assumption that potential victims are ambivalent about the act. That is, the wish to die is strong, but there is also a wish to live. Potential rescuers are trained to exert their efforts to preserve life. Part of their success in the prevention process is the ability to assess a client's suicide **lethality**—the probability that the person chooses to end his or her life (Bryan & Rudd, 2006; Rudd et al., 2004).

Working with a potentially suicidal individual is a three-step process that involves (1) knowing which factors are highly correlated with suicide; (2) determining whether there is high, moderate, or low probability that the person will act on the suicide wish; and (3) implementing appropriate actions (Table 8.3; Isaac,

lethality the probability that a person chooses to end his or her life

TABLE 8.3 Risk and Protective Factors in Suicide Assessment and Intervention

RISK FACTORS	PROTECTIVE FACTORS
• Previous suicide attempt	• Effective resources for clinical care for mental, physical, and substance-use disorders
• Mental disorders such as depression and bipolar disorder	• Easy access to a variety of clinical interventions and support for seeking help
• Co-occurring mental disorders and alcohol- or substance-use disorders	• Restricted access to lethal means of suicide
• Family history of suicide	• Family and community support
• Hopelessness	• Good skills in problem solving, conflict resolution, and nonviolent means of handling disputes
• Impulsive or aggressive tendencies	• Cultural and religious beliefs that discourage suicide and support self-preservation instincts
• Barriers to accessing mental health treatment	
• Relational, social, work, or financial loss	
• Physical illness	
• Easy access to lethal methods, especially guns	
• Unwillingness to seek help because of social stigma	
• Family members, peers, or favored celebrities who have died from suicide	
• Cultural or religious beliefs that suicide is a noble resolution	
• Local epidemics of suicide that have a contagious influence	
• Isolation	

Source: Bryan & Rudd (2006); USPHS (1999) *The Surgeon General's call to action to prevent suicide.* Washington, DC: Author.

et al., 2009). People trained in working with clients who are suicidal often attempt to quantify the seriousness of factors. For example, a person with a clear suicidal plan who has the means (e.g., a gun) to carry out a suicide threat is considered to be in a more lethal state than a recently divorced and depressed person.

Clues to Suicidal Intent

The prevention of suicide depends very much on a therapist's ability to recognize its signs. Clues to suicidal intent may be demographic or specific. We have already discussed a number of demographic factors, such as the fact that men are 3 times more likely to kill themselves than are women, and that older age is associated with an increased probability of suicide (Bryan & Rudd, 2006). And although the popular notion is that frequent suicidal gestures are associated with less serious intent, most people who commit suicide do have a history of making suicide threats; to ignore them is extremely dangerous. Any suicidal threat or intent must be taken seriously (A. L. Berman, 2006).

General characteristics often help detect potential suicides, but individual cases vary from statistical norms. What does one look for in specific instances? The amount of detail involved in a suicide threat can indicate its seriousness. A person who provides specific details, such as method, time, and place, is more at risk than one who describes these factors vaguely. Suicide potential increases if the person has direct access to the means of suicide, such as a loaded pistol. Also, sometimes a suicide may be preceded by a precipitating event. The loss of a loved one, family discord, or chronic or terminal illness may contribute to a person's decision to end his or her life.

A person contemplating suicide may verbally communicate the intent. Some people make very direct statements: "I'm going to kill myself," "I want to die," or "If such and such happens, I'll kill myself." Others make indirect statements: "Goodbye," "I've had it," "You'd be better off without me," and "It's too much to put up with." On the other hand, some cues are frequently very subtle.

Behavioral clues can be communicated directly or indirectly. The most direct clue is a "practice run," an actual suicide attempt. Even if the act is not completed, *it should be taken seriously*; it often communicates deep suicidal intent that may be carried out in the future. Indirect behavioral clues can include actions such as putting one's affairs in order, taking a lengthy trip, giving away prized possessions, buying a casket, or making out a will, depending on the circumstances. In other words, the more unusual or peculiar the situation, the more likely it is that the action is a clue to suicide. Clinicians often divide up warning signs into two categories: (a) early signs, such as depression, statements or expressions of guilt feelings, tension or anxiety, nervousness, insomnia, loss of appetite, loss of weight, and impulsiveness; and (b) critical signs, such as sudden changes in behavior (calmness after a period of anxiety), giving away belongings or putting affairs in order, direct or indirect threats, and actual attempts.

Crisis Intervention Suicide prevention can occur at several levels, and the mental health profession has now begun to move in several coordinated directions. At the clinical level, mental health institutions and even schools are educating staff to recognize conditions and symptoms that indicate potential suicides (Brown & Grumet, 2009; Isaac et al., 2009). For example, mental health professionals should recognize a single man who is older than 50 and experiencing a sudden acute onset of depression and expressing hopelessness as being at high risk.

When a psychiatric facility encounters someone who fits a particular risk profile for suicide, crisis intervention strategies are likely to be used to abort or ameliorate the processes that could lead to a suicide attempt. Crisis intervention is aimed at providing intensive short-term help to a client in resolving an immediate life crisis. Unlike traditional psychotherapy, in which sessions are spaced out and treatment is provided on a more leisurely long-term basis, crisis intervention recognizes the immediacy of the patient's state of mind. The client may be immediately hospitalized, given medical treatment, and seen by a psychiatric team for 2–4 hours every day until the client is stabilized and the immediate crisis has passed. In these sessions, the team is very active not only in working with the patient but also in taking charge of the client's personal, social, and professional life outside of the psychiatric facility. Many suicide intervention strategies have been developed through clinical work rather than research, because the nature of suicide demands immediate action (Bryan & Rudd, 2006). Waiting for empirical studies is not a luxury the clinician can afford. Figure 8.2 summarizes the process of assessing risk and determining lethality.

After clients return to a more stable emotional state and the immediate risk of suicide has passed, they are then given more traditional forms of treatment, on either an inpatient or an outpatient basis. In addition to the intense therapy clients receive from the psychiatric team, relatives and friends may be enlisted to help monitor them when they leave the hospital. In these cases, the responsible relatives or friends are provided with specific guidelines about how to deal with the client between treatment team contacts, whom to notify if problems arise outside of the hospital, and so forth.

Suicide Prevention Centers

Crisis intervention can be highly successful if a client who is potentially suicidal either is already being treated by a therapist or has come to the attention of one through the efforts of concerned family or friends. Many people in acute distress,

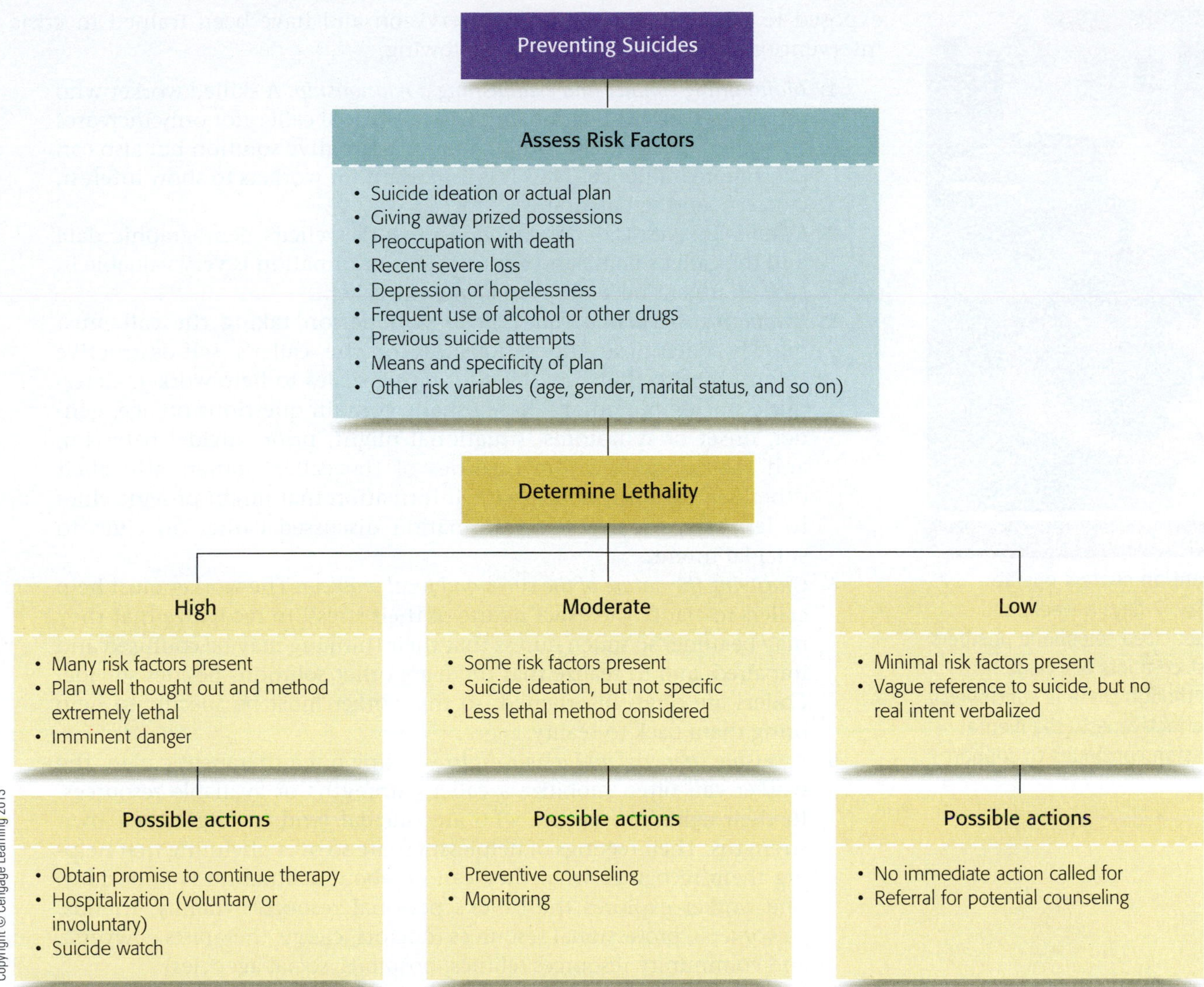

Preventing Suicides
Assess Risk Factors
• Suicide ideation or actual plan
• Giving away prized possessions
• Preoccupation with death
• Recent severe loss
• Depression or hopelessness
• Frequent use of alcohol or other drugs
• Previous suicide attempts
• Means and specificity of plan
• Other risk variables (age, gender, marital status, and so on)
Determine Lethality
High
• Many risk factors present
• Plan well thought out and method extremely lethal
• Imminent danger
Moderate
• Some risk factors present
• Suicide ideation, but not specific
• Less lethal method considered
Low
• Minimal risk factors present
• Vague reference to suicide, but no real intent verbalized
Possible actions
• Obtain promise to continue therapy
• Hospitalization (voluntary or involuntary)
• Suicide watch
Possible actions
• Preventive counseling
• Monitoring
Possible actions
• No immediate action called for
• Referral for potential counseling

FIGURE 8.2

The Process of Preventing Suicide

Suicide prevention involves the careful assessment of risk factors to determine lethality—the probability that a person will choose to end his or her life. Working with an individual who is potentially suicidal is a three-step process that involves (1) knowing what factors are highly correlated with suicide; (2) determining whether there is high, moderate, or low probability that the person will act on the wish; and (3) implementing appropriate actions.

however, are not formally being treated. Although contact with a mental health agency may be highly desirable, many people are unaware of the services available to them. Recognizing that suicidal crises may occur at any time and that preventive assistance on a much larger scale may be needed, a number of communities have established suicide prevention centers.

Telephone Crisis Intervention Suicide prevention centers typically operate 24 hours a day, 7 days a week. Because most suicide contacts are by phone, a well-publicized telephone number is made available throughout the community for calls at any time of the day or night. Furthermore, many centers provide inpatient or outpatient crisis treatment. Those that lack such resources develop cooperative programs with other community mental health facilities. Most telephone hotlines are staffed by paraprofessionals. All workers have been

Geri Engberg Photography/The Image Works

Intervening Before It Is Too Late

Suicide prevention centers operate 24 hours a day, 7 days a week, and have well-publicized telephone numbers because most contacts are made by phone. Even though there is controversy about their effectiveness, the mental health profession continues to support these centers.

exposed to crisis situations under supervision and have been trained in crisis intervention techniques such as the following:

1. *Maintaining contact and establishing a relationship.* A skilled worker who establishes a good relationship with a suicidal caller not only increases the caller's chances of working out an alternative solution but also can exert more influence. Thus it is important for workers to show interest, concern, and self-assurance.
2. *Obtaining necessary information.* The worker elicits demographic data and the caller's name and address. This information is very valuable in case an urgent need arises to locate the caller.
3. *Evaluating suicidal potential.* The staff person taking the call must quickly determine the seriousness of the caller's self-destructive intent. Most centers use lethality rating scales to help workers determine suicide potential. These usually contain questions on age, gender, onset of symptoms, situational plight, prior suicidal behavior, and the communication qualities of the caller. Staffers also elicit other demographic and specific information that might provide clues to lethality, such as the information discussed earlier on clues to suicidal intent.
4. *Clarifying the nature of the stress and focal problem.* The worker must help callers to clarify the exact nature of their stress, to recognize that they may be under so much duress that their thinking may be confused and impaired, and to realize that there are other solutions besides suicide. Callers are often disoriented, so the worker must be specific to help bring them back to reality.
5. *Assessing strengths and resources.* In working out a therapeutic plan, the worker can often mobilize a caller's strengths or available resources. In their agitation, people who are suicidal tend to forget their own strengths. Their feelings of helplessness are so overwhelming that helping them recognize what they can do about a situation is important. The worker explores the caller's personal resources (family, friends, coworkers), professional resources (doctors, clergy, therapists, lawyers), and community resources (clinics, hospitals, social agencies).
6. *Recommending and initiating an action plan.* Besides being supportive, the worker is highly directive in recommending a course of action. Whether the recommendation entails immediately seeing the person, calling the person's family, or referring the person to a social agency the next day, the worker presents a plan of action and outlines it step by step.

This list implies a rigid sequence, but in fact both the approach and the order of the steps are adjusted to fit the needs of the individual caller.

Today, approximately 200 suicide prevention centers function in the United States, along with numerous suicide hotlines in mental health clinics. Little research has been done on their effectiveness, however, and many of their clients want to remain anonymous. Despite this lack, there is always the possibility that suicide prevention centers do help. Because life is precious, the mental health profession continues to support them.

CHECKPOINT REVIEW

1. Name some potential clues to suicidal intent.
2. How do suicide crisis centers and suicide hotlines work?
3. Describe what actions you would take if your roommate in college expressed suicidal thoughts.

The Right to Suicide: Moral, Ethical, and Legal Issues

In September 2003, after the release of his book *I Ask the Right to Die*, 21-year-old Vincent Humbert's mother administered an overdose of sedatives into his intravenous line, causing his death (C. S. Smith, 2003). Hubert, a French citizen, was seriously injured in a traffic accident in which nearly every organ of his body was affected; he was, however, able to hear, think and reason. He spent 9 months in a coma and his only means of communication was with his thumb. With that one thumb, he pointed to letters of the alphabet and wrote a special appeal to French president Jacques Chirac asking for the right to die. The case of Vincent Humbert set off a national debate about the morality and legality of euthanasia.

Do people have the right to end their lives if their continued existence would result in psychological and physical deterioration? Surveys of the U.S. public indicate that a majority believe terminally ill individuals should be allowed to take their own lives; in a 1995 survey of physicians working with AIDS patients, over half indicated that they had prescribed lethal doses of narcotics to suicidal patients (Clay, 1997; Drane, 1995). Advocates contend that people should be allowed the choice of dying in a dignified manner, particularly if they have a terminal or severely incapacitating illness that would cause misery for their families and friends (Rosenfeld, 2004).

The act of suicide seems to violate much of what most of us have been taught regarding the sanctity of life. Many segments of the population consider it immoral and maintain strong religious sanctions against it. Suicide is both a sin in the canonical law of the Catholic Church and an illegal act according to the secular laws of most countries. Within the United States, many states have laws against suicide. Of course, such laws are difficult to enforce, because the victims are not around to prosecute.

Many are beginning to question the legitimacy of such sanctions, however, and are openly advocating a person's right to suicide. In November 1998, Oregon voters passed a physician-assisted suicide act granting physicians the legal right to help end the lives of terminally ill patients. In 2001, however, U.S. Attorney General John Ashcroft issued a directive intended to invalidate the law. In October 2005, the United States Supreme Court ruled 6–3 in favor of upholding the law. From its passage until 2008, 401 patients used the act. The average age of patients was 70, with 81.8 percent having malignant neoplasms (cancer), and all involved ingestion of lethal medication. No complications were reported.

Recent legislation has intensified the debate over whether it is morally, ethically, and legally permissible to allow relatives, friends, or physicians to provide support, means, and actions to carry out a suicide (Rosenfeld, 2004). Two high-profile individuals have fueled the debate by virtue of their actions. Derek Humphry, the former director of the Hemlock Society (an organization that advocates people's right to end their lives), published the best-selling book *Final Exit* (1991). It is a manual that provides practical information such as drug dosages needed to end one's life; when published, it created a national stir. Another individual who became a household name is Dr. Jack Kevorkian, a physician who helped nearly 130 people to end their own lives using a device he called a "suicide machine." Those who saw Kevorkian as a courageous physician willing to help others in their search for a dignified death called him a savior; those who opposed his actions referred to him as "Dr. Death."

Did You Know?

We are witnessing increased openness in discussing issues of death and dying, the meaning of suicide, and the right to take one's own life. Some individuals have even gone so far as to advocate a right to suicide and the legalization of assisted suicide. In January 2006, the U.S. Supreme Court upheld the first law in the nation (in Oregon) authorizing doctors to help their patients with terminal illness commit suicide.

CONTROVERSY:

Do People Have a Right to Die?

On November 22, 1998, over 15 million viewers of *60 Minutes* watched in either horror or sadness the death by lethal injection of 52-year-old Thomas Youk. This was not, however, a death sentence carried out for a murder conviction, but the enactment of a conscious desire and decision of a man in the latter stages of Lou Gehrig's disease.

Youk's wife stated, "[I am] so grateful to know that someone would relieve him of his suffering . . . . I consider it the way things should be done." The man who videotaped the event was Dr. Jack Kevorkian, a retired physician who carried on a 10-year battle with U.S. legal systems and society over the right to die.

It is estimated that since 1989, Kevorkian assisted in the suicides of nearly 130 people (most of them women) with chronic debilitating diseases. The early means of death used by Kevorkian was a "suicide machine," composed of bottles containing chemicals that could be fed intravenously into the arm of the person. The solution could bring instantaneous unconsciousness and quick, painless death. His first client, Janet Adkins, had Alzheimer's disease. She did not want to put her family through the agony of the disease, believed that she had a right to choose death, stated that her act was that of a rational mind, and had the consent of her husband. Many others whom Kevorkian helped commit suicide did not have diseases that threatened to kill them in the immediate future.

Carlos Osorio/epa/Corbis

Fighting for the Right to Choose Life or Death

Dr. Jack Kevorkian, a Michigan physician, was a lifelong advocate for the repeal of laws against assisted suicide. Convicted of the second-degree murder of Thomas Youk, who had Lou Gehrig's disease, Kevorkian was released in June 2007 after serving 8 years of his sentence. He died in 2011.

Before the *60 Minutes* taping, charges of homicide had been brought against Kevorkian four previous times; in each case either the charges were ultimately dropped or he was found not guilty. Because of his actions, a Michigan law outlawing physician-assisted suicides was passed and used to charge him with manslaughter. Prosecutors contended that Kevorkian's actions in the death of Youk went far beyond what many consider assistance: Because Youk was too weak to administer the dose himself, Kevorkian administered it for him. For that act, in 1999 the retired physician was charged with and convicted of second-degree murder, criminal assistance to a suicide, and delivery of a controlled substance. After serving 8 years in prison, he was released in 2007 because of failing health, after promising not to engage in assisted suicides.

For Further Consideration

1. Did Thomas Youk have a right to end his own life? What reasons lead you to your answer? Does a doctor—or, for that matter, anyone—have a right to help others terminate their lives?
2. What might motivate someone like Dr. Kevorkian to risk censure and imprisonment to help others die? Would you be in favor of legislation that would legalize physician-assisted suicides? Why or why not?

Ironically, the success of medical science has added fuel to the right-to-die movement. As a part of its remarkably successful efforts to prolong life, U.S. society has also begun to prolong the process of dying. And this prolongation has caused many people who are elderly or terminally ill to fear medical decision makers who are intent only on keeping them alive, giving no thought to their desires or dignity. They and many others find it abhorrent to impose on a dying patient a horrifying array of respirators, breathing tubes, feeding tubes, and repeated violent cardiopulmonary resuscitations—procedures that are often futile and against the wishes of the patient and his or her family. Humane and sensitive physicians who believe that the resulting quality of life will not merit such heroic measures but whose training impels them to sustain life are caught in the middle of this conflict. A civil or criminal lawsuit may be brought against a physician who agrees to allow a patient to die.

Proponents of the right to suicide believe that it can be a rational act and that mental health and medical professionals should be allowed to help such patients without fear of legal or professional repercussions. Others argue, however, that suicide is not rational, that many suffer from a mental disorder, or that determining rationality is fraught with hazards. Some are voicing the fear that one result of legalizing suicide may be that patients will fall victim to coercion from relatives intent either on collecting inheritances or on convincing patients that they will overburden their loved ones and friends or become a financial drain on them. Other critics of assisted suicide fear that in this time of medical cost control, medical professionals might encourage people who are terminally ill to choose to die, and that those who are poor and disadvantaged would receive the most encouragement.

Major problems also exist in defining the subjective terms *quality of life* and *quality of humanness* as the criteria for deciding between life and death. At what point do we consider the quality of life sufficiently poor to justify terminating it? Should people who have been severely injured or scarred (through loss of limbs, paralysis, blindness, or brain injury) be allowed to end their own lives? What about people who are mentally disabled or emotionally disturbed? Could it be argued that their quality of life is equally poor? Moreover, who decides whether a person is terminally ill? There are many recorded cases of "incurable" patients who recovered when new medical techniques or treatments arrested, remitted, or cured their illnesses.

Such questions deal with ethics and human values, and they cannot be answered easily. Yet mental health practitioners cannot avoid these questions. Like their medical counterparts, clinicians are trained to save people's lives. They have accepted the philosophical assumption that life is better than death and that no one has a right to take his or her own life. Strong social, religious, and legal sanctions support this belief. Therapists work not only with clients who are terminally ill clients and wish to take their own lives but also with clients who are disturbed and may have suicidal tendencies. These latter clients are not terminally ill but may be suffering severe emotional or physical pain; their deaths would bring immense pain and suffering to their loved ones. Moreover, as noted previously, most people who attempt suicide do not want to die, are ambivalent about the act, or find that their suicidal urges pass when their life situations improve.

Clearly, suicide and suicide prevention involve a number of important social and legal issues, as well as the personal value systems of clients and their families, mental health professionals, and those who devise and enforce our laws (Rosenfeld, 2004). And just as clearly, we need to know much more about the causes of suicide and the detection of people who are at high risk for suicide, as well as the most effective means of intervention (Rudd et al., 2004). Life is precious, and we need to do everything possible—within reason—to protect it.

CHECKPOINT REVIEW

1. Provide arguments for and against the right to die. What are your personal thoughts on this matter?
2. What makes it so difficult to provide clear criteria for when people should be allowed to end their lives?

Summary

1 What do we know about suicide?

- Suicide is the intentional, direct, and conscious taking of one's own life. In the past, it has often been kept hidden, and relatives and friends of victims did not speak of it.
- Much is known about the *facts* of suicide, but little about the reasons is understood. Men are more likely to kill themselves than women, although the latter make more attempts; people who are elderly are at high risk for suicides; religious affiliation, marital status, and ethnicity all influence suicides; and firearms are the most frequent method used.

2 What are the major explanations of suicide?

- Suicides appear to arise from an interaction of biological, psychological, social, and sociocultural factors.
- Genetics and biochemical factors are implicated in suicides.
- Psychological factors include mental disturbance, depression, hopelessness, and excessive alcohol consumption.
- Lack of positive social relationships can lead to feelings of loneliness and disconnection. Loss of significant others or lack of a life partner increases the chances of suicide.
- Race, culture, ethnicity, social class, gender, and other demographic variables can either increase or decrease the risk of suicide.
- Suicide is the result of a complex interaction of these four dimensions.

3 How does suicide affect specific populations?

- In recent years, childhood and adolescent suicides have increased at an alarming rate. Suicide among college students is also a serious concern. Suicide is highest among the elderly age group.

4 How can we intervene or prevent suicides?

- The best way to prevent suicide is to recognize its signs and intervene before it occurs. Recognizing signs of risk is crucial to suicide prevention.
- Crisis intervention concepts and techniques have been used successfully to treat clients who contemplate suicide. Intensive short-term therapy is used to stabilize the immediate crisis.
- Suicide prevention centers operate 24 hours a day to provide intervention services to all people who are potentially going to attempt suicide, especially those who are not undergoing treatment. Telephone hotlines are staffed by well-trained paraprofessionals who work with anyone who is contemplating suicide. In addition, these centers provide preventive education to the public.

5 Are there times and situations in which suicide should be an option?

- This question is difficult to answer, particularly when a person is terminally ill and wishes to end his or her suffering. Nevertheless, therapists, like physicians, have been trained to preserve life, and they have a legal obligation to do so.

Key Terms

suicide 206
suicidal ideation 207
psychological autopsy 207
suicidologist 215
lethality 220

Media Resources

Psychology CourseMate

Access an interactive e-Book and chapter-specific interactive learning tools, including:

- flashcards
- quizzes
- videos

and more in your Psychology CourseMate.

Go to **CengageBrain.com.**

AP Photo/Remy de la Mauviniere

9

Eating Disorders

CHAPTER OUTLINE

I'm not anorexic, I do eat. Three meals a day, almost every day. Breakfast, lunch, dinner. . . . It's amazing how much lettuce you can eat and keep below 100 calories, the soups you can make at 50–100 calories per serving. I'm 5′6″ and 99 pounds. I know I'm skinny. . . . I'm still safe, there is no reason to stop yet. (Anonymous 5, 2008)

I purge about 4 times a day. . . . I have to be skinny, I want to be skinny. . . . I feel guilty and stupid if I don't purge everything out of my stomach. . . . I'm really scared. I don't want to die, but I don't know who to go to. (lcouvrely@yahoo.com, 2009)

My friends and I put on weight our first semester of college. . . . We ate dinner as a group, trying to stick to salad and grilled chicken, until one of us said "screw it," and we shared a heaping bowl of our favorite makeshift dessert: marshmallow fluff and butter melted in the dining hall microwave and mixed with sugary cereal and chocolate chips. (Kapalko, 2010)

FOCUS QUESTIONS

1 What kinds of eating disorders exist?

2 What are some causes of eating disorders?

3 What are some treatment options for eating disorders?

4 What causes obesity and how is it treated?

D*isturbed eating patterns* such as bingeing, purging, and excessive dieting are increasing in frequency. In this chapter we attempt to determine the reasons for the increase in disordered eating patterns and consider the characteristics, causes, and treatment of eating disorders such as anorexia nervosa, bulimia nervosa, binge-eating disorder, and eating conditions not elsewhere classified. We also include a discussion of obesity, another condition with serious physical and psychological consequences (V. H. Taylor et al., 2012; Volkow & O'Brien, 2007).

Eating Disorders

In the United States, eating disorders and disordered eating patterns are becoming increasingly prevalent, even among children and adolescents. These behaviors are often linked to dissatisfaction with one's weight or body size, a common characteristic among adolescents. For example, unhappiness with weight and body shape was found among 41.5% of girls and 24.9% of boys in a sample of 4,745 middle and high school students (Ackard, Fulkerson, & Neumark-Sztainer, 2007). Nearly 50 percent of adolescent girls and 20 percent of adolescent boys diet to control their weight. Weight concerns are so great that 13.4 percent of girls and 7.1 percent of boys have engaged in disordered eating patterns (Table 9.1). Unfortunately, disordered eating patterns are often accompanied by depression, substance use, and suicidal ideation (Neumark-Sztainer, Hannan, & Stat, 2000; T. D. Wade, 2007).

Paradoxically, despite the increasing societal emphasis on thinness—especially for women—the population of the United States is becoming heavier. As of 2012, 68 percent of adults are overweight; 35% of that fraction are obese, as are 17 percent of children and adolescents (Flegal, Carroll, Kit, & Ogden, 2012; Ogden, Carroll, Kit, & Flegal, 2012). Weight and body shape concerns are now common not only among young white women and girls (the group most affected by eating disorders) but also among older women and members of ethnic minorities (S. C. Gilbert, 2003; S. A. McLean, Paxton, & Wertheim, 2010). Rates of eating disorders are high among Latina/Hispanic American and Native American women and girls and are increasing among Asian immigrant and Asian American women and girls (S. C. Gilbert, 2003; H.-Y. Lee & Lock, 2007; Sherwood, Harnack, & Story, 2000). Although African American women are less likely than white women to have eating disorders, the incidence is also increasing among this group (Talleyrand, 2006).

Men and boys are also demonstrating more behaviors associated with body dissatisfaction, such as exercising excessively and obsessively monitoring their weight (Boodman, 2007). When Dennis Quaid, the actor, lost 40 pounds to play a movie role and then kept his weight low, he termed his condition "manorexia." Actor Billy Bob Thornton battled anorexia nervosa, losing 59 pounds. However, weight dissatisfaction in men and boys most frequently involves a desire to be heavier and more muscular (Farquhar & Wasylkiw, 2007; Ricciardelli & McCabe, 2004).

In a cross-cultural study in Germany, France, and the United States (H. G. Pope, Gruber, et al., 2000), pictures of men differing in size and

TABLE 9.1 Prevalence of Weight Concerns of Youth in Grades 5–12

	GIRLS	BOYS
Very important not to be overweight	68.5%	54.3%
Ever been on a diet	45.4%	20.2%
Diet recommended by parent	14.5%	13.6%
Diet to "look better"	88.5%	62.2%
Engage in binge/purge behaviors	13.4%	7.1%
Binge/purge at least once a day	8.9%	4.1%

Source: Data from Neumark-Sztainer, Hannan, & Stat (2000)

muscularity were shown to male college students. The students were asked to choose images that represented their own bodies, the bodies they would like to have, and the male body they thought women preferred. In all three countries, the men picked an ideal body that was about 28 pounds more muscular than their own. Similarly, participants believed that women preferred a very muscular male body. (In actuality, women preferred ordinary male bodies without added muscle.) The extreme dissatisfaction with one's muscularity sometimes seen in men is called **muscle dysphoria** (S. B. Murray, Rieger, Touyz, & De la Garza Garcia, 2010).

As with women, body dissatisfaction in men may be due to social comparison processes involving media images portraying body types that few can achieve. A study of advertisements in *Sports Illustrated* magazine from 1975 to 2005 revealed an increase in muscular and lean male models. Male adolescents and college-age men exposed to these types of images are more likely to evaluate themselves negatively (Farquhar & Wasylkiw, 2007; Hobza & Rochlen, 2009). These unrealistic images may be responsible for the fact that over 4 percent of high school boys have taken steroids to gain more muscle mass (Centers for Disease Control and Prevention [CDC], 2010b).

Preoccupation with weight and body dimensions can become extreme and lead to eating disorders such as anorexia nervosa, bulimia nervosa, or binge-eating disorder (Table 9.2). The lifetime prevalence rates for anorexia nervosa, bulimia nervosa, and binge-eating disorder are 0.9, 1.5, and 3.5 percent, respectively, for women and 0.3, 0.5, and 2 percent, respectively, for men (Hudson, Hiripi, Pope, & Kessler, 2007). In addition, many people, including over half of those treated in eating disorder programs, exhibit disordered eating that does not quite meet the criteria for the other eating disorders (Dalle Grave & Calugi, 2007; Fairburn, Cooper, Bohn, et al., 2007). We begin our discussion of eating disorders with a focus on a life-threatening condition: anorexia nervosa.

Anorexia Nervosa

Case Study

Portia DeGeneres, known for her starring roles in the television shows *Ally McBeal, Arrested Development*, and *Better Off Ted*, weighed 82 pounds at 5 ft. 7 in. tall in her mid-20s. In her quest to become a model, she became consumed with bingeing, purging, exercising, dieting, and laxatives. In her autobiography *Unbearable Lightness: A Story of Loss and Gain*, DeGeneres recounts eating only 300 calories per day, taking up to 20 laxatives a day, and exercising for hours. She received a "wake-up call" when her brother broke down and said he was afraid she was going to die. When she collapsed on a movie set, her doctors said her organs were close to failing. These events helped her make changes in her life. With the development of self-confidence and self-acceptance, and coming out as a lesbian, DeGeneres now maintains a normal weight (de Rossi, 2010).

One of the most obvious symptoms of **anorexia nervosa** is extreme thinness. Individuals with this puzzling disorder literally engage in self-starvation, showing a relentless pursuit of thinness and an unwillingness to maintain a normal healthy weight. Their body image is distorted (e.g., they see themselves as fat) and they deny the seriousness of the physical effects of their low body weight (National Institute of Mental Health [NIMH], 2011b).

muscle dysphoria extreme dissatisfaction with one's muscularity

anorexia nervosa an eating disorder characterized by low body weight, an intense fear of becoming obese, and body image distortion

DISORDERS CHART EATING DISORDERS

TABLE 9.2

Disorder	Symptoms	Prevalence (%) and Gender Difference	Age of Onset
Anorexia nervosa types: • Restricting • Binge-eating/ purging	• Restricted caloric intake resulting in body weight significantly below the minimum normal weight for one's age and height • Intense fear of becoming obese, which does not diminish even with weight loss • Body image distortion (not recognizing one's thinness) or self-evaluation unduly influenced by weight	0.5–0.9; about 75% are female	Usually after puberty or late adolescence
Bulimia nervosa	• Recurrent episodes of binge eating • Loss of control of eating behavior when bingeing • Use of vomiting, exercise, laxatives, or dieting to control weight • One or more binges a week, occurring for 3 or more months • Excessive concern with body weight and shape	1–2; about 67% are female	Late adolescence or early adulthood
Binge-eating disorder (BED)	• Recurrent episodes of binge eating • Loss of control of eating when bingeing • No regular use of inappropriate compensatory activities to control weight • One or more binges a week for 3 months • Concern about the effect of bingeing on body shape and weight • Marked distress over binge eating	0.7–4; 1.5 times more prevalent in females than in males; about 30% in weight control clinics have this disorder	Late adolescence or early 20s

Source: Data from DSM-5 Work Groups, 2012; Hudson, Hiripi, Pope, & Kessler (2007)

Anorexia nervosa has been recognized for more than 100 years. It occurs primarily in adolescent girls and young women, although now 25 percent of those with this condition are male (Hudson, Hiripi, et al., 2007). A very frightening characteristic of anorexia nervosa is that most people with the disorder, even when clearly emaciated, continue to insist they are overweight. Some may acknowledge that they are thin but maintain that some parts of their bodies are too fat. In most cases, the body image disturbance is profound. As one researcher noted more than 30 years ago, people with this disorder "vigorously defend their often gruesome emaciation as not being too thin. . . . They identify with the skeleton-like appearance, actively maintain it, and deny its abnormality" (H. Bruch, 1978, p. 209).

Subtypes of Anorexia Nervosa Although the popular view of an individual with anorexia nervosa is a person who eats very little, there are actually two subtypes of the disorder: the restricting type and the binge-eating/purging type. The restricting type accomplishes weight loss through severe dieting or exercising. The binge-eating/purging type loses weight through the use of self-induced vomiting, laxatives, or diuretics, often after binge eating. Although both groups vigorously pursue thinness, they differ in some aspects. Those with the restricting type of anorexia nervosa are more introverted and tend to deny feelings of hunger or psychological distress. Those with the binge-eating/purging type are more extroverted; report more anxiety, depression, and guilt; admit more frequently to having a strong appetite; and tend to be older (Halmi et al., 2000).

Physical Complications Anorexia nervosa is associated with serious medical complications. The mortality rate is 6 times higher than that of the general population due to suicide, substance abuse, and the physiological effects of starvation (A. E. Andersen, 2007; Papadopoulous, Ekbom, Brandt, & Ekselius,

2009). Self-starvation produces a variety of physical problems such as irregular heart rate and low blood pressure. In addition, the heart becomes damaged and weakened when it and other muscles are used as a source of energy during starvation. Other physical changes include extreme tiredness, dry skin, brittle hair, and low body temperature

Those who purge often show enlargement of the salivary glands with a resultant chipmunklike face (NIMH, 2011b). Bone loss is a common side effect of low caloric intake (Olmos et al., 2010). Portia DeGeneres experienced osteoporosis (weakening of the bones) and cirrhosis of the liver and was near death as a result of her self-starvation. Unfortunately, even with the severe health and emotional damage associated with the disorder, Web sites advocating anorexia as a lifestyle choice continue to appear on the Internet (see the Controversy box "Anorexia's Web"; Borzekowski, Schenk, Wilson, & Peebles, 2010; J. L. Wilson, Peebles, Hardy, & Litt, 2006).

Portia DeGeneres

Portia DeGeneres' eating disorder had its roots in attempts to meet an idealized standard of beauty and turmoil over her sexual identity.

Course and Outcome The course of anorexia nervosa is highly variable and can range from full recovery after one episode to a fluctuating pattern of weight gain and relapse to a chronic and deteriorating course ending in death (American Psychiatric Association, 2006; Speranza, Loas, Wallier, & Corcos, 2007). In follow-up studies, about 20% of those with anorexia nervosa remained severely ill, with over 50% continuing to display disordered eating patterns. Purging, vomiting, and obsessive-compulsive features are associated with an unfavorable outcome. There is a high rate of death among those with anorexia nervosa, including those who commit suicide (Steinhausen, 2009). In a 5-year follow-up study of 95 female adolescents and adults with anorexia nervosa, more than 50 percent no longer had a diagnosable eating disorder, although most still showed disturbed eating patterns, poor body image, and psychosocial difficulties (Ben-Tovim et al., 2001).

Associated Characteristics Depression, anxiety, impulse control problems, loss of sexual interest, and substance use often occur concurrently with anorexia nervosa (Hudson, Hiripi, et al., 2007; Pinheiro et al., 2010). For some women, the overcontrol seen in restricted eating may result from feelings of powerlessness: "I'm not eating now and it's kind of a control thing. . . . At least I have control over what I'm eating" (Budd, 2007, p. 100).

Obsessive-compulsive behaviors and thoughts that may or may not involve food are often reported by those with anorexia nervosa (R. L. Rogers & Petrie, 2001). For example, one woman worried that touching or even breathing around food would cause her to gain weight (Bulik & Kendler, 2000). The manner in which these symptoms are related to anorexia nervosa is unclear because of the possibility that malnutrition or starvation may cause or exacerbate obsessive symptoms. The actor Billy Bob Thornton reported that he engaged in repetitive, compulsive rituals long before developing anorexia nervosa.

Personality disorders and other emotional difficulties have been linked to anorexia nervosa, although the restricting and binge-eating/purging types differ in the characteristics with which they are linked. As noted earlier, the restricting type tends to display introversion, conformity, perfectionism, and rigidity, as well as traits consistent with an obsessive-compulsive personality, whereas the binge-eating/purging type is frequently associated with extroverted, impulsive, or emotionally unstable personalities (Sansone & Sansone, 2011).

Interpreting these relationships has been difficult, as they could (a) represent the misfortune of having two or more disorders by chance, (b) indicate that anorexia nervosa is an expression of a personality disorder, or (c) be the result of common environmental or genetic factors that underlie both anorexia nervosa and the personality disorder (Westen & Harnden-Fischer, 2001).

CONTROVERSY:

Anorexia's Web

- Drink ice-cold water ("Your body has to burn calories to keep your temperature up") and hot water with bouillon cubes ("only 5 calories a cube, and they taste wonderful") (Springen, 2006).
- "Starvation is fulfilling. . . . The greatest enjoyment of food is actually found when never a morsel passes the lips" (Irizarry, 2004).
- "I will be thin, at all costs, it is the most important thing, nothing else matters" (Bardone-Cone & Cass, 2007).

Tips to reduce caloric intake, testimonials regarding the satisfaction of not eating, ways to conceal thinness from friends and family members, and rules to remain thin are part of pro-ana (anorexia) and pro-mia (bulimia) Web sites (Borzekowski et al., 2010). Some of the screen names used in online discussion groups include "thinspiration," "puking pals," "disappearing acts," "anorexiangel," and "chunkeee monkeee." Participants on the Anorexic Nation Web site talk about how it is important to have friends who are like them, and argue that anorexia is a lifestyle choice and not an illness. In one study, 43 percent of those who visited the Web sites indicated that they received emotional support: "I kind of lost all of my friends at school and in my neighborhood but I still have my pro-ana and pro-mia friends" (Csipke & Horne, 2007, p. 202).

Such Web sites are visited by thousands of people each day, including many adolescents experimenting with disordered eating (Rouleau & von Ranson, 2011; J. L. Wilson et al., 2006). Medical experts are deeply concerned that the sites are increasing the incidence of eating disorders, especially among susceptible individuals.

For Further Consideration

1. How much danger do you feel these Web sites pose to people with and without eating disorders?
2. What types of messages from these Web sites might resonate with young girls?
3. What kinds of restrictions, if any, should be placed on pro-ana and pro-mia Web sites?

Deze foto is zooo motiverend!
Ik heb precies dat zelfde jurkje alleen als ik het
Ik wil er precies zo uitzien !!

Koen Suyk/ANP/Newscom

Bulimia Nervosa

Case Study

"At first, after eating too much, I would just go to the toilet and make myself sick. I hadn't heard of bulimia. . . . I started eating based on how I was feeling about myself. If my hair looked bad, I'd stuff down loads of candy. After a while, I started exercising excessively because I felt so guilty about eating. I'd run for miles and miles and go to the gym for three hours." (Dirmann, 2003, p. 60)

bulimia nervosa an eating disorder in which episodes involving rapid consumption of large quantities of food and a loss of control over eating are followed by purging (vomiting, use of laxatives, diuretics, or enemas) or excessive exercise or fasting in an attempt to compensate for binges

Bulimia nervosa is an eating disorder characterized by recurrent episodes of binge eating (rapid consumption of large quantities of food); the binge eating and related feelings of loss of control over food occur at least once a week for 3 months. Eating episodes sometimes continue until abdominal pain develops or vomiting is induced (DSM-5 Work Groups, 2012). Some individuals with bulimia nervosa engage primarily in purging and regularly vomit or use laxatives, diuretics, or enemas, while others use excessive exercise or fasting in an attempt to compensate for binges.

People with bulimia realize that their eating patterns are not normal, and are frustrated by that knowledge. They become disgusted and ashamed of their eating and hide it from others. The binges typically occur in private. Some individuals eat nothing during the day but lose control and binge in the late afternoon or evening. When the consequences of binge eating are controlled through vomiting or the use of laxatives, the temporary relief (from physical discomfort or fear of weight gain) is followed by feelings of shame and despair. Binge-eating episodes are often followed by a commitment to fasting, severely restricting eating, or engaging in excessive exercising or physical activity (NIMH, 2011b).

Bulimia is much more prevalent than anorexia nervosa. Almost 2 percent of women have bulimia at some point in their lifetime, while an additional 10 percent of women report some symptoms but do not meet all the criteria for the diagnosis (Hudson, Hiripi, et al., 2007; Van Hoeken, Seidell, & Hoek, 2003). The incidence of bulimia appears to be increasing; the disorder is especially prevalent in urban areas. Fewer men and boys exhibit the disorder, presumably because there is less cultural pressure for them to remain thin, although up to 25 percent of those affected by this disorder are males (Hudson, Hiripi, et al., 2007).

Victor Chavez/WireImage

Body Revolution 2013

Aware of societal pressures on weight, Lady Gaga, who struggled with bulimia and anorexia in her teens, launched a project called Body Revolution 2013 to help her fans accept their bodies rather than focus on perceived shortcomings. Lady Gaga recently gained weight but reports feeling happier than ever with her body.

Physical Complications As noted earlier, people with bulimia use a variety of measures—fasting, self-induced vomiting, diet pills, laxatives, and exercise—to control the weight gain that accompanies binge eating. Side effects from self-induced vomiting or from excessive use of laxatives include erosion of tooth enamel from vomited stomach acid; dehydration; swollen salivary glands; and lowered potassium, which can weaken the heart and cause heart irregularities and cardiac arrest (Nashoni, Yaroslavsky, Varticovschi, Weizman, & Stein, 2010). Other possible gastrointestinal disturbances include inflammation of the esophagus, stomach, and rectal area.

Associated Characteristics Individuals with bulimia often use eating as a way of coping with distressing thoughts or external stressors (C. B. Peterson et al., 2010). As one woman stated, "Purging was the biggest part of my day. . . . It was my release from the stress and monotony of my life" (Erdely, 2004, p. 117). There is a close relationship between emotional states and disturbed eating. For example, among individuals with bulimia nervosa, the highest rates of binge eating occur during negative emotional states, including periods of anger or depression (Crosby et al., 2009). In a sample of university women, those who tended to respond emotionally when facing stressful situations (e.g., "Get angry," "Wish I could change what happened") were more preoccupied with weight than were women who responded in a task-oriented style (e.g., "Outline my priorities," "Think about how to solve the problem"; Denisoff & Endler, 2000). A task-oriented approach may diminish stress and, therefore, reduce the need to use food to cope with stressful emotions.

Course and Outcome Bulimia nervosa has a somewhat later onset than anorexia nervosa, beginning in late adolescence or early adult life. The mortality and suicide rates for this disorder are relatively high, similar to those found in anorexia nervosa (Crow, Mitchell, et al., 2009; Crow, Peterson, et al., 2009). Outcome studies have shown a mixed course, although the prognosis is more positive than for anorexia nervosa. In one recent follow-up study, about one third of individuals showed complete remission, one third showed partial remission, and the remaining third continued to meet the criteria for bulimia nervosa (Zeeck, Weber, Sandholz, Joos, & Hartmann, 2011). Based on an analysis of the results of 27 studies involving 5,653 individuals with bulimia nervosa, approximately 45 percent made a full recovery, 27 percent demonstrated considerable improvement,

Did You Know ?

The Middleton sisters, Kate and Pippa, have been prominently displayed on pro-ana and pro-mia websites as "thinspiration" models to inspire viewers to lose weight. As one girl stated after viewing the photos, "Awesome post, she's so thin".

Source: (Chernikoff, 2011)

and 23 percent showed little or no improvement. Those with better emotional functioning and positive social support had better outcomes, whereas psychosocial stress and low social status increased the likelihood of continued difficulties (Steinhausen & Weber, 2009).

Binge-Eating Disorder

Case Study

Ms. A, a 38-year-old African American woman, was single, lived alone, and was employed as a personnel manager. She weighed 292 pounds. Her chief reason for coming to the clinic was that she felt her eating was out of control, and as a result, she had gained approximately 80 pounds over the previous year. A typical binge episode consisted of the ingestion of two pieces of chicken, one small bowl of salad, two servings of mashed potatoes, one hamburger, one large serving of french fries, one large chocolate shake, one large bag of potato chips, and 15 to 20 small cookies—all within a 2-hour period. She was embarrassed by how much she was eating, and felt disgusted with herself and very guilty after eating. (Goldfein, Devlin, & Spitzer, 2000, p. 1052)

Binge-eating disorder (BED) is similar to bulimia nervosa in that it involves bingeing (i.e., consuming large amounts of food within a 2-hour period), an accompanying feeling of loss of control, and marked distress over eating during the episodes (Grilo & White, 2011). However, the binges are not followed by compensatory behaviors such as vomiting, excessive exercising, or fasting (Mond, Peterson, & Hay, 2010). As in the case of bulimia nervosa, individuals with BED eat large amounts of food even when not hungry, are secretive about their eating, and often feel guilty or ashamed afterwards. They are also overly preoccupied with weight or body shape (Grilo, Masheb, & White, 2010).

To be diagnosed with BED, an individual must have a history of binge-eating episodes at least once a week for a period of 3 months (DSM-5 Work Groups, 2012). Women and girls are one and a half times more likely to have this disorder than are men and boys; the lifetime prevalence rate is 3.5 percent in women and 2 percent in men (Hudson, Hiripi, et al., 2007). White women make up the vast majority of those seeking treatment, whereas in community samples, the percentages of African American and white women with BED are roughly equal (Wilfley, Pike, Dohm, Striegel-Moore, & Fairburn, 2001). Differences have been found between African American and white women with BED. For example, African American women are more likely to be obese but are less likely to receive treatment for eating problems or report weight concerns or psychiatric distress related to their eating (see Figure 9.1; K. M. Pike, Dohm, Striegel-Moore, Wilfley, & Fairburn, 2001).

Associated Characteristics In contrast to those with bulimia nervosa, individuals with binge-eating disorder are likely to be overweight (Bull, 2004). About 20–40 percent of individuals in weight control programs have BED. Binges are often preceded by poor mood, decreased alertness, feelings of poor eating control, and cravings for sweets (Hilbert & Tuschen-Caffier, 2007). When experiencing weight or shape concerns, women with BED are more likely than control participants to report negative emotions and an increased craving for food (Svaldi, Caffier, Blechert, & Tuschen-Caffier, 2009). Complications from BED include medical conditions associated with obesity, such as high blood pressure, high cholesterol levels, and type 2 diabetes. People with BED are also likely to suffer from depression

binge-eating disorder (BED) an eating disorder that involves the consumption of large amounts of food over a short period of time with accompanying feelings of loss of control and distress over the excess eating; behaviors to compensate for overeating are not typically seen with this disorder

(T. D. Wade, 2007). (See Table 9.3 for questions used to assess for an eating disorder.)

Course and Outcome The onset of BED is similar to that of bulimia nervosa in that it typically begins in late adolescence or early adulthood. There is limited information on the natural course of BED. In one study, most individuals with BED made a full recovery over a 5-year period, even without treatment, with only 18 percent continuing to demonstrate an eating disorder of clinical severity. However, their weight remained high and 39 percent were eventually considered obese (Fairburn, Cooper, Doll, Norman, & O'Connor, 2000).

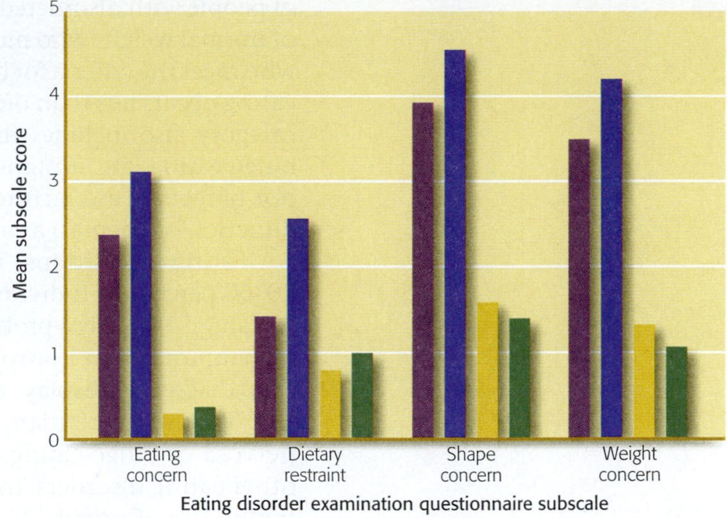

FIGURE 9.1

Binge-Eating Disorder

The comparison of scores on subscales of the Eating Disorder Questionnaire reveal differences between African American and white women with and without binge-eating disorder.

Source: Pike, Dohm, Striegel-Moore, Wilfley, & Fairburn (2001)

Eating Conditions Not Elsewhere Classified

The category **eating conditions not elsewhere classified** includes seriously disturbed eating patterns that do not fully meet the criteria for anorexia nervosa, bulimia nervosa, or binge-eating disorder. This is the most common eating disorder diagnosis (Swanson, Crow, LeGrange, Swendsen, & Merikangas, 2011). Examples

eating conditions not elsewhere classified a diagnostic category involving problematic eating patterns that do not fully meet the criteria for one of the eating disorders

TABLE 9.3 Do You Have an Eating Disorder?

QUESTIONS FOR POSSIBLE ANOREXIA NERVOSA
1. Are you considered to be underweight by others? What is your weight? (Screening question. If yes, continue to next questions.)
2. Are you intensely fearful of gaining weight or becoming fat even though you are underweight?
3. Do you feel that your body or a part of your body is too fat?
4. If you had periods previously, have they stopped?
QUESTIONS FOR POSSIBLE BULIMIA NERVOSA
1. Do you have binges in which you eat a lot of food? (Screening question. If yes, continue to next questions.)
2. When you binge, do you feel a lack of control over eating?
3. Do you make yourself vomit, take laxatives, or exercise excessively because of overeating?
4. Are you very dissatisfied with your body shape or weight?
QUESTIONS FOR POSSIBLE BINGE-EATING DISORDER
1. Do you have binges in which you eat a lot of food?
2. When you binge, do you feel a lack of control over eating?
3. When you binge, do three or more of the following apply? a. You eat more rapidly than usual. b. You eat until uncomfortably full. c. You eat large amounts even when not hungry. d. You eat alone because of embarrassment from overeating. e. You feel disgusted, depressed, or guilty about binge eating.
4. Do you feel great distress regarding your binge eating?

Note: These questions are derived from the diagnostic criteria for eating disorders (DSM-5 Work Groups, 2012).

of people with disordered eating that would fit in this category include individuals of normal weight who meet the other criteria for anorexia nervosa and individuals who meet the criteria for bulimia nervosa or binge-eating disorder except that binge eating occurs less than once a week or has been present for less than 3 months. The category also includes those with *night-eating syndrome* (a distressing pattern of binge eating late at night or after awakening from sleep) and individuals who do not binge but use recurrent purging (self-induced vomiting, misuse of laxatives, diuretics, or enemas) as a means to control weight (DSM-5 Work Groups, 2012).

Eating conditions not elsewhere classified, the diagnosis received by 40–60 percent of individuals in eating disorder treatment programs (Dalle Grave & Calugi, 2007), is a problematic diagnostic category because it includes a variety of symptoms and nonspecific symptom severity. Many individuals who receive this diagnosis display a number of emotional and physiological problems (J. J. Thomas, Vartanian, & Brownell, 2009) and continue on to develop bulimia nervosa or binge-eating disorder (Stice, Marti, Shaw, & Jaconis, 2009). As with other eating disorders, individuals in this category show increased mortality and higher risk of suicide (Crow, Peterson, et al., 2009).

CHECKPOINT REVIEW

1. What symptoms are needed for a diagnosis of anorexia nervosa?
2. In what ways are bulimia nervosa and binge-eating disorder similar to and different from one another?
3. What are the physical complications of each of the eating disorders?

Etiology of Eating Disorders

The search for the causal factors associated with eating disorders is complicated because biological, psychological, social, and sociocultural factors interact to produce vulnerability to these disorders (W. Kaye, 2009). We examine each of these influences to determine how they might explain the development of the severe dieting, bingeing, and purging behaviors found in eating disorders. Understanding etiology involves looking for conditions that both precede the development of disordered eating and maintain the disorder (A. Hartmann, Zeeck, & Barrett, 2010). Keeping this in mind, we use the multipath model (Figure 9.2) to consider the risk factors associated with eating disorders.

Psychological Dimension

A number of psychological risk factors have been found to increase an individual's chances of developing an eating disorder. These include body dissatisfaction, perfectionism, depression, dysfunctional beliefs, low levels of interpersonal competence, and use of control as a method of dealing with stress (T. A. Myers & Crowther, 2009).

Body dissatisfaction arises when someone's weight or body shape differs significantly from an imagined ideal. Up to one third of young people and a large percentage of women between the ages of 35 and 65 have significant levels of body dissatisfaction (Crow, Eisenberg, Story, & Neumark-Sztainer, 2008; McLean et al., 2010; Mission Australia, 2010). Women with high body dissatisfaction are more likely to compare their bodies to those of other women and report lower self-satisfaction after this process (Trampe, Stapel, & Siero, 2010). Similarly, men who score high on appearance orientation report lower body satisfaction when exposed to commercials portraying muscular men (Hargreaves & Tiggemann,

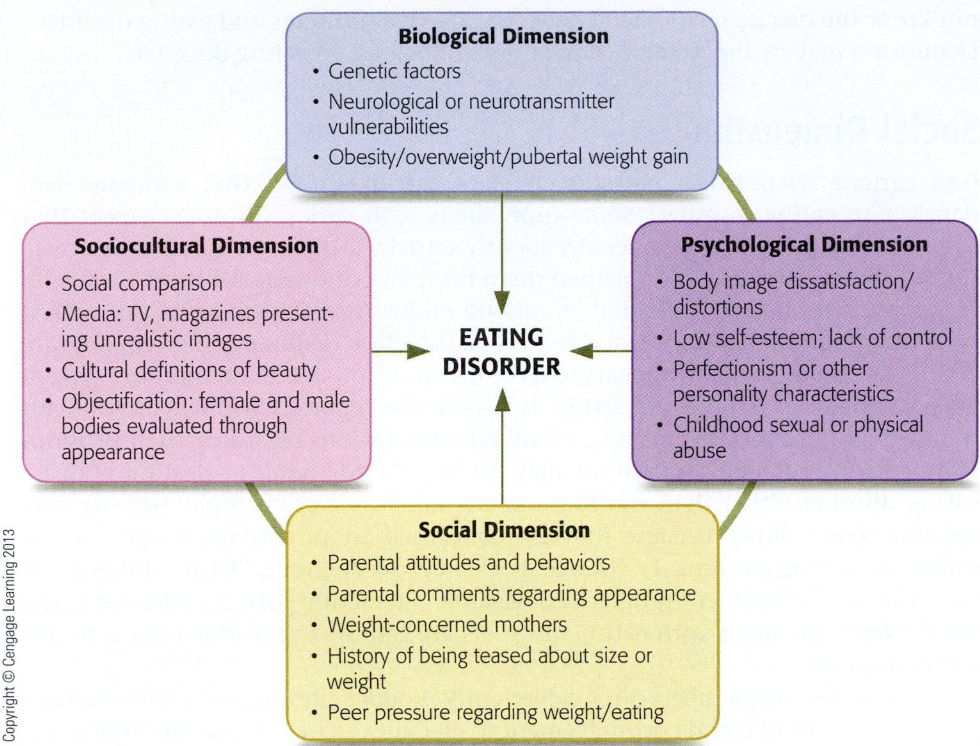

FIGURE 9.2

Multipath Model of Eating Disorders
The dimensions interact with one another and combine in different ways to result in an eating disorder.

2009). Body dissatisfaction is a robust risk factor in the development of eating disorders in longitudinal studies (Wade, George, & Atkinson, 2009).

Maladaptive perfectionism has also been identified as a risk factor; it may interact with body dissatisfaction to predict not only anorexia nervosa but also other eating disorders. Maladaptive perfectionism is composed of two dimensions: (a) inflexible high standards and (b) negative self-evaluations following mistakes. When these perfectionist standards are imposed on weight, shape, or dieting, disordered eating often results (Bardone-Cone & Cass, 2007; Bardone-Cone, Sturm, Lawson, Robinson, & Smith, 2010; Boone, Soenens, Braet, & Goossens, 2010).

Individuals with eating disorders also appear to use food or weight control as a means of handling stress or anxiety (Budd, 2007). Dieting also may be used to demonstrate self-control and improve self-esteem and body image (C. Jones, Leung, & Harris, 2007). One woman stated, "We can be told what to do and what to think. We can be pressured in all sorts of ways. But we decide what, if anything, crosses our lips" (L. Carroll, 2011). In contrast, binge eating is sometimes used as a source of comfort and to counteract depression and other negative emotions (Bergstrom & Neighbors, 2006).

Perceived or actual inadequacies in interpersonal skills are also associated with eating disorders. Individuals with eating disorders often perceive low levels of social support, which may be due to a passive interpersonal style (Bodell, Smith, Gordon, Holm-Denoma, & Joiner et al., 2011). For both men and women, higher scores on characteristics such as passivity, low self-esteem, dependence, and nonassertiveness were associated with higher scores on inventories of disordered eating (Budd, 2007; A. Hartmann, Zeeck, & Barrett, 2010). Perceived social incompetence, particularly when combined with maladaptive perfectionism, has been linked with disordered eating patterns (Ferrier-Auerbach & Martens, 2009).

Mood disorders such as depression often accompany eating disorders (Abbate-Daga et al., 2011; Mischoulon et al., 2011). Rates of depression are higher in relatives of individuals with eating disorders than in control populations: Eating disorders may represent an expression of a mood disorder. At this point, we still do

Did You Know?

Most women do not wish to be ultrathin.

- The amount of weight overweight or obese women would "ideally" like to lose would still place them in the overweight category.
- Women of normal weight want to lose only a few pounds, not the amount needed to be extremely thin.
- Underweight women believe they are at the ideal weight, suggesting that this group is most responsive to messages regarding thinness.

Source: L. Neighbors & Sobal (2007)

Did You Know? Protective variables against the impact of media on body image include strong social bonds and social support, personality variables such as self-determination and autonomy, social competence, and viewing attractiveness as only one of many qualities that are deemed important.

Source: Ferrier-Auerbach & Martens (2009); Pelletier & Dion (2007)

not know the precise relationship between affective disorders and eating disorders. Depression may be the result, not the cause, of having an eating disorder.

Social Dimension

Can certain relationship patterns increase the likelihood that someone will develop an eating disorder? Some individuals with eating disorders report that their parents or family members frequently criticized them, had a negative reaction to their eating issues, or blamed them for their condition (Di Paola, Faravelli, & Ricca, 2010). It is possible that childhood maltreatment produces a self-critical style that results in depression and body dissatisfaction (Dunkley, Masheb, & Grilo, 2010). Childhood trauma appears to have the most impact on the purging type of anorexia nervosa (Jaite et al., 2012). However, the reported findings are difficult to interpret. Most depend on the individual's perceptions regarding their relationships—family interaction patterns may, in fact, be the *result* of dealing with an eating disorder rather than the cause of the disorder. For example, parents may become "controlling" because they are concerned about extreme weight loss or unhealthy eating patterns (Le Grange, Lock, Loeb, & Nicholls, 2010). At this point we do not know whether the described negative interaction patterns reported in the families of individuals with eating disorders are causal factors or reactions to disordered eating.

Peers or family members can inadvertently produce pressure to be thin through discussions of weight and encouragement to diet or exercise (Annus, Smith, Fischer, Hendricks, & Williams, 2007; T. Jackson & Chen, 2010). Similarly, mothers who diet are indirectly transmitting the message of the importance of slimness and a thin-ideal to their daughters. Also, teasing and criticism about body weight or shape by family members have been found to predict body dissatisfaction, dieting, and eating problems (Vincent & McCabe, 2000). Peer relationships can also produce pressure to lose weight. In a longitudinal study, girls who reported that their friends were very focused on dieting at the beginning of the study were most likely to engage in extreme dieting and unhealthy weight control behaviors 5 years later (Eisenberg & Neumark-Sztainer, 2010).

Myrleen Ferguson Cate/PhotoEdit

Body Consciousness

Women and girls are socialized to be conscious of their bodies. Although most of the attention has been directed to concerns over appearance among young white girls, rates of disordered eating and body dissatisfaction are also high among Latina/Hispanic American and American Indian girls.

Sociocultural Dimension

A great deal of research has focused on the influence of sociocultural norms and values in the etiology of eating disorders. In the United States and most Western cultures, physical appearance is considered a very important attribute, especially for women and girls. Teenage girls describe an "ideal" body as being 5 ft 7 in. tall, weighing 110 lb, and fitting into a size 5 dress. Although this body type is far from the norm, it is consistent with body images portrayed in the media. Table 9.4 provides data on the average weights of adults in the United States.

Women are socialized to be conscious of their body shape and weight. At an early age, girls are sexualized and objectified through television, music videos, song lyrics, magazines, and advertising (American Psychological Association, Task Force on the Sexualization of Girls, 2007). Following exposure to these messages, girls begin to (a) believe that their primary value comes from being attractive, (b) define themselves according to the body standards shown in media, and (c) see themselves as objects rather than as having the capacity for independent action and decision making. As girls and women adopt these unrealistic standards, many internalize a *thin-ideal* and begin to agree with statements such as "slender women are more attractive" or "I would like to look like the women that appear in TV shows and movies" (J. K. Thompson & Stice, 2004, p. 99). In a random sample of 100 teenage girls, more than 60 percent reported trying to change their appearance to resemble that of a celebrity (Seitz, 2007).

What kind of predisposition or characteristic leads some people to interpret images of thinness in the media as evidence of their own inadequacy? Are people who develop eating disorders chronically self-conscious to begin with, or do they develop eating disorders because their social environment makes them chronically self-conscious? How does exposure to portrayals of thinness in the mass media influence the values and norms of young people? The development of disordered eating and preoccupation with body image appears to involve multiple processes (Figure 9.4; T. A. Myers & Crowther, 2009; Tylka & Subich, 2004).

TABLE 9.4 Average Weight for Women and Men 20–74 Years (in Pounds) for 1994–2006

	1994	2006
Women	153.0	164.7
Men	181.3	194.7
By ethnicity and gender		
White women	151.4	163.7
African American women	169.7	184.8
Mexican American women	152.6	162.2
White men	183.7	197.4
African American men	181.2	199.8
Mexican American men	172.3	180.5

Source: Ogden, Fryar, Carroll, & Flegal (2004); McDowell, Fryar, Ogden, & Flegal (2008)

A process of *social comparison* occurs in which women and girls begin to evaluate themselves according to external standards. Because these standards are unattainable for the vast majority of women, body dissatisfaction occurs. Self-consciousness and frequent monitoring of one's external appearance can lead to anxiety or shame about the body. When women compare their body shape or weight with other women's, those with high body dissatisfaction report increased feelings of guilt and depression. Thoughts of "solutions" such as dieting, purging, and extreme exercise increase. Interestingly, these reactions also occur in women with low body dissatisfaction, but less frequently (Leahey, Crowther, & Ciesla, 2011). Thus, social comparison appears to be a strong risk factor for eating disorders, especially among women who are dissatisfied with their bodies. Although societal emphasis on thinness may increase disordered eating, it does not explain why only a small percentage of individuals in our media-conscious society develop eating disorders.

As noted in the beginning of the chapter, mass media portrayals of lean, muscular male bodies are increasing. There appears to be a gradual shift away from traditional measures of masculinity, such as wealth and power, to physical appearance. Given this trend, is body image dissatisfaction among men increasing? In fact, more men are reporting body fat dissatisfaction (A. R. Smith, Hawkeswood, Bodell, & Joiner, 2011) and displeasure with their musculature (Cafri et al., 2005; Farquhar & Wasylkiw, 2007).

The gay male subculture places a great deal of value on physical attractiveness, resulting in more concern over body size and appearance and a greater prevalence of disturbed eating patterns than are found among heterosexual males (Blashill & Vander Wal, 2009). Body fat dissatisfaction is strongly associated with disordered eating in gay men (Blashill, 2010; A. R. Smith, Hawkeswood, Bodell & Joiner, 2011). Gay men appear to be particularly vulnerable to the influence of media on appearance-related anxiety and disordered eating (Carper, Negy, & Tantleff-Dunn, 2010). Subcultural influences on attractiveness are also apparent in the fact that lesbians appear to be less concerned about physical appearance and to have a better body image than other women and girls (Boehmer, Bowen, & Bauer, 2007).

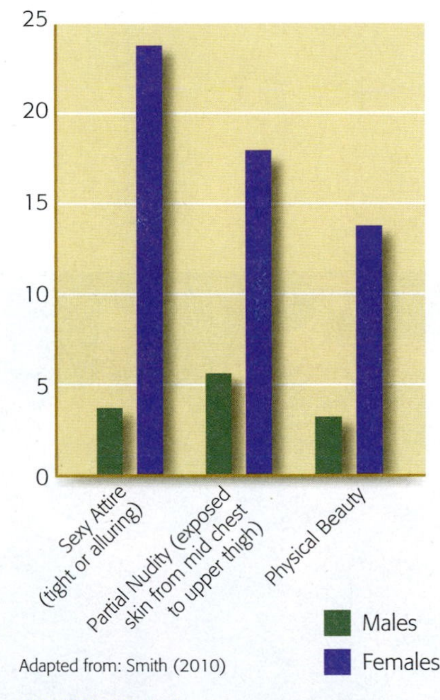

FIGURE 9.3

Objectification of Women and Girls
In family films (those with a G, PG, or PG-13 rating), women and girls often are "scantily clad" and very attractive, and have an unrealistic body shape. Does this contribute to the objectification of girls and women?
Source: S. L. Smith & Choueiti (2010)

Ethnic Minorities and Eating Disorders Do cultural values and standards affect body dissatisfaction and eating disorders among ethnic minorities? In a meta-analysis of the impact of ethnicity and body dissatisfaction among women in the United States, S. Grabe and Hyde (2006) came to the following conclusions: First, body dissatisfaction is not just a problem among white women; it also exists among women in ethnic minorities. Second, Latina/Hispanic and Asian American

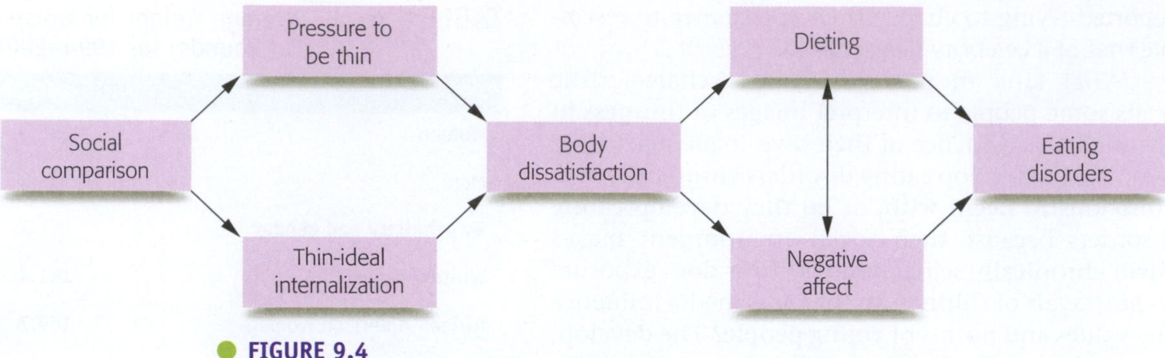

FIGURE 9.4

Route to Eating Disorders
Social comparison can lead to the development of eating disorders.
Source: Adapted from Stice (2001)

women have levels of body dissatisfaction equal to that of white women. Third, African American women show much less body dissatisfaction than all other comparison groups. Although African American girls and women are heavier, on average, than their white counterparts, they tend to be more satisfied with their body size, weight, and appearance and less interested in being thin (Chandler-Laney et al., 2009; S. M. Harris, 2006). Table 9.5 compares some differences in body image and weight concerns between African American and white women.

Why is it that African American women and girls appear to be somewhat insulated from unrealistic standards of thinness? It is possible that most are protected by several cultural factors. First, because many do not identify with white women and girls, media messages of thinness may have less influence. Second, the definition of attractiveness within the African American community encompasses dress, personality, and confidence, rather than focusing primarily on physical characteristics such as body shape and weight. Third, African American women are generally less influenced by gender-restrictive messages. For example, their assertiveness and belief in egalitarian relationships allow them to have important roles in the home and community.

Ideal Male Bodies?
Most men and boys would prefer to be heavier and more muscular. Will the increased media focus on physically powerful men increase body image distortion and dissatisfaction among men?

However, not all African American women and girls are immune to majority-culture messages (Rogers-Wood & Petrie, 2010). African American girls do, for example, diet, binge, and purge, but with less frequency than other groups. For example, approximately one third of African American girls diet, compared to over half of white girls (Story, Neumark-Sztainer, Sherwood, Stang, & Murray, 1998). The prevalence among African American women of eating conditions not elsewhere classified appears to be equivalent to that found in white U.S. women (Mulholland & Mintz, 2001). And although fewer African American women appear to have either anorexia nervosa or bulimia nervosa, they are as likely as other groups of women to have binge-eating disorder (Lovejoy, 2001; Striegel-Moore, Dohm, et al., 2003).

In general, acculturation to mainstream U.S. values appears to be a risk factor for developing an eating disorder (Talleyrand, 2010). This relationship is greatest among those who have internalized societal values concerning attractiveness (S. Grabe & Hyde, 2006). Some studies have shown that American Indian, Asian American, and Latina/Hispanic American girls show greater body image dissatisfaction than white girls, possibly due to attempts to fit into societal definitions of beauty (S. C. Gilbert, 2003). Thus it appears that

TABLE 9.5 Differences in Body Image and Weight Concerns Among African American and White Women and Girls

	AFRICAN AMERICAN	WHITE
Satisfied with current weight or body shape	70%	11%
Body image	Perceived selves to be thinner than they actually were	Perceived selves to be heavier than they actually were
Attitude toward dieting	Believed that it is better to be a little overweight than underweight	Believed in the importance of dieting to produce a slender body; feared being overweight
Definition of beauty	Good grooming, "style," and overall attractiveness; beauty is the right "attitude and personality"	Slim; 5′7″; 100–110 lb; a perfect body can lead to success and the good life
Being overweight	Of those who were overweight, 40% considered their figures attractive or very attractive	Those who believed they did not have a weight problem were 6–14 lb underweight
Age and beauty	Believed they would get more beautiful with age	Believed that beauty is fleeting and decreases with age

Source: Boyington, et al. (2008); Desmond, Price, Hallinan, Smith (1989); Lovejoy (2001); Parker, Nichter, Vuckovic, Sims, & Ritenbaugh (1995)

ethnic minorities are becoming increasingly vulnerable to societal messages regarding attractiveness; the fact that an increasing number of children and adults from ethnic minorities, especially females, are overweight may further increase the risk of eating disorders (Madsen, Weedn, & Crawford, 2010).

© Mango Productions/Corbis

Beauty Standards

African American females have a greater acceptance of heavier body sizes than white women. In addition, they adopt a broader definition of beauty that includes attitude, personality, and "style."

Cross-Cultural Studies on Eating Disorders Far fewer reports of eating disorders are found in Latin American, South American, and Asian countries than in European countries, Israel, and Australia (M. N. Miller & Pumariega, 2001). Of concern is the finding that countries or groups that have been exposed to Western values report a rising incidence of body dissatisfaction and disordered eating in females (Becker, 2004; Steiger & Bruce, 2007). Although the standard of beauty among women in South Africa has traditionally been based on fuller figures, black teenage girls in this region, exposed to Western standards of thinness, have shown a dramatic increase in eating disorders (Simmons, 2002). Asian countries that are exposed to Western media have also reported increases in body shape concerns and distorted eating attitudes (Liao et al., 2010).

Cultural values and norms affect views on body shape and size. Weight normalcy is influenced by cultural beliefs and practices. For example, Micronesians view thinness as a sign of illness. As one parent responded, "The culture on Saipan, the fat one is the healthy one . . . but when they are skinny, 'Oh, my goodness, nobody is feeding that child'" (Bruss, Morris, & Dannison, 2003). Feeding is considered to be an extension of love and care from parents toward their children. Historically, eating disorders in Chinese populations have been rare because plumpness in women and girls has been considered desirable and attractive. In a Hong Kong study, adolescent girls picked an ideal female body size that was somewhat larger than that preferred by boys (H. W. Marsh, Hau, Sung, & Yu, 2007). However, S. Lee, Lam, Kwok, and Fung (2010) found that individuals with eating disorders in Hong Kong were increasingly demonstrating a fat phobic pattern similar to that seen in Western countries.

What happens when other cultures are exposed to Western standards of beauty? Becker (2004) reported on the impact of television on adolescent girls living in a rural community in western Fiji. Traditional cultural norms support robust appetites and body sizes. Food and feasts are socially important, and plump bodies are considered to be aesthetically pleasing. After 3 years of exposure to Western television programs, girls revealed admiration for Western standards: "The actresses and all those girls, especially those European girls, I just like, I just admire them and want to be like them. I want their body, I want their size" (p. 546). The girls also paid attention to TV commercials advertising exercise equipment, which portrayed the ease with which weight could be lost. "When they show exercising on TV . . . I feel I should . . . lose my weight" (p. 542). This media exposure dramatically increased body dissatisfaction and purging among Fijian girls (Becker, Burwell, Herzog, Hamburg, & Gilman, 2002).

CONTROVERSY:

Should Underweight Models and Digitally "Enhanced" Photos Be Banned From Advertisements?

Former Ralph Lauren model Filippa Hamilton was fired for being too fat. She was 5 ft 10 in. tall, weighed 120 pounds, and wore size 4 clothing. "They fired me because they said I was overweight and I couldn't fit in their clothes anymore," she said (Melago, 2009, p. 1). Later, Hamilton was shocked when she encountered a digitally retouched advertisement in which her hips appeared smaller than her head. (Ralph Lauren has since apologized for this action.) Similarly, singer Kelly Clarkson was digitally slimmed for the cover of *Self* magazine, as was country singer Faith Hill for *Redbook*. Altering photos to make women on magazine covers and in advertisements appear slimmer and "flawless" is a common practice (Carmichael, 2010).

By using models in a "state of unnourishment" or airbrushed photos, the fashion industry has created an unattainable image of the "ideal" woman (Lis, 2011). The American Medical Association (2011) and the Royal College of Psychiatrists in the United Kingdom (Berman, 2010) have called for the cessation of practices such as the use of underweight models and airbrushed photos because of their link with unhealthy body image and eating disorders (Berman, 2010). Young women exposed to these types of images show increases in depression and body dissatisfaction that can lead to eating disorders (S. Grabe, Ward, & Hyde, 2008).

Do you believe we should ban the use of ultrathin models and digitally manipulated images? Would this reduce the incidence of body dissatisfaction and eating disorders? How could the mass media help youth develop more realistic and healthy body images?

Splash/Newscom

© Joe Seer/Shutterstock.com

Kate Winslet Photoshopped?

Actress Kate Winslet, pictured on the right, has frequently been the target of image manipulation. *Harper's Bazaar* has been accused of grafting Winslet's head onto another woman's body for the cover shot on the left. Why do magazines go to such lengths in their portrayal of thinness?

Biological Dimension

At this point, we have considered psychological, social, and sociocultural dimensions associated with eating disorders. However, an unanswered question remains: "If all young girls are exposed to these sociocultural pressures, why do only a small fraction go on to develop anorexia nervosa and bulimia nervosa?" (Striegel-Moore & Bulik, 2007, p. 188). A proposed answer to this question is that we need to look at gene × environment interaction. For example, if someone has a genetic predisposition toward severe dieting, the risk of developing an eating disorder is increased by exposure to environmental risk factors (e.g., family or societal emphasis on being thin). Conversely, those without the predisposition would find severe dieting to be extremely aversive. In this section we consider possible genetic influences on eating disorders.

Disordered eating appears to run in families, especially among female relatives (Steiger & Bruce, 2007). Strober, Freeman, Diamond, and Kaye (2000) examined the lifetime rates of anorexia nervosa and bulimia nervosa among close relatives of individuals with and without eating disorders. Support was found for a genetic contribution to disordered eating patterns. Whereas anorexia nervosa and bulimia nervosa were relatively rare among the relatives of the never-ill group, these disorders occurred with much greater frequency among close relatives of those with eating disorders. Heritability estimates from twin studies are 41 percent for binge-eating disorder, 46–76 percent for anorexia nervosa, and 50–83 percent for bulimia nervosa (Bulik, Thornton, et al., 2010; Striegel-Moore & Bulik, 2007).

Genetic influences may be triggered by physical changes such as puberty. In a sample of twins, heritability appeared to be low among preadolescent teens but was substantial after puberty. This suggests that either puberty itself or social processes associated with puberty (e.g., increasing awareness of sexuality and body shape) may influence the expression of genes for disordered eating through gene × environment interaction. In other words, the eating disorder only shows up when certain environmental factors interact with the presence of genetic risk factors (Culbert, Burt, McGue, Iacono, & Klump, 2009; Klump, Suisman, Burt, McGue, & Iacono, 2009).

Genetics may influence the neurotransmitters and brain structures, such as the hypothalamus, which are involved in eating behaviors. Research has focused on dopamine, which is thought to be the primary neurotransmitter involved in the reinforcing effects of food (Bello & Hajnal, 2010). Low levels of dopamine can increase the desire to consume food, whereas increased dopamine concentrations can decrease appetite (Y. Lee & Lin, 2010). Having genes that lower dopamine availability may interact with adverse childhood rearing experiences to result in emotional eating patterns (van Strien, Snoek, van der Zwaluw, & Engels, 2010). Differences in dopamine levels may explain why those with bulimia nervosa are more attentive to food stimuli and why individuals with anorexia nervosa show less appetitive response to food images (S. Brooks, Prince, Stahl, Campbell, & Treasure, 2011).

People with lower levels of dopamine may need greater quantities of food or other rewarding substances, such as drugs, to obtain pleasure. The possible influence of dopamine in eating disorders is being further investigated by examining medications that affect dopamine levels. For example, some stimulant medications such as methylphenidate appear to decrease appetite by increasing dopamine availability (L. H. Epstein, Leddy, Temple, & Faith, 2007). Although dopamine seems like a promising lead in explaining eating disorders, other brain regions and neurotransmitters such as serotonin also appear to be involved. More research is needed to determine the precise relationship between genetic factors, brain structures, neurotransmitters, and environmental influences.

In lesbian magazines (e.g., *Curve*, *Girlfriends*, and *Out*), models are more varied in age and weight compared to models in mainstream women's magazines (e.g., *Glamour*, *Elle*, *Mademoiselle*). Women models in lesbian magazines frequently advertise activities such as biking or travel, whereas models in mainstream magazines are more likely to wear revealing clothing and advertise products such as clothing or cosmetics

Source: Milillo, 2008.

CHECKPOINT REVIEW

1. Describe four psychological and three social factors that are related to eating disorders.
2. In what ways do sociocultural factors influence disordered eating?
3. Why might some men with body dissatisfaction develop anorexia nervosa while others attempt to gain muscle mass?

Treatment of Eating Disorders

Although there are some similarities in treatment strategies used for anorexia nervosa, bulimia nervosa, and binge-eating disorder (Stice & Shaw, 2004), the approach, priorities, and physical effects addressed differ among the disorders.

Treatment of Anorexia Nervosa

Case Study

A young woman who began treatment for anorexia nervosa weighing 81 lb reported:

I did gain 25 pounds, the target weight of my therapist and nutritionist. But every day was really difficult. I would go and cry. A big part of anorexia is fear. Fear of fat, fear of eating. But [my therapist] taught me about societal pressures to be ultra-thin that come from the media, TV, advertising. . . . She talked me through what I was thinking and how I had completely dissociated my mind from my body. . . . I'm slowly reintroducing foods one thing at a time. I'd like to think I am completely better, but I'm not. I'm still extremely self-conscious about my appearance. But I now know I have a problem and my family and I are finding ways to cope with it. (K. Bryant, 2001)

As you have seen, eating disorders, especially anorexia nervosa, can be life threatening. Weight gain is vital for a successful outcome in the treatment of anorexia nervosa (Brewerton & Costin, 2011). Because anorexia nervosa is a complex disorder, there is a need for teamwork between physicians, psychiatrists, and therapists. Treatment can be delivered in an outpatient therapy setting or in a hospital, depending on the weight and health of the individual. Regardless of the setting, developing a strong therapeutic relationship with treatment providers and demonstrating readiness for change are important predictors of successful treatment (M. D. McHugh, 2007).

Because an individual being treated for anorexia nervosa is starving, the initial goal is to restore weight and address the physical complications associated with starvation, a process requiring a great deal of psychological support. During the re-feeding process, the individual's feelings of apathy may begin to fade. Those with anorexia nervosa are often terrified of gaining weight and need the opportunity to discuss these reactions in therapy. During the weight restoration period, new foods are introduced, supplementing food choices that are not sufficiently high in calories. The physical condition of the person is carefully monitored, because sudden and severe physiological reactions can occur during re-feeding. Additionally, a dental exam is often conducted to assess for damage from purging.

Psychological interventions are used to help the client (a) understand and cooperate with nutritional and physical rehabilitation, (b) identify and understand the dysfunctional attitudes related to the eating disorder, (c) improve interpersonal and social functioning, and (d) address other psychological disorders or conflicts that reinforce disordered eating behavior (American Psychiatric Association, 2006; B. T. Walsh & Devlin, 1998).

Family therapy is often an important component of the treatment plan, as seen in the case of one 18-year-old woman who did not respond to inpatient treatment, dietary training, and cognitive-behavioral therapy (L. A. Sim, Sadowski, Whiteside, & Wells, 2004). Her family was enlisted to participate in family therapy. The therapy involved (a) having the parents assist in the refeeding process by planning meals, (b) reducing parental criticism by helping them understand that anorexia nervosa is a serious disease, (c) and learning new family relationship patterns. The parents were encouraged to help their daughter develop skills, attitudes, and activities appropriate to her developmental stage. This form of family therapy resulted in the woman's gaining more than 22 pounds.

Overall, family therapy is an important component in the treatment of anorexia nervosa and more effective than individual therapy alone (Halvorsen & Heyerdahl, 2007; Lock et al., 2010; Paulson-Karlsson, Engstrom, & Nevonen, 2009).

Gregg DeGuire/FilmMagic/Gettyimages.com

Plus Size Models—A Passing Fad?

Fashion model Whitney Thompson, an ambassador for the National Eating Disorders Association, is worried that the use of full-figured models is only a temporary phenomenon. Is she right?

Treatment of Bulimia Nervosa

During the initial assessment of individuals with bulimia nervosa, conditions that result from purging are identified and treated; these may include dental erosion, muscle weakness, cardiac arrhythmias, dehydration, electrolyte imbalance, or gastrointestinal problems involving the stomach or esophagus. As with anorexia nervosa, treatment involves an interdisciplinary team that includes a physician and a psychotherapist. One of the primary goals of treatment is to normalize eating patterns and to eliminate the binge/purge cycle.

Antidepressant medications such as selective serotonin reuptake inhibitors have been helpful in treating this condition (NIMH, 2011b; G. T. Wilson & Shafran, 2005). Cognitive-behavioral approaches can also help individuals with bulimia develop a sense of self-control (Crow, Mitchell, et al., 2009). Common components of cognitive-behavioral treatment plans involve encouraging the consumption of three or more balanced meals a day, reducing rigid food rules and body image concerns, identifying triggers for bingeing, and developing coping strategies. Even with these approaches, only about 50 percent of those with the disorder fully recover (Agras, Crow, et al., 2000). Adding exposure and response prevention (i.e., exposure to bingeing or cues associated with bingeing followed by prevention of purging) to cognitive-behavioral strategies appears to improve long-term outcomes for individuals with bulimia nervosa (McIntosh, Carter, Bulik, Frampton, & Joyce, 2010).

Treatment of Binge-Eating Disorder

Treatments for binge-eating disorder are similar to those for bulimia nervosa, although binge-eating disorder presents fewer physical complications because of the lack of purging. Individuals with binge-eating disorder do differ in some ways from those with bulimia nervosa. Most are overweight and have to deal with societal prejudices regarding their weight. Due to the health consequences of excess weight, many therapy programs also focus on healthy approaches to weight loss.

In general, treatment follows two phases (Ricca, Mannucci, Zucchi, Rotella, & Faravelli, 2000; Shelley-Ummenhofer & MacMillan, 2007). First, factors that

FOCUS ON RESILIENCE

Preventing Eating Disorders

A variety of prevention programs have been developed to reduce the incidence of eating disorders and disordered eating patterns among women and girls. They target protective factors such as social support and strong social bonds and characteristics such as self-determination, autonomy, and social competence (Ferrier-Auerbach & Martens, 2009). Girls who have a sense of personal power and recognize the positive attributes of their bodies are less likely to exhibit disordered eating or become obsessed with their weight or body shape (L. Phelps, Johnston, & Augustyniak, 1999; Steck, Abrams, & Phelps, 2004). Programs designed to reduce body dissatisfaction have resulted in women demonstrating increased acceptance of their overall appearance as well as their body weight (T. Wade et al., 2009). Interventions generally focus on (a) increasing awareness of societal messages of what it means to be female and the role the media plays in creating unrealistic views of an ideal body, (b) developing a more positive body image by reducing "fat talk" and teasing about body size, (c) developing healthier eating and exercise habits, (d) increasing comfort in openly expressing feelings to peers and family members, (e) developing healthy ways of coping with stress and pressure, and (f) increasing assertiveness skills. These topics are addressed through group discussions and the use of videos, magazines, and examples from mass media (C. Chapman, Gilger, & Chestnutt, 2010; Richardson & Paxton, 2010).

PhotoDisc

There has been less focus on preventing eating disorders in men and boys. One program attempting to fill this gap (S. Friedman, 2007) focuses on

- expanding the definition of masculinity to include prosocial characteristics such as caring, nurturance, and cooperation;
- examining beliefs regarding what it means to be male (e.g., needing to be brave and strong, not showing emotions, taking charge) and understanding how these beliefs affect men's feelings about their bodies;
- identifying and developing a positive sense of self that include qualities other than appearance;
- developing a broader range of emotions and feelings and learning to express them in a healthy manner; and
- developing skills to effectively deal with stressors.

It is hoped that bolstering protective factors such as social support, critical evaluation of unrealistic societal messages, and coping and communications skills will help stem the tide of eating disorders.

trigger overeating are determined; then clients are taught strategies to reduce eating binges, as seen in the following case study.

Case Study

Mrs. A. had very rigid rules concerning eating that, when violated, would result in her "going the whole nine yards." Two types of triggers were identified for her binges—emotional distress (anger, anxiety, sadness, or frustration) and work stress (long hours, deadlines). Interventions were applied to help her develop more flexible rules regarding eating and to deal with her stressors. Information about obesity, proper nutrition, and physical exercise was provided. Her body weight was recorded weekly, and a healthy pattern of three meals and two snacks a day was implemented. She used a food diary to record the type and amount of food consumed and her psychological state preceding eating. Second, cognitive strategies were employed to change distorted beliefs about eating. Mrs. A. was asked to prepare a list of "forbidden" foods and to rank them in order of "dangerousness." Gradually these foods were introduced

Case Study—cont'd

into normal eating routines, beginning with those perceived as being less dangerous. Mrs. A. was asked to observe her body in a mirror to help reduce or eliminate cognitive distortions. The prejudices of society about body size were discussed, and realistic expectations about change were addressed. She was asked to observe attractive individuals with a larger body size so that she could consider positive qualities rather than focusing solely on the body. After performing this "homework," Mrs. A. discovered that overweight women can look attractive, and she began to buy more fashionable clothes for herself. She was astonished at the positive reactions and comments from friends and coworkers, and attributed the attention to her confidence and improved body image. (Goldfein et al., 2000)

Cognitive-behavioral therapy can produce significant reductions in binge eating but is less successful in reducing weight (Hilbert et al., 2012; Shelley-Ummenhofer & MacMillan, 2007; Vocks et al., 2010).

CHECKPOINT REVIEW

1. What are the main components of eating disorder treatment programs?
2. Describe the steps involved in the treatment of anorexia nervosa.
3. Describe the similarities and differences in the treatment of bulimia nervosa and binge-eating disorder.

Obesity

Case Study

When I'm uptight, I often overeat. I know that I often use food to calm me when I'm upset and even find myself feeling that when things don't go my way, I'll just have my way by eating anything and all I want. Like an alcoholic who can't stop drinking once he or she starts, I don't seem to be able to stop myself from eating once I start. (LeCrone, 2007, p. 1)

Obesity is defined as having a **body mass index (BMI)** greater than 30. BMI is an estimate of body fat calculated on the basis of a person's height and weight. DSM-5 does not yet recognize obesity as a specific disorder, despite its devastating medical and psychological consequences. Some researchers believe that forms of obesity that are characterized by an excessive drive for food should be recognized as a "food addiction" (Volkow & O'Brien, 2007). We include obesity in this chapter because it is a condition that is often accompanied by depression and anxiety disorders, low self-esteem, poor body image, and unhealthy eating patterns (Eddy, Tanofsky-Kraff, et al., 2007; Rofey et al., 2009). In one study, the majority of obese women surveyed had engaged in binge eating (Bulik & Reichborn-Kjennerud, 2003). Also, obese individuals are five times more likely to display behaviors characteristic of night-eating syndrome—consuming at least 25% of their food after their evening meal (Stunkard et al., 2009; Vander Wal, 2012).

obesity a condition involving a body mass index greater than 30

body mass index (BMI) an estimate of body fat calculated on the basis of a person's height and weight

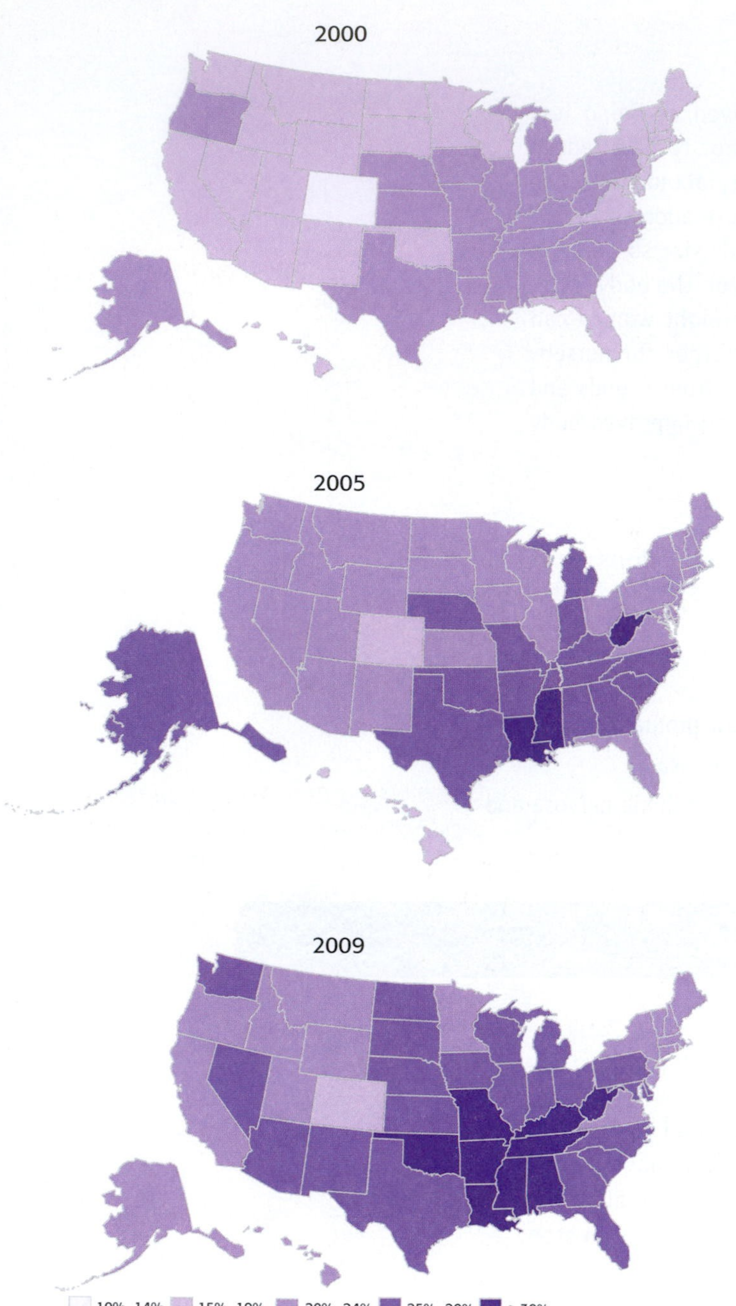

FIGURE 9.5

State-Specific Increase in Obesity Prevalence Among Adults, 2000–2009
These maps show the percentage of adults age 18 and older considered obese, by state.

Source: Centers for Disease Control and Prevention (2010d)

Obesity is a worldwide phenomenon that affects more than 300 million individuals (WHO, 2010). According to BMI standards, 68 percent of U.S. adults are overweight; of that fraction, 35 percent are obese (Flegal, Carroll, Kit, & Ogden, 2012). Almost one third of children and adolescents in the United States are either overweight or obese (Ogden, Carroll, Curtin, Lamb, & Flegal, 2010). Figure 9.5 shows the increase in obesity from 2000 to 2009. In the United States, the prevalence of overweight and obesity has doubled since the 1970s, and it is estimated that by 2015, 75 percent of adults and 24 percent of children and adolescents will fall into one of these categories. Statistics for African Americans, Mexican Americans, American Indians, and women show even higher rates of obesity (CDC, 2009a; Y. Wang & Beydoun, 2007).

Obesity is second only to tobacco use as a preventable cause of disease and death. Being overweight or obese increases the risk of high cholesterol and triglyceride levels, type 2 diabetes, cancer, coronary heart disease, stroke, gallbladder disease, arthritis, sleep apnea, and respiratory problems (CDC, 2010a, c) and is associated with a reduction in life expectancy of 5 years or more (Fontaine, Redden, Wang, Westfall, & Allison, 2003). Childhood obesity also has a significant health impact, especially for girls. Girls who are obese are 9 times more likely to develop high blood pressure compared to their peers who are not obese, whereas boys have a threefold increase in risk (Ortiz, 2011). Being overweight or obese in childhood is related to an increased risk of coronary heart disease in adulthood (J. L. Baker, Olsen, & Sorensen, 2007). As compared to children with normal weight, children who are overweight are more likely to report that they worry a lot, are concerned about how they look, have trouble falling asleep, have headaches, feel angry, and get into fights (American Psychological Association, 2010b).

Etiology of Obesity

Obesity stems from many causes, including genetic and biological factors; our sedentary modern-day lifestyle combined with easy access to attractive, high-calorie foods; and some of the same disturbed eating patterns seen in eating disorders.

Thus, obesity is a product of biological, psychological, social, and sociocultural influences, as shown in Figure 9.6. How these dimensions interact is still being investigated. For example, one theory, termed the "thrifty genotype" hypothesis, points to the role of both genetics and the environment in accounting for the rapid rise in obesity. According to this perspective, certain genes helped our ancestors survive famines by storing fat. These same genes, however, may be dysfunctional in an environment in which high-fat foods are now plentiful (CDC, 2010c). Although "thrifty" genes and access to foods can account for some cases of obesity, other factors must be involved, because rates of obesity also vary according to variables such as class, gender, and race or ethnicity.

Biological Dimension Genes can influence eating behaviors through brain structures and neurochemistry. Brain regions that both motivate and inhibit food consumption are believed to be involved in obesity (Volkow & O'Brien, 2007). The hormone leptin, which regulates appetite, has also been implicated in obesity. A group of children who weighed more than 200 lb by age 10 were found to have a chromosomal abnormality that affected nine of the genes that influence leptin production (Bochukova et al., 2010).

L. H. Epstein and colleagues (2007) found that about 50 percent of people carry a gene variation affecting the neurotransmitter dopamine. As previously mentioned, low levels of dopamine can increase attention to food and the desire to eat (Bello & Hajnal, 2010; S. Brooks et al., 2011; Y. Lee & Lin, 2010). Individuals who are obese have been found to possess fewer dopamine receptors than people of normal weight; the fewer receptors they have, the higher their BMI (G. J. Wang et al., 2001). Similar findings regarding dopamine receptors were found among genetically lean and obese rats (Thanos, Michaelides, Piyis, Wang, & Volkow, 2008). It is not clear, however, whether reduced dopamine receptor levels are a cause or an effect of obesity.

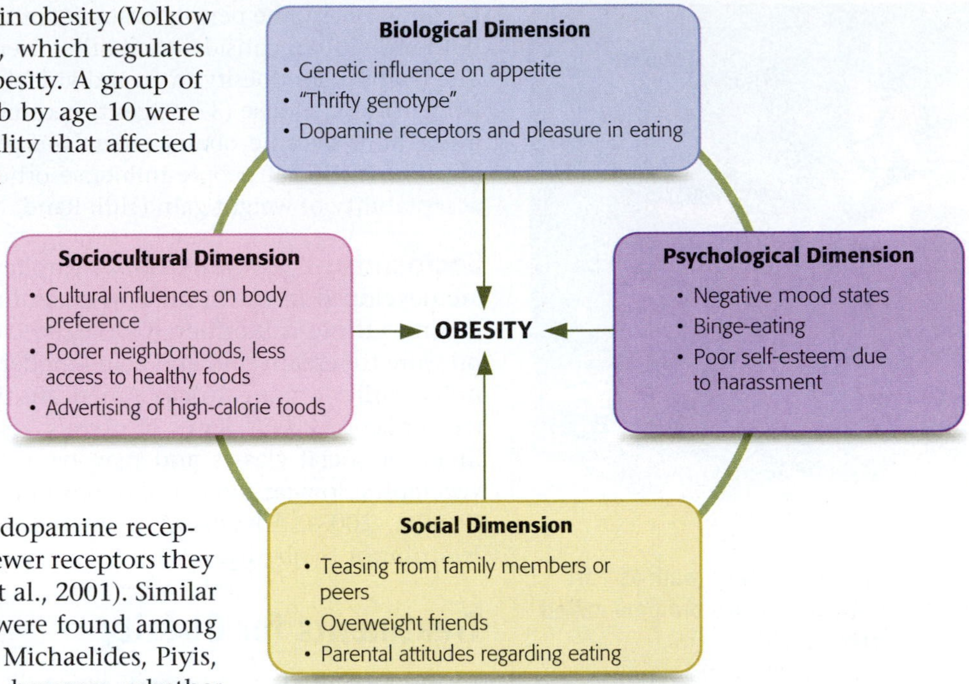

FIGURE 9.6

MULTIPATH MODEL FOR OBESITY

The dimensions interact with one another and combine in different ways to result in obesity.

Psychological Dimension Individuals who are obese often report feeling anxious or depressed. These responses are likely affected by the weight stigma that exists in society and the resultant harassment and discrimination in school, work, and hiring practices (Levi, Vinter, St. Laurent, & Segal, 2010; Obesity Action Coalition, 2007). The stigmatization faced by children who are obese from peers, parents, and teachers is pervasive and often unrelenting (Puhl & Heuer, 2009). Among a sample of 122 overweight youth, many reported being teased about their weight, suffering from mood and anxiety disorders, and internalizing a thin-ideal; more than one third had engaged in recent binge eating (Eddy, Tanofsky-Kraff, et al., 2007). It is not clear whether negative mood states are a cause of being overweight, but it is easy to imagine how they can be a result of societal responses to excess weight.

Social Dimension Stress within the family has been associated with excess weight during childhood, adolescence, and even adulthood. Individuals who had a "poor relationship" with their mother between the ages of 1 and 3 were twice as likely to become obese during adolescence compared to those who had a good relationship with their mother (Anderson, Gooze, Lemeshow, & Whitaker, 2012). Teasing by family members about weight issues is also associated with obesity (Eddy, Tanofsky-Kraff, et al., 2007). Parental eating patterns and attitudes may influence food intake in children (Bruss et al., 2003). In families in which a positive mealtime atmosphere was reported, adolescents were less likely to engage in disordered eating (Neumark-Sztainer, Wall, Story, & Fulkerson, 2004).

In an interesting study, Christakis and Fowler (2007) followed the social networks of 12,067 adults over a period of 32 years to determine social factors associated with obesity. They wanted to see if a person's friends, siblings, spouses, or neighbors had an impact on weight gain. Some of the findings were quite surprising. If someone a person considers a friend

MYTH VS REALITY

MYTH Body mass index standards represent unvarying thresholds that remain constant from year to year.

REALITY In 1998, the BMI scores were lowered for all weight classes. This resulted in an increased prevalence of individuals considered overweight or obese. For example, the BMI cutoff score for the category of overweight was lowered from 27 to 25. This resulted in 29 million Americans being added to the overweight category—an overnight increase of 42 percent.

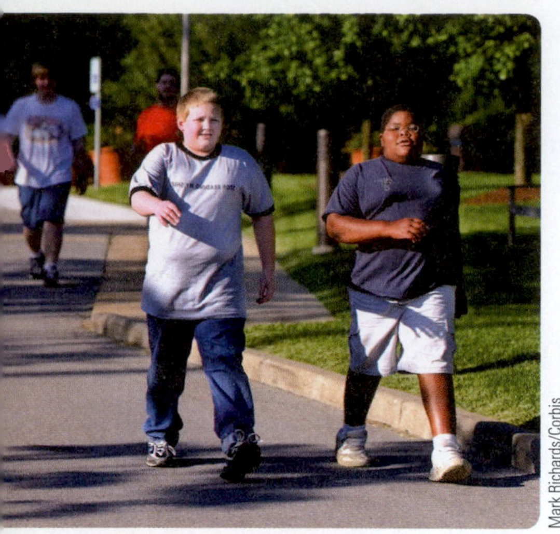
Mark Richards/Corbis

Childhood Obesity

Overweight boys speed walk as part of a childhood obesity program called "Committed to Kids."

becomes obese, the person's chances of becoming obese increase by 57 percent. If both individuals consider each other friends, the chances increase by 171 percent. The chances for obesity in an individual also increased when an adult sibling (40 percent) or a spouse (37 percent) became obese. There was no increase for when a neighbor became obese, unless the people were also friends. The researchers hypothesized that people influence others in their social network regarding the acceptability of weight gain (Hill, Rand, Nowak, & Christakis, 2010).

Sociocultural Dimension Attitudes regarding food and acceptable weight are developed in the home and community. Rates of obesity tend to be highest among ethnic minorities (CDC, 2009a). In some ethnic groups, there is less pressure to remain thin and being moderately overweight is not a big concern. As noted earlier, among African Americans there is greater acceptance of fuller figures (Foster-Scott, 2007). Rates of obesity also tend to be higher among individuals in lower social classes and may be a product of limited availability of fruits, vegetables, low-fat food, and opportunities for exercise in poorer neighborhoods (Peralta, 2003). Advertising of high-calorie foods is also seen by some to be a contributor to obesity.

Treatments for Obesity

Treatments for obesity have included dieting, lifestyle changes, medications, and surgery. In general, dieting alone may produce short-term weight loss but tends to be ineffective in the long term; some individuals gain back more weight than was lost. Dieting may be somewhat more successful for children (Moens, Braet, & Van Winckel, 2010). T. Mann and colleagues (2007) concluded that most adults would be better off not dieting, because of the stress on the body as a result of weight cycling. Indeed, the "yo-yo" effect in dieting (cycles of weight gain and loss) is associated with increased risk of cardiovascular disease and stroke and decreased immune functioning. Among those with a genetic predisposition to obesity, physical activity can reduce the risk of becoming overweight (Kilpelainen et al., 2011). Comprehensive intervention programs appear to be the most promising. In a meta-analysis of studies incorporating "rigorous randomized trials" of obesity treatments that have included a minimum of 2 years of follow-up, L. H. Powell, Calvin, and Calvin (2007) concluded that lifestyle interventions (low-calorie diets and exercise) were successful in producing moderate and sustained reductions in weight.

Did You Know ? Fitness may counter some of the health problems associated with obesity. In a 12-year study of American adults 60 years and older, those who were obese but fit had similar survival rates to individuals with normal weight.

Source: Sui et al., 2007

CHECKPOINT REVIEW

1. What are the health consequences of obesity?
2. What are some psychological, social, and sociocultural influences on obesity?
3. Describe different treatment strategies for obesity.

Summary

1 What kinds of eating disorders exist?

- Individuals with anorexia nervosa exhibit severe body image distortion. They are afraid of getting fat and engage in self-starvation. There are two subtypes of anorexia nervosa: the restricting type and the binge-eating/purging type.
- Individuals with bulimia nervosa are generally of normal weight, engage in recurrent binge eating, feel a loss of control over eating, and use vomiting, exercise, or laxatives to attempt to control weight.
- Individuals with binge-eating disorder also engage in recurrent binge eating and feel a loss of control over eating; however, they do not regularly use purging or exercise to counteract the effects of overeating. Most people with this disorder are overweight.
- Individuals who show atypical patterns of severely disordered eating that do not fully meet the criteria for anorexia nervosa, bulimia nervosa, or binge-eating disorder are given the diagnosis of eating conditions not elsewhere classified.

2 What are some causes of eating disorders?

- Genetics and neurotransmitter abnormalities are implicated in eating disorders. Research currently is focusing on the role of dopamine in eating disorders.
- It is believed that societal emphasis on thinness may contribute to the increasing incidence of eating disorder.
- Parental attitudes regarding the importance of thinness can contribute to disordered eating. Peer attitudes about body size and weight can also influence disturbed eating patterns.
- Countries that are influenced by Western standards have seen an increasing incidence of eating disorders.

3 What are some treatment options for eating disorders?

- Many of the therapies for eating disorders attempt to teach clients to identify the impact of societal messages regarding thinness and encourage them to develop healthier goals and values.
- For individuals with anorexia nervosa, medical as well as psychological treatment is necessary, because the body is in starvation mode. The goal is to help clients gain weight, normalize their eating patterns, understand and alter their thoughts related to body image, and develop healthier methods of dealing with stress.
- With both bulimia nervosa and binge-eating disorder, therapy involves normalizing eating patterns, developing a more positive body image, and dealing with stress in a healthier fashion.
- With bulimia nervosa, medical assistance may be required because of the physiological changes associated with purging.
- Because many people with binge-eating disorder are overweight or obese, weight reduction strategies are often included in treatment.

4 What causes obesity and how is it treated?

- The causes of obesity vary from individual to individual and involve combinations of biological predispositions and psychological, social, and sociocultural influences.
- In general, lifestyle changes that include reduced intake of high-calorie foods combined with exercise have proven to be the most effective treatment for obesity.

Key Terms

muscle dysphoria 233
anorexia nervosa 233
bulimia nervosa 236
binge-eating disorder (BED) 238
eating conditions not elsewhere classified 239
obesity 251
body mass index (BMI) 251

Media Resources

Psychology CourseMate

Access an interactive e-Book and chapter-specific interactive learning tools, including:

- flashcards
- quizzes
- videos

and more in your Psychology CourseMate.

Go to **CengageBrain.com.**

Alina G/Shutterstock.com

10

Substance-Use Disorders

CHAPTER OUTLINE

Jim, a married father of two teenage sons, is also a 54-year-old alcoholic who recently lost his job. Jim began drinking in high school, hoping it would help him feel more relaxed; he disliked the taste of alcohol, but forced himself to continue drinking. Over the next several years, Jim acquired the ability to consume large amounts of alcohol and was proud of his drinking capacity. He remained anxious about social gatherings, but after a few drinks he was the "life of the party." His heavy drinking continued throughout college.

After graduate school, Jim married and began his career in the aerospace industry. Soon, he was drinking throughout the week, claiming drinking was the only way he could relax. He attributed his increased drinking to pressures at work and a desire to feel comfortable in social situations. Despite the loss of his job, frequent arguments with his wife and sons regarding alcohol use, and a physician's warning that alcohol was causing liver damage, Jim could not control his alcohol consumption.

FOCUS QUESTIONS

1 What are substance-use disorders?

2 What substances are involved in substance-use disorders?

3 Why do people develop substance-use disorders?

4 What kinds of interventions and treatments for substance-use disorders are most effective?

Substance-Use Disorders

Substance-use disorders can develop in many ways. However, Jim's story of problem drinking is typical in several respects. He initially found the taste of alcohol unpleasant, but he continued drinking. Heavy drinking served a purpose: It reduced his anxiety, particularly with respect to work and social situations. His alcohol consumption continued despite obvious negative consequences. His preoccupation with alcohol and deterioration in social and occupational functioning are also characteristic of problem drinkers. Alcohol use may have reduced work and social anxieties, but it also increased arguments with his wife and resulted in health problems. Why was he unable to limit his drinking? What led him on the path to alcoholism? Would things have turned out differently if Jim had sought professional help for his anxiety rather than trying to self-medicate with alcohol?

Throughout history, people have used a variety of chemical substances for the purpose of altering their mood, level of consciousness, or behavior. The pervasiveness of substance use in contemporary culture is apparent from our vast consumption of alcohol, tobacco, caffeine, prescription medications, and illegal drugs, and from frequent media reports about substance abuse. The Substance Abuse and Mental Health Services Administration (SAMHSA) obtains annual data regarding the use of alcohol, tobacco, and illicit drugs based on interviews with approximately 67,500 adolescents and adults. Based on 2009 interview data (SAMHSA, 2010c), researchers estimated that 21.8 million adolescents and adults (8.7 percent of the population) used illicit drugs including cannabis, cocaine, heroin, hallucinogens, inhalants, and illicitly obtained prescription drugs. The problem of illicit drug use occurs with greater frequency in some age groups and some ethnic groups (Figures 10.1 and Figure 10.2). Increases in the nonmedical use of prescription drugs as well as high rates of

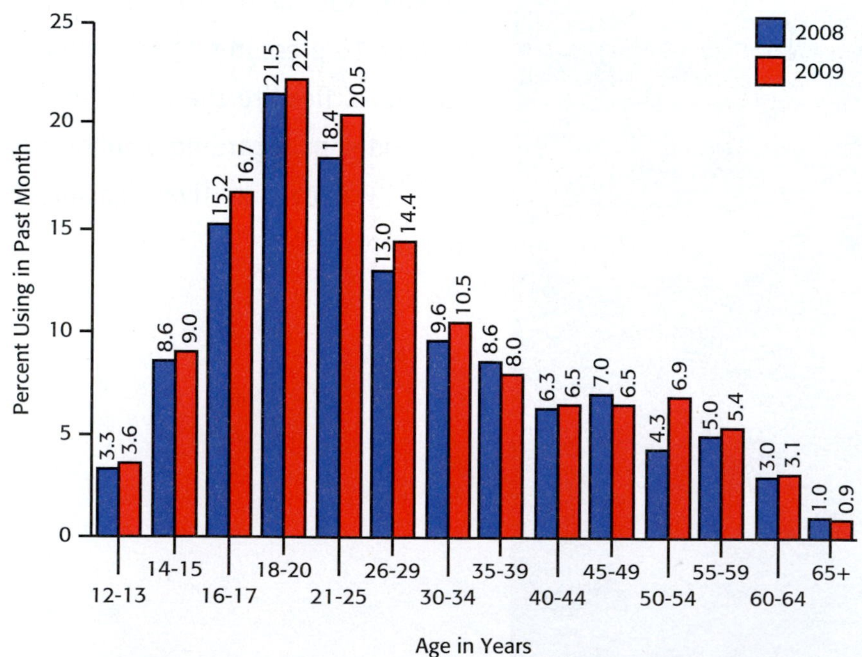

FIGURE 10.1

Two-Year Comparison of Past-Month Illicit Drug Use Across Age Groups

In comparing 2008 and 2009, increases in the use of illicit drugs (cannabis, cocaine, heroin, hallucinogens, inhalants, and prescription drugs used nonmedically) occurred in almost all age groups.

Source: Substance Abuse and Mental Health Services Administration (2010c)

heavy drinking and marijuana use reported by young adults (ages 18–25) are a particular concern.

Substance-use disorders arise when **psychoactive substances**—substances that alter moods, thought processes, or other psychological states—are used excessively. Heavy substance use induces changes in the brain that result in the behaviors that characterize addiction (Kalivas & O'Brien, 2008). **Addiction** involves compulsive drug-seeking behavior and a loss of control over drug use. Once addiction develops, it is difficult to stop using the substance, not only because of the pleasurable feelings associated with use, but also because of the **withdrawal** symptoms—negative psychological and physiological effects such as shaking, irritability, or emotional distress—that occur when use is discontinued. This is because chronic exposure to a substance often results in **physiological dependence**—the body adapts and begins to accept the presence of the substance as normal. Evidence of either withdrawal symptoms or **tolerance**, which involves progressive decreases in the effectiveness of the substance, indicates that physiological dependence has developed.

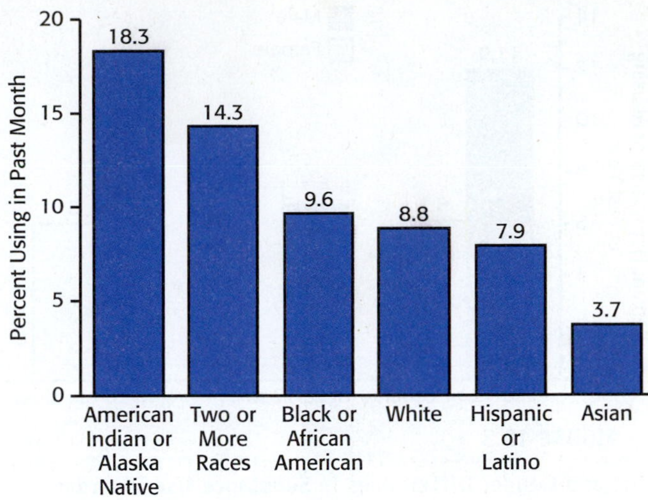

FIGURE 10.2

Comparison of Past-Month Illicit Drug Use Across Ethnic Groups

In 2009, there were significant differences among ethnic groups in the use of illicit drugs (cannabis, heroin, cocaine, hallucinogens, inhalants, and prescription drugs used nonmedically).

Source: Substance Abuse and Mental Health Services Administration (2010c)

The following characteristics are often present in individuals diagnosed with a substance-use disorder:

- an inability to control use of the substance, despite harmful physical, psychological, or interpersonal effects, including difficulty fulfilling work, school, or family obligations;
- a craving for and preoccupation with obtaining and using the substance;
- the development of tolerance—a need for increasing quantities of the substance to achieve the desired effect; and
- withdrawal symptoms that occur with reduction or cessation of substance intake and often precipitate resumption of substance use.

The DSM-5 differentiates substance-use disorders according to the specific substance used, such as alcohol-use disorder and cannabis-use disorder. All of the substance-use disorders involve a maladaptive pattern of recurrent use, extending over a period of at least 12 months. **Substance abuse** causes notable impairment or distress and continues despite social, occupational, psychological, or physical problems. Substance-use disorders can also cause legal difficulties, jeopardize the safety of the user or others, and affect social relationships and obligations at work, school, or home.

It is likely that you know someone with a substance-use disorder. Not only substance use is pervasive in our society; so is serious substance abuse. In 2009, an estimated 22.5 million adolescents and adults (8.9 percent of the population) met the criteria for a substance-use disorder at some time during the year; of this group, 3.2 million abused alcohol *and* illicit drugs, 3.9 million abused illicit drugs but not alcohol, and 15.4 million abused only alcohol. Marijuana was the most commonly abused illicit drug, followed by pain relievers and cocaine. Substance abuse is twice as prevalent in men and boys, although abuse rates are almost equal for girls and boys ages 12–17 (Figure 10.3). Additionally, the rate of illicit drug use is much higher among adolescents (with 61 percent reporting illicit drug use) than among those ages 18–25 (38 percent) and 26 or older (25 percent; SAMHSA, 2010c).

psychoactive substance a substance that alters mood, thought processes, or other psychological states

addiction compulsive drug-seeking behavior and a loss of control over drug use

withdrawal adverse physical and psychological symptoms that occur after reducing or ceasing intake of a substance

physiological dependence state of adaptation that occurs after chronic exposure to a substance; can result in craving and withdrawal symptoms

tolerance decreases in the effects of a substance that occur after chronic use

substance abuse pattern of excessive or harmful use of any substance for mood-altering purposes

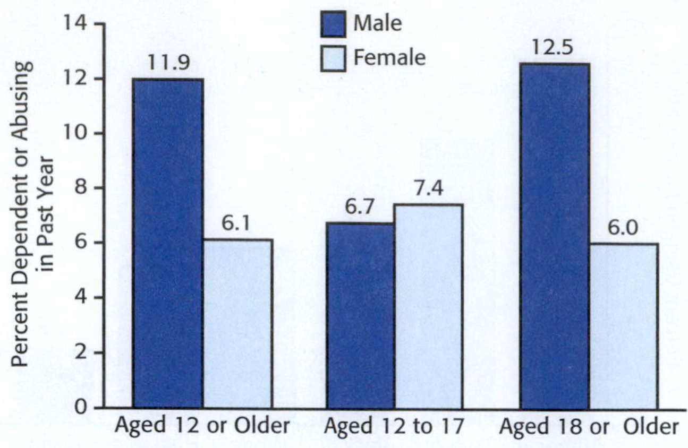

FIGURE 10.3

Age and Gender Differences in Substance-Use Disorder Diagnosis

With the exception of those ages 12–17, the incidence of past-year substance-use disorder diagnosis is about twice as high for males as for females.

Source: Substance Abuse and Mental Health Services Administration (2010c)

You may wonder which substances are considered the most dangerous. A recent analysis concluded that heroin, crack cocaine, and methamphetamine present the greatest danger for the user, but that alcohol is the most dangerous drug when both personal and societal ramifications are considered (Nutt, King, & Phillip, 2010). As you proceed through this chapter, we hope you consider the personal and societal effects of the substances discussed, as well as the vast number of people affected directly and indirectly by substance abuse. We first examine the various substances involved in substance-use disorders. We then use the multipath perspective to understand possible causes of addiction. We conclude by discussing addiction treatment and the importance of relapse prevention.

CHECKPOINT REVIEW

1. What characteristics are seen in individuals diagnosed with a substance-use disorder?
2. How common is substance abuse?
3. What demographic groups are most likely to use and abuse substances?

Substances Associated With Abuse

> Our national prescription drug abuse problem cannot be ignored. I have worked in the treatment field for the last 35 years, and recent trends regarding the extent of prescription drug abuse are startling. We must work with prescribers, the pharmaceutical industry, and families to help us fight this scourge.
>
> *Thomas McLellan, Deputy Director, Office of National Drug Control Policy, 2010.*

Misuse of a number of substances can lead to a substance-use disorder. Substances that are abused include prescription medications used to treat anxiety, insomnia, or pain; legal substances such as alcohol, caffeine, tobacco, and household chemicals; and illegal substances such as methamphetamine, cocaine, and heroin. Each of the substances discussed in this chapter can create significant physical, social, psychological, and, sometimes, legal problems. We discuss a variety of substances—including those that tend to overly relax the central nervous system such as alcohol, opioids, tranquilizers, sleeping pills, and antianxiety medications. We also discuss central nervous system stimulants (including caffeine, cocaine, amphetamines, and methamphetamine), hallucinogens (including LSD), dissociative anesthetics (including PCP, ketamine, and dextromethorphan), and substances with multiple effects, including nicotine, cannabis, Ecstasy, and inhalants. Table 10.1 lists these substances and their effects as well as their addictive potential.

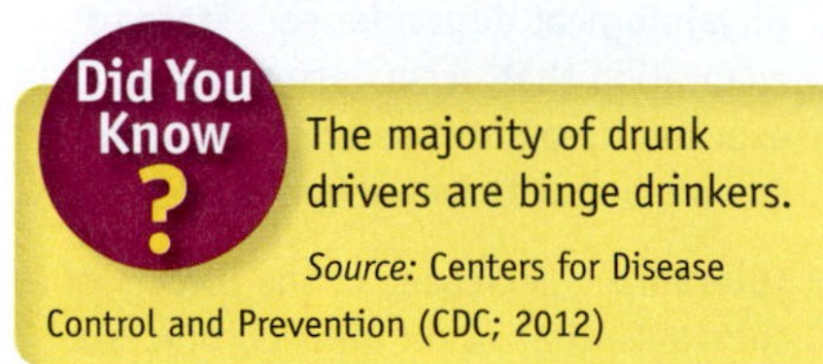

The majority of drunk drivers are binge drinkers.

Source: Centers for Disease Control and Prevention (CDC; 2012)

depressant a substance that causes a slowing of responses and generalized depression of the central nervous system

Depressants

Depressants cause generalized depression of the central nervous system and a slowing down of responses. Individuals taking depressants may feel relaxed and

TABLE 10.1 Commonly Abused Substances

SUBSTANCE	SHORT-TERM EFFECTS[a]	ADDICTIVE POTENTIAL
Central nervous system depressants		
Alcohol	Relaxation, loss of inhibitions	High
Opioids	Pain relief, sedation, drowsiness	High
Sedatives, hypnotics, anxiolytics	Sedation, drowsiness, reduced anxiety, impaired judgment	Moderate to high
Central nervous system stimulants		
Caffeine	Energy, enhanced attention	Moderate
Amphetamines	Energy, euphoria, enhanced attention	High
Cocaine	Energy, euphoria	High
Hallucinogens		
LSD, psilocybin, mescaline, salvia	Altered perceptions, sensory distortions	Low
Dissociative anesthetics		
Phencyclidine (PCP)	Confusion, sensory distortions, feelings of detachment	Moderate
Ketamine, methoxetamine (MXE)	Confusion, sensory distortions, feelings of detachment	Moderate
Dextromethorphan (DXM)	Confusion, sensory distortions, feelings of detachment	Moderate
Substances with multiple effects		
Nicotine	Energy, relaxation	High
Cannabis	Relaxation, euphoria	Moderate
Inhalants	Disorientation	Variable
Ecstasy (MDMA)	Energy, heightened senses	Moderate
Gamma hydroxybutyrate (GHB)	Relaxation, euphoria, enhanced strength	High

[a] Specific effects depend on the quantity used, the extent of previous use, and other substances concurrently ingested, as well as on the experiences, expectancies, and personality of the person using the substance.

sociable due to lowered interpersonal inhibitions. Let's examine in more detail one of the most widely used depressants—alcohol—and then discuss other depressants, including tranquilizers, sleeping pills, and antianxiety medications.

Alcohol Slightly more than half of all adolescent and adult U.S. Americans report being current drinkers of alcohol. We begin our discussion of alcohol by clarifying terminology. One drink is defined as 12 oz. of beer, 5 oz. of wine, or 1.5 oz. of hard liquor. The term **moderate drinking** is typically used to describe lower-risk patterns of drinking, generally no more than one drink for women or two drinks for men. **Heavy drinking** refers to chronic drinking, usually an average of more than two drinks per day for men and more than one drink per day for women (although the SAMHSA survey defines heavy drinking as binge drinking five or more days per month). **Binge drinking** refers to episodic drinking involving five or more drinks on a single occasion for men and four or more drinks for women.

About 70 percent of adults do not drink excessively, because they either abstain or drink in moderation (Hasin, Stinson, Ogburn, & Grant, 2007). However, nearly one fourth of Americans aged 12 or older binge drink, including 7 percent who binge at least five days per month. Males in all age groups are more likely to consume alcohol and engage in binge and heavy drinking compared to females.

Binge drinking accounts for more than 50 percent of the alcohol consumed by adults and 90 percent of the alcohol consumed by teens.

Source: CDC (2012)

moderate drinking a lower-risk pattern of alcohol intake (no more than one or two drinks per day)

heavy drinking chronic alcohol intake of more than two drinks per day for men and more than one drink per day for women

binge drinking episodic intake of five or more alcoholic beverages for men or four or more drinks for women

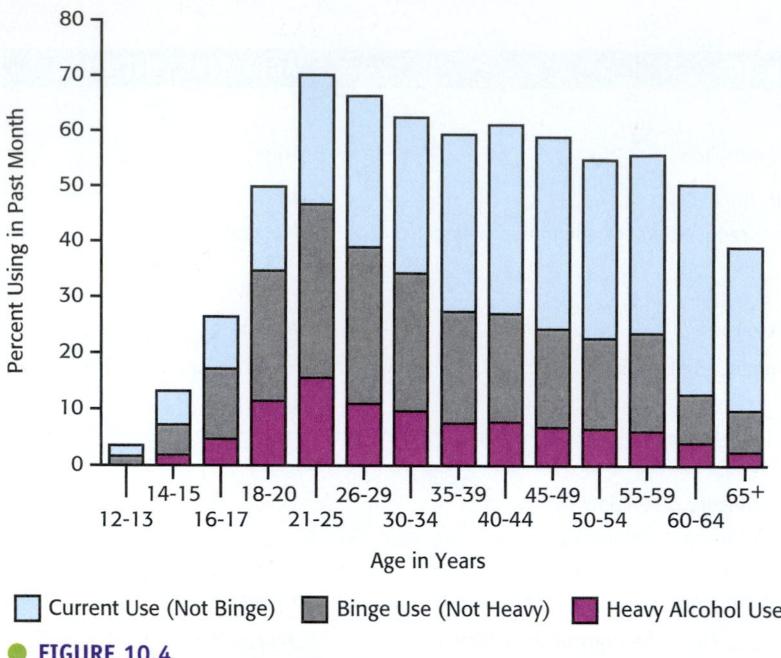

FIGURE 10.4

Comparisons of Alcohol Use Across Age Groups

Almost half of those ages 18–20 reported underage alcohol use in the previous month, including 23 percent who reported binge drinking and 11 percent who were heavy alcohol users. The highest level of binge drinking and heavy alcohol use is seen in the 21–25 age group.

Source: Substance Abuse and Mental Health Services Administration (2010c)

Ethnic group data reveal that Asian Americans (followed by African Americans) have the lowest levels of heavy and binge drinking (SAMHSA, 2010b). Native Americans of both genders demonstrate the earliest onset of drinking and highest weekly alcohol consumption, whereas Latino/Hispanic men have the highest rates of daily alcohol consumption (Chartier & Caetano, 2010).

Let's focus on statistics for the college-age population. As illustrated in Figure 10.4, binge drinking and heavy drinking are especially problematic among those ages 21–25. Among young adults (ages 18–25), the rate of binge drinking is 42 percent, with heavy drinking reported by 14 percent (SAMHSA, 2010b). Heavy drinking occurs more frequently in men and women ages 18–22 who attend college full-time than in those who do not (Figure 10.5). A recent online survey revealed that 83 percent of first-year students at one university reported recently consuming alcohol, half reported binge drinking, and many reported drinking at least six days during the month (C. Sloane, Burke, Cremeens, Vail-Smith, & Woolsey, 2010).

Approximately 5 percent of those who use alcohol are physiologically dependent (Koob, Kandel, & Volkow, 2008). Alcohol withdrawal symptoms vary and can include headache, fatigue, sweating, body tremors, and mood changes. Severe withdrawal can produce a life-threatening condition called **delirium tremens**, which begins with profound anxiety, agitation, and confusion followed by seizures, disorientation, hallucinations, or extreme lethargy. The lifetime prevalence of alcohol-use disorder is 18 percent. Whites, Native Americans, males, and those who are younger and unmarried with lower incomes are most likely to become **alcoholic** (Hasin, Stinson, et al., 2007). Although men are twice as likely to develop an alcohol-use disorder, **alcoholism** in women progresses more rapidly (Anthenelli, 2010).

Once swallowed, alcohol is quickly absorbed into the bloodstream and begins to depress central nervous system functioning. When the blood alcohol level, or alcohol content in the bloodstream, is about 0.1 percent—for many, the equivalent of drinking 3 oz. of whiskey or three glasses of beer—muscular coordination and judgment are impaired. Higher levels of blood alcohol, 0.3 percent in some individuals, can result in a loss of consciousness or even death.

Our bodies produce "cleanup" enzymes, including aldehyde dehydrogenase (ALDH), to counteract toxins that build up as alcohol is metabolized. Production of ALDH is affected by gender (males, especially younger males, produce more than females), genetic makeup (some groups, especially Asians, produce less ALDH), and food or medications concurrently in the body. Carbonated beverages and aspirin hasten alcohol absorption and reduce the efficiency of the cleanup, whereas food slows absorption, giving the enzymes more time to work. Body weight and the period of time during which alcohol was consumed also affect intoxication. Large amounts of alcohol consumed rapidly can result in impaired breathing, coma, and death; this condition, known as **alcohol poisoning**, can be exacerbated by the vomiting and dehydration that occur as the body attempts to rid itself of excess alcohol.

There are multiple physiological consequences associated with excessive alcohol use. Tolerance to alcohol develops rapidly, so drinkers wanting to

College-age binge drinkers are much more likely to show deficits with information processing and working memory compared to alcohol drinkers who do not binge.

Source: Courtney & Polich (2009)

delirium tremens life-threatening withdrawal symptoms that can result from chronic alcohol use

alcoholic person who has become dependent on alcohol and who exhibits characteristics of an alcohol-use disorder

alcoholism broad term referring to a condition in which the individual is dependent on alcohol and has difficulty controlling drinking

alcohol poisoning toxic effects resulting from rapidly consuming alcohol or ingesting a large quantity of alcohol; can result in impaired breathing, coma, and death

feel the effects of alcohol often increase their intake. Unfortunately, tolerance does not decrease the toxicity of alcohol, so heavy drinkers progressively expose their brains and bodies to greater physiological risk. Neurological effects include impaired motor skills, reduced reasoning and judgment, memory deficits, distractibility, and reduced motivation (E. V. Sullivan, Harris, & Pfefferbaum, 2010). Additionally, alcohol affects the liver and the entire cardiovascular system. People with alcoholism who continue to drink demonstrate declines in neurological functioning; sustained abstinence can lead to cognitive improvement, although heavy drinkers demonstrate ongoing impairment (Fortier et al., 2011; Yeh, Gazdzinski, Durazzo, Sjöstrand, & Meyerhoff, 2007).

In stark contrast to the stereotype of the skid row alcoholic, many people with alcoholism are able to function without severe disruption to their life—these so-called high-functioning alcoholics work, raise families, and maintain social relationships. Although aware of the negative physical and social consequences of their drinking, and distressed over their inability to control alcohol intake, they often deny they have a problem with alcohol or hide their drinking (Willenbring, 2010). It is not uncommon for individuals with alcoholism to alternate between periods of excessive drinking and sobriety, often in an attempt to prove they can abstain (E. V. Sullivan et al., 2010).

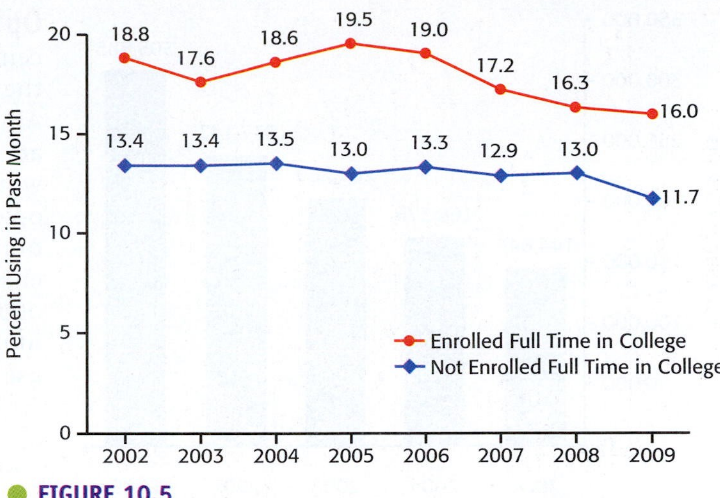

FIGURE 10.5

Trends in Heavy Alcohol Use Among 18- to 22-Year-Olds

There are significant differences in heavy alcohol use between 18- to 22-year-olds who attend college full-time and those who attend part-time or not at all, with college attendees consistently reporting higher rates of heavy drinking.

Source: Substance Abuse and Mental Health Services Administration (2010c)

CONTROVERSY:

Is There a Need for More Balance in Societal Messages About Alcohol Use?

What messages are we sending regarding alcohol use in contemporary society? Alcohol advertising and media glamorization of alcohol is pervasive. The myth persists that "everyone drinks," despite the fact that the majority of American adults consume alcohol only occasionally or not at all. Although efforts to prevent alcohol abuse stress the personal and societal risk of excess alcohol consumption and the risk of underage drinking, these messages receive only minimal attention. Should there be more effort to balance marketing and social media messages with information regarding the potential dangers of alcohol?

Professionals focused on addiction prevention fervently attempt to nullify societal messages that normalize and even glamorize alcohol use and to heighten awareness of risk factors, especially among those who are particularly vulnerable to addiction—adolescents and young adults. Scientists have demonstrated that alcohol (along with other substances) has a strong effect on the developing brain and that the effects of alcohol use on neurological development are most profound through the mid-20s. The college years are a particularly high-risk period for beginning the addiction process (Beseler, Taylor, Kraemer, & Leeman, 2012). College students who participate in underage alcohol use often drink heavily. Although college-bound high school students are less likely to binge drink, this trend reverses after college entrance; additionally, students with the greatest genetic risk of developing alcoholism tend to drink the most (Timberlake et al., 2007). Given the data on heavy-drinking college students, there is an apparent need for more information regarding alcohol and the addiction process. Although alcohol-abuse prevention campaigns are attempting to correct social misperceptions about the frequency of drinking (H. W. Perkins, Linkenbach, Lewis, & Neighbors, 2010), it may be difficult to reverse the trend of increasing alcohol abuse as long as societal messages make alcohol consumption look normative.

What messages have you encountered related to alcohol use since entering college? Do you feel the college environment plays a role in decisions to participate in heavy or underage drinking? What aspects of alcohol abuse do you think are most relevant to college students, and how can these be incorporated into prevention messages? What kinds of prevention efforts do you think would be the most effective on your college campus?

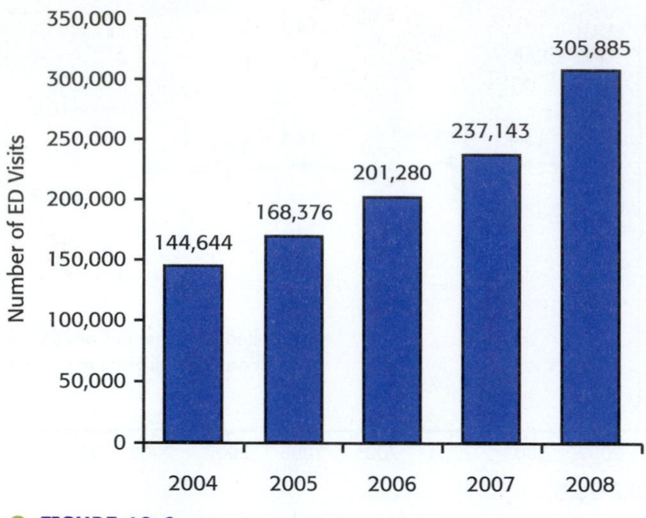

FIGURE 10.6

Emergency Department Visits Related to Illicit Use of Prescription Opioids

The number of emergency department visits due to illicit use of prescription pain medications increased 111 percent between 2004 and 2008, more than doubling in all age groups and for both males and females.

Source: Substance Abuse and Mental Health Services Administration (2010a)

Opioids **Opioids** are painkilling agents that depress the central nervous system. Heroin and opium, both derived from the opium plant, are the best-known of the illicit opioids. All opioids (including morphine, codeine, and oxycodone) are highly addictive and require careful medical management when prescribed for pain and anxiety. Use of prescription opioids obtained through illegal purchase or solicitation of multiple prescriptions is rising (Gilson & Kreis, 2009; Paulozzi et al., 2012). Nonmedical use of pain relievers is a leading form of drug abuse, second only to marijuana (SAMHSA, 2010c). The number of emergency department visits due to non-medical use of pain medications increased 111 percent between 2004 and 2008 (Figure 10.6), led by a 152 percent increase in oxycodone-related visits (SAMHSA, 2010a). Similarly, between 1998 and 2008 there was a 400 percent increase in adolescent and adult treatment admissions for prescription opioid abuse (SAMHSA, 2010d). Most opioid overdose deaths are accidental and involve concurrent use of alcohol or other drugs (Okie, 2010).

Long-term misuse of prescription opioids is linked with significant social problems (S. F. Butler, Black, Serrano, Wood, & Budman, 2010). Many people who abuse opioids begin their habit with prescribed medication, eventually buying prescription drugs illegally or trying a less expensive and even more lethal opioid—heroin (Canfield et al., 2010). Those who misuse prescription opioids often rationalize their use because the substances are prescribed medications (Daniulaityte, Falck, & Carlson, 2012). Prescription opioids are considered by some to be the new **gateway drug**—a substance leading to the use of more dangerous drugs.

Did You Know ? The number of deaths due to prescription drug overdoses (36,000 fatalities in 2008) has tripled in the past decade. Almost two thirds of overdose deaths involve prescription opioids.

Source: CDC (2011d)

Opioids produce both euphoria and drowsiness. Tolerance builds quickly, resulting in dependency and a need for increased doses to achieve desired effects. Withdrawal symptoms (including restlessness, muscle pain, insomnia, and cold flashes) are often severe. Symptoms of lethargy, fatigue, anxiety, and disturbed sleep may persist for months, and drug craving can persist for years.

Sedatives, Hypnotics, and Anxiolytics **Sedatives**, including hypnotics (sleeping pills) and anxiolytics (antianxiety medications), have calming effects and are used in the treatment of agitation, muscle tension, insomnia, and anxiety. **Hypnotics** induce sleep and are used during surgical procedures and to combat insomnia. **Anxiolytics** are used to treat anxiety; they are sometimes referred to as minor tranquilizers, so named to distinguish them from the major tranquilizing medications used with psychotic disorders. The drug classes of barbiturates, such as Seconal and phenobarbital, and benzodiazepines, such as Valium, Ativan, and Xanax, can provide rapid anxiety-reducing effects when used in moderate doses; higher doses are prescribed to produce hypnotic, or sleep-inducing, effects.

A sedative, hypnotic, or anxiolytic substance-use disorder can develop with high prescription doses or when these medications are misused or obtained illegally. Nonmedical use of sedatives, anxiolytics, and hypnotics is highest in the 26–35 age group (Sola, Chopra, & Rastogi, 2010). Individuals who have difficulty dealing with stress or who experience anxiety or insomnia are particularly prone to overusing and becoming dependent on sedatives. Additionally, some use sedatives recreationally or to counteract cocaine withdrawal symptoms (Sola et al., 2010).

opioid a painkilling agent that depresses the central nervous system, such as heroin and prescription pain relievers

gateway drug a substance that leads to use of additional substances that are even more lethal

sedatives a class of drugs that have a calming or sedating effect

hypnotics a class of medications that induce sleep

anxiolytics a class of medications that reduce anxiety

Sedatives are quite dangerous when misused. Even in low doses, they cause drowsiness, impaired judgment, and diminished motor skills. As with opioids, their legal use is carefully monitored due to known risks regarding drug dependence; however, their availability via illegal drug markets makes misuse difficult to control. Excessive use of sedatives can lead to accidental overdose and death. Combining alcohol with sedatives can be especially dangerous because alcohol compounds their depressant effects, slowing breathing and increasing risk of coma or lethal outcomes.

There is high potential for tolerance and physiological dependence with all sedatives; when they are discontinued, withdrawal symptoms can include insomnia, nervousness, headache, and drowsiness. Due to concerns regarding addictive potential and lethality with overdose, many medical practitioners avoid prescribing sedatives to treat anxiety, choosing to instead prescribe antidepressants. This stance is supported by data from a 35,000-participant national survey revealing that individuals prescribed sedatives for anxiety are twice as likely as those not prescribed sedatives to abuse these drugs (Fenton, Keyes, Martins, & Hasin, 2010). The risk of sedative dependence is greatest when doses are high, sedatives are used for more than one month, or there is a personal or family history of substance abuse (Sola et al., 2010).

The well-known sedative Rohypnol significantly interferes with cognitive functioning, balance, and short-term memory. Rohypnol is known as a "date rape" drug because unsuspecting individuals given the drug may feel sedated and uninhibited and not remember their activities. It is also used as a recreational drug in combination with alcohol, heroin, or cocaine.

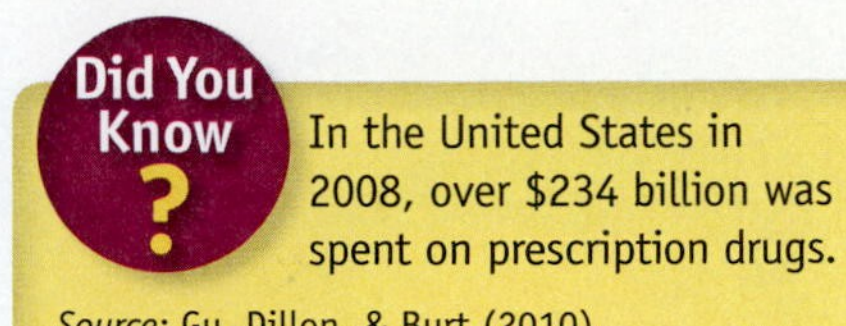

In the United States in 2008, over $234 billion was spent on prescription drugs.

Source: Gu, Dillon, & Burt (2010)

Stimulants

Stimulants, substances that speed up central nervous system activity, are used for a variety of reasons: to produce feelings of euphoria and well-being, improve mental and physical performance, reduce appetite, and prevent sleep. Unwanted physiological effects include heart arrhythmias, dizziness, tremors, and sweating. Psychological side effects can include anxiety, restlessness, agitation, hostility, and paranoia. Binge use of illicit stimulants is common, with sequential high doses leading to exhaustion and acute psychotic symptoms. Tolerance rapidly leads to increased drug use; withdrawal can result in depression, anxiety, and extreme fatigue. Our discussion begins with a commonly used mild stimulant, caffeine, and then concentrates on amphetamines (including methamphetamine) and cocaine.

Did You Know ?

Due to increased concern about prescription drug abuse, many states have implemented monitoring programs that track sales of addictive prescription medications. Electronic databases are used to prevent illegal drug sales and to identify and encourage treatment for individuals abusing prescription substances.

Caffeine

Case Study

I use energy drinks to stay awake while I study at night. I am noticing that I need more and more energy drinks to stay awake and keep alert. It's getting to the point where I need over four of five cans to get through a night, when normally it would take me only one can.

Caffeine is a stimulant found in coffee, chocolate, tea, and soft drinks. It is the most widely consumed psychoactive substance in the world, prized by almost every culture for increasing attentiveness. In North America, about

stimulant a substance that energizes the central nervous system

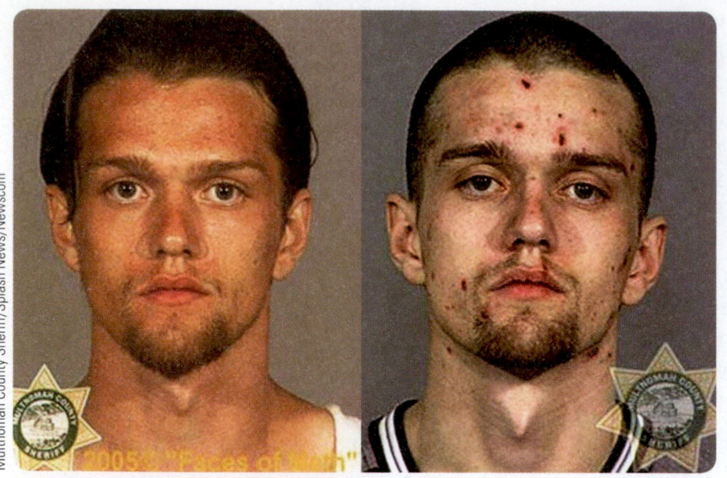

Multnomah County Sheriff/Splash News/Newscom

Methamphetamine Effects

This pair of mugshots is part of the Faces of Meth project started when justice officials noticed the significant physical decline among methamphetamine users arrested more than once. As seen here, many of the second, later mugshots clearly demonstrate the gauntness and facial lesions associated with ongoing methamphetamine use.

90 percent of adults use caffeine every day. Caffeine can produce restlessness, nervousness, insomnia, gastrointestinal disturbance, and cardiac arrhythmia. Although caffeine is generally consumed in moderate doses (a cup of tea has 40–60 mg, coffee 70–175 mg, and cola 30–50 mg), widespread marketing and consumption of energy drinks have resulted in increased caffeine consumption. Energy drinks, now a billion-dollar industry, typically have 80–150 mg of caffeine in addition to sweeteners and energy-boosting additives (Bigard, 2010). Frequent consumption of energy drinks can produce caffeine intoxication, tolerance, and withdrawal (Reissig, Strain, & Griffiths, 2009). Heavy consumption of energy drinks has been associated with new-onset seizures in some individuals (Duchan, Patel, & Feucht, 2010). Additionally, there has been a dramatic increase in emergency department visits associated with intoxication from energy drinks, particularly when combined with alcohol or illicit drugs (SAMHSA, 2011).

Amphetamines Amphetamines, also known as "uppers," significantly speed up central nervous system activity. Prescription amphetamines used to treat attention and sleep disorders (such as Ritalin, Benzedrine, and Dexedrine) are increasingly used illicitly (L. Wu, Pilowsky, Schlenger, & Galvin, 2007), particularly among white adolescents and young adults (Kroutil et al., 2006). About 2 percent of U.S. adults have experienced an addiction to amphetamines. Addiction is most common in those who take amphetamines intravenously or nasally ("snorting") and in high doses. Although amphetamines can induce feelings of euphoria and confidence, agitation and assaultive or suicidal behaviors also occur. Heavy doses can trigger delusions of persecution that resemble paranoid schizophrenia. Brain damage can result from chronic stimulant abuse (S. M. Berman, Kuczenski, McCracken, & London, 2009).

Methamphetamine, a particularly dangerous drug that is taken orally, snorted, injected, or heated and smoked in rock "crystal" form, is used by 0.2 percent of the population (SAMHSA, 2010c). Popular due to its low cost and rapid euphoric effects, methamphetamine has serious health consequences, including permanent damage to the heart, lungs, and immune system (Hauer, 2010). Although many are aware of the profound dental and aging effects of methamphetamine (Mooney et al., 2009), profound psychological changes also occur, including psychosis, depression, suicide, and violent behavior (Kaye, Darke, McKetin, & Duflou, 2008). As with other stimulants, methamphetamine has high potential for abuse and addiction.

Cocaine

Kevin Mazur/AMA2009/Getty Images

Death Linked to Cocaine

Actress and singer Whitney Houston is pictured here attending an American Music Awards ceremony several years before her death. Houston's death was the result of accidental drowning due to the effects of chronic cocaine use and atherosclerotic heart disease, a common side effect of stimulant use.

Case Study

A 49-year-old woman, previously diagnosed with congestive heart failure, was admitted to the hospital with a severe cough and labored breathing. She reported that she had never smoked cigarettes, consumed alcohol, or used drugs other than cocaine, which she had been smoking for 30 years. Due to her severe emphysema and continued cocaine use, she was not a candidate for heart transplantation. She died from respiratory failure and cardiac arrest (Vahid & Marik, 2007).

Cocaine, a stimulant extracted from the coca plant, induces feelings of energy and euphoria. Crack is a potent form of cocaine produced by heating cocaine with other substances ("freebasing"); it is sold in small, solid pieces ("rocks") and is typically smoked. Crack produces very immediate but short-lived effects. In 2009, there were an estimated 1.6 million cocaine users (0.7 percent of the population), with a large number of them (1.1 million) demonstrating a stimulant-use disorder (SAMHSA, 2010c).

Cocaine has a high potential for addiction, sometimes after only a short period of use. Approximately 20 percent of those who use cocaine become rapidly dependent on the drug (Koob et al., 2008). Due to cocaine's intense effects, withdrawal causes lethargy and depression; users often take multiple doses in rapid succession trying to recreate the high.

The constant desire for cocaine can impair social and occupational functioning. The high monetary cost of the substance, coupled with the need for increased doses to achieve a high, can cause users to resort to crime to feed their habit. Because cocaine stimulates the sympathetic nervous system, irregular heartbeat, stroke, and death may occur. Cocaine users sometimes experience acute psychiatric symptoms such as delusions, paranoia, and hallucinations; more chronic difficulties such as anxiety, depression, sexual dysfunction, and sleep difficulties also occur.

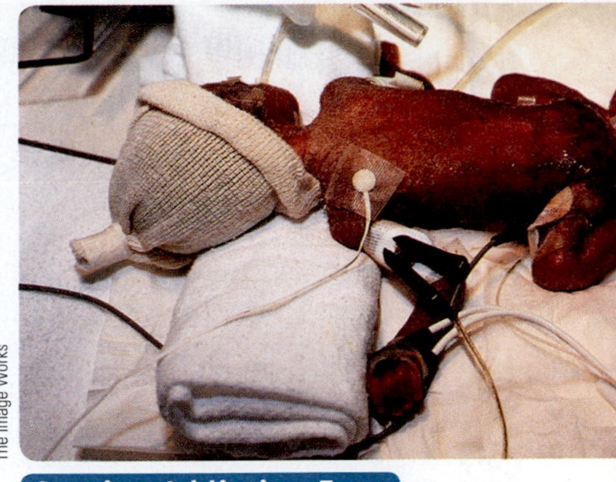

The Image Works

Cocaine Addiction From Mother to Child

Women who use drugs during pregnancy sometimes give birth to drug-addicted, underweight babies who are at risk for serious developmental problems. Pictured here is a newborn baby being monitored as it goes through cocaine withdrawal symptoms.

Hallucinogens

Hallucinogens are substances that produce vivid sensory awareness, heightened alertness, perceptions of increased insight, and sometimes hallucinations. The altered state produced by hallucinogens is sometimes pleasant, but can be an extremely traumatic experience. "Good trips" are associated with sharpened visual and auditory perception, heightened sensation, and perceptions of profound insight. "Bad trips" can produce severe depression, disorientation, delusions, and sensory distortions that result in fear and panic. Some users also experience flashbacks, the recurrence of hallucinations or other sensations days, weeks or even years after drug intake (Espiard, Lecardeur, Abadie, Halbecq, & Dollfus, 2005). Substances that have primarily hallucinogenic effects—including lysergic acid diethylamide (LSD), psilocybin, mescaline, and salvia—are discussed in this section. Drugs that have hallucinogenic effects combined with other properties (such as PCP, ketamine, and Ecstasy) are discussed later in the chapter. Hallucinogen use including Ecstasy was estimated to involve 1.3 million people (0.5 percent of the adolescent and adult population) in 2009 (SAMHSA, 2010c).

Traditional hallucinogens are derived from natural sources: LSD from a grain fungus, psilocybin from mushrooms, mescaline from the peyote cactus, and salvia from an herb in the mint family. Naturally occurring hallucinogens such as mescaline and psilocybin have been used in cultural ceremonies and religious rites for thousands of years. LSD, however, gained notoriety in the mid-1960s, praised by users as a potent consciousness-expanding psychedelic drug. National surveys reveal that LSD use is not common; mescaline, psilocybin, and salvia are also used infrequently. The effects and emotional reactions that result from hallucinogens can vary significantly, even for the same person using the same drug. Hallucinogens are not addictive and therefore do not cause compulsive drug-seeking behavior. However, tolerance does develop, so users frequently need larger quantities to re-create the initial effects of the drug. In one sample, nearly 1 in 4 hallucinogen users showed signs of hallucinogen dependence

MYTH VS REALITY

MYTH It is possible to be vaccinated against cocaine abuse.

REALITY Researchers are testing a vaccine (called TA-CD) to help individuals who are dependent on cocaine. Antibodies produced from the vaccine prevent cocaine from reaching the brain, thus reducing any pleasurable effects. Unfortunately, some users given the vaccine responded by using massive doses of cocaine, desperately trying to reach a high (B. M. Kinsey, Kosten, & Orson, 2010).

hallucinogen a substance that induces perceptual distortions and heightens sensory awareness

CONTROVERSY:

Using Stimulants to Improve Performance: A New Source of Addiction?

The nonmedical use of prescription medications is on the rise, including illicit use of stimulant medications by high school and college students and young professionals who want to enhance their performance and outperform the competition (Wilens et al., 2008). Eighteen percent of one group of undergraduates reported such use, and another 26 percent of students with attention-deficit/hyperactivity disorder reported overuse of their own medication (Arria et al., 2008); many of these same students also reported extensive marijuana and alcohol use. Medical students, a group who should clearly understand the consequences of nonmedical use of prescription stimulants, are also a high-risk population for illicit stimulant use (Tuttle, Scheurich, & Ranseen, 2010). The topic of using stimulants to avoid sleep or enhance performance has generated much debate, due to ethical as well as medical concerns. What ethical issues arise from the illicit use of prescription medication to improve performance?

(L. Wu, Ringwalt, Weiss, & Blazer, 2009). Large doses are not typically fatal, although there are reports of people who have unwittingly committed suicide while under the influence of hallucinogens.

Dissociative Anesthetics

Case Study

A 20-year-old man, tied in ropes, was brought to the hospital by his four brothers, who explained, "He came home crazy, threw a chair through the window, tore a gas heater off the wall, and ran into the street." Police tried to apprehend him as he stood naked, directing traffic at a busy intersection; his brothers were finally able to subdue him and bring him to the hospital, where he remained agitated, his mood fluctuating between fear and anger. He was unable to walk without staggering and his speech was slurred. He continued to behave in a violent and disorganized manner, with unpredictable bouts of intense anger, suspiciousness, and slurred speech punctuated by intervals of lucid thought. Once calm, he denied behaving violently or acting in an unusual manner; he could not remember how he got to the hospital. His blood and urine tested positive for PCP, a finding that did not surprise his brothers. (Adapted from Spitzer, Gibbon, Skodol, Williams, & First, 1994, pp. 121–122)

Phencyclidine (known as PCP) and ketamine (sometimes referred to as Special K), both highly dangerous and potentially addictive substances, are classified as **dissociative anesthetics**; developed for use as anesthetics in veterinary medicine, they produce a dreamlike detachment in humans. Dextromethorphan (DXM), an active ingredient in many over-the-counter cough suppressants, is another frequently misused dissociative anesthetic.

PCP and ketamine (and a related drug, methoxetamine) are very similar chemically. They have dissociative, stimulant, depressant, amnesic, and hallucinogenic properties. PCP and ketamine are among the most dangerous of the so-called club drugs, a term that comes from the popular use of certain drugs at dance clubs or raves. These drugs cause disconnection, perceptual distortion,

dissociative anesthetic a substance that produces a dreamlike detachment

euphoria, and confusion, as well as delusions, hostility, and violent psychotic behavior, as seen in the case study. The cognitive and memory deficits seen in frequent ketamine users increase with ongoing use. Additionally, frequent users demonstrate depressive, dissociative, and delusional symptoms; delusions can persist even after cessation of ketamine use (C. J. Morgan, Muetzelfeldt, & Curran, 2010).

Health officials are concerned about the increased abuse of DXM, readily available in over-the-counter cold medications and cough suppressants. Despite industry efforts to control misuse of these products, approximately 5 percent of high school teens report using cough and cold medicines to get high (Johnston, Bachman, & O'Malley, 2009). Effects of DXM abuse can include disorientation, confusion, and sensory distortion. The large quantities consumed by those who misuse DXM can result in **hyperthermia** (elevated body temperature), high blood pressure, and heart arrhythmia; as with PCP and ketamine, health consequences are intensified when DXM is combined with alcohol or other drugs.

Did You Know? The designer drug MDPV, marketed as a bath salt, has both stimulant and hallucinogenic properties; an international alert was issued due to the cardiac and neurological danger of the substance.

Source: Coppola & Mondola (2012)

Substances With Mixed Chemical Properties

A number of abused substances have varied effects on the brain and central nervous system. We begin by briefly discussing nicotine, an addictive drug with both depressant and stimulant features. We then discuss cannabis, inhalants, and Ecstasy, as well as the unique dangers involved when substances are combined.

Nicotine Nicotine, the widely used addictive substance found in tobacco, is most commonly associated with cigarette smoking. Nicotine is a stimulant in low doses and a relaxant in higher doses. In 2009, almost 70 million adults and adolescents (28 percent of the population) used tobacco products, primarily cigarettes. As seen in Figure 10.7, nicotine use increases significantly during late adolescence, peaking in the 20s. More males (34 percent) than females (22 percent) use tobacco, particularly noncigarette products. Although full-time college students (27 percent) are less likely to smoke than their age peers (41 percent), smokeless tobacco, used by 13 percent of males attending college, is increasing in popularity (SAMHSA, 2010c). Many current tobacco users find it extremely difficult to quit due to the strength of their nicotine addiction (Boardman et al., 2011).

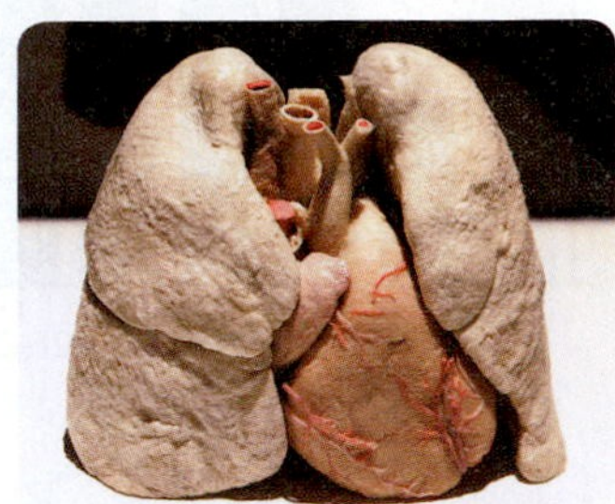

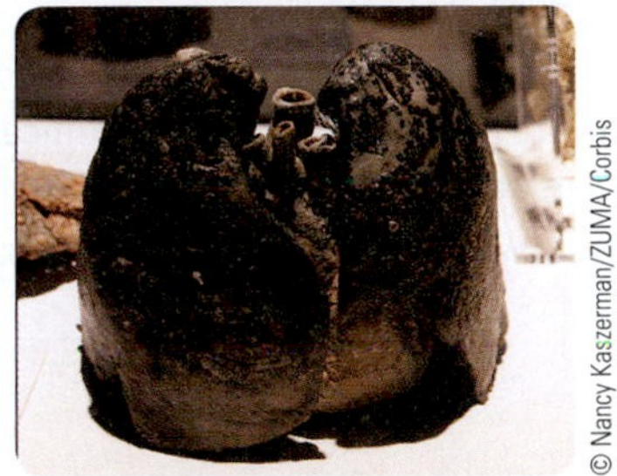

© Nancy Kaszerman/ZUMA/Corbis

Smoking's Effects on the Lungs

A New York City exhibit of real, whole human body specimens provides an actual view of the healthy lungs and heart of a nonsmoker versus the blackened lungs and heart of a smoker. The human body specimens are preserved through a revolutionary technique called polymer preservation. All bodies are from people who died of natural causes.

Nicotine causes both the release of adrenaline, which gives a burst of energy, and the release of dopamine, resulting in feelings of pleasure. A smoker's first cigarette of the day produces the greatest stimulant effect; as the day progresses, euphoric effects decrease and tolerance and withdrawal symptoms increase (Benowitz, 2010). As tolerance develops, cravings occur and more nicotine is needed to experience the same energy, pleasure, and relaxation. Nicotine withdrawal symptoms include difficulty concentrating, restlessness, anxiety, depressed mood, and irritability. Smoking results in health conditions that cause almost 1.5 million deaths annually in the United States (Benowitz, 2010) and is considered the single most preventable cause of premature death (American Cancer Society, 2007).

Cannabis Cannabis is the botanical name for a plant that contains a chemical (delta-9-tetrahydrocannabinol, referred to as THC) that can produce stimulant, depressant, and hallucinogenic effects. Marijuana is derived from the leaves and flowering top of the cannabis plant, whereas hashish, which contains particularly high levels of THC, comes from the pressed resin of the plant. Growing conditions influence the THC content as well as other chemicals in the plant. Concern about the dangers of synthetic marijuana (made from a combination of herbs and chemicals) has resulted in federal efforts to ban chemicals used in its manufacture.

hyperthermia significantly elevated body temperature

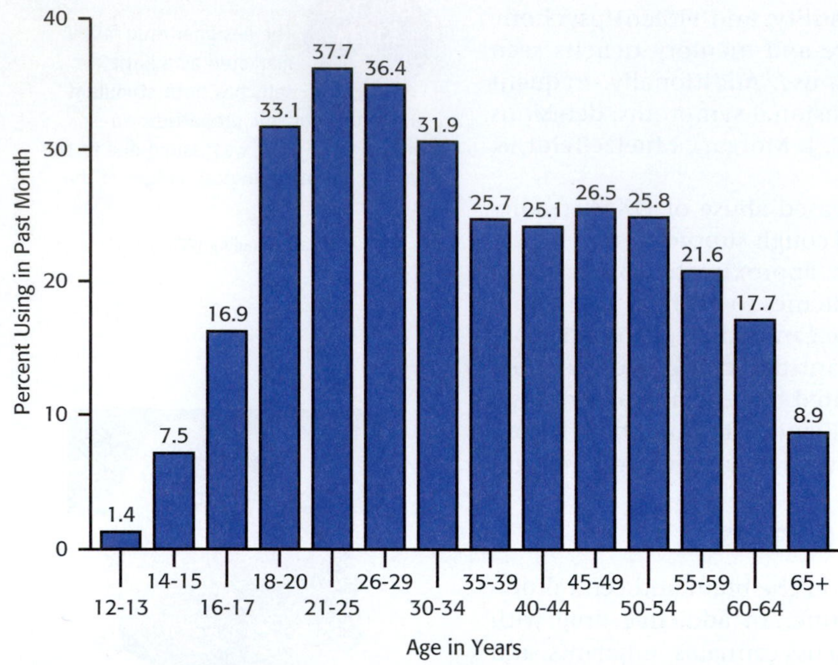

FIGURE 10.7

Past-Month Cigarette Use Among Adolescents and Adults Across Age Groups
Cigarette smoking increases significantly during late adolescence and peaks between ages 21 and 29.

Source: Substance Abuse and Mental Health Services Administration (2010c)

Marijuana is the most commonly used illicit drug both worldwide (United Nations Office on Drugs and Crime, 2010) and in the United States, where almost 17 million adults and adolescents report current use. Males are more likely than females to use marijuana (8.6 percent vs. 4.8 percent). As seen in Figure 10.8, of the 3.1 million adolescents and adults who first used illicit drugs in 2009, 59 percent reported the first drug they experimented with was marijuana (SAMHSA, 2010c). Marijuana use is particularly widespread among adolescents and young adults, with 21 percent of those ages 18–25 reporting current use (SAMHSA, 2010c). The Monitoring the Future annual survey revealed that 27 percent of 10th graders and 33 percent of 12th graders used marijuana in the previous year (Johnston et al., 2009); additionally, daily marijuana use among 8th, 10th, and 12th graders continues to increase (Johnston, O'Malley, Bachman, & Schulenberg, 2012).

Marijuana is the drug most frequently associated with a substance-use disorder diagnosis; more than four million adolescents and adults demonstrated a cannabis-use disorder in 2009 (SAMHSA, 2010c). A unique characteristic of marijuana dependence is a pervasive lack of concern regarding the consequences of drug use (Munsey, 2010). Cannabis is considered a gateway drug associated with later use of other illicit substances, especially among those who begin using during adolescence (SAMHSA, 2010c; Van Gundy, Cesar, & Rebellon, 2010). Cannabis produces feelings of euphoria, tranquility, and passivity combined with mild perceptual and sensory distortions, but can also increase anxiety and depression in females (Fattore & Fratta, 2010). Marijuana use can cause impaired memory, motor coordination, and concentration, as well as hallucinations and short-term psychotic reactions. Some individuals develop chronic psychotic symptoms following cannabis use, especially when use occurs at a young age (Degenhardt et al., 2009). Adolescents who use cannabis have an increased risk of developing schizophrenia (Large, Sharma, Compton, Slade, & Nielssen, 2011).

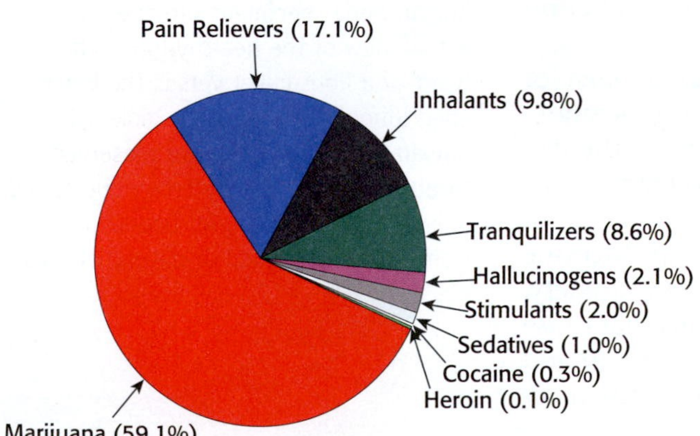

FIGURE 10.8

Drugs Involved in First-Time Illicit Drug Use in 2009
Among the 3.1 million adolescents and adults who first used an illicit drug during 2009, more than half reported their first drug was marijuana, followed by prescription medications—which accounted for over 25 percent of first drug experiences.

Source: Substance Abuse and Mental Health Services Administration (2010c)

The American Psychiatric Association (DSM-5 Work Groups, 2012) recently recognized cannabis withdrawal as a diagnostic category, citing:

- clear patterns of withdrawal, especially for those using cannabis three or more times per week (Copersino et al., 2006; Milin, Manion, Dare, & Walker, 2008);
- strong similarities between cannabis withdrawal and tobacco withdrawal (Budney, Vandrey, Hughes, Thostenson, & Bursac, 2008); and
- a clear link between severity of withdrawal symptoms and both severity of cannabis dependence (T. Chung, Martin, Cornelius, & Clark, 2008; Hasin, Keyes, et al., 2008) and relapse (Cornelius, Chung, Martin, Wood, & Clark, 2008).

Approximately 10 percent of those who use marijuana become dependent on the drug (Koob et al., 2008; Munsey, 2010). Withdrawal symptoms include irritability, anxiety, insomnia, restlessness, and depression as well as distressing physical symptoms such as stomach pain, tremors, sweating, fever, and headache (DSM-5 Work Groups, 2012). Withdrawal symptoms cause many users to return to cannabis use (Agrawal, Pergadia, & Lynskey, 2008) or resort to using other drugs (Copersino et al., 2006).

The risk of having a car accident is doubled after marijuana use; this risk is further increased when the driver has also consumed alcohol.

Source: M. Li et al. (2012)

Long-term use of cannabis is associated with impaired judgment, memory, and concentration. Diminished cognitive functioning involving attention, memory, and learning often lasts for days after marijuana use (Schweinsburg, Brown, & Tapert, 2008). Adolescents who engage in frequent marijuana use have lower academic achievement (Martins & Alexandre, 2009) and impaired attention, learning, and cognitive processing, as well as subtle abnormalities in brain structure (Jacobus, Bava, Cohen-Zion, Mahmood, & Tapert, 2009). These cognitive effects may be more pronounced and persistent in adolescents because their brains are undergoing a critical period of development, thus increasing vulnerability to the effects of drug use (Schweinsburg et al., 2008). Negative outcomes increase when marijuana is combined with other drugs, such as Ecstasy (L. Wu, Parrott, Ringwalt, Yang, & Blazer, 2009).

There is speculation that cannabis use is increasing because legalization efforts in many areas of the country are normalizing use of marijuana. Cannabis use (even when prescribed for medical purposes) remains illegal at the federal level. However, multiple states and municipalities, in an effort to allow law enforcement efforts to focus on other priorities, have decriminalized the possession of small quantities of marijuana. Various states also allow production and distribution of marijuana for legitimate medical use, such as treating side effects from chemotherapy. There has been much debate about the consequences of cannabis use. Some proclaim that cannabis use poses limited physical or psychological risk. However, researchers in the field of substance abuse believe that if marijuana is legalized, more prevalent use will lead to increased prevalence of cannabis-use disorder (Munsey, 2010).

Inhalants

Case Study

"I started when I was eleven. My cousin and his buddies would go down by the creek, and huff, so I would go with them. That's how I learned how to do it."

. . .

"The spray makes me talk slow. Besides the headache I get when I'm not doing it, it makes me slower. The high is good but it makes me slow. When it's wearing off, it makes me like I am stupid. I have to talk slow because the words don't come out."

. . .

"Sometimes I get suicidal. I don't know why. I just do. I just don't give a damn. I just get out in the street in front of cars. Sometimes I remember that I'm doing it and sometimes I don't know it. When I do know it, I don't give a damn. I just want to stop my life because the headaches I get when I stop the spray paint just make me crazy." (Ramos, 1998, pp. 14, 24, 28)

Inhalant abusers become intoxicated from chemical vapors found in a variety of common household products, including solvents (paint removers, gasoline,

Did You Know? Feeling "relaxed" immediately after the first puff of a cigarette was the leading predictor of becoming dependent on cigarettes and being unable to quit. About 29 percent of adolescents interviewed said they had experienced such a feeling after their first cigarette.

Source: DiFranza et al. (2007)

lighter fluid), office supplies (marker pens, correction fluids), aerosol sprays (spray paints, hair spray), and compressed air products (computer and electronics duster sprays). Inhalation of these substances (known as "huffing") is accomplished through sniffing fumes from containers, bags, or balloons; directly inhaling aerosol sprays; or using inhalant-soaked rags. One group of adolescents reported inhaling gasoline (22 percent), permanent markers (15 percent), computer cleaning spray (15 percent), and spray paint (12 percent; M. O. Howard, Balster, Cottler, Wu, & Vaughn, 2008).

Inhalant use is most common amongst those ages 12–17 (SAMHSA, 2010c). The use of inhalants by children and adolescents is considered a silent epidemic. In the 2009 Monitoring the Future survey, lifetime use of inhalants was reported by 15 percent of 8th graders, 12 percent of 10th graders, and 10 percent of 12th graders (Johnston, O'Malley, Bachman, & Schulenberg, 2010b). Experimental use of inhalants in younger adolescents typically occurs before experimentation with tobacco or alcohol. Fortunately, experimentation with inhalants does not appear to be a gateway to more serious drug use, although those who chronically abuse inhalants often initiate marijuana and cocaine use. Although boys and girls experiment about equally with inhalants, chronic users are more likely to be male. Most inhalant users are white, although Native Americans and low-income Latino/Hispanic Americans are increasing rates of use (Ding, Chang, & Southerland, 2009).

The intoxicating effects of inhalants are brief, resulting in repeated huffing to extend intoxication. The immediate effects of inhalants vary depending on the chemicals involved; typical effects include impaired coordination and judgment, euphoria, dizziness, and slurred speech. Hypoxia (oxygen deprivation) results in both acute and persistent cognitive deficits such as severe memory impairment and slow information processing. Any episode of inhalant use, even in first-time users, can result in stroke, acute respiratory distress, or sudden heart failure (referred to as "sudden sniffing death"). Fatal outcome is most common with compressed air products, aerosol sprays, air fresheners, butane, propane, and nitrous oxide (M. T. Hall, Edwards, & Howard, 2010; Marsolek, White, & Litovitz, 2010).

Inhalant use produces a number of emotional and interpersonal difficulties, including paranoid thinking and suicidal ideation. In one sample of inhalant abusers, 67 percent had contemplated suicide and 20 percent had attempted suicide (M. O. Howard, Perron, Sacco, et al., 2010). Additionally, chronic inhalant abuse is associated with high levels of anxiety and depression as well as antisocial behavior and interpersonal violence (M. O. Howard, Balster, et al., 2008; Howard, Perron, Vaughn, Bender, & Garland, 2010; Perron & Howard, 2009).

Ecstasy Ecstasy (methylenedioxymethamphetamine, or MDMA) has both stimulant and hallucinogenic properties. Between 2008 and 2009, there was a significant increase in first-time Ecstasy use, with an estimated 1.1 million new users (SAMHSA, 2010c); use has increased significantly among high school students (Johnston, O'Malley, Bachman, & Schulenberg, 2010b). Short-term effects of Ecstasy, including euphoria, mild sensory and cognitive distortion, and feelings of intimacy and well-being, are often followed by intense depression. Users frequently experience hyperthermia or the need to suck on lollipops or pacifiers to counteract involuntary jaw spasms and teeth clenching.

Ecstasy appears to have unique chemical properties that accelerate the development of physiological dependence, even among those who do not use it regularly (Bruno et al., 2009). In fact, characteristics of hallucinogen dependence were seen in almost 12 percent of one sample of occasional Ecstasy users (L. Wu, Ringwalt, Mannelli, & Patkar, 2008). In another study, 59 percent of Ecstasy users met the criteria for dependence, with many reporting withdrawal symptoms and continued use despite physical or psychological problems (Cottler, Leung, & Abdallah, 2009). Among another sample of adolescent Ecstasy users, 39 percent reported symptoms of considerable dependence (L.Wu, Ringwalt, Weiss, et al., 2009). Those withdrawing from Ecstasy report feeling depressed, irritable, and unsociable. Ecstasy has been linked to long-lasting damage in brain areas critical for thought and memory. Ecstasy use reduces the ability to complete challenging cognitive tasks, even with multiple practice opportunities (J. Brown, McKone, & Ward, 2010). Thus, it is not surprising that Ecstasy use has been strongly associated with low academic achievement in adolescents (Martins & Alexandre, 2009).

A review of 82 cases in which Ecstasy was a cause of death revealed the following: 83 percent of the decedents were male; the median age was 26; Ecstasy was the sole cause of death in 23 percent of the cases; combined drug toxicity caused 59 percent of deaths; and significant cardiovascular changes contributed to the remaining deaths. Surprisingly, despite the youth of the decedents, *atherosclerosis* (hardening of the arteries, a condition typically associated with aging) was found in 58 percent of decedents, with 23 percent demonstrating moderate to severe atherosclerosis. This effect, typically seen in cocaine and methamphetamine users, may relate to the stimulant properties of Ecstasy (S. Kaye, Darke, & Duflou, 2009).

Ecstasy is considered a club drug because it is often used in a club or party context. Some of the substances we have already discussed (PCP, ketamine, Rohypnol) are also considered club drugs. Additionally, cocaine is used within the club drug culture. In one large sample of individuals using drugs in a club context, 90 percent reported cocaine use; in fact, 59 percent demonstrated cocaine dependence (Parsons, Grov, & Kelly, 2009). Another common club drug with high addictive potential is GHB (gamma hydroxybutyrate), a substance used primarily by males because of its purported strength-enhancing properties. GHB, a central nervous system depressant with strong sedative effects, is particularly dangerous when combined with alcohol.

Club drugs are often used to induce energy and excitement, reduce inhibitions, and create feelings of well-being and connection with others, as well as magnify the effects of the high-energy events known as raves. Unfortunately, energy exertion in a warm environment intensifies harmful side effects, particularly hyperthermia and dehydration. Although positive effects may last for hours, they are typically followed by a crash—lethargy, low motivation, and fatigue. Extreme depression and anxiety (as well as acute physical symptoms due to dehydration or changes in blood pressure and heart rhythm) can occur, particularly when drugs are combined or taken with alcohol.

Combining Multiple Substances

Case Study

Kelly M., age 17, lived with her divorced mother. Kelly was hospitalized after her mother found her unconscious from an overdose of tranquilizers; her blood alcohol level was 0.15. The overdose was apparently accidental. Kelly had regularly used tranquilizers for over a year to help her relax and relieve her stress. Arguments with her mother would precipitate heavy use of the drugs. Eventually she found she needed more of the pills to relax, sometimes stealing money to buy them from classmates. She sometimes used alcohol as a substitute for or in combination with the tranquilizers. Her mother reported that she had no knowledge of her daughter's drug or alcohol use, although she had noticed that Kelly was increasingly isolated and sleepy. Hospital personnel informed Kelly of the dangers of sedatives, especially when combined with alcohol, and recommended she begin drug treatment.

The practice of combining substances can be extremely dangerous. Chemicals taken simultaneously may exhibit a **synergistic effect**, interacting to multiply one another's effects. For example, when tranquilizers are combined with alcohol, both depress the central nervous system, and the synergistic effect can result in respiratory distress or even death. Furthermore, some substances (such as alcohol) may reduce judgment, resulting in excessive (or lethal) use of other substances. Equally dangerous is the use of one drug to counteract the effects of another substance, such as taking stimulants to feel alert and later taking a sleeping pill to counteract insomnia from the stimulant.

Of particular concern is multiple drug use involving Ecstasy. One group of rave attendees taking Ecstasy tested positive for an average of four other drugs; those who illicitly manufacture drugs such as Ecstasy often adulterate them with other substances, a factor that may have affected the findings (D. L. Black et al., 2009). Consistent with the forensic toxicology findings we previously discussed regarding deaths associated with Ecstasy, polysubstance use was implicated in the majority of 49 deaths associated with GHB; the mean age was 26 years for male decedents and 21 years for females (Kugelberg, Holmgren, Eklund, & Jones, 2010). Youth advocates continue to focus on educating the public about the harmful effects of polysubstance use.

Concern about premixed, flavored alcoholic energy drinks that combine alcohol and high levels of caffeine led to a U.S. Food and Drug Administration ban on the products and a warning that "the combination of caffeine and alcohol . . . poses a public health concern" because high levels of caffeine combined with alcohol mask intoxication cues (2010b). Additionally, the diuretic effect of using alcohol and caffeine together causes dehydration, which increases intoxication. Research suggesting that college students who combine alcohol and caffeine have more heavy-drinking episodes, drunkenness, and alcohol-related consequences (sexual assault, physical injury, driving while intoxicated) lends validity to this concern (M. C. O'Brien, McCoy, Rhodes, Wagoner, & Wolfson, 2008).

CHECKPOINT REVIEW

1. Name the major categories of abused substances.
2. Describe the short-term and long-term effects of the various substances discussed.
3. Why is polysubstance use so dangerous?

Etiology of Substance-Use Disorders

Why do people abuse substances, despite knowing that the alcohol and drug abuse can have devastating consequences? In general, the progression from initial substance use to substance abuse follows a typical sequence (H. J. Walter, 2001). First, an individual decides to experiment with alcohol or drugs—perhaps to satisfy curiosity, enhance self-confidence, rebel against authorities, imitate others, or conform to social pressure. Second, the substance begins to serve an important purpose (such as reducing anxiety, producing feelings of pleasure, or enhancing social relationships) and so consumption continues. Third, brain chemistry becomes altered from chronic use. In many cases, physiological dependency develops, resulting in withdrawal symptoms and craving for the substance; it also becomes difficult to experience pleasure without the substance. Fourth, lifestyle changes occur due to chronic substance use. These changes may include loss of interest in previous

synergistic effect the result of chemicals (or substances) interacting to multiply one another's effects

activities and social relationships and preoccupation with opportunities to use the substance (Figure 10.9). Consistent with the multipath model, in all four phases, biological, psychological, social, and sociocultural influences are involved (Figure 10.10).

Psychological Dimension

Coping with psychological stress and emotional symptoms appears to be a major motive for substance use. Of the 20 million adults with a substance-use disorder in 2010, 45 percent had a concurrent psychiatric disorder. The use of illicit drugs is much higher among individuals with mental illness (26 percent) than among those without such difficulties (12 percent; SAMHSA, 2012). Individuals with psychiatric symptoms often use drugs and alcohol to self-medicate and compensate for emotions such as depression and anxiety. Stress is thought to play an important role in marijuana use (C. L. Fox, Towe, Stephens, Walker, & Roffman, 2011) and the development of alcoholism (Anthenelli, 2010). Individuals with post-traumatic stress disorder report using drugs and alcohol to cope with distressing symptoms (Leeies, Pagura, Sareen, & Bolton, 2010). In one study of individuals participating in drug treatment, those with the most severe post-traumatic stress disorder symptoms—especially hyperarousal and re-experiencing the trauma—reported the greatest dependence on marijuana, supporting the self-medication hypothesis (Villagonzalo et al., 2011). Those who use heroin have been noted to lack coping strategies, whereas those who use marijuana deal with stress by detaching and distancing themselves from others (Schindler, Thomasius, Petersen, & Sack, 2009).

Internalizing disorders such as depression and anxiety can precede substance use and abuse (O'Neil, Conner, & Kendall, 2011) or occur concurrently. In fact, anxiety and depressive symptoms that begin in early childhood and persist into adulthood appear to increase risk of alcohol abuse, particularly when accompanied by social withdrawal (Hussong, Jones, Stein, Baucom, & Boeding, 2011). For example, 24 percent of people who called a monitored smoking "quitline" had major depression and 17 percent had symptoms of mild depression (Hebert, Cummins, Hernández, Tedeschi, & Zhu, 2011). Anxiety diagnoses are also common among smokers seeking treatment (M. E. Piper, Cook, Schlam, Jorenby, & Baker, 2010). Almost half of a large sample of individuals who were dependent on methamphetamine had a concurrent mental illness, most commonly mood or anxiety disorders; those with psychiatric difficulties had more severe drug use and greater functional impairment (Glasner-Edwards et al., 2010).

Adolescent girls have an increased risk of nonmedical use of prescription medications (Johnston, O'Malley, et al., 2010b) including stimulants to lose weight and pain medications to deal with stress and depression. Similarly, adolescent girls with eating disorders often use nicotine and stimulants to suppress appetite, and

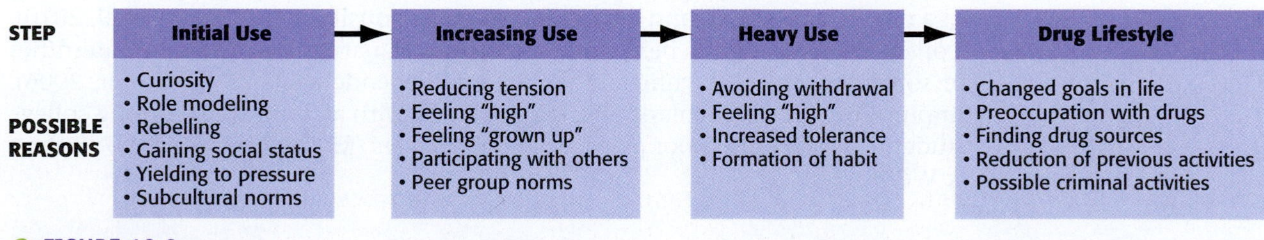

STEP
Initial Use
Increasing Use
Heavy Use
Drug Lifestyle
POSSIBLE REASONS
• Curiosity
• Role modeling
• Rebelling
• Gaining social status
• Yielding to pressure
• Subcultural norms
• Reducing tension
• Feeling "high"
• Feeling "grown up"
• Participating with others
• Peer group norms
• Avoiding withdrawal
• Feeling "high"
• Increased tolerance
• Formation of habit
• Changed goals in life
• Preoccupation with drugs
• Finding drug sources
• Reduction of previous activities
• Possible criminal activities

FIGURE 10.9

Typical Progression Toward Drug Abuse or Dependence

The progression from initial substance use to substance abuse typically begins with curiosity about a drug's effects and casual experimentation.

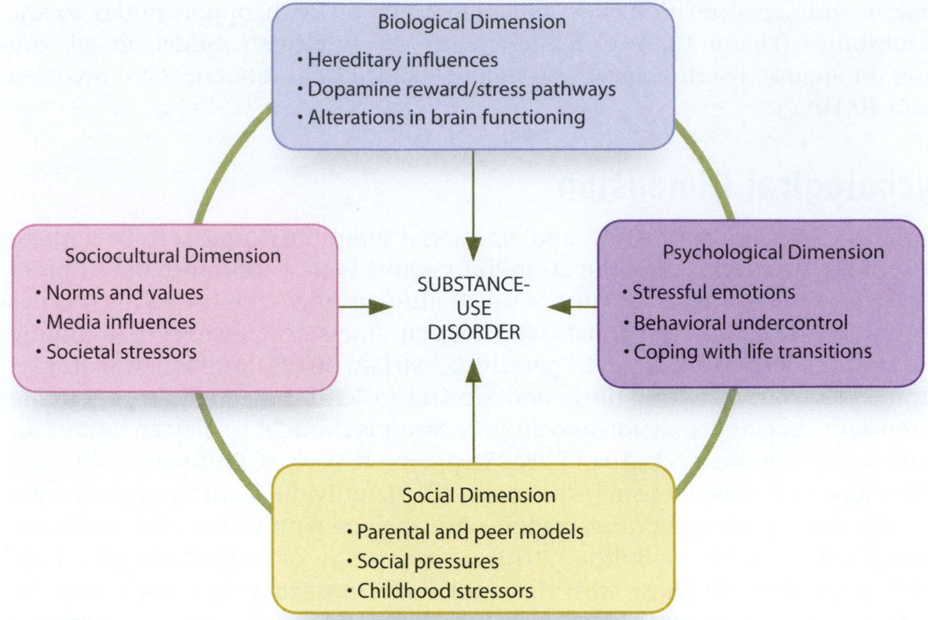

FIGURE 10.10

Multipath Model of Substance-Use Disorders

The dimensions interact with one another and combine in different ways to result in a substance-use disorder.

Copyright © Cengage Learning 2013

depressants to cope with bulimic urges (J. H. Baker, Mitchell, Neale, & Kendler, 2010). Adolescent girls also report using substances to help "forget troubles" or "deal with problems at home" (Partnership for a Drug-Free America & MetLife Foundation [PFDFA/MET], 2010).

The personality characteristic of **behavioral undercontrol**, associated with rebelliousness, novelty seeking, risk taking, and impulsivity, increases risk of substance use and abuse. Individuals with these traits are more likely to experiment with substances and continue use because they find the effects rewarding and exciting (Beseler et al., 2012). An investigation of possible genetic links between substance abuse and impulsivity revealed that siblings of people who used stimulants chronically tended to be highly impulsive, suggesting that impulsivity may be a behavioral *endophenotype* that increases risk for stimulant dependence (Ersche, Turton, Pradhan, Bullmore, & Robbins, 2010). Similarly, researchers have linked a propensity to risk taking with neurological responses (decreased activation of the ventral striatum during reward anticipation) associated with substance abuse (S. Schneider et al., 2012).

What psychological factors might account for drug and alcohol use in college students? Undergraduates use drugs and alcohol to cope with anxiety and depression (V. V. Grant, Stewart, O'Connor, Blackwell, & Conrod, 2007); academic, social, and financial pressures; and being away from home for the first time, living in a new environment, and having increased responsibility (C. Sloane et al, 2010). College students high in behavioral undercontrol, particularly those in fraternities or sororities, are most vulnerable to alcohol dependence (Grekin & Sher, 2006). Impulsivity has a particularly strong association with alcohol abuse among college students who are also poor planners and risk takers (Mackillop et al., 2007; Siebert & Wilke, 2007).

Social Dimension

behavioral undercontrol personality trait associated with rebelliousness, novelty seeking, risk taking, and impulsivity

The influence of social factors on substance abuse varies across the life span, exerting different effects at different ages (K. J. Sher, Dick, et al., 2010). Victimization and stressful events in childhood, especially child neglect, are strongly associated with substance use later in life, especially for those with multiple victimization experiences (H. T. McCabe, Wilsnack, West, & Boyd, 2010). Many individuals receiving residential treatment for substance abuse and mental health issues report childhood trauma (N. S. Wu, Schairer, Dellor, & Grella, 2010). Stress during adolescence can also influence substance use. Inner-city adolescents exposed to environmental stressors were more likely than those living in less stressful environments to use substances (J. A. Epstein, Banga, & Botvina, 2007). Adolescents with parents who were alcoholic reported drinking heavily and drinking alone, with the goal of becoming intoxicated in order to forget their problems (Chalder, Elgar, & Bennett, 2006).

As you might expect, adolescence and early adulthood are particularly vulnerable periods with respect to social influences on substance use, even for those without other life stressors. A variety of social factors affect decisions to drink alcohol or experiment with drugs, including pressure from peers, a wish to fit in socially or enhance social interactions, attempts to rebel and challenge authority, friendships with peers who have limited parental supervision, a desire to assert independence or escape from societal or parental pressures for achievement, and a desire to have fun or take risks. Adolescent boys often report that drugs help them "relax socially" and "have more fun at parties" (PFDFA/MET, 2010). Association with friends who get drunk increases high-risk drinking (Siebert & Wilke, 2007). Friends with a high social status can exert a particularly strong influence with respect to substance use (J. P. Allen, Chango, Szwedo, Schad, & Marston, 2012).

Family attitudes and behaviors about drinking and drugs (including the use of prescription medication) affect adolescents' likelihood of experimenting with substances. Additionally, adolescents who receive less parental monitoring have increased substance use, as do those whose parents feel unable to enforce rules or influence decisions related to substance use and those whose parents believe cultural myths such as "all adolescents experiment" or "it's okay to have teens drink at home" (K. D. Wagner et al., 2010).

College presents its own unique set of sociocultural influences. The first year of college is a particularly vulnerable transitional period (Grekin & Sher, 2006), due to abrupt changes in levels of parental supervision, increased competition and pressure for academic achievement, and exposure to "wet environments" (social or residential settings with easy access to low-cost alcohol) and heavy drinking (Weitzman, Nelson, & Wechsler, 2003). Unofficial social events that promote partying and peers who minimize the consequences of drinking contribute to college drinking (C. M. Lee, Geisner, Patrick, & Neighbors, 2010; Paschall & Saltz, 2007). Social media may play a role in increasing the acceptability and frequency of alcohol use in college: Recent research shows that 85 percent of male undergraduates in one sample had referenced alcohol in their Facebook postings (Egan & Moreno, 2011). Additionally, first-year college students overestimate the social acceptability of drinking and the quantity of alcohol consumed by peers (LaBrie, Hummer, Grant, & Lac, 2010). In one study, 91 percent of respondents estimated that their peers drank more than themselves (Broadwater, Curtin, Martz, & Zrull, 2006). Negative events associated with drinking—such as sexual assault, embarrassment over behavior while intoxicated, and poor academic performance—can exacerbate the cycle of college drinking or drug use (Dams-O'Conner, Martens, & Anderson, 2006).

Eating disorders and associated risks, such as stimulant use for appetite control, are also encountered in college. Some students skip meals and cut calories so they can drink more or get drunk faster. "Drunkorexia" is a term coined by the media in reference to a trend among college women—self-imposed starvation in order to compensate for high-caloric binge drinking. This practice not only hastens intoxication but stresses the body and increases risk of dehydration, blackouts, seizures, or cardiac arrest. In one sample of first-year college students, 15 percent reported fasting before drinking; of this subgroup, 70 percent were female. The restriction of food for weight control was endorsed by only 39 percent of those who limited food intake, whereas 69 percent reported a desire to hasten intoxication (C. Sloane et al, , 2010).

Sociocultural Dimension

Substance use varies according to sociocultural factors such as gender, age, socioeconomic status, ethnicity, religion, and nationality. Looking at alcohol use, we know that males and young adults consume more alcohol than females and older adults, respectively. Interestingly, alcohol consumption tends to increase with socioeconomic status, although alcoholism is more frequent in the middle socioeconomic classes (SAMHSA, 2007). In terms of religious affiliation, heavier drinking is found among Catholics than among Protestants or Jews.

As we have seen from prevalence data, certain substances—alcohol, nicotine, and, to some extent, marijuana and prescription drugs—are an accepted part of U.S. culture. It is common to see marketing messages regarding tobacco, alcohol, and prescription drug products, as well as depictions of these products in songs, movies, television, and social media. Exposure to positive drug and alcohol information on the Internet is increasing, whereas warnings from parents, schools, and antidrug advertising are decreasing (PFDFA/MET, 2010). Public debate regarding legalization of marijuana appears to be normalizing its social acceptability, with resultant increases in use (Johnston, O'Malley, et al., 2010b). Factors such as perceived prevalence of smoking, exposure to smokers, and exposure to tobacco advertising are all associated with smoking in young adults (Hanewinkel, Isensee, Sargent, & Morgenstern, 2011; Ling, Neilands, & Glantz, 2009). Similarly, exposure to episodes of smoking in movies increases risk of current smoking (Song, Ling, Neilands, & Glantz, 2007), and exposure to movies depicting alcohol use is associated with increased drinking (Stoolmiller, Wills, et al., 2012).

The data suggest that both drug and alcohol use are gaining acceptance among adolescents and are becoming a normative part of adolescent culture. Teen reports of declining concern about personal risk from substance use (Johnston, O'Malley, et al., 2010a) and increasing peer approval for getting high have been linked to increased use of substances associated with social situations and party environments (PFDFA/MET, 2010). Adolescents whose peer group lacks school commitment and connectedness are particularly prone to substance use (Latimer & Zur, 2010). Not having a high school diploma and not having a job are strong predictors of later substance use (Van Gundy et al., 2010).

As we have discussed, use and abuse of alcohol and illicit drugs varies both within and between ethnic groups. Cultural values affect not only the substances used and amount consumed but also the cultural tolerance of substance abuse. African Americans adolescents show lower rates of substance use than whites and Latino/Hispanic Americans; in the 8th grade, Latino/Hispanic Americans have the highest prevalence of use in all drug categories except stimulants, and they have the highest levels of crack and methamphetamine use in the 12th grade (Johnston, O'Malley, et al., 2010a). A recent study evaluating racial differences in adolescent substance use concluded that among middle school students, Latino/Hispanic Americans are more likely to smoke cigarettes, consume alcohol, and use marijuana compared to other racial groups, whereas Asian American middle-school students were least likely to engage in these activities. Latino/Hispanic American students reported less concern about potential negative consequences of substance use and less confidence using refusal skills. Asian American students reported that few of their friends and siblings used substances and that they wanted to respect parental expectations regarding substance use (Shih, Miles, Tucker, Zhou, & D'Amico, 2010).

Additional factors affecting variability among ethnic groups include racial discrimination; increased availability of alcohol in urban areas with high ethnic populations; decreased community safety; social and economic disadvantage, including limited job opportunities and inadequate health care; and stress related to acculturation, particularly for Latino/Hispanic Americans (Chartier & Caetano, 2010). Interviews conducted within the Filipino American community revealed a connection between perceptions of unfair treatment and illicit drug use and alcohol dependence (Gee, Delva, & Takeuchi, 2007). Similarly, the experience of unfair treatment and racial discrimination among Asian Americans with low ethnic identification increased the chances of alcohol dependence (Chae et al., 2008). African American adolescents who perceived racial discrimination reported subsequent willingness to use drugs to cope with their feelings of anger (F. Gibbons et al., 2010). Gay, lesbian, and transgender youth and adults, also targets for discrimination, have increased risk for substance use and abuse (S. E. McCabe, Hughes, Bostwick, West, & Boyd, 2009), especially when there is a history of childhood abuse or victimization (H. T. McCabe et al., 2010).

Events impacting a society, such as a recession, can increase substance use as individuals cope with unemployment or other financial stressors at a time when public health resources devoted to prevention and treatment are reduced. Although psychological, social, and sociocultural influences have a pronounced effect on both the initiation and the continuation of substance use, the question remains: Why are some individuals able to use drugs or alcohol in moderation, whereas others succumb to heavy use and addiction? Biological explanations provide considerable insight into this issue, as we see in the following section.

Biological Dimension

Biological factors affect the development of substance-use disorders in various ways. First, sex differences in the physiological effects of substances are frequently observed. Investigation into the neurobiological basis of sex differences in drug dependence, craving, and relapse has implicated the effects of hormonal influence on women's susceptibility to the reinforcing effects of addictive substances (M. E. Roth, Cosgrov, & Carroll, 2004; Fattore, Fadda, & Fratta, 2009). Additionally, physiological differences may influence the more rapid progression to alcoholism seen in females (Fattore & Fratta, 2010). Women tend to weigh less, have more fat tissue and less muscle mass, produce fewer enzymes to metabolize alcohol, possess less total body fluid to dilute alcohol in the blood, and be more likely to limit food intake, which can further increase toxicity from alcohol (C. Sloane et al., 2010). Additionally, sex differences in physiological reactions to stress (combined with differential exposure to traumatic life events) may help explain the more severe course of alcoholism in women (Anthenelli, 2010).

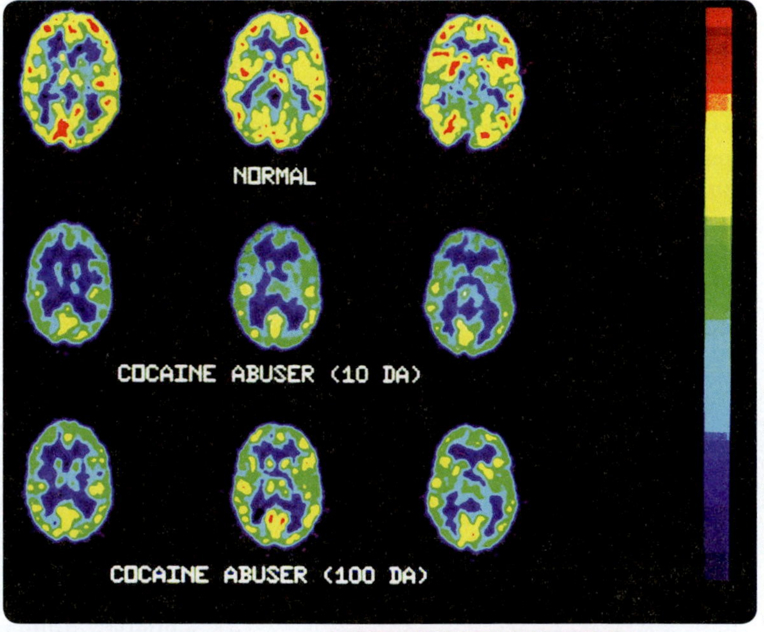

Brookhaven National Laboratory/Photo Researchers, Inc.

Effects of Cocaine Use

These positron emission tomography scan images compare the cerebral metabolic activity of a control subject (top row) with those of a person who formerly abused cocaine at 10 days after discontinuing the substance (middle row) and after 100 days of abstinence (bottom row). Red and yellow areas reveal efficient brain activity, whereas blue regions indicate minimal brain activity. As you can see, after 100 days of abstinence, brain activity is improved but remains far from normal.

As we have discussed, substance abuse changes brain chemistry and structure (Kalivas & O'Brien, 2008). Chronic substance use alters the normal dopamine reward and stress pathways—the brain is flooded with far more dopamine than is secreted normally. Feelings of euphoria or pleasure ensue. Eventually, substance use crowds out other pleasures and turns into an all-consuming, compulsive desire. As addiction develops, the chronic flooding of dopamine eventually results in the depletion of it and other neurotransmitters involved in stress and reward (Brower, 2006). Consequently, drugs and alcohol (as well as other normally pleasurable activities) bring limited pleasure. Simultaneously, drug tolerance develops and more and more of the substance is needed (Nestler & Malenka, 2004).

Furthermore, substance-induced changes in the area of the brain known as the frontal cortex result in impaired judgment and decision making. When cravings occur, compulsive drug-seeking behavior ensues without consideration of negative consequences (Crews & Boettiger, 2009). Adolescence through early adulthood is a critical

© Kurt Krieger/Corbis

Family Ties

Drew Barrymore entered a rehabilitation program at the age of 13 to deal with her addiction to drugs and alcohol. Although it is difficult to separate environmental and genetic influences in cases of alcohol abuse, both were likely operating in Barrymore's case. Not only did she experience the stress of young stardom, but she also had a family history of alcohol abuse—her grandfather drank himself to death and her father abused alcohol and drugs.

period for nuanced development of the frontal cortex; drug or alcohol use affecting this process can result in lifelong disruptions in reasoning, goal setting, and impulse control, which can then lead to further substance abuse (Crews, He, & Hodge, 2007).

Genetic factors also play an important role in the development of substance abuse. For example, there is strong evidence that alcoholism runs in families based on twin studies demonstrating higher rates of alcoholism among identical twins compared to fraternal twins (Agrawal & Lynskey, 2008), as well as analyses of family patterns of alcoholism (Gelernter & Kranzler, 2009). It is estimated that genetics accounts for approximately 50–60 percent of the risk of developing alcoholism (Foroud, Edenberg, & Crabbe, 2010). However, because family members usually share both genetic and environmental influences, researchers face the challenge of somehow separating the contributions of these two sets of factors (K. J. Sher, Dick, 2010). Kendler and Prescott (2006), using data from more than 4,500 pairs of identical and fraternal twins to isolate genetic and environmental factors involved in substance abuse, concluded the following:

- Genetic factors accounted for 56 percent of the risk of alcohol dependence and 55 percent of the risk of nicotine dependence.
- Genetic factors accounted for 75 percent of the risk of illicit drug abuse, with cannabis dependence having the strongest genetic risk.

Although collective findings support the importance of heredity in the etiology of substance use, the task of identifying the specific genes involved is complex (Wall, Shea, Luczak, Cook, & Carr, 2005). Genetic influences on alcohol dependence include the protective effects of variations in genes that produce the cleanup enzyme ALDH (Foroud et al., 2010). In individuals whose genetic makeup causes impaired production of ALDH, toxins from metabolized alcohol accumulate and cause unpleasant physical reactions; this naturally occurring effect makes alcohol consumption aversive and thus reduces risk of alcoholism (Eng, Luczak, & Wall, 2007). The protective effects of ALDH variations are quite strong—up to a sevenfold lowered risk in some Asian populations (Foroud et al., 2010). Similar protective genetic variations are seen in certain regions of the Middle East and Africa.

Overall, substance-use disorders are genetically influenced in the following manner:

- Genes affect individual responses to specific drugs (one person may have susceptibility to alcoholism, whereas another has genetic risk of marijuana dependence).
- Genetic variations influence the degree of pleasure (or aversion) experienced during initial drug use as well as the negative and positive effects of ongoing drug use.
- Genetics influences personality traits that increase risk, including impulsivity, risk taking, and novelty seeking, as well as protective characteristics such as self-control (Kendler & Prescott, 2006).

In summary, it is clear that genetic predispositions, as well as physiological changes that result from heavy or chronic substance exposure, influence susceptibility to addiction. However, there are many factors beyond physiological effects that contribute to the development and maintenance of substance abuse (Enoch, 2012). The psychological, social, and sociocultural factors previously discussed provide substantial insight into forces involved in decisions to initiate substance use as well as factors affecting continued use.

CHECKPOINT REVIEW

1. Describe how psychological, social, and sociocultural factors influence both substance use and abuse.
2. Describe how biological factors influence the addiction process.

FOCUS ON RESILIENCE

Curbing the Tide of Substance Abuse

Substance-use disorders are unique among mental disorders because they are completely preventable—refraining from substance use *guarantees* that a substance-use disorder will not occur. In fact, some individuals with parents who compulsively smoke or abuse alcohol or illicit drugs decide to never tempt fate—to never use substances—thus halting familial patterns of addiction (M. R. Pearson, D'Lima, & Kelley, 2011). Unfortunately, because substance abuse is a complex issue affected by a variety of processes operating over time, the solution is often not so simple (Masten, Faden, Zucker, & Spear, 2008).

We know that each day in the United States, approximately 8,500 adolescents or adults experiment with illicit drugs for the first time (SAMHSA, 2010a). Thus, a key to developing resilience is providing youth with the tools to refrain from such experimentation. Programs developed to increase resilience (and prevent substance use and abuse) often target critical periods of change—especially transitions during adolescence and early adulthood, when physiological addiction processes proceed most rapidly. Because youth develop within the broader context of family, school, community, and cultural groups, programs supporting healthy development typically aim at enhancing protective factors in a variety of areas (M. E. O'Connell, Boat, & Warner, 2009; Hawkins et al., 2012; C. Jackson, Geddes, Haw, & Frank, 2012), including:

- Family—encouraging parents to build strong family relationships; articulate expected behavior (including abstinence from substance use); monitor activities and friendships; and interact with schools and other institutions
- Individual assets—helping youth develop a positive identity, understand the importance of education, acquire positive values, and build strong social competencies (especially self-control, self-efficacy, and assertiveness)
- Schools—providing students with effective learning opportunities; interactive prevention education regarding abused substances and how substance-use disorders develop (including peer and media influences); and skills for making positive decisions resisting peer pressure
- Community connections—developing community activities that build connection and assist youth to develop a sense of purpose and commitment beyond the self

Prevention and early intervention efforts are crucial if we hope to reduce the prevalence of substance abuse, especially among individuals with multiple risk factors. Interventions to prevent early experimentation with substances can have far-reaching consequences, not only in terms of decreasing the likelihood of substance abuse but also in terms of preventing detrimental effects on the academic and social competence of youth (Masten et al., 2008).

PhotoDisc

Methods and Effectiveness of Treatment for Substance-Use Disorders

Half of all the adults and older adolescents in the United States know someone recovering from addiction to alcohol, illicit drugs, or prescription drugs (SAMHSA, 2008). However, there is a huge disparity between the estimated 23.5 million who need substance-use treatment and the 2.6 million who receive treatment; more than one million youth ages 12–17 need drug treatment, with an additional 1.2 million in need of alcohol treatment (SAMHSA, 2010c). Many who recognize that they have a serious substance-abuse problem are unable to initiate treatment; cost is often a significant barrier (Figure 10.11). As seen in Figure 10.12, treatment is most frequently sought for alcohol abuse (2.9 million), followed by cannabis abuse (1.2 million).

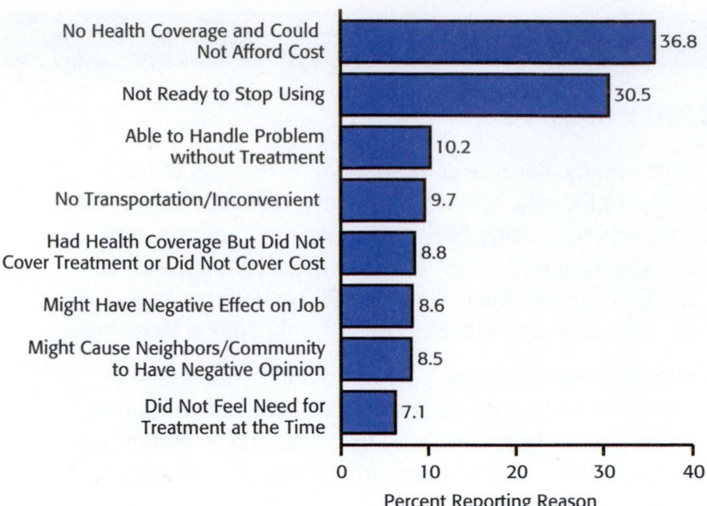

FIGURE 10.11

Reasons Given for Not Receiving Substance-Use Treatment
Among individuals with a substance-abuse problem who indicated that they would like to receive needed treatment, the most prevalent reason given for not initiating treatment was lack of health care coverage and inability to afford treatment.
Source: SAMHSA (2010c)

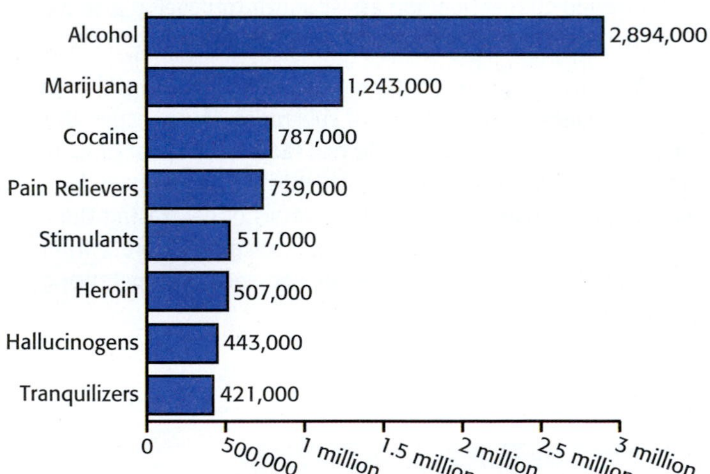

FIGURE 10.12

Substances for Which Treatment Was Received
In 2009, U.S. Americans sought treatment most frequently for alcohol abuse (2.9 million), followed by cannabis use (1.2 million).
Source: SAMHSA (2010c)

Treatment and supportive intervention take place in a variety of settings, including self-help groups, mental health clinics, and inpatient or outpatient drug and alcohol treatment centers. Self-help group meetings are the most common means of substance-abuse intervention in the United States, with almost 2.5 million individuals participating in groups like Alcoholics Anonymous (AA) and Narcotics Anonymous (SAMHSA, 2010c). Self-help groups commonly use fellowship and spiritual awareness to support abstinence. These groups provide a supportive approach to addiction rather than specialized treatment. A quality review of traditional drug and alcohol treatment programs produced findings that the authors called "unambiguous and disturbing." Not only were the majority of programs not implementing evidence-based care, but many programs relied on a model of treatment that has received minimal research support—AA or Narcotics Anonymous program attendance combined with lectures and group counseling provided by individuals recovering from addiction (McLellan & Meyers, 2004). This reliance on poorly trained staff using outdated methods rather than interventions derived from medical and psychological addiction research greatly jeopardizes treatment outcome (Willenbring, 2010). Additionally, these models do not provide the integrated care necessary for those with underlying emotional difficulties (Kuehn, 2010).

Effective treatment requires strategies and pharmaceutical interventions that are research based (Haaga, McCrady, & Lebow, 2006). In general, broad-spectrum interventions that include different treatment modalities are considered more effective than treatment that is confined to a single modality. Proponents of multimodal approaches recognize that no single kind of treatment is likely to be totally effective and that successful treatment outcomes require major life changes.

Goals of treatment include achieving sustained abstinence, maintaining a drug-free lifestyle, and functioning productively in family, work, and other environments. This requires changing habits, minimizing thoughts of drugs and drug-related social activities, and learning to cope with daily activities and stressors without the use of drugs. Therefore, effective treatment helps create a lifestyle that supports abstinence as well as develops a sense of self-efficacy and well-being with respect to educational, career, and leisure activities. Additionally, because drugs so often disrupt multiple aspects of an individual's life, there is a need to rebuild family, friend, and work relationships.

Most alcohol and drug treatment programs have two phases: first, removal of the abusive substance, and second, long-term maintenance without it. In the first phase, called **detoxification**, the user is immediately or gradually prevented from using the substance. Coping with withdrawal symptoms is a significant focus early in the treatment process. In the second phase, intervention programs focus on preventing **relapse**, a return to use of the substance. Individuals who have undergone detoxification frequently relapse when ongoing support for recovery is not in place.

detoxification phase of alcohol or drug treatment during which the body is purged of intoxicating substances

relapse a return to drug or alcohol use after a period of abstention

Understanding and Preventing Relapse

Relapse prevention considers both physiological effects such as withdrawal symptoms and neurological changes that affect pleasure, motivation, impulsivity, learning, and memory. **Neuroplasticity**, the ability of the brain to change its structure and function in response to experience, is an important concept in addiction treatment. Just as the brain became conditioned to need a substance, therapy can help recondition the brain, create new neural pathways, and undo changes caused by addiction. Initial abstinence results in transient alterations in neural functioning, but sustained abstinence is necessary for permanent neurological changes to occur and is thus essential for maximizing treatment results.

Because many individuals with substance-use disorders discontinue treatment, especially when drug craving occurs, relapse prevention is a critical component of effective treatment (Kalivas & O'Brien, 2008). Although a longer period of initial abstinence reduces the likelihood of relapse, a single lapse in abstinence often leads to complete relapse (B. A. Moore & Budney, 2003). Many therapists view relapse not as a treatment failure but as an indicator that treatment needs to be intensified. To help minimize withdrawal symptoms and prevent relapse, medications are sometimes prescribed; the goal is to disrupt the physiological mechanisms underlying substance abuse (Jupp & Lawrence, 2010). Medications prescribed vary depending on the substance abused. Currently, most medications produce only modest effects. Therefore, substantial research activity is directed toward the development of new medications to treat addiction (Montoya & Vocci, 2008). Additionally, pharmacological investigations are beginning to address sex differences in the physiological effects of substances (Fattore & Fratta, 2010). It is important to remember that although medication can assist with cravings and withdrawal, medication alone—given the complexities of addiction—is not sufficient to prevent relapse.

Contingency management procedures in which participants receive either voucher or cash incentives for verified abstinence, adherence to treatment goals, or compliance with a prescribed medication plan can significantly reduce relapse (Stitzer & Petry, 2006; Vandrey, Bigelow, & Stitzer, 2007). Incentives can also increase treatment participation and goal-related behaviors that are incompatible with substance use, such as exercising, attending school, or learning new job skills (Stitzer, Petry, & Peirce, 2010). Verifying abstinence via toxicology screening is an important component of these interventions (N. M. Petry, Alessi, et al., 2006).

An approach that is often used to set the stage for successful treatment and prevent relapse is **motivational enhancement therapy** (Rollnick, Miller, & Butler, 2008). This method addresses ambivalence about giving up substance use. Unless this ambivalence is resolved, change is slow and short-lived. Motivational interviewing helps clients overcome ambivalence by considering both the advantages and disadvantages of making a change and of the status quo; once there is a commitment to change, relapse risk is reduced and therapy moves forward with an emphasis on life modifications required for abstinence (K. M. Carroll & Onken, 2005).

As we have seen from our exploration of the multiple contributors to substance abuse, the development of addiction is a complicated process made even more complex by the addictive characteristics of different substances. What all substances have in common are the long-lasting, difficult-to-reverse physiological and psychological changes that occur with chronic use. Thus, effective treatment targets the involuntary activation of reward circuits in response to drug-associated cues and the resultant drug craving (Kalivas & O'Brien, 2008) as well as the psychological, social, and sociocultural factors that led to initial substance use. In the following sections we discuss research-validated treatment for the most commonly abused substances: alcohol, opioids, stimulants (including cocaine), cannabis, and nicotine.

The rate of alcohol-related treatment admissions is much higher among college students than among their nonstudent peers; almost half (46.6 percent) of all treatment admissions in 2010 involving students ages 18–24 were due to alcohol abuse.

Source: SAMHSA (2011)

Life changes needed for long-term recovery include:

- eliminating cues associated with substance use;
- learning to manage drug craving;
- developing skills to cope with stress, depression, or anxiety;
- learning effective interpersonal skills;
- rebuilding family relationships;
- cultivating friendships with those who are not using substances;
- developing new hobbies and activities;
- addressing financial issues; and
- enhancing job skills.

neuroplasticity the ability of the brain to change its structure and function in response to experience

motivational enhancement therapy a therapeutic approach that addresses ambivalence and helps clients consider the advantages and disadvantages of continuing substance use

Treatment for Alcohol-Use Disorder

Participation in AA is a common intervention for alcoholism. AA regards alcoholism as a disease and advocates total abstinence. Comparing the effects of AA with mental health treatment, Moos and Moos (2006) found AA participation is more strongly associated with positive long-term outcomes than is professional treatment alone although the best outcome occurred for those who participated in both interventions. Recent research has highlighted a strong association between regular attendance at AA meetings, increased spirituality, and decreased alcohol use. Additionally, AA members reported new friendships and enhanced mood as well as increased coping skills and motivation for abstinence (J. F. Kelly et al., 2011).

Consistent with the position of AA, alcoholism specialists who believe alcoholism is a disease argue that chronic alcoholism changes cerebral functioning in fundamental and long-lasting ways (Nestler & Malenka, 2004) and that people who are recovering from alcoholism must completely abstain from drinking because any consumption will set off the disease process (Wollschlaeger, 2007). On the other hand, proponents of controlled drinking assume that, under the right conditions, people with alcoholism can learn to limit their drinking to appropriate levels. There is evidence that controlled drinking may work for some people who abuse alcohol (Emmelkamp, 2004). A major task is to discover which individuals can handle controlled drinking without major relapse. In a comparison of individuals who had recovered from alcohol dependence and chose to engage in periodic heavy drinking, drink moderately, or abstain from drinking, abstinence significantly increased chances of continued recovery; 51 percent of those who drank heavily and 27 percent of those who drank moderately were once again dependent on alcohol in a 3-year follow-up, compared to 7 percent of those who abstained (D. A. Dawson, Goldstein, & Grant, 2007).

Medications are frequently used in the treatment of alcohol abuse. Antabuse (disulfiram), a medication that produces an aversion to alcohol by blocking the breakdown of alcohol and creating highly unpleasant symptoms if alcohol is consumed, has been used for decades. Unfortunately, people with alcoholism often avoid taking Antabuse due to its adverse effects, and few studies support its effectiveness (S. H. Williams, 2005). Similarly, the medication acamprosate, developed to reduce relapse rates and increase abstinence, does not reduce cravings for alcohol and has not received strong research support (Anton et al., 2006; K. C. Morley et al., 2006). Naltrexone, a medication used to reduce desire for and pleasure in using alcohol, is effective in reducing heavy drinking, especially among individuals with strong cravings for alcohol (Richardson et al., 2008), but less effective in sustaining abstinence (Ciraulo, Dong, Silverman, Gastfriend, & Pettinati, 2008; Pettinati et al., 2006).

Given the modest effects seen with pharmaceutical intervention, K. Mann and Hermann (2010) proposed an individualized approach to assessing the effectiveness of medications—assessing medication effects with subgroups of people with alcoholism based on biologically defined endophenotypes. They give the example of naltrexone being more effective with carriers of a specific gene variant and in those individuals with the strongest MRI evidence of brain reactivity in response to pictures of alcohol. Similarly, Ooteman and colleagues (2009) found that genetic characteristics of individuals undergoing alcohol treatment were associated with differential response to both acamprosate and naltrexone.

Overall, psychological and pharmacological approaches to alcohol treatment demonstrate only modest effects (K. Mann and Hermann, 2010). Interventions supported by research show the greatest promise. For example, a comprehensive analysis of interventions to decrease college drinking revealed that individual, face-to-face interventions using motivational interviewing and providing information correcting misperceptions of social norms regarding drinking yielded the greatest reduction in alcohol-related problems (K. B. Carey, Scott-Sheldon, Carey, & DeMartini, 2007). These methods combined with challenging positive expectancies regarding alcohol use successfully reduced heavy drinking in another group of students (M. D. Wood, Capone, Laforge, Erickson, & Brand, 2007).

Not only is there a need for continued research regarding treatments for alcoholism; there is a pressing need to increase access to alcohol treatment. This is particularly important because a decision to enter treatment appears to be a crucial change point for those with alcohol dependence (Willenbring, 2010). In 2009, almost 8 percent of adolescents and adults, more than 19 million individuals, needed treatment for an alcohol-use disorder; however, only about 3 million received treatment (SAMHSA, 2010c).

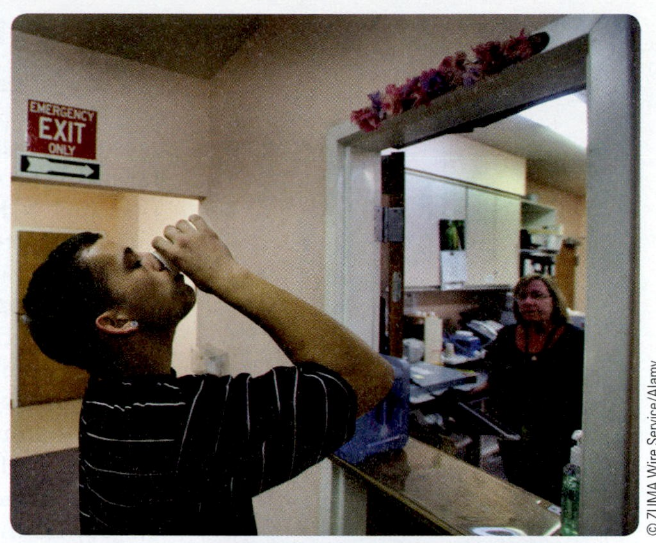

Methadone Treatment for Opioid Use Disorder

Michael Gomes, 20, takes methadone as part of his treatment for oxycodone addiction. His addiction began when, in his teens, he moved from experimenting with alcohol and marijuana to other substances.

Treatment for Opioid-Use Disorder

In 2009, almost three million Americans received some form of treatment for opioid dependence, including 739,000 individuals addicted to prescription opioids and 507,000 with heroin addiction (SAMHSA, 2010c). Early detoxification and treatment are critical with opioid dependence, because length of use strongly influences treatment outcome (S. F. Butler et al., 2010).

Methadone, a synthetic opioid that minimizes withdrawal symptoms and reduces cravings without producing euphoria, was initially considered a simple solution to the problem of prescription opioid abuse or heroin addiction. However, it has an important drawback—tolerance develops, resulting in an addictive need for methadone. Buprenorphine (a synthetic opioid similar to methadone) is a less addictive medication that assists with easing opioid withdrawal and preventing relapse (Vigezzi et al., 2006). Naltrexone (the medication designed to block pleasurable sensations in those who use alcohol) is sometimes used with opioid abuse, but a literature review has revealed limited effectiveness (Adi et al., 2007). Vivitrol, an injectable form of naltrexone, was recently approved to treat opioid dependence in those who have undergone detoxification (U.S. Food and Drug Administration, 2010a).

Opioid addiction is often associated with psychological drug dependence and feelings of being overwhelmed and unable to cope with daily activities. It is not surprising that being married and having a close relationship with one's spouse predicted better treatment outcome for heroin users (Heinz, Wu, Witkiewitz, Epstein, & Preston, 2009). Contingency management with incentives for abstinence (Bickel, Amass, Higgins, Badger, & Esch, 1997; K. M. Carroll & Onken, 2005) and behaviorally oriented individual and family counseling (Fals-Stewart & O'Farrell, 2003) have improved treatment outcomes.

Treatment for Stimulant-Use Disorder

Almost 1.5 million Americans received treatment for stimulant abuse in 2009, including almost 800,000 receiving treatment for cocaine dependence (SAMHSA, 2010c). There are currently no effective pharmacological interventions for stimulant abuse (Montoya & Vocci, 2008). Incentives for stimulant-free toxicology reports have increased rates of continuous abstinence in individuals receiving treatment for stimulant dependence (Peirce et al., 2006; Stitzer, Petry, et al., 2010). One group of researchers (Rohsenow, Monti, Martin, Michalec, & Abrams, 2000) found that training people who use cocaine to cope with temptations and high-risk situations was beneficial not only in lowering cocaine use but also in lowering the amount of cocaine used during a relapse. People who use cocaine, are married, and have a close spousal relationship have better treatment outcomes (Heinz et al., 2009).

Treatment for Cannabis-Use Disorder

In 2009, more than one million Americans received some form of treatment for cannabis abuse (SAMHSA, 2010c). Increases in treatment admissions and recent recognition of a cannabis withdrawal syndrome have led to a search for medications to assist in the withdrawal process and to help prevent relapse (Vandrey & Haney, 2009). Research efforts are focusing on the brain systems uniquely affected by marijuana use, particularly the cannabinoid system (Elkashef et al., 2008).

Psychological approaches such as brief therapy, cognitive and behavioral therapy, and motivational enhancement have shown promise with cannabis-use disorder (Benyamina, Lecacheux, Blecha, Reynaud, & Lukasiewcz, 2008). However, individuals who are dependent on marijuana experience difficulty both initiating and maintaining abstinence (B. A. Moore & Budney, 2003). Because of the ongoing cognitive and motivational deficits associated with marijuana use, some researchers advocate using short, frequent therapy sessions and focusing on increased self-efficacy (Munsey, 2010).

The use of vouchers to reinforce negative urine toxicology has shown some promise (Nordstrom & Levin, 2007). In one study, rewards for verified abstinence initially produced the highest rates of abstinence; however, those who participated in contingency management combined with motivational enhancement and cognitive behavioral therapy had higher abstinence in a later follow-up (Kaddena, Litt, Kabela-Cormiera, & Petrya, 2007). A review of outpatient therapies for cannabis dependence revealed low rates of abstinence even with cognitive and contingency management approaches; the researchers concluded that cannabis dependence may not be easily treated in outpatient settings (Denis, Lavie, Fatséas, & Auriacombe, 2006).

Treatment for Tobacco-Use Disorder

It has been estimated that one third to one half of those who smoke will die from smoking-related disease (Mitrouska, Bouloukaki, & Siafakas, 2007). Statistics like this highlight the importance of smoking cessation programs. Unfortunately, even once cessation occurs, relapse to smoking remains high, emphasizing the highly addictive nature of nicotine and the need for long-term treatment strategies (Hatsukami, Stead, & Gupta, 2008). Relapse rates and withdrawal-related discomfort are higher in people who smoke and have depression, anxiety, or other substance-use disorders (Weinberger, Desai, & McKee, 2010). Smoking cessation was much more difficult for individuals with major depression seeking help from a quitline than for those who were mildly depressed or not depressed, which emphasizes the importance of addressing underlying emotional issues (K. K. Hebert et al., 2011). Smoking cessation programs that provide emotional support and enhance readiness to change are most likely to result in ongoing abstinence (Grimshaw & Stanton, 2006).

Three pharmaceutical products are used for smoking cessation—nicotine replacement, bupropion, and varenicline. Nicotine replacement therapy (NRT) involves delivering increasingly smaller doses of nicotine using a patch, inhaler, nasal spray, gum, or sublingual tablet. This reduces withdrawal symptoms associated with smoking cessation, thus reducing the urge to smoke. NRT has been found to be fairly effective in smoking cessation (Silagy, Lancaster, Stead, Mant, & Fowler, 2003); those using NRT are much less likely to progress from a one-time smoking lapse to a full-blown relapse (Shiffman, Scharf, et al., 2006).

Bupropion (marketed under the name Zyban as an antismoking agent and Wellbutrin as an antidepressant) is frequently mentioned in the smoking cessation literature. Bupropion reduces activation of brain regions associated with craving, even in the presence of smoking-related cues (Culbertson et al., 2011). As with other antidepressant medications, caution is urged in the use of bupropion due to concerns about side effects, including agitation, depression, and suicidal ideation. Unfortunately, both NRT and bupropion have limited long-term effectiveness (Mitrouska et al., 2007) even when combined with psychological approaches.

A newer medication, varenicline (marketed as Chantix), has shown success in reducing cue-activated cravings and withdrawal symptoms as well as decreasing smoking satisfaction in healthy, adult smokers (T. Franklin et al., 2011; Garrison & Dugan, 2009). A smoker taking varenicline is 2 to 3 times more likely to achieve cessation four months after initiating treatment than is a smoker taking bupropion or using NRT (Cahill, Stead, & Lancaster, 2008). In one study, smokers taking varenicline had significantly higher continuous abstinence rates after 12–24 weeks of use compared to placebo, bupropion, or NRT; however, close monitoring for side effects involving agitation, depression, and suicidal thoughts is recommended for those taking varenicline, especially individuals with coexisting psychiatric disorders (Keating & Lyseng-Williamson, 2010).

A wide range of coping strategies have been helpful in reducing the urge to smoke, including learning to cope with negative emotions (K. A. O'Connell, Hosein, Schwartz, & Leibowitz, 2007). Relapse in smoking is strongly affected by a desire to terminate abstinence-induced negative mood; some smokers have particular difficulty tolerating negative moods (Lerman & Audrain-McGovern, 2010). Additionally, intervention to address anxiety issues is very important in smokers with anxiety disorders; they tend to have greater nicotine dependence and to be less likely to respond to standard pharmacological interventions (M. E. Piper et al., 2010). Smoking quitlines are usually free and thus easily accessible for those considering smoking cessation; the typically used, research-guided telephone counseling format has proven to be an effective intervention (Lichtenstein, Zhu, & Tedeschi, 2010). Interventions using the Internet also seem quite promising. Muñoz, Lenert, and colleagues (2006) evaluated the use of a Web-based brochure emphasizing reasons to stop smoking, how to prepare to quit, what to do in case of relapse, how to refuse cigarettes from friends and family, and information on pharmacological aids. Abstinence rates from the online program were similar to those found in traditional interventions such as psychotherapy.

Women have a more difficult time than men with smoking cessation; one variable that affects success is the phase of the menstrual cycle at the time of smoking cessation (S. S. Allen, Allen, & Pomerleau, 2009; S. S. Allen, Bade, Center, Finstad, & Hatsukami, 2008). Other factors that appear to make it more difficult for women to stop smoking include stress and negative mood (Shiffman & Waters, 2004), enjoyment of the routine of smoking, sensitivity to smoking cues (K. A. Perkins, 2009), and fear of weight gain. A study investigating methods to help women who were concerned about weight gain achieve cessation found success when bupropion was used in combination with cognitive-behavioral therapy focused on the issue of weight control (M. D. Levine et al., 2010).

CHECKPOINT REVIEW

1. What elements are important to consider in addiction treatment?
2. Discuss relapse prevention and its importance in addiction treatment.
3. Review treatment options for those addicted to alcohol, stimulants, cannabis, or tobacco.

Summary

1 What are substance-use disorders?

- People often use chemical substances that alter their mood, level of consciousness, or behavior. The use of such substances is considered a disorder when there is a maladaptive pattern of recurrent use over a 12-month period and the person is unable to reduce or cease intake of the substance despite social, occupational, psychological, medical, or safety problems.

2 What substances are involved in substance-use disorders?

- Substances are largely classified on the basis of their effects. Substances that are abused include depressants, stimulants, hallucinogens, dissociative anesthetics, and substances with multiple properties.
- Widely used depressants include alcohol, opioids (such as heroin and prescription pain relievers), and prescription medications that produce sedation and relief from anxiety.
- Stimulants energize the central nervous system, often inducing elation, grandiosity, hyperactivity, agitation, and appetite suppression. Amphetamines, cocaine, and caffeine are all considered stimulants.
- Hallucinogens, another category of psychoactive substances, produce altered states of consciousness, perceptual distortions, and sometimes hallucinations. Included in this category are LSD, psilocybin, and mescaline.
- Dissociative anesthetics are substances that produce a dreamlike detachment. Phencyclidine (PCP), ketamine, and dextromethorphan (DXM) are included in this category.
- Substances with multiple chemical properties include nicotine, cannabis, inhalants, and Ecstasy.

3 Why do people develop substance-use disorders?

- No single factor accounts for the development of a substance-use disorder. Biological, psychological, social, and sociocultural factors are all important.
- In terms of biological factors, heredity can significantly affect the risk of developing a substance-use disorder. Additionally, chronic drug or alcohol use alters brain chemistry, crowds out other pleasures, impairs decision making, and produces a compulsive desire for the substance.
- Psychological approaches to understanding substance-use disorders have emphasized personality characteristics such as behavioral undercontrol and self-medicating with substances to cope with stressful emotions and life transitions.
- Social factors are important in the initiation of substance use. Teenagers and adults use drugs because of parental models, social pressures from peers, and a desire for increased feelings of comfort and confidence in social relationships.
- Sociocultural factors affecting alcohol and drug use include media influences, cultural and subcultural norms, and societal stressors such as discrimination.

4 What kinds of interventions and treatments for substance-use disorders are most effective?

- The complex nature of addiction underscores the importance of a research-based, multifaceted treatment approach that is tailored to the individual's specific substance-use disorder and any concurrent social, emotional, or medical problems.
- Treatment for substance-use disorders has had mixed success. Intervening earlier in the addiction process increases success. Even after physiological withdrawal from a substance, individuals who abuse substances often relapse. Relapse prevention is enhanced through the use of motivational enhancement techniques to increase readiness for change, combined with pharmacological products to minimize withdrawal symptoms and with incentives for abstinence. Relapse indicates that longer-lasting or more intensive treatment is needed.

Key Terms

psychoactive substance 259
addiction 259
withdrawal 259
physiological dependence 259
tolerance 259
substance abuse 259
depressant 260
moderate drinking 261
heavy drinking 261
binge drinking 261
delirium tremens 262
alcoholic 262
alcoholism 262
alcohol poisoning 262
opioid 264
gateway drug 264
sedatives 264
hypnotics 264
anxiolytics 264
stimulant 265
hallucinogen 267
dissociative anesthetic 268
hyperthermia 269
synergistic effect 274
behavioral undercontrol 276
detoxification 282
relapse 282
neuroplasticity 283
motivational enhancement therapy 283

Media Resources

 Psychology CourseMate

Access an interactive e-book and chapter-specific interactive learning tools, including:

- flashcards
- quizzes
- videos

and more in your Psychology CourseMate.

Go to **CengageBrain.com**.

iStockphoto.com/Richard Johnson

11 Schizophrenia and Other Psychotic Disorders

CHAPTER OUTLINE

At the age of 8, Elyn Saks began to experience the hallucinations and fears of being attacked that have accompanied her throughout her life. She understood the importance of not talking openly about what ran through her mind, and she was able to hide her delusional thoughts and hallucinations and maintain top grades throughout college. In graduate school, she experienced full-blown psychotic episodes (e.g., believing that someone had infiltrated her research or dancing on the roof of the law library) that resulted in her hospitalization and subsequent diagnosis of schizophrenia. She once believed her therapist had been replaced by an evil person with an identical appearance. In her book *The Center Cannot Hold: My Journey Through Madness*, Saks recounts her lifelong struggle with mental illness, describing schizophrenia as a "slow fog" that becomes thicker over time (2007).

Saks's struggle with schizophrenia, as well as her experience with forced treatment, resulted in an intense interest in mental health and the law. Her doctors had painted a bleak picture of her future. They believed that she would not complete her degree nor be able to hold a job or get married. However, Saks did marry and complete graduate school. She is a professor of law, psychology, and psychiatry at the University of Southern California, where she also has served as an associate dean.

FOCUS QUESTIONS

1. What are the symptoms of schizophrenia?
2. How do other psychotic disorders differ from schizophrenia?
3. Is there much chance of recovery from schizophrenia?
4. What causes schizophrenia?
5. What treatments are currently available for schizophrenia, and are they effective?

Firsthand Experience

Elyn Saks teaches mental health law, has academic appointments at the University of Southern California (USC) and the University of California, San Diego, and has served as an associate dean at USC.

schizophrenia a group of disorders characterized by severely impaired cognitive processes, personality disintegration, mood disturbances, and social withdrawal

psychosis condition involving loss of contact with or distorted view of reality

positive symptoms symptoms of schizophrenia that involve unusual thoughts or perceptions, such as delusions, hallucinations, disordered thinking, or bizarre behavior

Schizophrenia refers to a group of disorders characterized by **psychosis** (impaired sense of reality), severely impaired cognitive processes, personality disintegration, mood disturbances, and social withdrawal. It is a heterogeneous clinical syndrome with different etiologies and outcomes (Braff, 2007; Frankenburg, 2010; R. M. Roth, Flashman, Saykin, McAllister, & Vidaver, 2004). Like Elyn Saks, individuals with schizophrenia lose contact with reality, see or hear things that are not actually present, or develop false beliefs about themselves or others. A diagnosis of schizophrenia involves deterioration from a previous level of functioning in areas such as work, interpersonal relationships, or self-care, together with symptoms such as delusions, hallucinations, disorganized speech, or grossly abnormal psychomotor behavior. Diagnosis requires symptoms to be present most of the time for at least 1 month, and some of the time for at least 6 months (DSM-5 Work Groups, 2012). Neurocognitive disorders, substance use, and mood disorders must be ruled out as causes of the symptoms.

Schizophrenia receives a great deal of attention for several reasons. First, it can be a severely disabling disorder that has a profound impact on the individual and on family members and friends. The prognosis is often much different from the productive life experienced by Elyn Saks. Second, schizophrenia also receives considerable attention because the financial costs of hospitalization, treatment, and loss of productivity it causes are huge—an estimated $62.7 billion annually (E. Q. Wu et al., 2005). Because the lifetime prevalence rate of schizophrenia in the United States is about 1 percent, it affects millions of people (Saha, Chant, Welham, & McGrath, 2005; National Institute of Mental Health, 2009c). In addition, because the causes of schizophrenia are not well understood, it has been difficult to find effective treatments for all individuals diagnosed with the disorder. In this chapter, we present findings regarding the diagnosis, etiology, and treatment of schizophrenia. Other psychotic disorders involving hallucinations, delusions, or cognitive abnormalities are also presented and contrasted with schizophrenia.

The Symptoms of Schizophrenia

The symptoms of schizophrenia fall into four categories: *positive symptoms*, *psychomotor abnormalities*, *negative symptoms*, and *cognitive symptoms*.

Positive Symptoms

Case Study

I was convinced that a foreign agency was sending people out to get rid of me. I was so convinced because I kept receiving messages from them via a device planted inside my brain. . . . I decided to strike first: to kill myself so they wouldn't have a chance to carry out their plans and kill me. (Kean, 2011, p. 4)

Positive symptoms of schizophrenia involve unusual thoughts or perceptions known as hallucinations or delusions, disordered thinking, incoherent communication, and bizarre behavior. Symptoms can be influenced by the individual's mood and intensified with stress (B. Smith et al., 2006).

FOCUS ON RESILIENCE

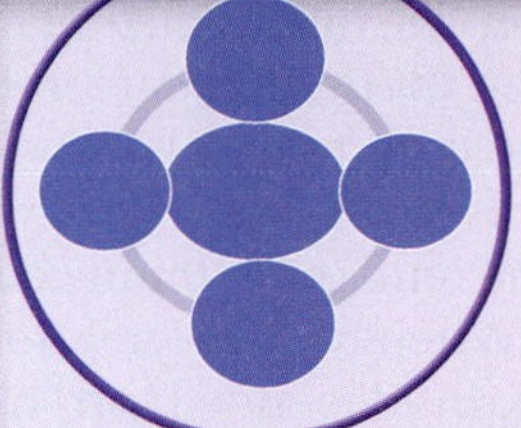

Instilling Hope After a Schizophrenia Diagnosis

I am no longer defined by myself or by others as my mental illness or disability, nor am I limited in opportunity, responsibility or direction. It is not who I am—though it may be a small part of me at times (Andresen, Oades, & Caputi, 2003, p. 588).

There has been a move away from the view that schizophrenia is a chronic disorder with an inevitably poor prognosis. This newer perspective, referred to as the recovery model, mobilizes optimism and collaborative support focused on recovery, and envisions substantial return of function for many individuals with schizophrenia. The model views schizophrenia as a chronic medical condition, such as diabetes or heart disease, which may interfere with optimal functioning but does not define the individual (R. Warner, 2009). The recovery model is based on the following assumptions (Bellack, 2006; Dilks, Tasker, & Wren, 2010):

- Recovery or improvement in functioning is possible.
- Healing involves separating one's identity from the illness and developing the ability to cope with psychiatric symptoms.
- Empowerment of the individual helps correct the sense of powerlessness and dependence that results from traditional mental health care.
- Establishing or strengthening social connections can facilitate healing.

Recovery may include—but does not require—the complete remission of symptoms. It is a process that involves overcoming the label of a "mental health patient" through personal growth, self-direction, identification and building upon of strengths, assumption of responsibility for self-care, and establishment of a personally fulfilling and meaningful life. It is learning to engage in new roles, such as partner, friend, spouse, worker, and parent (Frese, Knight, & Saks, 2009; Schrank & Slade, 2007).

The recovery model also supports social justice actions such as fighting policies that neglect the rights of individuals with schizophrenia, identifying the impact of stigma and discrimination on mental health, and promoting healing, growth, and respect for those affected by schizophrenia (Glynn, Cohen, Dixon, & Niv, 2006). Optimism about schizophrenia may be justified, as about 40 percent of people with the disorder show either complete recovery, defined as remission of symptoms and return to pre-illness function, or social recovery, which involves the return of independence and economic functioning (R. Warner, 2010).

Delusions **Delusions** are false personal beliefs that are firmly and consistently held despite disconfirming evidence or logic. Individuals experiencing delusions are not able to distinguish between their private thoughts and external reality. In the following case study, therapists attempt to confront the illogical delusion held by a graduate student in neuroscience that rats are inside his head, consuming a section of his brain.

Case Study

"Erin, you are a scientist," they'd begin. "You are intelligent, rational. Tell me then, how can you believe that there are rats inside your brain? They're just too big. Besides, how could they get in?" (Stefanidis, 2006, p. 422)

Erin had no explanation of how rats could enter his brain, but he was certain that he would soon lose functions controlled by the area of the brain that the rats

delusion a false belief that is firmly and consistently held

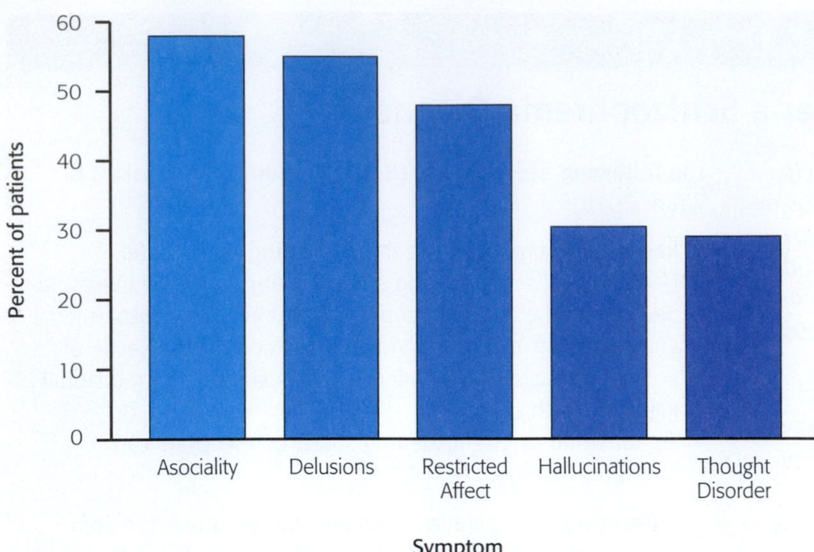

FIGURE 11.1

Lack of Awareness of Psychotic Symptoms in Individuals With Schizophrenia

Most individuals with schizophrenia are unaware or only somewhat aware that they have symptoms of the disorder. The symptoms they are most unaware of include delusions, disordered thinking, and blunt affect.

Source: Amador, X. (2003). Poor insight in schizophrenia: Overview and impact on medication compliance. Downloaded from http://www.xavieramador.com/file/cns-specialreport-on-insight.pdf. Used by permission of Dr. Xavier Amador.

were consuming. To prevent this from happening, he banged his head so that the "activated" neurons would "electrocute" the rats. Realizing he was not losing his sight even though the rats were eating his visual cortex, he entertained two possible explanations: Either his brain had a capacity for rapid regeneration or the remaining brain cells compensated for the loss. Whenever information became too discrepant, Erin depended on his enhanced thought processes or "Deep Meaning," a system he believed transcended scientific logic.

Although some individuals with schizophrenia, like Erin, attempt to maintain some sense of logic, most individuals are either unaware or only moderately aware of the illogical nature of their hallucinations or delusions (Figure 11.1). They may also attribute their symptoms to something other than mental illness (Amador, 2003; A. R. Mintz, Dobson, & Romney, 2003). *Poor insight*, a failure to recognize symptoms of one's own mental illness, is related to greater severity of illness and poorer functioning prior to the onset of the illness (Campos et al., 2011; Gilleen, Greenwood, & David, 2011).

A variety of delusional themes are seen in those with schizophrenia:

- *Delusions of grandeur.* Individuals may believe they are someone famous or powerful (from the present or the past).
- *Delusions of control.* Individuals may believe that other people, animals, or objects are trying to influence or take control of them.
- *Delusions of thought broadcasting.* Individuals may believe that others can hear their thoughts.
- *Delusions of persecution.* Individuals may believe that others are plotting against, mistreating, or even trying to kill them.
- *Delusions of reference.* Individuals may believe they are the center of attention or that all happenings revolve around them.
- *Delusions of thought withdrawal.* Individuals may believe that someone or something is removing thoughts from their mind.

MYTH VS. REALITY

MYTH Individuals experiencing delusions or hallucinations steadfastly accept them as reality.

REALITY The strength of hallucinations and delusions can vary significantly among individuals with schizophrenia. Some believe in them 100 percent, whereas others are less certain. Even without treatment, many people cope by developing means of reestablishing contact with reality or testing out the reality of their thinking. Some individuals with schizophrenia are able to combat delusions and hallucinations through a combination of conscious effort, cognitive skills, and medication.

The most common delusion in schizophrenia involves **paranoid ideation**, or suspiciousness about the actions or motives of others (Collip et al., 2010). Those with paranoid ideation often have high levels of anxiety and worry and experience **persecutory delusions** (i.e., beliefs of being targeted) as well as angry reactions to perceived persecution (Startup, Freeman, & Garety, 2006). Those with paranoid delusions often believe that others are plotting against them, talking about them, or out to harm them in some way. They are constantly suspicious, and their interpretations of the behavior and motives of others are distorted. A friendly, smiling bus driver is seen as someone who is laughing at them derisively. A busy clerk who fails to offer help is part of a plot to mistreat them. A telephone call that was a wrong number is an act of harassment or an attempt to monitor their comings and goings. Paranoid ideation may function to protect self-concept by turning personal problems into accusations that others are responsible for the bad things that are happening.

paranoid ideation suspiciousness about the actions or motives of others

persecutory delusions beliefs of being targeted by others

A rare delusion is *Capgras syndrome* (named after the person who first reported it). It is the belief in the existence of identical doubles who replace significant others, such as Elyn Saks's belief that her therapist had been replaced by an evil double (Dulai & Kelly, 2009). Similarly, the mother of one woman with delusions explained how her daughter would phone her, asking questions such as what she had worn as a Halloween costume at the age of 12 or who had attended a specific birthday party: "She was testing me because she didn't think I was her mother. . . . No matter what question I answered, she was just sobbing" (J. Stark, 2004). The daughter believed that her mother had been replaced by an impostor in a bodysuit and that her real mother had been kidnapped.

Delusions can produce strong emotional reactions such as fear, depression, or anger. Those with persecutory delusions may respond to perceived threats by leaving "dangerous" situations, avoiding areas where they might be attacked, or becoming more vigilant. Paradoxically, these "safety" behaviors may prevent them from encountering **disconfirmatory evidence** (information that contradicts the delusional belief), thus reinforcing the idea that the lack of catastrophe was due to their cautionary behaviors (Freeman, Garety, et al., 2007). Delusions may be unconnected or may involve a single theme. One woman had multiple delusions, including a belief that celebrities were talking to her through the television, that her deceased husband was still alive and cheating on her, and that her internal organs were getting infected (Mahgoub & Hossain, 2006). Delusions may vary from those that are plausible, such as being followed or spied on, to those that are bizarre (e.g., plots to remove internal organs or thoughts being placed in their minds). The strength of delusional beliefs and their effects on the person's life can vary significantly. Delusions have less impact when the individual can acknowledge that the belief may be incorrect and that others may question the accuracy of the belief, and when the individual can suggest an alternate hypothesis regarding the delusion (Islam, Scarone, & Gambini, 2011; Warman, Lysaker, Martin, Davis, & Haudenschield, 2007).

PrinzhornSammlung/Psychiatric University Clinic in Heidelberg

Paintings by People With Schizophrenia

The inner turmoil and private fantasies of people with schizophrenia are often revealed in their artwork. The paintings you see here were created by psychiatric patients in European hospitals. What do you think the paintings symbolize?

Hallucinations A **hallucination** is a sensory perception that is not directly attributable to environmental stimuli; it may involve a single sensory modality or a combination of modalities, including hearing (*auditory hallucination*), seeing (*visual hallucination*), smelling (*olfactory hallucination*), feeling (*tactile hallucination*), or tasting (*gustatory hallucination*). Auditory hallucinations are most common and can range from malevolent to benevolent or can involve both qualities (Copolov, Mackinnon, & Trauer, 2004; M. Hayward, Berry, & Ashton, 2011; Stip, 2009). Hallucinations are particularly distressing when they involve dominant, insulting voices or when the individual cannot communicate with the voices (Vaughan & Fowler, 2004).

Case Study

An individual describes his experience with auditory hallucinations while hospitalized for schizophrenia:

"You're alone," an insidious voice told me. "You're going to get what's coming to you." . . . No one moved or looked startled. It was just me hearing the voice. . . . I had seen others screaming back at their voices. . . . I did not want to look mad, like them. . . . Never admit you hear voices. . . . Never question your diagnosis or disagree with your psychiatrist . . . or you will never be discharged. (Gray, 2008, p. 1006)

disconfirmatory evidence information that contradicts a delusional belief

hallucination a sensory perception that is not directly attributable to environmental stimuli

CONTROVERSY:

Should We Challenge Delusions and Hallucinations?

The doctor asked a patient who insisted that he was dead: "Look. Dead men don't bleed, right?" When the man agreed, the doctor pricked the man's finger, and showed him the blood. The patient said, "What do you know, dead men do bleed after all." (Walkup, 1995, p. 323)

Clinicians are often unsure about whether to challenge psychotic symptoms. Some contend that delusions and hallucinations serve an adaptive function and that any attempt to change them would be useless or even dangerous. The example of the man who believed he was dead illustrates the apparent futility of using logic with delusions. However, many clinicians (Bak et al., 2003; A. T. Beck & Rector, 2000; Chadwick, Sambrooke, Rasch, & Davies, 2000; Freeman et al., 2007; K. Ross, Freeman, Dunn, & Garety, 2011) have also found that some clients respond well to challenges to their hallucinations and delusions. For example, Coltheart, Langdon, and McKay (2007) found that a "gentle and tactful offering of evidence" was successful in treating a man who believed his wife was not his wife but was, instead, his business partner. The man was asked to entertain the possibility that the woman was actually his wife. The therapist pointed out that the woman was wearing a wedding ring identical to the one he had bought for his wife. The man said that the woman probably bought the ring from the same shop. He was then shown the initials engraved in the ring—those of his wife. Within 1 week, he accepted the fact that the woman was his wife. This approach of gently presenting contradictory information and having clients consider alternative explanations appears to be a successful approach to weakening delusions.

For Further Consideration

1. Should we challenge psychotic symptoms? If so, what is the best way of doing so?
2. Might some hallucinations or delusions have an adaptive function?

Auditory hallucinations appear to be real to the individual experiencing them and sometimes involve relationship-like qualities (Chin, Hayward, & Drinnan, 2009). In one study involving individuals hospitalized with acute psychosis, 61 percent of respondents reported that the voice they heard had a distinct gender; 46 percent believed that the voice was that of a friend, family member, or acquaintance; and 80 percent reported having back-and-forth conversations with the voice. Most believed the voices were independent entities, and some had conducted "research" to test the reality of the voices. One said she initially thought that the voice might be her own but rejected it when the voice called her "mommy," something she would not call herself. Another woman explained, "They are not imaginary. They see what I do. They tell me that I'm baking a cake. They must be there. How else would they know what I'm doing?" (Garrett & Silva, 2003, p. 447).

Disorganized Thought and Speech Disordered thinking is a common characteristic of schizophrenia. During communication, individuals with schizophrenia may have difficulty focusing on one topic, speak in an unintelligible manner, or reply tangentially to questions. **Loosening of associations**, also referred to as *cognitive slippage*, is the continual shifting from topic to topic (without any apparent logical or meaningful connection between thoughts) that is characteristic of schizophrenia. Disorganized communication often involves the kind of incoherent speech or bizarre, idiosyncratic responses seen in the following case study.

Case Study

INTERVIEWER: "You just must be an emotional person, that's all."
PATIENT: "Well, not very much I mean, what if I were dead? It's a funeral age. Well, I . . . um. Now I had my toenails operated on. They got infected and I wasn't able to do it. But they wouldn't let me at my tools." (P. Thomas, 1995, p. 289)

loosening of associations continual shifting from topic to topic without any apparent logical or meaningful connection between thoughts

The beginning phrase in the patient's first sentence appears appropriate to the interviewer's comment. However, the reference to death is not. Slippage appears in the comments referring to a funeral age, having toenails operated on, and getting tools. None of these thoughts are related to the interviewer's comment, and they have no hierarchical structure or organization. People with schizophrenia may also respond to words or phrases in a very concrete manner and demonstrate difficulty with abstractions. A saying such as "a rolling stone gathers no moss" might be interpreted as meaning no more than "moss cannot grow on a rock that is rolling."

Individuals with schizophrenia also show overinclusiveness or abnormal categorization. When asked to sort cards with pictures of animals, fruit, clothing, and body parts into piles of things that go together, one man placed an ear, apple, pineapple, pear, strawberry, lips, orange, and banana together in a category he named "something to eat." When asked the reason for including the ear and lips in the "something to eat" category, he explained that an ear allows you to hear a person asking for fruit, and lips allow you to ask for and eat fruit (Doughty, Lawrence, Al-Mousawi, Ashaye, & Done, 2009).

Psychotic-type experiences are not uncommon among the general population. In a sample of 591 young adults:

- 38 percent endorsed the statement "Someone else can control my thoughts."
- 20 percent endorsed the statement "Others are aware of my thoughts."
- 18 percent endorsed the statement "I have thoughts that are not my own."
- 3 percent reported "hearing voices other people don't hear."

In most cases, these beliefs are transient and not clinically relevant, unless they become persistent, excessive, or associated with significant distress.

Source: Rossler et al. (2007)

Grossly Abnormal Psychomotor Behavior

The symptoms of schizophrenia that involve motor functions can be quite bizarre, as is evident in the following case study.

Case Study

At age twenty, patient A . . . was found sitting at the edge of the bed for hours, displaying simple repetitive movements of the right hand while simultaneously holding his left hand in a bizarre posture and repeating "I do, I do, I do." (Stober, 2006, pp. 38–39)

Some individuals with schizophrenia exhibit **catatonia**, a condition involving extremes in activity level (either unusually high or unusually low), peculiar body movements or postures, strange gestures and grimaces, or a combination of these (see Figure 11.2 for symptoms associated with catatonia; Caroff, Ungvari, Bhati, Datto, & O'Reardon, 2007; Enterman & van Dijk, 2011). People with *excited catatonia* are agitated and hyperactive. They may talk and shout constantly, moving or running until they drop from exhaustion. They sleep little and are continually on the go. Their behavior can become dangerous and involve violent acts.

In sharp contrast, people experiencing *withdrawn catatonia* are extremely unresponsive. They show prolonged periods of stupor and mutism, despite their awareness of all that is going on around them. Some may adopt and maintain strange postures and refuse to move or change position; stand for hours at a time, perhaps with one arm stretched out to the side; or lie on the floor or sit awkwardly on a chair, staring, aware of what is occurring but not responding or moving. Attempts to change the person's position may be persistently resisted. Others exhibit a waxy flexibility, allowing their bodies to be arranged in almost any position and then remaining in that position for long periods of time. The extreme withdrawal associated with a catatonic episode can be life-threatening when it results in inadequate food intake (Aboraya, Chumber, & Altaha, 2009).

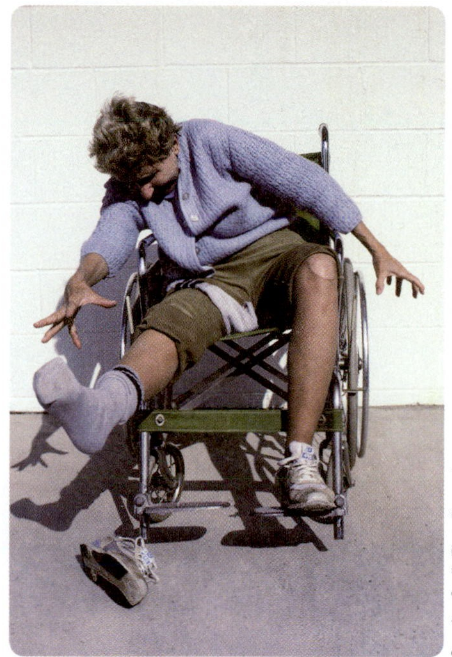

Grunnitus Studio/Photo Researchers

An Episode of Withdrawn Catatonia

The woman in the wheelchair is experiencing a form of catatonia that involves unresponsiveness and the adoption of a rigid body posture. Positions such as this are sometimes held for hours, days, weeks, or even months at a time.

catatonia a condition characterized by marked disturbance in motor activity—either extreme excitement or motoric immobility

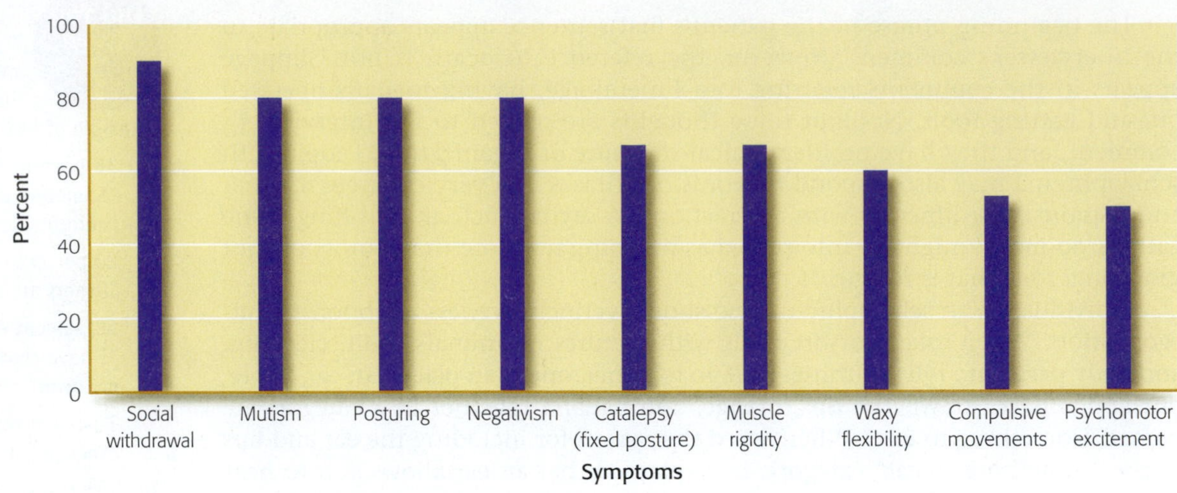

FIGURE 11.2

Prevalence of Symptoms in 30 Young Patients With Catatonia

Catatonic symptoms can vary significantly.

Source: Cornic, Consoli, & Cohen (2007)

Negative Symptoms

Negative symptoms of schizophrenia are associated with an inability or decreased ability to initiate actions or speech, express emotions, or feel pleasure (Messinger et al., 2011). Such symptoms include:

- **avolition**—an inability to take action or focus on goals;
- **alogia**—a lack of meaningful speech;
- **asociality**—minimal interest in social relationships; and
- **restricted affect**—severe or limited emotionality in situations in which emotional reactions are expected.

In clinical samples, approximately 15–25 percent of individuals diagnosed with schizophrenia display primarily negative symptoms (D. P. Johnson et al., 2009). Restricted affect is more common in men and is associated with poor prognosis and outcome (J. Addington & Addington, 2009; Gur, Kohler, et al., 2006). Negative symptoms are associated with poor social functioning. One group of individuals with schizophrenia with negative symptoms endorsed beliefs such as "Having friends is not as important as many say," "I attach very little importance to having close friends," "If I show my feelings, others will see my inadequacy," and "Why bother, I'm just going to fail" (Rector, Beck, & Stolar, 2005). These beliefs may contribute to a lack of motivation to interact with others.

negative symptoms symptoms of schizophrenia associated with an inability or decreased ability to initiate actions or speech, express emotions, or feel pleasure

avolition lack of motivation; an inability to take action or become goal oriented

alogia lack of meaningful speech

asociality minimal interest in social relationships

restricted affect severely diminished or limited emotional responsiveness

cognitive symptoms symptoms of schizophrenia associated with problems with attention and memory and with difficulty in developing a plan of action

Cognitive Symptoms

Cognitive symptoms of schizophrenia include problems with attention and memory and difficulty developing a plan of action. As compared with healthy controls, individuals with schizophrenia have moderately severe to severe cognitive impairment, as evidenced by poor executive functioning—deficits in the abilities to absorb and interpret information and make decisions based on that information, to sustain attention, and to retain and use recently learned information (Braw et al., 2008; Costafreda et al., 2011; National Institute of Mental Health, 2009c). Difficulties with social-cognitive skills, social perspective taking, and understanding one's own and other's thoughts, motivations, and emotions are also common. Cognitive symptoms are generally present even before the onset of the first psychotic episode (P. E. Bailey & Henry, 2010; Pflueger, Gschwandtner, Stieglitz, & Riecher-Rossler, 2007), tend to persist even with treatment, and are found (to a lesser degree) among nonpsychotic relatives of individuals with schizophrenia (Reichenberg & Harvey, 2007).

> **Did You Know?** In one study, individuals with schizophrenia and healthy controls wore a head-mounted virtual reality display that gave them the sense of going through a neighborhood, a shopping center, and a market. Fifty incoherencies such as a mooing dog, an upside-down house, and a red cloud were presented during the journey. Almost 90 percent of those with schizophrenia failed to detect these inconsistencies. Even when the inconsistencies were identified, about two thirds of the participants had difficulty explaining them
>
> *Source:* Sorkin, Weinshall, & Peled, (2008)

Cultural Issues

Culture may affect how symptoms of schizophrenia are viewed. In Japan, for example, schizophrenia is highly stigmatized. Part of the problem is that the condition is called *seishin-bunretsu-byou*, which roughly translates to "a split in mind or spirit." The term conjures up an irreversible condition. Because of this connotation, only about 20 percent of those with schizophrenia were told of their diagnosis in the years preceding 2000 (Y. Kim & Berrios, 2001). In 2002, the name was changed to *togo-shitcho-sho* (integration disorder), which is a less stigmatizing term. With this change, almost 70 percent of psychiatrists surveyed said they would now inform a patient of the diagnosis (Takahashi, Tsunoda, et al., 2011). Similarly, a negative reaction to the term *schizophrenia* is also part of the reason that many psychiatrists in Turkey will not mention the diagnosis to clients or family members (Ucok, 2007).

Immigrant groups, particularly those of African descent, have the highest rates of schizophrenia in Western Europe; similarly, follow-up of a large birth cohort in the United States revealed that African Americans were 2 to 3 times more likely to be diagnosed with schizophrenia than were whites (Bresnahan et al., 2007). It is not clear whether these differences reflect clinician bias or actual differences in rates of the disorder. Elevated rates for schizophrenia have been found for African Americans individuals even when assessment data are re-analyzed by clinicians unaware of the ethnicity of clients. It is possible that discriminatory experiences result in African Americans' responding in a manner that sounds psychotic to clinicians but actually represents normative responses to ongoing discrimination (Gara et al., 2012).

CHECKPOINT REVIEW

1. Describe the positive symptoms of schizophrenia.
2. Describe the negative and cognitive symptoms of schizophrenia.
3. How do cultural issues impact how symptoms are viewed and diagnosed?

Other Psychotic Disorders

Disorders in the group of other psychotic disorders are characterized by psychotic symptoms such as hallucinations, delusions, and disorganized speech but do not meet the diagnostic criteria for schizophrenia. They include brief psychotic disorder, schizophreniform disorder, delusional disorder, schizoaffective disorder, attenuated psychosis syndrome, and other specified psychotic disorder.

Brief Psychotic Disorder and Schizophreniform Disorder

Schizophrenic-type episodes that last less than 6 months are considered either a **brief psychotic disorder** (duration of at least 1 day but less than 1 month) or **schizophreniform disorder** (duration of at least 1 month but less than 6 months). Diagnosis of these disorders does not require impairment in social or occupational functioning (Bhalla & Ahmed, 2011; DSM-5 Work Groups, 2012). Psychological trauma can produce the short-term psychotic episodes seen in brief psychotic

brief psychotic disorder psychotic episodes with a duration of at least 1 day but less than 1 month

schizophreniform disorder psychotic episodes with a duration of at least 1 month but less than 6 months

Individuals with severe mental disorders such as schizophrenia have higher rates of violence than healthy people—if they also have other risk factors for violent behavior, such as substance abuse or a history of violence, physical abuse, or victimization. Severe mental illness alone does not predict violence

Source: Elbogen & Johnson (2009)

Cannabis use at a young age

- is related to earlier onset of psychotic symptoms,
- can lead to acute transient psychotic symptoms during intoxication,
- exacerbates pre-existing psychotic symptoms, and
- increases relapse in individuals with psychotic conditions.

Source: Dragt et al. (2010)

disorder. For example, among soldiers engaged in combat in Croatia, 20 percent reported hallucinations and delusions (Kastelan et al., 2007). Brief psychotic disorder has also been reported in cases of Guillain-Barré syndrome, a condition producing temporary paralysis of muscles, including those used for breathing. Among one group of individuals affected by this extremely distressing syndrome, 25 percent developed a brief psychotic reaction (H. Weiss, Rastan, Mullges, Wagner, & Toyka, 2002).

Brief psychotic disorder is relatively uncommon; it occurs more frequently in developing countries and among women (Memon & Bienenfeld, 2012). Schizophreniform disorder is found equally in men and women and shares some of the anatomical and neural deficits found in schizophrenia (Bhalla & Ahmed, 2011). The lifetime prevalence of schizophreniform disorder is 0.07 percent (Perala et al., 2007), while that of brief psychotic disorder is unknown; many brief psychotic episodes may not persist long enough for a diagnosis.

These disorders share many commonalities with schizophrenia (see Table 11.1). The diagnoses of brief psychotic disorder and schizophreniform disorder are often considered **provisional diagnoses**. For example, an initial diagnosis of brief psychotic disorder may change to schizophreniform disorder if symptoms last longer than 1 month and to schizophrenia if they last longer than 6 months and impair social or occupational functioning. In a follow-up study involving individuals with schizophreniform disorder, 46 percent later received a diagnosis of schizophrenia; 35 percent, a depressive or bipolar disorder; 18 percent, a nonschizophrenic psychotic disorder; and 2 percent, no disorder (Marchesi et al., 2007).

provisional diagnosis an initial diagnosis based on currently available information

delusional disorder persistent, nonbizarre delusions without other unusual or odd behaviors; tactile and olfactory hallucinations related to the delusional theme may be present

Delusional Disorder

Delusional disorder is characterized by persistent, nonbizarre delusions (i.e., beliefs that are false but could be plausible) that are not accompanied by other unusual or odd behaviors—other than those related to the delusional theme (Chopra & Bienenfeld, 2011). Delusional disorder is not considered a form of schizophrenia, due to the absence of additional disturbances in thoughts and perceptions or psychosocial impairment. The disorder is rarely diagnosed (the prevalence is 0.03–0.18 percent); however, it is believed that many with the disorder do not perceive they have a problem and therefore do not seek assistance (Chopra & Bienenfeld, 2011; Perala et al., 2007). People with delusional disorder behave normally when their delusional ideas are not being discussed. Common themes involved in delusional disorders include (Chopra & Bienenfeld, 2011) the following:

- *Erotomania*—the belief that someone is in love with the individual; this delusion typically has a romantic rather than sexual focus.

TABLE 11.1 Comparison of Brief Psychotic Disorder, Schizophreniform Disorder, and Schizophrenia

	BRIEF PSYCHOTIC DISORDER	SCHIZOPHRENIFORM DISORDER	SCHIZOPHRENIA
Duration	**Less than 1 month**	**Less than 6 months**	6 months or more
Psychosocial stressor	Likely present	Usually present	May or may not be present
Onset of symptoms	Abrupt onset of psychotic symptoms	Often abrupt psychotic symptoms	More gradual onset of psychotic symptoms
Outcome	Return to premorbid functioning	Possibly return to premorbid functioning	Occasionally return to premorbid functioning
Risk factors	More common in females	Some increased risk of schizophrenia among family members	Higher prevalence of schizophrenia among family members

Source: Bhalla & Ahmed, (2011); Memon & Bienenfeld. (2012)

CONTROVERSY:

Morgellons Disease: Delusional Parasitosis or Physical Disease?

More than 10 years ago, "Mary Leitao plucked a fiber that looked like a dandelion fluff from a sore under her two-year-old son's lips. . . . Sometimes the fibers were white, and sometimes they were black, red, or blue" (Devita-Raeburn, 2007). Leitao was frustrated by the inability of physicians to diagnose her son's skin condition. In fact, many of the professionals she consulted indicated that they could find no evidence of disease or infection. Frustrated by the medical establishment, Leitao put a description of the condition on a Web site in 2001, calling it Morgellons disease after a 17th-century French medical study involving children with similar symptoms (Mason, 2006).

The Web site has since compiled 11,000 worldwide reports of the condition among adults and children. Sufferers report granules and fiberlike threads emerging from the skin at the site of itching; sensations of crawling, stinging, or biting; and rashes and skin lesions that do not heal (M. Paquette, 2007). Some describe the fibers as "inorganic but alive" and report that the fibers pull back from a lit match (Browne, 2011). Symptoms of vision changes, joint pain, fatigue, mental confusion, and short-term memory difficulties have also been reported in connection with Morgellons disease (Centers for Disease Control, 2011c).

What could cause this disorder? Many dermatologists, physicians, and psychiatrists believe that Morgellons disease results from self-inflicted injury or is a somatic type of delusional disorder such as *delusional parasitosis*, a condition in which individuals (often those with psychosis or a substance-use disorder) maintain a delusional belief that they are afflicted with living organisms or other pathogens (Freudenmann & Lepping, 2009). Stephen Stone, past president of the American Academy of Dermatology, does not believe Morgellons is real disease. He argues that the Internet community is allowing individuals with somatic delusions to band together (Marris, 2006). Some physicians, however, believe there is an underlying physical disorder, citing those with Morgellons symptoms who test positive for Lyme disease or whose symptoms are alleviated with antibacterial or antiparasitic medications (Savely, Leitao, & Stricker, 2006). Others report that individuals with Morgellons symptoms show evidence of infectious disease such as immune system deficiency and markers of chronic inflammation (W. T. Harvey et al., 2009).

Because of the controversy and the increasing number of complaints, the Centers for Disease Control and Prevention initiated an investigation on the characteristics and epidemiologic data related to Morgellons, including psychological testing, environmental analysis, examination of skin biopsies, and laboratory study of fibers or threads obtained from people with the condition (CDC, 2011c). Researchers concluded that no medical condition or infection could be found to explain the reported symptoms and that the skin lesions were probably produced by scratching. Fibers found at the site of skin inflammation were cotton or nylon, not organisms. Psychological tests revealed that individuals studied were more likely to be depressed and attentive to physical symptoms than the general population, but that they were not delusional (Pearson et al., 2012). Some researchers believe that "the rapid rise of Morgellons could [not] have occurred without the internet . . . which can spread information—without regard for accuracy or usefulness" (Freudenreich, Kontos, Tranulis, & Cather, 2010, p. 456).

For Further Consideration

1. Are Internet Web sites on diseases such as Morgellons creating disorders among vulnerable individuals, or do they provide comfort for those with an actual disease?
2. How might a psychologist or a physician determine if an individual reporting symptoms of Morgellons was suffering from a somatic delusion?

- *Grandiosity*—the conviction that one has great, unrecognized talent, special abilities, or a relationship with an important person or deity.
- *Jealousy*—the conviction that one's spouse or partner is being unfaithful.
- *Persecution*—the belief that one is being conspired or plotted against.
- *Somatic complaints*—convictions of having body odor, being malformed, or being infested by insects or parasites.

Women are more likely to develop erotomanic delusions, whereas men tend to have paranoid delusions involving persecution (Chopra & Khan, 2009). The following cases illustrate some features of delusional disorders:

- A woman was convinced that people were watching her and following her because she saw the same people day after day in her neighborhood and in the stores where she shopped (Muller, 2006).

- A 37-year-old man was arrested for stalking and harassing Tyra Banks, a model and television personality. He had followed her for 2 months, appeared at her TV studio, made repeated phone calls, and sent multiple letters and flowers, claiming that they had a "thing together" (Serpe, 2009).

A decreased ability to obtain corrective feedback, combined with pre-existing personality traits of suspiciousness, may increase a person's susceptibility to developing delusional beliefs. For example, hearing impairment in early adolescence is associated with an increased risk of developing delusions (van der Werf et al., 2011). Delusional disorder can be treated with antipsychotic medications or cognitive-behavioral therapy (Chopra & Khan, 2009; Mercan, Altunay, Taskintuna, Ogutcen, & Kayaoglu, 2007).

Schizoaffective Disorder

Schizoaffective disorder involves the existence of both the psychotic features found in schizophrenia and major depressive or manic symptoms. Diagnosis is difficult, since the individual may actually have two separate mental disorders (schizophrenia and a depressive or bipolar disorder) or a depressive or bipolar disorder with psychotic characteristics. Schizoaffective disorder is relatively rare, occurring in only 0.32 percent of the population. Prognosis appears to be better than for schizophrenia but somewhat worse than with bipolar or depressive disorders. Treatment can involve both antipsychotic medication combined with mood stabilizers and individual and group psychotherapies (Brannon & Bienenfeld, 2012).

Attenuated Psychosis Syndrome

Attenuated psychosis syndrome involves distressing or disabling delusions, hallucinations, or disorganized speech that emerged or became progressively worse over the previous year; despite these symptoms, the individual is able to stay in touch with reality (Carpenter & Van Os, 2011; DSM-5 Work Groups, 2012). Whether these "milder" signs of psychosis should warrant a psychiatric diagnosis has been a matter of much debate. Those in favor make several arguments: (1) Symptoms of attenuated psychosis syndrome occurring in childhood and adolescence increase risk for psychiatric impairment in adulthood (Polanczyk et al., 2010); (2) rapid deterioration often occurs during the early years of psychosis, so early intervention and treatment might diminish the effects of the illness (Amminger et al., 2010; Carpenter Jr., 2010; Crumlish et al., 2009; McGlashan & Woods, 2011); and (3) this diagnosis allows treatment for people who are highly distressed by these milder psychotic symptoms.

Opponents of the attenuated psychosis syndrome diagnosis argue that many individuals with this diagnosis will not develop a psychotic disorder ("false positives") and that premature diagnosis could result in unnecessary stigma and unwarranted use of antipsychotic medications (Bola, Kao, & Soydan, 2012; Moncrieff, 2012). Psychotic-type experiences appear to be present not only in those with schizophrenia and related disorders but also in the general population (M. L. C. Campbell & Morrison, 2007; Freeman, McManus, et al., 2010; Kelleher & Cannon, 2010). For example, reports of psychotic symptoms such as beliefs of persecution, thought interference, and auditory hallucinations are common among adolescents but, in most cases, are only transitory (Dominguez, Wichers, Lieb, Wittchen, & Van Os, 2011; B. Nelson & Yung, 2011). Because of the controversy, the work group developing the DSM-5 deemed attenuated psychosis syndrome to be a "condition that requires further research" rather than a specific diagnostic category.

schizoaffective disorder a condition involving the existence of both symptoms of schizophrenia and major depressive or manic symptoms

attenuated psychosis syndrome condition being researched that involves distressing or disabling early signs of delusions, hallucination, or disorganized speech that emerged or became progressively worse over the previous year; reality testing remains relatively intact

Psychotic Disorder Not Elsewhere Classified

The category of "psychotic disorder not elsewhere classified" includes individuals who have psychotic symptoms (i.e., hallucinations, delusions, disorganized speech, grossly disorganized behavior, or catatonia) that are not significant enough to meet the criteria for a specific psychotic disorder (DSM-5 Work Groups, 2012). Examples are postpartum psychosis not associated with a depressive or bipolar disorder, persistent auditory hallucination in the absence of other symptoms, nonbizarre hallucinations that overlap with fluctuating mood symptoms, and psychotic symptoms of unknown etiology.

CHECKPOINT REVIEW

1. Compare and contrast brief psychotic disorder and schizophreniform disorder with each other and with schizophrenia.
2. What are the characteristics of delusional disorder?
3. Cite the pros and cons of adding attenuated psychosis symptom as a psychiatric diagnosis.

The Course of Schizophrenia

It is popularly believed that overwhelming stress can cause a well-adjusted and relatively normal person to experience a psychotic breakdown or develop schizophrenia. Although there are some cases of sudden onset of psychotic behaviors in previously well-functioning people (Kastelan et al., 2007), in most cases of schizophrenia, there is evidence of impairment in **premorbid** functioning; that is, individuals often show some abnormalities before the onset of major symptoms. Similarly, most people with schizophrenia recover gradually rather than suddenly. The typical course of schizophrenia consists of three phases: prodromal, active, and residual.

The *prodromal phase* includes the onset and buildup of schizophrenic symptoms. Social withdrawal and isolation, peculiar behaviors, inappropriate affect, poor communication patterns, and neglect of personal grooming may become evident during this phase. Of 11 individuals with schizophrenia who were interviewed in one study (Campo, Frederikx, Nijman, & Merckelbach, 1998), nine indicated that they had drastically changed their appearance (e.g., changing hairstyles; wearing multiple pants, dresses, coats, or other items of clothing at the same time) just before the onset of the schizophrenic episode. They said the changes were an attempt to maintain their identities. Friends and relatives often considered such behavior odd or peculiar.

Often, psychosocial stressors or excessive demands on an individual with schizophrenia in the prodromal phase result in the onset of prominent psychotic symptoms, or the *active phase* of schizophrenia. In this phase, the person shows full-blown symptoms of schizophrenia, including severe disturbances in thinking, deterioration in social relationships, and restricted or markedly inappropriate affect.

At some later time, the person may enter the *residual phase*, in which the symptoms are no longer prominent. In the residual phase, the symptom severity declines and the individual may show milder impairment similar to that seen in the prodromal phase. Although long-term studies have shown that many people with schizophrenia can lead productive lives, complete recovery is rare. (Figure 11.3 illustrates different courses schizophrenia may take.)

premorbid before the onset of major symptoms

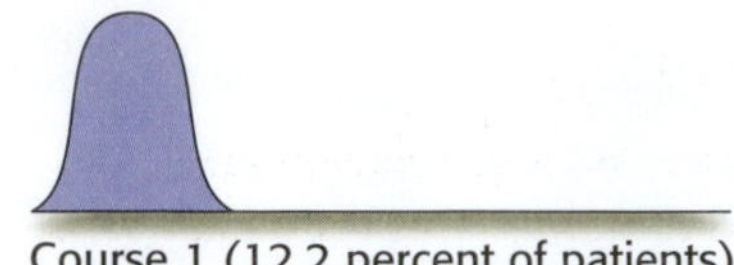

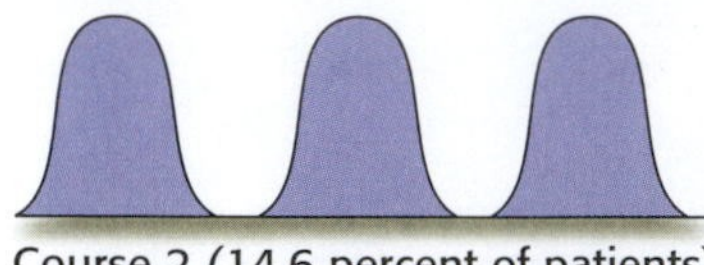

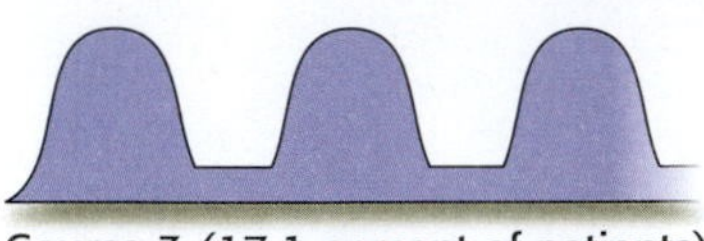

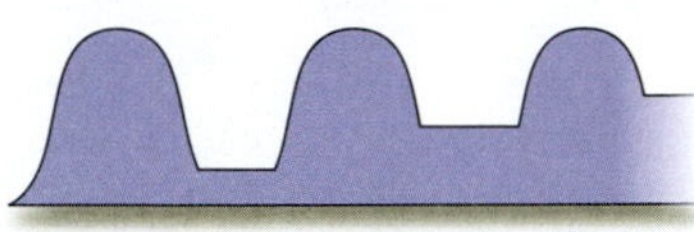

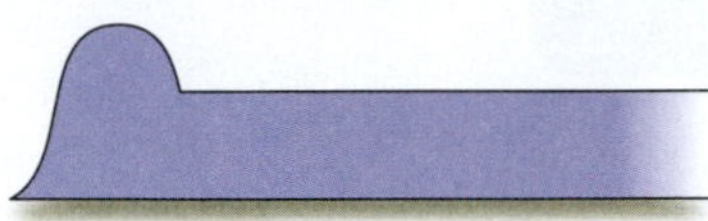

FIGURE 11.3

Varying Outcomes With Schizophrenia
This figure shows five of the many outcomes possible with schizophrenia in individuals during a 15-year follow-up study.

Source: Wiersma, Nienhuis, Sloof, & Giel (1998)

Long-Term Outcome Studies

What are the chances for recovery from or improvement in schizophrenia? The chances for improvement or recovery are difficult to definitively evaluate; recent developments in both psychotherapy and medication have led to increased optimism regarding the course of the disorder. In a 10-year follow-up study of individuals hospitalized for schizophrenia, the majority of participants improved over time, whereas a minority appeared to deteriorate (Rabinowitz, Levine, Haim, & Hafner, 2007). Similarly, during a 15-year follow-up involving individuals with schizophrenia, the following results were found (Harrow, Grossman, Jobe, & Herbener, 2005):

- More than 40 percent showed one or more periods of recovery (defined as the absence of psychotic activity and negative symptoms, working half-time or more, and no psychiatric hospitalization during the period of evaluation).
- A sizable minority were not on any medication.

Factors associated with a positive outcome include gender (women have a better outcome), higher levels of education, being married, and having a higher premorbid level of functioning (Irani & Siegel, 2006). In a 10-year follow-up study examining baseline predictors associated with recovery from schizophrenia, researchers found that fewer negative symptoms, a prior history of good work performance and ability to live independently, and lower levels of depression and aggression were all associated with improved outcome (Shrivastava, Shah, Johnston, Stitt, & Thakar, 2010). Having a social network and work opportunities and being single or married as opposed to separated or divorced are also associated with a more positive outcome (Sibitz, Unger, Woppmann, Zidek, & Amering, 2011; R. Warner, 2009).

CHECKPOINT REVIEW

1. Describe the prodromal, active, and residual phases of schizophrenia.
2. What are factors associated with a positive outcome in schizophrenia?

Etiology of Schizophrenia

Case Study

A 13-year-old boy who was having behavioral and academic problems in school was taking part in a series of family therapy sessions. Family communication was negative in tone, with a great deal of blaming. Near the end of one session, the boy suddenly broke down and cried out, "I don't want to be like her." He was referring to his mother, who had been receiving treatment for schizophrenia. He had often been frightened by her bizarre behavior, and he was concerned that his friends would find out about her condition. But his greatest fear was that he would inherit the disorder. Sobbing, he turned to the therapist and asked, "Am I going to be crazy, too?"

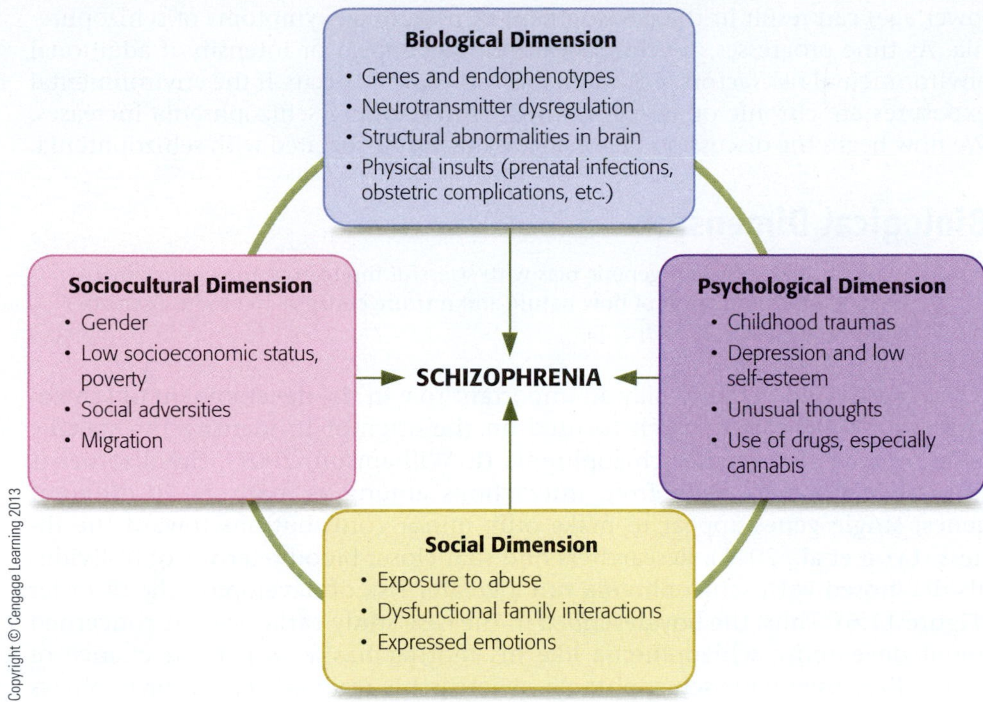

FIGURE 11.4

Multipath Model of Schizophrenia

The dimensions interact with one another and combine in different ways to result in schizophrenia.

If you were the therapist in the case study, how would you respond? At the end of this section on the etiology of schizophrenia, you should be able to reach your own conclusion about what to tell the boy.

Schizophrenia and other psychotic conditions are best understood using a multipath model that integrates heredity (genetic influences on brain structure and neurotransmitters), psychological characteristics, cognitive processes (e.g., faulty psychological processing of information), and social adversities (such as low social or economic status; van der Gaag, 2006). To develop an accurate etiological framework, all of these dimensions must be taken into consideration, as shown in Figure 11.4.

In this section, we discuss the biological, psychological, social, and sociocultural dimensions separately, keeping in mind that each dimension interacts with the others. For example, emotional or sexual abuse; cannabis use; and trauma (physical threat, serious accident) have all been hypothesized to affect dopamine levels and neurocognitive functioning in those susceptible to schizophrenia. In one sample, the probability of persistent psychotic symptoms was influenced by each of these factors, especially among individuals who were exposed to all three influences (Cougnard, Marcelis, et al., 2007).

The interactive model illustrated in Figure 11.5 demonstrates how an underlying biological vulnerability combined with other risk characteristics (e.g., male sex,

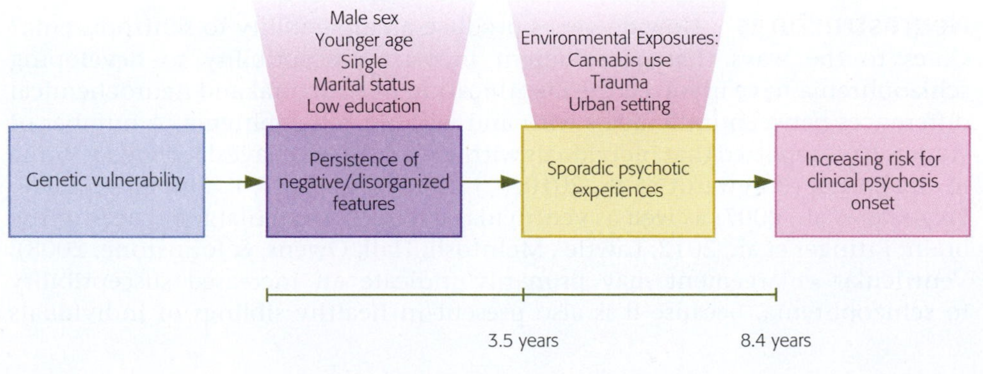

FIGURE 11.5

Interactive Variables and the Onset of Clinical Psychosis

This model shows how psychological and social factors may interact with genetic vulnerability to result in psychosis.

Source: Dominguez, M. D. G., Saka, M. C., Lieb, R., Wittchan, H.-U., & Van Os, J. (2010). Reprinted with permission from the *American Journal of Psychiatry*, copyright © 2010 American Psychiatric Association.

A meta-analysis of 35 studies reached the following conclusions:

- Risk of psychosis is increased by 40 percent in marijuana users.
- Being a "heavy pot user" increases the risk of psychosis by 50–200 percent.
- Psychotic symptoms are not due to the transitory effects of intoxication.
- It is estimated that 14 percent of the cases of psychosis might not have occurred if marijuana had not been used.

Source: T. H. M. Moore et al. (2007); Nordentoft & Hjorthoj (2007)

lower age) can result in the development of prodromal symptoms of schizophrenia. As time progresses, psychotic features may appear or intensify if additional environmental risk factors (e.g., cannabis use, trauma) occur. If the environmental exposures are chronic or severe, the risk of developing schizophrenia increases. We now begin the discussion of specific risk factors associated with schizophrenia.

Biological Dimension

> The coupling of sufficient genetic bias with stressful input from the environment is the modern formulation of how nature and nurture conspire to produce schizophrenia. (*Stahl, 2007, p. 583*)

Genetics and heredity play an important role in the development of schizophrenia. While past research focused on the attempt to identify the specific gene or genes that cause schizophrenia (P. Williamson, 2007), the disorder is now understood to result from interactions among as many as 20 different genes; single genes appear to make only minor contributions toward the illness (Lyon et al., 2011). Researchers find that closer blood relatives of individuals diagnosed with schizophrenia run a greater risk of developing the disorder (Figure 11.6). Thus, the boy described in the case study earlier who is concerned about developing schizophrenia like his mother has a 16 percent chance of being diagnosed with schizophrenia, whereas his mother's nieces or nephews have only a 4 percent chance. (It should be noted that the risk for the general population is 1 percent.) However, even among monozygotic (identical) twins, if one twin receives the diagnosis of schizophrenia, the risk of the second twin developing the disorder is less than 50 percent. This is because environmental influences also play a significant role in genetic expression of the disorder (Gottesman, 1978, 1991).

Endophenotypes The strategy in genetic research has moved from demonstrating that heredity is involved in schizophrenia to attempting to identify the genes that are responsible for specific characteristics or traits that are evident in this disorder. This approach involves the identification and study of **endophenotypes**—measurable, heritable traits (Braff, Freedman, Schork, & Gottesman, 2007). Endophenotypes are hypothesized to underlie heritable illnesses (such as schizophrenia) and exist in the individual before the disorder, during it, and following remission. It would be expected that these characteristics be found with higher frequency, although in milder forms, among "non-ill" relatives of individuals with schizophrenia (Gur, Calkins, et al., 2007). Researchers have identified several possible endophenotypes related to impairment in function both in those with schizophrenia and in their unaffected biological relatives. These traits include working memory, executive function, sustained attention, and verbal memory (Chan, Di, McAlonan, & Gong, 2011; Reichenberg & Harvey, 2007; Turetsky et al., 2007).

Neurostructures How do genes produce a vulnerability to schizophrenia? Clues to the ways that genes might increase susceptibility to developing schizophrenia have involved the identification of structural and neurochemical differences between individuals with and without schizophrenia. A number of studies have reported that individuals with schizophrenia have decreased volume in the cortex (Borgwardt et al., 2010; J. J. Kim et al., 2007; K. Sim et al., 2006; Tregellas et al., 2007) as well as ventricular enlargement (enlarged spaces in the brain; Ettinger et al., 2012; Lawrie , McIntosh, Hall, Owens, & Johnstone, 2008). Ventricular enlargement may primarily indicate an increased susceptibility to schizophrenia, because it is also present in healthy siblings of individuals

endophenotype measurable characteristics (neurochemical, endocrinological, neuroanatomical, cognitive, or neuropsychological) that can give clues regarding the specific genes involved in a disorder

with schizophrenia (Staal et al., 2001). In an interesting longitudinal study of brain changes among youth with and without schizophrenia, those with the disorder showed a striking loss of brain cells in the cortex over a period of 6 years. The loss was so rapid that it was likened to a "forest fire" (P. M. Thompson et al., 2001). Interestingly, healthy siblings of adolescents with child-onset schizophrenia also showed similar cortical loss (Gogtag, 2008).

How might decreased cortex volume and enlarged ventricles predispose someone to the development of schizophrenia? These structural characteristics may result in atypical or weak connectivity between the various brain regions, leading to reductions in the integrative function of the brain and impaired cognitive processing (Salgado-Pineda et al., 2007). Thus, ineffective communication within the different brain systems may lead to the cognitive symptoms (e.g., impairment in memory, decision making, and problem solving), negative symptoms (e.g., lack of drive or initiative), and positive symptoms (e.g., delusions and hallucinations) that are found in schizophrenia. However, the differences in brain structure between individuals with and without schizophrenia are relatively small. In addition, some of the abnormalities found in the brains of individuals with schizophrenia may result from the use of antipsychotic medication rather than the disorder itself (B.-C. Ho, Andreasen, Ziebell, Pierson, & Magnotta, 2011; Moncrieff & Leo, 2010).

Neurotransmitters Abnormalities in certain neurotransmitters (chemicals that allow brain cells to communicate with one another) including dopamine, serotonin, GABA, and glutamate have also been linked to schizophrenia (Benes, 2009; Tan et al., 2007). Considerable attention has been focused on the neurotransmitter dopamine (Borda & Sterin-Borda, 2006; Howes, Kambeitz, et al., 2012; Lyon et al., 2011). According to the **dopamine hypothesis**, schizophrenia may result from excess dopamine activity in certain areas of the brain. Support for the dopamine hypothesis has come from research with three types of drugs: phenothiazines, L-dopa, and amphetamines.

- *Phenothiazines* are conventional antipsychotic drugs that decrease the severity of disordered thinking, decrease social withdrawal, alleviate hallucinations, and improve the mood of individuals with schizophrenia. Phenothiazines reduce dopamine activity in the brain by blocking dopamine receptor sites.
- *L-dopa* is generally used to treat symptoms of Parkinson's disease, such as muscle and limb rigidity and tremors. As the body converts L-dopa to dopamine, schizophrenic-like side effects sometimes occur. (In contrast, the phenothiazines, which reduce dopamine activity, can produce side effects that resemble Parkinson's disease.)
- *Amphetamines* are stimulants that increase the availability of dopamine and norepinephrine (another neurotransmitter) in the brain. When individuals not diagnosed with schizophrenia are given continual doses of amphetamines, they sometimes show symptoms very much like those of acute paranoid schizophrenia. Also, even small doses of amphetamine can increase the severity of symptoms in individuals diagnosed with schizophrenia.

Thus one group of drugs that blocks dopamine reception has the effect of reducing the severity of schizophrenic symptoms, whereas two drugs that increase dopamine availability either produce or worsen these symptoms. Such evidence suggests that excess dopamine may be responsible for schizophrenic

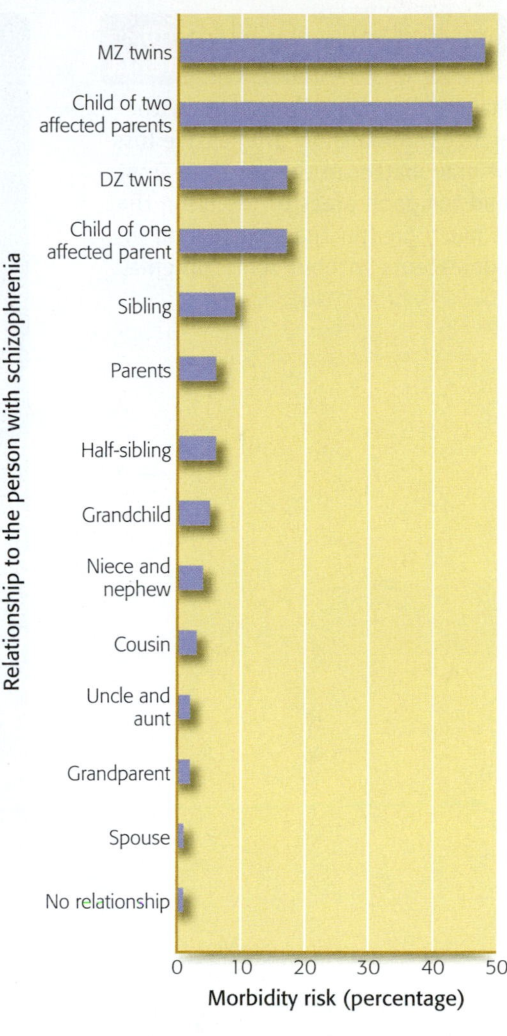

FIGURE 11.6

Risk of Schizophrenia Among Blood Relatives of Individuals Diagnosed With Schizophrenia

This figure reflects the estimate of the lifetime risk of developing schizophrenia—a risk that is strongly correlated with the degree of genetic influence.

Source: Data from Gottesman (1978, 1991)

dopamine hypothesis the suggestion that schizophrenia may result from excess dopamine activity at certain synaptic sites

Rate of Gray Matter Loss in Teenagers With Schizophrenia

Male and female adolescents with schizophrenia show progressive loss of gray matter in the parietal, frontal, and temporal areas of the brain that is much greater than that found in adolescents without schizophrenia.

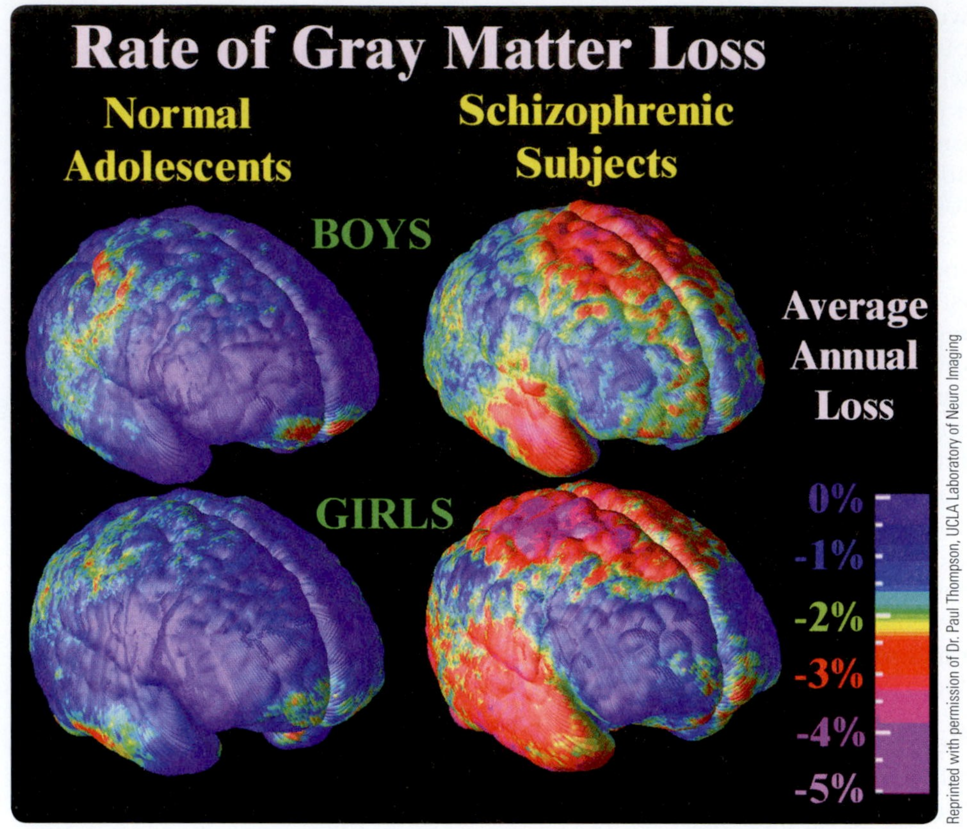

symptoms. The evidence is not clear-cut, however. Phenothiazines are not effective in treating many cases of schizophrenia, and newer antipsychotics work mainly by blocking serotonin receptors rather than dopamine receptors (Canas, 2005). This suggests that researchers may be looking for an oversimplified explanation by focusing on dopamine alone without considering the interactive functioning of the brain and the biochemical system as a whole. As was

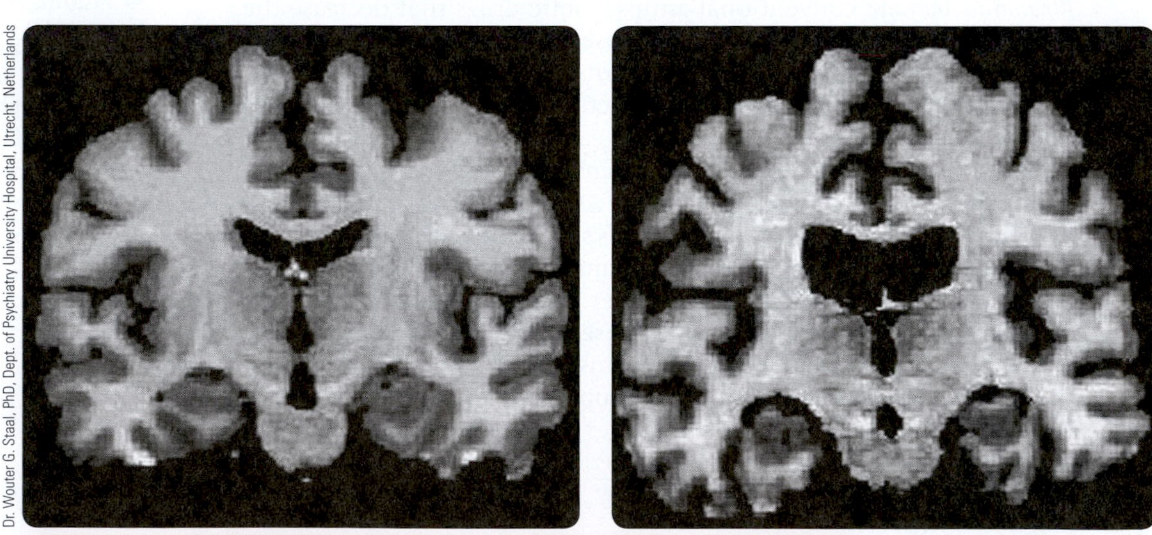

Coronal Sections of the Brain in a Patient With Schizophrenia

Structural brain abnormalities have been found in most individuals with schizophrenia. Patients with poor outcome (represented by the right photo) show significantly greater loss of cerebral gray matter and greater enlargement of the ventricles than those with less severe symptoms (represented by the photo on the left).

indicated earlier, other neurotransmitters also play a major role in schizophrenia (Tan et al., 2007).

Because the **concordance rate**—the likelihood that both members of a twin pair show the same characteristic—is less than 50 percent when one identical twin has schizophrenia, environmental influences (physical, psychological, social) that are not shared between the twins must also play a role. Conditions influencing prenatal or postnatal neurodevelopment that have been associated with schizophrenia include prenatal infections, obstetric complications, and head trauma (Compton, 2005; Jablensky, Morgan, Zubrick, Bower, & Yellachich, 2005; Mittal, Ellman, & Cannon, 2008; Stahl, 2007). Numerous studies have documented an association between early developmental delay and later development of schizophrenia; one large prospective population study recently reported that infants who later developed schizophrenia were slower to smile, lift their heads, sit, crawl, and walk than were infants who did not develop schizophrenia (Sørensen et al., 2010). Early behavioral disturbances and cognitive and language deficits have similarly been associated with development of the disorder (Welham, Isohanni, Jones, & McGrath, 2009).

Although a variety of biological influences appear to increase susceptibility to schizophrenia by changing or altering brain structures or neurotransmitters, specific psychological, social, and sociocultural variables can also influence development of schizophrenia. We now examine these influences as possible contributors to the disorder.

Did You Know?

Characteristics that sharply increase the likelihood of developing schizophrenia include: (a) genetic risk; (b) recent deterioration in functioning, such as withdrawing socially; (c) increasing frequency of unusual thoughts; (d) high levels of suspiciousness and paranoia; (e) social impairment; and (f) substance abuse.

Source: Cannon et al. (2008)

Psychological Dimension

The psychological dimension includes behaviors, attitudes, and attributes that contribute to the symptoms of schizophrenia by increasing the vulnerability of predisposed individuals. The use of cocaine, amphetamines, alcohol, and especially cannabis appears to increase the chances of developing a psychotic disorder (Callaghan et al., 2012; Zammit, Owen, Evans, Heron, & Lewis, 2012). The onset of psychosis is nearly 3 years earlier in cannabis users compared to nonusers (Large, Sharma, Compton, Slade, & Nielssen, 2011). Adolescents who use cannabis are more likely to report prodromal symptoms (e.g., "Something strange is taking place in me," "I feel that I am being followed," or "I am being influenced in a special way"; Miettunen et al., 2008).

Several possible interpretations can explain the relationship between cannabis use and psychosis: (1) the increased risk of developing psychosis may be due to the substance use itself; (2) individuals with a predisposition for psychosis may also have a predisposition to substance use; or (3) individuals with prodromal symptoms or psychotic-type experiences may use cannabis to self-medicate for these symptoms (Foti, Kotov, Guey, & Bromet, 2010; Thirthalli & Benegal, 2006). Additionally, cannabis may influence dopamine levels or increase vulnerability through interactions with environmental stressors associated with cannabis use (e.g., poor school or work performance).

Individuals who develop schizophrenia report certain cognitive patterns and unusual beliefs that precede the onset of psychotic symptoms (Solano & De Chavez, 2000). In many cases, milder disordered thinking (e.g., misattributions and catastrophic interpretations) evolves into more severe symptoms (Coltheart et al., 2007; Nothard, Morrison, & Wells, 2008). For example, negative symptoms such as avolition and restricted affect may be due to individuals' beliefs that they are worthless or failures and that their condition is hopeless (Rector et al., 2005). The combination of low expectancy for pleasure and success along with reduced expectancies due to their illness may maintain the negative symptoms. In fact, some researchers believe that it is primarily the interpretation of events that causes the distress and disability associated with schizophrenia

concordance rate the likelihood that both members of a twin pair show the same characteristic

TABLE 11.2 Negative Expectancy Appraisals Associated With Negative Symptoms

NEGATIVE SYMPTOM	LOW SELF-EFFICACY (SUCCESS)	LOW SATISFACTION (PLEASURE)	LOW ACCEPTANCE	LOW AVAILABLE RESOURCES
Restricted affect	If I show my feelings, others will see my inadequacy.	I don't feel the way I used to.	My face appears stiff and contorted to others.	I don't have the ability to express my feelings.
Alogia	I'm not going to find the right words to express myself.	I take so long to get my point across that it's boring.	I'm going to sound weird, stupid, or strange.	It takes too much effort to talk.
Avolition	Why bother, I'm just going to fail.	It's more trouble than it's worth.	It's best not to get involved.	It takes too much effort to try.

Source: Rector, Beck, & Stolar (2005), p. 254

(Garety, Bebbington, Fowler, Freeman, & Kuipers, 2007). These pessimistic interpretations can produce and maintain negative symptoms. See Table 11.2 for patterns of thinking associated with negative symptoms.

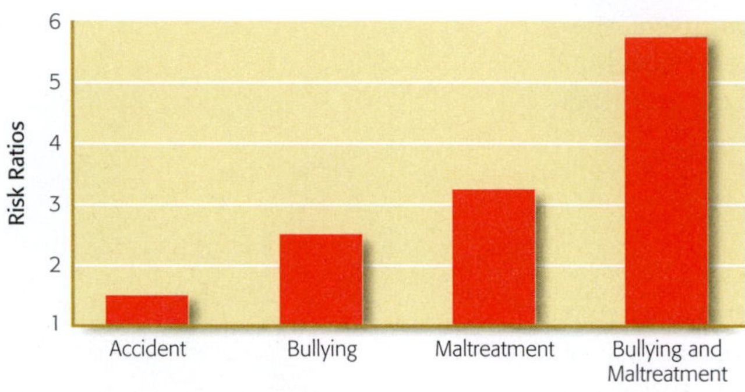

FIGURE 11.7

Risk of Psychotic Symptoms at Age 11 Associated With Cumulative Childhood Trauma

Youth exposed to both bullying and childhood maltreatment demonstrate a significantly increased risk of developing psychotic symptoms.

Source: Arseneault et al. (2011). Reprinted with permission from the *American Journal of Psychiatry*, copyright © 2011 American Psychiatric Association.

Social Dimension

Certain social events appear to influence the appearance of psychotic disorders (see Figure 11.7). For example, being in a traumatic accident has been associated with a slightly increased risk of psychotic symptoms (Arseneault et al., 2011). Individuals with psychosis were 3 times more likely to report severe physical abuse from mothers before 12 years of age than were individuals without psychosis (H. L. Fisher et al., 2010). In contrast, among adolescents with symptoms that appeared to put them "at imminent risk" for the onset of psychosis, positive remarks and warmth expressed by caregivers were associated with improvement in negative and disorganized symptoms and social functioning (M. P. O'Brien et al., 2006). Children at higher biological risk for schizophrenia may be more sensitive to the effects of both adverse and healthy child-rearing patterns (Aas et al., 2012; Tienari, Wynne, Sorri, et al., 2004). However, parenting style may also be influenced by how "sick" the child is, a possibility we consider later in the chapter.

In a longitudinal study focused on 2,232 twins, those who experienced maltreatment by an adult or bullying by peers had a higher risk of psychotic symptoms at the age of 12; children who reported being bullied were 2.5 times more likely to develop psychotic symptoms, and risk was 5.68 times greater for those exposed to both bullying and maltreatment. In another sample of 12-year-old children followed from the age of 7, the risk of psychotic symptoms doubled for those who were bullied between the ages of 8 and 10; the association was stronger with more severe or chronic forms of bullying (Schreier, Wolke, et al., 2009). Maltreatment during childhood may alter neurodevelopment in a manner that increases susceptibility to schizophrenia or other disorders.

Expressed emotion (EE), a negative communication pattern found among some relatives of individuals with schizophrenia, has been associated with higher relapse rates in individuals diagnosed with schizophrenia (Breitborde, Lopez, & Nuechterlein, 2009). EE is determined by the number of critical comments made by a relative (criticism); the number of statements of dislike or resentment directed toward the individual with schizophrenia by family members (hostility); and the number of statements reflecting emotional overinvolvement, overconcern, or overprotectiveness with respect to the family member with schizophrenia. For example, relatives high in EE are likely to make statements such as "You are a lazy person" or "You've caused our family a lot of trouble" (Rosenfarb, Goldstein, Mintz, & Nuechterlein, 1995).

expressed emotion (EE) a negative communication pattern found among some relatives of individuals with schizophrenia

Although high EE has been associated with an increased risk of relapse, the studies are correlational in nature and are therefore subject to different interpretations. Figure 11.8 indicates three possible interpretations:

- A high EE environment is stressful and may lead directly to relapse in the family member who has schizophrenia (Cutting & Docherty, 2000).
- An individual who is more severely ill has a greater chance of relapse and may cause more negative or high EE communication patterns in relatives. J. L. Schreiber, Breier, and Pickar (1995) hypothesized that expressed emotion may be a parental response to the "chronic disabling aspect of this illness" (p. 649).
- In the bidirectional model, odd behaviors or symptoms on the part of the individual with schizophrenia may cause family members to attempt to exert control and to react to the symptoms with frustration, which in turn produces increases in psychotic symptoms (Rosenfarb, Goldstein, et al., 1995).

Did You Know?

Individuals who recently experienced a psychotic breakdown attributed their emotional collapse to a variety of factors, including drug use (especially cannabis), adult trauma (e.g., sexual assault, violence, or abuse), personal sensitivity (e.g., not fitting in, bottling up feelings, discomfort around others), and developmental problems (e.g., being teased or bullied as a child, childhood abuse).

Source: Dudley, Siitarinen, James, & Dodson (2009)

The EE construct appears to have less meaning for different cultural groups; cultural factors may influence whether symptoms are appraised as burdensome by relatives as well as influencing the relationship among psychiatric symptoms, burden of care, and relatives' negative attitudes and behavior. For example, family criticism scores were not associated with relapse for Mexican Americans with schizophrenia (Lopez, Hipke, et al., 2004; Rosenfarb, Bellack, & Aziz, 2006). Among a sample of African Americans and white Americans with schizophrenia, high levels of critical and intrusive behavior by family members were associated with *better* outcomes for African American clients over a 2-year period, while white American clients had better outcomes with low levels of expressed emotion from family members. Among some African Americans, seemingly negative family communication may, in fact, be considered a reflection of caring and concern by the client (Rosenfarb, Bellack, et al., 2006). Lopez, Hipke, and associates (2004) concluded that different cultural groups interpret family communication processes such as emotional overprotection or overinvolvement differently. In fact, therapists who focus on reducing critical and intrusive communication patterns in culturally diverse families may inadvertently increase family stress.

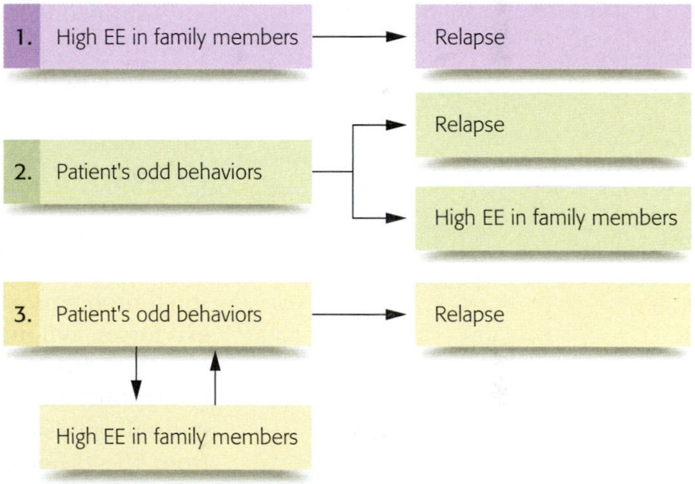

FIGURE 11.8

Possible Relationships Between High Rates of Expressed Emotion and Relapse Rates in Patients With Schizophrenia

This figure shows several ways in which expressed emotions and relapse rates can be related.

Sociocultural Dimension

Although the prevalence of schizophrenia is roughly equal between men and women, the age of onset is earlier in males than in females. The gender ratio shifts by the mid-40s and 50s, when the percentage of women receiving the diagnosis exceeds that of men. This trend is especially pronounced in the mid-60s and later (R. Howard, Rabins, Seeman, & Jeste, 2000; Thorup, Waltoft, Pedersen, Mortensen, & Nordentoft, 2007).

Researchers have hypothesized that the later age of onset found in women is due to the protective effects of estrogen, which diminish after menopause (Grigoriadis & Seeman, 2002; E. Hayes, Gavrilidis, & Kulkarni, 2012). In a study of premenopausal women with schizophrenia, significant improvements in psychotic symptoms were observed during the luteal phase of their menstrual cycle (the period after ovulation), when estrogen levels were higher (Bergemann, Parzer, Jaggy, et al., 2008). Estrogen may affect either dopamine levels or dopamine sensitivity, which have been associated with schizophrenia. Estrogen replacement therapy has improved cognitive functioning among women with schizophrenia (Bergemann, Parzer, Jaggy, et al., 2008).

© Nathan Benn/Alamy

Child Playing Outside Tenement Housing in St. Albans, Vermont

Schizophrenia is more prevalent among those living in poor neighborhoods. Some believe that the increased stress from living in poverty may be the cause. How might this environment be a risk factor?

A number of social factors have been identified as risk factors for schizophrenia, such as lower educational level of parents, lower occupational status of fathers, and residence in poorer areas at birth (Werner, Malaspina, & Rabinowitz, 2007; Wicks, Hjern, & Dalman, 2010). These forms of social adversity, especially in children who are exposed to other risk factors, appear to produce a threefold increase in the risk of developing schizophrenia compared to children who are exposed to none of these adversities (Wicks, Hjern, Gunnell, Lewis, & Dalman, 2005).

Experiences with social adversity during adulthood also increase risk of developing schizophrenia. Migration was identified as a risk factor for schizophrenia among first- and second-generation immigrants to the United Kingdom, especially for those with African ancestry (Bourque, van der Ven, & Malla, 2010; Schofield, Ashworth, & Jones, 2011; Selten, Cantor-Graae, & Kahn, 2007). Similarly, the incidence of schizophrenia has been found to be very high among several ethnic groups in the Netherlands, particularly Moroccan immigrants (Veling, Selten, Mackenbach, & Hoek, 2007). The stress of migration and experiences of discrimination as a member of a visible minority may act as additional stressors to predisposed individuals. How social stress might increase the risk for the disorder is not known, although there is a belief that stressors may affect levels of dopamine (Selten et al., 2007).

As noted throughout this book, the study of cross-cultural perspectives on psychopathology is important because indigenous belief systems influence views of etiology and treatment. In India, for example, the belief in supernatural causation of schizophrenia is widespread, leading to consultation and treatment by indigenous healers (G. Banerjee & Roy, 1998). In a study of individuals with schizophrenia from four ethnic groups (whites in the United Kingdom, African Caribbeans, Bangladeshi, and West Africans), distinct differences in explanatory models were found for the disorder (Table 11.3; R. McCabe & Priebe, 2004). The different models included biological (e.g., physical illness or substance abuse), social (e.g., interpersonal problems, stress, negative childhood events, personality), supernatural (e.g., evil forces, evil magic), and nonspecific explanations (do not know and other).

The white group as compared to the other ethnic groups was the most likely to attribute the condition to biological causes and least likely to identify supernatural causes—the explanation selected by a substantial minority of individuals from the other ethnic groups—as a potential causal factor. Differing views on etiology also influenced response to taking medication for their symptoms. Those who cited biological causes believed they were receiving the correct treatment (medication), whereas those who supported a supernatural explanation wanted alternative forms of treatment, such as religious activities. Thus views of etiology can affect an understanding of the disorder, including its severity, prognosis, and appropriate treatment.

TABLE 11.3 Explanatory Models of Illness in Schizophrenia Among Four Ethnic Groups

	BIOLOGICAL EXPLANATION	SOCIAL EXPLANATION	SUPERNATURAL EXPLANATION	NONSPECIFIC EXPLANATION
African Caribbean	6.7%	60%	20%	23.3%
Bangladeshi	0.0%	42.3%	26.9%	30.8%
West African	10.7%	31%	28.6%	21.4%
White (in the United Kingdom)	34.5%	31%	0.0%	34.5%

Source: McCabe & Priebe (2004)

CHECKPOINT REVIEW

1. Briefly describe the role of endophenotypes, neurostructures, and neurotransmitters in schizophrenia.
2. What are the psychological and social factors associated with schizophrenia?
3. What sociocultural risk factors have been found for schizophrenia?

The Treatment of Schizophrenia

Through the years, schizophrenia has been treated by a variety of means, including performing **prefrontal lobotomies**—a surgical procedure in which the frontal lobes are disconnected from the remainder of the brain—and "warehousing" severely disturbed patients in overcrowded asylums. Such inhumane treatment was generally abandoned in the 1950s, when the beneficial effects of antipsychotic drugs were discovered. Today schizophrenia is typically treated with antipsychotic medication, along with some type of psychosocial therapy. In recent years, the research and clinical perspective on people with schizophrenia has shifted from a focus on disease and deficit to one of recovery and promotion of health, competencies, independence, and self-determination (Bellack, 2006). This change of focus is affecting therapists' roles, their views of clients and their families, and appropriate treatments (Glynn et al., 2006). We first discuss medication in the treatment of schizophrenia, and then the psychological and social therapies.

Antipsychotic Medication

Case Study

Peter, a twenty-nine-year-old man, was diagnosed with chronic paranoid schizophrenia. . . . When on medication, he heard voices talking about him and felt that his phone was bugged. When off medication, he had constant hallucinations and his behavior became unpredictable. . . . He was on 10 milligrams of haloperidol (Haldol) three times a day. . . . Peter complained that he had been quite restless, and did not want to take the medication. Over the next six months, Peter's psychiatrist gradually reduced Peter's medication to 4 milligrams per day. . . . At this dose, Peter continued to have bothersome symptoms, but they remained moderate. . . . He was no longer restless. (Liberman, Kopelowicz, & Young, 1994, p. 94)

Did You Know? In a randomized, double-blind study (Amminger et al., 2010), 81 adolescents at very high risk for developing psychosis were given either omega-3 fatty acids (fish oil) or a placebo for 3 months and then followed for 12 months. In the placebo group, 11 developed psychosis as opposed to only 2 in the fish oil group. Could prevention be this easy?

Source: Amminger et al. (2010)

The use of medication in Peter's case (in the case study) illustrates several points. First, antipsychotic medications can reduce intensity of symptoms; second, dosage levels should be carefully monitored; and third, side effects can occur as a result of medication.

Many consider the 1955 introduction of *Thorazine*, the first **antipsychotic drug**, to be the beginning of a new era in treating schizophrenia. For the first time, a medication was available that sufficiently relaxed even those most severely affected by schizophrenia and helped organize their thoughts to the point that straitjackets were no longer needed for physical restraint. Although medications have improved the lives of many with schizophrenia, they do not cure the disorder. **First-generation antipsychotics** (also called conventional or typical

prefrontal lobotomy a surgical procedure in which the frontal lobes are disconnected from the remainder of the brain

antipsychotic drugs medications developed to counteract symptoms of psychosis

first-generation antipsychotics a group of medications originally developed to combat psychotic symptoms by reducing dopamine levels in the brain; also called *conventional* or *typical antipsychotics*

antipsychotics) are still viewed as effective treatments for schizophrenia, although their use has been largely supplanted by the newer **atypical antipsychotics**. Conventional antipsychotic medications (chlorpromazine/Thorazine, haloperidol/Haldol, perphenazine/Trilafon, and fluphenazine/Prolixin) have dopaminergic receptor-blocking capabilities (i.e., they reduce dopamine levels), which led to the dopamine hypothesis of schizophrenia.

The newer atypical antipsychotics (such as clozapine/Clozaril, risperidone/Risperdal, olanzapine/Zyprexa, quetiapine/Seroquel, and ziprasidone/Geodon) act on multiple dopamine and serotonin receptors and are purportedly less likely to produce side effects such as the rigidity, persistent muscle spasms, tremors, and restlessness that are found with the older antipsychotic medications (Caroff, Hurford, Lybrand, & Cabrina, 2011; Rummel-Kluge et al., 2012). However, questions are being raised about the side effects of these newer antipsychotic medications (Foley & Morley, 2011; Jeste et al., 2009; Lewin, Storch, & Storch, 2010; D. D. Miller et al., 2008).

Conventional and atypical antipsychotics effectively reduce the severity of the positive symptoms of schizophrenia, such as hallucinations, delusions, bizarre speech, and disordered thought. Most, however, offer little relief from the negative symptoms such as social withdrawal, apathy, and impaired personal hygiene (M. F. Green, 2007; Strous et al., 2004). Moreover, a "relatively large group" of people with schizophrenia does not benefit at all from antipsychotic medication, and many discontinue their medications for a variety of reasons, including side effects (Almerie, Matar, Essali, Alkhateeb, & Rezk, 2008).

Many individuals treated with antipsychotic medications develop **extrapyramidal symptoms** which include *parkinsonism* (muscle tremors, shakiness, and immobility), *dystonia* (slow and continued involuntary movements of the limbs and tongue), *akathisia* (motor restlessness), and *neuroleptic malignant syndrome* (muscle rigidity and autonomic instability, which can be fatal if untreated). Other symptoms may involve the loss of facial expression, immobility, shuffling gait, tremors of the hand, rigidity of the body, and poor postural stability; although many symptoms are reversible once medication is stopped, some symptoms (e.g., involuntary movements) can be permanent (D. E. Casey, 2006). Antipsychotic medications are also associated with increased risk of **metabolic syndrome** (a condition associated with obesity, diabetes, high cholesterol, and hypertension; Shirzadi & Ghaemi, 2006). (See the Controversy box "The Marketing of Atypical Antipsychotic Medications.")

Newer antipsychotic medications cost 10 times more than older antipsychotics. But are these newer antipsychotic medications safer and more effective than first-generation antipsychotics? In a comprehensive nationwide comparative drug study, the effectiveness of an older antipsychotic (perphenazine) was compared with that of several newer antipsychotic medications (olanzapine, quetiapine, risperidone, and ziprasidone) in the treatment of chronic schizophrenia (average length of illness in the participants was 14.4 years). Surprisingly, the older, less expensive medication (perphenazine) used in the study generally performed as well as the four newer medications and did not produce significantly more extrapyramidal symptoms (restlessness, involuntary movements, and muscular tension; Lieberman et al., 2005).

Most clinicians today agree that the most beneficial treatment for schizophrenia is a combination of antipsychotic medication and psychotherapy. Although medications can reduce many symptoms of schizophrenia, one vital fact is clear. Individuals with schizophrenia discharged from protective hospital environments often return to stressful home or work situations. Dealing with chronic stress can result in the return of psychotic symptoms and rehospitalization; medication alone is often not enough to help those with schizophrenia function in their natural environments.

atypical antipsychotics newer antipsychotic medications that are chemically different and less likely to produce the side effects associated with first-generation antipsychotics

extrapyramidal symptoms side effects such as restlessness, involuntary movements, and muscular tension produced by antipsychotic medications

metabolic syndrome a medical condition associated with obesity, diabetes, high cholesterol, and hypertension

CONTROVERSY:

The Marketing of Atypical Antipsychotic Medications

The woman in the Abilify ad says, "I'm taking an antidepressant but I think I need more help." According to the ad, two out of three individuals taking an antidepressant alone still have symptoms of depression. The ad goes on to suggest that Abilify can be helpful when combined with current antidepressant medications. Abilify is an atypical antipsychotic medication, but that fact is not mentioned (Westberg, 2010).

Surprisingly, the top selling class of medications in the United States is atypical antipsychotic medications, a drug class accounting for $13 billion of U.S. prescriptions in 2007, including more than $1 billion in annual sales for quetiapine (Seroquel), aripiprazole (Abilify), olanzapine (Zyprexa), and risperidone (Risperdal; G. C. Alexander, Gallagher, Mascola, Moloney, & Stafford, 2011). These profitable drugs are heavily promoted by the pharmaceutical companies, with resultant increases in the number of people taking both antidepressants and antipsychotics. However, many of these combinations are of "unproven efficacy" (Mojtabai & Olfson, 2010).

Even more problematic is that off-label use (i.e., prescribing medication for unapproved indications, such as for treatment of a different disorder or age group) of atypical antipsychotics has increased dramatically. Antipsychotics are increasingly prescribed for a range of mental disorders, including attentional, conduct, and anxiety disorders, although they have never been evaluated for use with these disorders (Crystal, Olfson, Huang, Pincus, & Gerhard, 2009). Among one sample of nursing home residents, 29 percent were prescribed at least one antipsychotic medication; many of this group had no clinical indication for the medication (Y. Chen et al., 2010). Findings such as this are of particular concern because the use of antipsychotic medication can compromise the health of individuals with dementia (Treloar et al., 2010). More than half of the prescriptions in 2008 for atypical antipsychotic medications were off-label and of "uncertain efficacy" (G. C. Alexander et al., 2011).

The increased use of atypical antipsychotic medications is of particular concern due to their association with troublesome side effects. After only 12 weeks on Abilify, Risperdal, Seroquel, or Zyprexa, children were found to gain up to 19 lb (Correll et al., 2010). In a 5-year study of atypical antipsychotics in middle-aged and older individuals with schizophrenia, 29.7 percent had serious adverse physical effects that were probably or possibly due to the medication. Increases in cholesterol levels and weight gain have been found in individuals taking atypical antipsychotic medications for as little as 3 months (Foley & Morley, 2011). The U.S. Food and Drug Administration (2011) has warned that infants born to mothers taking antipsychotic medications during the third trimester of pregnancy are at high risk of having abnormal muscle tone, tremors, sleepiness, severe difficulty breathing, and difficulty sucking.

Should regulations be in place to protect consumers from the increasing off-label use of antipsychotic medications? Should advertisements promoting atypical antipsychotic medications identify them as such? Should physicians and psychiatrists be required to inform patients about off-label prescriptions?

Psychosocial Therapy

Case Study

Philip's psychotic symptoms had been reduced with medication. However, he was unable to obtain employment because of cognitive and behavioral peculiarities. Philip did not seem to understand what were considered to be appropriate conversational topics and attire. His counselor suggested that his clothing (sweatshirt, exercise pants, headband, and worn sneakers) might be inappropriate for a job interview. Field trips were planned to allow Philip to observe attire worn by individuals in different businesses. He was trained in conversational topics and practiced job interviews with his counselor. After deciding to apply for landscape work, Philip wore a work shirt, blue jeans, and construction boots; he was hired by the landscaping contractor (Heinssen & Cuthbert, 2001).

Many individuals with schizophrenia behave "strangely," do not have positive conversational skills, and display faulty thinking. Social communication is problematic because many individuals exhibit deficits in emotional perception and in understanding the beliefs and attitudes of others (Combs et al., 2007). Heinssen and Cuthbert (2001) found that eccentricities in the appearance, attire, and communication patterns of individuals with schizophrenia, as well as lack of discretion in discussing their illness, can impede employment or the establishment of social networks. Psychotherapeutic approaches have been tailored to address these issues, allowing many individuals with schizophrenia to acquire employment.

Cognitive-Behavioral Therapy

Major advances have been made in the use of cognitive and behavioral strategies in treating the symptoms of schizophrenia, especially among those who have not been fully helped through medication. Therapists teach coping skills that allow clients to manage their positive and negative symptoms as well as the cognitive deficits found in schizophrenia (Hansen, Kingdon, & Turkington, 2006; Zimmermann, Favrod, Trieu, & Pomini, 2005). An 18-month follow-up of 216 individuals with persisting psychotic symptoms found that those receiving cognitive-behavioral therapy demonstrated 183 days of normal functioning, compared to 106 days of normal functioning for those who received treatment as usual consisting of pharmacotherapy and contact with a psychiatric nurse (van der Gaag et al., 2011).

The following case study provides an example of symptoms of schizophrenia that might be effectively addressed with cognitive-behavioral treatment strategies.

Case Study

A young African American woman with auditory hallucinations, paranoid delusions, delusions of reference, and a history of childhood verbal and physical abuse and adult sexual assault felt extremely hopeless about her prospects for developing social ties. She believed that her "persecutors" had informed others of her socially undesirable activities. . . . She often loudly screamed at the voices she was hearing. . . . When she did leave her home, she often covered her head with a black kerchief and wore dark sunglasses, partly in an effort to disguise herself from her persecutors. (Cather, 2005, p. 260)

Cognitive-behavioral treatment of schizophrenia often includes the following steps (J. Addington & Haarmans, 2006; Hansen et al., 2006):

- *Engagement.* The therapist explains the therapy and works to foster a safe and collaborative method of looking at causes of distress, drawing out the client's understanding of stressors and ways of coping.
- *Assessment.* Clients are encouraged to discuss their fears and anxieties; the therapist shares information about how symptoms are formed and maintained. In the preceding case study, the therapist helped the woman make sense of her persecutory experiences. It was explained that victims of abuse often internalize beliefs that they are responsible for the abuse, and that her view that she was "bad" led to expectations of negative reactions from others and the need to disguise herself.
- *Identification of negative beliefs.* The therapist explains to the client the link between personal beliefs and emotional distress, and the ways that

beliefs such as "Nobody will like me if I tell them about my voices" can be disputed and changed to "I can't demand that everyone like me. Some people will and some won't" (Hansen et al., 2006, p. 50). This reinterpretation often leads to less sadness and isolation.
- *Normalization.* The therapist works with the client to normalize and decatastrophize the psychotic experiences. Information that many people can have unusual experiences can reduce a client's sense of isolation.
- *Collaborative analysis of symptoms.* Once a strong therapeutic alliance has been established, the therapist begins critical discussions of the client's symptoms, such as "If voices come from your head, why can't others hear them?" Evidence for and against the maladaptive beliefs is discussed, combined with information about how beliefs are maintained through cognitive distortions or inferences.
- *Development of alternative explanations.* The therapist helps the client develop alternatives to previous maladaptive assumptions, using the client's ideas whenever possible.

Bruce Ayers/Getty Images

Family Communication and Education

Therapy that includes the family members of individuals with schizophrenia reduces relapse rates and is more effective than drug treatment alone.

More recently, instead of trying to eliminate or combat hallucinations, clients are taught to accept them in a nonjudgmental manner. In mindfulness training, clients are taught to let go of angry or fearful responses to psychotic symptoms; instead, they are taught to let the psychotic symptoms come into consciousness without reacting. This process enhances feelings of self-control and significantly reduces negative emotions (Chadwick, Hughes, Russell, Russell, & Dagnan, 2009; Dannahy et al., 2011). The approach was used with men who had heard malevolent and powerful voices for more than 30 years. Their attempts to stop the voices or to distract themselves were ineffective. After undergoing mindfulness training, the men were less distressed with the voices and more confident in their ability to live with them (K. N. Taylor, Harper, & Chadwick, 2009). Similarly, malevolent and persecuting voices became less disturbing when individuals with schizophrenia learned to access positive emotions such as warmth and contentment during psychotic episodes (Mayhew & Gilbert, 2008).

Interventions Focusing on Family Communication and Education

A serious mental illness such as schizophrenia can have a powerful effect on family members, who may feel stigmatized or responsible for the disorder. As one woman stated, "All family members are affected by a loved one's mental illness. The entire family system needs to be addressed" (Stalberg, Ekerwald, & Hultman, 2004).

More than half of those recovering from a psychotic episode return to live with their families, and new psychological interventions address this fact. Family intervention programs have not only reduced relapse rates but have also lowered the cost of care. They have been beneficial for families with and without negative communication patterns. Most programs include the following components (Glynn et al., 2006; Mueser et al., 2001):

- normalizing the family experience;
- demonstrating concern, empathy, and sympathy to all family members;
- educating family members about schizophrenia;
- avoiding blaming the family or pathologizing their coping efforts;
- identifying the strengths and competencies of the client and family members;
- developing skills in solving problems and managing stress;

AP Photo/Paul Sakuma

Artwork to Demonstrate Creative Talents

A self-portrait by artist William Scott is displayed at the Creative Growth Art Center in Oakland, California. The artist, diagnosed with schizophrenia and an autism spectrum disorder, has had his paintings and sculptures sold around the world in the trendiest galleries.

- teaching family members to cope with the symptoms of mental illness and its repercussions on the family; and
- strengthening the communication skills of family members.

Family approaches and social skills training are much more effective in preventing relapse than drug treatment alone (Xia, Merinder, & Belgamwar, 2011). Combining cognitive-behavioral strategies, family counseling, and social skills training seems to produce the most positive results (Penn et al., 2004). The use of medication combined with psychosocial interventions has provided hope for many of those with schizophrenia. In fact, recent research suggests that "optimism about outcome from schizophrenia is justified" and that "a substantial proportion of people with the illness will recover completely and many more will regain good social functioning" (R. Warner, 2009, p. 374).

CHECKPOINT REVIEW

1. Describe the pros and cons of using antipsychotic medications.
2. Describe the steps involved in cognitive-behavioral treatment of schizophrenia.
3. What are the common components in family interventions?
4. What are the most important components of treatment programs for schizophrenia?

Summary

1 What are the symptoms of schizophrenia?

- Positive symptoms of schizophrenia involve unusual thoughts or perceptions, such as delusions, hallucinations, disordered thinking, and bizarre behavior.
- Negative symptoms of schizophrenia include an inability or decreased ability to initiate actions (avolition) or speech (alogia), express emotions, or feel pleasure (restricted affect).
- Cognitive symptoms of schizophrenia include problems with attention, memory, and developing plans of action.

2 How do other psychotic disorders differ from schizophrenia?

- Brief psychotic disorder is usually associated with a stressor and is characterized by psychotic symptoms that last less than 1 month.
- Schizophreniform disorder is characterized by psychotic symptoms that are usually associated with a stressor and that last from 1 to 6 months.
- Delusional disorder is characterized by persistent nonbizarre delusions and the absence of other unusual or odd behaviors.
- Attenuated psychosis syndrome involves early, milder psychotic symptoms that have developed or increased over the past year.
- Psychotic disorder not elsewhere classified is a category characterized by disorders with psychotic symptoms that are not significant enough to meet the criteria for a specific psychotic disorder.

3 Is there much chance of recovery from schizophrenia?

- Prognosis for schizophrenia is variable and is associated with premorbid levels of functioning. Many individuals with schizophrenia experience minimal or no lasting impairment and recover enough to lead relatively productive lives.

4 What causes schizophrenia?

- The best conclusion is that genetics and environmental factors (physical, psychological, and social) combine to cause the disorder. Genetic factors may contribute to biological risk factors, such as abnormalities in neurotransmitters or brain structures. Early negative childhood experiences, use of substances such as cannabis and amphetamines, and sociocultural stressors may interact with genetic predisposition to produce schizophrenia.

5 What treatments are currently available for schizophrenia, and are they effective?

- Schizophrenia involves both biological and psychological factors; treatment programs that combine drugs with psychotherapy appear to hold the most promise.
- Drug therapy usually involves conventional antipsychotics or the newer atypical antipsychotics.
- The accompanying psychosocial therapy consists of either supportive counseling or behavior therapy, with an emphasis on cognitive and social skills training and facilitation of positive communication between those with schizophrenia and their family members.

Key Terms

schizophrenia 292
psychosis 292
positive symptoms 292
delusion 293
paranoid ideation 294
persecutory delusions 294
disconfirmatory evidence 295
hallucination 295
loosening of associations 296
catatonia 297
negative symptoms 298
avolition 298
alogia 298
asociality 298
restricted affect 298
cognitive symptoms 298
brief psychotic disorder 299
schizophreniform disorder 299
provisional diagnosis 300
delusional disorder 300
schizoaffective disorder 302
attenuated psychosis syndrome 302
premorbid 303
endophenotype 306
dopamine hypothesis 307
concordance rate 309
expressed emotion (EE) 310
prefrontal lobotomy 313
antipsychotic drugs 313
first-generation antipsychotics 313
atypical antipsychotics 314
extrapyramidal symptoms 314
metabolic syndrome 314

Media Resources

Psychology CourseMate

Access an interactive e-Book and chapter-specific interactive learning tools, including:

- flashcards
- quizzes
- videos

and more in your Psychology CourseMate.

Go to **CengageBrain.com.**

David Eulitt/MCT/Newscom

12

Neurocognitive Disorders

CHAPTER OUTLINE

Mr. C., age 42, was in a coma for 2 weeks after falling from a ladder. Before his fall, he was known for being respectful, reliable, and easygoing. After the fall, socially inappropriate and impulsive behaviors, such as getting into arguments and groping women, occurred frequently. Brain scans and psychological testing documented residual brain injury, including damage to the frontal lobe of his brain, an area associated with impulse control. Although additional rehabilitation resulted in significant improvement, lasting effects from the injury prevented complete recovery (Rao et al., 2007).

FOCUS QUESTIONS

1 How can we determine whether someone has a neurocognitive disorder?

2 What are the different types of neurocognitive disorders?

3 What are the causes of neurocognitive disorders?

4 What kinds of interventions are available to treat neurocognitive disorders?

Like many other individuals, Mr. C. suffers from a **neurocognitive disorder**—a condition resulting from transient (temporary) or permanent damage to the brain. Neurocognitive disorders involve changes in brain structure, function, or chemistry that affect thinking, memory, and perception (the ability to recognize and interpret stimuli). Changes in behavior and emotional functioning, as seen in the case of Mr. C., are commonly seen in neurocognitive disorders.

There are three major categories of brain disorders: (a) major neurocognitive disorder, (b) mild neurocognitive disorder, and (c) delirium (Table 12.1). Possible causes of neurocognitive disorders include degenerative conditions in which symptoms become worse over time (Table 12.2) and relatively sudden events such as stroke, head injury, or infection (Table 12.3). Although the symptoms of neurocognitive disorders result from the underlying brain condition, they are also influenced by social and psychological factors. People with similar types of brain damage may recover quite differently, depending on their personalities, their coping skills, and the availability of resources such as rehabilitation and family support systems. The disruptions in brain function seen in neurocognitive disorders can lead to a variety of behavioral and emotional changes that also can significantly affect progress, including apathy, depression, anxiety, and difficulty with impulse control (H. J. Rosen & Levenson, 2009). Furthermore, people with neurocognitive disorders are sometimes treated insensitively, which may add to their stress and hinder their recovery. This stress can exacerbate symptoms that stem from the **brain pathology** itself. Thus, biological, psychological, social, and sociocultural factors interact in complicated ways to produce the symptoms seen in neurocognitive disorders. We discussed the structure of the human brain in Chapter 2; in this chapter, we focus on the assessment of brain damage, types and causes of neurocognitive disorders, and treatment considerations.

TABLE 12.1 Neurocognitive Disorders

DISORDER	SYMPTOMS
Major neurocognitive disorder	Significant decline in performance in one or more cognitive areas; the deficits are severe enough to interfere with independence
Mild neurocognitive disorder[a]	Minor decline in performance in one or more cognitive areas; compensatory strategies may be required to maintain independence
Delirium[b]	Sudden changes in cognition, including diminished awareness and impaired attention and focus

[a]Mild and major neurocognitive disorder are sometimes earlier and later stages of the same disorder.
[b]Delirium can occur with major and mild neurocognitive disorder but can also occur independent of these disorders.
Source: DSM-5 Work Groups (2012)

TABLE 12.2 Neurodegenerative Disorders

ETIOLOGY	CHARACTERISTICS
Alzheimer's disease	Declining cognitive functioning, including early, prominent memory impairment
Lewy body dementia	Visual hallucinations, fluctuating cognitive impairment, decline in motor skills
Parkinson's disease	Tremor, muscle rigidity, slow movement, and possible cognitive decline
Huntington's disease	Involuntary movement, cognitive decline, and emotional instability
Frontotemporal lobar degeneration	Brain degeneration in frontal or temporal lobes that affects language and behavior
Vascular cognitive impairment	Brain degeneration due to cardiovascular factors
AIDS dementia complex	Cognitive decline due to HIV or AIDS

neurocognitive disorder a disorder that occurs when brain dysfunction affects thinking processes, memory, consciousness, or perception

brain pathology a dysfunction or disease of the brain

TABLE 12.3 Event Causes of Neurocognitive Disorders

ETIOLOGY	CHARACTERISTICS
Ischemic stroke	Blockage of blood flow in the brain
Hemorrhagic stroke	Bleeding within the brain
Traumatic brain injury	Head wound or trauma
Substance abuse	Results from intoxication, withdrawal, oxygen deprivation, or chronic substance use
Meningitis	Infection-produced inflammation of tissues surrounding the brain and spinal cord
Encephalitis	Infection-produced brain inflammation
Epilepsy	Seizures

electroencephalograph (EEG) a test that measures the firing of neurons via electrodes placed on the scalp

computerized axial tomography (CT or CAT) a neuroimaging technique that produces brain images using multiple cross-sectional X-rays of the brain

magnetic resonance imaging (MRI) a neuroimaging technique that produces brain images using a magnetic field

functional magnetic resonance imaging (fMRI) a specialized MRI that assesses brain structures and blood flow in different brain regions

The Assessment of Brain Damage

To screen for neurocognitive disorders, clinicians gather background information, keeping alert for information suggesting mental changes or declines in thinking or self-help skills. They carefully evaluate general functioning, personality characteristics, and coping skills, as well as behaviors and emotional reactions. They may conduct a mental status examination (see Chapter 3) to assess memory, attentional skills, and orientation to time and place. Psychologists also use a variety of tests and inventories to evaluate specific cognitive functions such as memory and thought processes. Comprehensive assessment provides the information needed for planning treatment or further evaluation.

Neurological testing is also used to assess neurocognitive functioning. The Glasgow Coma Scale, a screening tool used to objectively measure consciousness following head injury or stroke, helps localize and evaluate the extent of brain damage. Areas assessed are motor responsiveness, verbalization, and control over eye movements. A widely used means of examining the brain is the **electroencephalograph (EEG)**. Electrodes attached to the scalp record electrical activity (brain waves); EEGs can detect irregular electrical activity and brain wave patterns. Newer *neuroimaging techniques* allow medical professionals to noninvasively visualize brain structures and monitor activity within the brain. For example, the **computerized axial tomography (CT or CAT)** scan repeatedly takes X-rays of different areas of the brain and produces a three-dimensional, cross-sectional image of the structure of the brain. These images can provide a detailed view of brain abnormalities. **Magnetic resonance imaging (MRI)** also uses computer processing and a layer-by-layer scanning technique to produce highly detailed images of the brain (Burghart & Finn, 2010) without the radiation exposure and cancer risk seen with CT scans (Berrington de González et al., 2009; Brenner & Hall, 2007). Instead of radiation, MRI scans use a powerful magnetic field and radio frequency pulses to create brain images.

While CT and traditional MRI scans provide images of brain structure, nuclear imaging scans provide information on metabolic processes within the brain. **Functional magnetic resonance imaging (fMRI)** is a specialized MRI in which both brain structures and changes in blood flow in different brain regions can be

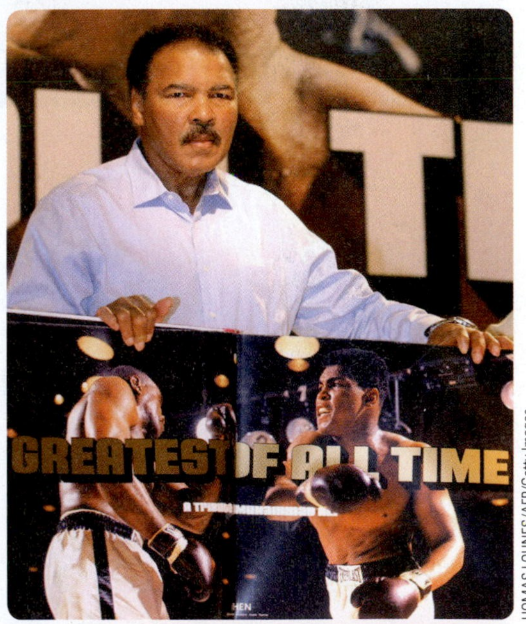

HOMAS LOHNES/AFP/Getty Images

Still a Champion, but at What Cost?

Muhammad Ali, a champion heavyweight boxer, developed symptoms of Parkinson's disease—such as slurred speech, a shuffling gait, expressionless facial appearance, and occasional memory lapses—in his early 40's. These symptoms are believed to be the result of chronic traumatic encephalopathy (also called boxer's dementia or punch-drunk syndrome), a condition that results from repeated blows to the head.

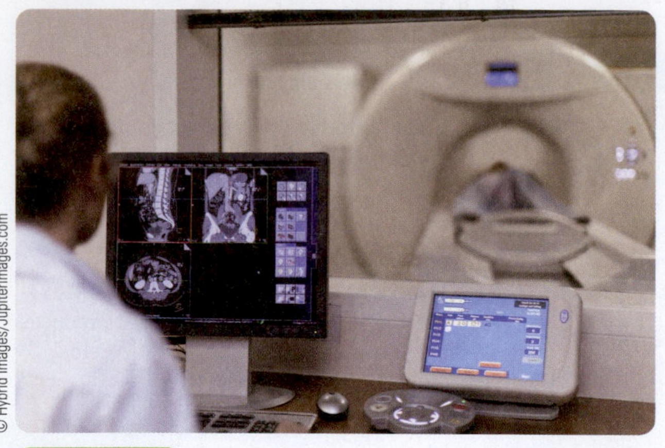

MRI Scans

A technician is observing the MRI scan of a patient. MRI uses a magnetic field and radio waves to produce detailed brain images and detect brain abnormalities. The procedure requires patients to remain perfectly still while the imaging is taking place.

observed. In a **positron emission tomography (PET)** scan, a radioactive substance is injected into the bloodstream and the metabolism of glucose in the brain is monitored. Computers then create three-dimensional images of physiological processes occurring within the brain. Through snippets of data regarding brain activity and subtle metabolic changes, PET imaging can determine if disease is active or dormant or if tumors are benign or malignant. **Single photon emission computed tomography (SPECT)** imaging is a less expensive technique that provides images of metabolic activity and blood flow patterns within the brain similar to those obtained through PET scans, but with less detail. Each of these neuroimaging techniques has strengths and weaknesses in terms of costs, benefits, and possible side effects. An appraisal of procedural risks and benefits guides decisions regarding which tools to use for diagnosis, treatment, and assessment of progress.

CHECKPOINT REVIEW

1. What kind of information is gathered when assessing possible brain damage?
2. What is the difference between a CT scan and an MRI scan?
3. What is the purpose of neurological assessment?

Types of Neurocognitive Disorders

There are three categories of neurocognitive disorder: major neurocognitive disorder, mild neurocognitive disorder, and delirium (DSM-5 Work Groups, 2012). Neurocognitive disorders most commonly result from specific medical conditions or from the use or abuse of certain drugs or alcohol. When they are known, clinicians indicate the underlying medical circumstances causing the disorder.

Major Neurocognitive Disorder

Case Study

Ms. B., an 80-year-old woman, became increasingly agitated, screaming, spitting, striking staff. . . . Her speech was loud, disarticulate. . . . She repeatedly yelled "get out." Ms. B. had recently moved to an assisted-living facility due to her declining language, social, and self-care skills (Bang, Price, Prentice, & Campbell, 2009, p. 379).

Individuals diagnosed with major neurocognitive disorder show significant decline in both of the following:

- one or more areas of cognitive functioning (Table 12.4), including attention, decision making, judgment, learning, memory, visual perception, or social behavior; and
- the ability to independently meet the demands of daily living

Direct observation, interviews, and psychological or neuropsychological testing are used to objectively document that skills are significantly lower than would

positron emission tomography (PET) a nuclear imaging scan that assesses glucose metabolism in the brain

single photon emission computed tomography (SPECT) a nuclear imaging scan that provides longer but less detailed images of metabolic activity within the brain

TABLE 12.4 Areas of Possible Neurocognitive Dysfunction

COGNITIVE DOMAIN	SKILLS AFFECTED
Complex attention	Planning, working memory
Executive ability	Decision making, mental flexibility
Learning and memory	Long-term, immediate, and recent memory
Language	Understanding and use of language
Visual-perceptual ability	Construction, visual perception
Social cognition	Recognition of emotions, behavioral regulation

Source: DSM-5 Work Groups (2012)

be expected based on the individual's age, gender, educational and cultural background, and levels of prior functioning. Although a significant deficit in only one cognitive area is needed for diagnosis, deficits in multiple areas are common. The cognitive slowing sometimes seen in normal aging is different from declines seen in major neurocognitive disorder (see comparisons in Table 12.5); for example, periodic memory difficulties (e.g., forgetting names or phone numbers, misplacing objects) are common occurrences and not signs of a neurocognitive disorder.

Dementia is a term used to describe the memory impairment and declining cognitive functioning resulting from degenerative brain conditions. People with dementia may forget the names of significant others or past events. They may also display difficulties with problem solving and impulse control. Dementia typically has a gradual onset followed by continuing cognitive decline. Age is the best studied and the strongest risk factor for dementia. The longer a person lives, the greater the chance of developing dementia. Women usually live longer than men, so they are more likely to develop dementia. Among 65-year-olds, the

Did You Know? Due to an aging population, lifestyle factors that affect brain health, and increased emphasis on early diagnosis, it is estimated that the number of people affected by dementia worldwide will nearly double every 20 years—increasing from 35.6 million in 2010 to 115.4 million in 2050.

Source: Prince et al, (2011)

TABLE 12.5 Normal Aging or Neurocognitive Disorder?

NORMAL AGING	MAJOR NEUROCOGNITIVE DISORDER
Is independent in most activities	Requires assistance with daily activities
Occasionally misplaces things and locates them after searching	Places items in unusual locations; may not recall objects are missing
Occasionally forgets a name, word, or appointment	Frequently forgets words or recently learned information; uses incorrect words
Usually follows written or verbal directions without difficulty	Has difficulty following written or verbal directions
Is slower to complete mental or physical activities	Has difficulty performing familiar tasks
Shows concern about occasional forgetfulness	Is unaware or unconcerned about memory difficulties
Experiences occasional distractibility	Exercises poor judgment; fails to remember important details
Continues interacting socially; occasionally feels tired	Exhibits decreasing social skills, declining social interest, and passivity
Occasionally gets lost	Experiences increasing disorientation and confusion
Undergoes normal changes in mood	Has personality changes and drastic mood shifts

dementia syndrome of symptoms involving deterioration in cognition and independent functioning

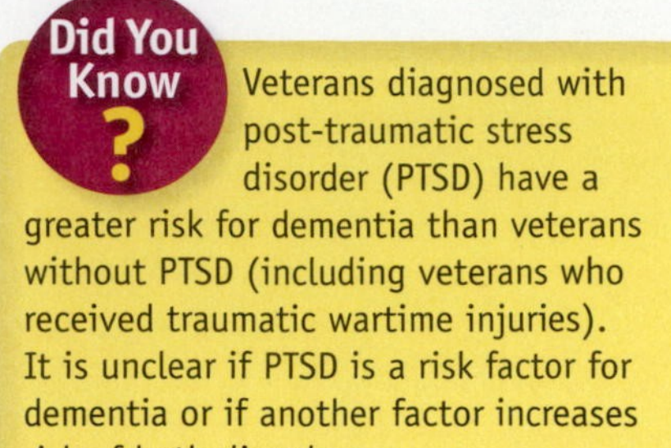

Veterans diagnosed with post-traumatic stress disorder (PTSD) have a greater risk for dementia than veterans without PTSD (including veterans who received traumatic wartime injuries). It is unclear if PTSD is a risk factor for dementia or if another factor increases risk of both disorders.

Source: Qureshi et al, (2010)

lifetime risk of developing dementia is estimated to be 11 percent for men and 19 percent for women (Gatz, 2007). Unfortunately, many cases of dementia go undiagnosed, and therefore those affected do not have the benefit of receiving practical information about the condition or the opportunity to plan for future care (Prince, Bryce, & Ferri, 2011).

Mild Neurocognitive Disorder

A mild neurocognitive disorder also involves deficits in at least one major cognitive area (see Table 12.4), although the degree of impairment is less severe than that seen in major neurocognitive disorder. Individuals with a mild neurocognitive disorder are often able to participate in their normal activities, although they may struggle to complete more complex tasks. Although extra effort to maintain independence may be required (e.g., keeping lists or hiring someone to manage finances), overall independent functioning is not compromised. The deficits seen in mild neurocognitive disorder are sometimes viewed as an intermediate stage between normal aging and dementia. In general, individuals with mild cognitive impairment decline by about 10 percent each year. However, early diagnosis and treatment of nonprogressive conditions can, in fact, result in a return to normal functioning (R. C. Petersen, 2011).

The primary distinction between major and mild neurocognitive disorder is the severity of decline in cognitive and independent functioning. In fact, mild and major neurocognitive disorders are sometimes earlier and later stages of the same disorder (R. C. Petersen, 2011). For example, someone in the early stages of a progressive disorder such as Alzheimer's disease may initially remain independent and display only minor declines in cognitive functioning; as the disease progresses, symptoms may increase in severity or affect additional cognitive areas. On the other hand, a diagnosis may change from major to mild neurocognitive disorder if recovery from stroke, traumatic brain injury, infection-induced brain damage, or substance abuse decreases impairment. Individuals with either major or mild neurocognitive disorder can show an abrupt change in functioning if they experience an episode of delirium, the third type of neurocognitive disorder.

Delirium

Case Study

Police brought an eighteen-year-old high school senior to the emergency department after he was picked up wandering in traffic. He was angry, agitated, and aggressive. In a rambling, disjointed manner he explained that he had been using "speed." In the emergency room he had difficulty focusing his attention, frequently needed questions repeated, and was disoriented as to time and place (Spitzer, Gibbon, Skodol, Williams, & First, 1994, p. 162).

delirium an acute state of confusion involving diminished awareness, disorientation, and impaired attentional skills

Delirium is an acute state of confusion characterized by diminished awareness (including disorientation) and impaired attentional skills. Although delirium can emerge in the context of a major or mild neurocognitive disorder, it can also appear independently. Delirium is distinguished from mild and major neurocognitive disorder based on its core characteristics (disturbance in awareness and inability to direct, focus, sustain, and shift attention) as well as its rapid onset and fluctuating course. Delirium typically develops rather rapidly. Symptoms can be mild or quite severe. Someone experiencing delirium may show confusion regarding the time of the day or where he or she is. Disorganized thinking and rambling, irrelevant, or incoherent speech may be present. Psychotic symptoms such as delusions or hallucinations may also occur. Symptoms of delirium fluctuate and can range from agitation and combativeness to drowsy, unresponsive behavior.

Treatment of delirium involves identifying the underlying cause, which may include high fever; severe dehydration or malnutrition; acute infection; side effects of medication; synergistic (interactive) effects of multiple medications; alcohol, drug, or inhalant intoxication; physiological withdrawal from alcohol, sedatives, or sleeping medications; or brain changes associated with a neurocognitive disorder. Additionally, when people are ill or elderly, they are more likely to develop delirium with medical illness, severe stress, or surgical procedures (American Geriatric Society, 2010; Wise, Hilty, & Cerda, 2001). Given the multiple stressors experienced during hospitalization (illness, recovery from surgery, use of new medications, sleep deprivation), episodes of hospital-associated delirium are not uncommon (R. R. Miller & Ely, 2007). Delirium associated with hospitalization is illustrated in the following case studies.

Did You Know?

Many people wonder if individuals with dementia can competently operate an automobile. In a simulated driving experiment, individuals with dementia received more speeding tickets, ran more stop signs, and were involved in more accidents than individuals of a similar age and gender with no dementia.

Source: de Simone, Kaplan, Patronas, Wassermann, & Grafman (2006)

Case Study

Following a lung cancer diagnosis, Annie, a smoker since age 18, had surgery to remove the diseased portion of her lung. After her surgery, she was quite agitated, begging to leave immediately, convinced that the doctors and nurses were trying to kill her. Annie's confusion and paranoia continued for the next few days, but resolved when she returned home.

Case Study

Justin Kaplan, an alert 84-year-old Pulitzer Prize–winning historian hospitalized after contracting pneumonia, describes an episode of delirium in which he fought with aliens: "Thousands of tiny little creatures, some on horseback, waving arms, carrying weapons like some grand Renaissance battle." In an attempt to "attack the aliens," Kaplan fell out of bed, injuring himself. He later threatened to kill his wife and kicked a nurse who was trying to restrain him. Once his medical condition improved, the delirium subsided (Belluck, 2010).

The severe symptoms of hospital delirium can distress loved ones, especially because there is usually no prior history of such behavior. Hospital delirium can result in longer hospital stays and lower rates of survival as well as increased risk of persistent cognitive impairment in older individuals (Girard, Pandharipande, & Ely, 2008). Fortunately, many hospitals attempt to detect and intervene with delirium in its earliest stages to prevent these consequences (American Geriatric Society, 2010).

CHECKPOINT REVIEW

1. What is the main distinction between a major and a mild neurocognitive disorder?
2. What is dementia?
3. What is delirium?

Etiology of Neurocognitive Disorders

Neurocognitive disorders result from a variety of medical conditions. Rather than an etiological discussion using our multipath model, we focus on some of the *sources* of neurocognitive disorders. We do this because neurocognitive disorders involve conditions in which the cause and expected symptoms and course of the disorder are already known. We also discuss factors that increase the risk of developing a neurocognitive disorder. From the perspective of our multipath model, the specific brain pathology is the primary biological factor for each condition; however, other factors interact with the neurological condition to affect outcome, as shown in Figure 12.1.

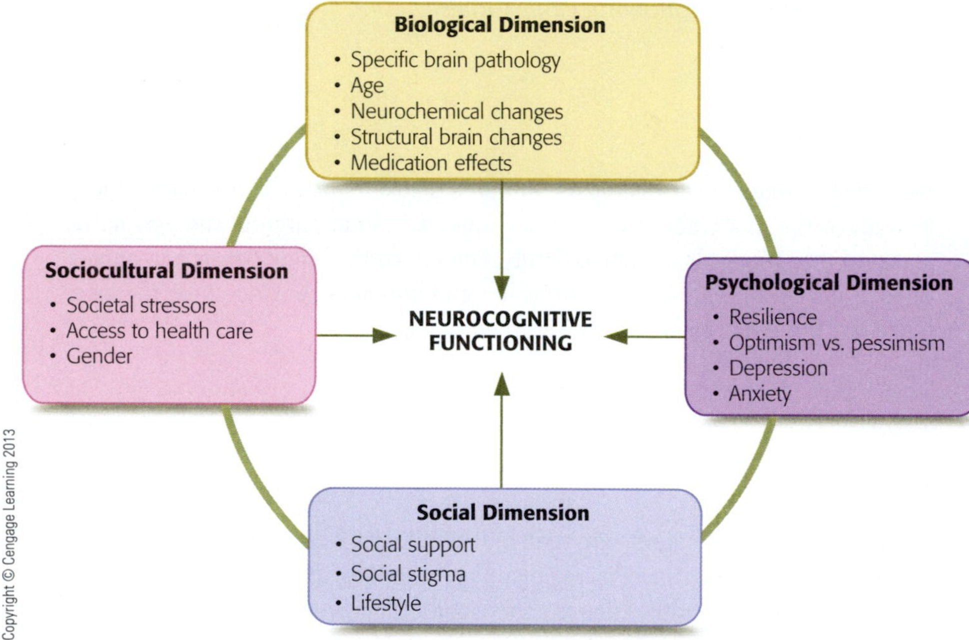

FIGURE 12.1

Multipath Model of Neurocognitive Disorders

The dimensions interact with specific brain pathology to produce the symptoms and pattern of recovery seen in various neurocognitive disorders.

CONTROVERSY:

Head Injury: What Do Soldiers Need to Know?

- A 28-year-old soldier with six separate blast-related concussions reports that he has daily headaches and difficulty performing simple mental tasks.
- After a bomb explosion hurled an Army enlistee against a wall, he continued working despite being dazed and suffering shrapnel wounds. Confusion, headaches, and problems with balance persisted for months; he later developed seizures.
- The driver of a vehicle hit by a roadside bomb did not appear to be seriously injured. However, in the months following the explosion, his speech was slurred and he had difficulty reading and completing simple tasks. (T. C. Miller & Zwerdling, 2010)

A confidential survey conducted by the Rand Corporation (2010) revealed that almost 20 percent of veterans returning from Iraq and Afghanistan reported experiencing probable traumatic brain injury (TBI) during combat; injuries often involved blasts from hidden land mines and improvised explosive devices. These explosions cause complex brain damage including (a) scattered brain injury resulting from shock waves that bruise the brain and damage nerve pathways, (b) penetrating injury from fragments of shrapnel or flying debris, and (c) injury from being thrown by the blast (Champion, Holcomb, & Young, 2009; Taber, Warden, & Hurley, 2006). Just what are the long-term risks from head injuries sustained in combat? The answer depends on many factors,

(continued)

including the source, location, and intensity of the injury, as well as interventions following the injury. Civilians treated for TBI are encouraged to allow the brain to rest to facilitate full recovery. However, in combat situations, mild head injuries are often not recognized, documented, and treated; soldiers return immediately to combat (Murray et al., 2005).

Soldiers may not be receiving quality, evidence-based care for their brain injuries in a timely manner (T. C. Miller & Zwerdling, 2010). Additionally, because the long-term consequences of brain injury resulting from blast exposure are unknown, some researchers wonder if soldiers exposed to multiple blast injuries are at risk for degenerative neurocognitive conditions such as *chronic traumatic encephalopathy* (Gavett, Stern, Cantu, Nowinski, & McKee, 2010). Should standard recommendations for TBI for civilians also apply to soldiers? What protocols might be beneficial to ensure that soldiers in combat receive appropriate care for TBI sustained in battle?

Traumatic Brain Injury

Case Study

United States representative Gabrielle Giffords, age 40, was shot in the head at point-blank range on January 8, 2011. The bullet entered into and exited from the left side of her brain. Following surgery, Representative Giffords remained in a **medically induced coma**, a state of deep sedation that allows time for the brain to heal. Part of her skull was removed to accommodate the anticipated swelling of her brain and to prevent further damage. Giffords' purposeful movements and responsiveness to simple commands were early, encouraging signs. Although extensive therapy helped Giffords regain many language and motor skills, one year after the shooting she officially resigned her congressional seat, recognizing that she needed to continue to participate in specialized cognitive and physical rehabilitation in order to maximize her recovery.

Jeff Siner/Charlotte Observer/MCT via Getty Images

Recovery from Traumatic Brain Injury

Gabrielle Giffords waves to the delegates at the 2012 Democratic National Convention. Giffords captivated the audience by reciting the Pledge of Allegiance in a halting but strong voice while holding her right hand over her heart with the help of her stronger left hand.

Case Study

At age 53, H. N. sustained multiple injuries, including mild bleeding in the brain, when he was hit by a car. Although his initial delirium subsided, other behavioral changes, including pervasive apathy punctuated by angry outbursts, persisted for months. Subsequent MRI scans revealed damage in the orbitofrontal cortex, an area of the brain involved in emotion and decision making (adapted from Namiki et al., 2008, p. 475).

Case Study

P. J. M., a 38-year-old woman, remained in a coma for several weeks after a bicycle accident. After regaining consciousness, she had severe short- and long-term memory deficits (including no recall of the year before her accident) and difficulty using the right side of her body. Despite some improvement, P. J. M. remains unable to drive or return to her work as a university professor (adapted from Rathbone, Moulin, & Conway, 2009, pp. 407–408).

medically induced coma a deliberately induced state of deep sedation that allows the brain to rest and heal

Did You Know? Individuals seeking emergency care for mild TBI demonstrated significantly reduced response time and diminished hazard perception on a simulated driving test; this suggests that it may be hazardous to drive immediately after sustaining a TBI.

Source: Preece, Horswill, & Geffen (2010)

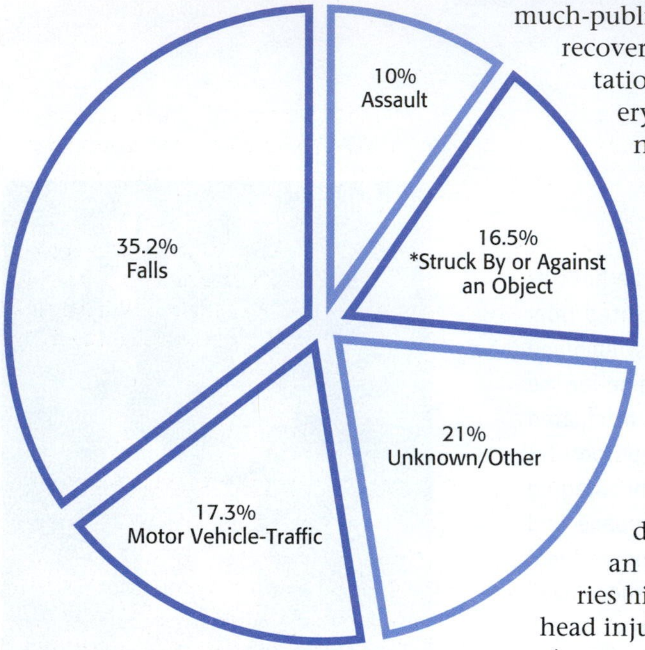

Traumatic brain injury (TBI) can result from a bump, jolt, blow, or physical wound to the head. Each year in the United States, approximately 1.7 million people receive emergency room care for TBI; infants and young children, older adolescents, and older adults are most likely to sustain a TBI (Centers for Disease Control and Prevention [CDC], 2011e). Head injury contributes to almost one third of injury-related deaths (Faul, Xu, Wald, & Coronado, 2010). Falls, vehicle accidents, and striking or being struck by objects are the leading causes of TBI (Figure 12.2).

Effects of TBI can be temporary or permanent and can result in mild to severe cognitive impairment. We are often amazed by stories of remarkable recovery of brain function following TBI. United States representative Gabrielle Giffords' much-publicized progress after her injury reinforces the capacity for brain recovery, particularly given immediate intervention, an excellent rehabilitation program, personal resilience, and social support during the recovery process. Similar conditions facilitated the recovery of well-known news anchor Bob Woodruff following a life-threatening brain injury he sustained when a roadside bomb exploded while he was covering the war in Iraq. After surgery, he spent 36 days in a **medically induced coma**. He underwent extensive rehabilitation and has since returned to work. In both cases, almost immediate medical attention and surgery played an important role in survival and recovery. A far different outcome resulted from what initially appeared to be a minor head injury sustained by actress Natasha Richardson. Her first symptom, a headache, did not appear until almost an hour after she hit the back of her head during a ski lesson; however, unrecognized neurological injury (i.e., bleeding between the skull and brain) resulted in her rapid and unexpected death. Sometimes referred to as the "talk and die" syndrome, such an injury can have severe, even fatal, consequences. All of these stories highlight the importance of immediate medical intervention when a head injury occurs.

FIGURE 12.2

Leading Causes of Traumatic Brain Injury

These data do not include injuries occurring during military deployment.

Source: Faul, Xu, Wald, & Coronado (2010)

As seen in the case studies, the severity, duration, and symptoms of TBI can vary significantly depending on the extent and location of the brain damage. Symptoms can include headaches, disorientation, confusion, memory loss, deficits in attention, poor concentration, fatigue, and irritability, as well as emotional and behavioral changes. Generally, the greater the tissue damage, the more impaired the functioning.

Chronic traumatic encephalopathy (CTE) is a progressive, degenerative condition diagnosed when autopsy reveals diffuse brain damage resulting from ongoing head trauma. CTE is seen in individuals who have had multiple episodes of head trauma, such as athletes who participate in sports such as boxing or football. CTE is associated with psychological symptoms such as depression and poor impulse control as well as a significantly increased risk of dementia in later adulthood (Gavett et al., 2010).

Acute head injuries include concussions, contusions, and cerebral lacerations. **Concussion**, the most common form of traumatic brain injury, refers to trauma-induced changes in brain functioning, typically caused by a blow to the head. The injury affects the functioning of neurons and causes disorientation or loss of consciousness. Symptoms of concussion can include headache, dizziness, nausea, impaired coordination, and sensitivity to light. Once a more severe brain injury is ruled out, individuals with a concussion are advised to rest, minimize stimulation and mentally challenging activities, refrain from any activity that can produce subsequent head injury, and immediately report any significant cognitive changes (Schatz & Moser, 2011). Symptoms are usually temporary, lasting no longer than a few weeks; however, in some cases they persist for much longer.

traumatic brain injury (TBI) a physical wound or internal injury to the brain

chronic traumatic encephalopathy (CTE) a progressive, degenerative condition involving brain damage resulting from multiple episodes of head trauma

concussion trauma-induced changes in brain functioning, typically caused by a blow to the head

A **cerebral contusion** (bruising of the brain) results when the brain strikes the skull with sufficient force to cause bruising. Unlike the disruption in cellular functioning seen in a concussion, contusions involve actual tissue damage in the areas bruised. Symptoms are similar to those seen with a concussion. Contusions and concussions commonly occur together. When someone receives a blow to the head, brain injury often occurs both at the site of impact and on the opposite side of the brain (i.e., the initial blow causes the brain to move and hit the other side of the skull). Brain imaging is frequently used to document specific areas of brain damage and monitor swelling. Unfortunately, brain imaging cannot always detect the more subtle changes caused by damage to neurons (a concussion), mild bruising of brain tissue (a contusion), or mild bleeding within the brain.

A **cerebral laceration** is an open head injury in which brain tissue is torn, pierced, or ruptured, usually from a skull fracture or an object that has penetrated the skull. As with a contusion, damage is localized and immediate medical care focuses on reducing bleeding and preventing swelling. As with other brain injuries, symptoms of cerebral lacerations can be quite serious, depending on the extent of damage to the brain tissue, the amount of hemorrhaging or swelling within the brain, and the medical care received. Severe brain trauma can have long-term effects, and recovery does not always ensure a return to prior levels of functioning. Along with the physical or cognitive difficulties produced by the injury, emotional reactions can also affect recovery.

Did You Know?

Recreational activities associated with the greatest risk of traumatic brain injury include bicycling; using a playground; football, basketball, and soccer; horseback riding; ice skating; golfing; and sledding and riding all-terrain vehicles.

Source: CDC, 2011e

cerebral contusion bruising of the brain, often resulting from a blow that causes the brain to forcefully strike the skull

cerebral laceration open head injury in which brain tissue is torn, pierced, or ruptured, usually from a skull fracture or an object that has penetrated the skull

CONTROVERSY:

Just How Safe Are Contact Sports?

How important is it for those involved in sports to know about concussion? Injuries resulting from team sports are just beginning to spark public concern. The suicide of Pennsylvania college football player Owen Thomas, age 21, garnered attention when his autopsy revealed evidence of the degenerative brain condition chronic traumatic encephalopathy (CTE), likely resulting from chronic head injury incurred while playing football. In fact, CTE has been found on autopsy in at least 20 former professional football players, including several who committed suicide (A. Schwartz, 2010). After dying from fall-related head trauma, former Cincinnati Bengals player Chris Henry, age 26, was also found to have CTE. Amazingly, neither Thomas nor Henry had ever been diagnosed with a concussion during their years in football. How could such significant brain damage occur at such a young age, particularly with no history of concussion?

A groundbreaking study involving a high school football team (Talavage et al., 2010) shed some light on the issue. Researchers compared cognitive testing and brain imaging of the players (obtained before, during, and after the football season) with data regarding the frequency and intensity of head impact during the football season (obtained by equipping the players' helmets with special impact-monitoring sensors). As expected, players who had experienced a concussion during the season showed MRI changes and related cognitive declines. However, so did half of the other players; data from the impact-monitoring sensors revealed that the players who experienced brain changes but no recorded concussions had sustained *multiple* impacts during the season. For example, one affected player had experienced 1,600 significant head blows during the season.

Professional medical organizations have created guidelines for school-age athletes who are suspected of having a concussion. Recommendations include immediate removal from play, restriction of physical activity for at least 7–10 days, and evaluation by a physician knowledgeable about head injury before return to play (American Academy of Neurology, 2010; Halstead & Walter, 2010). If followed, these guidelines could significantly increase safety for athletes. Careful monitoring of athletes with possible neurological damage (e.g., headache, confusion, poor balance, speech, vision or hearing difficulties) is certainly a step in the right direction. However, are adequate protections in place for those who experience a blow to the head but show no symptoms of a concussion? Are the potential dangers of concussion and head injuries in contact sports and other activities such as basketball, soccer, baseball, hockey, cycling, and motorbiking receiving sufficient attention?

Danger Is Just a Tumble Away
Millions of Americans receive head injuries each year. In order to reduce the risk of head injuries, the use of helmets is advised for activities such as skateboarding, in-line skating, and bicycling. If you engage in these activities, do you wear a helmet?

Vascular Neurocognitive Disorders

Case Study

Kate McCarron's stroke symptoms started on a Friday, with a little tingle in her leg. On Saturday, McCarron, age 46, felt uncharacteristically tired. Sunday she seemed a bit under the weather. Monday, her left side felt numb. Tuesday morning, she couldn't move her left side. She was rushed to the hospital. A small blood vessel leading to a deep part of her brain was closing, choking off a region of her brain that controlled motion (A. Dworkin, 2009).

Vascular neurocognitive disorders can result from a one-time **cardiovascular** event such as a stroke or from unnoticed, ongoing disruptions to the cardiovascular system. The majority of vascular neurocognitive disorders begin with **arteriosclerosis**, clogging of the arteries resulting from a buildup of plaque. This **plaque** (composed of fat, cholesterol, and other substances) accumulates over time, thickens, and narrows artery walls; blood flow and oxygen to the brain and other organs is reduced as a result.

A **stroke** occurs when there is an obstruction in blood flow to or within the brain. The sudden halt of blood flow that occurs during a stroke results in a loss of brain function. An **ischemic stroke** is caused by a clot or severe narrowing of the arteries; approximately 85 percent of strokes are ischemic (Lloyd-Jones et al., 2009). A **transient ischemic attack (TIA)** is a "mini-stroke" resulting from temporary blockage of arteries; TIAs produce temporary symptoms, but no long-term damage. Seeking medical attention for a TIA reduces risk of a major stroke. Additionally, if emergency medical care is sought immediately following a clot-produced ischemic stroke, medications can dissolve the clot and prevent serious brain damage. A **hemorrhagic stroke**, unrelated to plaque buildup, involves leakage of blood into the brain. In both ischemic and hemorrhagic strokes, brain damage occurs when brain cells are deprived of blood and oxygen (Figure 12.3). Stroke is the fourth leading cause of death in the United States; about 127,000 deaths result from stroke every year (CDC, 2011d; Heron et al., 2009). Careful monitoring and management of neurological complications from stroke (e.g., bleeding or swelling within the brain) reduces mortality and improves prognosis (Balami, Chen, & Grunwald, 2011).

Those younger than 50 years of age who experience a stroke often have risk factors such as hypertension, diabetes, high cholesterol, smoking, or exposure to secondhand smoke (Balci, Utku, Asil, & Celik, 2011). Cigarette smoking is believed to be a major contributor to about 1 in 4 strokes; however, when young adults experience a stroke, the contribution of smoking approaches 50 percent. Use of oral contraceptives (i.e., "the pill") can increase stroke risk, particularly when combined with smoking (Girot, 2009). Worldwide data regarding stroke risk point to stress, poor eating and sedentary lifestyles, and heavy or binge drinking as other major contributors to stroke (O'Donnell et al., 2010). Additionally, depression is associated with a 34 percent increase in risk for stroke; it is possible that unhealthy lifestyle factors associated with both disorders are the cause of this increased risk (Pan, Sun, Okereke, Rexrode & Hu, 2011).

Stroke is not only a leading cause of death but also a significant cause of disability (J. A. Young & Tolentino, 2011). Prompt medical intervention decreases the chances of death and vastly improves prognosis (N. Ahmed et al., 2010;

vascular involving blood vessels

cardiovascular pertaining to the heart and blood vessels

arteriosclerosis clogging of the arteries resulting from a buildup of plaque

plaque sticky material (composed of fat, cholesterol, and other substances) that builds up on the walls of veins or arteries

stroke a sudden halting of blood flow to a portion of the brain, leading to brain damage

ischemic stroke a stroke due to reduced blood supply caused by a clot or severe narrowing of the arteries supplying blood to the brain

transient ischemic attack (TIA) a "mini-stroke" resulting from temporary blockage of arteries

hemorrhagic stroke a stroke involving leakage of blood into the brain

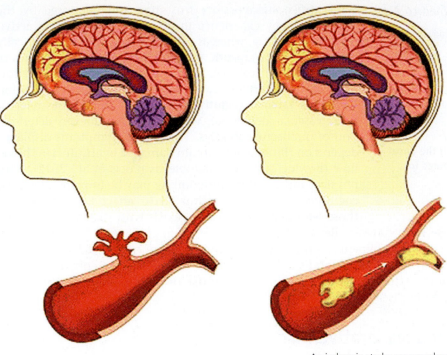

FIGURE 12.3

Types of Stroke

Ischemic strokes resulting from a blocked artery account for approximately 85 percent of all strokes.

A hemorrhagic stroke occurs when a blood vessel bursts within the brain.

An ischemic stroke occurs when a blood clot blocks the blood flow in an artery within the brain.

Roger et al., 2011); this underscores the importance of recognizing a stroke (Table 12.6). Because many people do not recognize stroke symptoms (e.g., slurred speech, blurry vision, or numbness on one side of the body), or hesitate to treat these symptoms as an emergency, public health campaigns continue to stress the importance of immediate intervention (Fussman, Rafferty, Lyon-Callo, Morgenstern, & Reeves, 2010). Additionally, many are unaware that women may display unique stroke symptoms, including sudden nausea, hiccups, facial pain, overall weakness, and shortness of breath (National Stroke Association, 2012).

Stroke survivors who do not receive immediate intervention often require long-term care because a variety of physical and psychological symptoms impair independent functioning. Strokes damaging the left side of the brain typically affect speech and language proficiency as well as physical movement on the right half of the body. Strokes occurring within the right hemisphere can increase impulsivity and impair judgment, short-term memory, and motor movement on the left side of the body. Visual problems (blurry or double vision) are sometimes seen in those with a right-hemisphere stroke. Cognitive, behavioral, and emotional changes that occur following stroke depend not only on the area affected by the stroke and the extent of brain damage but also on the individual's personality, emotional resilience, and coping skills.

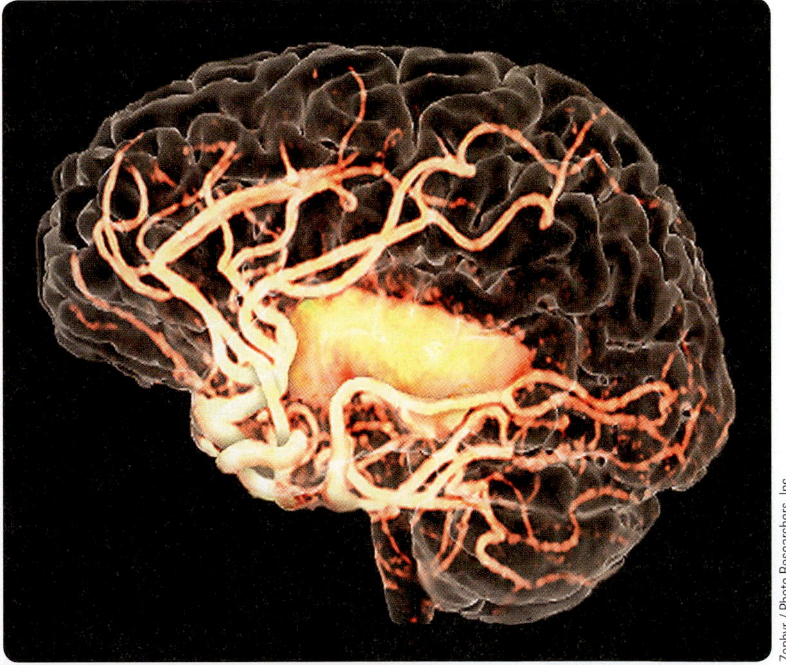

Results of a Stroke on the Brain

The brain damage associated with a stroke is caused by blockages that cause an interruption in the brain's blood supply or by the leakage of blood through blood vessel walls. Here, a three-dimensional magnetic resonance angiogram scan shows a human brain after a stroke. Major arteries are shown in white. The central region in yellow is an area in which bleeding occurred.

TABLE 12.6 Stroke Symptoms: Know When to Act

- Numbness or weakness, especially on one side of the body
- Confusion, trouble speaking or understanding speech
- Vision difficulty in one or both eyes
- Sudden dizziness, loss of balance, or difficulty with coordination
- Severe headache with no known cause

Emergency medical attention immediately following the onset of stroke symptoms can significantly improve outcomes for both ischemic and hemorrhagic strokes.

Some stroke survivors are frustrated and depressed by the difficulties they experience in attempting to perform activities of daily living, whereas others actively and optimistically participate in therapeutic rehabilitation activities. A series of small strokes (microbleeds) or a chronic decrease in blood flow from narrowed arteries can lead to a degenerative condition known as **vascular cognitive impairment** (sometimes referred to as vascular dementia), which involves uneven deterioration of intellectual abilities. The specific symptoms displayed depend on the area of the brain damaged by insufficient blood flow (Bowler, 2007) or microbleeds (Poels et al., 2012). Both physical and cognitive functioning may be impaired. Vascular cognitive impairment, estimated to affect 8–15 percent of those with dementia, often coexists with Alzheimer's disease, because both have similar lifestyle risk factors (Jellinger, 2008). Recent analyses concluded that hypertension (Sharp, Aarsland, Day, Sonnesyn, & Ballard, 2010), diabetes (Launer, 2009), and smoking (Rusanen, Kivipelto, Quesenberry, Zhou, & Whitmer, 2010) all significantly increase the risk of both vascular dementia and Alzheimer's disease.

Neurodegenerative Disorders

In contrast with the recovery often seen in cases of stroke or traumatic brain injury, individuals with neurodegenerative disorders show decline in function rather than improvement. **Neurodegeneration** refers to declining functioning due to progressive loss of brain structure, neurochemical abnormalities, or the death of neurons. We focus on a variety of disorders with very different symptoms, including some that appear in later life and some that can occur during early adulthood. Neurodegenerative disorders vary greatly in terms of age of onset, skills affected, and course of the disorder. We begin our discussion with the best-known neurodegenerative disorder: Alzheimer's disease.

Alzheimer's Disease

Alzheimer's disease (AD), the most prevalent neurodegenerative disorder, affects about five million Americans. AD is the sixth leading cause of death in the United States (CDC, 2011d). The cost of care for those currently diagnosed with AD is $172 billion per year. It has been estimated that by 2030 almost 8 million adults in the United States will have AD, with the prevalence reaching 16 million by 2050 (Alzheimer's Association, 2010). Although AD can strike adults in their 30s, 40s, or 50s, risk of the disease significantly increases with age; those who are 65 have a 1 percent risk, whereas those who are 95 have a 40–50 percent risk (X. P. Wang & Ding, 2008).

AD usually begins gradually and involves a pattern of ongoing cognitive decline. Although the main feature of AD is memory impairment, caution is used in making an AD diagnosis based only on signs of memory impairment; unless the individual has clear physiological indicators (e.g., evidence of genetic mutations or brain changes associated with AD), it is still not possible to reliably predict who among those with mild cognitive decline might eventually develop AD (Ballard, Corbett, & Jones, 2011). Individuals who seek treatment for impaired memory develop AD at a rate of 12–15 percent per year; however, individuals with memory impairment in the general population (i.e., not just those who seek treatment) are less likely to develop AD, and in some cases show a reversal of symptoms (DSM-5 Work Groups, 2012). Recent advances involving cerebrospinal fluid abnormalities found among individuals with AD (Ringman et al., 2012) and those with mild cognitive impairment who later developed AD (Buchhave et al., 2012) may lead to methods for successful detection and treatment of AD at an earlier stage.

vascular cognitive impairment decline in cognitive skills that occurs when damage to the cardiovascular system reduces blood flow to the brain; also called *vascular dementia*

neurodegeneration declining brain functioning due to progressive loss of brain structure, neurochemical abnormalities, or the death of neurons

Alzheimer's disease (AD) dementia involving memory loss and other declines in cognitive and adaptive functioning

FOCUS ON RESILIENCE

Lifelong Prevention of Brain Damage

Given the serious consequences of neurocognitive disorders, a question that is frequently asked is "Is there anything that can be done to reduce the chances of experiencing a stroke, suffering a head injury, or developing a degenerative disorder?" The answer is yes, especially when prevention efforts begin at an early age. For example, the use of car seats and seat belts can help prevent head injury in children, as can the use of safe practices and properly fitting protective headgear during sports (Rivara et al., 2011). Similarly, allowing the brain to rest and recover after a blow to the head or a concussion can reduce the likelihood of long-term brain damage (Schatz & Moser, 2011).

Lifestyle changes focused on maintaining a healthy cardiovascular system can significantly reduce the risk of both stroke and dementia. This can be accomplished by exercising regularly and eating a well-balanced diet (Aarsland, Sardahaee, Anderssen, & Ballard, 2010; O'Donnell et al., 2010; Rolland, van Kan, & Vellas, 2010); a healthy lifestyle protects against dementia not only by reducing risk factors but also by forming new brain cells and promoting efficient brain functioning through exercise and good nutrition (Lazarov, Mattson, Peterson, Pimplika, & van Praag, 2010). Prevention efforts focus on modifiable risk factors (e.g., avoiding smoking and excessive consumption of salt, sugar, saturated fats, and alcohol), because these unhealthy behaviors account for almost 90 percent of the risk of stroke (Hankey, 2011) and much of the risk of dementia (L. D. Baker et al., 2010). Regular participation in cognitively stimulating activities across the life span (especially during early and middle adulthood) is also associated with fewer pathological brain changes later in life (Landau et al., 2012). Prevention efforts really can make a difference in maintaining brain health.

PhotoDisc

Characteristics of Alzheimer's Disease AD symptoms typically begin quite subtly, followed by a progressive decline in cognitive, physical, and social functioning (Gatz, 2007). The physiological processes that produce AD begin years before the onset of symptoms (L. G. Brooks & Loewenstein, 2010). As early symptoms—memory dysfunction, irritability, and cognitive impairment—gradually worsen, other symptoms such as social withdrawal, depression, apathy, delusions, impulsive behaviors, and neglect of personal hygiene often appear. Some individuals with AD become loving and childlike, whereas others become increasingly agitated and combative. At present, no curative or disease-reversing interventions exist for AD. From the time of diagnosis, those with AD survive only half as long as those of similar age without dementia (E. B. Larson et al., 2004). However, slower rates of cognitive decline predict longer survival (Doody et al., 2010).

Case Study

Elizabeth R., a forty-six-year-old woman diagnosed with AD, is trying to cope with her increasing memory difficulties. She writes notes to herself and rehearses conversations, anticipating what might be said. After reading only a few sentences, she forgets what she has read. She sometimes forgets where the bathroom is located in her own house and is depressed by the realization that she is becoming a burden to her family (M. Clark et al., 1984, p. 60).

The deterioration of memory is one of the most disturbing symptoms for those who have AD. Initially, they may forget appointments, phone numbers,

AP Photo/Ron Schumacher

Did Alzheimer's Disease Affect His Presidency?

Former president Ronald Reagan was diagnosed with Alzheimer's disease at age 83. Many believe he began to show symptoms of the disease, such as memory difficulties, while still in office. Five years prior to the diagnosis, Reagan was treated for a traumatic head injury that occurred when he was thrown from a horse. Some have speculated that this head injury accelerated the progression of his Alzheimer's disease.

and addresses, but as AD progresses, they lose track of the time of day, have trouble remembering recent and past events, and forget who they are. But even when memory is gone, emotions remain. In fact, researchers have found that although those with AD may forget details of an emotional event (such as the plot of a sad movie), the emotions of the experience continue (Feinstein, Duff, & Tranela, 2010).

Other Factors Affecting Memory Loss A common concern of older adults is whether occasional memory lapses are signs of AD. Memory loss occurs for a variety of reasons. It can, in fact, be a symptom of AD or other neurodegenerative disorders. However, occasional lapses of memory are common in healthy adults. As we age, neurons are gradually lost, our brains become smaller, and information is processed more slowly. This normal process is why some older adults experience declines in memory and difficulty learning new material as they age (Mormino et al., 2008); more rapid shrinking of the brain is associated with more rapid cognitive decline (D. A. Smith et al., 2010). Many older adults experience only minimal decline in cognitive function despite shrinking of the brain; this is because, as we age, the brain reorganizes itself in a way to make it work as efficiently as possible (Population Reference Bureau, 2007).

Memory loss and confusion can also result from temporary conditions such as infections or reactions to prescription drugs. Medications sometimes interact with one another or with certain foods to produce side effects, including memory impairment. In addition, various physical conditions and nutritional deficiencies can produce memory loss and symptoms resembling dementia. This type of memory loss can usually be reversed once the medical condition is diagnosed and treated.

Alzheimer's Disease and the Brain Comparing the brains of individuals with AD and those without AD reveals a number of differences. First, those with AD have increased shrinkage of brain tissue. Second, the brains of those with AD are clogged with two abnormal structures, *neurofibrillary tangles* and *senile plaques*. Neurofibrillary tangles, found inside nerve cells, are twisted masses of protein fibers. Senile plaques are composed of parts of disintegrated neurons (e.g., patches of degenerated nerve endings) surrounding a group of proteins called beta-amyloid deposits. Both conditions, which are detected on autopsy, are believed to produce AD symptoms by causing inflammation, disrupting the transmission of impulses between neurons, and creating other changes in the brain that eventually result in the death of neurons and shrinking of the brain.

Although a person may have multiple indicators suggestive of AD (e.g., memory loss, brain scans showing brain shrinkage), it has not been possible to definitively diagnose AD before autopsy. However, the Food and Drug Administration is close to approving use of a special dye that allows senile plaques to be detected via PET imaging. Being able to know exactly who has AD will help researchers develop medications that slow or halt AD progression.

Did You Know ? Difficulty identifying smells such as lemon, banana, and cinnamon may be the first sign of Alzheimer's disease (R. S. Wilson, Schneider, et al., 2007). However, it is not clear if this difficulty is because changes occur in brain regions related to smell or because individuals with Alzheimer's disease cannot remember the words associated with the odors.

Source: Razani, Nordin, Chan, & Murphy (2010)

Etiology of Alzheimer's Disease AD is believed to be caused by both hereditary and environmental factors (Rocchi, Orsucci, Tognoni, Ceravolo, & Siciliano, 2009). A number of factors (or interaction between factors) increase the risk of AD.

The risk of developing AD is 1.8–4.0 times higher for those with a family history of the disorder than for those without (Gatz, 2007). In a comparison of fraternal and identical twins with AD, a couple of important findings emerged: (a) Heritability for the disease is high and (b) environmental influences (e.g., mental stimulation, social engagement, diet and exercise patterns) are also important and should be the focus of interventions to reduce risk or delay onset of the disease (Gatz et al., 2006). A small number of families have a very rare genetic mutation that results in a generational pattern of what is called *autosomal-dominant Alzheimer's disease*; any family member who inherits this mutation will develop early-onset AD (Zetzsche, Rujescu, Hardy, & Hampel, 2010). Those with the mutation typically develop AD between the ages of 30 and 50.

A much more common gene that increases risk for later-onset AD is the APOE-e4 gene. Those with this *risk gene* (thought to contribute to approximately 25 percent of all AD) have an increased *likelihood* of developing AD but will not necessarily develop it; risk is further increased when the gene is inherited from both parents. Carriers of this gene who show no AD symptoms have been found to have atypical connections within their brains and differences in how their brains metabolize glucose (Sheline et al., 2010; Zetzsche et al., 2010). Understanding why some people have brain changes associated with AD (e.g., neurofibrillary tangles) but show no symptoms is of great interest to researchers (Driscoll & Troncoso, 2011). Interestingly, among one group of adults with early-stage AD, those with good cardiovascular fitness had less brain atrophy than those who did not exercise regularly (Honea et al., 2009). Efforts to detect the genes and biological processes associated with AD continue, with the hope that someday this devastating disease can be prevented or successfully treated (Bateman et al., 2011; L. G. Brooks & Loewenstein, 2010).

Did You Know?

Various studies have found that depression (especially multiple episodes of depression) is associated with an increased risk of both Alzheimer's disease and other dementias. Some researchers believe this is because depression and dementia have similar risk factors (e.g., poor diet, little exercise), while others contend that depression that begins later in life may, in fact, represent an early symptom of dementia.

Source: Dotson, Beydoun, & Zonderman (2010); Saczynski et al. (2010); G. Li et al. (2011)

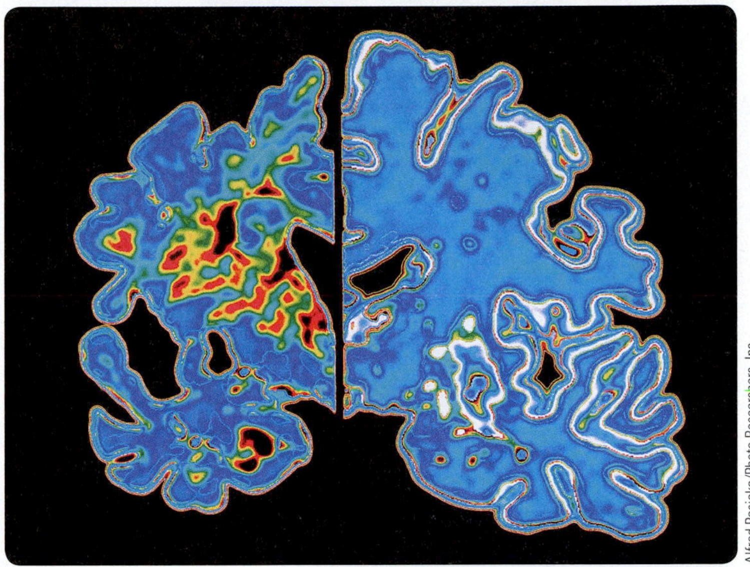

Alfred Pasieka/Photo Researchers, Inc.

Healthy Brain and Alzheimer's Brain

This image shows a computer graphic of a vertical slice through the brain of a person with Alzheimer's disease (at left) compared with a healthy brain (at right). The brain of the person with Alzheimer's disease is considerably shrunken, due to the degeneration and death of nerve cells. Symptoms of Alzheimer's disease include memory loss, disorientation, and personality change.

Lewy Body Dementia (LBD)

Lewy body dementia (LBD), the second most common form of dementia, results in cognitive decline similar to that seen in AD combined with the development of unusual movements (similar to those seen in Parkinson's disease, a disorder we discuss later in the chapter). Although LBD tends to develop more rapidly than AD, the two diseases have a similar survival period of approximately 8 years after diagnosis. Characteristics of LBD include (a) significant fluctuations in attention and alertness (e.g., staring spells and periods of extreme drowsiness); (b) recurrent, detailed visual hallucinations; (c) impaired mobility, including frequent falls, a shuffling gait, muscular rigidity, and slowed movement; and (d) sleep disturbance, including acting out dreams (Lewy Body Dementia Association, 2008). Depression is frequently seen in those with LBD. Compared to the cognitive deficits associated with AD, memory and language skills are unusually more intact in those with LBD, whereas visual-spatial tasks (such a reproducing a drawing) are more impaired.

Individuals with LBD have the same irregularities in brain cells (those affecting cognition and motor movement) that are seen in Parkinson's disease (Goldmann, Siderowf, & Hurtig, 2008). These unique cell structures are called Lewy bodies after the researcher, Frederick Lewy, who first discovered them. These abnormal neurons are found in the midbrain of those with Parkinson's disease and in the cortex and midbrain of individuals with LBD. Individuals with LBD often have the plaques and tangles characteristic of AD, and some with AD also have Lewy bodies. LBD can only be confirmed by autopsy, because brain imaging techniques cannot yet detect Lewy bodies (National Institute of Neurological Disorders and Stroke, 2011).

LBD is estimated to account for up to 30 percent of all dementias; however, prevalence data may be inaccurate because of the overlap in symptoms with other dementias and with Parkinson's disease. Additionally, professionals who are not dementia specialists are often less familiar with LBD. Although researchers have not yet identified any genes associated with LBD, the disorder has been found to occur more frequently in some families (Nervi et al., 2011).

Lewy body dementia (LBD) dementia involving visual hallucinations, cognitive fluctuations, and atypical movements

Mike Coppola/Getty Images for the Michael J. Fox Foundation for Parkinson's Research

Parkinson's Disease

Actor Michael J. Fox, who has Parkinson's disease, performs at a benefit for the Michael J. Fox Foundation for Parkinson's Research in New York City.

Frontotemporal Lobar Degeneration **Frontotemporal lobar degeneration (FTLD)**, the fourth leading cause of dementia, is characterized by progressive declines in language and behavior; these deficits result from degeneration in the frontal and temporal lobes of the brain (Rabinovici & Miller, 2010). FTLD presents in three distinct ways, depending on the area of the brain in which neurons are dying: (a) significant changes in behavior and personality (e.g., extreme impulsivity or intense apathy), (b) progressive difficulty using words and naming objects, or (c) difficulty forming words and using language. The average age of onset is in midlife, making it the second leading cause of dementia in those younger than age 65 (J. K. Johnson et al., 2005). The diagnosis and treatment of FTLD are complicated by the large variety of cognitive areas and physiological processes involved in the disorder. FTLD has a significant genetic component (Bigio, 2008). Recently, scientists were able to identify biomarkers of FTLD in cerebrospinal fluid, a finding that will further FTLD research (Borroni et al., 2010; Rabinovici & Miller, 2010).

Parkinson's Disease **Parkinson's disease (PD)** is a progressive disorder characterized by four primary symptoms: (a) tremor of the hands, arms, legs, jaw, or face; (b) rigidity of the limbs and trunk; (c) slowness in initiating movement; and (d) postural instability or impaired balance and coordination (National Institute of Neurological Disorders and Stroke, 2007). Cognitive impairment and dementia are common in the later stages of PD (A. W. Willis et al., 2012), eventually affecting up to 75 percent of those with the disorder; risk for dementia is highest in those who develop PD later in life (Aarsland, Andersen, Larsen, Lolk, & Kragh-Sorensen, 2003). Neurological changes in those with PD often affect the ability to recognize emotional cues, such as an upset face or voice—a factor that can strain interpersonal interactions (H. M. Gray & Tickle-Degnen, 2010). Many individuals with PD, especially those with more severe motor symptoms and those diagnosed at younger ages, are affected by depression and anxiety (Dissanayaka et al., 2010). Psychotic symptoms may also be present, particularly among those with dementia (Weintraub, Comella, & Horn, 2008).

PD is associated with Lewy bodies in the motor area of the brain stem, accelerated aging of neurons, and loss of dopamine-producing brain cells (Goldmann et al., 2008). The disease is the second most common neurodegenerative disorder in the United States (Dobkin, Allen, & Menza, 2006), affecting about 500,000 individuals. PD strikes about 50 percent more men than women, but the reasons for this discrepancy are unclear. Because genetic mutations account for only 5 percent of PD cases, researchers are trying to learn more about what causes the pattern of brain cell death seen in the disease (Stoessl, 2011; Syed et al., 2011). In some people, the disorder may result from infections of the brain, toxins, cerebrovascular disorders, or brain trauma. PD occurs more frequently in the northern Midwest and the Northeast and in urban settings; this geographic distribution has raised questions about whether environmental toxins common to these areas increase risk of PD (A. W. Willis, Bradley, et al., 2010). Twin studies have revealed that occupational exposure to certain toxins (contained in solvents and household cleaners) increases the risk of PD (Goldman et al., 2012).

Although medication can help control some PD symptoms, pharmacological treatment is often delayed until it is certain that the benefits clearly outweigh the risks. Side effects of medications for physical symptoms can produce or worsen hallucinations and other psychotic symptoms, and medications for psychotic symptoms can increase difficulties with movement (Weintraub & Hurtig, 2007). For some patients, the use of electrodes that continuously stimulate certain areas of the brain has helped improve symptoms (Shah et al., 2010).

frontotemporal lobar degeneration (FTLD) degeneration in the frontal and temporal lobes of the brain that results in ongoing declines in language and behavior

Parkinson's disease (PD) a progressive disorder characterized by poorly controlled motor movements

Huntington's Disease **Huntington's disease (HD)** is a rare, genetically transmitted degenerative disorder characterized by involuntary movement, progressive dementia, and emotional instability. Age of onset is variable, ranging from childhood to late in life; onset most typically occurs during midlife (Roos, 2010). Initial physical symptoms of HD can include facial grimaces or twitches in the fingers. As the disorder progresses, abrupt, repetitive movements often develop. Changes in personality and emotional stability are frequently seen soon after diagnosis; many individuals with HD become uncharacteristically moody and quarrelsome. Other psychiatric symptoms include agitation, hypersexuality, and psychosis. Cognitive deficits and dementia are often the last symptoms to appear. As the disease progresses, the severity of motor and cognitive impairment results in total dependency and the need for full-time care (Roos, 2010). Severity of depression and impairment in day-to-day functioning have the strongest influence on quality of life for those with HD (A. K. Ho, Gilbert, Mason, Goodman, & Barker, 2009). Medication can sometimes help reduce the severity of symptoms, including depression associated with the disorder. HD cannot be cured; death typically occurs 15–20 years after the onset of symptoms. Suicide is a common cause of death among those with HD (Roos, 2010).

Because HD is transmitted from parent to child through a dominant genetic mutation, offspring of someone with HD have about a 50/50 chance of developing the disorder. Symptoms are more severe in those who inherit the disease from their father. Predictive genetic testing is available for family members who want to know if they will develop HD. Genetic counseling is extremely important in preventing transmission of the disease.

Did You Know? Evidence of a genetic mutation that causes Huntington's disease has been found in some individuals whose primary symptom is major depression.

Source: Perlis, Smoller, et al. (2010)

AIDS Dementia Complex The general public knows about the serious consequences of AIDS (acquired immune deficiency syndrome), including susceptibility to diseases, physical deterioration, and death. Relatively few people, however, know that dementia may be the first sign of HIV infection or AIDS. Symptoms can include an inability to concentrate, difficulty with complex mental tasks, tremors, poor balance, and increasing apathy and lethargy. In more serious cases, a diagnosis of *AIDS dementia complex* (ADC) is made. The prevalence of ADC among individuals with HIV infection is between 10 and 20 percent in Western countries (I. Grant, Sacktor, & McArthur, 2005).

ADC develops when HIV becomes active within the brain and begins to affect mental processes. Also, because AIDS affects the immune system, AIDS-related infections can cause cells to release toxic substances that cause changes in brain functioning. Fortunately, the antiretroviral therapy used to aggressively treat HIV infection and AIDS can prevent or delay the onset of ADC. Strengthened immune system functioning is a key to decreasing the impact of HIV on neurocognitive functioning; however, antiretroviral therapy itself carries a risk of contributing to HIV-associated dementia (E. J. Wright, 2009). There are currently no medications proven to improve symptoms once ADC has developed (Uthman & Abdulmalik, 2008).

Other Diseases and Infections of the Brain

A variety of diseases and infections can lead to the development of neurocognitive disorders. In the following section, we discuss a few of these conditions.

Meningitis and Encephalitis Meningitis and encephalitis can both develop as a result of a viral or bacterial infection. Some types of bacterial meningitis and encephalitis are contagious. **Meningitis** is an inflammation of the *meninges*, the membrane that surrounds the brain and spinal cord, whereas **encephalitis** is inflammation of the brain itself. The symptoms of meningitis vary with age. In young infants, the symptoms are nonspecific (jaundice, lethargy, poor eating, and irritability), making diagnosis difficult. In patients older than 1 year,

Huntington's disease (HD) a genetic disease characterized by involuntary twitching movements and eventual dementia

meningitis inflammation of the membrane surrounding the brain and spinal cord

encephalitis inflammation of the brain

CONTROVERSY:

Genetic Testing: Helpful or Harmful?

DNA testing is now available to provide information regarding risk for a variety of neurocognitive disorders. Genotyping (gathering information about specific genes by examining an individual's DNA) brings up a number of interconnected issues. When genotyping is performed on individuals who have a family member with a *genetically determined* condition such as Huntington's disease (HD) or early-onset Alzheimer's disease (AD), the outcome of the test reveals life-changing information—they know *with certainty* if they will develop the disorder afflicting their parent or other family members. In cases where genetic tests only indicate *possible* risk (e.g., the APOE-e4 genotype associated with later-onset AD), clinicians often discourage genetic testing due to concerns that knowledge of *possible risk* can be more harmful than helpful (K. L. Howard & Filley, 2009; Howe, 2010). For example, someone who learns that he or she has the APOE-e4 genotype knows there is a 25 percent chance of developing AD—not the 100 percent risk revealed through genotype analysis involving HD or early onset AD.

Those who discourage genetic testing are concerned about the social and economic stigma associated with HD and AD (The Lancet Neurology, 2010) and the lack of specific treatments or interventions if HD or AD mutations are detected. Those who encourage genetic testing for individuals who may carry *deterministic genes* (e.g., for HD or early-onset AD) emphasize benefits such as being able to plan for the future, including decisions about whether or not to have children. Those who support genetic testing involving *possible* risk of AD (e.g., the APOE-e4 genotype) believe that learning about an increased risk of AD may motivate lifestyle changes that ultimately reduce the risk of developing the disease. Additionally, research involving individuals with the APOE-e4 genotype may help determine which interventions are most effective at preventing or slowing the progression of AD or other neurodegenerative diseases (Sleegers et al., 2010). Once such interventions exist, some of the debate may subside.

For Further Consideration

1. If your parent had Huntington's disease or early-onset Alzheimer's disease, would you want to know if you would eventually develop the disorder?
2. If your family members had later-onset Alzheimer's disease, would you want to know if you carried the APOE-e4 genotype and had a 25 percent risk of developing the disorder?

symptoms often include stiffness of the neck, headache, sudden high fever, and sensitivity to light and noise (Curtis, Stobart, Vandermeer, Simel, & Klassen, 2010). Diagnosis of suspected meningitis is confirmed through microscopic analysis of cerebrospinal fluid. Meningitis can result in the destruction of brain tissue at the site of infection; severity is greatest with bacterial meningitis and with meningitis contracted soon after birth. Lingering effects of bacterial meningitis can include partial or complete hearing loss and ongoing cognitive difficulties. Those with meningitis who experience seizures are more likely to have a serious outcome (Zoons et al., 2007). The availability of vaccines has helped reduce the incidence of bacterial meningitis (Hunt, 2010); however, death and disability remain a significant concern for those who contract it (Gammelgaard, Colding, Hartzen, & Penkowa, 2011).

Encephalitis can produce mild symptoms that resemble the stomach flu. Severe encephalitis can create lethargy, drowsiness, fever, vomiting, and delirium. The infection that results in encephalitis can come from a variety of sources, including viruses (including the herpes virus) and insect bites. Although seizures, headache, fatigue, memory difficulties, and impaired decision making can be long-term effects of encephalitis, many individuals make a complete recovery.

Epilepsy **Epilepsy** is a chronic neurological condition characterized by *seizures*—intermittent periods of altered consciousness resulting from uncontrolled electrical discharge within the brain. Epilepsy is the most common neurological disorder: 1–2 percent of the population has had at least one epileptic seizure. Epilepsy affects an estimated 2.7 million people in the United States and costs about $15.5 billion in medical expenses and lost or reduced earnings and productivity each year (CDC, 2012).

epilepsy disorder involving seizures that result from uncontrolled electrical discharge from brain cells

Epilepsy is most frequently diagnosed during childhood. It can be without an apparent cause or it can arise from such causes as brain tumors, injury, degenerative diseases, and substance abuse. Head trauma is the most common cause of new-onset epilepsy in young adults (Raymont et al., 2010). Epileptic seizures and unconsciousness may last from a few seconds to several hours; they may occur only a few times during the patient's entire life or many times in one day. Seizures can produce very subtle momentary changes in consciousness or violent convulsions lasting for hours. Researchers continue to look for ways to help the approximately 30 percent of individuals with epilepsy whose seizures do not improve with medication (French & Friedman, 2011; Radwa et al., 2010).

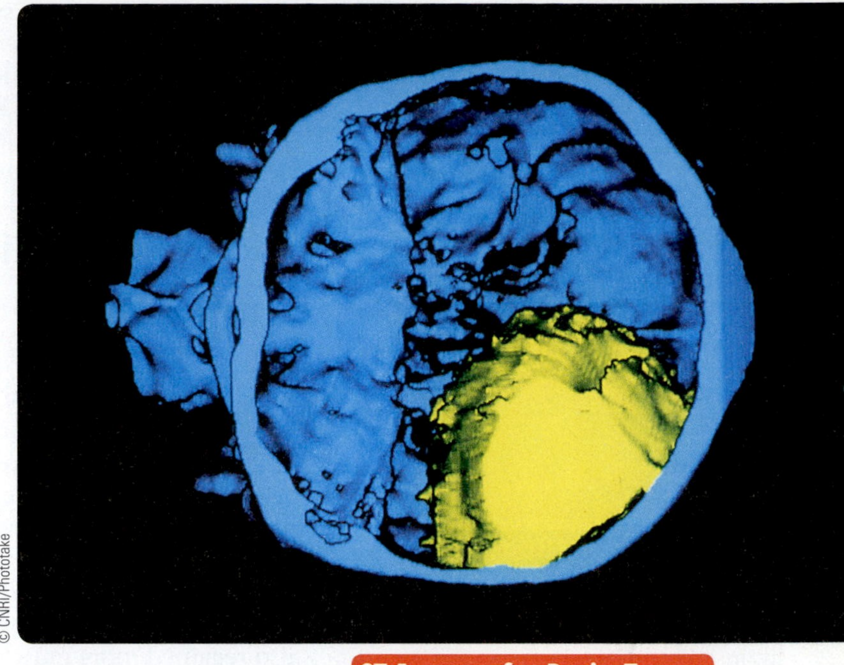

© CNRI/Phototake

CT Image of a Brain Tumor

The neuroimaging technique of computerized axial tomography (known as a CT or CAT scan) involves analysis of cross-sectional X-rays of the brain taken from various angles. CT scans can detect a variety of brain abnormalities, including cerebral tumors such as the one shown in this image. Cerebral tumors result from abnormal tissue growing within the brain. Symptoms depend on the size and location of the tumor.

Substance Abuse Use or abuse of drugs or alcohol can result in delirium or the chronic brain dysfunction seen in major and mild neurocognitive disorders. Significant neurocognitive dysfunction can occur when large quantities of drugs or alcohol are ingested, when multiple substances are taken simultaneously, or when inhalants are used (due to oxygen deprivation or the toxicity of substances inhaled). Substance-induced neurocognitive disorders are most common among individuals with a history of heavy substance use. Delirium can occur during acute intoxication or during drug or alcohol withdrawal. Some of the neurological damage caused by substance abuse can be reversed; however, older individuals and chronic users demonstrate less recovery of brain function (Yeh, Gazdzinski, Durazzo, Sjöstrand, & Meyerhoff, 2007).

CHECKPOINT REVIEW

1. What kinds of events can cause a traumatic brain injury?
2. What causes chronic traumatic encephalopathy?
3. What factors affect the long-term outcome following a stroke?
4. What are some factors that increase the risk of having a stroke or developing a degenerative neurocognitive disorder?

Treatment Considerations

Because neurocognitive disorders have many different causes and are associated with different symptoms and dysfunctions, treatment approaches vary widely. In general, the major interventions for neurocognitive disorders include rehabilitation services, medication, cognitive and behavioral treatment, lifestyle changes, and environmental support.

Rehabilitation Services

The key to recovery is often participation in comprehensive, sustained rehabilitation services. Physical, occupational, speech, and language therapy help individuals relearn skills or compensate for lost abilities. Rehabilitative interventions are often guided by the individual's strengths as well as deficits. The individual's commitment to and participation in therapy also plays an important role in recovery. Depression, pessimism, and anxiety can stall progress. Fortunately, in many

AP Photo/Al Grillo

Effective Rehabilitation

Sgt. Dan DaRosa plays a game to help with his memory at the traumatic brain injury clinic on Elmendorf Air Force base in Anchorage, Alaska. Structured activities such as this can play a key role in the recovery of cognitive skills.

cases survivors are encouraged when the brain begins to reorganize and skills return. Brain changes achieved through rehabilitation are sometimes documented with imaging techniques (J. A. Young & Tolentino, 2011); in fact, imaging studies can help determine which physical and occupational therapies best enhance brain recovery (K. C. Lin et al., 2010).

Medication

Medications can help prevent, control, or reduce the symptoms of some neurocognitive disorders. Some medications target physical symptoms of conditions such as epilepsy, PD, or LBD, whereas others help delay the inevitable cognitive decline associated with dementia. Medication can also help prevent recurrence of stroke by treating hypertension or diabetes. Antidepressants are sometimes used to alleviate the depression associated with neurocognitive disorders. In one study, individuals with moderate to severe motor impairment resulting from an ischemic stroke took an antidepressant (fluoxetine) for 3 months. This group not only reported fewer depressive symptoms than did individuals in a placebo control group but also regained more muscle function; the antidepressant may have enhanced progress by reducing brain inflammation, improving neurotransmitter functioning, or enhancing participation in physical therapy due to improved mood (Chollet et al., 2011). Although low doses of antipsychotic medication are sometimes used to reduce neurocognitive symptoms such as paranoia, hallucinations, and agitation, the use of antipsychotic medications for the treatment of dementia is discouraged (Treloar et al., 2010). As mentioned previously, it is often necessary to balance the positive effects and side effects of medications, taking particular care to monitor medication response and potential interactions of multiple medications.

Cognitive and Behavioral Treatment

Cognitive deficits resulting from neurocognitive disorders (e.g., emotional reactivity and diminished ability to concentrate) can hinder recovery and interfere with well-being; psychotherapy can enhance coping and participation in rehabilitation efforts. For example, a cognitive-behavioral treatment targeting depression in individuals with PD included identifying life stressors and teaching the participants self-care, stress management, and relaxation techniques. The treatment was found to be both feasible and effective (Dobkin et al., 2006). Cognitive and behavioral techniques are also used to reduce the frequency or severity of problem behaviors such as aggression or socially inappropriate conduct. Strategies may include teaching the individual social skills, reducing complex tasks (e.g., dressing or eating) into simpler steps, or simplifying the environment to avoid confusion.

Lifestyle Changes

Lifestyle changes can help prevent or reduce progression of some neurocognitive disorders. For example, to minimize the risk of further damage, treatment for vascular neurocognitive disorders often targets smoking cessation, weight reduction, and blood sugar, cholesterol, or blood pressure control (Gatz, 2007).

Mental stimulation has been found to both prevent and reduce cognitive decline in some individuals. In a population-based study of elderly individuals in Taiwan, researchers found that participating in social activities (e.g., playing games or volunteering) helped preserve cognitive function over a 7-year follow-up period (Glei et al., 2005). Another large-scale study concluded that mental exercises can improve

G. Paul Burnett/ The New York Times

Living With Alzheimer's Disease

Residents of an Alzheimer's care facility tend to flowers with the help of a staff member. Some researchers say the best way to treat Alzheimer's disease is with a broad approach that emphasizes meaningful activities, regular exercise, and a healthy environment.

memory, reasoning ability, and information-processing speed in older adults (S. L. Willis et al., 2006). Beneficial activities include playing computer games (Tárraga et al., 2006), reading newspapers, visiting the library, playing games such as chess or checkers (R. S. Wilson, Scherr, Schneider, Tang, & Bennett, 2007), and being exposed to novel and cognitively challenging tasks (Greenwood & Parasuraman, 2010).

Environmental Support

Although rehabilitation can be very effective with acute conditions such as TBI or stroke, neurodegenerative disorders involving dementia are irreversible and best managed by providing a supportive environment. In many cases, care within a nursing or assisted-living facility is required as independent living skills deteriorate. There are many ways to help those with declining abilities to feel happier and live comfortably and with dignity. Bright lighting has been shown to improve mood and slow cognitive decline in those with dementia (Riemersma-van der Lek et al., 2008). Techniques such as writing answers to questions that are repeatedly asked or labeling family photos can decrease frustration resulting from memory difficulties. Family visits enhance the lives of those with dementia because emotional memories (e.g., happiness at seeing a loved one) persist even when the visit itself is no longer recalled (Feinstein, Duff, et al., 2010). Modifying the environment can increase safety and comfort while decreasing confusion and agitation.

Family and friends who provide care may themselves need support. They may feel overwhelmed, helpless, frustrated, anxious, or even angry at having to take care of someone with neurocognitive impairment. Sometimes, agonizing decisions must be made about whether the affected individual can live at home or with relatives versus in a nursing home or assisted-living facility.

CHECKPOINT REVIEW

1. Describe various treatment options for nonprogressive neurocognitive disorders.
2. Why is it important to balance the positive effects and side effects of medications when treating neurocognitive disorders?
3. Describe support options for those with degenerative neurocognitive disorders.

Summary

1 How can we determine whether someone has a neurocognitive disorder?

- The effects of brain damage vary greatly. The most common symptoms include confusion, attentional deficits, and impairments in consciousness, memory, and judgment.
- The assessment of brain damage is performed using interviews, psychological tests, neurological tests, and other observational or biological measures.

2 What are the different types of neurocognitive disorders?

- There are three main types of neurocognitive disorders: major neurocognitive disorder, mild neurocognitive disorder, and delirium. In major neurocognitive disorder, significant declines in independent-care skills and cognitive functioning are noted. In mild neurocognitive disorder, cognitive declines are more minor and independent functioning is not compromised.
- Delirium is an acute condition characterized by diminished awareness (including disorientation) and impaired attentional skills.

3 What are the causes of neurocognitive disorders?

- Various events or conditions can cause neurocognitive disorders, including head injuries, substance abuse, lack of blood flow to the brain, and diseases that destroy brain tissue (e.g., meningitis, encephalitis, AIDS).
- The incidence of memory problems and cognitive disorders increases with age. However, many older adults do not experience any significant cognitive decline.
- Neurocognitive disorders caused by neurodegenerative processes include conditions involving dementia (e.g., Alzheimer's disease, vascular cognitive impairment, Lewy body dementia, frontotemporal lobar degeneration) and disorders such as Parkinson's disease and Huntington's disease that begin with symptoms involving motor dysfunction.

4 What kinds of interventions are available to treat neurocognitive disorders?

- Treatment strategies include physical rehabilitation and cognitive and behavioral therapy. Medication is sometimes used to control the symptoms of the various neurocognitive disorders.

Key Terms

Media Resources

Psychology CourseMate

Access an interactive e-Book and chapter-specific interactive learning tools, including:

- flashcards
- quizzes
- videos

and more in your Psychology CourseMate.

Go to **CengageBrain.com.**

Medioimages/Photodisc/Jupiterimages

13 Sexual Dysfunction, Gender Dysphoria, and Paraphilic Disorders

CHAPTER OUTLINE

Christina and Jeremiah had been referred for sex therapy by their primary care physician after only 8 months of marriage. Both were extremely dissatisfied with their lovemaking: Jeremiah complained that Christina never initiated sex, found excuses to avoid it, and appeared to fake her orgasms during intercourse; and Christina complained that Jeremiah's lovemaking was often brief, perfunctory, and without affection. During the therapy sessions, it became clear that Christina had never had a strong interest in sex and would seldom become aroused during intercourse. Although Jeremiah had never had difficulty with maintaining an erection, sex with Christina had become progressively worrisome, as he often had difficulty getting hard enough for penetration. Before initiating sex, Jeremiah drank heavily to give him "courage" to approach Christina and to alleviate his guilt at "forcing her to have sex." These encounters were often humiliating, as he felt that Christina only agreed to sex out of pity and sufferance.

FOCUS QUESTIONS

1 What are normal and abnormal sexual behaviors?

2 What does the normal sexual response cycle tell us about sexual dysfunctions?

3 What is panic disorder, what produces it, and how is it treated?

3 What causes sexual dysfunctions?

4 What types of treatment are available for sexual dysfunctions?

5 How does aging affect the sexual activity of people who are elderly?

6 What causes gender dysphoria, and how is it treated?

7 What are paraphilic disorders, what causes them, and how are they treated?

8 Is rape an act of sex or aggression?

The case of Christina and Jeremiah illustrates one of the three major groups of sexual disorders discussed in this chapter: *sexual dysfunctions*, which involve problems in the normal sexual response cycle that affect sexual interest, arousal, and response. The two others are *gender dysphoria* (an incongruity or conflict between one's anatomical sex and one's psychological feeling of being male or female) and *paraphilic disorders* (sexual urges and fantasies about situations, objects, or people that prove problematic).

What Is "Normal" Sexual Behavior?

Compared to all other psychological disorders, distinguishing between abnormal behavior and harmless variations in preferences and tastes is the most difficult for sexual disorders and dysfunctions (Balon, Segraves, & Clayton, 2007). The definitions of normal sexual behavior vary widely and are influenced by both moral and legal judgments. Up until 2003, some states had laws that define oral-genital sex as a "perversion" and a "crime against nature," punishable by imprisonment.

Today it is difficult to classify oral sex as a "perversion." In one of the most comprehensive studies conducted on the sexual behavior of U.S. Americans—with 5,865 participants—53 percent of men ages 20–24 reported giving oral sex to female partners and 63 percent reported receiving, and 74 percent of women ages 20–24 reported giving oral sex to male partners and 70 percent reported receiving, over a 1 year period (Herbenick et al., 2010).

Determining normal and abnormal behavior becomes especially difficult when one compares Western and non-Western cultures or different time periods within a particular culture (Rathus, Nevid, & Fichner-Rathus, 2005). For example, adults in Japan have 70 percent less sexual intercourse than do adults in the United States, as is the case in many Asian countries (Durex, 2005). Should we conclude that Asians are more prone to sexual interest/arousal disorders, or do cultural factors account for the lower rate? In ancient Greece, homosexuality was not only accepted but encouraged. In many countries, sex with animals is fairly common among rural youths but is rare among urban boys. Thus it is clear that definitions of sexual disorders are also strongly influenced by cultural norms and values.

Sexual activities vary widely among people of different ages, marital status, and nationalities (Durex, 2001, 2005):

- Worldwide, people have sex an average of 97 times a year.
- 59 percent claim to have sex at least once a week; 4 percent have sex every day.
- 21- to 34-year-olds have sex the most (113 times per year, compared with 70 for those older than 45).
- Unmarried people living together have more sex (113 times per year) than people who are married (100) or single (86).
- 1 in 10 people has never had sex.

The Study of Human Sexuality

Because sexual behavior is such an important part of our lives and because so many taboos and myths surround it, people have great difficulty dealing with the topic in an open and direct manner (Ohl, 2007). Freud made the discussion of sexual topics more acceptable when he made sex (libido) an important part of psychoanalytic theory. His knowledge of sexual practices and behavior, however, was largely confined to his clinical cases and his speculations based on the understanding of social mores.

Our contemporary understanding of human sexual physiology, practices, and customs is based on the works of Alfred Kinsey and his colleagues (A. C. Kinsey, Pomeroy, & Martin, 1948; A. C. Kinsey, Pomeroy, Martin, & Gebhard, 1953); William Masters and Virginia Johnson's seminal works *Human Sexual Response* (1966) and *Human Sexual Inadequacy* (1970); the *Janus Report on Sexual Behavior* (Janus & Janus, 1993); the findings of the National Survey of Sexual Health and Behavior (M. Reese et al., 2010); and the work of other contemporary sex researchers.

Copyright © Jeff Greenberg/PhotoEdit Inc.

Glowimages/Getty Images

Cultural Influences and Sexuality

Sexuality is influenced by how it is viewed in different cultures. Some societies have very rigid social, cultural, and religious taboos associated with exposure of the human body, whereas other societies are more open. Note the dress and behavioral differences between a group of Muslim and U.S. born American young women shown here.

The Sexual Response Cycle

Treating human sexual dysfunction requires an understanding of the normal sexual response cycle, which traditionally consists of four stages: appetitive (interest and desire), arousal, orgasm, and resolution (Figure 13.1). Empirical findings suggest that it is difficult to distinguish between the desire of the appetitive stage and subjective arousal, because they seem to overlap. Desire and interest, for example, may precede or follow arousal (Brotto, 2009; C. A. Graham, Sanders, Milhausen, & McBride, 2004; U. Hartmann, Heiser, Ruffer-Hesse, & Kloth, 2002). Although we maintain a four-stage description, it is best to perceive the appetitive and arousal stages as intertwined and interactive.

1. The *appetitive phase* is characterized by the person's interest in sexual activity. The person begins to have thoughts or fantasies surrounding

Did You Know?

In a national survey of 18- to 44-year-olds (Mosher, Chandra, & Jones, 2005), 90 percent of men identified themselves as heterosexual, 2.3 percent homosexual, 1.8 percent bisexual, and 3.9 percent something else; 1.8 percent did not respond. For women the responses were nearly identical: 90 percent heterosexual, 1.3 percent homosexual, 2.8 percent bisexual, and 3.8 percent something else; 1.8 percent did not answer.

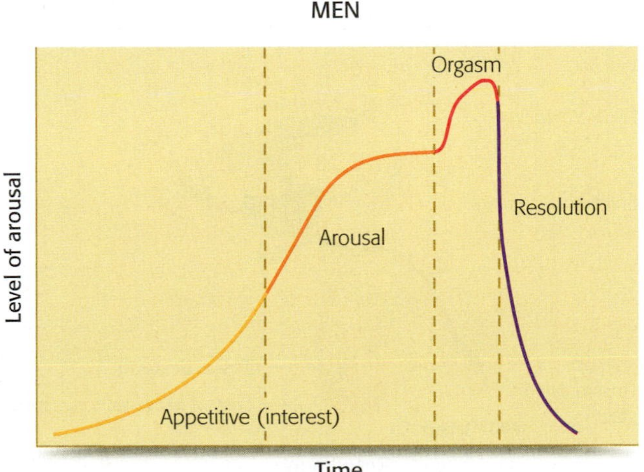

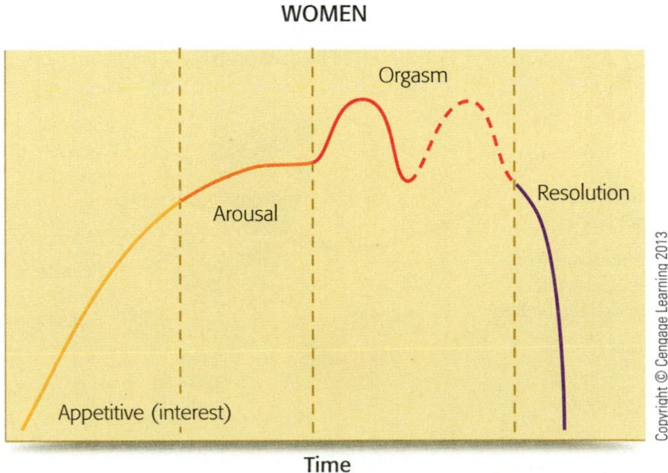

Copyright © Cengage Learning 2013

FIGURE 13.1

Human Sexual Response Cycle

The studies of Masters and Johnson reveal similar normal sexual response cycles for men and women. Note that women may experience more than one orgasm. Sexual disorders may occur at any of the phases, but seldom at the resolution phase.

sex. He or she may begin to feel attracted to another person and to daydream increasingly about sex.

2. The *arousal phase*, which may follow or precede the appetitive phase, is heightened and intensified when specific and direct—but not necessarily physical—sexual stimulation occurs. In a male, blood flow increases in the penis, resulting in an erection (Figure 13.2). In a female, the breasts swell, nipples become erect, blood engorges the genital region, and the clitoris expands (Figure 13.3).
3. The *orgasm phase* is characterized by involuntary muscular contractions throughout the body and the eventual release of sexual tension. In a male, muscles at the base of the penis contract, propelling semen through the penis. In a female, the outer third of the vagina contracts rhythmically.
4. The *resolution phase* is characterized by relaxation of the body after orgasm. Males enter a refractory period during which they are unresponsive to sexual stimulation. Heart rate, blood pressure, and respiration return to normal. However, females are capable of multiple orgasms with continued stimulation.

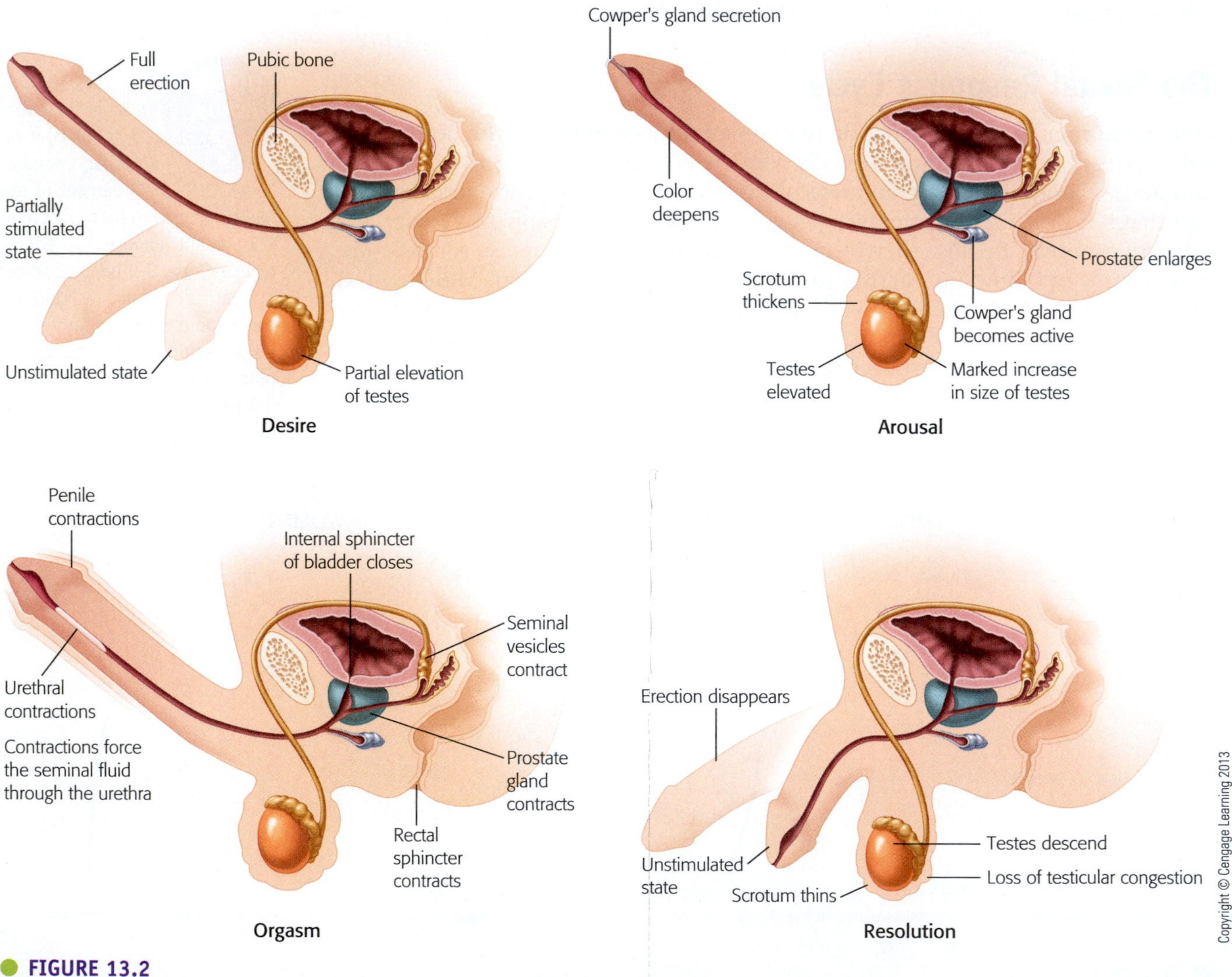

FIGURE 13.2

Genital Changes Associated With Stages of the Male Sexual Response Cycle

Although people often focus on the differences between men and women, Masters and Johnson found that the physiological responses of both to sexual stimulation are quite similar. (Compare this figure with Figure 13.3.)

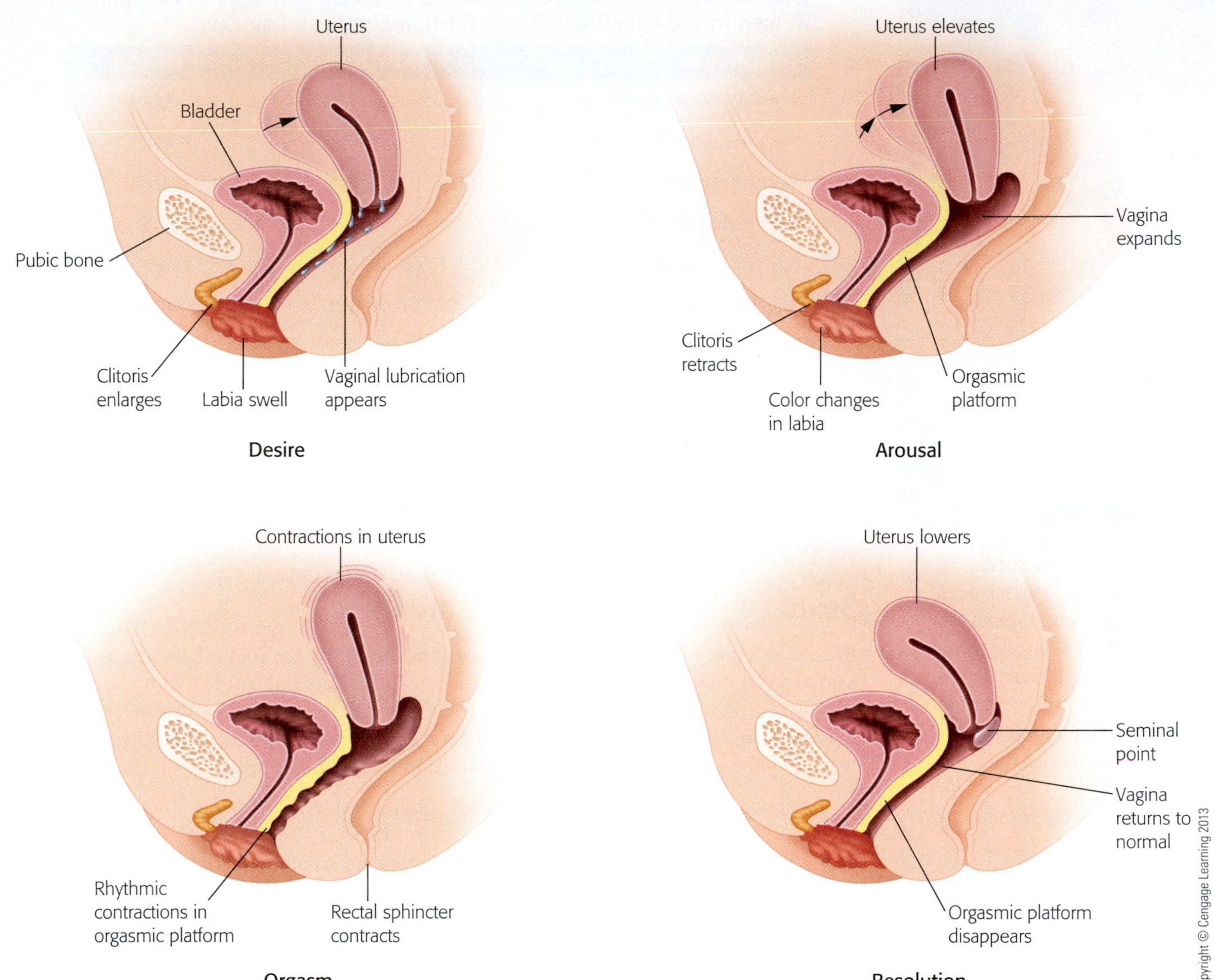

FIGURE 13.3

Genital Changes Associated With Stages of the Female Sexual Response Cycle
Compare this figure with Figure 13.2.

Sexual Dysfunctions

Problems may occur in any of the phases of the sexual response cycle, although they are rare in the resolution phase. If problems related to interest, arousal, or orgasm are recurrent and persistent, they may be diagnosed as dysfunctions. A **sexual dysfunction** is a disruption of any part of the normal sexual response cycle that affects sexual interest, arousal, or response. Epidemiological data suggest that 40–45 percent of adult women and 20–30 percent of adult men have at least one sexual dysfunction (R. W. Lewis et al., 2004). The lifetime prevalence of sexual problems in adults at some time in their lives is summarized in Table 13.1.

sexual dysfunction a disruption of any part of the normal sexual response cycle that affects sexual desire, arousal, or response

Photo by NBC/NBCU Photo Bank via Getty Images

Understanding Sexuality

Through their clinical research and well-known publications *Human Sexual Response* (1966) and *Human Sexual Inadequacy* (1970), William Masters and Virginia Johnson have done much to further understanding of and dispel myths about human sexuality.

TABLE 13.1 Lifetime Prevalence of Sexual Disorders in Men and Women in the 40–80 Age Range for Non-European Countries

CONDITION	WOMEN (%)	MEN (%)
Lack of interest in sex	32.9	17.6
Inability to reach orgasm	25.2	14.5
Orgasm reached too quickly	10.5	27.4
Pain during sex	14.0	3.5
Sex not pleasurable	21.5	12.1
Trouble lubricating	27.1	N/A

Source: Laumann, Glasser, Neves, & Moreira (2009)

To be diagnosed as a dysfunction, the disruption must be recurrent and persistent. The DSM-IV-TR also requires that such factors as frequency, chronicity, subjective distress, and effect on other areas of functioning be considered in the diagnosis. As indicated in Table 13.2, the DSM-IV-TR categories for sexual dysfunctions are *sexual desire disorders*, **sexual arousal disorders**, *orgasmic disorders*, and *sexual pain disorders*.

Sexual Interest/Arousal Disorders

Sexual interest/arousal disorders in women and men are related to the appetitive and arousal phases and are characterized by a lack of sexual interest or arousal over a prolonged period of time. These disorders are problems that occur during the excitement phase and relate to difficulties with feelings of sexual pleasure or with the physiological changes associated with sexual excitement. In the DSM-IV-TR they include:

- **hypoactive sexual desire disorder**, characterized by little or no interest in sexual activities, either actual or fantasized;
- *sexual aversion disorder*, characterized by an avoidance of and aversion to sexual intercourse; and
- **female sexual arousal disorder**, characterized by an inability to attain or maintain physiological response and/or psychological arousal during sexual activity.

The DSM-5 Work Groups (2012) are proposing to (a) remove *sexual aversion disorder* from this category and (b) make distinct, separate, and parallel diagnoses for *sexual interest/arousal disorders in women* and *sexual interest/arousal disorders in men*.

Whatever the direction the work groups elect to take, sexual interest/arousal disorders in men and women can be lifelong, acquired, generalized, or situational, and can be caused by relationship factors or a combination of psychological and biological factors (Hackett, 2008; Perlman, Martin, Hirdes, & Curtin-Telegdi, 2007; van Lankveld, 2008). For women, this disorder is often the result of negative attitudes about sex or early sexual experiences. Receiving negative information about sex, having been sexually assaulted or molested, and having conflicts with a sexual partner can contribute to the disorder (Perlman et al., 2007).

Some clinicians estimate that 40–50 percent of all sexual dysfunctions involve deficits in interest; these are now the most common complaint of couples seeking sex therapy (Laumann, Glasser, Neves, & Moreira, 2009; McAnulty & Burnette, 2004). Although people with sexual interest/arousal disorders are often capable of experiencing orgasm, they claim to have little interest in, or to derive no pleasure from, sexual activity.

sexual arousal disorder a disorder characterized by problems occurring during the excitement phase of the sexual response cycle and relating to difficulties with feelings of sexual pleasure or with the physiological changes associated with sexual excitement

hypoactive sexual desire disorder a sexual dysfunction that is related to the appetitive phase of the sexual response cycle and is characterized by a lack of sexual desire

female sexual arousal disorder the inability to attain or maintain physiological response or psychological arousal during sexual activity

erectile disorder (ED) an inability to attain or maintain an erection sufficient for sexual intercourse or psychological arousal during sexual activity

Erectile Disorder In men, inhibited sexual excitement takes the form of an **erectile disorder (ED)**, an inability to attain or maintain an erection sufficient for

DISORDERS CHART SEXUAL DYSFUNCTIONS

TABLE 13.2

Dysfunction	Symptoms	Prevalence	Age of Onset	Course
Sexual interest disorders	Problems during the appetitive phase **Hypoactive sexual desire disorder** Absent or low sexual interest or desire **Sexual aversion disorder** Avoidance of or aversion to sexual intercourse	20% of adult population; women have higher rates (20–35%) than men (15%)	Usually noticed in adulthood by a partner who complains	May be lifelong or acquired; treatment may help
Sexual arousal disorders	Problems of sexual pleasure or physiological changes involving sexual excitement **Erectile disorder (ED)** Inability to attain or maintain an erection sufficient for sexual intercourse or psychological arousal during sexual activity **Female sexual arousal disorder** Inability to attain or maintain physiological response or psychological arousal during sexual activity	10% of men report ED; some 50% have experienced "transient" conditions; 10–50% of women suffer from arousal lubrication problems	Can occur at age of sexual maturity but increases with age, especially in men	Most can be helped by psychological or medical treatment
Orgasmic disorders	Problems with the orgasm phase **Female/male orgasmic disorder** Persistent delay or inability to achieve orgasm after reaching excitement phase **Early (premature) ejaculation** Ejaculation with minimal sexual stimulation before, during, or shortly after penetration	Estimated 30–50% for early (premature) ejaculation; 3–10% of men in the nonclinical population suffer from orgasm disorder; 10% of women have never experienced an orgasm	Age of sexual maturity	In men, often related to performance anxiety; in women, lack of foreplay is the most frequent reason
Genital-pelvic pain/penetration disorders	**Dyspareunia** Genital pain in a man or woman not primarily due to lack of lubrication in the vagina or to vaginismus **Vaginismus** Involuntary spasm of the outer third of the vaginal wall that prevents or interferes with sexual intercourse	Dyspareunia is relatively rare in men but more common in women (17–19%); vaginismus occurs in less than 1% of females	Can occur because of medical problems (such as injury to the pelvis) or traumatic event	Most have physical causes and can be treated

Source: Data from American Psychiatric Association (2000); Hooper (1998); LoPiccolo (1995, 1997); Paik & Laumann (2006); Spector & Carey (1990)

sexual intercourse or psychological arousal during sexual activity (Segraves, 2010). The man may feel fully aroused, but he cannot finish the sex act. In the past, such a dysfunction has been attributed primarily to psychological causes ("It's all in the head"). However, studies indicate that from 30 percent to as many as 70 percent of erectile dysfunctions are caused by some form of vascular insufficiency, such as diabetes, atherosclerosis, or traumatic groin injury, or by other physiological factors (R. W. Lewis et al., 2004; Lewis, Yuan, & Wang, 2008).

Distinguishing between erectile dysfunctions that are primarily biological and those that are primarily psychological has been difficult (Lewis, Yuan, & Wang, 2008). For example, one procedure involves recording nocturnal penile tumescence. During sleep, men have frequent erections. If, however, they have an organic problem, they are not able to have erections during the waking state. Psychological distress is minimized during sleep and should not impair erections. Thus men who do not display adequate spontaneous erections during sleep have an organic impairment, and psychological causes are therefore thought to predominate in these men. Unfortunately, considerable overlap in nocturnal penile tumescence scores has been found between samples of diabetic men with erectile difficulties and men in control groups without them (Lewis, Yuan, & Wang, 2008; Lue, 2002). Therefore, some people diagnosed with organic impotence may actually have a psychologically based impotence. The reverse could also be true.

Primary erectile dysfunction is the diagnosis for a man who has never been able to engage successfully in sexual intercourse. This difficulty often has a clear psychological origin, because many men with this dysfunction can get an erection and reach orgasm during masturbation and can show erection during the rapid eye movement phase of sleep. In *secondary erectile dysfunction*, the man has had at least one successful instance of sexual intercourse but is currently unable to achieve an erection and penetration in 25 percent or more of his sexual attempts (Masters & Johnson, 1970).

Case Study

A 20-year-old college student was experiencing secondary erectile dysfunction. His first episode of erectile difficulty occurred when he attempted sexual intercourse after drinking heavily. Although to a certain extent he attributed the failure to alcohol, he also began to have doubts about his sexual ability. During a subsequent sexual encounter, his anxiety and worry increased. When he failed in this next coital encounter, even though he had not been drinking, his anxiety level rose even more. He sought therapy after the discovery that he was unable to have an erection even during petting.

Did You Know ? Men think about sex significantly more often than women do.

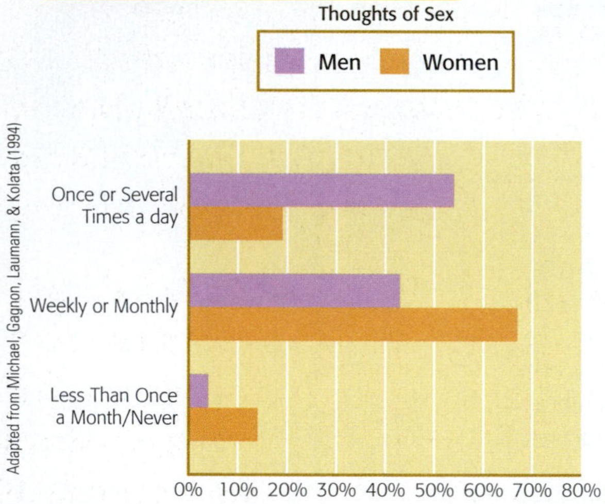

Thoughts of Sex

Men | Women

Once or Several Times a day

Weekly or Monthly

Less Than Once a Month/Never

0% 10% 20% 30% 40% 50% 60% 70% 80%

Adapted from Michael, Gagnon, Laumann, & Kolata (1994)

The prevalence rate of ED is difficult to determine because it is often unreported. Clinicians estimate that approximately 50 percent of men have experienced transient impotence (H. A. Feldman, Goldstein, Hatzichristou, Krane, & McKinlay, 1994).

Hypersexual Disorder?

Can a person be "oversexed" and have a sexual appetite that requires frequent sex in order to be satisfied? Golfer Tiger Woods, actor David Duchovny (*The X-Files*), and TV reality star Jesse James (ex-husband of actor Sandra Bullock) have admitted to sex addiction and entered rehabilitation centers for treatment. In all three cases, their "compulsions" to have sex with multiple partners resulted in marital or pair-bond dysfunctions or negative personal or professional consequences. Is sexual addiction a real disease or simply an excuse?

Most sex therapists are in agreement that some individuals seem obsessed with sex, feel compelled to engage in frequent sexual activity, and find that their behavior causes them personal distress. Terms such as *hypersexuality*, *erotomania*, *nymphomania*, and *satyriasis* refer to this phenomenon. More than 4 percent of people claim to have sex every day; 2 percent of married men and 1 percent of married women have intercourse more than once a day (Durex, 2001, 2005). By statistical standards, would these people be considered abnormal?

Sufficient clinical and research findings support the existence of a **hypersexual disorder**. People who have it seem to exhibit recurrent sexual fantasies, urges, and behaviors manifested in the following ways: (a) excessive time consumed by sexual urges and thoughts; (b) repetitive engagement in sexual fantasies and behaviors in response to depression, anxiety, boredom, and irritability; (c) repetitive engagement in sexual urges and behaviors due to stressful life events; (d) repetitive unsuccessful attempts to reduce or control sexual urges, activities, and fantasies; and (c) repetitive engagement in sexual urges and behaviors while disregarding the risk for physical or emotional harm to the self or others (DSM-5 Work Groups, 2012).

hypersexual disorder a craving for constant sex at the expense of relationships, work productivity, and daily activities

In addition to personal psychological distress (guilt, shame, anxiety, depression, and loss of control), the consequences of the disorder may include relationship problems, divorce or separation, an increased rate of sexually transmitted disease, unintended pregnancies, excessive spending on sexual services, and school or employment dysfunction (Kafka, 2009; McBride, Reece, & Sanders, 2008; R. C. Reid, Harper, & Anderson, 2009).

Did You Know ? A strong libido is often valued by our society because it connotes potency, power, attractiveness, sensual pleasure, and health. Indeed, the search for aphrodisiacs in the form of powdered animal genitals, herbs, secret concoctions, and even drugs such as Viagra is a multibillion-dollar industry.

Orgasmic Disorders

Orgasmic disorders affect both men and women. There may be a marked delay, infrequency, or inability to achieve a satisfactory orgasm after entering the excitement phase and receiving adequate sexual stimulation. How orgasm disorders are manifested in men and women may differ slightly.

Female Orgasmic Disorder

A woman with **female orgasmic disorder** experiences persistent delay or inability to achieve an orgasm with stimulation after entering the excitement phase that is "adequate in focus, intensity, and duration." If an orgasm occurs, she may report it as "greatly diminished in intensity and pleasure."

Female orgasmic disorders may be termed *primary*, to indicate that orgasm has never been experienced, or *secondary*, to show that orgasm has been experienced. It is the second most frequently reported sexual problem for women (Meston, Seal, & Hamilton, 2008). Primary orgasmic dysfunction is considered relatively common in women: Approximately 10 percent of all women have never achieved an orgasm (Rosen & Leiblum, 1995). This disorder is not equivalent to primary orgasmic disorder in males, who often can achieve orgasm through masturbation or by some other means.

Delayed Ejaculation (Male Orgasmic Disorder)

Delayed ejaculation (male orgasmic disorder) is the persistent delay or inability to achieve an orgasm after the excitement phase has been reached and sexual activity has been adequate in focus, intensity, and duration. The DSM-5 Work Groups (2012) are considering renaming male orgasmic disorder to "delayed ejaculation," because it is a more accurate descriptor. The term is usually restricted to the delay or inability to ejaculate within the vagina, even with full arousal and penile erection. As noted, men who have this dysfunction can usually ejaculate when masturbating. Inhibited orgasm in males is relatively rare, and little is known about it (McAnulty & Burnette, 2004). Because this definition appears heterosexist, it is important to note that inability to ejaculate within the anus should probably also be included.

Early Ejaculation

The inability to satisfy a sexual partner is a source of anguish for many men. **Early ejaculation** (also known as *premature ejaculation*) is ejaculation with minimal sexual stimulation before, during, or shortly after penetration. It is believed to be the most common type of male sexual dysfunction, affecting 21–33 percent of men (Walling, 2007). Table 13.3 provides comparison responses between groups of men with and without early ejaculation problems. Sex researchers and therapists differ in their criteria for prematurity. H. S. Kaplan (1974) defined it as the inability of a man to tolerate high (plateau) levels of sexual excitement without ejaculating reflexively. Masters and Johnson (1970) contended that a man who is unable to delay ejaculation long enough during sexual intercourse to produce an orgasm in the woman 50 percent of the time exhibits premature ejaculation. The difficulty with the latter definition is the possibility that a man may be "premature" with one partner but entirely adequate for another.

female orgasmic disorder a sexual dysfunction in which the woman experiences persistent delay or inability to achieve an orgasm with stimulation after entering the excitement phase that is adequate in focus, intensity, and duration

delayed ejaculation (male orgasmic disorder) persistent delay or inability to achieve an orgasm after the excitement phase has been reached and sexual activity has been adequate in focus, intensity, and duration; usually restricted to an inability to ejaculate within the vagina

early ejaculation ejaculation with minimal sexual stimulation before, during, or shortly after penetration; also known as *premature ejaculation*

TABLE 13.3 Mean Responses of Men With and Without Early Ejaculation

ITEM	WITH	WITHOUT
1. Over the past month, how was your control over ejaculation during sexual intercourse? (0 = very poor; 4 = good)	0.9	3.0
2. Over the past month, how was your satisfaction with sexual intercourse? (0 = very poor; 4 = very good)	1.9	3.3
3. How distressed are you by how fast you ejaculate during intercourse? (4 = extremely distressed; 0 = not at all)	2.9	0.7
4. To what extent does how fast you ejaculate cause difficulty in your relationship with your partner? (4 = extremely; 0 = not at all)	1.9	0.3

Source: Rowland, Tai, & Brummett (2007)

Genital-Pelvic Pain/Penetration Disorder **Genital-pelvic pain/penetration disorders** can be manifested in both males and females in a condition termed **dyspareunia**, which is a recurrent or persistent pain in the genitals before, during, or after sexual intercourse. It is estimated that the lifetime prevalence rate is 17–19 percent (Paik & Laumann, 2006). Dyspareunia is not caused exclusively by lack of lubrication or by **vaginismus**, which is an involuntary spasm of the outer third of the vaginal wall that prevents or interferes with sexual intercourse. Vaginismus is considered very rare. The DSM-5 Work Groups (2012) have observed that differentiating between dyspareunia and vaginismus is difficult and unreliable. Thus, they are proposing that these conditions be described under a broader overarching umbrella: genital-pelvic pain/penetration disorder.

CHECKPOINT REVIEW

1 Why is it so difficult to determine normal and abnormal sexual behavior?

2 Describe the four phases of the human sexual response cycle.

3 Can you name the types of sexual dysfunctions most likely to arise from each of the phases?

Etiology of Sexual Dysfunctions

There is perhaps no other group of mental disorders in which the interaction of biological, psychological, social, and sociocultural dimensions is as clearly demonstrated as in sexual dysfunctions (Lussier, McCann, & Beauregard, 2008; Ohl, 2007). Let's return to the case of Jeremiah and Christina from the chapter opening to illustrate how various etiological factors can contribute to sexual dysfunctions. (You may wish to reread the case in order to follow this multipath analysis.)

Recall that both came for sex therapy because Christina did not seem to desire or enjoy sex and Jeremiah was experiencing erection difficulties during their lovemaking. Christina was diagnosed as having a sexual interest arousal disorder and Jeremiah an erectile disorder. The possibility that Christina could also be experiencing an orgasmic disorder was entertained but eliminated as therapy progressed. It appeared that she was quite capable of being aroused and orgasmic under the right conditions.

Studies suggest that sexual interest and desire are due to a combination of biological, psychological, social, and sociocultural factors (Heard-Davison, Heiman,

genital-pelvic pain/penetration disorder physical pain or discomfort associated with intercourse or penetration; fear, anxiety, and distress are also usually present; includes previous diagnoses of vaginismus and dyspareunia

dyspareunia recurrent or persistent pain in the genitals before, during, or after sexual intercourse

vaginismus involuntary spasm of the outer third of the vaginal wall that prevents or interferes with sexual intercourse

& Briggs, 2004; Nanda, 2008). On the biological level, hormones such as prolactin, testosterone, and estrogen affect high or low levels of sexual desire (Hyde, 2005; van Lankveld, 2008). On a psychological level, negative childhood experiences such as sexual abuse, strict moralistic upbringing, and positive or negative attitudes toward sex affect fantasy and desire (University of Granada, 2007). Likewise, social and sociocultural factors such as a dysfunctional partner or a marital relationship that is full of anger or resentment and gender scripts ("Good girls do not initiate sex" or "They enjoy it as much as men") can affect desire.

A similar analysis can be applied to Jeremiah and his problems with maintaining an erection during intercourse. His past sexual history reveals no significant erectile problems until his marriage to Christina. Although his increasing ED seems more related to psychological causes, his heavy drinking affects his biological sexual response cycle. Although consumption of alcohol might decrease inhibition (and thereby increase his courage), it is a central nervous system suppressant that makes it more difficult for any man to achieve an erection. For Jeremiah, it is clear that he is also feeling guilt, humiliation, and anger toward Christina, whom he may blame for his problem. As a man, he may also operate from a *cultural script*—a social and cultural belief and expectation that guides our behaviors regarding sex—that equates masculinity with sexual potency. Given these facts, the following multipath explanation of the couple's sexual difficulties might be operative (Figure 13.4).

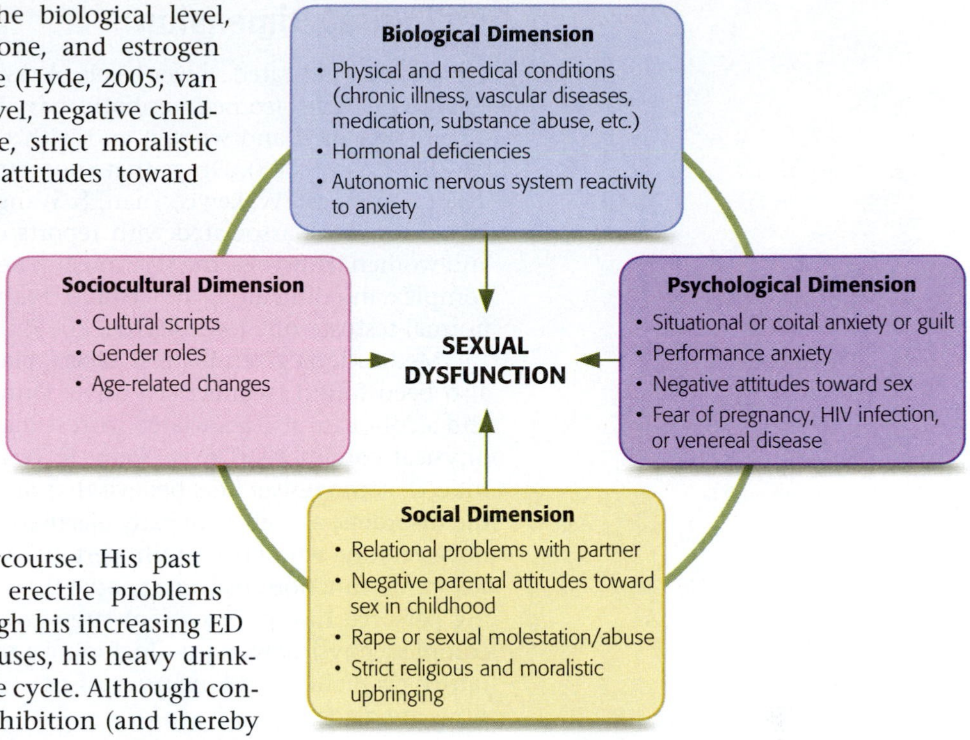

Biological Dimension
- Physical and medical conditions (chronic illness, vascular diseases, medication, substance abuse, etc.)
- Hormonal deficiencies
- Autonomic nervous system reactivity to anxiety

Sociocultural Dimension
- Cultural scripts
- Gender roles
- Age-related changes

SEXUAL DYSFUNCTION

Psychological Dimension
- Situational or coital anxiety or guilt
- Performance anxiety
- Negative attitudes toward sex
- Fear of pregnancy, HIV infection, or venereal disease

Social Dimension
- Relational problems with partner
- Negative parental attitudes toward sex in childhood
- Rape or sexual molestation/abuse
- Strict religious and moralistic upbringing

FIGURE 13.4

Multipath Model of Sexual Dysfunctions The dimensions interact with one another and combine in different ways to result in a specific sexual dysfunction.

Case Study Analysis

Jeremiah and Christina's sexual disorders are intertwined in their relationship (social) and cannot be viewed in isolation (interactive). Christina's low sexual interest (biological) makes Jeremiah doubt his own sexual attractiveness (psychological) and increases his anxiety levels so that it affects his ability to achieve an erection. He drinks heavily to reduce his anxiety and to decrease his inhibitions about initiating sex. Alcohol and anxiety affect his ability to achieve and maintain an erection (biological). When he does achieve an erection, he quickly enters Christina for fear of losing it (psychological), and in turn becomes "brief" and "perfunctory" in lovemaking. The brevity of the sexual encounter does not allow Christina to become sexually aroused, to become sufficiently lubricated (biological; intercourse becomes painful), or to achieve an orgasm, so she fakes it in order to please him. Jeremiah, however, knows it is faked and not only blames himself for the failure (psychological) but feels humiliated by what he sees as her pity. He may begin to equate his inability to satisfy Christina with "not being a real man" (sociocultural). Both find the encounter unpleasant (social). The cycle then repeats itself.

Biological Dimension

As has been indicated, lower levels of testosterone and higher levels of estrogens such as prolactin (sometimes both) have been associated with lower sexual interest in both men and women and with erectile difficulties in men (Hyde, 2005; van Lankveld, 2008). Drugs that suppress testosterone appear to decrease sexual desire in men (R. W. Lewis, Yuan, & Wang, 2008). Conversely, the administration of androgens is associated with reports of increased sexual desire in both men and women. However, the relationship between hormones and sexual behavior is complex and difficult to understand. Many people with sexual dysfunctions have normal testosterone levels (Hyde, 2005).

Medications given to treat ulcers, glaucoma, allergies, and convulsions have also been found to affect sex drive. Drugs such as antihypertensive medication and alcohol are also associated with sexual dysfunctions, as are illnesses and other physical conditions (Lewis, Yuan, & Wang, 2008; McAnulty & Burnette, 2004). Indeed, some researchers believe that alcohol abuse is the leading cause of erectile disorders, as well as of early ejaculation (Arackal & Benegal, 2007). But again, not everyone who takes antihypertensive drugs, consumes alcohol, or is ill has a sexual dysfunction. In some people these factors may combine with a predisposing personal history or current stress to produce problems in sexual function. A complete physical workup—including a medical history, physical exam, and laboratory evaluation—is a necessary first step in assessment before treatment decisions are made.

For some, a lack of sexual desire may be physiological (Paik & Laumann, 2006). Penile hypersensitivity to physical stimulation has been found to affect sexual functioning in men. Men who ejaculate early seem to have difficulty determining when ejaculation is inevitable once the sympathetic nervous system is triggered, and seem to be "hardwired" to have a sensitive and more easily triggered sensory and response system (Rowland & McMahon, 2008).

The amount of blood flowing into the genital area is also associated with orgasmic potential in women and erectile functioning in men. In women, masturbation training and Kegel exercises (tightening muscles in the pelvis) may increase vascularization of the labia, clitoris, and vagina. In men, vascular surgery to increase blood flow to the penis is successful when used appropriately. Unfortunately, if the problem is due to arteriosclerosis that affects a number of the small blood vessels, vascular surgery meets with little success.

Psychological Dimension

Sexual dysfunctions may be due to psychological factors alone or to a combination of psychological and biological factors. They may be mild and transient or lifelong and chronic. Psychological causes for sexual dysfunctions may include predisposing or historical factors as well as more current problems and concerns. Guilt, anger, or resentment toward a partner; fear of pregnancy; fear of catching a sexually transmitted disease; and anxiety can all interfere with sexual performance (Westheimer & Lopater, 2005).

Traditional psychoanalysts have stressed the role of unconscious conflicts in sexual dysfunctions. For example, erectile difficulties and early ejaculation are said to represent a man's hostility to women due to unresolved early developmental conflicts involving his parents. Likewise, a woman's lack of desire or arousal may also represent repressed hostility toward her partner or an attempt to punish him.

Cognitive theorists stress the interaction of performance anxiety and the spectator role in the etiology of sexual dysfunctions. For example, a man may experience a rare erection problem and begin to worry that it will happen again. Instead of enjoying the next sexual encounter and becoming aroused, he monitors or observes his own reactions ("Am I getting an erection?") and becomes a spectator who is anxious and detached from the situation. The result is potential failure and greater anxiety for future sexual encounters. Men with psychological erectile dysfunction often report anxiety over sexual overtures, including a fear of failing sexually, a fear of being seen as sexually inferior, and anxiety over the size of their genitals.

Early psychosexual experiences may shape a man's expectations and sexual responses as well. Men with early ejaculation, for example, have been found to have less sexual intercourse than their counterparts without early ejaculation (Rowland & McMahon, 2008). Even in men without sexual dysfunctions, longer intervals between sex result in greater excitement when intercourse occurs. For men with early ejaculation, it is possible that fewer sexual experiences predispose them to higher excitement and arousal, and they have fewer opportunities to learn how to delay an ejaculatory response. It is important to note that one successful form of sexual therapy for early ejaculation directs patients to attend more to somatic feedback and to adjust their cognitions and behaviors to influence an impending ejaculation.

© Jupiterimages

Sexual Flirtation Common Among Teens

Direct expressions of sexual interest are often discouraged in various cultures. Flirting, however, allows for indirect, playful, and romantic sexual overtures toward others. It may occur through verbal communication (tone of voice, pace, and intonation) or body language (eye contact, open stances, hair flicking, or brief touching).

Situational or coital anxiety can also interrupt sexual functioning in women. Factors associated with orgasmic dysfunction in women include having a sexually inexperienced or dysfunctional partner; a crippling fear of performance failure, of never being able to attain orgasm, of pregnancy, or of sexually transmitted disease; an inability to accept the partner, either emotionally or physically; and misinformation or ignorance about sexuality or sexual techniques.

Social Dimension

Social upbringing and current relationships have been identified as important in sexual functioning. It seems plausible that the attitudes parents display toward sex and affection and toward each other can influence their children's attitudes. Being raised in a strict religious environment is also associated with sexual dysfunctions in both men and women (Masters & Johnson, 1970). Traumatic sexual experiences involving incestuous abuse during childhood or adolescence or rape are also factors to consider (Lussier et al., 2008). Adults who have been molested as a children or women who have been raped may suffer from post-traumatic stress disorder, distrust men, find it difficult to establish intimacy, and exhibit sexual dysfunctions (Lussier et al., 2008).

Relationship issues are often at the forefront of sexual disorders among and between men and women. As we saw in the case of Jeremiah and Christina, current marital or relationship problems may interfere with sexual function. Marital satisfaction, for example, is associated with greater levels of sexual arousal and frequency between partners (C. A. Graham et al., 2004), whereas relationship dissatisfaction is linked to sexual difficulties (interest, arousal, and orgasm) among couples (Laumann, Gagnon, Michael, & Michaels, 1994). Specifically, relationships that are caring, warm, and affectionate and in which there is more communication about sex and sexual activities seem to predict much more sexual satisfaction (Meston et al., 2008). It is important to note that sexual satisfaction may be defined differently between the sexes. For women it is determined more by closeness to a partner than by the number or orgasms or the intensity of sexual arousal.

Frequency of yearly sex varies among countries, nationalities, and regions (Durex, 2001, 2005):

- U.S. Americans have the most sex (124 times per year), followed by Greeks (117 times per year), South Africans and Croatians (116 times per year), and New Zealanders (115 times per year).
- People in Japan (36 times per year), Hong Kong (63 times per year), Taiwan (65 times per year), and China (72 times per year) have the least sex.

Sociocultural Dimension

From our earlier discussion, it is clear that sexual behavior and functioning are influenced by gender, age, cultural scripts, educational level, and country of origin. Although the human sexual response cycle is similar for women and men, gender differences are clearly present: Women are capable of multiple orgasms, entertain different sexual fantasies than men do, have a broader arousal pattern to sexual stimuli, are more attuned to relationships in the sexual encounter, and take longer than men to become aroused (Northwestern University, 2003; Safarinejad, 2006; University of Granada, 2007).

Cultural scripts are the social and cultural beliefs and expectations that guide our behaviors regarding sex; they can have a major impact on sexual functioning. Some domestic scripts for men in the United States may be "sexual potency in men is a sign of masculinity" (implying that "impotence" is a sign of not being a "real man"); "the bigger the sex organ, the better"; and "strong and virile men do not show feelings." For women, scripts include "nice women don't initiate sex"; "nice women are restrained and proper in lovemaking"; and "it is the woman's responsibility to take care of contraception." Cultural scripts also exist in other nations. For example, people in Asian countries consistently report the lowest frequency of sexual intercourse. It would be a serious mistake to believe that an entire nation can suffer from a sexual interest/arousal disorder. Rather, some suggest that these countries are more conservative, restrained, and restrictive in their attitudes toward sex (D. W. Sue & Sue, 2013).

Likewise, sexual dysfunctions differ because of biological differences and gender role expectations: Women are more likely than men to be diagnosed as suffering from sexual interest disorders, and they differ as to the manifestation of arousal disorders (erectile disorder for men vs. lubrication problems for women). In U.S. society, men are taught to be sexually assertive whereas women are taught not to initiate sex directly, but rather in a more subtle and indirect manner. It is important to note that sex researchers and clinicians who do not consider biological differences and cultural scripts may unfairly portray women as having sexual interest disorders.

Sexual orientation is also an important sociocultural influence on understanding sexual responsiveness among gays and lesbians. Although there are no physiological differences in sexual arousal and response between lesbians and gay men on the one hand and heterosexuals on the other, it is also important to note that sexual issues may differ quite dramatically. For example, problems among heterosexuals most often focus on sexual intercourse, whereas sexual concerns among lesbians and gay men focus on other behaviors (e.g., aversion toward anal eroticism or cunnilingus). Lesbians and gay men must also deal with societal or internalized homophobia, which often inhibits open expression of their affection toward one another (M. S. Schneider, Brown, & Glassgold, 2002). Finally, gay men are forced to deal with the association between sexual activity and HIV infection. These broader contextual issues may create diminished sexual interest or desire, sexual aversion, and negative feelings toward sexual activity (Croteau, Lark, Lidderdale, & Chung, 2005).

Treatment of Sexual Dysfunctions

Many approaches have been used to treat sexual dysfunctions, including biological interventions and psychological treatment approaches.

Biological Interventions

Biological interventions may include hormone replacement and special medications or mechanical means to improve sexual functioning. For example, men with organic erectile dysfunction may be treated with vacuum pumps, suppositories, or penile implants. The penile prosthesis is an inflatable or semirigid device that, once inflated, produces an erection sufficient for intercourse and ejaculation. Approximately 89 percent of men with penile implants and 70 percent of their partners expressed satisfaction with the implants (Center for Male Reproductive Medicine and Microsurgery, 2005), and most said that they would choose the treatment again.

Another form of medical treatment for ED is the injection of substances into the penis (Lewis, Yuan, & Wang, 2008). Within a very short time the man gets a very stiff erection, which may last from 1 to 4 hours. Although men using the method have reported general satisfaction with it, as have their mates, it does have some side effects. There is often bruising of the penis and development of nodules. Some men find the prolonged erection disturbing in the absence of sexual stimulation.

Oral medications such as Viagra, Levitra, and Cialis have been found to be an attractive alternative in minimizing the negative effects of injection therapy. Viagra made headlines in 1998 as a "miracle cure" for the 30 million men with erectile dysfunctions (Tuller, 2004). The early clinical trials on 4,500 men indicated between 50 and 80 percent effectiveness; users' testimony of its "instantaneous success" has added to the hype (Hooper, 1998; Leland, 1997).

Unlike injectables, Viagra and its competitors do not produce an automatic erection in the absence of sexual stimuli. If a man becomes aroused, the drugs enable the body to follow through the sexual response cycle to completion. Urologists claim that for individuals with no sexual dysfunction, taking Viagra, for example, does not improve their erections; in other words, Viagra does not provide physiological help that will enable normally functioning men to improve their sexual functioning, nor does it lead to a stiffer erection. These drugs may aid sexual arousal and performance by stimulating men's expectations and fantasies; this psychological boost may then lead to subjective feelings of enhanced pleasure.

Psychological Treatment Approaches

In addition to biological forms of treatment, most general psychological treatment approaches include the following components:

- *Education.* The therapist replaces sexual myths and misconceptions with accurate information about sexual anatomy and functioning.
- *Anxiety reduction.* The therapist uses procedures such as desensitization or graded approaches to keep anxiety at a minimum. The therapist explains that constantly observing and evaluating one's performance can interfere with sexual functioning.
- *Structured behavioral exercises.* The therapist gives a series of graded tasks that gradually increase the amount of sexual interaction between the partners. Each partner takes turns touching and being touched over different parts of the body except for the genital regions. Later the partners fondle the body and genital regions without making demands for sexual arousal or orgasm. Successful sexual intercourse and orgasm are the final stage of the structured exercises.
- *Communication training.* The therapist teaches the partners appropriate ways of communicating their sexual wishes to each other and also teaches them conflict resolution.

Some specific nonmedical treatments for other dysfunctions are as follows:

- *Female orgasmic dysfunction.* Both structured behavioral exercises and communication training have been successful in treating sexual arousal disorders in women. Masturbation appears to be the most effective way for women with orgasmic dysfunction to have an orgasm. The procedure involves education about sexual anatomy, visual and tactile self-exploration, use of sexual fantasies and images, and masturbation, both individually and with a partner. High success rates have been reported with this procedure for women with primary orgasmic dysfunction. This approach does not necessarily lead to a woman's ability to achieve orgasm during sexual intercourse.

- *Early ejaculation.* In one technique, the partner stimulates the penis until the man feels the sensation of impending ejaculation. At this point, the partner stops the stimulation for a short period of time and then continues it again. This pattern is repeated until the man can tolerate increasingly greater periods of stimulation before ejaculation. Masters and Johnson (1970) and Kaplan (1974) used a similar procedure, called the "squeeze technique." They reported a success rate of nearly 100 percent. The treatment is easily learned. Although the short-term success rate for treating early ejaculation is very high, relapses are common.
- *Vaginismus.* The results of treatment for vaginismus have been uniformly positive. The involuntary spasms or closure of the vaginal muscle can be deconditioned by first training the woman to relax and then inserting successively larger dilators while she is relaxed.

Aging, Sexual Activity, and Sexual Dysfunctions

Aging has been found to be one of the most powerful predictors of changing sexual functioning (decreases in sexual interest, arousal, and activity), even when the effects of illness, medication, and psychopathology are controlled for (Gooren, 2008). In the most comprehensive study of sexuality and health among older U.S. adults—ages 57 to 85—3,005 participants (1,550 women and 1,455 men) were surveyed, with the following findings (Lindau et al., 2007):

- Sexual activity declined with age (73 percent among 57- to 64-year-olds; 53 percent among 65- to 74-year-olds; 25 percent among 75- to 85-year-olds).
- Women were far more likely to report less sexual activity at all ages.
- Among men and women who were sexually active, approximately 50 percent reported at least one bothersome sexual problem.
- The most frequently reported sexual problems for women included low sexual interest or desire (43 percent), problems with vaginal lubrication (39 percent), and inability to climax (34 percent).
- Among men the most frequent problems were erectile difficulties (37 percent).

David Young-Wolff/PhotoEdit

Sexual Behavior Among Seniors

Contrary to the belief that people who are elderly lose their sexual desire, studies reveal that sexual desire, activity, and enjoyment remain high in the older population.

It is important for us to understand how the aging process affects sexuality. When women reach menopause, estrogen levels drop, and women may experience vaginal dryness and thinning of the vaginal wall (Brotto & Luria, 2008). This may result in discomfort during sexual activity. Likewise, older men are at higher risk for prostate problems that may increase the risk of ED (Gooren, 2008). Both sexes are also at higher risk for illnesses that affect sexual performance and interest (diabetes, high blood pressure, rheumatism, and heart disease). Hormone replacement therapy, drugs for ED (Cialis, Levitra, and Viagra), and other medical procedures may help minimize the effects of these organic problems on sexual activity. For example, older men and women who rate their health as poor are less likely to be sexually active, and 14 percent of men report using medication to improve their sexual performance (Lindau et al., 2007).

Despite the problems of aging, sexual activity and enjoyment among the older population remains surprisingly high. Studies reveal that the sexual activity of people ages 65 and older declined little from that of their 30- to 40-year-old counterparts, their ability to reach orgasm and have sex diminished very little from their early years, and their desire to continue a relatively active sex life was unchanged (Janus & Janus, 1993; National Council on Aging, 1998).

CHECKPOINT REVIEW

1. Apply the multipath model to explain sexual dysfunctions.
2. What evidence exists that supports a biological, psychological, social, and sociocultural explanation of sexual dysfunctions?
3. How does age affect sexual behavior and functioning?

MYTH VS. REALITY

MYTH Sex is unimportant to people who are elderly. They are averse to being sexually active and are conservative in sexual behavior.

REALITY Although sexual activity does decline with age, a major survey of adults ages 57 to 85 (Lindau, 2007) found that many older people are sexually active well into their 60s, 70s, and 80s. Fifty-four percent reported having sex at least twice a month, and 23 percent reported once a week or more. Approximately 50 percent of men and women younger than age 75 had engaged in oral sex in the previous 2 months.

Gender Dysphoria

In contrast to the sexual dysfunctions, which involve any disruption of the normal sexual response cycle, **gender dysphoria**—previously called *gender identity disorder (GID)* or *transsexualism*—is characterized by a marked incongruence between one's experienced or expressed gender and one's assigned gender as a male or female (Meyer-Bahlburg, 2009). It is important to note that gender dysphoria and sexual orientation are not the same thing—the sexual orientation of a transgender person can thus be heterosexual, gay, lesbian, bisexual, or asexual (Zucker & Cohen-Ketteris, 2008).

Gender dysphoria involves experiencing strong and persistent dislike of or desire to be rid of one's sexual anatomy. Gender dysphoria may or may not be manifested in significant impairment in social, occupational, or other important areas of functioning. People with this disorder hold a lifelong conviction that nature has placed them in a body of the wrong sex. This feeling produces a preoccupation with eliminating the physical and behavioral sexual characteristics associated with the body's sex and acquiring those of the person's experienced gender instead (Lawrence, 2008).

People with gender dysphoria tend to exhibit gender-role incongruence at an early age and to report conflicted gender-role feelings in childhood, some as early as two years old (McAnulty & Burnette, 2004; Zucker, 2009). A boy may claim that he will grow up to be a woman, demonstrate disgust with his penis, and be exclusively preoccupied with interests and activities considered "feminine." Boys with this disorder are frequently labeled "sissies" by their male peers. They prefer playing with girls and generally avoid the rough-and-tumble activities in which boys are traditionally encouraged to participate. They are more likely than other boys to play with "feminine" toys.

Girls with gender dysphoria may insist that they have a penis or will grow one and may exhibit an avid interest in rough-and-tumble play. Women with gender dysphoria report being labeled "tomboys" during their childhoods. Although it is not uncommon for girls to be considered tomboys, the strength, pervasiveness, and persistence of the gender incongruence are the distinguishing features. Children who may engage in traditional role activities of the other sex (feminine or masculine) should not be prematurely diagnosed as having gender dysphoria. Nonconformity to stereotypical sex role behavior should not, for example, be confused with the pervasiveness of the wishes, interests, and activities regarding the other gender that characterize gender dysphoria.

gender dysphoria a disorder characterized by conflict between a person's anatomical sex and his or her gender identity, or self-identification as male or female

Etiology of Gender Dysphoria

The etiology of gender dysphoria is unclear. Because it is quite rare, investigators have focused more attention on other sexual disorders. Gender dysphoria appears to be more common in males than in females and may appear in both adults and children (Lawrence, 2008). In all likelihood, a number of variables interact to produce gender dysphoria. Again, a multipath analysis reveals multiple influences, but biological factors seem to be strongly implicated.

Biological Influences The research in this area suggests that neurohormonal factors, genetics, and possible brain differences may be involved in the etiology of gender dysphoria. In animal studies, for example, the presence or absence of testosterone early in life appears to influence the organization of brain centers that govern sexual behavior. In human females, early exposure to male hormones has resulted in a more masculine behavior pattern. Thus it does appear that gender orientation can be influenced by a lack or excess of sex hormones.

Genetics and differences in areas of the hypothalamus have also been found in some studies to correlate with the development of gender dysphoria (Henningsson et al., 2005; Zhou, Hofman, Gooren, & Swaab, 1995). These studies suggest that gender dysphoria may run in families and that there are differences in the size of brain clusters in regions of the hypothalamus between men with and men without gender dysphoria (Swaab, 2005).

It is important to note, however, that limited research in this area makes conclusions about hormonal, genetic, and brain structure explanations very hazardous. Some researchers believe that gender identity is malleable. For example, most transgender children have normal hormone levels, and their gender orientation raises doubt that biology alone determines masculine and feminine behaviors. Although neurohormonal levels are important, their degree of influence on gender identity in human beings may be minor.

Psychological and Social Influences Psychological and social explanations of gender dysphoria must also be viewed with caution. Some researchers have hypothesized that childhood experiences influence the development of gender dysphoria (Zucker & Cohen-Ketteris, 2008). Factors proposed to contribute to the disorder in boys include parental encouragement of feminine behavior, discouragement of the development of autonomy, excessive attention and overprotection by the mother, the absence of an older male as a model, a relatively powerless or absent father figure, a lack of exposure to male playmates, and encouragement to cross-dress.

Jim Smeal/WireImage/Getty Images

AP Photo/Matt Sayles

An Example of Sex Reassignment

Chaz Bono (named Chastity at birth) is the only child of famous entertainers Sonny and Cher. In 2008, Bono began undergoing a physical gender transition from female to male. He made a documentary film about his transition, *Becoming Chaz,* which premiered at the 2011 Sundance Film Festival. The photo on the top is from before Bono's transition. On the bottom, Bono is seen in a practice session with his partner on the fall 2011 season of *Dancing With the Stars*.

Treatment of Gender Identity Disorder

Psychotherapy and hormone therapy have been used for many people with gender dysphoria. Some, however, choose sex reassignment surgeries. According to DSM-IV, 1 in 30,000 adult males and 1 in 100,000 adult females seek sex reassignment. For men, the genital surgeries involve altering the male genitalia through what can be described as "penis inversion." The plastic surgeon constructs female genitalia, including a vagina and clitoris. The skin of the penis is used in this construction because the sensory nerve endings that are preserved enable the experience of orgasm. The male-to-female operations are nearly perfected, and affirms the gender identity of the individual. Research suggests that genital surgery can produce happier lives. People who want their sex reassigned to male generally request operations to remove their breasts, and some ask for an artificial penis to be constructed. This procedure is much more complicated and more expensive than the male-to-female reassignment.

CONTROVERSY:

Do Transgender People Have a Mental Disorder?

Do you believe that people who are labeled male or female at birth but who experience themselves as members of a different gender and desire to live their lives as such are normal? Or do you believe they qualify as having a mental disorder? The DSM-IV-TR classifies transgender people as having a gender identity disorder (now called *gender dysphoria*).

Labeling gender dysphoria as a disorder stirs up major conflicts and issues regarding the accuracy of psychological diagnosis, the scientific foundations of the disorder, the challenge it brings to our bimodal concepts of gender identity, inherent social stigma, and even civil rights issues (Frese & Myrick, 2010). Critics of the DSM inclusion of gender dysphoria point out the oppressive harm it works on people: (a) The maligning terminology is hurtful and damaging because it disregards their experienced gender identities, denies affirmed gender roles, and relegates them to their assigned birth sex; (b) it pathologizes ordinary behaviors and confuses cultural nonconformity with mental illness; and (c) it potentially denies equal access and opportunity to transgender people (Granderson, 2010; Winters, 2007).

This latter concern is evident in sports, where for years—until 2004—the International Olympic Committee denied transgender people the right to compete (unless they had undergone sex reassignment and had at least 2 years of postoperative hormone-replacement therapy). Discrimination in health care, employment, and education are often experienced due to prejudice and discrimination. Transgender people are often portrayed as less than human, an anomaly, and referred to as "shims" or "shemales."

Like the struggle to remove homosexuality as a mental disorder, the battle being waged by many transgender people contains numerous parallels too similar to ignore. First, many who allegedly have gender dysphoria do not regard their feelings and desires as abnormal (Granderson, 2010; Winters, 2007). Second, in May 2009, after years of study and debate, the government of France declared that a transsexual gender identity is not a psychiatric condition: "It is not a mental illness" ("La transsexualité ne sera plus," 2009).

Third, with the next revision of the DSM, some experts have advocated the removal of gender dysphoria as a psychiatric diagnosis (Winters, 2007). They cite the following in support of their contention: (a) There is a lack of reliability and validity supporting the diagnostic criteria; (b) the psychological distress experienced by sons and daughters who are themselves diagnosed with gender dysphoria is often created by negative societal reactions rather than being the result of pathology; (c) some therapeutic approaches are often similar to "reparative therapies"; and (d) there is little evidence of pathology in children who are diagnosed with the condition (Hausman, 2003).

Finally, there are some who believe that gender identity can best be conceptualized along a spectrum rather than as a bimodal quality. Like sexual orientation, gender identity is a basic and important aspect of our total being. Gender dysphoria challenges our basic notions of the dichotomy between male and female identities.

For Further Consideration

1. What makes a person a man or a woman? Is it based on anatomy?
2. With the removal of homosexuality as a mental disorder, what are your thoughts about removing transgender identity as a disorder?
3. What criteria should be used to determine whether being transgender is normal or abnormal?

Some studies of transgender people indicate positive outcomes for sex reassignment. Most individuals who transitioned to male expressed satisfaction over the outcome of the surgeries, although those who transitioned to female were less likely to feel satisfied (Lawrence, 2008). It has been suggested that adjusting to life as a man is easier than adjusting to life as a woman, or perhaps others may react less negatively to woman-to-man transitions than man-to-woman transitions (American Psychiatric Association, 2000).

CHECKPOINT REVIEW

1. Define gender dysphoria.
2. What are the major explanations for gender dysphoria?
3. What evidence exists that gender dysphoria may not be a mental disorder?
4. What types of treatments have been used for male-to-female or female-to-male transitions?

Paraphilic Disorders

Paraphilic disorders are sexual disorders of at least 6 months' duration in which the person has either acted on or is severely distressed by recurrent urges or fantasies involving any of the following three categories (Table 13.4): (a) nonhuman objects, as in fetishistic and transvestic disorders; (b) nonconsenting others, as in exhibitionistic, voyeuristic, frotteuristic (rubbing against others for sexual arousal), and pedohebephilic disorders; and (c) real or simulated suffering or humiliation, as in sexual sadism and sexual masochism disorders.

paraphilic disorders sexual disorders of at least 6 months' duration in which the person has either acted on or is severely distressed by recurrent urges or fantasies involving nonhuman objects, nonconsenting individuals, or suffering or humiliation

The DSM-5 Work Groups (2012) are proposing to make a distinction between paraphilias and paraphilic disorders. A paraphilia in and of itself may not cause personal distress or harm to others, thus psychiatric intervention is not justified. Such a distinction would prevent labeling a non-normative behavior as pathological. Thus, they propose adding the word *disorder* to all the paraphilias. Just as a person may gamble for recreational purposes, the activity must be distinguished from a gambling addiction.

DISORDERS CHART PARAPHILIC DISORDERS

TABLE 13.4

Paraphilia Category	Symptoms	Prevalence	Age of Onset	Course
Nonhuman objects	**Fetishistic disorder** Sexual attraction and fantasies involving nonliving objects, such as female undergarments	Primarily a disorder in males; rare in women; exact figures are unavailable	Usually adolescence	Causes are difficult to pinpoint; conditioning and learning seem likely
	Transvestic disorder Intense sexual arousal from cross-dressing	Exact figures are difficult to obtain, because cross-dressing often goes unreported and is acceptable in many societies	As early as puberty	Cross-dressing is not usually associated with major psychiatric problems
Nonconsenting people	**Exhibitionistic disorder** Urges, acts, or fantasies that involve exposing the genitals to a stranger	Mostly among males; best estimates are 4.1% of men and 2.1% of women	The teens; exhibitionism is most likely in the 20s	A man may doubt his masculinity or like to shock others; many have an erection during the act; most masturbate after exposure
	Voyeuristic disorder Urges, acts, or fantasies that involve observing an unsuspecting person disrobing or engaging in sexual activity	Difficult to determine; 11.4% of men and 3.9% of women	Around age 15; tends to be chronic	Mostly young males; they may masturbate during or after the episode
	Frotteuristic disorder Urges, acts, or fantasies that involve touching or rubbing against a nonconsenting person	Difficult to determine; mostly a disorder in men	Adolescence or earlier	Usually decreases after age 25
	Pedohebephilic disorder Urges, acts, or fantasies that involve sexual contact with a prepubescent child	Primarily in men; exact figures not available	Must be at least 16; tends to occur in the late 20s and 30s	Individuals prefer children between 5 and 13 years old; individuals often have poor social skills
Pain or humiliation	**Sexual sadism disorder** Sexually arousing urges, fantasies, or acts that involve inflicting physical or psychological suffering	Usually in males; rates are unknown, but 22% of men and 12% of women in one study reported some sexual arousal from sadistic stories	Early childhood, beginning with sexual fantasies	Fantasies begin in childhood; overt acts usually develop in adulthood and can stay at the same level of cruelty or, more rarely, increase to problematic proportions
	Sexual masochism disorder Sexual urges, fantasies, or acts that involve being humiliated, bound, or made to suffer	Precise figures unknown	Males report first interests around 15, and women at 22	Not all suffering arouses—usually it must be produced in a specific way; classical conditioning is strongly implicated as causal

Paraphilic Disorders Involving Nonhuman Objects

Under this category, two forms of paraphilic disorders are evident: fetishistic disorder, which involves attraction or arousal related to a nonliving object (the fetish), and transvestic disorder, which involves cross-dressing.

Fetishistic Disorder **Fetishistic disorder** comprises an extremely strong sexual attraction to and fantasies involving inanimate objects, such as undergarments. The fetish is often used as a sexual stimulus during masturbation or sexual intercourse. The disorder causes significant distress to the self or others and is most common in men; it is rare among women.

Case Study

Mr. D. met his wife at a local church and was strongly attracted to her because of her strong religious convictions. When they dated, occasional kissing and petting took place but never any other sexual contact. He did not masturbate before marriage, because he had been taught by moralistic parents who believed it a sin. Although Mr. and Mrs. D. loved each other very much, he was unable to have sexual intercourse with her because he could not obtain an erection. However, he had fantasies involving an apron and was able to get an erection while wearing one. Mrs. D. was upset over this discovery but was persuaded to accept it because she wanted children. Using the apron allowed them to consummate their marriage, but Mrs. D. was distressed about what she considered to be a perversion. Mr. D. remembers, during his childhood years, being forced by his mother to wear an apron and help her in the kitchen. As time went by, Mrs. D. could no longer tolerate the situation; both sought sex therapy.

Many heterosexual males find the sight of female undergarments sexually arousing and stimulating; this does not constitute a fetish. An interest in such inanimate objects as panties, stockings, bras, and shoes becomes a sexual disorder when the person is often sexually aroused to the point of erection in the presence of the fetish item, needs this item for sexual arousal during intercourse, chooses sexual partners on the basis of their having the item, or collects these items. To qualify as a paraphilic disorder, it must also cause the individual or others significant distress. In many cases the fetish item is enough by itself for complete sexual satisfaction through masturbation, and the person does not seek contact with a partner. Common fetishes include aprons, shoes, undergarments, and leather or latex items.

Transvestic Disorder A diagnosis of fetishistic disorder is not made if the inanimate object is an article of clothing used only in cross-dressing. In such cases, the appropriate diagnosis would be **transvestic disorder**—intense sexual arousal obtained through cross-dressing (wearing clothes appropriate to a different gender). This disorder should not be confused with gender dysphoria, in which the individual identifies with a different gender. Although some transgender people and some lesbians and gay men cross-dress, most people who cross-dress are exclusively heterosexual and married. Again, to be diagnosed with transvestic disorder, the person must have clinically significant distress or impairment in important areas of functioning.

The incidence of transvestic disorder is much higher among men than women. Many individuals with the disorder believe that they have alternating masculine

fetishistic disorder sexual attraction and fantasies involving inanimate objects, such as female undergarments

transvestic disorder intense sexual arousal obtained through cross-dressing (wearing clothes appropriate to a different gender); not to be confused with gender dysphoria

Craig Barrit/Getty Images

Not Necessarily What You Might Think

The etiology and behavioral symptoms of gender dysphoria go far beyond enjoying dressing as someone of a different gender; more important are persistent transgender identification and discomfort with one's own anatomical sex.

and feminine personalities. In a feminine role, they can play out such behavior patterns as buying nightgowns and trying on fashionable clothes. They may introduce their wives to their female personalities and urge them to go on shopping trips together as women. Others cross-dress only for the purposes of sexual arousal and masturbation and do not fantasize themselves as members of a different sex. Men with transvestic disorder often wear feminine garments or undergarments during sexual intercourse with their wives.

Paraphilic Disorders Involving Nonconsenting Persons

This category of disorders involves persistent and powerful sexual fantasies about unsuspecting strangers or acquaintances. The targets are nonconsenting in that they do not choose to be the objects of the attention or sexual behavior.

Exhibitionistic Disorder **Exhibitionistic disorder** is characterized by urges, acts, or fantasies that involve exposing one's genitals to a stranger, often with the intent of shocking the unsuspecting target. Individuals with the disorder are clinically distressed with their behavior and may experience impairment in important areas of life functioning.

Case Study

A 19-year-old single white college student reported that he had daily fantasies of exposing himself and had actually done so on three occasions. The first occurred when he masturbated in front of the window of his dormitory room when women would be passing by. The other two acts occurred in his car; in each case he asked young women for directions and then exposed his penis and masturbated when they approached. He felt a great deal of anxiety in the presence of women and dated infrequently. (S. C. Hayes, Brownell, & Barlow, 1983)

Did You Know? The United States is often considered an exhibitionistic and voyeuristic society that contributes to such disorders. Reality television and access to the Internet (MySpace, Facebook, YouTube, etc.) encourage people to reveal intimate aspects of their lives to strangers. Modern architecture that reflects the "peekaboo effect" (glass-walled condominiums and office buildings) allows residents to see out and be seen.

Exhibitionistic disorder is relatively common. Individuals who have it are most often male, and their targets female. A high number of young women have been targets of exhibitionists, although most women did not report any long-lasting psychological traumas associated with the episodes. It is more likely to cause moderate distress, although a smaller number believed the incidents had negatively affected their attitudes toward men (Lussier et al., 2008).

The main goal in exhibitionistic disorder seems to be the sexual arousal that comes from exposing oneself; most individuals with the disorder want no further contact. They may expect to produce surprise, sexual arousal, or disgust in the victim. The act may involve exposing a limp penis or masturbating an erect penis. Most individuals with the disorder are in their 20s—far from being the "dirty old men" of popular myth—and most are married.

Voyeuristic Disorder **Voyeuristic disorder** comprises urges, acts, or fantasies that involve observing an unsuspecting person disrobing or engaging in sexual activity. "Peeping," as voyeurism is sometimes termed, is considered aberrant when it includes serious risk, is done in socially unacceptable circumstances, or is preferred to coitus. Most people with voyeuristic disorder are not interested in looking at their spouses or partners; an overwhelming number of voyeurism acts involve strangers. Observation alone produces sexual arousal and excitement, and the individual often masturbates during this surreptitious activity. It is estimated that approximately 11% of men and 4% of women can be classified as voyeurs.

exhibitionistic disorder urges, acts, or fantasies that involve exposing one's genitals to strangers

voyeuristic disorder urges, acts, or fantasies that involve observing an unsuspecting person disrobing or engaging in sexual activity

Voyeuristic disorder is like exhibitionistic disorder in that sexual contact is not the goal; viewing an undressed body is the primary motive. However, an individual with the disorder may also exhibit or use other indirect forms of sexual expression. Because the act is repetitive, arrest is predictable. Usually an accidental witness or a victim notifies the police.

The increase of television programs with sexual content, "romance" paperbacks, explicit sexual magazines, and R-rated movies all point to the voyeuristic nature of our society. A growing number of clubs feature male exotic dancers and are attended by women, and female interest in the male body has become quite common and acceptable.

© Bettman/Corbis

Jerry Lee Lewis: Suffering from Pedohebephilia?

When musician Jerry Lee Lewis married a 13-year-old girl in the 1950s, it created a furor in the United Kingdom, where many considered him a pedophiliac. The public's outrage resulted in the cancellation of many of his concerts, forcing him to return to New York. Lewis was 22 at the time of this marriage and not yet divorced from his second wife.

Frotteuristic Disorder

Whereas physical contact is not the goal in voyeuristic disorder, it is the primary motive in **frotteuristic disorder**, which comprises recurrent and intense sexual urges, acts, or fantasies that involve touching or rubbing against a nonconsenting person. The touching, not the coercive nature of the act, is the sexually exciting feature. As in the case of the other paraphilic disorders, the diagnosis is made when the person has acted on the urges or is markedly distressed by them.

Pedohebephilic Disorder

Pedohebephilic disorder involves an adult obtaining erotic gratification through urges, acts, or fantasies that involve sexual contact with a prepubescent or early pubescent child. According to the DSM-IV-TR, a person must be at least 16 years of age to be diagnosed with this disorder (although the DSM-5 Work Groups recommend 18 years) and at least 5 years older than the victim. People with this disorder may victimize children within and outside of their families. Despite the large number of high-profile cases of abuse of boys by Catholic priests and in scouting, most individuals with pedohebephilic disorder prefer girls.

Sexual abuse of children is common (A. Phillips & Daniluk, 2004). Between 20 and 30 percent of women report having had a childhood sexual encounter with an adult man. And contrary to the popular view of child molesters as strangers, most people who act on pedohebephilic disorder are relatives, friends, or casual acquaintances of their victims (Lussier et al., 2008). In most cases of abuse, only one adult and one child are involved, but cases involving several adults or groups of children have been reported.

Child victims of sexual abuse show a variety of physical symptoms, such as urinary tract infections, poor appetite, and headaches. Reported psychological symptoms include nightmares, difficulty sleeping, decline in school performance, acting-out behaviors, and sexually focused behavior. Some child victims show symptoms of post-traumatic stress disorder. The effects of sexual abuse can be lifelong. One study of women who were victims of childhood sexual abuse revealed a "contaminated identity" characterized by self-loathing, shame, and powerlessness (A. Phillips & Daniluk, 2004).

Incest

The DSM-IV-TR considers childhood **incest** to be a form of pedohebephilic disorder. Incest, however, can also occur between adults too closely related to marry legally; it is nearly universally taboo in society. The cases of incest most frequently reported to law enforcement agencies are those between a father and daughter or stepdaughter. However, the most common incestuous relationship is brother–sister incest, not parent–child incest. Mother–son incest seems to be rare. Sexual activities between siblings are relatively frequent.

Although brother–sister incest is more common, most research has focused on father–daughter incest. This type of incestuous relationship generally begins when the daughter is between 6 and 11 years old. Unlike sex between siblings (which may or may not be exploitative), father–daughter incest is always exploitative. The girl is especially vulnerable because she depends on her father for emotional support. As

frotteuristic disorder recurrent and intense sexual urges, acts, or fantasies that involve touching or rubbing against a nonconsenting person

pedohebephilic disorder a disorder in which an adult obtains erotic gratification through urges, acts, or fantasies that involve sexual contact with a prepubescent or early pubescent child

incest a form of pedohebephilic disorder; can also be sexual relations between people too closely related to marry legally

TABLE 13.5 Sadomasochistic Activities Ranked by Samples of Male and Female Participants

ACTIVITY	MALE (%)	FEMALE (%)
Spanking	79	80
Master–slave relationships	79	76
Oral sex	77	90
Bondage	67	88
Humiliation	65	61
Restraint	60	83
Anal sex	58	51
Pain	51	34
Whipping	47	39
Use of rubber or leather	42	42
Enemas	33	22
Torture	32	32
Golden showers (urination)	30	37

Note: These sadomasochistic sexual preferences were reported by both male and female respondents. Many more men express a preference for sadomasochistic activities, but women who do so are likely to engage in these forms of sexual behavior more frequently and with many more partners.
Source: Data from Brewslow, Evans, & Langley (1986)

a result, victims often feel guilty and powerless. Their problems continue into adulthood and are reflected in their high rates of drug abuse, sexual dysfunction, and psychiatric problems (McAnulty & Burnette, 2003).

Paraphilic Disorders Involving Pain or Humiliation

Pain and humiliation do not appear to be related to normal sexual arousal. In sadism and masochism, however, they play a prominent role. **Sexual sadism disorder** is a paraphilic disorder in which sexually arousing urges, fantasies, or acts involve inflicting physical or psychological suffering on others. The word *sadism* was coined from the name of the Marquis de Sade (1740–1814), a French nobleman who wrote extensively about the sexual pleasure he received from inflicting pain on women. The marquis was so cruel to his sexual victims that he was declared insane and jailed for 27 years. Sadistic behavior may range from the pretended or fantasized infliction of pain through mild to severe cruelty toward partners to an extremely dangerous pathological form of sadism that may involve mutilation or murder.

Sexual masochism disorder is another paraphilic disorder, in which sexual urges, fantasies, or acts involve being humiliated, bound, or made to suffer. The word *masochism* is derived from the name of a 19th-century Austrian novelist, Leopold von Sacher-Masoch, whose fictional characters obtained sexual satisfaction only when pain was inflicted on them. Because of their passive roles, people who are masochistic are not considered dangerous to others.

For some people who are sadistic or masochistic, coitus becomes unnecessary; pain or humiliation alone is sufficient to produce sexual pleasure. As with other paraphilic disorders, the DSM-IV-TR specifies that to receive the diagnosis, a person must have acted on the urges and must be markedly distressed by them.

Most men and women who are sadomasochistic engage in and enjoy both submissive and dominant roles (Lussier et al., 2008). Only 16 percent are exclusively dominant or submissive. Many have engaged in spanking, whipping, and bondage (see Table 13.5). Approximately 40 percent have engaged in behaviors that caused minor pain using ice, hot wax, biting, or face slapping. Fewer than 18 percent have engaged in more harmful procedures, such as burning or piercing. Nearly all respondents reported sadomasochistic activities to be more satisfying than "straight" sex. Most people who are masochistic and have been studied have reported that they do not seek harm or injury but that they find the sensation of utter helplessness appealing (Baumeister, 1988). Sadomasochistic activities are often carefully scripted and involve role-playing and mutual consent by the participants. In addition, fantasies involving sexual abuse, rejection, and forced sex are not uncommon among both male and female college students. Most sadomasochistic behavior among college students involves very mild forms of pain (such as in biting or pinching) that are accepted in our society.

Sadomasochistic behavior is considered problematic when pain, either inflicted or received, is necessary for sexual arousal and orgasm. According to Kinsey and his associates (1953), 22 percent of men and 12 percent of women reported at least some sexual response to sadomasochistic stories. Janus and Janus (1993) reported that 14 percent of men and 11 percent of women have had at least some sadomasochistic experiences.

In addition to the paraphilic disorders covered here, the DSM-IV-TR lists many others under the category of paraphilia "not otherwise specified." They include making obscene telephone calls (*telephone scatalogia*) and sexual urges involving corpses (*necrophilia*), animals (*zoophilia*), or feces (*coprophilia*).

sexual sadism disorder sexually arousing urges, fantasies, or acts that involve inflicting physical or psychological suffering on others

sexual masochism disorder sexual urges, fantasies, or acts that involve being humiliated, bound, or made to suffer

Etiology and Treatment of Paraphilic Disorders

As the multipath model suggests, there are multiple contributing causes to paraphilic disorders, but the state of our knowledge provides only partial answers. Earlier, we noted that investigators have attempted to find genetic, neurohormonal, and brain anomalies that might be associated with sexual disorders. Some of the research findings conflict with each other; others need replication and confirmation. There is evidence, however, that some men may be biologically predisposed to pedohebephilic disorder (Centre for Addiction and Mental Health, 2007), as they have been found to have deficits in brain activation and less white matter. Even if biological factors are found to be important in the causes of sexual disorders, psychological factors are also likely to contribute in important ways.

Among early attempts to explain paraphilic disorders, psychodynamic theorists proposed that all sexual deviations symbolically represent unconscious conflicts that began in early childhood (Schrut, 2005). Castration anxiety in men, for example, is hypothesized to be an important etiological factor underlying transvestic fetishism, exhibitionistic disorder, sexual sadism disorder, and sexual masochism disorder. A man with exhibitionistic disorder, for example, exposes himself to reassure himself that castration has not occurred. The shock that registers on the faces of others assures him that he still has a penis. A man with sexual sadism disorder may protect himself from castration anxiety by inflicting pain (power equals penis). A man with sexual masochism disorder may engage in self-castration through the acceptance of pain, thereby limiting the power of others to castrate him. The psychodynamic treatment of sexual deviations involves helping the patient understand the relationship between the deviation and the unconscious conflict that produced it.

Learning theorists stress the importance of early conditioning experiences in the etiology of sexually deviant behaviors. For example, if a person with poor social skills masturbates while engaged in sexually deviant fantasies, the conditioning may hamper the development of normal sexual patterns. A young boy may develop a fetish for women's panties after he becomes sexually excited watching girls come down a slide with their underpants exposed. He begins to masturbate to fantasies of girls with their panties showing and may develop a fetish into adulthood. Accidental association between sexual arousal and exposure to situations, events, acts, or objects may result in the development of paraphilias or paraphilic disorders. In other words, classical conditioning, operant conditioning, or observational learning can account for the development of paraphilias.

Learning approaches to treating sexual deviations have generally involved one or more of the following elements: (a) weakening or eliminating the sexually inappropriate behaviors through processes such as extinction or aversive conditioning; (b) acquiring or strengthening sexually appropriate behaviors; and (c) developing appropriate social skills. The following case study illustrates this multiple approach.

Case Study

A 27-year-old man with a 3-year history of pedophilic sexual activities (fondling and cunnilingus) with 4- to 7-year-old girls was treated through the following procedure: He first masturbated to orgasm while exposed to stimuli involving adult females. He then masturbated to orgasm while listening to a relaxation tape, and then masturbated (but not to orgasm) to deviant stimuli. The procedure allowed the strengthening of normal arousal patterns and

Continued

Case Study—cont'd

lessened the ability to achieve an orgasm while exposed to deviant stimuli (extinction). Measurement of penile tumescence when he was exposed to the stimuli indicated a sharp decrease in reaction to pedophilic stimuli and high arousal from adult stimuli. These changes were maintained over a 12-month follow-up period (Alford, Morin, Atkins, & Schuen, 1987).

CHECKPOINT REVIEW

1. Distinguish between paraphilias and paraphilic disorders.
2. Name the three categories of paraphilic disorders and give examples of each type.
3. What are some explanations of paraphilias?

Rape

Although it is not considered a DSM disorder, we believe that the magnitude and seriousness of problems related to rape in U.S. society warrant such discussion. Public awareness of these problems has heightened in the wake of highly publicized allegations of sexual assault or harassment made against public figures such as basketball player Kobe Bryant, boxer Mike Tyson (convicted), NFL quarterback Ben Roethlisberger, talk show host Bill O'Reilly, Supreme Court justice Clarence Thomas, and Dominique Strauss-Kahn, the former director of the International Monetary Fund.

Rape is a form of sexual aggression that refers to *sexual activity* (oral-genital sex, anal intercourse, or vaginal intercourse) performed against a person's will through the use of force, argument, pressure, alcohol or drugs, or authority (McAnulty & Burnette, 2004). With a child younger than the age of consent, however, the law recognizes what is called *statutory rape*. Rape is an act surrounded by many myths and misconceptions (see Table 13.6). Considerable controversy exists over whether rape is primarily a crime of violence or of sex. Feminists have challenged the belief that rape is an act of sexual deviance; they make a good case that it is truly an act of violence and aggression against women. The principal motive, they believe, is that of power, not sex (J. C. Marsh, 1988).

Did You Know? Early explanations attributed rape to an unusually quick sexual arousal response and impulsivity that was considered a natural reaction. Even still, excuses were made for men: "Boys will be boys." Conversely, women are often blamed for enticing rape through flirtatious behaviors or revealing dress. In reality, most rapists are deliberate and often plan their attacks.

The number of rapes in the United States has risen dramatically, with an average of 1.3 rapes every minute, 78 rapes in one hour, 1,872 rapes in one day, 56,160 rapes each month, and 683,280 rapes each year (Coalition Educating About Sexual Endangerment, 2011). It is estimated that 1 in 3 women will be sexually assaulted in their lifetime. However, in past decades, only about 16 percent of reported cases resulted in a conviction for rape, with another 4 percent of those cases producing convictions for lesser offenses. This low conviction rate and the humiliation and shame of a rape trial keep many women from reporting rapes, so the actual incidence of the crime is probably much higher than reported.

rape a form of sexual aggression that involves sexual activity (oral-genital sex, anal intercourse, or vaginal intercourse) performed against a person's will through the use of force, argument, pressure, alcohol or drugs, or authority

Most rape victims are young women in their teens or 20s; in approximately half of all rape cases, the victim is at least acquainted with the rapist and is attacked in the home or in an automobile. One in seven women will be raped by their husband. About 90 percent of rapists attack people of the same race; the most frequent form of rape reported is "acquaintance" or "date" rape. Between 8 and 25 percent of female college students have reported that they had "unwanted sexual intercourse," and studies have generally found that most college women

TABLE 13.6 The Facts About Rape

- Anyone can be raped. Rape happens among all age groups, from infants to elderly women; among all economic classes, from rich to poor; among all ethnic groups and races of people; and in heterosexual and same-sex relationships.
- Rape happens to both males and females. Statistics show that 1 in 4 girls and 1 in 6 boys are sexually assaulted before they reach the age of 18. About 1 in 6 women and 1 in 11 men are raped after turning 18.
- Rape is not sex. Rape is an act of violence. Rape is used as a way of dominating, humiliating, and terrifying another person.
- Rape is never the fault of the victim. It has nothing to do with what the victim wore, where the victim went, what the victim did, or whether the victim is "attractive." Only the person committing the assault is to blame. Rape is painful, humiliating, and hurtful. No one ever asks to be raped.
- A rapist can be someone you know. Most rapes happen between people of the same race or ethnicity. You are much more likely to be raped by someone you know than by a stranger. Approximately 75 percent of rapes are committed by someone the victim knows.
- You have the right to say no anytime. You can be raped by someone you have had sex with before, even your spouse or partner. Each time you are asked to have sex, you have the right to say no, even if you have said yes before. You also have the right to stop having sex at any time.
- Rape is against the law. Not only is rape always wrong, it's also a crime.

Source: "Facts and Information" (n.d.)

experienced some unwanted sexual activity (Abuse, Rape, and Domestic Violence Aid and Resource Collection, 2011).

Men who try to coerce women into intercourse share certain characteristics (G. C. Hall, Windover, & Maramba, 1998; Lussier et al., 2008). They tend to

(a) actively create the situation in which sexual encounters may occur;
(b) interpret women's friendliness as provocation or their protests as insincerity;
(c) try to manipulate women into sexual encounters by using alcohol (some 70 percent of rapes are associated with alcohol intoxication) or "date rape drugs";
(d) attribute failed attempts at sexual encounters to perceived negative features of the woman, thereby protecting their egos;
(e) come from environments of parental neglect or physical or sexual abuse;
(f) initiate coitus earlier in life than men who are not sexually aggressive; and
(g) have more sexual partners than men who are not sexually aggressive.

Many men who do not rape may also have these characteristics.

- Approximately one third of college males reported some likelihood that they would rape if assured that they would not be caught and punished!
- Approximately 2 of every 3 rapes occur in the victim's home or that of a friend, relative, or neighbor.

Source: Coalition Educating About Sexual Endangerment (2011)

Effects of Rape

Rape victims may experience a cluster of emotional reactions known as the **rape trauma syndrome**; they include psychological distress, phobic reactions, and sexual dysfunction (Gijs, 2008; Lussier et al., 2008). These reactions appear consistent with post-traumatic stress disorder. Two phases have been identified in rape trauma syndrome (Koss, 1993):

1. *Acute phase: Disorganization.* During this period of several or more weeks, the rape victim may have feelings of self-blame, fear, and depression. Victims may believe they were responsible for the rape (for example, by

rape trauma syndrome a two-phase syndrome that rape victims may experience, involving such emotional reactions as psychological distress, phobic reactions, and sexual dysfunction

STR/AFP/Getty Images

Protesting Rape

Feminist leaders and activists hold a protest in front of the International Monetary Fund (IMF) Headquarters demanding that IMF Managing Director Dominique Strauss-Kahn be removed from his post in Washington, DC, on May 18, 2011. Strauss-Kahn resigned his post via a letter sent from jail on May 18. (AFP PHOTO/STR)

not locking the door, by wearing provocative clothing, or by being overly friendly toward the attacker). Victims may have a fear that their attackers will return and fear they may again be raped or even killed. The victim may express these emotional reactions and beliefs directly as anger, fear, rage, anxiety, or depression, or conceal them, appearing amazingly calm. Beneath this exterior, however, are signs of tension, including headaches, irritability, restlessness, sleeplessness, and jumpiness.

2. *Long-term phase: Reorganization*. This second phase may last for several years. Victims begin to deal directly with their feelings and attempt to reorganize their lives. Lingering fears and phobic reactions continue, especially to situations or events that remind the victim of the traumatic incident. A host of reactions may be present. Many victims report one or more sexual dysfunctions as the result of the rape; fear of sex and lack of desire or arousal appear most common. Some recover quickly, but others report problems years after the rape. Victims may experience selective fears involving things such as darkness and enclosed places—conditions likely to be associated with rape. Duration and intensity of fear also appear to be related to perceptions of danger. Many women's feelings of safety and personal vulnerability are drastically altered; the women feel unsafe in many situations and over an extended period of time. It is clear that rape has long-lasting consequences and that family, friends, and acquaintances need to exercise patience and understanding of victims as they go through the healing process.

Etiology of Rape

A variety of views of the motivations for rape have been proposed. Some claim that rape is an act of aggression; others indicate it is an act of sex; still others believe it to be due to a mental disorder. In an influential study of 133 rapists that supported the aggression viewpoint, Groth, Burgess, and Holstrom (1977) distinguished three motivational types:

- The *power rapist*, comprising 55 percent of those studied, is primarily attempting to compensate for feelings of personal or sexual inadequacy by intimidating his victims.
- The *anger rapist*, comprising 40 percent of those studied, is angry at women in general; the victim is merely a convenient target.
- The *sadistic rapist*, comprising only 5 percent of those studied, derives satisfaction from inflicting pain and may torture or mutilate the victim.

These findings are used to support the contention that rape has more to do with power, aggression, and violence than with sex. More recent formulations and findings (Abel & Rouleau, 1990; LeVay & Valente, 2006; Lussier et al., 2008) suggest that there is, however, support that rape is partially sexually motivated: (a) Although women with all degrees of physical attractiveness are raped, most victims are in their teens or 20s (considered most sexually attractive), (b) most rapists name sexual motivation as the primary reason for their actions, and (c) many rapists seem to have multiple paraphilias. Thus it appears that sexual motivation may play some role in some rapes.

Researchers have also raised questions about the effect that media portrayals of violent sex, especially in pornography, have on rape rates. Exposure to such material may affect attitudes and thoughts and influence patterns of sexual arousal. These media portrayals may reflect and affect societal values concerning violence

FOCUS ON RESILIENCE

Resilience in the Aftermath of Rape

In 1989, while jogging through New York's Central Park, Trisha Meili was raped, sodomized, and beaten so savagely that she lost 75 percent of her blood before she was found. At the hospital, doctors believed she would not live, but Meili fought valiantly for her life and survived the ordeal. She became known as the "Central Park Jogger," and her case generated a national debate about rape and violence in society. After years of recovery, she finally wrote a book—*I Am the Central Park Jogger: A Story of Hope and Possibility* (Meili, 2003)—which quickly rose to the *New York Times* best seller list. The book is less about the rape and assault than about resilience: the hope, healing, and courage of the human spirit.

The story of Trisha Meili exemplifies many of the basic principles that psychologists have discovered about resilience and post-traumatic growth after a rape (Bonanno, 2004; 2005; J. K. Hill, 2011; Westphal & Bonanno, 2007). Her story is about positive coping, the strengths and assets used by victims of crime to move forward, and the inner resources used to reconnect with loved ones, significant others, communities, and society at large. Similar to many women after a sexual assault, Meili expressed the following beliefs: (a) "I have no control over my life," (b) "The world is an unsafe place," (c) "I am unworthy," and (d) "People are not to be trusted" (Mena, 2012).

Resilience research indicates that the ability to overcome adversity especially in cases of rape involves intersecting elements that challenge these beliefs: (a) finding a meaningful purpose in life, (b) regaining control over the environment and events, (c) having positive social support, and (d) moving from defining oneself as a "victim" to a "survivor" (Hill, 2011; Bonanno, 2005).

Finding meaning in life and re-establishing control over one's life are manifested in many different ways. Meili, for example, wrote her book to help others overcome a sexual assault. She frequently speaks to groups and organizations about rape recovery and is an active advocate for survivors of rape. These activities have no doubt given her meaning in life, hope for the future, and a strong sense of control and influence in bettering society. For rape survivors, empowerment activities may include pressing charges, testifying in court, taking self-defense classes, becoming an activist, and seeking spiritual meaning in life. In essence, these actions may not only foster a sense of control and purpose in life but may have a larger altruistic goal of creating a safer and more predictable world.

PhotoDisc

Rape can alter a person's perception of relationships with others. This is compounded by the fact that most rapists are acquaintances and not strangers. Intimate relationships may be adversely affected, and often existing social support networks are not accessed when the person is most in need. Those who have positive social relationships with significant others are more resilient after a sexual assault. For those who might not have had strong social networks, re-establishing and strengthening them is imperative. Social support from family, friends, and caregivers has been found to be among the strongest protective factors. Social support (a) provides survivors with a sense of worth; (b) validates that others love, respect, and value them; (c) allows them to process their thoughts and feelings in a safe and understanding environment; and (d) provides an opportunity to dislodge their victim mentality.

With respect to the last point, how a woman defines her identity in relationship to the sexual assault is crucial to recovery. One of the most potent changes that aided Meili in her healing journey was redefining herself as a survivor rather than a victim. Resilient people do not overdefine themselves as victims, but see themselves as survivors. The former term seems to imply helplessness, lack of personal control, and a passive rather than an active stance. Being a survivor, however, acknowledges the trauma but defines the self as overcoming adversity, being in control, and perceives the self as active rather than passive. The stories of trauma women tell about themselves in relationship to the rape can be used to define them as victims or survivors. Research suggests that this cognitive shift in self-definition is all-important in the healing journey (Bonanno, 2004, 2005)

Meichenbaum (2012) has further outlined 10 ways to draw on attributes or protective factors that help recovery from sexual assaults and abuse:

1. Establish and nurture a supportive social network.
2. Be optimistic.
3. Be flexible in reframing stressful life events like rape.
4. Develop a moral or spiritual compass.
5. Be altruistic.
6. Find a resilient role model.
7. Learn to be adaptive in facing your fears.
8. Develop active coping skills.
9. Have a sense of humor.
10. Keep fit.

and women. A "cultural spillover" theory—namely, that rape tends to be high in cultures or environments that encourage violence—has been proposed (L. Baron, Straus, & Jaffee, 1988). The investigators studied the relationship between cultural support for violence and demographic characteristics and rates of rapes in all 50 states. Results indicated that cultural support for violence was significantly related to the rate of rape: When violence is generally encouraged or condoned, there is a "spillover" effect on rape. Interestingly, the United States has been described as a violent and sexually oriented society; it has the highest rape rate of countries reporting such statistics (Coalition Educating About Sexual Endangerment, 2011). This rate is 4 times higher than Germany's, 13 times higher than the United Kingdom's, and 20 times higher than Japan's.

Treatment for Rapists

Many people believe that sex offenders are not good candidates for psychiatric or treatment or rehabilitation. High recidivism rates are often associated with sexual aggression, and the most frequent response is imprisonment. However, the majority of convicts receive little or no treatment in prison. Behavioral treatment for sexual aggressors (rapists and child abusers) generally involves the following steps (Fedoroff, 2008; Lussier et al., 2008):

1. assessing sexual interests through self-report and measuring erectile responses to different sexual stimuli,
2. reducing deviant interests through aversion therapy (e.g., administering an electric shock when deviant stimuli are presented),
3. reconditioning orgasm or retraining masturbation to increase sexual arousal to appropriate stimuli,
4. training in social skills to increase interpersonal competence, and
5. assessing again after treatment.

Although treatment is becoming more sophisticated, questions remain about the effectiveness of these programs. Some treatment programs have been effective with child molesters and people with exhibitionistic disorder, but treatment outcomes have tended to be poor for rapists.

Surgical castration has been used to treat sexual offenders in many European countries, and results indicate that rates of relapse have been low (Fedoroff, 2008). Rapists, child molesters of various sexual orientations, and a sexual murderer, who were all surgically castrated, did report a decrease in sexual intercourse, masturbation, and frequency of sexual fantasies. However, some of these men remained sexually active.

Chemical therapy, usually involving the hormone Depo-Provera, reduces self-reports of sexual urges in child molesters but not the ability to show genital arousal. Drugs appear to reduce psychological desire more than actual erectile capability. The effectiveness of biological treatment such as surgery and chemotherapy is not known, and controversy obviously continues over the appropriate treatment for child molesters and rapists.

CHECKPOINT REVIEW

1. How is rape defined?
2. Discuss the findings regarding the frequency of rape.
3. What evidence indicates that rape is an act of aggression?
4. Describe the effects of rape.
5. What have researchers found about resilience and rape recovery?

Summary

1 What are normal and abnormal sexual behaviors?

- It is often difficult to diagnose abnormal sexual behavior by measuring it against the wide-varying standard of normal sexual behavior. No attempt to establish such criteria has been completely successful.

2 What does the normal sexual response cycle tell us about sexual dysfunctions?

- The human sexual response cycle has four stages: the appetitive, arousal, orgasm, and resolution phases. Sexual dysfunctions are disruptions of the normal sexual response cycle. They are fairly common in the general population, and treatment programs are generally successful.

3 What causes sexual dysfunctions?

- The multipath model illustrates how biological (hormonal variations and medical conditions), psychological (performance anxieties), social (parental upbringing and attitudes), and sociocultural (cultural scripts) dimensions contribute to sexual dysfunctions.

4 What types of treatment are available for sexual dysfunctions?

- Depending on the specific dysfunction, treatments vary: Biological interventions may include hormone replacement for low sexual desire; penile implants or drugs like Viagra for erectile dysfunction; education and communication training; and structured sexual exercises.

5 How does aging affect the sexual activity of people who are elderly?

- Despite myths to the contrary, sexuality extends into old age. However, sexual dysfunction becomes increasingly prevalent with aging, and the frequency of sexual activity typically declines.

6 What causes gender dysphoria, and how is it treated?

- Gender dysphoria involves strong and persistent transgender identification. Biological explanations seem strongly implicated.
- Some transgender people seek sex reassignment surgeries, although behavioral therapies are increasingly being used.

7 What are paraphilic disorders, what causes them, and how are they treated?

- Paraphilic disorders are characterized by (a) an orientation toward nonhuman objects for sexual arousal, (b) repetitive sexual activity with nonconsenting partners, or (c) the association of real or simulated suffering with sexual activity.
- Biological factors such as hormonal or brain processes have been studied as a cause of paraphilic disorders. Psychological factors also play a role.
- Treatments are usually behavioral and are aimed at eliminating the disordered behavior while teaching more appropriate behaviors.

8 Is rape an act of sex or aggression?

- There appears to be no single motivation for rape, and rapists seem to have different motivations and personalities.
- Some researchers feel that sociocultural factors can encourage rape and violence against women; others believe that biological factors coupled with sociocultural factors are important in explaining rape.

Key Terms

sexual dysfunction 351
sexual arousal disorder 352
hypoactive sexual desire disorder 352
female sexual arousal disorder 352
erectile disorder (ED) 352
hypersexual disorder 354
female orgasmic disorder 355
delayed ejaculation (male orgasmic disorder) 355
early ejaculation 355
genital-pelvic pain/penetration disorder 356
dyspareunia 356
vaginismus 356
gender dysphoria 363
paraphilic disorders 366
fetishistic disorder 367
transvestic disorder 367
exhibitionistic disorder 368
voyeuristic disorder 368
frotteuristic disorder 369
pedohebephilic disorder 369
incest 369
sexual sadism disorder 370
sexual masochism disorder 370
rape 372
rape trauma syndrome 373

Media Resources

Psychology CourseMate

Access an interactive e-book and chapter-specific interactive learning tools, including:

- flashcards
- quizzes
- videos

and more in your Psychology CourseMate.

Go to **CengageBrain.com**.

Blend Images/DreamPictures/Jupiterimages

14

Personality Psychopathology

CHAPTER OUTLINE

Aaron Kopinsky was known as a loner by classmates. He seldom participated in social activities, had few friends in his dormitory, and even avoided socializing with his roommate. His favorite pastime seemed to be sitting in front of the TV and watching programs in the lounge. Few things seemed to interest Aaron; he did not read the newspaper, did not go to movies, and had few hobbies or activities that seemed to give him joy. Yet he did not appear lonely. As his college major was in forestry, he frequently went on outings that required long periods of time in the forests. While his classmates would huddle around a campfire during the evenings for companionship, Aaron preferred to be by himself.

Jennifer Wang, a project manager for a small technology start-up company, was described by family, friends, and coworkers as excessively compulsive. At team meetings she was demanding, insistent that things be done correctly in a prescribed manner, and would drive employees "crazy" with her detailed lists, tasks, and posted schedules. Team members were expected to check off tasks posted on the bulletin board (always written in red marker) when completed. They had to do so with a blue marker; no other color would do. Jennifer would become upset when even the most trivial tasks or schedules were not completed or followed. Everything had to be done flawlessly without errors or faults.

Jordan Mitchell was "clubbing" with friends in San Francisco when he met an attractive prostitute who invited him to a nearby hotel for sex. Despite being warned by friends to use a condom because of the high incidence of HIV infection in the neighborhood, he failed to do so. Throughout his life, Jordan exhibited a high degree of recklessness and impulsivity. He enjoyed risky and dangerous activities such as racing his car against other willing drivers and discharging his firearm into the sky at night. Jordan bored easily and needed constant excitement. His impulsivity, distractibility, and constant need for change made completing life tasks difficult.

FOCUS QUESTIONS

1 Can one's personality be pathological?

2 What criteria are used to assess personality disorders?

3 Are there certain personality disorder types?

4 How does the multipath model explain antisocial personality disorder?

5 What types of therapy are used in treating antisocial personality disorder?

6 What personality traits are important in determining pathology?

Aaron, Jennifer, and Jordan's behaviors, thoughts, and feelings typify how they generally respond to life situations. These behavioral and mental characteristics make each of them unique and are said to form the basis of their personalities. In psychology, *personality* means three things. First, it refers to an individual's recognizable behaviors in which a pattern, order, and regularity can be identified. Aaron, for example, prefers spending time by himself; he is a loner, probably introverted, and avoids almost all social interactions or situations. Jennifer might be described as detail oriented, perfectionistic, and quite inflexible. Jordan, however, is impulsive, a thrill seeker and a risk taker. Essentially, all three exhibit a consistency in how they respond to similar, or even different, situations. Second, personality is a psychological construct, but it is influenced by biological processes and needs (J. R. Kuo & Linehan, 2009; Sterzer, 2010). People have, for example, been found at birth to exhibit different levels of physiological reactivity to outside stimulation (Glenn, Raine, Venables, & Mednick, 2009). This may account for why some people seek or avoid new and novel situations. Third, personality is an influence on how we respond in the world and a *cause* of some of our actions.

If we assume that Aaron, Jennifer, and Jordan do not have any forms of mental disorder, can their personalities be pathological? That is, can people's characteristic style of responding to situations prove problematic to themselves or others? Certainly, social isolation and friendlessness may be bothersome to most of us, but Aaron does not appear bothered by it. He prefers solitary tasks and situations, and perhaps his major in forestry and desire to become a forest ranger may be the perfect occupational match for him. Jennifer's compulsivity may be irksome to coworkers, but there are upsides and downsides to this prominent trait. Being orderly and attentive to detail are assets in many situations (accurate record keeping, accounting, etc.). Being governed by rules and habits, however, may mean a sacrifice of creativity and adaptability to unexpected problems or situations. On the other hand, Jordan's need for excitement, impulsivity, and risk taking may place both him and others in danger. His personality traits are more likely to become problematic than Aaron's or Jennifer's.

When personality characteristics result in an adaptive failure in life, when they cause personal problems to the self or others, and when they are quite pronounced, the person may have personality psychopathology or a **personality disorder**. People with personality psychopathology often function well enough to get along without aid from others. They often fall under the radar and are described simply as odd, peculiar, dramatic, or unusual. They may not see themselves as having a problem.

personality disorder a disorder characterized by impairment in self and interpersonal functioning and the presence of pathological personality traits that are relatively inflexible and long-standing

Indeed, as we have mentioned, some pronounced personality traits may actually be an asset in certain situations. For these reasons, many people with personality psychopathology rarely come to the attention of mental health professionals, seldom seek help, and often terminate therapy prematurely (Millon, Grossman, Millon, Meagher, & Ramnath, 2004). As a result, the incidence of personality disorders has been difficult to ascertain, but available statistics indicate that these disorders account for 5–15 percent of admissions to hospitals and outpatient clinics. The overall lifetime prevalence of personality disorders is 9–13 percent, which suggests that these disorders are relatively common in the general population (Lenzenweger, Lane, Loranger, & Kessler, 2007; K. A. Phillips, Yen, & Gunderson, 2004).

Diagnosing Personality Psychopathology

A person can prompt a diagnosis of personality disorder through two different routes: (a) showing characteristics from one of six specific personality disorder types or (2) possessing certain specific personality traits that impair functioning. Both personality types and descriptive personality traits must be pronounced and a good match with the individual. Further, the person's impairment or problem in adaptation must be relatively stable across time and situations (i.e., its manifestation can be traced to at least adolescence). Adaptive failures or problems related to personality must not be due to the presence of another mental disorder or to the physiological effects of substance use or a general medical condition. Figure 14.1 outlines the two major paths by which a diagnosis of a personality disorder may be made.

Most of us have a degree of consistency and predictability in our outlook on life and in how we approach people and situations (Millon et al., 2004). Yet all of us possess a degree of flexibility in how we respond to similar or different situations. A shy coworker, for example, is not necessarily shy in all situations or when he or she gets to know people. Individuals with personality psychopathology, however, possess rigid patterns of responding that are inflexible, long-standing, and enduring, and can extend into the elderly years (Abrams & Bromberg, 2007); they are shy and withdrawn in nearly all situations and continue to be uncomfortable even with people they know well. Personality disorders begin early in life and generally become evident in adolescence (Weston & Riolo, 2007). There are frequently telltale signs of personality disorders in childhood (Gao et al., 2010; Lahey, Loeber, Burke, & Applegate, 2005; Sterzer, 2010).

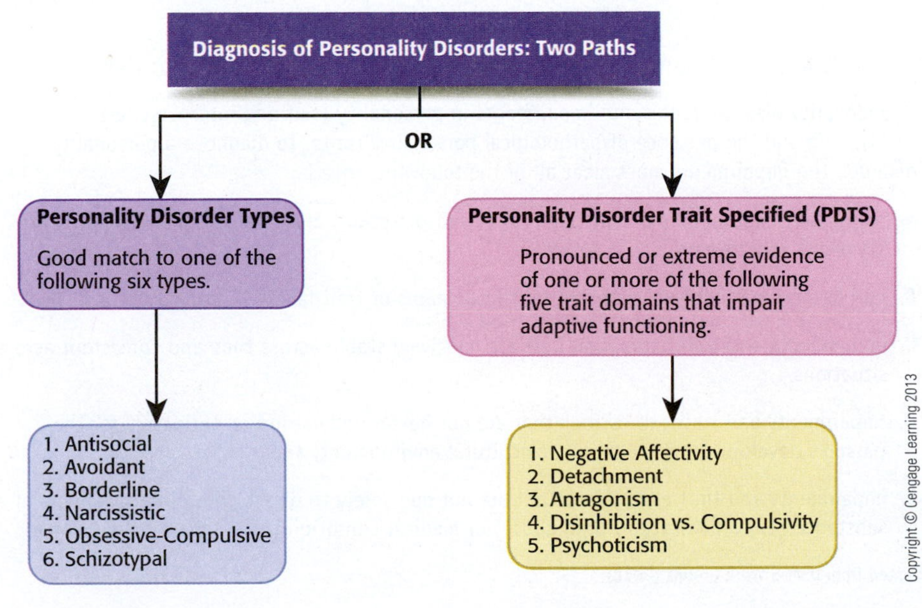

FIGURE 14.1

Diagnosing Personality Disorders: Two Paths

Levels of Personality Functioning

According to the DSM-5, personality disorders significantly impair an individual's *self functioning* (identity and self-direction issues) and his or her ability to engage in *effective interpersonal functioning* (empathy and intimacy issues). In other words, the key element in this definition is impairment and adaptive failure, because both concepts implicitly acknowledge that everyone has a personality and that how it is used determines whether it is adaptive or maladaptive.

The possible *interpersonal failures* of Aaron, Jennifer, and Jordan are quite apparent. Problems of intimacy (Aaron), co-operativeness (Jennifer), and social responsibility (Jordan) may ultimately result in dysfunctional relationships with others. All three also seem to possess potential *self-identity problems* (e.g., identity integration, integrity of self-concept, and self-directedness). A case can be made, for example, that Jordan's adaptive failure in self-identity is a lack of direction, meaning, and purpose in life. He possesses low self-directedness and is unable to set or achieve satisfying and rewarding goals. The general diagnostic criteria in the DSM-5 for a personality disorder are outlined in Table 14.1.

Did You Know? Franz Joseph Gall (1758–1828), a Viennese physician, believed that one could divine the character or personality of a person from the size and shape of the person's skull. Phrenology was a science of character divination, based on the belief that the brain consisted of different "organ regions" that correlated with personality traits. The size and shape of each organ region affected the shape of the human skull. Phrenologists would use instruments to measure these regions or would simply feel the head with their hands for bumps and indentations. It was believed, for example, that a large skull or a broad forehead indicated power and force. Although it has been discredited by the scientific community, groups still exist that believe in phrenology.

Clinicians would approach the task of diagnosing a personality disorder by asking the following questions: Does the person have impairment in personality functioning? If so, how severe is it? Is it manifested in one of the six personality disorder types or in one of the five domains of personality disorder trait specified (see Figure 14.1)?

The absence or degree of impairment in personality functioning is measured on the 5-point Levels of Personality Functioning scale: 0 = no impairment, 1 = mild impairment, 2 = moderate impairment, 3 = serious impairment, and 4 = extreme impairment. Impairment is assessed in self (identity and self-direction) and interpersonal (empathy and intimacy) functioning. For Aaron, Jennifer, and Jordan, a clinician would use these criteria to determine the degree of impairment each one experiences on the continuum for self and interpersonal functioning.

Sociocultural Considerations

In diagnosing a personality disorder, the DSM-5 recognizes the importance of culture and ethnicity by stressing that what is considered impaired or adaptive is based on the individual's contextual norms and expectations. It acknowledges that culture shapes habits, customs, values, and personality characteristics, so that expressions of personality in one culture may differ from those in another culture.

TABLE 14.1 General Diagnostic Criteria for Personality Disorder

A personality disorder represents impairments in personality (self and interpersonal) functioning and the presence of pathological personality traits. To diagnose a personality disorder, the impairments must meet all of the following criteria:
A. significant impairments in self (identity or self-direction) and interpersonal (empathy or intimacy) functioning,
B. one or more pathological personality trait domains or trait facets,
C. impairments and trait expression that are relatively stable across time and consistent across situations,
D. impairments and trait expressions that are not better understood as normative for the person's developmental stage or sociocultural environment, and
E. impairments and trait expressions that are not due solely to direct physiological effects of a substance (e.g., medication, drug abuse) or medical condition (e.g., severe head trauma).

Adapted from DSM-5 Work Groups (2012)

Asians in Asia, for example, are more likely to exhibit shyness and collectivism, whereas U.S. Americans are more likely to show assertiveness and individualism (D. W. Sue & Sue, 2013). Japanese people and Asian Indians (South Asians) often display more overt dependent, submissive, and social conformance behaviors than U.S. Americans or Europeans. In essence, these three traits in U.S. society often possess negative connotations. Does this mean that people in Japan and India are more likely to have a personality disorder? In all probability, the high incidence of these behaviors reflects the influence of cultural values that make such traits more acceptable in Asian societies.

In one study conducted in the United Kingdom, it was found that white clients were 2.8 times more likely to be given a diagnosis of antisocial personality disorder than African Caribbean clients (Mikton & Grounds, 2007). The diagnosis varied not only with the race of the client but also with that of the clinician. The three possible explanations of bias were (a) a belief that antisocial and criminal behavior is more "normal" among African Caribbean men, (2) a tendency to attribute antisocial behavior in black clients to environmental factors, and (3) a reluctance to attribute pathology to black clients because of sensitivity to risks of prejudice and stigmatization. Anyone making judgments about personality functioning and disturbance must consider the individual's cultural, ethnic, and social background (DSM-5 Work Groups, 2012).

Gender implications are also important in diagnosing personality disorders. One major study found that men were more likely than women to be diagnosed with antisocial personality disorder (B. F. Grant et al., 2004); women, on the other hand, more often receive diagnoses of borderline personality disorder (J. R. Kuo & Linehan, 2009), psychopathological traits associated with excessive dependency, and emotional lability (Millon et al., 2004; Torgersen, Kringlen, & Cramer, 2001). The existence of gender differences in the diagnosis of certain personality disorders is widely known in the profession. The question, however, is whether these differences are attributable to biases (Widiger & Coker, 2002).

Gender bias occurs when diagnostic categories are not valid and when they have a differential impact on men and women. The mere fact that men and women have different prevalence rates for a particular disorder is not sufficient to prove gender bias: Rates may differ because of actual biological conditions (e.g., a genetic predisposition) or social conditions (e.g., stressors) that affect one gender more than another. For the diagnostic system to be biased, the differences must be attributable to errors or problems in the categories or diagnostic criteria. Debate over what these differences mean continues.

Personality Disorder Types and Personality Disorder Trait Specified: A Hybrid Approach

In the past, the multiaxial classification of mental disorders listed all the clinical disorders on Axis I, whereas personality disorders, mental retardation, and long-standing defenses were noted on Axis II. In the DSM-5, this separation appears less important, although the distinction between personality psychopathology and the clinical disorders remains: (a) Personality disorders are chronic, developmental, and relatively inflexible patterns of responding that are less likely to be successfully changed in treatment; and (b) it is entirely possible for a personality disorder to coexist with one or more clinical disorders. For example, a person with a personality disorder may also be diagnosed with schizophrenia or alcohol-use disorder. Usually, people with personality disorders are hospitalized only when a co-occurring clinical disorder (e.g., schizophrenia, depression, etc.) so impairs social functioning that they require inpatient care. In fact, the treatment outcome for people with clinical disorders who also have personality disorders is worse than for those who have only clinical disorders (Benjamin & Karpiak, 2002; Clarkin & Levy, 2004).

The DSM-5 uses a hybrid approach in conceptualizing personality disorders. There is recognition that some disorders are more categorical in nature, whereas others are more accurately described on a continuum of traits. We discuss the personality disorder trait specified means of determining personality impairment shortly, but we first concentrate on personality disorder types.

CHECKPOINT REVIEW

1. Describe criteria used to diagnose personality disorders.
2. What are the two paths to diagnosing a personality disorder? How do they differ from one another?
3. Why do personality disorders often go undiagnosed in people?
4. Describe ways in which culture may affect the diagnosis of a personality disorder.

Personality Disorder Types

One path by which a person may be diagnosed as having a personality disorder is through matching a categorical type (see Figure 14.1). Research supports the existence of six specific personality disorder types (Table 14.2): schizotypal, borderline, avoidant, narcissistic, obsessive-compulsive, and antisocial. To diagnose a personality disorder type, clinicians use a brief DSM-5 description of the disorder and determine the degree of match with the individual.

Schizotypal Type

schizotypal type a personality disorder characterized by peculiar thoughts and behaviors and by poor interpersonal relationships

People with the **schizotypal type** of personality disorder manifest odd, eccentric, peculiar thoughts and behaviors and have poor interpersonal relationships. Many believe they possess magical abilities or special powers (e.g., "I can predict what people will say before they say it"), and some are subject to recurrent illusions (e.g., "I feel that my dead father is watching me"). Speech oddities, such as frequent

TABLE 14.2 DISORDERS CHART PERSONALITY DISORDER TYPES

Disorder	Symptoms	Gender Differences	Prevalence (%)
Schizotypal type	• Peculiar thoughts and behaviors; poor interpersonal relationships	More common in males	2.0–4.0
Borderline type	• Intense fluctuations in mood, self-image, and interpersonal relationships	More common in females	1.0–5.9
Avoidant type	• Fear of rejection and humiliation; reluctance to enter into social relationships	None	0.3–2.0
Narcissistic type	• Exaggerated sense of self-importance; exploitativeness; largely superficial relationships	More common in males	1.0–2.0
Obsessive-compulsive type	• Perfectionism; controlling interpersonal behavior; devotion to details; rigidity	More common in males	1 (American Psychiatric Association, 2008a); 7.9 (B. F. Grant et al., 2004)
Antisocial type	• Failure to conform to social or legal codes; lack of anxiety and guilt; irresponsible behaviors	More common in males	2.0–3.6

Note: In all of the personality disorders, early symptoms appear in childhood or adolescence. Personality disorders tend to be stable and to endure over time, although symptoms of antisocial and borderline personality disorders tend to remit with age. Prevalence figures and gender differences have varied from study to study, and investigators may disagree on these rates. Because the definition of personality psychopathology has moved to a continuous description of types, it is possible that these rates will change in future prevalence studies.

Source: Based on American Psychiatric Association (2000); Bollini & Walker (2007); B. F. Grant et al. (2004); J. R. Kuo & Linehan (2009); B. P. O'Connor (2008)

digression or vagueness in conversation, are often present. Again, the evaluation of individuals must take into account their cultural milieu. Superstitious beliefs, delusions, and hallucinations may be condoned or encouraged in certain religious ceremonies or cultures.

The peculiarities seen in schizotypal type stem from distortions or difficulties in cognition (Bollini & Walker, 2007; Goodman, Triebwasser, Shah, & New, 2007). That is, individuals seem to have problems in thinking and perceiving. People with this disorder often show social isolation, hypersensitivity, and inappropriate affect (emotions). They seem to lack pleasure from social interactions (Blanchard, Gangestad, Brown, & Horan, 2000). The prevailing belief among clinicians is that the disorder is defined primarily by cognitive distortions and that affective and interpersonal problems are secondary. Research shows that people with schizotypal type personality disorder have abnormalities in cognitive processing that explain many of their symptoms (Goodman, Triebwasser, et al., 2007; M. H. Stone, 2001).

The man described in the following case study was diagnosed as having schizotypal personality disorder type.

Case Study

A forty-one-year-old man was referred to a community mental health center's activities program for help in improving his social skills. He had a lifelong pattern of social isolation, with no real friends, and spent long hours worrying that his angry thoughts about his older brother would cause his brother harm. During one interview, the patient was distant and somewhat distrustful. He described in elaborate and often irrelevant detail his rather uneventful and routine daily life. . . . For two days he had studied the washing instructions on a new pair of jeans—Did "wash before wearing" mean that the jeans were to be washed before wearing the first time, or did they need, for some reason, to be washed each time before they were worn? . . . He asked the interviewer whether, if he joined the program, he would be required to participate in groups. He said that groups made him very nervous because he felt that if he revealed too much personal information, such as the amount of money that he had in the bank, people would take advantage of him or manipulate him for their own benefit. (Spitzer et al., 1994, pp. 289–290)

The man's symptoms included absence of close friends, magical thinking (worrying that his thoughts might harm his brother), being distant in the interview, and social anxiety. These symptoms are associated with schizotypal type.

Many characteristics of schizotypal type resemble those of schizophrenia, although in less serious form. For example, people with schizophrenia exhibit problems in personality characteristics, psychophysiological responses, and information processing—deficits that have also been observed among people with schizotypal personality disorder type (Goodman, Triebwasser, et al., 2007; Lenzenweger, 2001). Some research has suggested a genetic link between the two disorders (Bollini & Walker, 2007). There appears to be a higher risk of schizotypal personality disorder type among relatives of people diagnosed with schizophrenia than among members of a control group. Despite the possibility of genetic influence in the disorder, early environmental enrichment for children (i.e., 2 years of enhanced nutrition, education, and physical exercise) has been found to reduce schizotypal personality disorder type and symptoms compared with a nonenriched group of children (Raine, Mellingen, Liu, Venables, & Mednick, 2003).

Did Princess Diana Have Borderline Personality Disorder Type?

Princess Diana, smiling happily in this picture, was known to experience rapid mood swings, depression, and suicide attempts. Her emotional and behavioral traits, such as impulsiveness, marked fluctuations in mood, chronic feelings of emptiness, and unstable and intense interpersonal relationships, are consistent with a diagnosis of borderline personality disorder type. Why do women receive this diagnosis far more frequently than men do?

Various psychotherapies have been used to treat schizotypal personality disorder type, such as dynamic therapy, supportive therapy, and cognitive-behavioral approaches, as well as group psychotherapy. For clients who are experiencing a great deal of anxiety, small doses of anxiolytics (a class of antianxiety drugs) may be used (M. H. Stone, 2001).

Borderline Type

Individuals with the **borderline type** of personality disorder have a very fragile self-concept that may become easily disrupted and fragmented under stress. Self-identity is amorphous or lacking. Borderline type is also characterized by intense fluctuations in mood, self-image, and interpersonal relationships (Selby & Joiner, 2009). People with this disorder are impulsive, have chronic feelings of emptiness, and form unstable and intense interpersonal relationships (Goodman, Triebwasser, et al., 2007). They may be quite friendly one day and quite hostile the next.

Many individuals with borderline personality disorder type exhibit recurrent suicidal behaviors or gestures (Yen et al., 2003), and the probabilities of suicide attempts and completions are higher than average among those who have this disorder (Sherry & Whilde, 2008). Self-destructive behaviors, such as suicide attempts and self-harm (cutting and self-mutilation), are often triggered by interpersonal conflicts and events (Welch-Shaw, & Linehan, 2002; see Focus on Resilience Box). Sexual difficulties, such as sexual preoccupation, dissatisfaction, and depression, have also been observed (Zanarini, Parachini, Frankenburg, & Holman, 2003). Although no single feature defines borderline personality disorder type, its essence can be captured in the capriciousness of behaviors and the lability of moods (Millon et al., 2004).

This is the most commonly diagnosed personality disorder in both inpatient and outpatient settings (Oldham, 2006). Some researchers believe that the prevalence of the disorder is increasing because our society makes it difficult for people to maintain stable relationships and a sense of identity. People who have a borderline personality disorder type may exhibit psychotic symptoms, such as auditory hallucinations (e.g., hearing imaginary voices that tell them to commit suicide), but the symptoms are usually transient (Sieswerda & Arntz, 2007). They are recognized by the individuals as unacceptable, alien, and distressing (Oldham, 2006). By contrast, a person with a psychotic disorder may not realize that his or her hallucinations are pathological.

Some well-known individuals may have had borderline personality disorder type—Adolf Hitler, Marilyn Monroe, and even Princess Diana of the United Kingdom.

Source: Bedell-Smith, 1999

Some researchers (Trull et al., 2008) have found that individuals with borderline personality features are more likely to show dysfunctional moods, interpersonal problems, poor coping skills, and cognitive distortions than are people without borderline personality features (J. C. Franklin, Heilbron, Guerry, Bowker, & Blumenthal, 2009). It is important to note that borderline type may be better viewed on a continuum rather than as a distinct categorical disorder (Gunderson, 2010; Rothschild, Cleland, Haslam, & Zimmerman, 2003; Widiger & Mullins-Sweatt, 2005).

As in most disorders, psychodynamic explanations of borderline personality disorder type stress early childhood experiences of neglect, rejection, and abuse as causing adult emotional fluctuations and lack of trust in and connection with others (Kernberg, 1976). Contemporary explanations, however, point to mood regulation as central to the disorder (J. R. Kuo & Linehan, 2009). Emotional dysregulations have been observed in different populations of people with this disorder, including adolescents (Gratz, Rosenthal, Tull, Lejuez, & Gunderson, 2009; Santisteban, Muir, Mena, & Mitrani, 2003). Biological factors may be responsible for the emotional dysregulation among individuals with borderline personality disorder type. In fact, magnetic resonance imaging and positron emission tomography scans reveal structural abnormalities in the prefrontal cortex, and a different pattern of activation in the amygdala in the working brain, for people with borderline personality disorder (Goodman, Triebwasser, et al., 2007; Prossin, Love, Koeppe, Zubieta, & Silk, 2010). Both are implicated in mood and motor disinhibition.

borderline type a personality disorder characterized by intense fluctuations in mood, self-image, and interpersonal relationships

There appear to be two core aspects of borderline personality: difficulties in regulating emotions, and unstable and intense interpersonal relationships (J. C. Franklin et al., 2009; Oldham, 2006). According to the cognitive-behavioral approach, these two aspects are affected by distorted or inaccurate attributions (explanations for others' behaviors or attitudes). Cognitive-behavioral therapy for borderline personality disorder type, therefore, attempts to change the way clients think about and approach interpersonal situations (Sieswerda & Arntz, 2007). Aaron Beck, a cognitive theorist, has argued that an individual's basic assumptions (that is, thoughts) play a central role in influencing perceptions, interpretations, and behavioral and emotional responses (Beck, Freeman, & Davis, 2004). Individuals with borderline personality disorder type seem to have three basic assumptions: (1) "The world is dangerous and malevolent," (2) "I am powerless and vulnerable," and (3) "I am inherently unacceptable." Believing in these assumptions, individuals with this disorder become fearful, vigilant, guarded, and defensive. For these reasons, they are difficult to treat, and they also prematurely drop out of treatment (Gunderson & Links, 2001).

Dialectical behavior therapy (DBT), developed by Linehan (1993), is specifically for clients with borderline personality disorder. Patients are taught skills that include emotional regulation, distress tolerance, and interpersonal effectiveness (Benjamin & Karpiak, 2002; Harned et al., 2009). The goals of DBT, in descending order of priority, are to change (1) suicidal behaviors, (2) behaviors that interfere with therapy, (3) behaviors that interfere with quality of life, (4) acquisition of behavioral skills, (5) post-traumatic stress behavior, and (6) self-respect behaviors. Averting possible suicidal behaviors in clients and strengthening the therapist–client relationship are targeted as priorities in DBT. This treatment has been found to decrease dropping out and suicidal behaviors and to be generally effective (Emmelkamp, 2004). Because of positive treatment outcomes, DBT has been increasingly used as a treatment procedure (Harned et al., 2009).

FOCUS ON RESILIENCE

Dr. Marsha Linehan: Portrait of Resilience

A 17-year-old girl was institutionalized at the Institute of Living, a psychiatric facility in Hartford, Connecticut. Doctors considered her among the most seriously disturbed patients they had ever seen (B. Carey, 2011). She habitually cut and burned herself, and would use any sharp object to slash her arms, legs, and midsection. She expressed a desire to die and made attempts at suicide (Grohol, 2011). Because of her constant attempts at self-harm, she was locked in a seclusion room free of any object that she could possibly use to hurt herself. This did not, however, prevent her from injuring herself, since she constantly and violently banged her head against the floor or walls.

Peter Yates/New York Times

She was given hours of Freudian analysis, large doses of psychiatric drugs, and, as a last resort, electroconvulsive shock treatments. According to medical records, she received 14 shocks during the first session and another 16 during a second (B. Carey, 2011). At her discharge, some 2 years later, doctors gave her little chance of survival outside the hospital.

This is the true story of Dr. Marsha Linehan, a world-renowned psychologist who developed a groundbreaking form of psychotherapy called dialectical behavior therapy (DBT) that has been found to successfully treat people with borderline personality disorder type and suicidal tendencies. At age 68, standing before a packed audience of family, friends, and doctors (at the very institution in which she was first hospitalized), Linehan for the first time revealed that she was the 17-year-old patient who in 1961 seemed so out of control and destined to spend the rest of her life with a debilitating mental disorder.

Continued

FOCUS ON RESILIENCE

Dr. Marsha Linehan: Portrait of Resilience—cont'd

Yet, having been diagnosed with borderline personality disorder, Linehan seemed to have found the answers to the problems that haunted her and drove her to thoughts of suicide. She went on to receive her PhD in psychology at Loyola University in 1971 and is now on the faculty at the University of Washington, where the psychological community has embraced her work on DBT (a combination of cognitive-behavioral therapy with other forms of treatment). Her self-healing journey is truly inspirational and speaks to the courage, inner fortitude, and resilience of the human condition. In her own recovery, Linehan has outlined lessons she learned that involve components of a resilient and peaceful life (Emel, 2011):

1. **Real change is possible.** According to conventional wisdom, people with personality disorders have great difficulty changing; some people even go so far as to say that very little can be done, especially for those with borderline type. Yet Linehan is a prime example that change is possible, and her DBT incorporates the notion that learning new skills and changing behavior ultimately changes perceptions and emotions. The transformation cannot happen overnight, but is best framed as a day-to-day development.
2. **Accept life as it is, not as it is supposed to be.** Linehan calls this "radical acceptance" and uses her own recovery as an example. The gulf between who she was and what she wanted to be made her hopeless, desperate, and depressed. She despised herself, and her self-harm behaviors symbolized this hatred. People who are suicidal seem to also experience this gulf. Linehan believes that accepting oneself as one truly is represents the first step to combating feelings of self loathing because it (a) eliminates the discrepancy between an unrealistic ideal and the current state of the person, (b) allows realistic and positive views of the self to develop, and (c) fosters incremental changes in emotional and behavioral growth.
3. **A diagnosis of borderline personality disorder or any disorder is not a life sentence.** According to Linehan, receiving a psychiatric diagnosis often fosters a victim mentality that produces helplessness, dependency, and hopelessness. The person begins to believe that little can be done to overcome the disorder, that the diagnosis is a life sentence of misery and suffering. Linehan teachers her clients to think of themselves as survivors, or people who can control their destiny in life and are capable of overcoming challenges. Such a fundamental change in thinking moves clients from a passive to an active stance. Linehan's own battle with borderline personality disorder models how people with a disorder can lead productive and happy lives.
4. **Find faith and meaning in life.** Linehan's religion and faith in God played an important role in her recovery. Throughout all her treatments that seemingly were ineffective, it was her Catholicism that gave her meaning and allowed her to experience an epiphany in 1967 that ultimately led her to develop the core principles of DBT. Since that event, Linehan has found a mission in life to help others through the challenges and agonies of mental disorders.

Avoidant Type

The essential features of the **avoidant type** of personality disorder are fears of rejection and humiliation and a reluctance to enter into social relationships. People with this disorder tend to have a negative sense of self, low self-esteem, and a strong sense of inadequacy. They tend to avoid social situations and relationships and are perceived as socially inept, shy, and withdrawn. They are overly sensitive to criticism, fear humiliation, blame themselves for things that go wrong, and seem to find little pleasure in life.

avoidant type a personality disorder characterized by a fear of rejection and humiliation and a reluctance to enter into social relationships

In some studies, as children, people with avoidant personality disorder engaged in fewer extracurricular activities, hobbies, and leadership roles; had less athletic ability; and were less popular in school (Rettew, Zanarini, & Yen, 2003; Weston & Riolo, 2007). Unlike some individuals who avoid others because they lack interest, these people crave affection and an active social life. They want—but fear—social contacts, and this ambivalence may be reflected in different ways. For example, many people with this disorder engage in intellectual pursuits, wear fine clothes, or are active in the artistic community. Their need for contact and relationships is often woven into their activities. Thus a person with avoidant personality disorder may write poems expressing the plight of people who are lonely or a need for human intimacy. A primary defense mechanism is fantasy, whereby wishes are fulfilled to an excessive degree in the person's imagination (Millon et al., 2004).

People with this disorder are caught in a vicious cycle: Because they are preoccupied with rejection, they are constantly alert to signs of derogation or ridicule. This concern leads to many perceived instances of rejection, which cause them to avoid others. Their social skills may then become deficient and invite criticism from others. In other words, their very fear of criticism may lead to criticism. People with avoidant personality disorder often feel depressed, anxious, angry at themselves, inferior, and inadequate into their elderly years (Mahgoub & Hossain, 2007).

Case Study

Jenny L., a 27-year-old bank teller, showed several features of avoidant personality disorder. Although she functioned adequately at work, Jenny was extremely shy, sensitive, and quiet with fellow employees. She perceived others as being insensitive and gross. If the bank manager joked with other tellers, she felt that the manager preferred them to her. Although Jenny tried to be friendly, she did not interact much with anyone because of the possibility of their criticizing or rejecting her.

Jenny had very few hobbies. A great deal of her time was spent watching television and eating chocolates. As a result, she was about 40 pounds overweight. Television romances were her favorite programs; after watching one, she tended to daydream about having an intense romantic relationship. Jenny eventually sought treatment for her depression and loneliness.

Some researchers believe that avoidant personality disorder is on a continuum with social anxiety disorder, whereas others see it as a distinct disorder that simply has features in common with social phobia. It may be that the avoidant type results from a complex interaction of early childhood environmental experiences and innate temperament. For example, parental rejection and censure, reinforced by rejecting peers, may contribute to the disorder.

Because of the fear of rejection and scrutiny, clients may be reluctant to disclose personal thoughts and feelings. It is important for the therapist to establish rapport and a therapeutic alliance, or the client may fail to return for treatment. A number of different therapies have been used, such as cognitive-behavioral, psychodynamic, interpersonal, and psychopharmacological treatments.

Narcissistic Type

The clinical characteristics of **narcissistic personality disorder** are an exaggerated sense of self-importance, an exploitative attitude, and a lack of empathy. People with this disorder require constant attention and admiration, and have difficulty accepting personal criticism. In conversations, they talk mainly about themselves and show a lack of interest in others. Many have fantasies about power or influence, and they constantly overestimate their talents and importance.

narcissistic type a personality disorder characterized by an exaggerated sense of self-importance, an exploitative attitude, and a lack of empathy

Case Study

Roberto J. was a well-known sociologist at the local community college. He was flamboyant, always seeking attention, and was known for frequently bragging about himself to anyone who would listen. His wardrobe, which cost him a fortune, was extremely eye-catching and colorful, although it was inappropriate for most college events. Most people found him superficial and so self-centered that any type of meaningful conversation was nearly impossible. His expertise was in critical race theory, and he had published a few minor articles on topics of racism in professional journals. He saw himself as a great scholar and would often talk about his "accomplishments" to colleagues; Roberto frequently nominated himself for numerous awards, and asked colleagues to write letters on his behalf. Because his accomplishments were considered mediocre by academic standards, Roberto seldom received any of the awards. Nevertheless, he continued to present himself as a giant and a pioneer in the field of race relations.

Roberto came for couples counseling at the request of his wife, a former undergraduate student of his. In his classes, she was attracted to his apparent confidence, outgoing nature, sense of humor, and supposed achievements. After several months of marriage, however, she found his self-centered behavior and constant self-orientation alienating. After nearly a year of therapy without significant change in Roberto, his wife filed for divorce.

Narcissistic traits are common among adolescents and do not necessarily imply that a teenager has the disorder (American Psychiatric Association, 2000). However, it has been found that people later diagnosed with the disorder were more likely to experience feelings of invulnerability, to display risk-taking behavior, and to have strong feelings of uniqueness as adolescents (Weston & Riolo, 2007). As is the case with most of the personality disorders, no controlled treatment studies for narcissistic personality disorder have been conducted, and treatment recommendations are therefore based on clinical experience (Groopman & Cooper, 2001). Individual psychotherapy and group therapy have been used and are generally recommended. Unfortunately, narcissistic personality disorder is

20TH CENTURY FOX/WETCHER, BARRY/Album/Newscom

Narcissistic Behavior

Miranda Priestly (Meryl Streep) in the movie *The Devil Wears Prada* illustrates some of the symptoms of narcissistic personality disorder, including an exaggerated sense of self-importance, an excessive need for admiration, and an inability to accept criticism or rejection. Do you think that narcissistic personality disorder is increasing among young people?

considered very difficult to treat; most forms of therapy try to increase empathic abilities, focus on the opinion of others, and break self-involvement (Beck, Freeman, & Davis, 2004; R. L. Leahy, Beck, & Beck, 2005). Unfortunately, none of these treatments have met with much success.

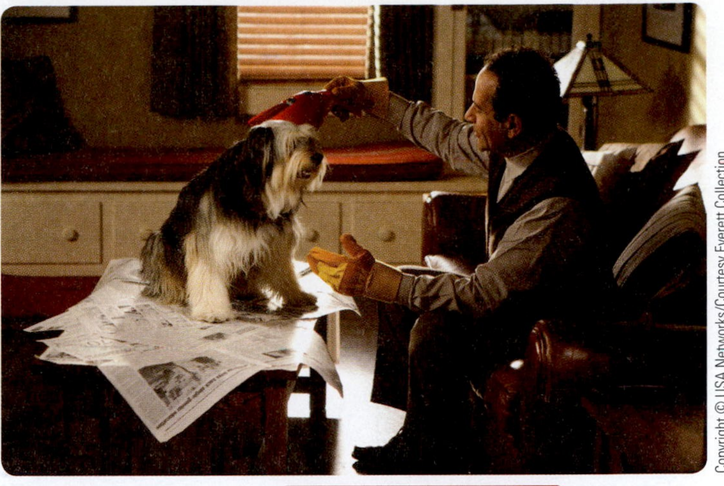

Compulsive Behavior

TV detective Adrian Monk, played by Tony Shalhoub in the once popular TV series "Monk", suffers from compulsive habits that involve excessive cleanliness.

Obsessive-Compulsive Type

The characteristics of the **obsessive-compulsive type (OCT)** of personality disorder are perfectionism, a marked tendency to be interpersonally controlling, strong devotion to details, and rigidity. Again, these traits are also found in many people without a personality disorder. Unlike those people, however, individuals with obsessive-compulsive personality disorder show marked impairment in occupational or social functioning. Their relationships with others may be quite stiff, formal, and distant (P. K. McCullough & Maltsberger, 2001). Further, the extent of character rigidity is greater among people who have this disorder.

OCT as presented in this chapter is distinct from obsessive-compulsive disorder, discussed in Chapter 4. The two disorders have similar names, but their clinical manifestations are quite different. OCT is a pervasive character disturbance. People with the disorder genuinely see their way of functioning as the correct way. Their overall style of relating to the world around them is processed through their own strict standards. Research also shows that OCT symptoms are related to anger and depression, and that those with these symptoms are more prone to suppress their anger (Whiteside & Abramowitz, 2004).

The preoccupation with details, rules, and possible errors leads to indecision and an inability to see the big picture. There is a heightened concern with being in control, not only over the details of one's own life but also over emotions and other people. Coworkers may find individuals with this disorder too demanding, inflexible, miserly, and perfectionistic. Individuals may actually be ineffective on the job, despite long hours of devotion, as in the following case study.

Case Study

Cecil, a third-year medical student, was referred by his graduate adviser for therapy. The adviser said Cecil was in danger of being expelled from medical school because of his inability to get along with patients and other students. Cecil often berated patients for failing to follow his advice. In one instance, he told a patient with a lung condition to stop smoking. When the patient indicated he was unable to stop, Cecil angrily told the patient to go for medical treatment elsewhere—that the medical center had no place for such a "weak-willed fool." Cecil's relationships with others were similarly strained. He considered many members of the faculty to be "incompetent old deadwood," and he characterized fellow graduate students as "partygoers."

The graduate adviser said that Cecil had not been expelled only because several faculty members thought that he was brilliant. Cecil studied and worked 16 hours a day. He was extremely well read and had an extensive knowledge of medical disorders. Although he was always able to provide a careful and detailed analysis of a patient's condition, it took him a great deal of time to do so. His diagnoses tended to cover every disorder that each patient could conceivably have, on the basis of all possible combinations of symptoms.

obsessive-compulsive type (OCT) a personality disorder characterized by perfectionism, a tendency to be interpersonally controlling, devotion to details, and rigidity

Did You Know? This table shows the primary differences and similarities between OCT and OCD.

CHARACTERISTIC	OCT	OCD
Rigidity in personality	Yes	Not usual
Preoccupation in thinking	Yes	Yes
Orderliness	Yes	Not usual
Control	Yes	Not usual
Perfectionism	Yes	Not usual
Indecisiveness	Yes	Not usual
Intrusive thoughts or behaviors	Not usual	Yes
Need to perform acts	Not usual	Yes
Recognition of irrationality	Not usual	Yes

Cognitive-behavioral therapy, as well as supportive forms of psychotherapy, has helped some clients (Barber, Morse, Krakauer, Chittams, & Crits-Cristoph, 1997; Beck, Freeman, & Associates, 1990). No medications specific to obsessive-compulsive type are currently available (P. K. McCullough & Maltsberger, 2001).

Antisocial Type

The characteristics of the **antisocial type** are arrogance, self-centeredness, feelings of entitlement, and an exaggerated sense of self-importance (Decuyper, De Pauw, De Fruyt, De Bolle, & De Clercq, 2009). Those with this disorder seek power over others and like to manipulate, deceive, exploit, and con others for their own needs and purposes. Chronic antisocial behavioral patterns, such as a failure to conform to social or legal codes, a lack of anxiety and guilt, and irresponsible behaviors, typify this type. People with this disorder show little guilt for their wrongdoing, which may include lying, using other people, and perpetrating aggressive sexual acts. Their relationships with others are superficial and fleeting and involve little loyalty.

Antisocial personality disorder, suggests some research, is composed of three factors (Cooke & Michie, 2001):

- arrogant and deceitful interpersonal style,
- deficient affective experience, and
- impulsive and irresponsible behavioral style.

Did You Know? Historically, people have been interested in antisocial personalities. An early-19th-century British psychiatrist, J. C. Prichard, described them this way:

The moral and active principles of the mind are strongly perverted or depraved; the power of self-government is lost or greatly impaired; and the individual is found to be incapable, not of talking or reasoning upon any subject proposed to him . . . but of conducting himself with decency and propriety in the business of life. (1837, p. 15)

Paramount Pictures/Getty Images

Anthony Neste/Time Life Pictures/Getty Images

Crime Bosses and Antisocial Personality Disorders

Vito Corleone (played by Marlon Brando) in *The Godfather* and Tony Soprano (played by James Gandolfini) in the TV series *The Sopranos* are both characters who exhibit many of the traits of antisocial personality disorder. Both evidence a callous disregard for the rights of others and show little regret or remorse for cheating, lying, breaking the law, or even killing. However, they also reveal characteristics that are at odds with the diagnosis. Both have deep family relationships, reveal intense loyalty and emotional commitment to their families, and evidence flashes of guilt; Tony Soprano even seeks psychiatric help for his anxiety attacks.

antisocial type a personality disorder characterized by a failure to conform to social and legal codes, a lack of anxiety and guilt, and irresponsible behaviors

People with this disorder are prone to engage in unlawful and criminal behavior and have no compunction about violating moral, ethical, or legal codes of conduct (Hare & Neumann, 2009). The following case study of Robert T. exemplifies many of these characteristics.

Case Study

The epitome of a hard-driven, successful businessman, Robert T. seemed to have it all: enormous financial wealth, influence with politicians, a private jet, an apparently healthy marriage, and, despite his reputation as a ruthless corporate raider, high regard from associates for his business acumen. Then, in less than a year, he lost everything—including his marriage, since Mrs. T. filed for divorce. Stockholders raised questions about nonstandard accounting practices, inappropriate personal use of funds for family vacations, and unauthorized purchase of properties in the name of his wife. When banks refused to loan him funds on a prospective takeover bid and creditors demanded repayment of loans, Robert's financial world collapsed. Lawsuits from investors against him and his company followed, with the trustees finally demanding his resignation. Robert refused to resign and launched a campaign against his own board of directors, accusing them of pursuing a personal vendetta and of conspiring against him. He hired a private detective to dig up dirt on certain trustees and their families, and tried to use that information to intimidate and discredit them. In cases where embarrassing information was lacking, he had no qualms about spreading false rumors. These attempts, however, failed, and Robert was eventually removed from his post.

Only with his downfall did the facts about Robert's tendency to exaggerate and distort the truth become known. He was not a graduate of the Wharton School, as his resume had indicated; he had told people that he had been divorced once, but in fact he had been married four times (two of the marriages ended in divorce before age 20); and his fortune did not come from "old money," but from a series of questionable business schemes in real estate that often left investors holding bad debts, which he referred to as "collateral damage." People who had known him in the past often described him as arrogant, deceitful, cunning, and calculating. He showed a disregard for the rights of others, manipulated them, and then discarded them when they served no further use to him. These attributes were evident even in his early years. For example, he married a 16-year-old from a wealthy family, but when her father refused to support them, Robert blamed his wife and constantly belittled her until their divorce 3 months later.

He never expressed regret or remorse for any of his actions, but operated from a belief that "this is a dog-eat-dog world" and that a person has to "do unto others before they do unto you." He had never been in therapy, but school records revealed a pattern of juvenile alcohol use, poor grades, frequent lying, and petty theft. At age 14, he was tentatively diagnosed with a conduct disorder when school officials became concerned with his fascination for setting fires in the restroom toilets. Nevertheless, it is interesting that the school psychologist described Robert as "charming, very bright, persuasive, and with high potential for future success."

Robert T. typifies our definition of an individual with antisocial personality disorder. He exhibits little empathy for others, views them as objects to be manipulated, and has difficulty establishing meaningful and intimate relationships. He

Behavior Patterns, Context, and Diagnosis

Bernard L. Madoff exhibits all the traits of a person with antisocial personality disorder and has often been labeled "a successful psychopath." He lied to family, friends, and investors, manipulated people, experienced feelings of grandiosity, and had a callous disregard for his victims. A seemingly respected power broker on Wall Street and in Washington, he is reported to have bilked investors out of some $50 billion dollars. He was convicted on 17 felony counts and, on June 29, 2009, sentenced to 150 years in prison.

DON EMMERT/AFP/Getty Images

also seems to suffer from problems with self-identity integration, in that he believes that the self he presents to the world is a façade or a fake. Robert pushes the boundaries of social convention and often violates moral, legal, and ethical rules for his own personal gain, with little regard for the feelings of others. His characteristic way of handling things is long-standing and developmental in nature, evident in his early teens (Dolan & Fullam, 2010; Weston & Riolo, 2007). Although these traits can be quite functional in some settings, they inevitably bring about personal and social difficulties (Millon et al., 2004). People with antisocial type often display temperamental deficiencies or aberrations (Robert's tendency to blame others), rigidity in dealing with life problems (making the same mistake over and over), a callous orientation toward people (deceiving others through lying, exaggeration, and manipulation), and defective perceptions of the self and others ("Do unto others before they do unto you").

Antisocial personality disorder is much more frequent in urban environments than in rural ones, and in lower socioeconomic groups than in higher ones. Rates of antisocial personality disorder appear comparable among whites, African Americans, and Latino/Hispanic Americans (Robins, Tipp, & Przybeck, 1991), although one study in the United Kingdom suggested significantly lower rates among African Caribbeans than among whites (Mikton & Grounds, 2007). Although African Americans have a higher rate of incarceration for crimes, their rates of antisocial personality type are either equal to or lower than those of other groups.

Did You Know?

Are there differences between those with antisocial personality disorder who are caught breaking the law (criminals) and those who break the law but elude capture (often called "successful")? The latter group has been found to exhibit higher-order cognitive functioning, be less likely to come from economically disadvantaged backgrounds and more likely to work in white-collar jobs, and have greater cardiovascular reactivity to stress (greater vigilance of danger; J. R. Hall & Benning, 2006). These attributes are believed to make them less susceptible to capture.

The behavior patterns associated with antisocial personality disorder are different and distinct from impulse control problems like pyromania and kleptomania (see Table 14.3) and from behaviors involving social protest or criminal lifestyles. People who engage in civil disobedience or violate the conventions of society or its laws as a form of protest are not, as a rule, people with antisocial personalities. Such people can be quite capable of forming meaningful interpersonal relationships and of experiencing guilt. They may perceive their violations of rules and norms as acts performed for the greater good.

Similarly, engaging in delinquent or adult criminal behavior is not a necessary or sufficient condition for being diagnosed with antisocial personality disorder. Although many convicted criminals have been found to have antisocial characteristics, many

Did You Know?

Beck, Freeman, and their associates (1990) have provided thumbnail sketches of the behavioral approaches to life (strategies) and beliefs that characterize three DSM-5 personality disorders:

DISORDER	STRATEGY	EXAMPLE BELIEF
Antisocial type	Predatory	"Others are patsies."
Avoidant type	Withdrawal	"People will reject the real me."
Obsessive-compulsive type	Ritualistic	"Details are crucial."

DISORDERS CHART IMPULSE CONTROL DISORDERS

TABLE 14.3

Definitions of personality disorders include the major characteristic of impulsivity. Yet certain impulse control disorders occupy a distinct category and are not considered personality disorders. Three such disorders are recognized under impulse control disorders.

1. People with **intermittent explosive disorder**
   - experience separate and discrete episodes of loss of control over their aggressive impulses that results in physical assaults or property damage,
   - display an aggressiveness that is grossly out of proportion to any precipitating stress that may have occurred, and
   - show no signs of general aggressiveness between episodes and may genuinely feel remorse for their actions.
2. People with **kleptomania**
   - chronically fail to resist impulses to steal;
   - do not need the stolen objects for personal use or monetary value, since they usually have enough money to buy the objects and typically discard them, give them away, or surreptitiously return them; and
   - feel irresistible urges and tension before stealing, followed by an intense feeling of relief or gratification after stealing.
3. People with **pyromania**
   - deliberately and purposefully set fires on more than one occasion;
   - are fascinated by and get intense pleasure or relief from setting the fires, watching things burn, or observing firefighters and their efforts to put out fires; and
   - have fire-setting impulses driven by this fascination rather than by motives involving revenge, sabotage, or financial gains.

There has been a controversial move to declare Internet addiction a new impulse control disorder. Fifteen percent of client youths described being addicted to the Internet and said they used the Internet so frequently that they isolated themselves from family and friends (Cynkar, 2007). Opponents believe that an overly broad approach to the definition of addiction opens the floodgates to declaring every compensatory behavior an impulse control disorder, such as fingernail biting, frequent sexual activity, or even excessive use of cell phones.

others have not. They may come from a subculture that encourages and reinforces criminal activity; hence, in perpetrating such acts, they are adhering to group mores and codes of conduct.

People with antisocial personality disorder are a difficult population to study because they do not voluntarily seek treatment. Only 1 out of 7 ever discusses his or her problems with a doctor, and concurrent problems are usually the reason for participation in treatment (Meloy, 2001). Consequently, investigators often seek research participants in prison populations, which presumably contain a relatively large proportion of people with antisocial personality disorder.

Former Personality Disorders

Originally, 10 personality disorders were identified by DSM-IV-TR; but scientific and clinical evidence did not support four of them: paranoid personality disorder, schizoid personality disorder, histrionic personality disorder, and dependent personality disorder. Justification for their removal is based primarily on three lines of evidence: (a) There is an absence of research on these disorders, making their existence as distinct entities questionable (Skodol & Bender, 2009; Widiger & Trull, 2007); (b) excessive co-occurrence means clients are often diagnosed with more than one disorder, making differentiation impossible (Zimmerman, Rothschild, & Chelminski, 2005); and (c) arbitrary diagnostic thresholds (Grilo, Shea, et al., 2004) make for questionable reliability and validity. The DSM-5 no longer recognizes these as distinct categorical types but believes they are better described in terms of a continuum of personality traits (Skodol & Bender, 2009).

Does eliminating certain personality types mean there are no longer paranoid or dependent people who qualify as having a personality disorder? The answer is no. Table 14.4 outlines the four personality disorders that have been removed, provides their DSM-IV-TR definitions, and contrasts how the DSM-5 personality

TABLE 14.4 Former DSM-IV-TR Personality Disorders Versus DSM-5 Domain-Trait Descriptions

	DSM-IV-TR CATEGORICAL DIAGNOSIS	DSM-5 CONTINUUM TRAIT DESCRIPTION
Paranoid personality disorder	People with paranoid personality disorder • show unwarranted suspiciousness, hypersensitivity, and reluctance to trust others; and • interpret others' motives as being malevolent, question their loyalty or trustworthiness, persistently bear grudges, or are suspicious of the actions of others. The categorical nature of this diagnosis is that a person has or does not have the disorder, depending on whether he or she meets an arbitrary threshold.	• Paranoid personality type is not recognized in the DSM-5. • The person is described in terms of personality disorder traits such as *suspiciousness*, *intimacy avoidance*, *hostility*, and *unusual beliefs*.
Schizoid personality disorder	People with schizoid personality disorder • exhibit social isolation, emotional coldness, and indifference to others; • have a long history of impairment of social functioning; • are reclusive and withdrawn; • do not desire or enjoy close relationships, and have few activities that provide pleasure; and • are perceived as peculiar and aloof and therefore inadequate as dating or marital partners due to lack of capacity or desire to form social relationships. The categorical nature of this diagnosis is that a person has or does not have the disorder, depending on whether he or she meets an arbitrary threshold.	• Schizoid personality type is not recognized in the DSM-5. • The person is described in terms of personality disorder traits such as *social withdrawal*, *social detachment*, *intimacy avoidance*, *restricted affectivity*, and *anhedonia*.
Histrionic personality disorder	People with histrionic personality disorder • engage in self-dramatization, exaggerated expression of emotions, and attention-seeking behaviors; • behave flamboyantly or flirtatiously for attention; • are typically shallow and egocentric, in spite of superficial warmth and charm; and • display emotions well beyond acceptable cultural norms. The categorical nature of this diagnosis is that a person has or does not have the disorder, depending on whether he or she meets an arbitrary threshold.	• Histrionic personality type is not recognized in the DSM-5. • The person is described in terms of personality disorder traits such as *emotional lability* and *histrionism*.
Dependent personality disorder	People with dependent personality disorder • lack self-confidence and subordinate their needs to those of the people on whom they depend; • are fearful of taking the initiative on most matters; • are afraid of disrupting their relationships with others; • see themselves as inherently inadequate and unable to cope; • believe they should find someone who can take care of them; and • often experience feelings of depression, helplessness, and suppressed anger. The categorical nature of this diagnosis is that a person has or does not have the disorder, depending on whether he or she meets an arbitrary threshold.	• Dependent personality type is not recognized in the DSM-5. • The person is described in terms of personality disorder traits such as *submissiveness*, *anxiousness*, and *separation insecurity*.

disorder trait specified domains would be used to describe such individuals. We provide a more thorough description of personality disorder trait specified later, in assessing personality psychopathology.

CHECKPOINT REVIEW

1. Describe and distinguish the six personality disorder types.
2. Give several etiological explanations of borderline personality disorder.
3. Give several etiological explanations of antisocial personality disorder.

Multipath Analysis of One Personality Disorder: Antisocial Type

Although research on personality disorders has been quite limited, information about antisocial personality disorder type is more developed, because of its higher visibility and association with criminality (Millon et al., 2004). We use our multipath model to explain how the biological, psychological, social, and sociocultural dimensions interact and contribute to the development of antisocial type, as shown in Figure 14.2. In this way, we hope to provide a prototype for understanding the multidimensional development of other personality disorders as well.

Biological Dimension

An extraordinary amount of research has been devoted to trying to uncover the biological basis of antisocial type. Early researchers concentrated primarily on using genetics, central nervous system abnormalities, and autonomic nervous system abnormalities to explain the disorder.

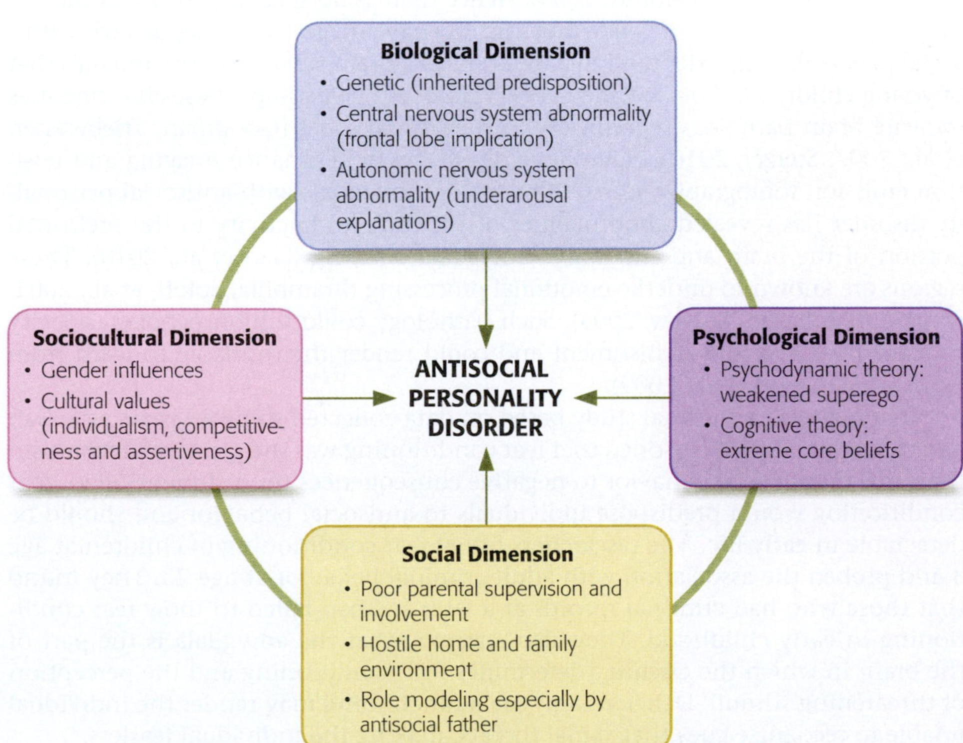

FIGURE 14.2
Multipath Model of Antisocial Personality Disorder
The dimensions interact with one another and combine in different ways to result in antisocial personality disorder.

Genetic Influences Throughout history, many people have speculated that some individuals are born to "raise hell." It is not uncommon for casual observers to remark that people with antisocial personalities, criminal backgrounds, or those suffering from sociopathy appear to have an inborn temperament toward aggressiveness, sensation seeking, impulsivity, and disregard for others. These speculations are difficult to test, because of the problems involved in distinguishing between the influences of environment and heredity on behavior (Sterzer, 2010). Nevertheless, considerable support indicates genetic influences on antisocial behavior, even across childhood and adolescence (Van Hulle et al., 2009).

Support for a genetic influence in antisocial behavior is evident in studies comparing concordance rates for identical or monozygotic twins and those for fraternal or dizygotic twins. Most studies show that monozygotic twins do tend to have a higher concordance rate than dizygotic twins for antisocial tendencies, delinquency, and criminality (Eley, Lichtenstein, & Moffitt, 2003; Gottesman & Goldsmith, 1994). Further, individuals who had been separated from their biological parents with antisocial personalities and had been raised by adoptive parents without such a diagnosis still exhibited higher rates of antisocial characteristics.

Although this body of evidence seems to show a strong causal pattern, it should be examined carefully for several reasons. First, many of the studies have drawn research participants from distinctly criminal populations. People with antisocial personality disorder from noncriminal populations have been relatively absent in such investigations. Second, the fact that crime has increased fivefold or more in most industrialized Western countries over the past 50 years has to be attributed to environmental influences, because gene pools cannot change that quickly. Third, studies indicating that genetic factors are important do not provide much insight into how antisocial type is inherited. Genetic factors do not influence crime and antisocial behavior directly, but they seem to affect the probability that such behavior occurs (Moffitt, 2005). Hence there is no specific gene for crime.

MYTH VS. REALITY

MYTH Problems of antisocial personality type are primarily caused by genetic factors.

REALITY Although genetic factors are related to antisocial type, a wide range of family patterns can influence the development of the disorder. For example, dysfunctional aspects of family life, such as severe parental discord, a parent's maladjustment or criminality, overcrowding, and even large family size, can predispose a child to antisocial personality disorder, especially if the child does not have a loving relationship with at least one parent (Millon et al., 2004).

Some investigators have suggested that adults with antisocial personality disorder tend to have abnormal brain wave activity similar to that of young children (Elliott & Gillett, 1992; Hare, 1993). Perhaps these abnormalities indicate brain pathology, specifically in the frontal lobes (Goodman, Triebwasser, et al., 2007; Sterzer, 2010). Neuroimaging (magnetic resonance imaging and positron emission tomography scans) of brains of individuals with antisocial personality disorder has revealed abnormalities of structure and activity in the prefrontal portion of the brain and the limbic amygdala circuitry (Gao et al., 2010). These regions are known to underlie emotional processing (Brambilla, Soloff, et al., 2004; Frankle, Lombardo, & New, 2005). Such pathology could inhibit people's capacity to learn how to avoid punishment and could render them unable to learn from experience (Glenn et al., 2009).

In a major longitudinal study based on data collected some 20 years ago, Gao and colleagues (2010) reasoned that fear conditioning was the primary mechanism that linked antisocial behavior to negative consequences (punishment). Poor fear conditioning would predispose individuals to antisocial behavior and should be detectable in early life. The researchers tested fear conditioning in children at age 3 and probed the association with adult criminal behavior at age 23. They found that those who had criminal records at a later age had failed to show fear conditioning in early childhood. They also reasoned that the amygdala is the part of the brain in which the circuitry determines fear conditioning and the perception of threatening stimuli. Deficient amygdala functioning may render the individual unable to recognize cues that signal threats, making the individual fearless.

This explanation is plausible, but there simply is not enough evidence to support its unconditional acceptance. Many people diagnosed with antisocial personality disorder do not show activity abnormalities in these regions of the brain. In addition, physiological measures of conditioning (e.g., skin conductance, heart rate, and electroencephalogram) are imprecise diagnostic correlates. Abnormal brain wave activity in people with antisocial personality disorder, for example, may simply be correlated with, rather than a cause of, disturbed behavior.

Autonomic Nervous System Abnormalities Other interesting research points to the involvement of the autonomic nervous system (ANS) in the prominent features of antisocial personality disorder: the inability to learn from experience, the absence of anxiety, and the tendency to engage in thrill-seeking behaviors (Glenn et al., 2009). Two lines of investigation can be identified, both based on the assumption that people with antisocial personality disorder have ANS deficiencies or abnormalities (Crozier et al., 2008). The first states that ANS abnormalities make people with antisocial personality disorder less susceptible to anxiety and therefore less likely to learn from their experiences in situations in which aversive stimuli (or punishment) are involved. The second explanation suggests that ANS abnormalities could keep people with antisocial personality disorder emotionally underaroused. To achieve an optimal level of arousal or to avoid boredom, underaroused individuals might seek excitement and thrills and fail to conform to conventional behavioral standards. The two premises—lack of anxiety and underarousal—may, of course, be related, because underarousal could include underaroused anxiety (J. P. Newman, Curtin, et al., 2010).

Genetic Predisposition to Fearlessness or Lack of Anxiety Lykken (1982) was among the first to maintain that genetic predisposition affects people's levels of fearlessness. Antisocial behavior may develop because of fearlessness or low anxiety levels (J. P. Newman, Curtin, et al., 2010). People who have high levels of fear avoid risks, stress, and strong stimulation; relatively fearless people seek thrills and adventures. Fearlessness is associated with heroes (such as those who volunteer for dangerous military action or who risk their lives to save others) as well as with individuals with antisocial personality disorder who may engage in risky criminal activities or impulsively violate norms and rules (Gao et al., 2010; Sterzer, 2010).

Because people with antisocial personality disorder do not become conditioned to aversive stimuli as readily as nonpsychopaths do, they fail to acquire avoidance behaviors, experience little anticipatory anxiety, and consequently have fewer inhibitions about engaging in antisocial behavior. There is evidence that low anxiety among psychopaths is associated with more errors in learning tasks (J. P. Newman & Schmitt, 1998), inhibited social learning, and poor fear conditioning (Gao et al., 2010).

Did You Know? It is possible that heroes and people suffering from antisocial personality disorder are two sides of the same coin, because they both share one characteristic: fearlessness. They tend to choose frightening or challenging situations, push the boundaries of acceptable behavior, and may use deception to attain goals. The difference seems to be that heroes channel their fearlessness into socially approved activities and are socialized in families that emphasize loving relationships rather than punishment.

Arousal, Sensation Seeking, and Behavioral Perspectives There is also the possibility that individuals with antisocial personality disorder may have deficiencies in learning because of lower anxiety. Because they have less fear about the consequences of their actions, they are less likely to learn appropriate and inappropriate behaviors. Safeguards against social transgressions and even criminal acts are poorly conditioned (learned). Another line of research proposes that people with antisocial personality disorder simply have lower levels of ANS reactivity and are underaroused (Glenn et al., 2009). According to this view, the sensitivity of individuals' reticular cortical systems varies, although there is an optimal level for each person. The system regulates the tonic level of arousal in the cortex, so that some people have high and some have low levels of arousal. Those with low sensitivity need more stimulation to reach an optimal level of arousal. If psychopaths are underaroused, it may take a more intense stimulus to elicit

© Greg Epperson/Shutterstock.com

Risk-Taking and Thrill-Seeking Behaviors

Lykken (1982) theorized that people with low anxiety levels are often thrill seekers. The difference between a risk-taking psychopath and an adventurer may largely be a matter of whether the thrill-seeking behaviors are channeled into destructive or constructive acts. It is believed that men are more likely to be risk takers than women. Do you believe there are gender differences in thrill-seeking behaviors? If so, what can account for the gender differences?

a reaction in them than in nonpsychopaths (J. P. Newman, Curtin, et al., 2010). The lowered levels of reactivity may cause psychopaths to show impulsive, stimulus-seeking behaviors to avoid boredom.

Zuckerman (1996) believes that a trait he calls *impulsive unsocialized sensation seeking* can help explain not only antisocial personality disorders but also other disorders. Those with this trait want to seek adventures and thrills and are disinhibited and susceptible to boredom. Psychopaths score high for this trait. Earlier, Farley (1986) proposed that people vary in their degree of thrill-seeking behaviors. At one end of the thrill-seeking continuum are the "Big Ts"—the risk takers and adventurers who seek excitement and stimulation. Because of their low levels of CNS or ANS arousal, Big Ts need stimulation to maintain an optimal level of arousal. On the other end of the continuum are "Little t's"—people with high arousal who seek low levels of stimulation to calm their hyped-up nervous systems. In contrast to Big Ts, Little t's prefer certainty, predictability, low risk, familiarity, clarity, simplicity, low conflict, and low intensity.

Psychological Dimension

Psychological explanations of personality disorders, and specifically antisocial type, tend to fall into three camps: psychodynamic, cognitive, and social learning.

Psychodynamic Perspectives According to psychodynamic approaches, faulty superego development (Fenichel, 1945) may cause a person suffering from antisocial personality disorder to experience little guilt so they are more prone to frequent violation of moral and ethical standards. Although the ego develops adequately, the personalities of people with antisocial personality disorder are dominated by id impulses that operate primarily from the pleasure principle in seeking immediate (impulsive) gratification with minimal regard for others (egocentricity). Because the infantile id is dominated primarily by sex and aggression, so are people with this disorder who act out these impulses on others (Millon et al., 2004). People exhibiting antisocial behavior patterns presumably did not adequately identify with their parents and thus did not internalize the morals and values of society. It is believed that frustration, rejection, or inconsistent discipline resulted in fixation at an early stage of development.

Cognitive Perspectives Certain core beliefs, and the ways they influence behavior, are emphasized in cognitive explanations of antisocial personality disorder (Beck, Freeman, & Associates, 1990). These core beliefs operate on an unconscious level, occur automatically, and influence emotions and behaviors. Beck and colleagues summarized the typical cognitions most likely found in people with antisocial personality disorder (p. 361):

- I have to look out for myself.
- Force or cunning is the best way to get things done.
- We live in a jungle and the strong person is the one who survives.
- People will get at me if I don't get them first.
- It is not important to keep promises or honor debts.
- Lying and cheating are OK as long as you don't get caught.
- I have been unfairly treated and am entitled to get my fair share by whatever means I can.
- Other people are weak and deserve to be taken.
- If I don't push other people, I will get pushed around.

- I should do whatever I can get away with.
- What others think of me doesn't really matter.
- If I want something, I should do whatever is necessary to get it.
- I can get away with things, so I don't need to worry about bad consequences.
- If people can't take care of themselves, that's their problem.

These thoughts arise from what Beck and colleagues refer to as a "predatory strategy." It is built around a need to perceive oneself as strong and independent, necessary attributes for survival in a competitive, hostile, and unforgiving world.

Learning Perspectives Learning theories suggest that people with antisocial personality disorder (1) have inherent neurobiological characteristics that delay or impede learning, (2) lack positive role models in developing prosocial behaviors, or (3) have poor role models. In all cases, whether we are speaking about classical conditioning, operant conditioning, or social modeling, it is proposed that biology or social and developmental factors combine in unique ways to influence the development of antisocial personality disorder.

As we have seen, some researchers believe that learning deficiencies among individuals with antisocial personality disorder are caused by the absence of anxiety and by lowered autonomic reactivity. If so, is it possible to improve their learning by increasing their anxiety or arousal ability? In a now classic study, researchers designed two conditions in which psychopaths, a mixed group, and nonpsychopaths would perform an avoidance learning task, with electric shock as the unconditioned stimulus (Schachter & Latané, 1964). Under one condition, participants were injected with adrenaline, which presumably increases arousal; under the other, they were injected with a placebo. Psychopaths receiving the placebo made more errors in avoiding the shocks than did nonpsychopaths; psychopaths receiving adrenaline, however, tended to perform better than nonpsychopaths. These findings imply that psychopaths do not react to the same amount of anxiety as do nonpsychopaths and that their learning improves when their anxiety is increased.

The *kind* of punishment used in avoidance learning is also an important consideration in evaluating psychopaths' learning deficiencies. Whereas psychopaths may show learning deficits when faced with physical (electric shock) or social (verbal feedback) punishments, they learn as well as nonpsychopaths when the punishment is monetary loss.

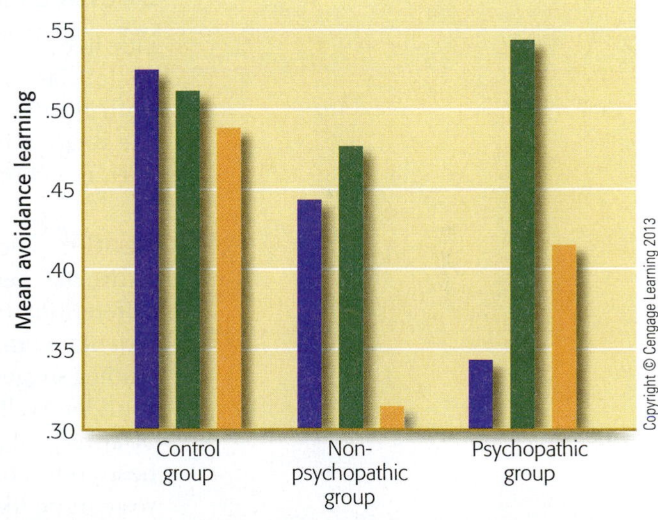

FIGURE 14.3

Effect of Type of Punishment on Psychopaths and Others

The effects of three different types of punishment on an avoidance learning task are shown for three groups of participants. Although physical or social punishment had little impact on psychopaths' learning, monetary punishment was quite effective.

Source: Schmauk (1970)

Social Dimension

Among the many factors that have been implicated in the development of personality disorders, relationships within the family—the primary agent of socialization—are paramount in the development of antisocial patterns. A number of social factors and conditions have been implicated in increased antisocial behaviors and lowered prosocial behaviors among children (S. M. Coyne, Nelson, Graham-Kevan, Keister, & Grant, 2009; J. C. Franklin, et al., 2009; Jaffee, Moffitt, Caspi, Taylor, & Arsenault, 2002). For children, rejection or deprivation by one or both parents means little opportunity to learn socially appropriate behaviors or the value of people as socially reinforcing agents. Children from impoverished backgrounds are twice as likely to develop antisocial personality disorder as are those from higher socioeconomic status (Lahey, Loeber, et al., 2005). Poor parental supervision and involvement are predictors of antisocial behaviors (Loeber, 1990). Children's risk of psychosocial dysfunction increases when they are part of families in which adults exhibit antisocial behavior, including neglect, hostility, maltreatment, and abuse (Jaffee, Moffitt, Caspi, & Taylor, 2004). Children from such environments learn that the world is cold, unforgiving, and punitive. Struggle and survival become part of their outlook on life, and they respond in an aggressive fashion to control and manipulate the world.

There is also evidence that family structure, predictability of expectations, and dependability of family roles are related to lower antisocial tendencies (Tolan, Gorman-Smith, Huesmann, & Zelli, 1997). Parental separation or absence and assaultive or inconsistent parenting are related to antisocial personality disorder (K. A. Phillips & Gunderson, 1999). Children may have been traumatized or subjected to a hostile environment during the parental separation, or the hostility in such families may result in interpersonal hostility among the children. Such situations may lead to little satisfaction in close or meaningful relationships with others. Individuals with antisocial type tend to misperceive the motives and behaviors of others and have difficulty being empathetic (Benjamin, 1996).

It has been long established that people with antisocial personality disorder can learn and use social skills very effectively, as shown in their adeptness at manipulating, lying, and cheating and their ease at being charming and sociable. The difficulty is that, in many areas of learning, these individuals do not pay attention to social stimuli (J. P. Newman, Curtin, et al., 2010), and their schedules of reinforcement differ from those of most other people. Perhaps this relatively diminished attention stems from inconsistent reinforcement from parents or inadequate feedback on behaviors.

Sociocultural Dimension

Our lives are influenced by the values, traditions, and institutions of our society. Social class, race, gender, and other sociodemographic variables are important in both normal and abnormal development (D. W. Sue & Sue, 2013). Determining the relative impact of specific sociocultural factors on antisocial disorders, however, is a complicated procedure.

Gender Because males are more likely to exhibit both conduct disorders and antisocial personality disorder than females, there is a strong possibility that different pathways to development exist along gender lines. For example, although parental conflict and disharmony are often implicated in antisocial development, studies suggest that they predict antisocial behavior for women but not for men (Mulder, Wells, Joyce, & Bushnell, 1994). Further, the specific manner of expression of antisocial personality disorder seems influenced by gender as well: Men have been found to exhibit job problems, violence, and traffic offenses, whereas women were more likely to report relationship problems, job problems, and violence.

Because the gender role for women emphasizes a less assertive and more people-focused orientation, the term *relational aggression* has been coined to describe the behavior of females with antisocial personality disorder (Millon et al., 2004). Whereas men are believed to engage in direct acting-out behaviors (e.g., physical aggression), women express themselves by more indirect or passive means (e.g., spreading rumors or false gossip and rejecting others from their social group).

Children often copy the behaviors of a parent who socializes them into the values of the larger society. The parental influence on antisocial behaviors in children may be a result of traditional gender-role training. Males have traditionally received more encouragement to engage in aggressive behaviors than females, and antisocial patterns are more prevalent among men than among women. As gender roles change, one might reasonably expect that antisocial tendencies will increase among females and that mothers will play a greater role in the development of antisocial behaviors in children.

Cultural Values To be born and raised in the United States is to be exposed to the standards, beliefs, and values of U.S. society. One dominant value is that of rugged individualism, which is composed of two assumptions: (a) Healthy functioning is equated with individualism and independence, and (b) people can and should master and control their own lives and the universe (D. W. Sue & Sue, 2013). Striving, competition, and ability to manipulate the environment are considered pathways to success; achievements are measured by surpassing the attainment of others. In the extreme, this psychological orientation may cause or fuel the aggressive and violent behavior of people with antisocial personality disorder.

Other societies, such as those in some Asian countries, possess values and beliefs that are often at odds with individualistic values: Collectivism and interdependence are valued, concern is with development of the group rather than the self, and harmony with the universe is preferred over mastery of it. Some have observed that antisocial behavior (e.g., crime and violence) is less likely to occur in Japan and China than in the United States because of these countries' collectivistic orientation, in which harmony and relationship with others are valued (Ivey, D'Andrea, Ivey, & Simek-Morgan, 2007). Because traditional Asian values, for example, emphasize harmony, subtlety, and restraint of strong feelings, Asian American clients who seek therapy are less likely than their European American counterparts to evidence acting-out disorders (e.g., overt expressions of anger, physical aggression, verbal hostility, substance abuse, and criminal behavior; D. W. Sue & Sue, 2013). Thus it is clear that the sociocultural dimension is a powerful determinant in the etiology and manifestation of personality disorders.

Treatment of Antisocial Personality Disorder

Because people with antisocial personality disorder feel little anxiety, they are less motivated to change themselves or seek treatment. They are unlikely to see their behaviors as bad. If they do seek treatment, they may try to manipulate or con therapists. Thus, traditional treatment approaches, which require the genuine cooperation of the client, may be ineffective for antisocial personality disorder. Few treatment outcome studies have been conducted for this disorder.

It appears that successful treatment can occur only in a setting in which behavior can be controlled. That is, treatment programs may need to provide enough control that those with antisocial personality disorder cannot avoid confronting their inability to form close and intimate relationships and the effect of their behaviors on others. Such control is sometimes possible for psychopaths who are imprisoned for crimes or who, for one reason or another, are hospitalized. Intensive group therapy may then be initiated to help clients with antisocial personality disorder in the required confrontation.

Some behavior modification programs have been tried, especially with delinquents who behave in antisocial ways. The most useful treatments are skill based and behavioral (Meloy, 2001). Money and tokens that can be used to purchase items have been given as rewards to young people who show appropriate behaviors (e.g., discussion of personal problems, good study habits, punctuality, and prosocial and nondisruptive behaviors). Historically, this use of material rewards has been fairly effective in changing antisocial behaviors (Van Evra, 1983). Once the young people leave the treatment programs, however, they are likely to revert to antisocial behavior unless their families and peers help them maintain the appropriate behaviors.

Cognitive approaches have also been used. Individuals with antisocial personalities may be influenced by dysfunctional beliefs about themselves, the world, and the future, so their ability to anticipate and act on the possible negative

Mary Kate Denny/PhotoEdit

Treating Antisocial Behaviors

Peers and family are critically important in the treatment of youth with antisocial personality disorder and in maintaining progress made in treatment. Here, a group led by a peer counselor is exploring some of the issues troubling these young people. What would you do as a peer counselor to help these youth open up and talk about their own problems?

outcomes of their behaviors varies. Beck, Freeman, and their associates (1990) have advocated that the therapist build rapport with the client, attempting to guide the client away from thinking only in terms of self-interest and immediate gratification and toward higher levels of thinking. These higher levels would include, for example, recognizing the effects of one's behaviors on others and developing a sense of responsibility. Because cognitive and behavioral approaches assume that antisocial behaviors are learned, treatment programs may target these behaviors by setting rules and enforcing consequences for rule violations, substituting new behaviors for undesirable ones, and learning to anticipate consequences of behaviors (Meloy, 2001).

Current treatment options for people with antisocial personality disorder are somewhat ineffective. Since longitudinal studies show that the prevalence of this disorder diminishes with age as individuals become more aware of the social and interpersonal maladaptiveness of their behavior, new strategies should focus on antisocial youth amenable to treatment (K. A. Phillips & Gunderson, 1999). Treatment programs should also broaden the base of intervention to involve not only young clients but also their families and peers. Because people with antisocial personality disorder may seek thrills (Big Ts), they may respond to intervention programs that provide the physical and mental stimulation they need (Farley, 1986).

CHECKPOINT REVIEW

1. Describe how the biological, psychological, social, and sociocultural dimensions explain antisocial personality disorders.
2. What is the relationship between underarousal, learning, and punishment in explaining antisocial personality disorder?
3. Why is treating people with antisocial personality disorder so difficult? What has been found most effective?

Personality Disorder Trait Specified

An exclusive categorical approach has limitations because it uses an all-or-none method of classification (Reed, 2010). In the larger context, it means that a person either has or does not have a personality disorder; it fails to recognize that people may possess varying amounts of a characteristic trait. Further, it is based on arbitrary diagnostic thresholds and does not recognize the continuous nature of personality traits (Westen et al., 2010). In reality, people may have a personality trait or disorder in varying degrees or at various times. We all exhibit some of the traits that characterize personality disorders—for example, suspiciousness, dependency, sensitivity to rejection, or compulsiveness.

For this reason, many investigators (Bienenfeld, 2007; Skodol & Bender, 2009; Widiger, 2007) prefer to view personality disorders as the extremes of underlying dimensions of normal personality traits. They argue that dimensions such as extraversion (sociability), agreeableness (nurturance), neuroticism, conscientiousness, and openness to experience may be used to describe personality disorders (Costa & McCrae, 2005). Because people differ in the extent to which they possess a trait, a clinician may have trouble deciding when a client exhibits a trait to a degree that could be considered a symptom of a disorder (Millon et al., 2004). For example, rather than considering the existence of a schizoid personality disorder in a client, it is more accurate to describe that person as possessing varying degrees of personality traits such as social withdrawal, social detachment, intimacy avoidance, and so forth. These can be assessed on a scaled continuum. Even with disorders that seem to better fit a type category (high validity and reliability), the DSM-5 uses a 5-point degree of match between the description of a personality disorder type and the client (see the Controversy box).

Another argument against a solely categorical approach to assessing personality psychopathology lies in the issue of diagnostic accuracy. Although diagnosticians show excellent reliability in diagnosing *whether* a particular client has a personality disorder, they show much lower reliability when they must classify clients as to the precise *type* of personality disorder (Costa & McCrae, 2005; Reed, 2010; Zimmerman et al., 2005). Co-occurrence is common in that a person diagnosed with one personality disorder often meets criteria for others as well (Rothman, Ahn, Sanislow, & Kim, 2009; Widiger, 2007). Because people can have more than one type of personality disorder, the problems in accurately distinguishing these disorders are formidable. Moreover, although the distinction between personality disorders and other disorders is valid, many individuals have symptoms that do not neatly characterize a particular disorder and that overlap with different disorders (Westen et al., 2010).

The DSM-5 Work Groups (2012) use an overarching dimensional diagnostic system of five domain traits for assessing other personality disorders. The use of the word *trait* refers to a specific personality characteristic possessed by an individual (distractibility, anxiousness, perfectionism, etc.). Traits may be organized around a *domain*, which represents a higher order or superordinate grouping of related traits like introversion (includes traits of social withdrawal, social detachment, intimacy avoidance, etc.). The term *dimension* simply refers to a scaled continuum that can be used to measure (match) the degree to whether a person possesses certain traits. The five domain traits are outlined in Table 14.5 and briefly described. The existence of one or more of these domain traits that impair self or interpersonal functioning is sufficient to indicate a personality disorder.

AP Images

Eluding Capture: Aided by a Personality Disorder?

It took many years for authorities to track down and arrest Ted Kaczynski, the Unabomber, who killed many people over an 18-year period. Formerly a math professor at the University of California, Berkeley, Kaczynski is believed to have a personality disorder and to have eluded capture because of his hermitlike existence. He was a loner and did not seem interested in socializing with people. He was finally arrested in his isolated cabin, where he had lived alone for many years.

TABLE 14.5 DSM-5 Domain Traits

1. *Negative affectivity* refers to a wide range of negative emotions—such as anxiety, depression, guilt, shame, worry, and so forth—and the behavioral or interpersonal manifestations of those experiences. The specific traits associated with this domain are
   - emotional lability, anxiousness, separation insecurity, perseveration, submissiveness, hostility, depressivity, suspiciousness, and restricted affectivity.
2. *Detachment* involves withdrawal from others, whether the relationships are with intimate acquaintances or strangers. It includes restricted or limited affective experiences and expressions, as well as limited hedonic capacity (i.e., an inability to experience pleasure or joys in life). The specific traits associated with this domain are
   - restricted affectivity, depressivity, suspiciousness, withdrawal, anhedonia, and intimacy avoidance.
3. *Antagonism* refers to negative feelings and behaviors toward others and a corresponding exaggerated sense of self-importance. The specific traits associated with this domain are
   - manipulativeness, deceitfulness, grandiosity, attention seeking, callousness, and hostility.
4. *Disinhibition* involves seeking immediate gratification, orientation to the present, and response primarily to immediate or current internal and external stimuli. The past (past learning) and the future (future consequences) appear to be minimally important in motivation or behavior. Compulsivity is the opposite end of this domain. The specific traits associated with this domain are
   - irresponsibility, impulsivity, distractibility, risk taking, and rigid perfectionism or lack of it.
5. *Psychoticism* includes behaviors and cognitions (perception, content, and belief) considered odd, unusual, or bizarre. The specific traits associated with this domain are
   - unusual beliefs and experiences, egocentricity, and cognitive and perceptual dysregulation.

CONTROVERSY:

What Domain Traits Best Apply to This Man?

The following case study describes the behavior of a teenager, Roy W. He exhibits some very prominent personality traits that appear bothersome. After reading the case, look closely at the five domains in Table 14.5 to determine which domain(s) you believe to be applicable. Use the following scale to ascertain the degree of match between the descriptions given and the behaviors of Roy W.: 0 = very little or not at all, 1 = mildly descriptive, 2 = moderately descriptive, and 3 = extremely descriptive.

For Further Consideration:

1. A rating of moderately or extremely descriptive for one or more of the trait domains would suggest a personality disorder. What are your conclusions?
2. Which of the two trait domains are most applicable to Roy?
3. Does Roy better fit a diagnosis of personality disorder trait specified or a personality disorder type? Why?

Case Study

Roy W. was an 18-year-old high school senior who was referred by the court for diagnosis and evaluation. He was arrested for stealing a car, something he had done on several other occasions. The court agreed with Roy's mother that he needed evaluation and perhaps psychotherapy. During his interview with the psychologist, Roy was articulate, relaxed, and even witty. He said that stealing was wrong but that none of the cars he stole was ever damaged. The last theft occurred because he needed transportation to a beer party (which was located only a mile from his home) and his leg was sore from playing basketball. When the psychologist asked Roy how he got along with young women, he grinned and said that he was very outgoing and could easily "hustle" them. He then related the following incident:

"About three months ago, I was pulling out of the school parking lot real fast and accidentally sideswiped this other car. The girl who was driving it started to scream at me. God, there was only a small dent on her fender! Anyway, we exchanged names and addresses and I apologized for the accident. When I filled out the accident report later, I said that it was her car that pulled out from the other side and hit my car. How do you like that? Anyway, when she heard about my claim that it was her fault, she had her old man call me. He said that his daughter had witnesses to the accident and that I could be arrested. Bull, he was just trying to bluff me. But I gave him a sob story—about how my parents were ready to get a divorce, how poor we were, and the trouble I would get into if they found out about the accident. I apologized for lying and told him I could fix the dent. Luckily he never checked with my folks for the real story. Anyway, I went over to look at the girl's car. I really didn't have any idea of how to fix that old heap, so I said I had to wait a couple of weeks to get some tools for the repair job.

"Meanwhile, I started to talk to the girl. Gave her my sob story, told her how nice I thought her folks and home were. We started to date and I took her out three times. Then one night I laid her. The crummy thing was that she told her folks about it. Can you imagine that? Anyway, her old man called and told me never to get near his precious little thing again. She's actually a slut.

"At least I didn't have to fix her old heap. I know I shouldn't lie, but can you blame me? People make such a big thing out of nothing."

CHECKPOINT REVIEW

1. In what ways is the use of domain traits to describe personality disorders important?
2. List the five domains and briefly describe them.
3. How do you determine whether a domain trait is sufficiently strong to warrant a personality diagnosis?

Summary

1 Can one's personality be pathological?

- Yes. Personality disorders are enduring, inflexible, longstanding personality traits or types that cause impairment or adaptive failure in the person's everyday life. They are usually extreme and manifest in adolescence and continue into adulthood.

2 What criteria are used to assess personality disorders?

- Impairments in self and interpersonal functioning are used to diagnose a personality disorder. They must meet criteria for a personality disorder type or be sufficiently extreme in one of the five personality domain traits as to cause impairment.
- Personality types or traits must also be relatively stable across time and consistent across situations, not be better explained by norms of the person's culture, and not be due to a physiological or medical condition.

3 Are there certain personality disorder types?

- Yes. Research and therapeutic findings support the existence of six types of personality disorders: schizotypal, borderline, avoidant, narcissistic, obsessive-compulsive, and antisocial.

4 How does the multipath model explain antisocial personality disorder?

- Because personality is at the core of the disorder, etiological explanations focus on factors that influence personality. Genetics and neurobiological factors (e.g., underarousal of the ANS and low anxiety), psychodynamics, cognitive and learning formulations, social or parental and family environments, and sociocultural factors (e.g., gender, race, and culture) all seem to contribute in a highly complex fashion.

5 What types of therapy are used in treating antisocial personality disorder?

- Traditional treatment approaches are not particularly effective with antisocial personality disorder. It may be that successful treatment can occur only in a setting in which behavior can be controlled so that those with the disorder cannot avoid confronting their inability to form close and intimate relationships and the effect of their behaviors on others.

6 What personality traits are important in determining pathology?

- Increasingly, personality disorders are being viewed less categorically but rather in a dimensional manner (e.g., as extremes on a continuum of normal personality traits).
- The five domain traits used to determine personality psychopathology are negative affectivity, detachment, antagonism, disinhibition versus compulsivity, and psychoticism. Numerous specific traits are associated with each domain.

Key Terms

personality disorder 382
schizotypal type 386
borderline type 388
avoidant type 390
narcissistic type 391
obsessive-compulsive type (OCT) 393
antisocial type 394

Media Resources

Psychology CourseMate

Access an interactive e-Book and chapter-specific interactive learning tools, including:

- flashcards
- quizzes
- videos

and more in your Psychology CourseMate.

Go to **CengageBrain.com.**

Jaimie Duplass/Shutterstock.com

15 Disorders of Childhood and Adolescence

CHAPTER OUTLINE

"No, I Won't"

Ten-year-old Cassie's parents are frustrated by Cassie's continuing defiance and constant arguments. Today Cassie is refusing to come out of her bedroom to meet friends and relatives attending her mother's surprise birthday party. She shouts at her parents, "You can't make me do anything!"

Diagnosis: oppositional defiant disorder

"Sit Still and Pay Attention"

Sitting in the psychologist's office, the mother explains that ever since he was in preschool, her son Tyrone (now 10) has disrupted classroom instruction. He has difficulty concentrating, is often reprimanded for talking, and is failing most subjects. Throughout the session, Tyrone fidgets in his seat and interrupts his mother.

Diagnosis: attention-deficit/hyperactivity disorder

"All Alone"

Five-year-old Ahmed sits apart from the other children, spinning the wheels of a toy truck and humming aloud as if to mimic the sound. Ahmed seems to live in a world of his own, interacting with those around him as if they are inanimate objects.

Diagnosis: autism spectrum disorder

FOCUS QUESTIONS

1 What internalizing disorders occur in childhood and adolescence?

2 What are the characteristics of externalizing disorders?

3 What are neurodevelopmental disorders, and what are their characteristics?

In this chapter, we discuss childhood and adolescent psychological disorders. Accurate assessment of childhood disorders requires understanding of normal child development and child **temperament**, as well as knowledge about psychiatric disorders. Familiarity with **child psychopathology** (how psychological disorders manifest in children and adolescents) is essential because characteristics that signify mental illness in adults often occur in normally developing children. Additionally, symptoms of some disorders are quite different in children compared to adults.

Anxiety about a parent leaving, oppositional behavior, or high levels of activity combined with a short attention span are viewed quite differently depending on the age of the child. These behaviors would be considered rather typical in a 2- or 3-year-old, but would be of concern in a 10-year-old. Additionally, children differ in their natural temperament; some are cautious and slow to warm to new situations, whereas others are energetic, strong willed, and intense in their reactions. To determine if a child has an actual disorder, clinicians consider the child's age and developmental level as well as environmental factors, asking questions such as: Is the child's behavior significantly different from that of other children the same age? Are the symptoms likely to subside as the child matures? Are the behaviors present in most contexts or only in particular settings? Are the symptoms occurring because adults are expecting too much or too little of the child? Diagnoses are approached cautiously; the effects of "labeling" on a child's future development are weighed against the knowledge that untreated disorders can develop into lifelong patterns that create ongoing distress.

Childhood disorders are not rare; about 1 in 5 children has a serious emotional or behavioral problem (Koppelman, 2004). Face-to-face diagnostic assessment of a representative sample of more than 10,000 U.S. adolescents (ages 13–18) found that almost half had experienced significant mental health concerns. Nearly one third (31.9 percent) reported symptoms of an anxiety disorder, 19.1 percent demonstrated a behavior disorder, and 14 percent reported symptoms of a depressive or bipolar disorder. Twenty-two percent of the sample reported severe impairment due to their symptoms. Depressive and bipolar disorder symptoms caused the greatest distress. (See Table 15.1 for prevalence,

TABLE 15.1 Lifetime Prevalence of Psychiatric Disorders in Youth Ages 13–18

DISORDER	FEMALES (%)	MALES (%)	PERCENTAGE WITH SEVERE IMPAIRMENT
Generalized anxiety disorder	3.0	1.5	30
Social phobia	11.2	7.0	14
Specific phobia	22.1	15.7	3
Panic disorder	2.6	2.0	9
Post-traumatic stress disorder	8.0	2.3	30
Depression	15.9	7.7	74
Bipolar disorder	3.3	2.6	89
Attention-deficit/hyperactivity disorder	4.2	13.0	48
Oppositional defiant disorder	11.3	13.9	52
Conduct disorder	5.8	7.9	32

Source: Merikangas, He, Burstein, Swanson, et al. (2010)

temperament innate emotional predisposition or personality traits

child psychopathology the emotional and behavioral manifestation of psychological disorders in children and adolescents

CONTROVERSY:

Are We Overmedicating Children?

Many medications are prescribed to treat childhood disorders, including tranquilizers, stimulants, and antipsychotics (Parens & Johnston, 2010). As with adults, medication prescriptions for children and adolescents have increased dramatically (Mojtabai & Olfson, 2010). Controversy continues regarding overdiagnosis of some childhood disorders, the "quick fix" nature of medication, and the tendency to use medication without first attempting psychotherapy or other interventions (S. M. Berman, Kuczenski, McCracken, & London, 2009). Additionally, many medications prescribed for youth have only been tested on adults; thus, there is insufficient information regarding how these medications might affect the extensive brain development that occurs throughout childhood and adolescence (S. E. Kern, 2009).

Many believe that medication should be considered only after comprehensive diagnostic evaluation and implementation of alternative interventions. Certainly if medication is prescribed, it is important to educate parents about the specific symptoms being treated and the plan for monitoring progress and possible side effects (American Academy of Child and Adolescent Psychiatry, 2009). How can we determine if medications are prescribed too freely and if their use with children is safe? How can we ensure that adequate assessment and consideration of nonpharmaceutical interventions occur before medication is prescribed?

severity, and gender comparisons of specific disorders.) Females reported more depression and post-traumatic stress disorder, whereas males demonstrated more inattention and hyperactivity symptoms; more than 40 percent of those surveyed met diagnostic criteria for more than one disorder (Merikangas, He, Burstein, Swanson, et al., 2010). Like adults, children and adolescents often have coexisting disorders (Yoo, Brown, & Luthar, 2009). Unfortunately, in a national sample of 6,483 adolescents (ages 13–18), almost two thirds of those with mental illness received no treatment (Merikangas, He, Burstein, Swendsen, et al., 2011). Of particular concern are the low treatment rates for youth experiencing major depression; this lack of intervention is particularly pronounced for African American, Latino/Hispanic American, and Asian American adolescents (J. R. Cummings & Druss, 2011).

Sociocultural factors can significantly affect definitions and characteristics of childhood disorders. For example, in Thailand, where parenting techniques prolong dependence and slow psychological maturation, children display problems involving dependence and immaturity that are not seen in the United States.

Source: Weisz, Weiss, Suwanlert, & Chaiyasit (2006)

Psychiatric disorders are diagnosed only when symptoms cause significant impairment in daily functioning over an extended period of time. We begin our discussion with internalizing (i.e., emotions directed inward) and externalizing (i.e., disruptive) disorders. We conclude with a look at neurodevelopmental disorders (childhood disorders involving impaired neurological development). The field of child psychopathology is extensive. In this chapter, we address characteristics, etiology, and treatment of some of the most significant disorders.

Internalizing Disorders of Childhood

Disorders involving emotional symptoms that are directed inward are referred to as **internalizing disorders**. As with adults, children and adolescents with internalizing disorders display heightened reactions to trauma, stressors, or negative events as well as difficulty regulating their emotions. Anxiety and depressive disorders are prevalent in early life (see Table 15.1) and are of particular concern because they often lead to substance use and abuse and suicide (Hussong, Jones, Stein, Baucom, & Boeding, 2011; O'Neil, Conner, & Kendall, 2011; Substance Abuse and Mental Health Services Administration, 2012). Certain patterns among youth with internalizing disorders, such as abrupt changes in behavior or self-destructive or sexualized behavior, can signal the need for assessment of possible sexual abuse (Floyed, Hirsh, Greenbaum, & Simon, 2011).

internalizing disorders conditions involving emotional symptoms directed inward

Anxiety, Trauma, and Stressor-Related Disorders in Early Life

Anxiety, trauma, and stressor-related disorders in childhood or adolescence typically result from a combination of innate reactivity and exposure to environmental influences. Anxiety disorders are the most prevalent mental health disorder in childhood and adolescence (Rockhill et al., 2010). Among the 32 percent of adolescents who have experienced an anxiety disorder, specific phobias (19 percent) and social phobia (9 percent) are most common (Merikangas, He, Burstein, Swanson, et al., 2010). Specific phobias often begin in early to middle childhood, whereas social phobias typically begin in early to middle adolescence (Rapee, Schniering, & Hudson, 2009). Social phobia can be an extremely disabling condition that persists into adulthood if untreated (Burstein, He, et al., 2011).

Childhood anxiety can significantly affect academic, social, and interpersonal functioning (Sakolsky & Birmaher, 2008) and can lead to adult anxiety disorders (Essex, Klein, Slattery, Goldsmith, & Kalin, 2010). An inhibited, fearful temperament increases risk for anxiety disorders in childhood, particularly when exacerbated by overprotective or controlling parenting practices, low parental warmth, or perceived parental rejection (Bayer et al., 2011; Lindhout et al., 2009). Anxiety disorders specific to childhood include:

- **school phobia**—fear of attending school;
- **separation anxiety disorder**—severe distress about leaving home, being alone, or being separated from a parent; and
- **selective mutism**—consistent failure to speak in certain situations.

Children with these disorders display exaggerated autonomic responses and are apprehensive in new situations, preferring to stay at home or in other familiar environments (Kossowsky, Wilhelm, Roth, & Schneider, 2012). Childhood phobias and anxiety disorders are most effectively treated with individual, group, and family-focused cognitive-behavioral therapy (W. K. Silverman, Pina, & Viswesvaran, 2008).

Post-Traumatic Stress Disorder in Early Life The effects of trauma and resultant post-traumatic stress disorder (PTSD) can be particularly distressing in childhood, as illustrated in the following case study.

Case Study

Several months after witnessing her father seriously injure her mother during a domestic dispute, Jenna remained withdrawn; she spoke little and rarely played with her toys. Although a protection order prevented her father from returning home, Jenna became startled whenever she heard the door open and frequently woke up screaming "Stop!" She refused to enter the kitchen, the site of the violent assault.

Youth with PTSD experience recurrent, distressing memories of a shocking experience. The trauma that precipitates PTSD can include threats of or direct experience with death, serious injury, or sexual violation. Witnessing or hearing about the victimization of others can also result in PTSD, especially when a primary caregiver is involved. Memories of the event may entail (a) distressing dreams, (b) intense physiological or psychological reactions to thoughts or cues associated with the event and avoidance of such cues, (c) episodes of playacting

school phobia fear of attending school

separation anxiety disorder severe distress about leaving home, being alone, or being separated from a parent

selective mutism consistent failure to speak in certain situations

the event (sometimes without apparent distress), or (d) dissociative reactions, in which the child appears to re-experience the trauma or appears unaware of present surroundings. Children who have been traumatized often display social withdrawal, diminished positive affect, and disinterest in activities they previously enjoyed. Behavioral evidence of PTSD includes angry, aggressive behavior or temper tantrums; difficulty sleeping or concentrating; and exaggerated startle response or vigilance for possible threats (DSM-5 Work Groups, 2012). Lifetime prevalence of PTSD among adolescents is 8 percent for girls and 2.3 percent for boys; approximately one third report severe PTSD symptoms (Merikangas, He, Burstein, Swanson, et al., 2010). Trauma-focused cognitive-behavioral therapies have proven to be effective in treating childhood PTSD (Nixon, Sterk, & Pearce, 2012; W. K. Silverman, Ortiz, et al., 2008).

Depressive Disorders in Early Life

Depressive disorders affect many youth, particularly girls and older adolescents (Merikangas, He, Burstein, Swanson, et al., 2010). Children are especially vulnerable to environmental factors because they lack the maturity and skills to deal with stressors. Conditions such as childhood physical or sexual abuse, parental mental or physical illness, or loss of an attachment figure can increase vulnerability to depression (D. G. Rosenthal, Learned, Liu, & Weitzman, 2012). Like adults, youth with depressive disorders have more negative self-concepts and are more likely to engage in self-blame and self-criticism. Early onset of depressive symptoms tends to predict a more chronic and severe course (Merikangas, He, Burstein, Swanson, et al., 2010).

Evidence-based treatment for depression in youth includes individual, group, or school-based cognitive-behavioral therapy; parent involvement and programs focused on building resilience based on positive psychology principles are also beneficial (David-Ferndon & Kaslow, 2008). Intervention is critical because of the strong association between depressive disorders and adolescent suicidal ideation and suicide attempts (Chronis-Tuscano et al., 2010). However, concerns about selective serotonin reuptake inhibitors (SSRIs) increasing suicidality led to U.S. Food and Drug Administration warnings regarding the use of certain antidepressants for treatment of depression in youth (Hammad, Laughren, & Racoosin, 2006). Subsequent data analysis has indicated that although SSRIs may have only a moderate effect on milder depressive symptoms, they appear superior to some cognitive-behavioral therapies, especially in the first months of treatment, and that the benefits of using SSRIs (particularly fluoxetine) may outweigh the risk of increased suicidality, especially among youth who are severely depressed (Bridge et al., 2007; Vitiello, 2009). Best practices support careful monitoring of suicidality in all children and adolescents who are depressed, with particular attention to those taking antidepressants (J. M. Reid et al., 2010).

Nonsuicidal Self Injury

Case Study

For the past year, Maria has been secretly cutting her forearms and thighs with a razor blade. She has tried to stop, but when she feels anxious or depressed she thinks of the razor blade and the relief she experiences once she feels the cutting. She does not understand why she cuts; she just knows it is how she copes when she feels overwhelmed. The more life hurts, the more she cuts.

FOX via Getty Images

Demi Lovato

Singer and actress Demi Lovato engaged in disordered eating and nonsuicidal self-injury during early adolescence in an effort to cope with her emotions and in response to bullying from classmates. When receiving treatment for these conditions, it was discovered that her mood swings were also related to undiagnosed bipolar disorder.

Nonsuicidal self injury (NSSI) is a relatively new phenomenon that involves the induction of bleeding, bruising, or pain by means of intentional, self-inflicted injury. Youth who engage in NSSI cut, burn, stab, hit, or excessively rub themselves to the point of pain and injury, but without suicidal intent. Intense negative affect or cognitions (e.g., depressive, anxious, angry, or self-critical thoughts) and a preoccupation with engaging in self-harm (often accompanied by a desire to resist the impulse to self-injure) typically precede episodes of NSSI. Those engaging in NSSI often expect that it will improve their mood, and many report a respite from uncomfortable feelings or a temporary sense of calm and well-being following self-harm (DSM-5 Work Groups, 2012). Two thirds of those who engage in NSSI begin the behavior in adolescence. NSSI occurs with similar frequency in both genders, although males are more likely to hit or burn themselves, while females more frequently cut themselves. It is estimated that approximately 14–17 percent of adolescents and young adults have engaged in self-injury at least once; only a minority engage in repeated self-injury. Those who engage in repeated NSSI tend to be highly self-critical and have difficulty expressing their emotions (Klonsky & Glenn, 2011). NSSI is associated with increased risk of attempted suicide (Kerr, Muehlenkamp, & Turner, 2010), particularly among those who have more depressive symptoms, lower self-esteem, and limited parental support (Brausch & Gutierrez, 2010). Although adolescent self-harming behavior usually resolves spontaneously, underlying emotional issues such as depression or anxiety often persist (Moran et al., 2012). Treatment for those who engage in repeated NSSI often includes teaching problem-solving, coping, and emotional regulation skills as well as improving interpersonal relationship skills (Klonsky & Muehlenkamp, 2007); however, there is a need for additional research regarding effective interventions (Ougrin, Tranah, Leigh, Taylor, & Asarnow, 2012), especially given the increased suicide risk associated with the disorder.

Pediatric Bipolar Disorder

Careful monitoring of suicidality is also important in **pediatric bipolar disorder (PBD)**, a debilitating disorder that parallels the mood variability, depressive episodes, and significant departure from the individual's typical functioning characteristic of adult bipolar disorder (Algorta et al., 2011). PBD is illustrated in the following case study.

Case Study

Anna was a fairly cooperative, engaging child throughout her early years. However, around her 10th birthday, her behavior changed significantly. At times, she experienced periods of extreme moodiness, depression, and high irritability; on other occasions, she displayed boundless energy and talked incessantly, often moving rapidly from one topic to another as she described different ideas and plans. During her energetic periods, she could go for several weeks with minimal sleep.

nonsuicidal self injury (NSSI) intentional, self-inflicted injury without suicidal intent; can also involve a preoccupation with engaging in self-harm

pediatric bipolar disorder (PBD) a childhood disorder involving depressive and energized episodes similar to the mood swings seen in adult bipolar disorder

Youth with PBD typically display (a) recurring depression, (b) rapid mood changes, and (c) distinct periods of abnormally elevated mood involving diminished need for sleep, increased activity, distractibility, talkativeness, and inflated self-esteem (Table 15.2; Stringaris et al., 2010). Periods of uncharacteristic irritability and depression alternate with exaggerated pleasure-seeking and goal-directed

DISORDERS CHART DISRUPTIVE MOOD DYSREGULATION DISORDER AND PEDIATRIC BIPOLAR DISORDER

TABLE 15.2

Disorder	Symptoms	Prevalence	Age of Onset	Course
Disruptive mood dysregulation disorder (DMDD)	• Recurrent episodes of temper, including verbal rage or physical aggression • Anger response that is exaggerated in intensity and duration • Typically irritable, angry, or sad mood	3%; more frequently diagnosed in boys	Symptoms are present before age 10 and may be present in early childhood	May improve with maturity; may evolve into a depressive disorder
Pediatric bipolar disorder	• Distinct periods of abnormally elevated mood (i.e., manic or hypomanic symptoms) • Periodic mood and behavioral changes (e.g., irritability, depression, increased activity, distractibility, or talkativeness; inflated self-esteem)	3%; affects boys and girls equally	Onset is around age 10, about 5 years later than disruptive mood dysregulation disorder	Poor prognosis; often evolves into a chronic psychiatric disorder

Source: Brotman, Schmajuk, et al. (2006); DSM-5 Work Groups (2012); Merikangas, He, Burstein, Swanson, et al. (2010); S. E. Meyer et al. (2009)

activity during periods of **hypomania** (Dickstein, Nelson, et al., 2007). Males and females have equal incidence of PBD; lifetime prevalence in adolescents is estimated to be 3 percent, with 89 percent of those with PBD reporting severe impairment (Merikangas, He, Burstein, Swanson, et al., 2010). Emergency room visits and hospitalizations are common for youth with PBD (Berry, Heaton, & Kelton, 2011).

Youth with PBD often demonstrate rapid-cycling of moods combined with neurocognitively based difficulties in processing emotional stimuli and regulating behavior and social-emotional functioning (Olsavsky et al., 2012; H. R. Rosen & Rich, 2010). They also show elevated neurological responsiveness to emotional stimuli, reduced volume in the amygdala (Kalmar et al., 2009), and other brain abnormalities (A. James et al., 2011). Symptoms of PBD can develop gradually or emerge suddenly. PBD often occurs in families with a history of the illness and is likely to evolve into adult bipolar disorder or another chronic psychiatric disorder (B. I. Goldstein, 2012). Medications used with adult bipolar disorder are often combined with therapy and psychosocial intervention to treat PBD (Parens & Johnston, 2010); however, there is concern about the safety of lithium and antipsychotic medications for children and adolescents (T. Thomas, Stansifer, & Findling, 2011).

Attachment Disorders

Infants and children raised in stressful environments that lack predictable parenting and nurturing sometimes demonstrate difficulties with emotional attachments and social relationships (Gleason et al., 2011). Disrupted attachments can manifest in the inhibited responding seen in *reactive attachment disorder* or the excessive attention seeking seen in *disinhibited social engagement disorder*. These attachment disorders are diagnosed only when symptoms are apparent before age 5 and when early circumstances prevent the child from forming stable attachments. Situations that can disrupt attachment include frequent changes in primary caregiver, persistent neglect of physical or psychological safety (including physical abuse), and ongoing failure to provide care, stimulation, or affection.

Infants or children with **reactive attachment disorder (RAD)** appear to have little trust that their needs will be attended to and do not readily seek or respond to comfort, attention, or nurturing. They appear to use avoidance or ambivalence as a psychological defense, have great difficulty with age-appropriate response to

hypomania a milder form of mania involving increased energy and activity, sometimes combined with an elevated or irritable mood

reactive attachment disorder (RAD) an attachment disorder characterized by inhibited, avoidant social behaviors and reluctance to seek or respond to attention or nurturing

FOCUS ON RESILIENCE

Enhancing Resilience in Youth

Early life experiences, according to research, are critical in the development of mental illness. Can modifying a child's environment increase resilience, especially in children who are genetically or environmentally at risk? In other words, are there steps that can be taken to help decrease the likelihood that a child will develop a mental disorder in childhood or later in life? The answer is yes. Resilience occurs when human adaptive systems are operating optimally—when brain functioning has not been compromised; when children experience social, emotional, and physical security; and when the environment supports their capacity for self-efficacy and effective problem solving (Masten, 2009).

Some interventions increase resilience by reducing potential harm to the developing child. For example, prenatal care and the avoidance of neurotoxins help eliminate conditions that interfere with optimal brain functioning, thus reducing the risk of neurodevelopmental disorders. Other interventions increase resilience by reducing environmental stress—thus providing both biological and psychological benefits to young children (S. E. Taylor, 2011). For example, intervening with parents experiencing mental illness or engaged in child maltreatment can improve behavioral or emotional outcomes in their children (Cicchetti, 2010; D. G. Rosenthal et al., 2012). Similarly, early intervention when children are experiencing behavioral or emotional difficulties can prevent the downward emotional spiral seen with many disorders (Sapienza & Masten, 2011). With support, even children who have been exposed to trauma can experience post-traumatic growth (e.g., increased sense of personal strength, spiritual changes, or enhanced connection with others) in response to their experiences (Meyerson, Grant, Carter, & Kilmer, 2011). Given the epidemic of mental illness, continued research regarding the best methods for and developmental timing of interventions for promoting resilience in the face of adversity is a global priority (Masten & Narayan, 2012).

Resilience can also be enhanced by fostering competence and healthy development throughout childhood. Such an approach has the potential to promote positive developmental cascades; that is, increased personal competence not only provides the basis for coping with adversity but also promotes other positive outcomes (Masten, 2011). For example, stimulating home and preschool environments not only enhance cognitive development but also allow children to develop a sense of mastery and optimism. Additionally, positive attachment experiences, quality parenting, and ongoing supportive relationships with positive role models allow children to develop interpersonal trust and coping skills (Masten, 2009). Knowing how to solve problems or regulate emotions allows children to reduce biological reactivity in response to stress or adversity (S. E. Taylor, 2011). Additionally, promotion of a healthy lifestyle (e.g., ensuring adequate sleep, nutrition, and exercise; monitoring television and computer use) can serve an important role in enhancing physical and psychological resilience (M. E. O'Connell, Boat, & Warner, 2009). One thing is clear—when basic physical, social, and emotional needs are met, youth can develop the strengths that allow them not only to overcome adversity but also to flourish.

PhotoDisc

or initiation of social or emotional interactions, and often behave in a very inhibited, watchful, or avoidant manner, even with family and caregivers. Children with RAD often show limited positive emotion and may demonstrate irritability, sadness, or fearfulness when interacting with adults (DSM-5 Work Groups, 2012).

In stark contrast, children with **disinhibited social engagement disorder (DSED)** socialize effortlessly but indiscriminately, and readily become superficially "attached" to strangers or casual acquaintances. They easily approach and interact with unfamiliar adults in an overly familiar manner (both verbally and physically) and demonstrate such eagerness for interpersonal contact that they venture away from caregivers. Children with DSED often have a history of harsh punishment or inconsistent parenting in addition to emotional neglect and limited attachment opportunities (DSM-5 Work Groups, 2012). Children who are exposed to

disinhibited social engagement disorder (DSED) an attachment disorder characterized by indiscriminate, superficial attachments and desperation for interpersonal contact

maltreatment or maternal psychiatric hospitalizations are particularly vulnerable to DSED (Lyons-Ruth, Bureau, Riley, & Atlas-Corbett, 2009).

The course of these disorders depends on the severity of the social deprivation, abuse, neglect, or disruptions in caregiving, as well as subsequent events in the child's life. Symptoms of RAD often disappear if children are provided an opportunity for predictable caretaking and nurturance, whereas symptoms of DSED are more persistent (Zeanah & Gleason, 2010). Issues of mistrust and difficulties with intimate relationships may, in some cases, continue into adulthood. Once RAD or DSED is identified, therapeutic support can focus on building emotional security (Hornor, 2008). Effective intervention includes providing a stable, nurturing environment and opportunities to develop interpersonal trust and social-relational skills. It should be noted that many children raised under difficult circumstances do not show signs of these disorders.

CHECKPOINT REVIEW

1. Why is it important to intervene early with internalizing disorders?
2. Compare and contract RAD and DSED.
3. What is nonsuicidal self injury?

Externalizing Disorders of Childhood

Externalizing disorders (sometimes called *disruptive behavior disorders*) include disruptive mood dysregulation disorder, oppositional defiant disorder, and conduct disorder—conditions associated with symptoms that are socially disturbing and distressing to others. Parenting a child with externalizing behaviors can be challenging and can result in negative parent–child interactions, high family stress, and negative feelings about parenting; this can further exacerbate behavioral difficulties. Although early intervention can help interrupt the negative course of these disorders, diagnosing disruptive behaviors can be controversial, because it is difficult to distinguish externalizing disorders from one another and from the defiance and noncompliance that can typically occur during childhood and adolescence. Diagnosing externalizing disorders requires a pattern of behavior that is (a) atypical for the child's gender, age, and developmental level; (b) persistent (occurring consistently for at least 1 year); and (c) severe enough to cause significant impairment in social, academic, or vocational functioning.

Disruptive Mood Dysregulation Disorder

Case Study

As an infant and toddler, Juan was irritable and difficult to please. Temper tantrums, often involving attempts to hit his parents, occurred multiple times daily. Juan's parents had hoped he would outgrow this behavior; but now 8, Juan is still "grumpy" and has continued temper outbursts in many settings.

externalizing disorders disruptive behavior disorders associated with symptoms that are socially disturbing and distressing to others.

disruptive mood dysregulation disorder (DMDD) a childhood disorder involving chronic irritability and significantly exaggerated anger reactions

Disruptive mood dysregulation disorder (DMDD) is characterized by chronic irritability and severe mood dysregulation, including recurrent episodes of temper triggered by common childhood stressors (e.g., interpersonal conflict, being denied a request). Anger reactions (e.g., verbal rage and physical aggression toward people and property) are significantly exaggerated in both intensity and duration. DMDD is considered a depressive disorder; although behavioral symptoms are directed outwards, they are reflective of an irritable, angry, or sad mood state. Although behavior patterns associated with DMDD often begin in early childhood, this diagnosis is not made until a child is 6 years of age (DSM-5 Work Groups, 2012). This age requirement ensures that diagnosis is not based on the erratic moods associated with early childhood (e.g., "the terrible 2s"). The pervasive negative affect associated with DMDD is predictive of later depressive and anxiety disorders (Leibenluft, 2011). Clinicians making a diagnosis of DMDD need to rule out PBD, due to the overlapping symptoms involving depression and mood changes (see Table 15.2); this differential diagnosis is important because interventions for PBD are quite different from those for DMDD (Dickstein, Towbin, et al., 2009; Jairam, Prabhuswamy, & Dullur, 2012).

Oppositional Defiant Disorder

Case Study

Mark's parents and teachers know that when requests are made, Mark often refuses to comply. He has been irritable and oppositional since he was a toddler. His parents have given up trying to enlist co-operation; they vacillate between ignoring Mark's hostile, defiant behavior and threatening punishment. If punished, Mark finds ways to retaliate.

oppositional defiant disorder (ODD) a childhood disorder characterized by negativistic, argumentative, and hostile behavior patterns

Oppositional defiant disorder (ODD) is characterized by a negativistic, argumentative, and hostile behavior pattern. Children with this disorder often lose their temper, argue, and defy adult requests, but do not demonstrate pervasive antisocial behavior and serious violations of societal norms (Table 15.3). Defiant behavior is primarily directed toward parents, teachers, and others in authority. Angry, resentful, blaming, spiteful, and vindictive behaviors are common. Although ODD sometimes evolves into conduct disorder, the symptoms of ODD often resolve, especially with early intervention. ODD appears to have two components, one involving

TABLE 15.3 DISORDERS CHART OPPOSITIONAL DEFIANT DISORDER AND CONDUCT DISORDER

Disorder	Symptoms	Prevalence	Age of Onset	Course
Oppositional defiant disorder	• Angry, irritable mood • Hostile, defiant, and vindictive behavior • Frequent loss of temper, argumentation, and defiance of adult requests • Failure to take responsibility for actions; blaming of others	6–13%; more common in males	Childhood	May resolve, or evolve into a conduct disorder or depressive disorder
Conduct disorder	• Aggression and cruelty to people or animals • Frequent bullying, threats, or initiation of physical fights • Serious violations of rules and societal norms (e.g., lying, stealing, cheating, destroying property)	2–9%; more common in males and in urban settings	Childhood or adolescence	Prognosis poor, especially with childhood onset; often leads to criminal behaviors, antisocial acts, and problems in adult adjustment

Source: DSM-5 Work Groups (2012); Froehlich, Lanphear, Epstein, et al., (2007); Merikangas, He, Burstein, Swanson, et al. (2010); Tynan (2008, 2010)

negative affect (e.g., angry, irritable mood) and the other involving oppositional behavior; negative affect predicts future depressive symptoms, whereas oppositional behaviors are more predictive of conduct disorder (First, 2007). Additionally, approximately half of those with ODD also display inattention and hyperactivity (McBurnett & Pfiffner, 2009).

Did You Know?

Among a group of 3-year-olds followed longitudinally, those who demonstrated a limited sense of fear as young children had frequent arrests for criminal activity in early adulthood; individuals who are not inhibited by fear may have difficulty learning from negative consequences associated with inappropriate behavior.

Source: Gao, Raine, Venables, Dawson, & Mednick (2010)

Conduct Disorders

Case Study

Ben, a high school sophomore well known for his ongoing bullying and aggressive behavior, was expelled from school after stabbing another student. Two months later, he was arrested for armed robbery and placed in juvenile detention. Peer relationships at the facility were strained because of Ben's ongoing attempts to intimidate others.

Conduct disorders (CDs) are characterized by a persistent pattern of antisocial behavior that reflects dysfunction within the individual, and include serious violations of rules and social norms, cruelty and deliberate aggression toward people or animals, and theft, deceit, or vandalism. A **callous and unemotional subtype** refers to those with CD who display minimal guilt or remorse and are consistently unconcerned about the feelings of others, their own wrongdoing, or poor performance at school or work. With this subtype, emotional expression is very superficial and is used primarily to manipulate others (DSM-5 Work Groups, 2012). Cruelty, aggression, and a pervasive lack of remorse are commonly seen in this subgroup (R. E. Kahn, Frick, Youngstrom, Findling, & Youngstrom, 2012). Additionally, individuals with this subtype are usually unconcerned about their victims' suffering or about possible punishment for their behavior (Pardini & Byrd, 2012). Magnetic resonance imaging (MRI) documented this callousness in one sample of adolescents with CD—they demonstrated strong pleasure responses to video clips of people experiencing pain and distress (Decety, Michalska, Akitsuki, & Lahey, 2009). Callous and unemotional behaviors (lack of empathy, guilt, and shallow affect) are also found in youth who do not have a conduct disorder (Kumsta, Sonuga-Barke, & Rutter, 2012).

Bill Aron/PhotoEdit

A Troubled Teen

Conduct disorders involve a persistent pattern of antisocial behaviors. Here a teenager watches for security as he shoplifts in a music store.

Approximately 2–9 percent of youth meet diagnostic criteria for CD; incidence of CD increases from childhood to adolescence. Approximately 50 percent of those with CD also display inattention and hyperactivity. Boys with CD are often involved in confrontational aggression (e.g., fighting, vandalism), whereas girls are more likely to display truancy, substance abuse, or chronic lying. CD tends to be more persistent than other childhood disorders. In particular, childhood-onset CD is associated with chronic, serious offenses, criminal behavior, and substance abuse in adulthood. Those with callous disregard of societal rules and other individuals often exhibit antisocial personality disorder in adulthood (Byrd, Loeber, & Pardini, 2012; Lubit, 2012). The behaviors and criminal acts associated with CD present a significant concern to the public. Some youth advocates endorse widespread screening for CD among young children and maintain that early intervention and treatment can successfully modify the course of the disorder (P. Wilson, Minnis, Puckering, & Gillberg, 2009).

conduct disorder (CD) a persistent pattern of behavior that violates the rights of others, including aggression, serious rule violations, and illegal behavior

callous and unemotional subtype a form of conduct disorder characterized by minimal guilt, remorse, or empathy and manipulative, superficial emotional expression

Biological Dimension
- Abnormal neural circuitry
- Low MAOA genotype
- Reduced autonomic nervous system activity

Sociocultural Dimension
- Large family size
- Crowding
- Male gender
- Poverty

CONDUCT DISORDER

Psychological Dimension
- Poor processing of social information
- Limited fear response
- Oppositional temperament
- Frequent parent-child conflict

Social Dimension
- Early maternal rejection
- Childhood maltreatment
- Harsh or inconsistent discipline
- Behaviors create social isolation
- Parental marital discord

FIGURE 15.1

Multipath Model of Conduct Disorder The dimensions interact with one another and combine in different ways to result in a conduct disorder.

Etiology of Externalizing Disorders

Externalizing disorders often begin in early childhood. The etiology of these disorders involves an interaction between biological, psychological, social, and sociocultural factors. Biological factors appear to exert the greatest influence on the development of CD (Figure 15.1). Aggressive behavior has been linked to brain abnormalities associated with deficits in social information processing as well as reduced activity in the amygdala in situations associated with fear (Sterzer, 2010; Sterzer & Stadler, 2009); these deficits appear to decrease the ability to learn from punishment (Gao et al., 2010). Risk of CD is particularly increased when carriers of the genotype "low MAOA" (an allele associated with fear-regulating circuitry in the amygdala) are subjected to childhood maltreatment (First, 2007). Reduced activity of the autonomic nervous system (associated with increased need for stimulation to achieve optimal arousal) is also associated with CD in males; this may account for the increased risk taking associated with the disorder (El-Sheikh, Keiley, & Hinnant, 2009; van Goozen, Fairchild, Snoek, & Harold, 2007). Elevated stress hormones (cortisol) are associated with symptoms of impulsive aggression, whereas low cortisol levels have been linked with callous and unemotional traits and predatory aggression (Barzman, Patel, Sonnier, & Strawn, 2010).

Bullying Without Remorse

Children and adolescents with conduct disorder frequently engage in aggressive behavior, including making fun of other students. Due to the pervasiveness of bullying behaviors, many schools have implemented curricula aimed at encouraging students to take a stand against bullying.

Both family and social context play a large role in the development of externalizing disorders (Parens & Johnston, 2010). Disruptive behavior is associated with large families, marital breakdown, economic stress, crowded living conditions, harsh or inconsistent discipline, and maternal or peer rejection (Costello, Mustillo, Erkanli, Keeler, & Angold, 2003; van Goozen et al., 2007). Parents with depression, anxiety, or other psychiatric conditions may behave in a punitive, inconsistent, or impatient manner in response to typical demands of parenting. Parent–child conflict and power struggles can intensify disruptive behaviors. Disruptive behaviors are also exacerbated by limited parental supervision, permissive parenting and avoidance of conflict, excessive attention for negative behavior, inconsistent disciplinary practices, and failure to teach prosocial skills and use positive management techniques (Bernstein, 2012).

Difficult child temperament (e.g., irritable, resistant, or impulsive tendencies) contributes to behavioral conflict and increases the need for parents to learn and consistently apply appropriate management skills. Similarly, these temperamental tendencies can lead to rejection by peers and a blaming, negative worldview, sometimes accompanied by aggressive behavior. Underlying emotional issues are common in disruptive behavior disorders. For example, many youth with ODD have underlying anxiety disorders (Mireault, Rooney, Kouwenhoven, & Hannan, 2008), and depression frequently coexists with ODD and DMDD (First, 2007).

Treatment of Externalizing Disorders

Interventions that address the family and social context of behaviors as well as deficits in psychosocial skills can significantly improve externalizing behaviors (Parens & Johnston, 2010). CD is particularly difficult to treat (Lubit, 2012); treatment is most effective when implemented before patterns of disruptive behavior are firmly established. A well-established intervention for externalizing disorders is parent education (Eyberg, Nelson, & Boggs, 2008). Parent-focused interventions can improve both child behavior and parent mental health (Furlong et al., 2012). Behavior management programs teach parents to establish appropriate rules, consistently implement consequences, increase positive interactions, and encourage positive behaviors (Hanisch et al., 2010).

Psychosocial interventions that focus on assertiveness training, anger management techniques, and building skills in empathy, communication, social relationships, and problem solving can also produce marked and durable changes in disruptive behaviors (Eyberg et al., 2008). Mobilizing adult mentors who demonstrate empathy, warmth, and acceptance is another effective intervention (Kazdin, Whitley, & Marciano, 2006).

Did You Know?

Boys are more likely to show direct forms of bullying—intimidating, controlling, or assaulting other children—whereas girls demonstrate more relational aggression, such as using threats of social exclusion.

Source: S. S. Leff & Crick (2010)

CONTROVERSY:

Child Maltreatment

Because the 3-year-old boy had soiled his pants, his mother forced him to sit on the toilet. She told her son that he would not be allowed to get up or eat unless he had a bowel movement. When the son could not comply, the mother pulled him from the toilet seat and lashed his buttocks until they were raw and bleeding.

Child neglect and the physical, emotional, and sexual abuse of children remain a significant national problem (X. Fang, Brown, Florence, & Mercy, 2012). In the United States, 702,000 cases of child neglect or physical or sexual abuse were confirmed in 2009, including 1,770 deaths from child abuse (U.S. Department of Health and Human Services, 2010). As seen in Figure 15.2, many fatalities from abuse involve children age 3 or younger. No doubt many cases of abuse go unreported, particularly cases of child sexual abuse.

Why would parents abuse or neglect their own children? We know that multiple factors, including poverty, parental immaturity, and lack of parenting skills, contribute to child maltreatment, and that many adults who abuse were themselves abused as children. Many parents involved in maltreatment are young, high school dropouts, and under severe stress. Many have personality disorders and low tolerance for frustration, and abuse alcohol and other substances (Leventhal, Martin, & Gaither, 2012). In the case of child sexual abuse, perpetrators are often friends or other family members, and the parent is unaware of the abuse until it is disclosed.

Childhood physical or sexual abuse can result in a variety of internalized or externalized symptoms during childhood or adolescence, as well as lifelong physical and psychological consequences including hypertension and chronic headaches (D. J. Stein et al., 2010; Tietjen et al., 2010); other possible outcomes are depression, anxiety, somatic disorders, eating disorders, and PTSD (R. G. Bradley et al., 2008; L. P. Chen et al., 2010; Gillespie, Phifer, Bradley, & Ressler, 2009; Paras et al., 2009). The more maltreatment or trauma a child encounters, the greater the risk of subsequent psychiatric illness (Benjet, Borges, & Medina-Mora, 2010; J. G. Green et al., 2010; McLaughlin, Green, et al., 2010).

Many communities offer parent education and support groups, especially for at-risk families and for families whose children have been affected by sexual abuse. There is a particular need for programs to prevent the maltreatment of infants and young children (Turner, Finkelhor, Ormrod, & Hamby, 2010). What are additional short-term and long-term consequences of child maltreatment? Why might those who are mistreated as children have an increased risk of becoming abusive themselves?

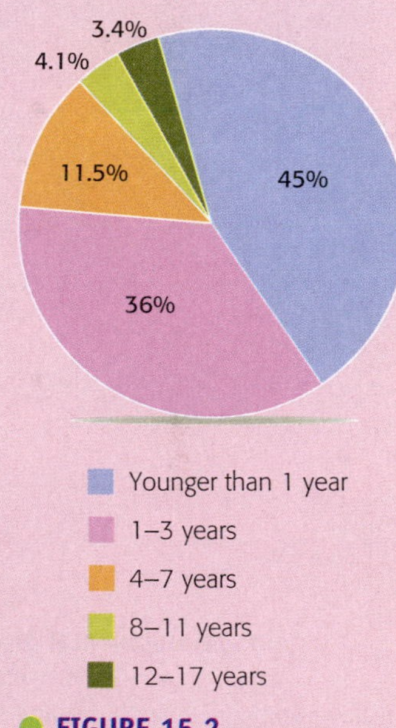

FIGURE 15.2

Fatalities From Child Abuse or Neglect by Age, 2004
The youngest are the most vulnerable.

Source: Child Welfare Information Gateway (2012)

CHECKPOINT REVIEW

1. What are three factors that need to be considered when diagnosing externalizing disorders?
2. Describe the various externalizing disorders.
3. Why is it important to intervene early with externalizing disorders?
4. Describe effective treatments for externalizing disorders.

Neurodevelopmental Disorders

Neurodevelopmental disorders (see Table 15.4) involve impaired development of the brain and central nervous system; symptoms such as difficulties with learning, communication, and behavior become increasing evident as the child grows and develops. Disorders include tic disorders (such as Tourette's disorder), attention-deficit/hyperactivity disorder, autism spectrum disorders, and intellectual and learning disorders.

Tics and Tourette's Disorder

Case Study

James Durbin, a contestant on *American Idol,* had facial and vocal tics as a child and was diagnosed with Tourette's disorder. During his school years he was bullied and teased because of his tics. However, when he would sing, he felt free because his tics completely disappeared (M. Healy, 2011).

Tics are involuntary, repetitive movements or vocalizations. **Motor tics** involve various physical behaviors including blinking, grimacing, jerking the head, tapping the feet, flaring the nostrils, and contracting the shoulders or abdominal muscles. **Vocal tics** include coughing, grunting, throat clearing, sniffling, and sudden, repetitive, and stereotyped outbursts of words. Short-term suppression of a tic is sometimes possible, but often results in subsequent increases in the tic. Some individuals report feeling tension build before a tic, followed by a sense of relief after the tic occurs. A physician with tics described it this way:

> "This urge comes in the form of a sensation . . . a sensation that is somehow incomplete. To complete and resolve the sensation, the tic must be executed, which provides almost instant relief. . . . The relief is very transient. . . . The sensation comes back again, but often more intensely than before. (Turtle & Robertson, 2008, p. 451)

neurodevelopmental disorders conditions involving impaired development of the brain and central nervous system that are evident early in a child's life

tic an involuntary, repetitive movement or vocalization

motor tic a tic involving physical behaviors such as eye blinking, facial grimacing, or head jerking

vocal tic an audible tic such as coughing, grunting, throat clearing, sniffling, or making sudden, vocal outbursts

Tourette's disorder (TD) a condition characterized by multiple motor tics and one or more vocal tics

Most tics in children are transient and disappear without treatment. Stress can increase the frequency and intensity of tics. When a tic has been present for less than a year, a diagnosis of *provisional tic disorder* is given; *chronic motor or vocal tic disorder* refers to tics lasting more than a year (DSM-5 Work Groups, 2012). Chronic tics sometimes continue throughout adolescence and into adulthood. Tic disorders are much more prevalent in boys (Robertson, 2010). In one sample of children, 2.6 percent met the criteria for provisional tic disorder, 3.7 percent had a chronic tic disorder, and 0.6 percent had Tourette's disorder (Wolanczyk et al., 2008).

Tourette's disorder (TD) is characterized by multiple motor tics (e.g., blinking, grimacing, shrugging, jerking the head or shoulders) and one or more vocal tics

DISORDERS CHART NEURODEVELOPMENTAL DISORDERS

TABLE 15.4

Disorder	Prevalence	Characteristics	Course
Tic disorder	2–5%; 4 times as common in males	Involuntary, repetitive movements or vocalizations	Sometimes persists into adulthood
Attention-deficit/ hyperactivity disorder	8–9%; twice as common in males	Inattention, hyperactivity, and impulsivity	Some symptoms may persist into adulthood
Autism spectrum disorder	0.6–1%; 4 times as common in males	Qualitative impairment in social communication; restricted, stereotyped interest and activities	Course depends on severity, presence of intellectual disability, and intervention
Intellectual developmental disorder	1–2%; more common in males	Mild, moderate, severe, or profound deficits in intellectual functioning and adaptive behavior	Lifelong
Learning disorder	5%; more common in males	Normal intelligence with significant deficits in basic reading, writing, or math skills	May improve with intervention or persist into adulthood

Source: Centers for Disease Control and Prevention (2009b, 2010b); Robertson (2010); U.S. Department of Education, National Center for Education Statistics (2010); Wolanczyk et al. (2008)

(e.g., repetitive throat clearing, sniffing, or grunting) that are present for at least 1 year, although not necessarily concurrently (DSM-5 Work Groups, 2012). Symptoms of TD can be severe or mild (Rivera-Navarro, Cubo, & Almazan, 2009). Usually the first symptoms are noticed between the ages of 7 and 10, with symptoms increasing in the middle teen years and improving in early adulthood; about 8 percent of those with TD eventually show a complete remission of symptoms (National Institute of Neurological Disorders and Stroke, 2010). **Coprolalia** (involuntary uttering of obscenities or inappropriate remarks) or motor movements involving self-harm (e.g., punching oneself) occur in about 10 percent of those with TD (Singer, 2005). Comorbid conditions include poor anger control, attention-deficit/ hyperactivity disorder, obsessive-compulsive disorder, impulsive behavior, and poor social skills (Dugdale, Jasmin, & Zieve, 2010).

Both chronic tic disorder and TD appear to be genetically transmitted. Because TD is highly comorbid with obsessive-compulsive disorder, similar physiological mechanisms involving the basal ganglia and orbital frontal cortex are likely involved (Mathews & Grados, 2011). Because some antipsychotic medications reduce the severity of TD symptoms, abnormalities involving neurotransmitters are hypothesized to be involved in the disorder (Robertson, 2010). Although antipsychotic medication is sometimes used to treat severe vocal tics (Kuwabara, Kono, Shimada, & Kano, 2011), medication is not typically used to treat tic disorders. Psychotherapy can help with the distress caused by tic symptoms. Additionally, the technique of **habit reversal**, which involves teaching a behavior that is incompatible with the tic, is an effective treatment (Bate, Malouff, Thorsteinsson, & Bhullar, 2011).

Attention-Deficit/Hyperactivity Disorder

Case Study

Ron, always on the go as a toddler and preschooler, has had many injuries resulting from his continual climbing and risk taking. In kindergarten, Ron talked incessantly and could not stay seated for group work. In the first grade, his distractibility and off-task behavior persisted despite ongoing efforts to help him focus. As part of a comprehensive assessment, his parents took him for a psychological evaluation and a complete physical examination.

coprolalia involuntary utterance of obscenities or inappropriate remarks

habit reversal a therapeutic technique in which a client is taught to substitute new behaviors for habitual behaviors such as a tic

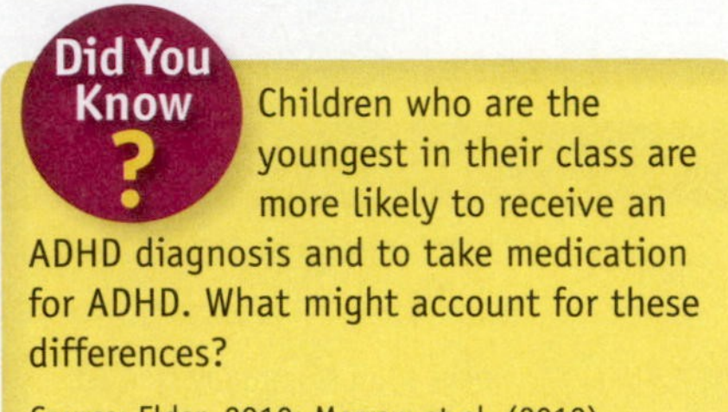

Children who are the youngest in their class are more likely to receive an ADHD diagnosis and to take medication for ADHD. What might account for these differences?

Source: Elder, 2010; Morrow et al. (2012)

Attention-deficit/hyperactivity disorder (ADHD) is characterized by attentional problems or impulsive, hyperactive behaviors that are atypical for the child's age and developmental level and that significantly interfere with social, academic, or occupational activities. An ADHD diagnosis requires that symptoms (see Table 15.5) begin before age 12 and persist for at least 6 months. Individuals with ADHD can have problems involving (a) inattention, (b) hyperactivity and impulsivity, or (c) a combination of these characteristics. The distractibility and intense focus on irrelevant environmental stimuli seen in ADHD are due to poor regulation of attentional processes (Contractor, 2012). Symptoms of hyperactivity and impulsivity involve a combination of excessive movement and a tendency to act without considering the consequences.

TABLE 15.5 Characteristics of Attention-Deficit/Hyperactivity Disorder

INATTENTION	HYPERACTIVITY AND IMPULSIVITY
Poor attention to detail	Fidgeting
Difficulty sustaining attention	Restlessness
Appearance of not listening	Excessive movement
Poor follow-through	Excessive loudness
Difficulty organizing tasks	Excessive talking
Avoidance of sustained mental effort	Blurting out answers
Misplacing of objects	Difficulty waiting for a turn
Distractibility	Interruption of or intrusion on others
Forgetfulness	Impatience

Note: With ADHD, these characteristics occur more frequently than would be expected based on age, gender, and developmental level.
Source: DSM-5 Work Groups (2012)

ADHD can be difficult to diagnose, especially in early childhood, when limited attentional skills and high levels of energy are common. Diagnosis relies on observations and input from parents, school personnel, and others knowledgeable about the child's behaviors. To receive a diagnosis of ADHD, a child must display symptoms in two or more settings (DSM-5 Work Groups, 2012). When presented with parental concern about ongoing inattentive, hyperactive, and impulsive behaviors, it is necessary to determine if the behaviors are (a) typical for the child's age, gender, and overall level of development; (b) a normal temperamental variant involving higher than average energy and impulsivity; or (c) an actual disorder involving significantly atypical behaviors that interfere with day-to-day functioning in multiple settings. *Hyperactive* is a confusing term because it is frequently used to describe all highly energetic children. In fact, family physicians often make ADHD diagnoses and prescribe medication when symptoms of inattention, hyperactivity, and impulsivity are not severe enough to meet DSM diagnostic criteria (Parens & Johnston, 2009).

ADHD is the most frequently diagnosed disorder in school-age children (T. D. Banerjee, Middleton, & Faraone, 2007). Prevalence in one national sample of youth (ages 8–15) was 8.7 percent (Froehlich, Lanphear, Epstein, et al., 2007), whereas in a broader sample, parent-reported prevalence (ages 6–17) was 8.2 percent (K. Larson, Russ, Kahn, & Halfon, 2011). Boys are more than twice as likely as girls to be diagnosed with ADHD (Bloom & Cohen, 2007; Centers for Disease Control and Prevention [CDC], 2010b). Although symptoms of ADHD often improve in late adolescence, follow-up studies suggest that between 30 and 50 percent of those diagnosed with ADHD experience continued symptoms of inattention or fidgeting, difficulty sitting still, and impulsive actions throughout adulthood (Montauk & Mayhall, 2010).

ADHD is associated with both behavioral and academic problems (K. Larson et al., 2011). Children with ADHD have the most difficulty in unstructured situations, activities demanding sustained attention, and circumstances involving insufficient stimulation (Kooistra, Crawford, Gibbard, Ramage, & Kaplan, 2010). Peer relationships and friendships are also challenging (CDC, 2010b). Data regarding more than 62,000 U.S. youth (ages 6–17) revealed that two thirds of those with ADHD had other mental health conditions (including CD, ODD, anxiety, and depression) or learning disabilities and other neurodevelopmental disorders; the risk of coexisting conditions is almost 4 times greater among children living in poverty (K. Larson et al., 2011). Youth with ADHD also have a high risk of smoking and use of alcohol and illicit drugs (Gudjonsson, Sigurdsson, Sigfusdottir, & Young, 2012),

attention-deficit/hyperactivity disorder (ADHD) childhood-onset disorder characterized by persistent attentional problems and/or impulsive, hyperactive behaviors

Etiology

As with many other disorders, symptoms of ADHD result from multiple etiological factors (Parens & Johnston, 2009). ADHD is an early-onset disorder with clear biological as well as psychological, social, and sociocultural etiology.

Biological Dimension ADHD is a highly heritable disorder, with up to 80 percent of symptoms explainable by genetic factors (Coghill & Banaschewski, 2009; Durston, 2010). The exact nature of genetic transmission is unclear, because no specific genes strongly link to ADHD symptoms (Faraone & Mick, 2010; Stergiakouli & Thapar, 2010); however, rare, inherited gene mutations (Elia, Gai, et al., 2010), chromosomal DNA deletions and duplications (N. M. Williams et al., 2010), and genes affecting the regulation of the neurotransmitters dopamine (Montauk & Mayhall, 2010) and glutamate (Elia, Glessner, et al., 2011) have been implicated. It is likely that many of the symptoms seen in ADHD involve multiple genes, each with small effects, and subsequent gene × gene or gene × environment interactions (Ficks & Waldman, 2009; Franke, Neale, & Faraone, 2009; Plomp, Van Engeland, & Durston, 2009).

Different hypotheses regarding neurological mechanisms that produce ADHD symptoms include the following:

- *Reduced activity in the prefrontal cortex when tasks require inhibition of responses.* This low arousal of inhibitory mechanisms can affect impulsivity, organizational planning, working memory, and attentional processes (Montauk & Mayhall, 2010).
- *Differences in brain structure and circuitry in the frontal cortex, cerebellum, and parietal lobes.* Neuroimaging has confirmed these differences (Cherkasova & Hechtman, 2009), including smaller frontal lobes in children with ADHD, especially those with more severe symptoms (Montauk & Mayhall, 2010). Additionally, some children with ADHD show slower development of the cerebrum, particularly prefrontal regions associated with attention and motor planning (P. Shaw et al., 2007); this delay (and subsequent catching up) in neurological developmental may explain why many children with ADHD eventually outgrow their disorder.
- *Inadequate dopamine and associated neurotransmitters that affect signal flow to and from the frontal lobes.* Medications used to treat ADHD target these neurotransmitters (T. J. Spencer, Biederman, & Mick, 2007; Stergiakouli & Thapar, 2010).

Other biological factors implicated in the development of ADHD include prematurity, oxygen deprivation during birth, and very low birth weight (Aarnoudse-Moens et al., 2009); exposure to lead and PCB (Abelsohn & Sanborn, 2010; Eubig, Aguiar, & Schantz, 2010); viral infections, meningitis, and encephalitis (Millichap, 2008); and maternal smoking or drug or alcohol use during pregnancy (Bandiera et al., 2011; Froehlich et al., 2009). Some researchers believe that certain food additives and unhealthy dietary patterns contribute to hyperactive behaviors (Millichap & Yee, 2012; Nigg et al., 2012).

AP Images

Interventions for Attention-Deficit/Hyperactivity Disorder

The 6-year-old boy shown here is enrolled in a study called Project Achieve, in which parents and teachers are taught strategies to help minimize problem behaviors. New research shows that providing more structure throughout a child's day can offer a nondrug alternative to help children with attention-deficit/hyperactivity disorder.

Psychological, Social, and Sociocultural Dimensions Many psychological, social, and sociocultural factors have been associated with ADHD. Sociocultural and social adversity (e.g., family stress, severe marital discord, low social class, family conflicts, maternal psychopathology, paternal criminality, maternal mental disorder, and foster care placement) seem to contribute to ADHD (G. T. Ray, Croen, & Habel, 2009; T. J. Spencer et al., 2007). Also, children who are inattentive, hyperactive, or impulsive often encounter negative reactions from others. These negative reactions and associated interpersonal conflict may result in psychological reactions (e.g., stress, low self-esteem, rebelliousness) that further exacerbate symptoms (Deault, 2010). Some argue that differing cultural and regional expectations regarding high activity, inattentiveness, and

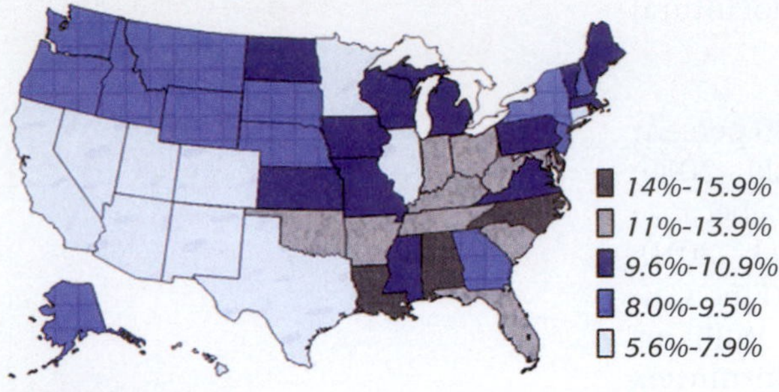

FIGURE 15.3

Prevalence of Attention-Deficit/Hyperactivity Disorder Among Youth (Ages 4–17) by State, 2007–2008

The prevalence of parent-reported attention-deficit/hyperactivity disorder (ADHD) varied significantly from state to state, ranging from a low of 5.6 percent in Nevada to a high of 15.6 percent in North Carolina. What might account for the variability in ADHD diagnoses from state to state?

Source: Centers for Disease Control and Prevention (2010b)

academic achievement can affect the prevalence of ADHD diagnosis (Figure 15.3). Similarly, parenting practices that encourage exercise and outdoor activity or help prevent children from getting overtired or overaroused may decrease the likelihood of ADHD symptoms (Parens & Johnston, 2009).

Treatment For decades, stimulants such as methylphenidate (Ritalin) have been used to treat ADHD symptoms (Findling, 2008); these medications continue to receive the most evidenced-based support for ADHD treatment (Greydanus, Nazeer, & Patel, 2009). Stimulants work by normalizing neurotransmitter functioning and increasing neurological activation in the frontal cortex, thereby increasing attention and reducing impulsivity. Some treatment trends have resulted in increased lifetime medication exposure (Parens & Johnston, 2009; Zuvekas & Vitiello, 2012), including emphasizing initiation of treatment at an early age, using medication throughout the day rather than just during school hours (Buitelaar & Medori, 2010), and continuing medication, if needed, during adolescence and throughout the life span. These trends, combined with increased rates of ADHD diagnoses, likely account for the continued increases in stimulant medication use in the United States (Figure 15.4). Due to the frequency of misuse and diversion (i.e., giving, selling, or trading) of prescribed short-acting stimulant medications (Arria et al., 2008; Wilens et al., 2008), the use of longer-acting stimulants or other medications with less abuse potential is increasing (Faraone & Wilens, 2007; Kollins, 2008).

Did You Know? The prevalence of ADHD diagnosis (based on parent report) ranges from 5.6 percent in Nevada to 15.6 percent in North Carolina, whereas the prevalence of children receiving medication for ADHD ranges from 2.1 percent in California to 6.5 percent in Arkansas.

Source: CDC (2010b)

There is strong and consistent evidence that behavioral and psychosocial treatments (e.g., parent education, classroom management strategies and reward systems, behavioral interventions involving peers, self-control training) are highly effective in producing both short-term and long-term reductions in ADHD symptoms (Fabiano, Pelham, Coles, et al., 2009; Verma, Balhara, & Mathur, 2011). In fact, some researchers have argued that these approaches should be used before considering medication, particularly for individuals with milder symptoms (Parens & Johnston, 2009). Additionally, modifying the environment or social context (e.g., allowing movement or opportunities to optimize cognitive stimulation) can enhance feelings of competence, motivation, and self-efficacy for those with ADHD (Gallichan & Curle, 2008). In fact, simply providing recess breaks can reduce inappropriate behaviors among children with ADHD (Ridgway, Northup, Pellegrin, LaRue, & Hightshoe, 2003).

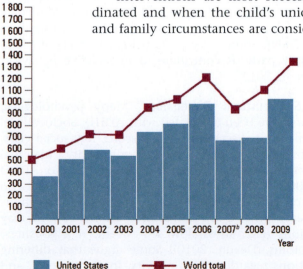

Interventions are most successful when services are coordinated and when the child's unique characteristics and social and family circumstances are considered (K. Larson et al., 2011). Some researchers have proposed that symptom severity should guide treatment decisions, with interventions ranging from environmental modifications for mild symptoms to intensive, combined treatment (e.g., behavior management, parenting strategies, and stimulant medication) for severe ADHD symptoms (Daly, Creed, Xanthopoulos, & Brown, 2007; Pelham & Fabiano, 2008).

Millions of S-DDD

1 800, 1 700, 1 600, 1 500, 1 400, 1 300, 1 200, 1 100, 1 000, 900, 800, 700, 600, 500, 400, 300, 200, 100, 0

2000 2001 2002 2003 2004 2005 2006 2007[b] 2008 2009

Year

United States — World total

FIGURE 15.4

Medical Consumption of Methylphenidate in the United States and Worldwide, 2000–2009

Methylphenidate is a medication frequently prescribed for attention-deficit/hyperactivity disorder (ADHD). This graph demonstrates that the United States accounts for a large percentage of the use of this medication worldwide, and that from 2000 to 2009 the amount of methylphenidate consumed more than doubled both in the United States and worldwide.

Source: International Narcotics Control Board (2010)

Autism Spectrum Disorders

Autism spectrum disorder (ASD) is characterized by significant impairment in social communication skills and by the display of stereotyped interests and behaviors (Ozonoff, Iosif, et al., 2010). ASD symptoms range from mild to severe. ASD, estimated to affect approximately 1 out of 100 to 110 children, has been increasing, and is four times as common in boys as in girls (CDC, 2009b; Landa, 2008; Kogan et al., 2009). We begin our discussion with an overview of characteristics of ASD.

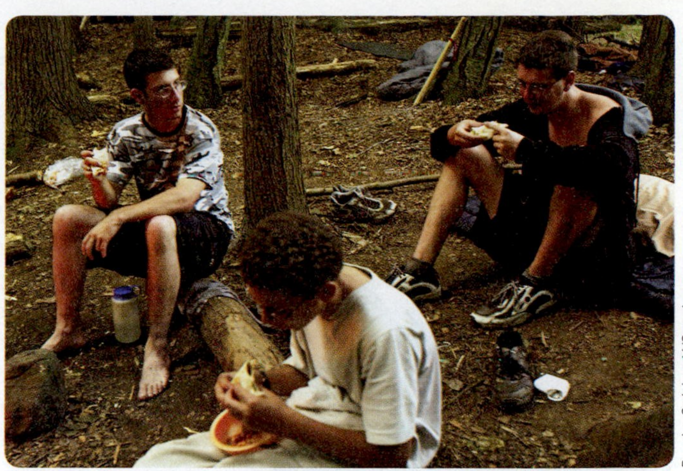
Brendan Smialowski/Getty Images

Interventions for Older Youth With Attention-Deficit/Hyperactivity Disorder

Students eat while camping out at the Center for Attention and Related Disorders camp in Connecticut. The 4-week camp matches one instructor with every two campers and provides structure, discipline, and social order that are helpful for children who have attention-deficit/hyperactivity disorder (ADHD) and similar disorders.

Symptoms of Autism Spectrum Disorder

Case Study

During the first and part of the second year of her life, Amy showed normal development—smiling, laughing, babbling, waving to parents, and playing peekaboo. By age 2, she was withdrawn and spoke no words except meaningless phrases from songs. She spent her time rocking back and forth or spinning her toys.

Case Study

Danny B. wants chicken and potatoes. He asks for it once, twice . . . ten times. . . . His mother patiently explains that she is fixing spaghetti. "Mom," he asks in a monotone, "why can't we have chicken and potatoes?" If Danny were a toddler, his behavior would be nothing unusual. But Danny is twenty years old. "That's really what life with autism is like," says his mom. "I have to keep laughing. Otherwise, I would cry." (Kantrowitz & Scelfo, 2006, p. 47)

At the beginning of this chapter, we introduced Ahmed, a young child with ASD. In the cases of Amy and Danny, we again get a glimpse of how ASD presents early in life and in early adulthood. In 1943, Leo Kanner, a child psychiatrist, identified a triad of behaviors that have come to define the essential features of ASD: extreme isolation and inability to relate to people, a need for sameness, and significant difficulties with communication. Kanner called the syndrome *infantile autism*, from the Greek *autos* ("self"), to reflect the profound aloneness and detachment of these children. At its core, ASD involves pervasive deficits in social communication (Tanguay, 2011).

ASD is diagnosed when a trained professional documents persistent evidence of the following characteristics (DSM-5 Work Groups, 2012):

1. Deficits in social communication and social interaction.
    - *Atypical social-emotional reciprocity.* Interest in social interaction may be limited or totally lacking. For example, infants with ASD are often content to be left alone and show no anticipatory responding when picked up. In adulthood, milder symptoms may include one-sided domination of conversation focused on narrow self-interests and failure to understand the back and forth of typical conversations.

autism spectrum disorder (ASD) a disorder characterized by impairment in social communication and restricted, stereotyped interests and activities

JODI COBB/National Geographic Stock

Identical Twins with Autism Spectrum Disorder

These identical twin boys were both diagnosed with autism spectrum disorder before their second birthday. However, the twins are at opposite ends of the autism spectrum. John, on the left, does not yet speak and engages in many repetitive behaviors such as hand-flapping. In contrast, Sam, on the right, possesses a wealth of information on specific topics such as trains, space and maps. Sam's greatest struggles involve social interactions, especially with other children.

- *Atypical nonverbal communication.* There may be little to no eye contact and an absence of meaningful gestures or facial expressions. Milder symptoms may include unusual nonverbal communication (e.g., pushing people aside), intrusive behavior, and poor social boundaries or failure to understand others' intentions.
- *Difficulties developing and maintaining relationships.* There may be a lack of interest in others or a failure to recognize people's identity or emotions, including treating people as objects, and a failure to seek physical or emotional responses from caretakers. Those with milder symptoms may have no interest in imaginative play, may be socially inept, and may have difficulty adjusting their behavior to the social context.

2. Repetitive behavior or restricted interests or activities involving at least two of the following:
   - *Repetitive speech, movement, or use of objects.* Rhythmic, repetitive, apparently purposeless movements (e.g., banging the head, flapping the arms, rocking the body, spinning objects, whirling in circles, rhythmically moving fingers) are common symptoms. Those with ASD sometimes repetitively stack or spin objects or move them from side to side. There may be repetitive use of language, including **echolalia** (echoing what has previously been said); incessant repetition of sounds, words, phrases, or nonsensical word combinations; or repetitive, one-sided conversations involving topics of fixated interest.
   - *Intense focus on rituals or routines and strong resistance to change.* Common rituals may involve objects (e.g., lining up or dropping toys) or insistence on the same foods, order of events, or routines. Even small changes in routine can produce intense reactions.
   - *Intense fixations or restricted interests.* This may involve fascination with certain objects or a repetitive focus on a narrow range of interests.
   - *Atypical sensory reactivity.* There may be a lack of reactivity (e.g., apparent indifference to pain, heat, or cold); over-reactivity to sensory input (e.g., aversion to touch or certain sounds); or an unusual focus on sensory aspects of objects (e.g., licking or smelling objects or exhibiting an intense interest in moving objects).

The symptoms seen in ASD are not simply developmental delays but reflect various differences in development that cause impairment in everyday functioning (Lord et al., 2012). Table 15.6 summarizes the range of symptoms found in ASD. Although some individuals with ASD have average or above-average cognitive skills and are considered "high-functioning," approximately two thirds have IQ scores lower than 70 (L. Kaufman, Ayub, & Vincent, 2010); some with low intellectual skills exhibit *splinter skills*—that is, they do well on isolated tasks such as drawing, puzzle construction, or rote memory but perform poorly on verbal tasks and tasks requiring language skills and symbolic thinking. These children are referred to as **autistic savants**.

Although ASD might seem easy to diagnose, given its unique characteristics, diagnosis can be complicated. Typical evaluation procedures include clinical observations, parent interviews, developmental histories, autism screening inventories, communication assessment, and psychological testing.

Although many children diagnosed with ASD show "differences" during infancy (Bolton, Golding, Emond, & Steer, 2012), ASD is often not diagnosed until age 3 or later (Barbaro & Dissanayake, 2009). Unlike typically developing infants, many infants with ASD symptoms fail to attend to human motion, such as a

echolalia repetition of vocalizations made by another person

autistic savant an individual with ASD who performs exceptionally well on certain tasks (e.g., superior rote memory, artistic, or musical skills)

TABLE 15.6 Continuum of Symptoms Associated With Autism Spectrum Disorder

LEVEL OF IMPAIRMENT	SOCIAL COMMUNICATION	RESTRICTED INTERESTS AND REPETITIVE BEHAVIORS
Severe (requires very substantial support)	Minimal or absent communication or response to attempts at social interaction	Ongoing repetitive behaviors; intense preoccupation with rituals; extreme distress upon interference with rituals
Moderate (requires substantial support)	Evident difficulties with social communication; noticeably atypical interactions	Fixated interests and frequent repetitive behaviors and rituals that significantly interfere with functioning
Mild[a] (requires support)	Atypical social interactions; difficulty initiating or responding to social communication	Repetitive behaviors and fixated interests that cause some interference with everyday functioning
Not severe enough for ASD diagnosis	Some atypical behaviors and mild deficits in social communication that do not limit or impair everyday functioning	Ritualized behavior, odd mannerisms, or excessive preoccupations that do not interfere with daily functioning
Variation of normal	Social isolation and awkwardness	Odd preoccupations or mannerisms

[a]Those who demonstrate milder symptoms are sometimes referred to as having high-functioning autism or Asperger's syndrome.
Adapted from DSM-5 Work Groups (2012)

parent's movement (Klin, Lin, Gorrindo, Ramsay, & Jones, 2009), or demonstrate interest in human faces (Chawarska, Volkmar, & Klin, 2010). ASD symptoms sometimes appear following a period of apparently normal social and intellectual development, with deterioration of skills beginning around 6–12 months of age (S. J. Rogers, 2009; Ozonoff, Iosif, et al., 2010). Children with this pattern of regression (referred to as *regressive autism*) often develop more severe symptoms compared to autistic children without this pattern (Meilleur & Fombonne, 2009).

Asperger's syndrome a condition with mild characteristics along the autism spectrum including intense focus on narrow interests and eccentric, one-sided social interactions

Etiology A great deal of research has focused on the causes of ASD, with the hope of developing early diagnostic procedures and interventions that can prevent, halt, or reverse symptoms (Zwaigenbaum, 2010). ASD is unique

CONTROVERSY

Eliminating the Asperger's Diagnosis: Why the Uproar?

I have aspergers (diagnosed) and my brother has classic autism. I can read and write, I've got a degree, I can dress myself in the morning. My brother however has no communication, bowel problems, he is a man in his 20s who is trapped with the mind of a two year old. He needs help with every aspect of his life. It doesn't do me any good or him any good by you trying to merge what we've got into one condition. (David, 2010)

Asperger's syndrome, a disorder involving characteristics on the mild end of the autism spectrum, is characterized by average to above-average cognitive skills, intense focus on narrow interests, and eccentric, one-sided social interactions (e.g., poor understanding of rules of social engagement and asking inappropriate or intrusive questions; Ghaziuddin, 2010; Newschaffer et al., 2007). Those revising the DSM-5 concluded that the social communication abnormalities (Hofvander et al., 2009), interpersonal relationship difficulties, desire for sameness, and narrow interests seen in Asperger's syndrome do not reflect a distinct disorder. Instead, the DSM-5 Work Group concluded that behaviors associated with Asperger's diagnosis are merely an extension of the ASD continuum and that a separate diagnostic category is redundant (DSM-5 Work Groups, 2012); thus, they have proposed eliminating the Asperger's diagnosis. This decision generated strong reactions from individuals diagnosed with Asperger's, who embrace their uniqueness and have found social connection within the Asperger's community. They argue that Asperger's is clearly distinct from ASD.

Some experts also supported maintaining the Asperger's category with modifications in diagnostic criteria to include unique features not previously identified, such as socially insensitive communication; verbose, one-sided conversations pertaining to areas of restricted interests; and difficulty with practical use of language (Ghaziuddin, 2010). Do individuals with Asperger's have a point—that they are different from those diagnosed with ASD and that including them on the ASD spectrum will result in increased stigma?

MYTH VS. REALITY

MYTH Childhood vaccinations cause autism spectrum disorder.

REALITY This widespread rumor, in part perpetuated by the coincidental timing of the administration of childhood vaccines and the onset of autistic symptoms, has been proven completely false. Although a 1998 study claimed the measles-mumps-rubella vaccine caused autistic symptoms, the study was deemed fraudulent when it was found that the lead author had manipulated the data for monetary gain. There is no evidence that vaccinations cause autism spectrum disorder (Godlee, Smith, & Marcovitch, 2011).

because symptoms sometimes appear following a period of relatively normal development and because, for some children, intervention has reversed progression of the disorder. Although psychological effects are important in understanding the course of the disorder, biological factors play the most critical role.

Biological Dimension Biological researchers are approaching the etiology of ASD from a variety of perspectives, including documenting biological processes involved in the development of the disorder, confirming genetic and environmental risk factors, and, most importantly, elucidating gene × environment interactions. There have been recent unprecedented advances in the identification of genes and risk alleles associated with ASD (Carayol et al., 2010; Oliver, Berg, Moss, Arron, & Burbidge, 2011). Although the exact mechanisms by which genetic defects translate into impaired brain functioning are not known, research has linked ASD with numerous neurological findings, including:

- unique patterns of metabolic brain activity (Lange et al., 2010),
- abnormally high levels of serotonin, particularly in males with ASD and those who are high-functioning (Brasic, 2010),
- differences in brain anatomy and connectivity in brain regions that are associated with autistic traits (J. S. Anderson et al., 2010; Ecker et al., 2012), and
- accelerated growth of the amygdala in early childhood (Nordahl, Scholz, et al., 2012); accelerated brain growth in boys with regressive autism began around 4–6 months of age, long before autistic symptoms appeared (Nordahl, Lange, et al., 2011)

Accelerated head growth may, in fact, be an endophenotype (biological marker) for ASD (Constantino et al., 2010). Male infants later diagnosed with ASD exhibited a pattern of rapid head growth 6–9 months after birth (Fukumoto et al., 2010). MRI with toddlers diagnosed with ASD has confirmed extra growth in multiple regions of the brain (Schumann et al., 2010). The period of accelerated head growth in infancy has been found to precede and overlap the onset of behavioral symptoms. Conversely, the increasingly severe autistic symptoms displayed by children with ASD in the second year of life correspond with a subsequent period of decelerated growth within the brain (G. Dawson, Munson, et al., 2007).

Genetic mutations have been implicated when ASD is diagnosed in multiple family members (Korvatska et al., 2011). Different genetic factors involving multiple brain regions, including the cerebellum and frontal and temporal lobes, appear to influence different autistic symptoms (Abrahams & Geschwind, 2010; Nijmeijer et al., 2010).

Concordance rates for ASD are much higher for monozygotic twins than dizygotic twins, with the heritability of ASD estimated to be around 0.73 percent for males and 0.87 percent for females (Taniai, Nishiyama, Miyachi, Imaeda, & Sumi, 2008). Furthermore, ASD affects up to 19 percent of the siblings of those who have it, a much higher prevalence than is seen in the rest of the population; the risk of recurrence is even higher for male infants (Ozonoff, Young, et al., 2011). Additionally, autistic traits have a high heritability (E. B. Robinson et al., 2011). Taken together, twin and family studies clearly establish that genetic susceptibility to ASD exists. However, because monozygotic concordance is less than 100 percent and the degree of impairment varies markedly among monozygotic twins with ASD, other factors are etiologically significant as well (Newschaffer et al., 2007).

Children who develop ASD appear to have an innate vulnerability that is triggered by environmental factors (Herbert, 2010). Environmental toxins associated with the development of ASD include exposure to mercury and other heavy metals (Dufault et al., 2009; Desoto & Hitlan, 2010; Geier, Kern, & Geier, 2009; J. K. Kern et al., 2011), certain pesticides (E. M. Roberts et al., 2007), maternal smoking, poor indoor ventilation, and PVC flooring (M. Larsson, Weiss, Janson, Sundell, & Bornehag, 2009). Why do environmental toxins cause ASD in some children and not others? A partial answer to this question may come from research showing that children with ASD and children who are developing typically appear to have similar blood levels of both lead (Tian et al., 2011) and mercury (Stamova et al., 2011); however, children with ASD appear to metabolize these toxins differently. It is unclear if toxins or other effects account for the demographic variance in ASD across the United States (Figure 15.5; Newschaffer et al., 2007).

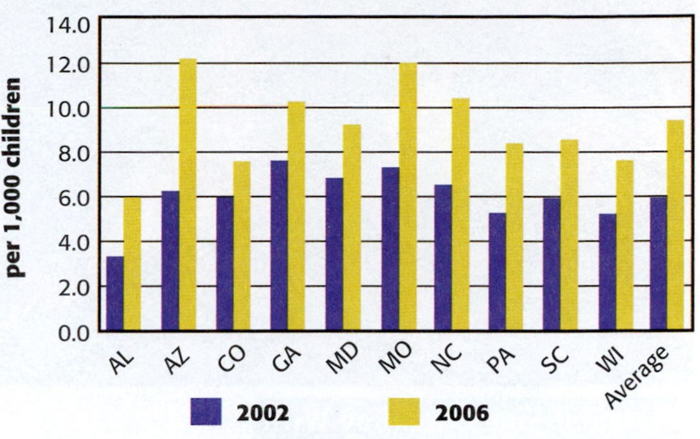

FIGURE 15.5

Changes in the Prevalence of Autism Spectrum Disorder Among 8-Year-Old Children in 10 U.S. States, 2002–2006 The prevalence of autism spectrum disorder among 8-year-old children increased between 2002 and 2006 in all 10 state sites monitored. What might account for these increases and the state-to-state variations in prevalence of the disorder?

Source: Centers for Disease Control and Prevention (2009b)

Other factors associated with ASD include nutritional deficiencies (Dufault et al., 2009), changes in the immune system (Careaga, Van de Water, & Ashwood, 2010; Chez & Guido-Estrada, 2010), low birth weight (Pinto-Martin et al., 2011), obstetric complications (Brasic & Holland, 2007), and closely spaced pregnancies (Cheslack-Postava, Liu, & Bearman, 2011). Biological mechanisms may also account for the fact that autistic symptoms sometimes improve and then abruptly return when a child with ASD has a fever (L. K. Curran et al., 2007). Most researchers agree that ASD is a heterogeneous disorder with multiple causes. Fortunately, biological researchers and experts in the field of ASD are working together to search for interventions that produce documentable biological changes (Llaneza et al., 2010); they are encouraged by the neuroplasticity seen in some children who have received intensive, early intervention (Landa, Holman, O'Neill, & Stuart, 2011).

Psychological Dimension From a psychological perspective, ASD affects the way a child interacts with the world, which in turn affects how others interact with the child. Many children with ASD seldom make eye contact, seek social connectedness, or bid for attention with gestures or vocalizations; instead, they prefer to be alone, do not engage in play, and ignore parental efforts at connection (C. P. Johnson, Myers, & Council on Children With Disabilities, 2007). All of these psychological characteristics affect interactions with peers and family members; without reciprocal social interaction, attempts to maintain social connection often diminish, further adding to the child's isolation. Additionally, behavioral characteristics associated with ASD often create stress and affect interactions within the family, particularly when parents have limited respite from the day-to-day demands of caretaking (J. L. Taylor & Seltzer, 2010a). It is now widely concluded that although psychological and social factors play a role in the manifestation of symptoms, ASD is primarily influenced by biological factors.

Intervention and Treatment

The prognosis for children with ASD is mixed. Most children diagnosed with ASD retain their diagnosis and require support throughout their lifetime. Although those with milder symptoms may be self-sufficient and successfully employed, and function reasonably well in adulthood, social awkwardness, restrictive interests, or atypical behaviors often persist (C. P. Johnson et al., 2007). In general, those with higher levels of cognitive-adaptive functioning fare better than those with intellectual disability and severe autistic symptoms. A significant degree of recovery has been seen in some children (including some with severe symptoms) who received early, intense intervention, such as comprehensive behavioral, speech, and occupational therapy focused on social and communication skills; the most impressive results have occurred

Did You Know ?

In a study involving 600,000 sibling pairs, children born less than 1 year after the birth of a sibling were almost 300 percent more likely to develop ASD compared to children born at least 4 years after a sibling.

Source: Cheslack-Postava et al. (2011)

AP Photo/The Day, Tim Martin

Therapist Signs to a Boy With Autism Spectrum Disorder

In a May 27, 2012 photo, Allissa Porter, right, 17, a senior at Stonington High School, communicates through sign language with her brother Robby, 14, who has autism and is deaf, in the living room of their Stonington, Conn., home. Her experiences growing up with Robby led Allissa Porter to do volunteer work with autistic children and to write and illustrate a children's book called "Why Doesn't Robby Love Me?" which she is now trying to get published.

among children with higher cognitive and language skills (G. Dawson, Rogers, et al., 2010; Mazurek, Kanne, & Miles, 2012). In fact, after intensive intervention, some children no longer meet ASD diagnostic criteria; however, even among children whose symptoms have remitted, comorbid conditions such as depression, anxiety, inattention, and hyperactivity often remain (Helt et al., 2008) and interfere with optimal performance in learning environments (Ashburner, Ziviani, & Rodger, 2010).

A variety of medications are used in an effort to decrease anxiety, repetitive behaviors, and hyperactivity in those with ASD, but with limited success (Oswald & Sonenklar, 2007); some medications (such as SSRIs) can, in fact, be harmful (K. Williams, Wheeler, Silove, & Hazell, 2010). Although some treatments (such as melatonin and antioxidants) have received substantial research support (Rossignol, 2009), only one medication—the antipsychotic risperidone—has received approval from the U.S. Food and Drug Administration for the treatment of ASD. Additionally, some preliminary research has found that that administration of **oxytocin**, a naturally occurring hormone that affects social bonding, can increase social interactions in adults and adolescents with mild ASD (Andari et al., 2010; Guastella et al., 2010).

ASD causes major disruption in families and unfulfilled lives for many affected children. However, comprehensive treatment programs have enabled many children with ASD to develop more functional skills (Eldevik et al., 2010). Because of the communication and social impairments associated with ASD, skill building in these areas is often a target of intervention. Interventions that result in the most significant gains involve emphasis on social communication, environmental enrichment, reinforcement of appropriate attention and response to social stimuli, prevention of repetitive behaviors, sustained practice of weaker skills, reduction of environmental stress, and cultivation of strategies to improve sleep and nutrition (Helt et al., 2008). Training age-level peers in strategies for interacting with children with ASD has also been effective in promoting social interaction (Kasari, Rotheram-Fuller, Locke, & Gulsrud, 2012).

Intellectual Developmental Disorder

Intellectual developmental disorder (IDD), formerly referred to as *mental retardation*, is characterized by significant limitations in intellectual functioning and adaptive behaviors, including

- significantly below-average general intellectual functioning (ordinarily interpreted as an IQ score of 70 or less on an individually administered IQ test) and
- deficiencies in **adaptive behavior** (e.g., self-care; understanding of health and safety issues; ability to live, work, or plan leisure activities and use community resources; functional use of academic skills) that are greater than would be expected based on age or cultural background.

IDD is diagnosed only when low intelligence is accompanied by impaired adaptive functioning. Psychologists have traditionally identified four distinct categories of IDD based on IQ score ranges and adaptive behaviors. These categories are (a) *mild* (IQ score 50–55 to 70), (b) *moderate* (IQ score 35–40 to 50–55), (c) *severe* (IQ score 20–25 to 35–40), and (d) *profound* (IQ score below 20–25). Table 15.7 summarizes functional characteristics associated with each of these categories; social, vocational, and adaptive behaviors can vary significantly not only between categories but also within a given category.

oxytocin a powerful hormone that affects social bonding

intellectual developmental disorder (IDD) a disorder characterized by limitations in intellectual functioning and adaptive behaviors

adaptive behavior performance on tasks of daily living including academic skills, self-care, and the ability to work or live independently

TABLE 15.7 Adaptive Characteristics Associated With Intellectual Developmental Disorder

LEVEL	APPROXIMATE IQ RANGE	CHARACTERISTICS
Mild	50–55 to 70	Daily living and social interactions skills are mildly affected; adaptive difficulties involve conceptual and academic understanding; the individual may need assistance with job skills or independent living; the individual may marry and raise children
Moderate	35–40 to 50–55	The individual may have functional self-care skills and the ability to communicate basic needs; the individual may read a few basic words; lifelong support and supervision are required (e.g., supervised meal preparation, sheltered work)
Severe	20–25 to 35–40	The individual may recognize familiar people; communication skills are limited; lifelong support is required
Profound	Below 20-25	Characteristics are similar to those of severe intellectual disability, with even more extensive care needs

The American Association on Intellectual and Developmental Disabilities (2012) asserts that, although IQ scores may be used to approximate intellectual functioning for diagnostic purposes, it is much more important to focus on adaptive functioning and the nature of psychosocial supports that are needed to maximize adaptive functioning. We know that the effects of IDD are variable and that individuals with mild or moderate IDD often function independently or semi-independently in adulthood. Additionally, with support and intervention, those with more severe IDD can make cognitive and social gains and have improved life satisfaction.

Approximately 1 percent of students in public schools in the United States are identified as having an IDD (U.S. Department of Education, National Center for Education Statistics, 2010). Low- and middle-income countries have double the prevalence of IDD compared to higher-income countries (Maulik, Mascarenhas, Mathers, Dua, & Saxena, 2011). Many individuals with IDD have coexisting conditions such as ASD or depression (Morin, Cobigo, Rivard, & Lépine, 2010); approximately one fourth have a seizure disorder (World Health Organization, 2011).

Etiology of Intellectual Developmental Disorder The etiology of IDD differs, to some extent, depending on the level of intellectual impairment. Mild IDD is often *idiopathic* (having no known cause), whereas more pronounced IDD

CONTROVERSY:

Risks of Substance Use in Pregnancy

It is common knowledge that alcohol and other drugs can affect a developing fetus. The effects depend on the timing (i.e., the stage of fetal development) as well as the type and amount of substance used. Pregnant women are advised to avoid alcohol throughout pregnancy to prevent the physical and cognitive abnormalities associated with fetal alcohol syndrome, the leading cause of preventable intellectual disability (J. D. Thomas, Warren, & Hewitt, 2010). Use of marijuana, cocaine, heroin, or methamphetamine can also lead to neurodevelopmental disorders (Campolongo, Trezza, Palmery, Trabace, & Cuomo, 2009; Delaney-Black, et al., 2010; Lu et al., 2009; Sowell et al., 2010). Of course, in utero substance exposure is often associated with other prenatal and childhood risk factors, such as poor nutrition, limited prenatal care, a chaotic home environment, and abuse, neglect, or other stressors that can affect brain development (B. M. Lester et al., 2010).

Researchers are attempting to find diagnostic tools to detect drug or alcohol use during pregnancy and to identify newborns affected by maternal substance use; their hope is that early detection will allow for early intervention (Ismail, Buckley, Budacki, Jabbar, & Gallicano, 2010). What are the health, legal, and moral implications of these efforts to detect substance use? Are there other ways to reach out to women who are using substances during pregnancy?

is typically related to genetic factors, brain abnormalities, or brain injury. Although a variety of biological factors are implicated in intellectual disability, psychological, social, and sociocultural dimensions also play a role in intellectual development and adaptive functioning.

Genetic Factors In up to 80 percent of cases of IDD, the underlying cause is unknown (L. Kaufman et al., 2010; Xiang et al., 2008). It is believed that genetic factors that have not yet been identified are responsible for many of these cases; in particular, researchers are working to identify genes that are related to learning and memory. Genetic factors that exert an influence on IDD include both *genetic variations* and *genetic abnormalities*. IDD caused by normal genetic variation reflects the fact that in a normal distribution of any trait (such as intelligence), some individuals fall in the lower range. The normal range of intelligence is considered to lie between the IQ scores of 70 and 130; some individuals with IDD have an IQ that falls at or slightly below the lower end of this normal range (70 or slightly lower) but are otherwise physically and emotionally healthy and have no specific physiological anomaly associated with their cognitive and adaptive difficulties.

The genetic anomalies associated with IDD include chromosomal abnormalities as well as conditions resulting from inheritance of a single gene. Although genetic abnormalities can result in varying degrees of IDD, many individuals who are genetically affected have significant impairment (Raymond et al., 2007). The most common inherited form of IDD is **fragile X syndrome**, a condition resulting in limited production of proteins required for brain development. Fragile X syndrome results in mild to severe IDD. Females generally have less impairment; males are prone to having communication and social difficulties including anxious, inattentive, fearful, or aggressive behavior. Autistic behavior and hyperactivity occur in some individuals with fragile X syndrome (Oliver et al., 2011).

Down syndrome (DS) is the most common and most easily recognized chromosomal disorder resulting in IDD (M. Shin et al., 2009). In the vast majority of cases, an extra copy of chromosome 21 originates during gamete development (involving either the egg or the sperm); this extra chromosome produces the physical and neurological characteristics associated with DS (Gardiner et al., 2010). DS occurs once in approximately every 800–1,000 live births ("Down Syndrome," 2007). The chance of an egg containing an extra copy of chromosome 21 increases significantly with increasing maternal age. The incidence of DS births to women younger than 30 is less than 1 in 1,000; the incidence increases to 1 in 400 at age 35, 1 in 60 at age 42, and 1 in 12 at age 49. However, because more than 90 percent of all pregnancies occur in women younger than age 35, over 75 percent of the babies born with DS have young mothers (National Institute of Child Health and Human Development, 2011a).

Distinctive physical characteristics associated with DS include a single crease across the palm of the hand, slanted eyes, a protruding tongue, and a harsh voice. The majority of individuals with DS have mild to moderate IDD; however, negligible intellectual impairment or severe impairment is also possible. With support, many adults with DS have jobs and live semi-independently. Individuals with DS have significantly increased incidence of childhood leukemia and infectious diseases, hearing loss, congenital heart disease, and premature aging (National Institute of Child Health and Human Development, 2011b). Although medical intervention has improved health outcomes and increased life expectancy (Weijerman & de Winter, 2010), those with DS continue to have a significantly increased risk of early dementia, including early-onset Alzheimer's disease (National Down Syndrome Society, 2012).

Prenatal detection of DS is possible through different techniques, including **amniocentesis**, a screening procedure involving withdrawal of amniotic fluid from the fetal sac. This procedure, performed between the 14th and 18th weeks

fragile X syndrome an inherited condition involving limited production of proteins required for brain development resulting in mild to severe intellectual disability

Down syndrome (DS) a chromosomal disorder (most frequently involving an extra copy of chromosome 21) that causes physical and neurological abnormalities

amniocentesis a prenatal screening procedure involving withdrawal of amniotic fluid from the fetal sac

of pregnancy, involves some risk for both mother and fetus, so it is employed primarily when the chance of finding DS is high (e.g., with women 35 or older).

Nongenetic Biological Factors IDD can result from a variety of environmental influences during the prenatal (from conception to birth), perinatal (just prior to and during the birth process), or postnatal (after birth) period. Many of the circumstances that can cause IDD (as well as other neurodevelopmental disorders) are preventable or controllable (Table 15.8). During the prenatal period, the developing fetus is susceptible to viruses and infections (e.g., tuberculosis or German measles), drugs and alcohol, radiation, and poor nutrition. Some risk factors can cause IDD both prenatally and after birth. For example, iodine deficiency either during pregnancy or during early infancy can impair intellectual development (World Health Organization, 2011).

TABLE 15.8 Preventable or Controllable Causes of Neurodevelopmental Disorders

PRENATAL (BEFORE BIRTH)
Severe malnutrition
Alcohol or illicit drugs; prescription medications
Iodine or folic acid deficiency[a]
Maternal infections such as rubella[a] or syphilis
Toxoplasma parasites (from cat feces, undercooked meats, or unwashed produce)
Exposure to radiation
Blood incompatibility (Rh factor)
Maternal chronic disease (heart or kidney disease, diabetes)
Untreated phenylketonuria
PERINATAL (JUST BEFORE OR DURING BIRTH)
Severe prematurity
Birth trauma
Asphyxia (lack of oxygen)
INFANCY AND CHILDHOOD
Untreated phenylketonuria
Nutritional deficiencies[a]
Iodine deficiency
Severe lack of stimulation
Chronic lead exposure[a]
Other environmental toxins[a]
Brain infections (e.g., meningitis and encephalitis)
Head injury

[a]These factors have also been implicated in the etiology of autism spectrum disorder.

Adapted from the World Health Organization (2011)

Alcohol intake can significantly affect embryonic and fetal development. Although there is a continuum of detrimental neurological and behavioral effects resulting from alcohol consumption during pregnancy (referred to as **fetal alcohol spectrum effects**), the greatest concern is for those children who have **fetal alcohol syndrome (FAS)**. Although FAS is estimated to occur in less than 1 percent of live births, 2–5 percent of the United States population is estimated to have fetal alcohol spectrum effects (P. A. May et al., 2009). Fetal alcohol spectrum effects include reduced cognitive functioning, attentional difficulties, slower information processing, and poor working memory (Kodituwakku, 2009), whereas FAS results in retarded growth, facial abnormalities, and significant dysfunction of the central nervous system and brain (J. D. Thomas et al., 2010). Children with FAS experience difficulty with attention, learning, memory, regulation of emotions, and executive functioning, all of which are associated with the frontal lobe of the brain (C. R. Green et al., 2009); overstimulation has a particularly negative effect on children with FAS (Kooistra et al., 2010). Markedly delayed development in adaptive behavior, particularly skills of daily living, is also common (Crocker, Vaurio, Riley, & Mattson, 2009).

The most common perinatal birth conditions associated with IDD are prematurity and low birth weight. Although most premature infants develop normally, some have neurological problems resulting in learning disorders and IDD (Whitaker et al., 2006). During the postnatal period, factors such as head injuries, brain infections, tumors, and prolonged malnutrition can cause brain damage and consequent IDD. Exposure to environmental toxins is an increasing concern. Lead, a well-known neurotoxin, is associated with both IDD and hyperactivity (Abelsohn & Sanborn, 2010.

fetal alcohol spectrum effects a continuum of detrimental neurological and behavioral effects resulting from maternal alcohol consumption during pregnancy

fetal alcohol syndrome (FAS) a condition resulting from maternal alcohol consumption during gestation that involves central nervous system dysfunction and altered brain development; the leading cause of preventable intellectual disability

Psychological, Social, and Sociocultural Dimensions Psychological, social, and sociocultural factors can affect both intellectual and adaptive functioning. A child's genetic background interacts with environmental factors; children from socioeconomically advantaged homes are often provided enriching experiences that enhance cognitive development. In contrast, crowded living conditions, lack of adequate health care, poor nutrition, and inadequate educational opportunities place children living in poverty at an intellectual disadvantage and can influence whether they reach their genetic potential (Tucker-Drob, Rhemtulla, Harden, Turkheimer, & Fask, 2011). Similarly, children raised by parents with mild IDD

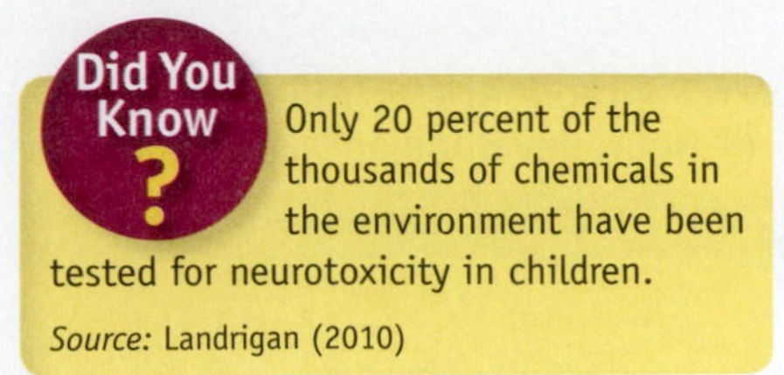

Only 20 percent of the thousands of chemicals in the environment have been tested for neurotoxicity in children.

Source: Landrigan (2010)

may begin their lives with less intellectual stimulation and learning opportunity, further contributing to a generational pattern of lower intellectual functioning. Additionally, the long-term effects of prematurity appear to be moderated by sociocultural factors such as socioeconomic status and parenting style; supportive parenting or increased socioeconomic resources can enhance ultimate cognitive functioning (P. J. Anderson & Doyle, 2008).

An enriching and encouraging home environment as well as ongoing educational intervention focused on targeted cognitive, academic, self-care, social, and problem-solving skills can have a strong and positive influence on the development of children with IDD (J. D. Thomas et al., 2010). Coping strategies and use of outside resources when raising a child with IDD can be highly influenced by sociocultural context. Additionally, religious or cultural beliefs may affect parents' perceptions of their child's condition; for example, some parents may attribute IDD to factors such as personal wrongdoing or a curse placed on their family, whereas others believe a child with special needs is a gift from God (Durà-Vilà, Dein, & Hodes, 2010).

Learning Disorders

A **learning disorder (LD)** is diagnosed when someone with at least average intellectual abilities demonstrates development of basic math, reading, or writing skills that is substantially lower than would be expected for the person's chronological age, educational background, and intellectual ability. LD primarily interferes with academic achievement and activities of daily living in which reading, writing, or math skills are required. As with any testing, when an assessment for LD is conducted, care is taken to ensure that testing procedures take the child's linguistic and cultural background into consideration. Specific learning disorders include **dyslexia** (significant difficulties with accuracy or fluency of reading), **dyscalculia** (significant difficulties in understanding quantities, number symbols, or basic arithmetic calculations), and disorders of written expression.

Approximately 5 percent of students in public schools in the United States are diagnosed with LD (U.S. Department of Education, National Center for Education Statistics, 2010); LD occurs twice as frequently in boys (CDC, 2011b). Many children with LD have concurrent ADHD. Some individuals appear to mature out of their academic difficulties, whereas for others LD is a lifelong condition. The severity of the disorder varies, and some individuals continue to cope with severe academic deficits in adulthood. Because adults with severe LD may experience problems with employment, it is beneficial when their career choice capitalizes on their abilities and strengths.

Etiology Little is currently known about the precise causes of LD. Children with LD that eventually resolves appear to have slower brain maturation (with eventual catching up). However, others have lifelong differences in neurological processing of information related to basic academic skills. Etiological possibilities for chronic LD include many of the same biological explanations for IDD and ADHD (see Table 15.8), such as prematurity (Aarnoudse-Moens et al., 2009) and maternal alcohol use during pregnancy (Kodituwakku, 2009). Additionally, LD tends to run in families, suggesting a genetic component.

learning disorder (LD) an academic disability characterized by deficits in reading, writing, and math skills that bring them substantially below levels that would be expected based on the person's age, intellectual ability, and educational background

dyslexia a condition involving significant difficulties with reading skills

dyscalculia a condition involving difficulties in understanding mathematical skills or concepts

Support for Individuals With Neurodevelopmental Disorders

Because many neurodevelopmental disorders produce lifelong disability, the goal of intervention is to build skills and develop each individual's potential to the fullest extent possible. For those with moderate to severe IDD or ASD, such support often begins in infancy and extends across the life span. In the case of

ASD, early targeted intervention can result in moderately to significantly improved linguistic, intellectual, adaptive, and social functioning (G. Dawson, Rogers, et al., 2010; Virués-Ortega, 2010). For children with ADHD, LD, mild IDD, or mild ASD, support may occur primarily in the school setting. Interventions for LD and mild IDD typically involve remedial interventions targeting the area of academic difficulty, whereas supports for ASD and more severe intellectual impairment are generally more comprehensive.

© Mika/Corbis

Work Opportunities for Individuals With Neurodevelopmental Disorders

Many people with Down syndrome and other neurodevelopmental disorders can function well in a supportive work environment. Here a baker's assistant is proudly displaying fresh bread.

Support in Childhood When ASD or IDD is identified early, children often participate in individualized home-based or school-based programs focused on decreasing inappropriate behaviors and maximizing skill development in areas such as movement; communication, and—when appropriate—pre-academic skills. Parent involvement is an integral part of early intervention programs; parents can help reduce maladaptive behaviors (Scahill et al., 2012) as well as enhance cognitive, social, and communication development.

In general, school services are individualized to meet the needs of the child and to maximize learning opportunities, including skills needed for independent or semi-independent living (National Dissemination Center for Children With Disabilities, 2012). Unfortunately, rates of improvement often decrease once school programs are completed; programs terminate following high school graduation, or at age 21 for those with more significant impairment (J. L. Taylor & Seltzer, 2010b).

Support in Adulthood A number of programs are available for young adults with moderate neurodevelopmental disabilities to learn vocational skills or to participate in work opportunities in a specialized setting. These programs focus on specific job skills, social skills for interacting with coworkers and supervisors, and completing work-related tasks with speed and quality. There is a clear need for more support for those with mild IDD or ASD as they make the transition from high school to out-of-school activities, especially for those who are unable to obtain employment without support (J. L. Taylor & Seltzer, 2010a).

Institutionalization of adults with neurodevelopmental disorders is rare. Many adults with special needs live with family members; others live independently or semi-independently within the community. The idea is to provide the least restrictive environment possible—that is, as much independence and personal choice as is safe and practical. Although group arrangements vary considerably from setting to setting (J. Perry & Felce, 2005), most normalized living arrangements produce benefits such as increased adaptive functioning, improved language development, and socialization. Many assisted-living environments promote social interaction with the larger community and continue to support the development of personal competence and independence.

CHECKPOINT REVIEW

1. Compare and contrast the various neurodevelopmental disorders.
2. What environmental influences can cause neurodevelopmental disorders?
3. Which neurodevelopmental disorders are influenced by genetic factors?

Summary

1 What internalizing disorders occur in childhood and adolescence?

- Anxiety disorders are the most common internalizing disorders in youth.
- Depressive and bipolar disorders can occur in childhood, but they are more prevalent during adolescence.
- Nonsuicidal self injury is most likely to emerge during adolescence.
- Attachment disorders develop early in life due to persistent neglect, abuse, or frequent changes in primary caregiver.

2 What are the characteristics of externalizing disorders?

- Disruptive mood dysregulation disorder involves negative affect and exaggerated responses to anger.
- Oppositional defiant disorder involves a pattern of hostile, defiant behavior toward authority figures.
- Conduct disorders involve serious antisocial behaviors and violations of the rights of others.

3 What are neurodevelopmental disorders, and what are their characteristics?

- Motor and vocal tic disorders and Tourette's disorder involve involuntary repetitive movements or vocalizations.
- Attention-deficit/hyperactivity disorder is characterized by inattention, hyperactivity, and impulsivity.
- Autism spectrum disorder involves impairment in social communication and restricted, stereotyped interests and activities.
- Intellectual developmental disorder involves limitations in intellectual functioning and adaptive behaviors.
- Learning disorders involve basic reading, writing, or math skills that are substantially below expectations based on age, intelligence, and educational experiences.

Key Terms

temperament 412
child psychopathology 412
internalizing disorders 413
school phobia 414
separation anxiety disorder 414
selective mutism 414
nonsuicidal self injury (NSSI) 416
pediatric bipolar disorder (PBD) 416
hypomania 417
reactive attachment disorder (RAD) 417
disinhibited social engagement disorder (DSED) 418
externalizing disorders 419
disruptive mood dysregulation disorder (DMDD) 419
oppositional defiant disorder (ODD) 420
conduct disorder (CD) 421
callous and unemotional subtype 421
neurodevelopmental disorders 424
tic 424
motor tic 424
vocal tic 424
Tourette's disorder (TD) 424
coprolalia 425
habit reversal 425
attention-deficit/hyperactivity disorder (ADHD) 426
autism spectrum disorder (ASD) 429
echolalia 430
autistic savant 430
Asperger's syndrome 431
oxytocin 434
intellectual developmental disorder (IDD) 434
adaptive behavior 434
fragile X syndrome 436
Down syndrome (DS) 436
amniocentesis 436
fetal alcohol spectrum effects 437
fetal alcohol syndrome (FAS) 437
learning disorder (LD) 438
dyslexia 438
dyscalculia 438

Media Resources

Psychology CourseMate

Access an interactive e-Book and chapter-specific interactive learning tools, including:

- flashcards
- quizzes
- videos

and more in your Psychology CourseMate.

Go to **CengageBrain.com.**

Bill Fritsch/Brand X/Jupiterimages

16 Law and Ethics in Abnormal Psychology

CHAPTER OUTLINE

On June 30, 2001, Andrea Yates waited until her husband left for work, filled the bathtub to the very top, and proceeded to kill her five children (ages 7 months to 7 years). She drowned the children in the bathtub, carried them to a bedroom, laid them out next to one another, and covered them with a sheet. Yates then called 911 and asked for the police. Afterward, she called her husband and stated, "You need to come home. . . . It's time. I did it." When asked what she meant, Yates responded, "It's the children . . . all of them." When the police arrived, Yates calmly explained how she had killed her five young children. Police report that the children struggled vigorously as she held each under the water until they drowned.

The case of Andrea Yates shocked the nation. How could a mother possibly commit such an unthinkable act? Her action was especially heinous because it involved five children and was carried out in such a methodical manner. During Yates's trial, the prosecution asked for the death penalty, but the defense contended that she was psychotic, had postpartum depression, was insane, and should not be held accountable for her actions. The jury, however, found her guilty. An appeals court subsequently overturned the verdict, and on July 26, 2006, another Texas jury found her not guilty by reason of insanity.

FOCUS QUESTIONS

1 What are the criteria used to judge insanity, and what is the difference between being insane and being incompetent to stand trial?

2 Under what conditions can a person be involuntarily committed to a mental institution?

3 What rights do mental patients have with respect to treatment and care?

4 What is deinstitutionalization?

5 What legal and ethical issues govern the therapist–client relationship?

6 What is cultural competence in the mental health profession?

How can we explain the actions of Andrea Yates? Was she so mentally disturbed that she was unaware of her actions or did not know right from wrong? How did psychologists determine her mental state and what criteria do they use to judge whether she was sane or insane? Is there a difference between insanity and mental illness?

Psychologists and mental health professionals are increasingly becoming involved in the legal system and must deal with the multiple questions posed here. Determining whether someone is sane or insane, however, is only a small part of their roles in the legal system. They help determine individuals' state of mind and participate in decisions and actions of the legal system that affect human relationships (R. I. Simon & Gold, 2004; Werth, Weifel, & Benjamin, 2009). In the past, psychologists evaluated competency in criminal cases such as those of Andrea Yates. Now, psychologists give expert opinions on child custody, organic brain functioning, traumatic injury, suicide, and even deprogramming activities (Table 16.1). The American Psychological Association has even taken on the role of *amicus curiae* (friend of the court) by filing briefs to act in an advisory capacity on how social psychological research can inform legal decisions (Clay, 2010). And just as psychologists influence decisions in the legal system, they are influenced by mental health laws passed at local, state, and federal levels (Pope & Vasquez, 2007).

In this chapter we cover many topics where psychology and the law intersect. We begin by examining some of the issues of criminal and civil commitment. Then we look at patients' rights and deinstitutionalization. We end by exploring the legal and ethical parameters of the therapist–client relationship and taking a final look at ethical issues related to cultural competence in mental health.

AP Photo/Greg Gilbert, Pool

The Insanity Defense

Naveed Haq, a Pakistani American, invaded the Jewish Federation of Greater Seattle, railing against Israel and the Iraq War. He fired at workers, killing one woman and wounding five. Haq pleaded not guilty by reason of insanity in April 2008. His family and a psychiatrist testified that he had a long history of mental illness and that he was in a manic state during the rampage. In June 2008, a mistrial was declared due to a deadlocked jury. Haq was retried and convicted in 2009.

TABLE 16.1 The Intersection of Psychology and the Law

Psychologists are finding that their expertise is being sought in the legal system and influenced by the law. A few of these roles and activities are included here.

Assessment of Dangerousness • Assess potential for suicide and homicide, child endangerment, civil commitment, and so on. • Be knowledgeable about the clinical and research findings affecting such determinations.	**Psychological Evaluations in Child Protection Matters** • Attempt to determine whether abuse or neglect has occurred, whether the child is at risk for harm, and what corrective action, if any, should be recommended.
Evaluation for Child Custody in Divorce Proceedings • Provide expertise to help courts and social services agencies determine the best interests of the child. • Possibly advise on parental arrangements, termination of parental rights, and issues of neglect and abuse in custody cases.	**Determination of Repressed, Recovered, or False Memories** • Determine the accuracy and validity of repressed memories—claims by adults that they have recovered memories of childhood abuse.
Civil Commitment Determination • Become involved in the civil commitment of an individual or the discharge of a person who has been so confined. • Determine whether the person is at risk of harm to the self or others, is too mentally disturbed to practice self-care, or lacks the appropriate resources for care if left alone.	**Jury Selection** • Aid attorneys in determining whether prospective jurors might favor one side of a case or the other. • Use clinical knowledge in an attempt to screen out individuals who might be biased against clients.

TABLE 16.1 The Intersection of Psychology and the Law—cont'd

Filing of Amicus Briefs • Use psychological science to help inform the court as to social science research that is relevant to a particular pending litigation. • Act as a friend of the court by filing amicus briefs (pleadings) that have psychological implications in court cases.	**Profiling of Serial Killers, Mass Murderers, or Specific Criminals** • Work hand in hand with law enforcement officials in developing profiles of criminals.
Determination of Sanity or Insanity • At the request of a court, prosecution, or defense, determine the sanity or insanity of someone accused of a crime. • Present findings via a private hearing to the judge or expert testimony in front of a jury.	**Testimony in Malpractice Suits** • Testify in a civil suit on whether another practicing clinician failed to follow the standards of the profession and is thus guilty of negligence or malpractice. • Determine whether the client bringing the suit incurred psychological harm or damage as a result of the clinician's actions.
Determination of Competency to Stand Trial • Determine whether an individual is mentally competent or sufficiently rational to stand trial and to aid in his or her defense.	**Protection of Patient Rights** • Become involved in seeing that patients are not grievously wronged by the loss of their civil liberties on the grounds of mental health treatment. • Advise on the right to receive treatment, to refuse treatment, and to live in the least restrictive environment.

Criminal Commitment

A basic premise of criminal law is that all of us are responsible beings who exercise free will and are capable of choices. If we do something wrong, we are responsible for our actions and should suffer the consequences. **Criminal commitment** is the incarceration of an individual for having committed a crime. Abnormal psychology accepts different perspectives on free will; criminal law does not. Yet criminal law does recognize that some people lack the ability to discern the ramifications of their actions because they are mentally disturbed. Although they may be technically guilty of a crime, their mental state at the time of the offense exempts them from legal responsibility. Let us explore the landmark cases that have influenced the evolution and application of insanity criteria. Standards arising from these cases and some other important guidelines are summarized in Figure 16.1.

The Insanity Defense

The concept of "not guilty by reason of insanity" (NGRI) has provoked much controversy among legal scholars, mental health practitioners, and the general public. The **insanity defense** is a legal argument used by defendants who admit they have committed a crime but plead not guilty because they were mentally disturbed at the time of the crime. The insanity plea recognizes that under specific circumstances, people may not be held accountable for their behavior.

The fear that a guilty individual might use such a plea to escape criminal responsibility has been frequently exploited in popular media for dramatic effect. For example, in the Hollywood film *Primal Fear*, Richard Gere plays a

criminal commitment incarceration of an individual for having committed a crime

insanity defense the legal argument used by defendants who admit that they have committed a crime but plead not guilty because they were mentally disturbed at the time of the crime

FIGURE 16.1

Legal Standards That Address the Mental State of the Defendant

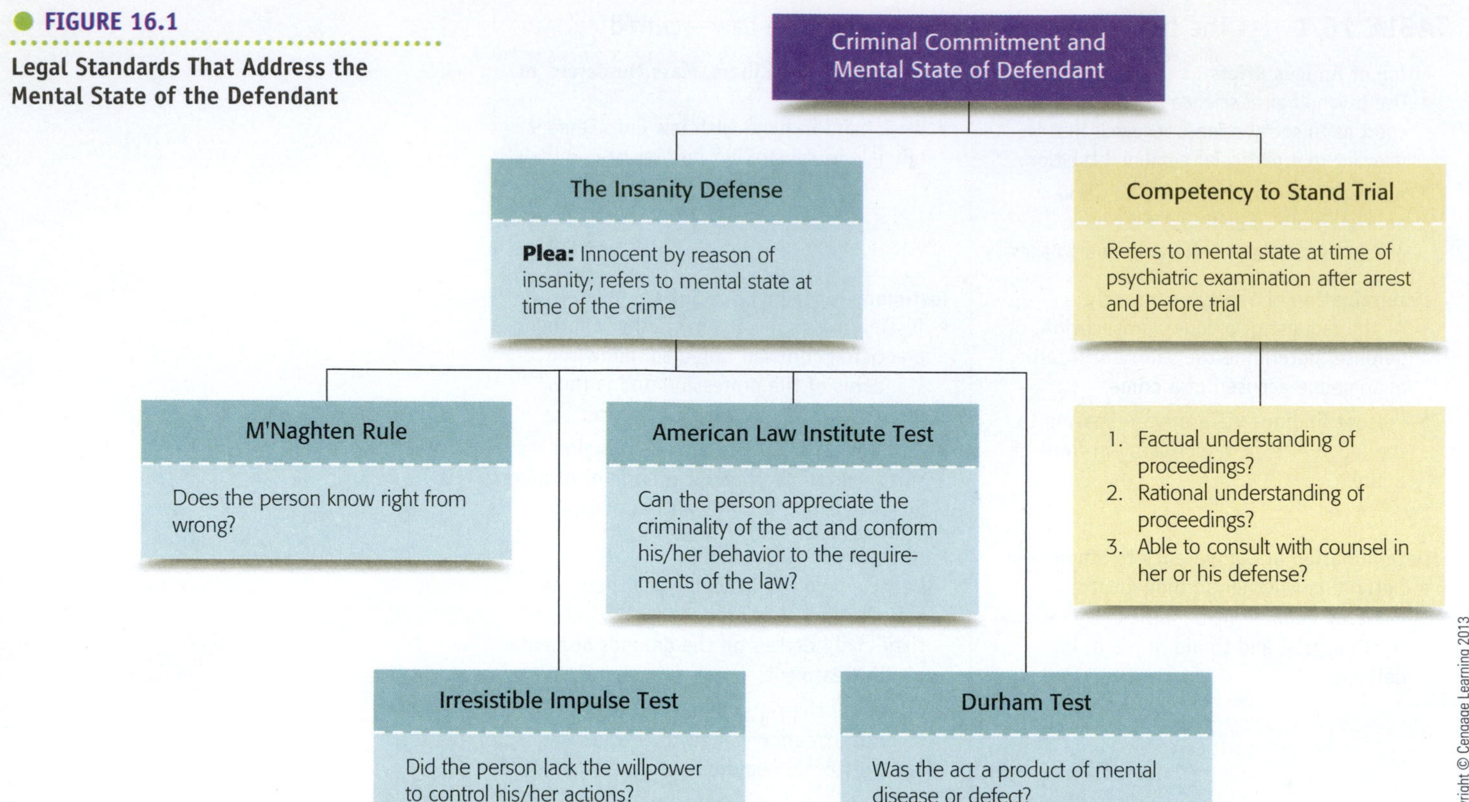

MYTH VS. REALITY

MYTH Defendants who are found not guilty by reason of insanity spend less time in custody (jail, mental health institution, or prison) than those who are convicted. That is the reason the plea is overused.

REALITY As a rule, defendants found NGRI spend significantly more time in custody than those who are convicted. They often face a lifetime of postrelease judicial oversight. Further, the plea is infrequently used (less than 1 percent of cases) and seldom successful.

high-powered attorney who is duped into believing that his client has dissociative identity disorder. The client is found NGRI at the trial, only to have Gere's character discover the ghastly truth: His client convincingly faked his insanity. In reality, less than 1 percent of defendants ever use an insanity defense and only 25 percent of NGRI defenses are successful ("Excuse: Insanity," n.d.). Many of the cases discussed in this chapter are the exceptions to the rule, but they are pivotal to the discussion of abnormal psychology and the law. These are the same cases that received media attention and helped construct the popular misconception that NGRI defenses are highly successful.

In real life, most defendants who plead NGRI have a long history of mental illness. Those who fake it are seldom successful. Confessed Hillside Strangler Kenneth Bianchi, for example, attempted to fake mental illness as mitigation for his part in raping, torturing, and murdering a number of girls and young women in the late 1970s. Wanting to use the insanity plea to get a reduced sentence, Bianchi tried to convince psychiatrists that he suffered from multiple personality disorder (now called dissociative identity disorder). Psychologist and hypnosis expert Dr. Martin Orne exposed his scheme as a fake, and Bianchi was found guilty of murder and sentenced to life in prison without parole.

Legal Precedents In the United States, a number of different standards are used as legal tests of insanity. One of the earliest is the *M'Naghten* rule. In 1843, Daniel M'Naghten, a grossly disturbed woodcutter from Glasgow, Scotland, claimed that he was commanded by God to kill the English prime minister, Sir Robert Peel. He killed a lesser minister by mistake and was placed on trial, where it became obvious that M'Naghten was quite delusional. Out of this incident emerged the **M'Naghten rule**, popularly known as the "right–wrong" test, which holds that people can be acquitted of a crime if at the time of the act, they (a) had such defective reasoning that they did not know what they were doing or (b) were unable to comprehend that the act was wrong. The *M'Naghten* rule has come under tremendous criticism from some who regard it as being exclusively a cognitive test (knowledge of right or wrong), which does not consider volition, emotion, or other mental activity. Further, it is often difficult to evaluate a defendant's awareness or comprehension.

The second major precedent that strengthened the insanity defense was the **irresistible impulse test**. In essence, this doctrine says that defendants are not criminally responsible if they lacked the willpower to control their behaviors. Combined with the *M'Naghten* rule, this test broadened the criteria for using the insanity defense. In other words, a verdict of NGRI could be obtained if it was shown that the defendant was unaware of or did not comprehend his or her actions or was irresistibly impelled to commit the acts. Criticisms of the irresistible impulse defense revolve around what constitutes an irresistible impulse. When, for example, is a person *unable* to exert control (irresistible impulse) rather than *choosing* not to exert control (unresisted impulse)? Is a man who rapes a woman unable to resist his impulses, or is he choosing not to exert control? Neither the mental health profession nor the legal profession has answered this question satisfactorily.

In the case of *Durham v. United States* (1954), a U.S. Court of Appeals for the District of Columbia Circuit broadened the *M'Naghten* rule with the so-called products test or ***Durham* standard**. An accused person is not considered criminally responsible if his or her unlawful act was the *product* of a mental disease or defect. The intent of the ruling was to (a) give the greatest possible weight to expert evaluation and testimony and (b) allow mental health professionals to define mental illness. The *Durham* standard also has its drawbacks. The term *product* is vague and difficult to define, because almost anything can cause anything (as you have learned by studying the many theoretical viewpoints in this text). Leaving the task of defining mental illness to mental health professionals often results in having to define mental illness in every case. In many situations, relying on psychiatric testimony serves only to confuse the issues, because both the prosecution and defense bring in psychiatric experts, who often present conflicting testimony (Koocher & Keith-Spiegel, 2008).

In 1962, the ***American Law Institute, Model Penal Code***, provided guidelines to help jurors determine the validity of the insanity defense on a case-by-case basis. The guidelines combined features from the previous standards (Sec. 401, p. 66):

1. A person is not responsible for criminal conduct if at the time of such conduct as a result of mental disease or defect he lacks substantial capacity either to appreciate the criminality of his conduct or to conform his conduct to the requirements of the law.
2. As used in the Article, the terms "mental disease or defect" do not include an abnormality manifested by repeated criminal or otherwise antisocial conduct.

It is interesting to note that the second point was intended to eliminate the insanity defense for people diagnosed as antisocial personalities.

In some jurisdictions, the concept of *diminished capacity* has also been incorporated into the American Law Institute standard. As a result of a mental disease or defect, a person may lack the *specific intent* to commit the offense. For example, a person under the influence of drugs or alcohol may commit a crime without premeditation or intent; a person who is grieving over the death of a loved one may harm the one responsible for the death. Although diminished capacity has been used primarily to guide the sentencing and disposition of the defendant, it is now introduced in the trial phase as well.

***M'Naghten* rule** a cognitive test of legal insanity that inquires whether the accused knew right from wrong when he or she committed the crime

irresistible impulse test a doctrine that states that a defendant is not criminally responsible if he or she lacked the willpower to control his or her behavior

***Durham* standard** a test of legal insanity also known as the *products test*—an accused person is not responsible if the unlawful act was the product of a mental disease or defect

American Law Institute Model Penal Code a test of legal insanity whose purpose is to give jurors increased latitude in determining the sanity of the accused

© Bettman/CORBIS

Not Guilty by Reason of Insanity

John Hinckley, Jr. (center), was charged with the attempted murder of President Ronald Reagan. His acquittal by reason of insanity created a furor among the U.S. public over use of the insanity defense. The outrage led Congress to pass the Insanity Defense Reform Act.

Such was the trial of Dan White, a San Francisco supervisor who killed Mayor George Moscone and supervisor Harvey Milk on November 27, 1978. White blamed both individuals for his political demise. During the trial, his attorney used the now-famous "Twinkie defense" (White gorged himself on junk food such as Twinkies, chips, and soda) as a partial explanation for his client's actions. White's attorney attempted to convince the jury that the high sugar content of the junk food affected White's cognitive and emotional state and was partially to blame for his actions. White was convicted only of voluntary manslaughter and was sentenced to less than 8 years in jail. Of course, the citizens of San Francisco were outraged by the verdict and never forgave White. Facing constant public condemnation, he eventually committed suicide after his release.

Guilty, but Mentally Ill Perhaps no other trial has more greatly challenged the use of the insanity plea than the case of John W. Hinckley, Jr. Hinckley's attempt to assassinate President Ronald Reagan and his subsequent acquittal by reason of insanity outraged the public, as well as legal and mental health professionals. Many had begun to believe that the criteria for the defense were too broadly interpreted.

For quite some time, the Hinckley case aroused such strong emotional reaction that calls for reform were rampant. As a result, Congress passed the Insanity Defense Reform Act of 1984, which based the definition of insanity totally on the individual's ability to understand what he or she did. The American Psychological Association's position on the insanity defense, however, ran counter to these changes: Even though a given verdict might be wrong, the standard is not necessarily wrong.

Nevertheless, in the wake of the Hinckley verdict, some states adopted alternative pleas, such as "culpable and mentally disabled," "mentally disabled, but neither culpable nor innocent," and "guilty, but mentally ill." These pleas are attempts to separate mental illness from insanity and to hold people responsible for their acts. Such pleas allow jurors to reach a decision that not only convicts individuals for their crimes and holds them responsible but also ensures that they are treated for their mental illnesses. Despite attempts at reform, however, states and municipalities continue to use different tests of insanity, with varying outcomes, and the use of the insanity plea remains controversial.

Competency to Stand Trial

Case Study

On June 5, 2002, 14-year-old Elizabeth Smart was kidnapped at knifepoint from her Salt Lake City, Utah, home by Brian David Mitchell. The incident set off a massive search effort, evoked intense media coverage, was showcased on the *America's Most Wanted* TV program, became the subject of a book, and resulted in a made-for-TV movie, *The Elizabeth Smart Story*. Smart was found 9 months later after enduring a horrendous experience that included a forced polygamous "marriage," frequent rapes, and constant threats to her life.

Case Study—cont'd

Mitchell, a former street preacher, was arrested for the crime, but claimed that God had commanded him to abduct Smart, to enter into a celestial marriage, and to form a religious society of younger females.

Despite his having been captured, arrested, and charged with kidnapping, Mitchell's trial did not begin for almost 9 years, finally occurring in November 2010. The delays in his trial were due to one primary reason: In three separate court hearings, Mitchell was judged "mentally incapable of assisting in his own defense." In the courtroom he would sing hymns and scream at the judge to "forsake those robes and kneel in the dust." His behavior was so bizarre that he was banished from the courtroom several times. As a result, Mitchell was ordered to be hospitalized indefinitely until he was capable of understanding the proceedings.

Finally, in a series of hearings that followed, Mitchell was found competent to stand trial. At the trial his insanity plea was rejected by the jury and he was found guilty. On May 25, 2011, Mitchell was sentenced to life imprisonment without the possibility of parole.

The term **competency to stand trial** refers to a defendant's mental state at the time of psychiatric examination after arrest and before trial. It has nothing to do with the issue of criminal responsibility, which refers to an individual's mental state or behavior at the time of the offense. Court-appointed psychiatrists who examined Mitchell declared him not competent to stand trial. Federal law states that an accused person cannot be tried unless three criteria are satisfied (Fitch, 2007):

- The defendant must have a factual understanding of the proceedings.
- The defendant must have a rational understanding of the proceedings.
- The defendant must be able to rationally consult with counsel in presenting his or her own defense.

Given this third criterion, for example, a defendant who experiences paranoid delusions could not stand trial, because a serious impairment exists. Many more people are committed to prison hospitals because of incompetency determinations than are acquitted on insanity pleas (Stafford & Wygant, 2005; Zapf & Roesch, 2006). It is estimated, for example, that some 40,000 people in the United States are evaluated each year for competency to stand trial, and as many as 75 percent are determined to be incompetent. Determination of competency to stand trial is meant to ensure that a person understands the nature of the proceedings and is able to help in his or her own defense. This effort is an attempt to protect people who are mentally disturbed and to guarantee preservation of criminal and civil rights. But being judged incompetent to stand trial may have unfair negative consequences as well. A person may be committed for a long period of time, denied the chance to post bail, and isolated from friends and family, all without having been found guilty of a crime.

Such a miscarriage of justice was the focus of a U.S. Supreme Court ruling in the 1972 case of *Jackson v. Indiana*. In that case, a man with severe mental retardation and brain damage who could neither hear nor speak was charged with robbery but was determined incompetent to stand trial. He was committed indefinitely—which in his case probably meant for life, because the severity of his disorders meant that he would never be competent. His lawyers filed a petition to have him released on the basis of deprivation of **due process**—the legal checks and

competency to stand trial a judgment that a defendant has a factual and rational understanding of the proceedings and can rationally consult with counsel in presenting his or her own defense; refers to the defendant's mental state at the time of the psychiatric examination

due process legal checks and balances that are guaranteed to everyone (e.g., the right to receive a fair trial, the right to face one's accusers, the right to present evidence, the right to have counsel, and so on)

balances that are guaranteed to everyone, such as the right to receive a fair trial, the right to face one's accusers, the right to present evidence, the right to have counsel, and so on.

The U.S. Supreme Court ruled that a defendant cannot be confined indefinitely solely on the grounds of incompetency. After a reasonable time, a determination must be made as to whether the person is likely or unlikely to regain competency in the foreseeable future. If, in the hospital's opinion, competency is unlikely, the hospital must either release the individual or initiate civil commitment procedures.

CHECKPOINT REVIEW

1. What is the difference between insanity and a mental disorder?
2. Compare and contrast the four criteria used for the insanity defense.
3. How is a verdict of "guilty, but mentally ill" different from insanity according to the four criteria?
4. What does being incompetent to stand trial mean? Does it differ from insanity?

Civil Commitment

Case Study

She was known only as BL ("Bag Lady") in the area of downtown Oakland, California. By night, she slept on any number of park benches and in storefronts. By day she could be seen pushing her Safeway shopping cart full of boxes, extra clothing, and garbage, which she collected from numerous trash containers. According to her only surviving sister, the woman had lived this way for nearly 10 years and had been tolerated by local merchants.

Over the previous 6 months, however, BL's behavior had become progressively intolerable. She had always talked to herself, but recently she had begun shouting and screaming at anyone who approached her. Her use of profanity was graphic, and she often urinated and defecated in front of local stores. Although she never physically assaulted anyone, her menacing behavior frightened many pedestrians, customers, and shopkeepers. She was occasionally arrested and detained for short periods of time by local law enforcement officials, but she always returned to her familiar haunts. Finally, her sister and several merchants requested that the city take action to commit her to a mental institution.

Action is required when people are severely disturbed and behave in bizarre ways that pose a threat to themselves or others. The government has a longstanding power of *parens patriae* ("father of the country" or "power of the state"), under which it has the authority to commit disturbed individuals for their own best interest. **Civil commitment** is the name of this action; it is the involuntary confinement of individuals judged to be a danger to themselves or others, even though they have not committed a crime. Factors relevant to civil commitment are displayed in Figure 16.2. The commitment of a person in acute distress may be viewed as a form of protective confinement and demonstration of concern for the psychological and physical well-being of that person or others. Hospitalization is considered when the situation involves potential suicide or assault, bizarre behavior, destruction of property, or severe anxiety leading to loss of impulse control.

civil commitment the involuntary confinement of a person judged to be a danger to the self or to others, even though the person has not committed a crime

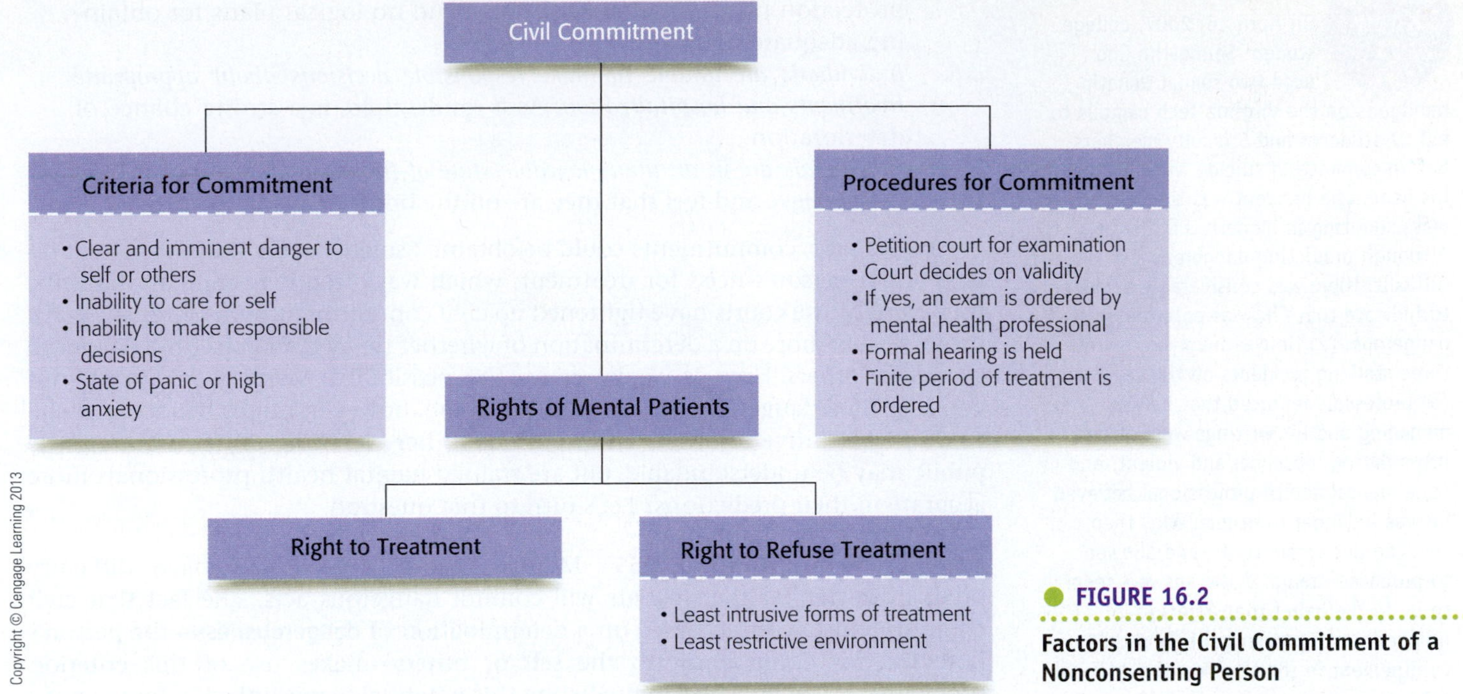

FIGURE 16.2

Factors in the Civil Commitment of a Nonconsenting Person

Involuntary hospitalization should, however, be avoided if at all possible, because it has many potentially negative consequences. It may result in the lifelong social stigma associated with psychiatric hospitalization, major interruption in the person's life, loss of control of one's life and dependency on others, and loss of self-esteem and self-concept. A possible loss or restriction of civil liberties is another consequence—a point that becomes even more glaring when we consider that the person has actually committed no crime other than being a nuisance or assailing people's sensibilities. In the case study, BL had committed no crime, although she had violated many social norms. But at what point do we confine people simply because they fail to conform to our standards of decency or socially appropriate behavior?

Criteria for Commitment

States vary in the criteria used to commit a person, but there are certain general standards. It is not enough that a person be mentally ill; any one or more of these additional conditions need to exist before hospitalization is considered (Corey, Callanan, & Corey, 2010).

- *Individuals present a clear and imminent danger to themselves or others.* An example is someone who is displaying suicidal or bizarre behavior (such as walking out on a busy freeway) that places the individual in immediate danger. Threats to harm someone else or behavior viewed as assaultive or destructive are also grounds for commitment.
- *Individuals are unable to care for themselves or do not have the social network to provide for such care.* Most civil commitments are based primarily on this criterion. The details vary, but states generally specify an inability to provide sufficient forms of food (the person is malnourished, food is unavailable, and the person has no feasible plan to obtain it), clothing (attire is not appropriate for the climate or is dirty or torn, and the person has no plans for obtaining other attire), or shelter (the person has no permanent residence, insufficient

Did You Know? On April 16, 2007, college student Seung-Hui Cho used two semiautomatic handguns on the Virginia Tech campus to kill 27 students and 5 faculty members before committing suicide with a shot to his head. The incident was the deadliest mass shooting in modern U.S. history. Although predicting dangerousness is difficult, there was considerable evidence to indicate that Cho was potentially dangerous: (a) He was involved in three stalking incidents on the campus; (b) professors reported that he was menacing and his writings were often intimidating, obscene, and violent; and (c) a mental health professional believed he was a danger to others. Why, then, was Cho not committed—and allowed to purchase firearms? The answers seem to lie in the belief that a person is innocent until proven guilty and that confinement in the absence of a criminal act violates a person's civil rights.

protection from climatic conditions, and no logical plans for obtaining adequate housing).

- *Individuals are unable to make responsible decisions about appropriate treatments and hospitalization.* As a result, there is a strong chance of deterioration.
- *Individuals are in an unmanageable state of fright or panic.* Such people may believe and feel that they are on the brink of losing control.

In the past, commitments could be obtained solely on the basis of mental illness and a person's need for treatment, which was often determined arbitrarily. Increasingly, the courts have tightened up civil commitment procedures and have begun to rely more on a determination of whether the person presents a danger to the self or others. How do we determine this possibility? Many people would not consider BL a danger to herself or others. Some, however, might believe that she could be assaultive to others and injurious to herself. Disagreements among the public may be understandable, but are trained mental health professionals more accurate in their predictions? Let's turn to that question.

Assessing Dangerousness Mental health professionals have difficulty predicting whether their clients will commit dangerous acts. The fact that civil commitments are often based on a determination of **dangerousness**—the person's potential for doing harm to the self or others—makes use of this criterion problematic. The difficulty in predicting this potential seems linked to four factors:

1. *The rarer something is, the more difficult it is to predict.* As a group, psychiatric patients are not dangerous! Although some evidence suggests that individuals with severe psychotic disorders may have slightly higher rates of violent behavior (Elbogen & Johnson, 2009; Junginger, 1996), the risk is not considered a major concern.
2. *Violence seems as much a function of the context in which it occurs as of the person's characteristics.* Although it is theoretically possible for a psychologist to accurately assess an individual's personality, we have little idea about the situations in which people find themselves. A person may be relatively meek and mild but, when driving in heavy traffic, experience uncontrollable road rage.
3. *The best predictor of dangerousness is probably past criminal conduct or a history of violence or aggression.* Such a record, however, is frequently ruled irrelevant or inadmissible by mental health commissions and the courts.
4. *The definition of dangerousness is itself unclear.* Most of us would agree that murder, rape, torture, and physical assaults are dangerous. But are we confining our definition to physical harm only? What about psychological abuse or even destruction of property?

Did You Know? A frequent misconception shared by both the public and the courts is that mental illnesses are in and of themselves dangerous. Studies have indicated that approximately 90 percent of people with mental disorders are neither violent nor dangerous (J. Swanson, Holzer, Ganju, & Jono, 1990), and few clients with psychosis are assaultive. Homicide is even rarer.

Procedures in Civil Commitment

Despite the difficulties in defining dangerousness, once someone believes that a person is a threat to himself or herself or to others, civil commitment procedures may be instituted. The rationale for this action is that it (a) prevents harm to the person or to others, (b) provides appropriate treatment and care, and (c) ensures due process of law (that is, a legal hearing). In most cases, people deemed in need of protective confinement can be persuaded to *voluntarily* commit themselves to a period of hospitalization. This process is fairly straightforward, and many believe that it is the preferred one. *Involuntary* commitment occurs when the person does not consent to hospitalization.

Involuntary commitment can be a temporary emergency action or a longer period of detention that is determined at a formal hearing. Although states vary

dangerousness a person's potential for doing harm to the self or to others

in the process and standards, all recognize that cases arise in which a person is so grossly disturbed that immediate detention is required (Bindman & Thornicroft, 2008). Because formal hearings may take a long time, delaying commitment might prove adverse to the person or to other individuals.

Formal civil commitment usually follows a similar process, regardless of the state in which it occurs. First, a concerned person, such as a family member, therapist, or family physician, petitions the court for an examination of the person. If the judge believes there is responsible cause for this action, he or she orders an examination. Second, the judge appoints two professionals with no connection to each other to examine the person. In most cases, the examiners are physicians or mental health professionals. Third, a formal hearing is held in which the examiners testify to the person's mental state and potential dangerousness. Others, such as family members, friends, or therapists, may also testify. The person is allowed to speak on his or her own behalf and is represented by counsel. Fourth, if it is determined that the person must enter treatment, a finite period may be specified; periods of 6 months to 1 year are common. Some states, however, have indefinite durations subject to periodic review and assessment.

A Tragic Case of Failure to Predict Dangerousness

Convicted serial killer Jeffrey Dahmer killed at least 17 men and boys over a period of many years. Besides torturing many of his victims, Dahmer admitted to dismembering and devouring their bodies. Although he had been imprisoned in 1988 for sexual molestation, it would have been difficult to predict his degree of dangerousness. Despite an attempt to use the insanity plea, Dahmer was found guilty in 1994 and imprisoned. Another inmate subsequently killed him.

Protection Against Involuntary Commitment We have said that involuntary commitment can lead to a violation of civil rights. Some have even argued that criminals are accorded more rights than people who are mentally ill. For example, a person accused of a crime is considered innocent until proven guilty in a court of law. Usually, he or she is incarcerated only after a jury trial, and only if a crime has been committed (not if there is only a possibility or even high probability of crime). Yet a person who is mentally ill may be confined without a jury trial and without having committed a crime, if it is thought possible that he or she might do harm to him- or herself or others. In other words, the criminal justice system will not incarcerate people because they *might* harm someone (they must already have done it), but civil commitment is based on possible future harm. It can be argued that in the former case, confinement is punishment, whereas in the latter case it is treatment (for the individual's benefit). For example, it is often argued that people who are mentally ill may be incapable of determining their own treatment, and that, once treated, they will be grateful for the treatment they received. If people resist hospitalization, they are thus being irrational, which is a symptom of their mental disorder.

Critics do not accept this reasoning. They point out that civil commitment is for the benefit of those initiating commitment procedures (society) and not for the individual. Even after treatment, people rarely appreciate it. These concerns have prompted and heightened sensitivity toward patient welfare and rights, resulting in a trend toward restricting the powers of the state over the individual.

CHECKPOINT REVIEW

1. Explain the difference between criminal commitment and civil commitment.
2. What criteria are used in civil commitment? What procedures are used by the court to commit a person?
3. Why is it so difficult to assess dangerousness?

Rights of Mental Patients

Many people in the United States are concerned about the balance of power among the state, our mental institutions, and our citizens. The U.S. Constitution guarantees certain rights such as trial by jury, legal representation, and protection

CONTROVERSY:

Predicting Dangerousness: Serial Killers and Mass Murderers

Seung-Hui Cho (the Virginia Tech shooter), Jeffrey Dahmer (killer of 17 men and boys), Kenneth Bianchi (one of the Hillside Stranglers), and Eric Harris and Dylan Klebold (the Columbine High School killers) were all either serial killers or mass murderers. Were there signs these individuals were potentially dangerous? Jeffrey Dahmer tortured animals as a small boy and was arrested in 1988 for molesting a child. Even though his father suspected that he was dangerous, Dahmer was released. And there appears to be sufficient evidence to suggest that Cho was a deeply disturbed young man who harbored great resentment and anger waiting to explode. Harris and Klebold created a Web site that seemed to foretell their proclivity toward violence. In all three situations, aberrant thoughts and behaviors appeared to go unrecognized or ignored.

Lest we be too harsh on psychologists and law enforcement officials, it is important to realize that few serial killers or mass murderers willingly share their deviant sexual or asocial fantasies. Furthermore, many of the problems in predicting whether a person will commit dangerous acts lie in (a) limited knowledge concerning the characteristics associated with violence, (b) the lack of a one-to-one correspondence between danger signs and possible violence, (c) an increasing knowledge that violent behavior is most often the result of many variables, and (d) the recognition that incarceration—both criminal and civil—cannot occur on the basis of potential danger alone. Nevertheless, our experiences with mass murderers and serial killers have produced patterns and profiles of interest to mental health practitioners and law enforcement officials. Although similar, the profiles of mass murderers and serial killers also differ in some major ways.

Profile of Serial Killers

Serial killers are usually white men, and they often suffer from some recognized psychiatric disorder, such as sexual sadism disorder, antisocial personality disorder type, extreme narcissistic personality disorder type, and borderline personality disorder type. Few are psychotic, and psychoses do not appear to be the cause of their compulsion to kill. Almost all, however, entertain violent sexual fantasies and have experienced traumatic sex at a young age. Their earlier years are troubled with family histories of abuse, alcoholism, and criminal activity. Dahmer, for example, was sexually molested as a youngster. Most serial killers seem to exhibit little remorse for their victims, have little incentive to change, and seem to lack a value system. The compulsion to kill is often associated with what have been described as "morbid prognostic signs" (Schlesinger, 1989): breaking and entering for nonmonetary purposes; unprovoked assaults and mistreatment of women; a fetish for female undergarments and destruction of them; hatred, contempt, or fear of women; violence against animals, especially cats; sexual identity confusion; a "violent and primitive fantasy life"; and sexual inhibitions and preoccupation with rigid standards of morality (Youngstrom, 1991).

Although we have come a long way in being able to compile a composite description of serial killers, some have challenged the accuracy of such profiles. In the 2002 Washington, DC, sniper attacks, in which 10 people were shot (eight fatally), John Allen Muhammad and teenager Lee Boyd Malvo did not fit the profile descriptions of the experts. They were originally thought to be angry white men, with no military background and probably local residents. As it turned out, the snipers were African Americans, one had combat experience, and they were drifters.

Profile of Mass Murderers

Mass murderers are usually men who are socially isolated and seem to exhibit inadequate social and interpersonal skills. They have been found to be quite angry and to be filled with rage. The anger appears to be cumulative and is triggered by some type of event, usually a loss. For example, they may view the end of a job or a relationship as a catastrophic loss. Most have strong mistrust of people and entertain paranoid fantasies, such as wide-ranging conspiracies against them.

They tend to be rootless and have few support systems such as family, friends, or religious or fraternal groups. Many researchers believe that the number of mass murders will increase as firearms proliferate in our society. Other social correlates affecting mass murders are an increasing sense of rootlessness in the country, general disenchantment, and loneliness. The more random the killings, the more disturbed, delusional, and paranoid the person is likely to be.

For Further Consideration

1. What criteria would you use to determine whether someone is dangerous or not?
2. Can you identify the weaknesses or possible dangers of using this set of criteria? Can you give specific examples of cases in which they would prove problematic to apply?
3. How does one balance applying and implementing criteria of dangerousness with the loss of civil liberties of citizens?

against self-incrimination. The mental health profession has great power, which may be used wittingly or unwittingly to abridge individual freedom. In recent decades, some courts have ruled that commitment for any purpose constitutes a major deprivation of liberty that requires due process protection.

In 1975 a U.S. district court issued a landmark decision in the case of *Dixon v. Weinberger*. The ruling established the right of individuals to the **least restrictive environment**. This means that people have a right to the least restrictive alternative to freedom that is appropriate to their condition. Only patients who cannot adequately care for themselves are committed to hospitals. Those who can function acceptably should be given alternative choices, such as boarding homes and other shelters.

Did You Know? The legal system uses three different standards of proof. *Beyond a reasonable doubt* is confined to criminal trials and is generally accepted to be 95 percent certainty; *clear and convincing evidence* is used in civil commitments (75 percent certainty); and *preponderance of the evidence* is generally used in civil actions (51 percent certainty). For mental health purposes, the standard of the burden of proof falls in between the two extremes.

Right to Treatment

One of the primary justifications for commitment is that treatment improves a person's mental condition and increases the likelihood that he or she will be able to return to the community. If we confine a person involuntarily and do not provide the means for release (therapy), is this not deprivation of due process? Several cases have raised this problem as a constitutional issue. Together, they have determined that mental patients who have been involuntarily committed have a **right to treatment**—a right to receive therapy that would improve their condition.

In 1966, in a lawsuit brought against St. Elizabeth's Hospital in Washington, DC (*Rouse v. Cameron*), the DC Circuit Court held that (a) the right to treatment is a constitutional right and (b) failure to provide treatment cannot be justified by lack of resources. In the Alabama federal case of *Wyatt v. Stickney* (1972), Judge Frank Johnson specified standards of adequate treatment, such as staff–patient ratios, therapeutic environmental conditions, and professional consensus about appropriate treatment. The court also made it clear that mental patients could not be forced to work (scrub floors, cook, serve food, wash laundry, and so on) or to engage in work-related activities aimed at maintaining the institution in which they lived. This practice, widely used in institutions, was declared unconstitutional. Moreover, patients who volunteered to perform tasks had to be paid at least the minimum wage to do them instead of merely being given token allowances or special privileges. This landmark decision ensured treatment beyond custodial care and protection against neglect and abuse.

Another important case (tried in a U.S. District Court in Florida), *O'Connor v. Donaldson* (1975), and affirmed by the U.S. Supreme Court that same year has also had a major impact on the issue of the right to treatment issue. It involved Kenneth Donaldson, who at age 49 was committed for 20 years to the Florida State Hospital in Chattahoochee on petition by his father. He was found to be mentally ill, unable to care for himself, easily manipulated, and dangerous. Throughout his confinement, Donaldson petitioned for release, but Dr. O'Connor, the hospital superintendent, determined that the patient was too "mentally ill." Finally, Donaldson threatened a lawsuit and was re luctantly discharged by the hospital after 14 years of confinement. He then sued both O'Connor and the hospital, winning an award of $20,000.

The monetary award is insignificant compared with the significance of the ruling. Again, U.S. Supreme Court reaffirmed the patient's right to treatment. It ruled that Donaldson did not receive appropriate treatment and said that the state cannot constitutionally confine a nondangerous person who is capable of caring for himself or herself outside of an institution or who has willing friends or family to help. Further, it said that physicians, as well as institutions, are liable for improper confinements.

least restrictive environment the least restrictive alternative to freedom that is appropriate to a person's condition

right to treatment the concept that mental patients who have been involuntarily committed have a right to receive therapy that would improve their condition

Right to Refuse Treatment

Brian David Mitchell, the man who kidnapped Elizabeth Smart, refused antipsychotic drugs over a period of 9 years. As you recall, he was declared incompetent

Did You Know? In the United States v Comstock (2010), the U.S. Supreme Court ruled that certain sex offenders can be civilly committed and confined even after finishing their prison sentence. The law allows the government to detain prisoners who have engaged in sexually violent conduct, have had a mental illness, and have difficulty controlling themselves. The ruling is believed by some to have dangerous implications for civil liberties implications and even to be unconstitutional (Liptak, 2010).

to stand trial, and he refused to take medication to make him competent. His attorneys, however, supported his right to refuse treatment and fought government officials on this point. It was only after a judge believed Mitchell was manipulating the system that he was judged competent in 2009.

The right to refuse treatment occasionally poses ironies. For example, a U.S. Supreme Court ruling (*Ford v. Wainwright*, 1986) concluded that the government cannot execute someone who is incompetent. Why would someone agree to take medication only to be executed? Some courts have ordered prisoners to take medication on the likelihood that they will improve. In June 2003, however, the U.S. Supreme Court (*Sell v. United States*) placed strict limits on the ability of the government to forcibly medicate defendants who are mentally ill to make them competent to stand trial. Such actions must be, according to the court, in the "best interest of the defendant." What this means will have to be played out in the future.

Although it may be easy for us to surmise the reason that Mitchell's attorneys supported his refusal of treatment to make him better, does it make sense for others? Patients frequently refuse medical treatment on religious grounds or because the treatment would only prolong a terminal illness. But should mental patients have a right to refuse treatment? Why commit patients for treatment and then allow them to refuse it? Is it not possible that mental patients may be incapable of deciding what is best for themselves?

Proponents of the right to refuse treatment argue, however, that many forms of treatment, such as medication or electroconvulsive therapy, may have long-term side effects, as discussed in previous chapters. They also point out that involuntary treatment is generally much less effective than treatment that is accepted voluntarily. People forced into treatment seem to resist it, thereby nullifying the potentially beneficial effects.

Courts have usually supported the right to refuse treatment, under certain conditions, and extended the principle of the least restrictive alternative to include the least intrusive forms of treatment. Generally, psychotherapy is considered less intrusive than somatic or physical therapies (e.g., electroconvulsive therapy and medication). Although this compromise may appear reasonable, other problems present themselves. First, how do we define intrusive treatment? Are insight therapies as intrusive as behavioral techniques (punishment and aversion procedures)? Second, if patients are allowed to refuse certain forms of treatment and if the hospital does not have alternatives for them, can they sue the institutions? These questions remain unanswered.

CHECKPOINT REVIEW

1. Why should we be concerned about the rights of mental patients?
2. Explain what the right to treatment is.
3. Explain what the right to refuse treatment is.
4. Define the least intrusive form of treatment.
5. What characteristics are similar and different between mass murderers and serial killers?

Deinstitutionalization

deinstitutionalization the shifting of responsibility for the care of mental patients from large central institutions to agencies within local communities

Deinstitutionalization is the shifting of responsibility for the care of mental patients from large central institutions to agencies within local communities. When originally formulated in the 1960s and 1970s, the concept excited many mental health professionals. Since its inception, the mental hospital population of patients has dropped 75 percent, the number of state-run mental hospitals has declined dramatically, and there has been a 75 percent decrease in the average daily number of committed patients (J. L. Geller, 2006; Lamb & Weinberger, 2005). The impetus behind deinstitutionalization came from several quarters.

First, there was (and still is) a feeling that large hospitals provide mainly custodial care, that they produce little benefit for the patient, and that they may even impede improvement. Court cases discussed earlier (*Wyatt v. Stickney* and *O'Connor v. Donaldson*) exposed the fact that many mental hospitals are no better than "warehouses for the insane." Institutionalization was accused of fostering dependency, promoting helplessness, and lowering self-sufficiency in patients. The longer patients were hospitalized, the more likely they were to remain hospitalized, even if they had improved. Further, symptoms such as flat affect and nonresponsiveness, which were thought to be clinical signs of schizophrenia, may actually result from hospitalization.

The Downside of Deinstitutionalization

Homelessness has become one of the great social problems of urban communities. Many believe that deinstitutionalization has contributed to the problem, although it is not clear what proportion of people who are homeless people are mentally ill and were previously institutionalized. Scenes such as this one, however, are becoming all too common in large urban areas.

Second, beginning in the 1970s, the issue of patient rights was receiving increased attention. Mental health professionals became very concerned about keeping patients confined against their will and began to discharge patients whenever they approached minimal competencies. It was believed that **mainstreaming**—integrating mental patients as soon as possible back into the community—could be accomplished by providing local outpatient or transitory services (such as board-and-care facilities, halfway houses, and churches). In addition, advances in tranquilizers and other drug treatment techniques made it possible to medicate patients, which made their conditions manageable once they were discharged.

Third, insufficiently funded state hospitals were almost forced to release patients back into communities. Overcrowded conditions made mental health administrators view the movement favorably; state legislative branches encouraged the trend, especially because it reduced state costs and funding.

What has been the impact of deinstitutionalization on people with mental illness? Its critics believe that deinstitutionalization is a policy that allows states to relinquish their responsibility to care for people who are unable to care for themselves. There are alarming indications that deinstitutionalization has been responsible for placing or "dumping" on the streets many former patients who should have remained institutionalized (Rosenberg & Rosenberg, 2006). Critics believe that the "bag lady" (BL) of Oakland, California, is an example of the human cost and tragedy of such a policy. Most of these people appear severely disabled, have difficulty coping with daily living, have schizophrenia, and are alcoholic. It appears that millions of mentally ill individuals have become homeless and that existing programs are woefully fragmented and inadequate in delivering needed services.

Thus it is becoming apparent that many people who are mentally ill are not receiving treatment. Many live on the streets, where conditions can be cruel and harsh and where they are prone to violent victimization. Others live in nursing homes, board-and-care homes, or group residences. The quality of care in many of these places is marginal, forcing continuing and periodic rehospitalization of their residents. It is estimated that 30 to 70 percent of the homeless population have a mental disorder (Cougnard, Grolleau, et al., 2006; Mojtabai, 2005).

Much of the problem with deinstitutionalization appears to be the community's lack of preparation and resources to care for people with chronic mental illness. Many patients lack family or friends who can help them make the transition back into the community; many state hospitals do not provide patients with adequate skills training; many discharged patients have difficulty finding jobs; many find substandard housing that is worse than the institutions from which

mainstreaming integrating mental patients as soon as possible back into the community

AP Photo/Shiho Fukada

Job Training for People With Intellectual Disabilities

Increasingly, it is recognized that the mentally challenged and individuals with mental disorders can be helped if they are taught functional self-care and employment-related skills. Here we see such a program in action, in which basic skills such as cooking are taught.

they came; many are not adequately monitored and receive no psychiatric treatment; and many become homeless.

It is difficult to estimate how many discharged mental patients have become homeless. We do know that homelessness in the United States, especially in large urban areas, is increasing at an alarming pace. Certainly, it is not difficult to see the number of people who live in transport terminals, parks, flophouses, homeless shelters, cars, and storefronts. It is hard to determine how many of these homeless people were deinstitutionalized before adequate support services were present in their community. We do know, however, that people who are homeless have significantly poorer psychological adjustment and higher arrests and conviction records (U.S. Department of Health and Human Services, 2003). The solution, although complex, probably is not a return to the old institutions of the 1950s but rather the provision of more and better community-based treatment facilities and alternatives.

For patients involved in alternative community programs, the picture appears somewhat more positive. A recent study concluded that programs providing permanent housing, special care, and concerned community treatment can reduce homelessness and improve well-being (G. Nelson, Aubry, & Lawrence, 2007; Padgett, Hawkins, Abrams, & Davis, 2006). These special programs are few, however, and much remains to be done if deinstitutionalized patients are to be provided with the best supportive treatment.

CHECKPOINT REVIEW

1. What is deinstitutionalization?
2. Identify the positive and negative aspects of deinstitutionalization.

The Therapist–Client Relationship

The therapist–client relationship involves a number of legal, moral, and ethical issues. Three primary concerns are issues of confidentiality and privileged communication, the therapist's duty to warn others of a risk posed by a dangerous client, and the therapist's obligation to avoid sexual intimacies with clients.

Confidentiality and Privileged Communication

Basic to the therapist–patient relationship is the premise that therapy involves a deeply personal association in which clients have a right to expect that whatever they say is kept private. Therapists believe that genuine therapy cannot occur unless clients trust their therapists and believe that they will not divulge confidential communications. Without this guarantee, clients may not be completely open with their thoughts and may thereby lose the benefits of therapy.

confidentiality an ethical standard that protects clients from disclosure of information without their consent; an ethical obligation of the therapist

Confidentiality is an ethical standard that protects clients from disclosure of information without their consent. The general public also agrees that confidentiality is important. In one study it was found that 74 percent of respondents thought everything told to a therapist should be confidential; indeed, 69 percent believed that whatever they discussed was never disclosed

(D. J. Miller & Thelen, 1986). Confidentiality, however, is an ethical, not a legal, obligation. **Privileged communication**, a narrower legal concept, protects privacy and prevents the disclosure of confidential communications without a client's permission (Corey, Callanan, et al., 2010). An important part of this concept is that the holder of the privilege is the client, not the therapist. In other words, if a client waives this privilege, the therapist has no grounds for withholding information. Our society recognizes how important certain confidential relationships are and protects them by law. These relationships are spousal, attorney–client, pastor–congregant, and therapist–client relationships. Psychiatric practices are regulated in all 50 states and the District of Columbia, and most of those jurisdictions have privileged-communication statutes.

Exemptions from Privileged Communication Although states vary considerably, they all recognize certain situations in which communications can be divulged (D. Brown & Srebalus, 2003). Corey and associates (Corey, Callahan, et al., 2010; Corey & Corey, 2010) summarized these conditions:

- In situations that deal with civil or criminal commitment or competency to stand trial, the client's right to privilege can be waived.
- Disclosure can also be made when a client sees a therapist and introduces his or her mental condition as a claim or defense in a civil action.
- When the client is younger than 16 or is a dependent elderly person and information leads the therapist to believe that the individual has been a victim of a crime (e.g., incest, rape, or abuse), the therapist must provide that information to the appropriate protective services agency.
- When the therapist has reason to believe that a client presents a danger to himself or herself (possible injury or suicide) or may potentially harm someone else, the therapist must act to ward off the danger.

Problems arise when we try to determine what the balance should be and how important various events and facts are in individual cases.

The Duty to Warn

Case Study

In 1968, Prosenjit Poddar—a graduate student from India studying at the University of California, Berkeley—sought therapy from the student health services for depression. Poddar was apparently upset over what he perceived to be a rebuff from another student, Tatiana Tarasoff, whom he claimed to love. During the course of treatment, Poddar informed his therapist that he intended to purchase a gun and kill Tarasoff. Judging Poddar to be dangerous, the psychologist breached the confidentiality of the professional relationship by informing the campus police. The police detained Poddar briefly but freed him because he agreed to stay away from Tarasoff. On October 27, 1969, Poddar went to Tarasoff's home and killed her, first wounding her with a gun and then stabbing her repeatedly with a knife. In the subsequent lawsuit filed by Tarasoff's family, the California Supreme Court made a landmark ruling in 1976 that established what is popularly known as the duty to warn; the therapist should have warned not only the police but the intended victim as well.

privileged communication a therapist's legal obligation to protect a client's privacy and to prevent the disclosure of confidential communications without a client's permission

AP Images

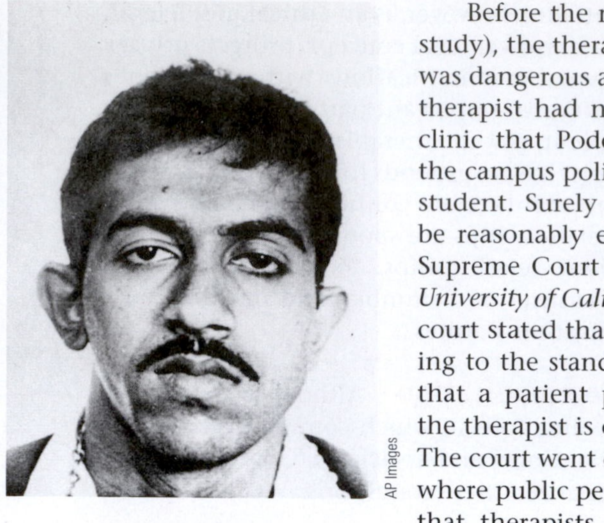

AP Images

A Duty to Warn

Tatiana Tarasoff, a college student, was stabbed to death in 1969 by Prosenjit Poddar, a graduate student at the University of California, Berkeley. Although Poddar's therapist had notified the university that he thought Poddar was dangerous, the California Supreme Court ruled that the therapist should have warned Tarasoff herself as well.

Before the murder of Tatiana Tarasoff (in the case study), the therapist had decided that Prosenjit Poddar was dangerous and likely to carry out his threat, so the therapist had notified the director of the psychiatric clinic that Poddar was dangerous. He also informed the campus police, hoping that they would detain the student. Surely the therapist had done all that could be reasonably expected. Not so, ruled the California Supreme Court (*Tarasoff v. the Board of Regents of the University of California*, 1976). In the ***Tarasoff* ruling**, the court stated that when a therapist determines, according to the standards of the mental health profession, that a patient presents a serious danger to another, the therapist is obligated to warn the intended victim. The court went on to say that protective privilege ends where public peril begins. In general, courts have ruled that therapists have a responsibility to protect the public from dangerous acts of violent clients, and have held therapists accountable for (a) failing to diagnose or predict dangerousness, (b) failing to warn potential victims, (c) failing to commit dangerous individuals, and (d) prematurely discharging dangerous patients from a hospital.

Criticism of the Duty to Warn The *Tarasoff* ruling seems to place the therapist in the unenviable role of being a double agent (Bednar, Bednar, Lambert, & Waite, 1991). Therapists have an ethical and legal obligation to their clients, but they also have legal obligations to society. Not only can these dual obligations conflict with one another, but they can also be quite ambiguous. Many situations exist in which state courts must rule to clarify the implications and uncertainties of the duty to warn.

When the *Tarasoff* ruling came out, M. Siegel (1979) loudly criticized it, stating that the outcome was a hollow victory for individual parties and was devastating for the mental health professions. He reasoned that if confidentiality had been an absolute policy, if it had been applied to all situations, Poddar might have been kept in treatment, thus ultimately saving Tarasoff's life. Other mental health professionals have echoed this theme in one form or another (Levin, 2008; Werth, et al., 2009). Hostile clients with pent-up feelings and emotions may be less likely to act out or become violent when allowed to vent their thoughts. The irony, according to critics, is that the duty to warn may actually be counterproductive to its intent to protect potential victims.

Past Crimes and the Requirement to Inform The *Tarasoff* ruling makes it clear that when clients disclose a potential to harm identifiable third parties, therapists have a legal obligation to take actions to ward off the danger. The duty to warn applies to *future threats of harm*. But what are the legal obligations of therapists who hear from clients that they have committed a *past crime*? What if clients disclose they have assaulted, raped, or even killed someone? Since there is no future threat of harm, are therapists obligated to report the crime?

These questions deal with not only legal issues but moral and ethical ones as well. It may be shocking to many students to know that the law is not clear on this matter. The prevailing consensus is that mental health professionals are not legally mandated to breach confidentiality when clients inform them that they have committed past crimes (Handelsman, Walfish, & Hess, 2001), and that doing so would in fact create liability for them.

But how often do therapists hear confessions from their clients about past criminal conduct? The answer is that although it is not common, it is not

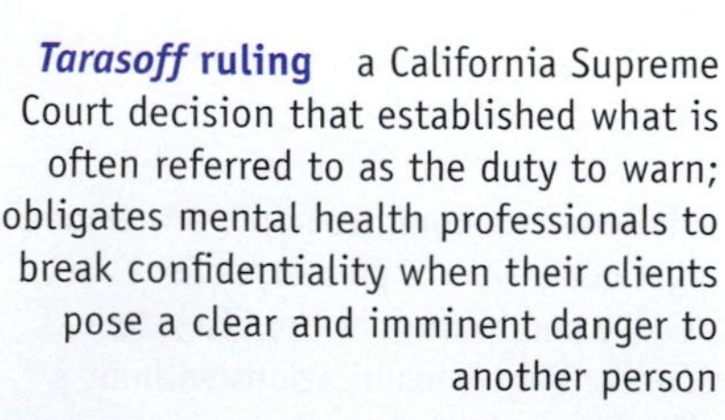

***Tarasoff* ruling** a California Supreme Court decision that established what is often referred to as the duty to warn; obligates mental health professionals to break confidentiality when their clients pose a clear and imminent danger to another person

infrequent either. In a recently conducted survey (Walfish, Barnett, Marlyere, & Zielke, 2010), incidents of clients informing their therapists of having committed violent crimes were reported. It is important to note that these crimes were never reported elsewhere. Out of a sample of 162 doctoral-level psychologists, mostly full-time psychotherapists, confessions of the following crimes were heard by the indicated number of respondents:

- Murder: 13 percent
- Sexual assault or rape: 33 percent
- Physical assault: 69 percent

In therapy, clients are likely to reveal very intimate secrets about their past feelings, thoughts, and actions. The likelihood that something shocking, distasteful, or even frightening may be disclosed is not low. It is important that therapists be prepared to respond in an appropriate legal, moral, and therapeutic manner.

The Family Educational Rights and Privacy Act and Confidentiality of College Student Life

Case Study

Elizabeth Shin, a 19-year-old sophomore at the Massachusetts Institute of Technology (MIT), died on April 14, 2000, after she was believed to have set fire to herself. Two years after her death, her parents filed a $27 million wrongful death suit against MIT, accusing the university of breach of contract, medical malpractice, and negligence on the part of university psychiatrists, student life staff, and campus police. The Shins contended that MIT knew that their daughter had made suicide attempts, cut herself frequently, and had depression, but failed to inform them of her deteriorating mental state. Had they done so, the family asserted, Shin might still be alive today. They further claimed that MIT broke the "business contract" with the family that they said was implied in Shin's college enrollment at MIT.

Not unlike the *Tarasoff* case, the outcome of the Shins' lawsuit (from the case study) had the power to set legal precedent; it could also radically change the Family Educational Rights and Privacy Act, which prevents colleges and universities from disclosing any personal information about students, even to their parents. Colleges and universities generally assume that students are adults. If they were required to report every problem to parents, they would infantilize students by sending the wrong message. Students might also be less inclined to share personal information with school officials if they knew that such information might be reported back to their parents. Yet institutions of higher education are very aware that they are grappling to minister to an undergraduate population that seems to require more mental health care than ever before. One national study of counseling center client problems over 13 years revealed that students are entering college with more severe problems than in the past (Benton, Robertson, Tseng, Newton, & Benton, 2003). The lawsuit never tested the issue of student confidentiality and privacy, because the case was settled out of court in 2005 for an undisclosed sum and with an agreement between MIT and the family that Shin died by accident rather than suicide.

Did You Know? Studies indicate that 1 to 17 percent of professionals have had some form of sexual contact with their clients. The actual incidence may be much higher, since therapists may be disinclined to admit such behaviors. The majority of these acts are between a male therapist and a female client, but the reverse has also been reported, as have acts in which the therapist and patient are of the same sex (National Board for Certification in Occupational Therapy, 2012).

Sexual Relationships With Clients

Therapeutic practice can be legally regulated by civil lawsuits brought by clients against their therapists for professional malpractice. To be successful, however, these lawsuits must satisfy four conditions: (a) The plaintiff must have been involved in a professional therapeutic relationship with the therapist, (b) there must have been negligence in the care of the client, (c) demonstrable harm must have occurred, and (d) there must be a cause-and-effect relationship between the negligence and harm. If these four conditions are demonstrated, a jury may find the therapist guilty and award the plaintiff monetary damages. Although malpractice claims can be brought in any number of situations, by far the most common type involves sexual intimacies with a current or former client (Corey et al., 2010; K. S. Pope & Vasquez, 2007).

Traditionally, mental health practitioners have emphasized the importance of separating their personal and professional lives. They reasoned that therapists need to be objective and removed from their clients because becoming emotionally involved with them was nontherapeutic. A therapist in a personal relationship with a client may be less confrontive, may fulfill his or her own needs at the expense of the client's, and may unintentionally exploit the client because of his or her position (Corey & Corey, 2010). Although some people question the belief that a social or personal relationship is necessarily antitherapeutic, matters of personal relations with clients, especially those dealing with erotic and sexual intimacies, are receiving increasing attention.

Sexual misconduct of therapists is considered one of the most serious of all ethical violations. Indeed, virtually all professional organizations condemn sexual intimacies in the therapist–client relationship. The American Psychological Association (2010a) states explicitly, "Psychologists do not engage in sexual intimacies with current therapy clients/patients."

But how do practitioners view sexual intimacies with clients? How often do such intimacies really occur? Who does what to whom? Being sexually attracted to a client or engaging in sexual fantasy about one is not uncommon among therapists (K. S. Pope & Vasquez, 2007). Furthermore, complaints to state licensing boards about sexual misconduct by therapists have increased significantly. Although these are indisputable facts, the vast majority of psychologists are able to control their sexual feelings and behave in a professional manner.

CHECKPOINT REVIEW

1. Distinguish between confidentiality and privileged communication.
2. Under what conditions can therapists breach confidentiality?
3. What is the *Tarasoff* decision (the duty to warn)?
4. Does the duty to warn apply to a client who admits to having committed a crime?
5. How does sexual contact with clients affect the therapeutic relationship?

Cultural Competence and the Mental Health Profession

Many mental health professionals assert that the prevailing concepts of mental health and mental disorders are culture bound and that contemporary theories of therapy are based on values specific to a middle class, white, highly individualistic, and ethnocentric population (American Psychological Association, 2003;

FOCUS ON RESILIENCE

Using Positive Psychology to Build Soldier Resilience: An Ethical Dilemma?

Throughout this text, we have extolled the virtues of positive psychology and the strength-based approach it takes to viewing the human condition. It has made many contributions to our understanding of resilience, hardiness, and protective factors that seem to immunize people against mental disorders. It has allowed us to focus on the positive aspects of mental health; to value prevention rather than remediation; and to view assets and strengths rather than the weaknesses of people. But can the basic tenets and principles of positive psychology be misused and misapplied? If so, does it not raise moral and ethical questions?

Such is the case of a major controversy now brewing in the psychological community, regarding the Comprehensive Soldier Fitness (CSF) program being implemented by the U.S. Army (G. W. Casey, 2011; Cornum, Matthews, & Seligman, 2011). Using research findings and principles derived from positive psychology (M. E. P. Seligman & Csikszentmihalyi, 2000), the U.S. Army has embarked on a program to increase the psychological strength and positive performance of soldiers and to reduce their maladaptive responses to military trauma and demands (constant threat of injury or death, sleep deprivation, separation from family and friends, extreme climates, taking the life of enemy combatants, etc.).

In the wars in Iraq and Afghanistan, it has been found that 70 percent of soldiers were exposed to "traumatic events," and high rates of post-traumatic stress disorder, alcohol abuse, suicide, and depression were reported among soldiers as a result of their combat experiences (Cornum et al., 2011). Just as physical training emphasizes the importance of physical fitness in military combat, CSF increases the mental fitness of soldiers by strengthening their psychological assets to meet high-risk actions (going on patrols, killing or injuring their enemies, interrogating captives, etc.) (Cornum et al., 2011). The training develops psychological resilience in soldiers using an evidence-based approach that strengthens emotional, social, family, and spiritual fitness to ward off the stresses of military life and combat. Considerable evidence exists that it can be highly effective (Algoe & Fredrickson, 2011; Cacioppo, Reis, & Zautra, 2011; Tedeschi & McNally, 2011).

Sergii Figurnyi/Shutterstock.com

On the surface, CSF appears to have very worthy goals. Who would not want the best treatment and care for our compatriots in the military? Yet a number of psychologists have raised serious moral and ethical objections with using positive psychology in the CSF program. They assert that the basic premise of the program is flawed and misguided (Eidelson, Pilisuk, & Soldz, 2011; Dyckman, 2011; J. Krueger, 2011; Phipps, 2011; Quick, 2011). Among their objections are the following:

- The use of positive psychology in the military operates under the assumption that war is unavoidable and that, as a result, it is the patriotic duty of psychologists to help the military make our men and women more resilient in combat. Critics vehemently question this assumption, and instead advocate the use of positive psychology principles to reduce conflict between nations, to prevent war, and to promote peace.
- War is horrific and exposes combatants to gruesome sights and situations. Responses of distress or repugnance are natural, healthy, and humane responses. To train soldiers to experience more death, destruction, and inhuman acts with less distress is a frightening prospect. To make soldiers, for example, feel better about killing or do a better job of it is morally and ethically reprehensible.
- Psychologists who use positive psychology to help the military are deceiving themselves. The CSF client is the Army and not the individual soldier. The Army demands discipline, efficiency, and obedience, and attempts to standardize behavior. It is credulous to think that if a soldier's need for self-actualization or spiritual development conflicts with the goals of the Army, the CSF program would consider that a positive development.

R. D. Laing, an existential psychiatrist once asked the question, "Is schizophrenia a 'sick' response in a 'healthy' society, or is it a 'healthy' response to a 'sick' one?" Psychologists who object to using psychological principles to aid the military seem to be asking a similar question about war and military objectives. If war is unnatural, unhealthy, and pathological, is positive psychology being used to adjust soldiers to a "sick" situation? Is it moral or ethical for psychologists to lend their considerable expertise in human behavior for military purposes if that leads to objectionable goals? The fact that psychological science exists means that it can be used for any number of purposes, both good and bad.

Changing Demographics and Therapy

The Teaching Tolerance program, founded in 1991 by the Southern Poverty Law Center, supports the efforts of K–12 teachers and other educators to promote respect for differences and appreciation of diversity. This photo was taken at the Mix It Up at Lunch day program, which encourages students to step outside their social boundaries through various activities.

D. W. Sue & Sue, 2013). There are strong concerns that the services offered to clients from different cultures are frequently antagonistic or inappropriate to the clients' life experiences, and that these services not only lack sensitivity and understanding but may also be oppressive and discriminatory toward minority populations. These assertions about counseling and psychotherapy are echoed by other marginalized groups (women, gay men and lesbians, people with disabilities, etc.) in our society as well.

The American Psychological Association (2010a), in its most recent *Ethical Principles of Psychologists and Code of Conduct*, has made it clear that working with clients from different cultures is unethical unless the mental health professional has adequate training and expertise in multicultural psychology. This position has been the result of incremental recognition about diversity's importance and reflected in the development of guidelines for providers of psychological services to ethnic, linguistic, and culturally diverse populations (American Psychological Association, 1993) and guidelines for psychotherapy with lesbian, gay, and bisexual clients (American Psychological Association, 2000).

In a historic move by the American Psychological Association, the Council of Representatives adopted the guidelines on multicultural education, training, research, practice, and organizational change for psychologists (2003). This document has now become the official policy of the American Psychological Association and extends to nearly every realm of psychological practice. One of the most comprehensive guidelines to be proposed on culturally sensitive work with racial and ethnic minorities, the document makes it clear that service providers need to become aware of how their own culture, life experiences, attitudes, values, and biases have influenced them. It also emphasizes the importance of cultural and environmental factors in diagnosis and treatment, and it insists that therapists respect and consider using traditional healing approaches that are intrinsic to a client's culture. Finally, it suggests that therapists learn more about cultural issues and seek consultation when confronted with culture-specific problems.

Inherent in all these documents is a call for cultural competence and the conclusion that psychotherapy may represent biased, discriminatory, and unethical treatment if the racial and cultural backgrounds of clients are ignored and if the therapist does not possess adequate training in working with a culturally diverse population. From this perspective, mental health professionals have a moral and professional responsibility to become culturally competent if they work with people who differ from them in terms of race, culture, ethnicity, gender, sexual orientation, and so forth. To become culturally competent requires mental health professionals to strive toward attaining three goals (D. W. Sue & Sue, 2013): (a) becoming aware of and dealing with the biases, stereotypes, and assumptions that affect their practice; (b) becoming aware of the values and worldview of a client from a different culture; and (c) developing appropriate intervention strategies that take into account the social, cultural, historical, and environmental influences on clients from different cultures. As we have seen, the increased awareness of multicultural influences in our understanding of abnormal psychology is reflected in the *Diagnostic and Statistical Manual of Mental Disorders* (American Psychiatric Association, 2000) and in the proposed DSM-5 (DSM-5 Work Groups, 2012).

CHECKPOINT REVIEW

1. Discuss ethical dilemmas that arise from applying positive psychology to build resilience among soldiers going to combat.
2. In what ways may traditional forms of mental health practice prove unethical and detrimental to clients from racial or ethnic minorities?
3. Define cultural competence.

Summary

1 What are the criteria used to judge insanity, and what is the difference between being insane and being incompetent to stand trial?

- Several criteria have been used. People can be acquitted of a crime if they (a) did not know right from wrong (*M'Naghten* rule), (b) were unable to control their behavior (irresistible impulse), or (c) acted out of a mental disease or defect (*Durham* decision). The American Law Institute guidelines attempt to combine aspects of these three standards.
- Competency to stand trial refers to defendants' mental state (whether they can rationally aid attorneys in their own defense) at the time they are being examined, not at the time of the offense.

2 Under what conditions can a person be involuntarily committed to a mental institution?

- People who have committed no crime can be confined against their will if it can be shown that they (a) present a clear and imminent danger to themselves or others, (b) are unable to care for themselves, (c) are unable to make responsible decisions about appropriate treatment and hospitalization, and (d) are in an unmanageable state of fright or panic.
- The concept of dangerousness is important in commitments. It is very difficult to predict dangerousness, because such acts often depend on many external situations and not solely on personal attributes.

3 What rights do mental patients have with respect to treatment and care issues?

- Because many practices and procedures seem to violate constitutional guarantees, court rulings have established important precedents in the right to treatment and the right to refuse treatment.

4 What is deinstitutionalization?

- Deinstitutionalization is the shifting of responsibility for the care of mental patients from large central institutions to agencies within the local community. Its implementation has often been not a positive experience for mental patients.

5 What legal and ethical issues govern the therapist–client relationship?

- Confidentiality and privileged communication are crucial to the therapist-client relationship. Exceptions involve (a) civil or criminal commitment and determinations of competency to stand trial, (b) a client's initiation of a lawsuit for malpractice or a civil action in which the client's mental condition is introduced, (c) the belief that child or elder abuse has occurred, or (d) the danger a client poses to himself or herself or to others.
- The *Tarasoff* decision makes therapists responsible for warning a potential victim in order to avoid liability.
- Sexual misconduct by therapists is considered to be one of the most serious of all ethical violations.

6 What is cultural competence in the mental health profession?

- It is important to consider culture, ethnicity, gender, and socioeconomic status as central to psychological practice. It unethical to treat members of marginalized groups without adequate training and expertise in multicultural psychology.

Key Terms

criminal commitment 445
insanity defense 445
***M'Naghten* rule** 447
irresistible impulse test 447
***Durham* standard** 447
American Law Institute Model Penal Code 447
competency to stand trial 449
due process 449
civil commitment 450
dangerousness 452
least restrictive environment 455
right to treatment 455
deinstitutionalization 456
mainstreaming 457
confidentiality 458
privileged communication 459
***Tarasoff* ruling** 460

Media Resources

Psychology CourseMate

Access an interactive e-book and chapter-specific interactive learning tools, including:

- flashcards
- quizzes
- videos

and more in your Psychology CourseMate.

Go to **CengageBrain.com.**

Glossary

abnormal behavior a behavioral or psychological syndrome or pattern that reflects an underlying psychobiological dysfunction, is associated with distress or disability, and is not merely an expectable response to common stressors or losses

abnormal psychology the scientific study whose objectives are to describe, explain, predict, and modify behaviors that are considered strange or unusual

acute stress disorder (ASD) disorder characterized by flashbacks, hypervigilance, and avoidance symptoms that occur within 1 month after exposure to a traumatic stressor

adaptive behavior performance on tasks of daily living including academic skills, self-care, and the ability to work or live independently

addiction compulsive drug-seeking behavior and a loss of control over drug use

agoraphobia an intense fear of being in public places where escape or help may not be readily available

alcohol poisoning toxic effects resulting from rapidly consuming alcohol or ingesting a large quantity of alcohol; can result in impaired breathing, coma, and death

alcoholic person who has become dependent on alcohol and who exhibits characteristics of an alcohol-use disorder

alcoholism broad term referring to a condition in which the individual is dependent on alcohol and has difficulty controlling drinking

alleles the gene pair responsible for a specific trait

alogia lack of meaningful speech

Alzheimer's disease (AD) dementia involving memory loss and other declines in cognitive and adaptive functioning

American Law Institute Model Penal Code a test of legal insanity that whose purpose is to give jurors increased latitude in determining the sanity of the accused

amniocentesis a prenatal screening procedure involving withdrawal of amniotic fluid from the fetal sac

amygdala brain structure associated with the processing, expression, and memory of emotions, especially anger and fear

analogue study investigative technique that attempts to replicate or simulate, under controlled conditions, a situation that occurs in real life

anorexia nervosa an eating disorder characterized by low body weight, an intense fear of becoming obese, and body image distortion

antipsychotic drugs medications developed to counteract symptoms of psychosis

antisocial type a personality disorder characterized by a failure to conform to social and legal codes, a lack of anxiety and guilt, and irresponsible behaviors

anxiety a fundamental human emotion that produces bodily reactions that prepare us for "fight or flight;" anxiety is anticipatory—the dreaded event or situation has not yet occurred

anxiety disorder fear or anxiety symptoms that interfere with an individual's day-to-day functioning

anxiety sensitivity trait involving fear of physiological changes within the body

anxiolytics a class of medications that reduce anxiety

anxious distress symptoms of motor tension, difficulty relaxing, pervasive worries, or feelings that something catastrophic will occur

arteriosclerosis clogging of the arteries resulting from a buildup of plaque

asociality minimal interest in social relationships

Asperger's syndrome a condition with mild characteristics along the autism spectrum including intense focus on narrow interests and eccentric, one-sided social interactions

assessment the process of gathering information and drawing conclusions about the traits, skills, abilities, emotional functioning, and psychological problems of an individual

asthma a chronic inflammatory disease of the airways in the lungs

atherosclerosis condition involving the progressive thickening and hardening of the walls of arteries due to an accumulation of fats and cholesterol along their inner linings

attention-deficit/hyperactivity disorder (ADHD) childhood-onset disorder characterized by persistent attentional problems and/or impulsive, hyperactive behaviors

attenuated psychosis syndrome condition being researched that involves distressing or disabling early signs of delusions, hallucination, or disorganized speech that emerged or became progressively worse over the previous year; reality testing remains relatively intact

atypical antipsychotics newer antipsychotic medications that are chemically different and less likely to produce the side effects associated with first-generation antipsychotics

aura a visual or physical sensation (e.g., tingling of an extremity or flashes of light) that precedes a headache

autism spectrum disorder (ASD) a disorder characterized by impairment in social communication and restricted, stereotyped interests and activities

autistic savant an individual with ASD who performs exceptionally well on certain tasks (e.g., superior rote memory, artistic, or musical skills)

avoidant type a personality disorder characterized by a fear of rejection and humiliation and a reluctance to enter into social relationships

avolition lack of motivation; an inability to take action or become goal oriented

axon extension on the neuron cell body that sends signals to other neurons, some a considerable distance away

behavioral inhibition shyness

behavioral models models of psychopathology concerned with the role of learning in abnormal behavior

behavioral undercontrol personality trait associated with rebelliousness, novelty seeking, risk taking, and impulsivity

binge drinking episodic intake of five or more alcoholic beverages for men or four or more drinks for women

binge-eating disorder (BED) an eating disorder that involves the consumption of large amounts of food over a short period of time with accompanying feelings of loss of control and distress over the excess eating; behaviors to compensate for overeating are not typically seen with this disorder

biofeedback training a physiological and behavioral approach in which an individual receives information regarding particular autonomic functions and is rewarded for influencing those functions in a desired direction

biological (organic) viewpoint the belief that mental disorders have a physical or physiological basis

blind design an experimental approach in which those helping are not aware of the details of the research

blood pressure the measurement of the force of blood against the walls of the arteries and veins

body dysmorphic disorder (BDD) condition involving a preoccupation with a perceived physical defect or excessive concern over a slight physical defect; often accompanied by frequently checking appearance, applying makeup to mask "flaws," and comparing appearance to those of others

body mass index (BMI) an estimate of body fat calculated on the basis of a person's height and weight

borderline type a personality disorder characterized by intense fluctuations in mood, self-image, and interpersonal relationships

brain pathology a dysfunction or disease of the brain

brief psychotic disorder psychotic episodes with a duration of at least 1 day but less than 1 month

bulimia nervosa an eating disorder in which episodes involving rapid consumption of large quantities of food and a loss of control over eating are followed by purging (vomiting, use of laxatives, diuretics, or enemas) or excessive exercise or fasting in an attempt to compensate for binges

callous and unemotional subtype a form of conduct disorder characterized by minimal guilt, remorse, or empathy and manipulative, superficial emotional expression

cardiovascular pertaining to the heart and blood vessels

case study intensive study of one individual that relies on clinical data, such as observations, psychological tests, and historical and biographical information

catatonia a condition characterized by marked disturbance in motor activity —either extreme excitement or motoric immobility

cathartic method a therapeutic use of verbal expression to release pent-up emotional conflicts

caudate nuclei brain region that regulates transmission of impulses warning that something is not right

cerebral contusion bruising of the brain, often resulting from a blow that causes the brain to forcefully strike the skull

cerebral laceration open head injury in which brain tissue is torn, pierced, or ruptured, usually from a skull fracture or an object that has penetrated the skull

child psychopathology the emotional and behavioral manifestation of psychological disorders in children and adolescents

chronic traumatic encephalopathy (CTE) a progressive, degenerative condition involving brain damage resulting from multiple episodes of head trauma

circadian rhythm an internal clock or daily cycle of internal biological rhythms that influence various bodily processes such as body temperature and sleep–wake cycles

civil commitment the involuntary confinement of a person judged to be a danger to the self or to others, even though the person has not committed a crime

classical conditioning a process in which responses to new stimuli are learned through association

cluster headache excruciating stabbing or burning sensations located in the eye or cheek

cognitive models models based on the assumption that conscious thought mediates an individual's emotional state or behavior in response to a stimulus

cognitive restructuring cognitive strategy that attempts to alter unrealistic thoughts that are believed to be responsible for phobias

cognitive symptoms symptoms of schizophrenia associated with problems with attention and memory and with difficulty in developing a plan of action

comorbid existing simultaneously with another condition

comorbidity co-occurrence of different disorders

competency to stand trial a judgment that a defendant has a factual and rational understanding of the proceedings and can rationally consult with counsel in presenting his or her own defense; refers to the defendant's mental state at the time of the psychiatric examination

compulsion the need to perform acts or dwell on thoughts to reduce anxiety

computerized axial tomography (CT or CAT) a neuroimaging technique that produces brain images using multiple cross-sectional X-rays of the brain

concordance rate degree of similarity between twins or family members with respect to a trait or disorder

concussion trauma-induced changes in brain functioning, typically caused by a blow to the head

conditioned response (CR) in classical conditioning, a learned response to a previously neutral stimulus that has acquired some of the properties of another stimulus with which it has been paired

conditioned stimulus (CS) in classical conditioning, a previously neutral stimulus that has acquired some of the properties of another stimulus with which it has been paired

conduct disorder (CD) a persistent pattern of behavior that violates the rights of others, including aggression, serious rule violations, and illegal behavior

confidentiality an ethical standard that protects clients from disclosure of information without their consent; an ethical obligation of the therapist

control group the group in an experiment that is similar to the experimental group except for exposure to the independent variable

conversion disorder (functional neurological symptom disorder) a condition involving sensory or motor impairment suggestive of a neurological disorder but with no underlying medical cause

coprolalia involuntary utterance of obscenities or inappropriate remarks

coronary heart disease (CHD) disease process involving the narrowing of cardiac arteries, resulting in the restriction or partial blockage of the flow of blood and oxygen to the heart

cortisol hormone released by the adrenal gland in response to stress

co-rumination extensively discussing negative feelings or events with peers or others

couples therapy a treatment aimed at helping couples understand and clarify their communications, role relationships, unfulfilled needs, and unrealistic or unmet expectations

criminal commitment incarceration of an individual for having committed a crime

cultural relativism the belief that lifestyles, cultural values, and worldviews affect the expression and determination of behavior

cultural universality the assumption that a fixed set of mental disorders exists whose obvious manifestations cut across cultures

culture the configuration of shared values, beliefs, attitudes, and behaviors that is transmitted from one generation to another by members of a particular group and symbolized by artifacts, roles, expectations, and institutions

dangerousness a person's potential for doing harm to the self or to others

defense mechanism in psychoanalytic theory, an ego-protection strategy that shelters the individual from anxiety, operates unconsciously, and distorts reality

deficit model early attempt to explain differences in minority groups that contended that differences are the result of "cultural deprivation"

deinstitutionalization the shifting of responsibility for the care of mental patients from large central institutions to agencies within local communities

delayed ejaculation (male orgasmic disorder) persistent delay or inability to achieve an orgasm after the excitement phase has been reached and sexual activity has been adequate in focus, intensity, and duration; usually restricted to an inability to ejaculate within the vagina

delirium an acute state of confusion involving diminished awareness, disorientation, and impaired attentional skills

delirium tremens life-threatening withdrawal symptoms that can result from chronic alcohol use

delusion a false belief that is firmly and consistently held

delusional disorder persistent, nonbizarre delusions without other unusual or odd behaviors; tactile and olfactory hallucinations related to the delusional theme may be present

dementia syndrome of symptoms involving deterioration in cognition and independent functioning

dendrite short, rootlike structure on the neuron cell body whose function is to receive signals from other neurons

dependent variable variable that is expected to change when an independent variable is manipulated in an experiment

depersonalization/derealization disorder dissociative condition characterized by feelings of unreality concerning the self and the environment

depressant a substance that causes a slowing of responses and generalized depression of the central nervous system

depression a mood state characterized by sadness or despair, feelings of worthlessness, and withdrawal from others

detoxification phase of alcohol or drug treatment during which the body is purged of intoxicating substances

diastolic pressure arterial force exerted when the heart is relaxed and the ventricles of the heart are filling with blood

disconfirmatory evidence information that contradicts a delusional belief

disinhibited social engagement disorder (DSED) an attachment disorder characterized by indiscriminate, superficial attachments and desperation for interpersonal contact

disruptive mood dysregulation disorder (DMDD) a childhood disorder involving chronic irritability and significantly exaggerated anger reactions

dissociative amnesia sudden partial or total loss of important personal information or recall of events due to psychological factors

dissociative anesthetic a substance that produces a dreamlike detachment

dissociative disorders a group of disorders, including dissociative amnesia, dissociative identity disorder, and depersonalization/derealization disorder, all of which involve some sort of dissociation, or separation, of a part of the person's consciousness, memory, or identity

dissociative fugue episode involving complete loss of memory of one's life and identity, unexpected travel to a new location, or assumption of a new identity

dissociative identity disorder (DID) a condition in which two or more relatively independent personality states appear to exist in one person, including experiences of possession; also known as *multiple-personality disorder*

dopamine hypothesis the suggestion that schizophrenia may result from excess dopamine activity at certain synaptic sites

double-blind design an experimental approach in which neither the participants nor those working directly with them are aware of experimental details

Down syndrome (DS) a chromosomal disorder (most frequently involving an extra copy of chromosome 21) that causes physical and neurological abnormalities

due process legal checks and balances that are guaranteed to everyone (e.g., the right to receive a fair trial, the right to face one's accusers, the right to present evidence, the right to have counsel, and so on)

***Durham* standard** a test of legal insanity also known as the *products test*—an accused person is not responsible if the unlawful act was the product of a mental disease or defect

dyscalculia a condition involving difficulties in understanding mathematical skills or concepts

dyslexia a condition involving significant difficulties with reading skills

dyspareunia recurrent or persistent pain in the genitals before, during, or after sexual intercourse

dysthymic disorder condition involving chronic depressive symptoms that are present most of the day for more days than not during a 2-year period with no more than 2 months symptom-free

early ejaculation ejaculation with minimal sexual stimulation before, during, or shortly after penetration; also known as *premature ejaculation*

eating conditions not elsewhere classified a diagnostic category involving problematic eating patterns that do not fully meet the criteria for one of the eating disorders

echolalia repetition of vocalizations made by another person

electroencephalograph (EEG) a test that measures the firing of neurons via electrodes placed on the scalp

elevated mood a mood state involving exaggerated feelings of energy and well-being

encephalitis inflammation of the brain

endophenotype measurable characteristics (neurochemical, endocrinological, neuroanatomical, cognitive, or neuropsychological) that can give clues regarding the specific genes involved in a disorder

epidemiological research study of the rate and distribution of mental disorders in a population

epigenetics field of biological research focused on understanding how environmental factors (e.g., trauma, toxins, or nutrition) influence or program gene expression

epilepsy disorder involving seizures that result from uncontrolled electrical discharge from brain cells

epinephrine hormone released by the adrenal gland in response to physical or mental stress; also known as adrenaline

erectile disorder (ED) an inability to attain or maintain an erection sufficient for sexual intercourse or psychological arousal during sexual activity

etiological model model developed to explain the cause of a disorder

etiology cause or origin of a disorder

euphoria exceptionally elevated mood; exaggerated feeling of well-being

exhibitionistic disorder urges, acts, or fantasies that involve exposing one's genitals to strangers

existential approach a set of attitudes that has many commonalities with humanism but is less optimistic, focusing (a) on human alienation in an increasingly technological and impersonal world, (b) on the individual in the context of the human condition, and (c) on responsibility to others as well as to oneself

exorcism treatment method used by the early Greeks, Chinese, Hebrews, and Egyptians in which prayers, noises, emetics, flogging, and starvation were used to cast evil spirits out of an afflicted person's body

experiment technique of scientific inquiry in which a prediction is made about two variables; the independent variable is then manipulated in a controlled situation and changes in the dependent variable are measured

experimental group the group in an experiment that is subjected to the independent variable

experimental hypothesis prediction concerning how an independent variable will affect a dependent variable in an experiment

exposure therapy treatment that involves gradually introducing the client to increasingly difficult encounters with a feared situation

expressed emotion (EE) a negative communication pattern found among some relatives of individuals with schizophrenia

externalizing disorders disruptive behavior disorders associated with symptoms that are socially disturbing and distressing to others

extrapyramidal symptoms side effects such as restlessness, involuntary movements, and muscular tension produced by antipsychotic medications

factitious disorder a disorder in which symptoms of illness are deliberately induced, simulated, or exaggerated, with no apparent external incentive

factitious disorder imposed on another a pattern of falsification or production of physical or psychological symptoms in another individual

family systems model model that assumes that the behavior of one family member directly affects the entire family system

fear an intense emotion experienced in response to a threatening situation

female orgasmic disorder a sexual dysfunction in which the woman experiences persistent delay or inability to achieve an orgasm with stimulation after entering the excitement phase that is adequate in focus, intensity, and duration

female sexual arousal disorder the inability to attain or maintain physiological response or psychological arousal during sexual activity

fetal alcohol spectrum effects a continuum of detrimental neurological and behavioral effects resulting from maternal alcohol consumption during pregnancy

fetal alcohol syndrome (FAS) a condition resulting from maternal alcohol consumption during gestation that involves central nervous system dysfunction and altered brain development; the leading cause of preventable intellectual disability

fetishistic disorder sexual attraction and fantasies involving inanimate objects, such as female undergarments

field study investigative technique in which behaviors and events are observed and recorded in their natural environment

first-generation antipsychotics a group of medications originally developed to combat psychotic symptoms by reducing dopamine levels in the brain; also called *conventional* or *typical antipsychotics*

flight of ideas rapidly changing or disjointed thoughts

flooding a technique that involves inducing a high anxiety level through continued actual or imagined exposure to a fear-arousing situation

fragile X syndrome an inherited condition involving limited production of proteins required for brain development resulting in mild to severe intellectual disability

free association psychoanalytic therapeutic technique in which the patient says whatever comes to mind for the purpose of revealing his or her unconscious

frontotemporal lobar degeneration (FTLD) degeneration in the frontal and temporal lobes of the brain that results in ongoing declines in language and behavior

frotteuristic disorder recurrent and intense sexual urges, acts, or fantasies that involve touching or rubbing against a nonconsenting person

functional magnetic resonance imaging (fMRI) a specialized MRI that assesses brain structures and blood flow in different brain regions

GABA gamma-aminobutyric acid, an inhibitory neurotransmitter involved in inducing sleep and relaxation

gateway drug a substance that leads to use of additional substances that are even more lethal

gender dysphoria a disorder characterized by conflict between a person's anatomical sex and his or her gender identity, or self-identification as male or female

generalized anxiety disorder (GAD) condition characterized by persistent, high levels of anxiety and excessive worry over many life circumstances

genetic linkage studies investigations regarding whether a disorder follows a genetic pattern

genital-pelvic pain/penetration disorder physical pain or discomfort associated with intercourse or penetration; fear, anxiety, and distress are also usually present; includes previous diagnoses of vaginismus and dyspareunia

genome all the genetic material in the chromosomes of a particular organism

genotype a person's genetic makeup

grandiosity an overvaluation of one's significance or importance

group therapy a form of therapy that involves the simultaneous treatment of two or more clients and may involve more than one therapist

habit reversal a therapeutic technique in which a client is taught to substitute new behaviors for habitual behaviors such as a tic

hallucination a sensory perception that is not directly attributable to environmental stimuli

hallucinogen a substance that induces perceptual distortions and heightens sensory awareness

heavy drinking chronic alcohol intake of more than two drinks per day for men and more than one drink per day for women

hemorrhagic stroke a stroke involving leakage of blood into the brain

hippocampus the part of the brain involved in forming, organizing, and storing memories

homeostasis state of metabolic equilibrium

humanism a philosophical movement that emphasizes human welfare and the worth and uniqueness of the individual

humanistic perspective the optimistic viewpoint that people are born with the ability to fulfill their potential and that abnormal behavior results from disharmony between a person's potential and his or her self-concept

Huntington's disease (HD) a genetic disease characterized by involuntary twitching movements and eventual dementia

hypersexual disorder a craving for constant sex at the expense of relationships, work productivity, and daily activities

hypertension a chronic condition, which increases risk of stroke and heart disease, characterized by a systolic blood pressure of 140 or higher or a diastolic pressure of 90 or higher

hyperthermia significantly elevated body temperature

hypervigilance state of ongoing anxiety in which the person is constantly tense and alert for threats

hypnotics a class of medications that induce sleep

hypoactive sexual desire disorder a sexual dysfunction that is related to the appetitive phase of the sexual response cycle and is characterized by a lack of sexual desire

hypomania a milder form of mania involving increased levels of activity and goal-directed behaviors combined with an elevated, expansive, or irritable mood

hypothalamic-pituitary-adrenal (HPA) axis the system involved in stress and trauma reactions and regulation of body processes such as "fight or flight" responses

hypothesis conjectural statement that usually describes a relationship between two variables

iatrogenic disorder a condition unintentionally produced by a therapist's actions and treatment strategies

illness anxiety disorder persistent health anxiety and concern that one has an undetected physical illness with no or minimal somatic symptoms

incest a form of pedohebephilic disorder; can also be sexual relations between people too closely related to marry legally

incidence number of new cases of a disorder that appear in an identified population within a specified time period

independent variable variable or condition that an experimenter manipulates to determine its effect on a dependent variable

inferiority model early attempt to explain differences in minority groups that contended that racial and ethnic minorities are inferior in some respect to the majority population

insanity defense the legal argument used by defendants who admit that they have committed a crime but plead not guilty because they were mentally disturbed at the time of the crime

intellectual developmental disorder (IDD) a disorder characterized by limitations in intellectual functioning and adaptive behaviors

internalizing disorders conditions involving emotional symptoms directed inward

interoceptive conditioning the production of fear and panic by the perception of bodily changes due to frequent pairing of changes in internal bodily sensations with fear responses

irresistible impulse test a doctrine that states that a defendant is not criminally responsible if he or she lacked the willpower to control his or her behavior

ischemic stroke a stroke due to reduced blood supply caused by a clot or severe narrowing of the arteries supplying blood to the brain

learned helplessness a learned belief that one is helpless and unable to affect outcomes

learning disorder (LD) an academic disability characterized by deficits in reading, writing, and math skills that bring them substantially below levels that would be expected based on the person's age, intellectual ability, and educational background

least restrictive environment the least restrictive alternative to freedom that is appropriate to a person's condition

lethality the probability that a person chooses to end his or her life

Lewy body dementia (LBD) dementia involving visual hallucinations, cognitive fluctuations, and atypical movements

lifetime prevalence the percentage of people in the population who have had a disorder at some point in their lives

localized amnesia lack of memory for a specific event or events

loosening of associations continual shifting from topic to topic without any apparent logical or meaningful connection between thoughts

***M'Naghten* rule** a cognitive test of legal insanity that inquires whether the accused knew right from wrong when he or she committed the crime

magnetic resonance imaging (MRI) a neuroimaging technique that produces brain images using a magnetic field

mainstreaming integrating mental patients as soon as possible back into the community

major depressive episode a period involving severe depressive symptoms that have impaired functioning for at least 2 full weeks

malingering feigning illness for an external purpose

managed health care the industrialization of health care, whereby large organizations in the private sector control the delivery of services

mania mental state characterized by very exaggerated activity and emotions including euphoria, excessive excitement or irritability, diminished need for sleep, and resultant impairment in social or occupational functioning

mass madness group hysteria in which a great many people exhibit similar symptoms that have no apparent physical cause

medically induced coma a deliberately induced state of deep sedation that allows the brain to rest and heal

meningitis inflammation of the membrane surrounding the brain and spinal cord

mental status examination procedure designed to evaluate cognitive, psychological, and behavioral functioning by means of questions, observations, and tasks posed to the client

metabolic syndrome a medical condition associated with obesity, diabetes, high cholesterol, and hypertension

migraine headache moderate to severe head pain resulting from abnormal brain activity affecting the cranial blood vessels and nerves

mixed episode concurrent hypomanic/manic and depressive symptoms

model an analogy used by scientists, usually to describe or explain a phenomenon or process they cannot directly observe

modeling process of learning by observing models (and later imitating them)

modeling therapy procedure involving observation of a non-phobic individual successfully coping with the phobic object or situation used to treat certain phobias

moderate drinking a lower-risk pattern of alcohol intake (no more than one or two drinks per day)

mood a prolonged emotional state

moral treatment movement movement instituted by Philippe Pinel that resulted in a shift to more humane treatment of people who were mentally disturbed

motivational enhancement therapy a therapeutic approach that addresses ambivalence and helps clients consider the advantages and disadvantages of continuing substance use

motor tic a tic involving physical behaviors such as eye blinking, facial grimacing, or head jerking

multicultural model contemporary attempt to explain differences in minority groups that suggests that behaviors be evaluated from the perspective of a group's value system, as well as by other standards used in determining normality and abnormality

multicultural psychology an approach that stresses the importance of culture, race, ethnicity, gender, age, socioeconomic class, and other similar factors in its effort to understand and treat abnormal behavior

multipath model a model of models that provides an organizational framework for understanding the numerous causes of mental disorders, the complexity of their interacting components, and the need to view disorders from a holistic framework

muscle dysphoria extreme dissatisfaction with one's muscularity

narcissistic type a personality disorder characterized by an exaggerated sense of self-importance, an exploitative attitude, and a lack of empathy

negative correlation increase in one variable accompanied by a decrease in a second variable

negative symptoms symptoms of schizophrenia associated with an inability or decreased ability to initiate actions or speech, express emotions, or feel pleasure

neurocognitive disorder a disorder that occurs when brain dysfunction affects thinking processes, memory, consciousness, or perception

neurodegeneration declining brain functioning due to progressive loss of brain structure, neurochemical abnormalities, or the death of neurons

neurodevelopmental disorders conditions involving impaired development of the brain and central nervous system that are evident early in a child's life

neuron nerve cell that transmits messages throughout the body

neuroplasticity the ability of the brain to change its structure and function in response to experience

neurotransmitter any of a group of chemicals that help transmit messages between neurons

nonsuicidal self injury (NSSI) intentional, self-inflicted injury without suicidal intent; can also involve a preoccupation with engaging in self-harm

normal blood pressure the normal amount of force exerted by blood against the artery walls; systolic pressure is less than 120 and diastolic pressure is less than 80

obesity a condition involving a body mass index greater than 30

observational learning theory theory that suggests that an individual can acquire new behaviors by watching other people perform them

obsession intrusive, repetitive thought or image that produces anxiety

obsessive-compulsive disorder (OCD) condition characterized by intrusive, repetitive anxiety-producing thoughts or a strong need to perform acts or dwell on thoughts to reduce anxiety

obsessive-compulsive type (OCT) a personality disorder characterized by perfectionism, a tendency to be interpersonally controlling, devotion to details, and rigidity

operant behavior voluntary and controllable behavior, such as walking or thinking, that "operates" on an individual's environment

operant conditioning theory of learning that holds that behaviors are controlled by the consequences that follow them

opioid a painkilling agent that depresses the central nervous system, such as heroin and prescription pain relievers

oppositional defiant disorder (ODD) a childhood disorder characterized by negativistic, argumentative, and hostile behavior patterns

optimal human functioning qualities such as subjective well-being, happiness, optimism, resilience, hope, courage, ability to cope with stress, self-actualization, and self-determinism

orbitofrontal cortex brain region associated with planning and decision making

oxytocin a powerful hormone that affects social bonding

panic attack episode of intense fear accompanied by symptoms such as a pounding heart, trembling, shortness of breath, and fear of losing control or dying

panic disorder disorder involving recurrent, unexpected panic attacks with apprehension over future attacks or behavioral changes to avoid attacks

paranoid ideation suspiciousness about the actions or motives of others

paraphilic disorders sexual disorders of at least 6 months' duration in which the person has either acted on or is severely distressed by recurrent urges or fantasies involving nonhuman objects, nonconsenting individuals, or suffering or humiliation

Parkinson's disease (PD) a progressive disorder characterized by poorly controlled motor movements

pediatric bipolar disorder (PBD) a childhood disorder involving depressive and energized episodes similar to the mood swings seen in adult bipolar disorder

pedohebephilic disorder a disorder in which an adult obtains erotic gratification through urges, acts, or fantasies that involve sexual contact with a prepubescent or early pubescent child

persecutory delusions beliefs of being targeted by others

personality disorder a disorder characterized by impairment in self and interpersonal functioning and the presence of pathological personality traits that are relatively inflexible and long-standing

phenotype observable physical and behavioral characteristics caused by the interaction between the genotype and the environment

phobia a strong, persistent, and unwarranted fear of a specific object or situation

physiological dependence state of adaptation that occurs after chronic exposure to a substance; can result in craving and withdrawal symptoms

placebo control group a group whose members are given either attention equivalent to that given to the experimental group or a medication capsule containing an inert drug

plaque sticky material (composed of fat, cholesterol, and other substances) that builds up on the walls of veins or arteries

pleasure principle the impulsive, pleasure-seeking aspect of our being, from which the id operates

polymorphic variation a common DNA mutation of a gene

positive correlation increase in one variable accompanied by an increase in a second variable

positive psychology the philosophical and scientific study of positive human functioning and the strengths and assets of individuals, families, and communities

positive symptoms symptoms of schizophrenia that involve unusual thoughts or perceptions, such as delusions, hallucinations, disordered thinking, or bizarre behavior

positron emission tomography (PET) a nuclear imaging scan that assesses glucose metabolism in the brain

possession the replacement of a person's sense of personal identity with a supernatural spirit or power

postpartum depression depressive symptoms beginning within 6 months of childbirth

post-traumatic stress disorder (PTSD) disorder characterized by flashbacks, hypervigilance, avoidance, and other symptoms that last for more than 1 month and that occur as a result of exposure to extreme trauma

predisposition a susceptibility to certain symptoms or disorders

prefrontal cortex the part of the brain involved in abstract thought and complex thinking, personality characteristics, and social functioning

prefrontal lobotomy a surgical procedure in which the frontal lobes are disconnected from the remainder of the brain

prehypertension a condition believed to be a precursor to hypertension, stroke, and heart disease, characterized by systolic blood pressure of 120 to 139 and diastolic pressure from 80 to 89

premorbid before the onset of major symptoms

pressured speech rapid, frenzied, or loud, disjointed communication

prevalence percentage of individuals in a targeted population who have a particular disorder during a specific period of time

privileged communication a therapist's legal obligation to protect a client's privacy and to prevent the disclosure of confidential communications without a client's permission

projective personality test involving responses to ambiguous stimuli, such as inkblots, pictures, or incomplete sentences

provisional diagnosis an initial diagnosis based on currently available information

psychiatric epidemiology the study of the prevalence of mental illness in a society

psychoactive substance a substance that alters mood, thought processes, or other psychological states

psychoanalysis therapy whose goals are to uncover repressed material, to help clients achieve insight into inner motivations and desires, and to resolve childhood conflicts that affect current relationships

psychodiagnosis assessment and description of an individual's psychological symptoms, including inferences about what might be causing the psychological distress

psychodynamic model model that views disorders as the result of childhood trauma or anxieties and that holds that many of these childhood-based anxieties operate unconsciously

psychogenic originating from psychological causes

psychological autopsy the systematic examination of existing information after a person's death for the purpose of understanding and explaining the person's behavior before death

psychological viewpoint the belief that mental disorders are caused by psychological and emotional factors rather than organic or biological ones

psychopathology the study of mental or behavioral disorders

psychophysiological disorder any physical disorder that has a strong psychological basis or component

psychosexual stages in psychodynamic theory, the sequence of stages—oral, anal, phallic, latency, and genital—through which human personality develops

psychosis condition involving loss of contact with or distorted view of reality

rape a form of sexual aggression that involves sexual activity (oral-genital sex, anal intercourse, or vaginal intercourse) performed against a person's will through the use of force, argument, pressure, alcohol or drugs, or authority

rape trauma syndrome a two-phase syndrome that rape victims may experience, involving such emotional reactions as psychological distress, phobic reactions, and sexual dysfunction

rapid-cycling the occurrence of four or more mood episodes per year

reactive attachment disorder (RAD) an attachment disorder characterized by inhibited, avoidant social behaviors and reluctance to seek or respond to attention or nurturing

reality principle an awareness of the demands of the environment and of the need to adjust behavior to meet these demands, from which the ego operates

relapse a return to drug or alcohol use after a period of abstention

relaxation training a therapeutic technique in which a person acquires the ability to relax the muscles of the body in almost any circumstance

reliability the degree to which a measure or procedure yields the same results repeatedly

remit diminish or disappear

repressed memory memory of a traumatic event has been repressed and is, therefore, unavailable for recall

resistance during psychoanalysis, a process in which the patient unconsciously attempts to impede the analysis by preventing the exposure of repressed material

response prevention treatment in which an individual with OCD is prevented from performing a compulsive behavior

response set tendency to respond to test items in a certain way regardless of content

restricted affect severely diminished or limited emotional responsiveness

right to treatment the concept that mental patients who have been involuntarily committed have a right to receive therapy that would improve their condition

rumination continually thinking about certain topics or reviewing events that have occurred

schema mental framework for organizing and interpreting information

schizoaffective disorder a condition involving the existence of both symptoms of schizophrenia and major depressive or manic symptoms

schizophrenia a group of disorders characterized by severely impaired cognitive processes, personality disintegration, mood disturbances, and social withdrawal

schizophreniform disorder psychotic episodes with a duration of at least 1 month but less than 6 months

schizotypal type a personality disorder characterized by peculiar thoughts and behaviors and by poor interpersonal relationships

school phobia fear of attending school

scientific method method of inquiry that provides for the systematic collection of data, controlled observation, and the testing of hypotheses

sedatives a class of drugs that have a calming or sedating effect

selective amnesia an inability to remember certain details of an event

selective mutism consistent failure to speak in certain situations

self-actualization an inherent tendency to strive toward the realization of one's full potential

self-concept an individual's assessment of his or her own value and worth

separation anxiety disorder severe distress about leaving home, being alone, or being separated from a parent

serotonin a neurotransmitter that regulates mood, sleep, and appetite

sexual arousal disorder a disorder characterized by problems occurring during the excitement phase of the sexual response cycle and relating to difficulties with feelings of sexual pleasure or with the physiological changes associated with sexual excitement

sexual dysfunction a disruption of any part of the normal sexual response cycle that affects sexual desire, arousal, or response

sexual masochism disorder sexual urges, fantasies, or acts that involve being humiliated, bound, or made to suffer

sexual sadism disorder sexually arousing urges, fantasies, or acts that involve inflicting physical or psychological suffering on others

single photon emission computed tomography (SPECT) a nuclear imaging scan that provides longer but less detailed images of metabolic activity within the brain

skin-picking disorder distressing and recurrent compulsive picking of the skin resulting in skin lesions

social anxiety disorder an intense fear of being scrutinized in one or more social or performance situations

somatic symptom disorder (SSD) condition involving a pattern of reporting distressing physical symptoms combined with extreme concern about health or fears of undiagnosed medical conditions

somatic symptom disorder (SSD) with pain features a subtype of SSD involving severe or lingering pain that appears to have no physical basis

somatic symptom disorder (SSD) with predominately somatic complaints a subtype of SSD involving chronic complaints of specific bodily symptoms that have no physical basis

somatic symptom disorders broad grouping of psychological disorders that involve physical symptoms or anxiety over illness including somatic symptom disorder, illness anxiety disorder, conversion disorder (functional neurological symptom disorder), and factitious disorder

somatic symptoms distressing physical or bodily symptoms

specific phobia an extreme fear of a specific object (such as snakes) or situation (such as being in an enclosed place)

spiritual being a person's animating life force that speaks to the thoughts, feelings, and behaviors related to a transcendent state or one's capacity for creativity, growth, and love

spirituality the animating life force or energy of the human condition that is broader than but inclusive of religion

standardization the use of identical procedures in the administration of tests, or the establishment of a norm or comparison group to which an individual's test performance can be compared

stimulant a substance that energizes the central nervous system

stress the internal psychological or physiological response to a stressor

stressor an external event or situation that places a physical or psychological demand on a person

stroke a sudden halting of blood flow to a portion of the brain, leading to brain damage

subjective taking place in the person's own mind

substance abuse pattern of excessive or harmful use of any substance for mood-altering purposes

suicidal ideation thoughts about suicide

suicide the intentional, direct, and conscious taking of one's own life

suicidologist a professional who studies the manifestation, dynamics, and prevention of suicides

sympathetic nervous system part of the nervous system that automatically performs functions such as increasing heart rate, constricting blood vessels, and raising blood pressure

synapse minute gap that exists between the axon of the sending neuron and the dendrites of the receiving neuron

syndrome certain symptoms that tend to occur regularly in clusters

synergistic effect the result of chemicals (or substances) interacting to multiply one another's effects

systematic desensitization exposure strategy that uses muscle relaxation to reduce the anxiety associated with specific and social phobias

systematized amnesia loss of memory for certain categories of information

systolic pressure force on blood vessels when the heart contracts

tarantism a mania or form of mass hysteria prevalent during the Middle Ages, characterized by wild raving, jumping, dancing, and convulsing; also known as *St. Vitus's dance*

***Tarasoff* ruling** a California Supreme Court decision that established what is often referred to as the duty to warn; obligates mental health professionals to break confidentiality when their clients pose a clear and imminent danger to another person

temperament innate emotional predisposition or personality traits

tension headache head pain produced by prolonged contraction of the scalp and neck muscles, resulting in constriction of the blood vessels and steady pain

therapy a program of systematic intervention whose purpose is to improve a person's behavioral, affective (emotional), or cognitive state

tic an involuntary, repetitive movement or vocalization

tolerance decreases in the effects of a substance that occur after chronic use

Tourette's disorder (TD) a condition characterized by multiple motor tics and one or more vocal tics

transference process by which a patient in psychoanalysis re-enacts early conflicts by applying to the analyst feelings and attitudes that the patient had toward significant others in the past

transient ischemic attack (TIA) a "mini-stroke" resulting from temporary blockage of arteries

transvestic disorder intense sexual arousal obtained through cross-dressing (wearing clothes appropriate to a different gender); not to be confused with gender dysphoria

traumatic brain injury (TBI) a physical wound or internal injury to the brain

trephining a surgical method from the Stone Age in which part of the skull was chipped away to provide an opening through which an evil spirit could escape

trichotillomania recurrent and compulsive hair pulling that results in hair loss and causes significant distress

unconditioned response (UCR) in classical conditioning, the unlearned response made to an unconditioned stimulus

unconditioned stimulus (UCS) in classical conditioning, the stimulus that elicits an unconditioned response

universal shamanic tradition (UST) set of beliefs and practices from non-Western indigenous psychologies that assume that special healers are blessed with powers to act as intermediaries or messengers between the human and spirit worlds

vaginismus involuntary spasm of the outer third of the vaginal wall that prevents or interferes with sexual intercourse

validity degree to which an instrument measures what it was developed to measure

vascular involving blood vessels

vascular cognitive impairment decline in cognitive skills that occurs when damage to the cardiovascular system reduces blood flow to the brain; also called *vascular dementia*

vocal tic an audible tic such as coughing, grunting, throat clearing, sniffling, or making sudden, vocal outbursts

voyeuristic disorder urges, acts, or fantasies that involve observing an unsuspecting person disrobing or engaging in sexual activity

withdrawal adverse physical and psychological symptoms that occur after reducing or ceasing intake of a substance

References

Aarnoudse-Moens, C. S., Weisglas-Kuperus, N., van Goudoever, J. B., & Oosterlaan, J. (2009). Meta-analysis of neurobehavioral outcomes in very preterm and/or very low birth weight children. *Journal of Pediatrics, 124*, 717–728.

Aarsland, D., Andersen, K., Larsen, J. P., Lolk, A. L., & Kragh-Sorensen, P. (2003). Prevalence and characteristics of dementia in Parkinson disease: An 8-year prospective study. *Archives of Neurology, 60*, 387–392.

Aarsland, D., Sardahaee, F. S., Anderssen, S., & Ballard, C. (2010). Is physical activity a potential preventive factor for vascular dementia? A systematic review. *Aging and Mental Health, 14*, 386–395.

Aas, M., Djurovic, S., Athanasiu, L., Steen, N. E., Agartz, I., Lorentzen, S., . . . Melle, I. (2012). Serotonin transporter gene polymorphism, childhood trauma, and cognition in patients with psychotic disorders. *Schizophrenia Bulletin, 38*, 15–22.

Abbate-Daga, G., Gramaglia, C., Marzola, E., Amianto, F., Zuccolin, M., & Fassino, S. (2011). Eating disorders and major depression: Role of anger and personality. *Depression Research and Treatment*, doi:10.1155/2011/194732.

Abdulhamid, I., & Pataki, C. (2011). Pediatric Munchausen syndrome by proxy. Retrieved from http://emedicine.medscape.com/article/917525-overview#aw2aab6b7

Abel, G. G., & Rouleau, J. L. (1990). The nature and extent of sexual assault. In W. L. Marshall, D. R. Laws, & H. E. Barbaree (Eds.), *Handbook of sexual assaults: Issues, theories and treatment of the offender* (pp. 9–22). New York, NY: Plenum.

Abelsohn, A. R., & Sanborn, M. (2010). Lead and children: Clinical management for family physicians. *Canadian Family Physician, 56*, 531–535.

Aboraya, A., Chumber, P., & Altaha, B. (2009). The treatment-resistant catatonia patient. *Current Psychiatry, 8*, 66–69.

Abrahams, B. S., & Geschwind, D. H. (2010). Connecting genes to brain in the autism spectrum disorders. *Archives of Neurology, 67*, 395–399.

Abramowitz, J. S., & Larsen, J. E. (2007). Exposure therapy for obsessive-compulsive disorder. In D. C. Richard & D. Lauterach (Eds.), *Handbook of exposure therapies* (pp. 185–208). New York, NY: Academic Press.

Abramowitz, J. S., Metzer-Brody, S., Leserman, J., Killenberg, S., Rinaldi, K., Mahaffey, B. L. . . . Pedersen, C. (2010). Obsessional thoughts and compulsive behaviors in a sample of women with postpartum mood symptoms. *Archives of Women's Mental Health, 13*, 523–530.

Abramowitz, J. S., Taylor, S., & McKay, D. (2010). Hypochondriasis and severe health anxiety. In D. McKay, J. S. Abramowitz, & S. Taylor (Eds.), *Cognitive-behavioral therapy for refractory cases: Turning failure into success* (pp. 327–346). Washington, DC: American Psychological Association Press.

Abrams, R. C., & Bromberg, C. E. (2007). Personality disorders in the elderly. *Psychiatric Annals, 37*, 123–127.

Abramson, L. Y., Seligman, M. E. P., & Teasdale, J. D. (1978). Learned helplessness in humans: Critique and reformulation. *Journal of Abnormal Psychology, 87*, 49–74.

Abreu, L. N., Lafer, B., Baca-Garcia, E., & Oquendo, M. A. (2009) Suicidal ideation and suicide attempts in bipolar disorder type I: An update for the clinician. *Journal of the Brazilian Psychiatric Association, 31*, 271–280.

Abuse, Rape, and Domestic Violence Aid and Resource Collection, An. (2011). Rape and sexual assault statistics. Retrieved from http://www.aardvarc.org/rape/about/statistics.shtml

Ackard, D. M., Fulkerson, J. A., & Neumark-Sztainer, D. (2007). Prevalence and utility of DSM-IV eating disorder diagnostic criteria among youth. *International Journal of Eating Disorders, 40*, 409–417.

Addington, J., & Addington, D. (2009). Three-year outcome of treatment in an early psychosis program. *Canadian Journal of Psychiatry, 54*, 626–630.

Addington, J., & Haarmans, M. (2006). Cognitive-behavioral therapy for individuals recovering from a first-episode psychosis. *Journal of Contemporary Psychotherapy, 36*, 43–49.

Adi, Y., Juarez-Garcia, A., Wang, D., Jowett, S., Frew, E., . . . Burls, A. (2007). Oral naltrexone as a treatment for relapse prevention in formerly opioid-dependent drug users: A systematic review and economic evaluation. *Health Technology Assessment, 11*(iii–iv), 1–85.

Adler, J., & Rogers, A. (1999, January 11). The new war against migraines. *Newsweek, 133*, 46–52.

Agras, W. S., Crow, S. J., Halmi, K. A., Mitchell, J. E., Wilson, G. T., & Kraemer, H. C. (2000). Outcome predictors for the cognitive behavior treatment of bulimia nervosa: Data from a multisite study. *American Journal of Psychiatry, 157*, 1302–1308.

Agrawal, A., & Lynskey, M. T. (2008). Are there genetic influences on addiction: Evidence from family, adoption and twin studies. *Addiction, 103*, 1069–1081.

Agrawal, A., Pergadia, M. L., & Lynskey, M. T. (2008). Is there evidence for symptoms of cannabis withdrawal in the national epidemiologic survey of alcohol and related conditions? *American Journal on Addictions, 17*, 199–208.

Ahmed, A. S. (2007). Posttraumatic stress disorder, resilience and vulnerability. *Advances in Psychiatric Treatment, 13*, 369–375.

Ahmed, N., Wahlgren, N., Grond, M., Hennerici, M., Lees, K. R., Mikulik, R., . . . Ringleb, P. (2010). Implementation and outcome of thrombolysis with alteplase 3–4.5 h after an acute stroke: An updated analysis from SITS-ISTR. *The Lancet Neurology, 9*, 866–874.

Akbaraly, T. N., Brunner, E. J., Ferrie, J. E., Marmot, M. G., Kivimaki, M., & Singh-Manoux, A. (2009). Dietary pattern and depressive symptoms in middle age. *British Journal of Psychiatry, 195*, 408–413.

Akinbami, L. (2006). Asthma prevalence, health care use and mortality: United States, 2003–2005. Retrieved from http://www.cdc.gov/nchs/data/hestat/asthma03-05/asthma03-05.htm

Akinbami, L. J., Moorman, J. E., & Liu, X. (2011). Asthma prevalence, health care use, and mortality: United States, 2005–2009. *National Health Statistics Report, 12*(32), 1–14.

Albert, M. A., Glynn, R. G., & Buring, J. (2010, November). *Women with high job strain have 40 percent increased risk of heart disease.* Presented at the Annual Meetings of the American Heart Association, Chicago, IL.

Alcantara, C., & Gone, J. P. (2008). Suicide in Native American communities. In F. Leong & M. M. Leach (Eds.), *Ethnic suicides* (pp. 173–199). New York, NY: Routledge.

Aldridge-Morris, R. (1989). *Multiple personality: An exercise in deception*. Hove, UK: Erlbaum.

Alexander, F. G., & Selesnick, S. T. (1966). *The history of psychiatry.* New York, NY: Harper & Row.

Alexander, G. C., Gallagher, S. A., Mascola, A., Moloney, R. M., & Stafford, R. S. (2011). Increasing off-label use of antipsychotic medications in the United States, 1995–2008. *Pharmacoepidemiology and Drug Safety, 20*(2), 177–184. doi:10.1002/pds.2082

Alford, G. S., Morin, C., Atkins, M., & Schuen, L. (1987). Masturbatory extinction of deviant sexual arousal: A case study. *Behavior Therapy, 18*, 265–271.

Algoe, S. B., & Fredrickson, B. L. (2011). Emotional fitness and the movement of affective science from lab to field. *American Psychologist, 66*, 35–42.

Algorta, G. P., Youngstrom, E. A., Frazier, T. W., Freeman, A. J., Youngstrom, J. K., & Findling, R. L. (2011). Suicidality in pediatric bipolar disorder: Predictor or outcome of family processes and mixed mood presentation? *Bipolar Disorder, 13*, 76–86.

Alim, T. N., Feder, A., Graves, R. E., Wang, Y., Weaver, J., & Westphal, M. (2008). Trauma, resilience, and recovery in a high-risk African-American population. *American Journal of Psychiatry, 165*, 1566–1575.

Allen, J. P., Chango, J., Szwedo, D., Schad, M., & Marston, E. (2012). Predictors of susceptibility to peer influence regarding substance use in adolescence. *Child Development, 83*, 337–350.

Allen, S. S., Allen, A. M., & Pomerleau, C. S. (2009). Influence of phase-related variability in premenstrual symptomatology, mood, smoking withdrawal, and smoking behavior during ad libitum smoking, on smoking cessation outcome. *Addictive Behavior, 34*, 107–111.

Allen, S. S., Bade, T., Center, B., Finstad, D., & Hatsukami, H. (2008). Menstrual phase effects on smoking relapse. *Addiction, 103*, 809–821.

Allenou, C., Olliac, B., Bourdet-Loubere, S., Brunet, A., Annie-Claude, D., Claudet, I., . . . Birmes, P. (2010). Symptoms of traumatic stress in mothers of children victims of a motor vehicle accident. *Depression and Anxiety, 27*, 652–657.

Allgulander, C., Hartford, J., Russell, J., Ball, S., Erickson, J., Raskin, J., & Rynn, M. (2007). Pharmacotherapy of generalized anxiety disorder: Results of duloxetine treatment from a pooled analysis of three clinical trials. *Current Medical Research and Opinion, 23*, 1245–1252.

Alloy, L. B., & Abramson, L. Y. (2010). The role of the behavioral approach system (BAS) in bipolar spectrum disorders. *Current Directions in Psychological Science, 19*, 189–194.

Alloy, L. B., Abramson, L. Y., Flynn, M., Liu, R. T., Grant, D. A., Jager-Hyman, S., & Whitehouse, W. G. (2009). Self-focused cognitive styles and bipolar spectrum disorders: Concurrent and prospective associations. *International Journal of Cognitive Therapy, 2*, 354–372.

Alloy, L. B., Abramson, L. Y., Walshaw, P. D., Gerstein, R. K., Keyser, J. D., . . . Harmon-Jones, E. J. (2009). Behavioral approach system (BAS)–relevant cognitive styles and bipolar spectrum disorders: Concurrent and prospective associations. *Journal of Abnormal Psychology, 118*, 459–471.

Almerie, M. Q., Matar, H. E.-D., Essali, A., Alkhateeb, H., & Rezk, E. (2008). Cessation of medication for people with schizophrenia already stable on chlorpromazine. *Schizophrenia Bulletin, 34*, 13–14.

Altshuler, L. L., Kupka, R. W., Hellemann, G., Frye, M. A., Sugar, C. A., . . . Suppes, T. (2010). Gender and depressive symptoms in 711 patients with bipolar disorder evaluated prospectively in the Stanley Foundation bipolar treatment outcome network. *American Journal of Psychiatry, 167*, 708–715.

Alzheimer's Association. (2010). *2010 Alzheimer's disease facts and figures*. Retrieved from http://www.alz.org/documents_custom/report_alzfactsfigures2010.pdf

Amador, X. (2003). Poor insight in schizophrenia: Overview and impact on medication compliance. Retrieved from http://www.xavieramador.com/files/cns-special-report-on-insight.pdf

American Academy of Child and Adolescent Psychiatry. (2009). Practice parameter on the use of psychotropic medication in children and adolescents. *Journal of the American Academy of Child & Adolescent Psychiatry, 48*, 961–973.

American Academy of Neurology. (2010). Practice parameter: The management of concussion in sports. Retrieved from http://www.aan.com/professionals/practice/guidelines/pda/Concussion_sports.pdf

American Association of Suicidology. (2012, August 28). *Fact Sheets: Reliable Information About Suicide*. Retrieved from http://www.suicidology.org/associations/1045/files/2005datapgs.pdf http://www.suicidology.org/stats-and-tools/suicide-fact-sheets

American Association on Intellectual and Developmental Disabilities. (2012). FAQ on Intellectual Disability. Retrieved from http://www.aaidd.org/content_104.cfm

American Cancer Society. (2007). Cigarette smoking. Retrieved from htpp://www.cancer.org/docroot/PED/content/PED_10_2X_Cigarette_Smoking.asp?sitearea5PED

American Geriatric Society. (2010, 3rd quarter). Preventing and effectively treating delirium in elderly can save seniors' lives and may also lower their risks of permanent cognitive loss. *AGS Newsletter*. Retrieved from ftp://ftp.frycomm.com/pub/old%20files/AGS%20Newsletter%202010-03-CS4-v1.pdf

American Heart Association. (2007). Cardiovascular disease statistics. Retrieved from http://www.americanheart.org/presenter.jhtml?identifier54478

Ameriçan Heart Association. (2010). *Heart disease and stroke statistics: 2010 update*. Dallas, TX: American Heart Association.

American Law Institute. (1962). *Model penal code: Proposed official draft*. Philadelphia, PA: Author.

American Medical Association. (2011, June 21). AMA adopts new policies at annual meeting. Retrieved from http://www.ama-assn.org/ama/pub/news/news/a11-new-policies.page

American Psychiatric Association. (2000). *Diagnostic and statistical manual of mental disorders* (4th ed., text rev.). Washington, DC: American Psychiatric Publishing.

American Psychiatric Association. (2006). Treatment recommendations for patients with eating disorders. *American Journal of Psychiatry, 163*, 5–54.

American Psychiatric Association. (2007). Practice guideline for the treatment of patients with obsessive-compulsive disorder. *American Journal of Psychiatry, 164*, 1–56.

American Psychiatric Association. (2011). DSM-5: The future of psychiatric diagnosis. Retrieved from http://www.dsm5.org/Pages/Default.aspx

American Psychological Association. (1993). Guidelines for providers of psychological services to ethnic, linguistic, and culturally diverse populations. *American Psychologist, 48*, 45–48.

American Psychological Association. (2000). Guidelines for psychotherapy with lesbian, gay, and bisexual clients. *American Psychologist, 55*, 1440–1451.

American Psychological Association. (2003). Guidelines on multicultural education, training, research, practice, and organizational change for psychologists. *American Psychologist, 58*, 377–402.

American Psychological Association. (2010a). *Ethical principles of psychologists and code of conduct*. Washington, DC: Author.

American Psychological Association. (2010b). *Stress in America*. Washington, DC: Author.

American Psychological Association, Task Force on the Sexualization of Girls. (2007). *Report of the task force on the sexualization of girls*. Retrieved from http://www.apa.org/pi/women/programs/girls/report.aspx

Amminger, G. P., Schafer, M. R., Papageorgiou, K., Klier, C. M., Cotton, S. M., . . . Berger, G. E. (2010). Long-chain omega-3 fatty acids for indicated prevention of psychotic disorders: A randomized, placebo-controlled trial. *Archives of General Psychiatry, 67*, 146–154.

Anastasi, A. (1982). *Psychological testing*. New York, NY: Macmillan.

Anda, R. F., Felitti, V. J., Bremner, J. D., Walker, J. D., Whitfield, C. H., . . . Giles, W. H. (2006). The enduring effects of abuse and related experiences in childhood: A convergence of evidence from neurobiology and epidemiology. *European Archives of Psychiatry and Clinical Neuroscience, 256*, 174–186.

Andari, E., Duhamel, J. R., Zalla, T., Herbrecht, E., Leboyer, M., & Sirigu, A. (2010). Promoting social behavior with oxytocin in high-functioning autism spectrum disorders. *Proceedings of the National Academy of Sciences, 107*, 4389–4394.

Andersen, A. E. (2007). Eating disorders and coercion. *American Journal of Psychiatry, 164*, 9–11.

Anderson, J. S., Druzgal, T. J., Froehlich, A., Dubray, M. B., Lange, N., Alexander, A. L., . . . Lainhart, J. E. (2011). Decreased interhemispheric functional connectivity in autism. *Cerebral Cortex, 21*(5), 1134–1146.

Anderson, K. W., Taylor, S., & McLean, P. H. (1996). Panic disorder associated with blood-injury reactivity: The necessity of establishing functional relationships among maladaptive behaviors. *Behavior Therapy, 27*, 463–472.

Anderson, P. J., & Doyle, L. W. (2008). Cognitive and educational deficits in children born extremely preterm. *Seminars in Perinatology, 32*, 51–58.

Anderson, S. E., Gooze, R. A., Lemeshow, S., & Whitaker, R. C. (2012). Quality of early maternal-child relationship and risk of adolescent obesity. *Pediatrics, 129*, 132–140.

Andrade, P., Noblesse, L. H., Temel, Y., Ackermans, L., Lim, L. W., Steinbusch, H. W., & Visser-Vandewalle, V. (2010). Neurostimulatory and ablative treatment options in major depressive disorder: A systematic review. *Acta Neurochirugia, 152*, 565–577.

Andreasen, N. C. (Ed.). (2005). *Research advances in genetics and genomics: Implications for psychiatry*. Washington, DC: American Psychiatric Publishing.

Andresen, R., Oades, L., & Caputi, P. (2003). The experience of recovery from schizophrenia: Towards an empirically validated stage model. *Australian and New Zealand Journal of Psychiatry, 37*, 586–594.

Andrews, G., Cuijpers, P., Craske, M. G., McEvoy, P., & Titov, N. (2010). Computer therapy for the anxiety and depressive disorders is effective, acceptable and practical health care: A meta-analysis. *PLoS One, 5*, e13196.

Andrews, G., Hobbs, J. J., Borkovec, T. D., Beesdo, K., Craske, M. G., . . . Stanley, M. A. (2010). Generalized worry disorder: A review of DSM-IV generalized anxiety disorder and options for DSM-V. *Depression and Anxiety, 27*, 137–147.

Annus, A. M., Smith, G. T., Fischer, S., Hendricks, M., & Williams, S. F. (2007). Associations among family-of-origin food-related experiences, expectancies, and disordered eating. *International Journal of Eating Disorders, 40*, 179–184.

Anonymous 5. (2008). Anorexia nervosa: Feeding the lie. Retrieved from http://www.eating.ucdavis.edu/speaking/told/anorexia/a37feeding.html

Anthenelli, R. M. (2010). Focus on: Comorbid mental health disorders. Retrieved from http://pubs.niaaa.nih.gov/publications/arh40/109-117.htm

Anton, R. F., O'Malley, S. S., Ciraulo, D. A., Cisler, R. A., Couper, D., . . . COMBINE Study Research Group. (2006). Combined pharmacotherapies and behavioral interventions for alcohol dependence: The COMBINE study: A randomized controlled trial. *Journal of the American Medical Association, 295*, 2003–2017.

Antony, M. M., Brown, T. A., & Barlow, D. H. (1997). Heterogeneity among specific phobia types in DSM-IV. *Behaviour Research and Therapy, 35*, 1089–1100.

Anttila, V., Stefansson, H., Kallela, M., Todt, U., Gisela, M., Terwindt, G. M., . . . Calafato, M. S. (2010). Genome-wide association study of migraine implicates a common susceptibility variant on 8q22.1. *Nature Genetics, 42*, 869–873.

Aoki, H., Kato, R., Hirano, K., Suzuki, T., Kato, K., & Inuma, M. (2003). A case of sudden unexplained nocturnal death from overlooked Brugada syndrome at a pre-employment check-up. *Journal of Occupational Health, 45*, 70–73.

Arackal, B. S., & Benegal, V. (2007). Prevalence of sexual dysfunction in male subjects with alcohol dependence. *Indian Journal of Psychiatry, 49*, 109–120.

Armstrong, J. G., Putnam, F. W., Carlson, E. B., Libero, D. Z., & Smith, S. R. (1997). Development and validation of a measure of adolescent dissociation: The Adolescent Dissociation Scale. *Journal of Nervous and Mental Disease, 185*, 491–497.

Arnett, J. J. (2008). The neglected 95%: Why American psychology needs to become less American. *American Psychologist, 63*, 602–614.

Arnold, I. A., de Waal, M. W. M., Eekhoff, J. A. H., & van Hemert, A. M. (2006). Somatoform disorder in primary care: Course and the need for cognitive-behavioral treatment. *Psychosomatics, 47*, 498–503.

Arnold, L. M. (2003). Gender differences in bipolar disorder. *Psychiatric Clinics of North America, 26*, 595–620.

Arria, A. M., Caldeira, K. M., O'Grady, K. E., Vincent, K. B., Johnson, E. P., & Wish, E. D. (2008). Nonmedical use of prescription stimulants among college students: Associations with attention-deficit-hyperactivity disorder and polydrug use. *Pharmacotherapy, 28*, 156–169.

Arseneault, L., Cannon, M., Fisher, H. L., Polanczyk, G., Moffitt, T. E., & Caspi, A. (2011). Childhood trauma and children's emerging psychotic symptoms: A genetically sensitive longitudinal cohort study. *American Journal of Psychiatry, 168*, 65–72.

Ashburner, J., Ziviani, J., & Rodger, S. (2010). Surviving in the mainstream: Capacity of children with autism spectrum disorders to perform academically and regulate their emotions and behavior at school. *Research in Autism Spectrum Disorders, 4*, 18–27.

Associated Press. (1998, August 14). Psychiatrist is sued over multiple bad personalities. *Seattle Post Intelligencer*, p. A12.

Associated Press. (2007a, January 26). Man loses memory, wanders for 25 days. Retrieved from http:////forum.psychlinks.ca/dissociative-disorders/6306-man-loses-memories-wanders-for-25-days.html

Associated Press. (2007b, August 10). Too many studies use college students as guinea pigs. Retrieved from http://online.wsj.com/article/SB118670089203393577.html

Association for Psychological Science. (2007, March 2). Genes and stressed-out parents lead to shy kids. *Science Daily*. Retrieved from http://www.sciencedaily.com/releases/2007/03/070302111100.htm

Asthma and Allergy Foundation of America. (2007). Asthma facts and figures. Retrieved from http://www.aafa.org/display.cfm?id=8&sub=42

Auerbach, J. G., Faroy, M., Ebstein, R., Kahana, M., & Levine, J. (2001). The association of the dopamine D4 receptor gene (DRD4) and the serotonin transport promoter gene (5-HTTLPR) with temperament in 12-month-old infants. *Journal of Child Psychology and Psychiatry, 42*, 777–783.

Autism decisions and background information. (2010). Retrieved from http://www.uscfc.uscourts.gov/node/5026

Avia, M. D., & Ruiz, M. A. (2005). Recommendations for the treatment of hypochondriac patients. *Journal of Contemporary Psychotherapy, 35*, 301–313.

Ayala, E. S., Meuret, A. E., & Ritz, T. (2009). Treatments for blood-injury-injection phobia: A critical review of current evidence. *Journal of Psychiatric Research, 43*, 1235–1242.

Ayers, C. R., Sorrell, J. T., Thorp, S. R., & Wetherell, J. L. (2007). Evidence-based psychological treatments for late-life anxiety. *Psychology and Aging, 22*, 8–17.

Azar, B. (2010). Your brain on culture. *Monitor on Psychology, 41*(10), 44–47.

Babiss, L. A., & Gangwisch, J. E. (2009). Sports participation as a protective factor against depression and suicidal ideation in adolescents as mediated by self-esteem and social support. *Journal of Developmental and Behavioral Pediatrics, 30*, 376–384.

Bailey, D. S. (2003). Help the media prevent copycat suicides. *Monitor, 34*, 14.

Bailey, P. E., & Henry, J. D. (2010). Separating component processes of theory of mind in schizophrenia. *British Journal of Clinical Psychology, 49*, 43–52.

Bak, M., Myin-Germeys, I., Hanssen, M., Bijl, R., Volleberg, W., Delespaul, P., & Van Os, J. (2003). When does experience of psychosis result in a need for care? A prospective general population study. *Schizophrenia Bulletin, 29*, 349–356.

Baker, J. H., Mitchell, K. S., Neale, M. C., & Kendler, K. S. (2010). Eating disorder symptomatology and substance use disorders: Prevalence and shared risk in a population based twin sample. *International Journal of Eating Disorders, 43*, 648–658.

Baker, J. L., Olsen, L. W., & Sorensen, T. I. A. (2007). Childhood body-mass index and the risk of coronary heart disease in adulthood. *New England Journal of Medicine, 357*, 2329–2337.

Baker, K. (2010). "It's not me" to "it was me, after all." *Psychoanalytic Social Work, 17*, 79–98.

Baker, L. D., Frank, K., Foster-Schubert, K., Green, P. S., Wilkinson, C. W., McTiernan, A., . . . Craft, S. (2010). Effects of aerobic exercise on mild cognitive impairment: A controlled trial. *Archives of Neurology, 67*, 71–79.

Bakker, A., Spinhoven, P., Van Balkom, A. J. L. M., & Van Dyck, R. (2002). Relevance of assessment of cognitions during panic attacks in the treatment of panic disorder. *Psychotherapy and Psychosomatics, 71*, 158–162.

Balami, J. S., Chen, R., & Grunwald, I. Q. (2011). Neurological complications of acute ischaemic stroke. *The Lancet Neurology, 10*(4), 357–371.

Balci, K., Utku, U., Asil, T., & Celik, Y. (2011). Ischemic stroke in young adults: Risk factors, subtypes, and prognosis. *Neurologist, 17*, 16–20.

Baldassano, C. F. (2006). Illness course, comorbidity, gender, and suicidality in patients with bipolar disorder. *Journal of Clinical Psychiatry, 67*(Suppl 11), 8–11.

Bale, T. L., Baram, T. Z., Brown, A. S., Goldstein, J. M., Insel, T. R., McCarthy, M. M., . . . Nestler, E. J. (2010). Early life programming and neurodevelopmental disorders. *Biological Psychiatry, 68*, 314–319.

Ballard, C., Corbett, A., & Jones, E. L. (2011). Dementia: Challenges and promising developments. *The Lancet Neurology, 10*, 7–9.

Ballenger, J. C., Davidson, J. R. T., Lecrubier, Y., Nutt, D. J., Borkovec, T. D., . . . Wittchen, H. U. (2000). Consensus statement on generalized anxiety disorder from the International Consensus Group on depression and anxiety. *Journal of Clinical Psychiatry, 62*, 53–58.

Ballew, L., Morgan, Y., & Lippmann, S. (2003). Intravenous diazepam for dissociative disorder: Memory lost and found. *Psychosomatics, 44*, 346–349.

Balon, R., Segraves, R. T., & Clayton, A. (2007). Issues of DSM-V: Sexual dysfunctions, disorder, or variation along normal distribution: Toward rethinking DSM criteria of sexual dysfunctions. *American Journal of Psychiatry, 164*, 198–200.

Bande, C. S., & Garcia-Alba, C. (2008). Munchausen syndrome by proxy: A dilemma for diagnosis. *Roschachiana, 29*, 183–200.

Bandiera, F. C., Richardson, A. K., Lee, D. J., He, J. P., & Merikangas, K. R. (2011). Secondhand smoke exposure and mental health among children and adolescents. *Archives of Pediatrics & Adolescent Medicine, 165*, 332–338.

Bandura, A. (1997). *Self-efficacy: The exercise of self-control*. New York, NY: Freeman.

Banerjee, G., & Roy, S. (1998). Determinants of help-seeking behaviour of families of schizophrenic patients attending a teaching hospital in India: An indigenous explanatory model. *International Journal of Social Psychiatry, 44*, 199–214.

Banerjee, T. D., Middleton, F., & Faraone, S. V. (2007). Environmental risk factors for attention-deficit hyperactivity disorder. *Acta Paediatrica, 96*, 1269–1274.

Bang, J., Price, D., Prentice, G., & Campbell, J. (2009). ECT treatment for two cases of dementia-related pathological yelling. *Journal of Neuropsychiatry and Clinical Neuroscience, 20*, 379–380.

Barbaro, J., & Dissanayake, C. (2009). Autism spectrum disorders in infancy and toddlerhood: A review of the evidence on early signs, early identification tools, and early diagnosis. *Journal of Developmental and Behavioral Pediatrics, 30*, 447–459.

Barber, J. P., Morse, J. Q., Krakauer, I. D., Chittams, J., & Crits-Cristoph, K. (1997). Change in obsessive-compulsive and avoidant personality disorders following time-limited supportive-expressive therapy. *Journal of Psychotherapy, 34*, 133–143.

Barboza, D. (June 6, 2010). After suicides, scrutiny of China's grim factories. The New York Times. Retrieved 9/29/12 at http://www.nytimes.com/2010/06/07/business/global/07suicide.html?pagewanted=all

Barbui, C., Cipriani, A., Patel, V., Ayuso-Mateos, J. L., & van Ommeren, M. (2011). Efficacy of anti-depressants and benzodiazepines in minor depression: Systematic review and meta-analysis. *British Journal of Psychiatry, 198*, 11–16.

Bardone-Cone, A. M., & Cass, K. M. (2007). What does viewing a pro-anorexia website do? An experimental examination of website exposure and moderating effects. *International Journal of Eating Disorders, 40*, 537–548.

Bardone-Cone, A. M., Sturm, K., Lawson, M. A., Robinson, D. P., & Smith, R. (2010). Perfectionism across stages of recovery from eating disorders. *International Journal of Eating Disorders, 43*, 139–148.

Barlow, M. R. (2011). Memory for complex emotional material in dissociative identity disorder. *Journal of Trauma and Dissociation, 12*, 53–66.

Barnhofer, T., Crane, C., Hargus, E., Amarasinghe, M., Winder, R., & Williams, J. M. G. (2010). Mindfulness-based cognitive therapy as a treatment for chronic depression: A preliminary study. *Behavior Research and Therapy, 47*, 366–373.

Baron, L., Straus, M. A., & Jaffee, D. (1988). Legitimate violence, violent attitudes, and rape: A test of the cultural spillover theory, *Annals of the New York Academy of Sciences, 528*, 79–110.

Barrera, T. L., & Norton, P. J. (2010). Quality of life impairment in generalized anxiety disorder, social phobia, and panic disorder. *Journal of Anxiety Disorders, 23*, 1086–1090.

Barsky, A. J., & Ahern, D. K. (2004). Cognitive behavior therapy for hypochondriasis: A randomized controlled trial. *Journal of the American Medical Association, 291*, 1464–1470.

Barton, J. (2004, September 29). Mental health centers feel storm surge: Calls for help climb after hurricanes. *Columbian* (Vancouver, WA), p. A3.

Barzman, D. H., Patel, A., Sonnier, L., & Strawn, J. R. (2010).Neuroendocrine aspects of pediatric aggression: Can hormone measures be clinically useful? *Journal of Neuropsychiatric Disease and Treatment, 6*, 691–697.

Baschnagel, J. S., Gudmundsdottir, B., Hawk, L. W., Jr., & Beck, J. G. (2009). Post-trauma symptoms following indirect exposure to the September 11th terrorist attacks: The predictive role of dispositional coping. *Journal of Anxiety Disorders, 23*, 915–922.

Bate, K. S., Malouff, J. M., Thorsteinsson, E. T., & Bhullar, N. (2011). The efficacy of habit reversal therapy for tics, habit disorders, and stuttering: A meta-analytic review. *Clinical Psychology Review, 31*, 865–871.

Bateman, R. J., Aisen, P. S., De Strooper, B., Fox, N. C., Lemere, C. A., Ringman, J. M., . . . Xiong, C. (2011). Autosomal-dominant Alzheimer's disease: A review and proposal for the prevention of Alzheimer's disease. *Alzheimers Research and Therapy, 3*, 1–13.

Bates, M. J., & Bowles, S. V. (2012). Review of well-being in the context of suicide prevention and resilience. Retrieved from http://ftp.rta.nato.int/public//PubFullText/RTO/MP%5CRTO-MP-HFM-205///MP-HFM-205-29.doc

Baum, A. E., Akula, N., Cabanero, M., Cardona, I., Corona, W., . . . McMahon, F. J. (2008). A genome-wide association study implicates diacylglycerol kinase eta (DGKH) and several other genes in the etiology of bipolar disorder. *Molecular Psychiatry, 13*, 197–207.

Baumeister, R. F. (1988). Masochism as escape from self. *Journal of Sex Research, 25*, 28–59.

Bayer, J. K., Rapee, R. M., Hiscock, H., Ukoumunne, O. C., Mihalopoulos, C., & Wake, M. (2011). Translational research to prevent internalizing problems early in childhood. *Depression and Anxiety, 28*, 50–57.

Bazalgette, L., Bradley, W., & Ouesbey, J. (2011). The truth about suicide. London: Demos.

Beard, C., Moitra, E., Weisberg, R. B., & Keller, M. B. (2010). Characteristics and predictors of social phobia course in a longitudinal study of primary-care patients. *Depression and Anxiety, 27*, 839–845.

Bearden, C. E., Woogen, M., & Glahn, D. C. (2010). Neurocognitive and neuroimaging predictors of clinical outcome in bipolar disorder. *Current Psychiatry Reports, 12*, 499–504.

Beck, A. T. (1976). *Cognitive therapy and emotional disorders*. New York, NY: International Universities Press.

Beck, A. T. (1985). Cognitive therapy, behavior therapy, psychoanalysis, and pharmacotherapy: A cognitive continuum. In M. Mahoney & A. Freeman (Eds.), *Cognition and psychotherapy* (pp. [illegible]7–220). New York, NY: Plenum Press.

Beck, A. T., Freeman, A. F., & Asso[illegible] *Cognitive therapy of personality diso*[illegible] NY: Guilford Press.

Beck, A. T., Freeman, A., & D[illegible] *Cognitive therapy of personal*[illegible] NY: Guilford Press.

Beck, A. T., & Rector, N[illegible] of schizophreni[illegible] lennium. *Ame*[illegible] 291–300.

Beck, A. T., Ward, C. H., [illegible] & Erbaugh, J. (1961). [illegible] ing depression. *Archives o*[illegible] 561–571.

Beck, A. T., & Weishaar, M. E. (2010). Co[illegible] apy. In R. J. Corsini & D. Wedding (Eds.), [illegible] *psychotherapies* (9th ed., pp. 301–322). Belmont, CA: Brooks/Cole.

Beck, C. T., & Indman P. J. (2005). The many faces of postpartum depression. *Journal of Obstetric, Gynecological & Neonatal Nursing, 34*, 569–576.

Becker, A. E. (2004). Television, disordered eating, and young women in Fiji: Negotiating body image and identity during rapid social change. *Cultural Medical Psychiatry, 28*, 533–559.

Becker, A. E., Burwell, R. A., Herzog, D. B., Hamburg, P., & Gilman, S. E. (2002). Eating behaviours and attitudes following prolonged exposure to television among ethnic Fijian adolescent girls. *British Journal of Psychiatry, 180*, 509–514.

Bedell-Smith, S. (1999). *Diana in search of herself.* New York, NY: Random House.

Bednar, R. L., Bednar, S. C., Lambert, M. J., & Waite, D. R. (1991). *Psychotherapy with high-risk clients: Legal and professional standards.* Pacific Grove, CA: Brooks/Cole.

Beers, C. W. (1948). *A mind that found itself.* Garden City, NY: Doubleday.

Bellack, A. S. (2006). Scientific and consumer models of recovery in schizophrenia: Concordance, contrasts, and implications. *Schizophrenia Bulletin, 32*, 432–442.

Bello, N. T., & Hajnal, A. (2010). Dopamine and binge eating behaviors. *Pharmacology, Biochemistry and Behavior, 97*, 25–33.

Belluck, P. (2010, June 20). Hallucinations in hospital pose risk to elderly. *New York Times.* Retrieved from http://www.nytimes.com

Benazzi, F. (2007). Bipolar II disorder: Epidemiology, diagnosis and management. *CNS Drugs, 21*, 727–740.

Bender, L. (1938). A visual motor gestalt test and its clinical use. *Research Monographs of the American Orthopsychiatric Association, 3*(11), 176.

Bender, R. E., & Alloy, L. B. (2011). Life stress and kindling in bipolar disorder: Review of the evidence and integration with emerging biopsychosocial theories. *Clinical Psychology Review, 31*, 383–398.

Benedict, J. G., & Donaldson, D. W. (1996). Recovered memories threaten all. *Professional Psychology: Research and Practice, 27*, 427–428.

Benes, F. M. (2009). Neural circuitry models of schizophrenia: Is it dopamine, GABA, glutamate, or something else? *Biological Psychiatry, 65*, 1003–1005.

Benjamin, L. S. (1996). *Interpersonal diagnosis and treatment of personality disorders.* New York, NY: Guilford Press.

Benjamin, L. S., & Karpiak, C. P. (2002). Personality disorders. In J. C. Norcross (Ed.), *Psychotherapy relationships that work* (pp. 423–440). New York, NY: Oxford University Press.

Benjet, C., Borges, G., & Medina-Mora, M. E. (2010). Chronic childhood adversity and onset of psychopathology during three life stages: Childhood, adolescence and adulthood. *Journal of Psychiatric Research, 44*, 732–740.

Bennett, M. P., & Lengacher, C. A. (2006). Humor and laughter may influence health. *Evidence Based Complementary Alternative Medicine, 3*, 61–63.

Bennett, M. P., Zeller, J. M., Rosenberg, L., & McCann, J. (2003). The effect of mirthful laughter on stress and natural killer cell activity. *Alternative Therapies in Health and Medicine, 9*, 38–45.

Bennett, S. A., Beck, J. G., & Clapp, J. D. (2009). Under-standing the relationship between posttraumatic stress disorder and trauma cognitions: The impact of thought control strategies. *Behaviour Research and Therapy, 47*, 1018–1023.

Benowitz, N. L. (2010). Nicotine addiction. *New England Journal of Medicine, 362*, 2295–2303.

Benton, S. A., Robertson, J. M., Tseng, W.-C., Newton, F. B., & Benton, S. L. (2003). Changes in counseling center client problems across 13 years. *Professional Psychology: Research and Practice, 34*, 66–72.

Ben-Tovim, D. I., Walker, K., Gilchrist, P., Freeman, R., Kalucy, R., & Esterman, A. (2001). Outcome in patients with eating disorders: A five-year study. *Lancet, 357*, 1254–1257.

Benyamina, A., Lecacheux, M., Blecha, L., Reynaud, M., & Lukasiewcz, M. (2008). Pharmacotherapy and psychotherapy in cannabis withdrawal and dependence. *Expert Reviews in Neurotherapy, 8*, 479–491.

Berenson, A. (2006, January 1). Study bolsters antidepression drugs. *Sacramento Bee*, p. A21.

Bergemann, N., Parzer, P., Jaggy, S., Auler, B., Mundt, C., & Maier-Braunleder, S. (2008). Estrogen and comprehension of metaphoric speech in women suffering from schizophrenia: Results of a double-blind, placebo-controlled trial. *Schizophrenia Bulletin, 34*, 1172–1181.

Berger, W., Mendlowicz, M. V., Marques-Portella, C., Kinrys, G., Fontenelle, L. F., . . . Figueira, I. (2009). Pharmacologic alternatives to antidepressants in posttraumatic stress disorder: A systematic review. *Progress in Neuropsychopharmacology and Biological Psychiatry, 33*, 169–180.

Bergstrom, R. L., & Neighbors, C. (2006). Body image disturbance and the social norms approach: An integrative review of the literature. *Journal of Social and Clinical Psychology, 25*, 975–1000.

Berk, L., Hallam, K. T., Colom, F., Vieta, E., Hasty, M., Macneil, C., & Berk, M. (2010). Enhancing medication adherence in patients with bipolar disorder. *Human Psychopharmacology, 25*, 1–16.

Berlim, M. T., & Turecki, G. (2007). Definition, assessment, and staging of treatment-resistant refractory major depression: A review of current concepts and methods. *Canadian Journal of Psychiatry, 52*, 46–54.

Berman, A. L. (2006). Risk management with suicidal patients. *Journal of Clinical Psychology: In Session, 62*, 171–184.

Berman, J. (2010, February 23). The media's contribution to eating disorders [Web log post]. Retrieved from http://doctorjenn.com/wordpress/2010/02/the-media%E2%80%99s-contribution-to-eating-disorders/

Berman, S. M., Kuczenski, R., McCracken, J. T., & London, E. D. (2009). Potential adverse effects of amphetamine treatment on brain and behavior: A review. *Molecular Psychiatry, 14*, 123–142.

Bernstein, E. B. (2012). Conduct disorder. Retrieved from http://emedicine.medscape.com/article/918213-overview

Berrington de González, A., Mahesh, M., Kim, K., Bhargavan, M., Lewis, R., Mettler, F., & Land, C. (2009). Projected cancer risks from computed tomographic scans performed in the United States in 2007. *Archives of Internal Medicine, 169*, 2071–2077.

Berrios, G. E. (1989). Obsessive-compulsive disorder: Its conceptual history in France during the 19th century. *Comprehensive Psychiatry, 30*, 283–295.

Berry, E. A., Heaton, P. T., & Kelton, C. M. (2011). National estimates of the inpatient burden of pediatric bipolar disorder in the United States. *Journal of Mental Health Policy and Economics, 14*, 115–123.

Beseler, C. L., Taylor, L. A., Kraemer, D. T., & Leeman, R. F. (2012). A latent class analysis of DSM-IV alcohol use disorder criteria and binge drinking in undergraduates. *Alcoholism: Clinical and Experimental Research, 36*, 153–161.

Bhalla, R. N., & Ahmed, I. (2011). Schizophreniform disorder. Retrieved from http://emedicine.medscape.com/article/2008351-overview

Bickel, W. K., Amass, L., Higgins, S. T., Badger, G. J., & Esch, R. A. (1997). Effects of adding behavioral treatment to opioid detoxification with buprenorphine. *Journal of Consulting and Clinical Psychology, 65*, 803–810.

Bienenfeld, D. (2007). Personality disorders. *Psychiatric Annals, 37*, 84–85.

Bienvenu, O. J., Davydow, D. S., & Kendler, K. S. (2011). Psychiatric 'diseases' vs. behavioral disorders and degree of genetic influence. *Psychological Medicine, 41*, 33–40.

Bigard, A. (2010). Risks of energy drinks in youth. *Archives of Pediatrics, 17*, 1625–1631.

Bigio, E. H. (2008). Update on recent molecular and genetic advances in frontotemporal lobar degeneration. *Journal of Neuropathology and Experimental Neurology, 67*, 635–648.

Bindman, J., & Thornicroft, G. (2008). Strategies for engagement and treatment. In K. T. Mueser & D. V. Jeste (Eds.), *Clinical handbook of schizophrenia* (pp. 516–523). New York, NY: Guilford Press.

Biondi, M., & Picardi, A. (2003). Attribution of improvement to medication and increased risk of relapse of panic disorder with agoraphobia: Reply. *Psychotherapy and Psychosomatics, 72*, 110–111.

Bjornsson, A. S., Dyck, I., Moitra, E., Stout, R. L., Weisberg, R., . . . Phillips, K. A. (2011). The clinical course of body dysmorphic disorder in the Harvard/Brown anxiety research project (HARP). *Journal of Nervous and Mental Disease, 199*, 55–57.

Black, D. L., Cawthon, B., Robert, T., Moser, F., Caplan, Y. H., & Cone, E. J. (2009). Multiple drug ingestion by ecstasy abusers in the United States. *Journal of Analytical Toxicology, 33*, 143–147.

Black, S. T. (1993). Comparing genuine and simulated suicide notes: A new perspective. *Journal of Consulting and Clinical Psychology, 67*, 699–702.

Blacker, K. J., Herbert, J. D., Forman, E. M., & Kounios, J. (2012). Acceptance- versus change-based pain management: The role of psychological acceptance. *Behavior Modification, 36*, 37–48.

Blanchard, J. J., Gangestad, S. W., Brown, S. A., & Horan, W. P. (2000). Hedonic capacity and schizotypy revisited: A taxometric analysis of social anhedonia. *Journal of Abnormal Psychology, 109*, 87–95.

Blashill, A. J. (2010). Elements of male body image: Prediction of depression, eating pathology and social sensitivity among gay men. *Body Image, 7*, 310–316.

Blashill, A. J., & Vander Wal, J. S. (2009). Mediation of gender role conflict and eating pathology in gay men. *Psychology of Men and Masculinity, 10*, 204–217.

Blier, P., Szabo, S. T., Haddjeri, N., & Dong, J. (2000). Orbitofrontal cortex–basal ganglia system in OCD. *International Journal of Neuropsychopharmacology, 3*, 1–14.

Bloom, B., & Cohen, R. A. (2007). Summary health statistics for U.S. children: National Health Interview Survey, 2006. *National Center for Health Statistics. Vital Health Statistics,* 10, 2007.

Bloomberg, D. (2000, January/February). Bennett Braun case settled: Two-year loss of license, five years probation. *Skeptical Inquirer*, 7–8.

Boardman, J. D., Blalock, C. L., Pampel, F. C., Hatemi, P. K., Heath, A. C., & Eaves, L. J. (2011) Population composition, public policy, and the genetics of smoking. *Demography, 48*, 1517–1533.

Bochukova, E. G., Huang, N., Keogh, J., Henning, E., Purmann, C., . . . Farooqui, I. S. (2010). Large, rare chromosomal deletions associated with severe early-onset obesity. *Nature, 463*, 666–669.

Bodell, L. P., Smith, A. R., Gordon, K. T., Holm-Denoma, J. M., & Joiner, T. E. (2011). Low social support and negative life events predict later bulimic symptoms. *Eating Behaviors, 12*, 44–48.

Boden, J. M., Fergusson, D. M., & Horwood, J. (2007). Anxiety disorders and suicidal behaviours in adolescence and young adulthood: Findings from a longitudinal study. *Psychological Medicine, 37*, 431–440.

Boehm, J. K., Peterson, C., Kivimaki, M., & Kubzansky, L. D. (2011). Heart health when life is satisfying: Evidence from the Whitehall II cohort study. *European Heart Journal, 32*, 2672–2677.

Boehmer, U., Bowen, D. J., & Bauer, G. R. (2007). Overweight and obesity in sexual-minority women: Evidence from population-based data. *American Journal of Public Health, 29*, 1134–1140.

Bohne, A., Keuthen, N. J., Wilhelm, S., Deckersbach, T., & Jenike, M. A. (2002). Prevalence of symptoms of body dysmorphic disorder and its correlates: A cross-cultural comparison. *Psychosomatics, 43*, 486–490.

Bohne, A., Wilhelm, S., Keuthen, N. J., Baer, L., & Jenike, M. A. (2002). Skin picking in German students: Prevalence, phenomenology and associated characteristics. *Behavior Modification, 26*, 320–339.

Bokszczanin, A. (2008). Parental support, family conflict, and overprotectiveness: Predicting PTSD symptom levels of adolescents 28 months after a natural disaster. *Anxiety, Stress, & Coping, 21*, 325–335.

Bola, J. R., Kao, D. T., & Soydan, H. (2012). Antipsychotic medication for early-episode schizophrenia. *Schizophrenia Bulletin, 38*, 23–25.

Boldrini, M., Underwood, M. D., Mann, J. J., & Arango, V. (2005). More tryptophan hydroxylase in the brainstem dorsal raphe nucleus in depressed suicides. *Brain Research, 104*, 19–28.

Bollini, A. M., & Walker, E. F. (2007). Schizotypal personality disorder. In W. O. Donohus, K. A. Fowler, & S. O. Lilienfeld (Eds.), *Personality disorders: Toward the DSM-V* (pp. 32–40). Los Angeles, CA: Sage.

Bolton, P. F., Golding, J., Emond, A., & Steer, C. D. (2012). Autism spectrum disorder and autistic traits in the Avon Longitudinal Study of Parents and Children: Precursors and early signs. *Journal of the American Academy of Child & Adolescent Psychiatry, 51*, 249–260.

Bonanno, G. A. (2004). Loss, trauma, and human resilience: Have we underestimated the human capacity to thrive after extremely aversive events? *American Psychologist, 59*, 20–28.

Bonanno, G. A. (2005). Resilience in the face of potential trauma. *Current Directions in Psychological Science, 14*, 135–138.

Bonde, J. P. (2008). Psychosocial factors at work and risk of depression: A systematic review of the epidemiological evidence. *Occupational and Environmental Medicine, 65*, 438–445.

Boodman, S. G. (2007, March 13). Eating disorders: Not just for women. *Washington Post*. Retrieved from http://www.washingtonpost.com/wp-dyn/content/article/2007/03/09/AR2007030901870.html

Boone, L., Soenens, B., Braet, C., & Goossens, L. (2010). An empirical typology of perfectionism in early-to-mid adolescents and its relation with eating disorder symptoms. *Behaviour Research and Therapy, 48*, 686–691.

Borch-Jacobsen, M. (1997). Sybil—The making of a disease: An interview with Dr. Herbert Spiegel. *New York Review of Books, 44*, 60–64.

Borda, T., & Sterin-Borda, L. (2006). Novel insight int o neuroimmunogenic factors in the etiology of schizophrenia. *Psychiatric Annals, 36*, 102–108.

Borgwardt, S. J., Picchioni, M. M., Ettinger, U., Toulopoulou, T., Murray, R., & McGuire, P. K. (2010). Regional gray matter volume in monozygotic twins concordant and disconcordant for schizophrenia. *Biological Psychiatry, 67*, 956–964.

Borkovec, T. D., & Ruscio, A. M. (2001). Psychotherapy for generalized anxiety disorder. *Journal of Clinical Psychiatry, 62*, 37–42.

Borroni, B., Alberici, A., Archetti, S., Magnani, E., Di Luca, M., & Padovani, A. (2010). New insights into biological markers of frontotemporal lobar degeneration spectrum. *Current Medical Chemistry, 17*, 1002–1009.

Borzekowski, D. L. G., Schenk, S., Wilson, J. L., & Peebles, R. (2010). E-ana and e-mia: A content analysis of pro-eating disorder Web sites. *American Journal of Public Health, 100*, 1526–1534.

Boudreault, S. (2011). Top six Charlie Sheen rantings, with analysis [Web log post]. Retrieved from http://celebs.gather.com/viewArticle.action?articleId=281474979115776

Bourque, F., van der Ven, E., & Malla, A. (2010). A meta-analysis of the risk for psychotic disorders among first- and second-generation immigrants. *Psychological Medicine, 41*(5), 897–910. doi:10.1017/S0033291710001406

Bowden, C. L. (2010). Diagnosis, treatment, and recovery maintenance in bipolar depression. *Journal of Clinical Psychiatry, 71*, e01.

Bowie, C. R., Depp, C., McGrath, J. A., Wolyniec, P., Mausbach, B. T., . . . Pulver, A. E. (2010). Prediction of real-world functional disability in chronic mental disorders: A comparison of schizophrenia and bipolar disorder. *American Journal of Psychiatry, 167*, 1116–1124.

Bowler, J. V. (2007). Modern concept of vascular cognitive impairment. *British Medical Bulletin, 83*, 291–305.

Boyington, J. E. A., Carter-Edwards, L., Piehl, M., Hutson, J., Langdon, D., & McManus, S. (2008). Cultural attitudes toward weight, diet, and physical activity among overweight African American girls. *Preventing Chronic Disease, 5*, 1–9.

Bradley, R. G., Binder, E. B., Epstein, M. P., Tang, Y., Nair, H. P., . . . Ressler, K. J. (2008). Influence of child abuse on adult depression: Moderation by the corticotropin-releasing hormone receptor gene. *Archives of General Psychiatry, 65*, 190–200.

Braff, D. L. (2007). Introduction: The use of endophenotypes to deconstruct and understand the genetic architecture, neurobiology, and guide future treatments of the group of schizophrenias. *Schizophrenia Bulletin, 33*, 19.

Braff, D. L., Freedman, R., Schork, N. J., & Gottesman, I. I. (2007). Deconstructing schizophrenia: An overview of the use of endophenotypes in order to understand a complex disorder. *Schizophrenia Bulletin, 33*, 21–25.

Brambilla, P., Bellani, M., Yeh, P. H., Soares, J. C., & Tansella, M. (2009). White matter connectivity in bipolar disorder. *International Review of Psychiatry, 21*, 380–386.

Brambilla, P., Soloff, P. H., Sala, M., Nocoletti, M. A., Keshavan, M. S., & Soares, J. C. (2004). Anatomical MRI study of borderline personality disorder patients. *Psychiatric Research: Neuroimaging, 131*, 125–132.

Brand, B., & Loewenstein, R. J. (2010, October). Dissociative disorders: An overview of assessment, phenomenology, and treatment. *Psychiatric Times*, 62–69. Retrieved from https://www.cmellc.com/landing/pdf/A10001101.pdf

Brand, B. L., Classen, C. C., McNary, S. W., & Zaveri, P. (2009). A review of dissociative disorders treatment studies. *Journal of Nervous and Mental Disease, 197*, 646–654.

Brand, B. L., Myrick, A. C., Loewenstein, R. J., Classen, C. C., Lanius, R., . . . Putnam, F. W. (2012). A survey of practices and recommended treatment interventions among expert therapists treating patients with dissociative identity disorder and dissociative disorder not otherwise specified. *Psychological Trauma: Theory, Research, Practice, and Policy,* Dec 5, 2011. doi: 10.1037/a0026487

Brand, M., Eggers, C., Reinhold, N., Fujiwara, E., Kessler, J., . . . Markowitsch, H. J. (2009). Functional brain imaging in 14 patients with dissociative amnesia reveals right inferolateral prefrontal hypometabolism. *Psychiatry Research: Neuroimaging, 174*, 32–39.

Brand, S., & Kirov, R. (2011). Sleep and its importance in adolescence and in common adolescent somatic and psychiatric conditions. *International Journal of General Medicine, 4*, 25–42.

Brandl, E. J., Muller, D. J., & Richter, M. A. (2012). Pharmacogenetics of obsessive-compulsive disorders. *Pharmacogenomics, 13*, 71–81.

Brannigan, G. G., Decker, S. L., & Madsen, D. H. (2004). *Innovative features of the Bender-Gestalt II and expanded guidelines for the use of the Global Scoring System* (Bender Visual-Motor Gestalt Test, 2nd ed., Assessment Service Bulletin No. 1). Itasca, IL: Riverside.

Brannon, G. E. (2011). History and mental status examination. Retrieved from http://emedicine.medscape.com/article/293402-print

Brannon, G. E., & Bienefeld, D. (2012). Schizoaffective disorder. Retrieved from http://emedicine.medscape.com/article/294763-overview

Brannon, G. E., & Dunayevich, E. (2011).Munchausen syndrome by proxy. Retrieved from http://emedicine.medscape.com/article/295258-overview#showall

Brasic, J. R., & Holland, J. A. (2007). A qualitative and quantitative review of obstetric complications and autistic disorder. *Journal of Developmental and Physical Disabilities, 19*, 337–364.

Brasic, J. R. (2010). PET scanning in autism spectrum disorders. Retrieved from http://emedicine.medscape.com/article/1155568-overview

Brausch, A. M., & Gutierrez, P. M. (2010). Differences in non-suicidal self-injury and suicide attempts in adolescents. *Journal of Youth and Adolescents, 39*, 233–242.

Braw, Y., Bloch, Y., Mendelovich, S., Ratzoni, G., Gal, G., . . . Levkovitz, Y. (2008). Cognition in young schizophrenia outpatients: Comparison of first-episode with multiepisode patients. *Schizophrenia Bulletin, 34*, 544–554.

Breese-McCoy, S. J. (2011). Postpartum depression: An essential overview for the practitioner. *Southern Medical Journal, 104*, 128–132.

Breier, A. (2011). Anxiety disorders and antipsychotic drugs: A pressing need for more research. *American Journal of Psychiatry, 168*, 1012–1014.

Breitborde, N. J. K., Lopez, S. R., & Nuechterlein, K. H. (2009). Expressed emotion, human agency, and schizophrenia: Toward a new model for the EE-relapse association. *Cultural and Medical Psychiatry, 33*, 41–60.

Brenner, D. J., & Hall, E. J. (2007). Computed tomography—An increasing source of radiation exposure. *New England Journal of Medicine, 357*, 2277–2284.

Brent, D. A. (2009a). In search of endophenotypes for suicidal behavior. *American Journal of Psychiatry, 166*, 1087–1089.

Brent, D. A. (2009b). Youth depression and suicide: Selective serotonin reuptake inhibitors treat the former and prevent the latter. *Canadian Journal of Psychiatry, 54*, 76–77.

Brent, D. A., & Melhem, N. (2008). Familial transmission of suicidal behavior. *Psychiatric Clinics of North America, 31*, 157–177.

Bresnahan, M., Begg, M. D., Brown, A., Schaefer, C., Sohler, N., . . . Susser, E. (2007). Race and risk of schizophrenia in a US birth cohort: Another example of health disparity? *International Journal of Epidemiology, 36*, 751–758.

Brewerton, T. D., & Costin, C. (2011). Treatment results of anorexia nervosa and bulimia nervosa in a residential treatment program. *Eating Disorders, 19*, 117–131.

Brewin, C. R. (2011). The nature and significance of memory disturbance in posttraumatic stress disorder. *Annual Review of Clinical Psychology, 7*, 203–227.

Brewslow, N., Evans, L., & Langley, J. (1986). Comparisons among heterosexual, bisexual, and homosexual male sadomasochists. *Journal of Homosexuality, 13*, 83–107.

Brezo, J., Klempan, T., & Turecki, G. (2008). The genetics of suicide: A critical review of molecular studies. *Psychiatric Clinics of North America, 31*, 179–203.

Bridge, J. A., Iyengar, S., Salary, C. B., Barbe, R. P., Birmaher, B., Pincus, H. A., . . . Brent, D. A. (2007). Clinical response and risk for reported suicidal ideation and suicide attempts in pediatric antidepressant treatment: A meta-analysis of randomized controlled trials. *Journal of the American Medical Association, 297*, 1683–1696.

Briggs, E. S., & Price, I. R. (2009). The relationship between adverse childhood experience and obsessive-compulsive symptoms and beliefs: The role of anxiety, depression, and experiential avoidance. *Journal of Anxiety Disorders, 23*, 1037–1046.

Brim, S. N., Rudd, R. A., Funk, R. H., & Callahan, D. B. (2008). Asthma prevalence among US children in underrepresented minority populations: American Indian/Alaska Native, Chinese, Filipino, and Asian Indian. *Pediatrics, 122*, 217–222.

Britton, J. C., Lissek, S., Grillon, C., Norcross, M. A., & Pine, D. S. (2011). Development of anxiety: The role of threat appraisal and fear learning. *Depression and Anxiety, 28*, 5–17.

Broadwater, K., Curtin, L., Martz, D. M., & Zrull, M. C. (2006). College student drinking: Perception of the norm and behavioral intentions. *Addictive Behaviors, 31*, 632–640.

Broeren, S., Lester, K. J., Muris, P., & Field, A. P. (2011). They are afraid of the animal, so therefore I am too: Influence of peer modeling on fear beliefs and approach–avoidance behaviors towards animals in typically developing children. *Behaviour Research and Therapy, 49*, 50–57.

Brooks, J. O., Goldberg, J. F., Ketter, T. A., Miklowitz, D. J., Calabrese, J. R., Bowden, C. L., & Thase, M. E. (2011). Safety and tolerability associated with second-generation antipsychotic polytherapy in bipolar disorder: Findings from the Systematic Treatment Enhancement Program for Bipolar Disorder. *Journal of Clinical Psychiatry, 72*, 240–247.

Brooks, L. G., & Loewenstein, D. A. (2010). Assessing the progression of mild cognitive impairment to Alzheimer's disease: Current trends and future directions. *Alzheimer's Research & Therapy, 2*, 28. Retrieved from http://alzres.com/content/2/5/28

Brooks, S., Prince, A., Stahl, D., Campbell, I. C., & Treasure, J. (2011). A systematic review and meta-analysis of cognitive bias to food stimuli in people with disordered eating behavior. *Clinical Psychology Review, 31*, 37–51.

Brotman, M. A., Schmajuk, M., Rich, B. A., Dickstein, D. P., Guyer, A. E., . . . Leibenluft, E. (2006). Prevalence, clinical correlates, and longitudinal course of severe mood dysregulation in children. *Biological Psychiatry, 60*, 991–997.

Brotto, L. A. (2009). The DSM diagnostic criteria for hypoactive sexual desire disorder. *Archives of Sexual Behavior, 7*, 2015–2030. doi:10.1007/s10508-009-9543-1

Brotto, L. A., & Luria, M. (2008). Menopause, aging, and sexual response in women. In D. Rowland & L. Incrocci (Eds.), *Handbook of sexual and gender identity disorders* (pp. 251–283). Hoboken, NJ: Wiley.

Brower, V. (2006). Loosening addiction's deadly grip. *EMBO Reports, 7*, 140–142.

Brown, D., & Srebalus, D. J. (2003). *Introduction to the counseling profession*. Boston, MA: Allyn & Bacon.

Brown, J., McKone, E., & Ward, J. (2010). Deficits of long-term memory in Ecstasy users are related to cognitive complexity of the task. *Psychopharmacology, 209*, 51–67.

Brown, M. M., & Grumet, J. G. (2009). School based suicide prevention with African American youth in an urban setting. *Professional Psychology: Research and Practice, 40*, 111–117.

Brown, R. J. (2004). Psychological mechanisms of medically unexplained symptoms: An integrative conceptual model. *Psychological Bulletin, 130*, 793–812.

Brown, R. J., & Lewis-Fernández, R. (2011). Culture and conversion disorder: Implications for DSM-5. *Psychiatry: Interpersonal and Biological Processes, 74*, 187–206.

Browne, B. (2011). Sinister secrets in the sky. Retrieved from http://coto2.wordpress.com/2011/02/05/sinister-secrets-in-the-ky-and-morgellons-disease/

Bruch, H. (1978). Obesity and anorexia nervosa. *Psychosomatics, 19*, 208–221.

Bruch, M. A., Fallon, M., & Heimberg, R. G. (2003). Social phobia and difficulties in occupational adjustment. *Journal of Counseling Psychology, 50*, 109–117.

Bruch, M. A., & Heimberg, R. G. (1994). Differences in perceptions of parental and personal characteristics between generalized and nongeneralized social phobics. *Journal of Anxiety Disorders, 8*, 155–168.

Bruno, R., Matthews, A. J., Topp, L., Degenhardt, L., Gomez, R., & Dunn, M. (2009). Can the severity of dependence scale be usefully applied to 'ecstasy'? *Neuropsychobiology, 60*, 137–147.

Brunoni, A. R., Fraguas, R., & Fregni, F. (2009). Pharmacological and combined interventions for the acute depressive episode: Focus on efficacy and tolerability. *Journal of Therapeutics and Clinical Risk Management, 5*, 897–910.

Brunoni, A. R., Teng, C. T., Correa, C., Imamura, M., Brasil-Neto, J. P., . . . Diwadkar, V. A. (2010). Neuromodulation approaches for the treatment of major depression: Challenges and recommendations from a working group meeting. *Arquivos de Neuro-Psiquiatria, 68*(3), 433–451.

Bruss, M. B., Morris, J., & Dannison, L. (2003). Prevention of childhood obesity: Sociocultural and familial factors. *Journal of the American Dietetic Association, 103*, 1042–1045.

Bryan, C. J., & Rudd, D. (2006). Advances in the assessment of suicide risk. *Journal of Clinical Psychology: In Session, 62*, 185–200.

Bryant, K. (2001, February 20). Eating disorders: In their own words. *Atlanta Journal-Constitution*, p. B4.

Bryant, R. A., Creamer, M., O'Donnell, M., Silove, D., & McFarlane, A. C. (2012). The capacity of acute stress disorder to predict posttraumatic psychiatric disorder (PTSD). *Journal of Psychiatric Research, 46*, 168–175.

Bryant, R. A., & Das, P. (2012). The neural circuitry of conversion disorder and its recovery. *Journal of Abnormal Psychology, 121*, 289–296.

Bryant, R. A., Felmingham, K. L., Falconer, E. M., Pe Benito, L., Dobson-Stone, C., Pierce, K. D., & Schofield, P. R. (2010). Preliminary evidence of the short allele of the serotonin transporter gene predicting poor response to cognitive behavior therapy in posttraumatic stress disorder. *Biological Psychiatry, 67*, 1217–1219.

Buchhave, P., Minthon, L., Zetterberg, H., Wallin, A. K., Blennow, K., & Hansson, O. (2012). Cerebrospinal fluid levels of β-amyloid 1-42, but not of tau, are fully changed already 5 to 10 years before the onset of Alzheimer dementia. *Archives of General Psychiatry, 69*, 98–106.

Budd, G. (2007). Disordered eating: Young women's search for control and connection. *Journal of Child and Adolescent Nursing, 20*, 96–106.

Budney, A. J., Vandrey, R. G., Hughes, J. R., Thostenson, J. D., & Bursac, Z. (2008). Comparison of cannabis and tobacco withdrawal: Severity and contribution to relapse. *Journal of Substance Abuse Treatment, 35*, 362–368.

Buitelaar, J., & Medori, R. (2010). Treating attention-deficit/hyperactivity disorder beyond symptom control alone in children and adolescents: A review of the potential benefits of long-acting stimulants. *European Child and Adolescent Psychiatry, 19*, 325–340.

Bulik, C. M., & Kendler, K. S. (2000). "I am what I (don't) eat": Establishing an identity independent of an eating disorder. *American Journal of Psychiatry, 157*, 1755–1760.

Bulik, C. M., & Reichborn-Kjennerud, T. (2003). Medical morbidity in binge eating disorder. *International Journal of Eating Disorders, 34*, S39–S46.

Bulik, C. M., Thornton, L. M., Root, T. L., Pisetsky, E. M., Lichtenstein, P., & Pedersen, N. L. (2010). Understanding the relation between anorexia nervosa and bulimia nervosa in a Swedish national twin sample. *Biological Psychiatry, 67*, 71–77.

Bull, C. B. (2004). Binge eating disorder. *Current Opinion in Psychiatry, 17*, 43–48.

Bullying statistics 2009. (2009). Retrieved from http://www.bullyingstatistics.org/content/bullying-statistics-2009.html

Buodo, G., Ghisi, M., Novara, C., Scozzari, S., Di Natale, A., & Sanavio, E. (2011). Assessment of cognitive functions in individuals with post-traumatic symptoms after work-related accidents. *Journal of Anxiety Disorders, 25*, 64–70.

Burgess, K., Rubin, K. H., Cheah, C., & Nelson, L. (2001). Socially withdrawn children: Parenting and parent-child relationships. In R. Crozier & L. E. Alden (Eds.), *The self, shyness and social anxiety: A handbook of concepts, research, and interventions* (pp. 137–158). New York, NY: Wiley.

Burghart, G., & Finn, C. A. (2010). *Handbook of MRI scanning*. New York, NY: Mosby.

Burke, S. C., Cremeens, J., Vail-Smith, K., & Woolsey, C. (2010). Drunkorexia: Calorie restriction prior to alcohol consumption among college freshman. *Journal of Alcohol & Drug Education, 54*, 17–34.

Burnham, J. J. (2009). Contemporary fears of children and adolescents: Coping and resiliency in the 21st century. *Journal of Counseling and Development, 87*, 28–33.

Burstein, M., & Ginsburg, G. S. (2010). The effect of parental modeling of anxious behaviors and cognitions in school-aged children: An experimental pilot study. *Behaviour Research and Therapy, 48*, 506–515.

Burstein, M., He, J. P., Kattan, G., Albano, A. M., Avenevoli, S., & Merikangas, K. R. (2011). Social phobia and subtypes in the National Comorbidity Survey—Adolescent Supplement: Prevalence, correlates, and comorbidity. *Journal of the American Academy of Child & Adolescent Psychiatry, 50*, 870–880.

Burt, V. L., Whelton, P., Roccella, E. J., Higgins, M., Horan, M. J., & Labarthe, D. (1995). Prevalence of hypertension in the U.S. adult population: Results from the Third National Health and Nutrition Examination Survey, 1988–1991. *Hypertension, 25*, 305–313.

Burton, C., McGorm, K., Weller, D., & Sharpe, M. (2010). Depression and anxiety in patients repeatedly referred to secondary care with medically unexplained symptoms: A case-control study. *Psychological Medicine, 41*(3), 555–563.

Butcher, J. N. (1990). *The MMPI-2 in psychological treatment*. New York, NY: Oxford University Press.

Butler, L. D., Duran, R. E. F., Jasiukaitis, P., Koopman, C., & Spiegel, D. (1996). Hypnotizability and traumatic experience. *American Journal of Psychiatry, 153*, 42–59.

Butler, S. F., Black, R., Serrano, J., Wood, M., & Budman, S. (2010). Characteristics of prescription opioid abusers in treatment: Prescription opioid use history, age, use patterns, and functional severity. *Journal of Opioid Management, 6*, 239–241, 246–252.

Butz, M. R., Evans, F. B., & Webber-Dereszynski, R. L. (2009). A practitioner's complaint and proposed direction: Munchausen syndrome by proxy, factitious disorder by proxy, and fabricated and/or induced illness in children. *Professional Psychology: Research and Practice, 40*, 31–38.

Buwalda, F. M., & Bouman, T. K. (2008). Predicting the effect of psychoeducational group treatment for hypochondriasis. *Clinical Psychology and Psychotherapy, 15*, 396–403.

Byrd, A. L., Loeber, R., & Pardini, D. A. (2012). Understanding desisting and persisting forms of delinquency: The unique contributions of disruptive behavior disorders and interpersonal callousness. *Journal of Child Psychology and Psychiatry, 53*, 371–380.

Bystritsky, A., Kerwin, L., Noosha, N., Natoli, J. L., Abrahami, N., . . . Young, A. S. (2010). Clinical and subthreshold panic disorder. *Depression and Anxiety, 27*, 381–389.

Cacioppo, J. T., Reis, H. T., & Zautra, A. J. (2011). The value of social fitness with an application to the military. *American Psychologist, 66*, 43–51.

Cafri, G., Thompson, J. K., Ricciardelli, L., McCabe, M., Smolak, L., & Yesalis, C. (2005). Pursuit of the muscular ideal: Physical and psychological consequences and putative risk factors. *Clinical Psychology Review, 25*, 215–239.

Cahill, K., Stead, L. F., & Lancaster, T. (2008). Nicotine receptor partial agonists for smoking cessation. *Cochrane Database of Systematic Reviews, 16*, CD006103.

Calikusu, C., Kucukgoncu, S., Tercer, O., & Bestepe, E. (2012). Skin picking in Turkish students: Prevalence, characteristics, and gender differences. *Behavior Modification, 36*, 49–66.

Callaghan, R. C., Cunningham, J. K., Allebeck, P., Arenovich, T., Sajeev, G., . . . Kish, S. J. (2012). Methamphetamine use and schizophrenia: A population-based cohort study in California. *American Journal of Psychiatry, 169*, 389–396.

Camara, W. J., Nathan, J. S., & Puente, A. E. (2000). Psychological test usage: Implications in professional psychology. *Professional Psychology: Research and Practice, 31*, 141–154.

Cameron, A., Palm, K., & Follette, V. (2010). Reaction to stressful life events: What predicts symptom severity? *Journal of Anxiety Disorders, 24*, 645–649.

Campbell, M. L. C., & Morrison, A. P. (2007). The role of unhelpful appraisals and behaviours in vulnerability to psychotic-like phenomenon. *Behavioural and Cognitive Psychotherapy, 35*, 555–567.

Campo, J. A., Frederikx, M., Nijman, H., & Merckelbach, H. (1998). Schizophrenia and changes in physical appearance. *Journal of Clinical Psychiatry, 59*, 197–198.

Campolongo, P., Trezza, V., Palmery, M., Trabace, L., & Cuomo, V. (2009). Developmental exposure to cannabinoids causes subtle and enduring neurofunctional alterations. *International Review of Neurobiology, 85*, 117–133.

Campos, M. S., Garcia-Jalon, E., Gilleen, J. K., David, A. S., Peralta, V., & Cuesta, M. J. (2011). Premorbid personality and insight in first-episode psychosis. *Schizophrenia Bulletin, 37*, 52–60.

Canapary, D., Bongar, B., & Cleary, K. M. (2002). Assessing risk for completed suicide in patients with alcohol dependence: Clinicans' views of critical factors. *Professional Psychology: Research and Practice, 33*, 464–469.

Canas, F. (2005). Mechanisms of action of atypical antipsychotics. *CNS Spectrums, 8*, 5–11.

Canavera, K. E., Ollendick, T. H., May, J. T. E., & Pincus, D. B. (2010). Clinical correlates of comorbid obsessive-compulsive disorder and depression in youth. *Child Psychiatry and Human Development, 41*, 583–594.

Canfield, M., Keller, C., Frydrych, L., Ashrafiuon, L., Purdy, Christopher, H., & Blondell, R. (2010). Prescription opioid use among patients seeking treatment for opioid dependence. *Journal of Addiction Medicine, 4*, 108–113.

Cannon, T. D., Cadenhead, K., Comblatt, B., Woods, S. W., Addington, J., . . . Heinssen, R. (2008). Prediction of psychosis in youth at high clinical risk: A multisite longitudinal study in North America. *Archives of General Psychiatry, 65*, 28–32.

Cantor, D. W., & Fuentes, M. A. (2008). Psychology's response to managed care. *Professional Psychology: Research and Practice, 39*, 638–645.

Caplan, P. J. (1995). *They say you're crazy*. Reading, MA: Addison-Wesley.

Carayol, J., Schellenberg, G. D., Torres, F., Hager, J., Ziegler, A., & Dawson, G. (2010). Assessing the impact of a combined analysis of four common low-risk genetic variants on autism risk. *Molecular Autism, 1, 4*. Retrieved from http://www.molecularautism.com/content/1/1/4

Cardena, E., & Weiner, L. A. (2004). Evaluation of dissociation throughout the lifespan. *Psychotherapy: Theory, Research, Practice, Training, 41*, 496–508.

Careaga, M., Van de Water, J., & Ashwood, P. (2010). Immune dysfunction in autism: A pathway to treatment. *Neurotherapeutics, 7*, 283–292.

Carels, R. A., Cacciapaglia, H., Perez-Benitez, C. I., Douglass, O., Christie, S., & O'Brien, W. H. (2003). The association between emotional upset and cardiac arrhythmias during daily life. *Journal of Consulting and Clinical Psychology, 71*, 613–618.

Carey, B. (2011, June 23). Expert on mental illness reveals her own fight. *New York Times*. Retrieved from http://www.nytimes.com

Carey, K. B., Scott-Sheldon, L., Carey, M. P., & DeMartini, K. S. (2007). Individual-level interventions to reduce college student drinking: A meta-analytic review. *Addictive Behaviors, 32*, 2469–2494.

Carlson, L. E., Speca, M., Faris, P., & Patel, K. D. (2007). One year pre-post intervention follow-up of psychological, immune, endocrine and blood pressure outcomes of mindfulness-based stress reduction (MBSR) in breast and prostate cancer outpatients. *Brain and Behavioral Immunology, 21*, 1038–1049.

Carmichael, S. (2010, June 17). Debenhams reveals tricks of the trade and axes digitally enhanced models. *London Evening Standard*. Retrieved from http://www.standard.co.uk

Carney, R. M., Freedland, K. E., & Veith, R. C. (2005). Depression, the autonomic nervous system, and coronary heart disease. *Psychosomatic Medicine, 67*, 29–33.

Caroff, S. N., Hurford, I., Lybrand, J., & Cabrina, C. E. (2011). Movement disorders induced by antipsychotic drugs: Implications of the CATIE schizophrenia trial. *Neurologic Clinics, 29*, 127–148.

Caroff, S. N., Ungvari, G. S., Bhati, M. T., Datto, C. J., & O'Reardon, J. P. (2007). Catatonia and prediction of response to electroconvulsive therapy. *Psychiatric Annals, 37*, 57–64.

Carpenter, W. T., & Van Os, J. (2011). Should attenuated psychosis syndrome be a DSM-5 diagnosis? *American Journal of Psychiatry, 168*, 460–463.

Carpenter, W. T., Jr. (2010). Conceptualizing schizophrenia through attenuated symptoms in the population. *American Journal of Psychiatry, 167*, 1013–1016.

Carper, T. L, Negy, C., & Tantleff-Dunn, S. (2010). Relations among media influence, body image, eating concerns, and sexual orientation in men: A preliminary investigation. *Body Image, 7*, 301–309.

Carroll, K. M., & Onken, L. S. (2005). Behavioral therapies for drug abuse. *American Journal of Psychiatry, 162*, 1452–1460.

Carroll, L. (2011, July 6). Eating disorders stalk women into adulthood. Retrieved from http://today.msnbc.msn.com

Carter, J. S., & Garber, J. (2011). Predictors of the first onset of a major depressive episode and changes in depressive symptoms across adolescence: Stress and negative cognitions. *Journal of Abnormal Psychology, 120*, 779–796.

Cartwright, S. (1851). "Report on the Diseases and Physical Peculiarities of the Negro Race", *The New Orleans Medical and Surgical Journal*, 1851:691–715 (May).

Casey, B. J., Ruberry, E. J., Libby, V., Glatt, C. E., Hare, T., . . . Tottenham, N. (2011). Transitional and translational studies of risk for anxiety. *Depression and Anxiety, 28*, 18–28.

Casey, D. E. (2006). Implications of the CATIE trial on treatment: Extrapyramidal symptoms. *CNS Spectrums, 11*, 25–31.

Casey, G. W. (2011). Comprehensive Soldier Fitness: A vision for psychological resilience in the U.S. Army. *American Psychologist, 66*, 1–3.

Caspi, A., Sugden, K., Moffitt, T. E., Taylor, A., Craig, I. W., . . . Poulton, R. (2003). Influence of life stress on depression: Moderation by a polymorphism in the 5-HTT gene. *Science, 301*, 386–389.

Cassidy, F. (2010). Insight in bipolar disorder: Relationship to episode subtypes and symptom dimensions. *Journal of Neuropsychiatric Disease and Treatment, 6*, 627–631.

Catalina, M. L., Gomez, M. V., & de Cos, A. (2008). Prevalence of factitious disorder with psychological symptoms in hospitalized patients. *Actas Espanolas de Psiquiatria, 36*, 345–349.

Cather, C. (2005). Functional cognitive-behavioural therapy: A brief, individual treatment for functional impairments resulting from psychotic symptoms in schizophrenia. *Canadian Journal of Psychiatry, 50*, 258–263.

Cavedini, P., Zorzi, C., Piccinni, M., Cavallini, M. C., & Bellodi, L. (2010). Executive dysfunctions in obsessive-compulsive patients and unaffected relatives: Searching for a new intermediate phenotype. *Biological Psychiatry, 67*, 1178–1184.

Center for Male Reproductive Medicine and Microsurgery. (2005). Penile implants (prosthesis) surgery. Retrieved from http://www.maleinfertility.org/penileimplants.html

Centers for Disease Control and Prevention. (2007a). Obesity and overweight. Retrieved from http://www.cdc.gov/needphp/dnpa/obesity/index.htm

Centers for Disease Control and Prevention. (2007b). Suicide: Facts at a glance. Retrieved from http://www.cdc.gov/ncipc/dvp/suicide/

Centers for Disease Control and Prevention. (2007c). Suicide prevention: Youth suicide. Retrieved from http://www.cdc.gov/ncipc/dvp/Suicide/youthsuicide.htm

Centers for Disease Control and Prevention. (2009a). Difference in prevalence of obesity among black, white, and Hispanic adults—United States, 2006–2008. *Morbidity and Mortality Weekly Report, 58*, 740–744.

Centers for Disease Control and Prevention. (2009b). Prevalence of autism spectrum disorders—Autism and Developmental Disabilities Monitoring Network, United States, 2006. Retrieved from http://www.cdc.gov/mmwr/preview/mmwrhtml/ss5810a1.htm

Centers for Disease Control and Prevention. (2010a). *Health, United States, 2010*. Retrieved from http://www.cdc.gov/nchs/data/hus/hus10.pdf#066

Centers for Disease Control and Prevention. (2010b). Increasing prevalence of parent-reported attention-deficit/hyperactivity disorder among children—United States, 2003 and 2007. *Morbidity and Mortality Weekly Report, 59*, 1439–1443.

Centers for Disease Control and Prevention. (2010c). Vital signs: State-specific obesity prevalence among adults—United States, 2009. *Morbidity and Mortality Weekly Report, 59*, 1–5.

Centers for Disease Control and Prevention. (2010d). Youth risk behavior surveillance—United States, 2009. *Morbidity and Mortality Weekly Report Surveillance Summary, 59*(SS-5), 1–142.

Centers for Disease Control and Prevention. (2011a). About BMI for adults. Retrieved from http://www.cdc.gov/healthyweight/assessing/bmi/adult_bmi/index.html

Centers for Disease Control and Prevention. (2011b). Attention-deficit/hyperactivity disorder (ADHD): Data and statistics. Retrieved from http://www.cdc.gov/ncbddd/adhd/data.html

Centers for Disease Control and Prevention. (2011c). CDC investigation of unexplained dermopathy. Retrieved from http://www.cdc.gov/unexplained-dermopathy/

Centers for Disease Control and Prevention. (2011d). Leading causes of death. Retrieved from http://www.cdc.gov/nchs/fastats/lcod.htm

Centers for Disease Control and Prevention. (2011e). Nonfatal traumatic brain injuries related to sports and recreation activities among persons aged ≤ 19 years—United States, 2001–2009. *Morbidity and Mortality Weekly Report, 60*, 1337–1342.

Centers for Disease Control and Prevention. (2012). Epilepsy. Retrieved from http://www.cdc.gov/epilepsy/basics/faqs.htm

Centers for Disease Control and Prevention. (2012). Vital signs: Binge drinking prevalence, frequency, and intensity among adults—United States, 2010. *Morbidity and Mortality Weekly Report, 61*, 14–19.

Centers for Disease Control and Prevention Web-Based Injury Statistics Query and Reporting System. (2005). Injury statistics. Retrieved from www.cdc.gov/injury/wisqars/index.html.

Centers for Disease Control and Prevention Web-Based Injury Statistics Query and Reporting System. (2007a). Fatal injury reports. Retrieved from www.cdc.gov/injury/wisqars/index.html

Centers for Disease Control and Prevention Web-Based Injury Statistics Query and Reporting System. (2007b). Leading causes of death reports. Retrieved from www.cdc.gov/injury/wisqars.index.html

Centers for Disease Control and Prevention Web-Based Injury Statistics Query and Reporting System. (2010). Injury prevention and control: Data and Statistics. Retrieved from http://www.cdc.gov/injury/wisqars/index.html

Centre for Addiction and Mental Health. (2007, October 23). Are some men predisposed to pedophilia? *Science Daily*. Retrieved from www.sciencedaily.com/releases/2007/10/071022120203.htm

Cerullo, M. A., Adler, C. M., Delbello, M. P., & Strakowski, S. M. (2009). The functional neuroanatomy of bipolar disorder. *International Review of Psychiatry, 21*, 314–322.

Cha, C. B., Najmi, S., Park, J. M., Finn, C. T., & Nock, M. K. (2010). Attentional bias toward suicide-related stimuli predicts suicidal behavior. *Journal of Abnormal Psychology, 119*, 616–622.

Chadwick, P., Hughes, S., Russell, D., Russell, I., & Dagnan, D. (2009). Mindfulness groups for distressing voices and paranoia: A replication and randomized feasibility trial. *Behavioral and Cognitive Psychotherapy, 37*, 403–412.

Chadwick, P., Kaur, H., Swelam, M., Ross,. S., & Ellett, L. (2011). Experience of mindfulness in people with bipolar disorder: A qualitative study. *Psychotherapy Research, 21*, 277–285.

Chadwick, P., Sambrooke, S., Rasch, S., & Davies, E. (2000). Challenging the omnipotence of voices: Group cognitive behavior therapy for voices. *Behaviour Research and Therapy, 38*, 993–1003.

Chae, D. H., Takeuchi, D. T., Barbeau, E. M., Bennett, G. G., Lindsey, J. C., Stoddard, A. M., & Krieger, N. (2008). Alcohol disorders among Asian Americans: Associations with unfair treatment, racial/ethnic discrimination, and ethnic identification (the National Latino and Asian Americans Study, 2002–2003). *Journal of Epidemiology and Community Health, 62*, 973–979.

Chalder, M., Elgar, F. J., & Bennett, P. (2006). Drinking and motivations to drink among adolescent children of parents with alcohol problems. *Alcohol and Alcoholism, 41*, 107–113.

Challacombe, F., & Salkovskis, P. (2009). A preliminary investigation of the impact of maternal obsessive-compulsive disorder and panic disorder on parenting and children. *Journal of Anxiety Disorders, 23*, 848–847.

Champion, H. R., Holcomb, J. B., & Young, L. A. (2009). Injuries from explosions. *Journal of Trauma, 66*, 1468–1476.

Chan, R. C. K., Di, X., McAlonan, G. M., & Gong, Q.-y. (2011). Brain anatomical abnormalities in high-risk individuals, first-episode, and chronic schizophrenia: An activation likelihood estimation meta-analysis of illness progression. *Schizophrenia Bulletin, 37*, 177–188.

Chandler-Laney, P. C., Hunter, G. R., Ard, J. D., Roy, J. L., Brock, D. W., & Gower, B. A. (2009). Perception of others' body size influences weight loss and regain for European American but not African American women. *Health Psychology, 28*, 414–418.

Chandra, A., Martino, S. C., Collins, R. L., Elliott, M. N., Berry, S. H., Kanouse, D. E., & Mui, A. (2008). Does watching sex on television predict teen pregnancy? Findings from a national longitudinal survey of youth. *Pediatrics, 122*, 1047–1054.

Chapman, C., Gilger, K., & Chestnutt, A. (2010). The challenge of eating disorders on a college campus. *Counseling Today, 53*, 44–45.

Chapman, L. J., & Chapman, J. P. (1967). Genesis of popular but erroneous psychodiagnostic observations. *Journal of Abnormal Psychology, 72*, 193–204.

Chartier, K., & Caetano, R. (2010). Ethnicity and health disparities in alcohol research. *Alcohol Research & Health, 33*(1/2), 152–160. Retrieved from http://pubs.niaaa.nih.gov/publications/arh40/152-160.pdf

Chaturvedi, S. K., Desai, G., & Shaligram, D. (2010). Dissociative disorders in a psychiatric institute in India—A selected review and patterns over a decade. *International Journal of Social Psychiatry, 56*, 533–539.

Chawarska, K., Volkmar, F., & Klin, A. (2010). Limited attentional bias for faces in toddlers with autism spectrum disorders. *Archives of General Psychiatry, 67*, 178–185.

Chekoudjian, C. B. (2009). The subjective experience of PMS: A sociological analysis of women's narratives (Unpublished master's thesis). University of South Florida, Tampa, FL. Retrieved from http://scholarcommons.usf.edu/etd/1895

Chen, L. P., Murad, M. H., Paras, M. L., Colbenson, K. M., Sattler, A. L., . . . Zirakzadeh, A. (2010). Sexual abuse and lifetime diagnosis of psychiatric disorders: Systematic review and meta-analysis. *Mayo Clinic Proceedings, 85*, 618–629.

Chen, Y., Briesacher, B. A., Field, T. S., Tjia, J., Lau, D. T., & Gurwitz, J. H. (2010). Unexplained variation across US nursing homes in antipsychotic prescribing rates. *Archives of Internal Medicine, 170*, 89–95.

Chentsova-Dutton, Y. E., Tsai, J. L., & Gotlib, I. H. (2010). Further evidence for the cultural norm hypothesis: Positive emotion in depressed and control European American and Asian American women. *Cultural Diversity and Ethnic Minority Psychology, 16*, 284–295.

Cherkasova, M. V., & Hechtman, L. (2009). Neuroimaging in attention-deficit hyperactivity disorder: Beyond the frontostriatal circuitry. *Canadian Journal of Psychiatry, 54*, 651–664.

Chernikoff, L. (2011, July 14). Kate and anorexia. Retrieved from http://today.msnbc.msn.com

Cheslack-Postava, K., Liu, K., & Bearman, P. S. (2011). Closely spaced pregnancies are associated with increased odds of autism in California sibling births. *Pediatrics, 127*, 246–253.

Chez, M. G., & Guido-Estrada, N. (2010). Immune therapy in autism: Historical experience and future directions with immunomodulatory therapy. *Neurotherapeutics, 7*, 293–301.

Child Welfare Information Gateway. (2012). *Child abuse and neglect fatalities: Statistics and interventions.* Retrieved from http://www.childwelfare.gov/pubs/factsheets/fatality.cfm

Chin, J. T., Hayward, M., & Drinnan, A. (2009). 'Relating' to voices: Exploring the relevance of this concept to people who hear voices. *Psychology and Psychotherapy: Theory, Research and Practice, 81*, 1–17.

Chobanian, A. V., Bakris, G. L., Black, H. R., Cushman, W. C., Green, L. A., . . . National High Blood Pressure Education Program Coordinating Committee. (2003). Seventh report of the Joint National Committee on Prevention, Detection, Evaluation, and Treatment of High Blood Pressure. *Hypertension, 42*, 1206–1274.

Chodoff, P. (1987). [Letter to the editor]. *American Journal of Psychiatry, 144*, 124.

Choi, P. Y. L., Pope, H. G., Jr., Olivardia, R., & Cash, T. F. (2002). Muscle dysphoria: A new syndrome in weightlifters. *British Journal of Sports Medicine, 36*, 375–377.

Chollet, F., Tardy, J., Albucher, J., Thalamas, C., Berard, E., . . . Loubinoux, I. (2011). Fluoxetine for motor recovery after acute ischaemic stroke (FLAME): A randomised placebo-controlled trial. *The Lancet Neurology, 10*(2), 123–130. doi:10.1016/S1474-4422(10)70314-8

Chopra, S., & Bienenfeld, D. (2011). Delusional disorder. Retrieved from http://emedicine.medscape.com/article/292991-overview

Chorpita, B. F., & Barlow, D. H. (1998). The development of anxiety: The role of control in the early environment. *Psychological Bulletin, 124*, 3–21.

Christakis, N. A., & Fowler, J. H. (2007). The spread of obesity in a large social network over 32 years. *New England Journal of Medicine, 357*, 370–379.

Christie, A. M., & Barling, J. (2009). Disentangling the indirect links between socioeconomic status and health: The dynamic roles of work stressors and personal control. *Journal of Applied Psychology, 94*, 1466–1478.

Chronis-Tuscano, A., Brooke, S. G., Molina, W. E., Pelham, B., Applegate, A., . . . Lahey, B. B. (2010). Very early predictors of adolescent depression and suicide attempts in children with attention-deficit/hyperactivity disorder. *Archives of General Psychiatry, 67*, 1044–1051.

Chung, T., Martin, C. S., Cornelius, J. R., & Clark, D. B. (2008). Cannabis withdrawal predicts severity of cannabis involvement at 1-year follow-up among treated adolescents. *Addiction, 103*, 787–799.

Cicchetti, D. (2010). Resilience under conditions of extreme stress: A multilevel perspective. *World Psychiatry, 9*, 145–154.

Cicero, D. C., Kerns, J. G., & McCarthy, D. M. (2010). The Aberrant Salience Inventory: A new measure of psychosis proneness. *Psychological Assessment, 22*, 688–701.

Ciraulo, D. A., Dong, Q., Silverman, B. L., Gastfriend, D. R., & Pettinati, H. M. (2008). Early treatment response in alcohol dependence with extended-release naltrexone. *Journal of Clinical Psychiatry, 69*, 190–195.

Cisler, J. M., Adams, T. G., Brady, R. E., Bridges, A. J., Lohr, J. M., & Olatunji, B. O. (2011). Unique affective and cognitive processes in contamination appraisals: Implications for contamination fear. *Journal of Anxiety Disorders, 25*, 28–35.

Clark, D. A., & Beck, A. T. (2009). *Cognitive therapy for anxiety disorders.* New York, NY: Guilford Press.

Clark, M., Gosnell, M., Witherspoon, J., Huck, J., Hager, M., . . . Robinson, T. L. (1984, December 3). A slow death of the mind. *Newsweek, 104*(22), 56–62.

Clark, R. (2006). Perceived racism and vascular reactivity in black college women: Moderating effects of seeking social support. *Health Psychology, 25*, 20–25.

Clarkin, J. F., & Levy, K. N. (2004). The influence of client variables on psychotherapy. In M. J. Lambert (Ed.), *Bergin and Garfield's handbook of psychotherapy and behavior change* (pp. 194–226). New York, NY: Wiley.

Clatworthy, J., Bowskill, R., Parham, R., Rank, T., Scott, J., & Horne, R. J. (2009). Understanding medication non-adherence in bipolar disorders using a necessity-concerns framework. *Affective Disorders, 116*, 51–55.

Clay, R. A. (1997, April). Is assisted suicide ever a rational choice? *APA Monitor, 28*(1), 43.

Clay, R. A. (2010). Psychology's voice is heard. APA Monitor, 41, 22.

Clay, R. A. (2012). Protesting proposed changes to the DSM. *APA Monitor, 43*, 42–43.

Cloitre, M., Stovall-McClough, K. C., Nooner, K., Zorbas, P., Cherry, S., Jackson, C. L., . . . Petkova, E. (2010). Treatment for PTSD related to childhood abuse: A randomized control trial. *American Journal of Psychiatry, 167*, 915–924.

Cloninger, C. R., & Dokucu, M. (2008). Somatoform and dissociative disorders. In S. H. Fatemi & P. J. Clayton (Eds.), *The medical basis of psychiatry* (pp. 181–194). Totawa, NJ: Humana Press.

Cloud, J. (January 15, 2011). The troubled life of Jared Loughner. *Time.* Retrieved from http://www.time.com

Coaley, K. (2010). *An introduction to psychological assessment and psychometrics.* Thousand Oaks, CA: Sage.

Coalition Educating About Sexual Endangerment. (2011). Rape statistics. Retrieved from http://oak.cats.ohiou.edu/,ad361896/anne/cease/numberspage.html

Cody, M. G., & Teachman, M. W. (2011). Global and local evaluations of public speaking performance in social anxiety. *Behavior Therapy, 42*, 601–611.

Coelho, C. M., & Purkis, H. (2009). The origins of specific phobias: Influential theories and current perspectives. *Review of General Psychology, 13*, 335–348.

Coghill, D., & Banaschewski, T. (2009). The genetics of attention-deficit/hyperactivity disorder. *Expert Review of Neurotherapeutics, 9*, 1547–1565.

Cohen, N. (2009, July 28). A Rorschach cheat sheet on Wikipedia? *New York Times.* Retrieved from http://www.nytimes.com

Cohen, S., Frank, E., Doyle, W. J., Skoner, D. P., Rabin, B. S., & Gwaltney, J. M. (1998). Types of stressors that increase susceptibility in the common cold in healthy adults. *Health Psychology, 17*, 214–223.

Cohen, S., & Lemay, E. P. (2007). Why would social networks be linked to affect and health practices? *Health Psychology, 26*, 410–417.

Cole, M. (2006). Internationalism in psychology: Why we need it now more than ever. *American Psychologist, 61*, 904–917.

Coles, M. E., & Coleman, S. L. (2010). Barriers to treatment seeking for anxiety disorders: Initial data on the role of mental health literacy. *Depression and Anxiety, 27*, 63–71.

Collip, D., Oorschot, M., Thewissen, V., Van Os, J., Bentall, R., & Myin-Germeys, I. (2010). Social world interactions: How company connects to paranoia. *Psychological Medicine, 41*(5), 911–921. http://journals.cambridge.org/abstract_S0033291710001558

Collishaw, S., Pickles, A., Messer, J., Rutter, M., Shearer, C., & Maughan, R. (2007). Resilience to adult psychopathology following childhood mistreatment: Evidence from a community sample. *Child Abuse and Neglect, 31*, 211–229.

Coltheart, M., Langdon, R., & McKay, R. (2007). Schizophrenia and monothematic delusions. *Schizophrenia Bulletin, 33*, 642–647.

Combs, D. R., Adams, S. D., Penn, D. L., Roberts, D., Thiegreen, J., & Stem, P. (2007). Social cognition and interaction training (SCIT) for inpatients with schizophrenia spectrum disorders: Preliminary findings. *Schizophrenia Research, 91*, 112–116.

Comer, J. S., Mojtabai, R., & Olfson, M. (2011). National trends in the antipsychotic treatment of psychiatric outpatients with anxiety disorders. *American Journal of Psychiatry, 168*, 1057–1065.

Compas, B. E., Forehand, R., Thigpen, J. C., Keller, G., Hardcastle, E. J., . . . Roberts, L. (2011). Family group cognitive-behavioral preventive intervention for families of depressed parents: 18- and 24-month outcomes. *Journal of Consulting and Clinical Psychology, 79*, 488–499.

Compton, M. T. (2005). Risk factors and risk markers for schizophrenia. *Medscape Psychiatry and Mental Health, 8*, 1–5.

Comtois, K. A., & Linehan, M. M. (2006). Psychosocial treatments of suicidal behaviors: A practice-friendly review. *Journal of Clinical Psychology: In Session, 62*, 161–170.

Conradi, H. J., Ormel, J., & de Jonge, P. (2010). Presence of individual (residual) symptoms during depressive episodes and periods of remission: A 3-year prospective study. *Psychological Medicine, 8*, 1–10.

Constantino, J. N., Majmudar, P., Bottini, A., Arvin, M., Virkud, Y., Simons, P., & Spitznagel, E. J. (2010). Infant head growth in male siblings of children with and without autism spectrum disorders. *Neurodevelopmental Disorders, 2*, 39–46.

Contractor, Z. (2012). Attention deficit hyperactivity disorder. Retrieved from http:// emedicine.medscape.com F912633-medication&ei=ZiQ6UPauMeKEjALRq4GgDw&usg=AFQjCNFKIPVaqaTzGkVbuoZfOJwlwqhDqg&sig2=67bMZTfguRm__e_6Xkzs4A

Cooke, D. J., & Michie, C. (2001). Refining the construct of psychopathy: Towards a hierarchical model. *Psychological Assessment, 13*, 171–188.

Coons, P. M. (1986). Treatment progress in twenty patients with multiple personality disorder. *Journal of Nervous and Mental Disease, 174*, 715–721.

Coons, P. M. (1988). Misuse of forensic hypnosis: A hypnotically elicited false confession with the apparent creation of a multiple personality. *International Journal of Clinical and Experimental Hypnosis, 36*, 1–11.

Coons, P. M. (1994). Confirmation of childhood abuse in child and adolescent cases of multiple personality disorder and dissociative disorder not otherwise specified. *Journal of Nervous and Mental Disease, 182*, 461–464.

Copeland, W. E., Keeler, G., Angold, A., & Costello, E. J. (2010). Posttraumatic stress without trauma in children. *American Journal of Psychiatry, 167*, 1059–1065.

Copersino, M. L., Boyd, S. J., Tashkin, D. P., Huestis, M. A., Heishman, S. J., . . . Gorelick, D. A. (2006). Cannabis withdrawal among non-treatment-seeking adult cannabis users. *American Journal of Addiction, 15*, 8–14.

Copolov, D. L., Mackinnon, A., & Trauer, T. (2004). Correlates of the affective impact of auditory hallucinations in psychotic disorders. *Schizophrenia Bulletin, 30*, 163–169.

Coppola, M., & Mondola, R. (2012). 3,4-methylenedioxypyrovalerone (MDPV): Chemistry, pharmacology and toxicology of a new designer drug of abuse marketed online, *Toxicology Letters, 208*, 12–15.

Corcoran, J., & Walsh, J. (2010). *Clinical assessment and diagnosis in clinical social work practice*. New York, NY: Oxford University Press.

Cordova, M. J., Cunningham, L. L. C., Carlson, C. R., & Andrykowski, M. A. (2001). Social constraints, cognitive processing, and adjustment to breast cancer. *Journal of Consulting and Clinical Psychology, 69*, 706–711.

Corey, G. (2013). *Theory and practice of counseling and psychotherapy*. Belmont, CA: Brooks/Cole.

Corey, G., Callanan, P., & Corey, M. S. (2010). *Issues and ethics in the helping professions*. Belmont, CA: Brooks/Cole.

Corey, G., & Corey, M. S. (2010). *Codes of ethics for the helping professions*. Belmont, CA: Brooks/Cole.

Cormier, J. F., & Thelen, M. H. (1998). Professional skepticism of multiple personality disorder. *Professional Psychology: Research and Practice, 29*, 163–167.

Cornah, D. (2006). *The impact of spirituality on mental health: A review of the literature*. London, UK: Mental Health Foundation.

Cornelius, J. R., Chung, T., Martin, C., Wood, D. S., & Clark, D. B. (2008). Cannabis withdrawal is common among treatment-seeking adolescents with cannabis dependence and major depression, and is associated with rapid relapse to dependence. *Addictive Behavior, 33*, 1500–1505.

Cornic, F., Consoli, A., & Cohen, D. (2007). Catatonia in children and adolescents. *Psychiatric Annals, 37*, 19–26.

Cornish, M. A., & Wade, N. G. (2010). Spirituality and religion in group counseling: A literature review with practice guidelines. *Professional Psychology: Research and Practice, 41*, 398–404.

Cornum, R., Matthews, M. D., & Seligman, M. E. P. (2011). Comprehensive Soldier Fitness: Building resilience in a challenging institutional context. *American Psychologist, 66*, 4–9.

Correll, C. U., Manu, P., Olshanskiv, V., Napolitano, B., Kane, J. M., & Malhotra, A. K. (2010). Cardiometabolic risk of second-generation antipsychotic medications during first-time use in children and adolescents. *Journal of the American Medical Association, 302*, 1765–1773.

Corrigan, P. W., & Watson, A. C. (2005). Mental illness and dangerousness: Fact or misperception, and implications for stigma. In P. W. Corrigan (Ed.), *On the stigma of mental illness: Practical strategies for research and social change* (pp. 165–179). Washington, DC: American Psychological Association.

Cortina, L. M., & Kubiak, S. P. (2006). Gender and posttraumatic stress: Sexual violence as an explanation for women's increased risk. *Journal of Abnormal Psychology, 115*, 753–759.

Cosgrove, L., & Krimsky, S. (2012). A comparison of DSM-IV and DSM-5 panel members' financial associations with industry: A pernicious problem persists. *PLoS Medicine, 9*(3), e1001190. doi:10.1371/journal.pmed.1001190

Costa, P. T., Jr., & McCrae, R. R. (2005). A five-factor model perspective on personality disorders. In S. Strack (Ed.), *Handbook of personality and psychopathology* (pp. 442–461). Hoboken, NJ: Wiley.

Costafreda, S. G., Fu, C. H., Picchioni, M., Toulopoulou, T., McDonald, C., Walshe, M., . . . McGuire, P. K. (2011). Pattern of neural responses to verbal fluency shows diagnostic specificity for schizophrenia and bipolar disorder. *BioMed Central Psychiatry, 11*, 18. doi:10.1186/1471-244X-11-18

Costello, E. J., Mustillo, S., Erkanli, A., Keeler, G., & Angold, A. (2003). Prevalence and development of psychiatric disorders in childhood and adolescence. *Archives of General Psychiatry, 60*, 837–844.

Cottler, L. B., Leung, K. S., & Abdallah, A. B. (2009). Test-re-test reliability of DSM-IV adopted criteria for 3,4-methylenedioxymethamphetamine (MDMA) abuse and dependence: A cross-national study. *Addiction, 104*, 1679–1690.

Cougnard, A., Grolleau, S., Lamarque, F., Beitz, C., Brugere, S., & Verdoux, H. (2006). Psychotic disorders among homeless subjects attending a psychiatric emergency service. *Social Psychiatry and Psychiatric Epidemiology, 41*, 904–910.

Cougnard, A., Marcelis, M., Myin-Germeys, I., DeGraaf, F., Vollebergh, W., . . . Van Os, J. (2007). Does normal developmental expression of psychosis combine with environmental risk to cause persistence of psychosis? A psychosis proneness-persistence model. *Psychological Medicine, 37*, 513–527.

Courtney, K. E., & Polich, J. (2009). Binge drinking in young adults: Data, definitions, and determinants. *Psychological Bulletin, 135*, 142–156.

Cousins, N. (1979). *Anatomy of an illness*. New York, NY: Norton.

Cowley, G., & Underwood, A. (1997, May 26). Why Ebonie can't breathe. *Newsweek*, 58–63.

Cox, J. E., Buman, M., Valenzuela, J., Joseph, N. P., Mitchell, A., & Woods, E. R. (2008). Depression, parenting attributes, and social support among adolescent mothers attending a teen tot program. *Journal of Pediatric and Adolescent Gynecology, 21*, 275–281.

Coyne, J. C., Stefanek, M., & Palmer, S. C. (2007). Psychotherapy and survival in cancer: The conflict between hope and evidence. *Psychological Bulletin, 133*, 367–394.

Coyne, S. M., Nelson, D. A., Graham-Kevan, N., Keister, E., & Grant, D. M. (2009). Mean on the screen: Psychopathy, relationship aggression, and aggression in the media. *Personality and Individual Differences, 48*, 288–293.

Craske, M. G., Kircanski, K., Epstein, A., Wittchen, H.-U., Pine, D. S., Lewis-Fernández, R., & Hinton, D. (2010). Panic disorder: A review of DSM-IV panic disorder and proposals for DSM-5. *Depression and Anxiety, 27*, 93–112.

Crews, F., & Boettiger, C. A. (2009). Impulsivity, frontal lobes and risk for addiction. *Pharmacology Biochemistry and Behavior, 88*, 237–247.

Crews, F., He, J., & Hodge, C. (2007). Adolescent cortical development: A critical period of vulnerability for addiction. *Pharmacology Biochemistry and Behavior, 86*, 189–199.

Crimlisk, H. L., Bhatia, K., Cope, H., & David, A. (1998). Slater revisited: Six-year follow-up study of patients with medically unexplained motor symptoms. *British Medical Journal, 316*, 582–586.

Crocker, N., Vaurio, L., Riley, E. P., & Mattson, S. N. (2009). Comparison of adaptive behavior in children with heavy prenatal alcohol exposure or attention-deficit/hyperactivity disorder. *Alcoholism: Clinical and Experimental Research, 33*, 2015–2023.

Crosby, R. D., Wonderlich, S. A., Engel, S. G., Simonich, H., Smyth, J., & Mitchell, J. E. (2010). Daily mood patterns and bulimic behaviors in the natural environment. *Behaviour Research and Therapy, 47*, 181–188.

Croteau, J. M., Lark, J. S., Lidderdale, M. A., & Chung, Y. B. (2005). *Deconstructing heterosexism in the counseling professions*. Thousand Oaks, CA: Sage.

Crow, S., Eisenberg, M. E., Story, M., & Neumark-Sztainer, D. (2008). Suicidal behavior in adolescents: Relationship to weight status, weight control behaviors, and body dissatisfaction. *International Journal of Eating Disorders, 41*, 82–87.

Crow, S. J., Mitchell, J. E., Crosby, R. D., Swanson, S. A., Wonderlich, S., & Lancaster, K. (2009). The cost-effectiveness of cognitive behavioral therapy for bulimia nervosa delivered via telemedicine versus face to face. *Behaviour Research and Therapy, 47*, 451–453.

Crow, S. J., Peterson, C. B., Swanson, S. A., Raymond, N. C., Specker, S., Eckert, E. D., & Mitchell, J. E. (2009). Increased mortality in bulimia nervosa and other eating disorders. *American Journal of Psychiatry, 166*, 1342–1346.

Crozier, J. C., Dodge, K. A., Fontaine, R. G., Lansford, J. E., Bates, J. E., Pettit, G. S., & Levenson, R. W. (2008). Social information processing and cardiac predictors of adolescent antisocial behavior. *Journal of Abnormal Psychology, 117*, 253–267.

Cruess, D. G., Antoni, M. H., Schneiderman, N., Ironson, G., McCabe, P., . . . Kumar, M. (2000). Cognitive-behavioral stress management increases free testosterone and decreases psychological distress in HIV-seropositive men. *Health Psychology, 19*, 12–20.

Crumlish, N., Whitty, P., Clarke, M., Browne, S., Karnali, M., . . . O'Callahan, E. (2009). Beyond the critical period: Longitudinal study of 8-year outcome in first-episode non-affective psychosis. *British Journal of Psychiatry, 194*, 18–24.

Crystal, S., Olfson, M., Huang, C., Pincus, H., & Gerhard, T. (2009). Broadened use of atypical antipsychotics: Safety, effectiveness, and policy challenges. *Health Affairs, 28*, 770–781.

Csipke, E., & Horne, O. (2007). Pro-eating disorder websites: Users' opinions. *European Eating Disorders Review, 15*, 196–206.

Cuffe, S. P. (2007, Summer). Suicide and SSRI medications in children and adolescents: An update. *DevelopMentor.* Retrieved from http://www.aacap.org/cs/root/developmentor/suicide_and_ssri_medications_in_children_and_adolescents_an_update

Culbert, K. M., Burt, S. A., McGue, M., Iacono, W. G., & Klump, K. L. (2009). Puberty and the genetic diathesis of disordered eating attitudes and behaviors. *Journal of Abnormal Psychology, 118*, 788–796.

Culbertson, C. S., Bramen, J., Cohen, M. S., London, E. D., Olmstead, R. E., . . . Brody, A. L. (2011). Effect of bupropion treatment on brain activation induced by cigarette-related cues in smokers. *Archives of General Psychiatry, 68*(5), 505–515. doi:10.1001/archgenpsychiatry.2010.193

Cummings, J. R., & Druss, B. G. (2011). Racial/ethnic differences in mental health service use among adolescents with major depression. *Journal of the American Academy of Child & Adolescent Psychiatry, 50*, 106–107.

Curran, L. K., Newschaffer, C. J., Lee, L. C., Crawford, S. O., Johnston, M. V., & Zimmerman, A. W. (2007). Behaviors associated with fever in children with autism spectrum disorders. *Pediatrics, 120*, 1386–1392.

Curtis, S., Stobart, K., Vandermeer, B., Simel, D. L., & Klassen, T. (2010). Clinical features suggestive of meningitis in children: A systematic review of prospective data. *Pediatrics, 126*, 952–960.

Cutrona, C. E., Russell, D. W., Brown, P. A., Clark, L. A., Hessling, R. M., & Gardner, K. A. (2005). Neighborhood context, personality, and stressful life events as predictors of depression among African American women. *Journal of Abnormal Psychology, 114*, 3–15.

Cutting, L. P., & Docherty, N. M. (2000). Schizophrenia outpatients' perceptions of their parents: Is expressed emotion a factor? *Journal of Abnormal Psychology, 109*, 266–272.

Cynkar, A. (2007, November). Socially wired. *Monitor on Psychology, 38*(10), 47–49.

Dahlstrom, W. G., & Welsh, G. S. (1965). *An MMPI handbook.* Minneapolis: University of Minnesota Press.

Dalenberg, C. J., Brand, B. L., Gleaves, D. H., Dorahy, M. J., Loewenstein, R. J., Cardeña, E., . . . Spiegel, D. (2012). Evaluation of the evidence for the trauma and fantasy models of dissociation. *Psychological Bulletin, 138*(3), 550–588. doi:10.1037/a0027447

Dalle Grave, R., & Calugi, S. (2007). Eating disorder not otherwise specified in an inpatient unit: The impact of altering the DSM-IV criteria for anorexia and bulimia nervosa. *European Eating Disorders Review, 15*, 340–349.

Dalrymple, K. L., & Zimmerman, M. (2011). Age of onset of social anxiety disorders in depressed outpatients. *Journal of Anxiety Disorders, 25*, 131–137.

Daly, B. P., Creed, T., Xanthopoulos, M., & Brown, R. T. (2007). Psychosocial treatments for children with attention deficit/hyperactivity disorder. *Neuropsychological Review, 17*, 73–89.

Dams-O'Conner, K., Martens, M. P., & Anderson, D. A. (2006). Alcohol-related consequences among women who want to lose weight. *Eating Behaviors, 7*, 188–195.

Damsa, C., Ruether, K. A., Moussaly, K., Adam, E., Vaney, C., & Berclaz, O. (2009). Greater evidence of dissociative symptoms noted in general practitioners attending an educational session on dissociation. *American Journal of Psychiatry, 166*, 1190–1191.

Daniulaityte, R., Falck, R., & Carlson, R. G. (2012) "I'm not afraid of those ones just 'cause they've been prescribed": Perceptions of risk among illicit users of pharmaceutical opioids. *International Journal of Drug Policy, 122*, 201–207.

Dannahy, L., Hayward, M., Strauss, C., Turton, W., Harding, E., & Chadwick, P. (2011). Group person-based cognitive therapy for distressing voices: Pilot data from nine groups. *Journal of Behavior Therapy and Experimental Psychiatry, 42*, 111–116.

Dao, J. (2011, December 1). After duty, dogs suffer like soldiers. *New York Times.* Retrieved from http://www.nytimes.com

Dar, R., Rish, S., Hermesh, H., Taub, M., & Fux, M. (2000). Realism of confidence in obsessive-compulsive checkers. *Journal of Abnormal Psychology, 109*, 673–678.

Dardick, H. (2004, February 13). Psychiatric patient tells of ordeal in treatment. *Chicago Tribune*, p. 1.

Datta, D., Basu, J., & Bandyopadhyay, G. (2011). Depression, personality characteristics and gain among female patients suffering from somatoform disorder and chronic physical pain in comparison to normal controls. *Journal of Projective Psychology and Mental Health, 18*, 177–185.

Davey, G. C. L., McDonald, A. S., Hirisave, U., Prabhu, G. G., Iwawaki, S., . . . Reimann, B. C. (1998). A cross-cultural study of animal fears. *Behaviour Research and Therapy, 36*, 735–750.

David. (2010, March 19). Re: Autism and Asperger's in the DSM-V: Thoughts on clinical utility [Web log comment]. Retrieved from http://www.child-psych.org/2010/02/autism-and-aspergers-in-the-dsm-v-going-beyond-the-politics.html

David-Ferndon, C., & Kaslow, N. J. (2008). Evidence-based psychosocial treatments for child and adolescent depression. *Journal of Clinical Child & Adolescent Psychology, 37*, 62–104.

Davidson, K. W., Mostofsky, E., & Whang, W. (2010). Don't worry, be happy: Positive affect and reduced 10-year incident coronary heart disease: The Canadian Nova Scotia Health Survey. *European Heart Journal, 31*, 1065–1070.

Davis, L., Uezato, A., Newell, J. M., & Frazier, E. (2008). Major depression and comorbid substance use disorders. *Current Opinion in Psychiatry, 21*, 14–18.

Dawson, D. A., Goldstein, R. B., & Grant, B. F. (2007). Rates and correlates of relapse among individuals in remission from DSM-IV alcohol dependence: A 3-year follow-up. *Alcoholism: Clinical and Experimental Research, 31*, 2036–2045.

Dawson, G., Munson, J., Webb, S. J., Nalty, T., Abbott, R., & Toth, K. (2007). Rate of head growth decelerates and symptoms worsen in the second year of life in autism. *Biological Psychiatry, 61*, 458–464.

Dawson, G., Rogers, S., Munson, J., Smith, M., Winter, J., Greenson, J., . . . Varley, J. (2010). Randomized, controlled trial of an intervention for toddlers with autism: The Early Start Denver model. *Pediatrics, 125*, 17–23.

Day, S. X., & Rottinghaus, P. (2003). The healthy personality. In W. B. Walsh (Ed.), *Counseling psychology and optimal human functioning* (pp. 1–23). Mahwah, NJ: Lawrence Erlbaum Associates.

Deault, L. C. (2010). A systematic review of parenting in relation to the development of comorbidities and functional impairments in children with attention-deficit/hyperactivity disorder (ADHD). *Child Psychiatry and Human Development, 41*, 168–192.

Decety, J., Michalska, K. J., Akitsuki, Y., & Lahey, B. B. (2009). Atypical empathic responses in adolescents with aggressive conduct disorder: A functional MRI investigation. *Biological Psychology, 80*, 203–211.

De Coteau, T., Anderson, J., & Hope, D. (2006). Adapting manualized treatments: Treating anxiety disorders among Native Americans. *Cognitive and Behavioral Practice, 13*, 304–309.

Decuyper, M., De Pauw, S., De Fruyt, F., De Bolle, M., & De Clercq, B. J. (2009). A meta-analysis of psychopathy, antisocial PD- and FFM associations. *European Journal of Personality, 23*, 531–565.

Dedovic, K., D'Aguiar, C., & Pruessner, J. C. (2009). What stress does to your brain: A review of neuroimaging studies. *Canadian Journal of Psychiatry, 54*, 5–15.

Dedovic, K., Wadiwalla, M., Engert, V., & Pruessner, J.C. (2009). The role of sex and gender socialization in stress reactivity. *Developmental Psychology, 4*, 45–55.

De Geus, E. J. C., Kupper, N., Boomsma, D. I., & Snieder, H. (2007). Bivariate genetic modeling of cardiovascular stress reactivity: Does stress uncover genetic variance? *Psychosomatic Medicine, 69*, 356–364.

Degenhardt, L., Hall, W. D., Lynskey, M., McGrath, J., McLaren, J., Calabria, B., . . . Vos, T. (2009). Should burden of disease estimates include cannabis use as a risk factor for psychosis? *PLoS Medicine, 6*(9), e1000133. doi:10.1371/journal.pmed.1000133

Degnan, K. A., & Fox, N. A. (2007). Behavioral inhibition and anxiety disorders: Multiple levels of a resilience process. *Development and Psychopathology, 19*, 729–746.

de Jong, P. J., Vorage, I., & van den Hout, M. A. (2000). Counterconditioning in the treatment of spider phobia: Effects on disgust, fear and valence. *Behaviour Research and Therapy, 38*, 1055–1069.

Delahanty, D. L. (2007). Are we prepared to handle the mental health consequences of terrorism? *American Journal of Psychiatry, 164*, 189–191.

Delaney-Black, V., Chiodo, L. M., Hannigan, J. H., Greenwald, M. K., Janisse, J., Patterson, G., . . . Sokol, R. J. (2010). Prenatal and postnatal cocaine exposure predict teen cocaine use. *Neurotoxicology and Teratology,* 33, 110–119.

De Leo, D. (2009). Cross-cultural research widens suicide prevention horizons. *Crisis, 30*, 59–62.

DeLisi, L. E., Maurizio, A., Yost, M., Papparozzi, C. F., Flulchino, C., . . . Stevens, P. (2003). A survey of New Yorkers after the Sept. 11, 2001, terrorist attacks. *American Journal of Psychiatry, 160*, 780–783.

Dell, P. F., & Eisenhower, J. W. (1990). Adolescent multiple personality disorder: A preliminary study of eleven cases. *Journal of the American Academy of Child & Adolescent Psychiatry, 29*, 359–366.

Denis, C., Lavie, E., Fatséas, M., & Auriacombe, M. (2006). Psychotherapeutic interventions for cannabis abuse and/or dependence in outpatient settings. *Cochrane Database of Systematic Reviews, 19*, CD005336. doi:10.1002/14651858.CD005336.pub2

Denisoff, E., & Endler, N. S. (2000). Life experiences, coping, and weight preoccupation in young adult women. *Canadian Journal of Behavioural Science, 32*, 97–103.

de Rossi, P. (2010). *Unbearable lightness: A story of loss and gain.* Chicago, IL: Atria.

DeRubeis, R. J., Siegle, G. J., & Hollon, S. D. (2008). Cognitive therapy vs. medications for depression: Treatment outcomes and neural mechanisms. *National Review of Neuroscience, 9*, 788–796.

Deshmukh, A. (2012, November). Women more likely than men to develop 'broken heart syndrome.' Presented at the Meetings of the American Heart Association, Gainesville, FL.

de Simone, V., Kaplan, L., Patronas, N., Wassermann, E. M., & Grafman, J. (2006). Driving abilities in frontotemporal dementia patients. *Dementia and Geriatric Cognitive Disorders, 23*, 1–7.

Desmond, S., Price, J., Hallinan, C., & Smith, D. (1989). Black and white adolescents' perceptions of their weight. *Journal of School Health, 59*, 353–358.

Desoto, M. C., & Hitlan, R. T. (2010). Sorting out the spinning of autism: Heavy metals and the question of incidence. *Acta Neurobiologiae Experimentalis, 70*, 165–176.

Deutsch, A. (1949). *The mentally ill in America* (2nd ed.). New York, NY: Columbia University Press.

Devita-Raeburn, E. (2007). The Morgellons mystery. *Psychology Today*. Retrieved from http://www.psychologytoday.com

Diamond, A. (2009). The interplay of biology and the environment broadly defined. *Developmental Psychology, 45*, 1–8.

Dickerson, S. S., & Kemeny, M. E. (2004). Acute stressors and cortisol responses: A theoretical integration and synthesis of laboratory research. *Psychological Bulletin, 130*, 355–391.

Dickstein, D. P., Nelson, E. E., McClure, E., Grimley, M. E., Knopf, L., . . . Leibenluft, E. (2007). Cognitive flexibility in phenotypes of pediatric bipolar disorder. *Journal of the American Academy of Child & Adolescent Psychiatry, 46*, 341–355.

Dickstein, D. P., Towbin, K. E., Van Der Veen, J. W., Rich, B. A., Brotman, M. A., . . . Leibenluft, E. (2009). Randomized double-blind placebo-controlled trial of lithium in youth with severe mood dysregulation. *Journal of Child and Adolescent Psychopharmacology, 19*, 61–73.

Diekstra, R. F., Kienhorst, C. W. M., & de Wilde, E. J. (1995). Suicide and suicidal behaviour among adolescents. In M. Rutter & D. J. Smith (Eds.), *Psychological disorders in young people* (pp. 686–670). Chichester, UK: Wiley.

Dienstbier, R. A. (1989). Arousal and physiological toughness: Implications for mental and physical health. *Psychological Review, 96*, 84–100.

Diflorio, A., & Jones, I. (2010). Is sex important? Gender differences in bipolar disorder. *International Review of Psychiatry, 22*, 437–452.

DiFranza, J. R., Savageau, J. A., Fletcher, K., Pbert, L., O'Loughlin, J., . . . Wellman, R. J. (2007). Susceptibility to nicotine dependence: The Development and Assessment of Nicotine Dependence in Youth 2 study. *Pediatrics, 120*, 974–983.

DiGrande, L., Neria, Y., Brackbill, M., Pulliam, P., & Galea, S. (2011). Long-term posttraumatic stress symptoms among 3,271 civilian survivors of the September 11, 2001, terrorist attacks on the World Trade Center. *American Journal of Epidemiology, 173*, 271–281.

Dilks, S., Tasker, F., & Wren, B. (2010). Managing the impact of psychosis: A grounded theory exploration of recovery processes in psychosis. *British Journal of Clinical Psychology, 49*, 87–107.

Dimidjian, S., Hollon, S. D., Dobson, K. S., Schmaling, K. B., Kohlenberg, R., . . . Jacobson, N. S. (2006). Randomized trial of behavioral activation, cognitive therapy, and antidepressant medication in the acute treatment of adults with major depression. *Journal of Consulting and Clinical Psychology, 74*, 658–670.

Dimsdale, J. E. (2011). Medically unexplained symptoms: A treacherous foundation for somatoform disorders? *Psychiatric Clinics of North America, 34*, 511–513.

Ding, K., Chang, G. A., & Southerland, R. (2009). Age of inhalant first time use and its association to the use of other drugs. *Journal of Drug Education, 39*, 261–272.

Di Paola, F., Faravelli, C., & Ricca, V. (2010). Perceived expressed emotion in anorexia nervosa, bulimia nervosa, and binge-eating disorder. *Comprehensive Psychiatry, 51*, 401–405.

Dirmann, T. (2003, September 8). Ex-Spice Girl Geri Halliwell: How I beat my eating disorder. *US Weekly*, 60.

Dissanayaka, N., Sellbach, A., Matheson, M., O'Sullivan, J. D., Silburn, P. A., Byrne, G. J., . . . Mellick, G. (2010). Anxiety disorders in Parkinson's disease: Prevalence and risk factors. *Movement Disorders, 25*, 838–845.

Dixon v. Weinberger, 498 F. 2d 202 (1975).

Dobkin, R. D., Allen, L. A., & Menza, M. (2006). A cognitive-behavioral treatment package for depression in Parkinson's disease. *Psychosomatics, 47*, 259–263.

Dobson, K. S., Hollon, S. D., Dimidjian, S., Schmaling, K. B., Kohlenberg, R. J., . . . Jacobson, N. S. (2008). Randomized trial of behavioral activation, cognitive therapy, and antidepressant medication in the prevention of relapse and recurrence in major depression. *Journal of Consulting and Clinical Psychology, 76*, 468–477.

Dodick, D. W., & Gargus, J. J. (2008). Why migraines strike. *Scientific American, 299*(2), 56–63.

Dolan, M. C., & Fullam, R. (2010). Emotional memory and psychopathic traits in conduct disordered adolescents. *Personality and Individual Differences, 48*, 327–331.

Dominguez, M. D. G., Saka M. C., Lieb, R., Wittchan, H.-U. & Van Os, J. (2010). Early expression of negative/disorganized symptoms predicting psychotic experiences and sub-sequent clinical psychosis: a 10-year study. *Am J Psychiatry* 167, 1075-1082.

Dominguez, M. D. G., Wichers, M., Lieb, R., Wittchen, H.-U., & Van Os, J. (2011). Evidence that onset of clinical psychosis is an outcome of progressively more persistent subclinical psychotic experiences: An 8-year cohort study. *Schizophrenia Bulletin, 37*, 84–93.

Domschke, K., Stevens, S., Pfleiderer, B., & Gerlach, A. L. (2010). Interoceptive sensitivity in anxiety and anxiety disorders: An overview and integration of neurobiological findings. *Clinical Psychology Review, 30*, 1–11.

Dong, Q., Yang, B., & Ollendick, T. H. (1994). Fears in Chinese children and adolescents and their relations to anxiety and depression. *Journal of Child Psychology and Psychiatry, 35*, 351–363.

Doody, R. S., Pavlik, V., Massman, P., Rountree, S., Darby, E., & Chan, W. (2010). Predicting progression of Alzheimer's disease. *Alzheimer's Research & Therapy, 2*, 2. Retrieved from http://alzres.com/content/2/1/2

Dorahy, M. J., Shannon, C., Seagar, L., Corr, M., . . . Middleton, W. (2009). Auditory hallucinations in dissociative identity disorder and schizophrenia with and without a childhood trauma history: Similarities and differences. *Journal of Nervous and Mental Disease, 197*, 892–898.

Dorgan, B. L. (2010). The tragedy of Native American youth suicide. *Psychological Services, 7*, 213–218.

Dotson, V. M., Beydoun, M. A., & Zonderman, A. B. (2010). Recurrent depressive symptoms and the incidence of dementia and mild cognitive impairment. *Neurology, 75*, 27–34.

Doughty, O. J., Lawrence, V. A., Al-Mousawi, A., Ashaye, K., & Done, D. J. (2009). Overinclusive thought and loosening of associations are not unique to schizophrenia and are produced in Alzheimer's dementia. *Cognitive Neuropsychiatry, 14*, 149–164.

Dovidio, J. F., Kawakami, K., Smoak, N., & Gaertner, S. L. (2009). Implicit measures of attitudes. In R. Petty, R. Faxio, & P. Brinol (Eds.), *Implicit measures* (pp. 165–192). New York, NY: Psychology Press.

Dowdy, K. G. (2000). The culturally sensitive medical interview. *Journal of the American Academy of Physician Assistants, 13*, 91–104.

Down syndrome. (2007). Retrieved from http://ghr.nlm.nih.gov/condition/down-syndrome

Dragt, S., Nieman, D. H., Becker, H. E., van de Fliert, R., Dingemans, P. M., . . . Linszen, D. H. (2010). Age of onset of cannabis use is associated with age of onset of high-risk symptoms for psychosis. *Canadian Journal of Psychiatry, 55*, 165–171.

Drane, J. (1995). Physican-assisted suicide and voluntary active euthanasia: Social ethics and the role of hospice. *American Journal of Hospice and Palliative Care, 12*, 3–10.

Driscoll, I., & Troncoso, J. (2011). Asymptomatic Alzheimer's disease: A prodrome or a state of resilience? *Current Alzheimer Research, 8*, 330–335.

Drum, D. J., Brownson, C., Denmark, A. B., & Smith,S. E. (2009). New data on the nature of suicidal crisis in college students: Shifting the paradigm. *Professional Psychology: Research and Practice, 40*, 213–222.

DSM-5 Work Groups. (2012). DSM-5: The future of psychiatric diagnosis. Retrieved from http://www.dsm5.org

Duarte-Velez, Y. M., & Bernal, G. (2008). Suicide risk in Latino and Latina adolescents. In F. Leong & M. M. Leach (Eds.), *Ethnic suicides* (pp. 81–115). New York, NY: Routledge.

Duchan, E., Patel, N. D., & Feucht, C. (2010). Energy drinks: A review of use and safety for athletes. *The Physician and Sports Medicine, 38*, 171–179.

Dudley, R., Siitarinen, J., James, I., & Dodson, G. (2009). What do people with psychosis think caused their psychosis? A Q methodology study. *Behavioural and Cognitive Psychotherapy, 37*, 11–24.

Dufault, R., Schnoll, R., Lukiw, W. J., Leblanc, B., Cornett, C., . . . Crider, R. (2009). Mercury exposure, nutritional deficiencies, and metabolic disruptions may affect learning in children. *Behavior and Brain Functioning, 27*, 44.

Dugas, M. J., & Ladouceur, R. (2000). Treatment of GAD: Targeting intolerance of uncertainty in two types of worry. *Behavior Modification, 24*, 635–657.

Dugdale, D. C., Jasmin, L., & Zieve, D. (2010). Gilles de la Tourette syndrome. Retrieved from http://www.ncbi.nlm.nih.gov/pubmedhealth/PMH0001744

Dulai, R., & Kelly, S. L. (2009). A case of the body snatchers. *Current Psychiatry, 8*, 56–65.

Dunkley, D. M., Masheb, R. M., & Grilo, C. M. (2010). Child maltreatment, depressive symptoms, and body dissatisfaction in patients with binge eating disorder: The mediating role of self-criticism. *International Journal of Eating Disorders, 43*, 274–281.

Durà-Vilà, G., Dein, S., & Hodes, M. (2010). Children with intellectual disability: A gain not a loss: Parental beliefs and family life. *Clinical Child Psychology and Psychiatry, 5*, 171–184.

Durex. (2001). Global sex survey. Retrieved from http://www.durex.com/uk/globalsexsurvey/2005results.asp

Durex. (2005). Global sex survey 2005 results. Retrieved from www.durex.com/uk/globalsexsurvey/2005results.asp

Durham v. United States, 214 F. 2d 862, 874–875 (D.C. Cir. 1954).

Durkheim, É. (1951). *Suicide*. New York, NY: Free Press. (Original work published 1897)

Durston, S. (2010). Imaging genetics in ADHD. *Neuroimage, 53*, 832–838.

Dworkin, A. (2009, November 11). After stroke, Portland woman's brain on the rebound [Web log post]. Retrieved from http://www.oregonlive.com/health/index.ssf/2009/11/after_stroke_portland_womans_b.html

Dyckman, J. (2011). Exposing the glosses in Seligman & Fowler's Straw-Man arguments. *American Psychologist, 66*, 644–645.

Dyer, O. (2004). GlaxoSmithKline faces US lawsuit over concealment of trial results. *British Medical Journal, 328*, 1395.

Dzokoto, A. A., & Adams, G. (2005). Understanding genital-shrinking epidemics in West Africa: Koro, juju, or mass psychogenic illness? *Culture, Medicine and Psychiatry, 29*, 53–78.

Eaker, E. D., Sullivan, L. M., Kelly-Hayes, M., D'Agostino, R. B., Sr., & Benjamin, E. J. (2007). Marital status, marital strain, and risk of coronary heart disease or total mortality: The Framingham Offspring Study. *Psychosomatic Medicine, 69*, 509–515.

Eastwood, S. L., & Harrison, P. J. (2010). Markers of glutamate synaptic transmission and plasticity are increased in the anterior cingulate cortex in bipolar disorder. *Biological Psychiatry, 7*, 1010–1016.

Eaton, D. K., Kann, L., Kinchen, S. A., Ross, J. G., Hawkins, J., & Harris, W. A. (2006). Youth risk behavior surveillance—United States, 2005. *Morbidity and Mortality Weekly Report, 55*(No. SS-5), 1–108.

Eberhart, N. K. (2011). Maladaptive schemas and depression: Tests of stress generation and diathesis-stress models. *Journal of Social and Clinical Psychology, 30*, 75–104.

Ecker, C., Suckling, J., Deoni, S. C., Lombardo, M. V., Bullmore, E. T., Baron-Cohen, S., . . . Murphy, D. G. (2012). Brain anatomy and its relationship to behavior in adults with autism spectrum disorder: A multicenter magnetic resonance imaging study. *Archives of General Psychiatry, 69*, 195–209.

Eddy, K. T., Tanofsky-Kraff, M., Thompson-Brenner, H., Hertzog, D. B., Brown, T. A., & Ludwig, D. S. (2007). Eating disorder pathology among overweight treatment-seeking youth: Clinical correlates and cross-sectional risk modeling. *Behaviour Research and Therapy, 45*, 2360–2367.

Edvardsen, J., Torgersen, S., Røysamb, E., Lygren, S., Skre, I., Onstad, S., & Oien, P. A. (2008). Heritability of bipolar spectrum disorders: Unity or heterogeneity? *Journal of Affective Disorders, 106*, 229–240.

Edwards, S., & Dickerson, M. (1987). On the similarity of positive and negative intrusions. *Behaviour Research and Therapy, 25*, 207–211.

Egan, K. G., & Moreno, M. A. (2011). Alcohol references on undergraduate males' Facebook profiles. *American Journal of Men's Health, 5*, 413–420.

Ehringer, M. A., Rhee, S. H., Young, S., Corley, R., & Hewitt, J. K. (2006). Genetic and environmental contributions to common psychopathologies of childhood and adolescence: A study of twins and their siblings. *Journal of Abnormal Child Psychology, 34*, 1–17.

Ehrlich, S., Pfeiffer, E., Salbach, H., Lenz, K., & Lehmkuhl, U. (2008). Factitious disorder in children and adolescents: A retrospective study. *Psychosomatics, 49*, 392–398.

Eidelman, P., Talbot, L. S., Gruber, J., & Harvey, A. G.(2010). Sleep, illness course, and concurrent symptoms in inter-episode bipolar disorder. *Journal of Behavior Therapy and Experimental Psychiatry, 41*, 145–149.

Eidelson, R., Pilisuk, M., & Soldz, S. (2011). The dark side of Comprehensive Soldier Fitness. *American Psychologist, 66*, 643–644.

Eisen, A. R., & Silverman, W. K. (1998). Prescriptive treatment for generalized anxiety disorder in children. *Behaviour Therapy, 29*, 105–121.

Eisenberg, M. E., & Neumark-Sztainer, D. (2010). Friends' dieting and disordered eating behaviors among adolescents five years later: Findings from Project EAT. *Journal of Adolescent Health, 47*, 67–73.

Eisendrath, S. J., Delucchi, K., Bitner, R., Fenimore, P., Smit, M., & McLane, M. (2008). Mindfulness-based cognitive therapy for treatment-resistant depression: A pilot study. *Psychotherapy and Psychosomatics, 77*, 319–320.

Elbogen, E. B., & Johnson, S. C. (2009). The intricate link between violence and mental disorder. *Archives of General Psychiatry, 66*, 152–161.

Elder, T. (2010). The importance of relative standards in ADHD diagnosis: Evidence based on exact birth dates. *Journal of Health Economics, 29*, 641–656.

Eldevik, S., Hastings, R. P., Hughes, J. C., Jahr, E., Eikeseth, S., & Cross, S. (2010). Using participant data to extend the evidence base for intensive behavioral intervention for children with autism. *American Journal of Intellectual and Developmental Disabilities, 115*, 381–405.

Eley, T. C., Lichtenstein, P., & Moffitt, T. E. (2003). A longitudinal behavioral genetic analysis of the etiology of aggressive and nonaggressive antisocial behavior. *Development and Psychopathology, 15*, 383–402.

El-Gabalawy, R., Cox, B., Clara, I., & Mackenzie, C. (2010). Assessing the validity of social anxiety disorder subtypes using a nationally representative sample. *Journal of Anxiety Disorders, 24*, 244–249.

Elia, J., Gai, X., Xie, H. M., Perin, J. C., Geiger, E., . . . White, P. S. (2010) Rare structural variants found in attention-deficit hyperactivity disorder are preferentially associated with neurodevelopmental genes. *Molecular Psychiatry, 15*, 637–646.

Elia, J., Glessner, J. T., Wang, K., Takahashi, N., Shtir, C. J., Hadley, D., . . . Hakonarson, H. (2011). Genome-wide copy number variation study associates metabotropic glutamate receptor gene networks with attention deficit hyperactivity disorder. *Nature Genetics, 44*, 78–84.

Elkashef, A., Vocci, F., Huestis, M., Haney, M., Budney, A., Gruber, A., & el-Guebaly, N. (2008). Marijuana neurobiology and treatment. *Substance Abuse, 29*, 17–29.

El Khoury-Malhame, M., Lanteaume, L., Beetz, E. M., Roques, J., Reynaud, E., . . . Khalfa, S. (2011). Attentional bias in post-traumatic stress disorder diminishes after symptom amelioration. *Behaviour Research and Therapy, 49*, 796–801.

Elliott, C., & Gillett, G. (1992). Moral insanity and practical reason. *Philosophical Psychology, 5*, 53–67.

Ellis, A. (1989). Rational-emotive therapy. In R. J. Corsini & D. Wedding (Eds.), *Current psychotherapies* (pp. 197–238). Itasca, IL: Peacock.

Ellis, A. (2008). Rational emotive behavior therapy. In R. J. Corsini & D. Wedding (Eds.), *Current psychotherapies* (8th ed., pp. 187–222). Belmont, CA: Brooks/Cole.

Ellis, D. M., & Hudson, J. L. (2010). The metacognitive model of generalized anxiety disorder in children and adolescents. *Clinical Child and Family Psychology Review, 13*, 151–163.

Ellison-Wright, I., & Bullmore, E. (2010). Anatomy of bipolar disorder and schizophrenia: A meta-analysis. *Schizophrenia Research, 117*, 1–12.

Elsevier. (2010, August 18). Early life influences risk for psychiatric disorders. *Science Daily*. Retrieved from http://www.sciencedaily.com/releases/2010/08/100818090012.htm

El-Sheikh, M., Keiley, M., & Hinnant, J. B. (2009). Developmental trajectories of skin conductance level in middle childhood: Sex, race, and externalizing behavior problems as predictors of growth. *Biological Psychology, 83*, 116–124.

Elwood, L. S., Mott, J., Lohr, J. M., & Galovski, T. E. (2011). Secondary trauma symptoms in clinicians: A critical review of the construct, specificity, and implications for trauma-focused treatment. *Clinical Psychology Review, 31*, 25–36.

Emel, B. (2011, July 1). 2 key components to a resilient and peaceful life [Web log post]. Retrieved from http://www.thebounceblog.com/2011/07/01/2-key-components-to-a-resilient-and-peaceful-life/

Emmelkamp, P. M. (2004). Behavior therapy with adults. In M. J. Lambert (Ed.), *Bergin and Garfield's handbook of psychotherapy and behavior change* (5th ed., pp. 393–446). New York, NY: Wiley.

Eng, M. Y., Luczak, S. E., & Wall, T. L. (2007). ALDH2, ADH1B, and ADH1C genotypes in Asians: A literature review. *Alcohol Research and Health, 30*, 22–27.

Engelhard, I. M., de Jong, P. J., van den Hout, M. A., & van Overveld, M. (2009). Expectancy bias and the persistence of posttraumatic stress. *Behaviour Research and Therapy, 47*, 887–892.

Engh, J. J. (2006). *In the name of heaven: 3,000 years of religious persecution*. Amherst, NY: Prometheus Books.

Enoch, M. A. (2012). The influence of gene-environment interactions on the development of alcoholism and drug dependence. *Current Psychiatry Reports,14*, 150–158.

Enterman, J. H., & van Dijk, D. (2011). The curious case of a catatonic patient. *Schizophrenia Bulletin, 37*, 235–237.

Epstein, J. A., Banga, H., & Botvina, G. J. (2007). Which psychosocial factors moderate or directly affect substance use among inner-city adolescents? *Addictive Behaviors, 32*, 700–713.

Epstein, L. H., Leddy, J. J., Temple, J. L., & Faith, M. S. (2007). Food reinforcement and eating: A multilevel analysis. *Psychological Bulletin, 133*, 884–906.

Erdely, S. R. (2004, March). What women sacrifice to be thin. *Redbook, 202*(3), 114–120.

Eronen, M., Angermeyer, M. C., & Schulze, B. (1998). The psychiatric epidemiology of violent behavior. *Social Psychiatry and Psychiatric Epidemiology, 33*(Suppl 1), S13–S23.

Ersche, K. D., Turton, A. J., Pradhan, S., Bullmore, E. T., & Robbins, T. W. (2010). Drug addiction endophenotypes: Impulsive versus sensation-seeking personality traits. *Biological Psychiatry, 68*, 770–773.

Eschleman, K. J., Bowling, N. A., & Alarcon, G. M. (2010). A meta-analytic examination of hardiness. *International Journal of Stress Management, 17*, 277–307.

Eshun, S., & Gurung, R. A. R. (Eds.). (2009). *Introduction to culture and psychopathology, in culture and mental health: Sociocultural influences, theory, and practice*. Oxford, UK: Wiley-Blackwell.

Espiard, M., Lecardeur, L., Abadie, P., Halbecq, I., & Dollfus, S. (2005). Hallucinogen persisting perception disorder after psilocybin consumption: A case study. *European Psychiatry, 20*, 458–460.

Essex, M. J., Klein, M. H., Slattery, M. J., Goldsmith, H., & Kalin, N. H. (2010). Early risk factors and developmental pathways to chronic high inhibition and social anxiety disorder in adolescence. *American Journal of Psychiatry, 167*, 40–46.

Ettinger, U., Schmechtig, A., Toulopoulou, T., Borg, C., Orrells, C., Owens, S., . . . Picchioni, M. (2012). Prefrontal and striatal volumes in monozygotic twins concordant and disconcordant for schizophrenia. *Schizophrenia Bulletin, 38*, 192–203.

Eubig, P. A., Aguiar, A., & Schantz, S. L. (2010). Lead and PCBs as risk factors for attention deficit/hyperactivity disorder. *Environmental Health Perspectives, 118*, 1654–1667.

Evans, C., Mezey, G., & Ehlers, A. (2009). Amnesia for violent crime among young offenders. *Journal of Forensic Psychiatry and Psychology, 20*, 85–106.

Excuse: Insanity—Empirical data and myths. (n.d.). Retrieved from http://law.jrank.org/pages/1136/Excuse-Insanity-Empirical-data-myths.html

Eyberg, S. M., Nelson, M. M., & Boggs, S. R. (2008). Evidence-based psychosocial treatments for children and adolescents with disruptive behavior. *Journal of Clinical Child and Adolescent Psychology, 37*, 215–237.

Fabiano, G. A., Pelham, W. E., Coles, E. K., Gnagy, E. M., Chronis-Tuscano, A., & O'Connor, B. C. (2009). A meta-analysis of behavioral treatments for attention-deficit/hyperactivity disorder. *Clinical Psychology Review, 29*, 129–140.

Facts and Information. (n.d.). Retrieved from http://www.sfwar.org/facts.html

Fagiolini, A. (2008). Medical monitoring in patients with bipolar disorder: A review of data. *Journal of Clinical Psychiatry, 69*, e16.

Fairburn, C. G., Cooper, Z., Bohn, K., O'Connor, M. E., Doll, H. A., & Palmer, R. L. (2007). The severity and status of eating disorders NOS: Implications for DSM-V. *Behaviour Research and Therapy, 45*, 1705–1715.

Fairburn, C. G., Cooper, Z., Doll, H. A., Norman, P., & O'Connor, M. (2000). The natural course of bulimia nervosa and binge eating disorder in young women. *Archives of General Psychiatry, 57*, 659–665.

Fals-Stewart, W., & O'Farrell, T. J. (2003). Behavioral family counseling and naltrexone for male opioid-dependent patients. *Journal of Consulting and Clinical Psychology, 71*, 432–442.

Fama, J. M. (2010). Skin picking disorder fact sheet. Retrieved from http://www.ocfoundation.org/uploadedFiles/MainContent/Find_Help/Skin%20Picking%20Disorder%20Fact%20Sheet.pdf

Fang, C. Y., & Myers, H. F. (2001). The effects of racial stressors and hostility on cardiovascular reactivity in African American and Caucasian men. *Health Psychology, 20*, 64–70.

Fang, X., Brown, D. S., Florence, C. S., & Mercy, J. A. (2012). The economic burden of child maltreatment in the United States and implications for prevention. *Child Abuse and Neglect, 36*, 156–165.

Faraone, S. V., & Mick, E. (2010). Molecular genetics of attention deficit hyperactivity disorder. *Psychiatric Clinics of North America, 33*, 159–180.

Faraone, S. V., & Wilens, T. E. (2007). Effect of stimulant medications for attention-deficit/hyperactivity disorder on later substance use and the potential for stimulant misuse, abuse, and diversion. *Journal of Clinical Psychiatry, 68*(Suppl 11), 15–22.

Farina, B., Mazzotti, E., Pasquini, P., Nijenhuis, E., & Di Giannantonio, M. (2011). Somatoform and psychoform dissociation among students. *Journal of Clinical Psychology, 67*, 665–672.

Farley, F. (1986). World of the type T personality. *Psychology Today, 20*, 45–52.

Farquhar, J. C., & Wasylkiw, L. (2007). Media images of men: Trends and consequences of body conceptualization. *Psychology of Men and Masculinity, 8*, 145–160.

Farrell, H. M. (2011). Dissociative identity disorder: Medicolegal challenges. *Journal of the American Academy of Psychiatry and the Law, 39*, 402–406.

Farrugia, D., & Fetter, H. (2009). Chronic pain: Biological understanding and treatment suggestions for mental health counselors. *Journal of Mental Health Counseling, 31*, 189–200.

Fattore, L., Fadda, P., & Fratta, W. (2009). Sex differences in the self-administration of cannabinoids and other drugs of abuse. *Psychoneuroendocrinology, 34*(Suppl 1), S227–S236.

Fattore, L., & Fratta, W. (2010). How important are sex differences in cannabinoid action? *British Journal of Pharmacology, 160*, 544–548.

Faul, M., Xu, L., Wald, M. M., & Coronado, V. G. (2010). Traumatic brain injury in the United States: Emergency department visits, hospitalizations, and deaths 2002–2006. Atlanta, GA: Centers for Disease Control and Prevention, National Center for Injury. Retrieved from http://www.cdc.gov/traumaticbraininjury/tbi_ed.html

Fava, L., & Morton, J. (2009). Causal modeling of panic disorder theories. *Clinical Psychology Review, 29*, 623–637.

Fava, M., Hwang, I., Rush, A. J., Sampson, N., Walters, E. E., & Kessler, R. C. (2009). The importance of irritability as a symptom of major depressive disorder: Results from the National Comorbidity Survey Replication. *Molecular Psychiatry, 15*, 856–867.

Fedoroff, J. P. (2008). Treatment of paraphilic sexual disorders. In D. Rowland & L. Incrocci (Eds.), *Handbook of sexual and gender identity disorders* (pp. 563–586). Hoboken, NJ: Wiley.

Feinstein, J. S., Adolphs, R., Damasio, A., & Tranel, D. (2011). The human amygdala and the induction and experience of fear. *Current Biology, 21*, 1–5.

Feinstein, J. S., Duff, M. C., & Tranela, D. (2010). Sustained experience of emotion after loss of memory in patients with amnesia. *Proceedings of the National Academy of Sciences, 107*, 7674–7679.

Feldman, H. A., Goldstein, I., Hatzichristou, D. G., Krane, R. J., & McKinlay, J. B. (1994). Impotence and its medical and psychosocial correlates: Results of the Massachusetts Male Aging Study. *Journal of Urology, 151*, 54–61.

Fenichel, O. (1945). *The psychoanalytic theory of neuroses*. New York, NY: Norton.

Fenton, M. C., Keyes, K. M., Martins, S. S., & Hasin, D. S. (2010). The role of a prescription in anxiety medication use, abuse, and dependence. *American Journal of Psychiatry, 167*, 1247–1253.

Ferrier-Auerbach, A. G., & Martens, M. P. (2009). Perceived incompetence moderates the relationship between maladaptive perfectionism and disordered eating. *Eating Disorders, 17*, 333–344.

Ficks, C. A., & Waldman, I. D. (2009). Gene-environment interactions in attention-deficit/hyperactivity disorder. *Current Psychiatry Reports, 11*, 387–392.

Fiedorowicz, J. G., Leon, A. C., Keller, M. B., Solomon, D. A., Rice, J. P., & Coryell, W. H. (2009). Do risk factors for suicidal behavior differ by affective disorder polarity? *Psychological Medicine, 39*, 763–771.

Field, A. P., Ball, J. E., Kawycz, N. J., & Moore, H. (2007). Parent-child relationships and verbal information pathway to fear in children: Two preliminary experiments. *Behavioural and Cognitive Psychotherapy, 35*, 473–486.

Findling, R. L. (2008). Evolution of the treatment of attention-deficit/hyperactivity disorder in children: A review. *Clinical Therapy, 30*, 942–957.

Fink, M., Shorter, E., & Taylor, M. A. (2010). Catatonia is not schizophrenia: Kraepelin's error and the need to recognize catatonia as an independent syndrome in medical nomenclature. *Schizophrenia Bulletin, 36*, 314–320.

First, M. B. (2007). Externalizing disorders of childhood (attention-deficit/hyperactivity disorder, conduct disorder, oppositional defiant disorder, juvenile bipolar disorder). Retrieved from http://www.dsm5.org/Research/Pages/ExternalizingDisorders of-Childhood%28Attention-deficitHyper-activity Disorder,ConductDisorder,Oppositional-Defiant-Disorder,Juven.aspx

Fisher, H. L., Jones, P. B., Fearon, P., Craig, T. K., Dazzan, P., . . . Morgan, C. (2010). The varying impact of type, timing and frequency of exposure to childhood adversity on its association with adult psychotic disorder. *Psychological Medicine, 40*, 1967–1978.

Fitch, W. L. (2007). AAPL practice guidelines for the forensic psychiatric evaluation of competence to stand trial: An American legal perspective. *Journal of American Psychiatric Law, 35*, 509–513.

Flegal, K. M., Carroll, M. D., Kit, B. K., & Ogden, C. L. (2012). Prevalence of obesity and trends in the distribution of body mass index among US adults, 1999–2010. *Journal of the American Medical Association, 307*, 491–497.

Flink, I. K., Nicholas, M. K., Boersma, K., & Linton, S. J. (2009). Reducing the threat value of chronic pain: A preliminary replicated single-case study of interoceptive exposure versus distraction in six individuals with chronic back pain. *Behaviour Research and Therapy, 47*, 721–728.

Flores, E., Tschann, J. M., Dimas, J. M., Pasch, L. A., & de Groat, C. L. (2010). Perceived racial/ethnic discrimination, posttraumatic stress symptoms, and health risk behaviors among Mexican American adolescents. *Journal of Counseling Psychology, 57*, 264–273.

Floyed, R. L., Hirsh, D. A., Greenbaum, V. J., Simon, H. K. (2011) Development of a screening tool for pediatric sexual assault may reduce emergency-department visits. Pediatrics, *128*, 221–226.

Foa, E. B., Dancu, C. V., Hembree, E. A., Jaycox, L. H., Meadows, E. A., & Street, G. P. (1999). A comparison of exposure therapy, stress inoculation training, and their combination in reducing posttraumatic stress disorder in female assault victims. *Journal of Consulting and Clinical Psychology, 67*, 194–200.

Foa, E. B., & Kozak, M. J. (1995). DSM-IV field trial: Obsessive-compulsive disorder. *American Journal of Psychiatry, 152*, 90–96.

Fogel, E. R. (2003). Biofeedback-assisted musculoskeletal therapy. In M. S. Schwartz & F. Andrasik (Eds.), *Biofeedback: A practioner's guide* (3rd ed., pp. 515–544). New York, NY: Guilford Press.

Foley, D. L., & Morley, K. I. (2011). Systematic review of early cardiometabolic outcomes of the first treated episode of psychosis. *Archives of General Psychiatry, 68*, 609–616. doi:10.1001/archgenpsychiatry.2011.2

Fontaine, K. R., Redden, D. T., Wang, C., Westfall, A. O., & Allison, D. B. (2003). Years of life lost due to obesity. *Journal of the American Medical Association, 289*, 187–193.

Fontenelle, L. F., Telles, L. L., Nazar, B. P., de Menezes, G. B., do Nascimento, A. L., Mendlowicz, M. V., & Versiani, M. (2006). A sociodemographic, phenomenological, and long-term follow-up study of patients with body dysmorphic disorder in Brazil. *International Journal of Psychiatry in Medicine, 36*, 243–259.

Foote, B., Smolin, Y., Kaplan, M., Legatt, M. E., & Lipschitz, D. (2006). Prevalence of dissociative disorders in psychiatric outpatients. *American Journal of Psychiatry, 163*, 623–629.

Ford v. Wainwright, 477 U.S. 399 (1986).

Fornaro, M., & Giosue, P. (2010). Current nosology of treatment resistant depression: A controversy resistant to revision. *Clinical Practice and Epidemiology in Mental Health, 6*, 20–24.

Forno, E., & Celedón, J. C. (2009). Asthma and minorities: Socioeconomic status and beyond. *Current Opinion in Allergy and Clinical Immunology, 9*, 154–160.

Fornos, L. B., Mika, V. S., Bayles, B., Serrano, A. C., Jimenez, R. L., & Villarreal, R. (2005). A qualitative study of Mexican American adolescents and depression. *Journal of School Health, 75*, 162–170.

Foroud, T., Edenberg, H. J., & Crabbe, J. C. (2010). Genetic research: Who is at risk for alcoholism? Retrieved from http://pubs.niaaa.nih.gov/publications/arh40/64-75.htm

Forsyth, J. P., Eifert, G. H., & Thompson, R. N. (1996). Systemic alarms in fear conditioning: II. An experimental methodology using 20 percent carbon dioxide inhalation as an unconditioned stimulus. *Behavior Therapy, 27*, 391–415.

Fortier, C. B., Leritz, E. C., Salat, D. H., Venne, J. R., Maksimovskiy, A. L., Williams, V., . . . McGlinchey, R. E. (2011). Reduced cortical thickness in abstinent alcoholics and association with alcoholic behavior alcoholism. *Clinical and Experimental Research, 35*, 2193–2201.

Foster, C. J., Garber, J., & Durlak, J. A. (2008). Current and past maternal depression, maternal interaction behaviors, and children's externalizing and internalizing symptoms. *Journal of Abnormal Child Psychology, 36*, 527–537.

Foster, J. A., & MacQueen, G. (2008). Neurobiological factors linking personality traits and major depression. *La Revue Canadienne de Psychiatrie, 53*, 6–13.

Foster-Scott, L. (2007). Sociological factors affecting childhood obesity. *Journal of Physical Education, Recreation and Dance, 78*, 29–47.

Foti, D. J., Kotov, R., Guey, L. T., & Bromet, E. J. (2010). Cannabis use and the course of schizophrenia: 10 year follow-up after first hospitalization. *American Journal of Psychiatry, 167*, 987–993.

Fournier, J. C., DeRubeis, R. J., Hollon, S. D., Dimidjian, S., Amsterdam, J. D., & Fawcett, J. (2010). Antidepressant drug effects and depression severity: A patient-level meta-analysis. *Journal of the American Medical Association, 303*, 47–53.

Fox, C. L., Towe, S. L., Stephens, R. S., Walker, D. D., & Roffman, R. A. (2011). Motives for cannabis use in high-risk adolescent users. *Psychology of Addictive Behaviors, 25*, 492–500.

Fox, N. A., Henderson, H. A., Marshall, P. J., Nichols, K. E., & Ghera, M. M. (2005). Behavioral inhibition: Linking biology and behavior within a developmental framework. *Annual Review of Psychology, 56*, 235–262.

Fox, N. A., Nichols, K. E., Henderson, H. A., Rubin, K., Schmidt, L., . . . Pine, D. S. (2005). Evidence for a gene-environment interaction in predicting behavioral inhibition in middle childhood. *Psychological Science, 16*, 921–926.

Foxhall, K. (2001, March). How psychopharmacology training is enhancing some psychology practices. *Monitor on Psychology, 32*(3), 50–52.

Frances, A. (2009). A warning sign to the road to DSM-V: Beware of its unintended consequences. *Psychiatric Times, 26*, 1–4.

Franke, B., Neale, B. M., & Faraone, S. V. (2009). Genome-wide association studies in ADHD. *Human Genetics, 126*, 13–50.

Frankenburg, F. R. (2010). Schizophrenia. Retrieved from http://emedicine.medscape.com/article/288259-overview

Frankle, W. G., Lombardo, I., & New, A. S. (2005). Brain serotonin transporter distribution in subjects with impulsive aggressivity: A positron emission study [11C] McN 5652. *American Journal of Psychiatry, 162*, 915–923.

Franklin, J. C., Heilbron, N., Guerry, J. D., Bowker, K. B., & Blumenthal, T. D. (2009). Antisocial and borderline personality disorder symptomalogies are associated with decreased prepulse inhibition: The importance of optimal experimental parameters. *Personality and Individual Differences, 47*, 439–443.

Franklin, M. E., Abramowitz, J. S., Kozak, M. J., Levitt, J. T., & Foa, E. B. (2000). Effectiveness of exposure and ritual prevention for obsessive-compulsive disorder: Randomized compared with nonrandomized samples. *Journal of Consulting and Clinical Psychology, 68*, 594–602.

Franklin, T., Wang, Z., Suh, J. J., Hazan, R., Cruz, J., . . . Childress, A. R. (2011). Effects of varenicline on smoking cue–triggered neural and craving responses. *Archives of General Psychiatry, 68*(5), 516–526. doi:10.1001/archgenpsychiatry.2010.190

Frazier, P., Anders, S., Perera, S., Tomich, P., Tennen, H., Park, C., & Tashiro, T. (2009). Traumatic events among undergraduate students: Prevalence and associated symptoms. *Journal of Counseling Psychology, 56*, 450–460.

Freed, G. L., Clark, S. J., Butchart, A. T., Singer, D. C., & Davis, M. M. (2010). Parental vaccine safety concerns in 2009. *Pediatrics, 125*, 654–659.

Freeland, A., Manchanda, R., Chiu, S., Sharma, V., & Merskey, H. (1993). Four cases of supposed multiple personality disorder: Evidence of unjustified diagnoses. *Canadian Journal of Psychiatry, 23*, 245–247.

Freeman, D., Garety, P. A., Kuipers, E., Fowler, D., Bebbington, P. E., & Dunn, G. (2007). Acting on persecutory delusions: The importance of safety seeking. *Behaviour Research and Therapy, 45*, 89–99.

Freeman, D., McManus, S., Brugha, T., Meltzer, H., Jenkins, R., & Bebbington, P. (2010). Concomitants of paranoia in the general population. *Psychological Medicine, 41*(5), 923–936.

Freeston, M. H., & Ladouceur, R. (1993). Appraisal of cognitive intrusions and response style: Replication and extension. *Behaviour Research and Therapy, 31*, 185–191.

Freiberg, P. (1991). Suicide in family, friends is familiar to too many teens. *APA Monitor, 22*, 36–37.

Freinkel, A., Koopman, C., & Spiegel, D. (1994). Dissociative symptoms in media eyewitnesses of an execution. *American Journal of Psychiatry, 151*, 1335–1339.

French, J., & Friedman, D. (2011). Epilepsy: From newly diagnosed to treatment-resistant disease. *The Lancet Neurology, 10*, 9–11.

Frese, F. J. III, & Myrick, K. J. (2010). On consumer advocacy and the diagnosis of mental disorders. *Professional Psychology: Research and Practice, 41*, 495–501.

Frese, F. J. III, Knight, E. L., & Saks, E. (2009). Recovery from schizophrenia: With views of psychiatrists, psychologists, and others diagnosed with this disorder. *Schizophrenia Bulletin, 35*, 370–380.

Freud, S. (1938). The psychopathology of everyday life. In A. B. Brill (Ed.), *The basic writings of Sigmund Freud*. New York, NY: Modern Library.

Freud, S. (1949). *An outline of psychoanalysis*. New York, NY: Norton.

Freudenmann, R. W., & Lepping, P. (2009). Delusional infestation. *Clinical Microbiology Reviews, 22*, 690–732.

Freudenreich, O., Kontos, N., Tranulis, C., & Cather, C. (2010). Morgellons disease, or antipsychotic-responsive delusional parasitosis, in an HIV patient: Beliefs in the age of the internet. *Psychosomatics, 51*, 453–459.

Frewen, P. A., Evans, E. M., Maraj, N., Dozois, D. J. A., & Partridge, K. (2008). Letting go: Mindfulness and negative automatic thinking. *Cognitive Therapy Research, 32*, 758–774.

Freyer, T., Kloppel, S., Tuscher, O., Kordon, A., Zurowski, B., . . . Voderhotzer, U. (2011). Frontostriatal activation in patients with obsessive-compulsive disorder before and after cognitive behavior therapy. *Psychological Medicine, 41*, 211–216.

Friedman, J. H., & LaFrance, W. C., Jr. (2010). Psychogenic disorders: The need to speak plainly. *Archives of Neurology, 67*, 753–755.

Friedman, M. A., Detweiler-Bedell, J. B., Leventhal, H. E., Horne, R., Keitner, G. I., & Miller, I. W. (2004). Combined psychotherapy and pharmacotherapy for the treatment of major depressive disorder. *Clinical Psychology: Science and Practice, 11*, 47–68.

Friedman, R. A. (2004, October 18). A patient's suicide, a psychiatrist's pain. *New York Times*, p. F6.

Friedman, S. (2007). *Just for boys*. Vancouver, Canada: Salah Books.

Froehlich, T. E., Lanphear, B. P., Auinger, P., Hornung, R., Epstein, J. N., Braun, J., & Kahn, R. S. (2009). Association of tobacco and lead exposures with attention-deficit/hyperactivity disorder. *Pediatrics, 124*, e1054–e1063.

Froehlich, T. E., Lanphear, B. P., Epstein, J. N., Barbaresi, W. J., Katusic, S. K., & Kahn, R. S. (2007). Prevalence and treatment of ADHD in a national sample of U.S. children. *Archives of Pediatrics and Adolescent Medicine, 161*, 857–864.

Frohm, K. D., & Beehler, G. P. (2010). Psychologists as change agents in chronic pain management practice: Cultural competence in the health care system. *Psychological Services, 7*, 115–125.

Frojd, S., Ranta, K., Kaltiala-Heino, R., & Marttunen, M. (2011). Associations of social phobia and general anxiety with alcohol and drug use in a community sample of adolescents. *Alcohol and Alcoholism, 46*(2), 192–199. doi:10.1093/alcalc/agq096

Frye, M. A., Helleman, G., McElroy, S. L., Altshuler, L. L., Black, D. O, . . . Suppes, T. (2009). Correlates of treatment-emergent mania associated with antidepressant treatment in bipolar depression. *American Journal of Psychiatry, 166*, 164–172.

Fukumoto, A., Hashimoto, T., Mori, K., Tsuda, Y., Arisawa, K., & Kagami, S. (2010). Head circumference and body growth in autism spectrum disorders. *Brain Development*. Retrieved from http://www.ncbi.nlm.nih.gov/pubmed/20934821

Fullana, M. A., Mataix-Cols, D., Caspi, A., Harrington, H., Grisham, J. R., . . . Poulton, R. (2009). Obsessions and compulsions in the community: Prevalence, interference, help-seeking, developmental stability, and co-occurring psychiatric conditions. *American Journal of Psychiatry, 166*, 329–336.

Fulton, J. J., Marcus, D. K., & Merkey, T. (2011). Irrational health beliefs and health anxiety. *Journal of Clinical Psychology, 67*, 527–538.

Furer, P., & Walker, J. R. (2005). Treatment of hypochondriasis with exposure. *Journal of Contemporary Psychotherapy, 35*, 251–267.

Furlong, M., McGilloway, S., Bywater, T., Hutchings, J., Smith, S. M., & Donnelly, M. (2012). Behavioural and cognitive-behavioural group-based parenting programmes for early-onset conduct problems in children aged 3 to 12 years. *Cochrane Database of Systematic Reviews* Feb 15;2:CD008225

Furness, P., Glazebrook, C., Tay, J., Abbas, K., & Slaveska-Hollis, K. (2009). Medically unexplained physical symptoms in children: Exploring hospital staff perceptions. *Child Clinical Psychology and Psychiatry, 14*, 575–587.

Furr, S. R., Westefeld, J. S., McConnell, G. N., & Jenkins, J. M. (2001). Suicide and depression among college students: A decade later. *Professional Psychology: Research and Practice, 32*, 97–100.

Fussman, C., Rafferty, A. P., Lyon-Callo, S., Morgenstern, L. B., & Reeves, M. J. (2010). Lack of association between stroke symptom knowledge and intent to call 911: A population-based survey. *Stroke, 41*, 1501–1507.

Gabriel, T. (2010, December 19). Mental health needs seen growing at colleges. *New York Times*. Retrieved from http://www.nytimes.com

Galea, S., Ahern, J., Resnick, H., Kilpatrick, D., Bucuvalas, M., Gold, J., & Vlahov, D. (2002). Psychological sequelae of the September 11 terrorist attacks in New York City. *New England Journal of Medicine, 346*, 982–987.

Gallichan, D. J., & Curle, C. (2008). Fitting square pegs into round holes: The challenge of coping with attention-deficit hyperactivity disorder. *Clinical Child Psychology and Psychiatry, 13*, 343–363.

Gallup. (2009). Religion. Retrieved from http://www.gallup.com/poll/1690/Religion.aspx

Galvez, J. F., Thommi, S., & Ghaemi, S. (2011). Positive aspects of mental illness: A review in bipolar disorder. *Journal of Affective Disorders, 128*, 185–190.

Gammelgaard, L. K., Colding, H., Hartzen, S. H., & Penkowa, M. (2011). Meningococcal disease and future drug targets. *CNS & Neurological Disorders—Drug Targets, 10*, 140–145.

Gangwisch, J. E., Babiss, L. A., Malaspina, D., Turner, J. B., Zammit, G. K., & Posner, K. (2010). Earlier parental set bedtimes as a protective factor against depression and suicidal ideation. *Sleep, 33*, 97–106.

Gao, Y., Raine, A., Venables, P. H., Dawson, M. E., & Mednick, S. A. (2010). Association of poor childhood fear conditioning and adult crime. *American Journal of Psychiatry, 167*, 56–60.

Gara, M. A., Vega, W. A., Arndt, S., Escamilla, M., Fleck, D. E., Lawson, W. B., . . . Strakowski, S. M. (2012). Influence of patient race and ethnicity on clinical assessment in patients with affective disorders. *Archives of General Psychiatry, 69*, 593–600.

Garb, H. N., Wood, J. M., Lilienfeld, S. O., & Nezworski, T. (2005). Roots of the Rorschach controversy. *Clinical Psychology Review, 25*, 97–118.

Garber, J., Clarke, G., Weersing, V. R., Beardslee, W. R., Brent, D., Gladstone, T., . . . Iyengar, S. (2009). Prevention of depression in at-risk adolescents: A randomized controlled trial. *Journal of the American Medical Association, 301*, 2215–2224.

Garber, J., & Cole, D. A. (2010). Intergenerational transmission of depression: A launch and grow model of change across adolescence. *Developmental Psychopathology, 22*, 819–830.

Gardiner, K., Herault, Y., Lott, I. T., Antonarakis, S. E., Reeves, R. H., & Dierssen, M. (2010). Down syndrome: From understanding the neurobiology to therapy. *Journal of Neuroscience, 30*, 14943–14945.

Gardner, A. (2011, March 1). Is Charlie Sheen bipolar? *Health*. Retrieved from http://www.health.com

Garety, P. A., Bebbington, P., Fowler, D., Freeman, D., & Kuipers, E. (2007). Implications for neurobiological research of cognitive models of psychosis: A theoretical paper. *Psychological Medicine, 37*, 1377–1391.

Garrett, M., & Silva, R. (2003). Auditory hallucinations, source monitoring, and the belief that "voices" are real. *Schizophrenia Bulletin, 29*, 445–451.

Garrison, G. D., & Dugan, S. E. (2009). Varenicline: A first-line treatment option for smoking cessation. *Clinical Therapeutics, 31*, 463–491.

Gavett, B. E., Stern, R. A., Cantu, R. C., Nowinski, C. J., & McKee, A. C. (2010). Mild traumatic brain injury: A risk factor for neurodegeneration. *Alzheimer's Research & Therapy, 2*, 18. Retrieved from http://alzres.com/content/2/3/18

Gatz, M. (2007). Genetics, dementia, and the elderly. *Current Directions in Psychological Science, 16*, 123–127.

Gatz, M., Reynolds, C. A., Fratiglioni, L., Johansson, B., Mortimer, J. A., . . . Pederson, N. L. (2006). The role of genes and environments for explaining Alzheimer's disease. *Archives of General Psychiatry, 63*, 168–174.

Gawrysiak, M., Nicholas, C., & Hopko, D. R. (2009). Behavioral activation for moderately depressed university students: Randomized controlled trial. *Journal of Counseling Psychology, 56*, 468–475.

Gee, G. C., Delva, J., & Takeuchi, D. T. (2007). Relationships between self-reported unfair treatment and prescription medication use, illicit drug use, and alcohol dependence among Filipino Americans. *American Journal of Public Health, 97*, 933–940.

Geier, D. A., Kern, J. K., & Geier, M. R. (2009). A prospective blinded evaluation of urinary porphyrins versus the clinical severity of autism spectrum disorders. *Journal of Toxicology and Environmental Health, 72*, 1585–1591.

Gelernter, J., & Kranzler, H. R. (2009). Genetics of alcohol dependence. *Human Genetics, 126*, 91–99.

Geller, D. A. (2006). Obsessive-compulsive and spectrum disorders in children and adolescents. *Psychiatric Clinics of North America, 29*, 353–370.

Geller, J. L. (2006). A history of private psychiatric hospitals in the USA: From start to finish. *Psychiatric Quarterly, 77*, 1–41.

Gelson, C. J., & Woodhouse, S. (2003). Toward a positive psychotherapy: Focus on human strength. In W. B. Walsh (Ed.), *Counseling psychology and optimal human functioning* (pp. 171–197). Mahwah, NJ: Lawrence Erlbaum Associates.

Geschwind, N., Nicolson, N. A., Peeters, F., Van Os, J., & Wichers, M. (2011). Early improvement in positive rather than negative emotion predicts remission from depression after pharmacotherapy. *European Neuropsychopharmacology, 21*, 241–247.

Geschwind, N., Peeters, F., Van Os, J., Drukker, M., & Wichers, M. (2011). Mindfulness training increases momentary positive emotions and reward experience in adults vulnerable to depression. A randomized controlled trial. *Journal of Consulting and Clinical Practice, 79*, 618–628.

Ghaemi, S. N. (2010a). Levels of evidence. *Psychiatric Times, 27*, 1–4.

Ghaemi, S. N. (2010b). *The rise and fall of the biopsychosocial model: Reconciling art and science in psychiatry*. Baltimore, MD: Johns Hopkins University Press.

Gharaibeh, N. (2009). Dissociative identity disorder: Time to remove it from DSM-V? *Current Psychiatry, 8*, 30–37.

Ghaziuddin, M. (2010). Should the DSM-V drop Asperger syndrome? *Journal of Autism and Developmental Disorders, 40*, 1146–1148.

Ghisi, M., Chiri, L. R., Marchetti, I., Sanavio, E., & Sica, C. (2010). In search of specificity: "Not just right experiences" and obsessive-compulsive symptoms in non-clinical and clinical Italian individuals. *Journal of Anxiety Disorders, 24*, 879–886.

Gibbons, F., Etcheverry, P. E., Stock, M. L., Gerrard, M., Weng, C., . . . O'Hara, R. E. (2010). Exploring the link between racial discrimination and substance use: What mediates? What buffers? *Journal of Personality and Social Psychology, 99*, 785–801.

Giesbrecht, T., Lynn, S. J., Lilienfeld, S. O., & Merckelbach, H. (2008). Cognitive processes in dissociation: An analysis of core theoretical assumptions. *Psychological Bulletin, 134*, 617–647.

Gijs, L. (2008). Paraphilia and paraphilia-related disorders: An introduction. In D. Rowland & L. Incrocci (Eds.), *Handbook of sexual and gender identity disorders* (pp. 491–528). Hoboken, NJ: Wiley.

Gilbert, B. D., & Christopher, M. S. (2010). Mindfulness-based attention as a moderator of the relationship between depressive affect and negative cognitions. *Cognitive Therapy and Research, 34*, 514–521.

Gilbert, S. C. (2003). Eating disorders in women of color. *Clinical Psychology: Science and Practice, 10*, 1–16.

Gilleen, J., Greenwood, K., & David, A. S. (2011). Domains of awareness in schizophrenia. *Schizophrenia Bulletin, 37*, 61–72.

Gillespie, C. F., & Nemeroff, C. B. (2007). Corticotropin-releasing factor and the psychobiology of early-life stress. *Current Directions in Psychological Science, 16*, 85–89.

Gillespie, C. F., Phifer, J., Bradley, B., & Ressler, K. J. (2009). Risk and resilience: Genetic and environmental influences on development of the stress response. *Depression and Anxiety, 26*, 984–992.

Gillham, J. E., Chaplin, T. M., Reivich, K. J., & Hamilton, J. (2008). Preventing depression in early adolescent girls: The Penn Resiliency and Girls in Transition Programs. In C. LeCroy & J. Mann (Eds.), *Handbook of prevention and intervention programs for adolescent girls* (pp. 123–161). Hoboken, NJ: Wiley.

Gillham, J. E., Hamilton, J., Freres, D. R., Patton, K., & Gallup, R. (2006). Preventing depression among early adolescents in the primary care setting: A randomized controlled study of the Penn Resiliency Program. *Journal of Abnormal Child Psychology, 34*, 203–219.

Gillham, J. E., Reivich, K. J., Freres, D. R., Lascher, M., Litzinger, S., Shatté, A., & Seligman, M. E. P. (2006). School-based prevention of depression and anxiety symptoms in early adolescence: A pilot of a parent intervention component. *School Psychology Quarterly, 21*, 323–348.

Gilson, A. M., & Kreis, P. G. (2009). The burden of the nonmedical use of prescription opioid analgesics. *Pain Medication, Suppl 2*, S89–100.

Ginzburg, K., & Solomon, Z. (2010). Trajectories of stress reactions and somatization symptoms among war veterans: A 20-year longitudinal study. *Psychological Medicine, 41*, 353–362.

Girard, T. D., Pandharipande, P. P., & Ely, E. W. (2008). Delirium in the intensive care unit. *Critical Care, 12*(Suppl 3), S3.

Girot, M. (2009). Smoking and stroke. *La Presse Medicale, 38*, 1120–1125.

Glasner-Edwards, S., Mooney, L. J., Marinelli-Casey, P., Hillhouse, M., Ang, A., & Rawson, R. A. (2010). Psychopathology in methamphetamine-dependent adults 3 years after treatment. *Drug and Alcohol Review, 29*, 12–20.

Gleason, M. M., Fox, N. A., Drury, S., Smyke, A., Egger, H. L., Nelson, C. A., . . . Zeanah, C. H. (2011). Validity of evidence-derived criteria for reactive attachment disorder: Indiscriminately social/disinhibited and emotionally withdrawn/inhibited types. *Journal of the American Academy of Child & Adolescent Psychiatry, 50*, 216–231.

Gleaves, D. H. (1996). The sociocognitive model of dissociative identity disorder: A reexamination of the evidence. *Psychological Bulletin, 120*, 42–59.

Glei, D. A., Landau, D. A., Goldman, N., Chuang, Y., Rodríguez, G., & Weinstein, M. (2005). Participating in social activities helps to preserve cognitive function: An analysis of a longitudinal, population-based study of the elderly. *International Journal of Epidemiology, 34*, 864–871.

Glenn, A. L., Raine, A., Venables, P. H., & Mednick, S. A. (2009). Early temperamental and psychophysiological precursors of adult psychopathic personality. *Personality Disorders: Theory, Research, and Treatment, S*, 46–60.

Glozier, N., Martiniuk, A., Patton, G., Ivers, R., Li, Q., . . . Stevenson, M. (2010). Short sleep duration in prevalent and persistent psychological distress in young adults: The DRIVE study. *Sleep, 33*, 1139–1145.

Glynn, S. M., Cohen, A. N., Dixon, L. B., & Niv, N. (2006). The potential impact of the recovery movement on family interventions for schizophrenia: Opportunities and obstacles. *Schizophrenia Bulletin, 32*, 451–463.

Godfrin, K. A., & van Heeringen, C. (2010). The effects of mindfulness-based cognitive therapy on recurrence of depressive episodes, mental health and quality of life: A randomized controlled study. *Behaviour Research and Therapy, 48*, 738–746.

Godlee, F., Smith, J., & Marcovitch, H. (2011). Wakefield's article linking MMR vaccine and autism was fraudulent. *British Medical Journal, 342*, c7452. doi:10.1136/bmj.c7452

Godoy, A., & Haynes, S. N. (2011). Clinical case formulation. *European Journal of Psychological Assessment, 27*, 1–3.

Goes, F. S., Zandi, P. P., Miao, K., McMahon, F. J., Steele, J., . . . Potash, J. B. (2007). Mood-incongruent psychotic features in bipolar disorder: Familial aggregation and suggestive linkage to 2p11-q14 and 13q21-33. *American Journal of Psychiatry, 164*, 236–247.

Goff, D. C. (1993). Reply to Dr. Armstrong. *Journal of Nervous and Mental Disease, 181*, 604–605.

Goff, D. C., & Simms, C. A. (1993). Has multiple personality disorder remained consistent over time? *Journal of Nervous and Mental Disease, 181*, 595–600.

Gogtag, N. (2008). Cortical brain development in schizophrenia: Insights from neuroimaging studies in childhood-onset schizophrenia. *Schizophrenia Bulletin, 34*, 30–36.

Golafshani, N. (2003). Understanding reliability and validity in qualitative research. *The Qualitative Report, 8*, 597–607.

Goldapple, K., Segal, Z., Garson, C., Lau, M., Bieling, P., Kennedy, S., & Mayberg, H. (2004). Modulation of cortical-limbic pathways in major depression: Treatment-specific effects of cognitive behavior therapy. *Archives of General Psychiatry, 61*, 34–41.

Goldberg, C. (2009). The mental status exam (MSE). Retrieved from http://meded.ucsd.edu/clinicalmed/mental.htm

Goldberg, D. (2006). The aetiology of depression. *Psychological Medicine, 36*, 1341–1347.

Goldberg, D. P., Krueger, R. F., Andrews, G., & Hobbs, M. J. (2009). Emotional disorders: Cluster 4 of the proposed meta-structure for DSM-V and ICD-11. *Psychological Medicine, 39*, 2043–2059.

Goldberg, J. F. (2007). What psychotherapists should know about pharmacotherapies for bipolar disorder. *Journal of Clinical Psychology: In Session, 63*, 475–490.

Goldberg, J. F., Perlis, R. H., Bowden, C. L., Thase, M. E., Miklowitz, D. J., . . . Sachs, G. S. (2009). Manic symptoms during depressive episodes in 1,380 patients with bipolar disorder: Findings from the STEP–BD. *American Journal of Psychiatry, 166*, 173–181.

Golden, R. N., Gaynes, B. N., Ekstrom, R. D., Hamer, R. M., Jacobsen, F. M., . . . Nemeroff, C. B. (2005). The efficacy of light therapy in the treatment of mood disorders: A review and meta-analysis of the evidence. *American Journal of Psychiatry, 162*, 656–662.

Goldfein, J. A., Devlin, M. J., & Spitzer, R. L. (2000). Cognitive behavioral therapy for the treatment of binge eating disorder: What constitutes success? *American Journal of Psychiatry, 157*, 1051–1056.

Goldman, S. M., Quinlan, P. J., Ross, G. W., Marras, C., Meng, C., . . . Tanner, C. M. (2012). Solvent exposures and Parkinson disease risk in twins. *Annals of Neurology, 71*, 776–784.

Goldmann, G. R., Siderowf, A., & Hurtig, H. I. (2008). Cognitive impairment in Parkinson's disease and dementia with lewy bodies: A spectrum of disease. *Neuro-Signals, 16*, 24–34.

Goldstein, B. I. (2012). Recent progress in understanding pediatric bipolar disorder. *Archives of Pediatrics and Adolescent Medicine, 166*, 362–371.

Goldstein, G., & Beers, S. (2004). *Comprehensive handbook of psychological assessment, intellectual and neuropsychological assessment* (Vol. 1). New York, NY: John Wiley.

Goldston, D. B., Molock, S. D., Whitbeck, L. B., Murakami, J. L., Zayas, L. H., & Hall, G. C. N. (2008). Cultural considerations in adolescent suicide prevention and psychosocial treatment. *American Psychologist, 63*, 14–31.

Gonçalves, D. C., & Byrne, G. J. (2012). Interventions for generalized anxiety disorder in older adults: Systematic review and meta-analysis. *Journal of Anxiety Disorders, 26*, 1–11.

Gonsiorek, J. C., Richards, P. S., Pargament, K. I., & McMinn, M. R. (2009). Ethical challenges and opportunities at the edge: Incorporating spirituality and religion into psychotherapy. *Professional Psychology: Research and Practice, 40*, 385–395.

Goodman, M., Triebwasser, J., Shah, S., & New, A. S. (2007). Neuroimaging in personality disorders: Current concepts, findings, and implications. *Psychiatric Annals, 37*, 100–104, 107–108.

Goodwin, G. M., Anderson, I., Arango, C., Bowden, C. L., Henry, C., . . . Wittchen, H. U. (2008). ECNP consensus meeting: Bipolar depression. *European Neuropsychopharmacology, 18*, 535–549.

Gooley, J. J., Rajaratnam, S. M., Brainard, G. C., Kronauer, R. E., Czeisler, C. A., & Lockley, S. W. (2010). Spectral responses of the human circadian system depend on the irradiance and duration of exposure to light. *Science Translational Medicine, 2*, 31–33.

Gooren, L. (2008). Androgens and endocrine function in aging men: Effects on sexual and general health. In D. Rowland & L. Incrocci (Eds.), *Handbook of sexual and gender identity disorders* (pp. 122–153). Hoboken, NJ: Wiley.

Gorman, J. M., Kent, J. M., Sullivan, G. M., & Coplan, J. D. (2000). Neuroanatomical hypothesis of panic disorder, revised. *American Journal of Psychiatry, 157*, 493–505.

Gotlib, I. H., & Joormann, J. (2010). Cognition and depression: Current status and future directions. *Annual Review of Clinical Psychology, 6*, 285–312.

Gotlib, I. H., Joormann, J., Minor, K. L., & Hallmayer, J. (2008). HPA axis reactivity: A mechanism underlying the associations among 5-HTTLPR, stress, and depression. *Biological Psychiatry, 63*, 847–851.

Gottesman, I. I. (1978). Schizophrenia and genetics: Where are we? Are you sure? In L. C. Wynne, R. L. Cromwell, & S. Matthysse (Eds.), *The nature of schizophrenia: New approaches to research and treatment* (pp. 59–69). New York, NY: Wiley.

Gottesman, I. I. (1991). *Schizophrenia genesis*. New York, NY: Freeman.

Gottesman, I. I., & Goldsmith, H. H. (1994). Developmental psychopathology of antisocial behavior: Inserting genes into its ontogenesis and epigenesis. In C. A. Nelson (Ed.), *Threats to optimal development*. Hillside, NJ: Lawrence Erlbaum Associates.

Gottesman, I. I., & Gould, T. D. (2003). The endophenotype concept in psychiatry: Etymology and strategic intentions. *American Journal of Psychiatry, 160*, 636–645.

Gould, M. S. (2007). Suicide contagion (clusters). Retrieved from http://suicideandmentalhealthassociationinternational.org/suiconclus.html

Goyal, D., Gay, C., & Lee, K. (2009). Fragmented maternal sleep is more strongly correlated with depressive symptoms than infant temperament at three months postpartum. *Archives of Women's Mental Health, 12*, 229–237.

Grabe, H. J., Schwahn, C., Appel, K., Mahler, J., Schulz, A., . . . Freyberger, H. J. (2010). Childhood maltreatment, the corticotropin-releasing hormone receptor gene and adult depression in the general population. *American Journal of Medical Genetics Part B: Neuropsychiatric Genetics, 153B*, 1483–1493.

Grabe, S., & Hyde, J. S. (2006). Ethnicity and body dissatisfaction among women in the United States: A meta-analysis. *Psychological Bulletin, 132*, 622–640.

Grabe, S., Ward, L. M., & Hyde, J. S. (2008). The role of the media in body image concerns among women: A meta-analysis of experimental and correlational studies. *Psychological Bulletin, 134*, 460–476.

Graham, C. A., Sanders, S. A., Milhausen, R. R., & McBride, K. R. (2004). Turning on and turning off: A focus group study of the factors that affect women's sexual arousal. *Archives of Sexual Behavior, 33*, 527–538.

Graham, J. R. (2005). *MMPI-2: Assessing personality and psychopathology* (4th ed.). New York, NY: Oxford University Press.

Granderson, L. Z. (2010, December 3). Sports, gender, questions and hate. Retrieved from http://sports.espn.go.com/espn/commentary/news/story?id=5879536

Granello, D. H. (2010). The process of suicide risk assessment: Twelve core principles. *Journal of Counseling and Development, 88*, 363–370.

Granello, D. H., & Granello, P. F. (2007). *Suicide: An essential guide for helping professionals and educators*. Boston, MA: Allyn & Bacon.

Grann, M., & Langstrom, N. (2007). Actuarial risk assessment: To weigh or not to weigh? *Criminal Justice and Behavior, 34*, 22–36.

Grant, B. F., Stinson, F. S., Dawson, D. A., Chou, S. P., Dufour, M. C., . . . Kaplan, K. (2004). Prevalence and co-occurrence of substance use disorders and independent mood and anxiety disorders. *Archives of General Psychiatry, 61*, 807–816.

Grant, I., & Adams, K. M. (2009). *Neuropsychological assessment of neuropsychiatric and neuromedical disorders* (3rd ed.). New York, NY: Oxford University Press.

Grant, I., Sacktor, H., & McArthur, J. (2005). HIV neurocognitive disorders. In H. E. Gendelman, I. Grant, I. Everall, S. A. Lipton, & S. Swindells (Eds.), *The neurology of AIDS* (pp. 357–373). London, UK: Oxford University Press.

Grant, J. E., Kim, S. W., & Crow, S. J. (2001). Prevalence and clinical features of body dysmorphic disorder in adolescent and adult psychiatric inpatients. *Journal of Clinical Psychiatry, 62*, 517–522.

Grant, V. V., Stewart, S. H., O'Connor, R. M., Blackwell, E., & Conrod, P. J. (2007). Psychometric evaluation of the five-factor modified drinking motives questionnaire—revised in undergraduates. *Addictive Behaviors, 32*(11), 2611–2632.

Gratz, K. L., Rosenthal, M. Z., Tull, M. T., Lejuez, C. W., & Gunderson, J. G. (2009). An experimental investigation of emotion dysregulation in borderline personality disorder. *Personality Disorders: Theory, Research, and Treatment, S*, 18–26.

Gray, B. (2008). Hidden demons: A personal account of hearing voices and the alternative of the hearing voices movement. *Schizophrenia Bulletin, 34*, 1006–1007.

Gray, H. M., & Tickle-Degnen, L. (2010). A meta-analysis of performance on emotion recognition tasks in Parkinson's disease. *Neuropsychology, 24*, 176–191.

Graziottin, A., & Serafini, A. (2009). Depression and the menopause: Why antidepressants are not enough? *Menopause International, 15*, 76–81.

Green, C. R., Mihic, A. M., Nikkel, S. M., Stade, B. C., Rasmussen, C., Munoz, D. P., & Reynolds, J. N. (2009). Executive function deficits in children with fetal alcohol spectrum disorders (FASD) measured using the Cambridge Neuropsychological Tests Automated Battery. *Journal of Child Psychology and Psychiatry, 50*, 688–697.

Green, J. G., McLaughlin, K. A., Berglund, P. A., Gruber, M. J., Sampson, N. A., Zaslavsky, A. M., & Kessler, R. C. (2010). Childhood adversities and adult psychiatric disorders in the National Comorbidity Survey Replication I: Associations with first onset of DSM-IV disorders. *Archives of General Psychiatry, 67*, 113–123.

Green, M. F. (2007). Cognition, drug treatment, and functional outcome in schizophrenia: A tale of two transitions. *American Journal of Psychiatry, 164*, 992–994.

Greenberg, B. D., Altemus, M., & Murphy, D. L. (1997). The role of neurotransmitters and neurohormones in obsessive-compulsive disorder. *International Review of Psychiatry, 9*, 31–44.

Greenberg, P. E., Burnham, H. G., Lowe, S. W., & Corey-Lisle, P. K. (2003). The economic burden of depression in the United States: How did it change from 1990 to 2000? *Journal of Clinical Psychiatry, 64*, 1465–1475.

Greenberg, W. M. (2010). Obsessive-compulsive disorder. Retrieved from http://emedicine.medscape.com/article/287681-print

Greenberger, E., Chen, C., Tally, S. R., & Dong, Q. (2000). Family, peer, and individual correlates of depressive symptomatology among U.S. and Chinese adolescents. *Journal of Consulting and Clinical Psychology, 68*, 209–219.

Greene, R. L. (1991). *The MMPI-2/MMPI: An interpretive manual*. Boston, MA: Allyn & Bacon.

Greenwood, P. M., & Parasuraman, R. (2010). Neuronal and cognitive plasticity: A neurocognitive framework for ameliorating cognitive aging. *Frontiers in Aging Neuroscience, 2*, 150. Retrieved from http://www.frontiersin.org/aging_neuroscience/10.3389/fnagi.2010.00150/full

Greer, T. L., & Trivedi, M. H. (2009). Exercise in the treatment of depression. *Current Psychiatry Reports, 11*, 466–472.

Gregory, R. J., & Jindal, S. (2006). Factitious disorder on an inpatient psychiatry ward. *American Journal of Orthopsychiatry, 76*, 31–36.

Grekin, E. R., & Sher, K. J. (2006). Alcohol dependence symptoms among college freshmen: Prevalence, stability and person-environment interactions. *Experimental and Clinical Psychopharmacology, 14*, 329–338.

Greydanus, D. E., Nazeer, A., & Patel, D. R. (2009). Psychopharmacology of ADHD in pediatrics: Current advances and issues. *Journal of Neuropsychiatric Disease and Treatment, 5*, 171–181.

Grigoriadis, S., & Seeman, M. V. (2002). The role of estrogen in schizophrenia: Implications for schizophrenia practice guidelines for women. *Canadian Journal of Psychiatry, 47*, 437–442.

Grilo, C. M., Masheb, R. M., & White, M. A. (2010). Significance of overvaluation of shape/weight in binge eating disorder: Comparative study with overweight and bulimia nervosa. *Obesity, 18*(3), 499–504.

Grilo, C. M., Shea, M. T., Sanislow, C. A., Skodol, A. E., Gunderson, J. G., Sout, R. L., . . . McGlashan, T. H. (2004). Two-year stability and change of schizotypal, borderline, avoidant and obsessive-compulsive personality disorders. *Journal of Consulting and Clinical Psychology, 72*, 767–775.

Grilo, C. M., & White, M. A. (2011). A controlled evaluation of the distress criterion for binge eating disorder. *Journal of Consulting and Clinical Psychology, 79*(4), 509–514.

Grimshaw, G. M., & Stanton, A. (2006). Tobacco cessation interventions for young people. *Cochrane Database of Systematic Reviews, 18*(4), CD003289.

Grohol, J. (2011, June 27). Marsha Linehan acknowledges her own struggle with bornderline personality disorder [Web log post]. Retrieved from http://psychcentral.com/blog/archives/2011/06/27/marsha-linehan-acknowledges-her-own-struggle-with-borderline-personality-disorder/

Groopman, L. C., & Cooper, A. M. (2001). Narcissistic personality disorder. In G. O. Gabbard (Ed.), *Treatment of psychiatric disorders* (pp. 2309–2326). Washington, DC: American Psychiatric Publishing.

Groth, A. N., Burgess, A. W., & Holstrom, L. (1977). Rape: Power, anger, and sexuality. *American Journal of Psychiatry, 134*, 1239–1243.

Groth-Marnat, G. (2009). *Handbook of psychological assessment* (5th ed.). New York, NY: John Wiley.

Gu, Q., Dillon, C. F., & Burt, V. L. (2010). Prescription drug use continues to increase: U.S. prescription drug data for 2007–2008. NCHS Data Brief 42. Retrieved from http://www.cdc.gov/nchs/data/databriefs/db42.htm

Guastella, A. J., Einfeld, S. L., Gray, K. M., Rinehart, N. J., Tonge, B. J., Lambert, T. J., & Hickie, I. B. (2010). Intranasal oxytocin improves emotion recognition for youth with autism spectrum disorders. *Biological Psychiatry, 67*, 692–694.

Gudjonsson, G. H., Sigurdsson, J. F., Sigfusdottir, I. D., and Young, S. (2012). An epidemiological study of ADHD symptoms among young persons and the relationship with cigarette smoking, alcohol consumption and illicit drug use. *Journal of Child Psychology and Psychiatry, 53*, 304–312.

Guerry, J. D., & Hastings, P. D. (2011). In search of HPA axis dysregulation in child and adolescent depression. *Clinical Child and Family Psychology Review, 14*, 135–160.

Gujar, N., Yoo, S. S., Hu, P., & Walker, M. P. (2011). Sleep deprivation amplifies reactivity of brain reward networks, biasing the appraisal of positive emotional experiences. *Journal of Neuroscience, 31*, 4466–4474.

Gunderson, J. G. (2010). Revising the borderline diagnosis for DSM-V: An alternative proposal. *Journal of Personality Disorders, 24*, 694–708.

Gunderson, J. G., & Links, P. S. (2001). Borderline personality disorder. In G. O. Gabbard (Ed.), *Treatment of psychiatric disorders* (pp. 2273–2291). Washington, DC: American Psychiatric Publishing.

Gupta, S., & Bonanno, G. A. (2010). Trait self-enhancement as a buffer against potentially traumatic events: A prospective study. *Psychological Trauma: Theory, Research, Practice, and Policy, 2*, 83–92.

Gur, R. E., Calkins, M. E., Gur, R. C., Horan, W. P., Nuechterlein, K. H., Seidman, L. J., & Stone, W. S. (2007). The Consortium on the Genetics of Schizophrenia: Neurocognitive endophenotypes. *Schizophrenia Bulletin, 33*, 49–55.

Gur, R. E., Kohler, C. G., Ragland, J. D., Siegel, S. J., Lesko, K., Bilker, W. B., & Gur, R. C. (2006). Flat affect in schizophrenia: Relation to emotion processing and neurocognitive measures. *Schizophrenia Bulletin, 32*, 279–287.

Gutierrez, P. M., & Silk, K. R. (1998). Prescription privileges for psychologists: A review of the psychological literature. *Professional Psychology: Research and Practice, 29*, 213–222.

Guyll, M., Cutrona, C., Burzette, R., & Russell, D. (2010). Hostility, relationship quality, and health among African American couples. *Journal of Consulting and Clinical Psychology, 78*, 646–654.

Haaga, D. A., McCrady, B., & Lebow, J. (2006). Integrative principles for treating substance use disorders. *Journal of Clinical Psychology, 62*, 675–684.

Hackett, G. I. (2008). Disorders of male sexual desire. In D. Rowland & L. Incrocci (Eds.), *Handbook of sexual and gender identity disorders* (pp. 5–31). Hoboken, NJ: Wiley.

Haeffel, G. J. (2010). When self-help is no help: Traditional cognitive skills training does not prevent depressive symptoms in people who ruminate. *Behavior Research and Therapy, 48*, 152–157.

Haenen, M. A., de Jong, P. J., Schmidt, A. J. M., Stevens, S., & Visser, L. (2000). Hypochondriacs' estimation of negative outcomes: Domain-specificity and responsiveness to reassuring and alarming information. *Behaviour Research and Therapy, 38*, 819–833.

Hagen, M. A. (2003). Faith in the model and resistance to research. *Clinical Psychology: Science and Practice, 10*, 172–178.

Haggard-Grann, U. (2007). Assessing violence risk: A review and clinical recommendations. *Journal of Counseling and Development, 85*, 294–301.

Haley, J. (1963). *Strategies of psychotherapy*. New York, NY: Grune & Stratton.

Haley, J. (1987). *Problem-solving therapy* (2nd ed.). New York, NY: Jossey-Bass.

Haley, J. (2003, October 31). Defendant's wife testifies about his multiple personas. *Bellingham Herald*, p. B4.

Hall, G. C., Windover, A. K., & Maramba, G. C. (1998). Sexual aggression among Asian Americans: Risk and protective factors. *Cultural Diversity and Mental Health, 4*, 305–318.

Hall, J. R., & Benning, S. D. (2006). The "successful psychopath": Adaptive and subclinical manifestations of psychopathy in the general population. In C. J. Patrick (Ed.), *Handbook of psychopathy* (pp. 456–478). New York, NY: Guilford Press.

Hall, M. T., Edwards, J. D., & Howard, M. O. (2010). Accidental deaths due to inhalant misuse in North Carolina: 2000–2008. *Substance Use and Misuse, 45*, 1330–1339.

Hallak, J. E. C., Crippa, J. A. S., & Zuardi, A. W. (2000). Treatment of koro with citalopram. *Journal of Clinical Psychology, 61*, 951–952.

Halmi, K. A., Sunday, S. R., Strober, M., Kaplan, A., Woodside, D. B., . . . Kaye, W. H. (2000). Perfectionism in anorexia nervosa: Variation by clinical subtype, obsessionality, and pathological eating disorder. *American Journal of Psychiatry, 157*, 1799–1805.

Halstead, M. E., & Walter, K. D. (2010). Clinical report—Sport-related concussion in children and adolescents. *Pediatrics, 126*, 597–615.

Halvorsen, I., & Heyerdahl, S. (2007). Treatment perception in adolescent onset anorexia nervosa: Retrospective views of patients and parents. *International Journal of Eating Disorders, 40*, 629–639.

Hamer, M., O'Donnell, K., Lahiri, A., & Steptoe, A. (2010). Salivary cortisol responses to mental stress are associated with coronary artery calcification in healthy men and women. *European Heart Journal, 31*, 424–429.

Hamilton, B. E., Miniño, A. M., Martin, J. A., Kochanek, K. D., Strobino, D. M., & Guyer, B. (2007). Annual summary of vital statistics: 2005. *Pediatrics, 119*, 345–360.

Hammad, T. A., Laughren, T., & Racoosin, J. (2006). Suicidality in pediatric patients treated with antidepressant drugs. *Archives of General Psychiatry, 63*, 332–339.

Hammen, C. (2006). Stress generation in depression: Reflections on origins, research, and future directions. *Journal of Clinical Psychology, 62*, 1065–1082.

Handelsman, M., Walfish, S., & Hess, A. K. (Eds.). (2001). *Learning to become ethical: Succeeding in graduate school: The career guide for psychology students*. Mahwah, NJ: Erlbaum.

Hanewinkel, R., Isensee, B., Sargent, J. D., & Morgenstern, M. (2011). Cigarette advertising and teen smoking initiation. *Pediatrics, 127*(2), e271–e278. doi:10.1542/peds.2010-2934

Hanisch, C., Freund-Braier, I., Hautmann, C., Jänen, N., Plück, J., Brix, G., . . . Döpfner, M. (2010). Detecting effects of the indicated prevention Programme for Externalizing Problem behaviour (PEP) on child symptoms, parenting, and parental quality of life in a randomized controlled trial. *Behavioral and Cognitive Psychotherapy, 38*, 95–112.

Hankey, G. J. (2011). Stroke: Fresh insights into causes, prevention, and treatment. *The Lancet Neurology, 10*, 2–3.

Hankin, B. L. (2008). Rumination and depression in adolescence: Investigating symptom specificity in a multiwave prospective study. *Journal of Clinical Child and Adolescent Psychology, 37*, 701–713.

Hankin, B. L. (2009). Development of sex differences in depressive and co-occurring anxious symptoms during adolescence: Descriptive trajectories and potential explanations in a multiwave prospective study. *Journal of Clinical Child and Adolescent Psychology, 38*, 460–472.

Hansen, L., Kingdon, D., & Turkington, D. (2006). The ABCs of cognitive-behavioral therapy for schizophrenia. *Psychiatric Times, 23*, 49–53.

Hare, R. D. (1993). *Without conscience: The disturbing world of the psychopaths among us*. New York, NY: Pocket Books.

Hare, R. D., & Neumann, C. S. (2009). Psychopathy: Assessment and forensic implications. *Canadian Journal of Psychiatry, 54*, 791–802.

Hargreaves, D. A., & Tiggemann, M. (2009). Muscular ideal media images and men's body image: Social comparison processing and individual vulnerability. *Psychology of Men and Masculinity, 10*, 109–119.

Harned, M. S., Chapman, A. L., Dexter-Mazza, E. T., Murray, A., Comtois, K. A., & Linehan, M. M. (2009). Treating co-occurring Axis I disorders in recurrently suicidal women with borderline personality disorder: A 2-year randomized trial of dialectical behavior therapy vs. community treatment by experts. *Personality Disorders: Theory, Research, and Treatment, S*, 35–45.

Harold, G. T., Rice, F., Hay, D. F., Boivin, J., van den Bree, M., & Thapar, A. (2010). Familial transmission of depression and antisocial behavior symptoms: Disentangling the contribution of inherited and environmental factors and testing the mediating role of parenting. *Psychological Medicine, 22*, 1–11.

Harris, S. M. (2006). Body image attitudes, physical attributes and disturbed eating among African American college women. *Race, Gender and Class, 13*, 46–56.

Harrow, M., Grossman, L. S., Jobe, T. H., & Herbener, E. S. (2005). Do patients with schizophrenia ever show periods of recovery? A 15-year multi-follow-up study. *Schizophrenia Bulletin, 31*, 723–734.

Hartmann, A., Zeeck, A., & Barrett, M. S. (2010). Interpersonal problems in eating disorders. *International Journal of Eating Disorders, 43*, 619–627.

Hartmann, U., Heiser, K., Ruffer-Hesse, C., & Kloth, G. (2002). Female sexual desire disorders: Subtypes, classification, personality factors and new directions for treatment. *World Journal of Urology, 20*, 79–88.

Harvey, A. G. (2008). Sleep and circadian rhythms in bipolar disorder: Seeking synchrony, harmony and regulation. *American Journal of Psychiatry, 165*, 820–829.

Harvey, W. T., Bransfield, R. C., Mercer, D. E., Wright, A. J., Ricchi, R. M., & Leitao, M. M. (2009). Morgellons disease, illuminating an undefined illness: A case series. *Journal of Medical Case Reports, 3*, 8243.

Hashimoto, K., Sawa, A., & Iyo, M. (2007). Increased levels of glutamate in brains from patients with mood disorders. *Biological Psychiatry, 62*, 1310–1316.

Hasin, D. S., Goodwin, R. D., Stinson, F. S., & Grant, B. F. (2005). Epidemiology of major depressive disorder: Results from the National Epidemiologic Survey on Alcoholism and Related Conditions. *Archives of General Psychiatry, 62*, 1097–1106.

Hasin, D. S., Keyes, K. M., Alderson, D., Wang, S., Aharonovich, E., & Grant, B. F. (2008). Cannabis withdrawal in the United States: Results from NESARC. *Journal of Clinical Psychiatry, 69*, 1354–1363.

Hasin, D. S., Stinson, F. S., Ogburn, E., & Grant, B. F. (2007). Prevalence, correlates, disability, and comorbidity of DSM-IV alcohol abuse and dependence in the United States: Results from the National Epidemiologic Survey on Alcohol and Related Conditions. *Archives of General Psychiatry, 64*, 830–842.

Hathaway, S. R., & McKinley, J. C. (1943). *Manual for the Minnesota Multiphasic Personality Inventory*. New York, NY: Psychological Corporation.

Hatsukami, D. K., Stead, L. F., & Gupta, P. C. (2008). Tobacco addiction. *Lancet, 371*, 2027–2038.

Hauer, P. (2010). Systemic affects of methamphetamine use. *South Dakota Medicine: Journal of the South Dakota State Medical Association, 63*(8), 285–287.

Hausman, K. (2003). Controversy continues to grow over DSM's GID diagnosis. *Psychiatric News, 38*(14), 25.

Hawkins, J. D., Oesterle, S., Brown, E. C., Monahan, K. C., Abbott, R. D., Arthur, M. W., & Catalano, R. F. (2012). Sustained decreases in risk exposure and youth problem behaviors after installation of the Communities That Care prevention system in a randomized trial. *Archives of Pediatrics and Adolescent Medicine, 166*, 141–148.

Hayes, E., Gavrilidis, E., & Kulkarni, J. (2012). The role of oestrogen and other hormones in the pathophysiology and treatment of schizophrenia. *Schizophrenia Research and Treatment*. Retrieved from http://www.hindawi.com/journals/sprt/2012/540273/ref/ Hayes, S. C., Brownell, K. D., & Barlow, D. H. (1983).

Heterosexual skills training and covert sensitization: Effects on social skills and sexual arousal in sexual deviants. *Behaviour Research and Therapy, 21*, 383–392.

Haynes, S. N. (2001). Clinical applications of analogue behavioral observation: Dimensions of psychometric evaluation. *Psychological Assessment, 13*, 73–85.

Hays, P. A. (2009). Integrating evidence-based practice, cognitive-behavior therapy, and multicultural therapy: Ten steps for culturally competent practice. *Professional Psychology: Research and Practice, 40*, 354–360.

Hayward, M., Berry, K., & Ashton, A. (2011). Applying interpersonal theories to the understanding of and therapy for auditory hallucinations: A review of the literature and directions for further research. *Clinical Psychology Review, 31*, 1313–1323.

Headaches. (2006). *Journal of the American Medical Association, 295*, 2320–2322.

Healy, M. (2011). 'Idol' finalist Durbin is singing through Tourette's. *USA Today*. Retrieved from http://www.usatoday.com

Heard-Davison, A., Heiman, J. R., & Briggs, B. (2004). Sexual disorders affecting women. In L. J. Haas (Ed.), *Handbook of primary care psychology* (pp. 495–509). New York, NY: Oxford University Press.

Hebert, K. K., Cummins, S. E., Hernández, S., Tedeschi, G. J., & Zhu, S. (2011). Current major depression among smokers using a state quitline. *American Journal of Preventive Medicine, 40*, 47–53.

Heinssen, R. K., & Cuthbert, B. N. (2001). Barrier to relationship formation in schizophrenia: Implications for treatment, social recovery, and translational research. *Psychiatry, 64*, 126–132.

Heinz, A. J., Wu, J., Witkiewitz, K., Epstein, D. H., & Preston, K. L. (2009). Marriage and relationship closeness as predictors of cocaine and heroin use. *Addictive Behavior, 34*, 258–263.

Hellstrom, K., Fellenius, J., & Öst, L.-G. (1996). One versus five sessions of applied tension in the treatment of blood phobia. *Behaviour Research and Therapy, 34*, 101–112.

Helt, M., Kelley, E., Kinsbourne, M., Pandey, J., Boorstein, H., Herbert, M., & Fein, D. (2008). Can children with autism recover? If so, how? *Neuropsychological Review, 18*, 339–366.

Heng, S., Song, A. W., & Sim, K. J. (2010). White matter abnormalities in bipolar disorder: Insights from diffusion tensor imaging studies. *Journal of Neural Transmission, 117*, 639–654.

Henningsson, S., Westberg, L., Nilsson, S., Lundstrom, B., Ekselius, L., Bodlund, O., . . . Landén, M. (2005). Sex steroid-related genes and male-to-female transsexualism. *Psychoneuroendocrinology, 30*, 657–664.

Herbenick, D., Reece, M., Schick, V., Sanders, S. A., Dodge, B., & Fortenberry, J. D. (2010). Sexual behavior in the United States from a national probability sample of men and women ages 14–94. *Journal of Sexual Medicine, 7*, 255–265.

Herbert, M. R. (2010). Contributions of the environment and environmentally vulnerable physiology to autism spectrum disorders. *Current Opinions in Neurology, 23*, 103–110.

Hernandez, A., & Sachs-Ericsson, N. (2006). Ethnic differences in pain reports and the moderating role of depression in a community sample of Hispanic and Caucasian participants with serious health problems. *Psychosomatic Medicine, 68*, 121–127.

Heron, M. P., Hoyert, D. L., Murphy, S. L., Xu, J. Q., Kochanek, K. D., & Tejada-Vera, B. (2009). Deaths: Final data for 2006. *National Vital Statistics Reports, 57*, 1–15. Retrieved from http://www.cdc.gov/nchs/data/nvsr/nvsr57/nvsr57_14.pdf

Hesapcioglu, S. T., Aktepe, E., Zeynep, G., & Dandil, S. T. (2010). Sociodemographic, clinical features, and comorbid disorders of children and adolescents with conversion disorder. *Yeni Symposium, 48*, 184–190.

Hettema, J. M. (2010). Genetics of depression. *Focus, 8*, 316–322.

Hettema, J. M., Annas, P., Neale, M. C., Kendler, K. S., & Frederikson, M. (2003). A twin study of the genetics of fear conditioning. *Archives of General Psychiatry, 60*, 702–708.

Hicks, T. V., Leitenberg, H., Barlow, D. H., & Gorman, K. M. (2005). Physical, mental, and social catastrophic cognitions as prognostic factors in cognitive-behavioral and pharmacological treatments for panic disorder. *Journal of Consulting and Clinical Psychology, 73*, 506–514.

Hilbert, A., Bishop, M. E., Stein, R. I., Tanofsky-Kraff, M., Swenson, A. K., Welch, R. R., & Wilfley, D. E. (2012). Long-term efficacy of psychological treatments for binge eating disorder. *British Journal of Psychiatry, 200*, 232–237.

Hilbert, A., & Tuschen-Caffier, B. (2007). Maintenance of binge eating through negative mood: A naturalistic comparison of binge eating disorder and bulimia nervosa. *International Journal of Eating Disorders, 40*, 521–527.

Hill, A. L., Rand, D. G., Nowak, M. A., & Christakis, N. A. (2010). Infectious disease modeling of social contagion in networks. *PLoS Computational Biology, 6*(11), e1000968. doi:10.1371/journal.pcbi.1000968

Hill, C. E., & Lambert, M. J. (2004). Methodological issues in studying psychotherapy processes and outcomes. In M. J. Lambert (Ed.), *Bergin and Garfield's handbook of psychotherapy and behavior change* (pp. 84–135). New York, NY: Wiley.

Hill, J. K. (2011). *Victims of Crime Research Digest, issue no. 2*. Retrieved from http://www.justice.gc.ca/eng/pi/rs/rep-rap/rd-rr/rd09_2-rr09_2/p1.html

Hiller, W., Leibbrand, R., Rief, W., & Fichter, M. M. (2002). Predictors of course and outcome in hypochondriasis after cognitive-behavioral treatment. *Psychotherapy and Psychosomatics, 71*, 318–327.

Hirshfeld-Becker, D. R., Biederman, J., Henin, A., Faraone, S. V., Davis, S., Harrington, K., . . . Jerrold, F. (2007). Behavioral inhibition in preschool children at risk is a specific predictor of middle childhood social anxiety: A five-year follow-up. *Journal of Developmental and Behavioral Pediatrics, 28*, 225–233.

Ho, A. K., Gilbert, A. S., Mason, S. L., Goodman, A. O., & Barker, R. A. (2009). Health-related quality of life in Huntington's disease: Which factors matter most? *Movement Disorders, 24*, 574–578.

Ho, B.-C., Andreasen, N. C., Ziebell, S., Pierson, R., & Magnotta, V. (2011). Long-term antipsychotic treatment and brain volumes. *Archives of General Psychiatry, 68*, 128–137.

Hobza, C. L., & Rochlen, A. B. (2009). Gender role conflict, drive for muscularity, and the impact of ideal media portrayals on men. *Psychology of Men & Masculinity, 10*, 120–130.

Hoehn-Saric, R., McLeod, D. R., Funderburk, F., & Kowalski, P. (2004). Somatic symptoms and physiologic responses in generalized anxiety disorder and panic disorder: An ambulatory monitor study. *Archives of General Psychiatry, 61*, 913–921.

Hoehn-Saric, R., Pearlson, G. D., Harris, G. J., Machlin, S. R., & Camargo, E. E. (1991). Effects of fluoxetine on regional cerebral blood flow in obsessive-compulsive patients. *American Journal of Psychiatry, 148*, 1243–1245.

Hoffman, B. M., Papas, R. K., Chatkoff, D. K., & Kerns, R. D. (2007). Meta-analysis of psychological interventions for chronic low back pain. *Health Psychology, 26*, 1–9.

Hofmann, S. G., Meuret, A. E., Rosenfield, D., Suvak, M. K., Barlow, D. H., . . . Woods, S. W. (2007). Preliminary evidence for cognitive mediation during cognitive-behavioral therapy of panic disorder. *Journal of Consulting and Clinical Psychology, 75*, 374–379.

Hofmann, S. G., Moscovitch, D. A., Kim, H.-J., & Taylor, A. N. (2004). Changes in self-perception during treatment of social phobia. *Journal of Consulting and Clinical Psychology, 72*, 588–596.

Hofvander, B., Delorme, R., Chaste, P., Nydén, A., Wentz, E., Ståhlberg, O., . . . Leboyer, M. (2009). Psychiatric and psychosocial problems in adults with normal-intelligence autism spectrum disorders. *BMC Psychiatry, 9*, 35.

The holiday-suicide link: The myth persists. (2009, December 7). Retrieved from http://www.annenbergpublicpolicycenter.org/NewsDetails.aspx?myId=331

Hollon, S. D., Stewart, M. O., & Strunk, D. (2006). Enduring effects for cognitive behavior therapy in the treatment of depression and anxiety. *Annual Review of Psychology, 57*, 285–315.

Holt-Lunstad, J., Smith, T. B., & Layton, B. (2010). Social relationships and mortality risk: A meta-analytic review. *PLoS Medicine, 7*(7), e1000316. doi:10.1371/journal.pmed.1000316

Honda, K., & Goodwin, R. D. (2004). Cancer and mental disorders in a national community sample. *Psychotherapy and Psychosomatics, 73*, 235–242.

Honea, R. A., Thomas, G. P., Harsha, A., Anderson, H. S., Donnelly, J. E., Brooks, W. M., & Burns, J. M. (2009). Cardiorespiratory fitness and preserved medial temporal lobe volume in Alzheimer disease. *Alzheimer Disease and Associated Disorders, 23*, 188–197.

Hooper, J. (1998, August). Science in the sack: Beyond Viagra. *Health and Fitness, 30*(6), 108–113.

Hornor, G. (2008). Reactive attachment disorder. *Journal of Pediatric Health Care, 22*, 234–239.

Hosenbocus, S., & Chahal, R. (2011). SSRIs and SNRIs: A review of the discontinuation syndrome in children and adolescents. *Journal of the Canadian Academy of Child and Adolescent Psychiatry, 20*, 60–67.

Howard, K. L., & Filley, C. M. (2009). Advances in genetic testing for Alzheimer's disease. *Review of Neurological Diseases, 6*, 26–32.

Howard, M. O., Balster, R. L., Cottler, L. B., Wu, L., & Vaughn, M. G. (2008). Inhalant use among incarcerated adolescents in the United States: Prevalence, characteristics, and correlates of use. *Drug and Alcohol Dependence, 93*, 197–209.

Howard, M. O., Perron, B. E., Sacco, P., Ilgen, M., Vaughn, M. G., Garland, E., & Freedentahl, S. (2010). Suicide ideation and attempts among inhalant users: Results from the National Epidemiologic Survey on Alcohol and Related Conditions. *Suicide and Life Threatening Behavior, 40*, 276–286.

Howard, M. O., Perron, B. E., Vaughn, M. G., Bender, K. A., & Garland, E. (2010). Inhalant use, inhalant-use disorders, and antisocial behavior: Findings from the National Epidemiologic Survey on Alcohol and Related Conditions (NESARC). *Journal of Studies on Alcohol and Drugs, 71*, 201–209.

Howard, R. (1992). Folie à deux involving a dog. *American Journal of Psychiatry, 149*, 414.

Howard, R., Rabins, P. V., Seeman, M. V., & Jeste, D. V. (2000). International late onset schizophrenia group: Late-onset schizophrenia and very-late-onset schizophrenia-like psychosis—An international consensus. *American Journal of Psychiatry, 157*, 172–178.

Howe, E. (2010). What psychiatrists should know about genes and Alzheimer's disease. *Psychiatry, 7*, 45–51.

Howes, O. D., Kambeitz, J., Kim, E., Stahl, D., Slifstein, M., Abi-Dargham, A., & Kapur, S. (2012). The nature of dopamine dysfunction in schizophrenia and what this means for treatment. *Archives of General Psychiatry, 69*, 776–786. doi:10.1001/archgenpsychiatry.2012.169

Howland, R. H. (2011). Sleep interventions for the treatment of depression. *Journal of Psychosocial Nursing and Mental Health Services, 49*, 17–20.

Howlett, S., & Reuber, M. (2009). An augmented model of brief psychodynamic interpersonal therapy for patients with nonepileptic seizures. *Psychotherapy: Research, Practice, Training, 46*, 125–138.

Huang, J., Perlis, R. H., Lee, P. H., Rush, A. J., Fava, M., . . . Smoller, J. W. (2010). Cross-disorder genomewide analysis of schizophrenia, bipolar disorder, and depression. *American Journal of Psychiatry, 167*, 1254–1263.

Hudson, J. I., Hiripi, E., Pope, H. G., & Kessler, R. C. (2007). The prevalence and correlates of eating disorders in the National Comorbidity Survey Replication. *Biological Psychiatry, 61*, 348–358.

Hudson, J. I., Manoach, D. S., Sabo, A. N., & Sternbach, S. E. (1991). Recurrent nightmares in posttraumatic stress disorder: Association with sleep paralysis, hypnopompic hallucinations, and REM sleep. *Journal of Nervous and Mental Disease, 179*, 572–573.

Huijbregts, K. M., van der Feltz-Cornelis, C. M., van Marwijk, H. W., de Jonge, F. J., van der Windt, D. A., & Beekman, A. T. (2010). Negative association of concomitant physical symptoms with the course of major depressive disorder: A systematic review. *Journal of Psychosomic Research, 68*, 511–519.

Humphrey, D. (1991). Final Exit. New York: Dell.

Hunfeld, J., Perquin, C., Hazebroek-Kampschrueur, A., Passchier, J., Suiklekom-Smit, L., & van der Wouden, J. (2002). Physically unexplained chronic pain and its impact on children and their families: The mother's perception. *Psychology and Psychotherapy: Theory and Practice, 75*, 251–260.

Hunt, W. G. (2010). Meningitis and encephalitis in adolescents. *Adolescent Medicine State of the Art Review, 21*, 287–317, ix–x.

Hunter, R., & Macalpine, I. (1963). *Three hundred years of psychiatry, 1535–1860*. London, UK: Oxford University Press.

Huntjens, R. J. C., Peters, M. L., Woertman, L., van der Hart, O., & Postma, A. (2007). Memory transfer for emotionally valenced words between identities in dissociative identity disorder. *Behaviour Research and Therapy, 45*, 775–789.

Hussong, A. M., Jones, D. J., Stein, G. L., Baucom, D. H., & Boeding, S. (2011). An internalizing pathway to alcohol use and disorder. *Psychology of Addictive Behaviors, 25*, 390–404.

Hyde, J. S. (2005). *Biological substrates of human sexuality*. Washington, DC: American Psychological Association.

Iannelli, V. (2009, February 22). Suicide and suicide prevention: Teen suicides. Retrieved from http://pediatrics.about.com/od/suicide/a/808_suicide_prv.htm

International Narcotics Control Board. (2010). Psychotropic Substances: Statistics for 2009. Retrieved from http://www.incb.org/pdf/technical-reports/psychotropics/2010/Psychotropic_Substances_Publication_2010.pdf

International Society for the Study of Dissociation. (2005). Guidelines for treating dissociative identity disorder in adults. *Journal of Trauma and Dissociation, 6*, 69–149.

Irani, F., & Siegel, S. J. (2006). Predicting outcome in schizophrenia. *Psychiatric Times, 23*, 69–71.

Irizarry, L. (2004, August 8). Widespread starvation: A proliferation of Web sites are promoting anorexia, which shows that sometimes, there is no safety in numbers. *New Orleans Times-Picayune*, p. 1.

Irwin, H. J. (1998). Attitudinal predictors of dissociation: Hostility and powerlessness. *Journal of Psychology, 132*, 389–404.

Isaac, M., Elias, B., Katz, L. Y., Belik, S. L., Deane, F. P., Enns, M. W., . . . Swampy Cree Suicide Prevention Team (12 members). (2008). Gatekeeper training as a preventative intervention for suicide: A systematic review. *La Revue canadienne de psychiatrie, 54*, 260–268.

Islam, L., Scarone, S., & Gambini, O. (2011). First- and third-person perspectives in psychotic disorder and mood disorders with psychotic features. *Schizophrenia Research and Treatment*, retrieved from http://www.hindawi.com/journals/sprt/2011/769136/

Ismail, S., Buckley, S., Budacki, R., Jabbar, A., & Gallicano, I. (2010). Screening, diagnosing and prevention of fetal alcohol syndrome: Is this syndrome treatable? *Developmental Neuroscience, 32*, 91–100.

Ivey, A. E., D'Andrea, M., Ivey, M. B., & Simek-Morgan, L. (2007). *Theories of counseling and psychotherapy: A multicultural perspective*. 2nd edition. Boston, MA: Allyn & Bacon.

Jabben, N., Arts, B., Van Os, J., Krabbendam, L. (2010). Neurocognitive functioning as intermediary phenotype and predictor of psychosocial functioning across the psychosis continuum: Studies in schizophrenia and bipolar disorder. *Journal of Clinical Psychiatry, 71*, 764–774.

Jablensky, A. V., Morgan, V., Zubrick, S. R., Bower, C., & Yellachich, L.-A. (2005). Pregnancy, delivery, and neonatal complications in a population cohort of women with schizophrenia and major affective disorder. *American Journal of Psychiatry, 162*, 79–91.

Jacka, F. N., Kremer, P. J., Beark, M., de Silva-Sanigorski, A. M, Moodie, M., . . . Swinburn, B. A. (2011). A prospective study of diet quality and mental health in adolescents. *PLoS One, 6*(9), e24805. doi:10.1371/journal.pone.0024805

Jacka, F. N., Pasco, J. A., Mykletun, A., Williams, L. J., Hodge, A. M., . . . Berk, M. (2010). Association between Western and traditional diets and depression and anxiety in women. *American Journal of Psychiatry*, 167, 305–311.

Jackson, C., Geddes, R., Haw, S., & Frank, J. (2012). Interventions to prevent substance use and risky sexual behaviour in young people: A systematic review. *Addiction, 107*, 733–747.

Jackson, T., & Chen, H. (2010). Sociocultural experiences of bulimic and non-bulimic adolescents in a school-based Chinese sample. *Journal of Abnormal Child Psychology, 38*, 69–76.

Jackson vs. Indiana. 406 US (1972).

Jacobsen, P. B., Bovbjerg, D. H., Schwartz, M. D., Hudis, C. A., Gilewski, T. A., & Norton, L. (1995). Conditioned emotional distress in women receiving chemotherapy for breast cancer. *Journal of Consulting and Clinical Psychology, 63*, 108–114.

Jacobus, J., Bava, S., Cohen-Zion, M., Mahmood, O., & Tapert, S. F. (2009). Functional consequences of marijuana use in adolescents. *Pharmacology Biochemistry and Behavior, 92*, 559–565.

Jaffee, S. R. (2007). Sensitive, stimulating caregiving predicts cognitive and behavioral resilience in neurodevelopmentally at-risk infants. *Development & Psychopathology, 19*, 631–647.

Jaffee, S. R., Caspi, A., Moffitt, T. E., & Taylor, A. (2004). Physical maltreatment victim to antisocial child: Evidence of an environmentally mediated process. *Journal of Abnormal Psychology, 113*, 44–55.

Jaffee, S. R., Moffitt, T. E., Caspi, A., Taylor, A., & Arsenault, L. (2002). Influence of adult domestic violence on children's externalizing and internalizing problems: An environmentally informative twin study. *Journal of the American Academy of Child & Adolescent Psychiatry, 41*, 1095–1103.

Jagdeo, A., Cox, B. J., Stein, M. B., & Sareen, J. (2009). Negative attitudes toward help seeking for mental illness in 2 population-based surveys from the United States and Canada. *Canadian Journal of Psychiatry, 54*, 757–766.

Jain, R. (2009). The epidemiology and recognition of pain and physical symptoms in depression. *Journal of Clinical Psychiatry, 70*, e04.

Jairam, R., Prabhuswamy, M., & Dullur, P. (2012). Do we really know how to treat a child with bipolar disorder or one with severe mood dysregulation? Is there a magic bullet? *Depression Research and Treatment*. Retrieved from http://www.hindawi.com/journals/drt/2012/967302/967302

Jaite, C., Schneider, N., Hilbert, A., Pfeiffer, E., Lehmkuhl, U., & Salbach-Andrae, H. (2012). Etiological role of childhood emotional trauma and neglect in adolescent anorexia nervosa: A cross-sectional questionnaire analysis. *Psychopathology, 45*, 61–66.

James, A., Hough, M., James, S., Burge, L., Winmill, L., Nijhawan, S., . . . Zarei, M. (2011). Structural brain and neuropsychometric changes associated with pediatric bipolar disorder with psychosis. *Bipolar Disorders, 13*, 16–27.

Janjua, A., Rapport, D., & Ferrara, G. (2010). The woman who wasn't there. *Current Psychiatry, 9*, 62–72.

Jankovic, J. (2011). Diagnosis and treatment of psychogenic parkinsonism. *Journal of Neurology, Neurosurgery, and Psychiatry, 82*, 1300–1303.

Janssen, K. (1983). Treatment of sinus tachycardia with heart-rate feedback. *Psychiatry and Human Development, 17*, 166–176.

Janssens, T., Verleden, G., De Peuter, S., Van Diest, I., & Van den Bergh, O. (2009). Inaccurate perception of asthma symptoms: A cognitive-affective framework and implications for asthma treatment. *Clinical Psychology Review, 29*, 317–327.

Janus, S. S., & Janus, C. L. (1993). *The Janus report on sexual behavior*. New York, NY: Wiley.

Jellinger, K. A. (2008). Morphologic diagnosis of "vascular dementia"—A critical update. *Journal of Neurological Science, 270*, 1–12.

Jenike, M. A. (2001). A forty-five-year-old woman with obsessive-compulsive disorder. *Journal of the American Medical Association, 285*, 2121–2128.

Jeste, D. V., Jin, H., Golshan, S., Mudaliar, S., Glorioso, D., Fellows, I., . . . Arndt, S. (2009). Discontinuation of quetiapine from an NIMH funded trial due to serious adverse effects. *American Journal of Psychiatry, 166*, 937–938.

Jobes, D. A. (2006). *Managing suicidal risk: A collaborative approach*. New York, NY: Guilford Press.

Joelving, F. (2011). One in 16 U.S. surgeons consider suicide: Survey. *Archives of Surgery*, 146, 1, 54–62.

Johns, L. C., Cannon, M., Singleton, N., Murray, R. M., Farrell, M., Brugha, T., . . . Metzer, H. (2004). Prevalence and correlates of self-reported psychotic symptoms in the British population. *British Journal of Psychiatry, 185*, 298–305.

Johnson, C. P., Myers, S. M., & Council on Children With Disabilities. (2007). Identification and evaluation of children with autism spectrum disorders. *Pediatrics, 120*, 1183–1215.

Johnson, D. P., Penn, D. L., Fredrickson, B. L., Meyer, P. S., Kring, A. M., & Brantley, M. (2009). Loving-kindness meditation to enhance recovery from negative symptoms of schizophrenia. *Journal of Clinical Psychology: In Session, 65*, 499–509.

Johnson, D. W., & Johnson, F. P. (2003). *Joining together*. Boston, MA: Allyn & Bacon.

Johnson, J., Gooding, P. A., Wood, A. M., & Tarrier, N. (2010). Testing the schematic appraisals model. *Behavior Research and Therapy, 48*, 179–186.

Johnson, J. G., Cohen, P., Smailes, E. M., Kasen, S., & Brook, J. S. (2002). Television viewing and aggressive behavior during adolescence and adulthood. *Science, 295*, 2468–2471.

Johnson, J. K., Diehl, J., Mendez, M. F., Neuhaus, J., Shapira, J. S., . . . Miller, B. L. (2005). Frontotemporal lobar degeneration: Demographic characteristics of 353 patients. *Archives of Neurology, 62*, 925–930.

Johnson, S. L., Cuellar, A. K., Ruggero, C., Winett-Perlman, C., Goodnick, P., White, R., & Miller, I. J. (2008). Life events as predictors of mania and depression in bipolar I disorder. *Journal of Abnormal Psychology, 117*, 268–277.

Johnson, S. L., Edge, M. D., Holmes, M. K., & Carver, C. S. (2012). The behavioral activation system and mania. *Annual Review of Clinical Psychology, 8*, 243–267.

Johnston, L. D., Bachman, J. G., & O'Malley, P. M. (2009). *Monitoring the future: Questionnaire responses from the nation's high school seniors, 2008*. Ann Arbor, MI: Institute for Social Research.

Johnston, L. D., O'Malley, P. M., Bachman, J. G., & Schulenberg, J. E. (2010a). Demographic subgroup trends for various licit and illicit drugs, 1975–2009 (Monitoring the Future Occasional Paper No. 73). Ann Arbor, MI: Institute for Social Research. Retrieved from http://www.monitoringthefuture.org/pubs/occpapers/mtf-occ74.pdf

Johnston, L. D., O'Malley, P. M., Bachman, J. G., & Schulenberg, J. E. (2010b). Marijuana use is rising; ecstasy use is beginning to rise; and alcohol use is declining among U.S. teens. Ann Arbor, MI: University of Michigan News Service. Retrieved from http://www.monitoringthefuture.org

Johnston, L. D., O'Malley, P. M., Bachman, J. G., & Schulenberg, J. E. (2012). Monitoring the Future national results on adolescent drug use: Overview of key findings, 2011. Ann Arbor: Institute for Social Research, University of Michigan.

Joiner, T. E. (2005). *Why people die by suicide*. Cambridge, MA: Harvard University Press.

Joiner, T. E., Van Orden, K. A., Witte, T. K., Selby, E. A., Ribeiro, J. D., Lewis, R., & Rudd, M. D. (2009). Main predictions of the interpersonal-psychology theory of suicidal behavior: Empirical tests in two samples of young adults. *Journal of Abnormal Psychology, 118*, 634–646.

Joinson, C., Heron, J., Lewis, G., Croudace, T., & Araya, R. (2011). Timing of menarche and depressive symptoms in adolescent girls from a UK cohort. *British Journal of Psychiatry, 198*, 17–23.

Jones, C., Leung, N., & Harris, G. (2007). Dysfunctional core beliefs in eating disorders: A review. *Journal of Cognitive Psychotherapy: An International Quarterly, 21*, 156–171.

Jones, D. R., Harrell, J. P., Morris-Prather, C. E., Thomas, J., & Omowale, N. (1996). Affective and physiological responses to racism: The role of Afrocentrism and mode of presentation. *Ethnicity and Disease, 6*, 109–122.

Josselson, R., & Matilla, H. (2012). The humanity of the psychotic patient and the human approach by the therapist: A relational and intersubjective meeting. *Pragmatic Case Studies in Psychotherapy, 8*, 36–48.

Jovanovic, T., Norrholm, S. D., Blanding, N. Q., Davis, M., Duncan, E., Bradley, B., & Ressler, K. J. (2010). Impaired fear inhibition is a biomarker of PTSD but not depression. *Depression and Anxiety, 27*, 244–251.

Juang, L. P., & Cookston, J. T. (2009). Acculturation, discrimination, and depressive symptoms among Chinese American adolescents: A longitudinal study. *Journal of Primary Prevention, 30*, 475–496.

Juang, L. P., Syed, M., & Takagi, M. (2007). Intergenerational discrepancies of parental control among Chinese American families: Links to family conflict and adolescent depressive symptoms. *Journal of Adolescence, 30*, 965–975.

Judd, L. L., Schettler, P. J., Akiskal, H. S., Coryell, W., Leon, A. C., Maser, J. D., & Solomon, D. A. (2008). Residual symptom recovery from major affective episodes in bipolar disorders and rapid episode relapse/recurrence. *Archives of General Psychiatry, 65*, 386–394.

Junginger, J. (1996). Psychosis and violence: The case for a content analysis of psychotic experience. *Schizophrenia Bulletin, 22*, 91–103.

Jupp, B., & Lawrence, A. J. (2010). New horizons for therapeutics in drug and alcohol abuse. *Pharmacological Therapy, 125*, 138–168.

Kaddena, R. M., Litt, M. D., Kabela-Cormiera, E., & Petrya, N. M. (2007). Abstinence rates following behavioral treatments for marijuana dependence. *Addictive Behaviors, 32*, 1220–1236.

Kafka, M. P. (2009). Hypersexual disorder: A proposed diagnosis for DSM-V. *Archives of Sexual Behavior, 39*(2), 377–400. doi:10.1007/s10508-009-9574-7

Kahn, R. E., Frick, P. J., Youngstrom, E., Findling, R. L., & Youngstrom, J. K. (2012). The effects of including a callous–unemotional specifier for the diagnosis of conduct disorder. *Journal of Child Psychology and Psychiatry, 53*, 271–282.

Kalivas, P. W., & O'Brien, C. (2008). Drug addiction as a pathology of staged neuroplasticity. *Neuropsychopharmacology Reviews, 33*, 166–180.

Kalmar, J. H., Wang, F., Chepenik, L. G., Womer, F. Y., Jones, M. M., . . . Blumberg, H. P. (2009). Relation between amygdala structure and function in adolescents with bipolar disorder. *Journal of the American Academy of Child & Adolescent Psychiatry, 48*, 636–642.

Kamarck, T. W., Muldoon, M. F., Shiffman, S. S., & Sutton-Tyrrell, K. (2007). Experiences of demand and control during daily life are predictors of carotid progression among healthy men. *Health Psychology, 26*, 324–332.

Kamat, S. A., Rajagopalan, K., Pethick, N., Willey, V., Bullano, M., & Hassan, M. J. (2008). Prevalence and humanistic impact of potential misdiagnosis of bipolar disorder among patients with major depressive disorder in a commercially insured population. *Academy of Managed Care Pharmacy, 14*, 631–642.

Kanaan, R., Armstrong, D., & Wessely, S. (2009). Limits to truth-telling: Neurologists' communication in conversion disorder. *Parent Education and Counseling, 77*, 296–301.

Kannai, R. (2009). Munchausen by mommy. *Families, Systems, & Health, 27*, 105–112.

Kantrowitz, B., & Scelfo, J. (2006, November 27). What happens when they grow up? *Newsweek*, 47–53.

Kapalko, J. (2010, June 18). Pro-ana websites abound. *Salon*. Retrieved from http://www.salon.com

Kaplan, H. S. (1974). No nonsense therapy for six sexual malfunctions. *Psychology Today, 8*, 76–80, 83, 86.

Karch, D., Cosby, A., & Simon, T. (2006). Toxicology testing and results for suicide victims: 13 states, 2004. *Morbidity and Mortality Weekly Report, 55*, 1245–1248.

Karg, K., Burmeister, M., Shedden, K., & Sen, S. (2011). The serotonin transporter promoter variant (5-HTTLPR), stress, and depression meta-analysis revisited: Evidence of genetic moderation. *Archives of General Psychiatry, 68*(5), 444–454. doi:10.1001/archgenpsychiatry.2010.189

Karno, M., & Golding, J. M. (1991). Obsessive-compulsive disorder. In L. N. Robins & D. A. Regier (Eds.), *Psychiatric disorders in America: The Epidemiologic Catchment Area study* (pp. 204–219). New York, NY: Free Press.

Kasari, C., Rotheram-Fuller, E., Locke, J., & Gulsrud., A. (2012). Making the connection: Randomized controlled trial of social skills at school for children with autism spectrum disorders. *Journal of Child Psychology and Psychiatry, 53*, 431–439.

Kashdan, T. B., & Rottenberg, J. (2010). Psychological flexibility as a fundamental aspect of health. *Clinical Psychology Review, 30*, 865–878.

Kastelan, A., Franciskovic, T., Moro, L., Roncevic-Grzeta, I., Grkovic, J., . . . Girotto, I. (2007). Psychotic symptoms in combat-related posttraumatic stress disorder. *Military Medicine, 172*, 273–277.

Kato, K., Sullivan, P. F., Evengard, B., & Pedersen, N. L. (2009). A population-based twin study of functional somatic syndromes. *Psychological Medicine, 39*, 497–505.

Kato, T. (2007). Molecular genetics of bipolar disorder and depression. *Psychiatry and Clinical Neurosciences, 61*, 3–19.

Katon, W. J. (2006). Panic attacks. *New England Journal of Medicine, 354*, 2360–2368.

Katon, W. J. (2010). Asthma, suicide risk, and psychiatric comorbidity. *American Journal of Psychiatry, 167*, 1020–1022.

Katzer, A., Oberfeld, D., Hiller, W., Gerlach, A. L., & Witthoft, M. (2012). Tactile perceptual processes and their relationship to somatoform disorders. *Journal of Abnormal Psychology, 121*, 530–543.

Kaufman, L., Ayub, M., & Vincent, J. B. (2010). The genetic basis of non-syndromic intellectual disability: A review. *Journal of Neurodevelopmental Disorders, 2*, 182–209.

Kawa, I., Carter, J. D., Joyce P. R., Doughty, C. J., Frampton, C. M., . . . Olds, R. J. (2005). Gender differences in bipolar disorder: Age of onset, course, comorbidity, and symptom presentation. *Bipolar Disorders, 7*, 119–125.

Kaye, S., Darke, S., & Duflou, J. (2009). Methylenedioxymethamphetamine (MDMA)-related fatalities in Australia: Demographics, circumstances, toxicology and major organ pathology. *Drug and Alcohol Dependence, 104*, 254–261.

Kaye, S., Darke, S., Duflou, J., & McKetin, R. (2008). Methamphetamine-related fatalities in Australia: Demographics, circumstances, toxicology and major organ pathology. *Addiction, 103*, 1353–1360.

Kaye, W. (2009). Eating disorders: Hope despite mortal risk. *American Journal of Psychiatry, 166*, 1309–1311.

Kazdin, A. E., Whitley, M., & Marciano, P. L. (2006). Child-therapist and parent-therapist alliance and therapeutic change in the treatment of children referred for oppositional, aggressive, and antisocial behavior. *Journal of Child Psychology and Psychiatry, 47*, 436–445.

Kean, C. (2011). Battling with the life instinct: The paradox of the self and suicidal behavior in psychosis. *Schizophrenia Bulletin, 37*, 4–7.

Kearney, D. J., McDermott, K., Malte, C., Martinez, M., & Simpson, T. L. (2012). Association of participation in a mindfulness program with measures of PTSD, depression and quality of life in a veteran sample. *Journal of Clinical Psychology, 68*, 101–116.

Keating, G. M., & Lyseng-Williamson, K. A. (2010). Varenicline: A pharmacoeconomic review of its use as an aid to smoking cessation. *Pharmacoeconomics, 28*, 231–254.

Kelleher, I., & Cannon, M. (2010). Psychotic-like experiences in the general population: Characterizing a high-risk group for psychosis. *Psychological Medicine, 41*(1), 1–6. doi:10.1017/S0033291710001005

Keller, R. M., & Calgay, C. E. (2010). Microaggressive experiences of people with disabilities. In D. W. Sue (Ed.), *Microaggressions and marginality: Manifestation, dynamics and impact* (pp. 241–267). Hoboken, NJ: Wiley.

Kellner, R. (1985). Functional somatic symptoms and hypochondriasis. *Archives of General Psychiatry, 42*, 821–833.

Kelly, J. F., Stout, R. L., Magill, M., Tonigan, J. S., . . . Pagano, M. E. (2011). Spirituality in recovery: A lagged mediational analysis of Alcoholics Anonymous' principal theoretical mechanism of behavior change. *Alcoholism: Clinical & Experimental Research, 35*, 454–463.

Kelly, V. L., Barker, H., Field, A. P., Wilson, C., & Reynolds, S. (2010). Can Rachman's indirect pathways be used to un-learn fear? A prospective paradigm to test whether children's fears can be reduced using positive information and modeling a non-anxious response. *Behaviour Research and Therapy, 48*, 164–170.

Keltner, N. G., & Dowben, J. S. (2007). Psychobiological substrates of posttraumatic stress disorder: Part 1. *Perspectives in Psychiatric Care, 43*, 97–101.

Kendall, P. C., Holmbeck, G., & Verduin, T. (2004). Methodology, design, and evaluation in psychotherapy research. In M. J. Lambert (Ed.), *Bergin and Garfield's handbook of psychotherapy and behavior change* (pp. 16–43). New York, NY: Wiley.

Kendall, P. C., Khanna, M. S., Edson, A., Cummings, C., & Harris, M. S. (2011). Computers and psychosocial treatment for child anxiety: Recent advances and ongoing efforts. *Depression and Anxiety, 28*, 58–66.

Kendall-Tackett, K. (2009). Psychological trauma and physical health: A psychoneuroimmunology approach to etiology of negative health effects and possible interventions. *Psychological Trauma: Theory, Research, Practice, and Policy, 1*, 35–48.

Kendall-Tackett, K., & Klest, B. (2009). Causal mechanisms and multidirectional pathways between trauma, dissociation, and health. *Journal of Trauma, 10*, 129–134.

Kendler, K. S., & Prescott, C. A. (2006). *Genes, environment, and psychopathology: Understanding the causes of psychiatric and substance use disorders*. New York, NY: Guilford Press.

Kenny, M. A., & Williams, J. M. G. (2007). Treatment-resistant depressed patients show a good response to mindfulness-based cognitive therapy. *Behaviour Research & Therapy, 45*, 617–625.

Kent, M. M., & Haub, C. (2005). Global demographic divide. *Population Bulletin, 60*, 1–24.

Kern, J. K., Geier, D. A., Adams, J. B., Mehta, J. A., Grannemann, B. D., & Geier, M. R. (2011). Toxicity biomarkers in autism spectrum disorder: A blinded study of urinary porphyrins. *Pediatrics International, 53*, 147–153.

Kern, S. E. (2009). Challenges in conducting clinical trials in children: Approaches for improving performance. *Expert Review of Clinical Pharmacology, 2*(6), 609–617.

Kernberg, O. (1976). Technical considerations in the treatment of borderline personality organization.

Journal of the American Psychoanalytic Association, 24, 795–829.

Kerr, P. L., Muehlenkamp, J. J., & Turner, J. M. (2010). Nonsuicidal self-injury: A review of current research for family medicine and primary care physicians. *Journal of the American Board of Family Medicine, 23*, 240–259.

Kessing, L. V., Hellmund, G., Geddes, J. R., Goodwin, G. M., & Andersen, P. K. (2011). Valproate v. lithium in the treatment of bipolar disorder in clinical practice: Observational nationwide register-based cohort study. *British Journal of Psychiatry, 199, 57–63*.

Kessler, D., Lewis, G., Kaur, S., Wiles, N., King, M., Weich, S., . . . Peters, T. J. (2009). Therapist-delivered Internet psychotherapy for depression in primary care: A randomized controlled trial. *Lancet,* 374, 628–634.

Kessler, R. C. (2003). Epidemiology of women and depression. *Journal of Affective Disorders, 74*, 5–13.

Kessler, R. C., Akiskal, H. S., Ames, M., Birnbaum, H., Greenberg, P., . . . Wang, P. S. (2006). Prevalence and effects of mood disorders on work performance in a nationally representative sample of U.S. workers. *American Journal of Psychiatry, 163*, 1561–1568.

Kessler, R. C., Berglund, P., Demler, O., Jin, R., Koretz, D., . . . National Comorbidity Survey Replication. (2003). The epidemiology of major depressive disorder: Results from the National Comorbidity Survey Replication (NCS-R). *Journal of the American Medical Association, 289*, 3095–3105.

Kessler, R. C., Berglund, P., Demler, O., Jin, R., Merikangas, K. R., & Walters, E. E. (2005). Lifetime prevalence and age-of-onset distribution of DSM-IV disorders in the National Comorbidity Survey Replication. *Archives of General Psychiatry, 62*, 593–602.

Kessler, R. C., Chiu, W. T., Demler, O., & Walters, E. E. (2005). Prevalence, severity, and comorbidity of 12-month DSM-IV disorders in the National Comorbidity Survey Replication. *Archives of General Psychiatry, 62*, 617–627.

Ketter, T. A. (2010). Diagnostic features, prevalence, and impact of bipolar disorder. *Journal of Clinical Psychiatry, 71*, e14.

Kidd, T., Hamer, M., & Steptoe, A. (2011). Examining the association between adult attachment style and cortisol responses to acute stress. *Psychoneuroendocrinology, 36*, 771–779.

Kiecolt-Glaser, J. (2009). Is stress a risk factor for cancer? *U.S. News and World Report*. Retrieved from http://health.usnews.com/health-news/blogs/health-advice/2009/02/19/is-stress-a-risk-factor-for-cancer.html

Kiecolt-Glaser, J. K., Glaser, R., Cacioppo, J. T., MacCallum, R. C., Snydersmith, M., Kim, C., & Malarkey, W. B. (1997). Marital conflict in older adults: Endocrinological and immunological correlates. *Psychosomatic Medicine, 59*, 339–349.

Kikuchi, H., Fujii, T., Abe, N., Suzuki, M., Takagi, M., . . . Mori, E. (2010). Memory repression: Brain mechanism underlying dissociative amnesia. *Journal of Cognitive Neuroscience, 22*, 602–613.

Kilpatrick, D. G., Amstadter, A. B., Resnick, H. S., & Ruggiero, K. J. (2007). Rape-related PTSD: Issues and interventions. *Psychiatric Times, 24*, 1–3.

Kilpatrick, D. G., Koenen, K. C., Ruggiero, K. J., Acierno, R., Galea, S., . . . Gelernter, J. (2008). The serotonin transporter genotype and social support and moderation of posttraumatic stress disorder and depression in hurricane-exposed adults. *American Journal of Psychiatry, 164*, 1693–1699.

Kilpeläinen, T. O., Qi, L., Brage, S., Sharp, S. J., Sonestedt, E., Demerath, E., . . . Loos, R. J. F. (2011). Physical activity attenuates the influence of *FTO* variants on obesity risk: A meta-analysis of 218,166 adults and 19,268 children. *PLoS Medicine, 8*(11): e1001116. doi:10.1371/journal.pmed.1001116

Kim, J.-J., Kim, D.-J., Kim, T.-G., Seok, J.-H., Chun, J. W., Oh, M.-K., & Park, A. J. (2007). Volumetric abnormalities in connectivity-based subregions of the thalamus in patients with chronic schizophrenia. *Schizophrenia Research, 97*, 226–235.

Kim, S. Y., Chen, Q., Li, J., Huang, X., & Moon, U. J. (2009). Parent-child acculturation, parenting, and adolescent depressive symptoms in Chinese immigrant families. *Journal of Family Psychology, 23*, 426–437.

Kim, Y., & Berrios, G. E. (2001). Impact of the term schizophrenia on the culture of ideograph: The Japanese experience. *Schizophrenia Bulletin, 27*, 181–185.

King, C. A., & Merchant, C. R. (2008). Social and interpersonal factors relating to adolescent suicidality: A review of the literature. *Archives of Suicide Research, 12*, 181–196.

King, N. J., Clowes-Hollins, V., & Ollendick, T. H. (1997). The etiology of dog phobia. *Behaviour Research and Therapy, 35*, 77.

King, N. J., Eleonora, G., & Ollendick, T. H. (1998). Etiology of childhood phobias: Current status of Rachman's three pathways theory. *Behavior Research and Therapy, 36*, 297–309.

Kinsey, A. C., Pomeroy, W. B., & Martin, C. E. (1948). *Sexual behavior in the human male*. Philadelphia, PA: Saunders.

Kinsey, A. C., Pomeroy, W. B., Martin, C. E., & Gebhard, P. H. (1953). *Sexual behavior in the human female*. Philadelphia, PA: Saunders.

Kinsey, B. M., Kosten, T. R., & Orson, F. M. (2010). Anti-cocaine vaccine development. *Expert Review of Vaccines, 9*, 1109–1114.

Kisch, J., Leino, E. V., & Silverman, M. M. (2005). Aspects of suicidal behavior, depression and treatment in college students: Results from the spring 2000 National College Health Assessment Survey. *Suicide and Life Threatening Behavior, 35*, 3–13.

Klauke, B., Deckert, J., Reif, A., Pauli, P., & Domschke, K. (2010). Life events in panic disorder—An update on "candidate stressors." *Depression and Anxiety, 27*, 716–730.

Kleeman, J. (2011, February 25). Sick note: Faking illness online. *Guardian*. Retrieved from http://www.guardiannews.com

Kleinman, A. (2004). Culture and depression. *New England Journal of Medicine, 351*, 951–953.

Klin, A., Lin, D. J., Gorrindo, P., Ramsay, G., & Jones, W. (2009). Two-year-olds with autism orient to nonsocial contingencies rather than biological motion. *Nature, 459*, 257–261.

Kline, T. J. (2005). *Psychological testing: A practical approach to design and evaluation*. Thousand Oaks, CA: Sage.

Klonsky, E. D. (2011). Non-suicidal self-injury in United States adults: Prevalence, sociodemographics, topography, and functions. *Psychological Medicine, 41*, 1981–1986.

Klonsky, E. D., & Muehlenkamp, J. J. (2007). Self-injury: A research review for the practitioner. *Journal of Clinical Psychology: In Session, 63*, 1045–1056.

Klopfer, B., & Davidson, H. (1962). *The Rorschach technique*. New York: Harcourt, Brace & World.

Klott, J., & Jongsma, A. E. (2004). *The suicide and homicide risk assessment and prevention treatment planner*. Hoboken, NJ: Wiley.

Kluft, R. P. (1987). Dr. Kluft replies. *American Journal of Psychiatry, 144*, 125.

Klump, K. L., Suisman, J. L., Burt, S. A., McGue, M., & Iacono, W. G. (2009). Genetic and environmental influences on disordered eating: An adoption study. *Journal of Abnormal Psychology, 118*, 797–805.

Knabb, J. J., Vogt, R. G., & Newgren, K. P. (2011). MMPI-2 characteristics of the old order Amish: A comparison of clinical, nonclinical and United States normative samples. *Psychological Assessment, 23*, 865–875.

Knowlton, A. R., & Latkin, C. A. (2007). Network financial support and conflict as predictors of depressive symptoms among a disadvantaged population. *Journal of Community Psychology, 35*, 13–28.

Knox, S., Catlin, L., Casper, M., & Schlosser, L. Z. (2005). Addressing religion and spirituality in psychotherapy: Clients' perspectives. *Psychotherapy Research, 15*, 287–303.

Kodituwakku, P. W. (2009). Neurocognitive profile in children with fetal alcohol spectrum disorders. *Developmental Disabilities Research Reviews, 15*, 218–224.

Kogan, M. D., Blumberg, S. J., Schieve, L. A., Boyle, C. A., Perrin, J. M., . . . van Dyck, P. C. (2009). Prevalence of parent-reported diagnosis of autism spectrum disorder among children in the US, 2007. *Pediatrics, 124*, 1395–1403.

Kolassa, I.-T., Ertl, V., Eckart, C., Kolassa, S., Onyut, L. P., & Elbert, T. (2010). Spontaneous remission from PTSD depends on the number of traumatic event types experienced. *Psychological Trauma: Theory, Research, Practice, and Policy, 2*, 169–174.

Kolb, B., Gibb, R., & Robinson,T. E. (2003). Brain plasticity and behavior. *Current Directions in Psychological Science, 12*, 1–4.

Kollannoor-Samuel, G., Wagner, J., Damio, G., Segura-Pérez, S., Chhabra, J., Vega-López, S., & Pérez-Escamilla, R. (2011). Social support modifies the association between household food insecurity and depression among Latinos with uncontrolled type 2 diabetes. *Journal of Immigrant and Minority Health, 13*, 982–989.

Kollins, S. H. (2008). A qualitative review of issues arising in the use of psycho-stimulant medications in patients with ADHD and co-morbid substance use disorders. *Current Medical Research Opinions, 24*, 1345–1357.

Kong, L. L., Allen, J. J. B., & Glisky, E. L. (2008). Interidentity memory transfer in dissociative identity disorder. *Journal of Abnormal Psychology, 117*, 686–692.

Koob, G. F., Kandel, D., & Volkow, N. D. (2008). Pathophysiology of addiction. In A. Tasman, J. Kay, J. A. Lieberman, M. B. First, & M. Maj (Eds.), *Psychiatry* (Vol. 1, 3rd ed., pp. 354–378). Hoboken, NJ: Wiley.

Koocher, G. P., & Keith-Spiegel, P. (2008). *Ethics in psychology and the mental health profession: Standards and cases* (3rd ed.). Oxford, UK: Oxford University Press.

Kooistra, L., Crawford, S., Gibbard, B., Ramage, B., & Kaplan, B. J. (2010). Differentiating attention deficits in children with fetal alcohol spectrum disorder or attention-deficit-hyperactivity disorder. *Developmental Medicine & Child Neurology, 52*, 205–211.

Kopelman, M. D. (2002). Disorders of memory. *Brain, 125*, 2152–2190.

Koppelman, J. (2004, June 4). Children with mental disorders: Making sense of their needs and the systems that help them. *National Health Policy Forum Issue Brief*, no. 799, 1–23.

Korvatska, O., Estes, A., Munson, J., Dawson, G., Bekris, L. M., Kohen, R., . . . Raskind, W. H. (2011). Mutations in the TSGA14 gene in families with autism spectrum disorders. *American Journal of Medical Genetics: Part B Neuropsychiatric Genetics, 156B*, 303–311. doi:10.1002/ajmg.b.31162

Koss, M. P. (1993). Detecting the scope of rape: A review of prevalence research methods. *Journal of Interpersonal Violence, 8*, 198–222.

Kossowsky, J., Wilhelm, F. H., Roth, W. T., and Schneider, S. (2012). Separation anxiety disorder in children: Disorder-specific responses to experimental separation from the mother. *Journal of Child Psychology and Psychiatry, 53*, 178–187.

Koszewska, I., & Rybakowski, J. K. (2009). Antidepressant-induced mood conversions in bipolar disorder: A retrospective study of tricyclic versus non-tricyclic antidepressant drugs. *Neuropsychobiology, 59*, 12–16.

Koszycki, D., Taljaard, M., Segal, Z., & Bradwejn, J. (2011). A randomized trial of sertraline, self-administered cognitive behavior therapy, and their combination for panic disorder. *Psychological Medicine, 41*, 371–381.

Kraepelin, E. (1923). *Textbook of psychiatry* (8th ed.). New York, NY: Macmillan. (Original work published 1883)

Kramer, P. D. (2009). Antidepressants and suicide: WHO scientists weigh in [Web log post]. Retrieved from http://www.psychologytoday.com/blog/in-practice/200902/antidepressants-and-suicide-who-scientists-weigh-in

Kramer, U. (2009). Individualizing exposure therapy for PTSD: The case of Caroline. *Pragmatic Case Studies in Psychotherapy, 5*, 1–24.

Kraus, R. P., & Nicholson, I. R. (1996). AIDS-related obsessive compulsive disorder: Deconditioning based in fluoxetine-induced inhibition of anxiety. *Journal of Behavior Therapy and Experimental Psychiatry, 27*, 51–56.

Kroutil, L. A., Van Brunt, D. L., Herman-Stahl, M. A., Heller, D. C., Bray, R. M., & Penne, M. A. (2006). Nonmedical use of prescription stimulants in the United States. *Drug and Alcohol Dependence, 84*, 135–143.

Krueger, J. (2011). Shock without awe. *American Psychologist, 66*, 642–643.

Kubany, E. S., Hill, E. E., Owens, J. A., Iannce-Spencer, C., McCaig, M. A., Tremayne, K. J., & William, P. L. (2004). Cognitive trauma therapy for battered women with PTSD (CTT-BW). *Journal of Consulting and Clinical Psychology, 72*, 3–18.

Kubiszyn, T. W., Meyer, G. J., Finn, S. E., Eyde, L. D., Kay, G. G., Moreland, K. L., . . . Eisman, E. (2000). Empirical support for psychological assessment in clinical health care settings. *Professional Psychology: Research and Practice, 31*, 119–130.

Kuehn, B. M. (2010). Integrated care key for patients with both addiction and mental illness. *Journal of the American Medical Association, 303*, 1905–1907.

Kuehnle, K., & Connell, M. (2009). *The evaluation of child sexual abuse allegations: A comprehensive guide to assessment and testimony*. Hoboken, NJ: John Wiley.

Kugelberg, F. C., Holmgren, A., Eklund, A., & Jones, A.W. (2010). Forensic toxicology findings in deaths involving gamma-hydroxybutyrate. *International Journal of Legal Medicine, 124*, 1–6.

Kumari, V. (2006). Do psychotherapies produce neurobiological effects? *Acta Neuropsychiatrica, 18*, 61–70.

Kumsta, R., Sonuga-Barke, E., & Rutter, M. (2012). Adolescent callous–unemotional traits and conduct disorder in adoptees exposed to severe early deprivation. *British Journal of Psychiatry, 200*, 197–201.

Kung, W. W., & Lu, P. C. (2008). How symptom manifestations affect help seeking for mental health problems among Chinese Americans. *Journal of Nervous and Mental Disease, 196*, 46–54.

Kuo, C.-J., Chen, V. C.-H., Lee, W.-C., Chen, W. J., Ferri, C. P., . . . Ko, Y.-C. (2010). Asthma and suicide mortality in young people: A 12-year follow-up study. *American Journal of Psychiatry, 167*, 1092–1099.

Kuo, J. R., & Linehan, M. M. (2009). Disentangling emotion processes in borderline personality disorder: Physiological and self-reported assessment of biological vulnerability, baseline intensity, and reactivity to emotionally evocative stimuli. *Journal of Abnormal Psychology, 118*, 531–544.

Kupka, R. W., Luckenbaugh, D. A., Post, R. M., Suppes, T., Altshuler, L. L., . . . Nolen, W. A. (2005). Comparison of rapid-cycling and non-rapid-cycling bipolar disorder based on prospective mood ratings in 539 outpatients. *American Journal of Psychiatry, 162*, 1273–1280.

Kusek, K. (2001, May). Could a fear wreak havoc on your life? *Cosmopolitan, 230*(5), 182–184.

Kuwabara, H., Kono, T., Shimada, T., & Kano, Y. (2011). Factors affecting clinicians' decision as to whether to prescribe psychotropic medications or not in treatment of tic disorders. *Brain and Development, 34*(1), 39–44. doi:10.1016/j.braindev.2011.01.003

LaBrie, J. W., Hummer, J. F., Grant, S., & Lac, A. (2010). Immediate reductions in misperceived social norms among high-risk college student groups. *Addictive Behaviors, 35*, 1094–1101.

Lader, M., & Bond, A. J. (1998). Interaction of pharmacological and psychological treatments of anxiety. *British Journal of Psychiatry, 173*, 41–48.

Ladouceur, R., Freeston, M. H., Rheaume, J., Dugas, M. J.,Gagnon, F., . . . Fournier, S. (2000). Strategies used with intrusive thoughts: A comparison of OCD patients with anxious and community controls. *Journal of Abnormal Psychology, 109*, 179–187.

Lagerberg, T. V., Andreassen, O. A., Ringen, P. A., Berg, O., Larsson, S., . . . Melle, I. (2010). Excessive substance use in bipolar disorder is associated with impaired functioning rather than clinical characteristics: A descriptive study. *BMC Psychiatry, 10*, 9.

La Greca, A. M., & Silverman, W. K. (2006). Children and disasters and terrorism. In P. C. Kendall (Ed.), *Child and adolescent therapy: Cognitive-behavioral procedures* (3rd ed., pp. 356–382). New York, NY: Guilford Press.

La Greca, A. M., Silverman, W. K., Lai, B., & Jaccard, J. (2010). Hurricane-related exposure experiences and stressors, other life events, and social support: Concurrent and prospective impact on children's persistent posttraumatic stress symptoms. *Journal of Consulting and Clinical Psychology, 78*, 794–805.

Lahey, B. B., Loeber, R., Burke, J. D., & Applegate, B. (2005). Predicting future antisocial personality disorder in males from a clinical assessment in childhood. *Journal of Consulting and Clinical Psychology, 73*, 389–399.

Lahmann, C., Loew, T. H., Tritt, K., & Nickel, M. (2008). Efficacy of functional relaxation and patient education in the treatment of somatoform heart disorders: A randomized controlled clinical investigation. *Psychosomatics, 49*, 378–385.

Laing, R. D. (1969). *The politics of experience*. New York, NY: Pantheon.

Laje, G., Paddock, S., Manji, H., Rush, A. J., Wilson, A. F., Charney, D., & McMahon, F. J. (2007). Genetic markers of suicidal ideation emerging during citolopram treatment of major depression. *American Journal of Psychiatry, 164*, 1530–1538.

Lam, D. (2009). Can the behavioral approach system (BAS) dysregulation theory help us to understand psychosocial interventions in bipolar disorders? *Clinical Psychology: Science and Practice, 16*, 476–477.

Lam, R. W. (2008). Addressing circadian rhythm disturbances in depressed patients. *Journal of Psychopharmacology, 22*, 13–28.

Lam, R. W., Levitt, A. J., Levitan, R. D., Enns, M. W., Morehouse, R., Michalak, E. E., & Tam, E. M. (2006). The Can-SAD study: A randomized controlled trial of the effectiveness of light therapy and fluoxetine in patients with winter seasonal affective disorder. *American Journal of Psychiatry, 163*, 805–812.

Lamb, H. R., & Weinberger, I. E. (2005). One year follow up of persons discharged from a locked intermediate care facility. *Psychiatric Services, 56*, 198–201.

Lambert, K. G., & Kinsley, G. H. (2005). *Clinical neuroscience: Neurobiological foundations of mental health*. New York, NY: Worth.

The Lancet Neurology. (2010). Dispelling the stigma of Huntington's disease. *The Lancet Neurology, 9*, 751. doi:10.1016/S1474-4422(10)70170-8

Landa, R. J. (2008). Diagnosis of autism spectrum disorders in the first 3 years of life. *Nature Clinical Practice Neurology, 4*, 138–147.

Landa, R. J., Holman, K. C., O'Neill, A. H., & Stuart, E. A. (2011). Intervention targeting development of socially synchronous engagement in toddlers with autism spectrum disorder: A randomized controlled trial. *Journal of Child Psychology and Psychiatry, 52*, 22–23.

Landau, S. M., Marks, S. M., Mormino, E. C., Rabinovici, G. D., Oh, H., O'Neil, J. P., . . . Jagust, W. J. (2012). Association of lifetime cognitive engagement and low β-amyloid deposition. *Archives of Neurology, 69*, 623–629. doi:10.1001/archneurol.2011.2748

Landrigan, P. J. (2010). What causes autism? Exploring the environmental contribution. *Current Opinions in Pediatrics, 22*, 219–225.

Landro, L. (2010). Hidden heart disease. *Wall Street Journal*. Retrieved from http://online.wsj.com/articles/SB10001424052748703514904575602382290981078.html

Laney, C., & Loftus, E. F. (2005). Traumatic memories are not necessarily accurate memories. *Canadian Journal of Psychiatry, 50*, 823–828.

Lange, N., Du Bray, M. B., Lee, J. E., Froimowitz, M. P., Froehlich, A., . . . Lainhart, J. E. (2010). Atypical diffusion tensor hemispheric asymmetry in autism. *Autism Research, 3*(6), 350–358. doi:10.1002/aur.162

Lara, M. E., Klein, D. N., & Kasch, K. L. (2000). Psychosocial predictors of the short-term course and outcome of major depression: A longitudinal study of a nonclinical sample with recent-onset episodes. *Journal of Abnormal Psychology, 109*, 644–650.

Large, M., Sharma, S., Compton, M. T., Slade, T., & Nielssen, O. (2011). Cannabis use and earlier onset of psychosis: A systematic meta-analysis. *Archives of General Psychiatry, 68*, 555–561. doi:10.1001/archgenpsychiatry.2011.5

Larkin, K. T., & Zayfert, C. (1996). Anger management training with mild essential hypertensive patients. *Journal of Behavioral Medicine, 19*, 415–433.

La Roche, M. J., & Christopher, M. S. (2009). Changing paradigms from empirically supported treatments to evidence-based practice: A cultural perspective. *Professional Psychology: Research and Practice, 40*, 396–402.

Larson, E. B., Shadlen, M. F., Wang, L., McCormick, W. C., Bowen, J. D., Teri, L., & Kukall, W. A. (2004). Survival after initial diagnosis of Alzheimer disease. *Annals of Internal Medicine, 140*, 501–509.

Larson, K., Russ, S. A., Kahn, R. S., & Halfon, N. (2011). Patterns of comorbidity, functioning, and service use for US children with ADHD, 2007. *Pediatrics, 127*(3), 462–470. doi:10.1542/peds.2010-0165

Larsson, B., & Fischtel, Å. (2012). Headache prevalence and characteristics among school children as assessed by prospective paper diary recordings. *Journal of Headache and Pain, 13*, 129–136. doi:10.1007/s10194-011-0410-9

Larsson, M., Weiss, B., Janson, S., Sundell, J., & Bornehag, C. G. (2009). Associations between indoor environmental factors and parental-reported autistic spectrum disorders in children 6–8 years of age. *Neurotoxicology, 30*, 822–831.

Latimer, W., & Zur, J. (2010). Epidemiologic trends of adolescent use of alcohol, tobacco, and other drugs. *Child and Adolescent Psychiatric Clinics of North America, 19*, 451–464.

Laumann, E. O., Gagnon, J. H., Michael, R. T., & Michaels, S. (1994). *The social organization of sexuality*. Chicago, IL: University of Chicago Press.

Laumann, E. O., Glasser, D. B., Neves, R. C. S., & Moreira, E. D. (2009). A population-based survey of sexual activity, sexual problems and associated help-seeking behavior patterns in mature adults in the United States of America. *International Journal of Impotence Research, 21*, 171–178.

Launer, L. J. (2009). Diabetes: Vascular or neurodegenerative: an epidemiologic perspective. *Stroke, 40*, S53.

Lavakumar, M., Garlow, S. J., & Schwartz, A. C. (2011). A case of returning psychosis. *Current Psychiatry, 10*, 51–57.

Lavebratt, C., Sjöholm, L. K., Soronen, P., Paunio, T., Vawter, M. P., . . . Schalling, M. (2010). CRY2 is associated with depression. *PLoS One, 5*, e9407.

Lawrence, A. A. (2008). Gender identity disorders in adults: Diagnosis and treatment. In D. Rowland & L. Incrocci (Eds.), *Handbook of sexual and gender identity disorders* (pp. 423–456). Hoboken, NJ: Wiley.

Lawrie, S. M., McIntosh, A. M., Hall, J., Owens, D. G. C., & Johnstone, E. C. (2008). Brain structure and function changes during the development of schizophrenia: The evidence from studies of subjects at increased genetic risk. *Schizophrenia Bulletin, 34,* 330–340.

Lazarov, O., Mattson, M. P., Peterson, D. A., Pimplika, S. W., & van Praag, H. (2010). When neurogenesis encounters aging and disease. *Trends in Neuroscience, 33,* 569–579.

lcouvrely@yahoo.com. (2009, October 29). Re: Binging & Purging: Bulimia [Online forum comment]. Retrieved from http://www.caloriesperhour.com/forums/forum25/656.html

Leach, M. M. (2006). *Cultural diversity and suicide: Ethnic, religious, gender and sexual orientation perspectives.* Binghamton, NY: Haworth.

Leahey, T. M., Crowther, J. H., & Ciesla, J. A. (2011). An ecological momentary assessment of the effects of weight and shape social comparisons on women with eating pathology, high body dissatisfaction, and low body dissatisfaction. *Behavior Therapy, 42,* 197–210.

Leahy, R. L. (2007). Bipolar disorder: Causes, contexts, and treatments. *Journal of Clinical Psychology: In Session, 63,* 417–424.

Leahy, R. L., Beck, J., & Beck, A. T. (2005). Cognitive therapy for the personality disorders. In S. Strack (Ed.), *Handbook of personality and psychopathology* (pp. 442–461). Hoboken, NJ: Wiley.

Leary, P. M. (2003). Conversion disorder in childhood: Diagnosed too late, investigated too much? *Journal of the Royal Society of Medicine, 96,* 436–444.

LeBeau, R. T., Glenn, D., Liao, B., Wittchen, H.-U., Beesdo-Baum, K., Ollendick, T., & Craske, M. G. (2010). Specific phobia: A review of DSM-IV specific phobia and preliminary recommendations for DSM-V. *Depression and Anxiety, 27,* 148–167.

LeBel, E. P., & Peters, K. R. (2011). Fearing the future of empirical psychology: Bem's (2011) evidence of Psi as a case study of deficiencies in modal research practice. *Review of General Psychology, 15,* 371–379.

Leckman, J. F., Denys, D., Simpson, H. B., Mataix-Cols, D., Hollander, E., Saxena, S., . . . Stein, D. J. (2010). Obsessive-compulsive disorder: A review of the diagnostic criteria and possible subtypes and dimensional specifiers for DSM-V. *Depression and Anxiety, 27,* 507–527.

LeCrone, H. (2007). BED sometimes thought of as overeating takes over one's life. Retrieved from http://proquest.umi.com.ezproxy.library.wwu.edu/pqdweb?index52

Lee, C. C., & Armstrong, K. L. (1995). Indigenous models of mental health intervention: Lessons from traditional healers. In J. G. Ponterotto, J. M. Casas, L. A. Suzuki, & C. M. Alexander (Eds.), *Handbook of multicultural counseling.* Thousand Oaks, CA: Sage.

Lee, C. C., Oh, M. Y., & Montcastle, A. R. (1992). Indigenous models of helping in nonwestern countries: Implications for multicultural counseling. *Journal of Multicultural Counseling and Development, 20,* 1–10.

Lee, C. M., Geisner, I. M., Patrick, M. E., & Neighbors, C. (2010). The social norms of alcohol-related negative consequences. *Psychology of Addictive Behaviors, 24*(2), 342–348.

Lee, H.-Y., & Lock, J. (2007). Anorexia nervosa in Asian-American adolescents: Do they differ from their non-Asian peers? *International Journal of Eating Disorders, 40,* 227–231.

Lee, P., Zhang, M., Hong, J. P., Chua, H. C., Chen, K. P., . . . Dossenbach, M. (2009). Frequency of painful physical symptoms with major depressive disorder in Asia: Relationship with disease severity and quality of life. *Journal of Clinical Psychiatry, 70,* 83–91.

Lee, S., Lam, K., Kwok, K., & Fung, C. (2010). The changing profile of eating disorders at a tertiary psychiatric clinic in Hong Kong (1987–2007). *International Journal of Eating Disorders, 43,* 307–314.

Lee, S., Tsang, A., Kessler, R. C., Jin, R., Sampson, N., . . . Petukhova, M. (2010). Rapid-cycling bipolar disorder: Cross-national community study. *British Journal of Psychiatry, 196,* 217–225.

Lee, S., Tsang, A., Von Korff, M., de Graaf, R., Bejet, C., Haro, J. M., . . . Kessler, R. C. (2009). Association of headache with childhood adversity and mental disorder: Cross-national study. *British Journal of Psychiatry, 194,* 111–116.

Lee, Y., & Lin, P.-Y. (2010). Association between serotonin transporter gene polymorphism and eating disorders: A meta-analytic study. *International Journal of Eating Disorders, 43,* 498–504.

Leeies, T. M., Pagura, J., Sareen, J., & Bolton, J. M. (2010). The use of alcohol and drugs to self-medicate symptoms of posttraumatic stress disorder. *Depression and Anxiety, 27*(8), 731–736.

Leenaars, A. A. (2008). Suicide: A cross-cultural theory. In F. Leong & M. M. Leach (Eds.), *Ethnic suicides* (pp. 13–37). New York, NY: Routledge.

Leff, S. S., & Crick, N. R. (2010). Interventions for relational aggression: Innovative programming and next steps in research and practice. *School Psychology Review, 39,* 504–507.

Le Grange, D., Lock, J., Loeb, K., & Nicholls, D. (2010). Academy for eating disorders position paper: The role of the family in eating disorders. *International Journal of Eating Disorders, 43,* 1–5.

Lehrer, P. M., Vaschillo, E., Vaschillo, B., Lu, S.-E., Scardella, A., Siddique, M., & Habib, R. H. (2004). Biofeedback treatment for asthma. *Chest, 126,* 352–361.

Leibenluft, E. (2011). Severe mood dysregulation, irritability, and the diagnostic boundaries of bipolar disorder in youths. *American Journal of Psychiatry, 168,* 129–142.

Leiknes, K. A., Finset, A., Moum, T., & Sandanger, I. (2008). Overlap, comorbidity, and stability of somatoform disorders and the use of current versus lifetime criteria. *Psychosomatics, 49,* 152–162.

Lejoyeux, M., Huet, F., Claudon, M., Fichelle, A., Casalino, E., & Lequen, V. (2008). Characteristics of suicide attempts preceded by alcohol consumption. *Archives of Suicide Research, 12,* 30–38.

Lejuez, C. W., Hopko, D. R., Acierno, R., Daughters, S. B., & Pagoto, S. L. (2011). Ten year revision of the brief behavioral activation treatment for depression: Revised treatment manual. *Behavior Modification, 35,* 111–161.

Leland, J. (March 24, 1997). A risky Rx for fun. *Newsweek, 129,* 12, 74–78.

Lenzenweger, M. F. (2001). Reaction time slowing during high-load, sustained-attention task performance in relation to psychometrically identified schizotypy. *Journal of Abnormal Psychology, 110,* 290–296.

Lenzenweger, M. F., Lane, M. C., Loranger, A. W., & Kessler, R. C. (2007). Personality disorders in the National Comorbidity Survey Replication. *Biological Psychiatry, 62,* 553–564.

Leonard, B. E. (2010). The concept of depression as a dysfunction of the immune system. *Current Opinion in Immunology, 6,* 205–212.

Leonardo, E. D., & Hen, R. (2006). Genetics of affective and anxiety disorders. *Annual Review of Psychology, 57,* 117–137.

Leong, F. T., & Leach, M. M. (2008). *Ethnic suicides.* New York, NY: Routledge.

Lerman, C., & Audrain-McGovern, J. (2010). Reinforcing effects of smoking: More than feeling. *Biological Psychiatry, 67,* 699–701.

Lervolino, A. C., Perroud, N., Fullana, M. A., Guipponi, M., Cherkas, L., Collier, D. A., & Mataix-Cols, D. (2009). Prevalence and heritability of compulsive hoarding: A twin study. *American Journal of Psychiatry, 166,* 1156–1161.

Lespérance, F., Frasure-Smith, N., St-André, E., Turecki, G., Lespérance, P., & Wisniewski, S. R. (2011). The efficacy of omega-3 supplementation for major depression: A randomized controlled trial. *Journal of Clinical Psychiatry, 72,* 1054–1062.

Lester, B. M., Lagasse, L. L., Shankaran, S., Bada, H. S., Bauer, C. R., & Lin, R. (2010). Prenatal cocaine exposure related to cortisol stress reactivity in 11-year-old children. *Journal of Pediatrics, 157,* 288–295.

Lester, D. (2008). Theories of suicide. In F. Leong & M. M. Leach (Eds.), *Ethnic suicides* (pp. 39–53). New York, NY: Routledge.

Leuchter, A. F., Cook, I. A., Hunter, A., & Korb, A. (2009). Use of clinical neurophysiology for the selection of medication in the treatment of major depressive disorder: The state of the evidence. *Clinical EEG and Neuroscience, 40,* 78–83.

LeVay, S., & Valente, S. M. (2006). *Human sexuality.* Sunderland, MA: Sinauer Associates.

Leve, L. D., Kerr, D. C., Shaw, D., Ge, X., Neiderhiser, J. M., . . . Reiss, D. (2010). Infant pathways to externalizing behavior: Evidence of genotype × environment interaction. *Child Development, 81,* 340–356.

Levenson, J. C., Frank, E., Cheng, Y., Rucci, P., Janney, C. A., . . . Fagiolini, A. (2010). Comparative outcomes among the problem areas of interpersonal psychotherapy. *Depression and Anxiety, 27,* 434–440.

Leventhal, J. M., Martin, K. D., & Gaither, J. R. (2012). Using US data to estimate the incidence of serious physical abuse in children. *Pediatrics, 129,* 458–464.

Levi, J., Vinter, S., St. Laurent, R., & Segal, R. M. (2010). *F as in fat: How obesity threatens America's future.* Washington, DC: Trust for America's Health. Retrieved from http://healthyamericans.org/report/88/

Levin, A. (2008, June 20). Psychiatrists lack crystal balls to predict patient violence. *Psychiatric News, 43*(12), 4.

Levine, M. D., Perkins, K. A., Kalarchian, M. K., Cheng, Y., Houck, P. R., Slane, J. D., & Marcus, M. D. (2010). Bupropion and cognitive behavioral therapy for weight-concerned women smokers. *Archives of Internal Medicine, 170,* 543–550.

Levinson, D. F. (2006). The genetics of depression: A review. *Biological Psychiatry, 60,* 84–92.

Levinthal, C. F. (2005). *Drugs, behavior, and modern society.* New York, NY: Allyn & Bacon.

Levkovitz, Y., Harel, E. V., Roth, Y., Braw, Y., Most, D., & Zangen, A. (2009). Deep transcranial magnetic stimulation over the prefrontal cortex: Evaluation of antidepressant and cognitive effects in depressive patients. *Brain Stimulation, 2,* 188–200.

Lewin, A. B., Storch, E. A., & Storch, A. D. (2010). Risks from antipsychotic medications in children and adolescents. *Journal of the American Medical Association, 303,* 729–730.

Lewinsohn, P. M. (1974). A behavioral approach to depression. In R. J. Friedman & M. M. Katz (Eds.), *The psychology of depression: Contemporary theory and research.* New York, NY: Wiley.

Lewinsohn, P. M., Hoberman, H. M., Teri, L., & Hautzinger, M. (1985). An integrative theory of depression. In S. Reiss & R. R. Bootzin (Eds.), *Theoretical issues in behavioral therapy* (pp. 331–359). Orlando, FL: Academic Press.

Lewinsohn, P. M., Muñoz, R. F., Youngren, M. A., & Zeiss, A. M. (1994). *Control your depression* (rev. ed.). New York, NY: Fireside.

Lewis, C. M., Ng, M. Y., Butler, A. W., Cohen-Woods, S., Uher, R., . . . McGuffin, P. (2010). Genome-wide association study of major recurrent depression in the U.K. population. *American Journal of Psychiatry, 167,* 949–957.

Lewis, G., Rice, F., Harold, G.T., Collishaw, S., & Thapar, A. (2011). Investigating environmental links between parent depression and child depressive/anxiety symptoms using an assisted conception design. *Journal of the American Academy of Child & Adolescent Psychiatry, 50,* 451-459.

Lewis, R. W., Fugl-Meyer, K. S., Bosch, R., Fugl-Meyer, A. R., Laumann, E. O., Lizza, E., & Martin-Morales, A. (2004). Epidemiology/risk factors of sexual dysfunction. *Journal of Sexual Medicine, 1,* 35–39.

Lewis, R. W., Yuan, J., & Wang, R. (2008). Male sexual arousal disorder. In D. L. Rowland & L. Incrocci

(Eds.). *Handbook of sexual and gender identity disorders*. pp. 32–63. Hoboken, NJ: Wiley.

Lewis-Fernández, R., Hinton, D. E., Laria, A. J., Patterson, E. H., Hofmann, S. G., . . . Liao, B. (2010). Culture and the anxiety disorders: Recommendations for DSM-V. *Depression and Anxiety, 27*, 212–229.

Lewy Body Dementia Association. (2008). Current issues in Diagnosis and Treatment. Retrieved from http://www.lbda.org/node/425

Li, C. T., Bai, Y. M., Huang, Y. L., Chen, Y. S., Chen, T. J., Cheng, J. Y., & Su, T. P. (2012). Association between antidepressant resistance in unipolar depression and subsequent bipolar disorder: Cohort study. *British Journal of Psychiatry, 200*, 45–51.

Li, G., Wang, L. Y., Shofer, J. B., Thompson, M. L., Peskind, E. R., . . . Larson, E. B. (2011). Temporal relationship between depression and dementia: Findings from a large community-based 15-year follow-up study. *Archives of General Psychiatry, 68*, 970–977.

Li, M., Brady, J. E., DiMaggio, C. J., Lusardi, A. R., Tzong, K. Y., & Li, G. (2012). Marijuana use and motor vehicle crashes. *Epidemiological Review, 34*, 65–72.

Liao, Y., Knoesen, N. P., Castle, D. J., Tang, J., Deng, Y., . . . Liu, T. (2010). Symptoms of disordered eating, body shape, and mood concerns in the male and female Chinese medical students. *Comprehensive Psychiatry, 51*, 516–523.

Liberman, R. P., Kopelowicz, A., & Young, A. S. (1994). Biobehavioral treatment and rehabilitation of schizophrenia. *Behavior Therapy, 25*, 89–107.

Lichtenstein, E., Zhu, S., & Tedeschi, G. J. (2010). Smoking cessation quitlines: An underrecognized intervention success story. *American Psychologist, 65*, 252–261.

Lieberman, J. A., Stroup, T. S., McEvoy, J. P., Swartz, M. S., Rosenheck, R. A., . . . Clinical Antipsychotic Trials of Intervention Effectiveness (CATIE) Investigators. (2005). Effectiveness of antipsychotic drugs in patients with chronic schizophrenia. *New England Journal of Medicine, 353*, 1209–1223.

Lilienfeld, S. O., Lynn, S. J., Kirsch, I., Chaves, J. F., Sarbin, T. R., Ganaway, G. K., & Powell, R. A. (1999). Dissociative identity disorder and the sociocognitive model: Recalling the lessons of the past. *Psychological Bulletin, 125*, 507–523.

Lilienfeld, S. O., Lynn, S. J., & Lohr, J. M. (2004). *Science and pseudoscience in clinical psychology*. New York, NY: Guilford Press.

Lilienfeld, S. O., Wood, J. M., & Garb, H. N. (2000). The scientific status of projective techniques. *Psychological Science in the Public Interest, 1*, 27–61.

Lilliecreutz, C., & Josefsson, A. (2008). Prevalence of blood and injection phobia among pregnant women. *Acta Obstetrics and Gynecology Scandinavia, 87*, 1276–1279.

Lilly, M. M., Pole, N., Best, S. R., Metzler, T., & Marmar, C. R. (2009). Gender and PTSD: What can we learn from female police officers. *Journal of Anxiety Disorders, 23*, 767–774.

Lin, E. C., & Alavi, A. (2009). *PET and PET/CT: A clinical guide* (2nd ed.). New York, NY: Thieme Medical.

Lin, K. C., Chung, H. Y., Wu, C. Y., Liu, H. L., Hsieh, Y. W., . . . Wai, Y. Y. (2010). Constraint-induced therapy versus control intervention in patients with stroke: A functional magnetic resonance imaging study. *American Journal of Physical and Medical Rehabilitation, 89*, 177–185.

Lindau, S. T., Schumm, L. P., Laumann, E. O., Levinson, W., O'Muircheartaigh, C. A., & Waite, L. J. (2007). A study of sexuality and health among older adults in the United States. *New England Journal of Medicine, 357*, 762–774.

Lindhout, I. E., Markus, M. T., Borst, S. R., Hoogendijk, T. H., Dingemans, P. M., & Boer, F. (2009). Childrearing style in families of anxiety-disordered children: Between-family and within-family differences. *Child Psychiatry and Human Development, 40*, 197–212.

Linehan, M. M. (1993). *Cognitive-behavioral treatment of borderline personality disorder*. New York, NY: Guilford Press.

Ling, P. M., Neilands, T. B., & Glantz, S. A. (2009). Young adult smoking behavior: A national survey. *American Journal of Preventive Medicine, 36*(5), 389–394.

Linn, V. (2004, June 26). Headache "beast" holds tight grip on sufferers. *Seattle Post-Intelligencer*, p. A1.

Lipsitt, D., & Starcevic, V. (2006). Psychotherapy and pharmacotherapy in the treatment of somatoform disorders. *Psychiatric Annals, 36*, 341–348.

Lipsitz, J. D. (2006). Psychotherapy for social anxiety disorder. *Psychiatric Times, 23*, 53–58.

Liptak, A. (2010, May 17). Extended civil commitment of sex offenders is upheld. *New York Times*, p. A3.

Lipton, R. B., Bigal, M. E., Diamond, M., Freitag, F., Reed, M. L., & Stewart, W. F. (2007). Migraine prevalence, disease burden, and the need for preventive therapy. *Neurology, 68*, 343–349.

Lis, J. (2011, May 17). Ban on stick-thin models passes Knesset hurdle. *Haaretz*. Retrieved from http://www.haaretz.com

Liu, R. T., & Alloy, L. B. (2010). Stress generation in depression: A systematic review of the empirical literature and recommendations for future study. *Clinical Psychology Review, 30*, 582–593.

Llaneza, D. C., DeLuke, S. V., Batista, M., Crawley, J. N., Christodulu, K. V., & Frye, C. A. (2010). Communication, interventions, and scientific advances in autism: A commentary. *Physiology and Behavior, 100*, 268–276.

Lloyd-Jones, D., Adams, R., Carnethon, M., De Simone, G., Ferguson, T. B., Flegal, K., . . . Yuling Hong. (2009). Heart disease and stroke statistics—2009 update. A report from the American Heart Association Statistics Committee and Stroke Statistics Subcommittee. *Circulation, 119*, e21–e181. doi:10.1161/CIRCULATIONAHA.108.191261

Lock, J., LeGrange, D., Agras, S., Moye, A., Bryson, S. W., & Jo, B. (2010). Randomized clinical trial comparing family-based treatment with adolescent-focused individual therapy for adolescents with anorexia nervosa. *Archives of General Psychiatry, 67*, 1025–1032.

Loeber, R. (1990). Development and risk factors of juvenile antisocial behavior and delinquency. *Clinical Psychology Review, 10*, 1–42.

Loewenstein, R. J. (1994). Diagnosis, epidemiology, clinical course, treatment, and cost effectiveness of treatment for dissociative disorders and MPD: Report submitted to the Clinton Administration Task Force on Health Care Reform. *Dissociation, 7*, 3–11.

Loftus, E. F., Garry, M., & Feldman, J. (1994). Forgetting sexual trauma: What does it mean when 38 percent forget? *Journal of Consulting and Clinical Psychology, 62*, 1177–1181.

Lohoff, F. W. (2010). Overview of the genetics of major depressive disorder. *Current Psychiatry Reports, 12*, 539–546.

Lommen, M. J. J., Sanders, A. J. M. L., Buck, N., & Arntz, A. (2009). Psychosocial predictors of chronic post-traumatic stress disorder in Sri Lankan tsunami survivors. *Behaviour Research and Therapy, 47*, 60–65.

Lopez, S. R., & Hernandez, P. (1987). When culture is considered in the evaluation and treatment of Hispanic patients. *Psychotherapy, 24*, 120–126.

Lopez, S. R., Hipke, K. N., Polo, A. J., Jenkins, J. H., Karno, M., Vaughn, C., & Snyder, K. S. (2004). Ethnicity, expressed emotion, attributions, and course of schizophrenia: Family warmth matters. *Journal of Abnormal Psychology, 113*, 428–439.

LoPiccolo, J. (1995). Sexual disorders and gender identity disorders. In R. J. Comer (Ed.), *Abnormal psychology* (pp. 411–435). New York, NY: Freeman.

LoPiccolo, J. (1997). Sex therapy: A postmodern model. In S. J. Lynn & J. P. Garske (Eds.), *Contemporary psychotherapies: Models and methods* (pp. 485–494). New York, NY: Guilford Press.

Lord, C., Petkova, E., Hus, V., Gan, W., Lu, F., Martin, D. M., . . . Risi, S. (2012). A multisite study of the clinical diagnosis of different autism spectrum disorders. *Archives of General Psychiatry, 69*, 306–313.

Lovejoy, M. (2001). Disturbances in the social body: Differences in body image and eating problems among African American and white women. *Gender and Society, 15*, 239–261.

Low, C. A., Thurston, R. C., & Matthews, K. A. (2010). Psychosocial factors in the development of heart disease in women: Current research and future directions. *Psychosomatic Medicine, 72*, 842–854.

Lu, L. H., Johnson, A., O'Hare, E., Bookheimer, S., Smith, L. M., O'Connor, M. J., & Sowell, E. R. (2009). Effects of prenatal methamphetamine exposure on verbal memory revealed with functional magnetic resonance imaging. *Journal of Developmental & Behavioral Pediatrics, 30*(3), 185–192.

Lubit, R.H. (2012). Oppositional defiant disorder. Retrieved from http://emedicine.medscape.com/article/918095-overview

Lucas, M., Mekary, R., Pan, A., Mirzaei, F., O'Reilly, E.J., . . . Ascherio, A. (2011). Relation between clinical depression risk and physical activity and time spent watching television in older women: A 10-year prospective follow-up study. *American Journal of Epidemiology, 174*, 1017–1027

Ludwig, J., Marcotte, D. E., & Norberg, K. (2009). Anti-depressants and suicide. *Journal of Health Economics, 28*, 659–676.

Lue, T. F. (2002). Physiology of penile erection and pathophysiology of erectile dysfunction and priapism. In P. C. Walsh, A. B. Retik, & E. D. Vaughan, Jr. (Eds.), *Campbell's urology* (8th ed., pp. 1610–1696). Philadelphia, PA: Saunders.

Lussier, P., McCann, K., & Beauregard, E. (2008). The etiology of sexual deviance. In D. Rowland & L. Incrocci (Eds.), *Handbook of sexual and gender identity disorders* (pp. 529–562). Hoboken, NJ: Wiley.

Lyke, M. L. (2004, August 27). Once a "people person," vet couldn't leave home. *Seattle Post-Intelligencer*, p. A8.

Lykken, D. T. (1982). Fearlessness: Its carefree charm and deadly risks. *Psychology Today, 16*, 20–28.

Lynch, T. B. (2007). *PET/CT in clinical practice*. London, UK: Springer-Verlag.

Lyon, G. J., Abi-Dargham, A., Moore, H., Lieberman, J. A., Javitch, J. A., & Sulzer, D. (2011). Presynaptic regulation of dopamine transmission in schizophrenia. *Schizophrenia Bulletin, 37*, 108–117.

Lyons-Ruth, K., Bureau, J., Riley, C. D., & Atlas-Corbett, A. F. (2009). Socially indiscriminate attachment behavior in the strange situation: Convergent and discriminant validity in relation to caregiving risk, later behavior problems, and attachment insecurity. *Development and Psychopathology, 21*, 355–367.

Mace, C. J., & Trimble, M. R. (1996). Ten-year prognosis of conversion disorder. *British Journal of Psychiatry, 169*, 282–288.

Machover, K. (1949). *Personality projection in the drawing of the human figure: A method of personality investigation*. Springfield, IL: Thomas.

Mackenzie, S., Wiegel, J. R., Mundt, M., Brown, D., Saewyc, E., . . . Fleming, M. (2011). Depression and suicide ideation among students accessing campus health care. *American Journal of Orthopsychiatry, 81*, 101–107.

Mackillop, J., Mattson, R. E., Anderson, E. J., Mackillop, E. J., Castelda, B. A., & Donovick, P. J. (2007). Multidimensional assessment of impulsivity in undergraduate hazardous drinkers and controls. *Journal of Studies on Alcohol and Drugs, 68*, 785–788.

Maddi, S. R. (2002). The story of hardiness: Twenty years of theorizing, research and practice. *Consulting Psychology Journal, 54*, 173–185.

Madsen, K. A., Weedn, A. E., & Crawford, P. B. (2010). Disparities in the peaks, plateaus, and declines in prevalence of high BMI among adolescents. *Pediatrics, 126*, 434–442.

Maguen, S., Luxton, D. D., Skopp, N. A., & Madden, E. (2012). Gender differences in traumatic

experiences and mental health in active duty soldiers redeployed from Iraq and Afghanistan. *Journal of Psychiatric Research. 46,* 311–316.
Mahgoub, N., & Hossain, A. (2006). A 73-year-old woman with Parkinson's disease, psychotic symptoms. *Psychiatric Annals, 36,* 598–602.
Mahgoub, N., & Hossain, A. (2007). A 60-year-old woman with avoidant personality disorder. *Psychiatric Annals, 37,* 10–12.
Mahon, K., Burdick, K. E., & Szeszko, P. R. (2010). A role for white matter abnormalities in the pathophysiology of bipolar disorder. *Neuroscience and Biobehavioral Reviews, 34,* 533–554.
Mahoney, D. M. (2000). Panic disorder and self states: Clinical and research illustrations. *Clinical Social Work Journal, 28,* 197–212.
Maier, S. F., & Watkins, L. R. (2010). Role of the medial prefrontal cortex in coping and resilience. *Brain Research, 1355,* 52–60.
Maines, R. P. (1999). *The technology of orgasm: "Hysteria," the vibrator, and women's sexual satisfaction.* Baltimore, MD: Johns Hopkins University Press.
Mak, W. W., Ng, I. S., & Wong, C. C. (2011). Resilience: Enhancing well-being through the positive cognitive triad. *Journal of Counseling Psychology, 58,* 610–617.
Małyszczak, K., & Pawłowski, T. (2006). Distress and functioning in mixed anxiety and depressive disorder. *Psychiatry and Clinical Neuroscience, 60,* 168–173.
Mancebo, M. C., Eisen, J. L., Sibrava, N. J., Dyck, I. R., & Rasmussen, S. A. (2011). Patient utilization of cognitive-behavior therapy for OCD. *Behavior Therapy, 42,* 399–412.
Mancuso, C. E., Tanzi, M. G., & Gabay, M. (2004). Paradoxical reactions to benzodiazepines: Literature review and treatment options. *Pharmacotherapy, 24,* 1177–1185.
Mancuso, S. P., Knoesen, N. P., & Castle, D. J. (2010). Delusional versus nondelusional body dysmorphic disorder. *Comprehensive Psychiatry, 51,* 177–182.
Mann, J. J. (2003). Neurobiology of suicidal behavior. *Nature Reviews Neuroscience, 4,* 819–828.
Mann, J. J., Arango, V. A., Avenevoli, S., Brent, D. A., Champagne, F. A., . . . Wenzel, A. (2009). Candidate endophenotypes for genetic studies of suicidal behavior. *Biological Psychiatry, 65,* 556–563.
Mann, J. J., & Haghighi, F. (2010). Genes and environment: Multiple pathways to psychopathology. *Biological Psychiatry, 68,* 403–404.
Mann, K., & Hermann, D. (2010). Individualized treatment in alcohol-dependent patients. *European Archives of Psychiatry and Clinical Neuroscience, 2,* S116–S120.
Mann, T., Tomiyama, A. J., Westling, E., Lew, A.-M., Samuels, B., & Chatman, J. (2007). Medicare's search for effective obesity treatments: Diets are not the answer. *American Psychologist, 62,* 220–233.
Marangell, L. B., Dennehy, E. B., Miyahara, S., Wisniewski, S. R., Bauer, M. S., Rapaport, M. H., & Allen, M. H. (2009). The functional impact of subsyndromal depressive symptoms in bipolar disorder: Data from STEP-BD. *Journal of Affective Disorders, 114,* 58–67.
Marangell, L. B., Martinez, M., Jurdi, R. A., & Zboyan, H. (2007). Neurostimulation therapies in depression: A review of new modalities. *Acta Psychiatrica Scandinavica, 116,* 174–181.
Marchand, E., Ng, J., Rohde, P., & Stice, E. (2010). Effects of an indicated cognitive-behavioral depression prevention program are similar for Asian American, Latino, and European American adolescents. *Behavior Research and Therapy, 48,* 821–825.
Marchand, W. R., Lee, J. N., Garn, C., Thatcher, J., Gale, P., Kreitschitz, S., . . . Wood, N. (2011). Striatal and cortical midline activation and connectivity associated with suicidal ideation and depression in bipolar II disorder. *Journal of Affective Disorders, 133,* 638–645.
Marchesi, C., Paini, M., Ruju, L., Rosi, L., Turrini, G., & Maggini, C. (2007). Predictors of the evolution towards schizophrenia or mood disorder in patients with schizophreniform disorder. *Schizophrenia Research, 97,* 1–5.
Marcus, S. M., Gorman, J., Shear, M. K., Lewin, D., Martinez, J., . . . Woods, S. (2007). A comparison of medication side effect reports by panic disorder patients with and without concomitant cognitive behavior therapy. *American Journal of Psychiatry, 164,* 273–275.
Maris, R. W. (2001). Suicide. In H. S. Friedman (Ed.), *Specialty articles from the encyclopedia of mental health.* San Diego, CA: Academic Press.
Maris, R. W., Berman, A. L., & Silverman, M. M. (2000). *Comprehensive textbook of suicidology.* New York, NY: Guilford Press.
Markarian, Y., Larson, M. J., Aldea, M. A., Baldwin, S. A., Good, D., . . . McKay, D. (2010). Multiple pathways to functional impairment in obsessive-compulsive disorder. *Clinical Psychology Review, 30,* 78–88.
Markus, C. R., & De Raedt, R. (2011). Differential effects of 5-HTTLPR genotypes on inhibition of negative emotional information following acute stress exposure and tryptophan challenge. *Neuropsychopharmacology, 36,* 819–826.
Marr, A. J. (2006). Relaxation and muscular tension: A biobehavioristic explanation. *International Journal of Stress Management, 13,* 131–153.
Marris, E. (2006). Mysterious "Morgellons disease" prompts U.S. investigation. *Nature, 12,* 982.
Marsh, H. W., Hau, K. T., Sung, R. Y. T., & Yu, C. W. (2007). Childhood obesity, gender, actual-ideal body image discrepancies, and the physical self-concept in Hong Kong children: Cultural differences in the value of moderation. *Developmental Psychology, 43,* 647–662.
Marsh, J. C. (1988). What have we learned about legislative remedies for rape? *Annals of the New York Academy of Sciences,* 528, 79–110.
Marsh, W. K., Ketter, T. A., & Rasgon, N. L. (2009). Increased depressive symptoms in menopausal age women with bipolar disorder: Age and gender comparison. *Journal of Psychiatric Research, 43,* 798–802.
Marshall, R. D., Bryant, R. A., Amsel, L., Suh, E. J., Cook, J. M., & Neria, Y. (2007). The psychology of ongoing threat: Relative risk appraisal, the September 11 attacks, and terrorism-related fears. *American Psychologist, 62,* 304–316.
Marshall, S. A., Landau, M. E., Carroll, C. G., & Schwieters, B. (2008). Conversion disorders. Retrieved from http://emedicine.medscape.com/article/287464-overview
Marsolek, M. R., White, N. C., & Litovitz, T. L. (2010). Inhalant abuse: Monitoring trends by using poison control data, 1993–2008. *Pediatrics, 125,* 906–913.
Martin, A., & Rief, W. (2011). Relevance of cognitive and behavioral factors in medically unexplained syndromes and somatoform disorders. *Psychiatric Clinics of North America, 34,* 565–578.
Martin, P. R., & MacLeod, C. (2009). Behavioral management of headache triggers: Avoidance of triggers is an inadequate strategy. *Clinical Psychology Review, 29,* 483–495.
Martin, P. R., & Seneviratne, H. M. (1997). Effects of food deprivation and a stressor on head pain. *Health Psychology, 16,* 310–318.
Martinez-Taboas, A. (2005). Psychogenic seizures in an espiritismo context: The role of culturally sensitive psychotherapy. *Psychotherapy: Theory, Research, Practice, Training, 42,* 6–13.
Martins, S. S., & Alexandre, P. K. (2009). The association of Ecstasy use and academic achievement among adolescents in two US national surveys. *Addictive Behaviors, 34,* 9–16.
Martinson, A. A., Nangle, D. W., Boulard, N., & Sigmon, S. T. (2011). Old habits die hard: Treating a woman with a 20-year severcase of skin-picking disorder. *Clinical Case Studies, 10,* 411–426.
Maslow, A. H. (1954). *Motivation and personality.* New York, NY: Harper & Row.
Mason, M. (2006, October 24). Is it disease or delusion? U.S. takes on a dilemma. *New York Times.* Retrieved from http://www.nytimes.com
Masten, A. S. (2009). Ordinary magic: Lessons from research on resilience in human development. *Education Canada, 49,* 28–32. Retrieved from http://www.cea-ace.ca/education-canada/article/ordinary-magic-lessons-research-or-resilience-human-development
Masten, A. S. (2011). Resilience in children threatened by extreme adversity: Frameworks for research, practice, and translational synergy. *Development and Psychopathology, 23,* 493–506.
Masten, A. S., Faden, V. B., Zucker, R. A., & Spear, L. P. (2008). Underage drinking: A developmental framework. *Pediatrics, 121*(Suppl 4), S235–S251.
Masten, A.S., & Narayan, A.J. (2012). Child development in the context of disaster, war, and terrorism: Pathways of risk and resilience. *Annual Review of Psychology, 63,* 227–257.
Masters, W. H., & Johnson, V. E. (1966). *Human sexual response.* Boston, MA: Little, Brown.
Masters, W. H., & Johnson, V. E. (1970). *Human sexual inadequacy.* London, UK: Churchill.
Mathews, C. A., & Grados, M. A. (2011). Familiality of Tourette syndrome, obsessive-compulsive disorder and attention-deficit/hyperactivity disorder: Heritability analysis in a large sib-pair sample. *Journal of the American Academy of Child & Adolescent Psychiatry, 50,* 46–54.
Maulik, P. K., Mascarenhas, M. N., Mathers, C. D., Dua, T., & Saxena, S. (2011). Prevalence of intellectual disability: A meta-analysis of population-based studies. *Research on Developmental Disabilities, 32,* 419–436.
May, P. A., Gossage, J. P., Kalberg, W. O, Robinson, L. K., Buckley, D., Manning, M., & Hoyme, H. E. (2009). Prevalence and epidemiologic characteristics of FASD from various research methods with an emphasis on recent in-school studies. *Developmental Disabilities Research Reviews, 15,* 176–192.
Mayhew, S. L., & Gilbert, P. (2008). Compassionate mind training with people who hear malevolent voices: A case series report. *Clinical Psychology and Psychotherapy, 15,* 113–138.
Mayo, C., Kaye, A. D., Conrad, E., Baluch, A., & Frost, E. (2010). Update on anesthesia considerations for electroconvulsive therapy. *Middle Eastern Journal of Anesthesiology, 20,* 493–498.
Mazurek, M. O., Kanne, S. M., & Miles, J. H. (2012) Predicting improvement in social-communication symptoms of autism spectrum disorders using retrospective treatment data. *Research in Autism Spectrum Disorders, 6,* 535–545.
McAnulty, R. D., & Burnette, M. M. (2003). *Fundamentals of human sexuality: Making healthy decisions.* New York, NY: Allyn & Bacon.
McAnulty, R. D., & Burnette, M. M. (2004). *Fundamentals of exploring human sexuality: Making healthy decisions.* New York, NY: Allyn & Bacon.
McBride, K. R., Reece, M., & Sanders, S. (2008). Using the sexual compulsivity scale to predict outcomes of sexual behavior in young adults. *Sexual Addiction & Compulsivity, 15,* 97–115.
McBurnett, K., & Pfiffner, L. J. (2009). Treatment of aggressive ADHD in children and adolescents: Conceptualization and treatment of comorbid behavior disorders. *Postgraduate Medicine, 121,* 158–165.
McCabe, H. T., Wilsnack, S. E., West, B. T., & Boyd, C. J. (2010). Victimization and substance use disorders in a national sample of heterosexual and sexual minority women and men. *Addiction, 105*(12), 2130–2140. doi:10.1111/j.1360-0443.2010.03088.x
McCabe, R., & Priebe, S. (2004). Explanatory models of illness in schizophrenia: Comparison of four ethnic groups. *British Journal of Psychiatry, 185,* 25–30.
McCabe, R. E., Miller, J. L., Laugesen, N., Antony, M. M., & Young, L. (2010). The relationship between anxiety disorders in adults and recalled childhood teasing. *Journal of Anxiety Disorders, 24,* 238–243.

McCabe, S. E., Hughes, T. L., Bostwick, W. B., West, B. T., & Boyd, C. J. (2009). Sexual orientation, substance use behaviors and substance dependence in the United States. *Addiction, 104*, 1333–1345.

McCarron, R. M. (2006). Somatization in the primary care setting. *Psychiatric Times, 23*, 32–36.

McCloud, A., Barnaby, B., Omu, N., Drummond, C., & Aboud, A. (2004). Relationship between alcohol use disorders and suicidality in a psychiatric population. *British Journal of Psychiatry, 184*, 439–445.

McClung, C. A. (2007). Circadian genes, rhythms and the biology of mood disorders. *Pharmacology and Therapeutics, 114*, 222–232.

McCracken, L. M., & Larkin, K. T. (1991). Treatment of paruresis with in vivo desensitization: A case report. *Journal of Behavior Therapy and Experimental Psychiatry, 22*, 57–62.

McCullough, J. P., Klein, D. N., Borian, F. E., Howland, R. H., Riso, L. P., Keller, M. B., & Banks, P. (2008). Group comparisons of DSM-IV subtypes of chronic depression: Validity of the distinctions—Part II. *Journal of Abnormal Psychology, 112*, 614–622.

McCullough, P. K., & Maltsberger, J. T. (2001). Obsessive-compulsive personality disorder. In G. O. Gabbard (Ed.), *Treatment of psychiatric disorders* (pp. 2341–2351). Washington, DC: American Psychiatric Publishing.

McDaniel, S. H., & Speice, J. (2001). What family psychology has to offer women's health: The examples of conversion, somatization, infertility treatment, and genetic testing. *Professional Psychology: Research and Practice, 32*, 44–51.

McDowell, M. A., Fryar, C. D., Ogden, C. L. & Flegal, K. M. (2008). Anthropometric Reference Data for Children and Adults: United States, 2003–2006. *National Health Statistic Reports,* Number 10, Hyattsville, MD.

McGlashan, T. H., & Woods, S. (2011). Early antecedents and detection of schizophrenia. *Psychiatric Times, 28*, 1–6.

McGoldrick, M., Giordano, J., & Garcia-Preto, N. (2005). *Ethnicity and family therapy*. New York, NY: Guilford Press.

McGorm, K., Burton, C., Weller, D., Murray, G., and Sharpe, M. (2010). Patients repeatedly referred to secondary care with symptoms unexplained by organic disease: Prevalence, characteristics, and referral pattern. *Family Practice, 27*, 479–486.

McGrath, J., Welham, J., Scott, J., Varghese, D., Degenhardt, L., Hayatbakhsh, M. R., . . . Najman, J. M. (2010). Association between cannabis use and psychosis-related outcomes using sibling pair analysis in a cohort of young adults. *Archives of General Psychiatry, 67*, 440–447.

McHugh, M. D. (2007). Readiness for change and short-term outcomes of female adolescents in residential treatment for anorexia nervosa. *International Journal of Eating Disorders, 40*, 602–605.

McHugh, P. R. (2009). Multiple personality disorder (dissociative identity disorder). Retrieved from http://www.psycom.net/mchugh.html

McIntosh, V. V. W., Carter, F. A., Bulik, C. M., Frampton, C. M. A., & Joyce, P. R. (2010). Five-year outcome of cognitive behavioral therapy and exposure with response: Prevention for bulimia nervosa. *Psychological Medicine, 41(5)*, 1061–1071. doi:10.1017/S0033291710001583

McKibben, J. B., Bresnick, M. G., Wiechman Askay, S. A., & Fauerbach, J. A. (2008). Acute stress disorder and posttraumatic stress disorder: A prospective study of prevalence, course, and predictors in a sample with major burn injuries. *Journal of Burn Care and Research, 29*, 22–35.

McLaughlin, K. A., Green, J. G., Gruber, M. J., Sampson, N. A., Zaslavsky, A. M., & Kessler, R. C. (2010). Childhood adversities and adult psychiatric disorders in the National Comorbidity Survey Replication II: Associations with persistence of DSM-IV disorders. *Archives of General Psychiatry, 67*(2), 124–132.

McLaughlin, K. A., & Hatzenbuehler, M. L. (2009). Stressful life events, anxiety sensitivity, and internalizing symptoms in adolescents. *Journal of Abnormal Psychology, 118*, 659–669.

McLaughlin, K. A., Hatzenbuehler, M. L., & Keyes, K. M. (2010). Responses to discrimination and psychiatric disorders among black, Hispanic, female, and lesbian, gay, and bisexual individuals. *American Journal of Public Health, 100*, 1477–1484.

McLaughlin, K. A., Mennin, D. S., & Farach, F. J. (2007). The contributory role of worry in emotion generation and dysregulation in generalized anxiety disorder. *Behavior Research and Therapy, 45*, 1735–1752.

McLean, C. P., & Anderson, E. R. (2009). Brave men and timid women? A review of gender differences in fear and anxiety. *Clinical Psychology Review, 29*, 496–505.

McLean, S. A., Paxton, S. J., & Wertheim, E. H. (2010). Factors associated with body dissatisfaction and disordered eating in women in midlife. *International Journal of Eating Disorders, 43*, 527–536.

McLellan, A. T., & Meyers, K. (2004). Contemporary addiction treatment: A review of systems problems for adults and adolescents. *Biological Psychiatry, 56*, 764–770.

McNally, R. J. (2007). Dispelling confusion about traumatic dissociative amnesia. *Mayo Clinic Proceedings, 82*, 1083–1087.

McNally, R. J., Clancy, S. A., Schacter, D. L., & Pitman, R. K. (2000). Personality profiles, dissociation, and absorption in women reporting repressed, recovered, or continuous memories of childhood sexual abuse. *Journal of Consulting and Clinical Psychology, 68*, 1033–1037.

Medina, J. J. (2008). Neurobiology of PTSD: Part 1. *Psychiatric Times, 25*(1), 29–33.

Meeks, J. (2004). *AFPPA 2003: Headache management—Evaluation and treatment*. Retrieved from www.medscape.com/viewarticle/467744

Meichenbaum, D. (2007). Stress inoculation training: A preventative and treatment approach. In P. M. Lehrer et al. (Eds.), *Principles and practice of stress management* (pp. 497–518). New York, NY: Guilford Press.

Meichenbaum, D. (2012). *Important facts about resilience: A consideration of research findings about resilience and implications for assessment and treatment*. Retrieved from http://www.melissainstitute.org/documents/facts_resilience.pdf

Meili, T. (2003). *I am the Central Park Jogger: A story of hope and possibility*. New York, NY: Scribner.

Meilleur, A. A., & Fombonne, E. J. (2009). Regression of language and non-language skills in pervasive developmental disorders. *Intellectual Disabilities Research, 53*, 115–124.

Meiser-Stedman, R., Dalgleish, T., Gluckman, E., Yule, W., & Smith, P. (2009). Maladaptive cognitive appraisals mediate the evolution of posttraumatic stress reactions: A 6-month follow-up of child and adolescent assault and motor vehicle accident survivors. *Journal of Abnormal Psychology, 118*, 778–787.

Melago, C. (2009, October 15). Ralph Lauren firing of 'too fat' size 4 Filippa Hamilton raises ire of women, body-image experts. *New York Daily News*. Retrieved from http://www.nydailynews.com

Melka, S. E., Lancaster, S. L., Adams, L. J., Howarth, E. A., & Rodriguez, B. F. (2010). Social anxiety across ethnicity: A confirmatory factor analysis of the FNE and SAD. *Journal of Anxiety Disorders, 24*, 680–685.

Meloy, J. R. (2001). Antisocial personality disorder. In G. O. Gabbard (Ed.), *Treatment of psychiatric disorders* (pp. 2251–2271). Washington, DC: American Psychiatric Publishing.

Memon, M. A., & Bienenfeld, D. (2012). Brief psychotic disorder. Retrieved from http://emedicine.medscape.com/article/294416-overview

Mena, A. (2012). *Rape trauma syndrome: The journey to healing belongs to every one*. Retrieved from http://www.adkanenough.com/rape-trauma-syndrome.html

Mercan, S., Altunay, I. K., Taskintuna, N., Ogutcen, O., & Kayaoglu, S. (2007). Atypical antipsychotic drugs in the treatment of delusional parasitosis. *International Journal of Psychiatry in Medicine, 37*, 29–37.

Mercer, K. B., Orcutt, H. K., Quinn, J. F., Fitzgerald, C. A. Conneely, K. N., . . . Ressler, K. J. (2012). Acute and posttraumatic stress symptoms in a prospective gene × environment study of a university campus shooting. *Archives of General Psychiatry, 69*, 89–97.

Merikangas, K. R., Akiskal, H. S., Angst, J., Greenberg, P. E., Hirschfeld, R. M., Petukhova, M., & Kessler, R. C. (2007). Lifetime and 12-month prevalence of bipolar spectrum disorder in the National Comorbidity Survey Replication. *Archives of General Psychiatry, 64*, 543–552.

Merikangas, K. R., He, J.-P., Burstein, M., Swanson, S. A., Avenevoli, S., Cui, L., . . . Swendsen, J. (2010). Lifetime prevalence of mental disorders in U.S. adolescents: Results from the National Comorbidity Survey Replication–Adolescent Supplement (NCS-A). *Journal of the Academy of Child & Adolescent Psychiatry, 49*, 980–989.

Merikangas, K. R., He, J.-P., Burstein, M., Swendsen, J., Avenevoli, S., Case, B., . . . Olfson, M. (2011). Service utilization for lifetime mental disorders in U.S. adolescents: Results of the National Comorbidity Survey–Adolescent Supplement (NCS-A). *Journal of the American Academy of Child & Adolescent Psychiatry, 50*, 32–45.

Merikangas, K. R., Jin, R., He, J.-P., Kessler, R. C., Lee, S., . . . Zarkov, Z. (2011). Prevalence and correlates of bipolar spectrum disorder in the world mental health survey initiative. *Archives of General Psychiatry, 68*, 241–251.

Merritt, M. M., Bennett, G. G., Jr., Williams, R. B., Edwards, C. L., & Sollers, J. J., III. (2006). Perceived racism and cardiovascular reactivity and recovery to personally relevant stress. *Health Psychology, 25*, 364–369.

Merryman, K. (1997, July 17). Medical experts say Roberts may well have amnesia: Parts of her life match profile of person who might lose memory. *Tacoma News Tribune*, pp. A8–A9.

Merskey, H. (1995). Multiple personality disorder and false memory syndrome. *British Journal of Psychiatry, 166*, 281–283.

Merten, J., & Brunnhuber, S. (2004). Facial expression and experience of emotions in psychodynamic interviews with patients suffering from a pain disorder. *Psychopathology, 37*, 266–271.

Messer, S. B. (2001). Empirically supported treatments: What's a nonbehaviorist to do? In B. D. Slife, R. N. Williams, & S. H. Barlow (Eds.), *Critical issues in psychotherapy* (pp. 45–59). Thousand Oaks, CA: Sage.

Messinger, J. W., Tremeau, F., Antonius, D., Mendelsohn, E., Prudent, V., . . . Malaspina, D. (2011). Avolition and expressive deficits capture negative symptom phenomenology: Implications for DSM-V and schizophrenia research. *Clinical Psychology Review, 31*, 161–168.

Meston, C. M., Seal, B. N., & Hamilton, L. D. (2008). Problems with arousal and orgasm in women. In D. Rowland & L. Incrocci (Eds.), *Handbook of sexual and gender identity disorders* (pp. 188–219). Hoboken, NJ: Wiley.

Mewton, L., Slade, T., McBride, O., Grove, R., & Teesson, M. (2011). An evaluation of the proposed DSM-5 alcohol use disorder criteria using Australian national data. *Addiction, 106*(5), 941–950. doi:10.1111/j.1360-0443.2010.03340.x

Meyer, G. J., Finn, S. E., Eyde, L. D., Kay, G. G., Moreland, K. L., . . . Reed, G. M. (2001). Psychological testing and psychological assessment: A review of evidence and issues. *American Psychologist, 56*, 128–165.

Meyer, S. E., Carlson, G. A., Youngstrom, E., Ronsaville, D. S., Martinez, P. E., Gold, P. W., . . . Radke-Yarrow, M. (2009). Long-term outcomes of youth who manifested the CBCL-pediatric bipolar disorder phenotype during childhood and/or adolescence. *Journal of Affective Disorders, 113*, 227–235.

Meyer-Bahlburg, H. F. L. (2009). From mental disorder to iatrogenic hypogonadism: Dilemmas in conceptualizing gender identity variants as psychiatric conditions. *Archives of Sexual Behavior, 39*(2), 461–476. doi:10.1007/s10508-009-9532-4

Meyerbroker, K., & Emmelkamp, P. M. (2010). Virtual reality exposure therapy in anxiety disorders: A systematic review of process-and-outcome studies. *Depression and Anxiety, 27*, 933–944.

Meyerson, D. A., Grant, K. E., Carter, J. S., & Kilmer, R. P. (2011). Posttraumatic growth among children and adolescents: A systematic review. *Clinical Psychology Review, 31*, 949–964.

Mezulis, A. H., Priess, H. A., & Hyde, J. S. (2011). Rumination mediates the relationship between infant temperament and adolescent depressive symptoms. *Depression Research and Treatment*, 487873.

Michael, R. T., Gagnon, J. H., Laumann, E. O., & Kolata, G. (1994). *Sex in America: A definitive survey*. New York, NY: Little, Brown.

Midei, A. J., & Matthews, K. A. (2009). Social relationships and negative emotional traits are associated with central adiposity and arterial stiffness in health adolescents. *Health Psychology, 28*, 347–353.

Miettunen, J., Tormanen, S., Murray, G. K., Jones, P. B., Maki, P., . . . Veijola, J. (2008). Association of cannabis use with prodromal symptoms of psychosis in adolescence. *British Journal of Psychiatry, 192*, 470–471.

Mikton, C., & Grounds, A. (2007). Cross-cultural clinical judgment bias in personality disorder diagnosis by forensic psychiatrists in the UK: A case-vignette study. *Journal of Personality Disorders, 21*, 400–417.

Mikulas, W. L. (2006). Integrating the world's psychologies. In L. T. Hoshman (Ed.), *Culture, psychotherapy and counseling* (pp. 91–111). Thousand Oaks, CA: Sage.

Milillo, D. (2008). Sexuality sells: A content analysis of lesbian and heterosexual women's bodies in magazine advertisements. *Journal of Lesbian Studies, 12*, 381–386.

Milin, R., Manion, I., Dare, G., & Walker, S. (2008). Prospective assessment of cannabis withdrawal in adolescents with cannabis dependence: A pilot study. *Journal of the American Academy of Child & Adolescent Psychiatry, 47*, 174–178.

Miller, D. D., Caroff, S. N., Davis, S. M., Rosenheck, R. A., McEvoy, J. P., . . . Liberman, J. A. (2008). Extrapyramidal side-effects of antipsychotics in a randomized trial. *British Journal of Psychiatry, 193*, 279–288.

Miller, D. J., & Thelen, M. H. (1986). Knowledge and beliefs about confidentiality in psychotherapy. *Professional Psychology, 17*, 15–19.

Miller, G. A., & Keller, J. (2000). Psychology and neuroscience: Making peace. *Current Directions in Psychological Science, 9*, 212–215.

Miller, G. E., Chen, E., & Zhou, E. S. (2007). If it goes up, must it come down? Chronic stress and the hypothalamic-pituitary-adrenocortical axis in humans. *Psychological Bulletin, 133*, 25–45.

Miller, G. E., Lachman, M. E., Chen, E., Gruenewald, T. L., Karlamangla, A. S., & Seeman, T. E. (2011). Pathways to resilience: Maternal nurturance as a buffer against the effects of childhood poverty on metabolic syndrome at midlife. *Psychological Science, 22*, 1591–1599.

Miller, J. M., Brennan, K. G., Ogden, T. R., Oquendo, M. A., Sullivan, G. M., Mann, J. J., & Parsey, R. V. (2009). Elevated serotonin 1A binding in remitted major depressive disorder: Evidence for a trait biological abnormality. *Neuropsychopharmacology, 34*, 2275–2284.

Miller, M., & Kantrowitz, B. (1999, January 25). Unmasking Sybil. *Newsweek*, 66–68.

Miller, M. N., & Pumariega, A. J. (2001). Culture and eating disorders: A historical and cross-cultural review. *Psychiatry, 64*, 93–110.

Miller, R. R., & Ely, E. W. (2007). Delirium and cognitive dysfunction in the intensive care unit. *Current Psychiatry Reports, 9*, 26–34.

Miller, S. B., Friese, M., Dolgoy, L., Sita, A., Lavoie, K., & Campbell, T. (1998). Hostility, sodium consumption, and cardiovascular response to interpersonal stress. *Psychosomatic Medicine, 60*, 71–77.

Miller, T. C., & Zwerdling, D. (2010, June 9) With traumatic brain injuries, soldiers face battle for care. Retrieved from http://www.npr.org/templates/story/story.php?storyId=127542820

Millichap, J. G. (2008). Etiologic classification of attention-deficit/hyperactivity disorder. *Pediatrics, 121*, e358–e365.

Millichap, J. G., & Yee, M. M. (2012). The diet factor in attention-deficit/hyperactivity disorder. *Pediatrics, 129*, 330–337.

Millon, T., Grossman, S., Millon, C., Meagher, S., & Ramnath, R. (2004). *Personality disorders in modern life*. Hoboken, NJ: Wiley.

Milstone, C. (1997). Sybil minds. *Saturday Night, 112*, 35–42.

Mineka, S., & Zinbarg, R. (2006). A contemporary learning theory perspective on the etiology of anxiety disorders. *American Psychologist, 61*, 10–26.

Mintz, A. R., Dobson, K. S., & Romney, D. M. (2003). Insight in schizophrenia: A meta-analysis. *Schizophrenia Research, 61*, 75–88.

Minuchin, S. (1974). *Families and family therapy*. Cambridge, MA: Harvard University Press.

Mireault, G., Rooney, S., Kouwenhoven, K., & Hannan, C. (2008). Oppositional behavior and anxiety in boys and girls: A cross-sectional study in two community samples. *Child Psychiatry and Human Development, 39*, 519–527.

Mischoulon, D., Eddy, K. T., Keshaviah, A., Dinescu, D., Ross, S. L., Kass, A. E., . . . Herzog, D. B. (2011). Depression and eating disorders: Treatment and course. *Journal of Affective Disorders, 130*, 470–477.

Mission Australia. (2010). National survey of young Australians 2010. Retrieved from https://www.missionaustralia.com.au/document-downloads/category/28-2010

Mitrouska, I., Bouloukaki, I., & Siafakas, N. M. (2007). Pharmacological approaches to smoking cessation. *Pulmonary Pharmacological Therapy, 20*, 220–32.

Mittal, V. A., Ellman, L. M., & Cannon, T. D. (2008). Gene-environment interaction and covariation in schizophrenia: The role of obstetric complications. *Schizophrenia Bulletin, 34*, 1083–1094.

Modell, S., & Lauer, C. J. (2007). Rapid eye movement (REM) sleep: An endophenotype for depression. *Current Psychiatry Reports, 9*, 480–485.

Modestin, J. (1992). Multiple personality disorder in Switzerland. *American Journal of Psychiatry, 149*, 88–92.

Moens, E., Braet, C., & Van Winckel, M. (2010). An 8 year follow-up of treated obese children: Children's process and parental predictors of successful treatment. *Behaviour Research and Therapy, 48*, 626–633.

Moffitt, T. E. (2005). The new look of behavioral genetics in developmental psychopathology: Gene-environment interplay in antisocial behaviors. *Psychological Bulletin, 131*, 533–554.

Mohr, D. C., Cox, D., & Merluzzi, N. (2005). Self-injection anxiety training: Successful treatment for patients unable to self-inject injectable medication. *Multiple Sclerosis, 11*, 182–185.

Moisse, K., & Davis, L. (2012, January 27). Erin Brockovich launches investigation into tic illness affecting N. Y. teenagers. Retrieved from http://abcnews.go.com/Health/Wellness/erin-brockovich-launches-investigation-tic-illness-affecting-ny/story?id=15456672

Mojtabai, R. (2005). Perceived reasons for loss of housing and continued homelessness among homeless persons with mental illness. *Psychiatric Services, 56*, 172–178.

Mojtabai, R., & Olfson, M. (2010). National trends in psychotropic medication polypharmacy in office-based psychiatry. *Archives of General Psychiatry, 67*, 26–36.

Mommersteeg, P. M. G., Keijsers, G. P. J., Heijnen, C. J., Verbraak, M. J. P. M., & van Doornen, L. J. P. (2006). Cortisol deviations in people with burnout before and after psychotherapy: A pilot study. *Health Psychology, 25*, 243–248.

Moncrieff, J, & Leo, J. (2010). A systematic review of the effects of antipsychotic drugs on brain volume. *Psychological Medicine,* 40, 1409–1422.

Moncrieff, J. (2012). Questioning the 'neuroprotective' hypothesis: Does drug treatment prevent brain damage in early psychosis or schizophrenia? *British Journal of Psychiatry, 198*, 85–87.

Moncrieff, J., & Leo, J. (2010). A systematic review of the effects of antipsychotic drugs on brain volume. *Psychological Medicine, 40*, 1409–1422.

Mond, J. M., Peterson, C. B., & Hay, P. J. (2010). Prior use of extreme weight-control behaviors in a community sample of women with binge eating disorder or subthreshold binge eating disorder: A descriptive study. *International Journal of Eating Disorders, 43*, 440–446.

Monk, C. S., Nelson, E. E., McClure, E. B., Mogg, K., Bradley, B. P., . . . Pine, D. S. (2006). Ventrolateral prefrontal cortex activation and attentional bias in response to angry faces in adolescents with generalized anxiety disorder. *American Journal of Psychiatry, 163*, 1091–1097.

Monopoli, J. (2005). Managing hypochondriasis in elderly clients. *Journal of Contemporary Psychotherapy, 35*, 285–300.

Monot, M. J., Quirk, S. W., Hoerger, M., & Brewer, L. (2009). Racial bias in personality assessment: Using the MMPI-2 to predict psychiatric diagnosis of African American and Caucasian chemical dependency inpatients. *Psychological Assessment, 21*, 137–151.

Monteith, T., & Sprenger, T. (2010). Tension type headache in adolescence and childhood: Where are we now? *Current Pain and Headache Reports, 14*, 424–430.

Monteleone, P., & Maj, M. (2008). The circadian basis of mood disorders: Recent developments and treatment implications. *European Neuropsychopharmacology, 18*, 701–711.

Montoya, I. D., & Vocci, F. (2008). Novel medications to treat addictive disorders. *Current Psychiatry Reports, 10*, 392–398.

Moodley, R. (2005). Shamanic performances: Healing through magic and the supernatureal. In R. Moodley & W. West (Eds.), *Integrating traditional healing practices into counseling and psychotherapy* (pp. 2–14). Thousand Oaks, CA: Sage.

Mooney, L. J., Glasner-Edwards, S., Marinelli-Casey, P., Hillhouse, M., Ang, A., . . . Rawson, R. A. (2009). Health conditions in methamphetamine-dependent adults 3 years after treatment. *Journal of Addiction Medicine, 3*, 155–163.

Moore, B. A., & Budney, J. (2003). Relapse in outpatient treatment for marijuana dependence. *Journal of Substance Abuse Treatment, 25*, 85–89.

Moore, K. (2009, October 26). 'Amnesia girl' drained bank account before vanishing. Retrieved from http://www.king5.com/home/NYC-amnesia-teen-identified-as-Kitsap-Co-resident—65981942.html

Moore, T. H. M., Zammit, S., Lingford-Hughes, A., Barnes, T. R. E., Jones, P. B., Burke, M., & Lewis, G. (2007). Cannabis use and risk of psychotic or affective mental health outcomes: A systematic review. *Lancet, 370*, 319–328.

Moos, R. H., & Moos, B. S. (2006). Participation in treatment and Alcoholics Anonymous: A 16-year follow-up of initially untreated individuals. *Journal of Clinical Psychology, 62*, 735–750.

Moran, P., Coffey, C., Romaniuk, H., Olsson, C., Borschmann, R., Carlin, J. B., & Patton, G. C. (2012). The natural history of self-harm from adolescence to young adulthood: A population-based cohort study. *Lancet, 379*, 236–243.

Morgan, C. J., Muetzelfeldt, L., & Curran, H. V. (2010). Consequences of chronic ketamine self-administration upon neurocognitive function and psychological wellbeing: A 1-year longitudinal study. *Addiction, 105*, 121–133.

Morgan, W. J., Crain, E. F., Gruchalla, R. S., O'Connor, G. T., Kattan, M., . . . Inner-City Asthma Study

Group. (2004). Results of a home-based environmental intervention among urban children with asthma. *New England Journal of Medicine, 351,* 1068–1080.

Morillo, C., Belloch, A., & Garcia-Soriano, G. (2007). Clinical obsessions in obsessive-compulsive patients and obsession-relevant intrusive thoughts in non-clinical, depressed and anxious subjects: Where are the differences? *Behaviour Research and Therapy, 45,* 1319–1333.

Morin, D., Cobigo, V., Rivard, M., & Lépine, M. (2010). Intellectual disabilities and depression: How to adapt psychological assessment and intervention. *Canadian Psychology, 51,* 185–193.

Morley, K. C., Teesson, M., Reid, S. C., Sannibale, C., Thomson, C., Phung, N., . . . Haber, P. S. (2006). Naltrexone versus acamprosate in the treatment of alcohol dependence: A multi-centre, randomized, double-blind, placebo-controlled trial. *Addiction, 101,* 1451–1462.

Morley, T. E., & Moran, G. (2011). The origins of cognitive vulnerability in early childhood: Mechanisms linking early attachment to later depression. *Clinical Psychology Review, 31,* 1071–1082.

Mormino, E. C., Kluth, J. T., Madison, C. M., Rabinovic, G. D., Baker, S. L., . . . Jagust, W. J. (2008). Episodic memory loss is related to hippocampal-mediated beta-amyloid deposition in elderly subjects. *Brain, 132,* 1310–1323.

Morris, C. D., Miklowitz, D., & Waxmonsky, J. A. (2007). Family-focused treatment for bipolar disorder in adults and youth. *Journal of Clinical Psychology: In Session, 63,* 433–445.

Morris, M. C., Ciesla, J. A., & Garber, J. (2008). A prospective study of the cognitive-stress model of depressive symptoms in adolescents. *Journal of Abnormal Psychology, 117,* 719–734.

Morris, M. C., Ciesla, J. A., & Garber, J. (2010). A prospective study of stress autonomy versus stress sensitization in adolescents at varied risk for depression. *Journal of Abnormal Psychology, 119,* 341–354.

Morrow, R. L., Garland, E. J., Wright, J. M., Maclure, M., Taylor, S., & Dormuth, C. R. (2012). Influence of relative age on diagnosis and treatment of attention-deficit/hyperactivity disorder in children. *Canadian Medical Association Journal, 184,* 755–762.

Mosher, W. D., Chandra, A., & Jones, J. (2005, September 15). Sexual behavior and selected health measures: Men and women 15–44 years of age, United States, 2002. *Advance Data from Vital and Health Statistics,* no. 362. 1–55. Hyattsville, MD: National Center for Health Statistics.

Mostofsky, E., Maclure, M., Sherwood, J. B., Tofler, G. H., Muller, J. E., & Mittleman, M. A. (2012). Risk of acute myocardial infarction after the death of a significant person in one's life: The determinants of myocardial infarction onset study. *Circulation, 125,* 491–496.

Moukheiber, A., Rautureau, G., Perez-Diaz, F., Soussignan, R., Dubal, S., . . . Pelissolo, A. (2010). Gaze avoidance in social phobia: Objective measure and correlates. *Behaviour Research and Therapy, 48,* 147–151.

Mueller, A., Mitchell, J. E., Crosby, R. D., Glaesmer, H., & de Zwaan, M. (2009). The prevalence of compulsive hoarding and its association with compulsive buying in a German population-based sample. *Behaviour Research and Therapy, 47,* 705–709.

Mueser, K. T., Sengupta, A., Schooler, N. R., Bellack, A. S., Xie, H., Glick, I. D., & Keith, S. J. (2001). Family treatment and medication dosage reduction in schizophrenia: Effects on patient social functioning, family attitudes, and burden. *Journal of Consulting and Clinical Psychology, 69,* 3–12.

Muhlberger, A., Wiedemann, G., Herrmann, M. J., & Pauli, P. (2006). Phylo- and ontogenetic fears and expectations of danger: Differences between spider- and flight-phobic subjects in cognitive and physiological responses to disorder-specific stimuli. *Journal of Abnormal Psychology, 115,* 580–589.

Mulder, R. T., Wells, J. F., Joyce, P. R., & Bushnell, J. A. (1994). Antisocial women. *Journal of Personality Disorders, 8,* 279–287.

Mulholland, A. M., & Mintz, L. B. (2001). Prevalence of eating disorders among African American women. *Journal of Counseling Psychology, 48,* 111–116.

Mulkens, S. A. N., de Jong, P. J., & Merckelbach, H. (1996). Disgust and spider phobia. *Journal of Abnormal Psychology, 105,* 464–468.

Muller, R. J. (2006). A woman who refused treatment for a paranoid psychosis. *Psychiatric Times, 23,* 422–424.

Muñoz, R. F., Lenert, L. L., Delucchi, K., Stoddard, J., Pérez, J. E., Penilla, C., & Pérez-Stable, E. J. (2006). Toward evidence-based Internet interventions: A Spanish/English Web site for international smoking cessation trials. *Nicotine and Tobacco Research, 8,* 77–87.

Muñoz, R. F., Ying, Y. W., Bernal, G., Pérez-Stable, E. J., Sorenson, J. L., . . . Miller, R. S. (1995). Prevention of depression with primary care patients: A randomized controlled trial. *American Journal of Community Psychology, 23,* 199–222.

Munsey, C. (2010). Medicine or menace?: Psychologists' research can inform the growing debate over legalizing marijuana. *APA Monitor, 41*(6), 50.

Muris, P., & Dietvorst, R. (2006). Underlying personality characteristics of behavioral inhibition in children. *Child Psychiatry and Development, 36,* 437–445.

Muris, P., Merckelbach, H., & Clavan, M. (1997). Abnormal and normal compulsions. *Behaviour Research and Therapy, 35,* 249–252.

Muris, P., Merckelbach, H., & Collaris, R. (1997). Common childhood fears and their origins. *Behaviour Research and Therapy, 35,* 929–936.

Muris, P., van Zwol, L., Huijding, J., & Mayer, B. (2010). Mom told me scary things about this animal: Parents installing fear beliefs in their children via the verbal information pathway. *Behaviour Research and Therapy, 48,* 341–346.

Murray, C. K., Reynolds, J. C., Schroeder, J. M., Harrison, M. B., Evans, O. M., & Hospenthal, D. R. (2005). Spectrum of care provided at an Echelon II medical unit during Operation Iraqi Freedom. *Military Medicine, 170,* 516–520.

Murray, H. A., & Morgan, H. (1938). *Explorations in personality.* New York, NY: Oxford University Press.

Murray, S. B., Reiger, E., Touyz, S. W., & De la Garza Garcia, Y. (2010). Muscle dysmorphia and the DSM-V conundrum: Where does it belong? A review paper. *International Journal of Eating Disorders, 43,* 483–491.

Muscatell, K. A., Slavich, G. M., Monroe, S. M., & Gotlib, I. H. (2009). Stressful life events, chronic difficulties, and the symptoms of clinical depression. *Journal of Nervous and Mental Diseases, 197,* 154–c160.

Mustafa, B., Evrim, O., & Sari, A. (2005). Secondary mania following traumatic brain injury. *Journal of Neuropsychiatry and Clinical Neuroscience, 17,* 122–124.

Myers, T. A., & Crowther, J. H. (2009). Social comparison as a predictor of body satisfaction. *Journal of Abnormal Psychology, 118,* 683–698.

Nacasch, N., Foa, E. B., Fostick, L., Polliack, M., Dinstein, Y., . . . Zohar, J. (2007). Prolonged exposure therapy for chronic combat-related PTSD: A case report of five veterans. *CNS Spectrums, 12,* 690–695.

Nademanee, K., Veerakul, G., Nimmannit, S., Chaowakul, V., Bhuripanyo, K., . . . Tatsanavivat, P. (1997). Arrhythmogenic marker for sudden unexplained death syndrome in Thai men. *Circulation, 96,* 2595–2600.

Naeem, F., Waheed, W., Gobbi, M., Ayub, M., & Kingdon, D. (2011). Preliminary evaluation of culturally sensitive CBT for depression in Pakistan: Findings from Developing Culturally Sensitive CBT Project (DCCP). *Behavioral and Cognitive Psychotherapy, 39,* 165–173.

Nagano, J., Kakuta, C., Motomura, C., Odajima, H., Sudo, N., Nishima, S., & Kubo, C. (2010). The parenting attitudes and the stress of mothers predict the asthmatic severity of their children: A prospective study. *BioPsychoSocial Medicine, 4,* 12. doi:10.1186/1751-0759-4-12

Namiki, C., Yamada, M., Yoshida, H., Hanakawa, T., Fukuyama, H., & Murai, T. (2008). Small orbitofrontal traumatic lesions detected by high resolution MRI in a patient with major behavioral changes. *Neurocase, 14,* 474–479.

Nanda, S. (2008). Cross-cultural issues. In D. Rowland & L. Incrocci (Eds.), *Handbook of sexual and gender identity disorders* (pp. 457–485). Hoboken, NJ: Wiley.

Nanri, A., Kimura, Y., Matsushita, Y., Ohta, M., Sato, M., . . . Mizoue, T. (2010). Dietary patterns and depressive symptoms among Japanese men and women. *European Journal of Clinical Nutrition, 64,* 832–839.

Nardi, A. E., Freire, R. C., Mochcovitch, M. D., Amrein, R., Levitan, M. N., King, A. L., . . . Versiani, M. (2012). A randomized, naturalistic, parallel-group study for the long-term treatment of panic disorder. *Journal of Clinical Psychopharmacology, 32,* 120–126.

Nash, J. R., Sargent, P. A., Rabiner, E. A., Hood, S. D., Argyopoulos, S. V., . . . Nutt, D. J. (2008). Serotonin 5-HT receptor binding in people with panic disorder: Positron emission tomography study. *British Journal of Psychiatry, 193,* 229–234.

Nashoni, E., Yaroslavsky, A., Varticovschi, P., Weizman, A., & Stein, D. (2010). Alterations in QT dispersion in the surface electrocardiogram of female adolescent inpatients diagnosed with bulimia nervosa. *Comprehensive Psychiatry, 51,* 406–411.

National Academy of Sciences, National Academy of Engineering, & Institute of Medicine. (2006). *Beyond bias and barriers: Fulfilling the potential of women in academic science and engineering.* Washington, DC: National Academies Press.

National Board for Certification in Occupational Therapy. (2012). Sexual misconduct by professionals. Retrieved from http://www.nbcot.org/index.php?option=com_content&view=article&id=128%3Asexual-misconduct-by-professionals&catid=2&Itemid=119

National Center for Health Statistics. (2012). *Health, United States, 2011: With special feature on socioeconomic status and health.* Hyattsville, MD: Library of Congress.

National Council on Aging. (1998, September 29). Want to understand how Americans view long-term care? *San Francisco Chronicle,* p. A4.

National Dissemination Center for Children With Disabilities. (2012). Intellectual Disability. Retrieved from http://nichcy.org/disability/specific/intellectual

National Down Syndrome Society. (2012). Alzheimer's and Down syndrome. Retrieved from http://www.ndss.org/Resources/Health-Care/Associated-Conditions/Alzheimers-Disease-Down-Syndrome/

National Institute of Child Health and Human Development. (2011a). Down syndrome. Retrieved from http://www.nichd.nih.gov/health/topics/down_syndrome.cfm

National Institute of Child Health and Human Development. (2011b). Fragile X syndrome. Retrieved from http://www.nichd.nih.gov/health/topics/fragile_x_syndrome.cfm

National Institute of Mental Health. (2009a). *Anxiety disorders.* Retrieved from http://www.nimh.nih.gov/health/publications/anxiety-disorders/nimhanxiety.pdf

National Institute of Mental Health. (2009b). *Posttraumatic stress disorder (PTSD).* Retrieved from http://www.nimh.nih.gov/health/publications/post-traumatic-stress-disorder-ptsd/nimh_ptsd_booklet.pdf

National Institute of Mental Health. (2009c). *Schizophrenia.* Retrieved from http://www.nimh.nih.gov/health/publications/schizophrenia/schizophrenia-booklet-2009.pdf

National Institute of Mental Health. (2010a). *The numbers count: Mental disorders in America.* Bethesda, MD: Author.

National Institute of Mental Health. (2010b). Obsessive-compulsive disorder: When unwanted thoughts take over. Retrieved from http://www.nimh.nih.gov/health/publications/obsessive-compulsive-disorder-when-unwanted-thoughts-take-over/ocd-trifold.pdf

National Institute of Mental Health. (2011a). *Depression.* Retrieved from http://www.nimh.nih.gov/health/publications/depression/depression-booklet.pdf

National Institute of Mental Health. (2011b). *Eating disorders.* Retrieved from http://www.nimh.nih.gov/health/publications/eating-disorders/index.shtml

National Institute of Neurological Disorders and Stroke. (2007). *Parkinson's disease: Hope through research.* Retrieved from www.ninds.nih.gov/disorders/parkinsons_disease/detail_parkinsons_disease.htm

National Institute of Neurological Disorders and Stroke. (2010). Tourette syndrome fact sheet. Retrieved from http://www.ninds.nih.gov/disorders/tourette/detail_tourette.htm

National Institute of Neurological Disorders and Stroke. (2011). NINDS dementia with Lewy bodies information page. Retrieved from http://www.ninds.nih.gov/disorders/dementiawithlewybodies/dementiawithlewybodies.htm

National Institute of Neurological Disorders and Stroke. (2012). Headache: Hope through research. Retrieved from http://www.ninds.nih.gov/disorders/headache/detail_headache.htm

National Institutes of Health. (2010). Premenstrual dysphoric disorder. Retrieved from http://www.ncbi.nlm.nih.gov/pubmedhealth/PMH0004461/

National Stroke Association. (2012). Unique symptoms in women. Retrieved from http://www.stroke.org/site/PageServer?pagename=WOMSYMP

Neal-Barnett, A., Flessner, C., Franklin, M. E., Woods, D. W., Keuthen, N. J., & Stein, D. W. (2010). Ethnic differences in trichotillomania: Phenomenology, interference, impairment, and treatment efficacy. *Journal of Anxiety Disorders, 24,* 553–558.

Nedic, A., Zivanovic, O., & Lisulov, R. (2011). Nosological status of social phobia: Contrasting classical and recent literature. *Current Opinion in Psychiatry, 24,* 61–66.

Neerakal, I., & Srinivasan, K. (2003). A study of the phenomenology of panic attacks in patients from India. *Psychopathology, 36,* 92–97.

Neighbors, L., & Sobal, J. (2007). Prevalence and magnitude of body weight and shape dissatisfaction among university students. *Eating Behaviors, 9,* 429–439.

Nelson, B., & Yung, A. R. (2011). Should a risk syndrome for first episode psychosis be included in the DSM-5? *Current Opinion in Psychiatry, 24,* 128–133.

Nelson, G., Aubry, T., & Lawrence, A. (2007). A review of the literature on the effectiveness of housing and support, assertive community treatment, and intensive case management interventions for persons with mental illness who have been homeless. *American Journal of Orthopsychiatry, 77,* 350–361.

Nemeroff, C. B. (2008). Recent findings in the pathophysiology of depression. *Focus, 6,* 3–14.

Nemeroff, C. B., Mayberg, H. S., Krahl, S. E., McNamara, J., Frazer, A., . . . Brannan, S. K. (2006). VNS therapy in treatment-resistant depression: Clinical evidence and putative neurobiological mechanisms. *Neuropsychopharmacology, 31,* 1345–1355.

Nervi, A., Reitz, C., Tang, M. X., Santana, V., Piriz, A., . . . Mayeux, R. (2011). Familial aggregation of dementia with Lewy bodies. *British Archives of Neurology, 68,* 90–93.

Nestler, E. J., Barrot, M., DiLeone, R. J., Eisch, A. J., Gold, S. J., & Monteggia, L. M. (2002). Neurobiology of depression. *Neuron, 34,* 13–25.

Nestler, E. J., & Malenka, R. C. (2004). The addicted brain. *Scientific American, 290,* 50–57.

Neugebauer, R. (1979). Medieval and early modern theories of mental illness. *Archives of General Psychiatry, 36,* 477–483.

Neumark-Sztainer, D., Hannan, P. J., & Stat, M. (2000). Weight-related behaviors among adolescent girls and boys. *Archives of Pediatric Adolescent Medicine, 154,* 569–577.

Neumark-Sztainer, D., Wall, M., Story, M., & Fulkerson, J. A. (2004). Are family meal patterns associated with disordered eating behaviors among adolescents? *Journal of Adolescent Health, 35,* 350–359.

Neumeister, A., Bain, E., Nugent, A. C., Carson, R. E., Bonne, O., . . . Drevets, W. C. (2004). Reduced serotonin Type 1A receptor binding in panic disorder. *Journal of Neuroscience, 24,* 589–591.

Newman, J. P., Curtin, J. J., Bertsch, J. D., & Baskin-Sommers, A. R. (2010). Attention moderates the fearlessness of psychopathic offenders. *Biological Psychiatry, 67,* 66–70.

Newman, J. P., & Schmitt, W. A. (1998). Passive avoidance in psychopathic offenders: A replication and extension. *Journal of Abnormal Psychology, 107,* 527–532.

Newschaffer, C. J., Croen, L. A., Daniels, J., Giarelli, E., Grether, J. K., . . . Windham, G. C. (2007). The epidemiology of autism spectrum disorders. *Annual Review of Public Health, 28,* 235–258.

Nichols, M. P., & Schwartz, R. C. (2005). *The essentials of family therapy.* New York, NY: Allyn & Bacon.

Nierenberg, A. A., Akiskal, H. S., Angst, J., Hirschfeld, R. M., Merikangas, K. R., Petukhova, M., & Kessler, R. C. (2010). Bipolar disorder with frequent mood episodes in the National Comorbidity Survey Replication (NCS-R). *Molecular Psychiatry, 15,* 1075–1087.

Nigg, J. T., Lewis, K., Edinger, T., & Falk, M. (2012). Meta-analysis of attention-deficit/hyperactivity disorder or attention-deficit/hyperactivity disorder symptoms, restriction diet, and synthetic food color additives. *Journal of the American Academy of Child & Adolescent Psychiatry, 51,* 86–97.

Nijmeijer, J. S., Arias-Vasquez, A., Rommelse, N. N., Altink, M. E., Anney, R. J., Asherson, P., . . . Hoekstra, P. J. (2010). Identifying loci for the overlap between attention-deficit/hyperactivity disorder and autism spectrum disorder using a genome-wide QTL linkage approach. *Journal of the American Academy of Child & Adolescent Psychiatry, 49,* 675–685.

Nillni, Y. I., Rohan, K. J., Bernstein, A., & Zvolensky, M. J. (2010). Premenstrual distress predicts panic-relevant responding to a CO2 challenge among young adult females. *Journal of Anxiety Disorder, 24,* 416–422.

Nixon, R., Sterk, J., & Pearce, A. (2012). A randomized trial of cognitive behaviour therapy and cognitive therapy for children with posttraumatic stress disorder following single-incident trauma. *Journal of Abnormal Child Psychology,* 40, 327–337.

Nolen-Hoeksema, S. (1987). Sex differences in unipolar depression: Evidence and theory. *Psychological Bulletin, 101,* 259–282.

Nolen-Hoeksema, S. (1991). Responses to depression and their effects on the duration of depressive episodes. *Journal of Abnormal Psychology, 100,* 569–582.

Nolen-Hoeksema, S. (2004). Gender differences in depression. In T. F. Oltmanns & R. E. Emery (Eds.), *Current directions in abnormal psychology* (pp. 49–55). Upper Saddle River, NJ: Prentice Hall.

Nolen-Hoeksema, S., Girgus, J. S., & Seligman, M. E. (1992). Predictors and consequences of childhood depressive symptoms: A 5-year longitudinal study. *Journal of Abnormal Psychology, 101,* 405–422.

Norcross, J. C. (2004). Empirically supported treatments (ESTS): Context, consensus, and controversy. *Register Report, 30,* 12–14.

Nordahl, C. W., Lange, N., Li, D. D., Barnett, L. A., Lee, A., Buonocore, M. H., . . . Amaral, D. G. (2011). Brain enlargement is associated with regression in preschool-age boys with autism spectrum disorders. *Proceedings of the National Academy of Sciences U S A, 108,* 20195–20200.

Nordahl, C. W., Scholz, R., Yang, X., Buonocore, M. H., Simon, T., Rogers, S., & Amaral, D. G. (2012). Increased rate of amygdala growth in children aged 2 to 4 years with autism spectrum disorders: A longitudinal study. *Archives of General Psychiatry, 69,* 53–61.

Nordentoft, M., & Hjorthoj, C. (2007). Cannabis use and risk of psychosis in later life. *Lancet, 370,* 293–294.

Nordstrom, B. R., & Levin, F. R. (2007). Treatment of cannabis use disorders: A review of the literature. *American Journal of Addiction, 16,* 331–342.

Norfleet, M. A. (2002). Responding to society's needs: Prescription privileges for psychologists. *Journal of Clinical Psychology, 58,* 599–610.

Northwestern University. (2003, June 13). Study suggests difference between female and male sexuality. *Science Daily.* Retrieved from www.sciencedaily.com/releases/2003/06/030613075252.htm

Nothard, S., Morrison, A. P., & Wells, A. (2008). Identifying specific interpretations and exploring the nature of safety behaviours for people who hear voices: An exploratory study. *Behavioural and Cognitive Psychotherapy, 36,* 353–357.

Noveck, J., & Tompson, T. (2007). Poll: Family, friends make youths happy. Retrieved from http://www.usatoday.com/news/topstories/2007-08-19-1958101914_x.htm.

Noyes, R., Jr., Holt, C. S., Happel, R. L., Kathol, R. G., & Yagla, S. J. (1997). A family study of hypochondriasis. *Journal of Nervous and Mental Disease, 185,* 223–232.

Noyes, R., Jr., Stuart, S., Watson, D. B., & Langbehn, D. R. (2006). Distinguishing between hypochondriasis and somatization disorder: A review of the existing literature. *Psychotherapy and Psychosomatics, 75,* 270–281.

Nutt, D. J. (2001). Neurobiological mechanisms in generalized anxiety disorder. *Journal of Clinical Psychiatry, 62,* 22–27.

Nutt, D. J., King, L. A., & Phillip, L. D. (2010). Drug harms in the UK: A multicriteria decision analysis. *Lancet, 376*(9752), 1558–1565.

Oaten, M., Stevenson, R. J., & Case, T. I. (2009). Disgust as a disease-avoidance mechanism. *Psychological Bulletin, 135,* 303–321.

Obesity Action Coalition. (2007). Understanding Obesity Stigma brochure. Retrieved from http://www.obesityaction.org/weight-bias-and-stigma/understanding-obesity-stigma-brochure

O'Brien, M. C., McCoy, T. P., Rhodes, S. D., Wagoner, A., & Wolfson M. (2008). Caffeinated cocktails: Energy drink consumption, high-risk drinking, and alcohol-related consequences among college students. *Academic Emergency Medicine, 5*(5), 453–460.

O'Brien, M. P., Gordon, J. L., Bearden, C. E., Lopez, S. R., Kopelowicz, A., & Cannon, T. D. (2006). Positive family environment predicts improvement in symptoms and social functioning among adolescents at imminent risk for onset of psychosis. *Schizophrenia Research, 81,* 269–275.

O'Brien, W. H., & Carhart, V. (2011). Functional analysis in behavioral medicine. *European Journal of Psychological Assessment, 27,* 4–16.

O'Connell, K. A., Hosein, V. L., Schwartz, J. E., & Leibowitz, R. Q. (2007). How does coping help people resist lapses during smoking cessation? *Health Psychology, 26,* 77–84.

O'Connell, M. E., Boat, T., & Warner, K. E. (2009). *Preventing mental, emotional, and behavioral disorders among young people: Progress and possibilities.* Washington, DC: National Academies Press. Retrieved from http://www.nap.edu/catalog.php?record_id=12480

O'Connor v. Donaldson, 95 S. Ct. 2486 (1975).

O'Connor, B. P. (2008). Other personality disorders. In M. Hersen & J. Rosqvist (Eds.), *Handbook of psychological assessment, case conceptualization and treatment: Vol. 1. Adults* (pp. 438–462). Hoboken, NJ: Wiley.

Odlaug, B. L., Kim, S. W., & Grant, J. E. (2010). Quality of life and clinical severity in pathological skin picking and trichotillomania. *Journal of Anxiety Disorders, 24*, 823–829.

Odom, E. C., & Vernon-Feagans, L. (2010). Buffers of racial discrimination: Links with depression among rural African American mothers. *Journal of Marriage and Family, 72*, 346–359.

O'Donnell, M. J., Xavier, D., Liu, L., Zhang, H., Chin, S. L., Rao-Melacini, P., . . . Yusuf, S. (2010). Risk factors for ischaemic and intracerebral haemorrhagic stroke in 22 countries (the INTERSTROKE study): A case-control study. *Lancet, 376*, 112–123.

O'Donohue, W. T., Mosco, E. A., Bowers, A. H., & Avina, C. (2006). Sexual harassment as diagnosable PTSD trauma. *Psychiatric Times, 23*, 50–62.

Offman, A., & Kleinplatz, P. J. (2004). Does PMDD belong in the DSM? Challenging the medicalization of women's bodies. *Canadian Journal of Human Sexuality, 13*, 17–27. Retrieved from http://psychopathology.fiu.edu/Articles/Offman+Kleinplatz_2004.pdf

Ofshe, R. J. (1992). Inadvertent hypnosis during interrogation: False confession due to dissociative state; misidentified multiple personality and the satanic cult hypothesis. *International Journal of Clinical and Experimental Hypnosis, 40*, 125–156.

Ogden, C. L., Carroll, M. D., Curtin, L. R., Lamb, M. M., & Flegal, K. M. (2010). Prevalence of high body mass in US children and adolescents, 2007–2008. *Journal of the American Medical Association, 303*, 242–249.

Ogden, C. L., Carroll, M. D., Kit, B. K., & Flegal, K. M. (2012). Prevalence of obesity and trends in body mass index among US children and adolescents, 1999–2010. *Journal of the American Medical Association, 307*, 483–490.

Ogden, C. L., Fryar, C. D., Carroll, M. D., & Flegal, K. M. (2004). Mean body weight, height, and body mass index, United States 1960–2002: Advance data from vital and health statistics (no. 347). Hyattsville, MD: National Center for Health Statistics.

Ohl, L. E. (2007). Essentials of female sexual dysfunction from a sex therapy perspective. *Urologic Nursing, 27*, 57–63.

Okazaki, S. (1997). Sources of ethnic differences between Asian American and white American college students on measures of depression and social anxiety. *Journal of Abnormal Psychology, 106*, 52–60.

Okazaki, S., Liu, J. F., Longworth, S. L., & Minn, J. Y. (2002). Asian American–White American differences in expressions of social anxiety: A replication and extension. *Cultural Diversity and Ethnic Minority Psychology, 8*, 234–247.

Okie, S. (2010). A flood of opioids, a rising tide of deaths. *New England Journal of Medicine, 363*, 1981–1985.

Olatunji, B. O., Etzel, E. N., Tomarken, A. J., Ciesielski, B. G., & Deacon, B. (2011). The effects of safety behaviors on health anxiety: An experimental investigation. *Behaviour Research and Therapy, 49*, 719–728.

Oldham, J. M. (2006). Integrated treatment for borderline personality disorder. *Psychiatric Annals, 36*, 361–362, 364–369.

Olivardia, R., Pope, H. G., Jr., & Hudson, J. I. (2000). Muscle dysphoria in male weight-lifters: A case-control study. *American Journal of Psychiatry, 157*, 1291–1296.

Oliver, C., Berg, K., Moss, J., Arron, K., & Burbidge, C. (2011). Delineation of behavioral phenotypes in genetic syndromes: Characteristics of autism spectrum disorder, affect and hyperactivity. *Journal of Autism and Developmental Disorders, 41*, 1019–1032. doi:10.1007/s10803-010-1125-5

Ollendick, T. H., Öst, L.-G., Reuterskiold, L., Cosa, N., Cederlund, R., . . . Jarrett, M. A. (2009). One-session treatment of specific phobias in youth: A randomized clinical trial in the United States and Sweden. *Journal of Consulting and Clinical Psychology, 77*, 504–516.

Ollove, M. (2010, April 28). Bullying and teen suicide: How do we adjust school climate? The Christian Science Monitor. Retrieved 9/29/12 at http://www.csmonitor.com/usa/society/2010/0428/bullying-and-teen-suicide-how-do-we-adjust-school-climate

Olmos, J. M., Valero, C., Gomez del Barrio, A., Amando, J. A., Hernandez, J. L., Menendez-Arango, J., & Gonzalez-Macia, J. (2010). Time course of bone loss in patients with anorexia nervosa. *International Journal of Eating Disorders, 43*, 537–542.

Olsavsky, A. K., Brotman, M. A., Rutenberg, J. G., Muhrer, E. J., Deveney, C. M., Fromm, S. J., . . . Leibenluft, E. (2012). Amygdala hyperactivation during face emotion processing in unaffected youth at risk for bipolar disorder. *Journal of the American Academy of Child & Adolescent Psychiatry, 51*, 294–303.

Olshansky, S. J. (2011). Aging of US presidents. *Journal of the American Medical Association, 306*, 2328–2329.

Olsson, A., Nearing, K. I., & Phelps, E. A. (2007). Learning fears by observing others: The neural systems of social fear transmission. *Scan, 2*, 3–11.

O'Neil, K. A., Conner, B. T., & Kendall, P. C. (2011). Internalizing disorders and substance use disorders in youth: Comorbidity, risk, temporal order, and implications for intervention. *Clinical Psychology Review, 31*, 104–112.

Ooteman, W., Naassila, M., Koeter, M. W., Verheul, R., Schippers, G. M., Houchi, H., . . . van den Brink, W. (2009). Predicting the effect of naltrexone and acamprosate in alcohol-dependent patients using genetic indicators. *Addictive Biology, 14*, 328–337.

Oquendo, M. A., Currier, D., Liu, S. M., Hasin, D. S., Grant, B. F., & Blanco, C. (2010). Increased risk for suicidal behavior in comorbid bipolar disorder and alcohol use disorders: Results from the National Epidemiologic Survey on Alcohol and Related Conditions (NESARC). *Journal of Clinical Psychiatry, 71*, 902–909.

Ortiz, R. M. (2011, October). Physiology of cardiovascular disease: Gender disparities. Presented at the meeting of the American Physiological Society, Jackson, MS.

Osbourne, L. (2001, May 6). Regional disturbances. *New York Times Magazine*. Retrieved from http://www.nytimes.com/2001/05/06/magazine/06LATAH.html?pagewanted=all

Öst, L.-G. (1987). Age of onset in different phobias. *Journal of Abnormal Psychology, 96*, 223–229.

Öst, L.-G. (1992). Blood and injection phobia: Background and cognitive, physiological, and behavioral variables. *Journal of Abnormal Psychology, 101*, 68–74.

Öst, L.-G., & Hugdahl, K. (1981). Acquisition of phobias and anxiety response patterns in clinical patients. *Behaviour Research and Therapy, 19*, 439–447.

Ostchega, Y., Yoon, S. S., Hughes, J., & Louis, T. (2008). Hypertension awareness, treatment, and control—continued disparities in adults: United States, 2005–2006. *National Center for Health Statistics, 3*, 1–8.

Oster, T. J., Anderson, C. A., Filley, C. M., Wortzel, H. S., & Arciniegas, D. B. (2007). Quetiapine for mania due to traumatic brain injury. *CNS Spectrums, 12*, 764–769.

Oswald, D. P., & Sonenklar, N. A. (2007). Medication use among children with autism spectrum disorders. *Journal of Child and Adolescent Psychopharmacology, 17*, 348–355.

Otto, M. W., McHugh, R. K., Simon, N. M., Farach, F. J., Worthington, J. J., & Pollack, M. H. (2010). Efficacy of CBT for benzodiazepine discontinuation in patients with panic disorder: Further evaluation. *Behaviour Research and Therapy, 48*, 720–727.

Ougrin, D., Tranah, T., Leigh, E., Taylor, L., & Asarnow, J. R. (2012). Practitioner review: Self-harm in adolescents. *Journal of Child Psychology and Psychiatry, and Allied Disciplines, 53(4)*, 337–350.

Ozer, E. J., Best, S. R., Lipsey, T. L., & Weiss, D. S. (2003). Predictors of posttraumatic stress disorder and symptoms in adults: A meta-analysis. *Psychological Bulletin, 129*, 52–73.

Ozonoff, S., Iosif, A. M., Baguio, F., Cook, I. C., Hill, M. M., . . . Sigman, M. (2010). A prospective study of the emergence of early behavioral signs of autism. *Journal of the American Academy of Child & Adolescent Psychiatry, 49*, 256–266.

Ozonoff, S., Young, G. S., Carter, A., Messinger, D., Yirmiya, N., Zwaigenbaum, L., . . . Stone, W. L. (2011). Recurrence risk for autism spectrum disorders: A baby siblings research consortium study. *Pediatrics, 128*, e488–495. Epub 2011 Aug 15.

Padgett, D. K., Hawkins, R. L., Abrams, C., & Davis, A. (2006). In their own words: Trauma and substance abuse in the lives of formerly homeless women with serious mental illness. *American Journal of Orthopsychiatry, 76*, 461–467.

Paik, A., & Laumann, E. O. (2006). Prevalence of women's sexual problems in the USA. In I. Goldstein, C. M. Meston, S. R. Davis, & A. M. Traish (Eds.), *Women's sexual function and dysfunction* (pp. 23–33). London, UK: Taylor & Francis.

Pajonk, F.-G., Wobrock, T., Gruber, O., Scherk, H., Berner, D., Kaizi, I., . . . Falkai, P. (2010). Hippocampal plasticity in response to exercise in schizophrenia. *Archives of General Psychiatry, 67*, 133–143.

Palaniyappan, L., & Cousins, D. A. (2010). Brain networks: Foundations and futures in bipolar disorder. *Journal of Mental Health, 19*, 157–167.

Palmieri, P. A., Weathers, F. W., Difede, J., & King, D. W. (2007). Confirmatory factor analysis of the PTSD Checklist and the Clinician-Administered PTSD Scale in disaster workers exposed to the World Trade Center Ground Zero. *Journal of Abnormal Psychology, 116*, 329–341.

Pan, A., Sun, Q., Okereke, O. I., Rexrode, K. M., & Hu, F. B. (2011). Depression and risk of stroke morbidity and mortality: A meta-analysis and systematic review. *Journal of the American Medical Association, 306*, 1241–1249.

Papadopoulous, F. C., Ekbom, A., Brandt, L., & Ekselius, L. (2009). Excess mortality, causes of death and prognostic factors in anorexia nervosa. *British Journal of Psychiatry, 194*, 10–17.

Papakostas, G. I., & Fava, M. (2008). Predictors, moderators, and mediators (correlates) of treatment outcome in major depressive disorder. *Dialogues in Clinical Neuroscience, 10*, 439–451.

Paquette, M. (2007). Morgellons: Disease or delusions? *Perspectives in Psychiatric Care, 43*, 67–68.

Paras, M. L., Murad, M. H., Chen, L. P., Goranson, E. N., Sattler, A. L., Colbenson, K. M., . . . Zirakzadeh, A. (2009). Sexual abuse and lifetime diagnosis of somatic disorders: A systematic review and meta-analysis. *Journal of the American Medical Association, 302*, 550–561.

Pardini, D. A., & Byrd, A. L. (2012). Perceptions of aggressive conflicts and others' distress in children with callous-unemotional traits: 'I'll show you who's boss, even if you suffer and I get in trouble.' *Journal of Child Psychology and Psychiatry, 53*, 283–291.

Parens, E., & Johnston, J. (2009). Facts, values, and attention-deficit hyperactivity disorder (ADHD): An update on the controversies. *Child and Adolescent Psychiatry and Mental Health, 3*, 1–17.

Parens, E., & Johnston, J. (2010). Controversies concerning the diagnosis and treatment of bipolar disorder in children. *Childhood and Adolescent Psychiatry and Mental Health, 10*, 4–9.

Parish, B. S., & Yutzy, S. H. (2011). Somatoform disorders. In R. E. Hales, S. C. Yudofsky, & G. O. Babbard (Eds.), *Essentials of psychiatry* (3rd ed., pp. 229–254). Arlington, VA: American Psychiatric Publishing.

Parker, S., Nichter, M., Vuckovic, N., Sims, C., & Ritenbaugh, C. (1995). Body image and weight concerns among African-American and white adolescent females: Differences that make a difference. *Human Organization, 54*, 103–114.

Parsons, J. T., Grov, C., & Kelly, B. C. (2009). Club drug use and dependence among young adults recruited through time-space sampling. *Public Health Reports, 124*(2), 246–254.

Partnership for a Drug-Free America & MetLife Foundation. (2010). *2009 parents and teens attitude tracking study*. Retrieved from http://drugfreetexas.org/wp-content/files_mf/1267570941PATS_Full_Report_2009_PDF.pdf

Paschall, M. J., & Saltz, R. F. (2007). Relationships between college settings and student alcohol use before, during and after events: A multi-level study. *Drug and Alcohol Review, 26*, 635–644.

Pascoe, E. A., & Richman, L. S. (2009). Perceived discrimination and health: A meta-analytic review. *Psychological Bulletin, 135*, 531–554.

Patton, G. C., Tollit, M. M., Romaniuk, H., Spence, S. H., Sheffield, J., & Sawyer, M.G. (2011). A prospective study of the effects of optimism on adolescent health risks. *Pediatrics, 127*, 306–316.

Paulozzi, L., Baldwin, G., Franklin, G., Kerlikowske, R. G., Jones, C. M., Ghiya, N., & Popovic, T. (2012). CDC grand rounds: Prescription drug overdoses, a U.S. epidemic. *Morbidity & Mortality Weekly Report, 61*, 10–13.

Paulson-Karlsson, G., Engstrom, I., & Nevonen, L. (2009). A pilot study of a family-based treatment for adolescent anorexia nervosa: 18- and 36-month follow-ups. *Eating Disorders, 17*, 72–88.

Pearson, M. L., Selby, J. V., Katz, K. A., Cantrell, V., Braden, C. R., Parise, M. E., . . . Eberhard, M. L. (2012). Clinical, epidemiologic, histopathologic and molecular features of an unexplained dermopathy. *PLoS One, 7*, 1–23.

Pearson, M. R., D'Lima, G. M., & Kelley, M. (2011). Self-regulation as a buffer of the relationship between parental alcohol misuse and alcohol-related outcomes in first-year college students. *Addictive Behaviors, 36*, 1309–1312.

Peirce, J. M., Petry, N. M., Stitzer, M., Blaine, J., Kellogg, S., . . . Li, R. (2006). Effects of lower-cost incentives on stimulant abstinence in methadone maintenance treatment: A National Drug Abuse Treatment Clinical Trials Network study. *Archives of General Psychiatry, 63*, 201–208.

Pelham, W. E., & Fabiano, G. A. (2008). Evidence-based psychosocial treatment for ADHD: An update. *Journal of Clinical Child and Adolescent Psychology, 37*, 184–214.

Pelletier, L. G., & Dion, S. C. (2007). An examination of general and specific motivational mechanisms for the relations between body dissatisfaction and eating behaviors. *Journal of Social and Clinical Psychology, 26*, 303–333.

Pemberton, C. K., Neiderhiser, J. M., Leve, L. D., Natsuaki, M. N., Shaw, D. S., Reiss, D., & Ge, X. (2010). Influence of parental depressive symptoms on adopted toddler behaviors: An emerging developmental cascade of genetic and environmental effects. *Developmental Psychopathology, 22*, 803–818.

Penn, D. L., Mueser, K. T., Tarrier, N., Gloege, A., Cather, C., Serrano, D., & Otto, M. W. (2004). Supportive therapy for schizophrenia: Possible mechanisms and implications for adjunctive psychosocial treatments. *Schizophrenia Bulletin, 30*, 101–112.

Perala, J., Suvisaari, J., Saarni, S. I., Kuoppasalmi, K., Isometsa, E., . . . Lonnqvist, J. (2007). Lifetime prevalence of psychotic and bipolar I disorders in a general population. *Archives of General Psychiatry, 64*, 19–28.

Peralta, R. L. (2003). Thinking sociologically about sources of obesity in the United States. *Gender Issues, 21*, 5–16.

Perkins, H. W., Linkenbach, J. W., Lewis, M. A., & Neighbors, C. (2010). Effectiveness of social norms media marketing in reducing drinking and driving: A statewide campaign. *Addictive Behaviors, 35*, 866–874.

Perkins, K. A. (2009). Sex differences in nicotine reinforcement and reward: Influences on the persistence of tobacco smoking. *The Motivational Impact of Nicotine and its Role in Tobacco Use: Nebraska Symposium on Motivation, 55*, 1–27.

Perlis, R. H., Ostacher, M., Fava, M., Nierenberg, A. A., Sachs, G. S., & Rosenbaum, J. F. (2010). Assuring that double-blind is blind. *American Journal of Psychiatry, 167*, 250–252.

Perlis, R. H., Smoller, J. W., Mysore, J., Sun, M., Gillis, T., . . . Gusella, J. (2010). Prevalence of incompletely penetrant Huntington's disease alleles among individuals with major depressive disorder. *American Journal of Psychiatry,167*, 574–579.

Perlman, C. M., Martin, L., Hirdes, J. P., & Curtin-Telegdi, N. (2007). Prevalence and predictors of sexual dysfunction in psychiatric inpatients. *Psychosomatics, 48*, 309–318.

Perron, B. E., & Howard, M. O. (2009). Adolescent inhalant use, abuse and dependence. *Addiction, 104*, 1185–1192.

Perry, J., & Felce, D. (2005). Factors associated with outcome in community group homes. *American Journal on Mental Retardation, 110*, 121–135.

Petersen, R. C. (2011). Mild cognitive impairment. *New England Journal of Medicine, 364*, 2227–2234.

Peterson, C., & Seligman, M. (2005). *Character strengths and virtue: A handbook and classification*. New York, NY: Oxford University Press.

Peterson, C. B., Thuras, P., Ackard, D. M., Mitchell, J. E., Berg, K., . . . Crow, S. J. (2010). Personality dimensions in bulimia nervosa, binge eating disorder, and obesity. *Comprehensive Psychiatry, 51*, 31–36.

Peterson, R. A. (2001). On the use of college students in social science research: Insights from a second-order meta-analysis. *Journal of Consumer Research, 28*, 450–461.

Petry, N. M., Alessi, S. M., Carroll, K. M., Hanson, T., MacKinnon. S., Rounsaville, B., & Sierra, S. (2006). Contingency management treatments: Reinforcing abstinence versus adherence with goal-related activities. *Journal of Consulting and Clinical Psychology, 74*, 592–601.

Pettinati, H. M., O'Brien, C. P., Rabinowitz, A. R., Wortman, S. P., Oslin, D. W., . . . Dackis, C. A. (2006). The status of naltrexone in the treatment of alcohol dependence: Specific effects on heavy drinking. *Journal of Clinical Psychopharmacology, 26*, 610–625.

Pezawas, L., Meyer-Lindenberg, A., Drabant, E. M., Verchinski, B. A., Munoz, K. E., . . . Weinberger, D. R. (2005). 5-HTTLPR polymorphism impacts human cingulated amygdala interactions: A genetic susceptibility mechanism for depression. *Nature Neuroscience, 8*, 828–834.

Pezdek, K., Blandon-Gitlin, I., & Gabbay, P. (2006). Imagination and memory: Does imagining implausible events lead to false autobiographical memories? *Psychonomic Bulletin and Review, 13*, 764–769.

Pflueger, M. O., Gschwandtner, U., Stieglitz, R.-D., & Riecher-Rossler, A. (2007). Neuropsychological deficits in individuals with an at risk mental state for psychosis: Working memory as a potential trait marker. *Schizophrenia Research, 97*, 14–24.

Phelps, B. J. (2000). Dissociative identity disorder: The relevance of behavior analysis. *Psychological Record, 50*, 235–249.

Phelps, L., Johnston, L. S., & Augustyniak, K. (1999). Prevention of eating disorders: Identification of predictor variables. *Eating Disorders: The Journal of Treatment and Prevention, 7*, 99–108.

Phillips, A., & Daniluk, J. C. (2004). Beyond "survivor": How childhood sexual abuse informs the identity of adult women at the end of the therapeutic process. *Journal of Counseling and Development, 82*, 177–184.

Phillips, D. P., Van Voorhees, C. A., & Ruth, T. E. (1992). The birthday: Lifeline or deadline? *Psychosomatic Medicine, 54*, 532–542.

Phillips, K. A., & Gunderson, J. G. (1999). Personality disorders. In R. E. Hales, S. C. Yudofsky, & J. A. Talbott (Eds.), *Textbook of psychiatry* (pp. 795–823). Washington, DC: American Psychiatric Publishing.

Phillips, K. A., McElroy, S. L., Dwight, M. M., Eisen, J. L., & Rasmussen, S. A. (2001). Delusionality and response to open-label fluvoxamine in body dysmorphic disorder. *Journal of Clinical Psychiatry, 62*, 87–91.

Phillips, K. A., McElroy, S. L., Keck, P. E., Pope, H. G., Jr., & Hudson, J. I. (1993). Body dysmorphic disorder: Thirty cases of imagined ugliness. *American Journal of Psychiatry, 150*, 302–308.

Phillips, K. A., Pagano, M. E., Menard, W., & Stout, R. L. (2006). A 12-month follow-up study of the course of body dysmorphic disorder. *American Journal of Psychiatry, 163*, 907–912.

Phillips, K. A., & Rasmussen, S. A. (2004). Change in psychosocial functioning and quality of life of patients with body dysmorphic disorder treated with fluoxetine: A placebo-controlled study. *Psychosomatics, 45*, 438–444.

Phillips, K. A., Stein, D. J., Rauch, S. L., Hollander, E., Fallon, B. A., . . . Leckman, J. (2010). Should an obsessive-compulsive spectrum grouping of disorders be included in DSM-V? *Depression and Anxiety, 27*, 528–555.

Phillips, K. A., Wilhelm, S., Koran, L. M., Didie, E. R., Fallon, B. A., . . . Stein, D. J. (2010). Body dysmorphic disorder: Some key issues for DSM-V. *Depression and Anxiety, 27*, 573–591.

Phillips, K. A., Yen, S., & Gunderson, J. G. (2004). Personality disorders. In R. E. Hales & S. C. Yudofsky (Eds.), *Essentials of clinical psychiatry* (2nd ed., pp. 567–589). Washington, DC: American Psychiatric.

Phipps, S. (2011). Positive psychology and war: An oxymoron. *American Psychologist, 66*, 641–642.

Picardi, A. (2009). Rating scales in bipolar disorder. *Current Opinion in Psychiatry, 22*, 42–49.

Piefke, M., Pestinger, M., Arin, T., Kohl, B., Kastrau, F., Schnitker, R., . . . Flatten, G. (2007). The neurofunctional mechanism of traumatic and non-traumatic memory in patients with acute PTSD following accident trauma. *Neurocase, 13*, 342–357.

Pike, K. M., Dohm, F.-A., Striegel-Moore, R., Wilfley, D. E., & Fairburn, C. G. (2001). A comparison of black and white women with binge eating disorder. *American Journal of Psychiatry, 158*, 1455–1461.

Pincus, A. L. (2011). Some comments on nosology, diagnostic process, and narcissistic personality disorder in DSM-5: Proposal for personality and personality disorders. *Personality Disorders: Theory, Research, and Treatment, 2*, 41–53.

Pincus, D. B., May, J. E., Whitton, S. W., Mattis, S. G., & Barlow, D. H. (2010). Cognitive-behavioral treatment of panic disorder in adolescence. *Journal of Clinical Child and Adolescent Psychology, 39*, 638–649.

Pinheiro, A. P., Raney, T. J., Thornton, L. M., Fichter, M. M., Berrentini, W. H., . . . Bulik, C. M. (2010). Sexual functioning in women with eating disorders. *International Journal of Eating Disorder, 43*, 123–129.

Pinto-Martin, J. A., Levy, S. E., Feldman, J. F., Lorenz, J. M., Paneth, N., & Whitaker, A. H. (2011). Prevalence of autism spectrum disorder in adolescents born weighing <2000 grams. *Pediatrics, 128*, 883–891.

Piper, A., & Merskey, H. (2004). The persistence of folly: A critical examination of dissociative identity disorder. Part 1: The excesses of an improbable concept. *Canadian Journal of Psychiatry, 49*, 592–600.

Piper, M. E., Cook, J. W., Schlam, T. R., Jorenby, D. E., & Baker, T. B. (2010). Anxiety diagnoses in smokers seeking cessation treatment: Relations with tobacco dependence, withdrawal, outcome and response to treatment. *Addiction, 106*, 418–427. doi:10.1111/j.1360-0443.2010.03173.x

Pizarro, J., Silver, R. C., & Prause, J. (2006). Physical and mental health costs of traumatic war experiences among Civil War veterans. *Archives of General Psychiatry, 63*, 193–200.

Plomin, R., & McGuffin, P. (2003). Psychopathology in the postgenomic era. *Annual Review of Psychology, 54*, 205–228.

Plomp, E., Van Engeland, H., & Durston, S. (2009). Understanding genes, environment and their interaction in attention-deficit hyperactivity disorder: Is there a role for neuroimaging? *Neuroscience, 164*, 230–240.
Poels, M. M., Ikram, M. A., van der Lugt, A., Hofman, A., Niessen, W. J., . . . Vernooij, M. W. (2012). Cerebral microbleeds are associated with worse cognitive function. *Neurology, 78*, 326–333.
Polanczyk, G., Moffitt, T. E., Arseneault, L., Cannon, M., Ambler, A., Keefe, R. S. E., . . . Caspi, A. (2010). Etiological and clinical features of childhood psychotic symptoms: Results from a birth cohort. *Archives of General Psychiatry, 67*, 328–338.
Poleshuck, E. L., Gamble, S. A., Cort, N., Hoffman-King, D., Cerrito, B., Rosario-McCabe, L., & Giles, D. E. (2010). Interpersonal psychotherapy for co-occurring depression and chronic pain. *Professional Psychology: Research and Practice, 41*, 312–318.
Pollard, C. A., Pollard, H. J., & Corn, K. J. (1989). Panic onset and major events in the lives of agoraphobics: A test of continuity. *Journal of Abnormal Psychology, 98*, 318–321.
Ponterotto, J. G., & Casas, J. M. (1991). *Handbook of racial/ethnic minority counseling research*. Springfield, IL: Thomas.
Ponterotto, J. G., Utsey, S. O., & Pedersen, P. B. (2006). *Preventing prejudice*. Thousand Oaks, CA: Sage.
Pope, H. G., Jr., Barry, S., Bodkin, A., & Hudson, J. I. (2006). Tracking scientific interest in the dissociative disorders: A study of scientific publication output, 1984–2003. *Psychotherapy and Psychosomatics, 75*, 19–24.
Pope, H. G., Jr., Gruber, A. J., Mangweth, B., Bureau, B., deCol, C., Jouvent, R., & Hudson, J. I. (2000). Body image perception among men in three countries. *American Journal of Psychiatry, 157*, 1297–1301.
Pope, K. S., & Vasquez, M. J. T. (2007). *Ethics in psychotherapy and counseling*. Hoboken, NJ: Wiley.
Population Reference Bureau. (2007). Cognitive aging: Imaging, emotion, and memory. *Today's Research on Aging, 5*, 1–5.
Powell, L. H., Calvin, J. E., III, & Calvin, J. E., Jr. (2007). Effective obesity treatments. *American Psychologist, 62*, 234–246.
Powers, M. B., Halpern, J. M., Ferenschak, M. P., Gillihan, S. J., & Foa, E. B. (2010). A meta-analytic review of prolonged exposure for posttraumatic stress disorder. *Clinical Psychology Review, 30*, 635–641.
Prati, G., & Pietrantoni, L. (2009). Optimism, social support, and coping strategies as factors contributing to posttraumatic growth: A meta-analysis. *Journal of Loss and Trauma, 14*, 364–388.
Pratt, L. A., Brody, D. J., & Gu, Q. (2011). *Antidepressant use in persons aged 12 and over: United States, 2005–2008* (NCHS Data Brief No. 76). Hyattsville, MD: National Center for Health Statistics.
Preece, M. H., Horswill, M. S., & Geffen, G. M. (2010). Driving after concussion: The acute effect of mild traumatic brain injury on drivers' hazard perception. *Neuropsychology, 24*, 493–503.
President's New Freedom Commission on Mental Health. (2003). *Achieving the promise: Transforming mental health care in America. Final Report* (DHHS Publication No. SMA03-3832). Rockville, MD: U.S. Department of Health and Human Services.
Price, C. S., Thompson, W. W., Goodson, B., Weintraub, E. S., Croen, L. A., Hinrichsen, V. L., . . . DeStafano, F. (2010). Prenatal and infant exposure to thimerosal from vaccines and immunoglobulins and risk of autism. *Pediatrics, 126*, 656–664.
Price, J., Cole, V., & Goodwin, G. M. (2009). Emotional side effects of selective serotonin reuptake inhibitors: Qualitative study. *British Journal of Psychiatry, 195*, 211–217.
Prichard, J. C. (1837). *Treatise on insanity and other disorders affecting the mind*. Philadelphia, PA: Haswell, Barrington, & Haswell.
Prince, M., Bryce, R., & Ferri, C. (2011). *World Alzheimer report 2011: The benefits of early diagnosis and intervention*. London, UK: Alzheimer's Disease International. Retrieved from http://www.alz.co.uk/research/WorldAlzheimerReport2011.pdf
Prossin, A. R., Love, T. M., Koeppe, R. A., Zubieta, J. K., & Silk, K. R. (2010). Dysregulation of regional endogenous opioid function in borderline personality disorder. *American Journal of Psychiatry, 167*, 925–933.
Proudfoot, J., Doran, J., Manicavasagar, V., & Parker, G. (2010). The precipitants of manic/hypomanic episodes in the context of bipolar disorder: A review. *Journal of Affective Disorders*. doi: 10.1016/j.jad.2010.10.051.
Puhl, R. M., & Heuer, C. A. (2009). The stigma of obesity: A review and update. *Obesity, 17*, 941–964.
Purdon, C., & Clark, D. A. (2005). *Overcoming obsessional thoughts*. Oakland, CA: New Harbinger.
Queinec, R., Benjamin, C., Beitz, E., Lagarde, C. & Encrenaz, G. (2010). Suicide contagion in France: An epidemiologic study. Injury Prevention, 16, 11–36.
Quick, J. C. (2011). Missing: Critical and skeptical perspectives on Comprehensive Soldier Fitness. *American Psychologist, 66*, 645.
Qureshi, S. U., Kimbrell, T., Pyne, J. M., Magruder, K. M., Hudson, T. J., . . . Kunik, M. E. (2010). Greater prevalence and incidence of dementia in older veterans with posttraumatic stress disorder. *Journal of the American Geriatrics Society, 58*, 1627–1633. doi:10.1111/j.1532-5415.2010.02977.x
Rabinovici, G. D., & Miller, B. L. (2010). Frontotemporal lobar degeneration: Epidemiology, pathophysiology, diagnosis and management. *CNS Drugs, 24*, 375–398.
Rabinowitz, J., Levine, S. Z., Haim, R., & Hafner, H. (2007). The course of schizophrenia: Progressive deterioration, amelioration or both? *Schizophrenia Research, 91*, 254–258.
Rachman, S., Elliott, C. M., Shafran, R., & Radomsky, A. S. (2009). Separating hoarding from OCD. *Behaviour Research and Therapy, 47*, 520–522.
Rachman, S., Marks, I. M., & Hodgson, R. (1973). The treatment of obsessive compulsive neurotics by modeling and flooding in vivo. *Behaviour Research and Therapy, 11*, 463–471.
Radwa, A. B., Badawy, R. A., Macdonell, L., Berkovic, S. F., Newton, M. R., & Jackson, G. D. (2010). Predicting seizure control: Cortical excitability and antiepileptic medication. *Annals of Neurology, 67*, 64–73.
Raikkonen, K., Matthews, K. A., & Salomon, K. (2003). Hostility predicts metabolic syndrome risk factors in children and adolescents. *Health Psychology, 22*, 279–286.
Raine, A., Mellingen, K., Liu, J., Venables, P., & Mednick, S. A. (2003). Effect of environmental enrichment at ages 3–5 years on schizotypal personality and antisocial behavior at ages 17 and 23 years. *American Journal of Psychiatry, 160*, 1627–1635.
Ramos, R. (1998). *An ethnographic study of Mexican American inhalant abusers in San Antonio*. Austin, TX: Texas Commission on Alcohol and Drug Abuse. Retrieved from http://www.dshs.state.tx.us/sa/research/populations/Inhale98S.pdf
Rand Corporation. (2010). Invisible wounds: Mental health and cognitive care needs of America's returning veterans. Retrieved from http://www.rand.org/pubs/research_briefs/RB9336/index1.html
Rao, V., Handel, S., Vaishnavi, S., Keach, S., Robbins, B., Spiro, J., . . . Berlin, F. (2007). Psychiatric sequelae of traumatic brain injury: A case report. *American Journal of Psychiatry, 164*, 728–735.
Rapee, R. M., Schniering, C. A., & Hudson, J. L. (2009). Anxiety disorders during childhood and adolescence: Origins and treatment. *Annual Review of Clinical Psychology, 5*, 311–341.
Rashid, T., & Ostermann, R. F. (2009). Strength-based assessment in clinical practice. *Journal of Clinical Psychology, 65*, 488–498.
Rathbone, C. J., Moulin, C. J., & Conway, M. A. (2009). Autobiographical memory and amnesia: Using conceptual knowledge to ground the self. *Neurocase: The Neural Basis of Cognition, 15*, 405–418.
Rathus, S. A., Nevid, J. S., & Fichner-Rathus, L. (2005). *Abnormal psychology*. New York, NY: Allyn & Bacon.
Rauch, S. L., Shin, L. M., & Wright, C. I. (2003). Neuroimaging studies of amygdala function in anxiety disorders. *Annals of the New York Academy of Sciences, 985*, 389–410.
Rausch, S. M., Gramling, S. E., & Auerbach, S. M. (2006). Effects of a single session of large-group meditation and progressive muscle relaxation training on stress reduction, reactivity, and recovery. *International Journal of Stress Management, 13*, 273–290.
Ravindran, L. N., & Stein, M. B. (2010). Pharmacotherapy of post-traumatic stress disorder. *Current Topics in Behavioral Neuroscience, 2*, 505–525.
Ray, G. T., Croen, L. A., & Habel, L. A. (2009). Mothers of children diagnosed with attention-deficit/hyperactivity disorder: Health conditions and medical care utilization in periods before and after birth of the child. *Medical Care, 47*, 105–114.
Raymond, F. L., Tarpey, P. S., Edkins, S., Tofts, C., O'Meara, S., . . . Futreal, P. A. (2007). Mutations in ZDHHC9, which encodes a palmitoyltransferase of NRAS and HRAS, cause X-linked mental retardation associated with a marfanoid habitus. *American Journal of Human Genetics, 80*, 982–987.
Raymont, V., Salazar. A. M., Lipsky, R., Goldman, D., Tasick, G., & Grafman, J. (2010). Correlates of posttraumatic epilepsy 35 years following combat brain injury. *Neurology, 75*, 224–229.
Razani, J., Nordin, S., Chan, A., & Murphy, C. (2010). Semantic networks for odors and colors in Alzheimer's disease. *Neuropsychology, 24*, 291–299.
Rector, N. A., Beck, A. T., & Stolar, N. (2005). The negative symptoms of schizophrenia: A cognitive perspective. *Canadian Journal of Psychiatry, 50*, 247–257.
Reed, G. M. (2010). Toward ICD-11: Improving the clinical utility of WHO's International Classification of Mental Disorders. *Professional Psychology: Research and Practice, 41*, 457–464.
Reese, H. E., McNally, R. J., & Wilhelm, S. (2011). Reality monitoring in patients with body dysmorphic disorder. *Behavior Therapy, 42*, 387–398.
Reese, M., Herbenick, D., Schick, V., Sanders, S. A., Dodge, B., & Fortenberry, J. D. (2010). Background and considerations on the National Survey of Sexual Health and Behavior (NSSHB) from the investigators. *Journal of Sexual Medicine, 7*, 243–245.
Reichenberg, A., & Harvey, P. D. (2007). Neuropsychological impairments in schizophrenia: Integration of performance-based and brain imaging findings. *Psychological Bulletin, 133*, 833–858.
Reid, J. M., Storch, E. A., Murphy, T. K., Bodzin, D., Mutch, P. J., Lehmkuhl, H., . . . Goodman, W. K. (2010). Development and psychometric evaluation of the treatment-emergent activation and suicidality assessment profile. *Child and Youth Care Forum, 39*, 113–124.
Reid, R. C., Harper, J. M., & Anderson, E. H. (2009). Coping strategies used by hypersexual patients to defend against the painful effects of shame. *Clinical Psychology and Psychotherapy, 16*, 125–138.
Reinders, A. A. T. S., Nijenhuis, E. R. S., Paans, A. M. J., Korf, J., Willemsen, A. T. M., & den Boers, J. A. (2003). One brain, two selves. *Neuroimage, 20*, 2119–2125.
Reinhold, N., & Markowitsch, H. J. (2009). Retrograde episodic memory and emotion: A perspective from patients with dissociative amnesia. *Neuropsychologia, 47*, 2197–2206.
Reiss, S., Peterson, R. A., Gursky, D. M., & McNally, R. J. (1986). Anxiety sensitivity, anxiety frequency, and the prediction of fearfulness. *Behaviour Research and Therapy, 24*, 1–8.

Reissig, C. J., Strain, E. C., & Griffiths, R. R. (2009). Caffeinated energy drinks—A growing problem. *Drug and Alcohol Dependence, 99*, 1–10.

Ressler, K. J. (2010). Amygdala activity, fear, and anxiety: Modulation by stress. *Biological Psychiatry, 67*, 1117–1119.

Rettew, D. C., Zanarini, M. C., & Yen, S. (2003). Childhood antecedents of avoidant personality disorder: A retrospective study. *Journal of the American Academy of Child & Adolescent Psychiatry, 42*, 1122–1130.

Ricca, V., Mannucci, E., Zucchi, T., Rotella, C. M., & Faravelli, C. (2000). Cognitive-behavioral therapy for bulimia nervosa and binge eating disorder: A review. *Psychotherapy and Psychosomatics, 69*, 287–295.

Ricciardelli, L. A., & McCabe, M. P. (2004). A biopsychosocial model of disordered eating and the pursuit of muscularity in adolescent boys. *Psychological Bulletin, 130*, 179–205.

Richards, J. C., Alvarenga, M., & Hof, A. (2000). Serum lipids and their relationships with hostility and angry affect and behaviors in men. *Health Psychology, 19*, 393–398.

Richardson, K., Baillie, A., Reid, S., Morley, K., Teesson, M., Sannibale, C., . . . Haber, P. (2008) Do acamprosate or naltrexone have an effect on daily drinking by reducing craving for alcohol? *Addiction, 103*, 953–959.

Richardson, L. F. (1998). Psychogenic dissociation in childhood: The role of the counseling psychologist. *Counseling Psychologist, 26*, 69–100.

Richardson, S. M., & Paxton, S. J. (2010). An evaluation of a body image intervention based on risk factors for body dissatisfaction: A controlled study with adolescent girls. *International Journal of Eating Disorders, 43*, 112–122.

Ridgway, A. R., Northup, J., Pellegrin, A., LaRue, R., & Hightshoe, A. (2003). The benefits of recess for children with and without attention-deficit/hyperactivity disorder. *School Psychology Quarterly, 18*, 253–268.

Ridley, C. R. (2005). *Overcoming unintentional racism in counseling and therapy* (2nd ed.). Thousand Oaks, CA: Sage.

Rieber, R. W. (2006). *The bifurcation of the self: The history and theory of dissociation and its disorders.* New York, NY: Springer.

Rieker, P. P., & Bird, C. E. (2005). Rethinking gender differences in health: Why we need to integrate social and biological perspectives. *Journal of Gerontology, 60*, S40–S47.

Riemersma-van der Lek, R. F., Swaab, D. F., Twisk, J., Hol, E. M., Hoogendijk, W. J., & Van Someren, E. J. (2008). Effect of bright light and melatonin on cognitive and noncognitive function in elderly residents of group care facilities: A randomized controlled trial. *Journal of the American Medical Association, 299*, 2642–2655.

Rihmer, Z., & Gonda, X. (2011). Antidepressant-resistant depression and antidepressant-associated suicidal behaviour: The role of underlying bipolarity. *Depression Research and Treatment, 2011*, 906462. doi:10.1155/2011/906462

Rinck, M., & Becker, E. S. (2006). Spider fearful individuals attend to threat, then quickly avoid it: Evidence from eye movements. *Journal of Abnormal Psychology, 115*, 231–238.

Ringman, J. M., Schulman, H., Becker, C., Jones, T., Bai, Y., Immermann, F., . . . Wan, H. I. (2012). Proteomic changes in cerebrospinal fluid of presymptomatic and affected persons carrying familial alzheimer disease mutations. *Archives of Neurology, 69*, 96–104.

Riskind, J. H., Moore, R., & Bowley, L. (1995). The looming of spiders: The fearful perceptual distortion of movement and menace. *Behaviour Research and Therapy, 33*, 171–178.

Rivara, F. P., Koepsell, T. D., Wang, J., Temkin, N., Dorsch, A., . . . Jaffe, K. M. (2011). Disability 3, 12, and 24 months after traumatic brain injury among children and adolescents. *Pediatrics, 128*, e1129-e1138.

Rivera, R. P., & Borda, T. (2001). The etiology of body dysmorphic disorder. *Psychiatric Annals, 31*, 559–564.

Rivera-Navarro, J., Cubo, E., & Almazan, J. (2009). The diagnosis of Tourette's syndrome: Communication and impact. *Clinical Child Psychology and Psychiatry, 14*, 13–23.

Rizvi, S., & Zaretsky, A. E. (2007). Psychotherapy through the phases of bipolar disorder: Evidence for general efficacy and differential effects. *Journal of Clinical Psychology: In Session, 63*, 491–506.

Roberts, A. L., Austin, S. B., Corliss, H. L., Vandermorris, A. K., & Koenen, K. C. (2010). Pervasive traumatic exposure among US sexual orientation minority adults and risk of posttraumatic stress disorder. *American Journal of Public Health, 100*, 2433–2441.

Roberts, A. L., Gilman, S. E., Breslau, J., Breslau, N., & Koenen, K. C. (2010). Race/ethnic differences in exposure to traumatic events, development of post-traumatic stress disorder, and treatment-seeking for post-traumatic stress disorder in the United States. *Psychological Medicine, 41*(1), 71–83. doi:10.1017/S0033291710000401

Roberts, E. M., English, P. B., Grether, J. K., Windham, G. C., Somberg, L., & Wolff, C. (2007). Maternal residence near agricultural pesticide applications and autism spectrum disorders among children in the California Central Valley. *Environmental Health Perspectives, 115*, 1482–1489.

Robertson, W. C., Jr. (2010). Tourette syndrome and other tic disorders. Retrieved from http://emedicine.medscape.com/article/1182258-overview

Robins, L. N., Tipp, J., & Przybeck, T. (1991). Antisocial personality. In L. N. Robins & D. A. Regier (Eds.), *Psychiatric disorders in America: The Epidemiologic Catchment Area study* (pp. 258–290). New York, NY: Free Press.

Robinson, E. B., Koenen, K. C., McCormick, M. C., Munir, K., Hallett, V., Happé, F., . . . Ronald, A. (2011). Evidence that autistic traits show the same etiology in the general population and at the quantitative extremes (5%, 2.5%, and 1%). *Archives of General Psychiatry, 68*, 1113–1121.

Robison, E. J., Shankman, S. A., & McFarland, B. R. (2009). Independent associations between personality traits and clinical characteristics of depression. *Journal of Nervous and Mental Disease, 197*, 476–483.

Rocchi, A., Orsucci, D., Tognoni, G., Ceravolo, R., & Siciliano, G. (2009). The role of vascular factors in late-onset sporadic Alzheimer's disease. *Current Alzheimer Research, 6*, 224–237.

Rockhill, C., Kodish, I., DiBattisto, C., Macias, M., Varley, C., & Ryan, S. (2010). Anxiety disorders in children and adolescents. *Current Problems in Pediatric and Adolescent Health Care, 40*, 66–99.

Rodebaugh, T. L. (2009). Social phobia and perceived friendship quality. *Journal of Anxiety Disorders, 23*, 872–878.

Rodewald, F., Wilhelm-Gobling, C., Emrich, H. M., Reddemann, L., & Gast, U. (2011). Axis-I comorbidity in female patients with dissociative identity disorder and dissociative disorder not otherwise specified. *Journal of Nervous and Mental Disease, 199*, 122–131.

Rofey, D. L., Kolko, R. P., Iosif, A. M., Silk, J. S., Bost, J. E., . . . Dahl, R. E. (2009). A longitudinal study of childhood depression and anxiety in relation to weight gain. *Child Psychiatry and Human Development, 40*, 517–526.

Roger, V. L., Go, A. S., Lloyd-Jones, D. M., Adams, R., Berry, J. D., . . . Wylie-Rosett, J. (2011). American Heart Association's heart disease and stroke statistics—2011 update. *Circulation, 123*, e18-e209. doi:10.1161/CIR.0b013e3182009701

Rogers, C. R. (1951). *Client-centered therapy*. Boston, MA: Houghton Mifflin.

Rogers, C. R. (1959). A theory of therapy, personality, and interpersonal relationships, as developed in client-centered framework. In S. Koch (Ed.), *Psychology: A study of science* (Vol. 3, pp. 123–148). New York, NY: McGraw-Hill.

Rogers, C. R. (1961). *On becoming a person*. Boston, MA: Houghton Mifflin.

Rogers, J. R. (1992). Suicide and alcohol: Conceptualizing the relationship from a cognitive-social paradigm. *Journal of Counseling and Development, 70*, 540–543.

Rogers, R. L., & Petrie, T. A. (2001). Psychological correlates of anorexic and bulimic symptomatology. *Journal of Counseling and Development, 79*, 178–187.

Rogers, S. J. (2009). What are infant siblings teaching us about autism in infancy? *Autism Research, 2*, 125–137.

Rogers-Wood, N. A., & Petrie, T. A. (2010). Body dissatisfaction, ethnic identity, and disordered eating among African American women. *Journal of Counseling Psychology, 57*, 141–153.

Rohrmann, S., Hopp, H., & Quirin, M. (2008). Gender differences in psychophysiological responses to disgust. *Journal of Psychophysiology, 22*, 65–75.

Rohsenow, D. J., Monti, P. M., Martin, R. A., Michalec, E., & Abrams, D. B. (2000). Brief coping skills treatment for cocaine abuse: 12-month substance use outcomes. *Journal of Consulting and Clinical Psychology, 68*, 515–520.

Rolland, Y., van Kan, G. A., & Vellas, B. (2010). Healthy brain aging: Role of exercise and physical activity. *Clinics in Geriatric Medicine, 26*, 75–87.

Rollnick, S., Miller, W. R., & Butler, C. C. (2008). *Motivational interviewing in health care: Helping patients change behavior.* New York, NY: Guilford Press.

Roos, R. A. (2010). Huntington's disease: A clinical review. *Orphanet Journal of Rare Diseases, 5*, 40. doi:10.1186/1750-1172-5-40

Rosen, H. J., & Levenson, R. W. (2009). The emotional brain: Combining insights from patients and basic science. *Neurocase, 15*, 173–181.

Rosen, H. R., & Rich, B. A. (2010). Neurocognitive correlates of emotional stimulus processing in pediatric bipolar disorder: A review. *Postgraduate Medicine, 122*, 94–104.

Rosen, R. C., & Leiblum, S. R. (1995). Hypoactive sexual desire. *Psychiatric Clinics of North America, 13*, 107–121.

Rosenberg, J., & Rosenberg, S. (2006). *Community mental health: Challenges for the 21st century.* New York, NY: Routledge.

Rosenfarb, I. S., Bellack, A. S., & Aziz, N. (2006). Family interactions and the course of schizophrenia in African American and white patients. *Journal of Abnormal Psychology, 115*, 112–120.

Rosenfarb, I. S., Goldstein, M. J., Mintz, J., & Nuechterlein, K. H. (1995). Expressed emotion and subclinical psychopathology observable within the transactions between schizophrenic patients and their family members. *Journal of Abnormal Psychology, 104*, 259–267.

Rosenfeld, B. (2004). *Assisted suicide and the right to die.* New York, NY: Guilford Press.

Rosenhan, D. L. (1973). On being sane in insane places. *Science, 179*, 250–258.

Rosenstreich, D. L., Eggleston, P., & Kattan, M. (1997). The role of cockroach allergy and exposure to cockroach allergen in causing morbidity among inner-city children with asthma. *New England Journal of Medicine, 336*, 1356–1363.

Rosenthal, D. G., Learned, N., Liu, Y., & Weitzman, M. (2012). Characteristics of fathers with depressive symptoms. *Maternal and Child Health Journal.* Advance online publication. doi:10.1007/s10995-012-0955-5

Rosenthal, N. E. (2009). Issues for DSM-V: Seasonal affective disorder and seasonality. *American Journal of Psychiatry, 166*, 852–853.

Ross, C. A. (2011). Possession experiences in dissociative identity disorder: A preliminary study. *Journal of Trauma and Dissociation, 12*, 393–400.

Ross, C. A., Anderson, G., Fleisher, W. P., & Norton, G. R. (1991). The frequency of multiple personality disorder among psychiatric inpatients. *American Journal of Psychiatry, 148*, 1717–1720.

Ross, K., Freeman, D., Dunn, G., & Garety, P. (2011). Can jumping to conclusion be reduced in people with delusions? An experimental investigation of a brief reasoning training module. *Schizophrenia Bulletin, 37*, 324–333.

Rossignol, D. A. (2009). Novel and emerging treatments for autism spectrum disorders: A systematic review. *Annals of Clinical Psychiatry, 21*, 213–236.

Rossler, W., Riecher-Rossler, A. R., Angst, J., Murray, R., Gamma, A., . . . Gross, V. A. (2007). Psychotic experiences in the general population: A twenty-year prospective study. *Schizophrenia Research, 92*, 1–14.

Roth, M. E., Cosgrov, K. P., & Carroll, M. E. (2004). Sex differences in the vulnerability to drug abuse: A review of preclinical studies. *Neuroscientific Biobehavioral Review, 28*, 533–546.

Roth, R. M., Flashman, L. A., Saykin, A. J., McAllister, T. W., & Vidaver, R. (2004). Apathy in schizophrenia: Reduced frontal lobe volume and neuropsychological deficits. *American Journal of Psychiatry, 161*, 157–159.

Rothman, B. M., Ahn, W. K., Sanislow, C. A., & Kim, N. S. (2009). Can clinicians recognize DSM-IV personality disorders from five-factor model descriptions of patient cases? *American Journal of Psychiatry, 166*, 427–433.

Rothschild, L., Cleland, C., Haslam, N., & Zimmerman, M. (2003). A taxometric study of borderline personality disorder. *Journal of Abnormal Psychology, 112*, 657–666.

Rouleau, C. R., & von Ranson, K. M. (2011). Potential risks of pro-eating disorder websites. *Clinical Psychology Review, 31*, 525–531.

Rouse v. Cameron, 373 F. 2d 451 (D.C. Cir. 1966).

Rowland, D. L., & McMahon, C. G. (2008). Premature ejaculation. In D. L. Rowland & L. Incrocci (Eds.). pp. 68–95. *Handbook of sexual and gender identity disorders*. Hoboken, NJ: Wiley.

Rowland, D. L., Tai, W., & Brummett, K. (2007). Interactive processes in ejaculatory disorders: Psychophysiological considerations. In E. Janssen (Ed.), *The psychophysiology of sex* (pp. 227–243). Bloomington: Indiana University Press.

Roy, A., Carli, V., & Sarchiapone, M. (2011). Resilience mitigates the suicide risk associated with childhood trauma. *Journal of Affective Disorders, 133*, 591–594.

Roy-Byrne, P. P., Craske, M. G., & Stein, M. B. (2006). Panic disorder. *Lancet, 368*, 1023–1032.

Rozen, T. D. (2010). Cluster headache with aura. *Current Pain and Headache Reports, 15*, 98–100. doi:10.1007/s11916-010-0168-9

Rozen, T. D., & Fishman, R. S. (2012). Cluster headache in the United States of America: Demographics, clinical characteristics, triggers, suicidality, and personal burden. *Headache, 52*, 99–113. doi:10.1111/j.1526-4610.2011.02028.x

Rucker, J. H., & McGuffin, P. (2010). Polygenic heterogeneity: A complex model of genetic inheritance in psychiatric disorders. *Biological Psychiatry, 68*, 312–313.

Rudaz, M., Craske, M. G., Becker, E. S., Ledermann, T., & Margraf, J. (2010). Health anxiety and fear of fear in panic disorder and agoraphobia vs. social phobia: A prospective longitudinal study. *Depression and Anxiety, 27*, 404–411.

Rudd, M. D., Joiner, T., & Rajab, M. H. (2004). *Treating suicidal behavior*. New York, NY: Guilford Press.

Rudolph, K. D., Flynn, M., Abaied, J. L., Groot, A., & Thompson, R. (2009). Why is past depression the best predictor of future depression? Stress generation as a mechanism of depression continuity in girls. *Journal of Clinical Child and Adolescent Psychology, 38*, 473–485.

Rummel-Kluge, C., Komossa, K., Schwarz, S., Hunger, H., Schmid, F., . . . Leucht, S. (2012). Second-generation antipsychotic drugs and extrapyramidal side effects: A systematic review and meta-analysis of head-to-head comparisons. *Schizophrenia Bulletin, 38*, 167–177.

Rusanen, M., Kivipelto, M., Quesenberry, C. P., Zhou, J., & Whitmer, R. A. (2010). Heavy smoking in midlife and long-term risk of Alzheimer disease and vascular dementia. *Archives of Internal Medicine, 170*(14), 1191–1201. doi:10.1001/archinternmed.2010.393

Ruscio, J., & Ruscio, A. M. (2000). Informing the continuity controversy: A taxometric analysis of depression. *Journal of Abnormal Psychology, 109*, 473–487.

Russell, J. J., Moskowitz, D. S., Zuroff, D. C., Bleau, Z. P., & Young, S. N. (2010). Anxiety, emotional security and the interpersonal behavior of individuals with social anxiety disorder. *Psychological Medicine, 41*, 545–554. doi:10.1017/S0033291710000863

Rutter, M. (2006). Implications of resilience concepts for scientific understanding. *Annals of the New York Academy of Sciences, 1094*, 1–12.

Ryder, A. G., Yang, J., Zhu, X., Yao, S., Yi, J., . . . Bagby, R. M. (2008). The cultural shaping of depression: Somatic symptoms in China, psychological symptoms in North America? *Journal of Abnormal Psychology, 117*, 300–313.

Rynn, M., Puliafico, A., Heleniak, C., Rikhi, P., Ghalib, K., & Vidair, H. (2011). Advances in psychopharmacology for pediatric anxiety disorders. *Depression and Anxiety, 28*, 76–87.

Saczynski, J. S., Beiser, A., Seshadri, S., Auerbach, S., Wolf, P. A., & Au, R. (2010). Depressive symptoms and risk of dementia: The Framingham Heart Study. *Neurology, 75*, 35–41.

Safarinejad, M. R. (2006). Female sexual dysfunction in a population-based study in Iran: Prevalence and associated risk factors. *International Journal of Impotence Research, 18*, 382–395.

Saha, S., Chant, D., Welham, J., & McGrath, M. (2005). *A systematic review of the prevalence of schizophrenia*. Retrieved from http://www.plosmedicine.org/article/info:doi/10.1371/journal.pmed.0020141

Sajatovic, M., Ignacio, R. V., West, J. A., Cassidy, K. A., Safavi, R., Kilbourne, A. M., & Blow, F. C. (2009). Predictors of nonadherence among individuals with bipolar disorder receiving treatment in a community mental health clinic. *Comprehensive Psychiatry, 50*, 100–107.

Saklofske, D. H., Hildebrand, D. K., & Gorsuch, R. L. (2000). Replication of the factor structure of the Wechsler Adult Intelligence Scale—Third Edition with a Canadian sample. *Psychological Assessment, 12*, 436–439.

Sakolsky, D., & Birmaher, B. (2008). Pediatric anxiety disorders: Management in primary care. *Current Opinion in Pediatric Care, 20*, 538–543.

Saks, E. R. (2007). *The center cannot hold: My journey through madness*. New York, NY: Hyperion.

Sakuragi, S., Sugiyama, Y., & Takeuchi, K. (2002). Effect of laughing and weeping on mood and heart rate variability. *Journal of Physiological Anthropology and Applied Human Science, 21*, 159–165.

Salgado-Pineda, P., Caclin, A., Baeza, I., Junque, C., Bernardo, M., Blin, O., & Funlupt, P. (2007). Schizophrenia and the frontal cortex: Where does it fail? *Schizophrenia Research, 91*, 73–81.

Salvadore, G., Quiroz, J. A., Machado-Vieira, R., Henter, I. D., Manji, H. K., & Zarate, C. A., Jr. (2010). The neurobiology of the switch process in bipolar disorder: A review. *Journal of Clinical Psychiatry, 71*, 1488–1501.

Sammons, M. T. (2004). Healthcare trends. *Register Report, 30*, 16–18.

Samuels, J., Shugart, Y. Y., Grados, M. A., Willour, V. L., Bienvenu, O. J., . . . Nestadt, G. (2007). Significant linkage to compulsive hoarding on chromosome 14 in families with obsessive-compulsive disorder: Results from the OCD Collaborative Genetics Study. *American Journal of Psychiatry, 164*, 493–499.

Sánchez-Villegas, A., Delgado-Rodriguez, M., Alonso, A., Schlatter, J., Lahortiga, F., & Martínez-González, M. A. (2009). Association of the Mediterranean dietary pattern with the incidence of depression: The Seguimiento Universidad de Navarra/University of Navarra follow-up (SUN) cohort. *Archives of General Psychiatry, 66*, 1090–1098.

Sánchez-Villegas, A., Verberne, L., De Irala, J., Ruíz-Canela, M., Toledo, E., Serra-Majem, L., & Martínez-González, M. A. (2011). Dietary fat intake and the risk of depression: The SUN Project. *PLoS One, 6*(1), e16268. doi:10.1371/journal.pone.0016268

Sansone, R. A., & Sansone, L. A. (2011). Personality pathology and its influence on eating disorders. *Innovations in Clinical Neuroscience, 8*, 14–18.

Santiago-Rivera, A. L., Arredondo, P., & Gallardo-Cooper, M. (2002). *Counseling Latinos and la familia*. Thousand Oaks, CA: Sage.

Santisteban, D. A., Muir, J. A., Mena, M. P., & Mitrani, V. B. (2003). Integrative borderline adolescent family therapy: Meeting the challenges of treating adolescents with borderline personality disorders. *Psychotherapy: Theory, Research, Practice, Training, 40*, 251–264.

Sapienza, J. K., & Masten, A. S. (2011). Understanding and promoting resilience in children and youth. *Current Opinion in Psychiatry, 24*, 267–273.

Sarter, M., Bruno, J. P., & Parikh, V. (2007). Abnormal neurotransmitter release underlying behavior and cognitive disorders: Toward concepts of dynamic and function-specific dysregulation. *Neuropsychopharmocology, 32*, 1452–1461.

Satir, V. (1967). A family of angels. In J. Haley & L. Hoffman (Eds.), *Techniques of family therapy* (pp. 99–113). New York, NY: Basic Books.

Satow, R. (1979). Where has all the hysteria gone? *Psychoanalytic Review, 66*, 463–477.

Sauer, S. E., Burris, J. L., & Carlson, C. R. (2010). New directions in the management of chronic pain: Self-regulation theory as a model for integrative clinical psychology practice. *Clinical Psychology Review, 30*, 805–814.

Saunders, S. M., Miller, M., & Bright, M. M. (2010). Spiritually conscious psychological care. *Professional Psychology: Research and Practice, 41*, 355–362.

Savely, V. R., Leitao, M. M., & Stricker, R. B. (2006). The mystery of Morgellons disease: Infection or delusion? *American Journal of Clinical Dermatology, 7*, 1–5.s

Saxena, S. (2007). Is compulsive hoarding a genetically and neurobiologically discrete syndrome? Implications for diagnostic classification. *American Journal of Psychiatry, 164*, 380–384.

Saxena, S. (2011). Psychotherapy of compulsive hoarding. *Journal of Clinical Psychology: In Session, 67*, 477–484.

Saxena, S., Brody, A. L., Schwartz, J. M., & Baxter, L. R. (1998). Neuroimaging and frontal-subcortical circuitry in obsessive-compulsive disorder. *British Journal of Psychiatry, 35*, 26–37.

Scahill, L., McDougle, C. J., Aman, M. G., Johnson, C., Handen, B., Bearss, K., . . . Vitiello, B. (2012). Effects of risperidone and parent training on adaptive functioning in children with pervasive developmental disorders and serious behavioral problems. *Journal of the American Academy of Child & Adolescent Psychiatry, 51*, 36–46.

Schachter, S., & Latané, B. (1964). Crime, cognition, and the autonomic nervous system. *Nebraska Symposium on Motivation, 12*, 221–274.

Schatz, P., & Moser, R. S. (2011). Current issues in pediatric sports concussion. *Clinical Neuropsychology, 25*, 1042–1057.

Schaubroeck, J. M., Riolli, L. T., Peng, A. C., & Spain, E. S. (2011). Resilience of trauma exposure among soldiers deployed in combat. *Journal of Occupational Health Psychology, 16*, 18–37.

Schauer, M., & Elbert, T. (2010). Dissociation following traumatic stress: Etiology and treatment. *Journal of Psychology, 218*, 109–127.

Schindler, A., Thomasius, R., Petersen, K., & Sack, P. M. (2009). Heroin as an attachment substitute? Differences in attachment representations between opioid, ecstasy and cannabis abusers. *Attachment & Human Development, 11*, 307–330.

Schlesinger, L. (1989). *Sex murder and sex aggression.* New York, NY: Wiley.
Schmauk, F. J. (1970). Punishment, arousal, and avoidance learning. *Journal of Abnormal Psychology, 76*, 325–335.
Schmidt, N. B., & Harrington, P. (1995). Cognitive-behavioral treatment of body dysmorphic disorder: A case report. *Journal of Behavior Therapy and Experimental Psychiatry, 26*, 161–167.
Schmidt, N. B., Keough, M. E., Mitchell, M. A., Reynolds, E. K., MacPherson, L., . . . Lejuez, C. W. (2010). Anxiety sensitivity: Prospective prediction of anxiety among early adolescents. *Journal of Anxiety Disorders, 24*, 503–508.
Schmidt, N. B., Kotov, R., Bernstein, A., Zvolensky, M. J., Joiner, T. E., & Lewinsohn, P. M. (2007). Mixed anxiety depression: Taxometric exploration of the validity of a diagnostic category in youth. *Journal of Affective Disorders, 98*, 83–89.
Schmidt, N. B., Lerew, D. R., & Jackson, R. J. (1997). The role of anxiety sensitivity in the pathogenesis of panic: Prospective evaluations of spontaneous panic attacks during acute stress. *Journal of Abnormal Psychology, 106*, 355–364.
Schmidt, N. B., Richey, J., Buckner, J. D., & Timpano, K. R. (2009). Attention training for generalized social anxiety disorder. *Journal of Abnormal Psychology, 118*, 5–14.
Schneider, M. S., Brown, L. S., & Glassgold, J. M. (2002). Implementing the resolution on appropriate therapeutic responses to sexual orientation: A guide for the perplexed. *Professional Psychology: Research and Practice, 33*, 265–276.
Schneider, S., Peters, J., Bromberg, U., Brassen, S., Miedl, S. F., Banaschewski, T., . . . Büchel, C. (2012). Risk taking and the adolescent reward system: A potential common link to substance abuse. *American Journal of Psychiatry, 169*, 39–46.
Schneier, F. R. (2006). Social anxiety disorder. *New England Journal of Medicine, 355*, 1029–1037.
Schneier, F. R., Neria, Y., Pavlicova, M., Hembree, E., Suh, E. J., . . . Marshall, R. D. (2012). Combined prolonged exposure therapy and paraxetine for PTSD related to the World Trade Center attack: A randomized controlled trial. *American Journal of Psychiatry, 169*, 80–88.
Schnittker, J. (2010). Gene-environment correlations in the stress-depression relationship. *Journal of Health and Social Behavior, 51*, 229–243.
Schofield, P., Ashworth, M., & Jones, R. (2011). Ethnic isolation and psychosis: Re-examining the ethnic density effect. *Psychological Medicine, 41*, 1263–1269.
Schonfeldt-Lecuona, C., Connemann, B. J., Spitzer, M., & Herwig, U. (2003). Transcranial magnetic stimulation in the reversal of motor conversion disorder. *Psychotherapy and Psychosomatics, 72*, 286–290.
Schrank, B., & Slade, M. (2007). Recovery in psychiatry. *The Psychiatrist, 31*, 321–325.
Schreiber, F. R. (1973). *Sybil*. Chicago, IL: Regnery.
Schreiber, J. L., Breier, A., & Pickar, D. (1995). Expressed emotion: Trait or state? *British Journal of Psychiatry, 166*, 647–649.
Schreier, A., Wolke, D., Thomas, K., Horwood, J., Hollis, C., Gunnell, D., . . . Harrison, G. (2009). Prospective study of peer victimization in childhood and psychotic symptoms in a nonclinical population at age 12 years. *Archives of General Psychiatry, 66*, 527–536.
Schrut, A. (2005). A psychodynamic (nonOedipal) and brain function hypothesis regarding a type of male sexual masochism. *Journal of the American Academy of Psychoanalysis and Dynamic Psychiatry, 33*, 333–349.
Schulte, I. E., & Petermann, F. (2011). Familial risk factors for the development of somatoform symptoms and disorders in children and adolescents: A systematic review. *Child Psychiatry and Human Development, 42*, 569–583.
Schulte, I. E., Petermann, F., & Noeker, M. (2010). Functional abdominal pain in childhood: From etiology to maladaptation. *Psychotherapy and Psychosomatics, 79*, 73–86.
Schulz, A. J., Gravlee, C. C., Williams, D. R., Israel, B. A., Mentz, G., & Rowe, Z. (2006). Discrimination, symptoms of depression, and self-rated health among African American women in Detroit: Results from a longitudinal analysis. *American Journal of Public Health, 96*, 1265–1270.
Schumann, C. M., Bloss, C. S., Barnes, C. C., Wideman, G. M., Carper, R. A., . . . Courchesne, E. (2010). Longitudinal magnetic resonance imaging study of cortical development through early childhood in autism. *Journal of Neuroscience, 30*, 4419–4427.
Schuster, R., Bornovalova, M., & Hunt, E. (2012). The influence of depression on the progression of HIV: Direct and indirect effects. *Behavior Modification, 36*, 87–119.
Schwartz, A. (2010, September 13). Suicide reveals signs of a disease seen in N.F.L. *New York Times*. Retrieved from http://www.nytimes.com
Schwartz, A. J. (2006). Four eras of study of college student suicide in the United States: 1920–2004. *Journal of American College Health, 54*, 353–366.
Schwartz, A. J., & Whittaker, I. C. (1990). Suicide among college students: Assessment, treatment, and intervention. In S. J. Blumenthal and D. J. Kupfer (Eds.), *Suicide over the life cycle: Risk factors, assessment, and treatment of suicidal patients* (pp. 302–323). Washington, DC: American Psychiatric Publishing.
Schwartz, M. S., & Andrasik, F. (2003). *Biofeedback: A practitioner's guide*. New York, NY: Guilford Press.
Schwartzman, J. B., & Glaus, K. D. (2000). Depression and coronary heart disease in women: Implications for clinical practice and research. *Professional Psychology: Research and Practice, 31*, 48–57.
Schweckendiek, J., Klucken, T., Merz, C. J., Tabbert, K., Walter, B., . . . Stark, R. (2011). Weaving the (neuronal) web: Fear learning in spider phobia. *NeuroImage, 54*, 681–688.
Schweinsburg, A. D., Brown, S. A., & Tapert, S. F. (2008). The influence of marijuana use on neurocognitive functioning in adolescents. *Current Drug Abuse Reviews, 1*(1), 99–111.
Schweitzer, P. J., Zafar, U., Pavlicova, M., & Fallon, B. A. (2011). Long-term follow-up of hypochondriasis after selective serotonin reuptake inhibitor treatment. *Journal of Clinical Psychopharmacology, 31*, 365–368.
Scott, C., & Resnick, P. J. (2009). Assessing potential for harm: Would your patient injure himself or others? *Current Psychiatry, 24*, 26–33.
Scroppo, J. C., Drob, S. L., Weinberger, J. L., & Eagle, P. (1998). Identifying dissociative identity disorder: A self-report and projective study. *Journal of Abnormal Psychology, 107*, 272–284.
Seal, K. H., Bertenthal, D., Miner, C. R., Sen, S., & Marmar, C. (2007). Bringing the war back home. *Archives of Internal Medicine, 167*, 476–482.
Seemüller, F., Riedel, M., Obermeier, M., Bauer, M., Adli, M., . . . Möller, H. J. (2009). The controversial link between antidepressants and suicidality risks in adults: Data from a naturalistic study on a large sample of in-patients with a major depressive episode. *International Journal of Neuropsychopharmacology, 12*, 181–189.
Seery, M. D. (2011). Resilience: A silver lining to experiencing adverse life events? *Current Directions in Psychological Sicence, 20*, 390–394.
Seery, M. D., Holman, E. A., & Silver, R. C. (2010). Whatever does not kill us: Cumulative lifetime adversity, vulnerability, and resilience. *Journal of Personality and Social Psychology, 99*, 1025–1041.
Segerstrom, S. C., & Miller, G. E. (2004). Psychological stress and the human immune system: A meta-analytic study of 30 years of inquiry. *Psychological Bulletin, 30*, 601–630.
Segerstrom, S. C., & Sephton, S. E. (2010). Optimistic expectancies and cell-mediated immunity: The role of positive affect. *Psychological Science, 21*, 448–455.
Segraves, R. T. (2010). Considerations for diagnostic criteria for erectile dysfunction in DSMV. *Journal of Sexual Medicine, 7*, 654–660.
Segrin, C., Powell, H. L., Givertz, M., & Brackin, A. (2003). Symptoms of depression, relational quality, and loneliness in dating relationships. *Personal Relationships, 10*, 25–36.
Sehlmeyer, C., Dannlowski, U., Schoning, S., Kugel, H., Pyka, M., . . . Konrad, C. (2011). Neural correlates of trait anxiety in fear extinction. *Psychological Medicine, 41*, 789–798. doi:10.1017/S0033291710001248
Seidel, L., & Walkup, J. T. (2006). Selective serotonin reuptake inhibitor use in the treatment of non-obsessive compulsive anxiety disorders. *Journal of Child and Adolescent Psychopharmacology, 16*, 171–179.
Seitz, V. (2007). The impact of media spokeswomen on teen girls' body image: An empirical assessment. *Business Review, 7*, 228–236.
Selby, E. A., & Joiner, T. E., Jr. (2009). Cascades of emotion: The emergence of borderline personality disorder from emotional and behavioral dysregulation. *Review of General Psychology, 13*, 219–229.
Seligman, M. E. (1995). *The optimistic child: A proven program to safeguard children from depression and build lifelong resilience*. New York, NY: Houghton Mifflin.
Seligman, M. E., Ernst, R. M., Gillham, J., Reivich, K., & Linkins, M. (2009). Positive education: Positive psychology and classroom interventions. *Oxford Review of Education, 35*, 293–311.
Seligman, M. E. P. (1975). *Helplessness*. San Francisco, CA: Freeman.
Seligman, M. E. P. (2007). Coaching and positive psychology. *Australian Psychologist, 42*, 266–287.
Seligman, M. E. P., & Csikszentmihalyi, M. (2000). Positive psychology: An introduction. *American Psychologist, 55*, 5–14.
Sell v. United States, 539 U.S. 166. (2003).
Selten, J. P., Cantor-Graae, E., & Kahn, R. S. (2007). Migration and schizophrenia. *Current Opinion in Psychiatry, 20*, 111–115.
Serpe, G. (2009). Tyra's alleged stalker goes on trial. Retrieved from http://www.eonline.com/news/119280/tyra-s-alleged-stalker-goes-on-trial
Severeijns, R., Vlaeyen, J. W. S., van den Hout, M. A., & Picavet, H. S. J. (2004). Pain catastrophizing is associated with health indices in musculoskeletal pain. *Health Psychology, 23*, 49–57.
Sgobba, C. (2011). Frown towns. *Men's Health*. Retrieved from http://www.menshealth.com
Shah, R. S., Chang, S. Y., Min, H. K., Cho, Z. H., Blaha, C. D., & Lee, K. H. (2010). Deep brain stimulation: Technology at the cutting edge. *Journal of Clinical Neurology, 6*, 167–182.
Sharma, A., Chaturvedi, R., Sharma, A., & Sorrell, J. H. (2009). Electroconvulsive therapy in patients with vagus nerve stimulation. *Journal of ExtraCorporeal Technology, 25*, 141–143.
Sharma, V., Khan, M., Corpse, C., & Sharma, P. (2008). Missed bipolarity and psychiatric comorbidity in women with postpartum depression. *Bipolar Disorders, 10*, 742–747.
Sharp, S. I., Aarsland, D., Day, S., Sonnesyn, H., & Ballard, C. (2011). Hypertension is a potential risk factor for vascular dementia: Systematic review. *International Journal of Geriatric Psychiatry, 26*, 661–669.
Shaw, P., Eckstrand, K., Sharp, W., Blumenthal, J., Lerch, J. P., . . . Rapoport, J. L. (2007). Attention-deficit/hyperactivity disorder is characterized by a delay in cortical maturation. *Proceedings of the National Academy of Sciences, 104*, 19649–19654.
Shea, S. C. (2002). *The practical art of suicide assessment*. Hoboken, NJ: Wiley.
Sheehan, W., Sewall, B., & Thurber, S. (2005). Dissociative identity disorder and temporal lobe involvement: Replication and a cautionary note. *Psychiatry On-Line*. Retrieved from www.priory.com/psych.htm
Sheline, Y. I., Morris, J. C., Snyder, A. Z., Price, J. L., Yan, Z., . . . Mintun, M. A. (2010). APOE4 allele disrupts resting state fMRI connectivity in the

absence of amyloid plaques or decreased CSF Aβ42. *Journal of Neuroscience, 30*, 17035–17040.
Shelley-Ummenhofer, J., & MacMillan, P. D. (2007). Cognitive-behavioural treatment for women who binge eat. *Canadian Journal of Dietetic Practice and Research, 68*, 139–142.
Shelton, R. C., Osuntokun, O., Heinloth, A. N., & Corya, S. A. (2010). Therapeutic options for treatment-resistant depression. *CNS Drugs, 24*, 131–161.
Sher, K. J., Dick, D. M., Crabbe, J. C., Hutchison, K. E., O'Malley, S. S., & Heath, A. C. (2010). Consilient research approaches in studying gene × environment interactions in alcohol research. *Addiction Biology, 15*, 200–216.
Sherry, A., & Whilde, M. R. (2008). Borderline personality disorder. In M. Hersen & J. Rosqvist (Eds.), *Handbook of psychological assessment, case conceptualization, and treatment: Vol. 1. Adults* (pp. 403–437). Hoboken, NJ: Wiley.
Sherwood, N. E., Harnack, L., & Story, M. (2000). Weight-loss practices, nutrition beliefs, and weight-loss program preferences of urban American Indian women. *Journal of the American Dietetic Association, 100*, 442–446.
Shi, J., Wittke-Thompson, J. K., Badner, J. A., Hattori, E., Potash, J. B., . . . Liu C. (2008). Clock genes may influence bipolar disorder susceptibility and dysfunctional circadian rhythm. *American Journal of Medical Genetics: Part B: Neuropsychiatric Genetics, 147B*, 1047–1055.
Shibasaki, M., & Kawai, N. (2009). Rapid detection of snakes by Japanese monkeys (*Macaca fuscata*): An evolutionarily predisposed visual system. *Journal of Comparative Psychology, 123*, 131–135.
Shiffman, S., Scharf, D. M., Shadel, W. G., Gwaltney, C. J., Dang, Q., Paton, S. M., & Clark, D. B. (2006). Analyzing milestones in smoking cessation: Illustration in a nicotine patch trial in adult smokers. *Journal of Clinical and Consulting Psychology, 74*, 276–285.
Shiffman, S., & Waters, A. J. (2004). Negative affect and smoking lapses: A prospective analysis. *Journal of Consulting and Clinical Psychology, 72*, 192–201.
Shih, R. A., Miles, J., Tucker, J. S., Zhou, A. J., & D'Amico, E. J. (2010). Racial/ethnic differences in adolescent substance use: Mediation by individual, family, and school factors. *Journal of the Study of Alcohol and Other Drugs, 71*, 640–651.
Shin, M., Besser, L. M., Kucik, J. E., Lu, C., Siffel, C., Correa, A., & CSABA. (2009). Prevalence of Down syndrome among children and adolescents in 10 regions of the United States. *Pediatrics, 124*, 1565–1571.
Shirani, A., & St. Louis, E. K. (2009). Illuminating rationale and uses for light therapy. *Journal of Clinical Sleep Medicine, 15*, 155–163.
Shirzadi, A. A., & Ghaemi, S. N. (2006). Side effects of atypical antipsychotics: Extrapyramidal symptoms and the metabolic syndrome. *Harvard Review of Psychiatry, 14*, 152–164.
Shneidman, E. S. (1992). What do suicides have in common? Summary of the psychological approach. In B. Bongar (Ed.), *Suicide: Guidelines for assessment, management, and treatment* (pp. 3–15). New York, NY: Oxford University Press.
Shneidman, E. S. (1993). *Suicide as psychache: A clinical approach to self-destructive behavior*. Northvale, NJ: Aronson.
Shorter, E. (2010). Disease versus dimension in diagnosis: Response to Dr. van Praag. *Canadian Journal of Psychiatry, 55*, 63.
Shrivastava, A., Shah, N., Johnston, M., Stitt, L., & Thakar, M. (2010). Predictors of long-term outcome of first-episode schizophrenia: A ten-year follow-up study. *Indian Journal of Psychiatry, 52*, 320–326.
Shweder, R. A., Goodnow, J., Hatano, G., LeVine, R. A., Markus, H., & Miller, P. (2006). The cultural psychology of development: One mind, many mentalities. In W. Damon (Ed.), *Handbook of child development* (pp. 716–792). Chicago, IL: University of Chicago Press.
Sibitz, I., Unger, A., Woppmann, A., Zidek, T., & Amering, M. (2011). Stigma resistance in patients with schizophrenia. *Schizophrenia Bulletin, 37*, 316–323.
Sidhu, K. A. S., & Dickey, T. O. (2010). Hallucinations in children: Diagnostic and treatment strategies. *Current Psychiatry, 9*, 53–61.
Siebert, D. C., & Wilke, D. J. (2007). High-risk drinking among young adults: The influence of race and college enrollment. *American Journal of Drug & Alcohol Abuse, 33*, 843–850.
Siegel, D. M. (2009). Munchausen syndrome by proxy: A pediatrician's observations. *Families, Systems & Health, 27*, 113–115.
Siegel, M. (1979). Privacy, ethics, and confidentiality. *Professional Psychology, 10*, 249–258.
Sierra, M. (2009). *Depersonalization: A new look at a neglected syndrome*. New York, NY: Cambridge University Press.
Sieswerda, S., & Arntz, A. (2007). Successful psychotherapy reduces hypervigilance in borderline personality disorder. *Behavioral and Cognitive Psychotherapy, 35*, 387–402.
Silagy, C., Lancaster, T., Stead, L., Mant, D., & Fowler, G. (2003). Nicotine replacement therapy for smoking cessation, Cochrane Review, 3, CD000146.
Silberg, J. L., Maes, H., & Eaves, L. J. (2010). Genetic and environmental influences on the transmission of parental depression to children's depression and conduct disturbance: An extended children of twins study. *Journal of Child Psychology and Psychiatry, 51*, 734–744.
Silberstein, S. D. (1998). *Migraine and other headaches: A patient's guide to treatment*. Chicago, IL: American Medical Association.
Silverman, W. K., Ortiz, C. D., Viswesvaran, C., Burns, B. J., Kolko, D. J., Putnam, F. W., & Amaya-Jackson, L. (2008). Evidence-based psychosocial treatments for children and adolescents exposed to traumatic events: A review and meta-analysis. *Journal of Clinical Child & Adolescent Psychology, 37*, 156–183.
Silverman, W. K., Pina, A. A., & Viswesvaran, C. (2008). Evidence-based psychosocial treatments for phobic and anxiety disorders in children and adolescents: A review and meta-analyses. *Journal of Clinical Child & Adolescent Psychology, 37*, 105–130.
Sim, K., DeWitt, I., Ditman, T., Zalesak, M., Greenhouse, I., . . . Heckers, S. (2006). Hippocampal and parahippocampal volumes in schizophrenia: A structural MRI study. *Schizophrenia Bulletin, 32*, 332–340.
Sim, L. A., Sadowski, C. M., Whiteside, S. P., & Wells, L. A. (2004). Family-based therapy for adolescents with anorexia nervosa. *Mayo Clinic Proceedings, 79*, 1305–1308.
Simeon, D., Gross, S., Guralnik, O., Stein, D. J., Schmeidler, J., & Hollander, E. (1997). Feeling unreal: Thirty cases of DSM-III-R depersonalization disorder. *American Journal of Psychiatry, 154*, 1107–1113.
Simeon, D., Guralnik, O., Hazlett, E. A., Spiegel-Cohen, J., Hollander, E., & Buchsbaum, M. S. (2000). Feeling unreal: A PET study of depersonalization disorder. *American Journal of Psychiatry, 157*, 1782–1788.
Simmons, A. M. (2002, January 13). Eating disorders on rise for South African blacks. *Los Angeles Times*, p. A3.
Simon, R. I., & Gold, L. H. (Eds.). (2004). *The American Psychiatric Association Publishing textbook of forensic psychiatry*. Washington, DC: American Psychiatric Publishing.
Sin, N. L., & Lyubomirsky, S. (2009). Enhancing well-being and alleviating depressive symptoms with positive psychology interventions: A practice friendly meta-analysis. *Journal of Clinical Psychology, 65*, 467–487.
Singer, H. S. (2005). "Tourette's syndrome: from behaviour to biology". *Lancet Neurology, 4*(3), 149–159.
Singh, B. S. (1998). Managing somatoform disorders. *Medical Journal of Australia, 168*, 572–577.
Singh, S. P., & Lee, A. S. (1997). Conversion disorders in Nottingham: Alive but not kicking. *Journal of Psychosomatic Research, 43*, 425–430.
Sjöholm, L. K., Backlund, L., Cheteh, E. H., Ek, I. R., Frisén, L., . . . Nikamo, P. (2010). CRY2 is associated with rapid cycling in bipolar disorder patients. *PLoS One, 5*(9), e12632.
Skinner, B. F. (1990). Can psychology be a science of mind? *American Psychologist, 45*, 1206–1210.
Skodol, A. E., & Bender, D. S. (2009). The future of personality disorders in DSM-V? *American Journal of Psychiatry, 166*, 388–390.
Slavich, G. M., Way, B. M., Eisenberger, N. I., & Taylor, S. E. (2010). Neural sensitivity to social rejection is associated with inflammatory responses to social stress. *Proceedings of the National Academy of Sciences of the USA, 107*, 14817–14822.
Sleegers, K., Lambert, J. C., Bertram, L., Cruts, M., Amouyel, P., & Van Broeckhoven, C. (2010). The pursuit of susceptibility genes for Alzheimer's disease: Progress and prospects. *Trends in Genetics, 26*, 84–93.
Sloane, C., Burke, S. C., Cremeens, J., Vail-Smith, K., & Woolsey, C. (2010). Drunkorexia: Calorie restriction prior to alcohol consumption among college freshman. *Journal of Alcohol & Drug Education, 54*(2), 17–34.
Slotema, C. W., Blom, J. D., Hoek, H. W., & Sommer, I. E. (2010). Should we expand the toolbox of psychiatric treatment methods to include repetitive transcranial magnetic stimulation (rTMS)? A meta-analysis of the efficacy of rTMS in psychiatric disorders. *Journal of Clinical Psychiatry, 71*, 873–884.
Smith, A. D., Smith, S. M., de Jager, C. A., Whitbread, P., Johnston, C., Agacinski, G., . . . Refsum, H. (2010). Homocysteine-lowering by B vitamins slows the rate of accelerated brain atrophy in mild cognitive impairment: A randomized controlled trial. *PLoS One, 5*(9), e12244. doi:10.1371/journal.pone.0012244
Smith, A. R., Hawkeswood, S. E., Bodell, L. P. and Joiner, T. E. (2011). Muscularity versus leanness: An examination of body ideals and predictors of disordered eating in heterosexual and gay college students. *Body Image, 8*, 232–236.
Smith, B., Fowler, D. G., Freeman, D., Bebbington, P., Bashforth, H., . . . Kuipers, E. (2006). Emotion and psychosis: Links between depression, self-esteem, negative schematic beliefs and delusions and hallucinations. *Schizophrenia Research, 86*, 181–188.
Smith, C. (2002, August 7). Persecuted parents or protected children? *Seattle Post Intelligencer*, pp. A1, A10.
Smith, C. S. (2003, September 27). Son's wish to die, and mother's help, stir French debate. *New York Times*, pp. A1, A4.
Smith, G. C., Clarke, D. M., Handrinos, D., Dunsis, A., & McKenzie, D. P. (2000). Consultation-liaison psychiatrists' management of somatoform disorders. *Psychosomatics, 41*, 481–489.
Smith, L. (2010). *Psychology, poverty, and the end of social exclusion*. New York, NY: Teachers College Press.
Smith, L., & Reddington, R. M. (2010). Class dismissed: Making the case for the study of classist microaggressions. In D. W. Sue (Ed.), *Microaggressions and marginality: Manifestation, dynamics and impact* (pp. 269–285). Hoboken, NJ: Wiley.
Smith, P. N., Cukrowicz, K. C., Poindexter, E. K., Hobson, V., & Cohen, L. M. (2010). The acquired capability for suicide: A comparison of suicide attempters, suicide ideators, and non-suicidal controls. *Depression and Anxiety, 27*, 871–877.
Smith, S. L., & Choueiti, M. (2010). Gender disparity on screen and behind the camera in family films. Retrieved from http://www.theeenadavisinstitute.org/downloads/FullStudy_GenderDisparityFamilyFilms.pdf
Smoller, J., Shiedly, B., & Tsuang, M. T. (Eds.). (2008). *Psychiatric genetics: Applications in clinical practice*. Washington, DC: American Psychiatric Publishing.

Smyke, A. T., Koga, S. F., Johnson, D. E., Fox, N. A., Marshall, P. J., Nelson, C. A., . . . BEIP Core Group (2007). The caregiving context in institution-reared and family-reared infants and toddlers in Romania. *Journal of Child Psychology and Psychiatry, 48,* 210–218.

Snorrason, I., Smari, J., & Olafsson, R. P. (2011). Motor inhibition, reflection impulsivity, and trait impulsivity in pathological skin picking. *Behavior Therapy, 42,* 521–532.

So, J. K. (2008). Somatization as a cultural idiom of distress: Rethinking mind and body in a multicultural society. *Counselling Psychology Quarterly, 21,* 167–174.

Soares, S. C., Esteves, F., Lundqvist, D., & Ohman, A. (2009). Some animal specific fears are more specific than others: Evidence from attention and emotion measures. *Behaviour Research and Therapy, 47,* 1032–1042.

Sola, C. L., Chopra, A., & Rastogi, A. (2010). Sedative, hypnotic, anxiolytic use disorders. Retrieved from http://emedicine.medscape.com/article/290585-overview

Solano, J., Jr., & De Chavez, G. M. (2000). Premorbid personality disorders in schizophrenia. *Schizophrenia Research, 44,* 137–144.

Sollman, M. J., Ranseen, J. D., & Berry, D. T. R. (2010). Detection of feigned ADHD in college students. *Psychological Assessment, 22,* 325–335.

Solomon, D. A., Leon, A. C., Endicott, J., Coryell, W. H., Li, C., . . . Keller, M. B. (2009). Empirical typology of bipolar I mood episodes. *British Journal of Psychiatry, 195,* 525–530.

Song, A. V., Ling, P. M., Neilands, T. B., & Glantz, S. A. (2007). Smoking in movies and increased smoking among young adults. *American Journal of Preventive Medicine, 33,* 396–403.

Sørensen, H. J., Mortensen, E. L., Schiffman, J., Reinisch, J. M., Maeda, J., & Mednick, S. A. (2010). Early developmental milestones and risk of schizophrenia: A 45-year follow-up of the Copenhagen Perinatal Cohort. *Schizophrenia Research, 118,* 41–47.

Sorensen, P., Birket-Smith, M., Wattar, U., Buemann, I., & Salkovskis, P. (2011). A randomized clinical trial of cognitive behavioural therapy versus no intervention for patients with hypochondriasis. *Psychological Medicine, 41,* 431–441.

Soria, V., Martínez-Amorós, E., Escaramís, G., Valero, J., Pérez-Egea, R., . . . Urretavizcaya, M. (2010). Differential association of circadian genes with mood disorders: CRY1 and NPAS2 are associated with unipolar major depression and CLOCK and VIP with bipolar disorder. *Neuropsychopharmacology, 35,* 1279–1289.

Sorkin, A., Weinshall, D., & Peled, A. (2008). The distortion of reality perception in schizophrenia patients, as measured in virtual reality. *Studies in Health Technology and Informatics, 132,* 475–480.

Sowell, E. S., Leow, A. D., Bookheimer, S. Y., Smith, L. M., O'Connor, M. J., Kan, E., . . . Thompson, P. M. (2010). Differentiating prenatal exposure to methamphetamine and alcohol versus alcohol and not methamphetamine using tensor-based brain morphometry and discriminant analysis. *Journal of Neuroscience, 30,* 3876–3885.

Spanos, N. P. (1978). Witchcraft in histories of psychiatry: A critical analysis and an alternative conceptualization. *Psychological Bulletin, 85,* 417–439.

Spanos, N. P. (1994). Multiple identity enactments and multiple personality disorder: A sociocognitive perspective. *Psychological Bulletin, 116,* 143–165.

Sparrevohn, R. M., & Rapee, R. M. (2009). Self-disclosure, emotional expression and intimacy within relationships of people with social phobia. *Behaviour Research and Therapy, 47,* 1074–1078.

Spector, I. P., & Carey, M. P. (1990). Incidence and prevalence of sexual dysfunctions: A critical review of the empirical literature. *Archives of Sexual Behavior, 19,* 389–408.

Spence, S. H., Donovan, C. L., March, S., Gamble, A., Anderson, R., . . . Kenardy, J. (2008). Online CBT in the treatment of child and adolescent anxiety disorders: Issues in the development of BRAVE–ONLINE and two case illustrations. *Behavioural and Cognitive Psychotherapy, 36,* 411–430.

Spencer, T. J., Biederman, J., & Mick, E. (2007). Attention-deficit/hyperactivity disorder: Diagnosis, lifespan, comorbidities, and neurobiology. *Journal of Pediatric Psychology, 32,* 631–642.

Speranza, M., Loas, G., Wallier, J., & Corcos, M. (2007). Predictive value of alexithymia in patients with eating disorders: A 3-year prospective study. *Journal of Psychosomatic Research, 63,* 365–371.

Spiegel, D. (2006). Recognizing traumatic dissociation. *American Journal of Psychiatry, 163,* 566–568.

Spiegel, D., Loewenstein, R. J., Lewis-Fernández, R., Sar, V., Simeon, D., Vermetten, E., . . . Dell, P. F. (2011). Dissociative disorders in DSM-5. *Depression and Anxiety, 28,* 824–852.

Spitzer, R. L., Gibbon, M., Skodol, A. E., Williams, J. B., & First, M. B. (Eds.). (1994). *DSM-IV: Casebook.* pp. 121–122. Washington, DC: American Psychiatric Publishing.

Spodak, C. (2010, March 18). College on edge after recent wave of student suicides. Retrieved from http://articles.cnn.com/2010-03-18/us/cornell.suicides

Spradlin, L. K., & Parsons, R. D. (2008). *Diversity matters.* Belmont, CA: Thomson Wadsworth.

Springen, K. (2006, December 7). Study looks at pro-anorexia web sites. Retrieved from www.msnbc.msn.com/id/16098915/site/newsweek/print

Staal, W. G., Pol, H. E. H., Schnack, H. G., van Haren, N. E. M., Seifert, M., & Kahn, R. S. (2001). Structural abnormalities in chronic schizophrenia at the extremes of the outcome spectrum. *American Journal of Psychiatry, 158,* 1140–1142.

Stack, S. (1987). Celebrities and suicide: A taxonomy and analysis, 1948–1983. *American Sociological Review, 52,* 401–412.

Stafford, K. P., & Wygant, D. B. (2005). The role of competency to stand trial in mental health courts. *Behavioral Sciences and the Law, 23,* 245–258.

Stahl, S. M. (2007). The genetics of schizophrenia converge upon the NMDA glutamate receptor. *CNS Spectrums, 12,* 583–588.

Stahl, S. M., & Wise, D. D. (2008). The potential role of a corticotrophin-releasing factor receptor–1 antagonist in psychiatric disorders. *CNS Spectrums, 13,* 467–478.

Stalberg, G., Ekerwald, H., & Hultman, C. M. (2004). At issue: Siblings of patients with schizophrenia: Sibling bond, coping patterns, and fear of possible schizophrenia heredity. *Schizophrenia Bulletin, 30,* 445–451.

Stambor, Z. (2006). Stressed out nation. *Monitor on Psychology, 37,* 28–29.

Stamova, B., Green, P. G., Tian, Y., Hertz-Picciotto, I., Pessah, I. N., . . . Sharp, F. R. (2011). Correlations between gene expression and mercury levels in blood of boys with and without autism. *Neurotoxicity Research, 19,* 31–48.

Staniloiu, A., & Markowitsch, H. J. (2010). Searching for the anatomy of dissociative amnesia. *Journal of Psychology, 218,* 96–108.

Stanley, M. A., Beck, J. G., Novy, D. M., Averill, P. M., Swann, A. C., Diefenbach, G. J., & Hopko, D. R. (2003). Cognitive-behavioral treatment of late-life generalized anxiety disorder. *Journal of Consulting and Clinical Psychology, 71,* 309–319.

Starcevic, V. (2005). Fear of death in hypochondriasis: Bodily threat and its treatment implications. *Journal of Contemporary Psychotherapy, 35,* 227–237.

Stark, J. (2004, July 25). Twin sisters, a singular affliction. *Bellingham Herald,* p. A1.

Startup, H., Freeman, D., & Garety, P. A. (2006). Persecutory delusions and catastrophic worry in psychosis: Developing the understanding of delusion distress and persistence. *Behaviour Research and Therapy, 45,* 523–537.

Stathopoulou, G., Powers, M. B., Berry, A. C., Smits, J. A. J., & Otto, M. W. (2006). Exercise interventions for mental health: A quantitative and qualitative review. *Clinical Psychology: Science and Practice, 13,* 179–193.

Steadman, H. J., Monahan, J., Robbins, P. C., Appelbaum, P., Grisso, T., Klassen, D., Mulvey, E. P., & Roth, L. H. (1993). From dangerousness to risk assessment: Implications for appropriate research strategies. In S. Hodgins (Ed.), *Mental disorder and crime* (pp. 39–62). New York, NY: Sage.

Steck, E. L., Abrams, L. M., & Phelps, L. (2004). Positive psychology in the prevention of eating disorders. *Psychology in the Schools, 41,* 111–117.

Steele, C. M., & Josephs, R. A. (1990). Alcohol myopia: Its prized and dangerous effects. *American Psychologist, 45,* 921–933.

Steele, M. S., & McGarvey, S. T. (1997). Anger expression, age, and blood pressure in modernizing Samoan adults. *Psychosomatic Medicine, 59,* 632–637.

Stefanidis, E. (2006). Being rational. *Schizophrenia Bulletin, 32,* 422–423.

Steiger, H., & Bruce, K. R. (2007). Phenotypes, endophenotypes, and genotypes in bulimia spectrum eating disorders. *Canadian Journal of Psychiatry, 52,* 220–227.

Stein, A., Craske, M. G., Lehtonen, A., Harvey, A., Savage-McGlynn, E., Davies, B., . . . Counsell, N. (2012). Maternal cognitions and mother–infant interaction in postnatal depression and generalized anxiety disorder. *Journal of Abnormal Psychology.* Advance online publication. doi:10.1037/a0026847

Stein, D. J. (2001). Comorbidity in generalized anxiety disorder: Impact and implications. *Journal of Clinical Psychiatry, 62,* 29–34.

Stein, D. J., Scott, K., Haro Abad, J. M., Aguilar-Gaxiola S., Alonso, J., Angermeyer, M., . . . Von Korff, M. (2010). Early childhood adversity and later hypertension: Data from the World Mental Health Survey. *Annals of Clinical Psychiatry, 22*(1), 19–28.

Stein, M. B., Simmons, A. N., Feinstein, J. S., & Paulus, M. P. (2007). Increased amygdala and insula activation during emotional processing in anxiety-prone subjects. *American Journal of Psychiatry, 164,* 318–327.

Steinberg, J. S., Arshad, A., Kowalski, M., Kukar, A., Suma, V., . . . Rozanski, A. (2004). Increased incidence of life-threatening ventricular arrhythmias in implantable defibrillator patients after the World Trade Center attack. *Journal of the American College of Cardiology, 44,* 1261–1264.

Steinbrecher, N., & Hiller, W. (2011). Course and prediction of somatoform disorder and medically unexplained symptoms in primary care. *General Hospital Psychiatry, 33,* 318–326.

Steiner, T. J., MacGregor, E. A., & Davies, P. T. G. (2007). *Guidelines for all healthcare professionals in the diagnosis and management of migraine, tension-type, cluster and medication-overuse headache* (3rd ed.). Hull, UK: British Association for the Study of Headache.

Steinhausen, H. C. (2009). Outcome of eating disorders. *Child and Adolescent Psychiatric Clinics of North America, 18,* 225–242.

Steinhausen, H. C., & Weber, S. (2009). The outcome of bulimia nervosa: Findings from one-quarter century of research. *American Journal of Psychiatry, 166,* 1331–1341.

Steketee, G., Frost, R. O., Tolin, D. F., Rasmussen, J., & Brown, T. A. (2010). Waitlist-controlled trial of cognitive behavior therapy for hoarding disorder. *Depression and Anxiety, 27,* 476–484.

Stergiakouli, E., & Thapar, A. (2010). Fitting the pieces together: Current research on the genetic basis of attention-deficit/hyperactivity disorder (ADHD). *Journal of Neuropsychiatric Disease and Treatment, 6,* 551–560.

Sternberg, R. J. (2005). The theory of successful intelligence. *Interamerican Journal of Psychology, 39,* 189–202.

Sterzer, P. (2010). Born to be criminal? What to make of early biological risk factors for criminal behavior. *American Journal of Psychiatry, 167,* 1–3.

Sterzer, P., & Stadler, C. (2009). Neuroimaging of aggressive and violent behaviour in children and adolescents. *Frontiers in Behavioral Neuroscience, 3,* 35.

Stice, E. (2001). A prospective test of the dual-pathway model of bulimic pathology: Mediating effects of dieting and negative affect. *Journal of Abnormal Psychology, 110*, 124–135.

Stice, E., Marti, C. N., Shaw, H., & Jaconis, M. (2009). An 8-year longitudinal study of the natural history of threshold, subthreshold, and partial eating disorders from a community sample of adolescents. *Journal of Abnormal Psychology, 118*, 587–597.

Stice, E., & Shaw, H. (2004). Eating disorder prevention programs: A meta-analytic review. *Psychological Bulletin, 130*, 206–227.

Stice, E., Shaw, H., Bohon, C., Marti, C. N., & Rohde, P. (2009). A meta-analytic review of depression prevention programs for children and adolescents: Factors that predict magnitude of intervention effects. *Journal of Consulting and Clinical Psychology, 77*, 486–503.

Stip, E. (2009). Psychosis: A category or dimension. *Canadian Journal of Psychiatry, 54*, 137–139.

Stitzer, M., & Petry N. (2006). Contingency management for treatment of substance abuse. *Annual Review of Clinical Psychology, 2*, 411–434.

Stitzer, M., Petry, N., & Peirce, J. (2010). Motivational incentives research in the National Drug Abuse Treatment Clinical Trials Network. *Journal of Substance Abuse Treatment, 38*(Suppl 1), S61–S69.

Stober, G. (2006). Genetic correlates of the nosology of catatonia. *Psychiatric Annals, 37*, 37–44.

Stoessl, A. J. (2011). Movement disorders: New insights into Parkinson's disease. *The Lancet Neurology, 10*, 5–7.

Stone, L. B., Hankin, B. L., Gibb, B. E., & Abela, J. R. (2011). Co-rumination predicts the onset of depressive disorders during adolescence. *Journal of Abnormal Psychology, 120*, 752–757.

Stone, L. B., Uhrlass, D. J., & Gibb, B. E. (2010). Co-rumination and lifetime history of depressive disorders in children. *Journal of Clinical Child and Adolescent Psychology, 39*, 597–602.

Stone, M., Laughren, T., Jones, M. L., Levenson, M., Holland, P. C., . . . Rochester, G. (2009). Risk of suicidality in clinical trials of antidepressants in adults: Analysis of proprietary data submitted to US Food and Drug Administration. *British Medical Journal, 339*, b2880. doi:10.1136/bmj.b2880

Stone, M. H. (2001). Schizoid and schizotypal personality disorders. In G. O. Gabbard (Ed.), *Treatment of psychiatric disorders* (pp. 2237–2250). Washington, DC: American Psychiatric Publishing.

Stoolmiller, M., Wills, T. A., McClure, A. C., Tanski, S. E., Worth, K. A., Gerrard, M., & Sargen, J. D. (2012). Comparing media and family predictors of alcohol use: A cohort study of US adolescents. *British Medical Journal Open, 2*, e000543.

Story, M., Neumark-Sztainer, D., Sherwood, N., Stang, J., & Murray, D. (1998). Dieting status and its relationship to eating and physical activity behaviors in a representative sample of U.S. adolescents. *Journal of the American Dietetic Association, 98*, 1127–1135.

St-Pierre-Delorme, M.-E., Lalonda, M. P., Perreault, V., Koszegi, N., & O'Connor, K. (2011). Inference-based therapy for compulsive hoarding: A clinical case study. *Clinical Case Studies, 10*, 291–303.

Strakowski, S. M., Fleck, D. E, DelBello, M. P., Adler, C. M., Shear, P. K., Kotwal, R., & Arndt, S. (2010). Impulsivity across the course of bipolar disorder. *Bipolar Disorder, 12*, 285–297.

Strenziok, M., Krueger, F., Despande, G., Lenrook, R. K., van der Meer, E., & Grafman, J. (2010). Frontal-parietal regulation of media violence exposure in adolescents: A multi-method study. *Social Cognitive and Affective Neuroscience, 6*, 537–547. doi:10.1093/scan/nsq079

Striegel-Moore, R. H., & Bulik, C. M. (2007). Risk factors in eating disorders. *American Psychologist, 62*, 181–198.

Striegel-Moore, R. H., Dohm, F. A., Kraemer, H. C., Taylor, C. B., Daniels, S., Crawford, P. B., & Schreiber, G. B. (2003). Eating disorders in white and black women. *American Journal of Psychiatry, 160*, 1326–1331.

Stringaris, A., Baroni, A., Haimm, C., Brotman, M., Lowe, C. H., Myers, F., . . . Leibenluft, E. (2010). Pediatric bipolar disorder versus severe mood dysregulation: Risk for manic episodes on follow-up. *Journal of the American Academy of Child & Adolescent Psychiatry, 49*, 397–405.

Strober, M., Freeman, R., Diamond, C. L. J., & Kaye, W. (2000). Controlled family study of anorexia nervosa and bulimia nervosa: Evidence of shared liability and transmission of partial syndromes. *American Journal of Psychiatry, 157*, 393–401.

Strong, R. E., Marchant, B. K., Reimherr, F. W., Williams, E., Soni, P., & Mestas, R. (2009). Narrow-band blue-light treatment of seasonal affective disorder in adults and the influence of additional nonseasonal symptoms. *Depression and Anxiety, 26*, 273–278.

Stroud, C. B., Davila, J., Hammen, C., and Vrshek-Schallhorn, S. (2011). Severe and nonsevere events in first onsets versus recurrences of depression: Evidence for stress sensitization. *Journal of Abnormal Psychology, 120*, 142–154.

Strous, R. D., Alvir, J. M., Robinson, D., Gal, G., Sheitman, B., Chakos, M., & Lieberman, J. A. (2004). Premorbid functioning in schizophrenia, treatment response, and medication side effects. *Schizophrenia Bulletin, 30*, 265–272.

Stuart, S., & Noyes, R., Jr. (2005). Treating hypochondriasis with interpersonal psychotherapy. *Journal of Contemporary Psychotherapy, 35*, 269–283.

Stunkard, A. J., Allison, K. C., Geliebter, A., Lundgren, J. D., Gluck, M. E., & O'Reardon, J. P. (2009). Development of criteria for a diagnosis: Lessons from the night eating syndrome. *Comprehensive Psychiatry, 50*, 391–399.

Substance Abuse and Mental Health Services Administration. (2007). *Results from the 2006 National Survey on Drug Use and Health: National findings* (Office of Applied Studies, NSDUH Series H-32, DHHS Publication No. SMA 07-4293). Rockville, MD.

Substance Abuse and Mental Health Services Administration. (2008). *Caravan survey for SAMHSA on addictions and recovery: Summary report*. Rockville, MD: Author. Retrieved from http://www.samhsa.gov/attitudes/CARAVAN_LongReport.pdf

Substance Abuse and Mental Health Services Administration. (2010a, June 18). Trends in emergency department visits involving nonmedical use of narcotic pain relievers. *The DAWN Report*. Retrieved from http://www.oas.samhsa.gov/2k10/dawn016/opioided.htm

Substance Abuse and Mental Health Services Administration. (2010b). *Results from the 2009 National Survey on Drug Use and Health: Mental health findings* (Office of Applied Studies, NSDUH Series H–39, HHS Publication No. SMA 10–4609). Rockville, MD.

Substance Abuse and Mental Health Services Administration. (2010c). *Results from the 2009 National Survey on Drug Use and Health: Volume I. Summary of National findings* (DHHS Publication No. SMA 09–4434, NSDUH Series H–36). Rockville, MD: Author. Retrieved from http://www.oas.samhsa.gov/NSDUH/2k9NSDUH/2k9Results.htm

Substance Abuse and Mental Health Services Administration. (2010d). Substance abuse treatment admissions involving abuse of pain relievers: 1998–2008. *The TEDS Report*. Retrieved from http://oas.samhsa.gov/2k10/230/230PainRelvr2k10.cfm

Substance Abuse and Mental Health Services Administration. (2012). *Results from the 2010 National Survey on Drug Use and Health: Mental health findings* (NSDUH Series H-42, HHS Publication No. SMA 11-4667). Rockville, MD.

Sue, D. W. (2010). *Microaggressions in everyday life: Race, gender and sexual orientation*. Hoboken, NJ: Wiley.

Sue, D. W., & Sue, D. (2013). *Counseling the culturally diverse: Theory and practice* (6th ed.). Hoboken, NJ: Wiley.

Sugawara, J., Tarumi, T., & Tanaka, H. (2010). Effect of mirthful laughter on vascular function. *American Journal of Cardiology, 15*, 856–859.

Sui, X., LaMonte, M. J., Laditka, J. N., Hardin, J. W., Chase, N., Hooker, S. P., & Blair, S. N. (2007). Cardiorespiratory fitness and adiposity as mortality predictors in older adults. *Journal of the American Medical Association, 298*, 2507–2516.

Suicide Prevention Resource Center. (2012). Risk and protective factors for suicide. Retrieved from http://www.sprc.org/suicide_prev_basics/about_suicide.asp

Sullivan, E. V., Harris, R. A., & Pfefferbaum, A. (2010). Alcohol's effects on brain and behavior. Retrieved from http://pubs.niaaa.nih.gov/publications/arh40/127-143.htm

Sundel, M., & Sundel, S. S. (1998). Psychopharmacological treatment of panic disorder. *Research of Social Work Practice, 8*, 426–451.

Suominen, K., Mantere, O., Valtonen, H., Arvilommi, P., Leppämäki, S., & Isometsä, E. (2009). Gender differences in bipolar disorder type I and II. *Acta Psychiatrica Scandanavica, 120*, 464–473.

Surtees, P. B., Wainwright, N. W. J., Luben, R., Wareham, N. J., Bingham, S. A., & Khaw, K.-T. (2010). Mastery is associated with cardiovascular disease mortality in men and women at apparently low risk. *Health Psychology, 29*, 412–420.

Suzuki, K., Takei, N., Kawai, M., Minabe, Y., & Mori, N. (2003). Is Taijin Kyofusho a culture-bound syndrome? *American Journal of Psychiatry, 160*, 1358.

Svaldi, J., Caffier, D., Blechert, J., & Tuschen-Caffier, B. (2009). Body-related film clip triggers desire to binge in women with binge eating disorder. *Behaviour Research and Therapy, 47*, 790–795.

Svoboda, E. (2006, December 5). All the signs of pregnancy except one: A baby. *New York Times*. Retrieved from http://www.nytimes.com

Swaab, D. F. (2005). The role of hypothalamus and endocrine system in sexuality. In J. S. Hyde (Ed.), *Biological substrates of human sexuality* (pp. 21–74). Washington, DC: American Psychological Association.

Swann, A. C., Dougherty, D. M., Pazzaglia, P. J., Pham, M., Steinberg, J. L., & Moeller, F. G. (2005). Increased impulsivity associated with severity of suicide attempt history in patients with bipolar disorder. *American Journal of Psychiatry, 162*, 1680–1687.

Swann, A. C., Moeller, F. G., Steinberg, J. L., Schneider, L., Barratt, E. S., & Dougherty, D. M. (2007). Manic symptoms and impulsivity during bipolar depressive episodes. *Bipolar Disorders, 9*, 206–212.

Swann, A. C., Steinberg, J. L., Lijffijt, M., Moeller, G. F. (2009). Continuum of depressive and manic mixed states in patients with bipolar disorder: Quantitative measurement and clinical features. *World Psychiatry, 8*, 166–172.

Swanson, J. W. (1994). Mental disorder, substance abuse, and community violence: An epidemiological approach. In J. Monahan & H. J. Steadman (Eds.), *Violence and mental disorder: Developments in risk assessment* (pp. 101–136). Chicago, IL: University of Chicago Press.

Swanson, J., Holzer, C., Ganju, V., & Jono, R. (1990). Violence and psychiatric disorder in the community: Evidence from the Epidemiological Catchment Area Surveys. *Hospital Community Psychiatry, 41*, 761–770.

Swanson, S. A., Crow, S. J., LeGrange, D., Swendsen, J., & Merikangas, K. R. (2011). Prevalence and correlates of eating disorders in adolescents: Results from the National Comorbidity Survey Replication–Adolescent Supplement. *Archives of General Psychiatry, 68*, 714–723.

Syed, Z., Imam, S. Z., Zhou, Q., Yamamoto, A., Valente, A. J., . . . Senlin, L. (2011). Novel regulation of parkin function through c-Abl-mediated tyrosine phosphorylation: Implications for Parkinson's disease. *Journal of Neuroscience, 31*, 157–163.

Sykes, R. (2007). Somatoform disorders in DSM-IV: Mental or physical disorders. *Journal of Psychosomatic Research, 60*, 341–344.

Szasz, T. S. (1987). Justifying coercion through theology and therapy. In J. K. Zeig (Ed.), *The evolution of psychotherapy* (pp. 158–174). New York, NY: Brunner/Mazel.

Taber, K. H., Warden, D. L., & Hurley, R. A. (2006). Blast-related traumatic brain injury: What is known? *Journal of Neuropsychiatry and Clinical Neuroscience, 18*, 141–145.

Takahashi, T., Tsunoda, M., Miyashita, M., Ogihara, T., Okada, Y., . . . Amano, N. (2011). Comparison of diagnostic names of mental illnesses in medical documents before and after the adoption of a new Japanese translation of 'schizophrenia.' *Psychiatry and Clinical Neurosciences, 65*, 89–94.

Talavage, T. M., Nauman, E. A., Breedlove, E. L., Yoruk, U., Dye, A. E., Morigaki, K., . . . Leverenz, L. J. (2010). Functionally-detected cognitive impairment in high school football players without clinically-diagnosed concussion. *Journal of Neurotrauma*. Advance online publication. doi:10.1089/neu.2010.1512

Talleyrand, R. M. (2006). Potential stressors contributing to eating disorder symptoms in African American women: Implications for mental health counselors. *Journal of Mental Health Counseling, 28*, 338–352.

Talleyrand, R. M. (2010). Eating disorders in African American girls: Implications for counselors. *Journal of Counseling and Development, 88*, 319–325.

Tan, H.-Y., Chen, Q., Sust, S., Buckholtz, J. W., Meyers, J. D., . . . Callicott, J. H. (2007). Epistasis between catechol-*O*-methyltransferase and type II metabotropic glutamate receptor 3 genes on working memory brain function. *Proceedings of the National Academy of Sciences of the USA, 104*, 12536–12541.

Tanguay, P. E. (2011). Autism in DSM-5. *American Journal of Psychiatry, 168*, 1142–1144.

Taniai, H., Nishiyama, T., Miyachi, T., Imaeda, M., & Sumi, S.(2008). Genetic influences on the broad spectrum of autism: Study of proband-ascertained twins. *American Journal of Medical Genetics. Part B, Neuropsychiatric Genetics, 147B*, 844–849.

Tao, X., Chen, X., Yang, X., & Tian J. (2012). Fingerprint recognition with identical twin fingerprints. PLoS ONE 7(4): e35704. Retrieved from http://www.plosone.org/article/info:doi/10.1371/journal.pone.0035704

Tarasoff v. the Board of Regents of the University of California, 17 Cal. 3d 435, 551 P.2d 334, 131 Cal. Rptr. 14, 83 Ad. L. 3d 1166 (1976).

Targum, S. D., & Nierenberg, A. (2011). The complexity of "mixed" depression: A common clinical presentation. *Innovations in Clinical Neuroscience, 8*, 38–42.

Tárraga, L., Boada, M., Modinos, G., Espinosa, A., Diego, S., . . . Becker, J. T. (2006). A randomised pilot study to assess the efficacy of an interactive, multimedia tool of cognitive stimulation in Alzheimer's disease. *Journal of Neurology, Neurosurgery, and Psychiatry, 77*, 1116–1121.

Taylor, C. T., & Alden, L. E. (2010). Safety behaviors and judgmental biases in social anxiety disorder. *Behaviour Research and Therapy, 48*, 226–237.

Taylor, E. H. (1990). The assessment of social intelligence. *Psychotherapy, 27*, 445–457.

Taylor, J. L., & Seltzer, M. M. (2010a). Changes in the autism behavioral phenotype during the transition to adulthood. *Journal of Autism and Developmental Disorders, 40*, 431–446.

Taylor, J. L., & Seltzer, M. M. (2010b). Employment and post-secondary educational activities for young adults with autism spectrum disorders during the transition to adulthood. *Journal of Autism and Developmental Disorders, 41*, 566–574. doi:10.1007/s10803-010-1070-3

Taylor, K. N., Harper, S., & Chadwick, P. (2009). Impact of mindfulness on cognition and affect in voice hearing: Evidence from two case studies. *Behavioural and Cognitive Psychotherapy, 37*, 397–402.

Taylor, S., Asmundson, G. J. G., & Coons, M. J. (2005). Current directions in the treatment of hypochondriasis. *Journal of Cognitive Psychotherapy: An International Quarterly, 19*, 285–304.

Taylor, S., Jang, K. L., Stein, M. B., & Asmundson, G. J. G. (2008). A behavioral-genetic analysis of cognitive-behavioral model of hypochondriasis. *Journal of Cognitive Psychotherapy: An International Quarterly, 22*, 143–154.

Taylor, S., Thordarson, D. S., Maxfield, L., Fedoroff, I. C., Lovell, K., & Ogrodniczuk, J. (2003). Comparative efficacy, speed, and adverse effects of three PTSD treatments: Exposure therapy, EMDR, and relaxation training. *Journal of Consulting and Clinical Psychology, 71*, 330–338.

Taylor, S. E. (2010). Mechanisms linking early life stress to adult health outcomes. *Proceedings of the National Academy of Sciences of the USA, 107*, 8507–8512.

Taylor, S. E. (2010). How psychosocial resources enhance health and wellbeing. In S. Donaldson, M. Csikszentmihalyi, & J. Nakamura (Eds.), *Applied positive psychology*. New York, NY: Routledge.

Taylor, V. H., McIntyre, R. S., Remington, G., Levitan, R. G., Stonehocker, B., & Sharma, A. M. (2012). Beyond pharmacotherapy: Understanding the links between obesity and chronic mental illness. *Canadian Journal of Psychiatry, 57*, 5–12.

Teachman, B. A., Marker, C. D., & Clerkin, E. M. (2010). Catastrophic misinterpretations as a predictor of symptom change during treatment for panic disorder. *Journal of Consulting and Clinical Psychology, 24*, 300–308.

Tedeschi, R. G., & Kilmer, R. P. (2005). Assessing strengths, resilience, and growth to guide clinical interventions. *Professional Psychology: Research and Practice, 36*, 230–237.

Tedeschi, R. G., & McNally, R. J. (2011). Can we facilitate posttraumatic growth in combat veterans? *American Psychologist, 66*, 19–24.

Teicher, M. H., Andersen, S. L., Polcari, A., Anderson, C. M., & Navalta, C. P. (2002). Developmental neurobiology of childhood stress and trauma. *Psychiatric Clinics of North America, 25*, 397–426.

Terman, L. M., & Merrill, M. A. (1960). *Stanford-Binet intelligence scale*. Boston, MA: Houghton Mifflin.

Thanos, P. K., Michaelides, M., Piyis, Y. K., Wang, G. J., & Volkow, N. D. (2008). Food restriction markedly increases dopamine D2 receptor (D2R) in a rat model of obesity as assessed with in-vivo muPET imaging ([(11)C] raclopride) and in-vitro ([(3)H] spiperone) autoradiography. *Synapse, 62*, 50–61.

Thirthalli, J., & Benegal, V. (2006). Psychosis among substance users. *Current Opinion in Psychiatry, 19*, 239–245.

Thom, A., Sartory, G., & Johren, P. (2000). Comparison between one-session psychological treatment and benzodiazepine in dental phobia. *Journal of Consulting and Clinical Psychology, 68*, 378–387.

Thomas, J. D., Warren, K. R., & Hewitt, B. G. (2010). Fetal alcohol spectrum disorders: From research to policy. *Alcohol Research & Health, 33*, 118–126.

Thomas, J. J., Vartanian, L. R., & Brownell, K. D. (2009). The relationship between eating disorder not otherwise specified (EDNOS) and officially recognized eating disorders: Meta-analysis and implications for DSM. *Psychological Bulletin, 135*, 407–433.

Thomas, P. (1995). Thought disorder or communication disorder: Linguistic science provides a new approach. *British Journal of Psychiatry, 166*, 287–290.

Thomas, T., Stansifer, L., & Findling, R. L. (2011). Psychopharmacology of pediatric bipolar disorders in children and adolescents. *Pediatric Clinics of North America, 58*, 173–187.

Thompson, J. K., & Stice, E. (2004). Thin-ideal internalization: Mounting evidence for a new risk factor for body-image disturbance and eating pathology. In T. F. Oltmanns & R. E. Emery (Eds.), *Current directions in abnormal psychology* (pp. 97–101). Upper Saddle River, NJ: Prentice Hall.

Thompson, P. M., Vidal, C., Giedd, J. N., Gochman, P., Blumenthal, J., . . . Rapoport, J. L. (2001). Mapping adolescent brain change reveals dynamic wave of accelerated gray matter loss in very early-onset schizophrenia. *Proceedings of the National Academy of Sciences, 98*, 11650–11655.

Thoresen, C. E. (1998). Spirituality, health and science: The coming revival? In S. R. Roemer, S. R. Kurpius, & C. Carmin (Eds.), *The emerging role of counseling psychology in health care* (pp. 409–431). New York, NY: Norton.

Thorndike, R. L., Hagen, E. P., & Sattler, J. M. (1986). *The Stanford-Binet intelligence scale: Guide for administration and scoring* (3rd ed.). Chicago, IL: Riverside.

Thorpe, S. J., Barnett, J., Friend, K., & Nottingham, K. (2011). The mediating roles of disgust sensitivity and danger expectancy in relation to hand washing behaviour. *Behavioural and Cognitive Psychotherapy, 39*, 175–190.

Thorup, A., Waltoft, B. L., Pedersen, C. B., Mortensen, P. B., & Nordentoft, M. (2007). Young males have a higher risk of developing schizophrenia: A Danish register study. *Psychological Medicine, 37*, 479–484.

Thurston, R. C., & Kubzansky, L. D. (2009). Women, loneliness, and incident coronary heart disease. *Psychosomatic Medicine, 71*, 836–842.

Tian, Y., Green, P. G., Stamova, B., Hertz-Picciotto, I., Pessah, I. N., . . . Sharp, F. R. (2011). Correlations of gene expression with blood lead levels in children with autism compared to typically developing controls. *Neurotoxicity Research, 19*, 1–13.

Tienari, P., Wynne, L. C., Sorri, A., Lahti, I., Laksy, K., . . . Wahlberg, K. E. (2004). Genotype-environment interaction in schizophrenia-spectrum disorder: Long-term follow-up study of Finnish adoptees. *British Journal of Psychiatry, 184*, 216–222.

Tierney, J. (1988, July 3). Research finds lower-level workers bear brunt of workplace stress. *Seattle Post Intelligencer*, pp. K1–K3.

Tietjen, G. E., Brandes, J. L., Peterlin, B. L., Eloff, A., Dafer, R. M., Stein, M. R., . . . Khuder, S. A. (2010). Childhood maltreatment and migraine (part III): Association with comorbid pain conditions. *Headache, 50*(1), 42–51.

Tikhonova, I. V., Gnezditskii, V. V., Stakhovskaya, L. V., & Skvortsova, V. I. (2003). Neurophysiological characterization of transitory global amnesia syndrome. *Neuroscience and Behavioral Physiology, 33*, 171–175.

Timberlake, D. S., Hopfer, C. J., Rhee, S. H., Friedman, N. P., Haberstick, B. C., Lessem, J. M., & Hewitt, J. K. (2007). College attendance and its effect on drinking behaviors in a longitudinal study of adolescents. *Alcoholism: Clinical and Experimental Research, 31*, 1020–1030.

Tindle, H. A., Chang, Y.-F., Kuller, L. H., Manson, J. E., Robinson, J. G., . . . Matthews, K. A. (2009). Optimism, cynical hostility, and incident coronary heart disease and mortality in the Women's Health Initiative. *Circulation, 120*, 656–662.

*Tobin, J. J., & Friedman, J. (1983). Spirits, shamans, and nightmare death: S*urvivor stress in a Hmong refugee. American Journal of Orthopsychiatry, 53, 439–448.

Tolan, P. H., Gorman-Smith, D., Huesmann, L. R., & Zelli, A. (1997). Assessment of family relationship characteristics: A measure t*o explain risk for antisoci*al behavior and depression among urban youth. Psychological Assessment, 9, 212–223.

Tolin, D. F., Meunier, S. A., Frost, R. O., & Steketee, G. (2011). Hoarding among patients seeking treatment for anxiety disorders. *Journal of Anxiety Disorders, 25*, 43–48.

Tolin, D. F., Steenkamp, M. M., Marx, B. P., & Litz, B. T. (2010). Detecting symptom exaggeration in combat veterans using the MMPI-2 symptom validity scales: A mixed group validation. *Psychological Assessment, 22*, 729–736.

Tolin, D. F., & Villavicencio, A. (2011). Inattention, but not OCD, predicts the core features of hoarding behavior. *Behaviour Research and Therapy, 49*, 120–125.

Tollefson, G. D., Rampey, A. H., Potvin, J. H., Jenike, M. A., Rush, A. J., . . . Genduso, L. A. (1994). A multicenter investigation of fixed-dose fluoxetine in the treatment of obsessive-compulsive disorder. *Archives of General Psychiatry, 51*, 559–567.

Torgersen, S., Kringlen, E., & Cramer, V. (2001). The prevalence of personality disorders in a community sample. *Archives of General Psychiatry, 58*, 590–596.

Torpey, D. C., & Klein, D. N. (2008). Chronic depression: Update on classification and treatment. *Current Psychiatry Reports, 10*, 458–464.

Trampe, D., Stapel, D. A., & Siero, F. W. (2010). On models and vases: Body dissatisfaction and proneness to social comparison effects. *Journal of Personality and Social Psychology, 92*, 106–118.

La transsexualité ne sera plus classée comme affectation psychiatrique. (2009, May 16). *Le Monde*. Retrieved from http://www.lemonde.fr/societe/article/2009/05/16/la-transsexualite-ne-sera-plus-classee-comme-affectation-psychiatrique_1193860_3224.html

Trautmann, E., & Kroner-Herwig, B. (2010). A randomized controlled trial of Internet-based self-help training for recurrent headache in children and adolescents. *Behaviour Research and Therapy, 48*, 28–37.

Tregellas, J. R., Shatti, S., Tanabe, J. L., Martin, L. F., Gibson, L., Wylie, K., & Rojas, D. C. (2007). Gray matter volume differences and the effects of smoking on gray matter in schizophrenia. *Schizophrenia Research, 97*, 242–249.

Treloar, A., Crugel, M., Prasanna, A., Solomons, L., Fox, C., Paton, C., & Katona, C. (2010). Ethical dilemmas: Should antipsychotics ever be prescribed for people with dementia? *British Journal of Psychiatry, 197*, 88–90.

Trichotillomania. (2010). Retrieved from http://www.ncbi.nlm.nih.gov/pubmedhealth/PMH0002485

Triffleman, E. G., & Pole, N. (2010). Future directions in studies of trauma among ethnoracial and sexual minority samples. *Journal of Consulting and Clinical Psychology, 78*, 490–497.

Trivedi, M. H., Greer, T. L., Church, T. S., Carmody, T. J., Grannemann, B. D., . . . Blair, S. N. (2011). Exercise as an augmentation treatment for nonremitted major depressive disorder: A randomized, parallel dose comparison. *Journal of Clinical Psychiatry, 72*, 677–684.

Trivedi, M. H., Hollander, E., Nutt, D., & Blier, P. (2008). Clinical evidence and potential neurobiological underpinnings of unresolved symptoms of depression. *Journal of Clinical Psychiatry, 69*, 246–258.

Troxel, W. M., Matthews, K. A., Bromberger, J. T., & Tyrrell, K. S. (2003). Chronic stress burden, discrimination, and subclinical carotid artery disease in African American and Caucasian women. *Health Psychology, 22*, 300–309.

Trull, T. J., Selhan, M. B., Tragesser, S. L., Jahng, S., Wood, P. K., Piasecki, T. M., & Watson, D. (2008). Affective instability: Measuring a core feature of borderline personality disorder with ecological momentary assessment. Journal of Abnormal Psychology, 117, 647–661.

Tsai, G. E., Condie, D., Wu, M.-T., & Chang, I.-W. (1999). Functional magnetic resonance imaging of personality switches in a woman with dissociative identity disorder. *Harvard Review of Psychiatry, 7*, 119–122.

Tucker, B. T. P., Woods, D. W., Flessner, C. A., Franklin, S. A., & Franklin, M. E. (2011). The skin picking impact project: Phenomenology, interference, and treatment utilization of pathological skin picking in a population-based sample. *Journal of Anxiety Disorders, 25*, 88–95.

Tucker-Drob, E. M., Rhemtulla, M., Harden, K. P., Turkheimer, E., & Fask, D. (2011). Emergence of a gene × socioeconomic status interaction on infant mental ability between 10 months and 2 years. *Psychological Science, 22*, 125–133.

Tuller, D. (2004, June 21). Gentlemen, start your engines? *New York Times*, pp. F1, F11.

Tully, E. C., Iacono, W. G., & McGue, M. (2010). Changes in genetic and environmental influences on the development of nicotine dependence and major depressive disorder from middle adolescence to early adulthood. *Developmental Psychopathology, 22*, 831–848.

Tunks, E. R., Weir, R., & Crook, J. (2008). Epidemiologic perspective on chronicpain treatment. *Canadian Journal of Psychiatry, 53*, 235–242.

Turetsky, B. I., Calkins, M. E., Light, G. A., Olincy, A., Radant, A. D., & Swerdlow, N. R. (2007). Neurophysiological endophenotypes of schizophrenia: The viability of selected candidate measures. *Schizophrenia Bulletin, 33*, 69–78.

Turk, D. C., Swanson, K. S., & Tunks, E. R. (2008). Psychological approaches in the treatment of chronic pain patients—When pills, scalpels, and needles are not enough. *Canadian Journal of Psychiatry, 53*, 213–223.

Turner, E. H., Matthews, A. M., Linardatos, E., Tell, R. A., & Rosenthal, R. (2008). Selective publication of antidepressant trials and its influence on apparent efficacy. *New England Journal of Medicine, 358*, 252–257.

Turner, H. A., Finkelhor, D., Ormrod, R., & Hamby, S. L. (2010). Infant victimization in a nationally representative sample. *Pediatrics, 126*, 44–52.

Turtle, L., & Robertson, M. M. (2008). Tics, twitches, tales: The experiences of Gilles de la Tourette's syndrome. *American Journal of Orthopsychiatry, 78*, 449–455.

Tutkun, H., Sar, V., Yargic, L. I., & Ozpulat, T. (1998). Frequency of dissociative disorders among psychiatric inpatients in a Turkish university clinic. *American Journal of Psychiatry, 155*, 800–805.

Tuttle, J. P., Scheurich, N. E., & Ranseen, J. (2010). Prevalence of ADHD diagnosis and nonmedical prescription stimulant use in medical students. *Academic Psychiatry, 34*, 220–223.

Tylka, T. L., & Subich, L. M. (2004). Examining a multidimensional model of eating disorder symptomatology among college women. *Journal of Counseling Psychology, 51*, 314–328.

Tyre, P. (2004, September 27). Combination therapy. *Newsweek, 144*, 66–67.

Ucok, A. (2007). Other people stigmatize.... But, what about us? Attitudes of mental health professionals towards patients with schizophrenia. *Archives of Neuropsychiatry, 44*, 108–116.

Ulloa, R.-E., Nicolini, H., Avila, M., & Fernandez-Guasti, A. (2007). Age onset subtypes of obsessive-compulsive disorder: Differences in clinical response to treatment with clomipramine. *Journal of Child and Adolescent Psychopharmacology, 17*, 85–96.

Ungvari, G. S., Caroff, S. N., & Gerevich, J. (2009). The catatonia conundrum: Evidence of psychomotor phenomena as a symptom dimension in psychotic disorders. *Schizophrenia Bulletin, 36*, 231–238.

United Nations Development Programme (2006). *Human Development Report 2006: Beyond scarcity, power, poverty and global water crisis*. New York: United Nations Development Programme.

United Nations Office on Drugs and Crime. (2010). *World drug report*. New York, NY: United Nations. Retrieved from http://www.unodc.org/unodc/en/data-and-analysis/WDR-2010.html

University of Michigan. (2010, October 28). Friends with cognitive benefits: Mental function improves after certain kinds of socializing. *Science Daily*. Retrieved from http://www.sciencedaily.com/releases/2010/10/101028113817.htm

U.S. Department of Education, National Center for Education Statistics. (2010). Digest of Education Statistics, 2009 (NCES 2010-013). Retrieved from http://nces.ed.gov/pubs2010/2010013_0.pdf

U.S. Department of Health and Human Services. (2003). *Ending chronic homelessness*. Washington, DC: Author.

U.S. Department of Health and Human Services. (2010). *Child maltreatment 2009*. Retrieved from http://www.acf.hhs.gov/programs/cb/pubs/cm09/cm09.pdf

U.S. Food and Drug Administration. (2007).Antidepressant use in children, adolescents, and adults. Retrieved from http://www.fda.gov/NewsEvents/Newsroom/PressAnnouncements/2007/ucm108905.htm

U.S. Food and Drug Administration.(2010a, October 12). FDA approves injectable drug to treat opioid-dependent patients. Retrieved from http://www.fda.gov/NewsEvents/Newsroom/PressAnnouncements/ucm229109.htm

U.S. Food and Drug Administration. (2010b, November 17). FDA warning letters issued to four makers of caffeinated alcoholic beverages. Retrieved from http://www.fda.gov/NewsEvents/Newsroom/PressAnnouncements/ucm234109.htm

U.S. Food and Drug Administration. (2011). FDA drug safety communication: Antipsychotic drug labels updated on use during pregnancy and risk of abnormal muscle movements and withdrawal symptoms in newborns. Retrieved from http://www.fda.gov/Drugs/DrugSafety/ucm243903.htm

U.S. Public Health Service. (1991). *Depression: What you need to know* (NIMH Publication No. 60-FL-1481-0). Rockville, MD: U.S. Government Printing Office.

U.S. Public Health Service. (1999). *The Surgeon General's call to action to prevent suicide*. Washington, DC: Author.

United States v Comstock. 560 U S (2010).

University of Granada. (2007, June 28). Study confirms importance of sexual fantasies in experience of sexual desire. *Science Daily*. Retrieved from www.sciencedaily.com/releases/2007/06/070627223851.htm

Utsey, S. O., Stenard, P., & Hook, J. N. (2008). Understanding the role of cultural factors in relation to suicide among African Americans: Implications for research and practice. In F. Leong & M. M. Leach (Eds.), *Ethnic suicides* (pp. 57–80). New York, NY: Routledge.

Uthman, O. A., & Abdulmalik, J. O. (2008). Adjunctive therapies for AIDS dementia complex. *Cochrane Database of Systematic Reviews, 3*, CD006496. doi:10.1002/14651858.CD006496.pub2

Vahid, B., & Marik, P. E. (2007). Severe emphysema associated with cocaine smoking: A case study. *Journal of Respiratory Diseases*, September suppl: *12–20*.

Valderhaug, R., Larsson, G., & Gotestam, K. G. (2007). An open clinical trial of cognitive-behavioral therapy in children and adolescents with obsessive-compulsive disorder administered in regular outpatient clinics. *Behaviour Research and Therapy, 45*, 577–585.

Valentí, M., Pacchiarotti, I., Rosa, A. R., Bonnín, C. M., Popovic, D., . . . Vieta, E. (2011). Bipolar mixed episodes and antidepressants: A cohort study of bipolar I disorder patients. *Bipolar Disorders*, 13, 145–154.

Valsiner, J. (2007). *Culture in mind and societies*. New Delhi, India: Sage.

van der Gaag, M. (2006). A neuropsychiatric model of biological and psychological processes in the remission of delusions and auditory hallucinations. *Schizophrenia Bulletin, 32*, 113–122.

van der Gaag, M., Stant, A. D., Wolters, K. J. K., Burkens, E., & Wiersma, D. (2011). Cognitive behavioral therapy for persistent and recurrent psychosis in people with schizophrenia-spectrum disorder: Cost-effectiveness analysis. *British Journal of Psychiatry,* 198, 59–65.

Vander Wal, J. S. (2012). Night eating syndrome: A critical review of the literature. *Clinical Psychology Review, 32*, 49–59.

van der Werf, M., Thewissen, V., Dominguez, M. D., Lieb, R., Wittchen, H., & Van Os, J. (2011). Adolescent development of psychosis as an outcome of hearing impairment: A 10–year longitudinal study. *Psychological Medicine, 41*, 477–485.

Vandrey, R., Bigelow, G. E., & Stitzer, M. L. (2007). Contingency management in cocaine abusers: A dose-effect comparison of goods-based versus cash-based incentives. *Experimental and Clinical Psychopharmacology, 15*, 338–343.

Vandrey, R., & Haney, M. (2009). Pharmacotherapy for cannabis dependence: How close are we? *CNS Drugs, 23*, 543–553.

Van Evra, J. P. (1983). *Psychological disorders of children and adolescents*. Boston, MA: Little, Brown.

van Goozen, S. H., Fairchild, G., Snoek, H., & Harold, G. T. (2007). The evidence for a neurobiological model of childhood antisocial behavior. *Psychological Bulletin, 133*, 149–182.

Van Gundy, K., Cesar, J., & Rebellon, C. (2010). A life-course perspective on the "gateway hypothesis." *Journal of Health and Social Behavior, 51*, 244–259.

Van Hoeken, D., Seidell, J., & Hoek, H. W. (2003). Epidemiology. In J. Treasure, U. Schmidt, & E. Van Furth (Eds.), *Handbook of eating disorders* (pp. 11–34). Chichester, UK: Wiley.

Van Hulle, C. A., Waldman, I. D., D'Onofrio, B. M., Rodgers, J. L., Rathouz, P. J., & Lahey, B. B. (2009). Developmental structure of genetic influences on antisocial behavior across childhood and adolescence. *Journal of Abnormal Psychology, 118*, 711–721.

van Lankveld, J. (2008). Problems with sexual interest and desire in women. In D. Rowland & L. Incrocci (Eds.), *Handbook of sexual and gender identity disorders* (pp. 154–187). Hoboken, NJ: Wiley.

Van Noppen, B., & Steketee, G. (2009). Testing a conceptual model of patient and family predictors of obsessive compulsive disorder (OCD) symptoms. *Behaviour Research and Therapy, 47*, 18–25.

van Strien, T., Snoek, H. M., van der Zwaluw, C. S., & Engels, R. C. (2010). Parental control and the dopamine D2 receptor gene (DRD2) interaction on emotional eating in adolescence. *Appetite, 54*, 255–261.

Van Vlierberghe, L., Braet, C., Bosmans, G., Rosseel, Y., & Bogels, S. (2010). Maladaptive schemas and psychopathology in adolescence: On the utility of Young's schema theory in youth. *Cognitive Therapy and Research, 34*, 316–332.

Vasey, M. W., Vilensky, M. R., Heath, J. H., Harbaugh, C. N., Buffington, A. G., & Fazio, R. H. (2012). It was as big as my head, I swear! Biased spider estimation in spider phobia. *Journal of Anxiety Disorders, 26*, 20–24.

Vassilopoulos, S. P., Banerjee, R., & Prantzalou, C. (2009). Experimental modification of interpretation bias in socially anxious children: Changes in interpretation, anticipated interpersonal anxiety, and social anxiety symptoms. *Behaviour Research and Therapy, 47*, 1085–1089.

Vaughan, S., & Fowler, D. (2004). The distress experienced by voice hearers is associated with the perceived relationship between the voice hearer and the voice. *British Journal of Clinical Psychology, 43*, 143–147.

Veling, W., Selten, J.-P., Mackenbach, J. P., & Hoek, H. W. (2007). Symptoms at first contact for psychotic disorder: Comparison between native Dutch and ethnic minorities. *Schizophrenia Research, 95*, 30–38.

Velligan, D. I., Weiden, P. J., Sajatovic, M., Scott, J., Carpenter, D., Ross, R., & Docherty, J. P. (2009). The expert consensus guideline series: Adherence problems in patients with serious and persistent mental illness. *Journal of Clinical Psychiatry, 70*(Suppl 4), 1–46.

Verboom, C. E., Sentse, M., Sijtsema, J. J., Nolen, W. A., Ormel, J., & Penninx, B. W. (2011). Explaining heterogeneity in disability with major depressive disorder: Effects of personal and environmental characteristics. *Journal of Affective Disorders, 132*, 71–81.

Verdon, B. (2011). The case of thematic tests adapted to older adults. *Rorschachiana, 32*, 46–71.

Verma, R., Balhara, Y. P., & Mathur, S. (2011). Management of attention-deficit hyperactivity disorder. *Journal of Pediatric Neuroscience, 6*, 13–18.

Vermetten, E., Schmahl, C., Lindner, S., Loewenstein, R. J., & Bremner, J. D. (2006). Hippocampal and amygdalar volumes in dissociative identity disorder. *American Journal of Psychiatry, 163*, 630–636.

Vigezzi, P., Guglielmino, L., Marzorati, P., Silenzio, R., De Chiara, M., . . . Cozzolino, E. (2006). Multimodal drug addiction treatment: A field comparison of methadone and buprenorphine among heroin- and cocaine-dependent patients. *Journal of Substance Abuse Treatment, 31*, 3–7.

Vigod, S. N. (2009). Understanding and treating premenstrual dysphoric disorder: An update for the women's health practitioner. *Obstetric and Gynecological Clinics of North America, 36*, 907–924.

Vigod, S. N., & Stewart, D. (2009). Emergent research in the cause of mental illness in women across the lifespan. *Current Opinion in Psychiatry, 22*, 396–400.

Vilhauer, J. S., Young, S., Kealoha, C., Borrmann, J., Ishak, W. W., . . . Mirocha, J. (2011). Treating major depression by creating positive expectations for the future: A pilot study for the effectiveness of future-directed therapy (FDT) on symptom severity and quality of life. *CNS Neuroscience and Therapeutics, 18*, 102–109. doi:10.1111/j.1755-5949.2011.00235.x

Villagonzalo, K. A., Dodd, S., Ng, F., Mihaly, S., Langbein, A., & Berk, M. (2011). The relationship between substance use and posttraumatic stress disorder in a methadone maintenance treatment program. *Comprehensive Psychiatry, 52*, 562–566. doi:10.1016/j.comppsych.2010.10.001

Vincent, M. A., & McCabe, M. P. (2000). Gender differences among adolescents in family, and peer influences on body dissatisfaction, weight loss, and binge eating disorders. *Journal of Youth and Adolescence, 29*, 205–221.

Virués-Ortega, J. (2010). Applied behavior analytic intervention for autism in early childhood: Meta-analysis, meta-regression and dose-response meta-analysis of multiple outcomes. *Clinical Psychology Review, 30*, 387–399.

Vitiello, B. (2009). Treatment of adolescent depression: What we have come to know. *Depression and Anxiety, 26*, 393–395.

Vocks, S., Tuschen-Caffier, B., Pietrowsky, R., Rustenbach, S. J., Kersting, A., & Herpertz, S. (2010). Meta-analysis of the effectiveness of psychological and pharmacological treatments for binge eating disorder. *International Journal of Eating Disorders, 43*, 205–217.

Vogele, C., Ehlers, A., Meyer, A. H., Frank, M., Hahlweg, K., & Margraf, J. (2010). Cognitive mediation of clinical improvement after intensive exposure of agoraphobia and social phobia. *Depression and Anxiety, 27*, 294–301.

Vogt, D., Vaughn, R., Glickman, M. E., Schultz, M., Drainoni, M.-L., . . . Eisen, S. (2011). Gender differences in combat-related stressors and their association with post-deployment mental health in a nationally representative sample of U.S. OEF/OIF veterans. *Journal of Abnormal Psychology, 120*, 797–806.

Volkow, N. D., & O'Brien, C. P. (2007). Issues for DSM-V: Should obesity be included as a brain disorder? *American Journal of Psychiatry, 174*, 708–710.

Voon, V., Gallea, C., Nattori, N., Bruno, M., Ekanayake, V., & Hallett, M. (2010). The involuntary nature of conversion disorder. *Neurology, 74*, 223–228.

Vowles, K. E., McCracken, L. M., & O'Brien, J. Z. (2011). Acceptance and values-based action in chronic pain: A three-year follow-up analysis of treatment effectiveness and process. *Behaviour Research and Therapy, 49*, 748–755.

Wade, T., George, W. M., & Atkinson, M. (2009). A randomized controlled trial of brief interventions of body dissatisfaction. *Journal of Consulting and Clinical Psychology, 77*, 845–854.

Wade, T. D. (2007). A retrospective comparison of purging type disorders: Eating disorder not otherwise specified and bulimia nervosa. *International Journal of Eating Disorders, 40*, 1–5.

Wagner, J., & Abbott, G. (2007). Depression and depression care in diabetes: Relationship to perceived discrimination in African Americans. *Diabetes Care, 30*, 364–366.

Wagner, K. D., Ritt-Olson, A., Chou, C. P., Pokhrel, P., Duan, L., . . . Unger, J. B. (2010). Associations between parental family structure, family functioning, and substance use among Hispanic/Latino adolescents. *Psychology of Addictive Behaviors, 24*, 98–108.

Walfish, S., Barnett, J. E., Marlyere, K., & Zielke, R. (2010). "Doc, there's something I have to tell you": Patient disclosure to their psychotherapist of unprosecuted murder and other violence. *Ethics and Behavior, 20*, 311–323.

Walker, J. R., & Furer, P. (2008). Interoceptive exposure in the treatment of health anxiety and hypochondriasis. *Journal of Cognitive Psychotherapy, 22*, 367–380.

Walkup, J. (1995). A clinically based rule of thumb for classifying delusions. *Schizophrenia Bulletin, 21*, 323–331.

Wall, T. L., Shea, S. H., Luczak, S. E., Cook, T. A. R., & Carr, L. G. (2005). Genetic associations of alcohol dehydrogenase with alcohol use disorders and endophenotypes in white college students. *Journal of Abnormal Psychology, 114*, 456–465.

Walling, A. D. (2007). Potential new treatment for premature ejaculation. *American Family Physician, 75*, 555–556.

Walsh, B. T., & Devlin, M. J. (1998). Eating disorders: Progress and problems. *Science, 280*, 1387–1390.

Walsh, R., & Shapiro, S. L. (2006). The meeting of meditative disciplines and Western psychologies. *American Psychologist, 61*, 227–239.

Walter, H. J. (2001). Substance abuse and substance use disorders. In G. O. Gabbard (Ed.), *Treatment of psychiatric disorders* (pp. 325–338). Washington, DC: American Psychiatric Publishing.

Walter, K. H., Gunstad, J., & Hobfoll, S. E. (2010). Self-control predicts later symptoms of posttraumatic stress disorder. *Psychological Trauma: Theory, Research, Practice, and Policy, 2*, 97–101.

Wampold, B. E., Lichtenberg, J. W., & Waehler, C. A. (2002). Principles of empirically supported interventions in counseling psychology. *Counseling Psychologist, 30*, 197–217.

Wang, G. J., Volkow, N. D., Logan, J., Pappas, N. R., Wong, C. T., . . . Fowler, J. S. (2001). Brain dopamine and obesity. *Lancet, 357*, 354–357.

Wang, S.-J., & Fu, J.-L. (2010). The "other" headaches: Primary cough, exertion, stress and primary stabbing headaches. *Current Pain and Headache Reports, 14*, 41–46.

Wang, X. P., & Ding, H. L. (2008). Alzheimer's disease: Epidemiology, genetics, and beyond. *Neuroscience Bulletin, 24*, 105–109.

Wang, Y., & Beydoun, M. A. (2007). The obesity epidemic in the United States—Gender, age, socioeconomic, racial/ethnic, and geographic characteristics: A systematic review and metaregression analysis. *Epidemiologic Reviews, 29*, 6–28.

Ward, M. J. (1946). *The snake pit*. London, UK: Cassell.

Ward, M. P., & Irazoqui, P. P. (2010). Evolving refractory major depressive disorder diagnostic and treatment paradigms: Toward closed-loop therapeutics. *Frontiers in Neuroengineering, 3*, 7.

Warman, D. M., Lysaker, P. H., Martin, J. M., Davis, L., & Haudenschield, S. L. (2007). Jumping to conclusions and the continuum of delusional beliefs. *Behaviour Research and Therapy, 45*, 1255–1269.

Warner, R. (2009). Recovery from schizophrenia and the recovery model. *Current Opinion in Psychiatry*, 22, 374–380.

Warner, R. (2010). Does the scientific evidence support the recovery model? *The Psychiatrist, 34*, 3–5.

Wartik, N. (1994, February). Fatal attention. *Redbook*, 62–69.

Watkins, E. R., & Moberly, N. J. (2009). Concreteness training reduces dysphoria: A pilot proof-of-principle study. *Behavior Research and Therapy, 47*, 48–53.

Watkins, E. R., Taylor, R. S., Byng, R., Baeyens, C., Read, R., Pearson, K., & Watson, L. (2012). Guided self-help concreteness training as an intervention for major depression in primary care: A Phase II randomized controlled trial. *Psychological Medicine, 42*, 1359–1371. doi:10.1017/S0033291711002480

Watson, J. B., & Rayner, R. (1920). Conditioned emotional reactions. *Journal of Experimental Psychology, 3*, 1–14.

Watt, M. C., O'Connor, R. M., Stewart, S. H., Moon, E. C., & Terry, L. (2008). Specificity of childhood learning experiences in relation to anxiety sensitivity and illness/injury sensitivity: Implications for health anxiety and pain. *Journal of Cognitive Psychotherapy: An International Quarterly, 22*, 128–143.

Wechsler, D. (1981). *Wechsler adult intelligence scale*. New York, NY: Harcourt, Brace, Jovanovich.

Weems, C. F., Hayward, C., Killen, J., & Taylor, C. B. (2002). A longitudinal investigation of anxiety sensitivity in adolescence. *Journal of Abnormal Psychology, 111*, 471–477.

Weems, C. F., Pina, A. A., Costa, N. M., Watts, S. E., Taylor, L. K., & Cannon, M. F. (2007). Predisaster trait anxiety and negative affect predict posttraumatic stress in youth after Hurricane Katrina. *Journal of Counseling and Clinical Psychology, 75*, 154–159.

Weijerman, M. E., & de Winter, J. P. (2010). The care of children with Down syndrome. *European Journal of Pediatrics, 169*, 1445–1452.

Weinberger, A. H., Desai, R. A., & McKee, S. A. (2010). Nicotine withdrawal in U.S. smokers with current mood, anxiety, alcohol use, and substance use disorders. *Drug and Alcohol Dependence, 108*, 7–12.

Weiner, I. B., & Greene, R. L. (2008). *Handbook of personality assessment*. Hoboken, NJ: John Wiley & Sons.

Weintraub, D., Comella, C. L., & Horn, S. (2008). Parkinson's disease—Part 3: Neuropsychiatric symptoms. *American Journal of Managed Care, 14*(2 Suppl), S59–S69.

Weintraub, D., & Hurtig, H. (2007). Presentation and management of psychosis in Parkinson's disease and dementia with Lewy bodies. *American Journal of Psychiatry, 164*, 1491–1498.

Weiser, B. (2000, December 16). Judge rules defendant's amnesia is feigned in terror case. *New York Times*, p. B2.

Weishaar, M. E., & Beck, A. T. (1992). Clinical and cognitive predictors of suicide. In R. W. Maris, A. L. Berman, J. T. Maltsberger, & R. I. Yufit (Eds.), *Assessment and prediction of suicide* (pp. 467–483). New York, NY: Guilford Press.

Weiss, H., Rastan,V., Mullges,W.,Wagner, R. F., & Toyka, K. V. (2002). Psychotic symptoms and emotional distress in patients with Guillain-Barré syndrome. *European Neurology, 47*, 74–78.

Weissberg, M. (1993). Multiple personality disorder and iatrogenesis: The cautionary tale of Anna O. *International Journal of Clinical and Experimental Hypnosis, 41*, 15–34.

Weisz, J. R., Weiss, B., Suwanlert, S., & Chaiyasit, W. (2006). Culture and youth psychopathology: Testing the syndromal sensitivity model in Thai and American adolescents. *Journal of Consulting and Clinical Psychology, 74*, 1098–1107.

Weitzman, E. R., Nelson, T. F., & Wechsler, H. (2003). Taking up binge drinking in college: The influences of person, social group, and environment. *Journal of Adolescent Health, 32*, 26–35.

Welch-Shaw, S., & Linehan, M. M. (2002). High-risk situations associated with parasuicide and drug use in borderline personality disorder. *Journal of Personality Disorders, 16*, 561–569.

Welham, J., Isohanni, M., Jones, P., & McGrath, J. (2009). The antecedents of schizophrenia: A review of birth cohort studies. *Schizophrenia Bulletin, 35*, 603–623.

Wells, A. (2005). The metacognitive model of GAD: Assessment of meta-worry and relationship with DSM-IV generalized anxiety disorder. *Cognitive Therapy and Research, 29*, 107–121.

Wells, A. (2009). *Metacognitive therapy for anxiety and depression*. New York, NY: Guilford Press.

Wells, T. T., & Beevers, C. G. (2010). Biased attention and dysphoria: Manipulating selective attention reduces subsequent depressive symptoms. *Cognition and Emotion*, 24, 719–728.

Werner, S., Malaspina, D., & Rabinowitz, J. (2007). Socioeconomic status at birth is associated with risk of schizophrenia: Population-based multilevel study. *Schizophrenia Bulletin, 33*, 1373–1378.

Werth, J. L., Weifel, R., & Benjamin, G. A. H. (2009). *The duty to protect: Ethical, legal, and professional considerations for mental health professionals*. Washington, DC: American Psychological Association.

West, K. (2007). *Biofeedback*. New York, NY: Infobase.

Westberg, J. (2010, July 30). Abilify commercials: There's something missing—and it might make you even more depressed. Retrieved from http://www.examiner.com/article/abilify-commercials-there-s-something-missing-and-it-might-make-you-even-more-depressed

Westen, D., Defife, J. A., Bradley, B., & Hilsenroth, M. J. (2010). Prototype personality diagnosis in clinical practice: A viable alternative to DSM-5 and ICD-11. *Professional Psychology: Research and Practice, 41*, 482-487.

Westen, D., & Harnden-Fischer, J. (2001). Personality profiles in eating disorders: Rethinking the distinction between Axis I and Axis II. *American Journal of Psychiatry, 158*, 547–562.

Westheimer, R. K., & Lopater, S. (2005). *Human sexuality: A psychosocial perspective*. Baltimore, MD: Lippincott Williams & Wilkins.

Weston, C. G., & Riolo, S. A. (2007). Childhood and adolescent precursors to adult personality disorders. *Psychiatric Annals, 37*, 114–120.

Westphal, M., & Bonanno, G. A. (2007). Posttraumatic growth and resilience to trauma: Different sides of the same coin or different coins? *Applied Psychology: An International Review, 56*, 417–427.

Westrin, A., & Lam, R. W. (2007a). Long-term and preventative treatment for seasonal affective disorder. *CNS Drugs, 21*, 901–909.

Westrin, A., & Lam, R. W. (2007b). Seasonal affective disorder: A clinical update. *Annals of Clinical Psychiatry, 19*, 239–246.

Whitaker, A. H., Feldman, J. F., Lorenz, J. M., Shen, S., McNicholas, F., Nieto, M., . . . Paneth, N. (2006). Motor and cognitive outcomes in nondisabled low-birth-weight adolescents: Early determinants. *Archives of Pediatrics and Adolescent Medicine, 160*, 1040–1046.

White, K. S., Craft, J. M., & Gervino, E. V. (2010). Anxiety and hypervigilance to cardiopulmonary sensations in non-cardiac chest pain patients with and without psychiatric disorders. *Behaviour Research and Therapy, 48*, 394–401.

White, L., McDermott, J., Degnan, K., Henderson, H., & Fox, N. (2011). Behavioral inhibition and anxiety: The moderating roles of inhibitory control and attention shifting. *Journal of Abnormal Child Psychology, 39*, 735–747.

Whiteside, S. P., & Abramowitz, J. S. (2004). Obsessive-compulsive symptoms and the expression of anger. *Cognitive Therapy and Research, 28*, 259–268.

Wicks, S., Hjern, A., & Dalman, C. (2010). Social risk or genetic liability for psychosis? A study of children born in Sweden and reared by adoptive parents. *American Journal of Psychiatry, 167*, 1240–1246.

Wicks, S., Hjern, A., Gunnell, D., Lewis, G., & Dalman, C. (2005). Social adversity in childhood and the risk of developing psychosis: A national cohort study. *American Journal of Psychiatry, 162*, 1652–1657.

Widiger, T. A. (2007). Current controversies in nosology and diagnosis of personality disorders. *Psychiatric Annals, 37*, 93–99.

Widiger, T. A., & Coker, L. A. (2002). Assessing personality disorders. In J. N. Butcher (Ed.), *Clinical personality assessment: Practical approaches* (pp. 407–434). New York, NY: Oxford University Press.

Widiger, T. A., & Mullins-Sweatt, S. N. (2005). Categorical and dimensional models of personality disorders. In J. M. Oldham, A. E. Skodol, & D. S. Bender (Eds.), *American Psychiatric Publishing textbook of personality disorders* (pp. 35–53). Washington, DC: American Psychiatric Publishing.

Widiger, T. A., & Trull, T. J. (2007). Plate tectonics in the classification of personality disorder: Shifting to a dimensional model. *American Psychologist, 62*, 71–83.

Wiersma, D., Nienhuis, F. J., Sloof, C. J., & Giel, R. (1998). Natural course of schizophrenic disorders: A fifteen-year follow-up of a Dutch incidence cohort. *Schizophrenia Bulletin, 24*, 75–85.

Wilens, T. E., Adler, L. A., Adams, J., Sgambati, S., Rotrosen, J., Sawtelle, R., . . . Fusillo, S. (2008). Misuse and diversion of stimulants prescribed for ADHD: A systematic review of the literature. *Journal of the American Academy of Child & Adolescent Psychiatry, 47*, 21–31.

Wilfley, D. E., Pike, K. M., Dohm, F.-A., Striegel-Moore, R. H., & Fairburn, C. G. (2001). Bias in binge eating disorder: How representative are recruited clinic samples? *Journal of Consulting and Clinical Psychology, 69*, 383–388.

Wilhelm, S., Phillips, K. A., Fama, J. M., Greenberg, J. L., & Steketee, G. (2011). Modular cognitive-behavioral therapy for body dysmorphic disorder. *Behavior Therapy, 42*, 624–633.

Willenbring, M. L. (2010). The past and future of research on treatment of alcohol dependence. Retrieved from http://pubs.niaaa.nih.gov/publications/arh40/55-63.htm

Williams, K., Wheeler, D. M., Silove, N., & Hazell, P. (2010). Selective serotonin reuptake inhibitors (SSRIs) for autism spectrum disorders (ASD). *Cochrane Database of Systematic Reviews, 4*(8), CD004677.

Williams, M., Powers, M., Yun, Y. G., & Foa, E. (2010). Minority participation in randomized controlled trials for obsessive-compulsive disorder. *Journal of Anxiety Disorders, 24*, 171–177.

Williams, M. J., McManus, F., Muse, K., Williams, J., & Mark, G. (2011). Mindfulness-based cognitive therapy for severe health anxiety (hypochondriasis): An interpretative phenomenological analysis of patients' experiences. *British Journal of Clinical Psychology, 50*, 379–397.

Williams, M. T., Abramowitz, J. S., & Olatunji, B. O. (2012). The relationship between contamination cognitions, anxiety, and disgust in two ethnic groups. *Journal of Behavior Therapy and Experimental Psychiatry, 43*, 632–637.

Williams, N. M., Zaharieva, I., Martin, A., Langley, K., Mantripragada, K., . . . Thapar, A. (2010). Rare chromosomal deletions and duplications in attention-deficit hyperactivity disorder: A genome-wide analysis. *Lancet, 376*, 1401–1408.

Williams, P. G., Smith, T. W., & Jordan, K. D. (2010). Health anxiety and hypochondriasis: Interpersonal extensions of the cognitive behavioral perspective. In G. Beck (Ed.), *Interpersonal processes in the anxiety disorders: Implications for understanding psychopathology and treatment* (pp. 261–284). New York, NY: American Psychological Association.

Williams, S. H. (2005). Medications for treating alcohol dependence. *American Family Physician, 72*, 1775–1780.

Williamson, D., Robinson, M. E., & Melamed, B. (1997). Patient behavior, spouse responsiveness, and marital satisfaction in patients with rheumatoid arthritis. *Behavior Modification, 21*, 97–106.

Williamson, P. (2007). The final common pathway of schizophrenia. *Schizophrenia Bulletin, 33*, 953–954.

Willis, A. W., Bradley, A., Evanoff, M. L., Criswell, S. R., & Racette, B. A. (2010). Geographic and ethnic variation in Parkinson disease: A population-based study of US Medicare beneficiaries. *Neuroepidemiology, 34*, 143–151.

Willis, A.W., Schootman, M., Kung, N., Evanoff, B. A., Perlmutter, J. S., & Racette, B. A. (2012). Predictors of survival in patients with Parkinson disease. *Archives of Neurology, 69*, 601–607. doi:10.1001/archneurol.2011.2370

Willis, S. L., Tennstedt, S. L., Marsiske, M., Ball, K., Elias, J., . . . ACTIVE Study Group. (2006). Long-term effects of cognitive training on everyday functional outcomes in older adults. *Journal of the American Medical Association, 296*, 2805–2814.

Wilson, G. T., & Shafran, R. (2005). Eating disorders guidelines from NICE. *Lancet, 365*, 79–81.

Wilson, J. L., Peebles, R., Hardy, K. K., & Litt, I. F. (2006). Surfing for thinness: A pilot study of pro-eating disorder web site usage in adolescents with eating disorders. *Pediatrics, 118*, 1635–1643.

Wilson, P., Minnis, H., Puckering, C., & Gillberg, C. (2009). Should we aspire to screen preschool children for conduct disorder? *Archives of Disorders of Childhood, 94*, 812–816.

Wilson, R. S., Scherr, P. A., Schneider, J. A., Tang, Y., & Bennett, D. A. (2007). Relation of cognitive activity to risk of developing Alzheimer disease. *Neurology, 69*, 1911–1920.

Wilson, R. S., Schneider, J. A., Arnold, S. E., Tang, Y., Boyle, P. A., & Bennett, D. A. (2007). Olfactory identification and incidence of mild cognitive impairment in older age. *Archives of General Psychiatry, 64*, 802–808.

Windsor, T. D., Anstey, K. J., Butterworth, P., & Rogers, B. (2008). Behavioral approach and behavioral inhibition as moderators of the association between negative life events and perceived control in midlife. *Personality and Individual Differences, 44*, 1080–1092.

Wingo, A. P., Wingo, T. S., Harvey, P. D., & Baldessarini, R. J. (2009). Effects of lithium on cognitive performance: A meta-analysis. *Journal of Clinical Psychiatry, 70*, 1588–1597.

Winters, K. (2007, September 30). Issues of GID diagnosis for transsexual women and men. Retrieved from http://www.gidreform.org/GID30285a.pdf

Wise, M. G., Hilty, D. M., & Cerda, G. M. (2001). Delirium due to a general medical condition, delirium due to multiple etiologies, and delirium not otherwise specified. In G. O. Gabbard (Ed.), *Treatment of psychiatric disorders* (pp. 387–412). Washington, DC: American Psychiatric Publishing.

Wiseman, F. (Director). (1967). *Titicut follies* [Motion picture]. United States: Zipporah Films.

Witek-Janusek, L., Albuquerque, K., Chroniak, K. R., Croniak, C., Durazo-Arvizu, R., & Mathews, H. L. (2008). Effect of mindfulness based stress reduction on immune function, quality of life and coping in women newly diagnosed with early stage breast cancer. *Brain and Behavioral Immunology, 22*, 969–981.

Wittchen, H.-U., Gloster, A. T., Beesdo-Baum, K., Fava, G. A., & Craske, M. G. (2010). Agoraphobia: A review of the diagnostic classificatory position and criteria. *Depression and Anxiety, 27*, 113–133.

Wittchen, H.-U., & Hoyer, J. (2001). Generalized anxiety disorder: Nature and course. *Journal of Clinical Psychiatry, 62*, 15–21.

Witte, T. K., Timmons, K. A., Fink, E., Smith, A. R., & Joiner, T. E. (2009). Do major depressive disorder and dysthymic disorder confer differential risk for suicide? *Journal of Affective Disorders, 115*, 69–78.

Wittstein, I. S., Thiemann, D. R., Lima, J. A. C., Baughman, K. L., Schulman, S. P., . . . Champion, H. C. (2005). Neurohumoral features of myocardial stunning due to sudden emotional stress. *New England Journal of Medicine, 352*, 539–548.

Wolanczyk, S. R., Wolanczyk, T., Gawrys, A., Swirszcz, K., Stefanoff, E., . . . Brynska, A. (2008). Prevalence of tic disorder among school children in Warsaw, Poland. *European Child and Adolescent Psychiatry, 17*, 171–178.

Woliver, R. (2000, March 26). 44 personalities, but artist shines. *New York Times*, pp. 6–9.

Wollschlaeger, B. (2007). The science of addiction: From neurobiology to treatment. *Journal of the American Medical Association, 298*, 809–810.

Wolpe, J. (1958). *Psychotherapy by reciprocal inhibition*. Stanford, CA: Stanford University Press.

Wolpe, J. (1973). *The practice of behavior therapy*. New York, NY: Pergamon.

Wong, Q. J. J., & Moulds, M. L. (2009). Impact of rumination versus distraction on anxiety and maladaptive self-beliefs in socially anxious individuals. *Behaviour Research and Therapy, 47*, 861–867.

Wood, M. D., Capone, C., Laforge, R., Erickson, D. J., & Brand, N. H. (2007). Brief motivational intervention and alcohol expectancy challenge with heavy drinking college students: A randomized factorial study. *Addictive Behaviors, 32*, 2509–2528.

Woods, N. F., Mitchell, E. S., Percival, D. B., & Smith-DiJulio, K. (2009). Is the menopausal transition stressful? Observations of perceived stress from the Seattle Midlife Women's Health Study. *Menopause, 16*, 90–97.

Woolgar, M., & Tranah, T. (2010). Cognitive vulnerability to depression in young people in secure accommodation: The influence of ethnicity and current suicidal ideation. *Journal of Adolescence, 33*, 653–661.

Work Group on Obsessive-Compulsive Disorder. (2007). Practice guidelines for the treatment of patients with obsessive-compulsive disorder. *American Journal of Psychiatry, 164*, 1–56.

World Health Organization. (2010). Obesity and overweight. Retrieved from http://www.who.int/mediacentre/factsheets/fs311/en/index.html

World Health Organization. (2011). Mental retardation: From knowledge to action. Retrieved from http://www.searo.who.int/en/Section1174/Section1199/Section1567/Section1825_8090.htm

Worley, C. B., Feldman, M. D., & Hamilton, J. C. (2009). The case of factitious disorder versus malingering. *Psychiatric Times, 26*, 1–4.

Wright, E. J. (2009). Neurological disease: The effects of HIV and antiretroviral therapy and the implications for early antiretroviral therapy initiation. *Current Opinions on HIV and AIDS, 4*, 447–452.

Wright, M. O., Crawford E., & Del Castillo, D. (2009). Childhood emotional maltreatment and later psychological distress among college students: The mediating role of maladaptive schemas. *Child Abuse and Neglect, 33*, 59–68.

Wrosch, C., Schulz, R., Miller, G. E., Lupien, S., & Dunne, E. (2007). Physical health problems, depressive mood, and cortisol secretions in old age: Buffer effects of health engagement control strategies. *Health Psychology, 26*, 341–349.

Wu, E. Q., Birnbaum, H. G., Shi, L., Ball, D. E., Kessler, R. C., Moulism, M., & Aggarwal, J. (2005). The economic burden of schizophrenia in the United States in 2002. *Journal of Clinical Psychology, 66*, 1122–1129.

Wu, L., Ringwalt, C., Mannelli, P., & Patkar, A. (2008). Hallucinogen use disorders among adult users of MDMA and other hallucinogens. *American Journal on Addictions, 17*, 354–363.

Wu, L., Parrott, A. C., Ringwalt, C.. Yang, C. M., & Blazer, D. G. (2009). The variety of ecstasy/MDMA users: Results from the National Epidemiologic Survey on Alcohol and Related Conditions. *American Journal on Addictions, 18*, 452–461.

Wu, L., Pilowsky, D. J, Schlenger, W. E., & Galvin, D. M. (2007). Misuse of methamphetamine and prescription stimulants among youths and young adults in the community. *Drug and Alcohol Dependence, 89*, 195–205.

Wu, L., Ringwalt, C., Weiss, R. D., & Blazer, D. G. (2009). Hallucinogen-related disorders in a national sample of adolescents: The influence of ecstasy/MDMA use. *Drug and Alcohol Dependence, 104*, 156–166.

Wu, N. S., Schairer, L. C., Dellor, E., & Grella, C. (2010). Childhood trauma and health outcomes in adults with comorbid substance abuse and mental health disorders. *Addictive Behavior, 35*, 68–71.

Wyatt v. Stickney, 344 F. Supp. 373 (Ala. 1972).

Wyatt, S. (2006, May). *Positive influence of religion and spirituality on blood pressure in the Jackson Heart Study*. Paper presented at the annual Scientific Meeting of American Society of Hypertension, New York, NY.

Xia, J., Merinder, L. B., & Belgamwar, M.R. (2011). Psychoeducation for schizophrenia. *Cochrane Database Systemic Reviews*. doi: 10.1002/14651858.CD002831.pub2

Xiang, B., Li, A., Valentin, D., Nowak, N. J., Zhao, H., & Li, P. (2008). Analytical and clinical validity of whole-genome oligonucleotide array comparative genomic hybridization for pediatric patients with mental retardation and developmental delay. *American Journal of Medical Genetics, 146*, 1942–1954.

Xu, Y., Schneider, F., Heimberg, R. G., Princisvalle, K., Liebowitz, M. R., Wang, S., & Blanco, C. (2012). Gender differences in social anxiety disorder: Results from the National Epidemiologic Sample on Alcohol and Related Conditions. *Journal of Anxiety Disorders, 26*, 12–19.

Yadin, E., & Foa, E. B. (2009). How to reduce distress and repetitive behaviors in patients with OCD. *Current Psychiatry, 8*, 19–23.

Yalom, I. D. (2005). *The theory and practice of group psychotherapy*. New York, NY: Basic Books.

Yang, L. H., & WonPat-Borja, A. J. (2007). Psychopathology among Asian Americans. In F. T. L. Leong, A. Ebreo, L. Kinoshita, A. G. Inman, M., Fu, & Yang, L. H., (Eds.), *Handbook of Asian American psychology* (pp. 379–405). Thousand Oaks, CA: Sage.

Yates, W. R. (2010). Somatoform disorders. Retrieved from http://emedicine.medscape.com/article/294908-print

Yeh, P. H., Gazdzinski, S., Durazzo, T. C., Sjöstrand, K., & Meyerhoff, D. J. (2007). Hierarchical linear modeling (HLM) of longitudinal brain structural and cognitive changes in alcohol-dependent individuals during sobriety. *Drug and Alcohol Dependence, 91*, 195–204.

Yehuda, R., Cai, G., Golier, J. A., Sarapas, C., Galea, S., . . . Buxbaum, J. D. (2009). Gene expression patterns associated with posttraumatic stress disorder follow exposure to the World Trade Center attacks. *Biological Psychiatry, 66*, 708–711.

Yen, S., Shea, M. T., Sanislow, C. A., Grilo, C. M., McGlashan, T. H., . . . Morey, L. C. (2003). Axis I and Axis II disorders as predictors of prospective suicide attempts: Findings from the Collaborative Longitudinal Personality Disorders Study. *Journal of Abnormal Psychology, 112*, 375–381.

Yeung, A., & Deguang, H. (2002). Somatoform disorders. *Western Journal of Medicine, 176*, 253–256.

Yoo, J. P., Brown, P. J., & Luthar, S. S. (2009). Children with co-occurring anxiety and externalizing disorders: Family risks and implications for competence. *American Journal of Orthopsychiatry, 79*, 532–540.

Young, J. A., & Tolentino, M. (2011). Neuroplasticity and its applications for rehabilitation. *American Journal of Therapeutics, 18*, 70–80.

Young, K. A., Bonkale, W. L., Holcomb, L. A., Hicks, P. B., & German, D. C. (2008). Major depression, 5HTTLPR genotype, suicide and antidepressant influences on thalamic volume. *British Journal of Psychiatry, 192*, 285–289.

Youngstrom, N. (1991). Spotting serial killer difficult, experts note. *APA Monitor, 22*, 32.

Yu, K., Cheung, C., Leung, M., Li, Q., Chua, S., & McAlonan, G. (2010). Are bipolar disorder and schizophrenia neuroanatomically distinct? An anatomical likelihood meta-analysis. *Frontiers in Human Neuroscience, 4*, 189.

Zammit, S., Owen, M. J., Evans, J., Heron, J., & Lewis, G. (2012). Cannabis, *COMT* and psychotic experiences. *British Journal of Psychiatry*. Advance online publication. doi:10.1192/bjp.bp.111.091421

Zanarini, M. C., Parachini, E. A., Frankenburg, F. R., & Holman, J. B. (2003). Sexual relationship difficulties among borderline patients and Axis II comparison subjects. *Journal of Nervous and Mental Disease, 191*, 479–482.

Zapf, P. A., & Roesch, R. (2006). Competency to stand trial: A guide for evaluators. In A.K. Hess & J. B. Weiner (Eds.), *Handbook of forensic psychology* (pp. 305–331). Hoboken, NJ: Wiley.

Zeanah, C. H., & Gleason, M. M. (2010). *Reactive attachment disorder: A review for DSM-V*. Retrieved from http://www.dsm5.org/Proposed%20Revision%20

Attachments/APA%20DSM-5%20Reactive%20 Attachment%20Disorder%20Review.pdf

Zeeck, A., Weber, S., Sandholz, A., Joos, A., & Hartmann, A. (2011). Stability of long-term outcome in bulimia nervosa: A 3-year follow-up. *Journal of Clinical Psychology, 67*, 318–327.

Zerdzinski, M. (2008). Olfactory obsessions—individual cases or one of the symptoms of obsessive-compulsive disorder? An analysis of 2 clinical cases. *Archives of Psychiatry and Psychotherapy, 3*, 23–27.

Zetzsche, T., Rujescu, D., Hardy, J., & Hampel, H. (2010). Advances and perspectives from genetic research: Development of biological markers in Alzheimer's disease. *Expert Review of Molecular Diagnostics, 10*, 667–690.

Zhang, A. Y., & Snowden, L. R. (1999). Ethnic characteristics of mental disorders in five U.S. communities. *Cultural Diversity and Ethnic Minority Psychology, 5*, 134–146.

Zhang, T.-Y., & Meaney, M. J. (2010). Epigenetics and the environmental regulation of the genome and its function. *Annual Review of Psychology, 61*, 439–466.

Zhou, J. N., Hofman, M. A., Gooren, L. J. G., & Swaab, D. F. (1995). A sex difference in the human brain and its relation to transsexuality. *Nature, 378*, 68–70.

Zilboorg, G., & Henry, G. W. (1941). *A history of medical psychology.* New York, NY: Norton.

Zimmerman, M., Rothschild, L., & Chelminski, I. (2005). The prevalence of DSM-IV personality disorders in psychiatric outpatients. *American Journal of Psychiatry, 162*, 1911–1918.

Zimmermann, G., Favrod, J., Trieu, V. H., & Pomini, V. (2005). The effect of cognitive behavioral treatment on the positive symptoms of schizophrenia spectrum disorders: A meta-analysis. *Schizophrenia Research, 77*, 1–9.

Zinzow, H. M., Resnick, H. S., McCauley, J. L., Amstadter, A. B., Ruggiero, K., & Kilpatrick, D. G. (2010). The role of rape tactics in risk for posttraumatic stress disorder and major depression: Results from a national sample of college women. *Depression and Anxiety, 27*, 708–715.

Zohar, J., Hollander, E., Stein, D. J., Westenberg, H. G. M., & the Cape Town Consensus Group. (2007). Consensus statement. *CNS Spectrums, 12*, 59–63.

Zoons, E., Weisfelt, M., de Gans, J., Spanjaard, L., Koelman, J. H., Reitsma, J. B., & van de Beek, D. (2007). Seizures in adults with bacterial meningitis. *Neurology, 70*, 2109–2115.

Zucker, K. J. (2009). The DSM diagnostic criteria for gender identity disorder in children. *Archives of Sexual Behavior, 39*, 477–498. doi:10.1007/s10508-009-9540-4

Zucker, K. J., & Cohen-Ketteris, P. T. (2008). Gender identity disorder in children and adolescents. In D. Rowland & L. Incrocci (Eds.), *Handbook of sexual and gender identity disorders* (pp. 376–422). Hoboken, NJ: Wiley.

Zuckerman, M. (1996). Sensation seeking. In C. G. Costello (Ed.), *Personality characteristics of the personality disordered* (pp. 317–330). New York, NY: Wiley.

Zuvekas, S. H., & Vitiello, B. (2012). Stimulant Medication Use in Children: A 12-year perspective. *American Journal of Psychiatry, 169*, 160–166.

Zwaigenbaum, L. (2010). Advances in the early detection of autism. *Current Opinions in Neurology, 23*, 97–102.

Name Index

Subject Index